THE BRUMBACK LIBRARY

PRESENTED BY:

Van Wert County Fruit
Growers Association

COMMON-SENSE
PEST CONTROL

COMMON-SENSE
PEST CONTROL

William Olkowski • Sheila Daar • Helga Olkowski

The Taunton Press

Cover drawings: Steve Buchanan

Taunton
BOOKS & VIDEOS

for fellow enthusiasts

© 1991 by Olkowski, Daar and Olkowski
All rights reserved.

10 9 8 7 6
Printed in the United States of America

A FINE GARDENING Book

FINE GARDENING® is a trademark of The Taunton Press, Inc.,
registered in the U.S. Patent and Trademark Office.

The Taunton Press, 63 South Main Street, Box 5506,
Newtown, CT 06740-5506
e-mail: tp@taunton.com

Distributed by Publishers Group West

Library of Congress Cataloging-in-Publication Data

Olkowski, William.
    Common-sense pest control/William Olkowski,
Sheila Daar, Helga Olkowski.
        p.   cm.
    "A Fine Gardening book"—T.p. verso.
    ISBN 0-942391-63-2
    1. Pests—Control. I. Daar, Sheila. II. Olkowski, Helga.
III. Title.
SB950.D3   1991   90-26624
635.0496—dc20   CIP

This book is dedicated to Dave and Tosia Martin and Hazel "Murma" Paine, whose love and support have inspired us to keep pushing on.

CONTENTS

5: Pests Inside the House

6: Pests of Indoor Plants

7: Pests of the House Structure

8: Pests in the Garden

9: Pests of the Community

Preface

Since 1971 we have worked as professionals in the field of pest management. Our focus has been on the design and implementation of management programs for pests of indoor and outdoor landscapes, greenhouses and buildings. We also work on pests of people and their domestic animals, and on pest problems associated with farms, rangelands, pastures, rights-of-way, marinas, zoos, conservatories, levees, ditch banks and urban vegetable and fruit gardens. We always seek the least-toxic methods for managing these problems.

Although much of our work has been for municipal, county, state and federal agencies, we receive daily requests for help from individuals. This book is a response to those questions from the public.

Many people are becoming concerned about exposure to the large number of laboratory-synthesized materials used in the modern world. Laboratory-created foods with artificial flavors and colors, cleaning and cosmetic products, plasticizers and many other products and by-products of industrial technology form a long list of compounds that have become part of our global environment. This environment is very different from the one in which human beings evolved. Some of these materials provide unequivocal benefits — money savings, increased convenience, a better quality of life — but others, like so many of the new medicines, combine cures for certain problems with undesirable and often unanticipated side effects. Some of these materials may prove toxic to humans and other organisms, either upon exposure or over time.

Pesticides are designed specifically to interfere with life processes. This fact alone is good reason to treat them with great respect, and to minimize their use. Notice, however, that we do not say "eliminate." That does not seem to us to be a useful goal. First of all, under the general category of pesticides, there are many different compounds and mixtures. Some are quite benign with respect to humans and the broader environment, even though they are quite deadly to the targeted pest. Examples include insecticidal soaps, insect growth hormones and some microbial insecticides.

In certain situations, the use of a pesticide may be the only cost- and labor-effective solution to a problem. In our experience, however, this reasoning is only occasionally justified. More often, pesticides are used because people are not aware of reliable alternatives. There are such alternatives, and we think it makes good sense to seek them out and use them. Worldwide concern over the effects of conventional pesticides and increasing pest resistance to toxic materials due to their overuse have encouraged tremendous growth in research and field evaluation of less-toxic alternatives. Hardly a month goes by without publication of the results of tests of materials, techniques or devices that have proven environmentally benign.

In 1978, we established the nonprofit Bio-Integral Resource Center (BIRC) to search out, evaluate and publicize this information. Each month we review the scientific literature worldwide, including journals, government reports, conference proceedings and new technical books. We follow up by contacting authors of key scientific papers, pest control professionals, manufacturers and others to determine the immediate and potential usefulness of these new approaches. We publish this information in two periodicals: *The IPM Practitioner,* which surveys current developments in least-toxic pest

management, and *Common Sense Pest Control
Quarterly*, a less technical publication that provides
practical, in-depth recommendations on the
management of specific pests. We also store this
information in our computer data base and refer to it
when answering questions from our members
around the world.

If you have been looking for effective least-toxic
methods for managing pests in and around your
house, apartment, work place or community, or on
your person or pets, this book was written for you.
If you want to keep abreast of and encourage new
developments in this fast-changing field, you can
become a member of BIRC. For information on
membership, write to BIRC, P.O. Box 7414, Berkeley,
CA 94707, or call (415) 524-2567.

Members are welcome to contact us at BIRC for
updates on information contained in this book, for
advice on adapting methods described herein to a
particular situation or for information on pest
problems not addressed in this book.

William Olkowski
Sheila Daar
Helga Olkowski

Berkeley, California
May, 1991

Acknowledgments

We wish to thank The Taunton Press for believing in the importance of this book and making publication possible, and Steve Marlens for his careful reading of the manuscript and commitment to seeing the project through.

Thanks are also due to the following scientists, naturalists, horticulturists, pest management professionals and other specialists for contributing information and reviewing drafts of various chapters of this book: Roger Akre, Deborah Altschuler, Mike Atkins, Harriet Barlow, Jack and Jake Blehm, Sterling Bunnell, Amigo Bob Cantisano, Paul Catts, Everett Dietrick, Walter Ebeling, Don Elliott, Frank Ennig, Mary Lou Flint, Steven Frantz, Parker Gambino, Tim Gordon, Joel Grossman, Ken Hagen, Joe Hancock, Robert Kourik, Robert Lane, John MacDonald, James Madison, Patrick Marer, Arthur McCain, the late Bernie Nelson, George Poinar, John Poorbaugh, George Puritch, Don Ross, Neil Seldman, Roger Swain, Bill Todaro, Ruth Troetschler, Joop van Lenteren, Robert Washino, Clarence Weinman and the many biological control researchers/ practitioners at the universities and commercial insectaries with whom we have worked over the years.

We also thank the many people who helped us with research and administrative work associated with this book, including Marsha Greenblatt, Irene Juniper, Gennui Raffill, Pat Shell, Rhoda Slanger, Kathy Spalding, Laurie Swiadon, Paul Thiers and the entire staff at the Bio-Integral Resource Center, who assisted with and accommodated the preparation of a large book midst the daily functions of the center.

Last, but by no means least, we thank the members, volunteers and board of directors of the Bio-Integral Resource Center and the foundations, corporations and donors whose financial and moral support over the years have made it possible for the information in this book to come to light.

To anyone whose help during the eight years it took to write this book we have failed to acknowledge, please forgive the oversight and accept our heartfelt thanks.

Introduction

This book is about ways to manage your encounters with other living organisms you regard as pests. The emphasis is on concepts and techniques that help you to do so in a manner that is in harmony with the health of humans, pets, other domestic animals, wildlife and the general environment. Chances are good you are reading this book because you want help solving a specific pest problem. Below we suggest ways you can use the book for that purpose.

Magic, Science and Simple Solutions: Distinguishing Coincidence from Cause

In all the information we present, we make a concerted effort to distinguish science from "magic," and to guide you in the art of applying sound scientific principles to the solving of pest problems. For many people actively seeking a less ecologically disruptive pest control technology, magic holds a strong attraction. Most likely this is because they have become disillusioned with science and the often destructive products they associate with it, including toxic pesticides. This may be one major reason why until recently much of the commonly available advice on nontoxic pest control contained such a heavy dose of magic.

Magical thinking can be entertaining. It can also lead to creative insights through intuitive processes beyond conscious control. But as a source of practical pest management techniques it is not very reliable. Magical thinking often concludes that one event was caused by another just because the second event followed the first event in time. It does not distinguish between coincidence and cause. For example, someone tells you that planting marigolds in your garden keeps bad bugs away. You try it. That year it seems as though the pest problem is less severe. Were the marigolds responsible? Magical thinking would instantly conclude that they were.

But we might ask a few more questions before jumping to that conclusion. By what mechanism did the marigolds keep the bad bugs away? Is the effect repeatable? Magical thinking does not deal with mechanisms; in fact, much of its appeal lies in the mysterious, unexplainable ways in which it operates. Like other human pursuits of mystery, such as religion, it requires unquestioning faith.

However, when you persist in questioning magical explanations—exactly how is it that marigolds reduce pest problems in the garden?—suddenly the magic disappears and you find yourself in the world of science. In this book you might find a statement like this:

> Certain marigolds, including *Tagetes patula* and *Tagetes erecta* (the universal scientific names for these particular species), have a root exudate that can reduce the number of plant-parasitic nematodes in the soil. To obtain this effect, the area where the problem is known to exist must be planted solidly with marigolds for an entire season. Then the plants must be chopped up and incorporated into the soil.

This statement is specific as to pest, species of plant, technique and pest control mechanism—in this case, a substance exuded from the roots that suppresses pest nematode populations.

What We Mean by the Scientific Process

Science is a loaded word in our society because it means different things to different people. Often the word is used in contexts involving emotional and political issues. In this book we use science to refer to the process by which an effort is made to discover the mechanisms underlying phenomena observed in the natural world. We also use it to distinguish between causal relationships and events that follow one another in time but probably are associated only by coincidence.

The scientific process goes something like this. First an idea occurs to someone—you, us or perhaps a professional scientist. If it has to do with the subject of this book, it is probably a new and better way of managing a particular pest problem. We call this a treatment, or because treatment to some people means applying a chemical material, we call it more formally a treatment action.

Next, that idea, or treatment, is tested in an experiment. In a sound experiment, the new treatment action is repeated several times and/or in different places. The experiment includes an untreated control group, also called a check. (Control is a confusing word. In a scientific investigation, the control is the group on which you do *not* carry out the treatment action. To the layperson, however, the word seems to suggest just the opposite, so we prefer the term "check.")

To return to the marigold example, we might conduct an experiment by selecting three areas where pest nematodes are known to occur at similar concentrations in the soil. We would plant Area 1 solidly for a season with what was said to be the "right" species of marigolds and then plow them under, as suggested above. In Area 2, we might interplant a few marigolds with other plants. Or, as some people do, we might run a border of marigolds around the entire bed and plant other things within the bed. Area 3, our check area, would contain no marigolds. The following season, we would plant all three areas with a species of plant known to be susceptible to the pest nematode that was originally present in the soil. Then we would compare levels of harmful nematode infection in each area by pulling out plants and examining their roots.

By carrying out just such an experiment, investigators at the Connecticut Agricultural Experiment Station determined how planting marigolds might reduce nematode pests infesting susceptible plants. The recommendation given above is based on our reading of the literature published on the experiment-station studies.

How Reliable Are Our Recommended Treatment Actions?

When one has completed a scientific investigation such as that just described, the best one can say is that the treatment action works under the specified circumstances a certain amount of the time. To say that an idea is scientifically valid means that the same result will be achieved under the same conditions at least 95 out of 100 times it is tried, or 95% of the time.

The key words are "under the same conditions." It is important to realize that although conditions can be duplicated in the laboratory, no two pest situations are identical in the real world. This has important consequences for applying pest management advice. You can't simply repeat a recommended treatment by rote and get the predicted results, as you can under laboratory conditions (or as you supposedly can using magic formulas).

Your key to success in applying the scientifically derived pest management advice we offer in this book is to follow a three-part process that involves your own judgment, intelligence and a little creativity. First, you must understand the underlying concepts. Then, you must familiarize yourself with circumstances under which the desired results have been achieved elsewhere. And finally, you must adapt the general techniques recommended in this book to the precise situation you are trying to manage.

This adaptation to your own circumstances is where the creativity comes in. You must become part biologist, carefully observing the various life forms you are attempting to manipulate, and part ecologist, observing the environment in which they live. Because so many conditions—soil, microclimate and plant or pest variety (or strain), to name a few—vary from place to place even in your own house, yard or greenhouse, you may need to carry out a few experiments of your own before you can figure out how the prescribed technique will work for you.

Few Simple Solutions

Does that sound simple? Most people say no. That is why pesticides are so popular. Their use seems simple. They offer what appears to be a simple solution to a complex problem. This apparent simplicity is also the reason why pesticides are limited in their usefulness. They are too simple to solve the problem in a permanent way. It's a bit like kicking the television when it stops working. You may get lucky, and the sudden jarring could get things working again…for a while. But finding a permanent solution to the problem requires that you take the trouble to educate yourself on the subject, put your attention to it, diagnose the problem and then apply the appropriate remedy. With complex systems, something more subtle than a sledgehammer is required.

The Hardest Part of All

Minimizing your dependence on pesticides takes a little more time and effort initially. But the rewards include less trouble in the long run and reduced personal and environmental contamination with toxic materials. Because the alternatives to toxic chemicals require learning new things and changing behavior, they also require a greater commitment than applying the same old simple but temporary chemical solutions. In fact, you may find that where modification of your own behavior and/or that of your housemates is involved—as in controlling certain indoor pests such as ants and cockroaches—this is the hardest part of all.

We sympathize. Having changed our own lives substantially to try to bring them into harmony with our ideals, we know how long it takes to break old patterns and make new ones automatic. For those of you who would like to learn more about how to change individual, family or institutional behavior, we recommend the book *Communication of Innovations: A Cross-Cultural Approach* by E. Rogers and F.F. Shoemaker (London: Free Press, 1971).

What You Need to Know and How to Find it in This Book

Two quite different types of information are needed to achieve good pest management. The first is general. You need a procedure for analyzing the problem and you need criteria for selecting the right treatment. The second is highly specific. You must know about the life cycle of the particular organism, the role it plays in the larger scheme of things and the role you or other humans play in creating or supporting the problem.

Accordingly, the first three parts of the book cover basic concepts. Parts 1 through 3 should help you take the right approach in thinking about existing pest problems and their solutions. In so doing, they should also provide you with a preventive approach to pest management. Subsequent parts of the book (Parts 4 to 9) tackle specific problems. They provide some of the specific pest control solutions many people are seeking. We present them as programs with diverse elements. In truth, however, the number of actual pest organisms and pest situations in the real world is so great that to address them all specifically would take a multivolume encyclopedia. So even in the latter parts of the book it will sometimes be necessary for you to generalize from specific examples to other closely related species whose management is similar.

After the Emergency Is Over

We suspect most readers will reach for this book after a pest problem has assumed emergency proportions and no longer responds to previously tried methods. The sense of urgency about the problem is often made worse by a fear of the pest organism itself or of the rapid damage it may cause. That is to say, when the house appears to be burning down, one wants fire-fighting equipment, not a learned discussion on making the house fireproof. So, understandably enough, there will a temptation to skip the background material and get right to specifics. However, we hope that once you have applied the "band-aid" suggestions we include under each specific pest, you will take the time to consider the deeper and wider perspective on the problem the book also provides. In our own experience, band-aid solutions, where available, are usually only temporary. If you want to avoid similar crises in the future, you should develop long-term, nontoxic preventive management strategies before the emergencies arise again.

Unfortunately, in many areas of the country community pest management of rats, mosquitoes and other pests still relies exclusively on chemical controls. Part of the reason this pattern continues is that it is hard to get financial support for pest management programs until the public perceives an emergency. By then it is too late for less-toxic methods. We hope that this book will equip you with the facts you need to help develop a pest management policy in your community that emphasizes prevention rather than crisis management. Specific language for such a policy and tips on how to get it adopted are contained in our booklet, *IPM Policy and Implementation* (Berkeley, Calif.: BIRC, 1990).

A Nest of Boxes

This book is organized around the various environments in which pests are found. Try thinking of yourself and your environment as a nest of boxes, one inside the other (see the drawing below). At the core is your own body and the bodies of your pets. Surrounding these are your clothes and home furnishings, including house plants. Your house structure envelops these, and shares its pest problems with the other buildings in which you spend time. Surrounding these are a variety of other environments both private—such as flower, vegetable and fruit gardens—and semipublic, such as the lawn and the foundation plantings that face your neighbors. Finally, there are problems you share with other people in the community that can be solved only by enlightened, cooperative community efforts. For each of these environments, the book provides a discussion of the biology of the pests in question, the damage they cause and specific strategies for dealing with pest problems.

Three Ways to Identify Your Pest

The first step in solving a pest problem is to identify the organism causing the problem. We suggest three ways in which you can do this. The first involves noting which nested environment(s) the pest occurs in: indoors, outdoors, the house structure, and so on. Next, you note what part of that larger environment the pest affects: the kitchen, lawn, basement or other area. Then you turn to the appropriate section of the book. Once there, you will probably be able to identify the pest based solely on the symptoms of infestation and locations we describe.

Alternatively, you can take or send the pest to an expert (we discuss this procedure in the first part of the book). This usually takes more time. Or you can learn to identify the pest yourself based on its physical characteristics and the location in which it was found. Throughout this book we recommend other books that can help you learn to identify various organisms. Of course, if you already know what the pest is, you can simply turn to the index to locate a discussion of its management.

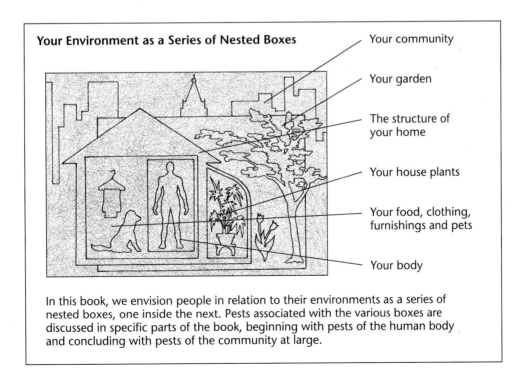

Your Environment as a Series of Nested Boxes

Your community

Your garden

The structure of your home

Your house plants

Your food, clothing, furnishings and pets

Your body

In this book, we envision people in relation to their environments as a series of nested boxes, one inside the next. Pests associated with the various boxes are discussed in specific parts of the book, beginning with pests of the human body and concluding with pests of the community at large.

How We Decided Which Pests to Include

As we mentioned earlier, a book that discussed every pest that bothers people would occupy many volumes. Therefore we had to be selective. In making the choices, we asked ourselves several questions: Is the pest common enough so that people in a large part of the country are familiar with it? Are reliable less-toxic alternatives to toxic methods of control now in common use? If a pest species is only regionally important, is it typical of a group of pests elsewhere whose least-toxic management is similar? Does the management program for the pest—or the common mismanagement of it—illustrate some important concept?

It was easy to pick the major pests. Some years ago we analyzed data on people who called us at the Bio-Integral Resource Center. Most callers were interested in alternatives to pesticides for just a few serious pests. No matter where the callers lived, what their educational level was, whether they were male or female or what they did for a living, they wanted to know about less-toxic controls for these organisms (listed in order of decreasing frequency): termites and other wood-boring insects, cockroaches, fleas, head lice, weeds, mosquitoes, ants, house-plant pests, mice and caterpillars such as the gypsy moth. Naturally we have included these pests (and many others) in the book.

If it's Not in This Book: Using the Chapter References

You may be disappointed to find that some less common pests are not in the book. Don't be discouraged. If you are serious about finding a relatively nontoxic solution, read Parts 1 through 3. Armed with the information on basic approaches and analogous situations you'll find there, you can turn to the section of the book that covers pests that fall into the same biological category or physical environment as yours. You can then adapt the recommendations to fit your situation. Each chapter ends with a section entitled "References and Readings." If you still have questions, the reference materials cited in this section will help you understand more about the biology and ecology of your pest.

A word about these references. We are always uneasy with information provided to the public by so-called "experts" who give no indication where they found it. If you are skeptical about some new idea you encounter in this book, you have the right to ask, "Who says so?" You should be able to determine whether our suggestions are based on our personal experience, technical literature, anecdotes from others or some other source. We have tried to make our sources clear.

On the other hand, to reference this book formally would require a citation for almost every statement and it would become a cumbersome scientific treatise—just the opposite of what we want it to be. Thus, we have limited ourselves to citing in the text only those books and articles we particularly want to draw to your attention; we also include some technical papers needed to substantiate recommendations that may be especially nontraditional or controversial. Full bibliographic citations for material quoted in the text are listed in each chapter's "References and Readings."

Don't be intimidated by the technical literature we cite. The papers require only concentration and common sense to understand. If you act seriously to change the way pests are managed around your home and community, sooner or later you will encounter authority figures—landlords, professional landscape and building maintenance workers, city public-works personnel, pest control operators—who are unfamiliar with or unsympathetic to what you are trying to do. This is where the technical literature helps, since most people are willing to try something new and different if you can show them it has worked elsewhere.

Standing on the Shoulders of Those Before Us

Furthermore, it is often essential to be able to turn to the source of the information to compare the original experiment with your own experimental results or to find additional clues. Checking your own results against the original experiment is one of the major ways progress is made through the scientific method. Science is a cumulative, cooperative effort to understand how things work. With the access to literature that a good library provides, you can go back in time or around the world to enhance your ability to manage problems that would otherwise be unsolvable.

You Can Help Us, Too

Much information in this book is the direct product of our own experience in pest management, but we learned most of what we know from the existing literature and from people we have tried to help. We have always appreciated feedback from our readers, and we do not hesitate to test and pass on novel approaches or techniques you suggest. If you are frustrated because your pest problem isn't addressed in this book, or if you have a comment on our recommendations, write to our nonprofit organization, the Bio-Integral Resource Center (BIRC), P.O. Box 7414, Berkeley, CA 94707.

We established BIRC in 1978 to identify and publicize scientifically based information on least-toxic pest management. We draw upon our staff's more than two decades of field work and applied research in integrated pest management (IPM), an extensive IPM data base and an international network of scientists, innovative farmers and other pest control professionals. BIRC members— membership is open to anyone who is interested— are kept up-to-date on least-toxic pest control through our magazine, *Common Sense Pest Control Quarterly*, and our international journal for pest control professionals, *The IPM Practitioner*. Members also use our consulting services by telephone or through correspondence for specific pest problems.

This book was written first and foremost for laypersons—home owners, apartment dwellers, gardeners and other individuals. We have done our very best to use nontechnical, everyday language, and to explain things as completely as possible. Yet we realize we may not always have been successful in this and welcome your suggestions as to how the book might be improved.

PART 1

Basic Concepts

CHAPTER 1
Naming Living Things and Understanding their Habits and Habitats

LINNAEUS' BRIGHT IDEA

In the early 1700s a brilliant young Swedish botanist, Carl von Linné, now better known as Carl Linnaeus, "undertook to classify the whole of nature—mineral, vegetable and animal—the Systema Naturae," as Url Lanham writes in his absorbing book, *Origins of Modern Biology* (which is listed under "References and Readings" on p. 29). Linnaeus, in his writings as well as in the sorting of his botanical collections, labored to bring order to the process of describing the vast number of organisms already recognized in the natural world. In so doing, he hit upon a system more enduring than even he himself appreciated.

Using the flower, or reproductive portion, of plants, he grouped them by similarity, first into large classes, then into finer divisions called genera (singular, genus) and finally into separate species within a genus. As Lanham points out:

Linnaeus had in his thinking... clearly separated the two functions of naming (or designating) and diagnosis (or description).... The 'name of the species' was to consist of the name of the genus to which it belonged, followed by the 'specific name,' which was a descriptive phrase-name.

This use of two names to describe each plant and animal is called binomial nomenclature, or simply, the scientific name. Lanham continues:

As a matter of fact, in finally coming to binomial nomenclature, Linnaeus had simply returned to the almost instinctive way of naming things that is used in everyday language. Thus, in designating different kinds of willow, we might use such names as red willow, black willow, sand willow, narrowleaf willow, etc., with 'willow' in each case corresponding to the generic name and the combination to the binomial. In English the qualifying adjective precedes the noun, but in Latin it follows.

This simple device for the precise naming of a specific organism using Latin words has become internationally accepted. It is an example of how within the sciences there is worldwide communication and a common body of information despite linguistic, political, religious and other cultural differences. For example, what the British call charlock, Americans call wild mustard. Yet if we use the Latin binomial *Brassica kaber*, we all know we are talking about the same organism. (Note: By convention, the genus name, in this case *Brassica*, is capitalized, and the species name begins with a lower-case letter. Both genus and species are italicized.) Binomial nomenclature is particularly important where the same common name is used to refer to two different organisms. For example, morningglory can denote the blue-flowered ornamental vine *Ipomoea purpurea*, or the pink- or white-flowered garden weed *Convolvulus arvensis*.

WHY NAMING THINGS IS IMPORTANT

The scientific name of an organism is the key to all the world's literature about its behavior, natural enemies and ways in which people have attempted to manage it. While two closely related species within a genus may have many common behaviors, the critical information for management purposes may lie in knowing which behaviors are different.

For example, in managing cockroaches, almost any brand of commercial roach trap can help you find a serious infestation *if* you have the German roach (*Blatella germanica*). But if you have the smokybrown roach (*Periplaneta fuliginosa)*, you must choose your trap carefully, because not all traps attract smokybrown roaches. Different bait preference is one of the many characteristics that distinguish the German roach from the smokybrown roach. As we shall see later in the book, trap effectiveness for a particular roach species often depends on the type of bait attractant used.

As another example, let's say you have a flea problem in your home. You have a large dog and a small cat. You would probably be tempted to pay more attention to the dog, as it is bigger and has more fleas. In truth, the cat should be the focus of your attention, because it is the so-called cat flea that is probably biting the cat, the dog and you. Here we are talking about the difference between the cat flea (*Ctenocephalides felis*) and the dog flea (*Ctenocephalides canis*).

Knowing the correct scientific name of an organism is so crucial to good pest management that we have taken great pains to give you the genus and species of every organism we mention. In some cases, however, the genera that compose larger families share enough traits to make their management similar. In these cases, we give you the family name instead.

Don't despair—you do not have to learn all the Latin names of all these organisms. We have organized the book so that you should be able to figure out what the pest is by considering the description in the text, the accompanying pictures and the environment in which you found the pest. However, we do delve a bit deeper into the subject of classification on pp. 13-14.

HOW TO DETERMINE THE SCIENTIFIC NAME OF A PLANT OR ANIMAL

If you have some doubt that the organism bothering you is the same as a particular organism described in this book, you should seek help in identifying it. We have seen many cases in which control measures have been applied to harmless or even beneficial insects because the insects were mistaken for a pest species.

The closest reliable source of information on common pests in your area is most likely the local office of the Cooperative Extension Service of the U.S. Dept. of Agriculture. The ser-

How To Preserve Plant Specimens

Find a stiff index card or piece of white poster board large enough for the specimen, then cut a piece of clear contact paper that overlaps the card ¾ in. (1.9 cm) on all sides. A sheet of aluminum foil or plastic wrap spread over the work surface will prevent the contact paper from sticking in the wrong place. Separate the backing from the paper and lay the paper over the plant, pressing out air bubbles by moving your hand from the bottom to the top (A in the drawing at right).

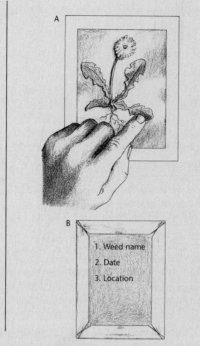

Cut off the corners of the contact paper, then fold the paper over the back of the card (B in the drawing at right). Write the name of the weed (if known), the date and the location where collected on the back.

(This method was suggested by Dr. David Bayer, a botanist at the University of California, Davis.)

vice, established in 1914, usually has an office in each county. Although their pest management advice has traditionally been pesticide oriented, more and more they are providing information on alternatives. Their many leaflets on the biology and ecology of pest species are excellent and easy to read. Reading about pest life cycles and environmental requirements can give you clues to nontoxic pest management tactics not explicitly mentioned in the extension-service literature.

If your pest problem is common in your area, cooperative-extension personnel may be able to confirm your identification over the phone just from your description of the organism and/or the damage it caused. Sometimes, however, they must inspect the specimen directly. If you must take or send a specimen, we recommend the following procedures.

Collecting Insects and Mites for Identification

Where possible, collect more than one insect or mite specimen. Larger organisms—those larger than aphids, for example—should be placed in an appropriately sized plastic container, such as a pill bottle or film canister. Do not use the original cap; instead, stopper the bottle tightly with cotton. The cotton prevents moisture from accumulating inside the container and encouraging mold, which can destroy important characteristics needed for identification. If the captured insects are still alive inside the bottle, place the container in the freezer for a day or two to kill them. It is not a good idea to send live in-

sects, because they may escape and cause a pest problem where you are sending them, particularly if they are not already present there. If you are mailing the bottle, place it in a box stuffed with crumpled newspaper.

Smaller organisms such as aphids or mites can be picked up with a paint brush and dropped into a small amount of rubbing alcohol in the container. The advantage of using alcohol is that the insects are killed almost instantly and cannot escape by tunneling around the cotton stopper, as they might in a dry container. They are also less likely to become entangled in the cotton stopper, which can impair identification. Alternatively, insects and mites, even soft-bodied species such as aphids, can be left to dry out in a container and rehydrated for study later. Details on specimen preservation are usually provided in reference works on particular insect groups; many of these books are listed at the end of the appropriate chapters in this book.

Collecting Plant Specimens for Identification

If you want to have a damaged plant inspected or a weed identified, place the plant and a moist paper towel inside a plastic bag. If you are unable to deliver the specimen in person, place the bag inside a padded mailing envelope. If you cannot mail the specimen immediately, however, it is likely to shrivel or mold. Use the process outlined in the sidebar at left instead.

Keeping a Record

If you send one sample specimen for identification, we suggest you keep another for your own reference, because samples are not always returned. Along with the sample, you should send and keep duplicate records of potentially important information about the situation or problem surrounding the specimen. We suggest you follow this format:

• Date the specimen was collected.
• Place or address where the specimen was collected.

Table 1.1
Three Examples Illustrating the Standard Taxonomic[a] Categories of the Hierarchical Classification System

Taxonomic level	Humans	Garlic	Northern House Mosquito
Kingdom	Animalia	Plantae	Animalia
Phylum (Division)[b]	Chordata	Angiospermophyta	Arthropoda
Subphylum[c]	Vertebrata	none	Mandibulata
Class	Mammalia	Monocotyledoneae	Insecta
Order	Primates	Liliales	Diptera
Family	Hominidae	Liliaceae	Culicidae
Genus	*Homo*	*Allium*	*Culex*
Species	*sapiens*	*sativum*	*pipiens*

[a] Taxonomy refers to the classification of organisms according to their natural relationships to each other. Closely related organisms are grouped together in families.

[b] Botanists use the term division instead of phylum.

[c] Intermediate taxonomic levels can be created by adding the prefixes "sub" and "super" to the name of any taxonomic level. The suffix "-oidea" is used to designate superfamilies, "-inae" designates subfamilies and "-ini" designates tribes, which are groups of genera smaller than a subfamily. No particular suffix is used to designate the subgenus or group of related species. Still other less well-defined levels are used, but they are not formalized with standard suffixes, e.g., "series," "divisions" and "cohort." There are also designations for subspecies, ecotypes, strains, varieties and races, although the latter term seldom is used today.

• Specific area where the specimen was collected (e.g., "closet floor, north side of house," "under stone," etc.).
• Maintenance practices that might have a bearing on the situation (e.g., "watered lawn two days before").
• Previous pest control efforts (e.g., "used insecticidal soap spray morning of problem").
• Host plant, if the insect was found on a plant.
• Weather, if it seems relevant (e.g., "rained night before").
• Time, if it seems relevant.

THE CLASSIFICATION OF LIFE FORMS

The binomial system is a very useful method for identifying organisms, but it does not tell us how one organism is related to another. These relationships are important for very practical reasons. For example, if you capture a fly that is identified as a member of the family Tachinidae, you can expect it to be parasitic on certain caterpillars even though you cannot determine its species name. This is because most tachinid flies are parasitoids of caterpillars.

Knowledge of these relationships helps you extend or extrapolate what is known about well-studied organisms to related but less well-studied organisms. Thus, when a new pest beetle is accidentally introduced into your area and little is known about its biology or management, reading about related beetles can give you clues to suppressing the new pest.

Another reason to know how an organism relates to all other life forms is to make categorization more efficient and accurate. Recent estimates of the number of different species on the planet go as high as ten million or more, even though the total number now known is at most two million. To handle storage of information about this mass of living things, one needs a classification or filing system with common nomenclature and enough flexibility to incorporate advances in knowledge about the identity, biology and relationships of organisms.

Until the late 1970s, all organisms were classified as either plants or animals. Table 1.1 above gives three examples of fully classified organisms. Every schoolchild learned that the first step in deciphering the "tree of life" was to place an organism in either the plant or the animal kingdom. Over the years, however, this simple two-kingdom view has come to be seen as rather limited because many organisms do not easily conform to the criteria used to define the two kingdoms. For example, the protozoan *Euglena* spp. possesses chlorophyll and photosynthesizes like a plant, but it has a nerve-like coordination system like an animal.

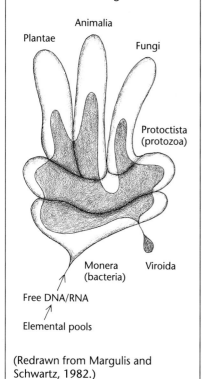
In general, protozoa, bacteria, fungi and viruses all seem to have some characteristics that fall outside the plant and animal kingdoms. Some viruses even defy the distinction between living and nonliving in that they can be dried out and broken apart but, after rehydration, can still infect other organisms.

The Five-Kingdom Model

In the 1970s, biologists Lynn Margulis and Karlene Schwartz proposed a five-kingdom classification system to represent what was known at that time about the complexity of living organisms. This system, presented as a model, will still require consider-able discussion within the scientific community before it is widely adopted.

Their new scheme set bacteria at the base of the tree, suggesting that bacteria are the most primitive forms of life and all other forms are derived from them. Next come the protozoa, and from these arise the plant, fungus and animal kingdoms. Note that viruses are not represented in this model since the authors did not consider them living things. This seems odd, since they are alive—as anyone with a cold will attest—even though they require another living organism, or host, in which to live.

More and more is being learned about viruses. Yet because of their small size, they remain largely a mystery, particularly when it comes to placing them on the tree of life. We speculate that a sixth kingdom representing the viruses will be proposed and that it will be conceptualized as residing within all the other kingdoms, since there are no known viruses that are free-living (see the drawing at left).

Within the animal kingdom there are about 20 major branches, called phyla. The phyla encompass the chordates (animals with backbones—humans, apes, mammals, birds, fish, reptiles and amphibians), mollusks (snails, slugs, squid, etc.), arthropods (insect-like animals), nematodes (the nematodes, or round-worms) and other divisions.

INTRODUCING THE ARTHROPODS

A rough survey of the species indicates that there are far more arthropods than all other animals combined. And there are more beetles within the arthropods than all other arthropods combined. This makes beetles the most numerous of living organisms. Most beetles are beneficial, playing key roles in the ecosystem such as recycling nutrients and, in the case of the lady beetles, suppressing pest organisms. Yet when most people see a beetle, they step on it or spray it. What prompts this reaction? Fear, and like many other fears, it must be addressed through education. Because arthropods are so numerous and because they also constitute the group with the most pest species, we feel it is important to provide a brief introduction to their classification and biology.

Arthropods comprise insects, mites, crabs, spiders, scorpions and similar animals. "Arthro" means jointed and "pod" means foot. It is the presence of legs that separates arthropods from earlier-evolved animal types without legs, especially the worms from which the arthropods are believed to have arisen. The other major characteristic that distinguishes arthropods from the animals from which they evolved is an external skeleton, or exoskeleton, made from chitin (a polysaccharide composed of simple sugars). The exoskeleton also separates arthropods from chordates (mammals, birds, etc.), which have an internal skeleton, and from mollusks, which usually have a calcium shell in place of a skeleton.

According to the five-kingdom model, arthropods are no longer a phylum but a collection of phyla with two large divisions. These occur between the insect-like organisms and the mite- or spider-like organisms. The divisions are based primarily on different types of mouthparts. The two largest arthropod groups are Mandibulata and Chelicerata.

The Mandibulata include those groups with mandibles, or opposed jaws, such as the insects and crustaceans. The Chelicerata, which include mites, ticks and spiders, have mouthparts called chelicerae. "Cheli" means cloven hoof or claw in Greek, and it refers to the paired appendages of the Chelicerata. Chelicerata lack antennae and have four pairs of walking legs. The presence of eight legs is one way to tell mites and spiders from six-legged (in three pairs) insects.

The chart on the facing page shows how the arthropod phyla and their finer divisions relate to the six-

The Arthropods and Their Place in the Living World [a]

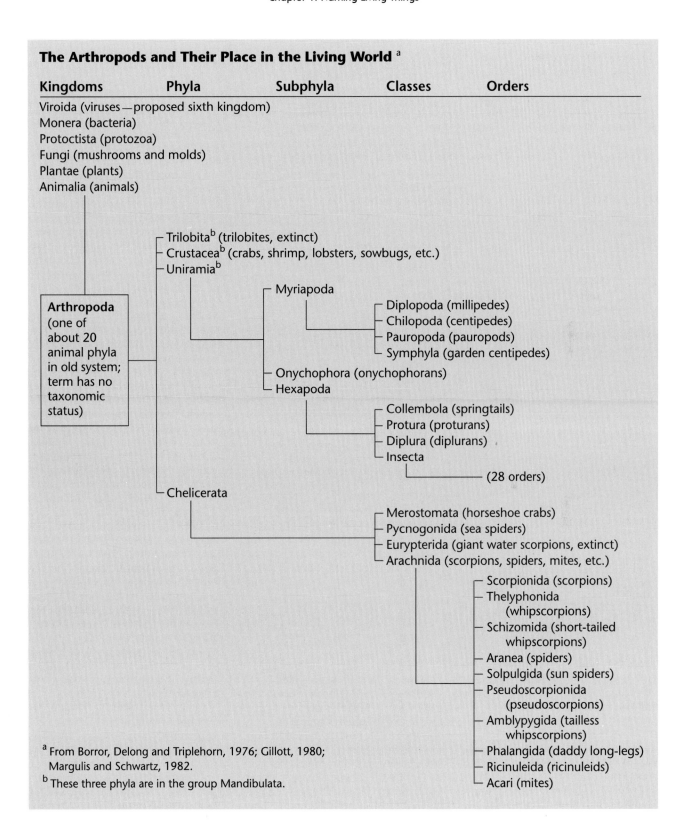

Kingdoms	Phyla	Subphyla	Classes	Orders

Viroida (viruses—proposed sixth kingdom)
Monera (bacteria)
Protoctista (protozoa)
Fungi (mushrooms and molds)
Plantae (plants)
Animalia (animals)

Arthropoda (one of about 20 animal phyla in old system; term has no taxonomic status)

Trilobita[b] (trilobites, extinct)
Crustacea[b] (crabs, shrimp, lobsters, sowbugs, etc.)
Uniramia[b]

Myriapoda

Diplopoda (millipedes)
Chilopoda (centipedes)
Pauropoda (pauropods)
Symphyla (garden centipedes)

Onychophora (onychophorans)
Hexapoda

Collembola (springtails)
Protura (proturans)
Diplura (diplurans)
Insecta

(28 orders)

Chelicerata

Merostomata (horseshoe crabs)
Pycnogonida (sea spiders)
Eurypterida (giant water scorpions, extinct)
Arachnida (scorpions, spiders, mites, etc.)

Scorpionida (scorpions)
Thelyphonida (whipscorpions)
Schizomida (short-tailed whipscorpions)
Aranea (spiders)
Solpulgida (sun spiders)
Pseudoscorpionida (pseudoscorpions)
Amblypygida (tailless whipscorpions)
Phalangida (daddy long-legs)
Ricinuleida (ricinuleids)
Acari (mites)

[a] From Borror, Delong and Triplehorn, 1976; Gillott, 1980; Margulis and Schwartz, 1982.

[b] These three phyla are in the group Mandibulata.

Table 1.2
Distinguishing among Major Groups of Arthropods[a]

Group[b]	Distinguishing Characteristics
Phylum: Crustacea (crabs) 26,000 species 30 orders	2 pairs antennae, 1 pair jaws, 2 pairs maxillae, 5 or more pairs of jointed legs, calcareous exoskeleton, gills, biramous (paired) appendages, wingless, aquatic; (includes shrimps, water fleas, barnacles, lobsters, crayfish, pill bugs)
Class: Insecta (insects) 2 million+ species 28 orders	1 pair antennae, usually 3 pairs legs and 2 pairs wings, mouthparts variable, chitinous exoskeleton, trachea, winged and wingless, all habitats; (includes beetles, butterflies, moths, flies, roaches, lice, fleas, termites, bees, wasps)
Class: Chilopoda (centipedes) 3,000 species 4 orders	1 pair antennae, body long and segmented (15-181 segments), with 1 pair legs per body segment, predacious—first pair legs contain poison glands, 1 pair jaws, trachea, wingless, terrestrial, nocturnal; (includes centipedes)
Class: Diplopoda (millipedes) 8,000 species 7 orders	1 pair antennae, body long, cylindrical, and segmented (9 to more than 100 segments), with 2 pairs of legs per body segment, wingless, prefers moist areas, terrestrial, decomposers; (includes millipedes)
Class: Arachnida (spiders, mites) 40,000 species 9 orders	no antennae, 4 pairs of legs, cephalothorax and abdomen, wingless, predacious, parasitic and detrivorous; (includes pseudoscorpions, sun spiders, jumping spiders, mites, ticks)

[a] Based on information from Storer and Usinger, 1965.

[b] All but the arachnids (which are in Chelicerata) are in the group Mandibulata.

kingdom model. In Table 1.2 above we characterize some common insect and non-insect arthropods.

The Insect Orders

As mentioned earlier, the names of the insect orders have Latin or Greek roots that usually describe the animals to which they refer. For example, the order name for the beetles is Coleoptera. "Pter-" means wing, as in the name of the extinct flying reptile, pterodactyl. "Cole" comes from the Greek word *koleos*, which means sheath. If you look at a ground beetle, it is apparent that it is a sheath-covered animal. The sheaths in this case are its hard wing covers, called elytra. These sheaths easily distinguish it from other insects like flies, which have two membranous wings (order Diptera), and moths and butterflies, which have scale-covered wings (order Lepidoptera). Table 1.3 on the facing page shows the insect orders as they are presently grouped; it also indicates the approximate numbers of species and families.

Insect Body Forms

The form of the body is another easy way to see how the major groups of arthropods are categorized. For example, adult insects have three body regions: the head, thorax (analogous to our chest) and abdomen. Spiders and mites have only two body segments: the head, which, because it is joined with the thorax, is called a cephalothorax, and abdomen. These and other characteristics useful for distinguishing insects from arachnids are shown in the top drawing on p. 18.

Because insects, spiders and mites are so different from humans, we tend to suffer from a kind of "specist bigotry." We dislike them because we don't understand them. Because we are apprehensive about their strangeness—and sometimes about their intentions toward us—we are often less willing than we should be to observe their structure, life stages and adaptive mechanisms. Some of the key characteristics we often overlook are the type of mouthparts (some insects have sucking mouthparts and others have chewing mouthparts; see the bottom drawing on p. 18), the presence, absence and number of wings, and whether the young look like the adults or are totally different. This information can be invaluable in helping us make the most of insect species we regard as beneficial and in helping us suppress those that compete with us.

There is great practical value in being able to distinguish one insect from another. For example, if pieces of your plant are missing and you see aphids on one of its remaining leaves, you might be tempted to blame the aphids for the damage. But aphids have sucking mouthparts, whereas

Table 1.3
The Insect Orders [a]

| | Number of Species | | Number of |
	World	North America	Families
PHYLUM UNIRAMIA			
class and order **Collembola** (springtails)	2,000	300	5
class and order **Protura** (proturans)	200	20	3
class and order **Diplura** diplurans)	600	25	3
class **Insecta**			
subclass **Apterygota**			
order **Microcoryphia** (bristletails)	250	20	3
order **Zygentoma** (silverfish, firebrats)	320	18	3
subclass **Pterygota**			
infraclass **Paleoptera**			
order **Ephemeroptera** (mayflies)	2,000	600	19
order **Odonata** (dragonflies and damselflies)	5,000	500	24
infraclass **Neoptera**			
division **Polyneoptera** (orthopteroids)			
order **Plecoptera** (stoneflies)	1,550	465	7
order **Embioptera** (webspinners)	2,000	29	8
order **Dictyoptera** (cockroaches and mantids)	5,500	49	7
order **Isoptera** (termites)	2,000	44	5
order **Grylloblattodea** (rock crawlers)	20	10	1
order **Dermaptera** (earwigs)	1,200	20	8
order **Phasmida** (stick insects)	2,500	29	2
order **Orthoptera** (grasshoppers, crickets)	20,000	601	14
order **Zoraptera** (angel insects)	20		1
division **Paraneoptera** (hemipteroids)			
order **Psocoptera** (barklice)	1,700	150	4
order **Phthiraptera** (lice)	4,000		15
order **Hemiptera** (true bugs)	55,000	3587	61 +
order **Thysanoptera** (thrips)	4,500	694	5
division **Oligoneoptera** (endopterygotes)			
Panorpoid complex			
order **Mecoptera** (scorpion flies)	480	68	7
order **Trichoptera** (caddis flies)	7,000	1,200	34
order **Lepidoptera** (butterflies and moths)	112,000	10,000	66 +
order **Diptera** (flies)	98,500	16,914	150 +
order **Siphonaptera** (fleas)	1,300	200	9
Hymenopteroidea			
order **Megaloptera** (alderflies and dobsonflies)	>100	50	2
order **Raphidioptera** (snakeflies)	100	20	2
order **Neuroptera** (lacewings, mantispids)	4,670	349	14 +
order **Coleoptera** (beetles)	300,000	23,701	150 +
order **Strepsiptera** (stylopids)	300	109	5
order **Hymenoptera** (bees, wasps, ants)	103,000	17,429	100 +
Total **28 orders**	**>737,810**	**77,201**	**737 +** [b]

[a] Sources: Gillott (1980), Arnett (1985).
[b] Estimates of the number of families and species are approximate.

the culprit, based on the evidence, was either a chewing insect, such as a beetle, caterpillar or grasshopper, or perhaps a snail, slug or bird. Beetle larvae, when feeding on a leaf, frequently scrape out portions between the veins with their chewing mouthparts, leaving behind a lace-like structure without the green portions; adults eat holes through the leaves.

Bees and syrphids (hover flies) are often confused because superficially they look quite similar. But bees have two pairs of wings and the ability to sting. Syrphids are flies, and the larvae of many syrphid species eat aphids and other pests. Adult syrphids may mimic bees or wasps in their coloration and in their interest in flowers, from which they take pollen and nectar. However, they are distinguished from bees by their single pair of wings and by their behavior. Similarly, people commonly confuse ants with termites. But ants are narrow-waisted and termites are broad-waisted. As another example, we admire adult lady beetles, but we kill their larvae because they look so different — and unappealing — compared to the adult form.

We have included many drawings in this book that introduce you to the appearance of the common species. We have also supplied many family names so that you can begin to get a working knowledge of the classification of the many groups of living things, especially the insects. To delve further into these areas, you must obtain and study the learning resources we list in "References and Readings" at the end of each chapter.

Insect Life Cycles

An insect begins life as an egg. Most eggs are fertilized by the male, but some aphids, wasps and others are able to give birth without fertilization, a process called parthenogenesis. Some insects, such as flesh flies and many aphids, produce living young; yet even they pass through an egg-like stage within the body of the female before being born alive.

Once the young insect hatches from the egg, it grows through a series of stages called instars. During the first instar, the insect eats until its skin cannot expand any further. At this point it sheds the skin, or molts, and grows a new one. After each molt, the insect is in its next instar; the number of instars varies among species, and can be affected by temperature, humidity and food availability. Juvenile hormones, also called

---

Distinguishing an Insect from an Arachnid

Because methods for solving insect problems may differ from those appropriate for arachnids (spiders or mites), it is important to be able to distinguish between the two classes of organisms.

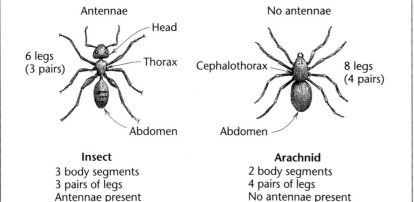

Insect	**Arachnid**
3 body segments	2 body segments
3 pairs of legs	4 pairs of legs
Antennae present	No antennae present

Insect Mouthparts

Knowing the type of mouthparts an insect has helps identify the order to which it belongs and the type of damage it causes. The four common mouthpart types are (A) chewing, (B) piercing/sucking, (C) sponging (typical of certain flies) and (D) siphoning. The siphoning is done through a retracting mouth tube, shown in its extended state and in its retracted, coiled state (dashed line).

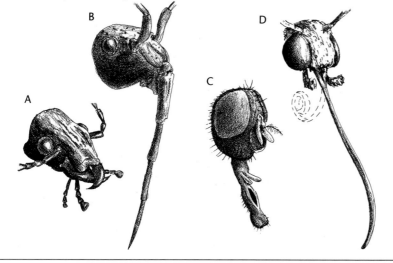

Insect Metamorphosis

Most insects, including the Indianmeal moth (A), begin life as an egg and evolve through several stages before reaching the adult form. This process is referred to as metamorphosis. A smaller group, including silverfish (B), emerge from the egg looking like a miniature version of their adult form. Such insects are considered to undergo no metamorphosis.

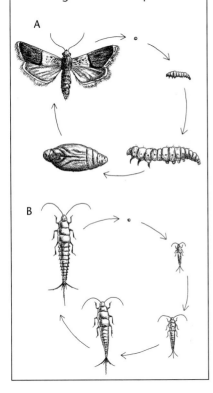

A Short Glossary of Terms Used in Table 1.4

Caudal filament: An antenna-like structure on the last abdominal segment.

Cerci: Segmented appendages at the rear end of certain groups.

Compound eyes: Eyes that have hundreds or more facets.

Decomposer: An organism that feeds on dead organisms.

Degenerate mouthparts: Mouthparts that do not have all the common components.

Ectoparasites: Parasites on the outside of the body of their host.

Filiform antennae: Antennae whose segments look like linked sausages.

Gregarious: Gathering together in a group; not solitary.

Halteres: Short structures near the base of the wings of certain flies that contribute to aerodynamic stability and control.

Hardened wings: Wings that are opaque, as opposed to soft, membranous wings.

Hindwings: The second pair of wings in certain orders.

Membranous wings: Wings that are flexible and clear.

Moniliform antennae: Antennae that look like strings of beads.

Mouthparts: Include two pairs of jaws (the mandibles and the maxillae) and other segmented appendages near the jaws used for holding food.

Ovipositor: An egg-laying structure.

Prolegs: Legs on the abdomen that are characteristic of caterpillars and sawflies.

Quiescent: Quiet, still or in a state of arrested development.

Simple eyes: Eyes with only a few facets.

Social insects: Insects that live together in a colony with well-developed castes, e.g., queen, workers, soldiers, etc. The most highly developed of these include the termites, ants, bees and wasps.

Vestigial: A structure with no apparent function that appears to be left over from an earlier stage of evolutionary development.

insect growth regulators (IGRs), trigger the change from one instar to the next. Synthetic versions of these juvenile hormones have been formulated into nontoxic pest control products for preventing the reproduction of fleas, cockroaches and a host of other pest insects. They are discussed on pp. 145-148.

The form the insect takes as it goes from egg to adult defines the type of metamorphosis it undergoes (see the drawing above). Some insects (e.g., silverfish) do not change structural form at all, or change only slightly (e.g., cockroaches) as they pass from young to adult; they merely become larger. Others undergo slight physical changes, as when a wingless nymphal damselfly becomes a winged adult. Still others undergo complete metamorphosis, as when a caterpillar hatches from an egg, spins a cocoon in the pupal stage, then emerges as a moth or butterfly.

In pest management, it is important to recognize these stages because different tactics must be devised for the different stages. Table 1.4 on pp. 20-23 describes the type of metamorphosis various insects undergo, and provides other important information on their form and habits. To keep the table compact, we have used more advanced terminology. The sidebar above provides informal working definitions of terms used in the table. You will undoubtedly begin to learn some of these terms through repetition as you become more experienced in pest control.

Table 1.4
A Synopsis of the Insect Orders [a, b]

Mouthparts	Metamorphosis	Antennae	Wings	Other Characteristics
class and order **Collembola** (springtails) ("coll" = glue; "embol" = wedge)				
chewing	none	46 segments	none	tube-like structure and spring on under surface; simple eyes; primarily decomposers
class and order **Protura** (proturans) ("prot" = first or primary; "ura" = tail)				
sucking	none	absent	none	thought to be fungus feeders; no eyes
class and order **Diplura** (diplurans) ("di" = two or double; "plur" = several)				
chewing	none	34 segments	none	tube-like structure and spring on under surface; no eyes

The Hexapods[c]

Mouthparts	Metamorphosis	Antennae	Wings	Other Characteristics
order **Coleoptera** (beetles) ("coleos" = sheath; "pter" = wing)				
chewing	complete	46 segments	2 pairs	first pair of wings hardened, second pair folded, membranous
order **Dermaptera** (earwigs) ("dermatos" = skin; "pter" = wing)				
chewing	gradual	long	2 pairs	abdomen has forcep-like cerci
order **Dictyoptera** (cockroaches, mantids) ("dicty" = net; "pter" = wing) The original name used for neuropteroids; its use is now established through common usage.				
chewing	gradual	filiform, long, multi-segmented	2 pairs, some wingless	compound eyes; short, multi-segmented cerci
order **Diptera** (flies) ("di" = two; "pter" = wing)				
sucking	complete	variable	1 pair, some wingless	hind wings reduced to knob-like halteres
order **Embioptera** (webspinners) ("embi" = long lived; "pter" = wing)				
chewing	simple	filiform	males 2 pairs, females none	live in silken tunnels; compound eyes; ancient group of insects

[a] With the new system of arthropod classes and orders, three of the more primitive orders now have a dual status as both orders and classes. These are the Collembola, Protura and Diplura.

[b] For definitions of technical terms used in this table, see the sidebar on p. 19.

[c] The summary below this point contains an alphabetical listing of 28 orders and their important distinguishing characteristics. These orders contain an estimated 737 families and 737,810 species. It is an estimate (based on the excellent introductory text by Cedric Gillott, 1980), because no one has made a sufficiently exhaustive count.

Table 1.4 (continued)

Mouthparts	Metamorphosis	Antennae	Wings	Other Characteristics
order **Ephemeroptera** (mayflies) ("ephemero" = for a day; "pter" = wing)				
vestigial	complete	short	2 pairs	abdomen with 2 long cerci and caudal filament; short adult life (hours to days)
order **Grylloblattodea** (rock crawlers) ("gryll" = cricket or grasshopper; "blatt" = an insect that shuns light)				
chewing	gradual	filiform, long	none	multi-segmented cerci; well-developed ovipositor
order **Hemiptera** (true bugs, aphids, scales, mealybugs, whiteflies) ("hemi" = one half; "pter" = wing) Half of the first pair of wings is hard, the other half is soft.				
sucking	gradual	variable	2 pairs, some wingless	this order now includes the orders Homoptera and Heteroptera
order **Hymenoptera** (bees, wasps, ants) ("hymen" = membrane; "pter" = wing)				
chewing	complete	variable	2 pairs	some females have ovipositor modified into a stinger; many groups social
order **Isoptera** (termites, white ants) ("iso" = equal; "pter" = wing)				
chewing	gradual	long, multi-segmented	2 pairs	cerci present; social insects
order **Lepidoptera** (butterflies, moths) ("lepido = scale; "pter" = wing)				
sucking and chewing	complete	variable	2 pairs	adult with coiled sucking mouthparts; larvae with chewing mouthparts
order **Mecoptera** (scorpion flies) ("meco" = long; "pter" = wing)				
chewing	complete	long, filiform in adult; short in larvae	2 pairs, some wingless	short cerci, prominent genitalia in males; larvae caterpillar-like with prolegs
order **Megaloptera** (alderflies, dobsonflies) ("mega" = great; "pter" = wing)				
chewing	complete	long	2 pair	no cerci, no ovipositor; large insects, formerly in order Neuroptera
order **Microcoryphia** (bristletails) ("micro" = small; "corypha" = head)				
chewing	none	long, multi-segmented	none	formerly in the order Thysanura, decomposer community; poorly studied

(continued on page 22)

Table 1.4 (continued)

Mouthparts	Metamorphosis	Antennae	Wings	Other Characteristics
order **Neuroptera** (lacewings, mantispids) ("neuro" = nerve; "pter" = wing)				
chewing	complete	long, filiform in adult; short in larvae	2 pairs	the aquatic species have gills
order **Odonata** (dragonflies, damselflies) ("odont" = tooth—refers to teeth on the mandibles)				
chewing	complete	short	2 pairs, some wingless	large compound eyes; larvae aquatic; well-studied order
order **Orthoptera** (grasshoppers, crickets) ("ortho" = straight; "pter" = wing)				
chewing	gradual	variable	2 pairs, some wingless	front pair wings hardened, hind pair membranous
order **Phasmida** (stick insects) ("phasm" = monster)				
chewing	gradual	variable	2 pairs	many look like their host plants; stick-like or leaf-like
order **Phthiraptera** (lice) ("phthir" = lice; "aptera" = without wings)				
chewing	gradual	short	none	dorsoventrally depressed (flattened); ectoparasites
order **Plecoptera** (stoneflies) ("pleco" = pleated; "pter" = wing)				
chewing	gradual	long, multi-segmented	2 pairs	compound eyes, larvae have gills
order **Psocoptera** (barklice) ("psoco" = to rub away, to grind; "pter" = wing)				
chewing	gradual	long, multi-segmented	2 pairs, some wingless	wings held roof-like, front wing bigger than hind wing; large head
order **Raphidioptera** (snakeflies) ("raphid" = needle-like; "pter" = wing)				
chewing	complete	long	2 pairs	long neck, no cerci; females with ovipositor; similar to Megaloptera
order **Siphonaptera** (fleas) ("siphon" = tube; "aptera" = wingless)				
piercing	complete	short	none	all are parasitic as adults; legs modified for jumping
order **Strepsiptera** (stylopids) ("strep = twisted; "pter" = wing)				
degenerate	complete	conspicuous	2 pairs in males, females wingless	females are parasitic, males free-living

Table 1.4 (continued)

Mouthparts	Metamorphosis	Antennae	Wings	Other Characteristics
order **Thysanoptera** (thrips) ("thysano" = fringe; "pter" = wing)				
rasping/ sucking	intermediate	short to medium	2 pairs, fringed	last 2 to 3 nymphal stages quiescent
order **Trichoptera** (caddis flies) ("tricho" = hair; "pter" = wing)				
vestigial	complete	variable scaled hairs	2 pairs	larvae aquatic, adults airborne
order **Zoraptera** (angel insects) ("zor" = pure, strong, sheer; "aptera" = wingless)				
biting	gradual	moniliform	wingless or winged	no ovipositor, short cerci; gregarious but not social;decomposers
order **Zygentoma** (=Thysanura) (silverfish, firebrats) ("zyg" = joining; "entom" = insect)				
chewing	none, up to 60 molts	long, multi-segmented	none	compound eyes small or absent, simple eyes absent, formerly in Thysanura

SYSTEMS AND ECOSYSTEMS

So far we have emphasized the importance of correctly identifying an organism that you want to manage. If your only interest is in using a pesticide to kill the pest, identifying the organism may be all you need to do. But if your aim is least-toxic pest management—and it should be—it is equally necessary to understand the role the organism plays in relation to the living and nonliving environments in which it is found. We call this larger view of a pest problem an ecosystem perspective. The advantage of taking the ecosystem perspective is that it reveals many pest control options you cannot perceive if you focus on just the pest organism.

The concepts of system and ecosystem are central to our thinking about pest management. When many components are linked together in such a way that something new emerges, we call this new entity a system. For example, your community probably has a system for managing garbage (see the drawing on the next page). Among the individual components of the system are the people who make decisions and/or contribute physical labor, the collection trucks and garbage cans, the sites to which and from which the garbage is taken, and so on. This is not an arbitrary example, even though it may superficially seem so. Systems for managing municipal solid wastes figure prominently in the control of community rat and fly problems, since both pests feed on garbage. In most cities, the rat is a component of the garbage-management system, although not usually an acknowledged or desirable one.

Each component is linked to and affects every other component. If you try to reduce rat problems but focus only on the rat itself, you are left with very few options—generally only poisoning or trapping. But by analyzing the systems of which the rat is a part—the garbage-management system is just one example—the number of options for reducing the rat population becomes large indeed.

By its very definition, everything in a system is connected to every-thing else; thus, changing any of the system components surrounding the pest modifies the problem. For example, you can reduce rat populations by changing the design or placement of individual garbage cans, thereby restricting rat access to food. To accomplish this you can raise the garbage cans more than 18 in. (46 cm) above the ground to prevent rusting and rat access, and you can use spring-fitted lids that stay closed even when the cans are knocked over (dogs regularly knock over garbage cans in urban areas, usually at night). Or you can try modifying the behavior of the people who are responsible for carrying the trash from a school or apartment building. They should be urged to do all they can to empty garbage containers into dumpsters without spilling the contents on the street or playground.

Another alternative involves approaching the decision-makers. Convincing city hall to allocate money for recycling centers and facilities that separate municipal organic wastes and compost them would make food

The Components of a Municipal Garbage-Collection System

This simplified view shows the components of a municipal garbage-collection system. A system is composed of a number of components linked together; a change in one component affects all the others.

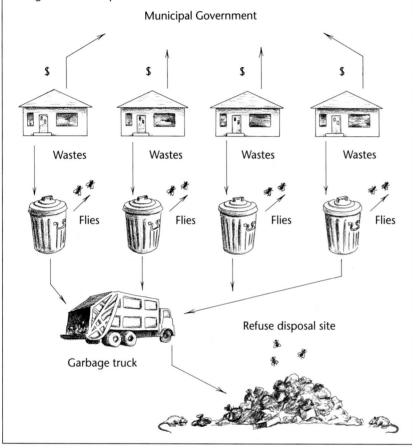

Municipal Government

$

Wastes

Flies

Garbage truck

Refuse disposal site

wastes less available to rats. This is another example of how changing part of the system—in this case, the political component—can influence the pest problem within the system.

The Pest's Ecosystem: At the Core of All Systems Surrounding It

Ecosystems are special types of systems. The largest example of an ecosystem is the planet Earth itself. We might refer to Earth as THE ECOSYSTEM, written in capital letters to distinguish it from the ecosytems with a small "e" that we examine in this book. By ecosystem,

we mean any system that has at least one living component that fixes energy from the sun. For example, if a specific green plant is at the core of a particular ecosystem, that ecosystem includes the animals, fungi and microbes that feed upon that plant and upon each other, as well as the minerals in various forms that cycle through and around these organisms.

To return to the rat example, the rat's ecosystem is at the core of all the other systems that surround it, such as the solid-waste-management system and the political system we discussed. This ecosystem core includes the plants upon which the rat feeds

(growing plants as well as plants in the form of organic wastes from human food), water, the gases in the air and the physical environment that provides the rat with places to nest and hide (see the chart on the facing page). These components of the rat's ecosystem form its life-support system. When any one of these components is changed, the rat's ability to survive is affected.

Modifying Ecosystem Components to Control the Pest

The concept of ecosystems is, of course, tremendously important to us. We now look at how ecosystem components can be manipulated to affect a pest organism.

Limiting Access to Food. Continuing with our example, if we deny the rat access to organic wastes in the garbage can, either by putting on a spring lid or by composting the organic component of the household wastes in a hot aerobic compost (described on p. 644), we manage the rat problem by reducing its life-support system. For example, since Norway, or "sewer," rats (*Rattus norvegicus*) particularly like to feed on wild blackberry bushes and certain species of ivy, reducing or eliminating these plants in the neighborhood reduces the Norway rat population.

Limiting Access to Shelter. To survive, rats need a safe place to hide and build nests. They like to burrow under wood and other debris, or under the cement foundations of buildings. Thus, eliminating piles of debris around the building foundations and placing L-shaped footings around structures are other means of modifying the life-support system to reduce the rat population in an area.

Encouraging Natural Enemies. In addition to its immediate life-support system—food, water and shelter—the rat's ecosystem includes its natural enemies, such as owls, cats, disease organisms and snakes, as well as other rats (with which it competes for space, food and mates). It also includes the natural enemies of its nat-

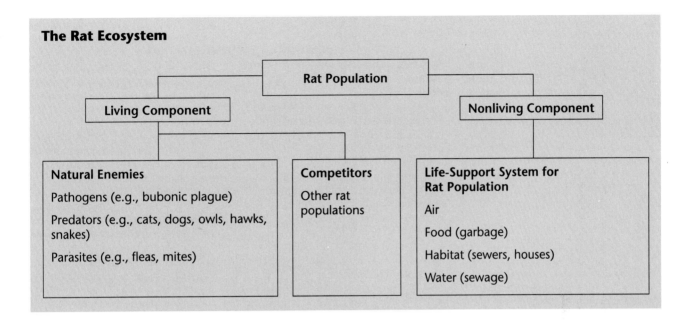

The Rat Ecosystem

Rat Population

Living Component

Nonliving Component

Natural Enemies

Pathogens (e.g., bubonic plague)

Predators (e.g., cats, dogs, owls, hawks, snakes)

Parasites (e.g., fleas, mites)

Competitors

Other rat populations

Life-Support System for Rat Population

Air

Food (garbage)

Habitat (sewers, houses)

Water (sewage)

ural enemies—most often humans and other animals. Encouraging populations of natural rat enemies helps reduce rat numbers. We return to this tactic below.

Limiting Energy. Because the complex food webs within an ecosystem are based on converting the sun's energy into sugars within green plants, and because heat, light and sugars can all be converted to calories, ecologists talk about "energy flow" through a system. They study the paths the energy takes and calculate the amount of energy (often called caloric or food energy) available to organisms within the system.

Returning to the rat example, the amount of energy available to the rat—or any organism that cannot convert the sun's energy directly into sugar—is the energy stored in the food it eats. The rat uses this energy to grow or repair tissue, produce body heat, move its muscles and reproduce. The farther the rat—or any pest—must go to find food (or water, if the pest species cannot get enough water from its food alone), the more of its energy is consumed in locomotion and heat instead of growth and reproduction. So by simply moving the food (the organic garbage, for example) farther away from the organism's preferred habitat (such as within a pile of broken concrete) we can reduce the number of pest organisms in an area.

Reducing the Carrying Capacity of a Site. We have found it useful when analyzing pest management problems to think of the pest's life-support system within its ecosystem and the multitude of human systems that may surround it as a series of concentric circles or boxes. The pest and its life-support system form the core. Around this core are the complex food webs that include the pest's natural enemies. Around these are the many human systems that envelop or support the pest (remember, it is the human value system that defines a "pest" in the first place). Together, these linked systems determine the carrying capacity, or the ability of a particular site to support the pest.

From this concept of carrying capacity come two very basic strategies in least-toxic pest management: reducing the site's carrying capacity with regard to the pest, and increasing its carrying capacity with regard to the pest's natural enemies.

By now, it should be clear that by taking an ecosystem perspective we become aware of the many ways to influence the pest situation and ensure that the role we humans play in the pest system is not overlooked. "Systems thinking," as it is sometimes called, particularly the concept of ecosystem, helps to identify pest control options because it provides a conceptual tool for analyzing the complex environments in which most pest problems occur.

We can now use systems thinking to examine the soundness of some more "conventional" means of pest control. Basic to systems thinking is the fact that minerals and other chemical elements of the air, water, rocks, microbes, plants and animals are continuously cycling on our planet. This is precisely why certain pesticides such as DDT remain toxic to living organisms even when they are broken down into simpler compounds. It also explains why they cause problems far from the site where they were applied and why they damage organisms quite different from those originally targeted.

Since the days when DDT was used in this country, a greater familiarity with the ecosystem perspective among lawmakers and other non-scientists has led to closer scrutiny of all new laboratory-synthesized compounds when they are released in the marketplace. It is now common for people to ask such questions as: Where will this material travel after I use it? Will it enter the water or the air? Are the breakdown products poisonous or benign? The pest control ramifications of this cycling of elements, known as the residue problem, are discussed further on pp. 93-95.

ENERGY AND THE FOOD CHAIN

Energy comes from the sun to this planet, flows through ecosystems and is then gradually lost again to outer space as heat. This phenomenon has important implications for pest management. Ultimately, it helps explain why pests are more abundant than their predators.

Let's return to the example of the rat to see what this means in practical terms. Plants in the rat's ecosystem incorporate some of the sun's energy that falls on the ecosystem. However, not all of that energy is available to the rat that eats the plants. Some of the sun's energy is used by the plants for growing and respiring (the process of taking in oxygen and giving out carbon dioxide) and some is lost as heat. To obtain enough energy for its needs, the rat must eat a great deal of plant material.

The predator that eventually eats the rat—an owl or hawk, for example—does not get all the energy that was in the food the rat ate, either. The rat uses some of that energy to grow and repair body tissues, sheds some in the form of hair and feces, and loses some as heat. So it takes many rodents to support one owl or hawk, which helps explain why a natural area may be able to support many rodents but only a few hawks or owls. Of course energy is not the only factor limiting the predators, but it is an important one.

Trophic Levels: What the Pest Eats and What Eats the Pest

It is also useful to sort ecosystems into their biotic and abiotic components. The abiotic, or nonliving, components of an ecosystem are the sun, air, water and the mineral portion of the soil. The biotic, or living, components are the plants, animals, bacteria and other life forms. Most of our pest problems arise when humans come into conflict with other biotic components. (The notable exceptions are certain human or plant diseases that occur when essential chemical elements—minerals, for example—are unavailable or are improperly metabolized.)

As noted in our example of the rat, when we attempt to determine the place of a living organism in the ecosystem, we are usually asking about its dining habits. What does it eat and by what is it eaten? In other words, we are asking about the food chains and webs of which it is a part and the trophic, or eating, levels on which it functions.

Rats eat almost everything; humans can also digest a wide range of materials. Thus, both rats and humans are omnivorous ("omni" means all and "vore" means eater). We eat both plant and animal matter. This flexibility in eating habits has undoubtedly helped us in our survival, just as it accounts in large part for the success of the rat. Other organisms with cosmopolitan eating habits, such as cockroaches, are equally good at surviving. On the other hand, many organisms with histories as ancient as the cockroach's and futures as rosy as the rat's are far more restricted in their eating habits.

In taking the ecosystem perspective on pest control, it helps to classify the organisms we encounter in and around our homes based on their eating habits (see the chart on the facing page).

Autotrophs ("auto" = self, "troph" = feeding). Autotrophs are the green plants that make their own food in

the presence of sunlight with the aid of air, water and minerals. They include food crops, ornamentals and wild plants both on land and in the sea. When they occur where we don't want them, we call them "weeds." When we think of ecosystems, we generally regard autotrophs as the base of the food web, or the primary level upon which all other life forms ultimately depend. Technically, they are also called primary producers.

Herbivores ("herbi" = grass, "vore" = eater). Herbivores are organisms that eat plants and may live in or on them. Because humans raise plants for sustenance and pleasure, a great many organisms that come into conflict with us fall into this category. But not all do. For those humans who eat meat, the vertebrate herbivores, such as cows, sheep and pigs, are important staples. And most people are aware of the importance of honeybees, which, like silkworms, are among the oldest of the domesticated herbivores. Herbivorous insects also play an important role in the control of weeds, as described in Chapter 27. However, when we think of herbivores in urban settings we are less likely to think of domesticated farm animals and desirable insects than of potential pests, such as caterpillars, gophers and starlings.

A few plant eaters, such as mistletoe, are plants themselves. Mistletoe may be delightful as a Christmas decoration, but foresters consider it a pest because its roots invade the nutrient-conducting tissue of the host tree. The terminology used to describe plants such as mistletoe is confusing. Because of its tree-invading nature, botanists may refer to it as a parasite. But in the popular press the term parasite is commonly used to refer to insects that feed on plants. To confuse things even more, plant pathologists may use parasite to refer to microbes—viruses, bacteria and other organisms—that cause plant disease. In this book we refer to disease-causing microbes as pathogens, we call tissue-invading plants such

A Simplified Ecosystem

This chart shows the relationships among the components of a simplified ecosystem and points out the key roles played by the community of recycling organisms in the maintenance of the ecosystem.

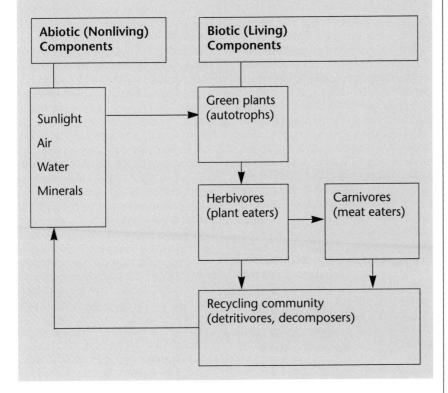

as mistletoe plant parasites, and we reserve the term parasite—or more accurately, parasitoid—for certain organisms that are discussed in the next category.

Carnivores ("carni" = meat, "vore" = eater). Carnivores are organisms that eat humans or other animals and may live in or on them. They can be predators, parasitoids, hyper-parasitoids or pathogens. We used the owl as an example of a carnivore in our rat ecosystem. As with herbivores, this level in the ecosystem contains both pests and beneficial organisms.

Carnivorous insects, mites, nematodes (microscopically small roundworms) and certain microbes play essential roles in the pest management strategy called biological control. From the human point of view, the beneficial microbes are those that cause disease in pest animals. We refer to these microbes as pathogens. Examples of carnivorous beneficial insects are the lady beetles and the small wasps that control many types of insect populations. Biological control is a strategy we want to encourage, and we describe many other beneficial carnivores later in the book. But there are also carnivorous animals we regard as pests, including fleas and scabies mites.

As we mentioned, the word "parasite" is confusing. It means different things to different people. To the general public it has an unpleasant connotation, but to a pest manager who specializes in biological control it usually refers to a beneficial organism that helps control a pest. The term parasite is most accurately used to indicate an organism that lives at the expense of another species (the host) but does not usually kill it. In this book we use the word in that sense only. The human pinworm described on pp. 154-157 is an example of a parasite in this sense of the word. Healthy humans frequently have intestinal parasites common to their geographical area without being aware of it. However, parasites may cause serious health problems in the very young, old or sick, or in travelers unaccustomed to them.

Scientists who study insects now use the term "parasitoid" when referring to beneficial insects that kill their host. This helps avoid confusion with parasites, which coexist with their hosts. Parasitoids are discussed further in the next chapter on biological controls, and again in Chapter 5 on beneficial insects.

In some ecosystems, especially in the sea, the food chains may become quite long before the energy runs out. There are carnivores that eat other carnivores. These are referred to, respectively, as secondary and tertiary carnivores. The highest carnivore—the animal that is eaten only by the detritivores, discussed in the next section—is referred to as the top carnivore.

Humans and predatory birds like the peregrine falcon are examples of top carnivores. Top carnivores may suffer, however, when poisons originally targeted at the autotrophs and herbivores at lower levels of the food chain become more and more concentrated as they move up the food webs until finally the dose ingested by the top carnivore is a damaging one. As we have shown, this occurs because each level of predator eats many prey during its lifetime, getting the cumulative dose of pesticide in all those prey. The next-higher-up

DDD Concentrations in the Clear Lake Food Chain

In Clear Lake in northern California, DDD, one of the breakdown products of DDT, was concentrated in plankton at 265 times its concentration in the lake water. In grebes, the concentration had risen to 80,000 times that of the water. (Source: Flint and van den Bosch, 1977.)

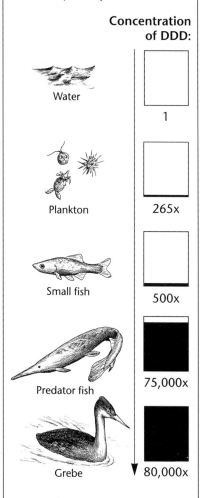

Concentration of DDD:

Water — 1

Plankton — 265x

Small fish — 500x

Predator fish — 75,000x

Grebe — 80,000x

carnivore eats many of these predators, and the cumulative dosage is compounded, as shown in the drawing above. This concentration of pesticide continues right up to the top carnivore, which may be us.

In the field of biological control of insect pests, the secondary carnivore (a parasitic wasp or primary parasitoid) that kills the primary carnivore is called a "hyperparasitoid." Whereas the primary parasitoid is regarded as beneficial because it kills the pest, the hyperparasitoid is regarded as undesirable because it kills the parasitoids of pests. When beneficial parasitoids are imported from other areas to control pests, great efforts are made to avoid importing hyperparasitoids that attack the beneficials. These points, very important to an understanding of naturally occurring and human-manipulated biological control, are discussed more thoroughly in Chapter 4.

Decomposers and Detritivores ("detritus" = decomposed material, "vore" = eater). These organisms, which eat the dead bodies of plants or animals, are some of our most notorious pests, including termites and clothes moths. But without the beneficial action of the myriads of fungi, mites and other organisms that are less easily recognized but also fall into this category, the wheel of life would come to a halt. These creatures, large and small, form the food webs ultimately responsible for breaking down all formerly living things into their original chemical compounds, which can then be used again by plants to build living systems.

The detritivores have a primarily physical effect upon the dead materials, breaking them down into smaller pieces that are not greatly changed from the original, except in size. For example, sowbugs function largely as detritivores; so does a dog when it breaks up a bone. In creating smaller pieces, these animals make more surface area available to true decomposers, which include many bacteria and fungi. Decomposers are the organisms that actually change the materials chemically, reducing them to simpler compounds. Eventually, the compounds are broken down to their basic constituents and can be absorbed by plant roots as nutrients.

Omnivores ("omni" = all, "vore" = eater). These are the organisms that eat living and dead plants, animals and/or their products. Some organisms deserve this designation because they feed on all three trophic levels: living plants, living animals and the dead bodies of the same. The Argentine ant *(Iridomyrmex humilis)* is a good example. It feeds on plant nectaries (non-flower plant glands that secrete nectar), flowers for nectar and pollen, and honeydew, a sweet deposit secreted onto the leaves of some plants by insects such as aphids, scales and mealybugs. It also feeds on many soil insects and the fly larvae that live in decomposing organic materials. And it eats dead insects and carrion. It will even cannibalize its own colonies when times get tough.

Another example is the skunk, which feeds on plant fruits, dead carcasses and living insects. So do rats and humans, as mentioned earlier. Even vegetarians may inadvertently eat an insect or insect part now and then, since many bugs are too small to notice!

THE ECOSYSTEM PERSPECTIVE: SUMMARY REVIEW

Why is it helpful to understand a pest's place in the local ecosystem (which may be your own kitchen, basement or lawn)? It is helpful because everything is connected to everything else. Knowing what a pest feeds upon, what feeds upon it and what other conditions are favorable or unfavorable to its survival reveals a multitude of strategies for influencing the pest's presence or absence.

By contrast, traditional pest control has been severely hampered by its narrow focus on the pest organism alone. If the pest organism is all you consider, your only options are to endure it or directly repel, remove or kill it. Traditional pest control techniques fall into just those categories.

By taking an ecosystem perspective, you can usually find a multitude of ways to affect the pest indirectly by modifying or removing conditions that support it, or by creating situations that encourage its natural controls. As you can see, the target organism is at the center, with the abiotic and biotic components of the ecosystem surrounding it, the human activities that maintain the ecosystem surrounding those and the sociopolitical realities of the larger society as the context in which all these systems occur.

The important fact to remember is this: Changing any one of the components in a system affects all the other components to some degree. That alone makes it plain that there must be numerous ways to achieve the objective of pest suppression besides spraying with a poison. This book emphasizes the many pest management options—some subtle and some obvious—that an ecosystem approach reveals.

REFERENCES AND READINGS

Arnett, R.H. 1985. *American insects: a handbook of the insects of America north of Mexico.* New York: Van Nostrand Reinhold. 850 pp.

An excellent, authoritative source of information on the subject.

Borror, D.J., D.M. Delong and C.A. Triplehorn. 1976. *An introduction to the study of insects.* New York: Holt, Rinehart and Winston. 852 pp.

This has been the standard entomology text for college students since the 1950s. Although often referred to as "boring and too long" by disrespectful students (a play on the senior authors' names), it is in fact fascinating reading for those who really want to learn about insects and a necessary reference for the budding amateur entomologist's library.

Borror, D.J., and R.E. White. 1970. *A field guide to the insects of America north of Mexico.* Boston: Houghton Mifflin. 403 pp.

This is part of the Peterson Field Guide series and contains a good section on collecting and preserving insects. It includes pictures, keys and descriptions of families and common individual insect species.

Carr, A. 1979. *Rodale's color handbook of garden insects.* Emmaus, Pa.: Rodale Press. 241 pp.

A useful tool for identifying pests and beneficials alike. Contains over 300 color photos of common garden insects.

Flint, M.L., and R. van den Bosch. 1977. *A source book on integrated pest management.* Oakland: University of California Press. 391 pp.

This was the source of the drawing on p. 28 showing concentrations of DDD in a lake in northern California.

Gillott, C. 1980. *Entomology.* New York: Plenum Press. 729 pp.

An introductory entomology text that discusses anatomy, physiology, systematics and relations of insects to humans. It includes a key to the orders and brief summaries of the taxonomic changes and arrangement of the classes, orders, superfamilies and families of insects.

Johnson, W.T., and H.H. Lyon. 1988. *Insects that feed on trees and shrubs.* Ithaca, N.Y.: Cornell University Press. 556 pp.

This book is the best tool a gardener can have for learning to recognize pest insects that attack trees and shrubs. Over 900 species and their damage symptoms are depicted in excellent color photos that facilitate identification by the layperson.

Lanham, U. 1968. *Origins of modern biology.* New York: Columbia University Press. 273pp.

A readable history of the development of modern biology.

Margulis, L., and K.V. Schwartz. 1982. *Phyla of the five kingdoms: an illustrated guide to the kinds of life on earth.* San Francisco: W.H. Freeman. 338 pp.

An in-depth presentation of the five-kingdom model of life on the planet for the layperson and college student. It contains well-illustrated, well-referenced introductions to each of the groups presented.

Storer, T.I, and R.L. Usinger. 1965. *General zoology.* 4th ed. New York: McGraw Hill. 741 pp.

An introductory text that has stood the passage of time very well. It was our source for information on many non-insect arthropods.

Wilcox, J.A. 1972. *Entomology projects for elementary and secondary schools.* Albany: The University of the State of New York (New York State Museum and Science Service Bulletin 422). 44 pp.

An excellent booklet with fine, explicit line drawings, good projects and an intelligent text that includes a simple key to winged insects.

CHAPTER 2
Natural Pest Controls

INTRODUCTION

In this chapter we look at the balance of nature and some of the fundamental ways in which living organisms control their own populations as well as populations of other living organisms. Obviously, when we look at all living organisms we are including that subset of organisms we regard as "pests." Therefore, included in this chapter is an examination of truly natural pest control—pest control that occurs in nature without any prompting from humankind. We humans have disturbed this great system and must now learn how to re-establish its effects.

Many of the micro-environments in which pest problems occur today are at least partially human-made or controlled, but the biological principles at work are still dictated by nature. Thus, understanding the natural principles discussed here will aid you tremendously in managing pest problems. Furthermore, many of the concepts in this chapter are critical to the development of a successful integrated pest management program, the subject of the next chapter.

Many animal and plant populations are capable of expanding very rapidly. For example, crabgrass (*Digitaria* spp.) can produce 2,000 seeds per square foot in a single season. The common housefly can lay 600 eggs, which mature in about six days in hot weather. Given that reproductive rate, over the course of one summer one original pair of flies could eventually lead to a layer of flies thousands of feet thick around the entire planet.

This has never happened, of course, because insects, like all other animal and plant populations, are under natural controls. The most important controls are climate and weather, food and habitat, pathogens (disease-causing organisms), predators, parasites and parasitoids. We now examine each of these factors in turn.

CLIMATE AND WEATHER

Climate is the long-term overview of temperature and humidity changes in a region; weather is the local and short-term variation in climate. Extremes of heat, cold, rainfall, dew or fog can limit a living population and influence its seasonal distribution. For example, whether the tomato hornworm is a pest in your area may be a function of climate, since warm summers favor the hornworm. But the weather in a given year—wet or dry—will determine whether the hornworm breaks out early or late in the season, and, to some extent, how large the outbreak is.

With many insects, warm weather speeds maturation from larvae to adult; cool weather retards it. Thus, weather can influence how quickly a population builds. Green bottle flies illustrate this well. As long as there is ample food, the flies can progress from egg to adult and be ready to mate and lay new eggs in as few as six days if the temperature is over 95°F (35°C). Practically speaking, this means that in the summertime a generation can easily mature in the garbage can between refuse collections without the householder being aware of it, particularly if garbage collection occurs only once a week.

FOOD AND HABITAT

Food and habitat can also be important limiting factors upon the growth of a pest population. It is obvious that without food, no organism can survive. Yet, when confronted with a pest problem, it is not always so obvious that limiting the pest's access to food can be the simplest nontoxic method of control.

For example, clothes moths eat animal-produced fibers such as wool and feathers. By placing garments made of these materials in sealed plastic bags when the clothes are not being worn, and by vacuuming cracks and crevices where pet hair and lint from clothes accumulate, you deny the moths food. The less food available to the moths, the fewer moths and problems with moths you will have (moth problems are discussed in detail on pp. 196-203).

There are many other pest control tactics that are based on the premise that food is a limiting factor. For example, placing nuts and grains in rubber-sealed jars keeps out kitchen pests, and setting the pet food dish in a larger bowl containing soapy water creates a "moat" that denies ants, cockroaches and other insects access to the food.

To a pest, availability of habitat is as important as food. For example, in some areas of California the ash aphid (*Prociphilus fraxinifolii*) is a common pest on Modesto ash trees. For reasons not entirely clear, the aphids' preferred habitat is the sucker growth around the base of the tree as well as suckers that grow from the trunk within the inner tree canopy. When these suckers are pruned away, the remaining aphid population may be so small as to be rarely noticed.

On the other hand, if the main outer branches are pruned severely in such a way as to encourage rapid, extensive sucker growth in the canopy, the pest problem may become severe. The aphids will curl up in the leaves and shower honeydew on cars and sidewalks beneath the trees. (Honeydew is a sticky substance derived from the sap of the tree and excreted by the aphids. It is as harmless to animals and plants as maple syrup, but the mold that grows on it may harm the finish on vehicles.)

The nutrient balance within a plant may also affect the selection of habitat by plant-feeding insects. Deciduous tree insects, such as the aphid just described, may go through two population peaks each season. These correspond to the periods when nitrogen levels are highest in the foliage. The first peak occurs in spring when the leaves unfold; the second comes in fall when the leaves are ready to drop. The insects need the nitrogen to form new tissue and produce young. It is important to bear this in mind when you use nitrogen-containing fertilizer, since you may unintentionally encourage aphids and other nitrogen-loving pests.

PATHOGENS

The effect of disease-causing pathogens on human populations over the centuries has been chronicled in *Plagues and Peoples* (listed under "References and Readings" on p. 36), in which William McNeill writes: "One can properly think of most human lives as caught in a precarious equilibrium between the microparasitism of disease organisms and the macroparasitism of large-bodied predators, chief among which have been other human beings." Overpopulation, leading to resource depletion, malnutrition and competition for habitat, has always led to disease and war, and clearly this model was well worked out in the plant and animal kingdoms before humans evolved.

That plants and animals commonly die of disease without human intervention is obvious to gardeners (see the drawing below). It is the basis for the folk pest control recipe for grinding up sick or dead insects and spraying the bug juice to spread the pathogens (microorganisms that cause disease) and kill more pest insects. However, spraying homemade bug juice around your house may not be a good idea, since some microorganisms and fungi found on the dead bodies of insects are pathogenic to humans and might get into the "juice." But the idea of using microbes that cause disease in plants and insects to control pests is not a bad one. A number of such microbial

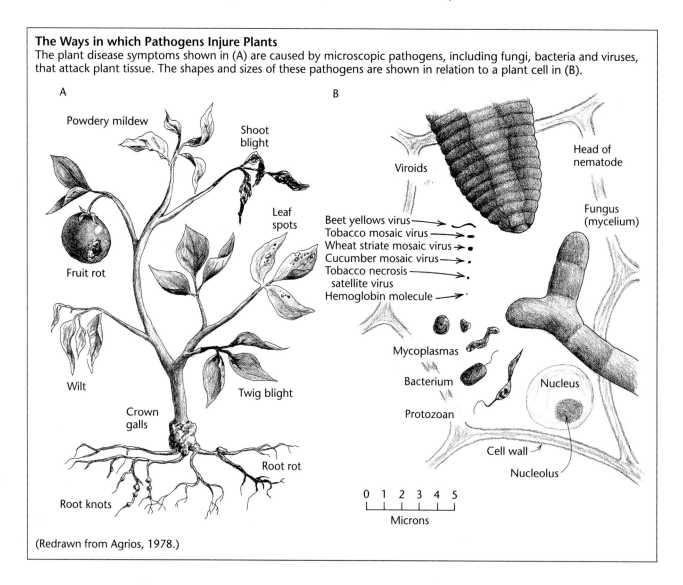

The Ways in which Pathogens Injure Plants
The plant disease symptoms shown in (A) are caused by microscopic pathogens, including fungi, bacteria and viruses, that attack plant tissue. The shapes and sizes of these pathogens are shown in relation to a plant cell in (B).

A

Powdery mildew
Shoot blight
Leaf spots
Fruit rot
Wilt
Twig blight
Crown galls
Root rot
Root knots

B

Viroids
Head of nematode
Beet yellows virus
Tobacco mosaic virus
Wheat striate mosaic virus
Cucumber mosaic virus
Tobacco necrosis satellite virus
Hemoglobin molecule
Fungus (mycelium)
Mycoplasmas
Bacterium
Nucleus
Protozoan
Cell wall
Nucleolus

0 1 2 3 4 5
Microns

(Redrawn from Agrios, 1978.)

products are available commercially. They are examined in detail in Chapter 7 and are mentioned throughout the book where they are applicable as controls for specific pests.

PREDATORS

Predators are often critical in the suppression of natural populations of animals and plants. Together with pathogens and parasitoids, they make up the fascinating study of biological control, discussed in greater detail in Chapter 4.

For the purpose of this book, predators, which can be mammals, arthropods or microorganisms such as fungi (see the drawing on the facing page), are defined as free-living, general feeders. Predators may eat a single prey at a meal, as do peregrine falcons when they feed on pigeons, or coyotes when they eat mice. Or they may consume many individuals, as does the convergent lady beetle *(Hippodamia convergens).*

The problem with predators such as lady beetles as pest control agents is that they frequently skim off the top of an abundant pest population, then move on without providing sufficient pest suppression. In enclosed environments such as screened greenhouses, however, their effectiveness can be substantial.

Predatory insects in the larval (worm, grub or nymph) stage often must consume several prey to attain maturity. Therefore, predator adults usually lay their eggs near populations of their prey, where the hatching young have a good chance of obtaining adequate food.

Spiders are an exception to this rule, however. They are among the most important predators of insects, and their role in controlling insect pests is often under-appreciated by humans. Rather than lay eggs near prey populations, many web-building spiders establish themselves in an environment in which their prey is likely to encounter them by accident. For example, one spider species likes to construct its webs over the holes of inverted flowerpots. Insects emerging from pupation in the soil fly toward the light and are caught by the spider as they come through the hole. Other spiders hunt by night, stalking their prey.

PARASITES AND PARASITOIDS

The difference between parasitoids, which are parasite-like organisms, and parasites is that parasitoids kill their hosts whereas parasites do not. Hence parasitoids provide more effective pest control. An example of an internal parasite is the ubiquitous pinworm (*Enterobius vermicularis* — see pp. 154-157), a common pest of young children. While the symptoms are annoying and in severely malnourished children may have serious consequences, they often come and go unnoticed and are not thought of as causing a serious affliction. Parasites cannot regulate a pest population, but they can debilitate it.

Parasitoids are the unsung heroes of naturally occurring insect pest control. Because they often are so tiny, their presence is generally not recognized and their effect is undervalued. They frequently have no common names, and their scientific names are long and difficult to pronounce and spell, so it is often hard to remember them even when they are noticed. We discuss them here at slightly greater length than predators because of their importance and the fact that they are generally not well known.

Many parasitoids are members of the insect order Hymenoptera, along with bees and wasps. Indeed, they look like minute wasps, and are called miniwasps. Parasitoids often provide good control of an insect population, even when the pest is present at very low densities, because many parasitoids are restricted in the number of species they can attack. Thus, they are called host-specific.

The advantage of host-specific parasitoids is that when they do find a population of the pest, they attempt to kill every last one they encounter. The adult parasitoid aggressively searches for prey. Unless it is confined to a cage with the pests, however, it never finds every last one. There are always a few prey that escape the parasitoid or wander in from outside the immediate area. This is not necessarily a bad thing. These prey reproduce and maintain enough of a population to ensure that the beneficial parasitoids have something to eat; otherwise the parasitoids would perish. Under ideal conditions, populations of parasitoid and prey rise and fall in natural cycles, just like local populations of coyotes and rabbits.

As shown in the drawing on p. 34. a common parasitoid life cycle starts with an adult female miniwasp laying her egg in or on another insect. Various parasitoids lay their eggs at various stages of the host's development. For example, one parasitoid lays its eggs in the eggs of the elm leaf beetle, another lays its eggs in the pupa (cocoon) stage. These parasitoids do not attack any other insect species; hence, they are species-specific and stage-specific biological controls.

Parasitoids such as those in the family Aphelinidae may feed upon and kill several aphids while selecting the one in which to lay an egg. They operate like predators, wounding the host with an egg-laying stinger without depositing an egg. They then feed on this wound, killing their host. This is called host-feeding.

Some parasitoids lay many eggs in or on the body of the host; others lay only one. Either way, the eggs develop into maggot-like larvae that begin to eat away at the prey and sooner or later cause its death. After killing the host, the larva of the miniwasp changes into a pupa. Aphid parasitoids may do this within the body of the aphid. These dead, parasitized aphids can be spotted easily among a colony of living ones because they are usually stiff, shiny and of a slightly different color than the live ones.

Other parasitoids may leave the dead host to spin a cocoon nearby.

Parasitoids of Insects

Parasitoids attack their hosts by laying eggs on or inside a specific developmental stage of the insect: egg, larva, pupa or adult. For example, *Tetrastichus galerucae* (A) lays its egg inside the egg stage of the elm leaf beetle, where it hatches and eats the beetle embryo. *Aphidius* species parasitoids (B) lay their eggs inside the adult stage of aphids. The egg develops into a larva, which eats the aphid from the inside, metamorphoses into an adult, cuts a hole in the dead aphid's body and then emerges (C). You can recognize a parasitized aphid by its hard, shiny body and the hole in its posterior.

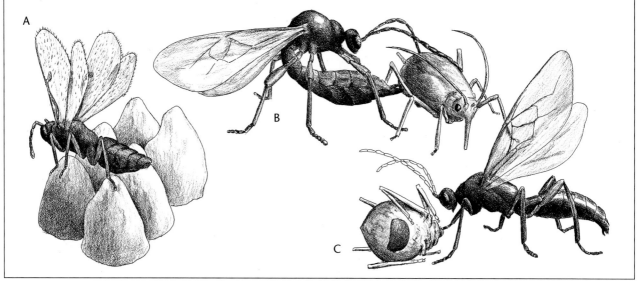

Within the pupal case, the insect changes, or metamorphoses, from a maggot-like form to a wasp-like adult form, as a caterpillar changes to a butterfly. In some species of parasitoids the newly emerged female adults must find males to mate with before they can lay fertile eggs, starting the cycle again; with others, mating is unnecessary, and with still others, males are unknown or are rarely found. We offer further details on these beneficial insects in Chapter 5.

For the layperson, the only clue that these fascinating natural controls exist may be the sight of a dead insect with tiny pinholes in it where the parasitoids have emerged. This is frequently seen in aphids and scales. Sometimes, too, a child will put a caterpillar cocoon or other insect in a jar, only to find some quite different and unexpected insects inside the jar later. These are the natural enemies of the original specimen that have emerged as adults to search for prey.

HOW NATURAL CONTROLS WORK

If natural controls are so great, why aren't they working, you may feel inclined to ask if you are battling some damaging or annoying pest. The answer is that natural controls do work, all the time. In fact, the number of species of plant-feeding insects is so great, and the number of individuals in each species so large that if most of these herbivores were not under good natural control they would have denuded the earth of plant life long ago, making their own further survival—along with ours—impossible. However, at certain times in certain places, specific insect, plant or animal populations grow so large that they become a problem. Why?

One reason is that sometimes their predators and parasitoids cannot find them. For example, aphids, mealybugs, whiteflies and spider mites can become a problem when plants are kept indoors, as discussed

in Part 6 of this book. If the house plants are set outdoors for a few days during warm weather, however, the natural enemies of the pests may find them and clean up the infestation.

All animal and herbaceous plant pest populations tend to fluctuate, rising and falling due to the natural controls we have just discussed (see the graph on the facing page). This fluctuation is particularly noticeable among insects. Occasionally, a native insect will become numerous enough outdoors during one or more seasons to cause aesthetic or economic damage. Then the outbreak will subside due to natural controls and the insect may hardly be noticed for a few or many years. Examples of insects that are famous for this kind of fluctuation are the southern pine beetle, eastern tent caterpillars and caterpillars of the gypsy moth and California oak moth. These insects do have pathogens, parasitoids and predators that usually keep them in check as

The Balance of Populations in Nature

Populations of all living organisms fluctuate in size over the short term. But over the long term—seasons or years—the average population size remains fairly stable.

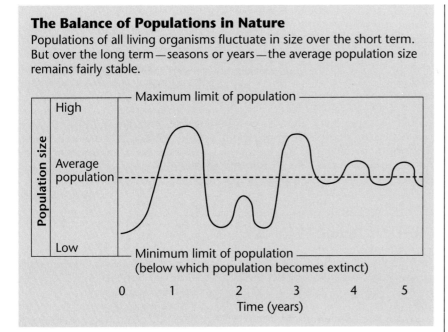

long as the plants they live on are not routinely treated with broad-spectrum insecticides.

Even with these natural controls, however, the populations of herbivores periodically rise to great numbers. For example, a native shade-tree insect such as the California oak moth is capable of completely defoliating oak trees during the one or two seasons when its populations are high. If this happens on trees near the house or in other highly visible locations, people may become upset, either because they believe something is wrong if the tree isn't green, or because they object to the sight of the caterpillars and their droppings. An infestation of this sort is hard to accept as a natural phenomenon.

Examining the California oak moth situation a little more, we see that the defoliation just described occurs in California's dry season, and thus reduces water loss through the leaves of these trees. Furthermore, the caterpillars process the leaves, which in many California native oak species are otherwise very slow to decompose. When the caterpillars eat the leaves, they leave behind their own droppings, a kind of "caterpillar manure" that releases the nutrients back to the tree when winter rains come. Thus, periodic defoliation of these native oaks may actually be more beneficial than harmful.

Similarly, deeper investigation into the rise and fall of other native animal pests usually reveals that these fluctuations are part of a natural cycle of events in their ecosystems. Consequently, we need to learn more about the ecological role these "pests" are playing, and adjust our aesthetic opinions and reactions accordingly.

A native insect population may fluctuate from year to year, but the invasion of a foreign insect may result in high populations every year. Our common indoor cockroaches, the gypsy moth, the Japanese beetle and the Mediterranean fruit fly are pests of exotic origin made familiar to nearly all citizens through first-hand experience or media attention. In these cases, the invading insect has usually left its most important natural enemies behind in its native area. Although in some cases predators and parasitoids of closely related insects may consume small numbers of the new invaders, the absence of specific controls usually permits the introduced species to reach population levels regarded as aesthetically or economically damaging.

Other well-known examples of introduced pests are the pathogens that cause Dutch elm disease and chestnut blight; rapidly spreading plants such as dandelions, kudzu and water hyacinth; and vertebrates like the English sparrow and the common rat and house mouse. In fact, as you will see throughout this book, many of our most serious pest problems arise through accidental—and occasionally deliberate but misguided—introductions of exotic species.

Another factor that may account for high pest populations on a particular plant is its greater genetic susceptibility to the pest than related strains or the plant's wild ancestors. "Old roses," for example, are far more disease-resistant than modern hybrid tea roses. In general, as traits that satisfy particular human desires and tastes are bred into vegetables, a number of traits that served to discourage insect attack may be eliminated. Strong oils, terpines, resins and hairiness are examples of such traits. A similar loss of pest resistance may occur as ornamentals are bred for aesthetic characteristics. As the new variety is developed, little or no emphasis is placed on retaining the plant's resistance to insects, pathogens and other pests.

Potential pest populations also may be encouraged, or their natural enemies discouraged, by attempting to grow a particular variety of plant in an environment not suited to it. It may simply be too hot, cold, wet or dry for the plant compared to its native home. Stressed by the new environment, the plant may be more susceptible to insect attack or less able to overcome insect damage when it occurs. For example, a London plane tree (Platanus acerifolia) planted in an unfavorable site is far more susceptible to anthracnose disease caused by the fungus *Gnomonia platani* than it would be if it were planted in a more favorable setting.

In horticultural plantings, species from many continents are often combined in close proximity, frequently with insufficient consideration of their individual native requirements. Even less thought is given to the requirements of the natural enemies of potential pests of the plant species selected. For example, free water from sprinklers, dew and other sources during dry periods, and nectar and pollen from shallow-throated flowers are required by parasitic insects, particularly the tiny ichneumonid wasps that parasitize many caterpillar species. Without this liquid and protein, the lives of many natural pest enemies are shortened, allowing pest numbers to rise. Given the wide lack of attention to the importance of natural controls and the details of how they relate to specific pest problems, it is not surprising that a stable mix of insect and other wildlife populations is rarely achieved in human-contrived landscapes.

Finally, the methods used to deal with pests may themselves cause the problem to become worse, or they may create entirely new problems. These undesirable results of human actions—which we hope to help you avoid—are discussed throughout the book under specific pest problems.

REFERENCES AND READINGS

Agrios, G.N. 1988. *Plant pathology.* San Diego: Academic Press. 803 pp.

This comprehensive text on plant diseases provides in-depth background on how pathogens attack plants. It is essential reading for anyone who wants to maximize the use of non-chemical controls for plant diseases.

Huffaker, C.B., and P.S. Messenger. 1976. *Theory and practice of biological control.* New York: Academic Press. 788 pp.

As well as reviewing the history and application of biological controls, this book contains an excellent discussion of biological control theory, especially the balance-of-nature concept.

McNeill, W.H. 1976. *Plagues and peoples.* Garden City, N.Y.: Anchor Press/Doubleday. 369 pp.

A marvelous history of the world that describes the impact on humans of infectious diseases and pests such as rats and lice.

CHAPTER 3
Introduction to Integrated Pest Management (IPM)

INTRODUCTION

In Chapter 2 we looked at some of the ways in which various organisms manage and control each other and themselves in nature. That understanding will help you immeasurably as you approach specific pest problems in and around your home. Chapter 2 was also important in showing you that many of the techniques used in integrated pest management—a fancy, new-sounding term—are in fact nothing new at all. We are simply borrowing and adapting processes that have existed in nature since time immemorial. With that in mind, we introduce the concept of integrated pest management, the cornerstone of this book.

WHAT IS IPM?

Integrated pest management, or IPM, is an approach to pest control that utilizes regular monitoring to determine if and when treatments are needed and employs physical, mechanical, cultural, biological and educational tactics to keep pest numbers low enough to prevent intolerable damage or annoyance. Least-toxic chemical controls are used as a last resort.

In IPM programs, treatments are not made according to a predetermined schedule; they are made only when and where monitoring has indicated that the pest will cause unacceptable economic, medical or aesthetic damage. Treatments are chosen and timed to be most effective and least disruptive to natural pest controls. The strategies for managing specific pests outlined later in this book are based on the IPM concept.

IPM, developed initially for agriculture, provides a process for identifying and reducing the factors causing pest problems; it is also designed to determine whether the cost of a particular pest management action is worth the result. Determining economic damage to a crop, where you have yield amounts and marketplace returns against which to measure re-

sults, is relatively straightforward. But putting a dollar amount on the revulsion or fear caused by a particular organism or on the media-inspired need for a "perfect lawn" is much more difficult. You must ask yourself whether preventing the damage is worth exposing your family and pets to the potentially health-impairing chemicals in "conventional" pesticides, or, alternatively, whether you are willing to put the requisite time and effort into less-toxic alternatives.

Clearly these are not straightforward questions, because both the costs and the benefits are harder to quantify than in traditional agriculture. Even in agriculture, the evaluation is becoming more difficult as costs that once were considered external to production—groundwater contamination, pesticide residues on and in food, regulatory requirements, educational activities, the purchase and use of safety equipment, occupational exposure to toxic materials—are beginning to be factored into the calculations.

The kinds of pest problems, the environments in which they occur and the personal values and community standards of those experiencing the problems vary enormously and change over time. The best we can do in this book is introduce you to some evaluative criteria and sources of information that will help you make up your own mind about when pest control is warranted and which methods to use. Ultimately, the decision about what is tolerable, either in terms of pest numbers or exposure to potentially hazardous materials, is yours. These decisions are not so very different from deciding whether you want to allow smoking in your house or whether riders in your car must buckle their seat belts.

PEST OR GUEST?

The question of when an organism becomes a pest is central to IPM. In *Unbidden House Guests* (listed under "References and Readings" on pp. 44-45), the brilliant, if eccentric, German pest management specialist Hugo Hartnack eloquently and sometimes humorously points out the thin line between when a specific creature is a valued member of the household and when it is despised. For example, the pet mouse is adored, but as a pantry visitor it is abhorred. Mealworms are purchased to feed tropical fish, but when they are found in the flour they precipitate a domestic crisis. In Hartnack's words, "No animal in itself is a pest. The way each of us feels about a visitor determines whether the animal is welcome or not, whether it is a pet or a pest, or, in the old Latin words, *hospes* or *hostis*, a guest or a foe."

A number of classic cases demonstrate how the same species may be regarded differently by various groups of people in the same society. This can precipitate lawsuits, legislative intervention and media attention. For example, during the 1970s when we were consultants to the National Park Service, we learned of a situation where the politically powerful and wealthy members of a suburban golf club adjacent to one of the parks petitioned the park to undertake mosquito control in a stream that bordered both properties. Club members complained that they were being bitten while pursuing their favorite recreational activities.

The Park Service proposed solving the problem by killing mosquito larvae in the stream with the microbial insecticide *Bacillus thuringiensis*, toxic only to mosquitoes and blackflies. When local farmers and low-income residents in the area learned about the plan, however, they vociferously opposed it and threatened to sue. Mosquito larvae were the primary source of food for the fish local residents caught to supplement their diet. Although Park Service personnel were conscientious in their choice of the least-toxic method of pest control, and were trying their best to be sensitive to the needs of all parties involved, the incident received much local press coverage that did not always cast the Park Service in the most favorable light.

It is plain from this and many other examples that we will discuss later in the book that there are few intrinsic characteristics that universally distinguish "good" from "bad" species of plants and animals. It is the human social context in which the organisms exist that determines whether a population is pestiferous. Moreover, it is almost always the size of that population, not merely the presence of an individual organism, that matters.

IS THE DAMAGE TOLERABLE?

Whether or not an organism is viewed as a pest is really an issue of whether its damage or annoyance is considered tolerable. Thus, when someone reports to us that they have observed a "pest" in their environment, our first impulse is to ask, "How bad is the damage," or, "How badly are you bothered by it?" As we just mentioned, it is important to realize that there is almost always some tolerable level of a pest population—even with organisms such as rats that are known to pose medical and public health risks. For most pest problems you are likely to experience, complete elimination of the pest is neither economically nor biologically feasible. Even if it were, the cost of eradication in terms of human health and environmental contamination would be prohibitive. Thus, the question of how large a pest population can or should be tolerated is a very important and practical one.

For example, a few fleas on the family dog are likely to be accepted as inevitable. But enough fleas to cause skin irritation on the pet or on us is more than most of us will tolerate. Cockroaches may be present in

the apartment house where you live, even though you do not see them. They are extremely light-shy and normally conceal themselves in small cracks or cluster in areas where you may rarely venture. The boiler room is a good example. But once you begin seeing them in the elevator or in your kitchen, you may become upset and want to do something about them. In this case, the mere fact that you are seeing the roaches is a sign that the population is large, since competition for food and space is causing them to brave the light and search for new territory. A pest manager would say that the roaches had risen above the tolerance level.

TYPES OF INJURY OR DAMAGE CAUSED BY PESTS

The broad categories of pest injury or damage include economic damage, medical damage, aesthetic damage and nuisance problems.

Economic Damage

Economic damage is most easily assessed in agriculture, forestry and similar occupational settings where pest activity affects the production of economic goods. Examples in and around the home might include boards that are so termite-eaten they must be replaced, cabbage seedlings that wilt and die from cabbage maggot infestations in the roots, a valuable wall hanging that has been destroyed by clothes moths or an old elm in your front yard that dies from Dutch elm disease, reducing the value of your property.

Medical Damage

Even in the United States, there remain serious pathogens that can be transmitted to humans by common wildlife. For example, the bubonic plague bacillus can be passed from certain wild rodents to humans, cats and domestic rats via species of fleas that carry the bacteria or through the coughs or sneezes of infected animals. Ground squirrels, chipmunks

and wild rabbits can also pass plague bacilli to humans.

The spirochete that causes Lyme disease is passed from wild mice, lizards and deer to cats, dogs and farm animals and thence to humans. In this case, the disease vector (the organism that transmits the pathogen causing the disease) is a tick. (See pp. 272-273 for more about ticks and Lyme disease.) Mosquitoes can transmit encephalitis and may pick up malaria brought in by travelers from areas of the world where it is common. Even the ubiquitous pigeon can spread the causal agents of histoplasmosis (an internal fungus infection), toxoplasmosis (an affliction of the central nervous system) and a host of other nasty pathogens. As you can see, the potential for passing pathogens to humans and domestic animals may be reason enough to control certain otherwise desirable wildlife species.

Aesthetic Damage

Aesthetic damage occurs when the mere presence of a plant or animal causes an undesirable change in the appearance of something. What constitutes an undesirable change is highly personal—one person may be repelled by a head of cabbage with signs of insect damage on its outer leaves while another finds it a welcome indication that the food is probably not covered with poisonous pesticide residues.

Concerns about aesthetic damage are in part a reflection of two prevalent attitudes in our society: the perception that nature is messy and needs to be cleaned up by humans in order to look beautiful, and a fear or lack of understanding of the natural world. For example, we don't like to see a leaf with a hole in it or a damaged bud, yet the plant itself may easily tolerate that damage without a significant loss of health. Many pest problems affecting ornamental plants fall into this category.

Sometimes the chief aesthetic complaint is the appearance of the pest itself. Insects and spiders often fall victim to this aesthetic judgment. Even though most spiders can be counted on to kill insect pests such as garbage flies in the house and plant-eating pests in the garden, many people kill them on sight simply because they find their appearance unappealing. Another example is the boxelder bug (see the drawing below), which some people simply don't like to look at despite the fact that it causes negligible damage to plants.

In some cases, people are frightened because insects like the boxelder bug are found massed together on walls, under foundation plantings or in other locations. Perhaps movies

The Boxelder Bug
The boxelder bug *(Leptocoris trivittatus)* is an example of a harmless organism that is nonetheless considered a pest. Its tendency to aggregate en masse on the exterior of homes near female boxelder trees, where it feeds on the seeds, makes some people fearful of it despite its harmlessness.

of insects attacking en masse have led people to fear large numbers of even innocuous organisms. We have observed that a small infestation of tent caterpillars can cause near hysteria in some persons.

Often it is the fear of future damage that causes concern. For example, although most aphids only feed on plants in one or a few closely related genera, some people worry that the aphids on their maple tree (genus *Acer)* will move onto their roses (genus *Rosa)* and damage the blossoms. Learning about the biology and ecology of the pest in question usually relieves these fears.

Sometimes the aesthetic problem is a product of the animal's activity. A dusty spider web along the ceiling (a sign that the web is no longer in use), aphids' honeydew drips on a parked car or scales on a tree are all examples. These problems can be solved by cleaning away the offending evidence but leaving the animal alone. That way the spider can continue to catch houseflies and other indoor pests, and the aphids can remain as food for the predators that keep the aphids and other plant-sucking insects under control.

In extreme cases, the fear engendered by the mere sight of insects can turn an aesthetic problem into a medical one, called entomophobia. This condition is surprisingly common. Public health personnel, who must sort out the real from the imaginary, recount many examples of people who complain that their houses are infested with insects and that they are being attacked and bitten repeatedly. But careful sleuthing fails to turn up any offending organism. Luckily, fear of insects—like other phobias—can be cured. In one case, we were able to help someone overcome a mild case of entomophobia simply by giving her a paper we had written on the subject.

Nuisance Problems
Because cities were created for humans with little thought to the wildlife and domestic animals that colonize such areas, many annoying pest problems arise when these three groups of animals attempt to coexist. Examples are fungus gnats that breed in house-plant soil, sparrows that nest in eaves and befoul buildings, squirrels that dig up lawns to bury nuts and free-roaming dogs that knock over garbage cans and defecate on the sidewalk. These organisms or the damage they cause may not be terribly destructive, but if you feel the nuisance strongly enough, you may take considerable pains to manage the problem.

Plants can become nuisances, too. For example, a generally desirable ornamental plant or vegetable may tend to "take over" and establish itself everywhere. This often happens in mild climates with calendulas, nasturtiums and chard. Seedling trees may pop up in your vegetable bed or lawn, as is often the case with elms, boxelders and maples.

DETERMINING TOLERABLE DAMAGE OR INJURY LEVELS
Total eradication of pest organisms is virtually impossible, and as mentioned earlier, it is usually undesirable because it often spells the demise of the pests' natural enemies and can upset the broader ecological balance. Although there are situations in which eradication is warranted, such as with newly invading species, it is usually better to determine the level of pest presence or pest-related damage you can tolerate without harm to your health and plants. This is called the injury or damage level.

Determining this level is a three-step process. First you decide how much aesthetic, medical or economic damage can be tolerated. Then you find out how large the pest population can grow before it causes that level of damage. And finally, you establish a treatment level that keeps the pest population small enough so it does not cause an unacceptable level of damage.

We can apply these three steps to the management of a familiar household pest: the common cat flea. Let's assume that your cat (or dog) is scratching noticeably. You begin combing the cat with a flea comb once a day, and you count the fleas you flick into a bowl of soapy water (this is the method we suggest in Chapter 15). You make a note of how many fleas you catch each day. After a week or so, it gets harder to find fleas, and the cat scratches much less. Now you comb every second or third day. Eventually you switch to once-a-week or once-a-month combing, still keeping track of the fleas. Suddenly a comparison of your recent flea catch with the earliest counts shows the infestation is recurring. The time has come to increase combing frequency and possibly institute other measures.

In this example, the amount of scratching the cat was doing and the number of fleas you removed with the comb constituted the damage or injury level. But you might also define the injury level as the impact the fleas have on you. As with all injury levels, this varies from pet to pet, household to household, season to season and owner to owner. Some pet owners ignore an almost constant scratching by their pets; others become alarmed at a mere indication the pet is itching. Some people hardly notice a flea bite or two, others scratch persistently afterward or feel discomfort after one bite.

In the cat example, the daily combing provides an approximate count of fleas. These numbers serve as a damage index and can suggest a level of fleas the cat can tolerate without much suffering. Efforts to eliminate *all* the fleas, however, may be more hazardous than helpful. Even if you do get rid of the fleas completely, others will ride in on the pet unless the pet is kept permanently indoors. And even that may not prevent humans from carrying in fleas.

The comb in the example functions much like a trap that allows you to approximate the flea population and ascertain whether it is rising or falling. This knowledge is essential to determining whether your control methods are working. A variety of traps for the same purpose are available commercially for a large number of pest organisms. The use of these traps is discussed in later chapters, along with the specific problems for which they are appropriate. In many cases, however, using traps is not necessary or even possible. Instead you can learn to correlate numbers of a given pest with levels of damage by regularly observing pest activity or damage and recording this information mentally or on paper. This process is called monitoring.

MONITORING THE PEST: RECORDS, TOOLS, TIMING, STRATEGIES

Being good at noticing things is critical to pest management. You particularly need to observe the connections among various elements of the environments in which you are working or living. You must become aware of how your own activities affect the other organisms, desirable and pestiferous, with which you share your indoor and outdoor space.

Monitoring can vary from the extremely casual to statistically strict, depending on how serious you feel the problem is. The levels of effort, listed from casual to strict, are:

1. Hearsay or other people's casual observation;
2. Casual looking with no keeping of records;
3. Casual looking with written observations;
4. Careful inspection with written observations;
5. Regular written observations and quantitative descriptions;
6. Quantitative sampling on a regular basis;
7. Statistically valid quantitative sampling.

The idea is that you match the level of monitoring effort to the importance of the problem. Levels 1 and 2 are the most common and least helpful; levels 3, 4 and 5 are most useful in the house or garden. Usually you start at level 3 and progress to level 5 only if you think the problem will become serious or recur. Level 6 is appropriate to situations like the greenhouse where you may be releasing beneficial insects and need to know where pest "hot spots" are and how effective beneficial insects have been in preying upon and controlling the pests (these procedures are described in Chapter 20).

Often, instead of recording numbers, you can use estimates such as "small," "medium" or "large" to describe the extent of the problem and the size of the pest population. Whether you use numbers or estimates, the important things are to get out and assess the situation, to do so at regular intervals and to make some record, no matter how informal, of what you see.

Unfortunately, monitoring may be complicated by the fact that pests and people don't always keep the same hours. Pests may be just becoming active when you're going to bed. In fact, the survival of a pest species in close proximity to humans may be partially dependent on the fact that our daily schedules are dissimilar. For this reason, a flashlight is often one of the most valuable monitoring tools you can have.

This difference in hours of activity is one of the common causes of misidentified pests. A great deal of effort may be expended with no reward. For example, when we started a garden for students at the University of California at Berkeley in 1970, we regularly blamed the substantial damage to our spring greens on snails and slugs, two pests common in our area. We were at our wits' end because no amount of hand removal of these pests could make a dent in the problem. The lettuce was being eaten to the nub.

In this particular instance, our early-evening examinations with a flashlight proved insufficient. Finally, one adventurous student took her sleeping bag to the garden and stayed there overnight. In the early morning she found birds raiding the vegetable patch with a vengeance. Our response was to place netting over the beds, which solved the problem immediately.

Another useful monitoring tool is a magnifying glass or hand lens (see the drawing below), since many pests and their natural enemies are difficult to see without enlargement. A lens that provides at least 6x enlargement is usually adequate, and a 15x lens allows you to distinguish among various mite species and other similarly small garden pests.

Don't forget a notebook and pencil for keeping records, and a plastic bag or small jar for holding specimens you want to examine more closely or have already identified. If you want to get really sophisticated, you can buy an aspirator or small vacuum for collecting specimens. These and other tools are discussed at appropriate points throughout the book; they can be purchased from supply houses listed in the Resource Appendix at the back of this book.

A maximum/minimum thermometer is another useful monitoring tool, because outdoor pests are greatly influenced by the weather. High temperatures may speed the development of certain pest populations or do just the opposite, causing them to go into a state of suspended activity (called aestivation in mammals and diapause in insects). An early or late freeze can affect the activity of pest organisms, as can a rainier or drier than usual spring or late summer. By reading the appropriate reference works recommended in this book and through careful observation, you can learn to anticipate these effects and put that knowledge to work in your management program.

The question of where to look for pests is not always as simple as it seems. As we just discussed, it can depend on the time of day you look. For example, you can spot a cutworm or armyworm quite easily when it is munching in the open at night. But during the day you would have to search in the first few inches of the soil or in the mulch closest to its last meal. German cockroaches often like to lay eggs near appliances where the electrical current generates warmth, so looking for them inside electric clocks, switches, electric typewriters and other appliances may prove useful. Just as you must learn about the impact of weather on a pest's activity, so you must learn where to look for the pest by reading about its life cycle and behavior and by making careful observations.

MONITORING THE PEST: WHAT YOU SHOULD LOOK FOR

In one sense, the question of what to look for presents a "chicken-and-egg" dilemma: To know where to look for the pest you must know something about its biology and ecology. But to find out more about its biology and ecology, you need to know what the pest is. Which comes first? It depends on what you already know.

If you are reasonably certain what the pest is, read about it. This will tell you more specifically what to look for when monitoring. On the other hand, if the main thing you find is the pest's damage and not the pest itself, a sleuthing job is in order. Try to answer as many of these questions as are relevant to the problem.

A Monitoring Tool Kit
These tools are useful for collecting samples of pests, their damage, and the beneficial organisms that attack them: hand lens (A), aspirator (B), sticky traps and pheromone traps (C), plastic vials and Ziploc® bags (D), hand trowel (E), flashlight (F), note pad (G) and pruning shears (H).

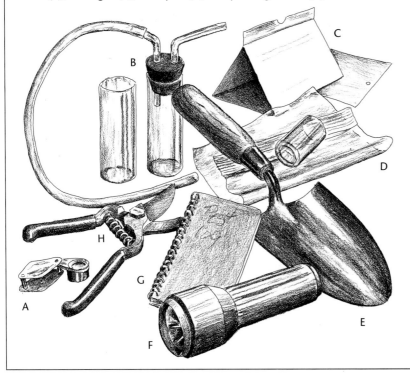

Evidence of Damage. If insects, weeds or pathogens are visible, are they causing any apparent damage? If so, what is the nature of the damage (honeydew drippings on the sidewalk, holes in the rose petals, brown spots in the lawn)? Where is the damage found (on buds, in clothing on upper shelves of closets)? What is the nature of the microenvironment (shady, damp, warm—near heater)? How many pests are present? This last piece of information might be recorded as precisely as "10 caterpillars on 1 ft. of branch 5 ft. off the ground on the north side of tree," or as generally as "many more than I can count along the branches."

If insects or other organisms are present but there is no apparent damage, record the date, site or plant, and presence of the organism. If you don't know the exact identity of the organism, use the general category —insect, for example—that best describes it. We offered tips for identifying the organism or having it identified on pp. 11-12. The entry might look something like this: "June 4— Many aphids on undersides of leaves of cucumber on fence by the driveway." Make a mental note to check again a few days later in hot weather, or in a week in cool weather to see if the population has gotten larger or smaller and if natural enemies are present.

Presence of Natural Enemies. Do you have any sense of what feeds on the pest or competes with it? Can you tell how many types of enemies are there and where they live? If you were to look at the cucumber plant in the example above a week later, the aphids you had observed might have disappeared altogether, or their numbers might have fallen dramatically if they were eaten by natural enemies such as lady beetles or syrphid fly larvae. Or they might have been parasitized by miniwasps (discussed in detail on pp. 75-76). In this case, the dead aphids would have turned into bronze "mummies," indicating that a miniwasp is—or was—inside them.

You would record any evidence of natural enemies, the date, whether or not the numbers of live aphids had dropped and whether any damage was apparent.

Relevant Human Activities. What regular human activities might be encouraging the pest? For example, how are plants watered, pruned and fertilized; how is food stored; how are wastes managed?

Other Potentially Contributing Activities. Are there any random or out-of-the-ordinary human or other events that might affect pest levels? For example, if your neighbor backed out of his garage and scraped some bark off your tree several months ago, it may explain why wood-boring insects are attacking it now.

Weather and Microclimate. How hot, cold, wet, dry or windy is it? How long has it been that way? Are there specific local variations? For example, is it windier outside the fence where the problem occurs, or is there less air circulation there?

WHERE AND WHEN TO TREAT
So far we have talked about monitoring as a means of helping initially to identify a pest problem and its significance. However, the long-term success of any treatment depends on its being timed and located properly. Ongoing monitoring tells you whether this is happening and lets you know if you are achieving your pest control objectives.

In timing treatment activities you often need to consider the life cycles and seasonal variations of both the pest and its natural enemies. As we saw in the flea example earlier, there is a time of year when fleas are more likely to be a problem. No doubt you have noticed the same is true with other pests. But you must also note the generation time of a pest, the time it takes to grow from seed or egg to adult. You can do this through first-hand observation or by reading about the pest. Generation time may be shorter or longer than the seasons,

and this has a bearing on the treatment schedule.

Bagworms, for example, should be treated before they have constructed their bags. Similarly, Japanese beetles are treated most effectively when they are still grubs in the lawn rather than once they have become beetles and are on the roses. Mosquitoes should be managed as larvae in their water source, not fogged after they emerge in the flying stage, as is still the practice in many communities. Soap-and-water treatments can be effective in reducing scale populations, but only if applied when young scales, called crawlers, are moving about on the plant. When predatory lady beetles are in the pupal stage, they are less vulnerable to soap-and-water sprays than when they are young larvae out on the leaves.

Correct timing is even more crucial in the application of the many newer, less-toxic commercial pesticide products, such as microbial controls and insect hormones. For example, *Bacillus thuringiensis*, known generically as BT and sold as Dipel®, Caterpillar Attack® and other products, is a bacterial product originally found to be potent in controlling various caterpillars without harming other insects or mammals.

Caterpillars are the young of moths and butterflies, and the BT must be eaten by the caterpillar to be effective. Thus, applying the material when the moths are flying is worthless. Even during the caterpillar stage, the insect is more susceptible to BT at certain times than at others. This important biological/chemical tool is discussed further on pp. 132-136 along with other microbial pesticides and insect growth regulators. Other examples illustrating the importance of proper timing of treatments are presented throughout the book.

Where you apply management tactics is also important, and it, too, hinges on knowledge of the biology and ecology of the pest. Treatment should be applied only where the problem is most severe and your actions will have the greatest impact. To illustrate this, we return to the flea example. The immature fleas are not on the pet, they are in its bedding and in the general household environment. Therefore, tactics that focus exclusively on the pet are bound to be less effective in the long run.

Spot Treatment

In every pest situation there are likely to be locations where the problem is more severe or less severe. Outdoors, where it is not possible to eliminate pests completely since more pests can walk, fly or be blown in, it is crucial to apply treatment specifically where the problem is worst. That way you leave a small, local, untreated residue of pests to feed the beneficial natural enemies of the pest, and the natural enemies are more likely to be around the next time the pest migrates into the area.

This very important basic approach —treating only the critical area—is known in IPM as spot treatment. This concept applies to cultural, physical, mechanical, biological and, most important, chemical controls. Obviously, it is far more conservative than the traditional approach of blanketing an area with a commercial pesticide. If you try to spot-treat with a commercial pesticide, you may run into problems. You may have to buy a gallon of pesticide when all you need is a cup's worth. What do you do with the rest, often considered "hazardous household waste" because it poses a threat to the environment? Even if your town has hazardous waste collection days, what can they do with it? It is tempting to use it up by spraying it around for preventive purposes. Sadly, this is often just what town or county agencies suggest. From an environmental point of view and from a pest control perspective this is often the worst thing to do.

Biological and environmental problems associated with spraying large quantities of pesticides over an area are discussed in Chapter 6. Fortunately, there are many alternative management options for pests. These are the subject of the next chapter.

REFERENCES AND READINGS

This list of recommended readings is taken from the leaflet *What is IPM?* by Helga Olkowski, published by the Bio-Integral Resource Center, P.O. Box 7414, Berkeley, CA 94707.

Bennett, G.W., and J.M. Owens, eds. 1986. *Advances in urban pest management.* New York: Van Nostrand Reinhold. 397 pp.

This volume reviews the current state of research in urban pest management. It contains 15 papers by different contributors that cover research on landscapes, food production, structural pests and public-health pests. However, there are few examples of programs that have reduced toxic pesticide use.

Bottrell, D.R. 1979. *Integrated pest managment.* Washington, D.C.: Council on Environmental Quality (U.S. Government Printing Office). 120 pp.

This report is broad in scope and depth, covering the federal role and government policy. It examines IPM as it relates to agriculture, forestry and medical and wildlife pests, and was written in response to a presidential directive that the council review IPM programs and recommend federal action to encourage IPM.

Flint, M.L., and R. van den Bosch. 1981. *Introduction to integrated pest management.* New York: Plenum Press. 240 pp.

This text is the best introduction to the concept of IPM in print. It covers basic ecological principles, the early history of pest control, the economic, social and evnvironmental costs of pest control and the philosophy of IPM. It then moves to practical procedures like monitoring and decision-making before discussing case histories and the role of the IPM specialist. Finally, there is a chapter on future possibilities for IPM implementation.

Goldstein, J., and R.A. Goldstein. 1978. *The least-is-best pesticide strategy: a guide to putting integrated pest management into action.* Emmaus, Pa.: JG Press. 205 pp.

This book explains why IPM is beneficial to consumers, farmers, students and policymakers.

Hartnack, H. 1943. *Unbidden house guests.* Tacoma, Wash.: Hartnack Publishing. 160 pp.

A fascinating book written by a learned European gentleman who continued his pest control career in the United States. He published and illustrated his own work, and provides a good view of urban pest control before the widespread use of "modern" insecticides both in this country and abroad.

Huffaker, C.B., and P.S. Messenger, eds. 1976. *Theory and practice of biological control.* New York: Academic Press. 788 pp.

Although this volume primarily discusses biological control, about a third of it focuses on integrated control strategies and tactics. It is important in demonstrating how IPM and biological control are intimately related.

Kilgore, W.W., and R.L. Doutt, eds. 1967. *Pest control: biological, physical and selected chemical methods.* New York: Academic Press. 477 pp.

This volume discusses various IPM strategies (biological, microbial, electromagnetic, radiation-induced sterilization, chemosterilants, pheromones, repellents, antifeedants and behavioral manipulation) and includes an excellent chapter on integrated control.

Knipling, E.F. 1979. *Basic principles of insect population suppression and management.* Washington, D.C.: U.S. Government Printing Office (Agricultural Handbook 512). 623 pp.

A comprehensive theoretical text that bridges population ecology and pest management.

Metcalf, R.L., and W. Luckmann, eds. 1982. *Introduction to insect pest management.* New York: Wiley-Interscience. 587 pp.

This basic text is divided into sections on principles, tactics, strategies and the application of IPM. The examples cover cotton, forage, tree fruit, forests, man and domestic animals. An epilogue discusses future directions. The book is good for gaining an understanding of ecological theory, sampling, modeling and specific crop systems.

National Academy of Sciences. 1969. *Insect pest management and control.* Washington, D.C.: N.A.S. 508 pp.

A comprehensive text on insect pest management, with discussions of identification, plant and animal resistance to pesticide, and biological, microbial, genetic, cultural, physical and chemical controls. Integrated systems and economic principles of pest mangement are also discussed. It is the third of six volumes on pest control.

Olkowski, H., and W. Olkowski. 1976. Entomophobia in the urban ecosystem. *Bulletin of the Entomological Society of America* 22(3):313-317.

This paper grew out of W. Olkowski's experiences on the staff of the California State Bureau of Vector Control and Solid Waste Management, where he encountered a number of cases of public hysteria regarding real or imagined insect problems. Such hysteria is the basis for a great deal of unnecessary pesticide use. This phenomenon needs to be understood better if pesticide reduction is to occur.

Perkins, J.H. 1982. *Insects, experts, and the insecticide crisis.* New York: Plenum Press. 304 pp.

This book is largely a discussion of how and why IPM developed.

Pimentel, D., ed. 1981. *Handbook of pest management in agriculture.* Boca Raton, Fla.: CRC Press.

This text, in three volumes, is technical and comprehensive. It discusses the crop ecosystem, the side-effects of pesticides and the developing science of IPM. It contains many case histories.

Stern, V.M., R.F. Smith, R. van den Bosch and K.S. Hagen. 1959. The integrated control concept. *Hilgardia* 29(2):81-101.

This paper, which still makes good reading, was the first to use the phrase "integrated control." Integrated control theory was the precursor of IPM.

CHAPTER 4
Pest-Treatment Strategies and Tactics

INTRODUCTION

Throughout this book we present programs for managing pests of homes, gardens, communities, pets and ourselves. Within these broad programs we recommend specific treatment strategies and tactics. If integrated pest management is to work for you, it is critical that you understand the terminology involved and approach your particular pest problem with a solid knowledge of all the strategies and tactics available.

It's not as imposing as it sounds. We're really talking about six strategies and 15 tactics, and it is not necessary at this point for you to jot them down or commit them to memory. The purpose of this chapter is simply to give you an idea of what kinds of tools are in the IPM practitioner's portfolio. This knowledge will make you far more resourceful when it comes to selecting the least-toxic methods for solving a specific pest problem.

CRITERIA FOR SELECTING A TREATMENT STRATEGY

A strategy is an overall approach to a problem, such as using habitat management to suppress a pest. A tactic is a specific action or series of actions within that strategy. For example, draining water from a depression in a field or cleaning out a clogged gutter that is retaining rainwater are tactics that might be part of a habitat-management strategy for mosquitoes.

An examination of the ecosystem of which the pest is part, as well as careful consideration of the natural control processes discussed in Chapter 2, usually suggests a variety of strategies and tactics you might use to suppress the target pest population below the intolerable injury or damage level. The objective is to design a program that uses more than one strategy. In doing this, we suggest you choose strategies that are:
• least disruptive of natural controls;
• least hazardous to human health;
• least toxic to nontarget organisms;

• least damaging to the general environment;
• most likely to produce a permanent reduction of the pest population;
• easiest to carry out effectively; and
• most cost-effective over the short and long terms.

These are the criteria we have applied throughout the book in making treatment recommendations. Frequently we also indicate why certain popular methods fall short of one or more of these criteria.

THE MAJOR TREATMENT STRATEGIES AVAILABLE

There are many strategies available to the pest manager who has a broad perspective. We outline these strategies in the chart below, and provide many examples under specific pest discussions in later chapters. As you read through these options, bear in mind one of the most important tenets of IPM: For most pest management problems, combined strategies are more effective in the long run than any one strategy used by itself.

To give you an idea of how we have organized things, there are two broad treatment strategy categories: Category I, indirect suppression, and Category II, direct suppression. Within these categories are specific strategies, which we have given letter designations; under these are various tactics, which we have numbered.

We should also say in advance that a seemingly disproportionate

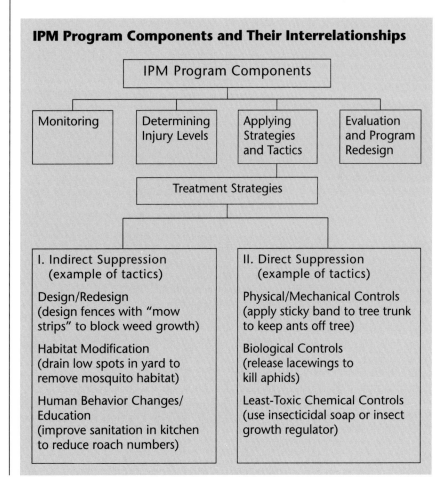

IPM Program Components and Their Interrelationships

IPM Program Components

Monitoring | Determining Injury Levels | Applying Strategies and Tactics | Evaluation and Program Redesign

Treatment Strategies

I. Indirect Suppression (example of tactics)

Design/Redesign (design fences with "mow strips" to block weed growth)

Habitat Modification (drain low spots in yard to remove mosquito habitat)

Human Behavior Changes/ Education (improve sanitation in kitchen to reduce roach numbers)

II. Direct Suppression (example of tactics)

Physical/Mechanical Controls (apply sticky band to tree trunk to keep ants off tree)

Biological Controls (release lacewings to kill aphids)

Least-Toxic Chemical Controls (use insecticidal soap or insect growth regulator)

amount of space in this chapter is devoted to one particular direct treatment strategy: biological control. We feel this reflects its relative importance in integrated pest management.

TREATMENT CATEGORY I: INDIRECT SUPPRESSION OF PESTS

The three indirect methods of pest suppression are design or redesign of the landscape or structure, modification of the habitat and changing human behavior.

Strategy A: Designing or Redesigning the Landscape or Physical Structure

The purpose of this strategy is to "design the pest out" of the system.

Tactic 1. Selection of food plants or structural materials that resist pests or prevent the development of predisposing conditions, support natural controls and enhance ecosystem diversity and processes.

Tactic 2. Use of landscape or structural designs that promote the health of the host plant or animal; help keep buildings structurally sound; are appropriate to the weather, soil, minerals, water, energy resources and systems (irrigation, waste management) at the site; and alter the microclimate to retard pests or enhance natural pest enemy populations.

We use the word "redesign" because so often pest-free maintenance is not emphasized in the original design of a new building, landscape or garden. Professional landscape and building architects and designers are often woefully untrained in or insensitive to the maintenance implications of various designs. Where potential pest problems were not considered at the outset it usually means some redesigning must be done once the unanticipated difficulties surface.

In some cases it almost seems as though the pest problems were deliberately designed into the situation initially. You still see wood porch stairs built in direct contact with the soil or very close to it—an open dinner invitation to termites. Even more frequently you see gardens where vegetables of the same kind are grown in the same area, with barren soil between the rows and fallen leaves and other debris cleaned away, as if the levels of neatness and cleanliness appropriate to a human dining room were equally desirable in the garden.

In reality, the bare soil is an open invitation to weeds. And if all plants of the same kind are clustered together it makes it easy for plant-specific pests to find new hosts and multiply. If all plant debris is cleaned away, there is no buffer against extremes of temperature at the soil surface and no hiding place for hunting spiders, lizards and toads, all of which are important predators of insect pests. Beneficial parasitoids often pupate inside the remains of dead pests while the pest is still attached to the leaf on the plant. When this leaf grows old, it may fall to the ground with the parasitoid still in place inside the pest. When the fallen leaves are swept away, the parasitoids emerge far from where they can continue to help in the garden by parasitizing more insect pests.

Contrast this "neat and clean" garden design with the gardens of many indigenous peoples. In *Plants, Man and Life* (listed under "References and Readings" on pp. 54-55), Edgar Anderson provides a vivid description of the gardens of Central American Indians. In the chapter entitled "Dump Heaps and the Origin of Agriculture," he writes:

The garden...was a small affair about the size of a small city lot in the United States. It was covered with a riotous growth so luxuriant and so apparently planless that any ordinary American or European visitor, accustomed to the puritanical primness of north European gardens, would have supposed (if he even chanced to realize that it was indeed a garden) that it must be a deserted one.

The garden was a vegetable garden, an orchard, a medicinal garden, a dump heap, and a bee yard. There was no problem of erosion though it was at the top of a steep slope; the soil surface was practically all covered and apparently would be during most of the year....In addition to the waste from the house, mature plants were being buried in between the rows when their usefulness was over....Plants of the same sort were so isolated from one another by intervening vegetation that pests and diseases could not readily spread from plant to plant.

Apparently the large number of plant species and varieties in these early Indian gardens, as well as the appropriateness of the species to the microclimate, soils and horticultural techniques of the gardeners, helped create a stable situation that was well buffered against the wild fluctuations associated with damaging pest and disease outbreaks. Two basic principles seem to underlie the design of such landscapes: avoiding bare soil and encouraging a diversity of organisms by incorporating ample organic materials below the ground and by growing a variety of plants above it.

Strategy B: Modifying the Habitat

This strategy involves changing the biophysical environment to reduce its carrying capacity with regard to the pest population. Carrying capacity describes the ability of an environment to support a population.

Tactic 1. Reduction of the pest's food, water, shelter, growing room and other needs.

Tactic 2. Enhancement of the environment required by the pest's predators, parasitoids and pathogens.

For example, reducing the number of cracks in which cockroaches can hide helps limit the number of cockroaches in the kitchen. When the cracks are caulked, the "roach carrying capacity" of the kitchen is reduced. It can also be reduced by limiting food, drinking water, temperature and relative humidity.

A companion to the concept of carrying capacity is that of limiting factors (see the drawing below). A site can support only a certain number of pests because one or more of the key requirements—food, water, shelter— is limited. When you are faced with a pest problem in a specific environment, the challenge is to decide which essential element(s) of the pest's life-support system can be modified to reduce the presence of the pest.

Conversely, you can raise the limit on certain limiting factors to promote populations of the pest's natural enemies. For example, many parasitoids of insect pests need free water. Although adult parasitoids get some

The Concept of Limiting Factors

The shortest barrel stave—the limiting factor—is the one that dictates how much water the barrel can hold, despite the fact that the other staves are much taller. In this representation, limited habitat is restricting the size of the pest population despite a relative abundance of food, water and other factors.

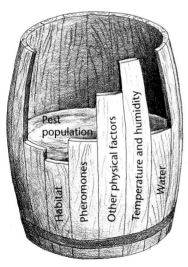

water from dew drops and from the food they consume, they may not satisfy all their water needs from these sources, particularly where it is arid. Thus, in the dry summer of the Mediterranean climate, such as exists in parts of the western or southwestern United States, an occasional sprinkling of garden plants with a hose provides water droplets from which the parasitoids can drink. This can increase the number of parasitoids in a specific location and lead to better control of certain plant pests such as aphids.

Temperature is a limiting factor in using certain parasitoids to control whiteflies in the greenhouse. The parasitoids work best at warmer temperatures than many unheated greenhouses maintain in winter, especially at night. Realizing that temperature is a limiting factor, you can figure out how to modify the habitat against the pest and in favor of its natural enemies. For example, you might use drums of water in the greenhouse which absorb solar radiation during the day and release it at night.

Strategy C: Changing Human Behavior

Tactic 1. Modification of horticultural practices. In pest management literature, this tactic is usually referred to as using "cultural controls," an abbreviation of the phrase "horticultural controls." It involves changing such practices as cultivating, mowing, watering, fertilizing, pruning and mulching.

Tactic 2. Modification of waste management and sanitation processes. This means adjusting the way cleaning is performed and the manner in which garbage and other wastes are managed.

Tactic 3. Inspection and quarantining of new plants, pets and materials that have the potential to transport pests. Inspection can prevent the importation of cockroaches and pantry pests into the house in package wrappings or on furniture, or house plant pests on new plants.

Tactic 4. Education. By educating yourself and others about pests and about the benefits of certain wildlife such as spiders and paper wasps, you can modify your own and others' perception, taste and judgment to avoid the unfortunate consequences of overzealous efforts to control organisms that are causing no harm. This may involve altering your definition of what constitutes cosmetic damage or readjusting your judgment as to how heavily manicured or defect-free a landscape must be before it is acceptable. Education can also influence how strongly one fears or is revolted by the physical appearance of a certain animal or plant.

TREATMENT CATEGORY II: DIRECT SUPPRESSION OF PESTS

Direct methods of destroying or excluding pests include physical and mechanical controls, biological controls and least-toxic chemical controls.

Strategy A: Physical and Mechanical Controls

Tactic 1. Manual removal or mechanical killing of pests (vacuuming up insects, using a hoe to remove weeds).

Tactic 2. The use of barriers, including screens, nets and caulking.

Tactic 3. The setting of traps, including electric and light traps.

Tactic 4. The use of heat or cold to destroy pests. This tactic includes the use of flamers in weed control, freezing to kill clothes moth eggs in furs and woolens, heating wood structures to kill wood-boring pests, microwaving to kill silverfish in books and linens, and similar strategies.

Strategy B: Biological Controls

This very important strategy, discussed at some length here, involves maximizing the impact of the pest's natural enemies, including predators, parasitoids, pathogens, antagonists and other competitors. The study and application of biological control

The Oldest Known Biological Control Program

The oldest example of the deliberate manipulation of a natural enemy species comes from ancient China. It involves collecting nests of yellow ants *(Oecophylla smaragdina)* and placing them on citrus trees to control caterpillars and other pests. Rope bridges allow the ants to commute from tree to tree. Moat barriers on the ground force these predatory ants to stay in the trees.

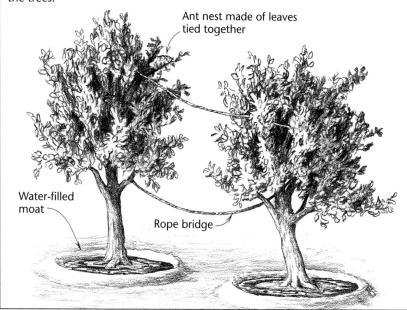

Ant nest made of leaves tied together

Water-filled moat

Rope bridge

techniques is most advanced in relation to the control of arthropods, specifically insects and mites.

Examples of the use of this strategy in agriculture and forestry are extensive and go back centuries, particularly in China (as shown in the drawing above).

The deliberate use of biological control techniques to manage agricultural pests in the United States can be traced to 1888, perhaps the most significant date in the early history of pest control in this country. In that year, the U.S. Department of Agriculture (USDA) imported the Vedalia lady beetle *(Rodolia cardinalis)* into California from Australia to control the cottony-cushion scale, which had been brought accidentally to the United States from Australia and was devastating the citrus industry in southern California. The lady beetle was so successful in permanently

controlling this pest that the citrus industry to this day is a strong supporter of biological controls. This early and important event is discussed further in the sidebar on the facing page. It is an example of "classical" biological control involving the release of natural enemies of pests, as distinguished from the recently developed biotechnological approaches in which tissue or cellular material is manipulated.

The Vedalia importation project is a classic example of the many benefits of biological control as a pest management tool. The few thousand dollars the USDA spent to import the beetles was a far smaller investment than that required of farmers using insecticides in their fruitless effort to control the scale. More recently, pest-management researchers Paul De-Bach and David Pimentel have documented that for every $1 invested in

biological control, $30 is earned in preserved crop yields and savings on conventional pesticides. By contrast, for every $1 invested in conventional pesticides, only $4 is earned in preserved crop yields.

Another advantage of biological control is that it can produce permanent pest suppression, as contrasted with pesticides, which must be reapplied on a regular basis. Except where pesticide use has killed the Vedalia beetles, they have kept pest scales under biological control in California citrus groves for the past 100 years.

We should also point out that the Vedalia project was undertaken by a nonprofit government agency, the USDA, acting in the interest of society at large. Since successful biological control importations generally produce permanent pest controls, farmers profit from the introduction of beneficial organisms, but the importers of the beneficials receive no direct monetary reward once the new organism becomes established in the environment. Pesticides, on the other hand, are generally developed by private industry, which expects to realize substantial profits from continuing sales and repeated use of their products. Absence of the long-term profit motive explains the relative neglect of the biological control strategy. It also emphasizes the need for the public to pressure the state and federal departments of agriculture as well as universities to undertake such projects and support the fledgling commercial insectary industry that produces beneficial organisms for sale.

The application of the science of biological control to weed pests is more recent, and its application to plant pathogens is most recent of all. In general, research into biological control is vastly underappreciated; therefore it is also underfunded. This is very unfortunate, because the potential economic, social and ecological benefits are so substantial.

Under the overall strategy of biological control we can identify four distinct approaches.

How A Lady Beetle Saved the American Citrus Industry

Although the Chinese have cultured and moved predatory ant species around for thousands of years, the modern importation of natural enemies to control insect pests began in late 1888 when USDA entomologist Albert Koebele shipped the Vedalia beetle *(Rodolia cardinalis;* see the photo below) from its native Australia to California to combat the cottony-cushion scale *(Icerya purchasi)*. In his very readable account of this project, Paul DeBach likens the establishment of the Vedalia beetle to the "shot heard around the world."

In the 1880s the cottony-cushion scale was devastating the booming citrus industry in southern California. Various insecticides, including cyanide gas, were used in attempts to control the scale, but with little effect and at great cost. The initial objective of Koebele's trip to Australia was the acquisition of the scale-eating parasitic fly *Cryptochaetum iceryae,* which Australian entomologist Frazer Crawford had discovered in 1886.

Koebele sent thousands of the flies back to the United States, and they were soon established in California. But he also sent back 524 Vedalia beetles, and they were used to start a series of field cultures in southern California. Through the efforts of farmers, insectaries (insect producers), government workers and researchers, the beetles were distributed throughout California, and later to other states and more than 50 countries.

Within a few weeks of introducing the beetles into citrus orchards, the scale population was reduced to negligible levels, and within one year virtually no cottony-cushion scale could be found in the state. (The parasitic fly also helped suppress scales, especially in coastal areas.) Today it is difficult to locate either the pest or the beetles in citrus orchards. The pest is evident only when there is heavy insecticide use or when an especially cold winter in the northern areas of its range kills the few predators needed to keep scale populations low.

A predatory red and black Vedalia lady beetle feeds on the cottony-cushion scale. (Photo by Max Badgley.)

Tactic 1. Conservation of biological controls. This involves protection of those biological controls already present in the environment. Since the natural enemies of the pest need some low level of prey in order to maintain their own numbers, complete elimination of the pest should almost never be your objective. (The exceptions are indoor pests of the human body, pets, food and fibers, since these pests rarely have natural enemies of significance inside the house.) Conservation is the approach of most importance to the layperson, and several very important guidelines are summarized here.

A. Treat only if injury levels will be exceeded. The size of the predator and parasitoid populations will always lag slightly behind that of the pest (see the graph on p. 52). This is only natural, because predators multiply as a result of finding food, not in anticipation of it. When their prey becomes plentiful, their own numbers increase. Thus, it is just before the pest reaches damaging numbers that the beneficials become abundant. If you apply a pesticide before you are certain treatment is necessary, it will damage natural enemy populations no matter how nontoxic the pesticide is to humans and pets. This can actually cause the pest problem to worsen.

B. Spot-treat to reduce the impact on the natural enemies of the pest. Restricting treatment to the very spot where the problem is serious and leaving adjacent areas untreated preserves the natural enemies of the pest. This ensures that some of these natural enemies survive to react quickly when the pests begin to multiply again.

C. Time treatments so they are least disruptive. Timing should take into account both the season and the life cycle of the pest's natural enemies. Because timing depends on a number of factors such as the organisms involved, the host plant or site and the geographic area, it is difficult to generalize about it. This is why it is so

Natural Enemy Populations Lag Behind Their Prey

Because natural enemies do not emerge until their food source—the pest—is abundant, there is always a lag between the pest population peak and that of its natural enemies. In many cases, the natural enemies keep the pest below damaging numbers despite this lag.

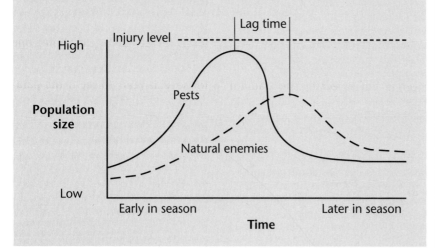

important to learn about the biology of the plant or animal and make careful observations of it.

D. Select the most species-specific, least broadly damaging treatment. Although few other techniques can match the specificity of traps, hand removal of pests, or host-specific parasitoids, this guideline does not exclude the use of certain pesticides. Some degree of specificity can be achieved with pesticides by carefully selecting compounds that are relatively focused in their effects and break down rapidly into nontoxic compounds. This is discussed at greater length in later chapters. Of course, pesticides should be used under the guidelines suggested here. If these guidelines are followed scrupulously, the specificity of the chemical compound may become less important. For example, when an herbicide is painted only on the cut stem of an offending plant rather than sprayed all over the weed and its surroundings, the application method itself is selective even though the herbicide is broad-spectrum or nonselective.

Tactic 2. Augmentation of natural enemies. This is the process of artificially increasing the numbers of specific predators, parasitoids or pathogens already present at the site in low numbers. Although augmentation has been used extensively in agriculture, it also has much to offer in many other situations. For example, brownbanded cockroaches have been controlled indoors through releases of large numbers of a parasitoid that is often already present and feeding on the roaches, but not in numbers high enough to achieve a desirable level of control.

Microbial controls developed from naturally occurring caterpillar pathogens have long been used for caterpillar control on ornamental plants and vegetables. A feature of some of these microbial pesticides, and to a lesser degree of augmentative releases generally, is that once released, the beneficial organisms may maintain themselves in the natural environment for several years. Two examples are *Bacillus popilliae*, a bacterium used to treat lawns for Japanese beetle grubs, and

Nosema lucustae, a protozoan used to control grasshoppers and locusts.

The variety of commercially available beneficial biological controls, including insects, mites, nematodes and various microbial species, is already quite large and can be expected to increase considerably in coming years. A list of producers of beneficials and the organisms they offer is provided in the Resource Appendix on pp. 683-686.

Tactic 3. Inoculation with natural enemies. This involves releasing natural enemies of the pest at the beginning of the season when they are not normally present and will not permanently colonize an area. Generally, natural enemies are not present early in the season because winter temperatures are too severe. As summer progresses, they fly in or get blown in. When unfavorable weather conditions return, they die off and do not reappear until the warm season is well underway the next year. By inoculating the pest population with beneficials earlier in the season year after year, both the current year's problem and the overwintering pest population can be reduced safely.

What distinguishes inoculation from augmentation is that natural enemies are released early in relatively low numbers before the pest population has built up rather than after the number of pests is already large. This procedure assumes that releases must be repeated regularly—at least once a season if not more often—because for some reason the natural enemies are unlikely to establish themselves permanently. The chapters on control of insect and mite pests in Part 6 describe in detail the procedures for inoculation with specific predators and parasitoids in houses, sun porches, greenhouses, enclosed shopping malls and other locations. Part 8 includes directions for releasing natural enemies outdoors.

Sometimes the natural enemy species native to the area where the pest occurs is not the species released. Instead, a related species is used because it is felt to be more effective or is more readily available. In China, Russia and many eastern European countries, inoculative releases of *Trichogramma* miniwasps are routinely used on a very large scale to control caterpillar pests in agriculture. A number of species of *Trichogramma* wasps, which parasitize the eggs of their hosts, are available commercially in the United States. We hope that augmentative releases of these beneficials will become more common here in the future.

Tactic 4. Importation of natural enemies. This involves bringing in and permanently establishing the appropriate natural enemies of a pest that has invaded a new area. The introduction of the new pest is usually accidental. Examples are the fruit flies that occasionally hitchhike onto the American mainland on produce from Hawaii, and the chestnut blight fungus, which came to North America on plants imported from Europe.

Occasionally, organisms that become pests are introduced deliberately by people who are nostalgic for old-country wildlife (the English starling, for example), or by people who want to study a species for possible commercial use. The most famous example of the latter is the importation of the gypsy moth in the hope that its silk would prove commercially valuable. A few moths escaped from their enclosures, and the species is now a major pest of trees in much of the northeastern United States.

When pet store customers tire of their exotic flora and fauna, they sometimes dump them in the nearest body of water or let them go free. Hydrilla and water hyacinth, both serious water weed pests, were originally sold as aquarium plants, and flocks of fruit-eating parakeets, probably descendants of former household pets, have naturalized themselves in some southern areas of the United States.

Insects as well as terrestrial and aquatic weeds have been suppressed by using the tactic of importation. We have already mentioned the

Vedalia beetle, the most famous and earliest example of the use of this approach against insect pests in the United States. The classic case in the field of weed management occurred in the 1940s with the control of Klamath weed (St. Johnswort), *Hypericum perforatum*. This plant, which is poisonous to cattle and sheep, was crowding out forage plants in the rangelands of the Northwest. Importation and establishment of other beetles, but especially the Klamath beetle *(Chrysolina quadrigemina),* wiped out 99% of the Klamath weed over millions of acres of rangeland in less than a decade.

Of all the approaches that come under the heading of biological control, importation, when successful, is probably the most spectacular in terms of results and the most economical in terms of money invested in research. Despite its obvious benefits, however, importation is greatly underutilized for a number of reasons. Perhaps the most important is the lack of potential for future commercial benefit. If the right natural enemy or combination of enemies is found and introduced, the pest problem virtually disappears. The natural enemies become established in the new area, the beneficial result is permanent. Thus, the controlling organism cannot be sold regularly for profit. In fact, once the biocontrol organism is working, few people even remember the prior pest problem or the fact that the natural enemy is still present and working.

We can illustrate this from our own experience. In the spring of 1972, William Olkowski released *Trioxys tenuicaudus*, an aphid parasitoid, to control aphids infesting elm trees in Berkeley, California. At the beginning of the project, the sticky honeydew exudate from the aphids was so thick on the sidewalk and on cars parked under the trees that people frequently complained about the problem. The fallen leaves, dirty from the mold that grows on the honeydew, stuck to shoes and were dragged

into houses, soiling floors and carpets. The honeydew also covered windshields and damaged the finish on cars.

The parasitoid was obtained from Czechoslovakia by the late Robert van den Bosch, who chaired the Division of Biological Control at the University of California at Berkeley. After it was released in the elms lining one city street, the site was monitored regularly during the growing season for several years to see if the parasitoid had become established. During 1972 and 1973 we found no sign of the parasitoids, although we searched the trees regularly, riding high in the bucket of a city lift truck. At the beginning of the third year, however, parasitized aphids were found on the tree where the initial releases had been made. Within a year, the aphid pests all but disappeared from the initial release site. As the parasitoid extended its range season by season, control was obtained block by block. As the aphid numbers declined, so did the sticky exudate, and to this day the sidewalk and cars beneath these trees remain free of honeydew. No further control action against aphids has ever been needed. Amazingly, no one seems to remember the honeydew problem!

Several important points can be drawn from this example. First, biological control importation projects must nearly always be supported by government agencies, commodity groups, such as the citrus farmers' cooperative mentioned earlier, or similar groups that stand to benefit directly from the result. Thus, there was no likelihood a business would have undertaken the Berkeley project. However, having been far-sighted enough to invest a few thousand dollars in importation in the 1970s, Berkeley has reaped the benefits of almost two decades of cost-free, nonpolluting pest control.

A second point is the length of time it took for the project's results to appear. During the two years that passed before it became evident that the parasitoid would be effective, residents had to endure sticky sidewalks and cars. Conventional pesticides could not be sprayed on the trees for fear of damaging the natural enemies. Thus, a considerable effort to educate residents was needed to persuade them to be patient—something people are not often willing to do when pest problems seem as severe as this one.

Although not a problem in our example, it should also be noted that it is often necessary to repeat an importation experiment several times before a strain of parasitoid appropriate to the local climate can be identified or before the right combination of natural enemies can be selected. The decades of ongoing effort by the federal government to find the best combination of natural enemies to control the gypsy moth is a good example.

Finally, it is important to note that the imported natural enemies are host-specific; that is, they live within one particular pest species but in no other. Because they depend on that single host species for survival, they are very good at seeking it out, even when populations are low. This is what makes them so effective.

We should also take a moment in this introductory discussion to answer the most commonly asked question about importation: What if an imported natural enemy starts feeding on something besides the pest and becomes a problem itself?

The first part of the answer is that the predators, parasitoids and pathogens used in biological control have adapted through eons of evolution to feed upon a specific pest or group of closely related pests. They are good at suppression of that particular pest exactly because they are unable to feed on anything else. Furthermore, to ensure that imported organisms do not become pests, an elaborate protocol is followed. Permits to import the species must first be obtained from the USDA's Animal and Plant Health Inspection Service (APHIS). Then the living material is reared in a federal quarantine laboratory with special drains, windows and doors to prevent accidental escape of the organisms. If there is any doubt about the identity of the organism being imported, it is tested in the laboratory by making sure it attacks the right host.

Projects involving the biological control of weeds operate under even more complex protocol because they deal with herbivores—organisms that eat plants and could possibly harm agriculture. An insect or mite found feeding and reproducing on a pest weed in its native country is a candidate for controlling the weed in a new area. But first it is tested against related horticultural and agricultural plants grown in the new area to make sure it is incapable of feeding on them. Only when it is clear that the herbivore depends for survival on

the pest plant alone is it considered for the new area.

Although you as a private citizen cannot import beneficial insects from outside the country, you can prompt government agencies and nonprofit organizations to do so by encouraging your legislators to support expenditures for research and development of importation. Becoming educated as to the potential of importation is the first step, and the bibliography below will help you in that regard.

Strategy C:
Least-Toxic Chemical Controls

Chemical compounds of various sorts have an important role to play in many environmentally sound pest-management efforts. If you disagree, perhaps you are defining the word "chemical" more narrowly than we are. It is important to realize that "chemical" describes not only the traditional, conventional pesticides that often find their way into soil, water, air, wildlife, food and ourselves, but also other less harmful compounds that are derived from plants and other "natural" sources or are synthesized in imitation of these compounds. Moreover, the line between what constitutes a nontoxic or less-toxic chemical compound and one that is too toxic to be acceptable may be drawn differently by different people. This complex and sensitive topic is covered in detail in Part 3 of this book.

REFERENCES AND READINGS

Anderson, E. 1971. *Plants, man and life.* Berkeley: University of California Press. 251 pp.

An inspiring account of the author's adventures as a botanist in the United States and Central America. He describes the diverse garden designs found among Central America's food-producing plots.

Askew, R.R. 1971. *Parasitic insects.* New York: American Elsevier. 216 pp.

A survey of insects that exhibit the parasitic (and parasitoid) lifestyle, with an emphasis on parasitism in contrast to parasitoidism.

Brooklyn Botanic Garden. 1974. *Handbook on biological control of plant pests* (Vol 16, No. 3). 97 pp.

An excellent introduction to the field of biological control. It includes good photographs and articles by many important figures in the field.

Clausen, P. 1972. *Entomophagous insects.* New York: Hafner. 688 pp.

A reprint of the classic 1940 book. It remains a useful source of information on many groups of predacious and parasitic insects.

Clausen, P. 1978. *Introduced parasites and predators of arthropod pests and weeds: a world review.* Washington, D.C.: United States Department of Agriculture (Agricultural Handbook No. 480). 545 pp.

A compendium of the results of previous importation projects that is an excellent starting place for learning about the biology of natural enemy species.

Davis, D.W., S.C. Hoyt, J.A. McMurty and M.T. AliNiazee. 1979. *Biological control and insect pest management.* Berkeley: Division of Agricultural Science, University of California (Publication 4096). 102 pp.

This publication introduces the field, provides current information and discusses directions future research should take.

DeBach, P., ed. 1964. *Biological control of insect pests and weeds.* London: Chapman and Hall. 844 pp.

A thoroughly documented research text that was for many years the major text used in graduate-level courses.

DeBach, P. 1974. *Biological control by natural enemies.* London: Cambridge University Press. 323 pp.

This introductory text describes the early history of the use of insects against other insects. It includes case histories, descriptions of organisms used in classical importation projects, a discussion of different types of biological controls and a chapter on the pesticide dilemma and how to escape from it. It was a source for the information on the economics of biological control versus chemical control cited in this chapter.

Howard, L.O. 1930. *A history of applied entomology.* Washington, D.C.: Smithsonian Institution (Miscellaneous Collection No. 84). 564 pp.

This book is the starting point for anyone interested in the historical development of biological control and entomology in the United States and worldwide. It is largely a collection of notes on various projects, subjects and pests by the "father of American entomology."

Hoy, M., and D.C. Herzog. 1985. *Biological control in agricultural IPM systems.* New York: Academic Press.

This book is the result of a three-day conference that explored the use of biological control in traditional U.S. commercial agriculture. It contains 31 papers on almost every aspect of the subject. The preface and overview contain powerful arguments for the wider use of biological controls that should also be read by those who need to be convinced of the validity of this strategy.

Huffaker, C.B., ed. 1971. *Biological control.* New York: Plenum Press. 511 pp.

The 20 chapters by different authors are divided into four sections: theory and ecology, outstanding examples of classical biocontrol, naturally occuring biological control and the key role of biological control in developing IPM programs.

Metcalf, R.L., and W. Luckman. 1975. *Introduction to insect pest management.* New York: John Wiley and Sons. 587 pp.

This excellent introduction to agricultural IPM emphasizes the role of biological control.

Papavizas, G.C. 1982. *Biological control in crop production.* Totaway, N.J.: Allanheld, Osmum Publications. 461 pp.

Contains an excellent series of short reviews of many current issues in the field.

Pimentel, D., ed. 1981. *CRC handbook of pest management in agriculture, vol. II.* Boca Raton, Fla.: CRC Press. 501 pp.

This comprehensive text contains a wealth of information on the pesticides used in agriculture and alternatives to them, particularly biological controls. It was one of the sources for information on the cost-effectiveness of biological control versus chemical control cited in this chapter.

Ridgeway, R.L., and S.B. Vinson. 1977. *Biological control by augmentation of natural enemies: insect and mite control with parasitoids and predators.* New York: Plenum Press. 480 pp.

An essential volume for anyone who is already using or is interested in rearing or using mass-reared insects or mites.

Samways, M.J. 1981. *Biological control of pests and weeds.* New York: Edward Arnold. 58 pp.

This short, well-written college-level text has many good examples of successful biological control programs worldwide.

Swan, L.A. 1964. *Beneficial insects.* New York: Harper and Row. 429 pp.

A survey of the field, with introductory chapters on different predatory and parasitic organisms.

van den Bosch, R. 1978. *The pesticide conspiracy.* New York: Doubleday. 226 pp.

A hard-hitting polemic by a man alarmed about the lack of attention given to the most powerful pest control strategy—biological control—and the logical framework for its implementation—IPM.

van den Bosch, R., P.S. Messenger and A.P. Gutierrez. 1982. *An introduction to biological control.* New York: Plenum Press. 247 pp.

A readable textbook-like introduction that is useful for the layperson but can also serve as an introduction for high-school and college students.

PART 2

Beneficial Organisms

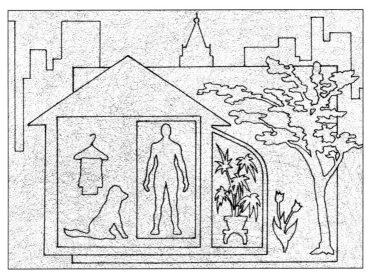

CHAPTER 5
Meet "the Beneficials"

INTRODUCTION

In Part 2 we introduce you to many of the beneficial organisms that help keep pest populations at low levels. They are listed in relative order of importance, starting with the non-insect arthropods—spiders, predatory mites and centipedes—then moving to the beneficial insects—lady beetles, ground beetles, rove beetles, lacewings, hover flies, predacious bugs, ants, bees and wasps. (Note that the discussion of beneficial nematodes is reserved for Chapter 8, on microbial insecticides.)

If you take a planetary view, the term beneficial insect (or "bennie," as we often say informally), frequently used when referring to insect biological control agents, is really a misnomer. The larger perspective makes plain that all insects are beneficial, just as are all other forms of life. Insects, mites and spiders are essential parts of complex food webs of the ecosystems that support life on earth. The larvae of mosquitoes, which are generally considered pests of humans, feed fish; the berries of mistletoe, which we often consider a plant pest, feed songbirds, and so on. In fact, everything feeds something else so that the great wheel of life can keep turning.

But, being human, sooner or later we want to know whether an organism furthers or hinders our human pursuits. It is very well to take the larger view and say that all species are beneficial, but what happens closer to home? When it comes right down to it, we might rewrite the old adage about equality: Some arthropods are more beneficial than others.

There are some groups, genera and species of arthropods that you really should become familiar with because of their great importance in controlling pest insects and mites. We introduce you to them here, but their numbers are so great and they are often so abundant in home and garden environments that we cannot do them complete justice. We hope that your interest in controlling pests naturally will motivate you to continue learning on your own. The chapter references and readings should help guide you.

A number of these beneficial organisms are available commercially for release in various situations. Many more organisms previously available only to large agricultural enterprises, or only in Canada and Europe, will become more widely available in the United States as the home-level market for nontoxic products grows. A list of producers and other distributors of beneficial organisms can be found in the Resource Appendix on pp. 681-689 (under "Biological Controls"). However, the field is expanding so rapidly that any list should be updated on a yearly basis. Updates are available from the Bio-Integral Resource Center, listed on p. 681 in the introduction to the appendix.

We should also note that some of these commercially available insects that make charming pets or educational subjects for school projects—such as the popular praying mantid shown in the drawing below—may have little impact on garden pest populations. Mantids, for example, are highly unselective in what they eat, consuming beneficial insects as well as pests and each other. These eating habits have led most U.S. researchers to dismiss mantids as effective agents of biological control. Recent information from China suggests that in certain agricultural settings some species of mantids can be useful in pest management, but there is as yet no American data supporting the effectiveness for direct pest control by our currently available species, *Tenodera aridifolia sinensis* and *Mantis religiosa*. We hope that the Chinese work will stir interest among American researchers in re-evaluating the role of mantids in pest control.

Predators and Parasitoids: How Many Are There?

During the discussion of natural and biological controls earlier in the book, we distinguished between parasitoids and predators. To give you some feeling for the numbers and importance of these groups of organisms, we quote from *An Introduction to Biological Control* (listed under "References and Readings" on pp. 77-79) by the great biological control specialist Robert van den Bosch, his colleague P.S. Messenger and former student A.P. Gutierrez:

> Parasitoids are recorded from five insect orders, with the bulk of species occurring in the Diptera [flies] and Hymenoptera [wasps].... Despite their restriction to only five orders, there are tremendous numbers of parasitoid species worldwide....Extrapolating from the numbers of described Coleoptera [beetles] and parasitic Hymenoptera in the well-studied British fauna (4,000 beetle species and 5,000 species of parasitic Hymenoptera),...up to 500,000 parasitic Hymenoptera might be described worldwide if that fauna were to be as well-studied as that of beetles....

> Predatory insects are the lions, wolves, sharks, barracudas, hawks and shrikes of the insect world. ...From the standpoint of feeding

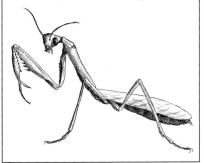

Praying Mantids
The European praying mantid *(Mantis religiosa)*, introduced into North America from Europe, has been widely distributed throughout the United States by insect collectors. (Actual size: 2 in. to 2½ in./5 cm to 6.5 cm)

habit, there are two kinds of predators: those with chewing mouthparts, e.g., lady beetles (Coccinellidae) and ground beetles (Carabidae), which simply chew up and bolt down their victims—legs, bristles, antennae, and all—and those with piercing mouthparts, e.g., assassin bugs (Reduviidae), lacewing larvae (Chrysopidae), and hover fly larvae (Syrphidae), which suck juices from their victims….

Predatory species occur in most insect orders, with the greatest number of species occurring in the Coleoptera. One order, the Odonata (dragonflies) is exclusively predacious, and others are nearly so. Predators may be polyphagous, having a broad host range (e.g., the green lacewing, *Chrysoperla =Chrysopa carnea);* oligophagous, having a restricted host range (e.g., aphid-feeding coccinellids and syrphids); or essentially monophagous, that is, highly prey specific (e.g., the Vedalia beetle, *Rodolia cardinalis*, which feeds only on cottony-cushion scale, *Icerya purchasi*, and its close relatives).

The greatest predators of the arthropods are not insects at all but spiders. It is with these that we begin our discussion of beneficial organisms.

SPIDERS
(Class Arachnida, order Araneae)

One day only! Greatest troupe of trained animals in the world! Don't miss this opportunity to see: death-defying parachutists, skilled performers on the flying trapeze, graceful and original dancers. These clever animals make their own apparatus for they are skilled engineers. See them spin and weave. Nothing like this has ever been presented before on any stage!

So begins *How to Know the Spiders* by B. J. Kaston. This magnificent spi-

Spiders: The True Pest Control Professionals

All spiders are predators, constantly searching for prey. Wolf spiders (*Lycosa* spp.) are particularly beneficial to farmers and gardeners because they attack many common garden pests. Here we see one dining on a captured fly. (Actual size of wolf spider: ½ in. to 1⅜ in./1.3 cm to 3.5 cm)

der show goes on all the time. Unfortunately, many people harbor unnecessary fears of spiders and don't appreciate the beneficial role they play in most settings. W. Gertsch in his classic work *American Spiders* discusses the enormous economic importance of spiders:

> Spiders are among the dominant predators of any terrestrial community. When the fauna of the soil and its plant cover is analyzed, they come to light in vast numbers, in such convincing abundance that it is evident that they play a significant part in the life of every habitat.

Gertsch provides some very impressive figures. For example, there were approximately 64,000 spiders per acre in a meadow near Washington, D.C., and 2,265,000 in a single acre of undisturbed grassland in England. That is about one spider every three square inches.

The primary food of most spiders is insects. Gertsch points out that although spiders are not often viewed as efficient agents of biological control, they can act that way. He cites a case where a predacious spider was credited with eradicating bedbugs in

Greek refugee camps. Hundreds of years later, he says, the same species was imported in a successful effort to control the same pest in German animal-rearing laboratories. There are examples of spiders controlling stored-grain pests, a caterpillar pest of the coconut palm, cotton worms, rice planthoppers, gypsy moths, pea aphids and others. We return to a discussion of spiders in Chapter 16, where we suggest how to remove unwanted spiders from the house.

PREDATORY MITES
(Class Arachnida, order Phytoseiidae)

Many people are familiar with pest mites that feed on plant leaves, but few are aware of the many species of beneficial mites that feed on pest mites, thrips and other organisms. Of the more than 200 mite families, predatory species are found in 13.

Like pest mites, the predatory mites (see the photo below) are small (usually less than ⅟₂₅ in./1 mm long) and tend to move rapidly. Some are white or cream-colored; a few are brightly colored. One of the most effective predators of pest mites on ornamental and food plants, *Phytoseiu-*

Predatory mites such as *Phytoseiulus persimilis,* with its distinctive red pear-shaped body, are used in agriculture and horticulture to control pest mites and thrips. (Photo by Jack Kelly Clark.)

lus persimilis, has a brilliant orange-red color. During the warm months, *P. persimilis* can complete its life cycle in just seven days—reproducing almost twice as fast as some pest mites (see the drawing below). This reproductive advantage enables the predator to keep pest mite populations at low levels.

Predatory mite species are abundant in the upper layers of soil and in moss, humus and animal manures, where they feed on insects and mites. Other mites are found on plants, where they primarily consume pest mites and their eggs. Still others inhabit aquatic systems (including hot springs!), where they feed on other mites, small crustaceans, isopods and insects. A few species occupy grain-storage facilities, where they attack a large number of insect species that damage the stored grain.

Predatory mites are used widely to control mites and thrips on food and ornamental crops in commercial greenhouses in Europe. The greenhouse nursery industry in North America is now beginning to use these beneficials. Predatory mites are also being used to control pests in orchards and vineyards in the United States, Canada and elsewhere.

We became very familiar with predatory mites while designing integrated pest management programs for pests of shade trees and in greenhouses. We learned how to rear and release them to suppress pest mites and thrips. Fortunately, many predatory mite species can now be purchased from commercial insectaries for release on indoor plants or in the garden or orchard. We discuss the use of predatory mites against pests of indoor plants in Chapter 20.

CENTIPEDES
(Class Chilopoda)

The chilopods, or centipedes (see the drawing at right), have one pair of legs per body segment, whereas millipedes, with which they are often confused, have two pairs of legs per body segment. All centipedes are predators, while millipedes are primarily detritivores (animals that break down dead plant materials). Both are commonly seen in the garden under boards resting on damp soil, or when the soil or compost is turned. Centipedes can generally move much faster than millipedes. The fastest centipedes have the fewest legs.

About 3,000 centipede species are known. All have poison glands that open through the jaws. Although none are dangerous, the bite of some southwestern species is painful tem-

A Predatory Centipede

The house centipede *(Scutigera coleoptrata)* hides in moist places during the day and seeks prey at night. It runs very rapidly, holding its body well elevated, then drops suddenly to the surface when it stops. Centipedes come in different sizes and colors. However, all have one pair of legs per body segment, as opposed to millipedes, which are usually dark and have two pairs of legs per body segment. (Actual size of house centipede: 1 in./2.5 cm)

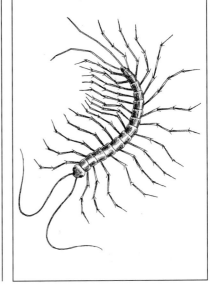

The Relative Reproductive Rates of the Two-Spotted Spider Mite and its Predator

When temperatures reach 70°F (21°C), many predatory mite species can reproduce twice as fast as pests such as the two-spotted spider mite *(Tetranychus urticae)*. It takes the two-spotted mite two weeks to mature from egg to adult, whereas its predator *(Phytoseiulus persimilis)* can go through two generations in the same time.

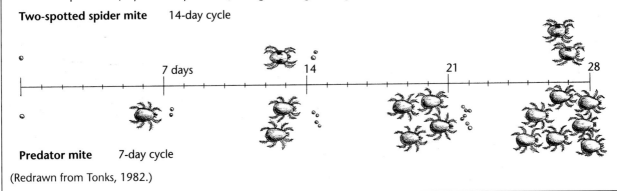

Two-spotted spider mite   14-day cycle

7 days   14   21   28

Predator mite   7-day cycle

(Redrawn from Tonks, 1982.)

porarily. Some centipedes are blind; all are predacious. A centipede frequently encountered indoors is the common house centipede, *Scutigera coleoptrata*. It is also found outdoors throughout the southern United States and Europe. It has 15 pairs of legs and long antennae, is about 1 in. (2.5 cm) long and can move rapidly along walls and floors when hunting flies and other insects, which it usually does at night. There are no reports of this species biting humans. Some people kill centipedes without realizing they provide good household insect control; other people are not even aware they are in the house. If you see a centipede indoors or out, don't kill it; let it help you control pest insects.

LADY BEETLES
(Order Coleoptera, family Coccinellidae)

Most predatory insects are beetles. The best known of these are the lady beetles in the family Coccinellidae, which children call ladybugs, not realizing that bugs and beetles are as different as elephants and tigers (more on that in a moment). Two other families are also seen regularly by gardeners and composters: the ground beetles (family Carabidae), and the rove beetles (family Staphylinidae). Some other families and their prey groups are listed in Table 5.1 at right.

Nearly everyone knows what a lady beetle looks like, but few of us know more than that. The Coccinellidae include about 400 North American beetle species and about 4,000 species worldwide. Except for one small subfamily, all members of this family prey in their larval and adult stages on aphids, mealybugs, scales, psyllids (jumping plant lice), whiteflies, mites and other insects.

Some of the more common predacious lady beetle species in the family Coccinellidae are listed in Table 5.2 on p. 63. Probably the most common beneficial species in North America is the convergent lady beetle *(Hippodamia convergens)*. All the lady beetles have similar life cycles. Eggs are laid in the early spring, producing larvae that feed for several weeks, pupate and then emerge as adults. The adults feed through the fall, then either lay eggs and die or hibernate over winter, emerging in spring to deposit eggs and die. The prey of the most common lady beetle species are listed in Table 5.3 on p. 63.

The Convergent Lady Beetle
(Hippodamia convergens)

"Ladybug, ladybug fly away home." So goes the children's rhyme about the most popular insect of all. Only the ladybug isn't a bug at all, it's a beetle. There is a big difference between the chewing insects of the order Coleoptera and the sucking insects of the order Hemiptera. Not only do members of these two groups have different ways of eating, and thus differently shaped mouthparts, they also have a distinctly different first pair of wings. Beetles have a hardened pair, whereas bugs have a

Table 5.1

Some Common Families of Predacious Beetles and Their Prey[a, b]

Common Name	Family Name	Prey
lady beetles	Coccinellidae	aphids, scales, mealybugs, white flies, mites
ground beetles	Carabidae	a wide variety of insects found in the same niche
rove beetles	Staphylinidae	scavengers; also prey on a variety of insects and mites; some are parasitic, others occur in ant and termite nests
tiger beetles	Cicindelidae	ants, flies, small beetles, bugs, caterpillars, spiders, aphids, fiddler crabs, marine fleas, grasshoppers
predacious diving beetles	Dytiscidae	tadpoles, snails, small frogs, fish, earthworms, immature dragonflies, mayflies, water bugs
whirligig beetles	Gyrinidae	dead and dying insects around water
carrion beetles	Silphidae	snails, caterpillars, fly larvae
hister beetles	Histeridae	principally scavengers; also prey upon beetles, flies, ants
lightning beetles	Lampyridae	cannibalistic; also prey upon snails and earthworms

[a] For further information on predacious beetles see Balduf, 1969.
[b] Listed in order of approximate effectiveness as predators.

Table 5.2
Common North American Lady Beetles[a]

Common Name	Scientific Name	Distinguishing Characteristics[b]
ash-grey lady beetle	*Olla abdominalis*	ash grey to pale yellow with black spots
black lady beetle	*Rhizobius ventralis*	shiny velvety black; reddish abdomen
California lady beetle	*Coccinella californica*	lateral white marks on thorax
convergent lady beetle	*Hippodamia convergens*	yellow-whitish slash marks on thorax
fifteen-spotted lady beetle	*Anatis quindecimpunctata*	head black, abdomen reddish-brown with 15 black spots
mealybug destroyer	*Cryptolaemus montrouzieri*	black head, reddish abdomen
red mite destroyer	*Stethorus picipes*	shiny black with white hairs
twice-stabbed lady beetle	*Chilocorus stigma*	shiny black with two red spots
two-spotted lady beetle	*Adalia bipunctata*	head black, two black spots on reddish abdomen
Vedalia lady beetle	*Rodolia cardinalis*	red, with irregular black marks

[a] From Swan and Papp, 1972.

[b] The term "abdomen" is used in place of "elytra," which means wing covers. The first pair of wings of the beetles is hardened, and technically is called the elytra. Distinguishing marks occur on these covers rather than on the abdomen proper.

half-hardened, half- membranous set, giving rise to the name Hemiptera ("hemi" = half).

The distinguishing characteristic of the convergent lady beetle is the two oblique, converging white lines on its thorax. The thorax is the second body segment, located behind the head and before the abdomen, as shown in the drawing on p. 64. You must look carefully for these markings, since the head of this beetle is partially hidden when viewed from above. This species may occur with orange, red or yellow wing covers and black circular spots. The number of black spots varies—sometimes they are absent entirely—so the white thoracic lines must be relied on for positive field identification.

The convergent lady beetle is a migrating species. Many individuals fly hundreds of miles to hibernating sites at higher elevations in the late spring after feeding. They return to the valleys the following early spring. For most of the year, they remain in

Table 5.3
The Prey of Common Lady Beetles[a]

Lady Beetle Genus	Common Name of Prey Group
Adalia	aphids, scales
Anatis	aphids
Chilocorus	scales
Coccinella	aphids
Cryptolaemus	mealybugs, aphids, scales
Hippodamia	aphids
Olla	aphids
Rhizobius	mealybugs, soft and armored scales
Rodolia	scales (cottony-cushion scale)
Stethorus	spider mites

[a] From Swan and Papp, 1972.

a quiescent state in large, spectacular aggregations. The aggregations shift during the year from the sides of creeks during the summer to mountainsides in fall and winter. During the aggregating phase, the beetles feed very little but do drink water.

They live largely off fat stored during the spring feeding phase.

If you find such an aggregation in the wild, stop to appreciate it but don't disturb or harvest it. There is a cottage industry that collects and sells these hibernating beetles for pest control purposes. Once released, many, if not most of the hibernating beetles fly away. Those that remain are sluggish and may even form aggregations again as if they were still hibernating. Several studies confirm what we have observed ourselves: released hibernating beetles do not feed. They must fly to burn off the stored fat before they can feed again. Thus, many may leave the area where released without benefiting the person who purchased them. Moreover, many of these beetles die soon after being relocated or even during storage prior to purchase.

In some areas, at the same time that purchased hibernating beetles are being released in gardens, naturally occurring beetles are also flying in from their hibernating sites. Although the artificially released beetles fly away, successful control of the aphid pests may result from predation by the naturally occurring beetles that have come out of hibernation and flown in themselves. The home owner often mistakenly assumes that the released beetles are solely responsible for the improvement, and this helps explain why the business of collecting hibernating beetles for sale persists.

Some commercial insectaries do sell adult convergent lady beetles that have been gathered in the spring during the feeding phase. These will feed heavily on an aphid population. When the number of aphid pests has been reduced to the point where there is no longer sufficient food for the beetles, they fly away to areas with more aphids. Proper timing of releases and the use of beetles that have used up their stored fat and are ready to feed are very important.

Outdoors, convergent lady beetles may not arrive until after plant damage has occurred. They are opportunistic, skimming off the top of the large aphid population but not staying long enough to do a good job of cleaning up the pests. Thus, successful aphid control with purchased convergent lady beetles is more likely

The Convergent Lady Beetle

The convergent ladybird beetle (*Hippodamia convergens*) is the most common species throughout North America. Its body is about ¼ in. (6 mm) long, with wing covers (elytra) that are yellow, orange or red and usually have small black spots. The larvae are small black or greyish grubs with indistinct orange spots on the back. Both the adult (A) and larval (B) stages feed on common pests such as aphids.

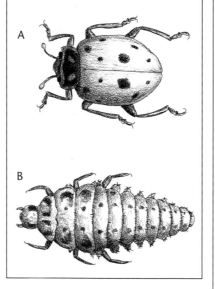

to be achieved inside a screened greenhouse than in a garden.

In addition to their aphid prey, convergent lady beetles should have access to a simulated honeydew or artificial yeast/sugar mixture (a by-product of the cheese industry; its formulation and use is discussed in Chapter 20). We generally do not recommend releasing adult lady beetles in the house because they fly to windows and tend to die in large numbers there. You can, however, import young beetle larvae from the garden and place them on aphid-infested house plants for some temporary help.

Perhaps the most important beneficial effect of releasing feeding convergent lady beetles in the garden,

however, is an indirect one: People who release beneficial insects are less likely to use disruptive pesticides in the same areas. This allows other less-visible or lesser-known biological controls to survive and provide the desirable control (even if the beetle does get all the credit).

H. convergens females can lay eggs from spring to late fall if there are adequate numbers of aphids and the temperature is high enough; usually, however, they and the males migrate by late spring. The yellow eggs are laid in groups of 5 to 50. (The maximum number of eggs laid by a female in the laboratory under ideal conditions is 2,500.) Eggs stand on end, each attached to the underside of a leaf, and they hatch in warm weather in about three to five days. The tiny black larvae that emerge cluster around the egg shells, sometimes eating the empty shells—and some of their brothers and sisters that are late in emerging.

When the dark, alligator-like larvae are very young, they have no conspicuous markings. But after they mature somewhat, colored markings begin to appear. Each coccinellid species in the larval stage has a characteristic design. *H. convergens* larvae have orange markings on a black background on the thoracic segment, and on the third, fourth and fifth abdominal segments.

After the larva has eaten 300 to 400 aphids and molted three times, a pupa (a quiescent, transitional stage between the larva and adult) forms. This pupa is black with reddish markings, and is usually found on upper leaf surfaces with its head pointing downward. Although attached to the leaf, the pupa is still capable of some movement. If you touch it with your finger or the end of a pencil, you will see it jerk. In five to seven days, the adult emerges from the pupal skin. The whole cycle from egg to adult takes about one month during the spring, and slightly less in summer. Mating, which is usually conspicuous, occurs several days after emergence from the pupa. After feeding on 200 to 500 medium-sized aphids, females produce their first eggs.

If you are washing aphids off a tree or shrub (see p. 571), timing the washing with the period when the lady beetles are in the pupal stage rather than in the larval or adult stages ensures that more of them remain on the tree. Lady beetle larvae that are washed to the ground may be damaged or eaten by predators; if they do survive, they may never find their way back to the infested plant.

GROUND BEETLES
(Order Coleoptera, family Carabidae)

Ground beetles, all of which are predacious in their larval and adult stages, are sometimes mistaken by the layperson for cockroaches, particularly in the warm, moist areas of the United States where cockroaches commonly occur outdoors in spring and summer. But cockroaches have long antennae and a different overall shape when seen from above.

As the common name implies, ground beetles are usually found on the ground. But they also tunnel under objects and surface debris, and search for prey on leaves and flowers. They are mostly nocturnal, preferring to hide during the day. Although sometimes seen flying to lights at night, they usually run rapidly, rather than fly, when disturbed.

Both larvae and adults—which usually occur in the same habitat — prey on a wide variety of organisms from mites, snails and earthworms to many of the insect orders. The well-known and rather large (1 in./2.5 cm) caterpillar hunter *Calosoma sycophanta,* shown in the drawing above right, was introduced from Europe to control the gypsy moth. Although it does feed on this pest, it cannot by itself control gypsy-moth outbreaks. It also feeds on a wide variety of other pest caterpillar species, including the satin moth, the brown-tailed moth and tussock moths. The adults have shiny

A Predatory Ground Beetle
The colorful ground beetles in the genus *Calosoma* climb trees and kill caterpillars such as gypsy moths. Members of this genus are large (1 in./2.5 cm), with well-developed jaws. They are black, green or bronze (or a combination of these colors), often with metallic iridescence.

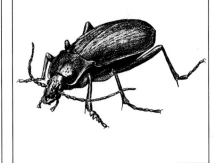

iridescent coloration. Compared to most insects, these beetles are long-lived, sometimes surviving as long as four years.

Learning about the feeding habits of predatory beetles is difficult, because they leave so little evidence of what they ate after they're done. Specially contrived laboratory or field studies are needed to determine their diet. In feeding experiments, *Pterostichus malidus* larvae (a European species of the common large black carabid genus beetles that occur widely throughout Europe and North America) consumed the following: nematodes, isopods (crustaceans), earthworms, thrips, bugs (Jassidae), caterpillars, larval craneflies and marchflies (Tipulidae and Bibionidae), ground-beetle eggs, larval water scavenger beetles, rove beetles and weevils. They also ate some species within the following groups: aphids, adult flies, springtails (Collembola), larval fruit flies and soldier flies, mites, spiders, silverfish and bristletails, slugs, larval ground beetles and soldier beetles, adult beetles and others. However, they would not touch

slug eggs, larval flower flies (Syrphidae), plant seeds, leaves of grasses and moss, strawberry fruit or apples. The studies indicate that this genus will eat a wide variety of other organisms—including its own species—that live within the same soil surface zone.

A few ground beetles are highly specific feeders that attack only certain arthropod groups; others feed on a range of plants. Many ground beetles are carrion feeders, some others are parasitic. An example of the latter is the large genus *Lebia*, which has species that parasitize the elm leaf beetle in southern Europe and the Colorado potato beetle.

Ground beetles are fed upon by an equally wide range of parasitic microorganisms and predators, including insectivores (hedgehogs, shrews, moles), bats, mice, birds, frogs, toads, spiders, predacious robber flies (Asilidae) and ants.

ROVE BEETLES
(Order Coleoptera, family Staphylinidae)

Most rove beetles are predators of other insects found in decaying organic matter such as dung and carrion. One group in the subfamily Aleocharinae has species that are parasitic on fleas, ants and termites. Rove beetles are easy to spot because they have wing covers so short that most of their abdominal segments are visible from above. Frequently these beetles carry their abdomen pointing upward.

Although rove beetles comprise one of the largest families of beetles, with about 3,000 North American species and 30,000 worldwide, they are poorly studied. They are found in a wide variety of habitats: in decaying vegetable matter, under stones, at the edges of creeks, in moss, fungi, dung and seaweed, on carrion, under bark, in caves and in the nests of birds and mammals. In the garden they can be seen in compost piles, in and under mulches and on flowers.

A Rove Beetle that Attacks Cabbage Root Maggots

A predatory rove beetle in the genus *Aleochara*, with its distinctive short wing covers just behind the head, is shown attacking a cabbage root maggot *(Delia [=Hylema] brassicae)*.

One large black species, *Ocypus olens*, with the ominous-sounding common name of devil's coachman, has recently been explored as a control for the brown garden snail *(Helix aspersa)*. This snail was introduced quite deliberately into California in the 1850s by a Frenchman who wanted to encourage its consumption by Americans. The snail never really did catch on as food here, but it has become a major pest in citrus groves and in domestic ornamental and food gardens (see Chapter 31). *Ocypus olens* preys on snails and other organisms in both the larval and adult stages. Where the beetle occurs, snail populations are lower. The devil's coachman is difficult to spot, but its presence can be detected by the small (⅛ in./3 mm) holes it leaves in empty snail shells.

We should note that research on this beetle species as a control for snails was recently eclipsed by newer work on the predatory decollate snail *(Rumina decollata)*, a beneficial snail that has been shown in field studies to be effective against the brown garden snail (see pp. 595-596). *R. decollata* is easier to rear than the staphylinid beetle. Nevertheless, where the beetle is present, it provides a valuable service in reducing snail populations, as damage to snails in our own area shows.

The cabbage root maggot *(Delia [= Hylema] brassicae)*, an accidentally introduced pest of brassicas (cabbage, turnips, broccoli, etc.), is preyed on by a staphylinid beetle, *Aleochara bilineata* (see the drawing above). The beetle was also accidentally introduced, probably about the same time as the pest. Adult staphylinid beetles lay their eggs in the soil near the roots of brassicas already infested by the pest root maggot. The young beetle larvae hatch in about 12 days and search out the maggot pupae, which by this time have left the roots. The beetles gnaw a hole in the pupal shell and feed on the developing pupae within. The beetles then pupate within the pupal shell (the entrance hole they chewed is sealed by their waste, called frass), and later emerge and mate. The adult beetles are strongly predacious on both the eggs and larvae of the root maggot.

LACEWINGS
(Order Neuroptera, families Chrysopidae and Hemerobiidae)

As the common name indicates, lacewings have two pairs of delicate lace-like wings in the adult stage. Another common name, aphis lions, implies that the lacewing's sole food is aphids, which is not so. Although many lacewings do feed on aphids, they also attack other pest insects including scales, mealybugs, whiteflies, caterpillars, leafhoppers, thrips, mites and others. The relatively well-known "ant lions" that dig a pit to capture ants are not lacewings at all, but related neuropterans (family Myrmeleontidae). The ant lion and some of the other related neuropteran families are listed in Table 5.4 on p. 67, along with their common names and usual prey species.

Two families of lacewings are known: the green lacewings (Chrysopidae) and the brown lacewings (Hemerobiidae). Chrysopidae, with over 1,500 species in 90 genera, is the largest neuropteran family and occurs on all the temperate continents and islands. The green lacewings are sometimes called goldeneyes. They lay eggs on the end of a thread of silk to protect them from predators, whereas brown lacewings lay eggs directly on leaves. Both families are widely distributed and are commonly seen by gardeners. Adults are sometimes observed flying to lights at night or against the outside of screened windows. Larvae are harder to find and frequently camouflage themselves by attaching debris to their backs.

The Green Lacewing (*Chrysoperla [=Chrysopa] carnea*)

The green lacewing (see the photos on the facing page) has become important as a commercial pest control agent in recent years; it has been mass-produced and released for control of aphids on many important greenhouse and agricultural crops.

Adult green lacewings are beautiful green or yellow-green insects about ¾ in. (1.9 cm) long with golden eyes. In the adult stage, this species of lacewing feeds only on pollen or honeydew (a sweet exudate of aphids, scales, mealybugs and some other hymenopterans derived from plant sap) or honeydew substitute, which we discuss further below. The larval stages prey on many types of soft-bodied insects and eggs of even more insects and mites. The larvae are very active and look like flat alligators, but with large, piercing, laterally opposed tusks. These hollow tusks, or mandibles, are used to pierce prey and suck out body fluids. The larger larvae do not hesitate to attack considerably larger pest insects, such as caterpillars. But they also eat smaller prey, such as pest mites.

The lacewing pupa is white and shaped like a small pearl. The strands of silk in the pupa are visible to the naked eye. After pupating for approximately two weeks, depending on the temperature, the adults emerge and look for mates. After mating, the females lay their eggs on short silky stalks, presumably to protect the late-hatchers from being eaten by the ear-

Table 5.4
Predacious Neuropterans and Their Prey[a, b]

Family	Common Name	Prey
Berothidae	beaded lacewings	after their first larval stage they become grub-like parasitoids of ants and termites
Coniopterygoidea	dusty-wings	mites, aphids, small arthropods
Corydalidae	dobsonflies, fishflies, hellgrammites, toe-biters	aquatic invertebrates, small fish, amphibians
Dilaridae	pleasing lacewings	soft-bodied insects in dead wood
Ithonidae	moth lacewings	soil-dwelling beetles, ooze from roots
Mantispidae	false mantids	predators until they find spider egg sac, then they become parasitoid-like
Myrmeleontidae	ant lions	ants, trapped in funnel-shaped pits in soil
Osmylidae	(none known)	soft-bodied organisms under bark; mayflies and larval diptera at streamsides
Polystoechotidae	giant lacewings	(poorly studied)
Sialidae	alderflies	aquatic prey (as Osmylidae, above)
Sisyridae	spongillaflies	organisms in sponges

[a] Snakeflies or the Raphidiidae or Raphidiodea, now considered a separate order, are sometimes included in Neuroptera.
[b] Adapted from Parker, 1982.

The alligator-like larval stage (left) of the green lacewing (*Chrysoperla carnea*) feeds on pest insects, piercing them with its sucking mouthparts. Adult lacewings (right) feed only on pollen and honeydew or honeydew substitute. (Photos by Max Badgley.)

ly ones, which are cannibalistic. The life cycle of the green lacewing is depicted in the drawing below.

In Chapter 20 (pp. 370-371), we discuss how to order lacewings from commercial insectaries and release them in greenhouses. Methods for conserving and augmenting lacewings in the garden are described in Chapter 31 (p. 570).

HOVER FLIES
(Order Diptera, family Syrphidae)

Hover flies or syrphids (see the photos below) are also called flower flies, because they frequently visit flowers. They are nectar- and pollen-feeders, and are important pollinators. For protection, many adults are brightly colored with yellow, black or metallic-looking markings that mimic the markings of wasps and bees. The range of feeding habits in this family is great. Syrphidae include plant-feeders, decomposers, predators and flies that live in ant, bee or wasp nests as inquilines (predators that enjoy the protection of the prey colony while feeding on the immature stages of the prey) or scavengers. The predacious species feed on aphids, caterpillars, beetles, thrips and larval sawflies.

Adults of the predacious species can usually be observed hovering around flowers or aphid colonies. They are easily mistaken for bees or wasps, but their hovering habit is steadier and more intense than members of these two groups. As dipterans, they have a single pair of wings. This distinguishes them from hymenopterans, or true bees, which have two pairs of wings. The males can be distinguished from the females (even while hovering) by the large eyes that cover most of their head.

After feeding on pollen for protein, the females are capable of laying eggs. Their white eggs are laid singly in a horizontal plane attached to leaf surfaces. (With a hand lens, these eggs can be distinguished from brown lacewing eggs, which have a short, raised cylindrical knob on one end.) The larvae that emerge are the important stage if you are relying on hover flies for aphid control. These larvae,

---

The Life Cycle of the Green Lacewing

The lacewing adult (*Chrysoperla carnea*), which lives 20 to 40 days, feeds on pollen and honeydew. Each female lays 10 to 30 eggs per day. The larvae that emerge in about five days are general predators of aphids, psyllids, mealybugs, moth eggs and larvae.

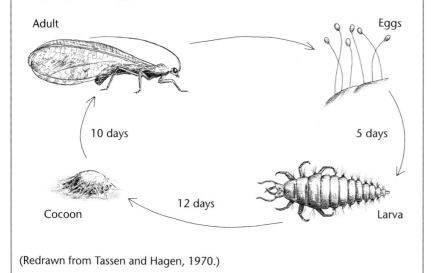

Adult — Eggs

10 days — 5 days

Cocoon — 12 days — Larva

(Redrawn from Tassen and Hagen, 1970.)

Syrphid fly larvae (left) are voracious predators of many pest insects. Adult syrphid flies (right), which superficially resemble yellowjackets, feed only on nectar and pollen. (Photos by Max Badgley.)

which lack jointed legs and are brownish or greenish in color, can frequently be seen moving about in aphid colonies, attacking aphids by puncturing their skins and sucking out the liquid contents.

After feeding and molting a number of times, the larvae form into tear- or barrel-shaped pupae, which are glued to the leaf. These pupae often resemble grape seeds. If you place one in a jar and let it emerge from its pupa, you can get a good look at an adult. But sometimes shiny, metallic-green miniwasps emerge instead of the adult hover fly. These are parasitic insects that have killed the developing hover-fly pupae; they belong to the hymenopteran genus *Diplazon* (family Ichneumonidae), and are sometimes called hyperparasites, or secondary parasitoids.

Like the bees whose markings and color they imitate, these valuable hover flies are especially at risk from insecticides used on flowering plants. You should let the hover flies eat your aphids; if you feel you must take further action against the aphids, try the plain water or soap-and-water wash described on pgs. 571 and 572 before using something more toxic that might harm the hover flies.

PREDACIOUS BUGS
(Order Hemiptera)
"Bug off," "you bug me," "bughouse" —bugs have found their way into the English language in many ways. And now they have invaded computer programs, which sometimes need debugging. We use the term loosely, even pejoratively in everyday language. But what does bug mean in the strict biological sense? As you have just read, ladybugs are not bugs at all, but beetles.

Scientifically speaking, hemipterans are the true bugs. But even the true bugs have suffered a confusing shift in nomenclature. Originally there were two orders, Hemiptera for bugs and Homoptera for aphids, scales, whiteflies, mealybugs, leaf-

hoppers, etc. Now both have been combined in a single large order, the Hemiptera, and the bugs that were in the original Hemiptera order now occupy the suborder Heteroptera, the true bugs.

More important than these fine points of nomenclature, however, is the fact that many Heteroptera are very important beneficial insects. For example, the spined soldier bug *(Podisus maculiventris —* see the photo below) is an important predator of the Mexican bean beetle and the Colorado potato beetle, two serious farm and garden pests that are largely resistant to insecticides. This suborder also contains phytophagous (plant-eating) species. We look more closely at pest bugs in Chapter 12, where we discuss bedbugs and conenose bugs. Some important Heteroptera families containing predatory species, together with their prey (if they are specif-

A spined soldier bug *(Podisus maculiventris)* is shown here attacking a Mexican bean beetle, a serious pest of food crops. (Photo courtesy USDA/ARS.)

ic), are listed in Table 5.5 on p. 70. The entire order contains more than 61 families.

ANTS, BEES AND WASPS
(Order Hymenoptera)
After spiders, probably no group of arthropods is as feared and under-appreciated as the organisms in the order Hymenoptera. Sadly, this may be an indication of how far we have moved away from our agricultural roots and how much we now control and limit our interaction with the natural systems that surround us.

The bad name is undeserved. In fact, hymenopterans comprise the greatest number of species that control pest insects through predation and parasitism. They are the most important plant pollinators, and many are detritivores. The hymenopterans in the latter group are particularly significant, as they break animal and plant tissues into smaller particles that eventually release nutrients crucial to the continued maintenance of life. If this order of insects had not evolved well before humans and other mammals, plant-feeding insects probably would have devoured everything in sight, making it impossible for us and many other species to have evolved.

Hymenoptera get their order name from "hymen" (membrane) and "ptera" (wings). They have two pairs of wings, but the second pair is often hard to see. This order is so big that it is difficult to capture its diversity in a brief review. Some of its species are virtually unnoticed and unstudied; others are so large or so common that most of us are very familiar with them. In fact, by the time most children reach kindergarten they have received so many warnings about bees and wasps that their curiosity has been replaced by fear of these marvelous creatures.

We can start by sorting the various Hymenoptera into ants, bees and wasps. But it is important to remember that their taxonomical grouping

Table 5.5
Important Families of Predatory Heteroptera[a]

Taxon and/or Family[b]	Common Name	Prey and/or Habitat
Series Geocorisae (terrestrial)		
Anthocoridae *Orius* spp.	minute pirate bugs or flower bugs	thrips, homopterans, hemipterans, lepidopterans, mites
Dipsocoridae	(none)	found in moss, leaf litter and ant nests
Enicocephalidae	(none)	found in litter, under stones and in rotting logs
Lygaeidae *Geocoris* spp.	big-eyed bugs	mites, Diptera larvae, aphids, leaf hoppers
Miridae *Deraeocoris* spp.	plant bugs	pentatomids, syrphid larvae, aphids
Nabidae *Nabis* spp.	damsel bugs	aphids, leaf hoppers
Pentatomidae	shield or stink bugs	lepidopterans, beetle larvae, bed bugs
Reduviidae	assassin bugs	aphids, leaf hoppers, caterpillars, fly larvae, bed bugs, other reduviids, bees
Series Hydrocorisae (aquatic—water surface)		
Gerridae	water striders	mosquitoes; feed on water surface
Hebridae	velvet water bugs	found on water surface on aquatic plants
Hydrometridae	(none)	found in water weeds and on surface
Mesoveliidae	water treaders	small invertebrates; found on water surface and in damp places
Veliidae	(none)	feed on surface in standing and rapid-moving water
Series Amphibicorisae (aquatic—underwater)		
Belostomatidae	giant water bugs	many insects, snails, fish, amphibians
Corixidae	water boatmen	small organisms (plant and animal), mosquito larvae
Nepidae	waterscorpions	found in still or slow-moving water
Notonectidae	backswimmers	mosquitoes, small crustaceans, small fish

[a] Adapted from Merritt and Cummins, 1978.
[b] "Taxon" refers to any taxonomic group. A "series" is a collection of families.

is more complicated. Technically the Hymenoptera are grouped into two large suborders. The first suborder contains sawflies and horntails, which are primarily plant-feeders, although one family is entirely parasitic on wood-boring beetles and the adults of other families are predators on other insects. The second suborder contains two divisions, one composed of the parasitoids, the other containing the ants, bees and predacious wasps.

It is important to understand that the few species of ants, bees and wasps that are considered pests also perform important predacious services, which we discuss when we address ants, carpenter bees and yellowjackets in later chapters. Table 5.6 on the facing page lists the superfamilies in the three hymenopteran suborders.

Ants
(Superfamily Formicoidea)

"Go to the ant...and consider her ways, and be wise" (Proverbs 6:68). The problem is, there are over 15,000 species of ants in nine subfamilies. Which one is the Bible suggesting we visit? George and Jeanette Wheeler actually try to answer this question (among others) in *The Ants of North Dakota*. After surveying various ants'

Table 5.6
The Superfamilies of the Hymenoptera[a]

Superfamilies	Common Names/Description
Suborder Symphyta	**Sawflies, horntails; stem, wood and leaf wasps**
Cephoidea Megalodontoidea Siricoidea Tenthredinoidea Xyeloidea	All these feed on plant and plant products except for some carnivorous adults in Tenthredinoidea, and one family in Siricoidea (Orussidae) which contains parasitoidic species that attack flat-headed wood-boring beetles in the family Buprestidae.
Suborder Apocrita	
Division: Parasitica	
Chalcidoidea	parasitoids and gall-makers[b]
Cynipoidea	one family, Cynipidae, contains gall-makers or gall inquilines[c]
Evanioidea	one family, Evaniidae, contains cockroach egg capsule parasitoids
Ichneumonoidea	parasitoids; the largest Hymnopteran family
Megalyroidea	parasitoids of wood-boring beetles
Proctotrupoidea	parasitoids with a diverse range of hosts
Trigonaloidea	hyperparasitoids[d] of sawfly and caterpillar larvae
Division: Aculeata	
Chrysidoidea	parasitoids of wasps and bees; Chrysididae comprises the cuckoo wasps
Apoidea	contains 11 families of bees
Bethyloidea	mostly parasitoids
Formicoidea	only one family, Formicidae, the ants
Pompiloidea	spider wasps, with one spider per nest cell
Scolioidea	parasitoids of beetles
Sphecoidea	digger wasps, the largest group of predatory wasps
Vespoidea	social wasps, yellowjackets, hornets, paper wasps

[a] From Krombein et al., 1979.

[b] Gall-makers produce external growths on plants.

[c] Gall inquilines live inside galls.

[d] Hyperparasitoids attack and develop on primary parasitoids.

modes of living, they concluded that the Bible must be talking about the harvest ant.

The ability to provide for the winter is just one reason ants deserve our respect. They are also very useful scavengers that not only clean up dead animals and debris in the garden (and house, if permitted), but also aerate the soil and prey on other insects. Certain ant species are used to control caterpillars in Chinese citrus orchards, and red ants are used in forest management in Europe because of their predatory habits. The fire ant kills boll weevils in U.S. cotton fields.

We have witnessed the power of Argentine ants *(Iridomyrmex humilis)* in killing subterranean termites. These ants, which are common throughout the southern United States from the eastern seaboard to California, can wipe out entire termite colonies overnight if humans allow them to enter the termite nest by opening the tunnels for them (see pp. 440-441). It seems clear that some measure of protection from new termite invasions is provided when the boundaries of a home or other wooden structure are patrolled constantly by ant species such as this one.

Table 5.7
Subfamilies of North American Ants[a]

Subfamily	Feeding Habits and Other Characteristics
Dolichoderinae	These ants are omnivorous, feeding on living and dead insects and honeydew, nectar and sugar. They include the Argentine ant *(Iridomyrmex humilis),* and the odorous house ant *(Tapinoma sessile).*
Dorylinae (army ants)	The only army ants in North America are two species of *Neivamyrmex* that prey exclusively on other ants in the southern United States from coast to coast.
Formicinae	This subfamily contains the largest ant genus, *Camponotus,* the carpenter ants, which live in decayed wood.
Myrmicinae	The harvester ants in this subfamily harvest seeds and grow fungi; some are parasitic. The largest subfamily, *Pogonomyrmex* spp., are serious agricultural pests and have vicious stings; the fire ants, *Solenopsis* spp., are in this subfamily.
Ponerinae	These ants are monomorphic (the reproductives and workers look alike) and carnivorous. They comprise 25 species found mostly in the southern United States.
Pseudomyrmecinae	These ants nest in plant cavities formed by other organisms or events. The five North American species are confined to the southern states.

[a] From Wheeler and Wheeler, 1973.

Of course, the Argentine ant and other ant species can be pests, too. Outdoors, Argentine ants protect honeydew-producing pests such as aphids from their natural enemies, and indoors they can become nuisances in the kitchen. Fire ants feed directly on plants and can inflict painful stings when they bite humans. The different ant subfamilies and their feeding habits are outlined in Table 5.7 above. Methods for managing pest ants indoors are described on pp. 233–239.

Bees
(Superfamily Apoidea)
In *Beekeeping in the United States*, M.D. Levin states:

Many of our fruits, vegetables, legumes, and oilseed crops are insect-pollinated. Although many kinds of insects visit flowers and effect accidental pollination, the amount is small. Bees are the most efficient and only dependable pollinators, because they visit flowers methodically to collect nectar and pollen and they do not destroy the plant by feeding on it in the pollination process. Although various species of bees contribute to the pollination of our crops, an estimated 80 percent of this pollination is done by the domesticated honeybee.

In *Venomous Animals of Arizona*, Robert Smith estimates that some 50 American crops with a total yearly value exceeding $7 billion rely solely on honeybees for pollination or are pollinated by a combination of honeybees and wild bees. He also points out that the stings people fear so much usually result from stepping on bees, inadvertently threatening their hive or brushing them away violently when they come to drink. (The sole intention of sweat bees in the family Halictidae, for example, is to drink moisture from your body.)

Although most bees are solitary, the common honeybee *(Apis mellifera)* is a social insect. The honeybee is one of the oldest domesticated animals; its honey and wax are still valuable commodities in societies that lack modern sugar- and oil-refining technology. Because of this bee's great value to humans and our fascination with its complex social behavior, a great deal is known about it.

Honeybees are considered the most highly evolved of the Hymenoptera. The key to the success of their complex, highly regulated society is that reproductive activities are delegated to a single member of the society: the queen. This theme—the segregation of reproductive functions among females—is the subject of a fascinating and ground-breaking book by Edward O. Wilson, *The Insect Societies*, which describes in great detail the biology and sociology of bees and the other major social insects: wasps, ants and termites.

The terms bee, wasp and hornet are often used interchangeably—and incorrectly. Table 35.1 on p. 652 explains how to distinguish among them; there is a discussion of how to treat stings on p. 655.

Social Wasps (Superfamily Vespoidea)

The social wasps are the insects people think of when they hear the term wasp, and they generate the same frightened reaction in some people that spiders do. All social wasps are predators; some are also scavengers. Thus, they are beneficial insects despite the fact that they can and occasionally do sting people.

The social wasps comprise the yellowjackets, hornets and paper wasps. The yellowjackets and hornets are great opportunists, feeding on almost any soft-bodied insect, spider or small animal, alive or dead. Yellowjackets have been seen preying on flies where the flies occur in large concentrations, as on cattle ranches. They also feed on economically injurious agricultural pests, including Lygus bugs, spittle bugs, various caterpillars, earwigs, beetles, grasshoppers and psyllids (jumping plant lice). However, studies documenting yellowjackets' prey habits and overall beneficial impact are few compared to those assessing damage caused by the injurious species.

All social wasps live in colonies, building their nests from a mixture of wood pulp, saliva and, sometimes, mud. They have worker castes that gather food, build and guard the nest and tend a queen and the young. The queen lays all the eggs for the colony; if a queen dies, a worker can take over the egg-laying function until a new queen is produced by the colony.

These social species only occur in Vespidae, one of the three families in the superfamily Vespoidea (see Table 5.8 at right). The other two families, Masaridae and Eumenidae, are solitary or subsocial wasps. These wasps and the paper wasps (subfamily Polistinae, family Vespidae) are much more docile than the aggressive yellowjackets and hornets in the subfamily Vespinae (family Vespidae).

The beneficial role of the paper, or umbrella, wasps (see the drawing on p. 74) has received more attention. Researchers have attempted to in-

Table 5.8
Classification of The Social Wasps[a]

Taxon	Characteristics
Superfamily Vespoidea	
Family Eumenidae	non-aggressive, solitary or subsocial; predacious on various insects, most often caterpillars
Family Masaridae	non-aggressive, solitary or subsocial; primarily pollen- and nectar-feeders; one genus predacious
Family Vespidae	aggressive and docile species; social; predacious
Subfamily Polistinae	docile
Tribe Polistini	worldwide distribution
Genus *Polistes*	docile paper wasps
Tribe Polybiini	found in tropical South America and Africa
Tribe Ropalidiini	found in tropics of the Old World
Subfamily Stenogastrinae	docile
Subfamily Vespinae	generally aggressive
Genus *Dolichovespula*	very aggressive hornets; four North American species; aerial nesting
Genus *Provespa*	nocturnal; three Southeast Asian species
Genus *Vespa*	only one North American species, the docile giant hornet (*Vespa crabro*)
Genus *Vespula*	aggressive yellowjackets; 12 North American species; large colonies

[a] From Edwards, 1980.

crease their numbers by building artificial nesting locations and measuring their predation rates. Studies have shown that more nesting sites can increase their impact on garden and agricultural pests such as the cabbage butterfly (*Pieris rapae*) and tobacco hornworm (*Manduca sexta*). Predation rates can be very high. For example, in starting up a new colony, individual wasp queens killed between one and eight cabbage-butterfly caterpillars a day. By the time the workers emerged in the new colony, the queens had already killed a total of 152 caterpillars on average. And after the workers emerged, the total caterpillars killed per wasp colony soared to 2,000.

The relatively docile paper wasps have thin waists that distinguish them from the more aggressive yellowjackets and hornets. Those found in the garden or around the house

The Nest of a Beneficial Paper Wasp

Beneficial paper wasps in the genus *Polistes* build an open, upside-down nest that is usually found attached to roof eaves or the ceilings of sheds. These wasps are more docile than their relatives, the yellowjackets, and feed on caterpillars and many soft-bodied insects, such as aphids.

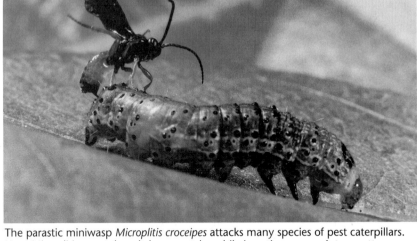

The parasitic miniwasp *Microplitis croceipes* attacks many species of pest caterpillars. Here *Microplitis* curves her abdomen under while inserting an egg into a cotton bollworm larvae. The egg will hatch into a tiny worm that will eat the caterpillar from the inside, later emerging as an adult miniwasp. (Photo courtesy USDA/ARS.)

probably belong to the paper wasp genus *Polistes*. If the waist is thin and long with bright yellow and black markings, the wasp is probably a mud-dauber, especially if it is seen flying to a mud nest. Mud-daubers prey on spiders.

Yellowjackets (subfamily Vespinae) are wasps about the size of bees (½ in. to ¾ in./13 mm to 19 mm long) with thick waists (or seemingly no waists at all) and yellow markings. They are often seen flying near garbage cans or picnic tables in search of food. These wasps can be quite pestiferous and may bite as well as sting. Fortunately, the bite is not as painful as the sting, and the effects are not as long-lasting. Yellowjacket management is discussed in Chapter 35.

Hornets (*Dolichovespula* spp.) also have thick waists, and their behavior is similar to that of yellowjackets; however, unlike yellowjackets, they usually live in aerial nests. The European hornet (*Vespa crabro*) was introduced accidentally from Europe. It is the largest vespine species, almost an inch long. Unlike yellowjackets, it is not pestiferous. This species is predacious, capturing large grasshoppers,

horseflies, flies, bees and yellowjackets. Its workers fly at night and are sometimes attracted to lighted windows, causing unwarranted alarm to the people inside.

This hornet has been reported to girdle (damage the cambium layer under the bark) twigs and branches of many trees and shrubs, including lilac, birch, ash, horsechestnut, dogwood, dahlia, rhododendron and boxwood, probably to obtain sap. Sometimes the plants are killed. *V. crabro* is also a pest of beehives, but it does not attack en masse like its relative, *V. mandariia*, a major pest of honeybees in the Mediterranean. In the United States, *V. crabro* is more beneficial than pestiferous, so it should be tolerated where possible.

Solitary Predatory Wasps

About 90% of predatory wasps are solitary species that hunt and sting insects in various groups. They provision their nest with the paralyzed prey, upon which they lay their own eggs. After hatching, the predatory wasp grub devours the prey, pupates and metamorphoses into an adult. The adults mate and the adult female

provisions her nest with insects, starting the cycle again. Generally the males do not hunt; they feed on nectar and pollen.

The females hunt and feed on specific insect groups. With a few exceptions, these are pest species. Evaniids, for example, attack only cockroaches; pompilids attack spiders. One well-known pompilid often seen in the southwestern United States is the large, striking, metallic-blue tarantula hawk (*Pepsis mildei*). This species, with its fiery red wings, is a favorite subject of nature films, which show the females attacking and paralyzing the much larger tarantula and then provisioning their nests with it.

The mud-dauber wasps that build clay nests belong to the largest predatory family, Sphecidae. They are also called thread wasps for their thin waist, which occurs between the thorax and abdomen. They are often seen around wooden buildings. They ferry mud to their nests, which they build in cavities, in attics and even on stored clothes. Wasps like these are fun to watch; they are so docile and so preoccupied with their work that they pose little hazard.

Table 5.9
The Prey of the Important Chalcid Families

Family Name	Parasitic on:
Aphelinidae[a]	scales, aphids
Chalcididae	lepidopteran pupae and Diptera (flies, most species), Hymenoptera (ants, wasps, etc.) and Coleoptera (beetles, some species)
Encyrtidae	most insect orders, ticks, and spider eggs
Eucharidae[b]	immature ants within nests
Eulophidae	Coleoptera, Lepidoptera, Diptera, Hymenoptera, mites, spider egg cases, Thysanoptera (thrips), and Homoptera; Eulophidae are primary and secondary parasitods
Eurytomidae	insect and spider eggs, gall-formers, Lepidoptera, Coleoptera, Diptera, Hymenoptera and psyllids in Homoptera; some are phytophagous (plant-feeders)
Eutrichosomatidae	weevils
Leucospidae	solitary bees
Mymaridae (fairy flies)	eggs of many species
Ormyridae	gall-forming Hymenoptera
Perilampidae[b]	dipteran and hymenopteran parasitoids of Lepidoptera, Coleoptera, Neuroptera; Perilampidae are primary and secondary parasitoids
Pteromalidae	Lepidoptera, Coleoptera, Diptera, Hymenoptera; Pteromalidae are primary and secondary parasitoids
Spalangiidae[b]	muscoid, calliphorid and drosophilid flies exclusively; attack pupae
Torymidae	gall-formers in Cynipidae, Cecidomyiidae, Diptera, Coleoptera, Lepidoptera, Hymenoptera, Orthoptera; plant-feeders and carnivorous
Trichogrammatidae	eggs of many Lepidoptera, Homoptera, Hemiptera, Orthoptera, Thysanoptera

[a] Aphelinidae, the most important family in classical biological control, is sometimes included in Encyrtidae.

[b] Some authors include these families as subfamilies in Pteromalidae.

Parasitic Wasps
(Division Parasitica)

Parasitic wasps are miniwasps that are busy controlling pest species all around you, indoors and out. You probably don't even notice them, but once someone with a trained eye points them out, you'll find them easy to spot, especially in the garden.

A common miniwasp nationwide is *Diaterella rapae*, a parasitoid of a common aphid that attacks brassicas. Since it is one of the larger miniwasps found on garden plants, chances are good you can spot it. Try watching a colony of aphids on any plants in the cabbage family for five minutes or so on a sunny day. Sooner or later, you will notice tiny winged insects flying and walking about among the aphids, jabbing their ovipositors into the aphids and laying eggs. In a very quick movement, the parasitoid curves the end of her abdomen under her body toward her head each time she deposits an egg (see the photo on the facing page).

The parasitic wasps fall mainly into two superfamilies: Ichneumonoidea and Chalcidoidea. Ichneumonoidea is divided into five families, three of which are minor. Most of the species in the two large families, Ichneumonidae and Braconidae, attack specific pest insect groups. They have been of major importance in the biological control of agricultural pests that have invaded from elsewhere; the chapter bibliography on pp. 77-79 recommends readings that contain some fascinating stories about these projects.

The ichneumonids have been studied extensively by Henry and Marjorie Townes, who have amassed what is probably the largest collection of worldwide parasitic wasp species and have published a long series of volumes on the family. According to the first volume, "The Ichneumonidae is one of the largest of all animal groups; it includes more species than the entire Vertebrata and more than any other family, with the possible exception of the Curculionidae [weevils]."

The ichneumonids comprise 5% to 10% of the insects in a particular geographical area and about 20% of all parasitic insects. Most of the world's species probably still remain to be described. Ichneumonids are mainly primary parasitoids—with a few hyperparasitoids—of all major insect orders. Some attack adult spiders as well as the egg sacs of spiders and pseudoscorpions. They also attack larvae and pupae of other insects, but not the adults or nymphs (the immature stage of orders that do not have pupae). The usual hosts are lepidopterans (caterpillars), sawflies and wood-boring beetles.

The braconids are primary internal parasitoids of caterpillars, but they attack most insect groups that undergo complete metamorphosis—Coleoptera (beetles), Diptera (flies) and Hymenoptera (bees and wasps), for example—as well as spiders. Worldwide, there are perhaps 40,000 species. Some species are hyperparasitoids, but these are relatively rare. Braconids have been used extensively in biological control projects. A former braconid subfamily that has been raised to family status (the family name is only used by Europeans), Aphidiidae, is important in the biological control of aphids.

The chalcids are the other large assemblage of hymenopterous parasitoids, with over 100,000 species worldwide. The superfamily Chalcidoidea includes some of the gall-formers, the fig wasps (without which some fig trees would not be pollinated), the well-known, commercially available parasitoids of caterpillar eggs in the family Trichogrammatidae, the fairy flies (Mymaridae), which are among the smallest known insects (all are egg parasitoids), and many other parasitoids.

One of the better-known chalcids is the whitefly parasitoid *Encarsia formosa*, which we discuss at length on pp. 384-387, along with the genus *Aphytis* in the family Aphelinidae, which is important in the biological control of scales. Table 5.9 on p. 75 summarizes the prey groups of the important chalcid families. Note that even though this table is rather general, you can see that certain parasitoid groups attack certain types of prey (or hosts). Host specificity is the key to successful use of these parasitoids against pests. The more host-specific a parasitoid is, the more it depends for survival on finding every individual of the pest species. But this also means that it will not switch to another pest species once it has decimated the first. It is obligated biologically to complete its life cycle on the particular host to which it is specific.

REFERENCES AND READINGS

Balduf, W.V. 1969. *The bionomics of entomophagous Coleoptera.* Hampton, England: E.W. Classey Ltd. 384 pp.

This classic but poorly known work, which was published in 1935 and reprinted in 1969, provides a detailed introduction to the families and species of predacious beetles.

Carr, A. 1979. *Rodale's color handbook of garden insects.* Emmaus, Pa.: Rodale Press. 241 pp.

This handy book's 300 color photos aid the gardener in recognizing insect allies.

Cloudsley-Thompson, J.L. 1968. *Spiders, scorpions, centipedes and mites.* Oxford, England: Pergamon Press. 278 pp.

This book includes one chapter each on woodlice, millipedes, centipedes, other myriapods, scorpions, false-scorpions, whip-scorpions, solifugae, harvest-spiders, spiders, mites and ticks.

Dillon, E.S., and L.S. Dillon. 1961. *The common beetles of eastern North America.* Evanston, Ill.: Row, Peterson. 884 pp.

Includes pictures of numerous beetles, with keys to all groups.

Edwards, R. 1980. *Social wasps.* West Sussex, England: Rentokil. 398 pp.

The most comprehensive book on social wasps (primarily yellowjackets) from a pest control perspective.

Erwin, T.L., G.E. Ball, D.R. Whitehead and A.L. Halpern. 1979. *Carabid beetles, their evolution, natural history, and classification.* Boston: Dr. W. Junk. 635 pp.

Surveys the natural history, systematics, classification, zoography, paleontology and techniques for collecting these beetles.

Evans, H.E. 1966. *The comparative ethology and evolution of the sand wasps.* Cambridge, Mass.: Harvard University Press. 526 pp.

A complete treatment of the biology of the Sphecid subfamily Nyssoniae, particularly the Bembicini, with an emphasis on the genus *Bembix*.

Evans, H.E. 1973. *Wasp farm.* Garden City, N.Y.: Anchor Press/Doubleday. 188 pp.

A reprint of the 1963 book recording observations of the natural history of predatory wasps on a farm in New York state.

Gertsch, W.J. 1957. *The ants.* Ann Arbor: University of Michigan Press. 173 pp.

A well-illustrated introduction to the biology of ants for laypersons and biologists alike.

Gertsch, W.J. 1979. *American spiders.* 2nd ed. New York: Van Nostrand Reinhold. 274 pp.

An introduction to the biology and behavior of spiders, with color and black-and-white photographs and many line drawings.

Greathead, D.J. 1986. Parasitoids in classical biological control. In *Insect parasitoids*, eds. D. Greathead and J. Waage. New York: Academic Press.

An essential introduction to the taxonomy, evolution, biology, ecology and manipulations (including augmentation and introduction) of parasitoids for agricultural pest control.

Hagen, K.S., and G.W. Bishop. 1979. Use of supplemental foods and behavioral chemicals to increase the effectiveness of natural enemies. In *Biological control and insect pest management*, eds. D.W. Davis, S.C. Hoyt, J.A. McMurty and M.T. AliNiazee, pp. 49-60. Berkeley: University of California (Agricultural Sciences Publication 4096). 102 pp.

This short work introduces and updates research in the field and suggests new directions that research efforts should take. It should be made more widely available, as it contains information hard to find elsewhere.

Hoy, M.A., G.L. Cummingham and L. Knutson, eds. 1983. *Biological control of pests by mites: proceedings of a conference held April 5-7, 1982, University of California, Berkeley.* Berkeley: Division of Agriculture and Natural Resources, University of California. 185 pp.

This scholarly text summarizes the use of predatory mites in a variety of agricultural, horticultural and grain-storage systems.

Kaston, B.J. 1972. *How to know the spiders.* Dubuque, Iowa: Wm. C. Brown. 289 pp.

An illustrated key with a short introduction to the biology and other aspects of spiders. Also describes collection techniques.

Krombein, K.V. 1967. *Trap-nesting wasps and bees: life histories, nests and associates.* Washington, D.C.: Smithsonian Press. 570 pp.

A thorough treatment that includes a family-by-family review of these organisms' biology and nest construction. It also looks at the other organisms found in their nests.

Krombein, K.V., P.D. Hurd. Jr., D.R. Smith and B.D. Burks. 1979. *Catalog of Hymenoptera in America north of Mexico, Vol. 2.* Washington, D.C.: Smithsonian Institute Press. 2,029 pp.

This is the source of the information in Table 5.6 on p. 71.

Larson, P.P., and M.W. Larson. 1976. *All about ants.* New York: Thomas Y. Crowell. 219 pp.

A study of ants that focuses on their social behavior.

Levin, M.D. 1971. Pollination. In *Beekeeping in the United States,* S.E. McGregor, pp. 77-85. Washington, D.C.: United States Department of Agriculture (Agricultural Handbook No. 335). 147 pp.

An introduction to beekeeping and the beekeeping industry.

Merritt, R.W., and K.W. Cummins. 1978. *An introduction to the aquatic insects of North America.* Dubuque, Iowa: Kendall/Hunt. 441 pp.

Contains a very good section on aquatic hemipteran predators, with illustrations and keys.

Miller, N.E. 1971. *The biology of the Heteroptera.* Hampton, England: E. W. Classey, Ltd. 206 pp.

The first part of this book is a broad introduction to the biology of the Heteroptera; the second part focuses on individual families.

Moore, I., and E.G. Legner. 1979. *An illustrated guide to the genera of the Staphylinidae of America north of Mexico, exclusive of the Aleocharinae (Coleoptera).* Berkeley: University of California Division of Agricultural Sciences (Publication 4093). 332 pp.

This publication is useful primarily for arthropod identification.

Morse, R.A. 1978. *Honeybee pests, predators, and diseases.* Ithaca, N.Y.: Cornell University Press. 430 pp.

A compilation of existing knowledge and literature about pests of the honeybee. Includes information about and references to the species of *Vespa* that attack bees.

Ondish, G. 1978. *The year of the ant.* New York: Charles Scribner's Sons. 139 pp.

An excellent introductory text.

Parker, S.P., ed. 1982. *Synopsis and classification of living organisms,* vols. 1 and 2. New York: McGraw-Hill. 1,165 and 1,232 pp., respectively.

Produced by 170 experts in 12 countries, these two volumes present all organisms—viruses, bacteria, algae, fungi, invertebrates and vertebrates—in taxonomic order. They include over 8,300 synopses of taxons, with short introductions to the life history, development, ecology and geographical distribution of each organism. The two volumes contain the scientific and common names of taxa, a 35,000-item index, outlines of taxonomic classification systems, an article on the process of biological classification and a discussion of kingdoms. References to relevant literature follow each family discussion.

Rau, P., and N. Rau. 1970. *Wasp studies afield.* New York: Dover Publications. 372 pp.

A reprint of a 1918 book with many observations on wasp predation.

Savory, T. 1964. *Arachnida.* New York: Academic Press. 291 pp.

An order-by-order introduction to spiders and mites for the biologist and taxonomist.

Shetlar, D.J., and V.E. Walter. 1982. Ants. In *Handbook of pest control,* 6th ed., ed. A. Mallis, pp. 425-487. Cleveland: Franzak and Foster.

A survey of the biology and management of pestiferous ants of North America.

Sims, R.W., ed. 1980. *Animal identification, a reference guide.* Vol. 1: *Marine and brackish water animals.* Vol. 2: *Land and freshwater animals.* Vol. 3: *Insects* (ed. D. Hollis). London: John Wiley and Sons. 111, 120 and 160 pp., respectively.

These three volumes provide lists of reference works, including catalogs and keys organized by biogeographical zone for families, orders and classes. They constitute a unique collection of resource materials for the biologist or ecologist who wants to learn about a particular group in greater depth.

Smith, R.L. 1982. *Venomous animals of Arizona.* Tucson: Cooperative Extension Service, College of Agriculture, University of Arizona. 134 pp.

An excellent practical survey of the venomous species in the animal kingdom and least-toxic approaches to their management.

Spradbery, J.P. 1973. *Wasps: an account of the biology and natural history of solitary and social wasps.* Seattle: University of Washington Press. 408 pp.

A broad approach to solitary and social wasps with an emphasis on British species.

Sudd, J.H. 1967. *An introduction to the behaviour of ants.* London: Edward Arnold Ltd. 200 pp.

An authoritative and detailed approach demonstrating many useful study methods.

Swan, L.A., and C.S. Papp. 1972. *The common insects of North America.* New York: Harper & Row. 750 pp.

Includes over 2,000 excellent line drawings with short descriptions useful for field identification.

Tassen, R. L., and K. S. Hagen. 1970. *Culturing green lacewings in the home and school.* Berkeley: University of California Cooperative Extension Service (Leaflet 2500). 2 pp.

This out-of-print leaflet is the source of the drawing of the life cycle of the green lacewing.

Thiele, H. 1977. *Carabid beetles in their environments.* New York: Springer-Verlag. 369 pp.

An eco-physiological approach to the distribution, predators, parasitoids, nutrition, importance, habitat selection, activity patterns, dispersal, evolution and speciation of carabid beetles. Includes a systematic index of cited families, subfamilies, tribes, genera and species.

Tonks, N.V., ed. 1982. *Pest problems in small greenhouses and indoor plantings.* Victoria, B.C.: Ministry of Agriculture and Food.

This is the source of the illustration comparing the life cycles of pest and predatory mites.

Townes, H. 1971. Ichneumonidae as biological control agents. In *Proceedings of the tall timbers conference on ecological animal control by habitat management, February, 1971*, pp. 25-27. 248 pp.

This reprint provides a good introduction to the biology of the largest family of parasitic insects.

van den Bosch, R., P.S. Messenger and A.P. Gutierrez. 1982. *An introduction to biological control.* New York: Plenum Press. 247 pp.

A readable, textbook-like introduction to the subject that is useful for the layperson but also can serve as an introduction for advanced high school or college students.

Wheeler, G.C., and J. Wheeler. 1963. *The ants of North Dakota.* Grand Forks, N. Dak.: University of North Dakota Press. 326 pp.

Wheeler, G.C., and J. Wheeler. 1973. *Ants of Deep Canyon.* Riverside: Philip L. Boyd Deep Canyon Desert Research Center, University of California. 162 pp.

These two books focus on local ants but also provide a great amount of information on the ant fauna of North America.

Wilson, E. O. 1971. *The insect societies.* Cambridge, Mass.: Harvard University Press. 548 pp.

A classic text on social insects, including chapters on bees, wasps, ants and termites.

PART 3

PESTICIDES

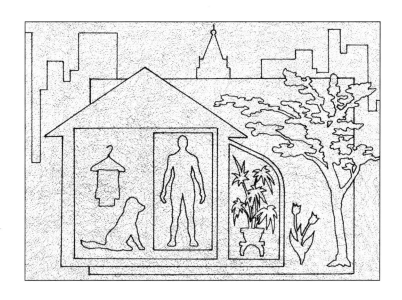

CHAPTER 6
Choosing the Right Chemical and Microbial Tools

OVERVIEW OF PART 3

This chapter and the next two chapters provide background information on the composition, application and impact of various pesticides, including the novel botanical and microbial materials we often recommend when pesticides are necessary. Because the primary focus of this book is on non-chemical methods, we are not trying to cover everything there is to know about pesticides; our goal is to provide enough information to enable you to select the safest, most effective material and apply it in a manner that protects both you and the general environment. Instead of discussing common insecticides such as malathion, herbicides like 2,4-D or fungicides such as benlate, we focus on the least-toxic pesticidal products, such as pesticidal soaps, horticultural oils and botanical compounds, as well as on insect growth regulators and microbes used to kill pests.

INTRODUCTION

The use of chemical compounds as tools in the competition among species predates the rise of humans. Plants have evolved chemical defenses against other plants (allelopathy) that are often expressed as root exudates or compounds leached from the leaves. Leaves or other tissues can also produce chemicals that repel or damage organisms that attempt to feed on them. Many familiar animals, such as toads, snakes and skunks, have incorporated repellent or poisonous materials into their skins, saliva or other fluids. And, among animals without backbones (invertebrates), the use of poisons against enemies is commonplace. Thus, it seems entirely natural that humans should also resort to chemical tools to rid themselves of their pests.

A BRIEF HISTORY OF THE USE OF CHEMICALS AGAINST PESTS

Before World War II, the pesticides in common use in the United States were predominantly inorganic materials, such as sulfur, lead, copper, arsenic, boron and mercury, as well as botanical (plant-derived) compounds, such as nicotine, pyrethrum, derris, rotenone, ryania and sabadilla.

The emergence of DDT, a "miracle" insecticide developed by the Swiss just before the war, changed the nature of pest control worldwide. The extraordinary effectiveness of DDT and the related materials that followed it in rapid succession — lindane, dieldrin, chlordane, 2,4-D and others — greatly slowed research and development of other, less-toxic methods of pest control, particularly biological controls (the use of the pests' natural enemies to control the pest). Even the gradual accumulation of evidence that the entire planet was becoming contaminated with these newly created materials and their breakdown products failed to impress upon many responsible people the real threat posed by this type of pollution.

Today there is a great deal of confusion about the toxicity of and necessity for pesticides. The good news is that there are some pesticides already on the market that are highly selective, meaning they kill only certain groups of pests, and are relatively harmless to humans and other non-target organisms. They also biodegrade rapidly. These materials, discussed in detail in chapters 7 and 8, are far more benign than such broad-spectrum insecticides as carbaryl, malathion and diazinon, which kill a wide range of organisms, including beneficial insects and microbes. Many broad-spectrum insecticides do not biodegrade readily into harmless materials and can contaminate groundwater and other resources.

THE REGISTRATION, NAMING AND CLASSIFICATION OF PESTICIDES

Pesticide selection is often complicated by technical terminology. This section should help clarify some of the important terms used by pest-control personnel and researchers.

Registration

The word "pesticide" is an umbrella term for all the sub-categories of materials used to suppress pests. These include insecticides, herbicides, fungicides and rodenticides. At present, a wide variety of commercially available chemical tools is used to control pests. Most are legally considered pesticides, although some are not. For example, when you use dish-washing detergent against aphids, it is acting as a pesticide; however, it is not legally registered as such.

If a product is sold as a pesticide it must be registered at the federal level by the Environmental Protection Agency and at the state level by an agency such as the state's department of agriculture. EPA-registered pesticides must carry labels describing the proper dosage and frequency of application for the control of specific pests. The label must also contain a list of the active ingredients (but not necessarily the "inert" ingredients, whose importance is discussed below), information about the product's relative toxicity to mammals, the name and address of the manufacturer, the net contents, an EPA registration number and cautions regarding hazards to humans and the environment. A sample label is shown on p. 84.

EPA registration implies that the pesticide has met standards set for health and environmental safety, although this is the subject of considerable controversy. Many people maintain that safety standards, testing methodology and testing compliance are far from adequate. These shortcomings are discussed more completely on pp. 89-92. There is no doubt, however, that the registration

Pesticide Labeling

All pesticides must be registered by the U.S. Environmental Protection Agency and must be packaged with a label. All labels must contain the kind of information shown on this sample.

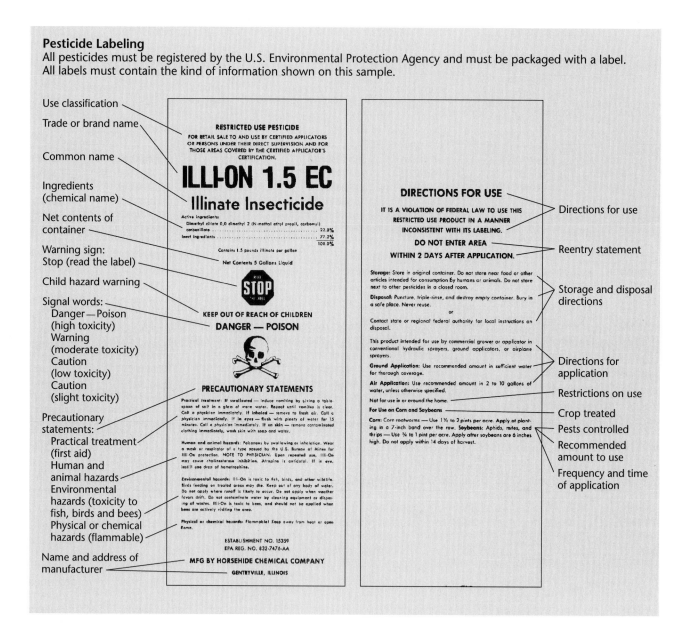

process is more stringent now than it was in the 1950s and 1960s, when most of the 35,000 pesticide products and over 600 active ingredients currently used as pesticides were registered. Unfortunately, the newer standards are still problematic. They are not comprehensive enough for those concerned about the hazards of pesticides, and they are too costly and too fraught with bureaucratic delays to suit manufacturers, particularly the small, innovative companies attempting to secure registration for novel, less-toxic pesticides.

Naming

A layperson may have considerable trouble obtaining and understanding information about pesticides, because each compound generally has at least two or three names. The generic name—carbaryl, for example—is the term used to refer to the chemical compound. It is frequently the name by which you must search for it in the technical literature to find out about its toxicity and effectiveness. There is also the chemical name, which describes the molecule. The chemical name for carbaryl, for example, is 1-naphthalenyl methylcarbamate. Sometimes there is more than one chemical name for a compound, depending on the conventions used to describe the molecule.

The trade or brand name is what you ask for in the store; it is also the name pest control professionals generally use when talking with the public. To continue the example, the best-known brand name for carbaryl is Sevin®. To confuse the issue even more, a substance may have several brand names when it is marketed in slightly different formulations.

Mode of Action and Formulation

Before exploring some of the ways in which pesticides are classified, it helps to understand two important terms: mode of action and formulation. The mode of action of a pesticide is the physiological mechanism by which it affects the pest. Many least-toxic pesticides operate physically or mechanically on the pest. For example, sorptive dusts like silica aerogel or diatomaceous earth abrade the waxy coating on the cuticle of insects, causing them to dehydrate and die. Insecticidal soap penetrates the waxy coating and disrupts the membranes surrounding the cells, allowing the cell contents to leak out, resulting in dehydration and death of the insect.

Other pesticides, including most conventional synthetic materials, have a biochemical mode of action, disrupting enzymes, hormones, nervous transmission or other biophysical processes of the target pest. The total impact on the organism and the environment of a pesticide with a biochemical mode of action is often difficult to predict, however, and unanticipated side effects are more often encountered with pesticides that operate this way than with pesticides whose mode of action is primarily physical and/or mechanical.

The formulation of a pesticide refers to the mixture of its active ingredient and the other ingredients that affect the active ingredient's solubility, its ability to stick to vegeta-

tion or insect bodies and other functions. Substances other than the active ingredient are referred to as adjuvants. An example of an adjuvant is a surfactant, also called a wetting agent or spreader. A surfactant enhances the coverage of a sprayed-on pesticide by reducing the surface tension of the spray droplets and allowing greater pesticide contact, enhancing the toxicity of the material. On the pesticide label these adjuvants are called "inert substances," certainly a misnomer since they generally are not inert, and in some cases are more toxic than the active ingredient itself.

The complete formulation of a pesticide—the active and "inert" ingredients together—is not tested by the registration agencies; only the active ingredients are tested. This is another area of controversy, since it is the entire mixture that people and other nontarget organisms are exposed to, not just the active ingredient.

Classification

Pesticides can be classified by their target pest group (see Table 6.1 above), formulation (see Table 6.2 on p. 86), chemical category (see tables 6.3 and 6.4 on p. 87) or function (see Table 6.5 on p. 88). Insecticides can also be classified according to the stage in the target insect's development at which they are effective. As described in Chapter 1, most insects go through four developmental stages: egg, larva (caterpillar, worm, grub or nymph), pupa (cocoon) and adult. Thus, an ovicide attacks eggs, a larvicide attacks the young and an adulticide attacks mature individuals. (Note that there are no pupicides.)

Another major point about pesticide classification is that within the major categories (insecticides, herbicides, fungicides, etc.) there are often subgroups peculiar to that group. For example, herbicides are frequently classified according to when they are

Table 6.1
Pesticide Groups Classified by Presumed Target Pest or Taxonomic Category[a]

Pesticide Group	Presumed Target Pest
acaricide	mites
algicide	algae
avicide	birds
bactericide	bacteria
fungicide	fungi
herbicide	plants
insecticide	insects
miticide	mites
molluscicide	snails, slugs
nematicide	nematodes
piscicide	fish
predacide	vertebrates
rodenticide	rodents
silvicide	trees and woody vegetation
slimicide	slime molds

[a] Many pesticides, although labeled as confined in their activity to a particular group of pests, may actually have broad toxicity over many types of organisms. Herbicides, for example, can damage insects and microbes.

Table 6.2
Pesticides Classified by Formulation

Formulation	Examples[a]
Baits (poison mixed with food or other attractant)	most rodenticides; ant baits such as boric acid in mint jelly for control of pharaoh ants
Dusts (finely ground mineral or pesticide combined with a dry carrier)	boric acid, diatomaceous earth, pyrethrum, silica aerogel, sulfur
Fumigants (poison gas)	CO_2
Granules (pesticide and carrier combined with a binding agent)	many insecticides and herbicides
Sprays	
Aerosols (very fine liquid droplets delivered from a pressurized can)	pyrethrins
Emulsifiable concentrates (petroleum-based liquid plus emulsifiers that enable it to mix with water)	many pesticides, either ready-to-use or concentrated
Flowables (combine the qualities of emulsifiable concentrates and wettable powders; require agitation when mixed and sprayed)	sulfur; copper compounds
Microencapsulated materials (pesticide particles surrounded by a plastic coating; active ingredients are released slowly as the plastic coating breaks down)	many pesticides
Slurry (thin, watery mixture of finely ground dusts)	Bordeaux mixture (hydrated lime and copper sulfate)
Water-soluble concentrates (liquid pesticides that dissolve in water)	insecticidal soaps
Wettable powders (water-insoluble active ingredient plus mineral clay ground into fine powder that can be mixed with water)	*Bacillus thuringiensis*
Oils (petroleum or botanical)	horticultural oil; weed oil

[a] These materials are discussed in greater detail in this and the next two chapters, and in later portions of the book are recommended in certain situations against specific pests.

Table 6.3
Insecticides Classified by Chemical Category

Category	Examples[a, b]	Category	Examples[a, b]
Inorganic	boric acid, borates, chlorates copper, cryolite, diatomaceous earth, silica aerogel	**Chlorinated hydrocarbons**	aldrin, chlordane, lindane, methoxychlor, pentachlorophenol
Organic botanical	garlic, limonene, neem, nicotine, pyrethrum, rotenone, ryania, sabadilla	**Organophosphates**	acephate (Orthene®), diazinon, malathion
microbial	*Bacillus thuringiensis, B. popilliae, Cephalasporium lecanii, Morrenia odorata, Nosema locustae*	**Synthetic pyrethroids** **Miscellaneous**	permethrin, resmethrin horticultural oils, insect growth regulators, insecticidalsoaps, insect pheromones
Carbamates	carbaryl (Sevin®), propoxur (Baygon®)		

[a] Most of these materials are discussed in greater detail in this and the next two chapters, and in later portions of the book are recommended in certain situations against specific pests.

[b] The names in parentheses are trade names that have become so common that the chemical or generic name is less known.

Table 6.4
Herbicides Classified by Chemical Category

Category	Examples[a]	Category	Examples[a]
Inorganic	borates, copper sulfate, sodium chlorate	phenoxy acetic acids	2,4-D; 2,4,5-T; Silvex® (2,4,5-TP)
Organic		phenyl ethers	nitrofen (TOK)
amino acids	glyphosate (Roundup®)	phthalic acids	DCPA (Dacthal®)
arsenicals	monosodium acid methanearsonate (MSMA)	pyridazinones	pyrazon (Pyramin®)
		pyridyls	picloram (Tordon®)
benzoic acids	dicamba (Banvel®)	substituted amides	alachlor (Lasso®)
benzonitriles	bromoxynil (Brominal®)	thio-carbamates	diallate (Avadex®)
carbamates	chlorpropham (Chloro-IPC®)	triazines	atrazine (Aatrex®), simazine (Princep®)
carbanilates	phenmedipham (Betanal®)		
dinitroanilines	trifluralin (Treflan®)	triazoles	amino-triazole (Amitrole™, Weedazol®)
dipyridyls	diquat		
halogenated aliphatic acids	dalapon (Dowpon®)	uracils	bromacil (Hyvar™)
		ureas	diuron (Karmex™)
phenols	dinoseb (Sinox®)		

[a] The names in parentheses are trade names that have become so common that the chemical or generic name is less known.

Table 6.5
Pesticides Classified by Function

Category	Examples
Attractants	compounds that attract pests to traps or poisons, including sex-based and food-based attractants, e.g., the food attractant in some cockroach traps
Repellents	compounds that repel the target pest, e.g., neem oil from the neem tree of India, which repels the Japanese beetle
Desiccants	compounds that kill by adhering to insect cuticle, abrading a hole and drying out the insect, e.g., diatomaceous earth, silica aerogel
Insect growth regulators (juvenile hormones)	compounds that mimic insect hormones that regulate development, e.g., methoprene, which prevents fleas from maturing
Poisons	
contact poisons	materials that penetrate the skin or outer membranes and disrupt the physiology of the organism, e.g., insecticidal soap, pyrethrins
stomach poisons	materials that attack the pest after it has ingested the poison, e.g., the microbial insecticide *Bacillus thuringiensis* (BT), boric acid
fumigants	respiratory poisons that kill by suffocation, e.g., CO_2, used to kill storage pests
pass-throughs or feed-throughs	poisons that pass through an animal's digestive system and kill insects that attempt to inhabit the dung
systemics	materials that are first absorbed by the plant or animal, then kill any organism that feeds upon the poisoned tissues, e.g., the insecticide metasystox-R, the fungicide benomyl
Sterilants	
insect	materials (in various stages of research) that sterilize an insect without killing it; no commercial products available at present
soil	compounds that kill many forms of life in the soil, e.g., methyl bromide, which is used to fumigate the soil where plant-infesting nematodes are a problem

applied in the life cycle of weeds. Pre-emergent herbicides are applied before the weed germinates; post-emergent herbicides are applied after weed growth is underway. Herbicides can also be classified according to their selectivity. A selective herbicide is intended to kill certain weeds but leave desirable plants. A nonselective herbicide is toxic to most plant material it encounters.

Herbicides classified according to their mode of activity usually fall into one of three main categories: contact, translocated or residual. Contact herbicides injure or kill plants on contact with their foliage. They are called "chemical mowers," because, like a lawn mower, they kill only that part of the plant with which they come into contact.

Translocated herbicides move through the entire plant system carried by water and food streams to the plant's active growth centers, which they damage or destroy. They can be applied to the soil around the plant or to the plant's foliage, and are usually selective in the range of plants they affect. Soil-residual herbicides are those that remain active in the soil for relatively long periods, depending on the dosage. To be effective, they must be sprayed directly on emerging plant shoots or washed into the soil, where they are taken up by the roots and carried to the leaves; they are relatively ineffective when sprayed on mature foliage.

Similar subcategories exist for all the major pesticide groups. Rodenticides, for example, are separated into single- and multiple-dose groups, fungicides into preventive and curative categories.

TOXICITY TO HUMANS

Toxicity questions about poisons usually fall into several broad categories: toxicity to humans; toxicity to plants (phytotoxicity); toxicity to organisms that may be exposed to the poison accidentally through drift, soil contamination, water contamination or magnification in the food chain (biomagnification); effectiveness against the pest; and procedures for using the poison as a pest management tool. We examine human toxicity first.

Measuring Toxicity

There are two general kinds of toxicity: acute and chronic. A given dose of a poison is said to have acute toxicity if it affects human health adversely after a relatively short term of exposure; it has chronic toxicity if it has an adverse impact after long-term exposure. Long-term exposure can range from days to years. A poison may be chronically toxic even at relatively low doses if there is prolonged exposure. Dizziness and, in more extreme cases, anaphylactic shock or a heart attack that occurs right after an individual sprays a pesticide indoors are examples of acutely toxic responses. The development of cancer or neurological problems from occupational exposure to pesticides over several decades is an example of a chronic toxicological response.

The most common method of measuring the acute toxicity of a pesticide is by giving test animals known doses of the poison and observing the results. This is the method by which the lethal dose, referred to as the LD_{50}, or the lethal concentration, commonly called the LC_{50}, of a compound is established. These measurements are used to predict the hazards to people and other nontarget organisms. Given the choice between two compounds, the higher LD_{50} rating indicates the less acutely poisonous —that is, the "safer"—compound.

The "50" in this expression refers to the dose of a given substance that kills 50% of the organisms exposed to it in tests (see the graph above). The

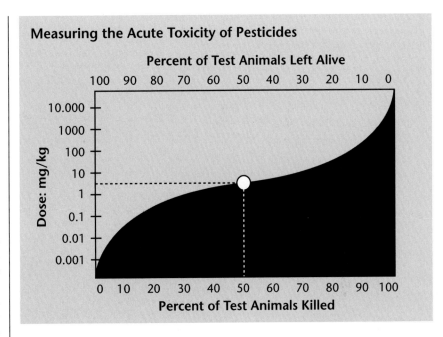

Measuring the Acute Toxicity of Pesticides

Percent of Test Animals Left Alive

Dose: mg/kg

Percent of Test Animals Killed

LD_{50} rating is usually expressed in milligrams of poison per kilogram of body weight, or mg/kg. For example, if a particular poison has an LD_{50} rating of 1.0 mg/kg and each individual in a group of 150-lb. (68-kg) men consumes approximately 68 mg of the pesticide, presumably half the individuals will die immediately. Here's how we arrive at that number mathematically: 1 mg/kg (the LD_{50} rating for the poison) x 150 lb. (the weight of each man) x 0.45 kg/lb. (the number of kilograms in each pound) = 68 mg, the dose that will kill one out of two men. However, this measurement has some serious limitations, as discussed on p. 90.

Acute toxicity can also be measured by the amount of pesticide vapor or dust in a given volume of air, or the amount diluted in waterways, that will cause the death of any specific proportion of a test-animal population. This measurement is the lethal concentration, or LC_{50}, and it is expressed in micrograms (one microgram equals one millionth of a gram) per liter of air or water mixture or solution.

Cautions on Pesticide Labels

If you look at a pesticide label—and you should always look at the label very carefully if you plan to use any pesticide—you will see one of these signal words: caution, warning or danger. By law, a signal word must be included on every pesticide label to give the user some indication of the acute toxicity of the material. Table 6.6 on p. 90 gives you an idea of what the various signal words mean. The word "caution" indicates a Category III or IV pesticide. Materials in this category are least-toxic based on their LD_{50}. Category I pesticides, as indicated by the signal word "danger," are the most toxic and are generally restricted to use by professional pest control operators.

It is important to remember that the tests that determine these ratings are performed primarily on rats and to a lesser degree on dogs, chickens, rabbits, monkeys, pheasants, ducks, sparrows and other animals. The reason for conducting the tests this way is obvious, but remember that humans may not react to the poison exactly as other animals do.

Table 6.6
Pesticide Toxicity Scale[a]

Hazard Level	I	II	III	IV
Indicators	Danger	Warning	Caution	Caution
oral LD_{50}	up to 50 mg/kg	50-500 mg/kg	500-5,000 mg/kg	>5,000 mg/kg
inhalation LC_{50}	up to 0.2 µg/l	0.2-2 µg/l	2-20 µg/l	>20 µg/l
dermal LD_{50}	up to 200 mg/kg	200-2,000 mg/kg	2,000-20,000 mg/kg	>20,000 mg/kg
eye effects	corrosive, corneal opacity not reversible within 7 days	corneal opacity reversible within 7 days; irritation persists 7 days	no corneal opacity; irritation reversible within 7 days	no irritation
skin effects	corrosive	severe irritation at 72 hours	moderate irritation at 72 hours	mild or slight irritation

[a] Adapted from Marer, 1988.

Routes of Pesticide Exposure

Routes of entry of pesticides into an organism can vary. They include oral, dermal (on the skin), interdermal (in the skin), interocular (in the eye), internasal (in the nose) and respiratory (in the lungs). Usually LD_{50} data is based on oral exposure as determined by feeding pesticides to test animals, but there can be large differences in the LD_{50} with different routes of entry. For example, the common organophosphate insecticide malathion has an oral LD_{50} (using rats as the test animal) of 2,800 mg/kg, but the dermal LD_{50} is only 4,100 mg/kg. Of the two exposure routes, the oral is the more toxic because it takes less material to kill 50% of the animals tested.

However, the respiratory route of entry is usually the most toxic of all, because pesticides are absorbed most rapidly through the lungs. They are quickly distributed throughout the body in the bloodstream, causing all organs and tissues to be exposed within minutes after inhalation. Unfortunately, studies of lung exposure to pesticides have been relatively few to date, and little or no comparative data are available.

Another organ that is highly susceptible to the absorption of pesticides is the eye, which is why it is important to wear goggles whenever pesticides are applied. The chart on the facing page illustrates the susceptibility of other body parts to the absorption of pesticides. Note that the scalp and scrotum are more susceptible than the hands. This is why we are concerned about the use of pesticides on the heads of young children to control head lice, as well as their use in the pubic area of children and adults to control pubic lice (for more on this subject, see Chapter 11).

The Limitations of Toxicity Ratings

The LD_{50} rating as a measure of how hazardous a material is has severe limitations since chronic, or long-term, effects are not indicated. Chronic effects may be carcinogenic (causing cancer), mutagenic (causing genetic changes) or teratogenic (causing birth defects). Furthermore, there is substantial variation in the impact of a toxic substance from individual to individual and from developmental stage to developmental stage in the same individual. For example, children, the elderly, pregnant women and the sick are more vulnerable than a younger but mature 150-pound man in the peak of health. Yet it is the latter for whom toxicity test data on animals are extrapolated.

Poisons can also produce a number of miscellaneous symptoms such as rashes, sleepiness or restlessness in sensitive individuals exposed over a period of time. Many of these symptoms are not easily associated with pesticide poisoning by doctors because they mimic other conditions. Often only the person suffering makes the connection. For example, the subject may observe that he or she is regularly exposed to pesticide treatments for cockroaches in the office, and that this coincides with headaches, rashes or other problems.

Data Gaps

Whereas data on acute toxicity is available for most registered pesticides, data on chronic toxicity is woefully inadequate or completely missing for most of the more than 600 registered active ingredients in pesticide products. It wasn't until the mid-1970s that chronic toxicity data was required by law, and the new legislation allowed all pesticides to remain on the market despite major data gaps on chronic toxicity. Although pesticide manufacturers are now required to produce the missing data, the EPA acknowledges that it will be

Rates of Absorption of Pesticides into the Human Body

Pesticides are absorbed through different parts of the body at different rates. This illustration shows the relative rates of absorption for the insecticide parathion.

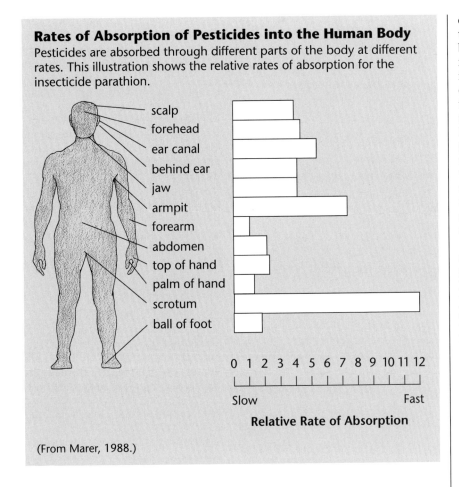

- scalp
- forehead
- ear canal
- behind ear
- jaw
- armpit
- forearm
- abdomen
- top of hand
- palm of hand
- scrotum
- ball of foot

0 1 2 3 4 5 6 7 8 9 10 11 12

Slow   Fast

Relative Rate of Absorption

(From Marer, 1988.)

well into the next century before testing is completed.

Another major problem is lack of toxicity data on the so-called "inert" ingredients in pesticide formulations. If you examine a pesticide label, you will see that these inert ingredients represent as much as 90% to 99% of the volume of the material in the package. In general, the inert ingredients are not identified, and there is little or no data on their toxicity. With the growing recognition that many inert ingredients are not inert at all, and in some cases may be more toxic than the pesticide's active ingredient (for example, the surfactant in the herbicide Roundup® is more toxic than its active ingredient, glyphosate), the EPA is beginning to require the listing of inert ingredients on the label and some level of testing. As with chronic-toxicity data, however, significant data on the impact of inert ingredients is still years away.

Synergism

Another potential danger not reflected in the LD_{50} rating is synergism. Synergism occurs when one compound enhances the effect of another many times beyond what would be experienced if either were encountered alone. This is why, for example, alcohol should not be combined with certain drugs. The interaction of the two substances can produce effects that are amplified in a totally unexpected manner.

To understand the implications of synergism, we must understand something about the nature and fre-

quency of our exposure to various toxic substances. There have always been natural hazards in the environment, and over the millennia it took for humans to evolve, man slowly developed various means of adapting to or managing these hazards. But now, suddenly, we live in a "soup" of human-created compounds. In a single morning, you may knowingly or unknowingly expose yourself to a wide variety of pesticides: flea collars and clothes-moth repellents at home, tree sprays on the way to work, cockroach treatment residues on the bus or in the office, and so on.

In addition, we may expose ourselves deliberately or passively to many other chemical hazards: alcohol; tars, nicotine and other compounds in tobacco and other recreational drugs; food preservatives; prescription and nonprescription antibiotics; and various cleaning agents. Finally, inside the house, at school, at work, in the garden and on the street we are unwillingly or unknowingly exposed to a vast variety of toxic materials that are by-products of our industrial world. This is especially true of air and water contaminants such as toxic gases that are emitted by synthetic building materials and furnishings or are the breakdown products of water-treatment chemicals and various aerosols. The list of pollutants in the air and drinking water is growing.

No one is examining in any systematic way how these many compounds, combined in the manner in which we are actually exposed to them, might produce undesirable health effects. Furthermore, the laboratory methods used to determine pesticide toxicity do not take into account the impact of mixtures of several pesticides and their additives, or pesticides plus other environmental toxicants. The human body can detoxify many poisons, but how much can be processed safely by different individuals cannot be stated clearly. Table 6.7 on p. 92 shows various pesticides that have been detected in hu-

Table 6.7
Pesticides and/or Their Metabolites Detected in Human Urine[a]

Pesticide (Active Ingredient)	Chemicals Present in Urine
carbaryl and naphthalene	alpha-naphthol
propoxur	isopropoxyphenol
carbofuran	carbofuran phenol and 3-ketocarbofuran
malathion	alpha-monocarboxylic acid (MCA),
pentachlorophenol, lindane, BHC	pentachlorophenol
methyl and ethyl parathion	paranitrophenol
2,4-D	2-4-D
2,4,5-T	2,4,5-T
chloropyrifos	3,5,6-trichloro-2-pyridinol (3,5,6-TC-2-P)
2,4,5-trichlorophenol	2,4,5-TCP
organophosphates	dimethyl phosphate (DMP) diethyl phosphate (DEP) dimethyl phosphorothionate (DETP) diethyl phosphorothionate (DETP) dimethyl phosphorodithionate (DMDTP) diethyl phosphorodithionate (DEDTP)

[a] From Kutz et al., 1978.

man urine. Table 6.8 on the facing page indicates chlorinated hydrocarbon pesticide levels in human adipose (fat) tissue.

The growing number of "chemically sensitive" individuals and individuals who believe or can document that they are suffering damage to their immune systems from chronic exposure to synthetic compounds such as pesticides is of increasing concern to health professionals. In fact, a new medical practice known as clinical ecology is developing to address this question.

Despite its limitations, and even though much research remains to be done, information on acute toxicity is nonetheless valuable. Table 6.9 on p. 94 lists some common pesticides and their LD_{50} ratings. Organizations that can provide information on the toxicity of common pesticides are listed in the sidebar on pp. 97-98.

Material Safety Data Sheets
One of the recent improvements in pesticide regulation is the requirement that manufacturers provide a material safety data sheet (MSDS) for each pesticide they produce. The MSDS describes the chemical characteristics of the active and other hazardous ingredients, and lists fire and explosion hazards, health hazards, reactivity and incompatibility characteristics and types of protective equipment needed for handling and storing the pesticide and cleaning up spills. LD_{50} ratings are given for vari-

ous test animals, and manufacturers' emergency phone numbers are listed.

Although the scope of the toxicity information on the MSDS still leaves much to be desired, and the data on chronic health effects and environmental impacts are minimal or missing entirely, there is more detail than is provided on the pesticide label. The manufacturer is required to provide an MSDS to anyone selling or using the material. If your local pesticide supplier does not have an MSDS for the pesticide you are contemplating using, obtain one from the manufacturer whose name and address are listed on the pesticide label.

TOXICITY IN THE ENVIRONMENT: BIOMAGNIFICATION
When considering how safe a material is, you must also look at its effects on the environment. With the exception of poison baits, which usually attract and kill just the pest, the application of most pesticides results in only a small amount—often as little as 1%—of the poison actually reaching the target pest. Most of the material lands in adjacent areas. Outdoors, this means it falls on nontarget organisms, plants, other animals, the soil and outdoor furniture.

Because a healthy garden is teeming with life above and in the soil, all kinds of undesired side effects can arise. For example, fungicides used against a plant disease may fall on and become incorporated into the soil. This may inhibit the growth of the beneficial fungi called mycorrhizae that are associated with plant roots and are important in helping the plant obtain nutrients. Decomposer organisms, which break down dead plant and animal litter so the nutrients are once again available for plant growth, may also be affected by insecticides that fall on garden soil.

Some pesticides accumulate in food chains. Small amounts of poison distributed over plants or plant-eating animals can become concentrated in

Table 6.8
Trends in Chlorinated Hydrocarbon Pesticide Levels in Human Fat Tissue[a]

Pesticides in Parts Per Million (ppm) in Fat Tissue [b]

Pesticide	1970	1971	1972	1973	1974	1975
BHC	0.37	0.34	0.23	0.27	0.21	0.27
DDT[c]	7.87	7.95	6.88	5.8	4.8	4.8
dieldrin	0.18	0.21	0.18	0.18	0.14	0.16
heptachlor epoxide	0.09	0.09	0.08	0.09	0.09	0.10
oxychlordane[d]	N/A	0.11	0.11	0.10	0.10	0.13
trans-Nonachlor [d]	N/A	N/A	N/A	N/A	0.10	0.15

[a] Data on DDT prior to 1970 from Kutz et al., 1974; data after 1972 from Kutz et al., 1978.

[b] The sample size was in excess of about 1,000, with the exception of trans-Nonachlor, where there were 47 samples in 1974, 683 in 1975.

[c] Total DDT equivalent = mixtures of DDT, DDD and DDE, the latter two of which are breakdown products of DDT.

[d] Oxychlordane and trans-Nonachlor are major mammalian metabolites of the insecticides chlordane and heptachlor. Aldrin readily epoxydizes to dieldrin; dieldrin residues indicate exposure to either or both pesticides.

the bodies of the organisms that eat those plants or animals. For example, organisms such as earthworms that are low on the food chain may eat many fallen leaves. Even though each leaf holds only a small amount of pesticide residue, the pesticide is concentrated in the earthworm's body because of the number of leaves it consumes. This concentrated dose is then passed on to the earthworm's predators, such as birds. Because a single bird eats many earthworms, the pesticide reaches even higher concentrations in the bird's body. Finally, at the top of the food chain, predators such as cats may ingest such high concentrations of poison that they become sick or suffer an impaired ability to reproduce.

In one classic case, plankton absorbed pesticides from contaminated waters through the microorganisms they fed upon. The plankton were eaten by small fish, and these were in turn fed upon by larger fish. The brown pelican, a fish-eating bird at the top of the food chain, suffered a serious population decline due to the effects of these accumulated poisons. Other fish- and rodent-eating birds, such as bald eagles and peregrine falcons, were also suffering declines. This is one reason why a whole series of long-lasting compounds, starting with DDT, was withdrawn from use by the federal government.

Because humans are at the top of numerous food chains on this planet, the long-term health consequences of using these pesticides are feared. DDT is a good example of a substance whose direct toxicity, when expressed as an LD_{50} measurement, does not reflect its tendency to biomagnify. If we consider its LD_{50} alone, we might be misled into thinking that DDT is not as potentially dangerous as it really is. Unfortunately, the current EPA registration process does not exclude substances that biomagnify.

RESIDUE, RESURGENCE, RESISTANCE AND SECONDARY PEST OUTBREAKS

"Three Rs and an S" is a mnemonic device we learned from Dr. Donald Dahlsten, an entomologist at the University of California at Berkeley, that helps you remember the main problems associated with pesticide use.

The first R stands for residue. Biomagnification is one aspect of the residue problem. But residues can also be a more direct problem. This is true in the house, for example, when pesticide sprays fall on dishes and other surfaces or mix with the air we breathe. Outdoors, pesticides often get into the groundwater or rivers. From there they can contaminate wells or have undesired effects on aquatic life. Over 50% of Americans rely on wells for drinking water. As of 1988, the EPA found groundwater in 38 states contaminated by 74 pesticides.

The EPA has set guidelines for permitted levels of residue for specific pesticides—a concept unacceptable to many clean-water advocates—and the pesticide levels in a significant

Table 6.9
Generic Names and Acute Toxicity Measurements for Some Common Pesticides[a]

Generic Name	Trade Name [b]	LD$_{50}$ (mg/kg)[c]	Route	Test Animal	Fish[d]	Honeybees[e]
acephate	Orthene®	866-945	oral	rats	—	—
atrazine	Gesaprim 50®, Pramitol A 50®	1,859-3,080	oral	rats	toxic	—
Bacillus thuringiensis	Caterpillar Attack®, Dipel®, Thuricide®	>10,000	oral	rats	—	—
bendiocarb	Ficam®	3,400	oral	rats	toxic	very toxic
benomyl	Benlate®	>10,000	oral	—	—	—
boric acid	Roach Prufe®	3,200	oral	rats	—	—
carbaryl	Sevin®	850	oral	rats	—	very toxic
chlordane	Octachlor®	457-590	oral	rats	—	—
chlorpyrifos	Dursban®	163	oral	rats	toxic	—
diazinon	Spectracide®	300,850	—	—	—	—
diphacinone	Ramik®	3	oral	rats	—	—
		3.0-7.5		dogs	—	—
		14.7	oral	cats	—	—
insecticidal soap	Safer™ Insecticidal Soap	>10,000	oral	rats	—	—
malathion	Cythion®	2,800	oral	rats	—	very toxic
methoprene	Precor®	5,100	oral	rats	—	—
methyl bromide	Dowfume®	65	resp.	humans	—	very toxic
naled	Dibrom®	430	oral	rats	—	—
neem oil	Margosan-O®	>13,000	oral	rats	—	—
nicotine	Black Leaf 40®	50-60	oral	rats	—	—
paraquat	Weedol®	157	oral	rats	—	—
		25-50	oral	dogs	—	—
pentachlorophenol	Permite®	210	oral	rats	toxic	—
propoxur	Baygon®	90	oral	rats	—	very toxic
pyrethrin aerosol	many products	584	oral	rats	—	—
pyrethroid	many products	430	oral	rats	—	—
pyrethrum	many products	>18,000	dermal	rats	—	—
silica aerogel	Dri-Die®	4,400	oral	rats	—	—
sodium octaborate	TIM-BOR®	2,000	oral	rats	—	—

[a] From Berg, 1980; Wiswesser, 1976; and Worthing, 1979.

[b] Most pesticides have many trade names; not all can be listed here. If no trade name is listed it means the material is best known by its generic name.

[c] Since LD$_{50}$ values may vary with the formulation, these values are given for comparative purposes only.

[d] Toxic to fish means that the substance should not be used where the material will enter waterways.

[e] Toxic to honeybees and other beneficial insects in the order Hymenoptera.

number of the wells tested exceeded these levels. Even in wells where residues from a specific pesticide fall within the guidelines, there may still be a problem since the guidelines fail to take into account the synergistic effect of the residues of several pesticides in the same well.

Residues constitute the one negative aspect of pesticide use that has most captured the public's attention. It is primarily the residue problem that inspired Rachel Carson's book *Silent Spring*. However, it is the other two Rs, resurgence and resistance, and the S, secondary pest outbreaks, that are of greater direct concern to the pest manager.

Resurgence occurs when the predators, parasitoids or pathogens that would naturally control the pests are temporarily removed or drastically reduced in number. The home gardener often experiences this phenomenon without realizing what is happening. In treating aphids on shrubs, for example, the first spraying may kill predators such as lacewings and syrphid flies, as well as the tiny parasitoids (miniwasps) that kill the aphids from within. Initially the aphids appear to have been wiped out by the pesticide. But some always escape the poison and others fly in from neighboring areas. In fact it is quite possible that what the gardener has thoroughly decimated is not the aphids, but their natural enemies. There are always fewer of these and they are slower to increase than the pests. Also, because of their greater mobility, they are more likely to be exposed to higher doses of the poison. The remaining aphids can now multiply with fewer restraints. After a time, the aphid problem is even worse than before.

Horrified at this new and more serious infestation, the gardener may spray again. This time the aphids bounce back even more quickly; their population has resurged. But the population of natural enemies does not bounce back to catch up with the pest. The reason has to do with the

state of things in the natural world as well as the nature of many human-designed pesticides.

Generally, there is a time lag between the appearance of the first noticeable populations of the pest and the development of sufficient numbers of their parasitoids or predators to reduce the pest population satisfactorily. This makes biological sense. The predators have evolved life cycles that ensure that when they emerge or are lured into an area, there is enough prey for them to eat. Populations of predators and parasitoids often take longer to build up than the pest because they produce fewer generations per season. The predators may compensate for this by living longer, as in the case of predacious ground beetles and spiders, by having more young, as with the parasitoids of caterpillars that produce multiple young from a single host, or by taking better care of their young, as with social insects such as wasps and many mammalian predators.

To illustrate this, we return to the example of the aphids and their predators. Aphids don't need to mate during the growing season. The insects you see on the plants are likely to be females carrying female embryos ready to be born in a short time. The parasitoids of aphids, however, must find a member of the opposite sex, mate, search out an aphid of the right kind and lay an egg within it to survive. Obviously this is a much slower, more complicated process than aphid reproduction. But eventually the parasitoids have a substantial impact on the pest population because each female parasitoid is capable of laying hundreds of eggs. If most of these beneficial insects have been killed by pesticides, however, it takes a long time for their population to recover.

There is another factor that explains why predators and parasitoids frequently do not bounce back as quickly as their prey after pesticide treatments. Sometimes the compounds used are more toxic to the

predators than to the pests. This is true, for example, of carbaryl (Sevin®), which is still popular with home gardeners and pest control professionals even though it is toxic to honeybees and the many beneficial insects closely related to them in the order Hymenoptera.

Pesticide use can also be responsible for the development of new, previously unimportant insect pests, which are sometimes called secondary pests—the S in the "3 Rs and an S." These multiply rapidly in the absence of their former competitors or other natural control organisms that have been killed by the chemicals. Although the gardener may be aware of only one or two types of insects present in large numbers on a particular plant, in actuality many other potential pest species are likely to be feeding there also. They are not obvious because their natural enemies keep their populations low.

When a pesticide is sprayed to kill pests such as caterpillars, the natural enemies of other potential pests may also be killed. Thus, the caterpillar problem is soon replaced, for example, by a damaging and sometimes more serious mite problem. As with the natural enemies of aphids, the natural enemies of mites (usually other, carnivorous mites) are very susceptible to many pesticides, often more so than are the pests.

The third R, resistance, is in some ways even more awesome in its potential for causing problems than residue or resurgence. Each time a pesticide is applied, some of the pests that survive to produce the next generation develop a means of avoiding or detoxifying the poison. This is very different from immunity, wherein the body develops antibodies to a disease organism (e.g., the polio virus) so that on subsequent exposure the body is far less or not at all susceptible to it. The resistance we are referring to is one of forced genetic selection. By creating a situation where only those organisms that can tolerate a pesticide survive and reproduce, we humans effectively select certain groups to continue that species. Normal genetic processes take centuries or longer to produce measurable differences in the gene pool; the changes produced in pest populations by pesticide applications over a few short years are a form of accelerated genetic selection.

With each treatment, the pests whose genetic composition allows them to tolerate the poison increase in number while those that are still susceptible to the poison die (see the drawing at right). Gradually, it becomes harder to reduce pest numbers through applications of the poison. In response, many people increase the frequency of treatment and the strength of the dose, only to have the pest population bounce back sooner and in greater numbers than before. This often happens with aphids, cockroaches, head lice and other garden, household and body pests that are treated frequently with pesticides.

In agriculture, resistance to pesticides has become a matter of worldwide concern. According to Cornell University entomologist David Pimentel, between the 1940s and 1974 crop losses due to insect pests in the United States alone actually increased nearly twofold from 7% to about 13%, despite a tenfold increase in the use of insecticides. The development of insect resistance to insecticides is a major factor in this increase.

Switching to a new compound may help, but the success may be short-lived due to the phenomenon known as cross-resistance. Once a pest has developed resistance to one class of chemicals, it usually develops resistance to others as well, often in a shorter time than it did to the first. This is the "pesticide treadmill" (described vividly by Robert van den Bosch in *The Pesticide Conspiracy*) in which sole reliance on pesticides leads to ever-increasing use until at some point no pesticide is effective against the pest.

The implications of this phenomenon for the field of public health are

Pesticide Resistance

This drawing shows how pesticide resistance builds up in a pest population. In (A), some individuals (shown in black) in the pest population have genetic traits that allow them to survive the pesticide spraying. In (B), a certain portion of these survivors' offspring have inherited the pesticide resistance trait. These individuals survive the next spraying. If spraying is frequent, the population soon consists mainly of resistant individuals (C).

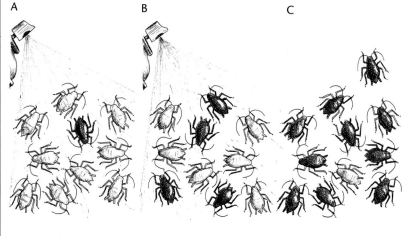

(Redrawn from Marer, 1988.)

particularly important. As with the antibiotics used to control human infections, casual or overly frequent use of powerful pesticides can render them powerless when they are really needed. For example, resistance has become a problem among certain mosquito species that carry the causal agents of malaria and encephalitis, and among rats whose fleas vector bubonic plague. There are always some cases of these diseases in humans in the United States, and as a nation we could face a major emergency if serious outbreaks of such diseases should occur.

More than 600 pest insects, weeds and plant pathogens are now resistant to one or more pesticides. Because pesticides cost much to develop and test, the loss of their use just when they are needed most is a double tragedy for the society that has invested so much in them.

It is important to understand that the problem of resistance is not related to the toxicity of the compound

to humans, other nontarget animals or the environment. Resistance can be expected to show up in any population of pests that is regularly exposed to a pesticide. This is so because a chemical compound cannot change or adjust in response to genetic changes in the pest population that help the pest tolerate the chemical. This is quite different from biological controls, where pest and predator or parasitoid have evolved together over millions of years, the population of each adjusting to changes in the other.

For this reason, chemical tools must always be regarded as temporary solutions to be resorted to only when other methods have failed and the pest problem truly threatens to become intolerable. Designing your home, garden and work environments to maximize the effect of natural enemies on the pest is always a more permanent and ultimately more cost-effective approach.

CRITERIA FOR SELECTING AND USING CHEMICAL AND MICROBIAL CONTROLS

As we mentioned earlier, a wide variety of new chemical tools are appearing on the market, largely in response to an increased understanding of the "3 Rs and an S." Some of these are believed to be far less toxic to humans and other mammals than the more traditional pesticides still in use. In this respect, the new materials are more acceptable for application around the home and garden. Nevertheless, most have not been around long enough for us to fully understand the long-term implications of their use, so caution is in order. We don't want to wait 10 or 30 years to find out that something has gone wrong, possibly irreversibly.

In order to minimize the hazards to yourself and the environment, and to maximize the immediate desired effect upon the pest and the long-term usefulness of the material, you should select the safest, most species-specific, most effective chemical or microbial material available. The sidebar at right describes the kind of information you should have about any pesticide before buying or using it.

APPLYING PESTICIDES

The pesticides recommended for use in this book can be applied by laypersons or professional pest control operators. Table 6.11 on pp. 100-101 depicts and describes the different types of equipment used to apply various kinds of pesticides. These tools are referred to throughout the book. The next section describes safety precautions you should follow whenever you use these pesticides.

Protecting Yourself when Applying Pesticides

The pesticides we discuss are the least-toxic pesticides currently available, but we nevertheless strongly recommend that you wear protective gear whenever applying any pesticide. Table 6.10 on p. 99 is an adapta-

Information You Should Obtain before Using a Pesticide and Where You Can Get It

I. What You Should Know

Safety. This means safety to you, other humans, pets, livestock, wildlife and the overall environment.

• Acute and chronic toxicity. What is the LD_{50} of the substance? Can or might it be carcinogenic (cancer-causing), mutagenic (causing genetic changes) or teratogenic (causing birth defects)?

• Mobility. Is the compound volatile, so that it moves into the air breathed by a building's occupants? Can it move through the soil into the groundwater?

• Residual life. How long does the compound remain toxic?

Species specificity. The best materials are species-specific; that is, they affect just the group of animals or plants you are trying to suppress. Avoid broad-spectrum materials because they are nonselective and can cause resurgence and secondary pest outbreaks in the long run. Where broad-spectrum materials must be used, apply them in as selective a way as possible (for more on this, see the discussion of spot treatment on p. 44).

Effectiveness. This issue is not as straightforward as it might seem, since it depends on how the effectiveness is being tested. For example, a pesticide can appear to be very effective in laboratory tests because it kills 99% of the test insects. But in field tests under more realistic conditions

it may also kill 100% of the pest's natural enemies. This will lead to serious pest outbreaks at a later date.

Endurance. A pesticide may have been effective against its target pest at the time it was registered, but if the pest problem is now recurring frequently, it may be a sign that the pest has developed resistance to the pesticide or, stated otherwise, that the pesticide has lost its endurance.

Speed. A quick-acting, short-lived, more acutely toxic material might be useful in emergencies; a slow-acting, longer lasting, less-toxic material might be preferable for a chronic pest problem.

Repellency. Some insecticides are effective more because of their repellency to insects than their ability to kill them. This is an important consideration in cockroach and subterranean termite control (see chapters 14 and 23, respectively).

Cost. This is usually measured as cost per volume of active ingredient used. You can find the percentage of active ingredient in the mixture by reading the product label. By multiplying the percentage of active ingredient by the number of times you need to apply the material, and then multiplying this product by the cost per volume of active ingredient, you can determine the cost-effectiveness of the pesticide.

(continued on page 98)

(continued from page 97)

Some of the newer, less-toxic microbial insecticides and insect growth regulators discussed in Chapter 8 may appear to be more expensive than some older, more toxic pesticides. But the newer materials tend to be effective in far smaller doses than the older materials—one container goes a long way. This factor, together with their lower impact on the environment, often makes them more cost-effective.

Other considerations. In addition to informing yourself about the characteristics of the material itself, it is important to:

• Observe all application directions on the label.

• Clothe yourself in neoprene gloves, goggles, respirator, hat and other protective clothing as necessary (see the discussion of protective clothing in the text and Table 6.10 on p. 99).

• Confine your use of the material to the area requiring treatment (see the discussion of spot treatment on p. 44).

• Store all materials under lock and key.

II. Sources of Information

You can find this information by consulting the references and readings at the end of this chapter. Authoritative acute toxicity data, including the LD_{50} ratings of various substances, is contained in Worthing (1979). Characteristics of different materials for the control of cockroaches, rats, mice and termites, including their toxicity to applicators and others, are compiled in Pinto and Spear (1980). Two books that provide an introduction to the pesticides are Ware (1978) and Bohmont (1981). Marer (1988) provides excellent information on safety precautions that should be followed when using pesticides.

You can also contact the organizations below by telephone or mail for more information on the toxicology and other aspects of specific pesticides:

• National Coalition Against the Misuse of Pesticides (NCAMP) 701 E Street S.E., Suite 200 Washington, DC 20003 (202) 543-5450

NCAMP maintains an extensive file of literature on the toxicology of pesticides. They can provide a summary of published data and tell you which pesticides lack the full range of health-hazard tests. This is a nonprofit organization, so please consider a donation when requesting information.

• The National Pesticide Telecommunications Network (NPTN) Texas Tech University Health Sciences Center School of Medicine Dept. of Preventive Medicine Lubbock, TX 79430 (800) 858-7378

NPTN operates a Pesticide Hotline funded by the Environmental Protection Agency and Texas Tech University. They can provide information on the proper use and toxicity of pesticides.

tion of the protective clothing and equipment guide developed by the California Department of Food and Agriculture. It indicates which pieces of protective gear are deemed necessary by various statements on a pesticide label. Although this chart was prepared for professional pest control personnel, it is a good guide for the nonprofessional as well. It, and a great deal of additional excellent advice on safety issues surrounding use of pesticides, are contained in *The Safe and Effective Use of Pesticides* by Patrick Marer.

Anyone planning to apply a pesticide should have on hand the following gear at the minimum:
• Full-length pants and a long-sleeved shirt made from tightly woven cotton fabric. Cotton overalls on top of these garments provide added protection and can be removed easily if there is a spill.
• A water-resistant or plastic wide-brimmed hat or a hooded waterproof jacket. Remember, the scalp readily absorbs pesticides.
• Waterproof gloves made from natural rubber, latex, butyl or neoprene. Do not use lined gloves since the fabric used for lining may absorb pesticides. Make sure the cuffs of the gloves are long enough to extend to the mid-forearm. Wear sleeves on the outside of gloves to keep pesticides from getting inside (unless spraying overhead, in which case sleeves should be tucked inside the gloves).
• Footwear made of rubber or synthetic materials such as PVC, nitrile, neoprene or butyl. Do not wear leather or fabric shoes since they absorb most pesticides.
• Goggles to protect the eyes, another highly absorptive area of the head.
• A respirator or disposable paper dust mask to protect the lungs and respiratory tract from airborne pesticides. Dust masks should be worn when applying pesticidal dusts. Buy masks that are capable of screening out micron-sized particles.

When liquid sprays are being applied, a cartridge respirator should be

Table 6.10
Guide to Protective Clothing and Equipment[a]

Protective clothing and equipment should be worn when applying any pesticide. This guide helps you decide which protective gear to wear based on the toxicity category and cautionary statements printed on the pesticide label.

Summary of Statement on Pesticide Label	Toxicity Category	
	I and II	**III and IV**
precautions to be taken to prevent exposure	B C F G H R[b]	C F H R[b]
protective clothing or equipment to be worn	B C F G H R[b]	C F H R[b]
clean clothing to be worn	C	C
contact with clothing to be avoided	B C	C
contact with shoes to be avoided	B	B
rubber boots or foot coverings to be worn	B	B
contact with skin to be avoided	B C F G	C F G[b] H
cap or hat to be worn	H	H
rubber gloves to be worn	G	G
contact with eyes to be avoided	F	F
goggles or face shield to be worn	F	F
avoid inhalation	R	M[c] R[b]
respirator to be worn	R[b]	R[b]

[a] Adapted from a California Department of Food and Agriculture document.

[b] Use this equipment when there is a likelihood of exposure to spray, mist, dust or vapors. If a Category III pesticide application is being made in an enclosed area such as a greenhouse, use the protective equipment guidelines for Category I-II pesticides.

[c] A dust mask can be used when applying sorptive dusts such as silica aerogel, but a cartridge respirator provides better protection.

Key

B   Wear waterproof boots or shoes made from rubber or synthetic material.

C   Clean overalls or outer clothing; wear waterproof pants and jacket if there is a chance of becoming wet from pesticide spray.

F   Wear face shield or goggles with side shields.

G   Wear waterproof unlined gloves made from rubber or synthetic material.

H   Wear waterproof wide-brimmed hat with non-absorbent headband.

M   Wear dust mask.

R   Wear cartridge-type respirator.

Table 6.11
Guide to Pesticide Application Equipment[a]

	Type	Uses	Suitable Formulations	Comments
	Aerosol can	insect control on house or patio plants, on pets, and in cracks, crevices and confined spaces	liquids must dissolve in solvent; some dusts available	very convenient, but high cost per unit of active ingredient; select a brand with a nonfluorocarbon propellant
	Hose-end sprayer	home garden and small landscaped areas; used for insect, weed and pathogen control	all formulations; wettable powders and emulsifiable concentrates require frequent shaking	a convenient, low-cost way of applying pesticides to small outdoor areas; cannot be sprayed straight up
	Trigger pump sprayer	indoor plants, pets and small yards; used for insect and pathogen control	liquid-soluble formulations best	low-cost and easy to use
	Compressed-air sprayer	many commercial and home-owner applications; can develop fairly high pressures; used for insect, weed and pathogen control	all formulations; wettable powders and emulsifiable concentrates require frequent shaking	good overall sprayer for many types of applications; needs thorough cleaning and regular servicing to keep sprayer in good working condition and prevent corrosion of parts
	Backpack sprayer	same uses as compressed-air sprayer	all formulations; wettable powders and emulsifiable concentrates require frequent shaking	durable and easy to use; requires periodic maintenance
	Wick applicator	used for applying contact herbicides to emerged weeds; agricultural and landscape uses	only water-soluble herbicides	simple and easy to use; permits spot treatment of weeds; must be cleaned frequently

Table 6.11 (continued)

	Type	Uses	Suitable Formulations	Comments
	Dust applicators bulb applicator	for forcing dusts into small cracks and crevices; also used to dust pets	dusts	simple and easy to use; avoid breathing dusts
	compressed-air duster	used to apply dusts in confined spaces such as wall voids	dusts	avoid breathing dusts
	mechanical duster (not shown)	for landscapes and small agricultural areas	dusts	avoid drift; do not breathe dust; may have bellows to disperse dust
	power duster	vine crops and some special applications; also used in buildings	dusts	equipped with blower to disperse dusts; considerable danger of drift
	Granule applicators hand-operated granule applicator	landscape, aquatic, and some agricultural uses	granules or pellets	easy to use and suitable for small areas
	mechanically driven granule applicator	turf and other landscaped areas; also commonly used in agricultural areas	granules or pellets	requires accurate calibration
	powered granule applicator	agricultural areas, usually row crops; some large landscape applications	granules or pellets	requires frequent servicing and cleaning; some units may have blowers to disperse granules; others may distribute granules along a boom

[a] From Marer, 1988.

The "Banana Oil" Respirator Fit Test[a]

The chemical isoamyl acetate, commonly referred to as "banana oil" because of its strong banana-like smell, is available from major chemical suppliers and is widely used to check the fit of respirators. It can be used with any pesticide respirator equipped with an organic vapor cartridge or canister. Some brands of respirators are available in small, medium and large sizes. If possible, have several different sizes on hand so you can determine which fits best; for the same reason, try respirators made by different manufacturers.

The drawing below (A) shows how the various elements of a respirator work to filter out toxic vapors. Since a respirator that does not fit properly does not protect you adequately, follow the test procedures described here carefully. You should have a partner to help you conduct the fit test, but it can be self-administered.

• Make sure there is no banana-oil odor already in the test area that would decrease the wearer's ability to detect it.

• Once the wearer has selected a respirator, have him or her adjust it until there is a good face-to-mask seal (as shown at B in the drawing below).

• Saturate a piece of cotton or cloth with banana oil. Use rubber gloves and avoid skin contact, since banana oil is a mild irritant.

• Pass the saturated material close to the respirator first in a clockwise, then in a counterclockwise motion. Have the wearer stand still and breathe normally and then deeply. If the wearer smells banana oil, adjust the respirator or select a different size or style before starting again.

• If the wearer cannot detect the odor while standing still, have him or her perform side-to-side and up-and-down head movements. Then have the wearer talk loudly enough to be heard by someone standing nearby (sometimes the movement of facial muscles disrupts the seal). Finally, have the person make other movements such as bending over that may occur during spray application.

• If the banana oil odor still cannot be detected, it indicates a satisfactory fit. Seal the respirator in a plastic bag marked with the wearer's name. Keep a record of when the fit test was conducted, along with the size and brand of respirator selected for each user.

• After each use, remove the cartridges and scrub the respirator with a toothbrush set aside for this purpose and warm soapy water to remove any pesticide residue. Let the respirator air-dry. Then rinse goggles, gloves and boots in warm soapy water and let them air-dry. Store all pesticide-application equipment in a plastic bag between uses. Proper laundering techniques for pesticide-contaminated clothing are described in the sidebar on the facing page.

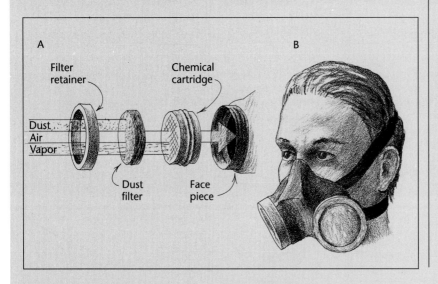

A

Filter retainer

Chemical cartridge

Dust
Air
Vapor

Dust filter

Face piece

B

[a] From Marer, 1988.

worn. The cartridge contains activated charcoal, which removes pesticide vapors when the wearer inhales. It is essential that respirators fit properly (i.e., seal tightly to the face). You should record the amount of time a cartridge is used so you know when to replace it. Store the record book with the respirator. Since beards and long sideburns impede a good seal, persons with facial hair should consider finding someone else to apply the pesticide. The best way to determine how well a respirator fits is to try the "banana oil" test described in the sidebar on the facing page.

WHAT TO REQUEST FROM A PEST CONTROL COMPANY

If you choose to hire a pest control company to solve your pest problem, it is important that you retain control over the methods and products used on your property. Try to find a company that is familiar with integrated pest management (IPM) approaches and will work cooperatively with you in selecting the least-toxic methods available. We have been helping an increasing number of pest control companies throughout the United States develop monitoring services, and it is becoming easier for consumers to find local firms offering this approach.

Our nonprofit organization, the Bio-Integral Resource Center, publishes a booklet for public agencies and consumers entitled "Contracting for Pest Control Services," which outlines in detail what to ask for when hiring a pest control firm and includes a discussion of contract language. We also publish a booklet for pest control companies entitled "Delivering IPM Services," which outlines IPM program components for common urban pests and shows how to bid on IPM-based contracts.

Traditionally, pest control companies have offered routine spray services, often on a monthly basis. This service is based on the idea that regular applications of pesticides, whether

---

How To Wash Pesticide-Contaminated Clothing[a]

• Keep pesticide-contaminated clothing separate from all other laundry (e.g, store it in a plastic bag until it can be laundered).

• Do not handle contaminated clothing with your bare hands; wear rubber gloves or shake clothing from the plastic bag into the washer.

• Wash only small amounts of clothing at a time. Do not combine clothing contaminated with different pesticides. Wash these in separate loads.

• Before washing, presoak clothes in a tub or automatic washer, or spray the garments outdoors with a garden hose. Use a commercial solvent soak product or apply prewash spray or liquid laundry detergent to soiled spots.

• Wash the garments in the washing machine, using the hottest water temperature, the full water level and a normal (12-minute) wash cycle. Use the maximum recommended amount of liquid laundry detergent. Neither bleach nor ammonia seems to enhance the removal of most pesticides. Never use bleach and ammonia at the same time.

• If garments still have a pesticide odor, spots or stains after washing, re-wash once or twice more as described in the previous step.

• Clean the washing machine before using it for other laundry by repeating the wash step, using the full-load setting, the hottest water, the normal wash cycle and laundry detergent, but no clothing.

• Hang the laundry outdoors on a clothesline to avoid contaminating the dryer.

[a] From Marer, 1988.

---

or not a pest is present, prevent pest problems. Today, there is both a need and great opportunity for a new kind of pest control service where the consumer pays a pest control professional to provide regular monitoring rather than regular spraying.

Biweekly or monthly monitoring reports from a pest control company reassure the consumer that a professional is overseeing pest prevention and management. Pest treatments occur only if the monitoring data shows a developing problem. Because monitoring serves as an early warning system, there is usually time to act preventively with non-chemical methods before pest numbers become high. Spot treatment with a least-toxic pesticide can be used as a backup.

If you have a pest emergency and cannot find a company that uses an IPM approach, show the company you hire the chapter in this book on managing the pest in question, then ask the company to use the methods described. If they resist and will only apply a pesticide, insist that they treat with the less-toxic substances recommended in this book. Remember that virtually all the least-toxic pesticides described here are available commercially, so even if the pest control operator (PCO) is not familiar with the material, he or she can order it from local chemical suppliers.

If the PCO is not willing to apply the materials suggested in this book, request the material safety data sheet (MSDS) described on p. 92 or ask to see the label for the pesticide(s) the operator plans to use. Both the MSDS and the label contain the generic and chemical names for the material. With this information in hand, call the organizations listed in the sidebar on p. 98 for information on toxicity. This will at least give you some background for choosing among the pesticides offered by the PCO. If you have any questions about the information conveyed by the PCO, call your county agricultural commissioner, the local Cooperative Extension office or your public-health agency to verify the information. The agricultural commissioner's office or state consumer protection agency can also tell you if there have been any complaints filed against the pest control company you are contemplating hiring.

When the pesticide is applied in your home or garden, insist that the spot-treatment approach described on p. 44 be used so that the pesticide is applied only where it is absolutely needed. Open your windows and doors and thoroughly air out the house for as long as possible after any indoor pesticide application. Most liquid pesticide formulations volatilize in the air, leading to respiratory exposure for the occupants. Remember that if you can smell a pesticide, your lungs are absorbing it.

If you or a PCO is going to apply a pesticide in your yard, it is a courtesy to give your neighbors advance warning. Many people suffer from chemical sensitivities to synthetic materials, including conventional pesticides. The inevitable drift of pesticides in the air can cause sufferers of this syndrome intense physical discomfort for long periods. If they know of the intended spraying in advance, they can take the necessary precautions.

REFERENCES AND READINGS

Berg, G. 1980. *Farm chemicals handbook.* Willoughby, Ohio: Meister Publishing. 400 pp.

A source of general information on commonly used pesticides.

Bohmont, B.L. 1981. *The new pesticide user's guide.* Fort Collins, Colo.: B and K Enterprises. 250 pp. (Available from: B and K, 1053 Montview Rd., Fort Collins, CO 80521.)

A handbook for the pesticide user that includes a wealth of general information on all classes of common pesticides but relatively little information on their chronic side effects.

Carson, R. 1962. *Silent spring.* Greenwich, Conn.: Fawcett. 304 pp.

Hailed as a great book by the lay press and condemned by pest control academics and professionals, this book marked a turning point in public awareness of the side effects of pesticide use. It still makes very interesting reading, since much of what was written then still applies today.

Craigmill, A.L. 1981. *Toxicology: the science of poisons.* Berkeley: University of California Division of Agricultural Science (Leaflet 21221). 15 pp.

A succinct introduction to the question of how pesticides are evaluated for toxicity.

Haiomes, Y.Y., and J.H. Synder. 1984. *Proceedings of the Engineering Foundation Conference, Groundwater Contamination, Santa Barbara, California, November 11-16, 1984.* New York: Engineering Foundation. 193 pp.

Some 37 participants from the United States discussed the detection, monitoring, prevention, abatement, containment, correction and restoration of groundwater contaminated by pesticides. An understanding of pesticide production chemistry is useful in understanding the connection between many of the industrial water contaminants and pesticide use.

Kutz, F.W., A.R. Yobs, W.G. Johnson and G.B. Wiersma. 1974. Pesticide residues in adipose tissue of the general population of the United States, FY 1970 survey. *Bulletin of the Society of Pharmacological and Environmental Pathologists* 2(3):(reprint).

This is the major source of the information presented in Table 6.8.

Kutz, F.W., R.S. Murphy and S.C. Strassman. 1978. Survey of pesticide residues and their metabolites in urine from the general population. In *Pentachlorophenol,* ed. K. R. Rao, pp. 363-369. New York: Plenum Press. 402 pp.

This is the source of the information presented in Table 6.7.

Maibach, H.I., R.J. Feldman, T.H. Milby and W.R. Serat. 1971. Regional variation in percutaneous penetration in man. *Archives of Environmental Health* 23:208-211.

The is the source of the skin pesticide penetration data in this chapter.

Marer, P.J. 1988. *The safe and effective use of pesticides.* Davis: University of California Statewide Integrated Pest Management Project, Division of Agriculture and Natural Resources (Publication 3324). 387 pp.

This is the best basic discussion of pesticide composition, behavior, toxicity and appropriate methods of use currently in print. Written for professionals but accessible to the layperson, it contains practical advice for the use of pesticides in an integrated pest management framework.

Mitchell, D.G. et al. 1987. Acute toxicity of Roundup® and Rodeo® herbicides to rainbow trout, chinook, and coho salmon. *Bulletin of Environmental Contamination Toxicology* 39:1028-1035.

This study indicates that the surfactant in these pesticide formulations is more toxic than the active ingredient, glyphosate.

***MSDS Reference for crop protection chemicals*, 2nd ed. 1979.** New York: John Wiley and Sons. 1,358 pp.

This book contains Material Safety Data Sheets for most companies in the United States that manufacture agricultural chemicals. They are indexed by manufacturer as well as by brand name. The publishers also include information on EPA reporting requirements and a list of extremely hazardous substances.

Olkowski, W., and H. Olkowski. 1983. *Contracting for pest control services: cockroaches, mice, rats and flies in public and private buildings.* Berkeley, Calif.: Bio-Integral Resource Center. 50 pp.

This booklet is written for the layperson planning to hire a pest control company. It describes the monitoring and least-toxic control strategies the consumer should request, and it discusses contract language.

Olkowski, W., and H. Olkowski. 1983. *Delivering integrated pest management services: pest control services for cockroaches, mice, rats and flies in public and private buildings.* Berkeley, Calif.: Bio-Integral Resource Center. 50 pp.

This booklet is written for the pest control professional interested in providing a high level of pest control with minimal use of pesticides. It describes monitoring methods and the use of least toxic-control tactics.

Perkins, J.H. 1982. *Insects, experts, and the insecticide crisis: the quest for new pest management strategies.* New York: Plenum Press. 304 pp.

An excellent introduction to the recent history of pesticide use and the conceptual framework and philosophical background for the development of integrated pest management as a general approach to pest control, primarily in agricultural settings.

Pimentel, D., ed. 1981. *CRC handbook of pest management in agriculture. Vol. II.* Boca Raton, Fla.: CRC Press. 501 pp.

Although primarily a reference tool on the use of biological controls in agriculture, this excellent book is also loaded with statistics on pesticide use on crops.

Pinto, L.J., and P.J. Spear. 1980. *Technical data for pesticides of the structural pest control industry.* Vienna, Va.: National Pest Control Association. 124 pp.

A reference book that provides information on the chemical and physical characteristics, fire and explosion hazards and toxicity to operators of pesticides. It is particularly useful to structural pest control operators.

Rudd, R L. 1964. *Pesticides and the living landscape.* Madison: University of Wisconsin Press. 320 pp.

A University of California zoology professor provides background information in support of Rachel Carson's book, *Silent Spring.* It is a lesser-known but important historical document about the pesticide crisis.

Sax, N.I., and R.J. Lewis, Sr. 1988. *Rapid guide to hazardous chemicals in the workplace.* New York: Van Nostrand Reinhold. 236 pp.

This book covers 700 highly hazardous industrial chemicals based on data from the U.S. Occupational Safety and Health Administration (OSHA), the American Conference of Governmental Industrial Hygienists and the German Research Society. It includes the most comprehensive set of workplace air-level guides published. The Department of Transportation's hazard class numbers and descriptions are included. Most of the 700 materials are in the highest class, and many pesticides are among the 700. Indexes are provided.

Shen, S. 1988. *Pesticide residues in food: technologies for detection.* Washington, D.C.: Office of Technology Assessment, Congress of the United States. 232 pp.

This review describes the technology for detecting pesticides in and on foods. New technologies not yet used in federal or state programs are evaluated and described, and gaps in detection capabilities are indicated.

Sherman, J. 1988. *Chemical exposure and disease.* New York: Van Nostrand Reinhold. 259 pp.

This book, written for physicians and public-health workers, contains a cogent explanation of toxicity testing protocols and procedures. It discusses the effects on humans of exposure to chemicals, including case histories; it also describes how to monitor for exposure. One chapter is devoted to information sources, but only a relatively small list of sources of pesticide exposure information is provided.

Trieff, N.M., ed. 1981. *Environment and health*. Ann Arbor, Mich.: Ann Arbor Science Publishers. 652 pp.

This book provides an overview of environmental pollution and pesticides as global contaminants.

United States Environmental Protection Agency. 1988. *Pesticide fact handbook*. Park Ridge, N.J.: Noyes Data Corporation. 810 pp.

The 130 pesticide fact sheets issued by the EPA and announced in the Federal Register through December, 1987, are collected in this book. They cover more than 550 trade-named pesticides, arranged alphabetically. The book includes a glossary and numerical list of the fact sheets, as well as indexes of common names, generic names and trade names. Individual entries include the description of the chemical, its use patterns and formulations, findings related to its toxicity, a summary of the EPA's regulatory position and rationale, a summary of major data gaps and a contact person at EPA. LD_{50} measurements cited here can be quoted as authoritative.

van den Bosch, R. 1978. *The pesticide conspiracy*. Garden City, New York: Doubleday. 226 pp.

Van den Bosch set out to change the pesticide industry. This, his last book, is a major contribution to that effort. It documents the underside of the industry, its stupidity and venality and the corruption behind major political decisions regarding pesticide use and regulation. The book also provides support for an accelerated change in direction away from sole reliance on pesticides. Van den Bosch was a major force in popularizing the concept of integrated pest management and he was a leader in the field of biological control.

Ware, G.W. 1978. *The pesticide book*. San Francisco: W.H. Freeman. 197 pp.

An informative layperson's introduction to pesticides, which unfortunately neglects to address side effects on humans, wildlife and the environment (except for its consideration of LD_{50} ratings).

Watterson, A. 1988. *Pesticide users' health and safety handbook: an international guide*. New York: Van Nostrand Reinhold. 504 pp.

This international source includes extensive documentation showing which pesticides have been incriminated as health hazards. It includes summaries of large-scale accidents involving pesticides and their effects on humans. Pesticide data sheets based on 25 sources compose more than half the book. One of the many appendices lists the pesticides banned or severely restricted in various countries, including the United States, Germany, Finland, Sweden, Portugal, Australia and Thailand.

Wiswesser, W.J., ed. 1976. *Pesticide index*. 5th ed. College Park, Md.: Entomological Society of America. 328 pp.

This is an authoritative source for LD_{50} information for all taxonomic classes of pesticides on the market as of the mid-1970s. Although in need of updating, it is still a useful index.

Worthing, C.R., ed. 1979. *The pesticide manual*. Worcester, England: British Crop Protection Council, BCPC Publication Sales. 665 pp.

This is the best overall source for LD_{50} data, sources of published toxicity data and physiochemical descriptions of pesticides.

CHAPTER 7
Some Useful Inorganics, Organics and Botanicals

INTRODUCTION

Now that we have given you abundant warnings about pest resistance, human health hazards and other potential problems associated with pesticide use, we would like to describe a variety of chemical tools we have found exceedingly useful in our work. We will also discuss others that we think will be very valuable once they arrive in the marketplace. We hope that by increasing the general knowledge about these products, we will help increase the demand for them. This, in turn, should increase their availability and use in place of more toxic materials.

In this and the following chapter, we introduce you to the least-toxic pesticides, since it is often difficult for the average consumer to obtain accurate information on their composition and use. Even though you may already be aware of some of the older pesticides, such as sulfur and oils, you may not be familiar with their full spectrum of use. This chapter focuses on inorganic materials, including sulfur and copper; insecticidal dusts, including silica aerogel, diatomaceous earth and boron; sodium hypochlorite, pesticidal soaps and horticultural oils; and botanicals, including pyrethrum, neem, limonene/linalool and garlic.

Chapter 8 discusses the frontiers of pesticide development, focusing on microbials, pheromones and insect growth regulators. It covers materials that only recently have become commercially available, as well as materials that are in the research stage but are very close to being registered. It also touches on some microbials that have been available for a long time but should be better known.

When reading about these pesticides, it is very important to remember that they should be used only within an overall pest management program that includes nontoxic methods. By taking this approach, you will maximize the effectiveness of your pest control efforts and minimize use of toxic materials.

Note that we do not take the space here to discuss many of the conventionally available pesticides, including the organophosphates such as malathion and diazinon and the carbamates such as carbaryl (Sevin®). There is already a large body of literature on these pesticides, and almost any Cooperative Extension publication on the subject of pest control will provide you with a surfeit of recommendations on their use. Only if one of these pesticides is commonly used for a specific pest problem and there is no alternative to it will we mention it in the section discussing the pest for which it is appropriate.

Least-Toxic Chemical Tools: Special Characteristics

Least-toxic pesticides have a number of special characteristics that must be kept in mind when using them. The first is the duration of effective action against the target pest. Although it is true that these substances may be more benign in relation to mammals (including humans) and less of a threat to the environment at large, the very qualities that make them better in that respect often mean they are not likely to last. Some are broken down quickly by sunlight and microbes. This is particularly true of the insecticidal soaps and many botanicals. For example, if you treat a plant for aphids with a soap-and-water spray, you will probably have to treat again after a shorter interval than if you used a more poisonous material. On the other hand, you won't have to take the same risks and safety precautions as with the more toxic substances.

A second apparent drawback is that least-toxic chemicals can be slower to show results than more commonly used pesticides—although they may be every bit as effective against the pest in the long run. Boric acid, for example, is a far more permanent control than most of the other insecticides used against cockroaches. But the roaches do not keel over the first day boric acid is used. Because most customers want to see roaches die immediately, pest control professionals have been reluctant to use boric acid. In addition, most boric acid is formulated as a powder or dust that is somewhat less convenient to apply than a liquid spray. This is why individuals who do their own pest control seem more willing to buy and use boric-acid dust than do pest control professionals. However, an aerosol formulation that has recently become available may increase the use of this less-toxic compound among professionals.

A third apparent drawback concerns the selectivity of the pesticide. The fact that a material is less toxic to mammals is no guarantee of selective toxicity to the pest alone. In fact, many of the materials discussed below, pyrethrum, for example, have a very broad spectrum of impact. Some of these materials kill the natural enemies of the pest or the enemies of other, potential pests just as much as more toxic materials do. With the pests' natural enemies decimated, the pest problem may actually become worse. However, when the material's residual life is short—meaning it is effectively gone in hours—the overall impact on the general living community can be minimized.

How you integrate these materials into a comprehensive program that includes nontoxic tactics first or simultaneously, and when and where you use least-toxic chemicals are questions that are just as important as they are with more conventional pesticides. We discuss this issue in later chapters devoted to specific pests.

One final caveat: Before you use any pesticide, *read the label*. Do not exceed the recommended dosage and observe all the listed precautions. The old adage, "If a little pesticide is good, a lot must be better," is absolute nonsense, and can lead at best to damaged plants or belongings and at worst to serious harm to human health and the environment.

INORGANIC PESTICIDES

Inorganic pesticides are those that do not contain carbon. They are among the oldest known pesticides, and may include the following elements: arsenic, boron, copper, lead, sulfur, barium, mercury, thallium, antimony, selenium or fluorine. Inorganic pesticides also include such sorptive dusts as silica aerogel, diatomaceous earth and the fluorine compound cryolite (sodium fluraluminate, sold as Kryocide®). Many inorganic pesticides take the form of tiny white crystals that resemble common table salt. They are very stable, do not volatilize and are often soluble in water.

The only elemental inorganic pesticides still in wide use today are arsenic, boron, copper and sulfur. Arsenic is used in herbicides (e.g., MSMA) and in ant baits as arsenic trioxide, but EPA registrations for most other materials have been withdrawn because of the potential for environmental contamination and the threat to human and animal health. Even though arsenic is registered for certain uses, extreme caution should be used when handling it, because it can be absorbed through the skin. Arsenic, mercury and lead are heavy metals that are potent disrupting agents in all living systems. These heavy metals are much more directly toxic than the lighter metals such as boron, copper and sulfur. Heavy metals can also become methylated or alkylated. When they do, they are more soluble and mobile in living systems, which only increases their threat to health. With the exception of boron, copper and sulfur, the inorganic light metals are no longer used because more effective, less-toxic substitutes are now available.

The information below, which describes the formulation, mode of action, safety and uses of inorganic pesticides, is drawn from a number of sources. Chief among them are *Fundamentals of Pesticides*, an excellent paperback by George W. Ware, *Pesticide Fact Book*, produced by the Environmental Protection Agency and *Handbook of Pest Management in Agriculture*, edited by David Pimentel. These books are listed under "References and Readings" on pp. 125-127.

Sulfur

Elemental sulfur without additives is probably the oldest effective pesticide in use today, and it remains popular because of its low toxicity to humans. Sulfur smoke was used to fumigate trees for aphids in the 1700s, and candles made from sulfur were burned in the late 1800s as a fumigant for bedbugs and as a general household disinfectant. Sulfur sprays for mildew control also became common in the 1800s. Today, sulfur is used widely as a fungicide and sometimes as a miticide. Gardeners can purchase finely ground sulfur products in most plant nurseries.

Properties. Sulfur is used as a pesticide both in its elemental form and as an important component of other pesticide compounds. The organosulfur compounds, which contain carbon and sulfur, are widely used as fungicides and miticides, but elemental sulfur, which occurs in nature as a yellow powder or crystal and produces a powerful odor when heated, has even wider use.

Mode of Action. Sulfur disrupts the metabolic processes of fungi and other target pests that absorb it and try to use it in place of oxygen.

Formulations. Sulfur is available in three major formulations. The first is sulfur dust, which has particles small enough to pass through a 325-mesh screen. It is mixed with 1% to 5% clay or talc to enhance the spread and adhesion of the dust. The second is wettable sulfur, which is composed of finely ground sulfur particles and a wetting agent to make the sulfur soluble in water. The third is colloidal sulfur, which has particle sizes so small it is formulated as a wet paste so it can be mixed with water. The small size is important in dispersing the sulfur evenly over the surface of a leaf so it can affect fungal pathogens before they penetrate the leaf tissue.

Sulfur in large particles—crystalline "flowers of sulfur," for example—leave spaces between particles through which fungi can attack the plant.

Safety. Sulfur is less toxic to humans than many conventional synthetic fungicides and miticides. However, precautions should be taken to prevent inhalation of the dust, which can damage the lungs, or skin or eye contact with sulfur compounds, which are strong irritants. A dust mask, goggles and the protective clothing described on pp. 97-103 should be worn.

Uses and Application. Sulfur is effective against powdery mildews, rusts, apple scab, brown rot of stone fruits, rose black spot and other plant diseases. Copper and oils can have a synergistic effect when used with sulfur that causes the sulfur to be more potent against plant pathogens. But this enhanced toxicity also increases the likelihood that the sulfur will burn the plant tissue. For this reason, sulfur sprays or dusts should not be applied within a month of an oil spray. Because heated sulfur can burn leaf tissue, it should not be applied when the air temperature is above 90°F (32°C).

Sulfur is toxic to arthropods, although mites are far more susceptible than insects. This relative selectivity means that sulfur can be used without causing undue disruption of many species of beneficial insects. We have used sulfur dusts to hold down populations of the broad mite *(Polyphagotarsenomus latus)* on gerberas in the greenhouse. However, we found a predatory mite, *Amblyseius limonicus*, more effective than sulfur. (In Chapter 10, we discuss the use of sulfur in a petroleum-jelly base to control the scabies mite of the human body.)

Because sulfur has a tendency to settle out when in liquid form, the spray tank must be agitated during application. Sulfur materials are abrasive to metal, so plastic sprayers should be used.

Copper

The growth of modern plant pathology was stimulated by a copper and lime combination called Bordeaux mixture. This mixture was used for the first time in 1878 by French viticulturists, whose grapes were being pilfered, particularly where they grew along roadways. In an attempt to discourage theft, the growers applied a poisonous-looking mixture of lime and copper sulfate to the roadside plants. A. Millardet, a researcher at the nearby Academy of Sciences in Bordeaux, noticed that the vines painted with this mixture suffered little or no downy mildew disease, which had been introduced inadvertently into Europe from America. But the vines without the compound were being defoliated. This observation led to widespread use of what became known as Bordeaux mixture. The fungicide was introduced into the United States in 1885.

Properties. Copper compounds in their solid state are blue, green, red or yellow powders that are virtually insoluble in water.

Mode of Action. The toxic action of copper is attributed to its ability to denature (change) the properties of cellular proteins and to deactivate enzyme systems in fungi and algae.

Formulations. Many copper compounds are used as fungicides. Among the most common is copper sulfate, also known as bluestone. It is available as a crystalline solid, wettable powder, liquid concentrate or dust. Bordeaux mixture, which in its solid state is a pale blue powder, is prepared by combining copper sulfate and hydrated lime. It can be purchased as a wettable powder at most plant nurseries.

Safety. Dilute copper solutions are considered to have moderately acute toxicity to humans; the LD_{50} of copper hydroxide in rats is 1,000 mg/kg. However, copper compounds are strong eye and skin irritants, so you should always wear protective clothing when applying these materials (see pp. 97-103 for details on protective clothing and equipment). Copper compounds are highly toxic to fish and aquatic invertebrates.

Uses and Application. Copper sulfate is primarily used as an algicide in lakes, ponds, reservoirs and irrigation systems, although it is also applied as a foliar fungicidal spray on fruit, nut, vegetable and ornamental plants. Copper hydroxide, cuprous oxide and other formulations are also used for this purpose.

Bordeaux mixture is used primarily as a fungicide, but it also has insecticidal and repellent properties. It was used in the 1940s to repel flea beetles on potatoes and tomatoes. It is also used to control common plant diseases, such as peach leaf curl, powdery mildew, black spot, rust, anthracnose, fire blight and bacterial leaf spots and wilts.

Because copper compounds can be toxic to plant tissue, the timing of Bordeaux mixture applications is very important. For example, if the mixture is used to prevent peach leaf curl—and it is still the best treatment for this problem—it should be applied just before leafing out occurs. If it is applied afterwards, it can damage the leaves. It is not safe to use on peaches during the growing season, and it may burn apples and cause them to russet. On rose leaves, it can cause red spotting, yellowing and leaf loss, symptoms that may be confused with black spot, an important disease of roses (see pp. 585-591). It may also defoliate Japanese plums. Injury is most prominent when the temperature drops below 50°F (10°C) and the humidity is high. Late summer use of Bordeaux mixture may increase the plant's susceptibility to early fall frosts. Read the label for additional cautions, and consult *Westcott's Plant Disease Handbook*.

Copper is also used as a wood preservative in the form of copper naphthanate (see p. 424), and copper sheets can be used as snail barriers, as discussed on p. 594.

INSECTICIDAL DUSTS

Many insects, particularly cockroaches, are repelled by dusts. Birds and animals know the value of dust in ridding themselves of lice, fleas and other ectoparasites. Powdered clay is used by some human tribes for the same purpose. Sulfur, which we have already discussed, is often applied as a dust to control fungi and mites on food and ornamental crops.

Certain dusts known as sorptive dusts have the ability to cling to or be absorbed by the waxy layer on the outside of the cuticle of insects. This waxy layer, which is the chief barrier to excessive loss of water, averages about 0.25 microns in thickness in most insects, although cockroaches have a layer of soft mobile grease about 0.6 microns thick. Some sorptive dusts are abrasive and scratch off the waxy material, whereas others remove the wax by absorbing it. Either way, the insect eventually dies through dehydration.

Among the many substances proven effective in disrupting the solid wax coating on the outside of the insect cuticle are activated gas-mask charcoal, alumina (aluminum oxide), diatomaceous earth, montmorillonite and kaolin acid-activated clays, amorphous precipitated silica and silica aerogels. If you are interested in precisely how these materials work on the insect cuticle, consult the article by Walter Ebeling (1971) listed in the chapter references.

Below we discuss the active ingredients of three dusts that are particularly useful as insecticides around the house: silica aerogel, diatomaceous earth and boric acid and borate compounds. None of these insecticidal dusts has received the attention it deserves from the public or from pest control professionals. This may be because special application equipment is often needed. Nonetheless, these dusts can be less toxic and more effective against certain insect groups.

Remember, however, that if you use dusts of any kind in your pest management programs, even dusts safe enough to eat, you should avoid getting them in your lungs or eyes. Protect yourself with goggles and a dust mask (see pp. 98-99). Once in place, these materials no longer pose the same hazard unless they are stirred up, as, for example, when a house is razed. Because sorptive dusts are inorganic and nonvolatile, they can remain active for years if kept dry and undisturbed.

Silica Aerogel

Silica aerogels are amorphous, non-abrasive, chemically inert materials that are used as insecticides and dehydrating agents. You have probably seen, for example, the small bags of silica aerogel that are put in electrical-equipment packages to prevent the accumulation of moisture during shipping or storage.

Properties. Silica aerogels are formed by a reaction of sodium silicate and sulfuric acid to form fluffy aerogels, whose small particles can absorb three times their weight in linseed oil—a substance similar to the waxy material on the cuticles of insects—and 5% to 100% of their weight in water.

Mode of Action. These aerogels absorb the waxy protective coating on an insect's cuticle, causing the insect to dehydrate and die.

Formulations. One silica-aerogel mixture, with 4.7% ammonium fluosilicate added to make it easier to grind, is formulated as an insecticide called Dri-Die®. A related product, Drione®, contains 40% amorphous silica aerogel and 1% pyrethrins as active ingredients, piperonyl butoxide as a synergist to boost the impact of the pyrethrins and a petroleum carrier to move the mixture to the target. This product supplies 60% more ammonium fluosilicate than Dri-Die®, producing a positive electrostatic charge on the silica-aerogel particles that lasts for several months, enabling the material to stick more tightly to the cuticles of insects and other surfaces. However, it must be kept dry to remain effective. For sources of these products, see the Resource Appendix under "Insect Management: Chemical Controls" on pp. 686-687.

Safety. Dri-Die® has been used for over 20 years with no adverse effect among those who manufacture, package and apply it. Laboratory studies show an LD_{50} in rats of more than 3,160 mg/kg of body weight, which is comparatively less toxic than most commonplace insecticides. No adverse health effects were noted in laboratory feeding tests, and no disease was observed in autopsies of laboratory rats fed up to 25,000 ppm of Dri-Die® for 28 days.

Drione® also has low acute toxicity, with an LD_{50} in rats of more than 8,000 mg/kg. It should be noted, however, that there has been some controversy over the safety of piperonyl butoxide (see p. 121) that has yet to be resolved.

Follow the label directions closely when using these materials, and always wear a dust mask and goggles because the particles can irritate the lungs and eyes. Note, however, that despite the similarity in names, silica aerogels do not cause silicosis, a lung disease associated with workers in industries using crystalline or "free" forms of silica. These free forms differ significantly from the amorphous silica aerogels used as insecticides.

Uses and Application. Silica aerogel, particularly Drione® (silica aerogel plus pyrethrum), is effective against those insects listed in the chart at left. It is particularly useful against pests in confined areas, including cockroaches in sewers and wall voids, drywood termites in attics and adult and larval fleas on pets. It also works around the yard. Because the formulated product is toxic to fish, it should not be used where it can contaminate lakes, streams or ponds.

Diatomaceous Earth

Properties. Diatomaceous earth is mined from the fossilized silica shell remains of unicellular or colonial algae in the class Bacillariophyceae, better known as diatoms. It has both abrasive and sorptive qualities.

Mode of Action. Like the silica aerogels, although to a lesser extent, diatomaceous earth absorbs the waxy layer on the surface of insect skins, causing the insect to desiccate (dry out). In addition to its desiccant action, it works abrasively to rupture insect cuticles, allowing cell sap to leak out.

Formulation. Diatomaceous earth is formulated as a dust, either alone or in combination with pyrethrin.

Safety. Diatomaceous earth is virtually nontoxic to mammals. The oral LD_{50} in rats is between 3,160 and 8,000 mg/kg, depending on the for-

Insects Killed by Drione®[a]

ants
bedbugs
bees
boxelder bugs
cadelles
cheese mites
cigarette beetles
cockroaches
confused flour beetles
crickets
dark meal worms
drug store beetles
firebrats
fleas
grain mites
granary weevils
red flour beetles
rice weevils
sawtoothed grain beetles
silverfish
spiders
ticks
wasps
yellow meal worms

[a] From Drione® label, provided by Fairfield American Corporation.

mulation. It is safe for human consumption in the small amounts that are mixed with grains for insect control. However, treated grain should be rinsed before cooking.

Both swimming-pool-grade (used as a filtering agent) and natural diatomaceous earth come from the same fossil sources, but they are processed differently. The natural grades are mined, dried, ground, sifted and bagged. The pool-grade diatomaceous earth is chemically treated and partially melted; consequently, it contains crystalline silica, which is a respiratory hazard. Thus it is imperative that only natural diatomaceous earth be used for insect control. The human body is not harmed by this noncrystalline form of silica. It can, however, irritate the eyes and lungs, so wear goggles and a dust mask when applying it.

Uses and Application. In the home, diatomaceous earth can be applied in wall voids, attics and other out-of-the-way places to kill insects such as ants, cockroaches, drywood termites and many of the other insects listed in the silica-aerogel section on p. 111. It can be sprinkled on carpets to kill fleas and be placed in jars with stored grains to kill insect pests. Diatomaceous earth can also be fed to animals to control intestinal parasites, where its mode of action is probably a mild scouring effect. It is used as a border around vegetable and ornamental plant beds to discourage slugs and snails. Sources of diatomaceous-earth products are listed in the Resource Appendix under "Insect Management: Chemical Controls" on pp. 686-687.

Boron

Boron is probably best known for the compounds borax and boric acid, which have many uses. Early Asian artisans used borax—the most common compound of elemental boron —in welding and brazing and in glazing pottery. It was also used in drugs and pharmaceuticals. Borax has long served as a mild antiseptic and fungicide, and boric acid is com-

monly used as an eyewash. Today, boron finds use primarily in glass-making, but it is also used in cleaners, soaps, contact-lens solutions, flame retardants, metal flux, control rods in atomic reactors and in agricultural and wood-product chemicals.

Properties. It is important to understand the difference between boron, borate, borax and boric acid. Boron, an element, is found naturally in combination with sodium, calcium or magnesium and oxygen as borates. Borax, or sodium tetraborate, is a combination of sodium, boron and oxygen, and is mined from the soil in its crude form. Boric acid is a crystalline material derived from borax.

Mode of Action. Boric acid acts as a stomach poison when ingested. The exact mechanism is not fully understood, but some researchers think boric acid disrupts the action of protozoa or bacteria in the insect's gut, inhibiting the functioning of the enzymes that break down food. This causes the insect to starve to death.

Formulations. Borate products used in pest control (primarily boric acid) come in many formulations, including powders, pastes, aerosols, tablets and liquid solutions. Common boric-acid powder, sold in most hardware stores for use against cockroaches, is ground to a very small particle size and combined with an anticaking agent. Materials that impart a colored tinge and a bitter taste are added to some formulations to ensure that boric acid is not mistaken for other household powders. The most effective formulations exhibit an electrostatic charge that makes the powder adhere more readily to insects and surfaces.

Safety. Judging from their LD_{50} rating in rats (from 3,200 to 6,000 mg/kg depending on the formulation), borate products have low toxicity to humans and other mammals. Boric acid has been used for over 80 years in low doses as an eyewash, and is found in many contact-lens cleaners. When ingested in high doses, however, boric acid can be

harmful. Therefore it must be kept away from food, children and pets. When inhaled, boric-acid powder can irritate the nose, throat and lungs. Boric acid and other borate compounds can also be absorbed through skin lesions and burns. You should wear a dust mask, gloves and eye protection when applying it. Keep boric acid in its original container and store in a safe place.

Uses and Application. Borax-based compounds are widely used in the United States as insecticides against ants, cockroaches, fleas, silverfish and other insects; as fungicides against molds on citrus; and as soil-sterilant herbicides. In Germany and other parts of Europe as well as in Australia and New Zealand, borates are used as wood preservatives. This use is increasing in the United States as well.

The most widely used borate material in pest control is boric acid. Although boric acid is effective against a number of insect pests, most research on this insecticide has been conducted in connection with cockroaches. Thus, the available boric-acid products tend to be directed at that market. When using these products against other insects, follow the same cautions and recommendations described for roaches. Remember that boric acid is only one component of the overall program for cockroach control discussed in Chapter 14.

In a series of studies testing the effectiveness of common insecticides against cockroaches, UCLA entomologist Walter Ebeling found that boric acid, which is virtually vaporless, was the only material that roaches were not repelled by, and was therefore the insecticide most likely to kill them. However, it can take 5 to 10 days before the cockroaches die, whereas some other commonly used insecticides take only one to four days. You must be patient. This delay often confuses novices, who assume that because they see roaches for a few days after using boric acid, it is not working. Although slower-acting initially, boric acid is certain to work.

This is quite different from other insecticides, which repel but do not kill roaches. If you can keep the boric acid dry, a single application will continue working for years.

Boric acid is most commonly sold as a dust or powder, but it can also be bought as an aerosol spray, as a paste for use as a caulk, in small plastic discs sold as roach or ant baits, in tablets that can be glued to walls or placed in hard-to-reach areas, as a water-soluble product for washing floors and walls and as a wood preservative. These various forms of boric acid are discussed below. Sources of boric-acid products are listed in the Resource Appendix under "Insect Management: Chemical Controls" on pp. 686-687.

Boric-Acid Powder. When purchasing boric acid as a powder, look for brands such as Roach Prufe®, made by Copper Brite, and Roach Kill®, made by R-Value, that contain an anticaking compound to help the boric acid resist the effects of moisture. Also look for brands that have an electrical charge that improves the powder's ability to adhere to the bodies of insects. The added safety features of a blue or green color and a bitter flavor help prevent children and pets from mistaking the substance for food.

To be most effective, boric-acid powder must be applied as a very thin film of dust on the target surface. The dust should be barely visible, as if you were salting food with it. When applied in piles, as from a teaspoon for example, the roaches avoid it. Piles also cake up fairly quickly and lose their effectiveness. When the boric acid is applied properly, however, roaches walk over the lightly dusted surfaces and pick up the powder on their legs, antennae and bodies. Their habit of frequent grooming (cockroaches are actually rather fastidious insects) leads to ingestion of the boric acid; thus, it also acts as a stomach poison.

The boric-acid container should be a plastic squeeze bottle with a pointed applicator tip that enables you to blow the powder into cracks and crevices where roaches and other insects hide. Unfortunately, Roach Prufe®, one of the most effective brands of boric acid, comes in a container without an applicator nozzle, and the directions call for applications by the teaspoon (just the opposite of what we suggested above). If you buy this brand, also purchase a bulb duster to apply it.

When used against cockroaches and ants indoors, boric acid is usually applied as a powder where habitat modification is difficult. Such locations include in and around stoves, in refrigerator engine cases, in electrical conduits, around ductwork and in false ceilings. It is used where caulk cannot be used or in wall voids that can be caulked shut afterward. It can be blown into voids or subfloor areas by drilling small holes in the wall or floor to allow penetration of the applicator nozzle. Do not use boric acid as a substitute for caulking, however.

In new construction, boric acid can be blown onto stud walls and subflooring before the finished wallboard and floor coverings are installed. This provides a long-lasting barrier against insects attempting to enter the house through cracks and crevices. In a test of four different materials used in the control of German roaches, boric acid/silica dust plus 0.1% Dri-Die® was found to be most effective when buildings were treated during construction. Eighteen months after a single treatment only two cockroaches were found in boric-acid-treated units, whereas untreated apartments averaged 31.

The time it takes to make large-scale applications of boric-acid powder can be reduced dramatically by using a variable-power duster called The Pest Machine®, marketed by Parker Pest Control (listed in the Resource Appendix under "Insect Management: Chemical Controls" on pp. 686-687). This machine dispenses the dust in a fine, light coating that optimizes roach control, and can shoot dust into small, confined areas. Conventional power dusters can dispense a large volume of material, but the dust often lands in piles that roaches detect and avoid. Conventional dusters also jam frequently. Parker's pneumatic duster operates under pressures as low as 2 psi for treatment below cabinets and in wall voids. It also imparts a strong electrostatic charge to the boric acid, which makes it adhere to surfaces and greatly increases the residual life of the application.

Boric-Acid Aerosol. To make boric acid easier to apply, particularly in crevices and other hard-to-reach places, R-Value has introduced an aerosol formulation called Borid Turbo®. This product contains 20% boric acid, a CO_2 propellant, a trichloroethane carrier and a silica-aerogel stabilizer. The Whitmire Company also produces an aerosol formulation, but it is available only to professionals. The convenience of aerosol formulations may help trigger serious interest in boric acid among pest control operators.

Boric-Acid Paste. Boric-acid baits, packaged in small covered plastic discs, contain a paste formulation that includes an attractant. Small holes in the disc allow roaches to enter and feed on the bait but deny access to children and pets. The paste can also be purchased in bulk from suppliers and applied to cracks and crevices with a caulking gun or spatula. Paste formulations are particularly useful in very moist areas.

Boric-Acid Tablets. Harris Roach Tablets®, with the active ingredient boric acid, was the first registered pesticide in the United States. These tablets are still sold in hardware and grocery stores, and they fill a gap in an IPM cockroach program where it is too wet to use dusts. They can be glued on wall surfaces or placed in hard-to-reach areas. Unfortunately, the small white tablets can be mistaken for candies or pills, so you must take care to place them where they are inaccessible to children and pets.

Water-Soluble Boric Acid. R-Value also markets a water-soluble product called Mop Up™ that can be added to water. It is used when mopping floors in food-preparation areas or to treat floors and walls in deteriorated structures that cannot be adequately caulked and screened to reduce roach breeding and migration. Boric-acid water washes can also be used on surfaces that do not come into direct contact with food, eating utensils, skin or pets, but are too vertical to retain a sufficient film of dust.

Borate Wood Preservatives. The disodium octaborate product TIM-BOR®, manufactured by U.S. Borax and Chemical Corporation, is registered for use as a wood preservative in the United States and is currently in the EPA registration process for use as a remedial control of wood-destroying pests. Studies in Australia and Europe have demonstrated that borax compounds provide wood used above ground and protected from rainfall with decades of protection from wood-boring beetles, termites and decay fungi. When borate-treated posts are placed in wet soil, however, the borate leaches out over time. In Germany, this problem is overcome by combining borate with copper and chrome (as copper/chrome/borate, or CCB), because these metals are far less likely to leach out. Scientists at U.S. Borax Research Corporation and a number of universities are currently working on other methods to reduce borate leaching, and new borate products able to protect wood in damp soil may reach the market in the future.

As health hazards associated with conventional wood preservatives such as pentachlorophenol, creosote and arsenical compounds restrict use of these materials, the United States' lumber industry is beginning to switch to pressure-treating building materials with borate products. Borax-treated wood is gradually becoming available at local lumber yards. For details on using TIM-BOR® to treat building foundations, see p. 425.

SODIUM HYPOCHLORITE

Most people are familiar with sodium hypochlorite as household bleach and use it to "whiten" their clothes or to keep their swimming pools and hot tubs free of algae. It is widely used as a disinfectant in water supplies, medical facilities and food processing plants. Sodium hypochlorite also serves as a fungicide in the nursery industry, and it is this application we focus on here.

Properties. Sodium hypochlorite is caustic in a water solution.

Mode of Action. Sodium hypochlorite is a strong oxidizing agent that kills organisms by chemically "burning," or oxidizing, their tissue. Hypochlorite compounds act by releasing chlorine-oxygen radicals.

Formulation. Sodium hypochlorite is sold as a colorless 5% solution.

Safety. In the dilute solution in which it is used, sodium hypochlorite is relatively safe for human use, although the undiluted material is quite toxic. Its oral LD_{50} in rats is 150 mg/kg. Bleach is a caustic eye and skin irritant, so it is important to wear gloves and eye protection when mixing it. Because it is highly reactive, it breaks down rapidly in soil.

Uses and Application. Bleach solutions are used to disinfect greenhouse benches, seedling flats and pots, and pruning tools to prevent fungal and bacterial infection of plants. They are also used to protect cuttings from disease organisms. In commercial nurseries, for example, the stems of rose and grape cuttings are dipped for 20 minutes in a 0.5% sodium hypochlorite solution (household bleach diluted at 1 part bleach to 9 parts water) to eliminate crown gall bacteria (*Agrobacterium tumefaciens*), which may be carried on the surface of the cuttings. A drench of 2% solution of household bleach (2½ oz. of bleach to 1 gal. of water) can also be used to arrest the development of damping-off fungi in flats of cuttings or seedlings.

Because bleach breaks down rapidly in soils, it provides little or no residual protection. Moreover, it is strongly alkaline and can raise the pH of soil. Therefore, you should apply an acidic drench of tea (the beverage type) or 25% vinegar (acetic acid) solution after every third bleach drench to counteract the alkaline effect.

PESTICIDAL SOAPS

Soaps, which are sodium or potassium salts combined with fish or vegetable oil, have been used as insecticides since the late 1700s and perhaps even earlier. Fish-oil soaps, the most widely used early insecticidal soaps, included those made with whale oil until recently, when public awareness that whales are endangered curtailed their use. Vegetable oil-based soaps, which did not have as disagreeable an odor as fish-oil soaps, were made with coconut, corn, linseed or soybean oil. "Green soap," a potassium/coconut oil soap used widely as a liquid hand soap in public restrooms years ago, has been used to control many soft-bodied insects such as aphids. Although the term "green soap" is no longer used, similar potassium/coconut oil soaps are still available on the market as hand soaps and shampoos.

Most of the research on and use of insecticidal soaps halted abruptly during World War II due to the increasing availability of inexpensive chlorinated hydrocarbon pesticides, such as DDT, which had broad toxicity. The soaps, though virtually nontoxic to humans, were relatively short-lived and could not match the persistence of the chlorinated hydrocarbons. Unfortunately, the long-term human health and environmental effects of the chlorinated hydrocarbons were not understood until years after their introduction. Today, pesticidal soaps are making a comeback.

Properties. A soap is a substance made from the action of an alkali such as sodium or potassium hydroxide on a fat. The principal components of fats are fatty acids. The old-fashioned way of making soap was by boiling animal fat and lye (sodium hydroxide). This converted the normally water-insoluble fat into a water-soluble soap. Commercial insecticidal soaps that are manufactured today contain a blend of selected fatty-acid chain lengths.

Mode of Action. When pesticidal soap touches the cuticle (outer body) of a susceptible insect, the fatty acids penetrate the insect's covering and dissolve into the membranes around its cells, disrupting their integrity. The cells leak and collapse, resulting in the dehydration and death of the insect. Susceptible insects become instantly paralyzed on contact with the soap; other insects become paralyzed for a short time, then recover. Soap can also penetrate the protective coating on plant tissue and fungi, causing dehydration and death.

Formulations. Pesticidal soaps are formulated as liquid concentrates and ready-to-use liquid sprays. A formulation of dry granules is currently being developed.

Safety. The principal value of soaps as pesticides is that they are virtually nontoxic to the user unless ingested in high doses. Even at high doses they have no serious systemic effects, although they can cause vomiting and general stomach upset. The LD_{50} in rats of Safer™ Insecticidal Soap is greater than 16,500 mg/kg, and Safer's other soap products show similarly large margins of safety. At the doses found in commercial formulations, including concentrates, no mortality has been observed in test animals. Pesticidal soaps biodegrade rapidly in the soil. Refer to pp. 97-103 for a rundown of the safety precautions you should follow when applying any pesticide.

Soaps show relative selectivity in the range of insects they affect. Soft-bodied mites and sucking insects such as aphids, scale crawlers, whiteflies and thrips are the most susceptible. Some insects, including adult beetles, bees, wasps, flies and grasshoppers, are relatively unaffected, apparently due to resistance factors in the chemical composition of their

Table 7.1
Some Organisms Susceptible to Safer™ Insecticidal Soap[a]

General Group	Specific Organisms[b]
aphids	cabbage, pea, bean, balsam wooly, spruce gall, many others
caterpillars	hemlock looper, tent caterpillars, Douglas-fir tussock moth
crickets	
earwigs	European earwig
fleas	cat flea, dog flea adults
flies	adult fruit flies, fungus gnats
grasshoppers	
lacebugs	
leafhoppers[c]	
mealybugs	
mites	two-spotted spider mite, red spider mite, bird mites, others
mosses, algae, lichens, liverworts	plant bugs
psyllids	pear psylla
sawflies	cherry, pear, and rose slugs (actually sawflies, not slugs)
scales	brown soft scale, some others
spittlebugs	
springtails[d]	
thrips	
whiteflies	greenhouse whiteflies, other whiteflies

[a] Sources: Product labels and research papers provided by Safer, Inc.
[b] If identified in the literature.
[c] Efficacy highly variable.
[d] When applied as a soil drench.

outer coverings. Slow-moving insects are more susceptible than highly mobile ones that can fly away from the spray. Thus, the adult forms of many beneficial insects, such as lady beetles, rapidly moving lacewings and syrphid flies, are not very susceptible; the flightless, soft-bodied pre-adult forms of these insects are more susceptible.

Uses and Application. Specific uses of soap sprays are discussed throughout the book under various pest problems. Table 7.1 above lists the organisms that are susceptible to insecticidal soap. For sources of pesticidal soap, see the Resource Appendix under "Insect Management: Chemical Controls" on pp. 686-687.

One limitation of earlier insecticidal soaps was the fact that their active ingredients and dosages varied widely due to a lack of standardization. Many of the insecticidal soaps were obtained from the commercial soap trade, where the blend of fatty acids was not quality-controlled. Therefore, there was little consistency from one batch to the next. A 1% to 2% solution of regular household soap or detergent can be used to kill insects, but its reliability is less predictable than soaps formulated as insecticides. Such solutions are also more likely to "burn" plants than are the commercial insecticidal products.

In recent years, the standardization of insecticidal soap has improved considerably, largely through the work of Dr. G.S. Puritch of Safer, Inc. In the 1970s, his published research indicated that the toxicity of fatty-acid salts (soaps) peaked when the saturated fatty-acid molecule contained about 10 carbon atoms, or 18 in an unsaturated molecule. Insecticidal soaps marketed today are standardized to maximize the number of 10-carbon or 18-carbon fatty acids in their formulations. As of this writing, pesticidal soaps are manufactured in the United States by two companies: Safer, Inc., and Ringer Corp.

Insects with relatively soft bodies, including aphids, adelgids (a type of aphid), mealybugs, whiteflies and pear psylla, are the most sensitive to these fatty acids. The lepidopteran defoliators, such as gypsy moths and winter moths, are less sensitive. Least affected of all are the beetles, including lady beetles, spruce beetles and black vine beetles. Pesticidal soaps are particularly useful indoors, where the toxicity of other pest control materials can pose a safety threat.

Safer, Inc., has also introduced a soap-based fungicide composed of fatty-acid salts and sulfur. It is effective against a variety of fungi that attack ornamental and food plants, including powdery mildew, black spot, brown canker, leaf spot and rust. It also controls mites, chiggers and ticks.

According to Dr. Puritch, the fungicide has both a preventive and an eradicant action on fungi. For example, properly timed sprays can prevent powdery mildew and rust from germinating, or they can eradicate existing infections. The fungicide also prevents the germination of black spot, but it cannot remove the damage symptoms (black spots) from individual leaves because the tissue is already dead.

Safer, Inc., markets a fatty-acid herbicide called Sharpshooter™, a nonselective material that kills or damages any plant it touches. The fatty acids are decomposed by soil microbes within 48 hours. This product is most effective when used against weeds in the seedling stage. Since it does not translocate to the roots, Sharpshooter™ is not very effective against mature perennial plants, particularly those with tap roots.

When using an insecticidal or fungicidal soap, test the dosage on a small number of plants or on the portion of the plant or animal to be treated to evaluate its toxic effects. In general, insecticidal soap is not phytotoxic. But plants such as African violets that have hairy leaves tend to hold the soap solution on their leaf surfaces, where it can cause burning. You can minimize this effect by rinsing the soap off the plant after the pests have died. This should be done within ten minutes to several hours after application, depending on the sensitivity of the plant, the temperature (the higher the temperature, the more likely the plant is to react negatively) and the strength of the soap solution. You will have to experiment to discover what works best.

HORTICULTURAL OILS

Written records of the use of oils as pesticides date from as early as the first century A.D., when the Roman scholar Pliny the Elder wrote that mineral oil controlled certain plant pests. It was also recognized that oils could damage plant tissue. By 1763, petroleum oil and turpentine were in common use as insecticides. Whale oil was used against scales as early as 1800 in the United States, and an oil mixture of kerosene, soap and water was used against caterpillars in the 1860s.

Oils can be petroleum-based (that is, they come from fossilized plants), they can be derived from living plants, as with the vegetable oils, or botanicals, described in the next section, or they can come from animal fat. Most pesticidal oils in use today are petroleum-based, and there has been a resurgence in their use as insecticides as a result of new refining techniques that reduce plant damage. Horticultural oils, which are insecticides, creosote, which is a fungicide/insecticide, and weed oil, a herbicide, are examples of petroleum oils used as pesticides. Petroleum-based oils are considered to be synthetic organic chemicals because they have been highly purified compared to the crude state in which they were extracted from underground oil deposits.

On the horizon are insecticidal oils extracted from safflower, corn and other crop plants. Recent research shows these materials to be effective insecticides, particularly against pests that have developed resistance to common chemical insecticides.

Properties. Horticultural oils are a complex mixture of hydrocarbons containing traces of nitrogen- and sulfur-linked compounds.

Mode of Action. In general, oils kill all stages of insects by blocking their breathing apparatus and smothering them. Oils kill eggs by penetrating the shells and interfering with metabolic processes, or by preventing respiration through the shells.

Formulation. Horticultural oils are sold as emulsified liquid concentrates. Because oils and water do not mix, a third material (such as soap) must be introduced to bring them together. Such materials are called emulsifiers. When oil and water are mixed by means of an emulsifier, the product is called an oil emulsion. It is made up of very minute and separate globules of oil surrounded by thin films of water.

Prior to the 1970s, most horticultural oils were "heavy," that is, they had a viscosity range of 100 to 220. They were used primarily as "dormant oils" on fruit and shade trees that had shed their leaves for the winter. When these heavy oils were used on trees in leaf, however, the oil would clog the stomata (breathing pores on leaves) and lenticles (breathing pores on stems), reducing the trees' ability to exchange gases with the air. This often resulted in burning of tissues and other damage, particularly if the tree was under water stress at the time of spraying.

Research between 1930 and 1970 identified the source of the phytotoxicity problem as the aromatic, unsaturated sulfonated compounds in crude oils. A new class of "superior" horticultural oils was developed to overcome the problem. These oils have had most of the sulfur compounds removed, and are lighter, with viscosities between 60 and 80. Under appropriate conditions they can be applied to most verdant plants without harm. Virtually all the horticultural oil sprays on the market today are these newer, highly refined oils, although they may be marketed under the old names, such as dormant oil and summer oil.

Safety. Oil operates physically on a plant or insect rather than by disrupting biochemical pathways, as do many other synthetic pesticides. Oil's mode of action places it toxicologically in a much safer class than a material that blocks biochemical processes similar to processes that occur in humans and other mammals. Oils also have a relatively short residual life and less impact on natural enemy populations than other synthetic products. They can, however, cause skin and eye irritation, so protective clothing, gloves and goggles should be worn during application.

Uses. Oils are used against a wide range of insects and mites, weeds and, to a lesser extent, certain fungi. An oil-based fungicide used in wood preservation is discussed in Chapter 22. The insects susceptible to horticultural oils are listed in Table 7.2 on p. 118. Sources of horticultural oils are listed in the Resource Appendix under "Insect Management: Chemical Controls" on pp. 686-687.

Oils as Insecticides

Oils are commonly used on ornamental plants and fruit trees to combat adelgids, aphids, cankerworms, leafhoppers, leafrollers, leaftiers, mealybugs, mites, mosquitoes, psyllids, scales, tent caterpillars and webworms, particularly the overwintering stages. Until recently, horticultural oils were most commonly used as dormant sprays applied during fall or winter when deciduous trees are leafless and insects and mites cling to the bark in their egg or other overwintering stage. This is when they are most susceptible to suffocation.

The labels on many dormant oils caution against spraying certain thinbarked species, such as maples, beeches and birches, and certain evergreen conifers with waxy or powdery (glaucous) leaves. According to Warren T. Johnson, an authority on horticultural oil sprays from whose work much of the information in this discussion is drawn (see "References and Readings" on pp. 125-127), these precautions are unfortunate holdovers from the days of heavy oils. The dormant oils available on the market today are the lighter "superior" type, and as of 1980, Johnson says he had found "no published literature that claims phytotoxicity to any species of deciduous tree or shrub, in the U.S. or Canada, from using a superior oil in the dormant stage." According to Johnson, the same is true of conifers, except for those such as blue spruces in which the oil removes the bluish frosted material from the needles. It takes two or three years before the normal color returns.

Johnson also disputes the label precautions against using oils on plants when temperatures fall below 40°F (4°C). "Field studies at the New York Agricultural Experiment Station have yielded no evidence that low-temperature oil applications, per se, will cause damage to dormant fruit trees....Any superior oil that remains in the liquid state at 20°F [–6.5°C] should be safe for all routine field applications."

The new horticultural oils can also be sprayed as a 2% solution against insects and mites on plants in full leaf if environmental conditions are right. Recent field tests of summer applications of oils on trees, shrubs and greenhouse-grown bedding and foliage plants have shown that the new oils can safely be applied to most common ornamental plants even at high temperature (see Table 7.3 on p. 120). The key is making sure that the plants are not under water stress when they are sprayed and that the relative humidity is low to moderate (45% to 65%) so the oil spray evaporates from the leaves fairly quickly.

"There are plenty of examples where oil has been applied to shade trees when the temperature was over 90°F [32°C] without injury symptoms," Johnson writes. He points out that it is not the high temperature itself that should be of concern, but the combination of high temperature and moisture stress. If oils are sprayed on foliated trees at high temperatures, damage (e.g., scorched leaves) will probably occur only if the trees do not have access to sufficient water to replace respired moisture. However, research by University of Maryland entomologists John Davidson, Stanton Gill and Mike Raupp during drought periods in the late 1980s demonstrated that even under moisture stress, shade trees have a surprisingly high tolerance for oil sprays at high temperatures. They sprayed oils on over 50 genera of trees and found

Table 7.2
Insects and Mites Killed or Repelled by Horticultural Oil Sprays[a]

Scientific Name	Common Name	Scientific Name	Common Name
Aphids and Adelgids		*Oligonychus bicolor*	oak mite
Aphis citricola	citrus aphid	*O. ununguis*	spruce spider mite
A. fabae	bean aphid	*Panonychus ulmi*	European red mite
A. pomi	apple aphid	*Phytoptus pyri*	pear leaf blister
Cinara spp.	pine aphids		mite
Eulachnus agilis	pine needle aphid	*Tetranychus urticae*	two-spotted spider
Hormaphis hamamelidis	witch hazel leaf gall		mite
	aphid	*Vasates aceriscrumena*	spindle gall mite
Macrosiphum liriodendri	tuliptree aphid	*V. quadripedes*	bladder gall mite
M. rosae	rose aphid		
Myzocallis granovsky	hemlock wooly	**Phylloxera and Psyllids**	
	adelgid	*Phylloxera* spp.	pecan phylloxera
		Psylla pyricola	pear psylla
Beetles			
Diabrotica spp.	corn rootworms	**Sawflies**	
Pyrrhalta luteola	elm leaf beetle	*Amauronemalus* spp.	locust sawflies
Bugs		**Scales**	
Stephanitis pyrioides	azalea lace bug	*Aonidiella aurantii*	California red scale
		Asterolecanium spp.	pit scales
Caterpillars		*Carulaspis juniperi*	juniper scale
Archips spp.	leafrollers	*Chionaspis pinifoliae*	pine needle scale
Heliothis zea	corn earworm	*Coccoidea* spp.	scales
Malacosoma americanum	eastern tent	*Coccus hesperidum*	brown soft scale
	caterpillar	*Gossyparia spuria*	European elm scale
Spodoptera frugiperda	fall armyworm	*Lecanium corni*	lecanium scale
Yponomeuta multipunctella	euonymus webworm	*Lepidosaphes gloveri*	Glover scale
		Macrosiphum liriodendri	tuliptree scale
Fungus Gnats and		*Melanaspis obscura*	obscure scale
Leafminers		*Neolecanium cornuparvum*	magnolia scale
Liriomyza spp.	leafminers	*Pulvinaria amygdali*	cottony peach scale
Lycoriella mali	fungus gnat	*P. innumerabilis*	viburnum cottony
			scale
Mealybugs		*Saissetia oleae*	black scale
Dysmicoccus wistariae	taxus mealybug	*Unaspis euonymi*	euonymus scale
Planococcus citri	citrus mealybug		
		Whiteflies	
Mites		*Bemesia tabaci*	sweet-potato
Aculus ligustri	privet rust mite		whitefly
Eotetranychus tillarum	linden spider mite	*Trialeurodes vaporariorum*	greenhouse
Epitrimerus pyri	pear rust mite		whitefly

[a] This list of species has been assembled from a number of research papers on the effectiveness of oils on various pest species. Many other insects and mites are no doubt also susceptible to oil sprays, so experimentation is encouraged.

very little damage to the leaves and other plant parts.

Despite this apparent latitude in spray conditions, prudence dictates that during hot weather, plants be irrigated before spraying with oils to minimize the potential for phytotoxicity. It is also wise to spray in the early morning or on cloudy days when it is cooler to reduce the likelihood of damage.

Horticultural oils are beginning to be used in commercial nurseries to control pests on bedding and house plants, and no doubt will become more common in the home garden on food and ornamental plants as well. As with any insecticide, you should always test the material on a small portion of the plant before treating the entire specimen. The cooler and shadier the conditions when the oil is applied, the better.

Oils are also used to kill mosquito larvae. The oil is spread on the surface of water in which mosquitoes develop. When the larvae, sometimes called "wigglers," push their breathing tubes through the surface of the water to take in oxygen, the oil adheres to the tubes, clogging them and suffocating the mosquitoes.

Recent changes in formulation have made commercial oils used against mosquitoes less toxic to other forms of wildlife than they were a decade or so ago. However, oils applied to the surface of water also kill or otherwise interfere with certain beneficial insects that inhabit the water surface, including water striders, which prey on mosquito larvae and pupae. Even so, most other mosquito larvicides kill a much wider range of aquatic species. Thus, oils can serve as one of the less-toxic insecticides in an overall mosquito control program. For a complete discussion of mosquito management, see Chapter 36.

Oils as Herbicides

Unlike the highly refined horticultural oils used on trees and shrubs, the best weed oils are cruder oils with a high percentage of the aromatic, unsaturated sulfonated compounds that are toxic to plants. The petroleum distillates with low flammability, called "Stoddard solvents," that are often used for dry-cleaning clothes can also be used for selective weed control in vegetable crops and on lawns. Cruder diesel oils are used as nonselective herbicides on railroad beds, roadsides and paths; however, these materials are potential soil contaminants, so it may be unwise to use them for this purpose.

In *Weed Science*, weed specialists Glenn Klingman and Floyd Ashton discuss the ways in which herbicidal oils act on plants. Oils penetrate the leaves, bark and roots, and move into intercellular spaces where they apparently dissolve the constituents of cell walls. This allows the cell sap to leak out, causing collapse of the cell. As a result, leaves sprayed with oil often look as if they are water-soaked.

Some plants, such as carrots, celery, parsnips, parsley and some conifer tree seedlings, have membranes that resist the dissolving action of Stoddard solvent-type oils and are not seriously damaged by treatments. In such cases, oil can be applied to kill common annual weeds without significant damage to the crop plant.

Although weed oils are used as contact sprays, they do have some translocating ability. However, they apparently move up and down plants through intercellular spaces rather than in the water- or starch-conducting vessels, as is the case with common chemical herbicides.

Weed oils are most effective when applied in hot weather. In the 1940s they were used to control the hard-to-eradicate puncturevine *(Tribulus terrestris)*. The oil was reported to kill not only the mature vine, but also the seeds, whose coating the oil was able to penetrate. Klingman and Ashton also report that "kerosene sprayed on bluegrass at proper rates will effectively remove dandelions; the dandelion is killed and the bluegrass is injured little or not at all."

BOTANICALS

Botanical pesticides are derived from plants. Common examples include pyrethrum, which is derived from a species of chrysanthemum, and nicotine, derived from the tobacco plant. There are several basic ways in which botanicals are derived from their source plants.

• Preparations made from the crude plant material. These are the dusts or powders made from ground and dried plant parts that have not been extracted or treated extensively. They are marketed at full strength or are diluted with carriers such as clays, talc or diatomaceous earth. Examples include dusts or wettable powders of cubé roots (rotenone), pyrethrum flowers, sabadilla seeds, ryania stems and neem leaves, fruits and bark.

• Plant extracts or resins. These are water or solvent extracts that concentrate the plant's insecticidal components. Such extracts or resins are formulated as liquid concentrates or are combined with dusts or wettable powders. Examples include pyrethrins, cubé resins (rotenone), citronella and other essential oils and neem seed extracts or oils.

• Pure chemicals isolated from plants. These are purified insecticidal compounds that are isolated and refined through a series of extractions, distillations and/or other processes, and are formulated as concentrates. They include d-limonene and linalool, nicotine and pyrethrin.

Hundreds of plants are known to have insecticidal properties, and the number of separate compounds is probably in the thousands. Like the inorganic pesticides described earlier, botanicals were in common use until the 1940s when they, too, were displaced by modern synthetic pesticides that seemed cheaper, easier to apply and longer-lasting. Pyrethrum, nicotine and rotenone continued to be used in small amounts by organic farmers and home gardeners, but sabadilla and ryania virtually disappeared from use. As awareness of the health and environmental haz-

Table 7.3

Ornamental Plants that Tolerate Summer Oil Sprays[a]

Scientific Name	Common Name	Scientific Name	Common Name
Trees and Shrubs		*P. serrulata* 'Kwanzan,' 'Tibetica'	Japanese flowering cherry
Acer griseum	paperback maple		
A. palmatum	Japanese maple	*P. subhirtella* 'Pendula'	higan cherry
A. platanoides 'Crimson King,' 'Debbie'	Norway maple	*P. yedoensis* 'Yoshino'	Japanese flowering cherry
		Pyrus calleryana 'Aristocrat,' 'Bradford,' 'Redspire'	ornamental pear
A. rubrum 'Embers'	red maple		
Betula pendula	weeping birch		
Cedrus atlantica 'Glauca'	blue atlas cedar	*Quercus palustris*	pin oak
Cornus florida	pink flowering dogwood, white flowering dogwood	*Syringa chinensis* 'Expansa'	Chinese lilac
		S. vulgaris	common lilac
Cryptomeria japonica	Japanese cedar	*Taxus cuspidata* 'Intermedia'	Japanese yew
Cupressocyparis leylandii	Leyland cyprus		
Euonymus alata 'Compacta'	winged spindle tree	*T. media* 'Hicksii'	Hicks' yew
		Tilia cordata 'Greenspire'	linden tree
Fraxinus pennsylvanica 'Marshall Seedless,' 'Autumn Applause'	green ash	*Tsuga canadensis*	Canadian hemlock
		Zelkova serrata 'Green Vase,' 'Village Green'	zelkova
Ginkgo biloba 'Prince Century'	maidenhair tree		
		Bedding and Potted Plants	
Gleditsia triacanthos inermis 'Shademaster'	honeylocust	*Ageratum houstonianum* 'Blue Puffs,' 'Madison'	floss flower
Ilex crenata 'Convexa'	Japanese holly	*Impatiens* 'Red Dazzler,' 'Dazzler White'	busy Lizzie
I. opaca	American holly		
Juniperus chinensis 'Pfitzerana-Glauca'	blue pfitzer juniper	*Petunia* 'Plum Madness,' 'White Dancer'	petunia
Laburnum anagyroides	golden chain tree	*Poinsettia* spp.	poinsettia
Magnolia stellata	star magnolia	*Salvia* 'Red Carabiniese,' 'Blue Carabiniese'	sage
Malus 'Indian Summer'	crab apple		
Oxydendrum arboreum	sourwood	*Tagetes* 'Bonanza Harmony,' 'Hero Flame'	marigold
Platanus acerifolia 'Bloodgood'	London plane tree	*Vinca* 'Little Bright Eyes,' 'Little Linda'	periwinkle
Prunus laurocerasus	cherry laurel		

[a] In tests conducted by University of Maryland researchers, these plants were sprayed one or more times with a 2% SunSpray™ UltraFine or SunSpray™ 6E Plus oil during summer months when temperatures ranged from 70°F to 100°F (21°C to 38°C). Plants were evaluated for phytoxic reactions, including leaf-spotting, discoloration, marginal burn and distortion.

Plants in this table showed little or no phytotoxic reaction, and none of the trees and shrubs listed showed damage. Among the bedding and potted plants listed, impatiens showed minor spotting or pitting on leaves or buds, but subsequent growth was unaffected and quickly covered the damage. Poinsettias showed no damage if sprayed prior to bract expansion. Additional oil-tolerant potted and bedding plants listed on the SunSpray™ label include azaleas, camellias, crowns of thorn, dieffenbachias, some ferns, gardenias, jade plants, some palms, philodendrons, portulacas and zinnias.

ards of synthetic petrochemical-based pesticides increases, however, and as pests become resistant to more and more of the synthetic compounds, interest in plant-derived pesticides is increasing.

It is important to realize, however, that just because a pesticide is derived from a plant does not mean that it is safe for humans and other mammals or that it cannot kill a wide variety of other life. For example, the botanical insecticide nicotine is a very poisonous compound that impedes neuromuscular functioning, causing insects to convulse and die. But the same fate can befall humans exposed to high doses of nicotine. Ryanodine, the active ingredient in the botanical insecticide ryania, is 20 times more toxic to mammals than to most insects. Strychnine, a botanical widely used against gophers and birds, is very dangerous if ingested by humans or other vertebrates. If the carcasses of strychnine-poisoned rodents and birds are fed on by other animals, they in turn can be killed.

Regardless of how poisonous they are, botanicals tend to break down into harmless compounds within hours or days in the presence of sunlight. Because they are chemically very close to the plants from which they are derived, they are also easily decomposed by a variety of microbes common in most soils. A list of common botanical pesticides is provided in Table 7.4 at right, along with the names of their plant sources and their toxicity ratings.

Synergists

Many botanical insecticides are formulated with synergists. These have no insecticidal effect of their own, but serve to enhance the insecticidal effect of the botanicals. Synergists help deactivate the enzymes in the bodies of insects and mammals that break down a wide variety of toxic substances. This increases the impact of the insecticide and reduces the amount of raw active ingredient needed to do the job. Synergists are usually combined with insecticides in ratios of from 2:1 to 10:1 (synergist: insecticide). In the presence of a synergist, a little active ingredient can go a long way.

Piperonyl butoxide (PBO), which is derived from sesame, is the most common synergist. It is used in most products containing pyrethrins but is also formulated with rotenone, ryania, sabadilla, citrus-oil derivatives and some synthetic pyrethroids. PBO is somewhat controversial because there are indications that chronic levels of human exposure to PBO can affect the nervous system. Thus, PBO-containing materials are often not allowed for use in organic certification programs. Recently, however, PBO was registered as a pesticide in its own right.

The botanicals described in detail below are the least toxic and most versatile currently available.

Pyrethrum and Its Derivatives

Pyrethrum is probably the most important insecticide ever developed. Details about the discovery and early commercial development of insecticidal powders from flowers of chrysanthemum species remain obscure, but peasants in Persia and the Caucasus made an insecticidal powder from the dried flowers of *Chrysanthemum roseum* and *C. carneum*. China, however, was probably the earlier source. In 1886, serious cultivation of *C. cinerariaefolium*, from which "Dalmatian powder" was prepared, was begun in Europe. This expanded until World War I, when Japan became the

Table 7.4
Some Well-Known Botanical Pesticides[a, b]

Active Ingredient	Plant Source	LD$_{50}$ (mg/kg)[c]	Route	Test Animal
derris, cubé, rotenone	*Derris* spp., *Lonchocarpus* spp.	132-1,500	oral	rats
hellebore	*Veratrum viride*	—	—	—
nicotine	*Nicotiana tabacum*	50-60 50	oral dermal	rats rabbits
pyrethrum	*Chrysanthemum cinerariaefolium*	200 >18,000	oral dermal	rats rats
quassia	*Quassia* spp.	low toxicity to mammals	—	—
red squill	*Urginea maritima*	0.7 0.43	oral oral	male rats female rats
ryania	*Ryania speciosa*	750-1,000 750	oral oral	rats dogs
sabadilla	*Schoenocaulon officinale*	>10,000	oral	rats

[a] Compiled in part from Shepard, 1939.

[b] All but red squill, which is a rodenticide, are insecticides.

[c] Toxicity ratings primarily from Worthing, 1979 (where available).

major supplier. Later, the growing of pyrethrum shifted to Kenya and Tanzania in eastern Africa, which remain the major sources today.

It will help you considerably throughout this book if you are clear about the meaning of the three names that relate to materials derived from the chrysanthemum flower. Pyrethrum refers to the dried, powdered flower heads of the plant. Pyrethrin refers to the active-ingredient compounds that occur in the flowers. Pyrethroid refers to synthetic compounds that resemble pyrethrins in chemical structure but are more toxic to insects. They are also far more stable in the presence of sunlight. Some formulations persist in the environment longer than either pyrethrum or pyrethrin, often lasting 10 days or more, compared to a few hours or days for the natural botanicals.

Properties. Pyrethrum is a mixture of compounds, including pyrethrins I and II and cinerin I and II. Pyrethrins comprise 0.9% to 1.3% of dried pyrethrum flowers. Pyrethroids are composed of synthetic compounds similar to pyrethrins.

Mode of Action. The toxic effect of pyrethrin, the active ingredient of natural pyrethrum, is attributed to its disruption of normal transmission of nerve impulses, causing virtually instant paralysis in insects. Some insects can detoxify pyrethrin and recover from the initial knockdown, so most pyrethrins are combined with the synergist PBO, which blocks the ability of insects to break down the toxin. Synthetic pyrethroids have a similar mode of action.

Formulations. Pyrethrum is available as a powder or, like pyrethrin and the pyrethroids, can be purchased as a liquid concentrate, wettable powder or aerosol "bug bomb." Aerosols with fluorocarbon propellants, created during the World War II era, soon became so popular that almost every home in the United States had them. Today, although the propellant in most products has been changed to CO_2 because fluorocarbons are now known to contaminate the upper atmosphere, many pyrethrin and pyrethroid products are still packaged as aerosols for home use. For sources of these materials, see the Resource Appendix under "Insect Management: Chemical Controls" on pp. 686-687.

In general, we do not recommend aerosol formulations, because so much material is released into the general environment rather than directly onto the target pest. In addition, the mist created by an aerosol is composed of very fine particles that stay suspended in the air longer than those from liquid applications. Thus, indoor aerosol sprays cause unnecessary respiratory exposure. Unfortunately, many aerosols contain pleasant perfume additives rather than the unpleasant odors that would alert people that they have just taken a breath of poison.

Some formulations contain microencapsulated pyrethrins that release their active ingredient slowly, prolonging the life of the insecticide when used indoors. Other pyrethrins are formulated with inorganic or other botanical insecticides so the quick knockdown from the pyrethrins is combined with slower but longer-term control from the other ingredients.

Safety. Pyrethrum, pyrethrin and some pyrethroids are low in mammalian toxicity; the oral LD_{50} of pyrethrin in rats is 1,200 to 1,500 mg/kg. In rats fed synthetic pyrethroids, acute toxicity ranged between 430 and 4,000 mg/kg for permethrin, depending on the solvent used as a carrier, and was 3,000 mg/kg for resmethrin. No genetic mutations or birth defects were found during the chronic-exposure tests. However, repeated contact with dusts may cause skin irritation or allergic reactions in humans.

Pyrethrin can be toxic to cats at doses above 0.04%, so you should follow the label directions closely when treating cats for fleas. Wear gloves, goggles and a respirator when applying these compounds, because inhalation places the poison directly in the bloodstream. (See pp. 97-103 for details on protective equipment.)

Uses and Application. Pyrethrum and related compounds are toxic to a wide range of household and garden insects including ants, aphids, beetles, caterpillars, cockroaches, fleas, flies, leafhoppers, lice, mosquitoes and tapeworms.

Neem

The tropical neem tree *(Azadirachta indica)* is widely distributed in Africa and Asia and is grown as a beautiful ornamental shade tree in the southern United States and other subtropical regions of the continent. Neem oil extracts have been used as medicinal preparations and pest control products in Asia and Africa for centuries. Recently, neem's insecticidal, fungicidal and bactericidal properties and its safety to mammals have aroused interest among researchers in Europe and the United States. A commercial insecticide called Margosan-O® has now reached the American market.

Properties. Neem oil is composed of a complex mixture of biologically active compounds. It has a strong, unpleasant odor and a bitter taste.

Mode of Action. The complex structure of neem oil makes it difficult to pinpoint its mode of action. The principal active ingredient is azadirachtin, but more than 25 other active compounds, including deacetylazadirachtinol, meliantriol, vepol and salannin, have also been isolated. Its various active ingredients act as repellents, feeding inhibitors, egg-laying deterrents, growth retardants, sterilants and direct toxins. These multiple modes of action make it unlikely that insects or pathogens will develop resistance to neem compounds because they affect the pests in so many ways.

Neem has both contact and systemic action in plants. When it is applied to the soil, some species absorb it through their roots and distribute (translocate) it throughout the plant. When sprayed on plant foliage, neem is only somewhat systemic, and only in certain species. Generally, flushes of new foliage must be sprayed periodically to ensure adequate protection.

Formulations. Margosan-O®, the only registered neem product in the United States, is an oil emulsion currently authorized for use on ornamental crops, although registration for food crops is pending. Several companies are planning to produce neem products for both food and ornamental crop pests, so the number of products should increase in the near future.

Safety. Neem-oil extracts show very low toxicity to mammals. The oral LD_{50} in rats is greater than 13,000 mg/kg. According to the Ames test, which uses bacteria as test organisms, neem oil is not mutagenic. Seed dust can irritate the lungs, but in most forms neem is not irritating to the skin. The active ingredients biodegrade rapidly in sunlight and within a few weeks in the soil.

Uses and Application. Because neem is so new to the American market, there is a lack of practical experience with it under conditions in the United States. However, research literature shows that neem extracts affect a wide variety of insects in various ways. Extracts have inhibited feeding in 170 insect species in seven orders. They have inhibited normal growth in species in four orders and have proven directly toxic to aphids, termites and various caterpillars. In a recent review of neem as an antifeedant and growth inhibitor, 20 species of Coleoptera (beetles), 5 species of Diptera (flies), 14 species of Hemiptera (bugs), 3 species of Homoptera (scales, mealybugs and whiteflies), 2 species of Isoptera (termites), 25 species of Lepidoptera (caterpillars), 5 species of Orthoptera (locusts and crickets) and one mite species showed responses to neem extracts. Table 7.5 above lists

Table 7.5
Selected Insects Affected by Neem Extracts

Scientific Name	Common Name
Acheta domestica	house cricket
Aphis fabae	bean aphid
Blatella germanica	German cockroach
Culex pipiens	northern house mosquito
Dacus dorsalis	oriental fruit fly
Diabrotica undecimpunctata	spotted cucumber beetle
Epilachna varivestis	Mexican bean beetle
Heliothis zea	corn earworm, bollworm
Leptinotarsa decemlineata	Colorado potato beetle
Liriomyza trifolii	serpentine leafminer
Locusta migratoria	migratory locust
Meloidogyne incognita	root-knot nematode
Musca autumnalis	face fly
Nilaparvata lugens	brown planthopper
Oncopeltus fasciatus	large milkweed bug
Pectinophora gossypiella	pink bollworm
Plutella xylostella	diamondback moth
Podagrica uniforma	flea beetle
Schistocera gregaria	desert locust
Spodoptera frugiperda	fall armyworm
Tetranychus urticae	two-spotted spider mite
Tineola bisselliella	webbing clothes moth
Tribolium confusum	confused flour beetle
Trichoplusia ni	cabbage looper

some major household and garden pests that are affected by neem.

The preliminary studies also indicate that certain beneficial insects such as hymenopteran parasitoids and predatory mites escape the effects of neem.

Limonene and Linalool (Citrus Peel Extract)

Tons of citrus peel are discarded regularly by the juice industry, yet they contain insecticidal compounds that appear to be of low toxicity to mammals. These insect-killing properties were brought to the attention of Dr. Craig Sheppard, an entomologist at

the Coastal Plains Experiment Station in Georgia, by a group of auto mechanics who reported that a hand cleaner called Dirt Squad™ killed fire ants. This hand cleaner contains orange-peel liquids, so Sheppard designed experiments to investigate the insecticidal properties of oil extracts from citrus peels.

The two most effective insecticidal compounds are d-limonene, a terpene that constitutes about 90% of crude citrus oil, and linalool, a terpene alcohol. Terpenes are hydrocarbons found in essential oils. They are used as solvents, fragrances and flavors in cosmetics and beverages.

Linalool can also be extracted from pine wood.

Properties. Citrus oils have a fresh floral odor and an oily consistency.

Mode of Action. Limonene and linalool are contact poisons, but research on their properties and modes of action is in its infancy. At this time it is thought that limonene heightens sensory nerve activity in insects, causing massive overstimulation of motor nerves that leads to convulsion and paralysis. Some insects, such as adult fleas, recover from the paralysis unless limonene is synergized by piperonyl butoxide (PBO), a controversial material discussed on p. 121. There is very little published research on the action of linalool on insects, although it has been determined that it is not a cholinesterase inhibitor (a nerve poison). As of this writing, linalool is also formulated with PBO.

Formulation. Limonene and linalool are available in aerosol and liquid products. They are marketed primarily as flea dips and shampoos but are also formulated with insecticidal soap for use as contact poisons against aphids and mites.

Safety. Limonene and linalool are used extensively in cosmetics, foods, soaps and perfumes. At low doses such as these, they are regarded as safe by the U.S. Food and Drug Administration. Limonene has an oral LD_{50} of more than 5,000 mg/kg in rats; linalool has an oral LD_{50} in male rats of 4,858 mg/kg and in female rats of 4,127 mg/kg. At the higher doses found in insecticides, greater caution is called for.

In summarizing preliminary toxicology literature on these materials, Henn and Weinzierl (1989) reported that when applied topically to some laboratory animals, both compounds could irritate the skin, eyes and mucous membranes. They also found that at both moderate and high doses, these substances could cause tremors, excess salivation, lack of coordination and muscle weakness. However, even at the higher doses the symptoms were temporary, lasting several hours to several days, and the animals recovered fully. Some cats may experience minor tremors and excess salivation for up to one hour after applications of limonene or linalool at recommended rates. Limonene was shown to promote tumor formation in mouse skin that had been previously sensitized to tumor initiation. Linalool is more active as a systemic toxin than as a skin irritant.

Although the vast majority of pets probably tolerate treatments with EPA-registered citrus-oil products with no adverse effects, these laboratory reports underscore the prudence of applying a small amount of the material to a portion of the pet before treating its entire body. If the pet shows an adverse reaction, discontinue use.

Uses and Application. Limonene and linalool are registered for use against fleas, aphids and mites. However, studies by Dr. Sheppard have shown that these compounds also kill fire ants, houseflies, stable flies, black soldier flies, paper wasps and house crickets. In a test using scarified (grated) limes, all the fruit flies were immobilized in 15 minutes, and all were dead in two hours. Flies on unscarified limes appeared to be unaffected after two hours. In California, preliminary tests of citrus oils on Argentine ants have shown them to be very effective in immediate toxicity, although they degrade rapidly.

Although to date these citrus oils have been incorporated only into flea-control products and sprays for aphids and mites, they have the potential for much wider use, including treatments for livestock and human ectoparasites, fumigation of food handling and storage facilities and household pest control.

The manufacturer of d-limonene and linalool products for flea control is Farnam Co., which markets the Flea Stop® line of citrus-based products (see the Resource Appendix under "Insect Management: Chemical Controls" on pp. 686-687).

Garlic Oil

Garlic *(Allium sativum)*, a member of the lily family, has been used for thousands of years in treating coughs, colds, chronic bronchitis, toothache, earache, dandruff, high blood pressure, arteriosclerosis and other ailments. The first detailed description of garlic as a medicinal plant was made by the Greek physician Dioscorides, who recommended it for destroying or expelling intestinal worms and as a diuretic. Chinese medicine uses garlic for diarrhea, amebic and bacterial dysentery, pulmonary tuberculosis, bloody urine, diphtheria, whooping cough, typhoid, hepatitis, trachoma, scalp ringworm, vaginal trichomoniasis and other disorders. Modern studies confirm that garlic oil exhibits antibacterial, antifungal, amebicidal and insecticidal qualities, although whether garlic is indeed effective against all the ailments listed above requires further research.

Encouraged by recommendations and anecdotes in the organic-gardening literature, gardeners have been using homemade garlic preparations as insecticides for many years. Take note, however, that although garlic does kill pest insects and some pathogens, it also kills beneficial insects and microbes. Thus, we do not recommend it as an all-purpose spray for garden use. We include it in the list of botanical materials discussed here due to its popularity with gardeners and the fact that current interest in botanicals among pesticide researchers may lead to the marketing of commercial garlic-based pesticides.

Properties. Garlic is a strong-scented plant whose bulb contains the volatile oil alliin (S-allyl-L-cysteine sulfoxide) and other compounds. Commercial garlic oil is obtained by steam distillation of crushed fresh bulbs; powdered garlic is derived from dried bulbs.

Mode of Action. Although the chemical structure of garlic compounds is not well studied, diallyl disulfide and diallyl trisulfide, both present in garlic oil, have been identified as causing mortality in mosquito larvae. Both natural and synthetic samples of these active ingredients were lethal at a dosage of five parts per million in water. Garlic oil also contains the volatile compounds allicin, citral, geraniol and linalool, which are known to have insecticidal properties. Extracts obtained with a water and alcohol mixture appear to have more fungicidal and bactericidal effects than does the essential oil.

Safety. Because garlic is a culinary staple, it is presumed safe for humans. When used as an insecticide, however, it has a broad-spectrum effect, killing both pests and beneficials. Because it is a naturally occurring plant, it can be presumed to biodegrade rapidly in the soil.

Formulation and Uses. Garlic is toxic to a broad range of organisms. Recently, laboratory studies have shown various extracts to be effective against two nematodes, *Aphelenchoides sacchari,* which attacks commercial mushrooms, and *Tylenchulus sempenetrans,* which attacks citrus. Garlic chips fed to baby chickens prevented the establishment of candidiasis, caused by the yeast *Candida albicans.* Aqueous extracts of commercially prepared garlic powder were shown in laboratory studies to inhibit clinical isolates of the yeast *Candida albicans* and the fungus *Cryptococcus neoformans.*

Garlic solutions have been reported to destroy four species of larval mosquitoes in the genera *Culex* and *Aedes,* as well as aphids, the cabbage-butterfly caterpillar *(Pieris brassicae,* a European species) and larvae of the Colorado potato beetle *(Leptinotarsa decemlineata).* It has also been reported to be toxic to the natural aphid enemies *Syrphus corollae,* a syrphid fly; *Chrysoperla carnea,* the green lacewing; and *Coccinella septempunctata,* a lady beetle. See Chapter 5 for a more complete discussion of these important beneficial insects.

We do not recommend garlic for aphid control since it kills the natural enemies of the aphids as well as the pests; insecticidal soaps are preferable. Because garlic seems to have broad-spectrum insecticidal effects, it should be limited to those home and garden applications where natural controls are rarely present.

REFERENCES AND READINGS

Agrios, G.N. 1969. *Plant pathology.* New York: Academic Press. 629 pp.

Contains information about sulfur as a fungicide.

Amonkar, S.V., and A. Banerji. 1971. Isolation and characterization of larvicidal principles of garlic. *Science* 174:1343-1344.

An important early paper reporting on the larvicidal effects of garlic extracts on mosquitoes.

Casida, J.E., ed. 1973. *Pyrethrum, the natural insecticide.* New York: Academic Press. 329 pp.

Reviews the chemistry and toxicology of natural pyrethrum and synthetic pyrethroids.

Davidson, J.A., S.A. Gill and M.J. Raupp. 1990. Foliar and growth effects of repetitive summer horticultural oil sprays on trees and shrubs under drought stress. *Journal of Arboriculture* 16(4):77-81.

This paper was the source of the information on plant species that tolerate oil sprays while under drought stress in hot summer weather.

Ebeling, W. 1971. Sorptive dusts for pest control. *Annual Review of Entomology* 16:123-158.

An early review paper on sorptive dusts, their action and their use as pest control agents.

Ebeling, W. 1975. *Urban entomology.* Los Angeles: University of California, Division of Agricultural Sciences. 695 pp.

A very useful source of information on silica aerogel, boric acid, other urban/suburban pesticides and the biology and management of urban pests.

Findlay, W.P.K. 1960. Boron compounds for the preservation of timber against fungi and insects. German Wood Research Association, 6th Wood Protection Congress, July 1959. In *Pest Technololgy* 2(6):124-127.

This is a general discussion of the development and efficacy of boron-containing wood preservatives.

Grossman, J. 1990. Horticultural oils: New summer uses on ornamental plant pests. *The IPM Practitioner* 12(8):1-9.

This review brings together the latest information about the uses of horticultural oils on ornamental plants and their pests.

Henn, T., and R. Weinzierl. 1989. *Botanical insectidies and insecticidal soaps.* Urbana-Champaign: University of Illinois Office of Agricultural Entomology (Circular 1296). 18 pp.

A short, comprehensive paper that updates a great deal of information.

Horst, R.K. 1979. *Westcott's plant disease handbook.* 4th ed. New York: Van Nostrand Reinhold. 803 pp.

A useful diagnostic guide for the layperson concerned about plant diseases in ornamental and food gardens. The treatment emphasis is on pesticides, however, and no references are provided.

Johnson, W.T. 1980. Spray oils as insecticides. *Journal of Arboriculture* 6(7):169-174.

A thorough discussion of modern horticultural-oil formulations and how to use them.

Johnson, W.T. 1982. Horticultural spray oils for tree pest control. *Weeds, Trees, and Turf* May:36-40.

This paper clears up many misconceptions about the formulation and application of horticultural oils.

Klingman, G.C., and F.M. Ashton. 1975. *Weed Science: principles and practices.* New York: John Wiley and Sons. 431 pp.

This basic text on weed control covers all the basic herbicide groups and provides information about using herbicides.

Leung, A.Y. 1980. *Encyclopedia of common natural ingredients used in food, drugs, and cosmetics.* New York: John Wiley and Sons. 409 pp.

A basic reference work that covers the common natural food ingredients, some of which are used in pesticidal products. The short general descriptions provide information on chemical composition, pharmacological or biological uses and commercial preparations. The book is thoroughly referenced.

Mallis, A. 1982. *Handbook of pest control.* 6th ed. Cleveland: Franzak and Foster. 1,101 pp.

A basic handbook for the pest control professional that contains much information about sorptive dusts and other pesticides.

***MSDS reference for crop protection chemicals.* 1989.** 2nd ed. New York: John Wiley and Sons. 1,358 pp.

This book contains Material Safety Data Sheets for most companies in the United States that manufacture agricultural chemicals. The chemicals are indexed by manufacturer as well as by brand name. The publishers have also included information on EPA reporting requirements and a list of extremely hazardous substances.

Mullison, W.R., ed. 1979. *Herbicide handbook.* 4th ed. Champaign, Ill.: Weed Science Society of America. 479 pp.

Although this book lacks a thorough review of the existing literature on chronic toxicity and includes largely producer information, it is very useful to those learning about the properties of herbicides and the limitations of their use. The herbicides are listed alphabetically, with information on physical and chemical properties, use, precautions, physiological behavior, behavior in or on soils and toxicological properties. The toxicity discussion includes the effects on wildlife, acute toxicity in different test animals and with different routes of exposure, sub-acute toxicity and chronic toxicity.

Nath, A., N.K. Sharma, S. Bhardway, and C.K. Thapa. 1982. Short communications. *Nematologica* 28: 253-255.

This paper discusses the garlic extracts that kill two nematode species.

National Institute of Occupational Safety and Health (NIOSH). 1974. *Criteria for a recommended standard for occupational exposure to crystalline silica.* Cincinnati: National Institute for Occupational Safety and Health (Centers for Disease Control Publication 75120). 121 pp.

This publication discusses exposure standards for crystalline silica.

National Institute of Occupational Safety and Health (NIOSH). 1978. *A recommended standard for occupational exposure to refined petroleum solvents.* Cincinnati: National Institute for Occupational Safety and Health. 10 pp. (Single copies available from: OSHA, Division of Technical Services, Publication Dissemination, 4676 Columbia Parkway, Cincinnati, OH 45226.)

This pamphlet recommends the use of an organic-vapor cartridge respirator for Stoddard solvents, mineral spirits and kerosene and specifies permissible exposure levels and types of protective equipment.

Nelson, R.H. 1975. *Pyrethrum flowers, 1945-1972.* 3rd ed. Minneapolis: McLaughlin Gormley King. 149 pp.

A good discussion of developments affecting the use and manufacture of pyrethrum flowers and pyrethrum extracts.

Pimentel, D., ed. 1981. *CRC handbook of pest management in agriculture: Vol III, major types of pesticides — chemical nature, modes of action, and toxicity.* Boca Raton, Fla.: CRC Press. 656 pp.

This exhaustively referenced volume provides a good overview of major pesticides used in agriculture and horticulture, together with IPM-oriented discussions of pest management in major crops.

Powers, K.A. 1985. Toxicological aspects of linalool: a review. *Veterinary and Human Toxicology* 27(6):484-486.

A summary of studies on the toxicity of linalool.

Puritch, G.S. 1981. *Pesticidal soaps and adjuvants: what are they and how do they work?* Proceedings of the 23rd Annual Lower Mainland Horticultural Improvement Association Grower's Short Course, February 11, 12 and 13, Abbotsford, B.C. (Available from Dr. G.S. Puritch, Safer's Ltd., 6761 Kirkpatrick Crescent, RR3, Victoria, BC V8X 3X1 Canada.)

Includes an introduction to the chemistry of pesticidal soaps.

Quraishi, M.S. 1977. *Biochemical insect control.* New York: John Wiley and Sons. 280 pp.

An introduction to pyrethroids, botanicals, attractants, pheromones, hormones and microbial insecticides.

Roe, F.J., and W.E. Field. 1965. Chronic toxicity of essential oils and certain other products of natural origin. *Food and Cosmetic Toxicology* 3:311-324.

This is the source of the information on tumor formation in mice treated with d-limonene.

Saleem, Z.M., and K. Al-Delaimy. 1981. Inhibition of *Bacillus cereus* by garlic extracts. *Journal of Food Protection* 45(11):1007-1009.

Documentation of some of the bacteriocidal effects of garlic extracts.

Schmutterer, H., K.R.S. Ascher and H. Rembold. 1981. *Natural pesticides from the neem tree* (Azadirachta indica). Proceedings of the First International Neem Conference, Rottach, Egern, Federal Republic of Germany, 16-18 June, 1980.

These conference proceedings contain research papers on neem, its mode of action and its impact on pests and nontarget organisms.

Shepard, H.H. 1939. *The chemistry and toxicology of insecticides.* Minneapolis, Minn: Burgess Publishing Co. 383 pp.

This is the source of the information in Table 7.4.

Smith, M.D. 1982. *The Ortho problem solver.* San Francisco: Ortho Information Services. 1,022 pp.

Although essentially a promotional effort for Ortho (Chevron Chemical Co.) products, this large book with many color photographs brings together a composite of Cooperative Extension Service recommendations for house-plant, household, garden, insect, weed and plant problems in the United States. It includes many nontoxic control methods.

Thomson, W.T. 1977. *Agricultural chemical handbook II: herbicides.* Fresno, Calif.: Thompson Publ. 264 pp.

This handbook includes two pages of information on petroleum oils and weed oils.

U.S. Environmental Protection Agency. 1988. *Pesticide fact book.* Park Ridge,N.J.: Noyes Data Corporation. 810 pp.

A collection of 130 pesticide fact sheets that summarize the properties, formulations, use patterns and toxicology of various chemicals. The "scientific findings" section on each fact sheet lists major toxicological data available, and perhaps more important, notes where data gaps on health and environmental effects occur.

Von Nasseh, O.M. 1982. Zur Wirkung von Knoblauchextrakt auf *Syrphus corollae F., Chrysopa carnea Steph.* und *Coccinella septempunctata. Zeitschrift für angewandte Entomologie* 94:123-126.

A paper in German describing the toxic effects of garlic extracts on a series of aphid predators.

Ware, G.W. 1986. *Fundamentals of pesticides: a self-instruction guide.* Fresno, Calif.: Thompson Publ. 274 pp.

An excellent introduction to pesticides and their chemistry.

Weir, R.J., Jr., and R.S. Fisher. 1971. Toxicologic studies on borax and boric acid. *Toxicology and Applied Pharmacology* 23:351-364.

A summary of feeding studies on rats showing low acute toxicity of borax products.

Westcott, C. 1971. *Plant disease handbook,* 3rd ed. New York: Van Nostrand Reinhold. 843 pp.

This book was a source of much of the information on sulfur, particularly its formulations and side effects.

Worthing, C. R. 1979. *The pesticide manual: a world compendium.* 6th ed. Croydon, England: British Crop Protection Council (BCPC) Publications. 655 pp.

This was one source for the LD_{50} and other toxicity information quoted in this chapter.

CHAPTER 8
New Frontiers: Microbials, Pheromones and Insect Growth Regulators

INTRODUCTION

During the 1970s and 1980s exponentially rising rates of pest resistance to conventional chemical controls, which we discussed in Chapter 6, and widespread public concern about the health and environmental hazards of many pesticides led researchers to seek novel materials that were effective against the pests but posed fewer hazards to other components of the ecosystem. As a result, three categories of "biological" or "biorational" pesticides entered—or re-entered—the marketplace: microbials, insect pheromones and insect growth regulators (IGRs). Microbial pesticides are used to suppress weeds and plant diseases as well as insects; pheromones and IGRs are used only against insects.

The biological pesticides discussed in this chapter deserve the special attention of those who are interested in less-toxic pest control, since they are at the forefront of a new wave of improved pest management tools. They combine increased effectiveness, safety and biodegradability with novel active ingredients and modes of action. In general, however, they also require greater sophistication and knowledge on the part of the user.

After defining the terms used to refer to the three groups of biorational pesticides, we examine each in turn, including how it works, the pests it controls, its special characteristics, its potential role in IPM programs and what developments must take place before it fulfills that potential.

• *Microbial pesticides* contain living microorganisms or the toxins they produce as active ingredients. Algae, bacteria, fungi, mycoplasms, parasitic nematodes, protozoa, rickettsia, viroids and viruses that kill their host organisms are referred to as microbials within the pesticide industry.

Many microbials are cultured in large industrial vats in much the same way as yeasts used to brew beer are cultured. They are collected at a certain stage of their development, such as the spore stage in the case of the microbial *Bacillus thuringiensis* and the infective juvenile stage in the case of nematodes. They are mixed with compounds that make them compatible with water and enhance their shelf life, and are then packaged for sale.

Microbials are formulated as sprays, dusts and granules, and are applied with the same equipment as conventional pesticides. If necessary, some microbials can be used in conjunction with synthetic chemical pesticides. The label indicates when this is the case.

• *Pheromones* are chemical signals emitted by insects and other organisms that enable the organisms to communicate with other members of the same species. Pheromones are sometimes referred to as "perfumes," particularly those pheromones used to attract members of the opposite sex for purposes of mating. In insect control, pheromones can be used to attract insects to traps. Or they can be applied in artificially large amounts over a crop to so confuse insects that they fail to find mates and thus fail to reproduce.

• *Insect growth regulators (IGRs)* are compounds that mimic or interfere with the natural hormones that regulate an insect's developmental stages: egg, larva, pupa and adult.

MICROBIAL PESTICIDES

The microbes currently marketed as insecticides, fungicides and herbicides are very effective against their target pests but are virtually nontoxic to humans, domestic animals, wildlife and the natural enemies of the pests. In other words, they are highly selective in their action. Selectivity refers to the ability of a pesticide to affect a pest organism but not the rest of the ecosystem. It is a very important factor in choosing pest control tools. For example, because currently available microbials are nontoxic to humans and other animals, they can be applied to food crops right before or during harvest.

Microbial pesticides have other advantages. First, they have less potential for environmental contamination than conventional pesticides because they are much more biologically fragile and are therefore more biodegradable. The use of microbials is also far less likely to produce pest resistance or pest resurgence, the twin banes of conventional pesticide technology that were discussed in Chapter 6. The explanation lies in their selectivity.

Most chemical pesticides are designed to kill insects on contact. Most microbials must be consumed before they become active. Thus, consumption determines which insects die from a microbial, whereas only resistant individuals will survive treatment with a chemical insecticide, which also tends to decimate the pest's natural enemies. Because microbials are generally harmless to a pest's natural enemies, pests that survive the microbial application are often subsequently killed by their existing predators or parasitoids, preventing resurgence. The microbial pesticide does not kill as high a proportion of a pest population, which ensures that the pest's gene pool contains individuals susceptible to the microbial, thereby slowing or preventing development of resistant pest populations.

Although microbial pesticides are often referred to as biological controls, they must be distinguished from the predators and parasitoids used to control pests in the kind of classical biological control programs described in Chapter 4. Many predator and parasitoid populations become established on a self-sustaining basis in the natural environment; they increase or decrease their numbers in response to the population density of their prey. In contrast, most microbial pesticides require repeated applications.

There are a few cases in which the introduction of a microbial species did suppress a pest with the same permanence shown by introduced parasitoids or predators. The classic example is the introduction of the myxoma virus *(Leporipoxvirus)* into Australia and France to control the European rabbit *(Oryctolagus cuniculus)*, which had become a serious pest in these countries. The virus became permanently established as one control element for these rabbits. The microbial insecticide *Bacillus popilliae*, also known as milky spore disease, is applied to turf to kill beetle grubs and can remain active in the soil for more than 25 years before another application is needed. Even this, however, does not equal the permanence of many successfully established predators or parasitoids.

Microbials have many advantages, but their use may require special care. For instance, many microbials are highly vulnerable to unfavorable environmental conditions. Although most are effective if applied in warm, moist conditions, coolness, insufficient moisture or exposure to ultraviolet radiation from sunlight can deactivate or kill them. It is important to pay close attention to the application directions on the label.

The fact that microbials are living organisms means that some have shorter shelf lives than some synthetic chemicals. Containers of synthetic pesticides can usually be stored for several years under a wide range of temperatures, whereas microbials are most effective when fresh. Their storage lives may be limited to a few weeks or months under optimum conditions, which may include refrigeration. In fact, some microbials must be kept in portable ice chests while being transported to the site where they will be used. You should buy only the amount of microbial you can use during its effective storage life; don't keep a supply on hand for the long term, as is often done with chemical products.

With microbials, the timing of applications to coincide with the vulnerable stage of the pest is usually far more critical than it is with synthetic chemical products. The latter are more likely to damage several or all life stages of the pest, whereas many microbials affect only one life stage. For example, the bacterial insecticide *Bacillus thuringiensis* (BT) kills only the larval (caterpillar) stage of moths and butterflies. If it is sprayed when adult moths are seen, it does nothing to prevent damage by the next generation of caterpillars that emerges from eggs laid by the moths.

Because a single microbial pesticide is toxic to a narrow range of pest species, only a portion of the pests occurring in a crop, garden or building will be affected by the application. Pests unaffected by the microbial will continue to cause damage unless additional measures are used to combat them. A single chemical pesticide does not kill all groups of pests either, but the range of host species killed is greater than with microbials. Thus, it is very important that microbials be combined with cultural, physical, mechanical and biological controls so that a wide range of mortality factors are brought to bear on any particular pest species.

Barriers to Registration

In the United States the Environmental Protection Agency (EPA) has responsibility for registration of pesticides as mandated by the Federal Insecticide, Fungicide and Rodenticide Act (FIFRA). In recent years, the EPA has been criticized severely for its registration policies regarding microbial and other biorational products. The term biorational, as used by the EPA, refers to pesticides composed of or analogous to naturally occurring organisms or substances, and includes most microbials, analogs of certain chemicals produced by pests (e.g., pheromones and juvenile hormones) and other naturally occurring biochemicals, such as allelotoxins (natural herbicides), that differ in their mode of action from most conventional pesticides. The bulk of the criticism has focused on the EPA's policy requiring extensive toxicology testing of biorational materials that, say

critics, are not warranted by their biochemical ingredients. Meanwhile, more toxic synthetic pesticides that have not been held to the same rigorous level of safety testing remain on the market. Critics agree that microbials should undergo some level of testing, but how much testing is a matter of intense debate at this time.

The registration process has recently been streamlined somewhat at the EPA level, but high production costs associated with the research and testing required for registration have prevented the registration of many seemingly benign microbial pesticides that could play an important role in least-toxic pest control. Thus, few new microbial products have reached the market in the last decade. Those that have tend to be biotechnologically altered microbes or their by-products. Currently, engineered organisms seem to be favored by the pesticide industry because they can be patented. We examine this issue next.

Microbial Pesticides and Biotechnology

Until recently, most microbial pesticides were formulated with naturally occurring microorganisms. With the advent of the biotechnology industry and its concomitant drive for profits from genetically altered and patented organisms, research emphasis has shifted. Now, instead of selecting the most effective pesticidal strain of bacteria or fungus from among the dozens or hundreds occurring naturally within a single species, researchers are focusing on artificially enhancing the toxicity of microbes by altering their genetic material. Not surprisingly, each of the approximately 20 new microbial insecticides awaiting EPA registration at the time of this writing is a genetically altered organism.

This approach has both potential advantages and drawbacks. The focus of much of this research is on increasing the speed with which microbials kill insects. Thus, a number of safe and effective microbial products may result from biotechnology. However, another line of research involves incorporating the toxic properties of microbials into the genetic composition of plants so insects will die when they eat the crop. This could lead to the development of insect resistance to microbes, a subject discussed further below.

One of the first bioengineered microbials registered for use was a *Bacillus thuringiensis*-based insecticide toxic to the Colorado potato beetle *(Leptinotarsa decemlineata)* and to the elm leaf beetle *(Pyrrhalta luteola)*. This product, called M-One®, consists of a natural plant bacterium whose genetic material is deliberately altered to contain genes from a BT strain that naturally kills beetles. The bacterium is killed prior to formulation so there is no danger of the engineered organism reproducing in the environment. It is incorporated into an improved formulation that is more persistent than the natural bacterium alone, yet is no more likely to encourage development of insect resistance than is natural *Bacillus thuringiensis*.

In tests, other engineered microbials are being released live onto target pests or incorporated into the genetic makeup of crop plants. These approaches are far more controversial because it is not known how the altered organisms will affect the environment in the long term. Of immediate concern is the possibility that current research on cloning *Bacillus thuringiensis* may lead to insect resistance to this safe, naturally occurring insecticide. Recently, the gene code for the BT toxin active against caterpillars was cloned and inserted into tobacco and tomato plants by researchers at Monsanto, Inc., a leading pesticide manufacturer. The resulting transgenic (genetically altered) plants produced their own BT toxin and were protected from feeding by larvae of the tobacco hornworm *(Manduca sexta)* and tomato fruitworm *(Heliothis zea)*, two target pests on these plants.

Critics worry that the wide use of genetically altered plants will rapidly lead to the rise of insects that are resistant to the BT toxin. According to Dr. Steve Welter, an entomologist at the University of California, Berkeley, "If all the plants in a field are producing the toxin continuously in all parts of the plant, there will be strong selection pressure for the insects to develop resistance. That may mean one of our safest insecticides would become useless." This and other cautions about the impact of biotechnology on pest control research are discussed further in the sidebar below.

Questions about the Appropriateness of Biotechnology to Integrated Pest Management[a]

Biotechnology holds great promise for solving many pest problems. But how well will these technologies fit into an integrated approach to pest management?

Certainly some of the applied research programs currently underway are consistent with IPM goals. The engineering of plants for virus resistance, for example, not only protects the crop from the disease, but should also reduce the use of pesticides. Reduced chemical use means a better environment for beneficial insects. Other research goals, however, do not seem to fit an IPM approach as clearly. One example is the effort to engineer organisms that tolerate environmental pollutants. The U.S. Forest Service is developing trees that tolerate damage from acid rain. The Department of Agriculture is developing honeybees that tolerate insecticides, and many private and public research groups are developing transgenic (genetically altered) plants that tolerate herbicides. All these technologies could increase the use of and dependence on toxic agricultural chemicals.

Another concern is the privatization of research. The development of biotechnology has been marked by a dramatic shift in the funding of agricultural research from the public to the private sector. According to Dr. Robert Goodman of Calgene, Inc., "The research is driven by economics."

Even public universities are not immune to this trend. Dr. Al Schmid, an economist at the University of Michigan, asserts that the race toward development of protected varieties among universities, which can get royalties, is making them "look like any private firm with patented varieties, returning royalties to finance more research" (*Ag Biotechnology News*, May/June 1988, p. 16). As the profit motive comes to the fore, concern about environmental quality may suffer. One must ask what happens to projects that do not hold promise of returning profit in such a profit-driven research environment.

In summary, genetic engineering is here to stay. It is a powerful technology and promises to change many aspects of our lives. Whether these changes are toward or away from environmentally sustainable systems will probably be determined more by political inertia and the desire for profits than by the technology itself.

[a] Adapted from Liebman, 1989.

Microbial Insecticides: Currently Registered Organisms

Of all the pest groups being studied for possible control with microbial pesticides, insects have received the greatest attention. There are more than 1,850 naturally occurring microorganisms or their by-products that hold promise for the control of major insect pests. These pathogens, found within insects, include nearly 100 species of bacteria, over 700 viruses, more than 750 fungi and at least 300 protozoan species. Currently, only a few of these candidates have been registered for use in the United States as microbial insecticides (see Table 8.1 on the facing page). Clearly these organisms are underexploited commercially.

Bacterial Insecticides

The active ingredients in most bacterial insecticides are rod-shaped bacteria in the genus *Bacillus*. Most of these bacterial species belong primarily to the families Enterobacteriaceae, Micrococcaceae, Pseudomonadaceae and Bacillaceae. About 100 species are reported to attack insects, and four of them—*Bacillus thuringiensis, B. popilliae, B. lentimorbus* and *B. sphaericus*—have been studied extensively as insect control agents. The chief advantages of bacterial species are their narrow host range and their lack of toxic effects on nontarget species, including humans and the natural enemies of the pests.

Bacterial species were the first commercial microbial pest control products. The earliest, called Doom® or milky spore disease, was registered in 1948 for use against Japanese beetle grubs. Composed of two bacterial species, *Bacillus lentimorbus* and *B. popilliae*, milky spore disease is still marketed today (see the Resource Appendix under "Insect Management: Biological Controls" on pp. 683-686). The second species to be marketed was *B. thuringiensis*, variety *kurstaki* (BTK), which is active against caterpillars. Since then, additional BT strains have been discovered and for-

mulated commercially for use against a variety of insects, and many others show potential. The mosquito pathogen *B. sphaericus* is also being studied as a commercial possibility.

These four *Bacillus* species are commonly found in soils, and all are spore-forming. The spore is the stage that tides the bacteria over from one favorable period to the next, and it has the ability to withstand degradation by ultraviolet light rays, drought and other unfavorable environmental conditions, at least for a short time. *B. thuringiensis* and *B. popilliae* also produce protein crystals within their sporulating cells. These crystals are their important toxic agents. Bacteria that do not form spores usually do not persist long enough to control pests once applied to a crop; consequently, they are considered poor candidates for development as insecticides.

Bacillus thuringiensis (BT).
Bacillus thuringiensis is a commercially available bacterial species that causes disease in certain insects. It is named after Thuringia, the town in Germany where it was discovered in 1911 in diseased Mediterranean flour moths. At least 35 BT varieties have now been identified, each of which attacks different groups of insect hosts via the toxic protein crystals contained in its spores. The total number of strains under investigation and isolates being held in culture for various uses is increasing as commercial interest grows. Some companies maintain hundreds or more cultures.

According to University of Illinois entomologists Rick Weinzierl and Tess Henn, authors of the excellent pamphlet "Microbial Insecticides,"

BT products are produced commercially in large industrial fermentation tanks. As the bacteria live and multiply in the right conditions, each cell produces (internally) a spore and a crystalline protein toxin called an endotoxin. Most commercial BT products contain the protein toxin and spores, but some are cultured in a

manner that yields only the toxin component....The nature of the crystalline protein endotoxin differs among BT subspecies and isolates, and it is the characteristics of these specific endotoxins that determine which insects will be poisoned by each BT product.

The first commercial BT product entered the market in 1958. It was formulated from the variety *kurstaki* (BTK) and was effective only against the caterpillar (larval) stage of moths and butterflies in the insect order Lepidoptera. Over the years, improved BTK strains have been formulated as a variety of products, which are listed in Table 8.1 on the facing page. In the 1980s, additional BT strains that kill insects in other orders were registered with the EPA. These include BT variety *israelensis* (BTI), which kills the larvae of certain mosquitoes, black flies and fungus gnats in the insect order Diptera, and BT varieties *san diego* and *tenebrionis*, which are toxic to certain beetles in the insect order Coleoptera.

Properties. BT appears as a fine tan to brown powder or reddish-orange granules consisting of spores or toxic crystals and inert ingredients.

Mode of Action. BT is a bacterial stomach poison that must be eaten by an insect to be toxic. All commercial BT products have similar modes of action. When the crystal entodoxin inside the spore is ingested by an insect with a highly alkaline gut that contains appropriate enzymes, the crystal dissolves. The components of the crystal attach to the gut wall, blocking the enzyme systems that protect the insect's gut from its own digestive juices. In a short time, holes appear in the gut wall, allowing the gut's contents to enter the insect's body cavity and bloodstream. This initial poisoning causes the insect to stop feeding and may also lead to paralysis. Then bacterial spores themselves invade the insect's body cavity through these holes, producing septicemia (blood poisoning), which

Table 8.1
Microbial Insecticides: A Product Summary

Pathogen	Product Name	Host Range
Bacteria		
Bacillus thuringiensis var. *kurstaki* (BTK)	Bactur®, Bactospeine®, Caterpillar Killer®, Dipel®, Futura™, Javelin®, SOK-Bt™, Thuricide®, Topside™, Tribactur™, Worm Attack®	caterpillars
B. thuringiensis var. *israelensis*	Bactimos®, Mosquito Attack®, Skeetal™, Teknar®, Vectobac®	mosquito larvae (*Aedes* and *Psorophora* spp.), black flies, fungus gnats
B. thuringiensis var. *san diego*	M-One®	larvae of Colorado potato beetle, elm leaf beetle adults
B. thuringiensis var. *tenebrionis*	Trident®	larvae of Colorado potato beetle
B. thuringiensis var. *aizawai*	Certan™	wax moth larvae
B. popilliae and *B. lentimorbus*	Doom®, Japidemic™, Milky Spore Disease™, Grub Attack®	Japanese beetle larvae and certain other lawn grubs
B. sphaericus	(under development)	mosquito larvae (*Culex, Psorophora, Culiseta* spp.)
Fungi		
Beauveria bassiana	(under development)	many soil-dwelling insects
Lagenidium giganteum	(under development)	mosquito larvae (most genera)
Protozoa		
Nosema locustae	NOLO Bait®, Grasshopper Attack®	grasshoppers, crickets
Viruses		
Gypsy moth nuclear polyhedrosis virus	Gypchek®	gypsy moth caterpillars
Tussock moth NPV	TM Biocontrol-1®	tussock moth caterpillars
Pine sawfly NPV	Neochek-S®	pine sawfly larvae
codling moth granulosis virus (GV)[a]	(experimental)	codling moth larvae
Nematodes		
Steinernema feltiae [b]	Biosafe™, Scanmask™	many larvae of soil-dwellers and wood-borers
Heterorhabditis heliothidis	Bioquest™, and products available from Hydrogardens, Pherotech and Praxis	many soil-dwelling insects

[a] The codling moth granulosis virus is no longer available commercially. Experimental-use permits have been issued for its production by the University of California at Berkeley under the direction of Dr. Louis Falcon, a pioneer in the development of this viral insecticide. Limited distribution has been arranged through a grower/member cooperative (see p. 139).

[b] The earlier name for this nematode was *Neoaplectana carpocapsae,* and various strains and even other nematode species may occur in the final product.

may kill the insect immediately or may take a few days to do so.

A caterpillar that ingests BT may live for several days. However, it does not continue feeding and therefore causes no further damage to plants. Dead and dying caterpillars turn a dark color, remaining attached to leaves for a few days, usually hanging at a 90° angle toward the ground (see the photo at right).

Although the BT multiplies within the body of the infected insect, spores and toxic crystals are almost never produced. Consequently, insects killed by BT do not serve as sources of new infections, and several applications of BT may be required to control an insect infestation, much as with a conventional insecticide. Also, when sprayed outdoors, BT is broken down within one to several days by ultraviolet radiation, another reason repeated applications may be necessary.

BT is nontoxic to the natural enemies of BT-susceptible insects. Thus, target pests that escape the effects of a BT application are often attacked afterward by their predators and parasitoids, further lowering the pest population and reducing the amount of pesticide needed.

Formulations. BT products are formulated as liquid concentrates, wettable powders and ready-to-use dusts, granules and briquettes. Recent advances in formulation promote adherence to leaves, increase drop density per unit of foliage surface area to improve coverage, reduce evaporation during aerial application, enhance palatability to pests, increase resistance to breakdown in sunlight and increase the ease of mixing. These improvements may mean that older studies suggesting that BT is ineffective against certain pests should not be relied on; instead, there should be new tests against such species using the improved formulations.

Safety. BT is generally considered harmless to humans and other species. The acute oral toxicity rating in rats varies from an LD_{50} of 400 mg/kg for

This caterpillar consumed *Bacillus thuringiensis* (BT) spores that were sprayed on the leaves of the plant and died within hours. BT-killed caterpillars are commonly seen hanging upside-down from vegetation for a day or two before their cadavers fall from the plant. (Photo by Helga Olkowski.)

BT technical grade (preformulation) powder to 8,100 mg/kg for the formulated product Dipel® 2X. After thorough testing for toxicity to humans, the Food and Drug Administration granted an "exemption from tolerance" for the use of BT on food crops. This means that there is virtually no level that causes toxicity in test animals, and BT can be sprayed on food crops without harm to humans. There is one report of a lab technician inadvertently getting BT

solution in his eye, but no dire consequences developed, and the infection was cleared up with an antibiotic.

When bacterial spores are inhaled or rubbed into the skin, they become "foreign proteins" and can cause serious allergic reactions in certain susceptible individuals. It is only common sense that you should wear a respirator or mask to avoid breathing mist from the spray or dust of various BT products. Goggles are also recommended, because mist or dust can irritate your eyes. Wear gloves, long-sleeved shirts and trousers when applying any pesticide, including microbials. See pp. 97-103 for a review of safety precautions.

Uses and Application. Because BT is a living organism, it must be protected from high temperature during storage. Ideally, BT packages should be stored in a refrigerator or cooler until used. When kept at 70°F to 75°F (21°C to 24°C), BT powders remain active for two to three years; storage at lower temperatures presumably prolongs their shelf life somewhat. When transporting BT, keep packages shaded and ventilated. BT should not be exposed to direct sunlight, and the container should not be left in a car trunk or other enclosed space on a hot day.

Because storage temperatures affect the viability and effectiveness of the product, be certain the package is fresh from the manufacturer through the distributor. Some distributors resell BT that has languished on retail shelves, where it may have been subjected to high temperatures and other conditions that reduce its effectiveness. If you have any doubt as to the product's age, note the batch number on the package and call the manufacturer directly.

Most BT formulations are mixed with water and applied as sprays. When mixing wettable powders, be sure to start with the water and add the BT while constantly stirring the mixture. Use water that is adjusted to pH 7 or less (making it more acidic), because an alkaline suspension of pH 8 or more destroys the toxic effect of the crystal. However, most formulations are buffered to minimize pH problems. The addition of a soap or detergent "sticker-spreader" will improve the flow of BT onto plants. Mix a fresh batch of BT for each use; mixtures lose their effectiveness in 12 to 72 hours, depending on which formulation you use. Shake the container of spray constantly during application to ensure that the BT remains in suspension.

Treating Caterpillars. *Bacillus thuringiensis* var. *kurstaki* products toxic to caterpillars (the larva of moths and butterflies) are listed in Table 8.1 on p. 133. Hundreds of species of caterpillars that feed on plants are susceptible to BTK, including the "worms" that attack vegetables such as broccoli, cabbage, corn and tomatoes, the "loopers" found on melons and lettuce, the armyworms and webworms that eat the leaves of lawn grasses, the oakworms, bagmoths, gypsy moth larvae and tent caterpillars found on trees and shrubs and the larvae of moths that attack stored grains and infest beehives. Table 8.2 at right lists some of the more common caterpillar pests that are susceptible to BT.

Table 8.2 also lists some caterpillars that cannot be controlled effectively by BT products currently available, primarily because they feed little or not at all on the treated surfaces of plants. These pests include larvae that live in the soil (e.g., certain cutworms), those that bore inside plant stems (e.g., fruit tree borers) and those that attack the inside of fruits (e.g., codling moths in apples and walnuts).

The labels on BTK products list many, but not all, the common caterpillars susceptible to the material. Additions to the label of susceptible species often lag months or years behind tests demonstrating efficacy against them. Therefore, if your caterpillar pest is not listed on the BTK product label, contact the manufacturer whose address is on the label.

Table 8.2
Susceptibility of Caterpillar Pests to *Bacillus thuringiensis* var. *kurstaki* (BTK)[a]

Common Name	Scientific Name
Susceptible	
bagworm	*Thyridopteryx ephemeraeformis*
cabbage looper	*Trichoplusia ni*
diamondback moth	*Plutella xylostella*
fall cankerworm	*Alsophila pometaria*
fall webworm	*Hyphantria cunea*
gypsy moth	*Lymantria dispar*
imported cabbageworm	*Pieris rapae*
Indianmeal moth	*Plodia interpunctella*
mimosa webworm	*Momadaula anisocentra*
spring cankerworm	*Paleacrita vernata*
spruce budworm	*Choristoneura fumiferana*
tent caterpillars	*Malacosoma* spp.
tomato/tobacco hornworm	*Manduca sexta*
Not susceptible[b]	
codling moth	*Cydia pomonella*
peachtree borer	*Synanthedon exitiosa*
squash vine borer	*Melittia curcurbitae*

[a] From Weinzierl and Henn, 1989.
[b] These species live in the plant interior and thus are not reached by BT spray.

As we mentioned earlier, BTK is a stomach poison and must be ingested by caterpillars to kill them. Because caterpillars often feed on different sides of or locations on leaves at different developmental stages, thorough coverage of both the upper and lower surfaces of leaves is necessary for good control. BTK degrades fairly rapidly in the presence of sunlight, so spray in the late afternoon or on cloudy (but not rainy) days to prolong the effectiveness. Special materials are added to most BT formulations to help them adhere to plants during rainfall.

BTK is most effective if applied on caterpillars during their first and second instars, when they are still small. Here, as with all safe, effective pest management, learning how to monitor your plants and recognize when insects are at various stages and most susceptible to various controls is critical. General monitoring techniques were introduced in Chapter 3; methods specific to garden caterpillars (pp. 576-579), caterpillars on shade trees (pp. 617-618) and moth larvae in stored grains (pp. 241-243) are discussed in later chapters.

Treating Mosquitoes, Blackflies and Fungus Gnats. *Bacillus thuringiensis* var. *israelensis* (BTI) products toxic to mosquitoes and the larvae of blackflies and fungus gnats are listed in Table 8.1 on p. 133. BTI is most effective against mosquitoes in the genera *Aedes* and *Psorophora*; higher than normal doses are required to kill

Anopheles and *Culex* species. BTI's effectiveness against flies is limited to aquatic blackflies in the family Simuliidae and fungus gnats in the genera *Megaselia, Lycoriella* and others (see pp. 395-398). BTI does not affect common houseflies or stable flies. This is perhaps because it is not available to their larval stages, which live in manure and other organically active environments in which BTI spores quickly decompose.

BTI can be applied to water sources where mosquitoes develop, such as ditches, standing ponds, catch basins, storm drains, pastures, salt marshes and rice fields, and to streams inhabited by blackfly larvae. It is most effective when used by mosquito-abatement districts on a community-wide basis. Chapter 36 provides a detailed discussion of community mosquito IPM programs.

BTI formulated with corn-cob granules is commonly used to control mosquitoes breeding in tree cavities, tires and other containers. The granules are more resistant to degradation by sunlight and can be blown efficiently into piles of tires and other breeding sites where good penetration and coverage are difficult to achieve by other means. BTI should be applied to clear, calm water, since turbidity and high levels of organic pollutants reduce its effectiveness.

For treating fungus-gnat larvae in greenhouses, BTI is mixed with water and applied as a drench to potted soil. Drenches can also be applied to the soil under greenhouse benches or in large planter boxes. For additional treatment tips, see pp. 396-397 on fungus gnat management.

Treating Beetles. *Bacillus thuringiensis* var. *san diego* (M-One®) and BT var. *tenebrionis* (Trident®) are toxic to a limited range of leaf-feeding beetle species, including larvae of the Colorado potato beetle *(Leptinotarsus decemlineata)* and the elm leaf beetle *(Pyrrhalta luteola)*. However, these products cannot control other common beetle larvae such as corn rootworms and wood-boring beetles,

which live in hidden sites. The application techniques are similar to those already discussed for the other BT products. See the package label for further details.

Other Insecticidal Bacterial Species. The milky spore disease of the Japanese beetle *(Popillia japonica)* was the first microbial control to be developed commercially. Milky spore is the name of the disease to which Japanese beetle larvae succumb when attacked by *Bacillus popilliae* and *B. lentimorbus*. These species combine to kill the larvae, and in so doing turn them milky white.

Between 1939 and 1951, the USDA applied milky spore powder to turf in 14 states and the District of Columbia in a successful effort to suppress the newly invaded Japanese beetle. At least 13 other species of beetle grubs that feed on turf are also known to be susceptible to various strains of *B. popilliae* and *B. lentimorbus*. At present, however, only products effective against Japanese beetles are available. For product names, see the Resource Appendix under "Insect Management: Biological Controls" on pp. 683-686. For details on using milky spore disease to control Japanese beetle grubs, see pp. 537-538.

There has recently been progress in research on another bacillus species, *B. penetrans*. This bacillus attacks the plant-parasitic roundworms known as root-knot nematodes, which cause extensive damage in many agricultural and garden crops. Research conducted by G.R. Stirling and M.F. Wachtelat at the South Australian Department of Agriculture's Research Center in Loxton indicates that a system that can mass-produce this nematode pathogen has been developed. This advance suggests that bacterial nematicides (pesticides that kill nematodes) may soon be available commercially.

Fungal Pesticides

Fungi are probably the most numerous insect and plant pathogens, so it seems logical to search among the

fungal species for commercial possibilities for insecticides, herbicides and other microbial pesticides. More than 750 fungal species representing approximately 100 genera have been reported to infect insects alone. Nearly all fungal groups and virtually every insect group is represented. Insect-attacking fungi have been found in approximately 175 host insect species in North America (see Table 8.3 on the facing page).

Mode of Action. Most of the fungi that attack insects and other organisms spread by means of asexual spores called conidia. Free water or high humidity is usually required before conidia can germinate and attack a susceptible host. Unlike bacterial spores or virus particles, fungi can penetrate the insect cuticle directly so they don't have to be ingested to infect insects. Thus they can be useful against sucking insects as well as against those that chew foliage. Likewise, fungi can enter plant tissues or other fungal organisms. The infected hosts die from toxins produced by the fungus.

Fungal Insecticides

In nature, fungal pathogens persist at low levels within insect populations, causing some amount of sickness and/or death in each insect generation. When conditions are optimal— meaning a high population of susceptible insects and appropriate temperature and humidity—the fungal pathogens multiply rapidly and explode into a disease outbreak called an epizootic by insect pathologists. This outbreak kills tens of thousands of insects within a few days or weeks. This phenomenon is common among many caterpillar pests of forest and ornamental trees, chinch bugs that attack grain crops and lawn grasses, beetles that attack potatoes and other food crops, and many other insect groups.

Unfortunately, epizootics generally don't occur until insect populations are high, which is often too late to prevent extensive plant damage.

In theory, fungal pesticide products that can be sprayed directly onto pests could trigger disease outbreaks when pest numbers are still low, before there is significant damage to plants.

The fungal species *Beauveria bassiana* has been applied against insect pests in field tests more frequently than any other fungus, and it is used as an insecticide in the Soviet Union, Eastern Europe and China. Currently, the Soviet Union applies five tons of *B. bassiana* each year, mostly against the Colorado potato beetle *(Leptinotarsa decemlineata)*. *B. bassiana* is currently under development as an insecticide for beetle control in the United States, and should become available commercially in the near future.

Beauveria tenella has shown promise in tests in France against the soil-inhabiting cockchafer grub *(Melolontha melolonthae)*. *Lagenidium giganteum*, a fungus that attacks the larvae of pest mosquitoes, is undergoing commercial development in the United States.

Vertalec® and Mycotal®. These products are microbial insecticides that contain spores of the fungus *Cephalosporium (=Verticillium) lecanii*. Natural epidemics of this fungus occur in insect populations in the tropics and subtropics. Both products have been registered in Europe for some years and are used in the greenhouse industry to control pests such as aphids and whiteflies. Vertalec® and Mycotal® were available in the United States in the 1980s, but unfortunately they were discontinued for reasons that are unclear. They are still available in Europe.

Cephalosporium lecanii does not infest or damage plants, and no toxic residues are produced. There are many strains of the fungus, some of which have been found attacking Coleoptera (beetles), Collembola (springtails), Diptera (flies), Homoptera (aphids, whiteflies, etc.), eriophyid mites (e.g., fuchsia mites) and one beneficial ichneumonid (miniwasp) species. Some strains are

Table 8.3
Fungal Genera Being Developed as Microbial Insecticides[a]

Fungus	Infective Stage	Host Insect
Chytridiomycetes		
Coelomomyces	motile zoospores	mosquitoes
Oomycetes		
Lagenidium	motile zoospores	mosquitoes
Zygomycetes		
Entomophthora	conidia[b]	caterpillars, aphids, flies
Deuteromycetes		
Ashersonia	conidia	whiteflies
Beauveria	conidia	beetles, caterpillars
Culincimomyces		
Clavosporus	conidia	mosquitoes, other diptera
Hirsutellia	conidia	mites
Metarhizium	conidia	leafhoppers, beetles, mites
Nomuraea	conidia	caterpillars
Paecilomyces	conidia	beetles
Cephalosporium (=*Verticillium*)	conidia	aphids, whiteflies, scales

[a] From National Academy of Sciences, 1979.
[b] Conidia are asexual spores of fungi.

parasites of other fungi, mostly rusts and powdery mildews.

Vertalec®, the C-3 strain of *Cephalosporium lecanii*, is specific to aphids and scales and is being used for the control of the ubiquitous green peach aphid *(Myzus persicae)*, among others. Mycotal® is specific to whiteflies and is being used against the greenhouse whitefly *(Trialeurodes vaporariorum)* in European greenhouses. Both products are designed to promote long-term insecticidal activity in the crop. In conditions of high humidity, the residual activity of the fungal insecticide may last several months.

It is best to apply these insecticides when the relative humidity is 85% or higher, causing a film of wa-

ter to remain on the leaves, and the temperature is between 60°F and 77°F (15°C and 25°C). They are most successful when used in greenhouses, where humidities tend to be high.

Insect mortality occurs 5 to 10 days after application. Thus, it is essential to detect potentially harmful infestations early through monitoring. If pest populations are allowed to rise too close to injury levels, it is too late to apply these fungal materials because they take days to have an impact. If such a situation does arise, the aphids or whiteflies should first be reduced with insecticidal soap, horticultural oil or a short-term, nonresidual contact insecticide like pyrethrum. Then the fungal insecticide can be applied while the pest population is small; it will be spread by the diseased insects themselves.

In field trials against aphids and whiteflies, *C. lecanii* was not observed to attack the two-spotted spider mite *(Tetranychus urticae)*, its predator *Phytoseiulus persimilis* or *Encarsia formosa*, the parasitoid that controls greenhouse whiteflies. Thus, a management program that integrates the fungus with these biological controls is probably feasible. Although *C. lecanii* can be used in combination with many conventional insecticides, it would be judicious to avoid combining it with conventional fungicides that might kill it.

Because *C. lecanii* cannot grow at the high internal temperatures typical of mammals and birds—97°F to 110°F (36°C to 43°C)—the likelihood of it infecting humans or other vertebrates is remote. This is confirmed by the fact that although widespread in nature, it has never been observed to infect humans or vertebrate wildlife. Moreover, there are no records of researchers having experienced injurious effects from the fungus.

Fungi that Protect against Plant Disease

Fungal products that control plant pathogens are also reaching the marketable stage. The registration of Galltrol-A® and Norbac 84® (see the Resource Appendix under "Plant Disease Management: Biological Controls" on p. 687) is a welcome development. These products contain the active ingredient *Agrobacterium radiobacter*, which is a fungal antagonist of the crown gall disease that affects many species of fruit and nut trees. Other microbial products containing beneficial fungi in the genera *Trichoderma* and *Gliocladium* are nearing commercialization.

Microbial Herbicides

Microbial herbicides are living organisms or their products that are useful in suppressing weed populations. They offer the same advantages as microbial insecticides: They are rela-

tively selective in their impact on plants and are safe to the user and the environment. Most of the microbial herbicides studied to date have been fungi. Thus, the term mycoherbicide ("myco" = fungus) has gained popularity as a label for the class of microbial products that uses fungi to suppress weeds. When a fungus is not the active agent, however, the proper term is bioherbicide.

Nematodes and other microbes are also under study as bioherbicides. The use of fungi as herbicides seems reasonable, because fungi exhibit great selectivity in the range of species they attack. Many rust fungi, for example, attack only one plant species. Two bioherbicides are commercially available: Devine® for controlling milkweed vine *(Morrenia odorata)* and Collego® for controlling northern jointvetch *(Aeschynomene virginica)*; for sources, see the Resource Appendix under "Weed Management: Biological Controls" on p. 689).

The initial emphasis was on the development of herbicides for control of weeds in rangeland and agriculture. But scientists are now also trying to find ways to use mycoherbicides to control the aquatic weeds that clog ponds, canals, drainage ditches and recreational lakes, as well as the artificial bodies of water that have become common features in urban residential and commercial developments. Eventually, we should have products that are more directly useful in lawn and other landscape care, particularly if there is increased interest in microbial controls among landscape maintenance professionals and home gardeners. Some mycoherbicides that are already registered or are currently under study are listed in Table 8.4 on the facing page.

Viral Insecticides

Insects, particularly in the larval stage, are susceptible to major outbreaks of viral diseases. Over 700 types of viruses have been found to infect insects, most of which fall into one of the following major viral

groups: nucleopolyhedrosis (NPV), cytoplasmic polyhedrosis (CPV), granulosis (GV), entomopox (EPV) and noninclusion viruses (NIV).

Like fungal diseases, viruses tend to be highly specific, attacking only a single insect genus or even a single species. The NPV and GV viral groups are the most promising candidates for development as commercial insecticides due to their specificity, safety, stability and virulence to insects. These virus groups infect caterpillars and the larval stages of sawflies. No hazards to nontarget organisms were found when these viruses were subjected to toxicological tests.

Mode of Action. Insects must ingest viruses to become infected. The viral particles (protein-coated bundles of DNA) can move into insect cells and lodge in the nucleus, thereby taking charge of genetic synthesis. Entomologists Rick Weinzierl and Tess Henn, in their pamphlet "Microbial Insecticides," explain how these viruses act on susceptible insects.

In sawfly larvae, virus infections are limited to the gut, and disease symptoms are not as obvious as they are in caterpillars. In caterpillars, virus particles pass through the insect's gut wall and infect other body tissues. As an infection progresses, the caterpillar's internal organs are liquefied, and its cuticle (body covering) discolors and eventually ruptures.

Caterpillars killed by virus infection appear limp and soggy. They often remain attached to foliage or twigs for several days, releasing virus particles that may be consumed by other larvae. The pathogen can be spread throughout an insect population in this way (especially when raindrops help to splash the virus particles to adjacent foliage) and by infected adult females depositing virus-contaminated eggs. Dissemination of viral pathogens is deterred by exposure to direct sunlight, because direct ultraviolet radiation destroys virus particles. Although

Table 8.4
Mycoherbicides Already Registered or Under Study[a]

Fungus	Target Weed Species	Producer
Colletotrichum gloeosporioides (Collego®)	northern jointvetch (*Aeschynomene virginica*), a pest of rice in southeastern U.S.	Ecogen, N. Langhorne, Pa.
Phytophthora citrophthora (Devine®)	milkweed vine (strangler vine, *Morrenia odorata*), a pest in Florida citrus groves	Abbott Labs, N. Chicago, Ill.
Cercospora rodmanii, *Uredo eichhorniae*	water hyacinth (*Eichhornia crassipes*)	USDA

[a] From Schroth and Hancock, 1981.

naturally occurring epidemics do control certain pests, these epidemics rarely occur before pest populations have reached outbreak levels.

Uses and Application. Four insect-attacking viruses are currently registered in the United States: Elcar®, the NPV of the cotton bollworm *(Heliothis zea)*; Biocontrol-1®, the NPV of the Douglas-fir tussock moth *(Orygia [=Hemerocampa] pseudotsugata)*; Gypchek®, the NPV of the gypsy moth *(Lymantria [=Porthetria] dispar)*; and Neochek-S®, the NPV of the red-headed pine sawfly *(Neodiprion lecontei)*. Elcar®, registered in 1975, was the first virus to receive EPA registration in the United States, and it is a landmark in microbial control. In Japan, Matsu-kemin®, a CPV of the pine caterpillar *(Dendrolimus spectabilis)*, was registered in 1974. The NPV of the European sawfly *(Neodiprion sertifer)* is registered in Finland and Canada as well as in the United States, and two NPVs for agricultural caterpillar pests are used commercially in South and Central America.

Decyde®, a CPV of the codling moth *(Cydia pomonella)*, was registered in the United States for a brief time in the 1980s but is no longer on the market. However, experimental quantities of the virus are available to member fruit growers from the Association for Sensible Pest Control (P.O. Box 1154, Lafayette, CA 94549-1154), a nonprofit organization that hopes to produce and distribute commercial quantities of the product in the near future. The cost of membership is nominal; write them for details.

With the exception of the codling moth CPV and the bollworm NPV Elcar®, which is marketed commercially by Sandoz Crop Protection (see the Resource Appendix under "Insect Management: Biological Controls" on pp. 683-686), viral insecticides registered in the United States are produced exclusively by the U.S. Forest Service and are used to treat forest pests. Other viruses that infect agricultural pests like cabbage loopers and worms, soybean and alfalfa loopers, and armyworms have been effective in field tests, but have not been registered commercially.

Several obstacles are hindering greater commercial development of viral insecticides. First, they must be produced in live hosts, which is an expensive process. Second, the fact that they are genus- or species-specific greatly limits their market. Moreover, they rapidly decompose in sunlight, do not tolerate high temperatures and tend to kill slowly. We hope that improvements in artificial media for rearing insect viruses as well as formulations that increase their residual life in the field are forthcoming and that more of these highly selective insecticides will become commercially available.

Protozoan Insecticides
Of the 35,000 protozoan species known, the approximately 300 insect-attacking species are in the orders Microsordia and Neogregarinida. Protozoan pathogens tend to produce chronic but not always fatal diseases in insects. Chronic infections generally result in reduced feeding and reproduction, although death can also occur. In toxicological tests, insect-attacking protozoa have shown no effect on humans or other mammals.

Like insect viruses, almost all protozoa of potential use as insecticides must be produced in living hosts, which makes them expensive. This is one factor accounting for the slow pace at which protozoan insecticides are being developed. Some of the most promising candidates for pest control are listed in Table 8.5 on p. 140.

At present, only one protozoan insecticide has been registered by the

EPA. It is *Nosema locustae*, a pathogen of grasshoppers. It is marketed by several companies under various trade names, which are listed in the Resource Appendix under "Insect Management: Biological Controls" on pp. 683-686.

Mode of Action. After being eaten by a grasshopper, *Nosema locustae* infects the fat tissue. Infection then spreads throughout the body of the grasshopper, disrupting circulation, excretion and reproduction, and leads to disfigurement and/or death. Infected eggs carry the disease from one generation to the next.

Uses. This species is known to infect 58 species of grasshoppers as well as the mormon cricket *(Anabrus simplex)*, a black field cricket *(Gryllus* spp.) and a species of pygmy locust.

Insect-Attacking Nematodes

Although nematodes are not microbials in the same sense as the bacteria, fungi, viruses and protozoa described above, their microscopic size and the fact that they release toxic bacteria into host insects have led to their being grouped with microbials in pest control terminology. Nematodes are tiny, mostly microscopic roundworms that belong to the phylum Nematoda. They are also called threadworms *(nema* in Greek means "thread"), and are among the oldest living multicellular life forms, dating to the Cambrian period 500 million years ago. Nematodes occupy all the basic habitats of the earth. They live in marine and fresh-water environments, in soil as free-living saprophytes (decomposers), in and on plants, on other animals and on humans.

Nematodes are well-known as pests of plants and humans, but there are also a large number of predatory nematode species that are natural enemies of insects. These nematodes are useful against the grubs (insect larvae) that attack lawns, shrubs, trees and agricultural crops. Over 400 pest insect species have proven susceptible to parasitic nematodes in laboratory and field studies; the major

Table 8.5

Some of the Most Promising Protozoan Insecticide Candidates[a]

Protozoa[b]	Host Insect
Adelina tribolii, Farinocystis tribolii	stored-product pests
Lambornella stegomyiae, L. clarki	mosquitoes
Malameba locustae	grasshoppers
Mattesia dispora, M. trogodermae	lepidopterans and coleopterans
Nosema algerae	anopheline mosquitoes
N. disstriae	forest tent caterpillar
N. fumiferanae	spruce budworm
N. gasti	boll weevil
N. melolonthae	European cockchafer
N. pyrausta	European corn borer
Vairimorpha necatrix	lepidopterous pests

[a] From National Academy of Sciences, 1979.

[b] Note that *Nosema locustae* is already registered for the control of grasshoppers.

groups in the phylum Nematoda are listed and described in Table 8.6 on the facing page.

Species of nematodes that have been mass-produced in quantities sufficient for use in field trials as insecticides fall into the following genera: *Delademus, Romanomermis, Heterorhabditis, Heterotylenchus* and *Steinernema (=Neoaplectana). Romanomermis culicivorax* was used widely against mosquito larvae in the 1950s but was displaced by synthetic insecticides. *Heterotylenchus autumnalis* has been used widely and successfully against the face fly *(Musca autumnalis).* Most current research on and commercial development of parasitic nematodes is focused on species in the genera *Heterorhabditis* and *Steinernema*, especially the latter. Commercial products containing *H. heliothidis* and *S. carpocapsae* are listed in Table 8.1 on p. 133 and in the Resource Appendix under "Insect Management: Biological Controls" on pp. 683-686.

Mode of Action. Parasitic nematodes kill their hosts by infecting

them with bacteria that poison the blood (see the photo on p. 142). The hardy third-stage infectious juveniles (J3), which can survive without feeding for long periods in moist soil, actively search for insect hosts by standing on their tails and waving back and forth. When they sense the presence of a host, they swim on a film of soil moisture to invade the host's body. They can jump many times the length of their bodies, which also helps them find a host.

Steinernema nematodes enter the host via the mouth, anus or other natural opening; *Heterorhabditis* nematodes enter through the same openings or use a hook-like appendage to bore directly into the insect cuticle. Once inside the host, they develop into adult males and females, mate and lay eggs. The eggs hatch and the nematodes continue reproducing inside the insect until crowding, lack of food or other unfavorable situation arises. At that point, the young nematodes develop into the J3 stage and exit the dead insect to seek a new host.

Table 8.6
Major Taxonomic Categories of the Phylum Nematoda, with Their Habitats and/or Prey[a]

Taxonomic Category		Habitat and/or Prey
Class Adenophorea		
Subclass Chromadoria		mostly marine forms
Subclass Enoplia		soil, aquatic; plant and animal parasites
Order Mermithida		
Superfamily Mermithoidea		
Family Mermithidae	*Romanomermis culicivorax*	mosquitoes
	Mermis nigrescens	orthoptera and others
	Pheromermis pachysoma	yellowjackets
	Pheromermis myopis	horseflies
	Hydromermis conopophaga	chironomid midges
	Mesomermis flumenalis	blackflies
	Filipjevimermis leipsandra	diabrotica beetles, other Coleoptera
Family Tetradonematidae	*Tetradonema plicans*	fungus gnats in Sciaridae and Mycetophilidae
	Heterogonema ovomasculis	nitidulid beetle
Class Secernentea		
Order Rhabditida		soil, aquatic; insects, mollusks, annelid and vertebrate parasites
Superfamily Diplogasteroidea		
Family Diplogasteridae	*Mikoletzkya aerivora*	termites, white-fringed beetle
Superfamily Rhabditoidea		
Family Rhabditidae	*Rhabditis insectivora*	cerambycid beetles
Family Steinernematidae	*Steinernema carpocapsae*	Coleoptera, Diptera, Heteroptera, Homoptera, Hymenoptera, Isoptera, Lepidoptera, Neuroptera, Odonata and Orthoptera
Family Heterorhabditidae	*Heterorhabditis bacteriophora, H. heliothidis*	originally found in Lepidoptera; experimental infections also occur in Coleoptera, Diptera and Orthoptera
Order Tylenchida		mostly plant parasites, some invertebrate parasites
Superfamily Neotylenchoidea		
Family Neotylenchidae		weevils and woodwasps
	Deladenus siricidicola	Hymenoptera, Siricidae, Coleoptera, Melandryidae
Superfamily Allantonematoidea		
Family Allantonematidae		Coleoptera, Diptera, Siphonaptera, Thysanoptera, Heteroptera
	Heterotylenchus autumnalis	face flies (*Musca autumnalis*)
	Howardula husseyi	mushroom phorid (*Megasalia halterata*)
Superfamily Sphaerularioidea		
Family Sphaerulariidae	*Tripius sciarae*	fungus gnats in the family Sciaridae
Order Strongylida		vertebrates
Order Ascaridida		vertebrates
Order Oxyurida		vertebrates and invertebrates
Order Spirurida		vertebrates

[a] From Poinar, 1983.

Tiny worm-like nematodes have just migrated out of the body of a dead termite and are seeking a new host. Infective juvenile nematodes enter an insect host through its body openings. Once inside, they feed on the insect and release toxic bacteria that produce lethal blood poisoning.
(Photo courtesy George Poinar.)

These infectious juvenile nematodes have mutually beneficial relationships with the bacteria *Xenorhabdus nematophilus* and *X. luminescens*, which they carry in their gut. Once inside the host, the bacteria are released from the anus of the nematode and multiply rapidly in the host's bloodstream. The insect host dies within 24 hours from blood poisoning caused by the bacteria, and the nematodes continue to use the bacteria as a food source within the insect's body.

Formulations. Mass production of nematodes has resulted in a number of commercial products containing J3 infective nematodes. These are mixed with water and are applied as drenches or sprays to the soil or other moist environments. The major factor limiting wider use of parasitic nematode species is the lack of a formulation that allows nematodes to survive for long periods under adverse—particularly dry—conditions. Additives that could solve this prob-

lem are now being researched. Encapsulation processes whereby nematodes are enclosed in a gelatin-like material have recently been developed. New developments in mass-rearing will probably lower production costs so nematodes will be even more commercially feasible.

Safety. After extensive toxicological testing, these nematodes and their bacteria have been found to be nontoxic to humans, animals and other nontarget organisms.

Uses and Application. At their present stage of development, parasitic nematodes are most effective when applied to moist soil to kill insects in the ground or in plant containers, or when injected into holes bored by insects in trees. Because commercial nematode species cannot survive naturally in dry environments, current formulations are not effective when sprayed on the leaves of plants. Nematodes applied this way quickly desiccate and die before finding a host.

Steinernema carpocapsae, the most widely available commercial nematode, has been shown to infect and kill about 300 species of insects in 17 families of Coleoptera (beetles), 9 families of Diptera (flies), 5 families of Heteroptera (bugs), 4 families of Homoptera (aphids, scales, mealybugs, whiteflies), 8 families of Lepidoptera (caterpillars), 1 family of Neuroptera (lacewings) and 5 families of Orthoptera (grasshoppers, crickets). With an organism that has such a wide host range, it may be necessary to devise baits, carriers and other delivery systems that ensure the nematode attacks the target pest selectively.

The same nematode has been shown to attack subterreanean termites *(Reticulitermes* spp.) in laboratory cultures. A product called SAF-T-Shield™, which contains *S. carpocapsae* as its chief ingredient, is now marketed to control these termites. However, field testing of this and other nematode products against subterranean termites is still underway. A number of private termite companies have been using the nematodes for

several years and report success; however, data from controlled studies of treatments applied to structures is needed before scientifically accurate assessments of nematode effectiveness can be made.

Parasitic nematodes have been shown to kill many horticultural and agricultural insect species in laboratory tests; however, when applied to plants or soil in field experiments, *S. carpocapsae* was effective in controlling only a few plant-boring insects, including carpenterworms (moths of the family Sesiidae) in figs, oak and other trees, and the wood-boring larvae of the western poplar clearwing moth *(Prionoxystus robinae)* in birches and willows in California. In these cases, the nematodes were mixed with water and pumped directly into the hole made by the borer, using either an oil-can applicator or a hand-operated plastic spray bottle. The nematodes can also be applied with traditional spraying equipment.

Another *Steinernema* species has been found effective in controlling a borer of currants in Australia; when used in conjunction with one or more species of *Heterorhabditis*, it has also been successful in controlling a few soil-inhabiting insects. *Steinernema* and *Heterorhabditis* are effective against root weevils such as the black vine weevil *(Otiorhynchus sulcatus)* and the strawberry root weevil *(O. ovatus).* (For application procedures in containerized soil, see p. 395.) Commercial cranberry growers have controlled the strawberry root weevil in cranberry bogs through aerial applications of nematodes. In lawns, nematodes have controlled white grubs such as the Japanese beetle (see p. 538), other beetles, cutworms and mole crickets.

PHEROMONES AND OTHER SEMIOCHEMICALS

Various pheromone products have had a great impact on pest control to date and offer great promise for the future. Pheromones are chemicals secreted and emitted by an organism that elicit responses in other individuals of the same species. The insect sex pheromones are the most widely known, probably because they have enjoyed good press and have captured the interest of the public. Large-scale detection programs for the gypsy moth that use sticky cardboard traps baited with their sex pheromones familiarized the public in many areas of the country with this new class of chemicals for manipulating pest populations.

There are other types of pheromones and related substances with potential for insect control. These include alarm pheromones, aggregation pheromones, food attractants, food stimulants and various repellents, deterrents and arrestants. In fact, pheromones are only one of at least three classes of chemicals called semiochemicals (see the sidebar at right) that are used by organisms to communicate with other species and the inanimate environment.

Awareness of the importance of semiochemicals is still relatively new, but research in this area may have a great impact on world affairs if it continues to grow and mature. After all, if human sex pheromones can influence human behavior just as insect sex pheromones affect insects—and there is now good evidence of this in humans as well as in other mammals —then a whole range of other classes of pheromones and semiochemicals may also be affecting humans without our being aware of it. This means that a whole new set of substances awaits discovery, industrial use and market exploitation.

Pheromones Used in Insect Control

The ability to synthesize insect pheromones in the laboratory has given rise to the seductive vision of total, species-specific pest control in a bottle. If we sound skeptical, it is not because we doubt the usefulness of these materials in pest control programs; it simply seems unwise to put

too much faith in a chemical control that is used repeatedly and in isolation. The likelihood of insect resistance or tolerance is too great. It is obvious to us that the value of these materials is as a complement to programs that integrate many strategies to make the habitat less desirable for pests.

Mode of Action. Insects can communicate via chemical stimuli produced in their bodies and emitted into the air. They detect these compounds by way of their chemoreceptors which detect messenger compounds at extremely low concentrations. Once a chemical message is detected, it may trigger a specific behavior or development process. Most pheromones currently used in pest control are synthetic versions of natural insect chemical compounds, chiefly sex pheromones, aggregation pheromones or feeding attractants.

Formulations. Pheromones are used as lures to attract insects to traps or baits containing insecticides. The most commonly used pheromones are the attractant chemicals that one insect gender uses to attract the other. For example, a pheromone secreted by female moths is placed in a trap to capture males of the same species (or vice versa). The chemical attractant is usually impregnated into or enclosed within a rubber or plastic lure or hollow tube that slowly releases the pheromone over a period of days or weeks. Sometimes several pheromones are combined in the lure. The lures are then placed in cardboard or plastic traps (see the drawing on p. 144) that use an adhesive-coated surface or funnel-shaped entrance to capture the target insect.

Uses and Application. Pheromone traps are used to monitor for the presence of pests, as control tools to capture insects, as confusants to disrupt insect mating and as lures to attract insects to insecticidal baits. Currently, the most important use of pheromones is as detection and monitoring tools. They make it possible to look for pests with a "chemical

Definitions of Various Classes of Chemical-Releasing Stimuli[a]

Semiochemical: A substance produced by an organism or inanimate object that elicits a response in another organism.

Pheromone: A substance produced by an organism that elicits a response in another individual of the same species.

Allelochemic: A substance produced by an organism that elicits a response in an individual of a different species.

  Allomone: A type of allelochemic that favors the emitter over the receiver.

  Kairomone: A type of allelochemic that favors the receiver over the emitter.

  Synomone: A type of allelochemic that favors both emitter and receiver.

Apneumonic: A substance produced by a nonliving thing that elicits a response from a living organism.

[a] From Nordlund, D. A., et al.,1981.

searchlight" that points out where and when the pest is occurring so other measures can be brought to bear on the pest and its environment. An excellent example is the use of traps in cockroach management.

Cockroach traps, now a common product, were virtually unknown 20 years ago. These traps use a food attractant together with an adhesive inside a box or triangle-shaped cardboard container designed to be thrown away after it fills with cockroaches. (We discuss this tool further in Chapter 14 on cockroach management.) The trap tells you where the roaches are most concentrated and

Pheromone Lures and Traps

Pheromones are impregnated in lures that slowly release the active ingredients over a period of days or weeks. Lures are placed in a variety of traps designed to attract specific groups of insects. Trap styles include wing traps (A), delta traps (B, which also shows a cross section of the Biolure™ pheromone dispenser), square cardboard traps (C) and funnel traps (D).

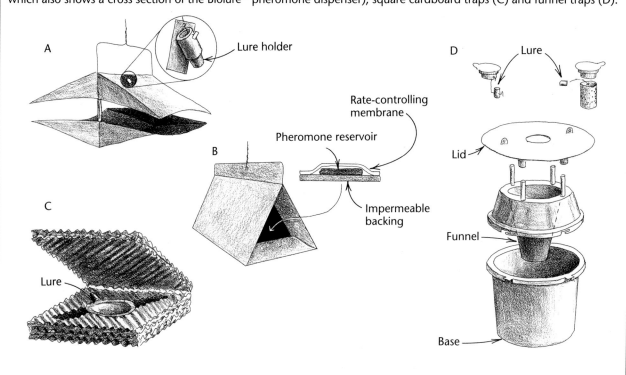

whether your control efforts are working or not. Despite advertisements that suggest differently, the traps are not a method of control. Certainly the roaches "check in but don't check out," but they don't all check in. Such traps have not been shown to be useful for control in field tests against large populations.

Different pheromone-baited traps also attract a large variety of other pest species indoors and in the garden. We mention these species in the appropriate sections of this book, including the discussions of stored-product pests in Chapter 14 and pests of lawns and ornamental plants in Part 8. But some general cautions about using pheromone-baited traps are in order here.

First, the synthesized materials are usually not perfect replicas of the natural product. Because the substances that insects and plants manufacture themselves are so complex, it is extremely difficult to copy them exactly. This means that the natural pheromones emitted by the living organism "out-compete" the human products in attractiveness to other members of the same species. The pulsed timing of the normal release and the need for a target with normal behaviors (a live partner) are also factors that make attractant traps less than effective in some species. Thus, what works on a very small scale, for example in one fruit tree in a back yard, may not necessarily be successful on a larger scale, such as in a suburban lot or small home orchard. In the latter situations, it may be difficult to provide an artificial scent in a trap that is as powerful as that emitted by live members of the same pest species.

Second, there is always the possibility that you will attract a pest into the area that was not already there, or attract it in greater numbers than would otherwise have been present. Thus, strategies have to be applied to limit drawing pests to an area, especially small-scale plantings. To do this, you must place the traps around the perimeter of the area being sampled, attaching the traps to plants that would not normally be attacked by the pest. For example, a codling-moth trap should be placed on a linden or elm tree, because these trees lack the fruit on which the moth normally lays its eggs. Apple or walnut trees, of which the moth is a pest, would be bad choices because traps set in them may attract more moths than they can catch. In such cases, the traps would actually exacerbate the pest problem.

The important exception to the above is the use of pheromone confusant systems. These are hollow plastic fibers that contain a pheromone sex attractant distributed en masse over many acres, usually by aircraft. Results to date have been very promising in large-scale agriculture and forestry against the pink bollworm (Pectinophora gossypiella), the tomato pinworm (Keiferia lycopersicella), the artichoke plume moth (Platyptilia carduidactyla) and the western pine shoot borer (Eucosma sonomana). The same approach has also been used against the gypsy moth (Lymantria [=Porthetria] dispar).

A slightly different type of pheromone system combines an aggregation stimulant, or a bio-irritant, and a conventional pesticide. The irritant encourages the pest insect to travel farther; the insect is thereby exposed to higher dosages of the insecticide than it would be without the stimulant. This system has proven effective against the boll weevil (Anthonomus grandis) and two tobacco and cotton pests, Heliothis virescens and H. zea, which are also vegetable pests in home gardens. This approach offers the potential for the reduction of the amount of insecticide applied to various crops.

Although most pheromone trap systems have been developed for the larger agricultural pest control market, they may also find use in home gardens. But gardeners troubled with agricultural pest problems on a small scale will have to do their own experimentation. In Table 8.7 on p. 146, we provide a list of insects that are susceptible to pheromone attractants that are commercially available as we go to press. If you see your pest on this list, write to one of the producers of the substance that attracts the pest to see whether the product can be made available to you or a local distributor. Major pheromone producers are listed in the Resource Appendix

under "Insect Management: Identification and Monitoring" on pp. 681-682. These producers can also provide information about techniques for trap placement and frequency of trap replacement.

A few pheromones attract an entire insect family instead of just one species or a few members of a single genus. For example, the pheromone that attracts the ash borer (Podosesia syringae) also attracts other members of the same family, the Sesiidae (Lepidoptera). If your pest is not on the list but another pest in the same genus is, the pheromone that works against it may also work against your pest.

INSECT GROWTH REGULATORS

Insect growth regulators (IGRs) are the insect hormones (or their synthetic mimics) that govern an insect's maturation processes and other vital functions. IGRs are sometimes referred to as third-generation insecticides. The first generation consisted of stomach poisons such as arsenic compounds. The second generation included the commonly used organochlorines, organophosphates and carbamates. The third generation, the IGRs, are the newest compounds on the scene, and there are great hopes for this class of pesticide, with its promise of selectivity of target pests and safety to nontarget organisms.

Insects, like other animals, can be viewed as biochemical factories, with each of their various glands producing specific compounds. These compounds function in reproduction, coordination of the nervous system, tissue protection and repair, molting and metamorphosis. Insects, like many other forms of life, are biochemically similar to humans and other mammals in certain ways, but differ significantly in other ways. The search for less-toxic insecticides has focused on substances such as IGRs that affect biochemical processes unique to arthropods, so that the po-

tential negative effects on humans and other mammals are minimized.

This motivation, coupled with adequate research support, has so far facilitated the exploitation of two classes of important insect hormones: ecdysone, which is responsible for insect molting, and juvenile hormones (JH) that prevent metamorphosis (the change from larva to adult). Scientists have mapped the biochemical pathways involved in their production and their impact on target tissues. Of the two, the juvenile hormones have received more commercial attention. The application of a natural JH and its synthetic mimics to juvenile insects in many orders arrests their development enough so that they cannot complete their life cycles and either die at an immature stage, or mature into sterile adults.

Formulations. Available IGRs are formulated as liquid concentrates or as aerosol sprays or foggers. The concentrates can be mixed and applied with standard spray equipment.

Safety. Because mammals do not molt or metamorphose as insects do, the chemical compounds in IGRs are unlikely to affect them. The LD_{50} of methoprene, the most widely used IGR, is greater than 34,000 mg/kg, indicating its wide margin of safety to humans and other mammals. In addition, the relatively narrow range of species affected by a given IGR results in low or zero toxicity to beneficial insects.

Uses. At least five IGRs have been registered: the JH analogs methoprene, hydroprene, kinoprene and fenoxycarb, and the chitin inhibitor diflubenzuron. Table 8.8 on p. 147 lists the target pests affected by these IGRs. Other materials are under development, so additional products can be expected.

Methoprene. Methoprene impedes insect maturation, causing sterility and death before insects can mature. Thus, like most JHs, it is useful only on insects such as fleas that are pests when adults, but whose immature stages are not pestiferous. Metho-

Table 8.7
Insects Susceptible to Commercially Available Pheromones

Common Name	Scientific Name	Common Name	Scientific Name
Coleoptera		fall armyworm	*Spodoptera frugiperda*
boll weevil	*Anthonomus grandis*	false codling moth	*Argyroploce leucotreta*
Japanese beetle	*Popillia japonica*	filbert leafroller	*Archips rosana*
khapra beetle	*Trogoderma granarium*	filbert worm	*Melissopus latiferreanus*
smaller European elm	*Scolytus multistriatus*	fruit tree leafroller	*Archips argyrospila*
bark beetle		fruit tree tortrix	*A. podana*
spruce bark beetle	*Ips typographus*	grape berrymoth	*Endopiza viteana*
		greater peachtree borer	*Synanthedon exitiosa*
Diptera		gypsy moth	*Lymantria dispar*
apple maggot	*Rhagoletis pomonella*	Indianmeal moth	*Plodia interpunctella*
black cherry fruit fly	*R. fausta*	lesser appleworm	*Graphiolitha prunivora*
cherry fruit fly	*R. cingulata*	lesser peachtree borer	*Synanthedon pictipes*
Mediterranean fruit fly	*Ceratitis capitata*	lilac borer	*Podosesia syringae*
red plum maggot	*Grapholita funebrana*	Mediterranean flour moth	*Anagasta kuehniella*
tentiform leafminer	*Lithocolletis blancardella*	Nantucket pine tip moth	*Rhyacionia frustrana*
walnut husk fly	*R. completa*	navel orangeworm	*Amyelois transitella*
		oblique-banded leafroller	*Choristoneura rosaceana*
Homoptera		omnivorous leafroller	*Platynota stultana*
California red scale	*Aonidiella aurantii*	orange tortrix	*Argyrotaenia citrana*
citrus mealybug	*Planococcus citri*	oriental fruit moth	*Graphiolitha molesta*
comstock mealybug	*Pseudococcus comstocki*	peach twig borer	*Anarsia lineatella*
San Jose scale	*Quadraspidiotus perniciosus*	pink bollworm	*Pectinophora gossypoiella*
		plum fruit moth	*Cydia funebrana*
Lepidoptera		potato tubermoth	*Phthorimaea operculella*
alfalfa looper	*Autographa californica*	redbanded leafroller	*Argyrotaenia velutinana*
angoumois grain moth	*Sitrotroga cerealella*	rhododendron borer	*Synanthedon rhododendri*
artichoke plume moth	*Platyptilia carduidactyla*		
ash borer	*Podosesia syringae*	smaller tea tortrix	*Adoxophyes fasciata*
bagworm	*Thyridopteryx ephemeraeformis*	soybean looper	*Pseudoplusia includens*
		spiny rollworm	*Earias insulana*
beet armyworm	*Spodoptera exigua*	spotted tentiform	*Phyllonorycter blancardella*
black cutworm	*Agrotis ipsilon*	leafminer	
bollworm/corn	*Heliothis zea*	spruce budworm	*Choristoneura fumiferana*
earworm			
cabbage looper	*Trichoplusia ni*	strawberry crown moth	*Synanthedon bibionipennis*
codling moth	*Cydia pomonella*		
common armyworm	*Pseudaletia unipuncta*	sugarcane borer	*Diatraea saccharalis*
cranberry girdler	*Chrysoteuchia topiaria*	summer fruit tortrix	*Adoxophyes orana*
diamondback moth	*Plutella xylostella*	sunflower headmoth	*Homoeosoma electellum*
dogwood borer	*Synanthedon scitula*	threelined leafroller	*Pandemis limitata*
Douglas-fir cone moth	*Barbara colfaxiana*	tobacco budworm	*Heliothis virescens*
Egyptian cotton leafworm	*Spodoptera littoralis*	tomato pinworm	*Keiferia lycopersicella*
European corn borer	*Ostrinia nubilalis*	tufted apple budmoth	*Platynota idaeusalis*
European grape	*Lobesia botrana*	variegated cutworm	*Peridroma saucia*
vine moth		variegated leafroller	*Platynota flavedana*
European pineshoot moth	*Rhyacionia buoliana*		

Table 8.8
Insecticide Products Containing Insect Growth Regulators[a]

Product	Target Pest (Scientific Name)	Affected Crop/ Target Area
Methoprene		
Altosid®	mosquitoes (Culex, Culiseta)	
Apex™	darkwinged fungus gnats (Sciaridae)	mushrooms
Dianex®	almond moth (Ephestia cautella)	stored products
	Indianmeal moth (Plodia interpunctella)	
	lesser grain borer (Rhyzopertha dominica)	
	sawtooth grain beetle (Oryzaephilus mercator)	
	red flour beetle (Tribolium castaneum)	
	confused flour beetle (T. confusum)	
Kabat®	cigarette beetle (Lasioderma serricorne)	on tobacco
	tobacco moth (Ephestia elutella)	
Mirex®	chrysanthemum leafminer (Liriomyza trifolii)	
Pharorid®	pharaoh ants (Monomorium pharaonis)	
Precor®, Flea Trol®	cat flea (Ctenocephalides felis)	
Kinoprene		
Enstar®	whiteflies (Trialeuroides spp.)	greenhouses
	aphids (many species)	indoor plants
	soft and armored scales (many species)	
	mealybugs (Planococcus)	
Hydroprene		
Gencor®	German cockroach (Blatella germanica)	buildings and yards
	American cockroach (Periplaneta americana)	
	Australian cockroach (P. australasiae)	
	brown cockroach (P. brunnea)	
	smokybrown cockroach (P. fuliginosa)	
	brown-banded cockroach (Supella longipalpa)	
	Surinam cockroach (Pycnoscelus [=Blatta] surinamensis)	
	Cuban cockroach (Panchlora nivea)	
	lobster cockroach (Nauphoeta cinerea)	
	oriental cockroach (Blatta orientalis)	
Diflubenzuron		
Dimilin®	gypsy moth (Lymantria dispar)	
	forest tent caterpillar (Malacosoma disstria)	
	Nantucket pine tip moth (Rhyacionia frustrana)	
	boll weevil (Anthonomus grandis)	
	mosquitoes (many species)	
	mushroom flies (many species)	
	darkwinged fungus gnats (many species)	
	beet armyworm (Spodoptera exigua)	

[a] From labels and other information supplied by Zoecon Corporation and Uniroyal Chemical Company.

prene is used widely against fleas and a few other economically important insects such as flies. The list of target pests should increase because methoprene has a relatively large host range. See p. 262 for details on using methoprene to control fleas.

Hydroprene. Hydroprene is marketed specifically for cockroach control. After being applied to young roaches, the JH eventually produces sterile adults with twisted wings. See pp. 226-228 for a discussion of using hydroprene as part of a program for controlling cockroaches.

Kinoprene. Kinoprene, which is toxic to both adult and larval insects, is an effective IGR for common pests of house plants and greenhouse-grown crops (e.g, aphids and scales). It was marketed in the 1970s under the brand name Enstar®, then dropped from the market in the 1980s. An improved formulation is currently available. This product could be very important in commercial greenhouses in helping make the transition to biological controls, because it does little damage to natural enemies.

Fenoxycarb. Fenoxycarb, through its JH analog activity, causes distortion of the wings and other parts of an insect, which indicates that it has caused the insect to become sterile. Part of fenoxycarb's molecular structure resembles a carbamate, but it does not inhibit cholinesterase (nerve transmission) as do carbamate insecticides. Fenoxycarb, which is more persistent in the environment than other JH analogs, is registered for use against cockroaches, fire ants, fleas and stored-product pests. Refer to the relevant sections on management of these pests for application details.

Diflubenzuron. This material is a chitin inhibitor. Chitin, a polysaccharide similar in structure to cellulose, is the main ingredient of insect skin. Because all insects contain chitin, concerns over the potential negative impact of the indiscriminate use of diflubenzuron on beneficial insects as well as its unusual stability have led the EPA to restrict its use to licensed pest control professionals.

REFERENCES AND READINGS

Batra, S.W.T. 1981. Biological control of weeds, principles and prospects. In *Biological control in crop production*, ed. G.C. Papavizas, pp. 45-60. Totowa, N.J.: Allanheld Osman Publishers. 461 pp.

A short but comprehensive review article in an important book.

Bowers, W.S. 1976. Hormone mimics. In *The future for insecticides: needs and prospects*, eds. R.L. Metcalf and J. J. McKelvey Jr., pp. 421-444. New York: John Wiley and Sons. 524 pp.

A short introduction to insect growth inhibitors. The book has many other papers on various aspects of pesticides, with a focus on designing new, less-toxic materials.

Burgess, H.D., ed. 1981. *Microbial control of pests and plant diseases, 1970-1980.* New York: Academic Press. 949 pp.

A comprehensive review of research on microbials for use against insect pests, as well as an authoritative source of information and an essential reference tool for those interested in the field.

Daar, S. 1985. Microbial control for grasshoppers. *The IPM Practitioner* 7(9):1-6.

This article reviews the use of *Nosema locustae* by the National Park Service. It provides background information on the pathogen and its effectiveness and points out how this potentially useful grasshopper control agent has been neglected by the Animal Plant Health Inspection Service (APHIS), the USDA's agency responsible for grasshopper control.

Daar, S. 1987. New federal IPM program for grasshoppers. *The IPM Practitioner* 9(4):1-3.

A description of a five-year demonstration IPM program, along with a summary of other developments since the earlier article (see previous listing).

Grossman, J. 1989. Biological control of weeds: What's happening, what's needed? Parts 1 and 2. *The IPM Practitioner* 9(6/7):1-11 and 9(8):1-8.

These review articles update information on past and current biological control importation projects against various agricultural weeds. They also cover newly developed mycoherbicides and the regulation of organisms used to control weeds.

Hummel, H.E., and T.A. Miller, eds. 1984. *Techniques in pheromone research.* New York: Springer-Verlag. 64 pp.

This technique-oriented book gives an idea of what is involved in working with pheromones in the laboratory and in the field.

Kaya, H.K. 1987. Diseases caused by nematodes. In *Epizootiology of insect diseases*, eds. J.R. Fuza and Y. Tanada, pp. 454-470. New York: John Wiley and Sons.

This paper reviews the more important nematode groups, their life cycles and their host interactions.

Kurstak, E., ed. 1982. *Microbial and viral pesticides.* New York: Marcel Dekker. 720 pp.

An excellent source book that provides entry into the theoretical and applied aspects of insect pathology.

Liebman, J. 1989. IPM and the genetic engineering of plants. *The IPM Practitioner* 11(10):4-7.

This was the source for the sidebar on biotechnology on p. 131.

Lipa, J.J. 1990. Microbial pest control in Eastern Europe. *The IPM Practitioner* 12(2):1-5.

This article reports that microbial control in Eastern Europe is well developed, and documents developments with BT, *Beauveria bassiana*, nematodes, various antibiotics, *Trichoderma* spp. and various viruses.

Martignoni, M.E. 1981. A catalogue of viral diseases of insects, mites and ticks. In *Microbial control of pests and plant diseases, 1970-1980*, ed. H.C. Burgess, Appendix 2, pp. 897-911. New York: Academic Press. 949 pp.

This catalog summarizes information from 3,400 publications and lists 826 host species, each reported to have one or more of 22 viral diseases or disease groups for a total of 1,271 host-virus records..

National Academy of Sciences Board on Science and Technology, National Research Council. 1979. Microbial insect control agents. In *Microbial processes: promising technologies for developing countries.* Washington, D.C.: National Academy of Sciences. 199 pp.

An excellent introduction that provides the good overview more technical sources often lack.

Nordlund, D.A., R.L. Jones, and W.J. Lewis, eds. 1981. *Semiochemicals: their role in pest control.* New York: John Wiley and Sons. 306 pp.

This book explains what semiochemicals are and reviews the research on their development and use.

Olkowski, W. 1988. Great expectations for non-toxic pheromones. *The IPM Practitioner* 10(6/7):1-9.

This article reviews early developments in pheromone synthesis and the literature to date concerning field studies on pheromones as trap components and mating disruptants. It speculates about the future of pheromones, and describes the need for changes in the EPA registration process for them.

Papavizas, G.C. 1981. *Biological control in crop production.* Totowa, N.J.: Allanheld Osman Publishers. 461 pp.

This book, the result of a 1980 symposium, contains many important papers about the use of microorganisms and other natural enemies of insects and weeds.

Poinar, G.O., Jr. 1979. *Nematodes for biological control of insects.* Boca Raton, Fla.: CRC Press. 277 pp.

This is the first comprehensive volume on the use of nematodes for insect control.

Poinar, G.O., Jr. 1983. *The natural history of nematodes.* Englewood Cliffs, N.J.: Prentice-Hall. 323 pp.

The best overall introduction to nematodes currently available.

Poinar, G.O., Jr. 1986. Entomophagous nematodes. In *Biological plant and health protection (Fortschrifte der Zoologie, Bd. 32)*, ed. H. Franz, pp. 95-121. New York: G. Fischer Verlag.

This article updates information in Poinar, 1979, with an emphasis on species in the genera *Neoaplectana* (=*Steinernema*), *Heterorhabditis* and others that have proven successful as control agents for insect pests.

Quraishi, M.S. 1977. *Biochemical insect control.* New York: John Wiley and Sons. 280 pp.

An introduction to pyrethroids, botanicals, attractants, pheromones, hormones and microbial insecticides.

Rice, E.L. 1983. *Pest control with nature's chemicals: allelochemics and pheromones in gardening and agriculture.* Norman, Okla.: University of Oklahoma Press. 224 pp.

A well-referenced history of research on allelochemics and their use in gardens and agriculture.

Ridgway, R.L., ed. 1990. *Behavior-modifying chemicals for insect management: applications of pheromones and other attractants.* New York: Marcel Dekker. 761 pp.

This is the most up-to-date volume on pheromones. It covers their research and development and dispenser designs, and includes practical case studies.

Schroth, M.N., and J.G. Hancock. 1981. Selected topics in biological control. *Annual Review of Microbiology* 35:453-76.

A short review of the use of microbes for weed control and as parasites of other pathogens.

Weinzierl, R., and T. Henn. 1989. *Microbial insecticides.* Urbana-Champaign: Office of Agricultural Entomology, University of Illinois (Circular 1295). 12 pp.

An excellent discussion, written for the layperson, of commercially available microbials, their impact on pests and how to use them.

Zoecon Professional Pest Management Division. 1985. *Proceedings of the First Insect Growth Regulator Symposium, 24 July 1985, Dallas.* Dallas, Tex.: Zoecon Corporation. 88 pp.

This publication documents the history of the development of IGRs and presents the results of field work with IGRs against cat fleas and cockroaches. It also covers other aspects of cockroach management.

PART 4

Pests of the Human Body

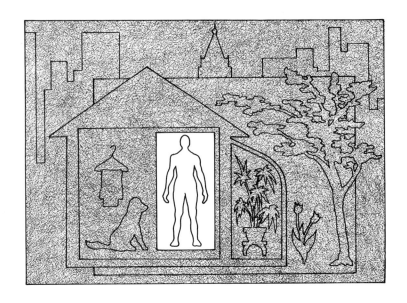

CHAPTER 9
Pinworms

OVERVIEW OF PART 4

It is a giant step from feeling a part of nature and understanding intellectually that all organisms are interconnected by the web of life to realizing that we ourselves support natural communities of living organisms on the interior and exterior of our bodies. Our body profoundly influences our self-image, and we like to think of its surface as a protective barrier between what is "us" and what is the rest of the world. In reality, our skin and the mucous membranes of our respiratory, alimentary and genitourinary systems are lively crossroads for many other forms of life. Most are far too minute for us to notice. Yet these microbial, mite, worm and insect fellow travelers have the power to help us feel well, annoy us and cause serious illness.

The number of species of internal and external fauna and flora of the skin is so large on even the healthiest persons in the temperate regions of the United States that a description of their biology and management could easily fill a volume several times the size of this one. Those we discuss in Part 4 are those about which we receive the most requests for advice; they are also those that are most frequently treated with materials that are more toxic than necessary.

Chapter 9 begins with a general introduction to the human body as an ecosystem, then continues with a specific discussion of pinworms that live in the intestines. Chapter 10 focuses on house dust mites that cause human respiratory problems, as well as scabies mites, which burrow into the skin. Head and pubic lice, which live on body hair, and body lice, which live in clothing, are the subject of Chapter 11. The final chapter in Part 4 is devoted to the biting bugs that live in the bedroom. This last group includes bedbugs, which can live on human blood alone, and conenose (kissing) bugs, which depend on blood from other animals to lay eggs. If you are experiencing symptoms of one of these body pests, the diagnostic key in the sidebar on page 154 should help lead you to the culprit.

INTRODUCTION

The body surface is an ecosystem, as shown in the drawing below. When we are not plagued by itches, bites or similar irritations—that is, when the ecosystem is in balance—we remain unaware of the intimate inhabitants of our body. But a surge in the number of a particular species or other changes in the condition of our body or the environment can suddenly draw these organisms to our attention.

There are variations in individual levels of tolerance of body pests and pest-related damage, just as there are differences in how much caterpillar defoliation different home owners are willing to tolerate. This tolerance variation is easiest to see when we compare cultures or look at the same society at different periods in history. Some cultures, for example, tolerate head lice to a far greater degree than do North Americans.

When we do become aware of the presence of these organisms, the first thought is almost always to find a chemical cure. Just as in the management of home, garden and community pests, chemical tools can be a valuable component of a program to suppress a pest population of the human body. But they are unlikely to be the total answer. The most important first step is learning something about the organism that is bothering you. Then you can see whether you can change the conditions that may be encouraging the pest or discouraging its natural enemies and/or more acceptable competitors.

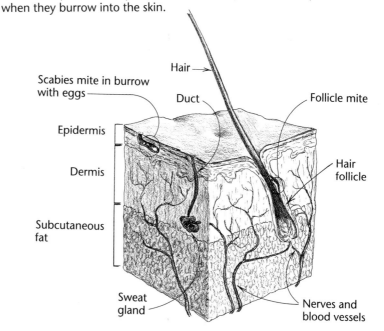

The Skin as an Ecosystem
The skin is composed of many parts, including pores, hair follicles and glands. Some arthropods (such as follicle mites) are normal inhabitants of human skin, but others (such as scabies mites) can cause major discomfort when they burrow into the skin.

Scabies mite in burrow with eggs

Hair

Duct

Follicle mite

Epidermis

Dermis

Hair follicle

Subcutaneous fat

Sweat gland

Nerves and blood vessels

Redrawn from Andrews, 1976.

Diagnostic Key to Pests of the Human Body

Pinworms

Symptoms: Intense itching of the anus at night.

Other Indicators: Small white worms visible to the naked eye, or microscopic eggs visible under the microscope. (Worms and/or eggs may be collected on cellophane tape pressed to the anus during or after periods of intense itching.)

House Dust Mites

Symptoms: Asthma (often suspected to be a dust allergy).

Other Indicators: Presence of mites in dust samples.

Scabies Mites

Symptoms: Intense itching on hands, arms, chest or elsewhere, particularly at night.

Other Indicators: No organisms visible to naked eye. Note, however, that scabies mites can be confused with many allergies, including poison oak, poison ivy and chiggers, that also cause dispersed itching accompanied by a rash and skin that becomes scabbed-over from scratching.

Head Lice or Pubic Lice

Symptoms: Intense itching of the scalp and/or pubic area; large amounts of dandruff on shoulders.

Other Indicators: Small white nits (lice eggs) glued to the hairs visible to the naked eye.

Bedbugs

Symptoms: Isolated bites received at night that result in swollen, itchy areas.

Other Indicators: Bug fecal matter on bed linen; small, fast-moving bugs seen in groups (occur most often in urban areas).

Conenose Bugs

Symptoms: Isolated bites received at night that result in swollen, itchy areas.

Other Indicators: No fecal matter on bedding; the discovery of large solitary bugs that can also fly, but usually walk slowly enough to catch (most likely to occur in suburban and rural areas where wood rats, opossums and raccoons are found).

PINWORMS
(Phylum Nematoda, superfamily Oxyuroidea: *Enterobius vermicularis*)

Pinworms are intestinal roundworms that live only in humans. Related species attack cats, dogs, horses, rats and mice but do not infect people. When pinworms infect one member of a household, they usually spread to others in the group.

Pinworm's sticky eggs, commonly found under the fingernails of infected children, are plentiful and infective almost as soon as they are laid. They are extremely light in weight and easily become airborne. Human females are infected three times as often as males, and persons up to 20 years old are infected more frequently than are older persons. Grade-school children are particularly susceptible, with their teachers running a close second. People in institutions also are infected frequently.

Pinworms probably come closest to what the average person thinks of when he hears the word "parasite."

The worms live what seems an effortless life, bathed in nutritious fluids and troubled with few dramatic changes in their environment. In *Rats, Lice and History*, Hans Zinsser notes:

> [There is a] widely prevalent tendency of all living creatures to save themselves the bother of building by their own efforts the things they require. Whenever they find it possible to take advantage of the constructive labors of others, this is the direction of the least resistance. The plant does the work with its roots and its green leaves. The cow eats the plant. Man eats both of them; and bacteria...eat the man....The principle is clear. Life on earth is an endless chain of parasitism which would soon lead to the complete annihilation of all living beings unless the incorruptible workers of the vegetable kingdom constantly renewed the supply of suitable nitrogen and carbon compounds which other living things filch....In the last analysis, man may be defined as a parasite on a vegetable.

While we humans feed on other things, various worms feed on us. None is more common than the pinworm, or seatworm. Pinworms are probably intestinal parasites of all human races, but they are particularly common in Caucasian children. Unlike the parasitic hymenoptera or parasitoids that kill their hosts, pinworms for the most part are relatively benign, causing no symptoms in the majority of infected adults and children. For those who do suffer irritating symptoms, pinworms are relatively easy to get rid of, although they are also easily reacquired.

Biology

Infections are acquired through the ingestion (swallowing) of eggs. Most of the eggs that start an infection are carried to the mouth on a finger or under a fingernail that has touched the anal region. The eggs hatch and develop into adult worms, which inhabit the large intestine (see the drawing at right). After mating and developing a large number of eggs, the female migrates to the lower bowel area. She leaves the anus at night and lays her eggs as she crawls along on the skin. This generally occurs from 15 to 40 days after the ingestion of eggs. The average number of eggs laid by each female is 11,000, with a range of 5,000 to 17,000. The female does not re-enter the intestinal canal.

Eggs can also be obtained from sleeping in the same bed or bedroom with an infected person or by touching contaminated objects, such as soiled bed linen, table tops and doorknobs. *E. vermicularis* eggs have been found on the fur of dogs and cats that share rooms and furniture with infected children. Because eggs easily become airborne, they can enter the mouth by inhalation and swallowing. This route of exposure helps explain the large number of persons who are lightly infected, since the degree of infection is proportional to the number of eggs ingested or the means by which they are conveyed to the mouth.

The Pinworm Life Cycle on Humans

The female pinworm (A) deposits an average of 11,000 eggs on the skin within several inches of the anus, then dies. The eggs (B) become attached to clothing or bedding, or move on the room air. They are carried to the mouth and ingested. Hatched worms live in the large intestine, where they feed on body fluids. Within 15 to 40 days after hatching, the worms mate and repeat the cycle. (Actual length of adult female: ¼ in./6 mm)

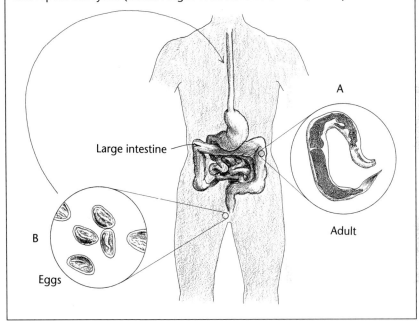

Large intestine

B

Eggs

A

Adult

Detection and Monitoring

Some people detect a pinworm infection at night, when intense anal itching occurs. The itching is a response of a person sensitized to the movement of the female worm in the anal area as she moves to lay her eggs. The scratching that follows sometimes leads to superficial secondary bacterial infections.

To confirm an infection, use cellophane tape to capture eggs from the anal region. Wrap a strip of tape, sticky side out, around an index finger or a round, long, narrow object such as a tongue depressor, the end of a spoon handle or a strip of stiff cardboard cut for this purpose (approximately ¾ in. wide and 5 in. or 6 in. long). Press the applicator firmly against first one and then the other side of the area where the anal opening and adjacent skin meet. Cover

the exposed portion of the tape with a second piece of tape, sticky side down, forming a sealed package. The best time to perform the test is after you wake up, but before you pass a stool or bathe. Take the tape to your physician, who will pull it apart and check for pinworm eggs under the microscope (they are not visible to the naked eye).

If children wake up and complain of anal itching, they should be examined for worms leaving the anus at that time. With the child lying face down, the parent should part the buttocks gently and examine the anal area with a flashlight. The wandering females are about ¼ in. (6 mm) long and ⅟₅₀ in. (0.5 mm) wide. They are light yellowish-white with long, thin, sharply pointed tails. Worms should be picked up with a cotton swab, placed in a small pill bottle contain-

ing rubbing alcohol or vinegar and taken to a doctor for identification. It is important to distinguish among pinworms and other worms that require different treatments.

Damage

Most people can tolerate a low population of pinworms without suffering any harm or showing any symptoms. When symptoms do occur, they generally do not go beyond local itching, which lasts a few weeks. In some children, however, a heavy infestation can produce intense scratching, resulting in poor sleep, inattention in school and/or self-consciousness and embarrassment. As mentioned earlier, scratching of the anal and surrounding skin may cause bacterial infection and local inflammation that subsides after the worm infection is cleared up.

Treatment:
Indirect Strategies
One of the biggest problems with pinworms is psychological. Parents and children may become embarrassed by infections and the need for monitoring the problem. Children who experience irritation of the anal region while in public places often fear being observed scratching.

Squeamishness, shame about certain parts of the body and fear of insects, worms or other common human parasites are largely learned responses. Children take their behavioral cues from parents. A matter-of-fact parental attitude will aid the child greatly in dealing with the problem and help relieve a potentially stressful situation. Explaining the facts about pinworms helps the child realize that there is no need to be embarrassed about being infected —most people are infected at least once during their lives. Older children, who are particularly susceptible to reinfestation, can learn to monitor themselves, squatting over a hand mirror and collecting eggs on a tape to take to the doctor.

Treatment:
Direct Physical Controls
In addition to education and parental attitude, there are also physical controls for treating pinworms.

1. Washing Linen. When a child complains of pinworms or shows symptoms, bed linen, sleepwear and underclothes should be washed in hot water daily to reduce the number of eggs. However, many clinicians do not believe that washing linen alone reduces the reinfection rate significantly because the worm produces so many eggs that are so easily distributed throughout the bedroom.

2. Drying the Room Air. Moisture and high relative humidity increase the survival rate of eggs, so using a dehumidifier to dry the air in the infected person's room may help.

3. Sunlight and Ultraviolet Light. Sunlight and ultraviolet light destroy pinworm eggs. Thus, daily sun drying of clothing and sheets used the previous night will reduce the number of eggs without the need for washing. Ultraviolet lamps may be used effectively in bedrooms of infested persons. A fan that produces a gentle breeze can be used to circulate the air in the room into the path of the light. However, because ultraviolet light also can damage human eyes and the skin, the lamp should be aimed away from room inhabitants. Special ultraviolet-protective goggles are recommended when ultraviolet lamps must be used for long periods; they are available from theatrical suppliers. Do not use the lamps where children are unsupervised.

4. Stepping out of Night Clothes. One investigator found that soiled night clothes often transferred eggs when they were drawn over the head in the morning. If your children have pinworms, choose night clothes that button or zip from the neck to the hem or have separate tops and bottoms. The child should be encouraged to step out of the night clothes rather than pass them over the face.

5. Frequent Hand Washing. Frequent washing of hands and brushing of fingernails may help reduce the reinfection rate. Irritated skin should be treated with an antiseptic ointment or tincture (e.g., an alcohol solution of Merthiolate® or other disinfectant) to reduce secondary bacterial infections. Petroleum jelly applied to the anal area will help relieve itching.

6. Warm-Water Enema. The least-toxic means of killing parasites inside the body is a warm-water enema — the worms swell up and die from the difference in osmotic (water) pressure. This method is recommended by Kaiser Permanente Hospitals in the San Francisco Bay Area; it is also discussed in *Medical Parasitology* by E. Markell, Professor of Family, Community and Preventive Medicine at Stanford University. Light infestations have been controlled through this technique without additional sanitary measures or medication.

The enema may have to be repeated if itching recurs, because this procedure does not eliminate small worms high in the intestine. Nor does it prevent reinfection from eggs already deposited and scattered in the environment. However, for persons who become infected repeatedly, it offers a quick, nontoxic means of eradicating an early light infection after initial symptoms are detected. It also reduces itching temporarily before taking medication.

Treatment:
Direct Chemical Controls
When itching is intolerable, a chemical control may be warranted. One type of prescription drug is absorbed through the intestine and circulates elsewhere in the body; another is not absorbed through the intestine. The latter type is the least toxic because it minimizes exposure of tissues and organs to the drug. In the past, physicians commonly prescribed multiple doses of piperazine salts (for example, Antepar®) but single-dose drugs such as pyrvinium pamoate (Povan®) are now the preferred medications.

Piperazines, which are absorbed through the intestine, usually are formulated in a sugary liquid to make repeated doses palatable to young children. Prolonged treatment schedules are needed because these drugs are not very effective against immature worms. A typical course of treatment involves ingestion of the drug for a week, a week of rest and a second week of treatment. The second course is aimed at worms that have survived the first course of treatment and have developed further during the rest period.

Povan® requires only a single dose and has the advantage of not being absorbed through the intestine. However, it is bright red and can stain undergarments and clothes; for that reason alone, some physicians do not prescribe it. Our experience is that staining is not a problem if the drug is handled with care. Povan® occasionally causes vomiting or diarrhea and, more rarely, a sensitivity to light.

Despite the use of medicines, children who are particularly susceptible —that is, those living in group situations or with a family history of infection—are likely to get repeat infections from the many eggs laid by the worms and dispersed in the environment. When pinworms are detected in one member of the family, some physicians recommend treatment of the entire family because re-transmission to children may occur from adults who are unaware they are infected.

Summary: Least-Toxic Pinworm Control

• Wash hands and brush fingernails frequently to reduce ingestion of pinworm eggs.

• Hang bedclothes and sleeping garments in the sun during the day to help reduce the number of eggs. Alternatively, wash bed linen, night clothes and underclothes in hot water daily during periods when anal itching indicates worm migration.

• Encourage susceptible children to step out of night clothes rather than pull them over their heads.

• Use a warm-water enema to manage a pinworm infestation, particularly a light infestation, before resorting to more toxic medications.

• If a drug is needed, choose one that is not absorbed by the intestine; for example, choose Povan® over piperazine salts.

REFERENCES AND READINGS

Andrews, M. 1977. *The life that lives on man.* New York: Taplinger Publishing Co. 183 pp.

We heartily recommend this book if you want to go deeper into the general subject of pests of the human body. Its discussion ranges from dandruff to natural bacterial protection against invading opportunistic organisms such as *Staphylococcus aureus*, which is associated with pimples and boils and is believed to be the pathogen involved in toxic-shock syndrome.

Beaver, P.C., R.C. Jung and E.W. Cupp. 1984. *Clinical parasitology.* 9th ed. Philadelphia: Lea and Fabiger. 825 pp.

This authorative textbook contains clinical and biological information on pinworms and other parasites for researchers and medical personnel.

Markell, E.K, and M. Voge. 1981. *Medical parasitology.* 5th ed. Philadelphia: W.B. Saunders. 374 pp.

This book recommends using warm-water enemas and, in difficult cases, the single-dose pesticide pyrvinium pamoate (Povan®).

Rippon, J. W. 1974. *Medical mycology: the pathogenic fungi and pathogenic actinomycetes.* Philadelphia: W. B. Saunders. 587 pp.

A good text on mycological health problems in humans.

Zinsser, H. 1935. *Rats, lice and history.* Boston: Little Brown. 301 pp.

A classic, easy-to-read book that provides numerous insights into public health, parasitism, rats and lice.

CHAPTER 10
Mites

INTRODUCTION

In Chapter 1, we indicated the close taxonomic relationship between mites and insects. Both are arthropods, because they have jointed legs. Yet it is important to realize that in an evolutionary sense, they parted company long ago.

Insects are in the class Insecta; mites are in the class Arachnida, along with spiders and scorpions. Within the Arachnida, the mites occupy the subclass Acari along with ticks. The distinguishing characteristics of the Acari are their eight legs, a head, thorax and abdomen that are fused into a single body, and their small size. Insects, on the other hand, have six legs, and their head, thorax and abdomen are distinct segments.

Mites are easy to overlook because of their small size, and this is no doubt a major reason for the lack of common knowledge about them. Their numbers are quite large— more than 30,000 species have been identified to date, according to G.W. Krantz's *A Manual of Acarology* (listed under "References and Readings" on p. 169). Mites are extremely important to humans and all other forms of life.

Because this book focuses on organisms regarded as pests by humans, it may tend—by implication —to reinforce the unwarranted bias against mites and insects. Although some mites do bother people, mites as a group are far from pestiferous. On the contrary, they are mainly beneficial detritivores (decomposers) that break down organic matter, making nutrients available for use by plants once again.

Mites exist at every trophic, or eating, level of the ecosystem. There are species that are herbivorous, carnivorous and saprophytic (living on dead material). We mention members of all three categories in various parts of the book (see the discussions of spider mites and their predators in Part 6, stored-product pests in Part 5 and the management of mites on plants outdoors in Part 8). In this chapter we examine two surprisingly common mite pests of the body: the dust mite, whose dead skin and feces may be inhaled and cause allergies, and the scabies mite, which burrows into the skin.

HOUSE DUST MITES
(Family Pyroglyphidae: *Dermatophagoides pteronyssinus* and *D. farinae)*

House dust consists of particles that can become airborne. A large part of it is human skin scales; these are some of the particles, often called "dust motes," that you see suspended in a sunbeam when it streams into a room. Dust also has other components, many of which are listed in the sidebar at right.

Although house dust has been known for thousands of years by residents of structures, it was not until 1694 that Antoni van Leeuwenhoek, the Dutchman credited with the development and use of the microscope, studied its constituents. His early investigation was directed at a dust mite that feeds on grains. Over time, the constituents of house dust have changed. For example, in the late 1800s it consisted primarily of dried horse manure swept into homes by the long dresses worn by women of the day. As fashions in clothing, furnishings and cleaning have changed, so has the dust itself.

Many species of insects and mites are regularly found indoors, even though human occupants may be unaware of their presence until their populations become large. Examples are cockroaches, fleas, bedbugs, ticks, parasitic mites of pets, wood-boring beetles, various stored-product pests and spiders. Many of these evolved initially in nests of animals that lived in the same types of sites inhabited by early man; later they moved into the homes of humans. Table 10.1 on p. 160 provides examples of insect and mite species collected from the nests of city pigeons. Many of these arthropods also live in house dust, including not only mites, but also sow-

bugs or "woodlice," booklice, centipedes, silverfish, dust lice, pseudoscorpions and other organisms (see the drawing on p. 160).

About 140 mite species have been isolated from house dust. Most are occasional intruders from outdoor ecosystems. Some are herbivorous, some are pet and human parasites and others live off stored foods. The remaining group either lives in the dust itself or occasionally visits house-dust deposits. Because many of these mites live in or on furniture, they are called furniture mites. Furni-

Constituents of House Dust [a]

ash, cigarette
ash, incinerator
combustion products
fiber, synthetic textile
fibers: wool, cotton, paper and silk
fingernail filings
food crumbs
glass particles
glue
graphite
hair, human and animal
insect fragments
oil soot
paint chips
plant parts
pollen
polymer foam particles
salt and sugar crystals
skin scales, humans
skin scales, pets
soil
spores, fungal
stone particles: limestone and quartz
tobacco
wood shavings

[a] Drawn primarily from van Bronswijk, 1981.

Table 10.1
The Most Abundant Insect and Mite Species Found in City Pigeon Nests[a]

Primary Decomposers[b]	Secondary Consumers	Tertiary Consumers
Insect Larvae	**Insect Parasitoids and Predators**	**Mite Predator**
fleas	*Apanteles carpatus*	*Cheyletus eruditus*
flies	*Metacoelus mansuetor*	
silverfish	*Lystocoris campestris*	
moths	*Scenopinus fenestralis*	
beetles		
Mites	**Mite Predators**	
Pyroglyphidae	*Cheyletus eruditus*	
Tyrophagus longior	*Acaropsis docta*	
Acarus siro		
Glycphagus domesticus		

[a] From van Bronswijk, 1981.

[b] Primary decomposers feed on the substances listed in the sidebar on p. 159; secondary consumers feed on primary decomposers, and so on.

ture mites are more common in moist areas, and live on the fungi that grow on bamboo or reed furniture or furniture padded with organic materials. Another group of dust mites preys on other mites. One species, *Cheyletus eruditus*, is probably cosmopolitan (meaning it is widely distributed throughout the world) and feeds on a wide range of mites (including its own kind), booklice and flea larvae.

All 15 pyroglyphid genera are associated with birds, mammals or stored products; 13 species in six of these genera inhabit house dust. The house dust mites in the Pyroglyphidae have received the most attention from researchers because they are a source of allergens and cause asthma and rhinitis (an inflammation of the tissues of the nose). Members of this family, commonly called floormites and bed mites, are the true house dust mites, because they feed directly on house dust.

The medical impact of house dust mites was discovered only recently. The first report associating asthmatic

Organisms Found in House Dust
This drawing shows the important allergen-producing organisms and relative amounts of their body parts and by-products found in one gram of house dust.

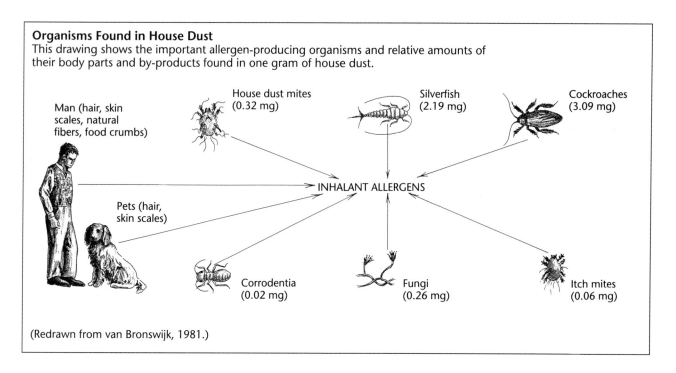

(Redrawn from van Bronswijk, 1981.)

or dermatological complaints by inhabitants and certain mites was in 1964. The work was done by Dr. R. Voorhorst and his co-workers. Since that time, much has been discovered about the arthropods in house dust, particularly the mite species, and especially the house dust mites in the family Pyroglyphidae.

To understand the significance of house dust mites, it was necessary first to make an association between house dust allergens and asthmatic conditions. Then came the discovery by Dutch and Japanese investigators that large numbers of mites lived in dwellings where there were problems with house dust allergens. Further studies indicated that the most potent house dust allergens could be extracted from organic debris produced by house dust mites that feed on human and animal danders (skin debris).

The pyroglyphid mite species are the most important and most widely occurring house dust allergen producers, but other mites in other families can produce the same or slightly different allergens. Some of these mites are associated with stored grains, and people who handle these grains often have allergic difficulties traceable to them (see pp. 239-251 on stored-product pests).

Biology

Every mature human being produces about 12 grams of skin scales per day. House dust mites live mostly on these scales, and control of these mites centers around reducing the amount of scales.

Three species of house dust mites occur throughout most of the world. The first is the European house dust mite *(Dermatophagoides pteronyssinus* —see the drawing above) found on human skin scales, rats, flying squirrels, small pets, dried animal skins and birds, as well as in bird nests and beehives. The second species is the American house dust mite *(D. farinae)* found in stored food, on human skin and in beehives. The third

---

The House Dust Mite
The European house dust mite (*Dermatophagoides pteronyssinus*) is found throughout most of the world and causes allergic reactions in susceptible humans. (Actual size: ⅛ in./3 mm)

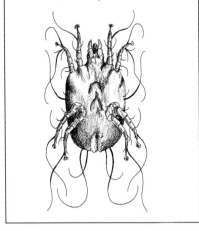

---

species is *Euroglyphus maynei*, found in stored food, on skins of small pets, on humans, in chicken houses, in chimpanzee, orangutan and gorilla cages at the zoo, in bird nests and in attics inhabited by the bat *Myotis dasycneme*. This species is not yet known in North America.

Anatomically, the Pyroglyphidae stand between parasitic and free-living mite forms. These mites are so tiny (⅛ in./3 mm long) that they are virtually invisible to the naked eye. They pass through six developmental stages, and the adult form may also molt once. The cream-colored elliptical eggs laid singly or in groups of three to five are coated with a sticky fluid that helps them adhere to substrate particles. Under optimal conditions, the cycle from egg to adult takes about one month.

The house dust mites in the genus *Dermatophagoides* feed on pollen, spores of microorganisms, fungi, bacteria, fibers of plant origin, lepidopteran (butterfly and moth) scales, animal dander and skin scales of birds. Human, cat, dog and horse dander have been used to raise these species

in the laboratory. They also feed on dried semen found in beds, doubling their egg production compared to mites in semen-free beds. (This suggests an additional reason for the use of condoms.)

The food consumption of these mites depends upon the humidity —more food is consumed at higher relative humidity. Growth occurs at temperatures between 50°F and 90°F (10°C and 32°C). The optimum temperature for *D. farinae* is about 86°F (30°C), and for *D. pteronyssinus*, about 77°F (25°C). One hour at 140°F (60°C) is lethal. Some mites are more resistant than others to low temperatures, however; six hours at –5°F (–20°C) kills 60% of *D. pteronyssinus* and 100% of *D. farinae*.

Dust mites do not drink; they get water from the surrounding air. At 70% relative humidity (RH) they lose as much water as they gain. Only 50% of starving *D. pteronyssinus* survived two days at 33% RH, but in the presence of food it took 22 days to kill all stages at 40% RH and 77°F (25°C). Because the mites seldom feed below 70% RH, the food must contain sufficient moisture to create a local, more moist environment. Laboratory cultures are successfully reared at 70% to 80% RH. This research suggests that reducing the humidity in a room may help reduce mite numbers.

Predators of pyroglyphid mites include silverfish, dust lice, pseudoscorpions and predatory mites. Among the predatory mites are *Cheyletus* mite species and others whose role is not yet fully known. Fungi are suspected pathogens of these mites.

Damage

The medical significance of house dust mites arises from the formation of the house dust allergen, which, when inhaled, triggers bronchial asthma, or rhinitis allergica (see the sidebar on p. 162 for definitions of common terms used to describe allergic reactions). The allergen itself seems to be composed of the fecal

Definitions of Common Terms Used To Describe Allergic Reactions

Allergen: A type of antigen that stimulates the organism to produce antibodies in the immunoglobulin IGE class.

Allergy: A hypersensitive reaction to a foreign substance that includes the release of histamine, which is thought to result from the formation of incomplete antibodies.

Antibody: A substance in the blood produced by plasma cells that is derived from white blood cells in lymph nodes and the spleen in response to the presence of a protein foreign to the body.

Antigen: Any substance that stimulates the production of antibodies.

Histamine: A substance that dilates capillaries, increases capillary permeability (leading to swelling) and causes spasms of smooth muscles under the influence of the autonomic nervous system. Smooth muscles are found in the digestive, reproductive, respiratory and urinary tracts, as well as in the iris of the eye, in arteries and veins, and elsewhere.

Immunoglobulin: That fraction of the protein component of the blood that contains the antibodies. Different types of immunoglobulin with different biochemical activity patterns are designated by letters—IGA, IGE, etc. IG is the abbreviation for immunoglobulin.

material from the mites, but it may also include their decomposing molted skins. This allergen may be involved in cases of atopic dermatitis (a skin disorder of infants, children and young adults), sudden infant death syndrome and pigmented purpuric dermatosis (skin lesions). Although house dust mites have been found on persons suffering from scabies *(Herpes farinosus)* and the ringworm fungi *Trichophyton*, they are doubtless there because they are attracted to the large amount of skin scales produced by these disorders.

Various standards have been proposed for what constitutes a tolerable concentration of mites in the house. These standards essentially correspond to the injury or tolerance levels cited by pest managers. One proposed concentration level is 24 mites per sq. yd. of mattress area and two mites per sq. yd. of floor surface. Theoretically, a higher population than this means abatement measures should be taken; remember, however, that these are still hypothetical numbers and are subject to variation based on local conditions.

Detection and Monitoring

If you or other family members are suffering from asthma or similar respiratory distress and you want to determine whether an allergy to house dust mites is responsible, you should consult a specialist. It will be necessary to collect and identify the mites to determine whether they are a cause or a contributing factor to a particular condition. Specialists may be found through dermatologists, teaching hospital clinics, colleges with medical entomologists and local and state public-health departments.

To perform the sampling yourself you will need a small (#1) artist's brush or a vacuum cleaner with a paper dust bag. Collect dust samples on and around the bed and take them to a physician or a specialist at the public-health department for examination under a microscope. If mites are found, they will need to be mounted on a microscope slide in a special fluid and examined under a compound microscope by someone familiar with mite taxonomy. Various methods used by researchers for detecting house dust mites are reviewed in *House Dust Biology* by Johanna van Bronswijk.

Treatment: Indirect Strategies

Detailed studies have examined various means of reducing sensitive persons' exposure to house dust allergens. Findings from this work and our own experience suggest the following measures be taken: habitat modification, including moisture reduction; physical controls, including special tools and techniques for allergen reduction; and direct suppression of house dust mite populations. Each of these is discussed below. Complete elimination of dust mites is not a realistic goal. However, if you determine that dust mites are causing problems, it does make sense to try to reduce their population. Sleeping areas deserve the most attention.

1. **Selecting Appropriate Furnishings.** The goal is to reduce organic debris that provides a habitat for house dust mites. When choosing furnishings, consider how much dust they produce and collect. Avoid furniture that uses textiles, fibers and softwood parts such as those made of pine or balsam. Also avoid wool, because it sheds particles that can be eaten by mites and other organisms. Use washable curtains, blinds that can be vacuumed and small rugs that

can be washed repeatedly. Furniture should be easy to clean, and it should be easy to move to clean behind. Surfaces should be kept free of clutter and knickknacks that collect dust and hinder cleaning.

2. Removing Cloth Furnishings. Reduce or eliminate wall-to-wall carpets, stuffed furniture and drapes. Enclose bed mattresses in plastic covers, because this decreases the number of mites in the bed. Ventflex™, a polyurethane coating that blocks mites and mite feces while letting in water vapor, was used to cover mattresses in a study by British researchers P. Harvey and R. May. Coated mattresses had 97% less mite allergen than uncoated mattresses. A source for Ventflex™ is listed in the Resource Appendix under "Insect Management: Physical Controls (Barriers)" on pp. 682-683.

3. Avoiding Furry or Feathered Pets. Pets that have fur or feathers contribute dander to the dust. Even fish can be a problem. Although they do not add to the house dust, large aquarium systems supply moisture, which is crucial to mite survival. If you already have pets, locate their sleeping quarters as far from yours as possible and arrange them so they can be cleaned easily.

4. Reducing Allergen-Producing Raw Materials. Some of the more important raw materials from which house dust mites produce allergens are the bodies, cast skins and fecal matter of various house-dwelling arthropods. You can reduce these by suppressing fleas, cockroaches and silverfish in the house. As mentioned above, you should also exclude dogs, cats and other animals that produce dander that is converted to allergens by house dust mites. Store grains and crackers in glass containers with good rubber seals that close by pressure; store these containers in the freezer. Replace feather pillows and down quilts with synthetic fibers. An electrostatic precipitator may also help reduce small particles in the air.

5. Low Humidity. The humidity in the house should be kept below 70%. In temperate regions, insulate under floors and place a plastic vapor barrier on the soil under foundations to reduce moisture that migrates upward from the soil under the house. Prune trees so that they do not shield the house; they transpire large amounts of water. Find all water leaks and repair or replace faulty fixtures. Prevent condensation on pipes by wrapping and insulating them. Install fans to improve ventilation during cooking, washing or bathing, and keep temperatures indoors as high as possible, since this helps dry out the air.

6. Reducing Air Infiltration. Air infiltration allows the entry of pollen, which is a food source for house dust mites. Cracks around windows, doors and other openings should be caulked or painted shut just as you would in a weatherizing program to reduce energy loss. Once infiltration of outside air has been greatly reduced, a dehumidifier can be used much more effectively to reduce the moisture content of the indoor air. It might not be practical to dehumidify the entire house, but it should be done in the sleeping areas, because these are frequently the places where dust mites accumulate. See the detailed suggestions on reducing house moisture under the discussion of house-structure pests in Chapter 21.

Treatment:
Direct Physical Controls

Direct physical controls for allergen reduction include vacuuming, cleaning and washing home furnishings and bedding, and exposing mites to extremes of heat and cold.

1. Vacuuming. The most important tool for managing house dust mites is the vacuum cleaner. Brooms remove only large particles and may make the situation worse by redistributing dust into areas that are harder to clean. Avoid wet-mopping, because it increases moisture at floor level and encourages mite popula-

tions. Where wet-mopping is necessary, as in kitchens and bathrooms, vacuum thoroughly first.

Vacuums with a water filter are preferable to those with a disposable paper bag. Our observations indicate that a water vacuum removes a greater range of particle sizes then paper-bag types. A simple comparison of the amounts of dust being distributed during vacuuming can be made by observing the suspended particles in a sunbeam while vacuuming with either type. The water vacuum pulls the sucked air through a water column that is whirled around in a container. The container is rinsed and refilled periodically. The bag-type vacuum actually passes the very fine dust particles through its paper-bag filter and exhausts them back into the room air. Much of this dust is relocated or resuspended rather then removed. A house vacuumed with a cloth or paper-bag-type vacuum can actually be dustier after vacuuming than before, as the vacuum picks up small particles of dust and reintroduces them into the air via the exhaust. There are a number of vacuums with highly efficient filters designed for use by people with allergies to dust. These and the water vacuums are listed in the Resource Appendix under "Insect Management: Physical Controls" on pp. 682-683.

It is better to vacuum thoroughly once a week rather than lightly on a daily basis. Light vacuuming removes only the large dust particles. It may be selectively more harmful to predatory mites, such as *Cheyletus eruditus*, which prey on house dust mites and flea larvae, than it is to the house dust mites or their food sources. Vacuum mattresses and padded furniture thoroughly; 20 minutes for each mattress is not too long.

2. Dusting, Shampooing and Dry-Cleaning. Dust furniture before you vacuum so the dust has time to settle on the floor, where it can be picked up by the vacuum. Special dust cloths or other cleaning implements that are treated chemically to hold rather than scatter dust may be helpful. Shampoo, steam-clean or beat large, nonwashable carpets once a year. This removes large particles missed by the vacuum. Wash sheets in soapy water at 140°F (60°C) every one or two weeks to kill all mites. Take your blankets to the dry cleaners, hang them outdoors once a year or wash them frequently.

According to Bruce Mitchell, immunology director at the Blackrock Clinic in Dublin, Ireland, a cleaning solution called Allerite® penetrates carpet fibers and when vacuumed up dislodges allergen-bearing mite feces. Houses severely infested with dust mites might require four vacuumings with Allerite® over a two-month period to reduce mite allergens to tolerable levels (less than two micrograms of allergen per gram of dust).

3. **Exposure to Heat or Cold.** Two other direct physical techniques can be used to reduce mite populations. In colder areas during the winter, the house or various interior artifacts (furniture, bedding, etc.) can be exposed to the outside cold for one or two days. A large-scale or walk-in freezer, if available, also works well. The opposite approach is also effective. One study showed that switching on an electric blanket for eight hours every day reduced mites in mattresses by 50% in one month. Another documented that heating blankets in a clothes dryer at 140°F (60°C) for six hours killed all mites. Investigators report that if this is done each month, with one annual dry-cleaning or wash, mites are held to a minimum. (Note: Temperatures in typical clothes dryers range from 135°F to 180°F [57°C to 82°C], depending on the number of temperature settings available on the particular machine. Check the appliance manual or hire an appliance repair technician to determine the temperature range of your dryer.)

Treatment:
Direct Chemical Controls

There is probably no need to resort to the use of pesticides, except in tropical areas where cleaning and nontoxic approaches have not proven sufficient. The least-toxic chemical materials found to be effective in laboratory tests include two insect growth regulators, Altosid® and Altonar®; the mosquito repellent diethyl-m-toluamide (DEET); and the herbal mixture Paragerm®, which contains solol, thymol, terpineol, citrus-fruit natural essence, natural essence of *Syringa* and *Nardus* spp. plants, two halogenized phenyl alcohols and light liquid paraffin. The herbal product did not affect asthmatics.

Summary: Least-Toxic Dust Mite Control

Reduce sources of food for dust mites by:

• selecting textile-free or synthetic-textile furnishings

• encasing mattresses in plastic

• excluding pets, especially from sleeping areas

• reducing humidity in the house

• reducing air infiltration

• vacuuming thoroughly once a week, preferably with a water vacuum

Kill mites directly by:

• vacuuming with a water vacuum or a vacuum with special dust filters

• washing bed linen in hot soapy water

• freezing or heating blankets

• using least-toxic pesticides if other approaches don't work

The organophosphates malathion and diazinon were also effective, although some people may become sensitive to them, as with other synthetic insecticides. Lindane should be avoided, however. Although it is effective at killing the mites, it is even more effective at killing the mite predator *Cheyletus eruditus*, and it is hazardous to humans. In moist tropical areas, silica aerogel has been used successfully on and under floor coverings, including tatami (rice straw) mats. Various sulfur mixtures and boric-acid products may also be effective in killing house dust mites, but these have not yet been tested.

SCABIES OR "ITCH" MITES
(Family Sarcoptidae:
Sarcoptes scabiei)

A scabies infection is caused by mites that burrow into the skin. These very infectious mites are particularly troublesome because a person may infect other people long before becoming aware of the problem. This can be true for several reasons. First, when a person is infested initially, there is an incubation period of about six weeks, which allows at least three generations of mites to develop in the host before any itching is detected. Mites may be transmitted to other people during this entire period. Second, one rare type of encrusted scabies, Norwegian scabies, does not itch and is therefore hard to detect in the early stages. And finally, the symptoms of scabies may be masked by steroid hormones, such as cortisone used to reduce itching, before the condition is properly diagnosed. Although scabies can affect anyone, it is a particular problem in residential institutions such as hospitals and nursing homes.

Bill Todaro, a medical entomologist for the Allegheny County Health Department in Pittsburgh, Pennsylvania, describes his personal encounters with scabies in nursing homes in an article in *The IPM Practitioner*:

In southwestern Pennsylvania, encrusted scabies cases were observed in eight of ten nursing homes, all of which had "itch hysteria" among patients and staff. Itch hysteria is characterized by growing numbers of nursing staff complaining of itch and papular rashes [small solid elevations of the skin] on upper arms, upper legs, and abdomen. Managerial staff try to eliminate the unknown cause of the itch by large-scale environmental insecticide applications, changes of laundry detergents, mass use of pediculicides [insecticides that kill lice] and/or scabicides (lindane in the form of Kwell®) and cortisone....In summary, cortisone treatments, given to the elderly for itches of undiagnosed cause that are actually due to scabies mites,...[suppress] the immune response, and once the urge to...scratch is removed, normal scabies progresses to encrusted scabies, which in these cases does not itch.

Dr. Milton Orkin, in *Scabies and Pediculosis*, cites the occurrence of scabies in an infant whose skin contained hundreds of burrows. Normal suppression of the mites by the infant's defenses had been overcome by fluorinated corticosteroids. Cortisone treatments are not always successful in stopping the itch of scabies. If a patient with a very itchy rash fails to respond to potent topical steroids, this itself suggests scabies.

Although the itching of scabies is intense, the small size of the mite makes it very easy to overlook. This often leads to misdiagnoses, such as "nervous eczema" and the like. It helps if the patient bears in mind that scabies is a possibility every time a persistent, intense skin itch occurs, particularly at night, and particularly when no other cause can be found.

The scabies mite is spread by any close, prolonged contact between human bodies; it is very difficult to transmit through clothing or bedding. The scabies mites of dogs, cats, cattle, sheep, goats, horses and poul-

try do not establish themselves and reproduce on people. However, they may infest humans for a few weeks, then die; reinfestations can occur.

There are few ways in which the scabies sufferer can modify the environment to suppress the scabies mite population. The good news is that there is an alternative—albeit a messy one—to using the commonly prescribed pesticides for scabies control. We discuss this alternative on p. 168.

Biology

Scabies mites (see the drawing below right) are tiny organisms whose mature females average a mere 1/50 in. (0.5 mm) in length. The young female burrows into the skin, where she is joined by a male. Copulation, which takes place in the burrow, occurs only once and renders the female fertile for life. After fertilization, the male apparently dies in the burrow while the female emerges on the skin surface and wanders at a speed of 1 in. (25 mm) per minute until she finds a suitable site for a permanent burrow.

The female then digs into the outer layer of the skin, taking about an hour to submerge herself. She feeds on liquids from cells she has ruptured. Within a few hours of starting the burrow, she begins to lay eggs and continues to do so at the rate of two to three per day. She expands the burrow from 1/50 in. to 1/5 in. (0.5 mm to 5 mm) each day. Burrows may reach over 1 in. in length. The female mite remains in the burrow for the rest of her life (30 days or more).

The eggs hatch in three to four days. The larva, after spending a day or so in the original burrow, move up to the surface of the skin, find a favorable site—such as within a hair follicle or the bottom of a skin fold—and burrow in again for shelter and food. After three days or more, the larva molts and begins its nymph stage. The mite at this stage lives on or beneath the skin surface. It molts twice more at approximately three-day intervals, with both males and fe-

males emerging from the last molt. Adults appear 10 to 14 days after the first egg is laid.

Studies show that the average number of mite females infesting a person is about 11. Half the scabies cases had between one and five females, and 4% had over 50 mites, mostly females. Occasionally, as in the description of the encrusted scabies infestations above, larger populations are observed—up to 500 mites or more—but these are rare. Theoretical calculations indicate that in two months, a population of a million

The Life Cycle of the Scabies Mite

After mating, the adult female scabies mite *(Sarcoptes scabiei)* burrows into the skin, where she feeds on cell liquids and lays a total of 10 to 25 eggs along the course of the burrow. The female remains in the burrow until death. The larvae emerge from the egg after three to four days, surface from the birth burrow and travel across the skin until they find a suitable place to create another burrow and repeat the cycle. (Actual size of adult: 1/50 in./0.5 mm)

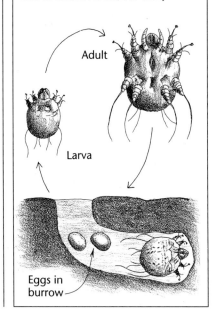

Adult

Larva

Eggs in burrow

mites can be obtained from a single female. But this rarely occurs because scratching and immune host reactions in response to the mites prevent the mite population from rising this high. Scratching can kill many mites; on the other hand, if the skin is opened, it can lead to secondary infections unless treated with an antiseptic. Bathing must also take a heavy toll on scabies mites on the skin surface.

The sites where mites are most commonly found are the hands and wrists (63%), elbows (11%), feet and ankles (9%), penis and scrotum (8% —only human males were included in the largest study on mite siting), buttocks (4%), armpits (2%) and all other areas (2%), except the back and neck, where no mites were found. In women, mites commonly attack the areas around the nipples and under the breasts. Interestingly, the common scabies rash that develops in response to the mites does not correspond with the burrowing described above. Rather, the rash is typically produced in areas of secondary infection, which may be a result of temporary excavations in thinner skin by mites in the earlier stages of development. It may also be the result of immunological sensitization in individuals previously infected.

Scabies mites that are off the host die when exposed to temperatures of 120°F (80°C) for 10 minutes in dry or moist air. At 77°F (25°C), the mites can survive two days in dry air at 30% RH, or for three days in moist air at 90% RH. The longest known survival period away from a host is 14 days at 54°F (12°C) in moist air— lower temperatures favor mite survival. Thus it becomes apparent that the mite is relatively easy to kill when off the host. Infested clothing passed through a clothes dryer for 10 minutes or longer can be disinfested.

Damage
Symptoms of scabies infections include development of rashes, particularly at the site of burrows in the skin, accompanied by itching, which can become severe. The itching is caused by the body's reaction to toxic mite secretions and excretions. Scratching can cause secondary infections, resulting in bleeding and leakage of lymph onto the skin. This can obscure the diagnosis.

In most individuals who have not been previously infested, little or no rash appears for several weeks. Nor is there much itching, redness or swelling at the sites of burrows in the early weeks of a first-time infestation. Itching generally starts four to six weeks after mites attack a new host.

Detection and Monitoring
The first indication that a scabies mite infestation has occurred is an intense itching that often keeps one awake at night; a characteristic rash that resembles tiny blisters will also be present. Although most dermatologists can identify scabies mites from superficial indications, proper identification is based on finding burrows, mites, eggs or mite feces. Usually a diagnosis is made by identifying burrows, the characteristic rash, past medical history and an assessment of the likelihood of exposure to scabies. This diagnostic approach is used because detecting the mites themselves is difficult even when the proper procedure is used.

The method for diagnosing scabies (see the sidebar on the facing page) involves technical procedures recommended for use by dermatologists, medical entomologists and other medical specialists.

Treatment: Indirect Strategies
A treatment program for scabies should involve the person with the itch or rash, the family or living group and any other intimate associates of the infected person, particularly if they sleep together. Close associates should be made aware that transmission of mites can occur before the itch becomes apparent. If possible, all potentially infested members of the group should sleep separately during the treatment period. The separation time depends on the type of treatment selected.

Treatment: Direct Physical Controls
Tests conducted during World War II on the effects of disinfecting clothing and blankets indicated that the procedure then recommended (sterilization of clothing and bedding sheets) was not justified given the results. Scabies is seldom spread by inanimate objects. Nevertheless, to eliminate any possibility of reinfestation, wash or dry-clean bedding and clothing after the last treatment.

It may be possible to remove the egg-laying females with a needle, fingernail or other tool (as described in the sidebar on the facing page), but the possibility of missing some females is great. Because of the likelihood of passing the infestation to others if the mites are not removed from the body, it is better to use a miticide. Fortunately, most mites are very susceptible to sulfur, a material that is relatively nontoxic to humans (sulfur is discussed below).

Treatment: Direct Chemical Controls
The most widely used pesticides for treating scabies mites are lindane, sulfur, crotamiton and permethrin.

1. **Lindane.** Lindane (Kwell®) is the most common pesticide used for scabies mites. However, we do not recommend it because of its potential hazards to human health (see the discussion under head lice on p. 177).

2. **Sulfur.** Sulfur is the best choice for treatment because it is safe, effective and widely available (see pp.109-110 for more details on this material). It is recommended by the U.S. Public Health Service's Centers for Disease Control as an alternative to lindane, particularly when treating pregnant women and young children.

The Chinese used sulfur against scabies mites as long ago as 1111 A.D. Today, an ointment containing 10%

Clinical Procedure for Diagnosing Scabies

Because over 80% of scabies infestations involve the hands, arms, elbows, feet and ankles, these areas should be inspected first for the short (less than 1 in. long) burrows that contain the females. The mite is visible at one end of the burrow as a raised whitish oval with dark pigmentation at the front. This dark pigmentation represents the mouthparts of the mite. The peppered appearance of the tunnels is due to the accumulation of fecal pellets. Although this is visible without a hand lens, it can be seen more clearly with a 10x or 15x lens.

You are most likely to find mites in burrows that have not been scratched and have no marks on the surface, that is, no crust. Such burrows will require some skill to detect; a penlight held obliquely to the skin helps in the search.

Another approach is to select an area that itches. Apply a small drop of fountain-pen ink (use nonpermanent ink) to the site and wipe off the excess. The ink will work into the burrow and stop at the mite, which you should then try to withdraw. The procedure is similar to removing a splinter. A needle, razor blade, scalpel or even a very sharp knife can be used to scrape the skin surface until the mite becomes stuck to the tool—dead and live mites stick readily to a needle. Again, although the process can be done with the naked eye, a 10x to 15x hand lens helps. Better still, a jeweler's glass leaves both hands free during the scraping process.

Whichever scraping tool you choose should first be sterilized by passing it through a flame several times quickly, without letting it become hot. Getting the tool too hot either delays its use or increases the chance of burning the skin; moreover, if you let it cool too long, it can become contaminated again.

You also can use the slightly different procedure shown in the drawing below. Sterilize or "flame" the knife blade as described above, then place a drop of sterile mineral oil —available at most drugstores— on the blade. Touch the tool to the papule (raised area) produced by the mite and allow the oil to run onto the skin surface (A in the drawing). Scrape six or seven times with the blade to remove the entire top of the papule. Tiny flecks of blood will appear in the oil. Deposit the oil from the blade onto a glass microscope slide (B in the drawing). Repeat the entire procedure four or five times, wiping and flaming the blade between each scraping. Examine the slide under a 50x to 100x microscope with or without a cover glass. Look for females, which are about $\frac{1}{50}$ in. (0.5 mm) long.

If an individual has had previous scabies or antiscabetic treatments, small reddish-brown nodules may appear with a new infestation. These may or may not be associated with burrows, and occur most commonly in the groin and armpit regions, as well as on the genitalia. Mites are no longer present in these nodules, which may persist for weeks, months or years after successful therapy. In previously infested persons the reaction to a new infestation will usually occur much more quickly, typically about 12 days after being invaded.

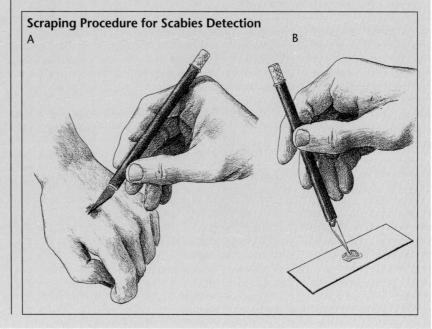

Scraping Procedure for Scabies Detection

A

B

precipitated sulfur is commonly used in the United States, although a recent review of treatments indicated that as little as a 6% concentration was also effective. A 2.5% concentration is recommended when treating infested infants. Because the sulfur is carried in a petrolatum (Vaseline®) base, the preparation is relatively messy. It can stain clothing and sheets and has a distinct odor. Nonetheless, its other attributes lead most patients to tolerate its shortcomings without complaint.

The mixture can be obtained from a pharmacist without a doctor's prescription. You can also make your own mixture from inorganic (precipitated) sulfur available from plant nurseries, or from technical-grade sulfur sold at chemical-supply houses. If you are hypersensitive to petroleum products, there are at least two alternative carriers you can experiment with: Eucerin™, which is not as sticky as Vaseline®, and Aquaaquphor™, which is water-washable. Sulfur can also be added to vanishing creams, available at pharmacies. These alternative carriers are more expensive than petrolatum jelly, but their advantages may outweigh the additional cost.

Two other sulfur drugs are often available from pharmacies. One is Mitigal™ (dimethyl diphenylene disulfide, which contains 25% organically combined sulfur); unfortunately, this drug tends to produce a sulfur dermatitis. The other is Tetmosol™ (tetraethylthiuram monosulfide), which is used on children but is slow to work. Tetmosol™ can also be combined with soap and used as a scabies prophylactic.

Apply the sulfur ointment each night for three successive nights; do not wash it off until the fourth day, when the treatment series is completed. On adults, miticides should be applied thoroughly from the neck down (scabies mites are not found on the heads of adults); on young children, they should be applied from the head down. Bathing in hot water

before applying a sulfur mixture may make the treatment more effective, but it is not necessary to rub the skin excessively during washing. Old pajamas, socks and cotton gloves can be worn to keep the ointment off the bedding.

3. Crotamiton. This scabicide is formulated as a 10% concentration of crotamiton in a vanishing cream base. Like sulfur, it is recommended by the Centers for Disease Control as an alternative to lindane. Two applications on successive nights, with washing 24 to 48 hours after the second application, are suggested. Crotamiton is formulated as the product Eurax®. It may cause irritation when used for a long period or when applied to skin that is already irritated from scratching. However, crotamiton also has an anti-itching effect.

4. Permethrin. At the time of writing, the synthetic pyrethroid insecticide permethrin has just been registered for use against scabies (see p. 122 for details on synthetic pyrethroids). It will be marketed under the trade name Elimate®, and will be sold in pharmacies. The advantage of this material is that generally only one application will be needed to kill the scabies mites. Thus, it will be more convenient to use than sulfur,

although permethrin is more acutely toxic than sulfur.

5. Other Drugs. Aspirin may help relieve the itching but it does not affect the mites. Avoid cortisone drugs, including hydrocortisone, if possible, at least until treatment has started —they may suppress physiological reactions that help limit the size of scabies infestations. Because the itch may persist after all the live mites have been eliminated, anti-itch treatments such as antihistamines may be needed during the healing process after treatment. The infested person can usually distinguish between itching due to the mites and the sensitization caused by them. If there is no recognizable change in the itching after treatment, retreatment may be needed, but this should be preceded by a search that includes scraping as previously discussed for the presence of mites.

Summary: Least-Toxic Scabies Mite Control

• Obtain a diagnosis from a dermatologist, parasitologist or medical entomologist who takes a skin scraping and is capable of identifying the mite and its signs.

• If you have scabies, tell others whom you may have infested, even though they may not yet have started to itch. That way, they will seek treatment if and when the first indication of a scabies problem appears.

• Encourage infested persons to sleep separately during treatment.

• A sulfur ointment is the least-toxic miticide. Apply the ointment nightly for three days. Wear old clothing to protect bedding from stains produced by the sulfur.

• Permethrin is the fastest-acting miticide. Generally only one application is needed, but it is more toxic than sulfur.

REFERENCES AND READINGS

Alexander, J.O. 1984. *Arthropods and human skin.* Berlin: Springer-Verlag. 442 pp.

The most authoritative text on all human ectoparasites, particularly scabies and dust mites.

Beaver, P.C., R.C. Jung and E.W. Cupp. 1984. *Clinical parasitology.* 9th ed. Philadelphia: Lea and Fabiger. 825 pp.

This authoritative parasitological text includes a summary of house dust mite information.

Bronswijk, J.H. van. 1981. *House dust biology, for allergists, acarologists and mycologists.* Zeist, The Netherlands: NIB Publishers. 316 pp. (Available from: NIB Publishers, Box 144, 3700 AC Zeist, The Netherlands).

This paperback was the major source of the information on house dust mites. It is a primary source and background document for anyone interested in house dust and house dust mites.

Friberg, H., V.A. Hall, P.K. Shaw and E.B. Smith. 1976. *Itch epidemic: exterminating the scabies mite.* Reprinted from *Patient Care*, May 1, 1976.

Particularly useful for diagnosis and treatment. Includes a discussion of post-treatment itching.

Harvey, P., and R. May. 1990. Matrimony, mattresses, and mites. *New Scientist* 125(1706):48-49.

This study shows that dried semen on mattresses serves as a food source for dust mites, doubling their production of eggs.

Krantz, G.W. 1978. *A manual of acarology.* Corvallis: Oregon State University Book Stores. 335 pp.

A comprehensive textbook for students of mites.

Mellanby, K. 1972. *Scabies.* Hampton, England: E.W. Classey. 81 pp.

A classic work on scabies and its management during World War II. Includes information about sulfur as well as another scabicide, benzyl benzoate, available in Europe.

Muller, G. 1973. Scraping for human scabies. *Arch. Dermatol.* 107:70.

This short article gives a clear description of the scraping procedure for scabies mites.

Orkin, M., H.I. Maibach, L.C. Parish and R.M. Schwartzman, eds. 1977. *Scabies and pediculosis.* Philadelphia: J.B. Lippincott . 203 pp.

This is the definitive work on scabies and lice. It reviews the history, biology, epidemiology, immunology and treatment of scabies. Secondary infections and treatment complications are also covered.

Todaro, W. 1982. Scabies in the elderly. *The IPM Practitioner* 4(7):2-3.

This article describes how steroid hormones such as cortisone suppress the human immune response that otherwise helps reduce scabies mite infestations. It also discusses the potentially dire consequences of using lindane (Kwell®) to treat elderly people.

CHAPTER 11
Lice

INTRODUCTION

Hans Zinsser, writing in *Rats, Lice and History*, reveals:

> The manner of living throughout the Middle Ages made general lousiness inevitable....The habit of shaving the head and wearing a wig was no doubt in part due to the effort to hold down vermin. Gentlemen and ladies all over Europe resorted to this but the wigs they wore were often full of nits....Even in the highest society, the questions of lice and scratching were serious problems; and the education of children, even in the highest circles, included a training of the young in relation to their vermin.
>
> Reboux, speaking of the education of a princess of France in the middle of the seventeenth century, says: "One had carefully taught the young princess that it was bad manners to scratch when one did it by habit and not by necessity, and that it was improper to take lice or fleas or other vermin by the neck to kill them in company, except in the most intimate circles."

In recent years, the number of people infested with head and pubic lice is believed to have increased. Estimates derived from the sale of insecticides or pediculicides (insecticides that are specifically intended to kill lice) — $35 million in 1987 — indicate that as many as six million cases of head and pubic lice occur each year.

In contrast, body lice are not common in the United States. This is fortunate, because body lice are significant vectors (transmitters) of human disease. These disease pathogens, particularly the deadly typhus caused by *Rickettsia prowazekii*, still occur in epidemic form on a number of continents. Body lice also can be vectors of epidemic relapsing fever, sometimes called louse-borne typhus (LBT), which is caused by the spirochete *Borrelia recurrentis*. LBT killed at least three million Russians during World War II; 81% of those who were in-

Table 11.1
Human-Disease-Causing Agents Transmitted by the Body Louse

Disease (Common Names)	Causal Pathogen	Significance
epidemic typhus (Brill-Zinsser disease, war fever, jail fever, European typhus)	*Rickettsia prowazekii* (rickettsia)	historically one of the large-scale killers of humans
trench fever (five-day fever)	*Rochalimaea quintana* (rickettsia)	widespread, usually latent[a], highly debilitating but non-fatal
epidemic relapsing fever (louse-borne typhus)	*Borrelia recurrentis* (spirochete)	pockets of infection remain in Africa, mortality low

[a] Not visible or apparent.

fected died. Table 11.1 above lists various diseases transmitted by the body louse.

Hot-water/detergent washing kills the eggs that female body lice lay on the host's clothing. Head and pubic lice, by contrast, lay their eggs only in the hair, and no amount of washing can dislodge or kill them. This makes their management difficult, particularly in light of the widespread resistance of the lice to insecticides. The social stigma of being infested with either head or pubic lice further complicates their management, and the hysteria that may surround the discovery that you or your child has lice can interfere with the rational choice of management strategies.

The application of insecticidal shampoos or ointments is the most common method of managing head and pubic lice. However, there are a number of problems with this approach. For example, the most popular pesticide for such treatments, lindane (Kwell®), may pose long-term health hazards (cautions are discussed on pp. 177-178). Moreover, its chronic overuse has rendered it inef-

fective in many cases because the lice have become resistant to it.

The traditional chemical "first strike" approach is inappropriate. Sound management of head and pubic lice involves prompt diagnosis and the use of nontoxic physical treatments, with insecticides only as a backup. Each of these elements requires that the person treating the lice problem have more precise information about the biology of lice than is usually available.

Biological Overview

There are only two groups of lice in the animal kingdom, the biting lice in the insect order Mallophaga, and the sucking lice in the order Anoplura. Biting lice are found on birds and some nonhuman mammals, such as chickens and goats. Sucking lice occur only on mammals, including humans. The three sucking-lice species that feed on humans are the head louse (*Pediculus humanus capitis*), the body louse (*P. humanus corporis*) and the pubic louse (*Phthirus pubis*).

The head louse and body louse are in the family Pediculidae, while the

Table 11.2
Some Biological Characteristics of the Three Human Lice Species

Lice Species	Microhabitat on Body	Most Commonly Affected Group	Where Eggs Laid
head	scalp, eyebrows; occasionally elsewhere	school-aged children	hair on head
body	body and clothing	indigent adults who habitually sleep in their clothes	adults' clothing
pubic	groin and armpits	sexually active young adults	pubic hair

pubic louse is in the family Phthiridae. Head and body lice are known to interbreed, resulting in intermediate forms, but pubic lice cannot mate with either of the other two other species. As Table 11.2 above shows, each species has a characteristic pattern of occurrence on the human body and a group of people with which it is most commonly associated.

Head lice are most often found on schoolchildren between the ages of three and ten, less often on older children or adults and sometimes among people in psychiatric facilities, jails and other institutions. The eggs, or nits, of head lice are glued tightly to hairs, most often around the back of the ears and at the nape of the neck. The adults are found in these and other areas of the head, including the eyelashes, and more rarely on other body hairs. Adult head lice have been found on headgear, combs, brushes and scarves.

Body lice, on the other hand, do not live on the head. They live on clothing, move to the body to feed and then return to the clothing to lay eggs. They are most common on indigent adults who habitually sleep in their clothes. Persons who regularly carry large infestations develop hard, pigmented skin areas, a condition known as vagabond's disease. Body

lice have been nicknamed cooties, graybacks or mechanized dandruff.

Body lice are relatively rare in the United States at this time, but with the recent rise in the number of homeless people, cases of body lice can be expected to increase. As mentioned above, body lice can be managed by washing clothes. Cases of head and pubic lice are much more common and are usually treated with toxic materials. Consequently, we focus our discussion on the management of these problem lice.

HEAD LICE
(Family Pediculidae:
Pediculus humanus capitis)
Managing head lice is a major task for parents, school personnel and health-care professionals worldwide. Approximately 10% of the elementary school population—as many as 6 million children—is treated for head-lice infestations (pediculosis) in the United States each year. The growing resistance of the lice to pediculicides, coupled with a surprising willingness of many families to tolerate head lice, is causing a manageable problem to become a major nuisance.

Biology
Head lice are exclusively human ectoparasites (meaning they live externally on the host). The louse spends its entire life on the human head; if it does move onto other surfaces, it must return to the head within a few hours to survive. Although lice are not known to reproduce naturally on other species, laboratory colonies of lice have been maintained on rabbits.

The six-legged, wingless adult head louse is $\frac{1}{16}$ in. to $\frac{1}{8}$ in. long (1.5 mm to 3 mm), and ranges from tan to greyish-white in color. Each of its six legs ends in a claw, which it uses to grasp the hair shaft. Female lice select hair for egg deposition that is round in cross section. This accounts for the lack of head lice in "kinky," or negroid, hair, which is oval in cross section. The eggs, or nits, of the louse are laid on the head hairs near the junction of the scalp and the hair shaft, one egg per hair (see the drawing on the facing page). The egg is coated with a glue-like substance that cements it to the hair. Most eggs are laid at night. Each female produces about six to eight eggs in a 24-hour period; estimates of the total eggs produced by a female range from 50 to 300.

Left undisturbed, over 90% of the eggs hatch within 7 to 11 days. Once hatched, developing lice take 8 or 9 days to become adults; after an additional day, the adult female can start laying eggs. Thus, about 16 days in all are required for an egg to give rise to a female capable of laying more eggs. Adults live for 9 to 10 days, making an approximate total lifespan of at least 24 days.

How long head lice survive away from the host depends on the temperature. At room temperature—73°F (23°C)—adults live up to 55 hours; at 59°F (15°C), adults survive up to 10 days. The eggs are the most resistant stage. Detailed studies of survival periods at different temperatures off the host indicate that infested clothing stored for one month at

The Life Cycle of the Head Louse

The adult female head louse lives about ten days and lays 50 to 300 eggs close to the scalp, attaching them to individual hairs with a glue-like secretion. Nymphal lice emerge from the eggs, feed on human blood, mature to adults within nine days, mate and repeat the cycle. (Actual size of adult: 1/16 in. to 1/8 in./1.5 mm to 3 mm)

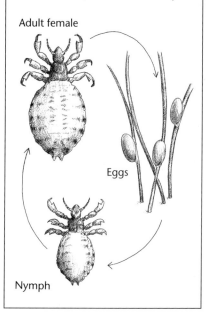

Adult female

Eggs

Nymph

room temperature could not possibly harbor living lice. At much higher temperatures, eggs succumb after much shorter periods. For example, at 131°F (55°C), they live no more than five minutes.

Head lice can move fairly rapidly, but cannot jump or fly. Most head lice are probably transmitted when an infested person comes into direct contact with another. For example, when children sleep or sit together, enough time and opportunity is provided for a louse to walk from head to head. Lice and their eggs can also be transferred between people via infested brushes, combs, caps, hats, scarves, coats, bedding, towels and upholstered furniture.

Damage

The louse bite itself is painless, but the saliva usually causes an allergic reaction that produces itching (although some people may not experience the itching for several weeks). If it is severe, the lice probably have been present for some weeks. Scratching can lead to excoriated skin, which creates an entryway for germs and lice feces and can lead to secondary infections such as impetigo and swollen glands. Severely infested individuals may experience fever and feel tired and irritable.

Although the symptoms of head lice are irritating, head lice have generally been regarded as little more than a nuisance by medical personnel. In the laboratory, head lice have been artificially infected with the deadly typhus rickettsiae (*Rickettsia prowazekii*) and the spirochetes of relapsing fever (*Borrelia recurrentis*). Fortunately, these serious human diseases have not been shown to be transmitted under natural conditions by the head louse. But recent concern about transmissible diseases carried in the blood is leading researchers to take another look at the head louse as a possible disease vector.

Detection and Monitoring

Excessive head scratching, sometimes leading to scalp damage and excoriated skin, or a note from the school nurse indicating your child has head lice are often the ways parents learn of lice presence. Red or blackish louse fecal specks may be visible on the child's shoulders or back.

Immature and/or active adult lice may be present on the head or in the eyebrows; the eggs themselves may be detected by careful observation of the hairs close to the scalp, around the ears and in the nape of the neck. A pair of lice sticks, which resemble long toothpicks, is useful for separating strands of hair when inspecting scalps for lice. For sources of these sticks, see the Resource Appendix under "Insect Management: Identification and Monitoring" (pp. 681-682).

In *Head Lice Infestation*, University of Miami parasitologists David Taplin and Terri Meinking write:

It has traditionally been thought that only nits within one-quarter inch of the scalp are viable. The rationale behind this theory is that female lice lay their eggs at the junction of scalp and hair shaft, and in the seven to ten days during which the egg incubates, the hair grows only one-quarter inch. Eggs past that point would presumably be past hatching time and therefore considered nonviable.

Recent research indicates, however, that in warmer climates viable nits are found farther than one-quarter inch from the scalp. Therefore the entire length of hair should be examined, and judgment about nit viability should be based on color and shape of the egg casing. A viable nit has a yellowish to grey color, darkening to a tan or coffee color as it matures. It is shaped like a tear drop. Empty egg casings are white. Nits that contain air pockets or have a shrunken or indented shape will not hatch.

Suspected nits should be examined under a microscope or a 10x hand lens. An empty egg case can be distinguished from a flake of dandruff or a particle of dried hair spray by the fact that it sticks to the hair, whereas the other particles can be flicked off. An empty egg case is easily detected by its white color, whereas viable nits are darker.

Under the microscope, viable eggs appear yellowish with a pearly luster that is probably due to light reflected from the illumination source. Empty louse eggs appear more transparent under magnification than when observed with the naked eye when they are still attached to a hair. The color of viable eggs changes from greyish white to yellow opalescent as the lice inside mature.

One quick, effective tool for school nurses on the lookout for head lice is a special light with a magnifying glass mounted in a flexible arm. A dual system of cool white fluorescent and long-wave ultraviolet bulbs is mounted around a center opening with three low-power magnifying lenses (1.75x, 3x and 8x). The special phosphors in the ultraviolet light often cause the lice to fluoresce (glow) yellow-green, and the live nits to stand out as opalescent white. These lights are available from medical supply houses. Hogil Corp. includes the light and other useful tools in its Innoscan pediculosis detection kit designed for use in schools and public-health facilities (see the Resource Appendix under "Insect Management: Identification and Monitoring" on pp. 681-682).

Treatment: Indirect Strategies

A combination of preventive practices — combing with a special comb, shampooing with nontoxic soaps and, if necessary, using the least-toxic insecticide (i.e., one that contains pyrethrin) as a backup — can control head lice successfully. We have personally observed the elimination of infestations on individuals and entire families with no pesticide other than the incidental insecticidal effects of ordinary soap shampoos.

Whether an infestation can be eliminated in a totally nontoxic manner depends on the motivation of the parents and the cooperation of the child. Reinfestation from playmates is common, regardless of the treatment used. Successfully avoiding reinfestation means educating the larger group of parents and the children with whom the child associates. This education should stress frequent bathing and hair-washing, because, in our experience, severe head lice cases are often associated with infrequent bathing.

There are two serious obstacles to implementing a nontoxic program for managing a head-lice outbreak. The first is the likelihood of the same individual becoming reinfested. If re-infestation occurs almost immediately after the initial treatment, which frequently happens, those responsible for management will often assume wrongly that the first treatment did not work because it was not strong enough. Consequently, they turn to something more toxic. The second problem is the repulsion many adults feel at the very thought of head lice. Often, panicked parents who would not normally expose their children to potentially hazardous materials will apply pesticides in haste, sometimes well beyond the recommended frequency and dosages. Both obstacles can be overcome through education.

1. Education. The education of as many members of the potentially affected community as possible is a critical component of a successful lice control program. Educational efforts can be hampered, however, by the extreme squeamishness of many adults. The reluctance of teachers to talk about the problem in a straightforward manner, coupled with the hysteria of parents who incorrectly associate head lice with the stigma of poverty and poor personal hygiene, are often major obstacles. Although hygiene and living conditions play a role in lice infestations, other factors appear to be more important, given the fact that head-lice outbreaks occur frequently in fashionable private schools as well as in low-income day-care centers.

To combat this ignorance and the emotional climate it generates, we recommend education even before a lice problem is detected. Every group of young children, except children with extremely kinky or negroid hair, is at risk for head lice. They and their parents should be educated about lice detection and treatment in the same tone and manner as one would inform people about first aid for mosquito bites or bee stings.

If the problem is already present, special meetings between teachers and parents may be needed. In our experience in developing head-lice programs for grade schools, we found that sometimes only a small group of families is responsible for the frequent reinfestation of an entire class. It is important to understand that there are some parents who do not regard head lice as a serious problem at all. Many cultures outside the United States accept head lice as a minor, constant inconvenience, and do not assume that head lice can be eliminated when infestations occur. Families with this attitude may need to be convinced of the feasibility of eliminating head lice.

The National Pediculosis Association (P.O. Box 149, Newton, MA 02161; (617) 449-NITS), a nonprofit organization that provides education on safe ways to manage head lice, recommends that schools establish a "No Nit" policy, which means that children are denied readmission to the classroom until their heads are free of lice eggs (nits). They base this recommendation on the fact that most parents and teachers cannot easily tell the difference between a live and hatched egg. A policy that tolerates nits allows infested children to return to school and unwittingly spread head lice to others.

Young children generally are not hesitant to talk about head lice — for them, it's just another learning experience. They are eager to learn about lice biology, how to remove the lice with special combs and noninsecticidal shampooing and how to avoid infecting each other. They appreciate the importance of storing headgear individually and not sharing combs, and we have found that they become very cooperative in combing and other efforts to reduce the problem. They like to look at lice and draw pictures of them. They learn that lice cannot fly, but must crawl from place to place. In our experience with school head-lice programs, it is the squeamish teachers, not the children, who constitute the major obstacle to a successful program.

2. Proper Storage of Garments. Transmission of head lice can be reduced through proper storage of garments that may carry stray louse females. Head lice are a particular problem among children in child-care programs, kindergarten and the early grades of grammar school. Facilities should be equipped with separate lockers or cubbyholes for each child. Headgear, scarves and other clothing that comes into contact with the hair should be stored separately, one cubby for each child. It is crucial that the parent or teacher clearly explains the importance of this procedure.

If, during head-lice outbreaks, permanent wooden or metal containers cannot be bought or constructed, large, sturdy plastic bags can be used. An identifying decal can be applied to individual bags so children know which is theirs. Bags with clothing inside should be doubled over and wrapped with a metal string tie; this process should be supervised to make sure the children are doing it properly. Torn bags should be replaced immediately. Setting the bags in the heat of direct sunlight or in the cold outdoors in winter may help kill some of the lice.

Treatment:
Direct Physical Controls

Least-toxic management of head lice requires that four tactics be carried out simultaneously: the application of heat, combing, washing clothing and bedding, and shampooing with soap. The first three tactics are discussed in this section. Shampooing is discussed with other insecticides under chemical controls, because certain soaps, although virtually nontoxic to humans, are known to have an insecticidal effect.

We have personally observed cases where these tactics were sufficient to eliminate the problem without more toxic chemicals. Success depends on several factors, including how determined the parents are not to use insecticide on their child's scalp, good relations between the parent and child and the length and texture of the child's hair.

1. Heat. Head lice are very sensitive to changes in the surface temperature of the host's skin. Perspiring persons, for example, are repellent to lice, and fevers drive lice from the head. This suggests that saunas or hair dryers may be effective in reducing lice numbers. However, there are no studies that indicate how much impact such treatments have. Nonetheless, it does make sense to use water as hot as tolerable when shampooing the hair—but remember that the scalps of young children are extremely sensitive to heat. Hotter water can be used on the heads of older children (7 to 10 years). In any case, do as you would on your own scalp: Start with lukewarm water and increase the temperature gradually so it is always comfortable.

The application of heat and combing should be combined with regular shampooing. Shampoos with added pesticides are generally not necessary. Shampooing must take place immediately before combing, because the hair must be soft and wet during the process. This allows the comb to pull the eggs, or nits, out of the hair without pulling out the hair itself. It also slows down any lice and aids in their removal. For more on shampoos, see p. 177.

Placing bedding, hats or other head-gear in a clothes dryer for 30 minutes at the highest setting should kill all stages of the lice, including the eggs, which die after five minutes at 131°F (55°C).

2. Combing. Eggs (nits) are often difficult to remove because female head lice make a strong glue with which they attach the eggs to individual hairs. Unfortunately, there is no safe solvent for this glue. Soap shampoos, though they may have an insecticidal effect on the young and adult lice, do not kill the eggs. Vinegar is sometimes recommended, but it doesn't seem to work. Pyrethrin-based insecticides may kill some eggs, but they do not kill all of them. Thus, the major value of the comb is in removing eggs from the hair.

A number of combs with specially tooled metal teeth designed to remove head lice and their eggs from the hair are available commercially. We particularly recommend the Derbac and Innomed combs (see the Resource Appendix under "Insect Management: Physical Controls" on pp. 682-683). Ordinary fine-toothed plastic combs are not adequate, even though they may be sold for this purpose along with various insecticides for the control of head lice.

Some lice combs are better suited to certain hair textures than others. Look for a comb that removes the nits but does not pull the hair unnecessarily. Be forewarned, however, that with very long and/or very curly hair, the length of time it takes to remove the lice eggs with a comb may be beyond the patience of parent and child. In such cases a shorter haircut may be advisable. An interesting television show or video can help hold a child's attention during the combing process. The sidebar on p. 176 outlines the combing procedure.

There is no denying that the combing process demands time and patience from parents and children. On the other hand, many parents tell us that their children grow to love the process and look forward to it—it feels good, and the child is the center of the parents' attention. Most other primates spend long periods grooming each other. Grooming rids their fur of parasites, provides the physical satisfaction of stroking and reinforces the social structure of the group.

Children eight years old and up can be encouraged to carry a head-lice comb for use whenever an "itch" occurs. Small new infestations can be caught and removed by the child before they become a serious problem. Ideally, after each pass through the hair, the child should rinse the comb in the hottest tap water available, following with a soap-and-water wash of hands and comb. However, regular combing and disposal of hair strands, lice and debris in the toilet may be all that is necessary.

Combing for Head Lice

A. You will need:

• A deep bowl of hot water with a squirt of soap or detergent added. Almost any kind of liquid or powdered detergent will do. This water is used to kill eggs and lice combed from the head.

• A box of tissue paper.

• A strong lamp with a flexible arm that allows you to rotate it to direct the light wherever you are working.

• Many large bobby pins or hair clips, if the hair is long, to pin up sections of hair that have been combed.

• Two large towels, one to wrap around the head after shampooing, and one to place around the shoulders during combing.

• Two comfortable seats, one for the child and one for you. It may be best to seat the child on a table or low counter unless you have a very high stool available for yourself.

• Entertaining, absorbing playthings, such as coloring books, other books and plastic clay, that do not require much physical activity. If the child has very long hair, which takes more time and tries the patience of the child, two people can work simultaneously on different parts of the head.

B. Follow these steps:

1. Wet the hair thoroughly with water that is as hot as tolerable, because lice are extremely vulnerable to high temperatures. Remember, however, that the scalp of a young child is extremely sensitive to heat. Always start with lukewarm water, then gradually increase its temperature; that way the child will not be uncomfortable.

2. Apply the shampoo and scrub the scalp and hair thoroughly. Rinse.

3. Repeat Step 2, this time leaving the shampoo in the hair.

4. Tie a towel around the lathered head and leave it on for 15 to 20 minutes.

5. Seat the child so that his or her head is just slightly below your eye level.

6. Give the child something interesting to do.

7. Remove the towel. The hair will be moist with soap. Leave it this way; do not rinse the soap out.

8. Comb the hair with a large-toothed regular comb to remove snarls and accumulations of suds and line up the hair strands for a more thorough combing with the fine-toothed, specially designed head-lice comb.

9. Separate a 1-in. mass of hair and hold it with one hand. Hold the comb in a slanting position with the other hand with the curved side of the teeth toward the head.

10. Insert the comb at the base of the hair mass as close to the scalp as possible, since the eggs are first laid within ⅟₂₅ in. (1 mm) of the scalp surface. Pull the comb through the hair toward your body, making an effort to remove all the eggs you can see.

11. Comb slowly, working a 1-in. section at a time. Check each section to make sure it is clean, then pin it out of the way, curling it flat against the head.

12. Periodically clean hair and other debris from the comb with a tissue. When the tissue becomes soiled, place it in the bowl of hot detergent water. When the bowl is full, flush its contents down the toilet and refill the bowl with hot detergent water.

13. If the hair dries during the combing process, wet it again with water. Wet, soapy hair reduces pulling and hair loss.

14. When all the hair has been combed, rinse it thoroughly with water that is as hot as tolerable, then dry.

15. Once the hair is completely dry, check the entire head for stray nits and remove them individually.

C. Cleaning up:

1. Soak the comb in hot soapy ammonia water (1 teaspoon of ammonia in two cups of hot water) for 15 minutes. Metal combs can be boiled in plain water for 15 minutes. A comb cleaned either way can be reused by many different children.

2. Scrub the teeth of the comb with a nail brush or an old toothbrush to remove debris. Remove dirt lodged between the teeth of the comb with dental floss or a small stiff brush.

Based on the life cycle of female head lice, and assuming your child is not immediately reinfested, the combing process should be repeated every week or 10 days during the period when head lice are a problem at school. If the child becomes reinfested before a week has elapsed, the process will have to be repeated sooner. See the discussion of timing shampoos under chemical controls below.

3. **Washing Clothing and Bedding.** Because lice may wander from the head to the pillow or head wear, washing these items at the time the child is treated initially is a good idea. Clothing or bedding will be fully deloused if immersed in hot (140°F/60°C) water for 10 minutes. Cold also kills lice, including their eggs, which die if subjected to –4°F (–20°C) for 5 hours, or 5°F (–15°C) for 10 hours. Longer exposure is necessary if the eggs are insulated from the cold by cloth. This susceptibility of lice to cold suggests that bedding could be placed in the freezer for a day or two for delousing.

In general, however, head lice do not leave the head. Some families have been known to go into a frenzy of laundering and dry-cleaning, washing furnishings and washing or spraying rooms. There is no scientific evidence that this is worthwhile. Experts such as the late Dr. Benjamin Keh, former director of the Vector Control Unit of the California Department of Public Health, have emphasized to us that, in their opinion, the time and energy spent in washing clothes and the home environment would be far better spent shampooing, combing out nits and educating the child and other parents and children with whom the child associates.

Treatment: Direct Chemical Controls

There is no evidence that insecticidal spraying of lockers, classrooms, homes, automobiles or other environments is effective at solving outbreaks of head lice. Shampoos with insecticidal properties are the only chemical controls recommended for use against head lice.

1. **Soap Shampoo.** There is strong evidence that certain fatty acids are effective insecticides. Fatty acids are the common ingredients in most soaps (but not in detergents). Straight-chain fatty acids with carbon chains of 10 and 18 atoms have recently been shown to be particularly useful as insecticides. Such fatty acids are found naturally in coconut and olive oils. Thus, it may be worthwhile to use soaps made from these oils regularly as shampoos on young children susceptible to head lice.

Oil-based shampoos are available where hair products are sold. If you cannot locate a coconut- or olive-oil-based shampoo, use soap made from these products. Periodic applications of conditioner to hair counteracts the drying effects of soap. Safer™ Insecticidal Soap, which we discuss on pp. 115-116, has been proven effective against lice on domestic animals; however, it is not yet registered for use on humans.

Most soaps kill all stages of the louse except the eggs. Two treatments, applied a week apart, will kill existing non-egg stages. Each shampoo will also kill young lice hatching from eggs. Thus, two to four weekly shampoos should theoretically kill all lice. Unfortunately, some lice may survive the shampoo, or the child may become reinfested right after a shampoo. Therefore, shampooing should be combined with combing (see the sidebar on the facing page). In addition, every effort should be made to educate the child as described on p. 174.

2. **Pyrethrins, Pyrethroids and Lindane.** If you decide to use an insecticide, you will be faced with the choice of a pyrethrin, a synthetic pyrethroid, or lindane (gammabenzene hexachloride). Table 11.3 below compares the effectiveness of these insecticides. For many years, lindane (Kwell®) was the treatment of choice; it is still recommended by some medical personnel who have not taken the time to acquaint themselves with its potential health hazards to humans. It is available only by prescription. We do not recommend its use.

Table 11.3
Comparison of the Effectiveness of Insecticides Against Lice[a]

Generic Name	Brand Name	Lice Killing Time	% Eggs Killed	% Lice Killed in 7 Days	% Lice Killed in 14 Days
lindane	Kwell®	several hours	45-70	91.9	85.2
synergized natural pyrethrin	Rid®, Barc®, R&C Shampoo®, A-200 Pyrinate®	10-23 min.	70-80	85.0	62.0
synthetic pyrethroid	NIX™ (permethrin)	10-15 min.	70-80	85.0	62.0

[a] Adapted from Taplin and Meinking, 1988.

According to a 1989 report by the U.S. Department of Health and Human Services, there is evidence that lindane is a carcinogen.

The pyrethrins and permethrin (a synthetic pyrethroid) are safer and more effective than lindane (see Chapter 7 for more details on these insecticides). In a 1988 study by David Taplin and Terri Meinking, four pyrethrin products killed all the lice within 10 to 23 minutes, whereas lindane took up to three hours to do the same thing. And subjects treated with lindane complained about the sensations caused by the twitching of slowly dying lice on their scalps.

When permethrin-treated subjects were compared to lindane-treated subjects 14 days after treatment, 97% of the permethrin subjects were louse-free, compared to only 43% of the lindane subjects and 6% of the placebo-treated subjects. In addition, permethrin killed 70% of the nits, whereas lindane killed only 45%, and the placebo, 14%. Because of its residual activity, permethrin treatments last longer than those involving either natural pyrethrins synergized with piperonyl butoxide or lindane. Pyrethrins are available over the counter in pharmacies; permethrin is available by prescription.

As mentioned earlier, there is evidence that some head-lice populations are already resistant to lindane, and there is every reason to assume that with increasing use of pyrethrins and pyrethroids, resistance to these will develop, too. This is another reason why other approaches should be tried first; pesticides should only be used when other methods don't work.

If and when resistance to pyrethrins and pyrethroids does occur, Cuprex® (copper oleatetetra hydronaphthalene) may come into use. Malathion powder or lotion has also been recommended on occasion. However, we do not recommend either material as long as insecticidal soaps or pyrethrins remain effective.

In using any poison, it is essential that you follow label directions exactly. Never re-treat with the chemical more frequently than the label allows. We would add the following cautions to those already on the label:
• Never treat infants with toxic insecticides, especially lindane.
• Minimize body exposure. Confine the insecticide to the head hair. Do not use a pesticide in the bath water or during a shower; use a basin or sink so pesticide residues do not reach other parts of the body. Wear rubber gloves to protect yourself if you are shampooing someone else.
• Minimize frequency of use. Regular or repeated use of insecticides, particularly lindane, on the heads of children can be dangerous. Many people, unaware of lindane's side effects, use it or recommend its use more often than eight days apart at higher dosages for longer periods over larger body surfaces than the label recommends. This practice constitutes a misuse of the insecticide and a risk to those exposed that is out of proportion to the hazard posed by the lice.
• Never apply an insecticide to anyone who has open cuts, scratches or head or neck inflammations. Check for such conditions before treatment.

Summary: Least-Toxic Head Lice Control

• Educate yourself, your child and others about the biology of head lice, the probability of infestations (which is always high) and appropriate nontoxic methods for eliminating the problem.

• When head-lice infestations are common at school, check your child's head nightly with a bright light and comb. Begin treatment with soap shampoos and combing as soon as infestations are detected.

• Provide each child with separate storage space for head coverings or other clothing at home and at school.

• Do not use pesticides in locker areas or other places where lice-infested children may come into contact with treated surfaces.

• Wash the bedding and clothing of the infested child or place them in a clothes dryer at the hottest setting at the same time treatment of the hair and scalp is undertaken. Dry-clean garments that cannot be washed. Note, however, that where time and energy are limited, you should concentrate on inspection and combing rather than on extra washing of clothing and bedding.

• Follow a program that combines hot shampoos with soap and combing out lice every week for at least three weeks. A specially designed head-lice comb should be used.

• Use insecticidal preparations only as a last resort after combing and shampooing with soap have proven ineffective.

• Pyrethrin-based pediculicides are less hazardous to humans than those containing lindane.

• Do not use lindane more than twice in any eight-day period.

Warning: Confusing nonviable eggs with living nits is common, as is prescribing insecticides over the phone without any inspection of the scalp or eggs with a lens or microscope. Both situations may result in unnecessary exposure to a pesticide and should not be tolerated.

• Store insecticides out of reach of young children, ideally in a locked cabinet. Treat insecticides as you would any other hazardous material.

• Do not use any head-lice insecticide preventively. Before you undertake any treatment, make sure live head lice or viable eggs are present. This is particularly important if you plan to use a toxic material.

• Never treat with lindane following a warm bath. If you feel you must use lindane, remember that it is absorbed through the skin and gets into the bloodstream; once absorbed, it can be carried throughout the body to tissues and organs. In a pregnant woman, it can even be carried across the placenta to the developing fetus. Absorption is greater when the skin is warm and blood vessels are dilated. There is no need for a bath prior to treatment. If you decide to use lindane, apply it to dry, cool skin.

PUBLIC LICE
(Family Phthiridae:
Phthirus pubis)

Pubic lice, also called crab lice, are a much rarer affliction than head lice, but infestations are becoming more common, perhaps because of changing sexual mores. Estimates indicate that 12 million cases occur in the United States annually. Young adults are the most commonly affected.

Pubic lice, like the closely related body and head lice, are generally found only on humans. They are transmitted primarily by sexual contact. Transmission to humans from objects such as sheets, blankets and toilet seats, or from mothers to children, is much less common. There is no evidence to date that pubic lice transmit human pathogens (disease-causing agents), but this louse is poorly studied compared to head and body lice.

Pubic lice are frequently associated with other sexually transmitted diseases. Therefore, if you discover that you have pubic lice, you should also seek medical attention to determine whether you have other common venereal diseases.

As with head lice, the most common treatment for pubic lice has been the use of the insecticide lindane (Kwell®). However, pyrethrins and synthetic pyrethroids are equally effective and much less toxic (see chemical controls on p. 180). Unfortunately, the embarrassment of having pubic lice can cause people to avoid seeking medical attention at all. The horror that people may feel on hearing the diagnosis also may discourage rational questioning of the toxicity of prescribed cures. It is recorded that women seek medical advice earlier than do men—perhaps they also can take the lead in pursuing least-toxic management.

Biology

Adult pubic lice inhabit the pubic areas, including the perianal region, the thighs and the abdomen. They are found less commonly in the armpits, and even more rarely in other hairy parts of the body, including the mustache, beard, eyelashes and head. These lice are less mobile than body and head lice, and they often remain attached at one point for days with their mouthparts in the skin.

Six to eight days are spent in the egg stage. After hatching, pubic lice pass through three more stages, each with a duration of about four to seven days. There is a molt at each stage, then they are adults, and they live for another month at the most. In all, it takes about 23 days from egg to adult —eight days for egg incubation, plus three stages of about five days each. Mating takes place during the ensuing 12 days, after which the eggs are laid. The females then cement 75 to 90 eggs to pubic hairs.

Most adults survive no more than one day after being removed from the host. But there are records of *Phthirus* being found on toilet seats and in beds, and there is also the possibility, however small, that lice or their eggs might be spread by loose hairs dropped from infested persons.

Damage

No diseases are known to be transmitted by pubic lice; however, the species is poorly studied, and there is always some risk when any blood-sucking species feeds. The inflammation that results from the injection of saliva causes intense itching, or pruritus, and can lead to further irritation when the wound is scratched. A skin discoloration can result if the infestation continues for some time.

Detection and Monitoring

The first symptom of pubic lice is usually an itch with subsequent scratching. The scratching can lead to a localized eczematous condition: red itching skin with oozing lesions that become scaly, crusted or hardened. Some people are relatively insensitive to the bites; in others, however, they can produce small, irregularly shaped blue spots. The spots, which appear some hours after the louse bites, are painless. They do not disappear when pressure is applied, and seem to be in the deeper skin layers.

Flecks of rust-colored excreta from the lice and excoriations from the scratching can indicate an infestation, as do dark specks on underclothes or tiny dandruff-like flakes among the pubic hairs. Finding the characteristic adult lice attached close to the base of the pubic hairs is the definitive indication of phthiriasis (the technical name for an infestation of pubic lice). The louse can be overlooked quite easily, so if intense itching occurs in the pubic area, the inspection should be very thorough.

Treatment:
Indirect Strategies

The stigma associated with pests of the pubic region is undoubtedly a product of a philosophy that views sex as sinful or dirty except when engaged in after a marriage ceremony sanctified by a religion. Adopting that view, any pests of the body transmitted through "immoral" sexual or intimate contact are doomed to be considered as shameful as the activity through which they were acquired. The taboos associated with the discussion of these pests—or even thinking about them privately—may delay diagnosis and treatment. Presumably, the extra suffering caused thereby is regarded as justified punishment by those who subscribe to the belief system just described.

If you do not subscribe to that belief system, spare yourself the unnecessary distress. These infestations are spread by contact with other humans just as is the common cold. There is no reason to delay treatment or accept a more-toxic treatment because you're too uncomfortable to discuss less-toxic alternatives. Moreover, you will need to warn those with whom you have had intimate contact so they can treat themselves before they spread the organism further.

Treatment:
Direct Physical Controls

Because pubic lice are occasionally found off the body on clothing and bedding, these should be washed in soapy water that is as hot as you can get it. Sexual partners, or others sharing sleeping quarters even briefly, should also launder their clothing. Placing clothing in a clothes dryer at the hottest setting for 30 minutes should kill all stages of lice.

If only a few pubic lice are present on the body, simply shaving the affected area and then washing the skin vigorously each day with hot soapy water may eliminate the lice. Coconut- or olive-oil-based soaps have insecticidal properties and should be used when available. Small infestations may also be combed out. Major Dale R. Westrom, M.D., from the Veterans' Administration's Letterman General Hospital in San Francisco, advises us that a solution of one part vinegar and one part water may soften the glue holding the eggs to the hair and make them easier to comb out.

Treatment:
Direct Chemical Controls

Lindane (Kwell®), long the most commonly prescribed treatment for pubic lice, is absorbed into the skin and constitutes an unnecessary hazard, given the alternatives. In recent studies, Rid®, a nonprescription liquid pediculicide containing 0.3% pyrethrins synergized by 3.0% piperonyl butoxide, was shown to be as effective as the more widely used lindane product. The pyrethrin solution does not penetrate the skin to the same degree and is faster-acting than lindane. A single 10-minute application of the pyrethrin liquid produced the same results as a single 12-hour application of the lindane solution. No side effects were observed in those treated with the pyrethrin product. Sexual partners should also be treated.

At the time of writing, NIX™, a synthetic pyrethroid product with the active ingredient permethrin, has been approved for head-lice treatment. It should also prove effective against pubic lice.

In the occasional instances where pubic lice infest the eyelashes, petrolatum jelly (Vasoline®) should be applied twice a day for a week, and the nits physically removed from the lashes. (This is also the advice of Major Westrom.)

Summary: Least-Toxic Pubic Lice Control

• If your pubic area itches, seek diagnosis immediately; there is no reason to suffer unnecessarily. Moreover, if you wait, you may infect others. Note, however, that itching does not necessarily indicate pubic lice—there are other, noninfectious causes of itching in this area.

• If pubic lice are diagnosed, wash bedding and clothing and/or place them in a hot clothes dryer at the same time you apply an insecticide to your pubic area.

• Pyrethrin pediculicides or the pyrethroid NIX™ are more effective than lindane (gammabenzene hexachloride) and are less toxic. Pyrethrins are available over the counter in local drug stores; NIX™ is available by prescription.

• Make sure your sexual partner(s) are alerted to the problem, educated about the organism and treated, if necessary.

REFERENCES AND READINGS

Keh, B. 1979. Answers to some questions frequently asked about pediculosis. *California Vector Views*, 26(5/6): 51-62.

A short review of all three human-lice species, with a discussion of the use of combs, lindane resistance and the ineffectiveness of treating the surrounding environment. This paper also indicates that eggs more than ¼ in. (6 mm) from the scalp do not survive.

Kluge, H.A. 1980. Management of head lice: an integrated approach. (Anoplura: Pediculidae) *Pest Management Papers*, No. 20. Burnaby, British Columbia: Simon Fraser University. 70 pp.

A comprehensive review of the literature on head lice.

Newson, J.H., J.L. Fiore, and E. Hackett. 1979. Treatment of infestation with *Phthirus pubis*: Comparative efficacies of synergized pyrethrins and gammabenzene hexachloride. *Sexually Transmitted Diseases* 6(3): 203-205.

This article presents the results of comparative studies of 30 outpatient adults aged 18 to 46 who were treated with 0.3% pyrethrins synergized by 3.0% piperonlyl butoxide (Rid® and 1% gammabenzene hexachloride (Kwell®). The results indicate that a single 10-minute application of the pyrethrin liquid produces the same results as a single 12-hour application of lindane.

Solomon, L.M., and D.P. West. 1977. Gamma benzene hexachloride toxicity. *Arch. Dermatol.* 113:353-357.

This paper reviews toxicity studies on laboratory animals and on humans. It also makes suggestions on how to minimize the use of lindane.

Taplin, D., and T.L. Meinking. 1988. *Head lice infestation: biology, diagnosis, management.* Miami: University of Miami School of Medicine. 31 pp.

A well-illustrated pamphlet on head lice and their management. Well-referenced studies compare pyrethrins, pyrethroids and lindane.

United States Department of Health and Human Services. 1989. *Fifth annual report on carcinogens: Summary 1989.* Washington, D.C.: U.S. Department of Health and Human Services. 340 pp. (Available from: Public Information Office, National Toxicology Program, B2-04, P.O. Box 12233, Research Triangle Park, NC 27709.)

The section on lindane and related compounds indicates that there is sufficient evidence that these compounds are carcinogens.

Zinsser, H. 1934. *Rats, lice, and history.* New York: Little Brown. 301 pp.

This book has become a parasitological classic. It is the first and best-known popular book to attempt to link the modern medical understanding of disease with historical events, and it is full of entertaining philosophical musings.

CHAPTER 12
Bedbugs and Conenose Bugs

INTRODUCTION

Evolutionary history appears to have begun with the emergence of large molecules with lifelike characteristics. From these macromolecules arose the microbes. Some of these developed the ability to fix sugars from sunlight and gave rise to the organisms we know as plants. Others, dependent on these sunlight-fixers for the manufacture of critical nutrients, became the plant-eaters or herbivores. Organisms that developed the ability to feed on the herbivores were the carnivores, or predators, and the parasites. Some of these became specialists in feeding on the carnivores themselves; we call these secondary carnivores. The scabies mites and head lice we discussed in chapters 10 and 11 are secondary carnivores because they feed on humans, who are primary carnivores.

This evolutionary overview is important, because understanding something about the evolution of blood-sucking insects like bedbugs and conenose bugs helps us figure out where to look for their other hosts. This in turn may help us eliminate infestations.

Blood-sucking insects probably evolved from carnivorous species that fed on other insects and then adapted to feed on mammals when mammals evolved. It is likely that some predatory insect with piercing mouthparts, such as the assassin bug that feeds upon a wide variety of insects, explored the skin of a vertebrate, possibly a young bird in a nest. After accidentally piercing the skin, the predator found the liquid beneath to its liking. This seems a highly plausible story, since many of the predatory bugs do indeed bite humans at times. Even plant-feeding "bugs" occasionally bite humans, probably in response to the moisture on our skin.

It is more likely that a predacious species gave rise to the ancestors of the bedbugs and conenose bugs, because animal tissues are more like human blood than are plant tissues.

A simple comparison between insect blood and plant fluids shows that insect blood has a greater amount of protein (in the form of amino acids). An accidental feeder might have gained an advantage from its occasional blood meals and increased its reproductive rate compared to closely related species that did not enjoy such a concentrated food source. Later, a species that could live on blood alone evolved from this accidental blood-feeder.

Thus, it is plausible that a stink-bug-like organism (a general plant-feeder) evolved into an assassin-bug-like organism (a general predator), and then into our present conenose bug, which is still dependent on finding the blood of another mammal in order to feed and reproduce. A similar line can be drawn upward along another evolutionary stem to the bedbugs, which are more advanced than the conenose bugs as they do not fly. Human bedbugs live primarily on human blood, whereas conenose bugs also frequently feed on wild species, especially rodents.

The two groups of biting bugs discussed in this chapter are intermittent blood-feeders. Both live relatively free of their hosts, visiting them only for an occasional meal. In this respect, they are more like micropredators that feed on blood than true parasites. Both can become residents of our bedrooms, and both can obtain blood from other mammals. Conenose bugs, however, are more opportunistic than bedbugs, commonly feeding on a wider range of other domestic species.

The blood-feeder that switches hosts is the greater health hazard, because it has the potential to transfer new microbial pathogens among different host organisms. Parasitologists know that it is the new pathogens that are the killers, not the parasites that have long been associated with their hosts. The host population has developed a means of dealing with the parasites. But the new pathogens can devastate a host population.

BEDBUGS
(Family Cimicidae: *Cimex lectularius* and other *Cimex, Oeciacus* and *Haematosiphon* spp.)

Some 74 bug species in the family Cimicidae are known to feed on humans and many species of bats and birds. Both bat bedbugs and human bedbugs feed on humans and bats. Some scientists speculate that bedbugs first evolved from bat bedbugs to feed on humans when humans were cave-dwellers. Others believe that human bedbugs evolved from bat bedbugs some time after bats adapted themselves to roost in human dwellings such as barns, churches and houses.

Bedbugs are not a common problem today, although they were severe 50 years ago. But infestations do still occur. As human populations increase, and cities with their attendant decay and squalor grow larger, we can expect bedbugs to become more common. (It should be noted, however, that slums are not a prerequisite for bedbugs.)

It is important to realize that species related to the human bedbug—swallow bedbugs, bat bedbugs, pigeon bedbugs and chicken bedbugs—also bite humans. Although bedbugs have long been associated with poor housekeeping, the original cause of a bedroom infestation may not be lack of cleanliness. The infestation may be associated with birds nesting on the exterior of the house, bats in the attic or a nearby chicken house. Information about the human bedbug and related species is summarized in Table 12.1 on p. 184.

Biology

All bugs in the family Cimicidae are wingless. The common bedbug rides from place to place on clothing, in baggage, in bedding, on beds and on furniture. Public places such as theaters, buses, trains and laundromats are common avenues for distribution. The bugs can also migrate actively from house to house and be-

Table 12.1
Common Blood-Sucking Bugs in the Family Cimicidae

Common Name	Scientific Name	Primary Host	Other Hosts	Distribution
African bedbug	*Leptocimex boueti*	humans	bats	tropical Africa
bat bug	*Cimex pilosellus*	bats	humans	North America
bat bug	*C. pipistrelli*	bats	humans	Europe
common bedbug	*C. lectularius*	humans	bats, chickens	worldwide
Indian bedbug	*C. hemipterus*	humans	chickens, bats	tropics
Mexican chicken bedbug	*Haematosiphon buginodorus*	great horned owl, California condor	chickens, eagles, humans	southwestern U.S. and Mexico
pigeon bug	*C. columbarius*	pigeons	humans	Europe
swallow bug	*Oeciacus hirundinis*	swallows	humans	Old World
swallow bug	*O. vicarius*	swallows	humans	New World

The Common Bedbug
The tiny, reddish-brown adult bedbug (A) lays her white eggs (B) in batches of 10 to 50 on bedding and in cracks and crevices on beds and adjacent walls. The young hatch in about 10 days and use their beak-like mouthparts to extract blood meals from hosts. It takes one to two months for eggs to mature into adults. Adults live another eight to nine months. (Actual size of adult: ⅛ in./5 mm)

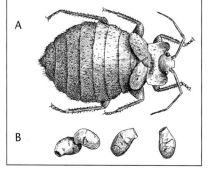

A

B

tween apartments by way of water pipes, wall voids and ducts. They may wander when apartments are vacated and hosts are unavailable. Travelers from hot countries where bedbugs are more prevalent may import them in luggage. Within a living unit, bedbugs are almost exclusively confined to bedrooms.

The adults are about ⅛ in. (5 mm) long. From above, they appear flattened and elliptical, and the head has beak-like mouthparts (see the drawing at left). They are reddish brown, but turn blood-colored after feeding. Nymphs are yellowish until they feed, after which they resemble animated drops of blood. Nymphs and adults generally feed during the night when the host sleeps, although they can also feed in subdued daylight. They engorge themselves with blood in 3 to 10 minutes, and feed an average of 45 times to reach maturity. During development they can feed daily, but once they become adults they feed less frequently.

Bedbugs hide in crevices during the day. Although capable of traveling considerable distances for blood meals, in their active stages they normally lodge as close as possible to their sleeping hosts. Favorite hiding places include seams of mattresses, cracks in the bed frame, and within box springs. The species is gregarious—eggs, nymphs and adults are all found together, sometimes in great numbers.

The female deposits small, white, elongated eggs in batches of 10 to 50. A total of 200 to 500 eggs are laid, with an average of 345. Given adequate food (two meals per week) egg-laying is almost continuous at about three eggs per day. As eggs are deposited, they are covered with a thin, quick-drying glue that cements them to various inanimate surfaces. About 10 days later (with a range of 4 to 21 days, depending on temperature), the young hatch and begin searching for a blood meal. Five molts, or 37 to 128 days later, they become adults and mate. One to two months with adequate food is required for an egg to mature into a fertile egg-laying adult.

Bedbugs at any stage of development are capable of withstanding starvation for 80 to 140 days; however, older stages are most starvation-resistant. With adequate food and normal development, the adult stage lives about 10 months. In unheated buildings without food, adults can live a year or longer. (It is an interesting characteristic of many blood-feeding organisms that they can actually live longer without food.)

Bedbugs are sensitive to extremes of heat and cold. If temperatures rise above 97°F (36°C) or drop below 48°F (9°C) they die. One physical control treatment (described on p. 186) is based on increasing or decreasing the room temperature.

Damage

As with other blood-sucking species, the bites of bedbugs produce a range of reactions in humans from virtually none at all to considerable pain and swelling. The welts and local inflammation are caused by an allergic reaction to an anticoagulant enzyme secreted by the bedbug's salivary glands and injected during feeding. Some people suffer from interrupted sleep caused by the irritation. Persistent feeding by large populations has been observed to reduce the hemoglobin count in affected persons.

In the laboratory, the bedbug has been shown to have the capacity to harbor and transmit many human pathogens. But in actual field settings, transmission of pathogens has not been confirmed; consequently, the bedbug is not now regarded as a vector of human disease. Suspicions remain, however, and repeated bites should not be tolerated.

Detection and Monitoring

In heavily infested rooms, bedbugs produce a characteristic disagreeable pungent odor. Clusters of tiny eggs in cracks and blood or fecal spots on sheets and pillow cases are other indicators of bedbug activity. Bedbugs have been found hiding alongside waterbed mattresses, so you should inspect small, warm spaces where they can congregate. Also look for eggs, nymphs, adults and/or black feces in cracks and spaces in the bed frame and bedstead, along baseboards, around windows and door frames, in picture frames, behind moldings, in light fixtures, under loose wallpaper and under upholstery. A flashlight helps during inspections and in catching adult bedbugs at night (they can move along at about 8 in./20 cm per minute).

Pest control experts sometimes use pyrethrin sprays to flush out insects during inspections. The spray infiltrates the smallest cracks and irritates the bugs so that they leave their harborage; it also kills many of them. However, use of this material should be considered only after other approaches have failed to locate the insects. Nonprofessionals can undertake this procedure, too, but must follow closely the safety precautions outlined on pp. 97-103.

If wingless bedbug-like specimens are found feeding in a bedroom, consider the possibility that they are ectoparasites that have moved in from a bat roost or bird nest elsewhere in the house. The bedbug species should be identified, which usually requires a specialist. Ask for help from your state or county public-health department. Some professional pest control operators also may be able to make identifications or give you the name of a specialist who can. Of course, evidence like a bat roost or bird's nest near the infested site is important in the analysis, particularly if bedbugs are found in the roost or nest as well.

Treatment: Indirect Strategies

To decide which strategy to pursue to reduce the infestation, you must first determine which species of bug is present. If the source of the infestation is a bird nest, bat roost or chicken house, you should consider eliminating or moving these animals' habitats. Alternatively, you can try to prevent the animals from gaining access to your house. An example of the first solution is changing the eaves or ornaments of the exterior of the house to discourage birds from nesting there; an example of the second solution is "tightening up" an attic so bats cannot enter (see p. 308).

If the culprit is the human bedbug, an intensive effort should be made to caulk and paint the bed and immediate environment so that all cracks and hiding places are sealed or eliminated. The procedures followed are exactly the same as those used to reduce cockroach habitats (see pp. 223-224).

Treatment: Direct Physical Controls

Bedbugs can be controlled directly by creating barriers, cleaning and/or replacing furnishings and modifying room temperature.

1. Barriers. Simple barriers can be employed to deny bedbugs access to beds. When using such barriers, however, be sure no portion of the bed is touching a wall, which would allow the bedbugs alternate access to the bed.

On a short-term emergency basis, the legs of an infested bed can be placed in containers such as cat-food cans that are filled with soapy water. This should be done after you have cleaned the bed of bugs by hand-picking or vacuuming, or if you suspect that there are bedbugs in the room even though you do not yet have direct evidence. The water-filled containers act as barriers, keeping bedbugs and other crawling pests from migrating into the bed at night. You might well encounter such situations when traveling in underdeveloped countries or even in poorly maintained motels in the United States. An emergency barrier can be made by coating the bed legs for a few inches with petroleum jelly.

Alternatively, the legs of the bed can be set into clean glass jars or polished metal cans. The bedbugs' feet, or tarsi, have claws that are useful in climbing vertical surfaces like paper, plaster or wood, but cannot cling to clean glass or polished metal.

Caulking cracks along moldings, floors and the bed frame also provides a barrier to bedbug movement and habitation. Another temporary means of avoiding these bugs is to sleep in a hammock while solving the problem with other methods.

2. Cleaning and/or Replacing Furnishings. Infested mattresses and beds should be replaced, steam-cleaned or taken outdoors for treatment with insecticides. Launder or dry-clean sheets and blankets. When transporting infested materials, enclose them in plastic bags to prevent inadvertent introduction of bugs into other areas. Second-hand furniture and appliances, particularly those from infested dwellings, should be steam-cleaned before being brought to clean locations. These measures are similar to those taken to prevent importation of cockroach egg cases from areas suspected of being infested (see pp. 223-224).

3. Exposure to Heat or Cold. Because bedbugs are very sensitive to heat at all stages of their development, artificially raising the temperature for several days within the room may be helpful as part of an overall strategy to eliminate the pest. The thermal death point for the common bedbug is 111°F to 113°F (44°C to 45°C); temperatures of 97°F to 99°F (36°C to 37°C) kill large numbers of the bug. Raising room temperature to these levels by using a high thermostat setting and supplemental heaters for an hour or so would probably eliminate an infestation.

Bedbugs are also killed by prolonged exposure to low temperatures (32°F to 48°F/0°C to 9°C). Eggs die at these temperatures within 30 to 60 days, although adults and nymphs die within hours. Thus, closing off an infested bedroom and leaving it unheated in cold weather might also eradicate a bedbug infestation.

Treatment:
Direct Biological Controls

Numerous house predators, such as spiders, mites and other bugs (including the reduviids, which are related to the conenose bugs discussed below), will prey on bedbugs, but there are two species of ants in the United States that can totally wipe out bedbug infestations when they find them. These are the pharaoh ant *(Monomorium pharaonis)* and the Argentine ant *(Iridomyrmex humulis)*. Unfortunately, the prejudice against ants in the house is so great that it seems doubtful that many people would tolerate them long enough for them to eliminate an infestation.

Treatment:
Direct Chemical Controls

The chemicals commonly recommended for bedbug control include insecticidal sprays with malathion, dichlorvos, ronnel or triclorophon. None of these is recommended here, because most infestations do not require their use. If insecticide treatments are judged necessary, we recommend instead the use of natural pyrethrum and related compounds, insecticidal soaps and sorptive dusts.

1. Pyrethrum and Related Compounds. Natural pyrethrum, pyrethrin and synthetic pyrethroids (e.g., permethrin) are less toxic to humans, pets and other mammals than other insecticides registered for bedbugs. (For details on these materials, see pp. 121-122; for sources, see the Resource Appendix under "Insect Management: Chemical Controls" on pp. 686-687.) Liquid or powder formulations can be used to treat infestations in seams of mattresses, box springs and other hard-to-reach areas.

Summary: Least-Toxic Bedbug Control

- Identify the type of bedbug.
- Steam-clean mattresses and used bedroom furnishings; launder bedding.
- Apply temporary barriers to bed legs.
- Caulk cracks in and around the bed and around wall moldings.
- If the bedbugs are other than human bedbugs, remove associated animal nests, roosts or access routes.
- If an insecticide is needed, the following are recommended (least toxic listed first): insecticidal soap, silica aerogel (with or without pyrethrin), natural pyrethrum, permethrin.

2. Soaps and Sorptive Dusts. An insecticidal soap, a strong cleaning solution made from soapy ammonia or a sorptive dust such as silica aerogel can also be used against bedbug infestations. For details on these materials, see Chapter 7 ; for sources, see the Resource Appendix under "Insect Management: Chemical Controls" on pp. 686-687.

CONENOSE BUGS
(Family Reduviidae, *Triatoma* spp.)

Conenose, or kissing, bugs are found in the western and southern United States and Central and South America. In Spanish-speaking areas, the bugs are called "vinchuca," "pito," "chinche," "chupon" and "chirmacha." Conenose bugs are blood-sucking species that feed on humans and a wide variety of domestic and wild animals. The common name "conenose" describes the elongated cone-shaped head characteristic of this group and the closely related predatory assassin bugs. The latter are all beneficial predators of other insects; however, a few of these beneficials can also inflict a painful bite if handled roughly.

Conenose bugs cause concern because they carry *Trypanosoma cruzi*, the agent of American sleeping sickness, which is also called Chagas' disease after Carlos Chagas, who discovered and described it in 1909. The protozoan pathogen *T. cruzi* is maintained in wild populations of various mammals, including marsupials, bats, rodents, rabbits, carnivores and primates. Probably the most important reservoir is the opossum, but in some areas, such as Texas, armadillos are more frequent carriers. Many parts of the United States are home to both conenoses and the pathogen *T. cruzi*, but, luckily, the disease is rarely encountered in the United States (the few reported cases have been in Texas and California).

T. cruzi is found in the feces of the bug; it is not transmitted directly

Table 12.2
Common Conenose Bugs Found in Houses in the United States[a]

Species	Common host and *T. cruzi* carrier	Range
Triatoma sanguisuga	raccoons, opossums, wood rats (*Neotoma* spp.)	Maryland south to Florida, west to Arizona
T. protracta	wood rats (*Neotoma* spp.)	Colorado and Utah, west to California, south to Arizona, New Mexico and Texas
T. gerstaeckeri	wood rats (*Neotoma* spp.)	New Mexico, Texas
T. lecticularia	wood rats (*Neotoma* spp.)	Pennsylvania south to Florida, west to California

[a] From Mallis, 1982.

The Conenose Bug

Adult conenose bugs are brown with yellowish-red markings on the abdomen and wing tips. They use their beak-like mouthparts to extract blood meals from hosts. Their conical heads and straight beaks give them their name. (Actual size of adult: ½ in. to 1 in./13 mm to 25 mm)

through the bite. The reason the disease is so rare in the United States but common and serious in Central and South America is thought to lie in the difference in behavior between species of bugs carrying the protozoan in these different areas. The most important vectors of the disease tend to defecate immediately after feeding. The human victim then scratches the bite, contaminating the fingers, which carry the trypanosome to the eye, nose, mouth or fresh wound. In contrast, the four most common carriers of the pathogen in the United States do not defecate immediately after biting, so inoculation through contaminated feces is much less likely.

Table 12.2 above summarizes the distribution and primary hosts of the four common conenose bugs found in the United States. Keep in mind that all of these bugs probably also feed on other vertebrates, such as rats, chickens, dogs, horses and many wild animals.

Even though Chagas' disease has so far proven rare in the United States, many people are hypersensitive to conenose bites, which cause reactions similar to severe reactions from other insect stings or bites. Even in people who are not hypersensitive, the bite may raise a substantial welt and itch for several days in the manner of a bad mosquito bite. These reactions are discussed in detail in the sidebar on pp. 188-189.

Biology

Adult conenose bugs (see the drawing below, left) are relatively large— ½ in. to 1 in. (13 mm to 25 mm) long —and dark brown with yellowish-red markings on the abdomen and wing tips. Their conical heads and straight beaks give them their name. They appear in the spring, lay eggs in summer, pass the winter as developing nymphs and molt into adults the following spring. Two generations per year are possible in some warm areas. Eggs are laid in crevices in and around nests of various host animals. The nymphs that hatch from these eggs require one full blood meal during each of their five stages until the winged adult stage is reached; however, they also prey on other insects. Both males and females suck blood.

There have been detailed laboratory studies of *Rodnius prolixus*, an important vector of Chagas' disease in Central and South America and a relative of the house-invading *Triatoma* spp. in the United States. Much of the information on the biology of all conenose bugs is based on these studies, because the two genera are assumed to be very similar.

According to one study, a single female *R. prolixus* specimen laid 701 eggs in 240 days while eating 26 blood meals. Adults take 20 to 30 minutes to complete a blood meal, and the bite is painless to humans. The egg incubation period is about 10 days at 93°F (34°C) . Blood-feeding occurs at night; during the day, the nymphs and adults form aggregations and hide. The bugs are found primarily in suburban areas near parks and other sites where they find non-human hosts; they are seldom if ever found in downtown areas. The adults are attracted to light at night.

Damage

Most persons feel nothing at the time of a conenose bite, but local reactions such as reddening, swelling or itching follow. About 5% of those bitten react severely when bitten a second time, having been sensitized by the

Conenose Bites: Allergic Reactions, Treatment, Chagas' Disease

I. Allergic Reactions to Conenose Bug Bites [a]

Allergic reactions to the bite of conenose bugs can vary from local mild itching to anaphylactic reactions such as shock, hives, fainting, vomiting, generalized itching, swelling of the eyes, angioneurotic edema, and tongue and laryngeal edema with difficulty in swallowing, speaking and breathing. Hypersensitive persons should have an arthropod anaphylaxis kit close at hand (see the Resource Appendix under "Insect Management: Chemical Controls" on pp. 686-687).

The bites can also produce the following types of skin lesions:

- Papular lesions with a central spot (a papule is a small, solid, usually conical elevation of the skin)

- Blisters ⅘ in. to 1⅕ in. (2 cm to 3 cm) in diameter

- Large, itchy areas with extensive swelling

- Blood-filled nodular to bulbous lesions on the hands or feet

II. A Triatoma-Bite Desensitization Program (for Physicians) [b]

Cases of anaphylactic shock or other serious allergic reactions in individuals due to *Triatoma* (conenose bug) bites continue to increase as rural foothill areas are developed residentially. Fortunately, a successful method for diagnosis and treatment of susceptible patients using a *Triatoma* salivary-gland extract has been developed recently by Neil Marshall and Donald Street. This immunotherapy program is now available to California residents on a limited basis through Dr. Andrew Saxon, Chief of Clinical Immunology and Allergy at the UCLA School of Public Health (Los Angeles CA 90024; [213] 825-3718). All arrangements for testing and desensitization must be made between the patient's physician and Dr. Saxon.

III. Chagas' Disease [c]

Common Names: Chagas' disease, American trypanosomiasis.

Causal Pathogen: *Trypanosoma (Schizotrypanum) cruzi.*

[a] From Nichols and Green, 1963.

[b] From Marshall et al., 1986.

[c] From Harwood and James, 1979.

first bite. Symptoms of a severe systemic reaction include itching of the scalp, palms and soles of feet that lasts from 30 minutes to five hours. Swelling of the tongue, larynx and trachea can make speaking, breathing and swallowing difficult for 10 to 12 hours after a bite. A few people experience welts and rashes for several hours, or nausea, vomiting, body aches and pain, fever, cramps, diarrhea or fainting.

These various allergic reactions are discussed in the sidebar above. The sidebar surveys potential reactions to conenose bites, presents information for physicians on obtaining immunotherapy (if you are hypersensitive, you may want to draw this information to your physician's attention) and describes symptoms of Chagas' disease.

Detection and Monitoring

Conenose bugs may enter the house down chimneys or through floor cracks, broken window screens or other openings. Within human habitats, they seek low daytime light intensities. They hide in cracks or crevices around doors and window screens, behind the face plates of wall light switches (if these are not perfectly flush against the wall) and in furniture, closets and other dimly lit locations. If they have been feeding on a sleeping person, they may hide in the folds of blankets or under the mattress during the day.

Conenose bugs are relatively large —about ¾ in. (19 mm) long—and uniformly black. Sometimes they can be seen walking along the floor, especially on light-colored surfaces. It is

A Homemade Conenose Bug Trap

A small cardboard box with accordion-folded paper sheets inside can be attached to the wall above the bed with tape, tacks or nails to trap conenose bugs.

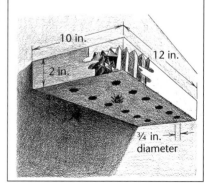

10 in.

12 in.

2 in.

¾ in. diameter

Potential Victims of Bites: Humans, dogs and other domestic and wild animals. There are about 100 recorded mammalian hosts.

Vectors (carriers): Mostly conenose bugs, especially *Panstrongylus megistus, Triatoma infestans, T. dimidiata* and *Rodnius prolixus.*

Reservoirs (where the disease is harbored): Asymptomatic humans; many mammals, including, in descending order of importance, opossums, armadillos, dogs, cats, rats, guinea pigs, mice, squirrels, bats, sloths and monkeys. Two South American lizard species are also known to become infected and are capable of passing the pathogen to the conenose bugs that feed on them.

Geographical Distribution: The American tropics and subtropics from northern Mexico (about 25°N latitude) to Rio Negro, Argentina (about 38°S latitude). However, some humans and mammals have been infected beyond these limits.

Importance: As of 1972, an estimated 10 million or more cases of the disease had occurred in South America, and cases have been recorded in Texas and other places along the United States' border with Mexico.

Symptoms: The most common external sign is unilateral swelling of the face or eyelid known as "the sign of Romana." High or moderate fever starts two weeks after the victim is bitten. Swelling of other body areas, including the adenoids, and sometimes nervous disorders are also present. If the patient recovers, chronic infection establishes itself four weeks later. The early acute and/or chronic phase may be asymptomatic. Cardiac damage, sudden death, loss of nervous control and injury to the alimentary tract can occur with chronic infections.

Transmission: Conenose bugs carrying the pathogen defecate during feeding, and the pathogen can be transferred by human fingers to the conjunctiva of the eyes or mucosa of the nose or mouth. From there, the pathogen enters the bloodstream. However, the pathogen can also be transmitted congenitally, through blood transfusions, through mothers' milk or by bug feces that drop onto victims' scratched, infected skin. Dogs, cats, raccoons and other animals can become infected by eating infected conenose bugs. The bugs themselves can become infected by feeding upon infected humans, pets, domestic animals, wild animals and other infected conenose bugs.

easier to spot them if you hold a flashlight nearly parallel to the floor, sweeping the beam across the surface; for this reason, floors without rugs or carpeting are easiest to monitor. If bugs are present, you will see their shadows. Your search should coincide with the most favorable temperatures for conenose activity: 60°F to 84°F (16°C to 29°C).

The western conenose species often moves very slowly and may be reluctant to fly; it is possible to capture bugs at night (we have done). You often awake as a bug is crawling up to begin feeding, or after it has just bitten. At that point, by throwing back the covers quickly and turning on a flashlight, you can usually find the bug and flick it into a jar filled with detergent water. You should kill the bug this way rather than crushing it with your fingers to avoid pathogens. Later, wash the container in which it was killed.

The box trap shown in the drawing on the facing page also works in detecting infestations. It can be made from a cardboard box 12 in. by 10 in. by 2 in. that is filled with six standard-bond paper sheets, each cut into four pieces and accordion-folded. Twelve holes, each about ¾ in. (19 mm) diameter, are made in the bottom of the box. The box is closed on top with adhesive tape and attached to the wall with nails, tape or picture-hanging hardware. The holes should face the floor. Bugs will hide in the folds during the day.

Since the average range of a conenose bug (*Rodnius prolixus* in this particular study) from its harborage is just under 7 ft. (2 m), the trap should be placed within a few feet of the bed. At least two boxes should be used per house, and they should be left in the house for about 28 weeks. The boxes should be inspected at night when the bugs are attracted to the house by its lights. Bugs, molted skins, eggs or feces in the trap are signs of bug presence.

Treatment:
Indirect Strategies
Treatment programs should include structural modifications to the building and preventive reduction of wild-animal nests. Bites should be washed with soap to remove bug feces. Hypersensitive persons should have an arthropod anaphylaxis kit close at

hand (for souces, see the Resource Appendix under "Insect Management: Chemical Controls" on pp. 686-687) and should make special efforts to protect themselves with mosquito netting at night until it is quite certain that the bedroom has been cleared of bugs and all entry points have been secured.

1. Placement of Outdoor Lghting. Conenose bugs are attracted to lights at night, so outdoor lighting should be installed away from doors. Where lighting is already near entrances, it should be used only briefly when necessary. For advice on catching bugs on screens at night, see "Direct Physical Controls," below.

2. Sealing and Caulking. To help prevent the entry and harborage of conenose bugs, seal the exterior skin of the dwelling, including windows, vent openings and the chimney, especially during warm weather when conenose bugs are active. Screens should be free of tears; gaps around doors and windows should be sealed with caulk such as silicone seal. Eliminate special pet entrances or weather-seal them.

3. Removal of Animal Nests and Nesting Material. Subfloors, attics and the exterior of the foundation should be checked carefully for rodent or other animal dens or nests; any wild animals or nests should be removed. Traps may aid in this effort. Piles of lumber, firewood, rock and miscellaneous debris should be cleared away from the house, since they can provide permanent or temporary refuge for the hosts of conenose bugs. Thinning shrubbery around the foundation may help, too.

If raccoons or opossums are seen frequently near your home, try to figure out what is attracting them, then eliminate the attractant or reduce access to it. For example, you can improve your outdoor garbage storage system (see pp. 630-631), remove pet food between feedings, collect fallen fruit, harvest ripe fruit promptly and install overhanging edges that protect fish in garden pools.

4. Mosquito Netting. Mosquito nets can be placed over beds to prevent bug access before or after the modifications suggested above have been made. Netting should be tucked in all around the mattress or sleeping pad, but it should not touch the sleeping person. When friends of ours were remodeling their bedroom in Sacramento Valley, California, they were attacked repeatedly by conenose bugs that had found their way into the house during construction. They solved the problem by sleeping in a small camping tent set up within the bedroom until they could finally "tighten" the house and eliminate the bugs that had already entered.

Treatment:
Direct Physical Controls

In many cases, the actual number of bugs entering the home is low, and they can be captured by hand or with the kind of trap recommended for detection on p. 189. During warm evenings in areas where these insects are known to be a problem, check the bed each night before going to sleep. Lift the mattress, looking under and around its edges, and check between all blankets and sheets. Keep a jar of soapy water handy to drop bugs into, or place them in an empty jar that you can later put in the freezer to kill them. Bear in mind that the bugs can bite if pinched or crushed, so any bugs that alight on your face or hands should be brushed gently into the jar. If they drop to the floor, you can crush them with your feet (assuming you're wearing shoes).

Because conenose bugs are attracted to light at night, it is not uncommon to find them on window screens and screen doors on warm summer evenings. Check screen doors before opening them to avoid admitting bugs. You can catch bugs on the outside of the screen by inverting a jar over them, then sliding a stiff piece of paper or a 3x5 index card between the lip of the jar and the screen until it scrapes the bug from the screen into the jar. Wash

out any container in which conenose bugs have been placed to remove feces and other contaminants.

Treatment:
Direct Chemical Controls

The non-chemical procedures outlined above should be sufficient to eliminate most conenose infestations. If you use insecticides without following the nonchemical strategies, you probably won't solve the problem. However, if after trying the nonchemical strategies you find them insufficient, follow the chemical-control recommendations listed under bedbugs on p. 186.

Summary: Least-Toxic Conenose Bug Control

• Seal or screen cracks and openings through which conenose bugs can enter.

• Put out traps to detect and catch bugs.

• Remove wild animals and their nests and clear debris from foundations, attics, basements and crawl spaces.

• Locate outdoor lighting away from doorways.

• Make a tent of mosquito netting over the bed if the entire bedroom cannot be made bug-tight.

• Check bedding before going to sleep each night.

• Use a flashlight to search for bugs on floors.

• Sleep with a flashlight and jar of soapy water near your bed.

REFERENCES AND READINGS

Agriculture Canada. 1981. *Control of bedbugs.* Ottawa: Information Services, Agriculture Canada (Publication 1293). 4 pp.

A succinct one-sheet flier on bedbugs and their management.

Brenner, R.R., and A. de la Merced Stoka, eds. 1987. *Chagas' disease vectors, Vols. I, II and III.* Boca Raton, Fla.: CRC Press. 155 pp.

These three volumes comprise the most comprehensive review of this disease currently in print.

Busvine, J.R. 1980. *Insects and hygiene: the biology and control of insect pests of medical and domestic importance.* 3rd ed. New York: Chapman and Hall. 568 pp.

This work is similar to the Harwood and James text listed below, but is written specifically for readers in the United Kingdom.

Gomez-Nunez, J.C. 1965. Desarolló de un nuevo metodo para evaluar la infestación intradomiciliaria por *Rodinus prolixus. Acta Cient. Venezuela* 16:26-31.

This paper (in Spanish) describes the conenose trap and its use.

Harwood, R.F., and M.T. James. 1979. *Entomology in human and animal health.* 7th ed. 548 pp.

This authoritative medical entomology text provides a good introduction to bedbugs and conenose bugs and their ecology.

Herms, W.B., and M.T. James. 1961. *Medical entomology.* New York: Macmillan. 616 pp.

This earlier edition of the Harwood and James text listed above has additional information about the control of bedbugs.

Mallis, A. 1982. *Handbook of pest control.* Cleveland: Franzak and Foster. 1,101 pp.

A standard reference text for urban pest control. It is full of useful information, although chemical controls receive the primary emphasis.

Marshall, N.A. 1982. Allergy to *Triatoma protracta* (Heteroptera: Reduviidae). II: antigen production in vitro. *Journal of Medical Entomololgy* 19(3):253-254.

The first description of growing insect tissues for antigenic properties on artificial hosts.

Marshall, N.A., et al. 1986. The prevalence of allergic sensitization to *Triatoma protracta* (Heteroptera: Reduviidae) in a Southern California, U.S.A., community. *Journal of Medical Entomology* 23(2):119-124.

In this article it is estimated that 30,000 people in California are at risk of serious or life-threatening reactions to the bite of conenose bugs.

Marshall, N.A., and D.H. Street. 1982. Allergy to *Triatoma protracta* (Heteroptera: Reduviidae). I: etiology, antigen preparation, diagnosis and immunotherapy. *Journal of Medical Entomololgy* 19(3):248-252.

A description of the successful use of a salivary gland extract in treating a woman with a hypersensitivity to *Triatoma* bites.

Miller, N.E. 1971. *The biology of the Heteroptera.* 2nd ed, rev. Hampton, England: E.W. Classey. 206 pp.

A good introduction to the biology and families of the Heteroptera that discusses evolutionary relationships between families.

Nichols, N., and T.W. Green. 1963. Allergic reactions to "kissing bug" bites. *Calif. Med.* 98:267-268.

A good source of additional information on allergies produced by conenose bites.

Usinger, R.L. 1944. *The Triatominae of North and Central America and the West Indies and their public health significance.* Rockville, Md.: United States Public Health Service (Public Health Reports Bulletin No. 288). 83 pp.

The authoritative taxonomic work on the Triatominae, with good information on their identification and distribution.

Wood, S. F. 1975. Home invasions of conenose bugs (Hemiptera: Reduviidae) and their control. *National Pest Control Operators News* 35:16-18.

An excellent survey of where conenose bugs are found in homes.

PART 5

Pests Inside the House

CHAPTER 13
Pests of Fabric, Feathers and Paper

OVERVIEW OF PART 5

Part 5 describes the management of some of the more common pests found on clothes and furnishings and in the kitchen and pantry. It also covers pests associated with dogs, cats and miscellaneous wildlife that become a nuisance when they find their way into the house.

Before looking at these pests individually, we will address two issues that affect them all: humidity and good housekeeping.

The Effect of Humidity on Indoor Pests

Humidity is a key factor in controlling pests indoors. Where it is extremely dry, cloth and other plant- or animal-derived materials can last centuries; where it is humid, pest problems multiply. The deserts and the tropics, with their respective paucity and multitude of living organisms, are the extremes that illustrate the effects of humidity on life forms.

In modern industrial nations we have available a variety of appliances and other means of dehumidifying our dwellings (as long as nonrenewable energy supplies hold out or can be switched to renewable sources). These technological solutions, along with house maintenance, repair and good initial design, can be crucial in managing a variety of pests, from the house dust mites we discussed in Chapter 10, to the indoor pests we cover in this part of the book and the pests of the house structure we discuss later.

Because we (and our house plants) like a certain amount of indoor humidity, we must strike a balance between our own physical comfort and the dryness that reduces pest problems. This can involve modifying the overall indoor environment, changing the climate in specific locations where the pest problem occurs or, even more locally, changing the moisture content of the materials that are affected or attacked by the pest. We discuss how this can be done throughout Part 5.

The Vacuum Cleaner: A Universally Useful Tool

The second important factor in controlling pests indoors is old-fashioned good housekeeping. In days past, control of household "vermin" was the main point of all the scrubbing, airing and repairing that made a 15-hour day for the conscientious homemaker—or kept a crew of servants working year-round for those in more fortunate circumstances (see the drawing at right). Although those days are gone for good—we hope—it is important to realize that modern pesticides contributed to their demise. So if you want to minimize the use of chemical pesticides, all members of your household must work cooperatively in a regimen of regular, constant home maintenance.

Toward that end, we must say a few words in praise of the vacuum cleaner. Through the attentive use of the vacuum you can learn where pests are, what they are living on and how you might change things to reduce their access to your home or specific items within it. Vacuuming around windows, doors, vents, rafters and eaves in the living and storage areas of the house helps reveal holes in the "skin" of the house that permit the entry of arthropods, rodents and other vertebrate pests. Often these cracks and crevices can be eliminated permanently through the use of caulk or paint inside or outside the house. It is also important to get into the habit of finding the little nooks and crannies where fabric lint, food particles, pet hair, human-skin dander and other miscellany accumulate, since these things are edible for a myriad of household pests. You may decide to eliminate certain furnishings because they are too difficult to keep clean.

Water vacuums (see the drawing at right) and dry vacuums with extremely fine filters, which were also discussed under house dust mites in Chapter 11, are the best kinds of vacuums to use because they do not spew out fine dust particles in their

Pest Control in the Middle Ages

In the late 1400s, professional beaters were employed in late August and early September to brush and beat furs and woolens to control clothes-moth larvae.

Source: Snetsinger, 1983.

Water Vacuum

Water vacuums are superior pest control tools because they trap dirt, dust and insects in a swirling water bath. Because they have no bag to hinder air flow, they are more powerful than ordinary vacuums and can suck up greater numbers of pests and the various foods pests eat.

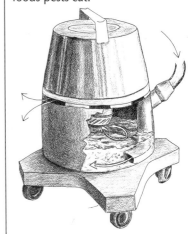

exhaust. Water vacuums also drown trapped insects in the water in the dust-collecting receptacle. If you use a dry vacuum, it should have disposable bags or be constructed so it can be emptied easily after each vacuuming. The contents should be disposed of by burning, burying in a hot compost, freezing for 24 hours, dumping in a solution of insecticidal soap that is drained before disposal or in other ways that prevent live insects and eggs from reinfesting the house.

Vacuums are also being used increasingly to control pests found in the garden. In agriculture, huge vacuums mounted on tractors remove lygus bugs and other pest insects from strawberries and vegetable crops. For the home garden, a Dustbuster® modified for collecting insect specimens is available (for sources of vacuums, see the Resource Appendix under "Insect Management: Physical Controls" on pp. 682-683).

INTRODUCTION

The clothes we wear and the furnishings we surround ourselves with, if made from once-living plants or animals, are potential food for a large number of fungi and insects that can reach pestiferous proportions. Few things made from natural materials are safe from natural decomposition and disintegration.

Because our clothing and interior furnishings cost us time and money, and are often important to our self-image, status and comfort, protecting them is a serious ongoing concern. However, the use of pesticides to protect them is particularly problematic, since these possessions frequently make direct contact with our skin and occupy the air we breathe.

The organisms discussed in this chapter, including clothes moths, carpet beetles, silverfish, firebrats and booklice, are sometimes referred to as fabric pests (although feathers and leather, which also are attacked by these pests, are not truly fabricated). Many of these insects can digest ker-

atin, the "hard" protein of which hair, horns, nails, claws, hoofs, feathers and the scales of reptiles, birds and mammals are formed. The known keratin-digesters comprise about 30 species of moth larvae, including the common clothes moths, the larvae of 15 beetle species, including the carpet beetles, and hundreds of bird lice species in the order Mallophaga.

These organisms can also attack a wide variety of other natural materials and even some synthetic ones, which they use for non-food purposes. They often use paper, starch, cotton or silk to build cocoons, or they simply pass the material through their gut along with fabric, food sources and other materials that are nutritious to them. From the human point of view, however, this is just as destructive as when fabric is being consumed.

Of all the fabric pests, the clothes moths (family Tineidae) and the carpet and hide beetles (family Dermestidae) are by far the most significant. Clothes moths are more common in southern areas, but are found widely enough to be considered cosmopolitan. Dermestid beetles are perhaps the most destructive of all because they attack a broader range of materials. They include species that attack stored grains.

Clothes moths and carpet beetles are a less common problem today than they were 50 years ago. Arnold Mallis, in the *Handbook of Pest Control*, suggests a number of factors that might explain why. It is worth considering these factors, because they can help us devise effective management strategies.

First, synthetic materials, which are not attractive to clothes moths, have replaced much of the wool used for clothing, upholstery and carpeting. Air-conditioning, central heating and insulation have lowered the humidity in the home, creating an environment unfavorable for clothes moths. Plywood flooring and concrete covered with tightly fitted squares of tile have replaced hard-

wood flooring, with its many crevices that were attractive to clothes moths. And newer, more powerful vacuum cleaners do a better job of pulling up larvae of clothes moths.

Not long ago, an additional factor was the widespread use of persistent chlorinated hydrocarbon insecticides, such as DDT, dieldrin, chlordane and lindane, as sheep dips. These insecticides permeated the wool used to make garments and carpets, providing long-lasting protection against moths and beetles. When the health hazards associated with these materials became better understood in the 1970s, however, their use was reduced. Other pesticides have fallen into disuse because of widespread insect resistance to them. As a result, fabric-eating insects are once again becoming major residential pests. Gradually people are noticing these pests and the damage they cause.

CLOTHES MOTHS
(Order Lepidoptera, family Tineidae)

It is the larvae of clothes moths that attack fabrics. In the wild, clothes-moth larvae feed on pollen, hair, feathers, wool, fur, dead insects and dried animal remains (the adult moths do not eat). In the house, they feed on wool, hair or feather products wherever they have access to them. Clothing, carpets, furs, blankets, upholstery, piano felts, brush bristles and a myriad of other items are subject to their attack. They also feed on synthetic fabrics and fabrics from botanical sources if they are mixed with wool.

There are three important facts around which any successful clothes-moth management program must be built: (a) clothes moths dislike direct sunlight, (b) the larvae are fragile, and (c) the moths cannot complete their normal life cycle on clean, processed wool; it must be contaminated with some nutritional supplement such as food, beverage, sweat or urine stains. Such stains provide the proteins, the mineral salts and the vitamin B complex essential to the moth.

The value of these facts in clothes-moth management is discussed in the section on treatment below.

Biology

The most common fabric-attacking moths are the webbing and the casemaking clothes moths. The webbing clothes moth *(Tineola bisselliella),* shown in the drawing at right, is common throughout the United States, whereas the casemaking moth *(Tinea pellionella)* is more common in the southern states. The adults of both species are about ¼ in. (6 mm) long with their wings folded, and have a wingspan of ½ in. to ¾ in. (13 mm to 19 mm). The webbing clothes moth is golden buff or yellowish grey with a satiny sheen; the hairs on its head are upright and reddish. The casemaking clothes moth is similar in size and shape, but has a browner hue and three indistinct dark spots on the wings, with lighter-colored hairs on the head.

The larvae of both moths are also similar, with pearly-white naked bodies and dark heads; they are about ⅜ in. (9.5 mm) long when fully grown. Their fecal matter is often the same color as the material they consume. The larvae of the webbing clothes moth sometimes spin characteristic silken tubes and mats under which they feed; the tubes can include parts of the fabric. Occasionally, the larvae crawl around unprotected for several days. The casemaking moth larva spins a small, silken cell-like case, which it carries as it feeds. When it is ready to pupate, it may seek a protected crevice in the wall or ceiling.

Adult moths of both species avoid light and attempt to hide when disturbed; this trait, which helps distinguish these moths from others, is discussed further in the section on detection below. However, they are occasionally seen flying in subdued light. Males fly more often than females, but both may fly considerable distances and can move from build-

---

The Life Cycle of the Webbing Clothes Moth
The adult webbing clothes moth *(Tineola bisselliella)* lives 10 to 28 days, but does not feed. It lays up to 200 eggs, which generally hatch in 3 to 21 days. It is the larval stage that feeds on natural fabrics, causing damage. Larvae live from 35 days to as much as 2½ years. The pupal cocoon lasts 8 to 40 days. (Wingspan of adult: ½ in. to ¾ in./13 mm to 19 mm)

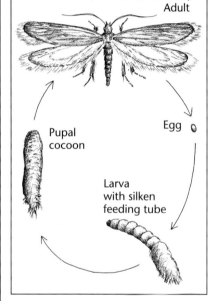

Adult

Pupal cocoon

Egg

Larva with silken feeding tube

---

ing to building in favorable weather. Adults can be seen flying at any time of year, but they are more common in spring and autumn, during periods of slightly higher humidity.

Adult females lay up to 200 eggs. Incubation takes from three days to three weeks or even longer. If conditions are good—meaning abundant food, temperatures around 75°F (24°C) and at least 75% relative humidity—a new generation can be produced in a month. However, it takes over a year when conditions are less favorable, and periods up to four years have been recorded in the laboratory. The larval and pupal stages combined may take 45 days to more than a year to complete. At ordinary

---

household temperatures, adult moths live from two to four weeks. The adults do not feed on fabrics.

In artificially heated buildings, the webbing clothes moth females can mate and lay eggs any month of the year. Some of these eggs will mature to adult moths, while others will die from desiccation (drying out), attack by natural enemies or other causes. The casemaking clothes moth generally produces one generation each year in the north and two generations in the south. The latter species particularly likes feathers, and may reduce stored garments, quilts or down pillows to masses of frass (insect fecal material); it also attacks many substances that might be thought to repel it, such as cayenne pepper, horseradish, ginger, black mustard seed and hemp *(Cannabis sativa),* as well as some botanicals that are poisonous to humans.

Damage

Clothes-moth larvae chew holes in fabrics (see the photo on p. 198). The holes appear to be scattered about the garment and are generally small. (Carpet-beetle holes, by contrast, usually seem to be concentrated in a few areas and can be quite large.)

Detection and Monitoring

If you find clothes-moth larvae, eggs or webbing in the material they are damaging, there can be no doubt as to their presence. But what do the little moths you see flying around indicate? It is easy to confuse clothes moths with the small moths that eat grain, dried fruit and other stored foods, or with moths that enter the house at night through open windows. Clothes moths do not fly to lights, as do many familiar outdoor moths, but they can be seen fluttering about in dimly lit areas. The fluttering flight itself is quite distinctive, and may be enough to distinguish them from food-infesting moths, which have a calmer, steadier flight.

Because clothes moths intersperse flying with landing and walking, it is

The adult and larval stages of the webbing clothes moth are shown here on moth-damaged fabric along with portions of debris-covered cocoons. (Photo by Stennett Heaton, courtesy of Van Waters and Rogers.)

not hard to catch them. You can capture them by inverting a jar or small vial over them, then coaxing them to fly up into the bottom of the container by slowly sliding a card under the open end. You can put the jar with the captured moth in the freezer or refrigerator overnight. Once the moth has quieted down or died, you should examine it with a hand lens. The tineid moths all have prominent hairs or scales on their heads, which present a crested appearance. They also have long fringed wings and long legs.

If it turns out that you have captured a stored-food pest, there is no reason to fear for your woolens, but you had better search out the source of the infestation in your kitchen. Table 13.1 on the facing page describes, depicts and compares clothes and grain moths; the latter are discussed in the next chapter.

You can use sticky traps as detection tools (they can also serve as controls). They may be more effective if they contain a bait attractive to moths. In the 1940s, entomologist H.F. Wilson reported that box traps and flypaper rolls containing "cloth pads treated with fish meal or an alcoholic extract of the same material" attracted both adult and larval clothes moths and carpet beetles. Sardine oil and meat scraps also show promise as baits.

You can make similar traps by purchasing sticky flypaper rolls or whitefly traps to catch moths, and box or sticky traps — sold for monitoring cockroaches — to catch moth larvae and adult and larval beetles. The flypaper and roach traps are sold in most hardware stores; whitefly traps are available from nurseries (they are also listed in the Resource Appendix under "Insect Management: Physical Controls" on pp. 682-683). The sidebar on p. 200 explains how to bait these traps and where to place them.

Treatment:
Indirect Strategies

Indirect treatment strategies for controlling clothes moths include proper storage of clothes, removal of nests and cleaning.

1. Storage in Tight Containers. If clean materials are placed into tightly closed containers — chests, boxes or bags — they will be safe from infestation. Note that the long-touted effectiveness of cedar chests in protecting against moths is due to their tight seal and the repellency of the cedar oil in keeping moths away, rather than from the moth-killing effects of the oil volatilizing from the wood. Although it is true that the cedar oil can kill small larvae, it cannot kill older, larger ones, and the cedar lumber used usually loses its oil within a few years after cutting.

The problem with closets and similar storage areas is that they are almost impossible to seal. When you consider that the female moth lays her eggs in tiny crevices and newly hatched larvae are so small they can crawl through any gap larger than 0.0004 in. (0.01 mm), you can see just how well taped or tight-fitting a container must be to be effective. Such a tight seal is so difficult to achieve that most people resort to repellents.

The military solved this problem by using heat-sealed brown kraft paper case liners backed with plastic, a specially fabricated combination, for their experimental study. After five years of testing, they concluded that woolens stored inside such plastic bags would stay insect-free. Entomologist Roy Bry of the USDA Stored Product Insects Laboratory in Savannah, Georgia, who has conducted research on moth-resistant clothing storage systems, thinks plain brown kraft paper alone could be an effective barrier, because clothes moths do not eat through kraft paper.

Bry suggests wrapping clean clothing in heavy brown paper and sealing it tightly closed with heavy-duty tape. As long as the package is not punctured or torn, clothing should be safe from attack for years. Bry also thinks that placing clean clothes in Ziploc® plastic bags or heavy-duty plastic garbage bags (10 mil or thicker, or a double bag) and sealing them tightly with tape would work.

2. Removal of Animal Nests. Fabric-damaging pests such as clothes moths sometimes move into homes from the abandoned nests of birds, rodents, bats, bees and wasps, as well as from the carcasses of dead animals.

Table 13.1
Distinguishing among Common Clothes Moths and Common Grain Moths

	Species	Distinguishing Characteristics
	webbing clothes moth (Tineidae: *Tineola bisselliella*)	wingspan ½ in. (13 mm); resting length ¼ in. (6 mm), wings without spots, body covered with shiny golden scales, usually with reddish hairs on head; adults fly in dark areas; cosmopolitan
	casemaking clothes moth (Tineidae: *Tinea pellionella*)	same size as webbing clothes moth but less common; resting length ¼ in. (6 mm); more brownish than webbing clothes moth, often with three indistinct dark spots on the wings (on older moths they may have rubbed off); larvae always in case; adults fly in dark areas; not common in northern states
	Mediterranean flour moth (Pyralidae: *Anagasta [=Ephestia] kuehniella*)	wingspan ⅘ in. (20 mm); hind wings dirty white, fore wings pale grey with transverse black wavy bars; at rest forebody distinctly raised; cosmopolitan
	Indianmeal moth (Pyralidae: *Plodia interpunctella*)	wingspan ⅝ in. (16 mm); resting length ½ in. (13 mm); broad greyish band across bronzy wings; favors dried fruit but will feed on many other stored products; cosmopolitan
	angoumois grain moth (Gelechiidae: *Sitotroga cerealella*)	same size as webbing clothes moth but with pale yellow fore wings and grey pointed hind wings; cosmopolitan

These sources should be located and removed. Rats and mice should be trapped rather than poisoned. If poisoned rodents die in inaccessible places, their carcasses can become food sources for fabric pests and flies.

3. **Vacuuming.** The vacuum cleaner can be a very important part of your strategy to reduce fabric pests. Accumulations of lint, human and pet hair, and other organic debris in cracks and crevices of floors, baseboards, closets and shelves constitute food for clothes moths. These areas should be cleaned thoroughly and regularly to prevent infestations. Particularly important places to clean are under furniture that is rarely moved; along baseboards, in cracks between floorboards and wherever debris collects; in closets where fabric items, furs and feather-filled materials are stored; and inside and behind heaters, vents and ducts.

Treatment: Direct Physical Controls

The following are the direct physical strategies recommended for controlling clothes moths:

1. **Cleaning Fabrics.** Clothes moths are attracted to the food, beverage, sweat and urine stains in woolens and other materials, not to the wool itself. For this reason, garments should be cleaned thoroughly before being stored.

Moth larvae and cocoons are very fragile. Thus, regular shaking, brushing and airing of woolens, fur and feather garments, blankets and other fabrics is very effective in preventing moth damage. Vigorous brushing, particularly under cuffs, collars and other protected areas, removes and

Baiting and Placing Sticky Traps for Clothes Moths[a]

To prepare bait for a sticky trap, saturate one side of several cotton balls in fish oil (e.g., sardine, tuna or cod-liver oil) and affix them to the sticky traps. Use two bait balls per flypaper trap, and one per whitefly or box trap, as shown in the drawing at right. Hang the flypaper or whitefly traps from ceilings of closets or storerooms to catch adult moths. Two traps are probably sufficient in the average 3-ft. by 3-ft. by 8-ft. closet. Place the box traps on the floor next to the walls to capture larvae.

Check the traps every few days for two weeks. Since the odor of the bait dissipates after two weeks, traps need to be replaced at that time. If you find moths and larvae on or in the traps, refer to the directions under the various treatments outlined in this chapter. Remember, however, that clothes-moth larvae can live on lint collected in floor and wall crevices. Thus, they may appear in the traps even where there are no woolen clothes or carpets. In such cases, vacuuming up lint and caulking crevices may eliminate the insects.

An obvious drawback of this trapping method is the fishy smell the bait emits where traps are placed. But people have long lived with the very strong chemical odor of mothballs, which are toxic to humans. Perhaps the nontoxic odor of fish oil can also become accepted. Better yet, we hope that an insect pheromone or other attractant for these pests will become available for use in traps. Pheromones are the chemical scents insects use to locate one another for mating. They are odorless to humans.

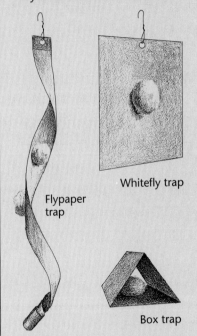

Whitefly trap

Flypaper trap

Box trap

[a] These suggestions are based on the literature and are offered here as a guide for experimentation.

moths are likely to be active throughout the year. Still, they are generally most damaging in summer when woolens and furs are in storage. Moths almost never attack garments that are worn frequently.

A thorough housecleaning involves strenuous physical labor. The custom of spring cleaning centered around a household with servants or women who kept house full-time. Nowadays, with few adult members of most households devoting themselves to unpaid housework, it might be best to hire professionals for a thorough once- or twice-yearly cleaning. The cleaning should include hanging out and brushing all wool garments and other items, vacuuming closets, and so on. If a professional spring cleaning is too expensive, the job of airing and brushing woolens might be hired out to a young person willing to follow specific instructions.

2. Exposure to Heat. Clothes moths can survive through their entire life cycle at 91°F (33°C), but as the temperature climbs above 95°F (35°C), various stages begin to die, depending on the duration of exposure. The eggs are the most heat-resistant, but after a week at 99°F (37°C), all moths at all stages die; only four hours at 106°F (41°C) does the same trick. Table 13.2 on the facing page summarizes the effects of various temperatures and exposure times on moths at different stages.

If you find it hard to imagine the circumstances under which clothing might be exposed to temperatures over 100°F (38°C) for many hours, think of the uninsulated portions of attics in many parts of the country where outdoor summer temperatures reach into the nineties. Under a dark-colored roof, an outside temperature of 90°F (32°C) can generate an attic temperature of 120°F (49°C). Woolens stored under such conditions are adequately protected from moths without other precautions.

A closet can be heat-treated by removing all garments and placing an

destroys moth eggs. The larvae are repelled by light and will drop from materials if they cannot find protection.

Spring cleaning once meant collecting all woolens and other susceptible materials, hanging them in the sun on the clothesline and brushing and beating them vigorously with a metal beater designed for the job. It was done in the spring because that was when the susceptible clothing would be put away for the summer. Unheated homes meant that moths were less likely to be active in the winter, but now, with houses kept at an even temperature year-round,

Table 13.2
Length of Heat Exposure Required to Produce 100% Clothes-Moth Mortality[a,b]

	95°F	97°F	99°F	100°F	102°F	104°F	106°F
egg			2 days		1 day		4 hours
larva			7 days	18 hours		3 hours	3 hours
pupa				1 day		3 hours	
adult	6 days	3 days	3 days	1 day	1 day	4 hours	

[a] Tests conducted at 70% relative humidity.
[b] Adapted from Rawle, 1951.

electric heater inside. Center the heater on the closet floor, put it on its hottest setting and monitor it with a baking thermometer. Keep the closet temperature at 120°F (49°C) for four hours to kill the insects. This method is based on research conducted by UCLA entomologist Walter Ebeling.

3. Exposure to Cold. Cold storage has long been used to protect furs from fabric pests, and it is useful for killing clothes moths, too. The question is, how cold for how long? Although it was once thought that temperatures from 40°F to 42°F (4°C to 5°C) would protect stored garments, it is now known that this does not always work if there are larvae in the garments when they are placed in cold storage. Apparently, it is not so much the cold temperature itself as sudden changes in the temperature that cause moth mortality. Thus, various schemes for alternating from room temperature to freezing and back have been developed.

In his *Handbook of Pest Control*, Arnold Mallis suggests that "if articles infested with clothes moths were refrigerated at 18°F [–8°C] for several days, then suddenly exposed for a short time to 50°F [10°C], and then returned to 18°F, and finally held permanently at about 40°F [4°C], all moth life in them would be killed ....During the winter if furniture is placed outdoors at 0°F [–18°C] for

several hours, it often results in good control." This suggests a strategy for the home owner that may work for smaller items. These should be bagged and moved in and out of bin-type freezers that are normally kept at 0°F to reduce deterioration of frozen foods. Cleaned garments can be placed in tightly closed plastic bags in a freezer for two to three days, since few insects can withstand this temperature. After that, they can be moved for long-term storage to closets or chests at room temperature.

4. Microwave Radiation. In laboratory studies, eggs, larvae and adults of webbing clothes moths were killed after four minutes at 2,450 MHz in a Sharp™ carousel microwave oven. The tests were conducted on a worsted wool gabardine cloth (2/1 twill at 7.1 oz/sq. yd.). The microwave did not affect the breaking strength or wrinkle recovery of the fabric, or the colorfastness of its natural and acid dyes. Although these tests indicate that microwave radiation is useful in destroying clothes moths, further work is necessary before a recommendation can be fashioned from this preliminary work. Additional studies should help determine the optimum depth of the material, since thick layers may shield the moths. Note: Any clothing with metal buttons, zippers or decorations should not be microwaved.

Treatment: Direct Biological Controls
There are many parasitoids, predatory flies, mites and spiders that may occur naturally in dwellings and prey upon the different stages of the clothes moth. They may be helpful in suppressing moth populations in organic debris in the cracks and crevices of the house, and this, in turn, may help prevent large moth populations from threatening woolens.

As long as susceptible garments are adequately cleaned and properly stored, the additional assistance of natural biological controls in the general environment may provide enhanced protection. However, biological control alone should not be relied upon for protection against the clothes moth—just one hole chewed by one larva can ruin a good piece of clothing. This is a case where the injury or damage level is too low for biological control alone to be of much direct help.

Treatment: Direct Chemical Controls
You can protect woolens and furs from clothes moths without using pesticides simply by cleaning them well before storing them and then sealing them in moth-tight containers; frequent wearing and airing of fabrics not stored is equally effective. However, where chemical controls are felt to be necessary, you may want to investigate some of the materials discussed below, listed in order from least to most toxic.

When using any pesticide, even one like pyrethrum, which is regarded as having low mammalian toxicity, protect yourself with a good-quality respirator, goggles, gloves and suitable outer garments. Chapter 6 provides details on buying and using protective equipment. Where possible, apply pesticides outdoors.

Regardless of the pesticide you use, we recommend washing or dry-cleaning stored material before and after storage. Cleaning beforehand eliminates food and sweat stains that might attract the moths during storage and ensures that clothing is not placed in storage with moths or eggs already in the garment. Garments treated with chemicals should be cleaned after removal from storage, because it is unwise to bring the pesticides into contact with your skin. Be advised, however, that neither washing nor dry-cleaning is likely to remove *all* pesticide residue from treated garments.

The objective in moth control is to prevent larvae—the stage that eats fabric—from damaging even one strand of stored material. Thus, a chemical control that has a repellent action is more effective than one that is a stomach poison or a fumigant, since, by the time the larva dies from the latter, it will have already ingested some of the cloth. Many materials recommended for repellency have proven worthless (examples are cayenne pepper, allspice, angelica root, black pepper, lime, sulfur, salt, quassia, borax, eucalyptus leaves, red cedar leaves, hellebore and sodium bicarbonate).

Of the three chemical controls commonly sold for protection from clothes moths—camphor, naphthalene and paradichlorobenzene (PDB) —only camphor is both an effective repellent and a fumigant. It is also less toxic than the other two chemical controls.

1. Camphor. Camphor is a natural product distilled from the camphor tree *(Cinnamomum camphora)*, which is grown almost exclusively in Formosa, Japan and southern China. Camphor has been known as an insect repellent since ancient times, and it is still sold as a moth repellent. Synthetic camphor, available in some drug stores, has properties identical to those of the natural product. It is produced from pine turpentine.

There is ample evidence that camphor is also effective as a fumigant for adult and larval clothes moths, but it is less effective than naphthalene or PDB (see below). Camphor imparts a smell to clothing, so gar-

ments must be aired out, but the same is true of traditional moth crystals composed of naphthalene or PDB. Some people prefer the odor of camphor to that of the other chemicals. Camphor should not be used with naphthalene or PDB; if mixed, they form a sticky mass that can damage clothing.

Despite its long history as a household medicine, camphor should not be treated lightly. It is a poison and a central-nervous-system stimulant capable of causing neurological disorders. Although we have not been able to locate information about the toxic effects of camphor vapor, accidental ingestion of camphor mothballs has caused death. No oral LD_{50} is available for camphor, but when injected into the body cavities of laboratory rats, 900 mg/kg of body weight killed 50% of the animals. Using this LD_{50} as a measure of toxicity, camphor is less toxic than PDB, and possibly even naphthalene. (Although the LD_{50} of injected camphor is about half that of the oral LD_{50} of naphthalene, one can expect a body injection route of exposure to be much more toxic than an oral route. The oral LD_{50} of camphor would be much higher. Remember, the higher the LD_{50}, the less toxic the pesticide).

Camphor for use against clothes moths can be purchased in ball, flake or cake form from a pharmacy or hardware store. Cakes should be broken up into small pieces about ½ in. (1.3 cm) square and, as with balls or flakes, scattered throughout the garment and its container. Sterling Bunnell, a Berkeley, California, physician, reported to us that when he compared stored woolens treated with camphor to those receiving no other chemical treatment, he found that camphor provided protection if the woolens were not infested when placed in storage.

2. Permethrin. Permethrin, a synthetic pyrethroid (see pp. 121-122), is another moth-proofing insecticide. It has been shown in laboratory tests that clothes dipped in permethrin so-

lutions were protected for at least six months. The insecticide withstood repeated washings, dry-cleanings, abrasion, perspiration, sea water and ultraviolet light. Permethrin is less toxic than PDB and comparable in toxicity to naphthalene. For sources of pyrethroids, see the Resource Appendix under "Insect Management: Chemical Controls" on pp. 686-687.

3. *Bacillus thuringiensis* (BT). Laboratory tests indicate that *Bacillus thuringiensis,* which is nontoxic to humans, is effective against clothesmoth larvae. However, we could not find published studies on its use for this purpose in home settings. See Chapter 8 for more details on BT.

4. Boric Acid. Boric acid, described in detail on pp. 112-114, may have a role to play in suppressing clothes moths. In a test by entomologists R. E. Bry and L. L. MacDonald, a 1% boric-acid solution applied directly to infested wool fabric produced little effect on clothes moths. Similarly, a 1% solution of imidazole did not provide satisfactory control. However, when a solution of 1% imidazole and 2% to 4% boric acid was used, control of clothes moths was achieved. The treatment did not persist through washing, but did provide satisfactory control after three dry-cleanings.

5. Naphthalene and Paradichlorobenzene (PDB). These are the two materials most often used for moth protection. Yet laboratory studies indicate that both naphthalene and PDB are ineffective as repellents. They are, however, effective as fumigants, killing primarily adult moths and early-stage larvae. When using these materials to protect clothes from moths, it is essential that they be used inside reasonably well-sealed containers, such as clothes bags or boxes. In a confined space, the vapors can build up to toxic levels and kill moths that enter. These vapors also impart a strong smell to clothing. Thus, treated clothing needs to be aired thoroughly before being worn.

Both naphthalene and PDB are sold in ball, flake and cake form in most variety and hardware stores. Generally, the consumer receives little guidance as to which to choose. You should always read the label on all anti-moth products carefully to learn what the active ingredients are. Because use of these products in drawers, closets and clothes storage bags usually means that residents of the house receive a respiratory dose of the active substances (sometimes for prolonged periods), it is worth examining their potential hazards.

We were unable to find a listing for the LD_{50} of naphthalene in humans; however, the oral LD_{50} in rats is 2,200 mg/kg. In contrast, PDB, with an oral LD_{50} of 500 mg/kg in rats, is much more toxic. Since benzene, the basic molecule from which PDB is built, is a potent human carcinogen, PDB with the addition of two chlorine atoms can be expected to be even more toxic. PDB is readily absorbed into the body through respiration; people chronically exposed to its vapors have relatively large amounts stored in their body fat. Our advice is to avoid PDB.

Naphthalene is made from coal tar, and its molecular structure is based on two benzene rings stuck together. This material is known to have a spectacular blood-destroying action in sensitive individuals, particularly those of dark-skinned races. This includes Native Americans and some African, Arab and other Semitic peoples, Mediterranean peoples, Caucasians of Latin extraction and some Asians. Highly sensitive individuals are believed to possess a sex-linked, genetically determined metabolic defect that finds full expression in males. Nonsensitive persons also are subject to toxic sensitization, but usually do not respond to as low a dose as those who are sensitive.

Naphthalene is toxic if ingested, but it can also cause damage when vapors are inhaled. Whole-body responses called systemic reactions have occurred after children were dressed in clothing stored with naphthalene mothballs. Studies have

shown naphthalene to contaminate a fetus after maternal exposure, indicating placental passage. Laboratory animals exposed to naphthalene developed corneal ulcers and cataracts. From this information, it seems that naphthalene, too, should be avoided.

If you do use either naphthalene or paradichlorobenzene, be advised that they impart a strong odor to clothing. It is important to air out treated clothing thoroughly before wearing it to minimize absorption of the active ingredients through the skin and respiratory system.

Summary: Least-Toxic Clothes Moth Control

• Clean susceptible materials before storing them and/or pass items through the freezer for several days before placing them in storage.

• Store items in heat-sealed or otherwise completely sealed plastic bags.

• The use of any common moth "repellent" in unsealed containers is probably ineffective, because most of these chemicals are actually fumigants rather than repellents and require tightly closed containers to retain their toxic vapors. Camphor may be the exception in that it has a repellent action.

• If you cannot store garments in sealed containers, store them with pieces of camphor or treat them with BT or permethrin and store them in containers that are taped closed. Treat carpets with boric acid, BT or permethrin, if a chemical control is needed.

• Use naphthalene only as a last resort. Bear in mind that naphthalene vapors can produce toxic reactions in sensitive individuals.

• Avoid the use of paradichlorobenzene (PDB) because it may be carcinogenic (cancer-causing).

• Clean garments after storage if a pesticide has been used.

• Vacuum up organic debris from cracks in floors, closets, etc., where clothes moths breed. Apply heat treatment to empty closets and small storerooms.

• Eliminate old birds' nests in or on the building, because they may be sources of moth infestations. In addition, remove plant growth that could encourage bird nesting.

• Trap rather than poison rodents. (Inaccessible dead carcasses can become a source of clothes moths and unpleasant odors).

CARPET AND HIDE BEETLES
(Order Coleoptera, family Dermestidae)

As part of the natural detritivore/decomposer community, dermestid beetles help recycle skin, hair, feathers, dead insects and similar materials back into their basic components so that the compounds can be taken up by plants as nutrients again. Like clothes moths, some dermestids can digest keratin, a substance not easily processed by other animals.

Dermestid beetles are a valuable resource to archaeologists and other museum workers who rely on them to chew the flesh from the bones of delicate specimens whose skeletons must be preserved. But to most other people they are pests. The same museum workers dread carpet beetles because they can destroy valuable animal, plant and human artifacts. Home owners, too, can suffer serious losses when the beetles attack clothing or carpets.

As a group, dermestids cause far more damage than clothes moths, since the range of substances they consume is much greater. Because of their significance as pests, there is a great deal of literature on their biology and control, although it emphasizes the use of toxic materials. These studies are summarized well in Arnold Mallis's *Handbook of Pest Control*, from which much of the following information about these beetles is abstracted.

Mallis points out that dermestids can be separated into three broad species categories based on what they consume. The first category eats only animal matter or materials containing animal proteins; the second category usually eats animal matter but can breed if fed only vegetable matter; and the third category (the warehouse beetle, *Trogoderma variabile*), usually eats only grains and cereal products. Most of the dermestids are carnivorous, which is believed to be the most primitive eating habit of the three. Table 13.3 on the facing page lists and depicts the significant carpet and hide beetles.

In general, the hide beetles may be a less serious problem in some residences than they used to be. Before refrigeration was common, home-cured and dried meat and fish products were available as food for the beetles. But there still are serious beetle infestations in some homes, and they continue to be a problem in warehouses, museum collections and wherever large amounts of their preferred foods can be found.

The discussions of biology and management below focus on carpet beetles. But it should be understood that to the extent that they damage the same materials in the home, the management of hide and carpet beetles is similar. Carpet beetles may become more significant now that the persistent chlorinated hydrocarbon insecticides are no longer used on livestock, woolens and leathers.

Biology

All dermestids have similar life histories. Adults lay eggs on the larval food source and the eggs hatch after less than two weeks. The larvae feed for varying periods, depending upon the species and the microenvironmental conditions. When ready to pupate, the larvae may burrow farther into the food or wander and burrow elsewhere. They may also pupate within their last larval skin if no other location is found.

The brownish, slow-moving larvae are characteristically hairy or bristly. The hairs are up to ¼ in. (6 mm) long and are arranged in a neat pattern. Unlike clothes moths, the larvae do not construct webs, but their shed skins and fecal pellets make it obvious where larvae have been feeding. Walter Ebeling points out that the cast skins look so much like live larvae that under casual inspection there may seem to be a far larger infestation than is actually present.

Some carpet-beetle species seek pollen and nectar in the adult stage; thus, they may be imported into the house on cut flowers. They are sometimes mistaken for lady beetles, because some species of carpet beetles are similarly round in shape. Other strains of the same carpet-beetle species apparently breed indoors year-round without access to pollen, living on fabrics inside the home.

Damage

Carpet beetles have been known to cause dermatitis, irritation of the nasal passages and sinuses and more generalized allergies. The small hairs on the larvae are the cause of the problems. Hide beetles are carcass- and hide-feeders, and, as Mallis points out, they can spread bacilli or spores of anthrax, a disease of cattle and sheep that can be passed to humans. Mallis reports that anthrax bacilli have been found in the feces of a dermestid. Although anthrax no longer occurs in the United States, we mention it to indicate the possibility of microbial dissemination by beetles in this group.

Nonetheless, these beetles are not primarily of public-health concern; it is their damage to household furnishings that causes them to be regarded as pests. They chew holes in carpets and fabrics (see the photo on p. 206). The damage is most likely to be concentrated in one area of the item — in contrast to moth damage, which

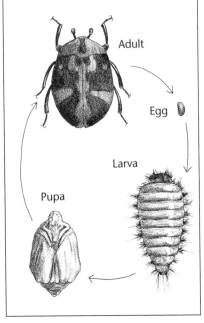

The Life Cycle of the Carpet Beetle
Carpet beetles undergo complete metamorphosis. The adult lives 20 to 60 days and lays 30 to 100 eggs, which hatch in 6 to 20 days. The larva lasts 60 to 325 days, and the pupa, 6 to 24 days. Both the larval and adult stages damage fabric. (Actual size of adult: ¹⁄₁₀ in. to ⅕ in./2.5 mm to 5 mm)

Adult

Egg

Larva

Pupa

Table 13.3
Important Carpet or Hide Beetles in the Family Dermestidae

	Common Name(s)	Scientific Name	Description of Adults
	furniture carpet beetle	*Anthrenus flavipes* (=*A. vorax*)	⅒ in. to ⅕ in. (2.5 mm to 5 mm) long; definite cleft at rear; mottled with black, white and yellow scales
	common carpet beetle[a], buffalo bug, buffalo moth	*A. scrophulariae*	⅛ in. (3 mm) long; blackish with varied pattern of white and orange scales on back; scalloped band of orange-red scales down middle of back
	varied carpet beetle	*A. verbasci*	⅛ in. (3 mm) long; mottled with white, brownish and yellowish scales
	black carpet beetle[a]	*Attagenus megatoma*	⅒ in. to ⅕ in. (2.5 mm to 5 mm) long; oval; shiny black and dark brown with brownish legs
	black larder beetle, incinerator beetle	*Dermestes ater* (=*D. cadaverinus*)	³⁄₁₀ in. to ⅖ in. (7.5 mm to 10 mm) long; black with yellowish grey hairs; black rounded and hook-shaped spots on underside of abdomen
	larder beetle	*D. lardarius*	³⁄₁₀ in. to ⅖ in. (7.5 mm to 10 mm) long; dark brown with pale greyish yellow hair; yellow band at base of wing covers with about six black spots
	hide beetle, leather beetle	*D. maculatus* (=*D. vulpinus*)	⅕ in. to ⅖ in. (5 mm to 10 mm) long; black with white hairs on sides and undersides; apex of each wing cover comes to a fine point
	warehouse beetle	*Trogoderma variabile*	⅛ in. (3 mm) long; brownish black

[a] Believed by some researchers to have been imported accidentally into the United States from Europe, but see Mallis, 1982, for a different opinion.

The spotted adults and hairy larvae of the carpet beetle feed on fabric. Note that the individual fabric strands are relatively cleanly cut and the area is free of accumulated debris. This contrasts with clothes-moth damage (shown in the photo on p. 198), which is more cluttered with fecal debris and cast-off pupal skins. (Photo by Stennett Heaton, courtesy of Van Waters and Rogers.)

usually appears as scattered holes. Table 13.4 on the facing page lists common food sources of carpet and hide beetles.

Detection and Monitoring

As with clothes moths, it is the larval stage of the Dermestidae that causes damage to fabrics. The larvae feed in dark, quiet locations. Unlike moth larvae, however, carpet-beetle larvae may be found wandering far from their food, particularly to pupate, so they are sometimes encountered on materials they do not actually eat. Also, unlike clothes moths, adult carpet beetles do not shun light and may be found crawling on windows. This is often the first place they are noticed.

If you find either active or dead adults at windows or elsewhere (such as in cabinets or closets), search for the primary source of the infestation. This is a two-step process. First, try to identify the insect. Either use Table 13.3 on p. 205 or seek help from your county cooperative extension agent.

Then consult Table 13.4 on the facing page, which lists common food sources of that species. Keep in mind that the list covers only the most likely foods; it is not exhaustive.

With the food list in mind, search in the most obvious places first:
• Around carpets or furniture covered or filled with susceptible materials. Infestations may be under the slip-covers, where it is dark and quiet, or in the pads under the carpet.
• Around accumulations of lint, hair from pets and other organic debris, particularly under and behind furniture that is rarely moved, in wall and floor cracks, in cracks behind shelves or other built-in items that may not be flush with the wall, behind baseboards, moldings and window trim, and in cold air and heater ducts.
• Around stored garments, blankets or other items made of susceptible materials that were not cleaned first and then stored in heat-sealed plastic containers (see the discussion under treatment for clothes moths on p. 198).

• Around bags or boxes of pet food, dried milk or other dry, nutritious foods that are not stored in glass jars with tight-sealing tops or in heavy, tight-sealing plastic or similar containers (see the discussion under treatment for cockroaches on p. 222). Carpet beetles can bore through cardboard and paper packaging. Once they have done this, they provide access to other stored-food pests.

If this procedure does not uncover the source of the beetles, try looking for some of the more exotic items listed as food sources for species other than the one you have in hand. If the infestation you find does not appear large enough to account for the number of beetles you see, or if cleaning up the infestation does not seem to diminish the number of beetles, then search for less obvious sources:
• bird, wasp, bee, squirrel or other animal nests on or very close to the walls of the house,
• animal carcasses or trophies, insect collections, or leather or horn goods,
• cut flowers brought from the garden, or blooming bushes near open, unscreened windows or doorways,
• incompletely incinerated garbage.

Traps may also be useful in some circumstances (see the description of traps on p. 198).

Treatment:
Indirect Strategies

Indirect treatment strategies for controlling dermestid beetles include:

1. Proper Storage. The storage methods recommended for clothes moths —placing clean materials in tightly sealed plastic bags (see p. 198) —also apply to carpet beetles. In fact, the studies undertaken by the military discussed in that section showed that materials were protected from all fabric pests for five years, which was the length of the study. Presumably the protection would have lasted indefinitely. All pet foods, grains, cereals and other susceptible substances or materials should be stored in tight-fitting containers to deny dermestid beetles access.

Table 13.4
Some Food Sources for Carpet and Hide Beetles[a]

furniture carpet beetle (*Anthrenus flavipes*)	horse-hair-filled furniture, wool, hair, fur, feathers, bristles, horn, tortoise shell, silk, animal excreta, stained linen, cotton, rayon, jute, softwood, leather, bags containing animal products, dried silkworm pupae and cocoons, dead mice, dead insects, dried cheese, old grain, casein, dried blood and the glue of book bindings
common carpet beetle (buffalo bug, buffalo moth) (*A. scrophulariae*)	carpets, fabrics, woolen and other animal products such as feathers, leather, furs, hairbrushes, silks, mounted museum specimens and pressed plant specimens; found in a chipmunk nest in the California mountains; adults found on *Spiraea*, *Ceanothus* (a chaparral shrub), wild buckwheat daisy and wild aster flowers; they enter homes on cut flowers
varied carpet beetle (*A. verbasci*)	nests of bees, wasps and spiders, carpets, woolen goods, skins, furs, stuffed animals, leather book bindings, feathers, horns, whalebone, hair, silk, fish manure, dried silkworm pupae, rye meal, cacao, corn, red pepper and dead insects in collections
black carpet beetle (*Attagenus megatoma*)	feathers, dead birds, birds' nests, bird manure, dry horse and cow carcasses, seeds, grains, cereals, woolen rugs, clothing, carpeting, felts, furs, skins, yarn, velvet, silk, hair-filled mattresses, upholstered furniture, wool-filled blankets, house insulation with sheep wool or cattle hair, meat, insect meal, kid leather, milk powders, casein, books, cayenne pepper, dried pupae of silkworms, pet food, spilled flours and pollen (for adults, particularly of *Spiraea*)
black larder beetle, incinerator beetle (*Dermestes ater*)	mouse cadavers in walls of buildings; partially burned food and other kitchen wastes in incinerators; pet foods
larder beetle (*D. lardarius*)	stored ham, bacon, meats, cheese, dried museum specimens, stored tobacco, dried fish, dog biscuits; can tunnel slightly in wood; can penetrate lead and tin but not zinc or aluminum; pest of silkworm cultures; reported to attack newly hatched chickens and ducklings
hide beetle, leather beetle (*D. maculatus*)	prefers hides and skins; used to clean carcasses; known to survive on smoked meat and dried cheese, but cannot live on fat alone; larvae can tunnel short distances into wood
warehouse beetle (*Trogoderma variabile*)	prefers barley, wheat, animal feeds, grains and pollen; also found in seeds, dead animals, cereals, candy, cocoa, cookies, corn, corn meal, dog food (dried and "burgers"), fish meal, flour, dead insects, milk powder, nut meats, dried peas, potato chips, noodles, spaghetti and dried spices

[a] From Mallis, 1982.

2. Avoiding Furnishings that Contain Materials of Animal Origin. Where dermestid beetles are a continuing and serious problem, it may be worthwhile to select furnishings that do not contain materials of animal origin. In addition, you may need to undertake some of the dust and lint reduction strategies suggested under management of house dust mites in Chapter 10. For example, choose small carpets that can be washed regularly rather than wall-to-wall carpets, and purchase furniture that is easy to dust and clean behind.

3. Screens. Where carpet beetles are coming in from blooming plants in the garden, window screens, screen doors and screened vents should be part of the house design. Some beetle species are more likely to invade from this source than others (see Table 13.4 on p. 207).

4. Removal of Animal Pests. Bird and other animal (including insect) nests in the eaves or close to the walls of the house can be a source of carpet beetles, so they should be removed. Usually, if problems with birds' nests occur, it will be after the nestlings have left and the beetles start to wander. Nests should be removed before the cold weather sets in and the beetles begin searching for sheltered hibernation spots.

5. Caulking. Because accumulations of hair, lint and other organic debris in cracks and crevices provide a breeding area for carpet beetles, caulking or otherwise repairing these areas should be carried out as a means of reducing the beetle carrying capacity of the environment. These same habitats are likely to be inviting to cockroaches; we discuss caulking in greater detail under cockroaches on pp. 223-224.

6. Trapping Mice and Rats. Mice and rats should be trapped rather than poisoned. When you trap a rodent, you can dispose of the carcass in a safe manner; when you poison rodents, particularly with the relatively slow-acting anti-coagulants, the rodent is likely to die within the

walls of the house or in other inaccessible places. Its decomposing carcass will breed flesh flies, clothes moths and carpet beetles, as well as generate unpleasant smells. See pp. 290-291 for tips on trapping rodents.

Treatment:
Direct Physical Controls

Direct physical strategies for controlling dermestid beetles focus on vacuuming and keeping fabrics clean.

1. Vacuuming. A good vacuum cleaner, particularly a water vacuum, is probably the most important tool in managing dermestids. See pp. 195-196 for details on vacuum models and their use.

2. Keeping Fabrics Clean. Steam-clean susceptible furniture and carpets that cannot be washed. Move furniture occasionally to allow a thorough cleaning of those floor areas where it generally remains dark and undisturbed. Garments, blankets and other susceptible materials should be cleaned well before being placed in storage. If a pesticide is used to protect them, they should also be

cleaned before being worn or used (see the discussion under clothes moths on pp. 201-202).

Fabrics and other items badly damaged by dermestids should be burned or, if salvageable, submerged in hot soapy water (at least 120°F/49°C) for two to four hours to kill the larvae and eggs. The microwave treatment suggested for clothes moths (see p. 201) may also be effective against dermestids.

Treatment:
Direct Chemical Controls

Using the strategies suggested above, you should be able to manage carpet beetles in your home without resort to any materials that are toxic to humans or pets. If you do decide that a pesticide is necessary, the recommendations given for clothes moths can also be followed for dermestid beetles. Of the materials discussed on pp. 201-203, BT, boric acid, camphor and permethrin are the least hazardous to mammals. Camphor acts both as an insect repellent and as a fumigant. However, it is slow-acting

---

Summary: Least-Toxic Carpet Beetle Control

- Identify the type of beetle.

- Find the primary source of the infestation and eliminate it, if possible.

- Dispose of badly infested articles in such a way as to avoid recontaminating the household.

- Clean and caulk or repair cracks and crevices in floors, walls, closets and other places where lint accumulates.

- Remove bird, wasp, bee and other animal nests that may be sources of infestations.

- Trap rather than poison rodents.

- Screen windows, doors and vents against beetles migrating from flowering plants.

- Vacuum and steam-clean susceptible carpets and furniture. Dispose of vacuumed debris in a way that avoids recontamination.

- Store cleaned garments and blankets inside tightly sealed plastic bags or other tightly sealed containers.

- Store pet food and other dried foods in tightly sealed glass containers.

- If a pesticide is necessary, use boric acid, camphor or permethrin.

and thus is best used as an addition to sealed storage containers in which thoroughly cleaned garments have been placed.

The eggs of the black carpet beetle are among the most pesticide-resistant stages of the common species of household-infesting dermestid beetles, and their presence may warrant the use of permethrin. As with all hazardous materials, you should protect yourself with a respirator, goggles, gloves and washable outer garments (see pp. 97-103). If possible, conduct spraying treatments outdoors and follow the label directions in every detail.

SILVERFISH AND FIREBRATS
(Order Thysanura [=Zygentoma], family Lepismatidae)

The remainder of this chapter is about the management of insects that eat paper or appear to do so. Silverfish and firebrats, discussed first, may eat paper with a vengeance, but what really attracts them is the paste in the binding of the book and the sizing (glue) in the paper. Booklice, or psocids (pronounced SO-sids), discussed next, are unlikely to eat paper. Although silverfish and firebrats are not closely related to booklice, we discuss them together because all three are found in similar environments within the home. Often one group is accused of causing damage done by the other, and their manage-

ment (see pp. 212-213) is essentially the same.

The presence of silverfish, firebrats or booklice is an indicator of excessive humidity. Even when they are doing little or no damage to household furnishings—the silverfish may be feeding on miscellaneous accumulations of cellulose in cracks and the booklice on molds—their presence should be taken as a warning that damp conditions exist. These damp conditions must be corrected, if possible, because they can lead to termite and carpenter-ant infestations and decay of the house structure itself.

Silverfish and firebrats are primitive, long-lived, wingless insects that evolved before insects developed wings and the ability to fly. They are entomologically rather odd in that they continue to molt as adults. Adults in laboratory colonies have been observed to molt as many as 80 times.

These insects are assumed to have originated in the humid tropics. In temperate climates they normally live in the soil under stones, under leaves or under tree bark, but they have adapted to human dwellings in which the environment is sufficiently warm and damp. Their primary conflict with humans arises because of their love of starch. Silverfish and firebrats also feed on a variety of substances as an extension of this preference: paste, glue (as in book bindings), starched cotton, linen, silk and

certain synthetic fabrics (particularly rayon), starched curtains, cereals, wallpaper paste and paper.

Silverfish and firebrats are frequently introduced into a home with boxes of materials that have been stored in damp basements or attics, but they can also wander in from the outdoors. They are fast-moving and may travel throughout a building in ventilators or heating conduits originating in damp basements. Once they find a good source of food, however, they stay close to it. In general, they do very little damage, but they may be seriously upsetting to people who are afraid of insects or think they are dangerous.

Firebrats prefer hotter areas than silverfish, but otherwise the two species are biologically and ecologically similar. Table 13.5 below lists the major silverfish and firebrat species that inhabit homes and may become pestiferous. The most common silverfish is *Lepisma saccharina*, the most common firebrat, *Thermobia domestica*. These insects are also known as bristletails, sugarlice, silver witches, sugar fish, wood fish and paper moths.

Biology

Silverfish and firebrats are nocturnal and are rarely seen unless disturbed during cleaning or moving. Occasionally, they are found in the bathtub and washbasin, or in china or glass utensils into which they have

Table 13.5
Common Pestiferous Silverfish and Firebrat Species

Common Name	Scientific Name	Distribution
silverfish	*Lepisma saccharina (=inquilinus)*	cosmopolitan
four-lined silverfish	*Ctenolepisma lineata*	eastern and western United States
grey silverfish	*C. longicaudata (=urbana)*	South, Midwest and southern California
firebrat	*Thermobia domestica*	cosmopolitan
(none)	*T. campbelli*	Ohio and Pennsylvania
(none)	*Acrotelsa collaris*	Florida

Silverfish and Firebrats

These insects are similar in shape, but differ in color—silverfish are greyish to green, whereas firebrats have a mottled black-and-white color. They are usually found in moist environments and feed on starchy substances such as book bindings or paper. (Actual size: ⅜ in. to ½ in./9.5 mm to 13 mm)

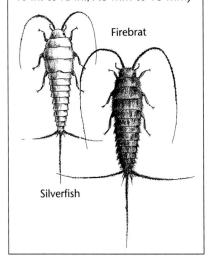

Firebrat

Silverfish

fallen but cannot climb out. When surprised at night, their first reaction is to remain motionless, then dart for harborage. Both prefer moist areas, and both leave yellowish stains on materials, especially linen.

Silverfish adults are about ⅜ in. to ½ in. (9.5 mm to 13 mm) long when fully grown. They are greyish to greenish in color, and their bodies have a flattened-carrot shape with two long antennae and three appendages attached to the tapered posterior end. Each appendage is about as long as the body. The silvery or metallic sheen and the rapid darting movements and fish-like undulating turns have given this household inhabitant its name.

Female silverfish lay eggs in any season, usually in secluded places. They lay only a few at a time in several batches over a period of weeks. Fewer than 100 eggs are laid by a single female. They are oval and about 1/32 in. (0.8 mm) long, and hatch in about 28 weeks, depending upon the temperature. The young resemble the

adults and grow slowly. Optimum developmental conditions include a temperature between 72°F and 80°F (22°C and 27°C) and a relative humidity of 75% to 97%. It takes 90 to 120 days for the insect to mature from egg to egg-laying female. Adults can live 2 to 2½ years at 90°F (32°C), or 1 to 1½ years at 99°F (37°C).

Outdoors, silverfish have been found in nests of insects, birds (especially pigeons) and mammals, and under the bark of trees. Silverfish like warm temperatures—about 80°F (27°C). Indoors, they may be found throughout the house. They are probably transported from house to house in furniture, food packages and other goods. Both silverfish and firebrats are hardy and can live without food for several months.

The common name "firebrat" is probably derived from the frequent occurrence of certain species in fireplaces, ovens, chimneys, furnace rooms, insulation around hot-water and heat pipes, and other warm areas. Their preference for temperatures around 100°F (38°C) makes them a particular problem in places like bakeries. They have a mottled appearance with patches of white and black, and are shaped similarly to silverfish.

Firebrats lay about 50 eggs at a time in several batches, but some individuals have been observed to lay up to 195 eggs. The shortest recorded time from egg to mature egg-laying female is 11 to 12 weeks at 97°F (36°C). At 90°F to 98°F (32°C to 37°C), the adults will live 1 to 2¼ years.

About 350 species of silverfish and firebrats in the family Lepismatidae are known, but only a few inhabit homes. Areas of the house where the different species are likely to be found are listed in Table 13.6 at left. As mentioned above, the management of firebrats, silverfish and booklice is essentially the same. To avoid repetition, we have included details on damage, detection, monitoring and treatment of all three pests in the next section, on booklice.

Table 13.6
Distribution of Silverfish and Firebrats within Homes

Species	Distribution within Homes
Silverfish	
Lepisma saccharina	in basements around water pipes; sometimes common in newly built homes before the masonry has dried; uncommon outdoors
Ctenolepisma lineata	in attics with wood-shingled roofs; can live outside, and has been found in mulch
C. longicaudata	throughout house, around water pipes in the bathroom; can live in drier areas such as crawl spaces under the house, or in the attic; often found in new homes; not found outdoors
Firebrats	
Thermobia domestica	in and around ovens, bakeries, book and paper storage areas
T. campbelli	in book covers

BOOKLICE OR PSOCIDS
(Order Psocoptera, family Liposcelidae)

Booklice, or psocids, are poorly named since they are in no way related to lice and they feed primarily on microscopic molds and not so much on books. If you find them on books, it is a sign that the books are moldy and need to be dried out, preferably in the hot sun. Outdoors, some species inhabit bark, where they feed on mosses and lichens, hence, their other common name, barklice.

Booklice can be found in grass, on leaves, on damp wood and in other areas where molds grow. They are sometimes seen in large numbers on house plants, but do not damage the plants. Such plant-inhabiting booklice may be feeding on honeydew (a protein-rich substance excreted by plant-eating insects such as aphids) or, more likely, on the sooty mold that grows on the honeydew. House-inhabiting booklice feed on molds growing on dead insects; they also feed occasionally on books and paper products.

Some of the 150 booklice species in the United States are pests of stored grains and other products. One species has been found feeding on pollen in a beehive. In the home, booklice seldom if ever cause damage, but their presence, particularly in high numbers, can upset people. Booklice may be a problem in new houses for a short time before all the plaster, stucco, cement and/or mortar has had a chance to dry, but they will die by themselves as conditions become drier. Table 13.7 above right lists booklice species commonly found in the United States.

Biology

Booklice (see the drawing at right) are small, soft-bodied insects. They have chewing mouthparts, undergo a gradual metamorphosis and occur as wingless and winged species. If winged, two pairs of wings are present, although booklice do not fly readily. The house-inhabiting species

Table 13.7
Common Booklice Species Found in the United States

Common Name	Scientific Name	Locations
common booklouse	*Liposcelis* spp.	on or in books, flowerpots, boards, loose wallpaper, cardboard boxes
larger pale trogiid or deathwatch trogiid	*Trogium pulsatorium*	in storage buildings under cloth storage bags

are wingless. From June to August in southern California, with daily temperatures ranging between 60°F and 90°F (16°C to 32°C), the average number of eggs per female is 57, and the egg-to-egg period averages 24 days. From October to January, with daily temperatures varying from 50°F to 87°F (10°C to 31°C), the number of eggs laid by the female of the common booklouse drops to 20, and the egg-to-egg period is 110 days.

Like the deathwatch beetle that attacks wood, the deathwatch psocid gets its name by making tapping sounds that can be heard at night when the house is otherwise silent. The psocid produces this ticking sound by banging its abdomen against the surface it is resting on, up to six taps per second. The taps are most audible when the insect is on paper, and may continue for as long as a minute. Since only the females produce these sounds, they are believed to be mating calls.

Damage
(Booklice, Silverfish and Firebrats)

Booklice cause little direct food loss because they feed chiefly on mold. Damage to books may be more direct, since they eat the starch sizing in the bindings and along the edges of pages.

The mouthparts of silverfish and firebrats are similar to those of cockroaches, and they are used for biting

The Booklouse

Booklice are small, greyish, soft-bodied insects whose shape superficially resembles that of head lice. They feed primarily on mold, and can damage books when they eat the starch sizing in the bindings. (Actual size: ¹⁄₂₅ in. to ¹⁄₁₂ in./1 mm to 2 mm)

off small particles or for scraping away at surfaces. Silverfish and firebrats eat material high in protein, sugar or starch, including cereals, moist wheat flour, starch in book bindings, sizing in paper and paper on which there is glue or paste. They often attack wallpaper, eating irregular holes though the paper to get to the paste. Silverfish may bite very small holes in various fabrics, including cotton, linen and silk. They can digest silk, but not wool, linen or cotton. Firebrats will feed extensively on rayon, whereas silverfish may only damage it slightly.

Detection and Monitoring

Groups of small insects in damp areas should be suspected of being booklice, particularly if mold is present or the area smells moldy. Booklice are considerably smaller (1/25 in. to 1/12 in./ 1 mm to 2 mm long) than silverfish (3/8 in. to 1/2 in./9.5 mm to 13 mm). Booklice lack the telltale three long bristles at the tail end that mark the silverfish. If you are not sure which you are looking at, use a hand lens.

Silverfish are found in bookcases, on closet shelves, behind baseboards, behind window or door frames and in wall voids, attics and subfloor areas. They prefer bathrooms and kitchens because of the moisture. If you suspect that damage to textiles, carpets, curtains, linens or other fabrics is due to silverfish or firebrats, confirm your suspicions using this test: Mix flour and water to form a paste the consistency of house paint. Coat one or more 3x5 index cards with the paste. Let it dry, and place the cards where you have spotted damage. If silverfish or firebrats are in the vicinity, they will be attracted to the card within a week and will feed on the paste. Characteristic feeding marks are minute scrapings in irregular patterns; the edge of the card may be notched.

These insects can also be detected by placing sticky cockroach traps in the area where damage is occurring. These traps, along with other homemade ones, can also be used for control purposes (see the discussion below under direct physical controls).

Treatment:
Indirect Strategies

As mentioned earlier, management of booklice, silverfish and firebrats is essentially the same. Indirect strategies for controlling these household pests focus on reducing humidity in the house.

Silverfish, firebrats and booklice are living indicators of excessive moisture. An occasional individual is not a pest, and is usually tolerated by most people. Nonetheless, its presence should be taken seriously. In rooms where these insects are found, some alteration to the habitat to reduce moisture production and accumulation should be undertaken. If moisture is not eliminated, it may bring more serious pests, such as termites, carpenter ants and wood rot.

If these insects are usually found around one particular window, for example, check the window for a hidden leak and fix it. If the window accumulates condensation repeatedly, then you need to take measures to reduce the condensation. Replacing a single-glazed window with a double-glazed window is one possibility. In rooms such as bathrooms that are regularly moist, a dehumidifier can reduce air moisture and lessen condensation.

Anhydrous calcium carbonate, a dehydrating agent sold in hardware stores for use in small packages, can also be used to absorb free moisture from wood and other surfaces in small areas of the house, particularly enclosed ones. It is a granular material that is often packaged in small cloth bags, which can be dried out in the oven when saturated, and reused. Diatomaceous earth can also be used as a dehydrating agent.

Other techniques for dehumidifying houses, such as altering drainage patterns outside the house, are discussed in Chapter 21 among the habitat modifications suggested to discourage pests of the house structure.

Treatment:
Direct Physical Controls

The direct physical controls for managing silverfish, firebrats and booklice include:

1. Vacuuming. Accumulations of cellulose lint in cracks and crevices should be vacuumed up regularly. Wherever possible, such potential hiding and feeding areas should then be sealed with patching plaster and/or caulk (see the discussion under cockroaches on pp. 223-224).

2. Exposure to Heat and Cold. Firebrats die when exposed to a temperature of 120°F (49°C) for one hour. Below freezing and above 112°F (44°C), nymphs (the young) are killed quickly. Thus, in local areas of the house where temperatures can be elevated, hot air can be tried as a lethal procedure. After you have made a general effort to reduce the source of the humidity, you can use a small heater to warm and dry the area where the eggs have been laid. Make sure you turn off the heat before the wood surface gets too hot to touch. Secondhand books and similar materials that are suspected sources of infestations should be placed inside a plastic bag with a dehydrating agent and placed in the freezer for a week to kill all stages of the insect.

3. Microwave Radiation. Silverfish and other insects that attack books can be killed by placing the book in a kitchen microwave oven for 30 to 60 seconds. According to Professor Jerry Brezner of the State University of New York at Syracuse, most books can undergo this treatment without any damage. The glue on paperback book bindings may soften initially, causing the book to curl a little, but if the book is set on a flat table it will soon flatten out again. Brezner does not recommend this treatment for very old books made of parchment or other fragile paper, or for those with color illustrations that may contain metallic salts in their paints—metals and microwaves don't mix.

4. Trapping. Silverfish can be trapped very easily in small glass jars, such as baby-food containers. Wash the jars thoroughly in hot water and detergent to remove all traces of food and oils; make sure the glass is clean and smooth on the inside. Wrap the outside with masking tape so the insects have something to grip as they climb up. Tests by UCLA entomologist Walter Ebeling showed that adding bait in no way enhances the trapping power of the glass jars— they work just as well completely empty. Set the upright jars in areas where silverfish have been seen. Silverfish can also be trapped in sticky cockroach traps. But remember, there is no point in trapping if the original moisture conditions are not corrected because pests will continue to migrate to the damp area.

5. Drying out Stored Articles. Periodic airing and drying out of articles stored in damp areas may help reduce the mold on which booklice feed. Disposing of moldy articles is often the simplest way of ridding the household of booklice infestations.

Treatment:
Direct Chemical Controls

It should not be necessary to use pesticides to control silverfish, firebrats and booklice. Instead, you should focus your attention on reducing humidity, and on heating or freezing infested articles.

If a pesticide is felt to be necessary, select materials that have a drying action, such as diatomaceous earth and silica aerogel. The latter is particularly effective in killing silverfish. Boric acid is also effective. All of these materials (discussed at length in Chapter 7) must be kept dry.

Dusts should be applied only in cracks and crevices, attics, crawl spaces and other areas that are relatively inaccessible to humans and pets. Although boric acid is regarded as a common and harmless household item, it is also a poison. Before using it, read pp. 112-114 and the discussion of cockroach management on pp. 226-227. Wear a dust mask or a professional-quality respirator to provide proper lung protection when applying any dust.

Because booklice are associated with molds, any of the household products used against these fungi, such as bleach or ammonia solutions, salt water and 2% formalin, can be used to eliminate the mold, depending on the situation. Pyrethrum (see pp. 121-122) is registered for the control of booklice.

Summary: Least-Toxic Silverfish, Firebrat and Booklouse Control

• Find the reason for the moist conditions and try to correct it.

• Use dehumidifiers, increase air flow or focus heat on the damp area to dry it out.

• Use desiccants such as anhydrous calcium carbonate, or drying dusts such as diatomaceous earth or silica aerogel to dry up damp areas.

• Heat or freeze infested articles to dry them out and kill insects.

• Clean and caulk cracks and crevices where lint accumulates and allows these insects to feed and breed.

• Use a household cleaning agent to reduce the mold that feeds booklice.

REFERENCES AND READINGS

Abbott, W.S., and S.C. Billings. 1935. Further work showing that paradichlorobenzene, naphthalene and cedar oils are ineffective as repellents against clothes moths. *Journal of Economic Entomology* 28:493-495.

This early study shows that woolens placed in boxes with these pesticides were contaminated after adult clothes moths were released in the rooms.

Baerg, W.J., and L.O. Warren. 1954. Biology and control of the webbing clothes moth. *Arkansas Agricultural Experiment Station Bulletin* 544. 19 pp.

A short review of the subject that is a source of information on least-toxic controls, natural enemies and webbing clothes moth biology.

Bry, R.E., R.E. Boatright and J.H. Lang. 1982. Permethrin: effectiveness of low deposits against three species of fabric insects. *Journal of the Georgia Entomological Society* 17(1): 46-53.

This study reveals that fabrics treated with synergized permethrin were protected for six months against the black carpet beetle (*Attagenus megatoma*), the webbing clothes moth (*Tineola bisselliella*) and the furniture carpet beetle (*Anthrenus flavipes*).

Bry, R.E., R.E. Boatright, J.H. Lang and R.A. Simonaitis. 1980. Spray applications of permethrin against fabric pests. *Pest Control* 47(4):14-16.

This paper reports on the effectiveness of the pesticide permethrin against fabric pests.

Bry, R.E., and L.L. McDonald. 1970. Moth-proofing investigations with imidazole. *Journal of Economic Entomology* 63:71.

This study reveals that adding boric acid to imidazole increases overall effectiveness and reduces the amount of imidazole needed to kill clothes moths.

Bry, R.E., L.L. McDonald and J.H. Lang. 1972. Protecting stored woolens against fabric-insect damage: a long-term nonchemical method. *Journal of Economic Entomology* 65(6): 1735-1736.

This study reports that heat-sealed kraft/polyethylene case liners were 100% effective in protecting stored military woolens for five years without other protection.

Busvine, J.R. 1980. *Insects and hygiene: the biology and control of insect pests of medical and domestic importance.* 3rd ed. New York: Chapman and Hall. 568 pp.

Although oriented primarily toward pests of Britain, this book is also an excellent source of information about pests in the United States and elsewhere.

Ebeling, W. 1975. *Urban entomology.* Los Angeles: University of California. 695 pp.

A classic text that we used extensively in the preparation of this book.

Freeman, P. 1980. *Common insect pests of stored food products: a guide to their identification.* 6th ed. London: British Museum of Natural History (Economic Series No. 15). 69 pp. (Available in the United States from: Rudolph W. Sabbot, Natural History Books, 5239 Tendilla Ave., Woodland Hills, CA 91364.)

A pamphlet of keys, photos and excellent line drawings of the insects of stored foods and related products. The closely related lepidoptera are distinguished in a key and photos.

Mallis, A. 1982. *Handbook of pest control.* Cleveland: Franzak and Foster. 1,101 pp.

This standard text is full of fascinating details about clothes moths, and includes a chapter describing an integrated pest management program for silverfish.

Rawle, S.G. 1951. The effect of high temperatures on the common clothes moth, *Tineola bisselliella. Bull. Ent. Res.* 42(1):29-40.

A detailed study of the way that clothes moths react to changes in temperature.

Reagan, B.M., Chiang-cheng Jaw-Hu and N.J. Streit. 1980. Effects of microwave radiation on the webbing clothes moth, *Tineola bisselliella* and textiles. *Journal of Food Protection* 43(8):658-663.

A study of the effectiveness of microwave radiation on wool samples infested with eggs, larvae and adults.

Snetsinger, R. 1983. *The ratcatcher's child: the history of the pest control industry.* Cleveland: Franzak and Foster. 294 pp.

This was the source for the drawing on p. 195 of clothes moth control in the Middle Ages.

Stojanovich, C.J., and H.G. Scott. 1967. Silverfish; pictorial key to domestic species. In *CDC pictorial keys: arthropods, reptiles, birds and mammals of public-health significance.* Atlanta, Ga.: U.S. H.E.W. Public-Health Service Department. 192 pp.

A pictorial key for identification of silverfish species in the United States.

Tittanen, K. 1971. The efficiency of pyrethrin aerosol against the larvae of the clothes moth *Tineola bisselliella. Pyrethrum Post* 11(1):15-17.

This article provides experimental evidence indicating that pyrethrins can be substituted for chlorinated hydrocarbons such as DDT and lindane.

Wilson, H.F. 1940. Lures and traps to control clothes moths and carpet beetles. *Journal of Economic Entomology* 33:651-653.

In this study, clothes moths and carpet beetles were attracted to box traps containing cloth pads treated with fish oil or an alcoholic extract of the same material.

Yamvrias, C., and T.A. Angus. 1969. Toxicity of *Bacillus thuringiensis* for larvae of the clothes moth, *Tineola bisselliella. Journal of Invertebrate Pathology* 14:423-424.

This article provides laboratory results indicating the susceptibility of the clothes moth to BT.

CHAPTER 14
Kitchen and Pantry Pests

INTRODUCTION

We have brought with us into the 20th century a number of ancient roommates that have shared our nests since the days of the cave. Not surprisingly, many of them tend to gravitate toward the kitchen and cupboard. Like guests who have come to dinner and overstayed their welcome, once inside these visitors are often very difficult to get rid of. The best strategy, of course, is to exclude them in the first place.

In this chapter, we focus on some of the least-liked creatures: cockroaches, ants and pests of stored food. (Pests that are occasionally found in the kitchen—mice, for example—but take up residence elsewhere as well are discussed in Chapter 16.)

In addition to excluding these pests from the house, or from the food in the house, the management of kitchen and pantry pests often involves changing the manner in which we store our organic wastes. Waste management has two aspects, both equally difficult to tackle because they involve changing life-long attitudes and habits of sanitation, cleanliness and garbage disposal. Because most of us live with other people, we must review not only our own actions, but also the habits of other house companions. Without the cooperation of all household occupants, any effort to control the pests discussed here will be difficult if not impossible to apply.

Even if pest exclusion is practiced to the best of one's ability—if wastes are stored out of reach of pests and kitchen cleanliness becomes a religion—there will still be many situations where additional modification of the habitat, as well as physical and chemical controls, will be needed. Fortunately, there are many relatively nontoxic options for the home owner that, in our experience, can withstand the test of even the most roach-infested inner-city apartment houses. It is our pleasure to share these tips with you.

COCKROACHES: OVERVIEW
(Order Blattoidea, family Blattidae)

Cockroaches are among the most disagreeable of household insects, often inducing psychological distress and embarrassment in those persons whose dwellings are infested. Cockroaches consume human foodstuffs and contaminate them with saliva and excrement; they also produce secretions that impart a characteristic fetid odor to materials.

Cockroaches have changed little since their beginnings in the Devonian period of the Paleozoic era 400 million years ago. Evidence of cockroaches found in an orangutan nest suggest that the present residential roach species evolved from roaches that inhabited primate nests. There are more than 3,500 known roach species in the world, 57 of them in the United States. As many as 4,000 additional species are believed to exist but have not yet been described. Cockroaches are found in caves, mines, animal burrows, ant and termite nests and human habitats.

Only five roach species are significantly pestiferous throughout the United States: the German, brownbanded, oriental, American and smokybrown. Table 14.1 on the facing page lists the colors and reproductive characteristics of these five.

The smokybrown cockroach has become a problem in the Gulf and southwestern states. It is a large cockroach, as are the American and the Australian roaches. The German and brownbanded roaches are small in comparison, whereas the oriental roach is medium in size.

The Asian cockroach *(Blattella asahinai)* is new to the United States, and has recently established itself in Florida. The infested area includes about 500 square miles as we go to press; however, because the roach flies very readily and has a greater reproductive potential than the German roach, it may become a serious pest in other areas in the future.

A number of other native and introduced roaches live primarily outdoors in the decaying vegetation of the garden and forest. Examples include the brown roach and the field cockroach. In areas where these roaches periodically come into the house, it is essential to clean decaying vegetation away from foundations, leaving a clean border. Outdoor planter boxes and other structures close to the house where moisture and decayed organic material collect should also be monitored.

Even roaches that are pests indoors have their preferred habitats. The Australian roach is more vegetarian than the others and may establish itself in greenhouses. The American roach likes moisture and the seafaring life—it is common on ships as well as in basements and sewers. The smokybrown roach is also found in sewers, but lives primarily outdoors. The oriental roach is another moisture-lover, while the brownbanded roach prefers the warm dryness of closet shelves and the upper stories of houses. Table 14.2 on p. 218 lists the five most important roach species and their preferred indoor habitats.

Cockroaches evolved as scavengers of dead plant material; as a result, they prefer carbohydrates to protein and fat. They will discriminate among foods if given a choice, but when hungry they eat almost anything. Some products not normally considered food—starch-based paints, wallpaper paste, envelope glue and bar soaps—contain carbohydrates, and hence are food for roaches.

Buildings provide roaches with microclimates similar to their native habitats. A source of moisture and warmth is most important to their survival, although some species, particularly the brownbanded roach, are adapting so that they need less water.

By this point it should be clear that the key to long-term cockroach management is reduction of sources of food, water and the harborage roaches need to survive. Nonetheless,

Table 14.1
Characteristics of Residential Cockroaches[a]

	Roach Species	Length	Color and Markings	Eggs[b]	Egg to Adult	Reproductive Characteristics
	German (Blattella germanica)	9/16 in. (14 mm)	light brown with two dark stripes on the pronotum (the section of the thorax behind the head)	37	55-68 days	female carries egg case until 12 days before hatching, then drops it anywhere
	brownbanded (Supella longipalpa)	9/16 in. (14 mm)	tan-golden with faint V-shaped lighter bands on wings	16	95-276 days	egg case glued to the ceilings, beneath furniture, or in closets or other dark places
	oriental (Blatta orientalis)	1¼ in. (32 mm)	dark red-brown-black throughout	14	300-800 days	egg case deposited in debris or food in a sheltered place
	American (Periplaneta americana)	1¾ in. (44 mm)	reddish brown throughout with a pale band on the edge of the pronotum; a very large roach	14	285-616 days	egg case carried up to six days; brown when laid but turns black in 1 to 2 days
	smokybrown (Periplaneta fuliginosa)	1½ in. (38 mm)	pronotum a solid dark brown to black; a very large roach	20	320-388 days	egg case carried for one day; will hatch from 24 to 70 days later

[a] Drawings show adults and egg cases.
[b] Average number per egg case.

it is still common to have an entire apartment or building treated with insecticides when cockroaches are present — over $1.5 billion is spent in the United States alone each year to spray roaches. This is rarely necessary or advisable. Time, energy and money are far more effectively spent determining the exact location of the cockroaches and applying pest control tactics just in those areas. If insecticides are needed, spot treatment just in the cracks and crevices where roaches hide reduces the likelihood of the roaches becoming resistant to the material, no matter what its toxicity. To determine where to direct your cockroach management efforts — or the work of anyone you hire — it is essential that you have a monitoring program in place. We discuss monitoring on pp. 219-221.

The German cockroach is the most troublesome domestic roach species in North America. Although the following discussion focuses on this roach, it should be stressed that the basic principles for managing all roaches indoors are the same. Where there are important differences in the management of various species, we draw them to your attention.

THE GERMAN COCKROACH
(Family Blattidae: Blattella germanica)

The German roach has the widest distribution of all domestic roaches. Outside, it is often found in dead leaves and rubbish heaps. It invades the indoors from outdoor habitats in

Table 14.2
Preferred Habitats of Common Pest Roaches

Roach Species	Habitat
German	found in warm, moist areas in food establishments and other buildings where food, warmth and moisture are readily available; prefers the kitchen and bathroom
brownbanded	found throughout the house; prefers high locations in heated homes, apartments and hospitals; also found in closets, under furniture, in appliances that generate heat, behind wallpaper, and in desks, dressers, boxes, piles of debris and material
oriental	found in crawl spaces and basements, under refrigerators, washing machines, in sewers, drains and sinks, usually below ground level
American	found in commercial structures such as food establishments, grocery stores, warehouses, office buildings, prisons and ships; prefers warm, moist areas around furnaces or heating ducts; usually found in basements or on first floor; flies more readily than others
smokybrown	prefers to live outdoors in woodpiles and other debris near homes, but can enter garages and other buildings; a southern U.S. species

summer but not in winter. In eastern and midwestern cities, it is the roach you most often see scurrying for the dark when you turn on the kitchen light at night. Austin Frishman, in his revision of the chapter on cockroaches in Arnold Mallis' standard reference work, the *Handbook of Pest Control*, quotes a poem by Christopher Morley:

Timid roach why be so shy?
We are brothers, thou and I.
In the midnight, like thyself,
I explore the pantry shelf!

Cockroach infestations can occur in any building, and their egg cases are often accidently introduced in shipped materials, groceries, beer and soft-drink cases, used appliances, rugs, furniture, and so forth. The German roach readily visits cartons, sacks and containers, and will enter open or empty bottles. It is the most common roach on ships and planes, and is found in commercial buildings such as grocery stores, warehouses, offices, prisons and schools. It prefers the warm areas around furnaces and heating ducts.

The German roach is usually found in basements and on first floors, and is the most common species seen in food-preparation areas in restaurants, cafeterias and other eating establishments, as well as in bathrooms. All these are microenvironments where the combination of food, moisture and warm temperature mimics the environment of its native East Africa. (Just how the German roach got its common name is lost in antiquity.)

The migratory ability of roaches is considerable. In apartment and office buildings, roaches can travel up elevator shafts and drains, through air and heating vents, through tiny cracks and crevices in walls that connect one unit with another, and above false ceilings. Some species enter buildings through ill-fitting doors of boiler rooms and other basement areas, through open windows, etc.

Roaches commonly radiate out from areas that provide a steady source of food: kitchens, pantries, snack bars, restaurants, and garbage collection or disposal areas. Where and when the weather is warm enough, roaches can migrate between structures outdoors along the outsides of buildings and from dumpsters to nearby living units. The very activities that are meant to reduce roach populations in one area, such as pesticide spraying and garbage cleanup, may send large numbers of adult roaches scurrying to attached units nearby. Some species, such as the smokybrown roach common in the southern states, spend much of their life outdoors, living in woodpiles and organic mulch in wooded areas. Cool weather or lack of food may drive them into garages, outbuildings or homes. Oriental roaches, commonly found in sewers, may enter basements through unscreened drains.

Biology

The life cycle of the German roach (see the drawing on the facing page) starts with the egg case, or ootheca, which is dropped by the female after she has carried it for most of the incubation period. Incubation takes 28 days at 76°F (24°C), 23 days at 85°F (29°C) and 16 days (with a reduced percentage that hatch) at 88°F (31°C). Between 35 and 43 nymphs emerge from the egg case, pass

The Life Cycle of the German Cockroach

The adult German cockroach lives more than 200 days. Females produce an average of four egg cases containing 30 to 50 eggs. The egg stage lasts 23 days and the nymphal stage 27 to 103 days, although in warm environments the life cycle can be completed in as few as 28 days. (Actual length of adult: 9/16 in./14 mm)

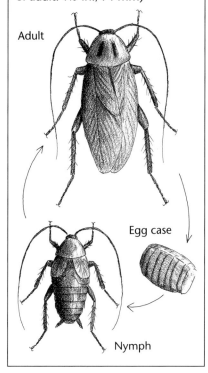

Adult

Egg case

Nymph

through six or seven instars and molt into adults. The average development period from nymph to adult is 103 days at 76°F (24°C) and 74 days at 85°F (29°C). Females can live more than 200 days and produce an average of four egg cases each. After maturing, it takes another 11 days before egg-laying starts. There are three or four generations per year; the German roach has the highest reproductive capability of all domestic cockroach species.

German cockroaches are thigmotactic; that is, they prefer squeezing into small cracks where their backs and undersides make contact with other surfaces. In heavily infested areas, roaches can often be observed backed into cracks with their heads sticking out and their antennae waving around, picking up chemical signals from the air. Their behavior is apparently more dependent on the interception of chemical stimuli than on vision or sound. These roaches generally become more active 20 minutes to two hours before dark, and increase their activity to a peak, which ends before daybreak. They are active in daylight only when populations are very high.

Damage

Cockroaches have not yet been proven to be involved in the natural transmission of any particular human pathogen, and the federal Centers for Disease Control recently removed roaches from their list of public-health pests. However, much evidence has been collected that clearly indicates the potential for cockroaches to transmit a long list of disease-causing organisms. Because roaches wander at will through all types of organic wastes, then travel with equanimity over kitchen counters, dinner plates and silverware, it is hard to regard the presence of roaches in the kitchen as benign.

Nonetheless, tolerance for cockroaches varies widely. If you live in a building that has a large roach population that is distributed throughout the structure, the best you can hope for is to keep the number of roaches in your apartment low enough so that you don't see them at night when you turn on the light. This can be done, but you will still occasionally trap one that has wandered under the entrance door or through some other crack you were unable to weatherstrip or caulk. Some people can tolerate far more than an occasional roach, and feel the extra work required to get the number so low that they can't be seen is not worth the trouble.

Detection and Monitoring

Efforts to control roaches should begin with a monitoring program to identify where most roaches are concentrated. This tells you where to focus your effort to reduce roach harborage (by caulking up crevices where they like to stay, for example). The second objective of monitoring is to determine whether your efforts have reduced the roach population.

When faced with a roach infestation, many people automatically assume that the insects are dispersed everywhere throughout the room or building. This is rarely the case. An interesting fact about German cockroaches is their tendency to occur in "patches" in a room. Once they have located a suitable harborage, they tend to concentrate there, leaving periodically to forage for food and water, then returning to the same place. Thus, the first step in monitoring is to locate these roach concentrations.

A monitoring technique commonly used by pest control operators is to use a pyrethrin spray to flush roaches out from their hiding places and make rough estimates of roach numbers on the basis of visual counts. We think a better method is to use nontoxic sticky traps. The traps provide more reliable information about where roaches are concentrated and whether or not a particular roach population is being reduced by various treatments.

The drawing on p. 220 shows several kinds of traps that can be used to monitor roaches. One variety of nontoxic trap that has become widely available throughout the United States consists of a small rectangular or triangular cardboard box. Inside the box are bands of sticky glue and, in some models, a dark strip of cockroach food. Such traps are sold in hardware stores under a variety of brand names.

You can also make your own trap. One effective model originally developed by UCLA entomologist Walter Ebeling consists of a quart-sized mason jar with a slice of white sandwich

Cockroach Traps

A variety of cockroach traps are available in grocery and hardware stores. Most are small and rectangular (A) or triangular (B) with sticky glue inside, but homemade traps made from jars whose inner rims are coated with petroleum jelly (C) also work. The traps should be placed along the edges of walls or counters where roaches normally travel (D). Only nontoxic traps should be used in cupboards.

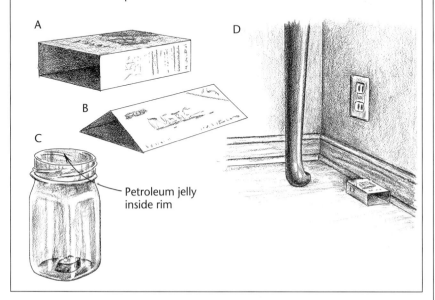

Petroleum jelly
inside rim

bread inside. In this design, the jar was coated on all inside surfaces with a fine clay material to prevent the roaches from escaping. The material is no longer available, but you can coat the inside of the jar mouth with Vaseline® or any other petroleum jelly, drop in the bread and set the jar upright in room corners. Cockroaches will fall into the jar to get the bait, but will not be able to cross the petroleum-jelly barrier to escape. You can kill the trapped roaches with hot, soapy water, or screw a lid on the jar and put it in the freezer overnight.

In one test comparing the homemade trap with the commonly available commercial traps, the homemade trap was shown to provide the most reliable sample of the roach population. To achieve this degree of reliability, however, the trap should be left in place for at least one week.

It is important to note that not all traps are equally effective against all roach species. If you take the time to identify the species you have, you can choose the best trap for monitoring. The homemade trap described above was originally tested against the German roach. If you make your own trap and use it for a different species, you may have to experiment with different baits. Table 14.3 on the facing page compares the effectiveness of four commercial traps against the five most common pest roaches.

Roaches prefer to congregate in tight or enclosed spaces within warm, moist environments. Such locations include cracks and crevices, the motor compartment under refrigerators, inside electric clocks or wall sockets, under the pilot light in stoves, and near leaky plumbing fixtures under the sink. Thus traps should be placed in drawers, closets and cupboards, under sinks and stoves, in the motor area of refrigerators and against walls where you think that roaches may

travel. Roaches prefer to move along the perimeter of walls and other objects (for example, where counters or floors intersect walls), so place the traps along such travel routes rather than out in the open. Roaches will not seek out traps located outside their normal travel routes.

Initially, put out as many traps as you can afford (for example, eight in the kitchen, three per bathroom). The more traps you use, the faster you will find out where the roaches are located. Later, you can use fewer traps for ongoing monitoring.

Trap data is helpful in three major ways. First, it tells you where management efforts should be directed. Check the traps 24 hours after setting them out, and count the number of roaches in each. This will suggest where the roach population is concentrated. Traps with the highest numbers of roaches indicate a nearby harborage, and this is where you should concentrate management efforts; traps with few or no roaches should be moved to other locations until you are certain you have pinpointed the main harborage areas.

Second, data from the traps tells you whether management efforts have been effective. To see how well your efforts are working, put out fresh traps a week or so after implementing the treatment methods described below, and count again 24 hours later. If the roach population has dropped considerably, you know you are on the right track. If not, greater efforts are needed.

Third, trap data tells you the level of infestation you can tolerate. To determine this, count the total number of roaches caught in 24 hours and divide by the total number of traps set out, whether or not they trapped roaches. The answer is the average number of roaches in the area. Use this data to establish your roach injury or tolerance level, that is, the relative number of roaches you will tolerate before an expenditure of time, labor and money is justified in controlling them.

Table 14.3
A Comparison of the Effectiveness of Different Sticky Roach Traps[a]

Sticky Trap (Commercial Name)	Description	Performance with Domestic Roach Species[b]				
		G	B	O	A	S
D-Con®	molasses bait inside in center of three sticky bands; rectangular in cross section, with ¾-in. wide internally directed flaps at both ends; black exterior, white interior	1	2	1	3	3
Holiday Roach Coach®	bait packet placed in trap by user; trapezoidal in cross section; brown wood-grain exterior, grey interior with sticky layer on bottom	2	1	1	2	2
Mr. Sticky®	no bait; triangular in cross section; yellow, blue and orange exterior, grey interior with sticky layer on bottom	2	3	2	3	4
Raid Roach Traps®	bait attractant; same size and shape as D-Con®; brown wood-grain exterior, black interior; sticky inside	1	2	1	1	1

Key:

G = German   B = brownbanded   O = oriental   A = American   S = smokybrown

[a] Based on work by Moore and Granovsky, 1983.

[b] 1 = best, 4 = worst

For example, in an experimental roach IPM program in a Washington, D.C., area school, the roach tolerance level was determined to be an average of less than one roach per trap. In a kitchen on an army base, however, the tolerance level was an average of two roaches per trap. At these population levels, roaches were never seen by staff, although the traps showed that some roaches were present.

Traps are logical tools for monitoring roach densities, and in certain limited situations they can also be used to reduce roach numbers. For example Art Slater and others at the University of California used sticky box traps to control roaches in animal-rearing rooms where no insecticides were allowed. Traps may also capture occasional roaches that were dislodged during construction, introduced into roach-free areas on furniture or packaging, or forced into the area when an adjacent room was sprayed with an insecticide.

When traps are used to reduce populations of roaches, you will want to leave them in place until they are full. In most situations, however, trapping alone will not produce sufficient control of roaches. It is best to regard traps as a tool for monitoring and focus management efforts on exclusion and other tactics that will reduce roach access to food, water and habitat, combined with judicious use of least-toxic chemical controls in the form of baits and dusts.

Treatment: Indirect Strategies

Entomologist Walter Ebeling has done much to show that roaches can be controlled through habitat management, reduction of access to water and food and the selective application of boric acid. The treatment strategies we describe here are based largely on Ebeling's work.

Published information on cockroach control around kitchen equipment focuses on commercial food service carts and walk-in refrigerators, which are particularly attractive to roaches. Unfortunately, there is little of practical use for the designer of household kitchen equipment and other furnishings. Kitchen cupboards and appliances can be made less inviting to roaches simply by eliminating the cracks built into trim and edges. If you are remodeling your kitchen, consider installing the fashionable stainless-steel open shelving units used in commercial kitchens. The round shape of the metal and the general openness of the design offer few hiding places to roaches.

1. Proper Storage of Food. Food should be kept in containers that close tightly and resist roach entry by chewing; paper and cardboard boxes should not be considered roach-proof. Glass containers with rubber gaskets and various plastic containers that seal by pressure resist roaches, so you should transfer packaged goods into them as soon as you get home. Buy a set of jars in a range of sizes. All the food you store should be in sealed containers within a refrigerator with a good seal around the door, in sealed glass jars or in plastic containers with snap-on lids.

Cough drops by the bed, a candy bar in the desk at the office, peanuts or crackers for snacking in the den—all these constitute potential roach food. Wherever there is food, a roach-proof storage container should be provided. These containers should be attractive, conveniently placed and easy to use. Children, visitors and all other household members must train themselves to clean up rigorously and use these containers.

2. Storage of Organic Waste. If you take the trouble to design your waste-management system correctly, you will take a large step toward reducing not only roaches but a number of other common household pests, such as ants, flies and rodents. It is important to develop a waste-storage system in which the organic wastes—the peelings and shells from food preparation and food scrapings from plates—are placed in a container that is inaccessible to roaches. We found gallon plastic containers with snap-on lids that were perfect for this in a variety store with a large plastic ware section. You will need at least two containers so one can air out or be disinfected with a weak bleach or soap solution while the other is in use.

Five-gallon plastic containers (obtainable from paint stores) can be adapted for this use. The container should be lined with a large but thin plastic bag so the lid can snap down tightly over it.

All debris from the preparation and cleanup of meals should go into this container, and the lid should be snapped down firmly after each use

---

Pest-Free Storage of Kitchen Waste
Indoors, organic kitchen garbage can be stored in plastic containers with tight lids (A) or between layers of sawdust (B), as described in the sidebar on the facing page. Outdoors, put garbage in metal containers with tight covers and lid fasteners (C).

 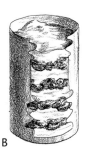 

A   B   C

(see the drawing above). This also reduces housefly problems. When the inner sack becomes full, it should be transferred immediately to the incinerator or to a large outdoor garbage can with a tight, snap-on lid. If you are storing the organic wastes to make batches of hot aerobic compost, follow the procedure described in the sidebar on the facing page. Bottles, cans, wrappings and other items that have food residues clinging to them should be washed out thoroughly in soapy water before being stored for recycling.

3. Screening Vents and Windows. Many apartments in roach-infested buildings are interconnected by a variety of unscreened ducts and vents through which roaches can and do travel. In apartments above furnace or laundry rooms you may find that in warm weather roaches travel the few feet up the outside of the building and enter the apartment through an open window. The answer is to design in or retrofit aluminum screening for vents and windows. This prevents roaches from using these as major highways for getting from one part of the building to another. It is often possible to remove existing grillwork over vents, place screening behind it and replace the grillwork, which is often quite attractive, so the

screen is hidden. Be sure to caulk around the edge of the screen to make a tight barrier.

4. Habitat Modification. Modify the environment to reduce roach access to food, shelter and water. If you use good-quality materials and do a careful job, the alterations will be permanent and make a similarly permanent change in the roach carrying capacity of the environment.

Studies have shown that without food and water, female German cockroaches survive only 13 days at 81°F (27°C) and 40% humidity. With water but no food, survival time increases to 42 days. With both food and water, females survive about 80 days. Survival time with food alone —about 12 days—is about the same as with no food or water. The survival time increases significantly if the relative humidity is higher. For example, six females survived 28 days at 70% RH with no food or water. One can conclude from this data that the German roach survives longer on water alone than on food alone. And it survives longer without food or water if the relative humidity is higher. Thus, the first priorities in habitat modification are reducing the available drinking water and humidity.

Roaches find drinking water in sink traps, drain pipes, wash basins,

Storing Organic Kitchen Garbage in Sawdust

1. Drain the organic kitchen wastes in a colander at the sink.

2. Transfer the wastes to a five-gallon container, such as a plastic garbage can, with a lid.

3. Cover each new layer of waste in the container with several inches of dry sawdust to eliminate the smells that attract roaches, flies, mice and other pests. Over time, this should result in alternating layers of waste and sawdust.

4. When the container is almost full, top it off with a final layer of sawdust, cover and set aside.

5. When enough containers have been filled to make a cubic yard of compost when added to grass clippings, leaves, weeds and other garden gleanings, empty them into a tightly constructed compost bin with a lid. For directions on constructing a "hot" compost system, see Olkowski et al.'s *The Integral Urban House Book.*

tubs, toilet bowls and flush tanks. Other sources are spillage, condensation on cold-water pipes and windows, leaky pipes and faucets, pet dishes, aquaria, vases, beverage bottles, drainage pans underneath refrigerators, and various high-moisture foods. Much can be done to cut back this supply through repairs and barriers. Fix dripping faucets and any other leaks. Provide drainage or ventilation to dry out moist areas. Do not leave water on kitchen surfaces, and remove pet water bowls at night or place them in a pan of soapy water as a barrier to roaches. Unfortunately, many moisture sources are virtually impossible to eliminate effectively; food-reduction strategies deserve extra attention in the vicinity of such moisture sources.

5. Cleaning. We have already discussed the importance of placing all foodstuffs in roach-proof containers and of developing a system for managing organic garbage so that roaches are denied access. In addition, you should give the kitchen a periodic, all-inclusive cleaning. Focus on areas where grease accumulates: drains, vents, ovens and stoves. After each meal or snack, wipe the surfaces clean, then wipe them dry. Sweep up crumbs and miscellaneous debris. Pick up pet food between feedings and store it in the refrigerator. Or, if you use dry kibble, serve it in a plastic bowl or other container that has a tight snap-on lid and seal it up between meals. Make a habit of submerging dirty dishes in a strong solution of detergent and water when you don't have time to wash them immediately. A small vacuum like a Dustbuster® kept in a handy place can help keep problem areas clean.

6. Sealing Cracks. The adult German cockroach can hide in cracks as narrow as ¹⁄₁₆ in. (1.5 mm), and first instar nymphs can squeeze through a gap as small as ¹⁄₂₅ in. (1 mm). To reduce the roach carrying capacity of your home, potential harborage must be caulked (as shown in the drawing at right), painted or sealed shut with whatever material is appropriate to the location.

In older dwellings, where there are numerous cracks, crevices and hard-to-reach places, you might feel that there are simply too many cracks to seal. Fortunately, you don't have to seal them all. This is where monitoring with traps pays off. Start by caulking where the traps indicate roach populations are highest, then work on other areas as time and energy allow. Remember that every foot of hiding place you plug up reduces the number of roaches the structure can support for as long as the plug lasts.

Caulking to Eliminate Cockroach Harborage

Use a caulking gun to seal cracks where roaches hide. Hold the gun at a 45° angle to the crack and squeeze the trigger to force caulk into the crack. The caulk should completely fill the crack and adhere firmly to both sides of it. Release the trigger just before reaching the end of the crack. Moisten your finger with soapy water (for latex caulk) or mineral spirits (for other caulks) and smooth the caulk over the crack.

Before beginning the sealing process, wash or vacuum and wash the area to eliminate all egg cases, fecal material and bits of food waste that may have accumulated there. Dispose of these vacuumings by burning the bag, burying it, placing it in a tightly closed container for disposal or composting it after freezing for one or two days. Once the areas to be sealed are clean, plug cracks around baseboards, wall shelves, cupboards, pipes, sinks, bathtub fixtures and similar furnishings in the locations suggested by trap results.

Paint can be used alone or in conjunction with putty or caulk. Large caulking jobs are best done before repainting. Three general types of caulk are available. Cartridge caulk, which requires an inexpensive caulking gun, is useful for big jobs such as along floor boards or behind cabinets. Squeeze-tube caulk is good for sealing around faucets, vents and similar openings. Rope-like caulk, which usually comes in coils, is most useful for quick, temporary seals. Large holes or cracks will require special cements or other substances that match existing materials, depending upon how visible the repairs will be.

Latex caulk is water-soluble before it dries, but cracks if flexed afterwards. Butyl caulk stays flexible, but is very sticky and requires special solvents to remove. Silicone seal is flexible and easy to apply. It comes in clear and colored forms, and manufacturers claim it will last for 50 years. But it is more expensive than other caulks. A cheaper grade of silicone seal has recently been developed, but its flexibility still needs evaluation.

You can repair small holes in window screens with silicone seal or a similar clear caulk. Weatherstrip around doors and windows where cockroaches may enter the house.

Urethane foams for sealing cracks are available in aerosol cans, but they are insufficient for small jobs as the can tends to seal itself after one use and cannot be reopened easily. However, urethane is excellent for filling openings larger than 3 in. (7.6 cm) wide that cannot be sealed in other ways. Look for small cans that you are likely to use up in a single job.

7. Steam-Cleaning Furniture. Upholstered furniture and kitchen appliances suspected of harboring roaches can be steam-cleaned. Furniture with wood veneer and/or plastic components should not be treated in this manner, however, as it may be damaged by moisture or heat.

8. Education. We do not suggest that all the above practices can be instituted overnight. It takes time for household members to learn new ways of doing things. These changes are particularly challenging if you live in an old building with many residents, including children and/or pets, that has a serious infestation. All members of the dwelling must be educated about the need to control the roaches and about the importance of reducing the food and water they need to survive.

Two popular misconceptions make this difficult. Some people feel the roach problem is hopeless, especially if they live in a building where all the other apartments also have roaches. To boost the morale of people with this attitude, we (the Olkowskis) would like to share our personal experience. For a time, our work required that we reside in Arlington, Virginia. Places to live that we could afford were hard to find. When we finally did find something suitable, we discovered after moving in that the apartment house was crawling with roaches. There were roaches in the hallways, in the elevators and in the laundry room. Worse, there were plenty in the apartment we moved into, judging by the skins and egg cases we saw in the cabinets under the sink.

We should point out that we are far more interested in our professional activities than in house-cleaning; we are probably among the world's worst housekeepers. But we followed the techniques outlined here. After initial cleaning with soap and water and a vacuum, we set out traps, caulked, screened, weatherstripped, set up a tight garbage system and trained ourselves either to clean up at night or to submerge dishes in soapy water overnight. Also, following the techniques described on pp. 226-227 under "Chemical Controls," we used boric acid in a few out-of-the-way places. Within a month we had reduced the roach population to such a low level that we hardly ever saw a roach in the two years we lived there. To our knowledge, nothing else changed in the apartment house; roaches were still common in other areas. If the world's worst housekeepers can do it, so can you.

Other people are under the misconception that the only way to handle roaches is to have the entire building treated with insecticides. In fact, we have seen many apartment houses and other buildings that are treated repeatedly but, after a period of time, end up with as many or more roaches than before. So they have to treat again...and again. In the end, they have a pesticide-residue problem as well as a roach problem.

Sooner or later roaches either learn to avoid the insecticide being used, or the population becomes resistant. The only permanent solution is to modify the environment and reduce its roach carrying capacity. Then, if you feel you need to use chemical controls to suppress the remaining roaches, the insecticides are far more likely to work, especially when used sparingly for spot treatment in those locations where you have detected the highest concentrations of roaches.

Treatment:
Direct Physical Controls

If you see a roach wandering about, squash it with a paper towel or soapy sponge rather than your hand so you don't pick up pathogens the roach may be carrying. Small, confined populations can often be trapped. Larger infestations can be killed using carbon dioxide, steam or vacuums.

1. Carbon Dioxide Fumigation. Cartons of roach-infested belongings can be sealed in plastic bags and fumigated with carbon dioxide gas. Chris Christiansen and colleagues at the University of Kentucky, whose vacuuming technique is discussed below, loaded cardboard boxes full of furnishings, clothing and papers from roach-infested apartments into 5-ft. by 3-ft. by 12-ft. (1.5 m by 0.9 m by 3.7 m) plastic bags, 6 mil in thickness. The bags are available from Urban Insect Solutions (listed in the Resource Appendix under "Suppliers" on pp. 690-696).

Once a bag was full, the end of a vacuum hose was inserted to suck as much air as possible out of the bag. The bag was then tightly sealed (using duct tape to reinforce all seams in the bag). Then a hose from a canister of CO_2 was inserted into a small opening cut in the top side of the bag. Enough undiluted CO_2 was released to fill the bag, then the canister was removed and the hole sealed with duct tape. When the bag was reopened, roaches were either dead or extremely sluggish, dying a short time later without further treatment.

2. Steam-Cleaning. Infested appliances can be steam-cleaned to kill roaches. Survivors driven out by the steam can be caught in traps placed nearby. A pest control company in southern California uses periodic steam-cleaning to keep garbage chutes in multistory apartment buildings free of roaches.

3. Vacuuming. A regular household vacuum, or a larger-capacity "shop vac," can be used to suck up roaches, including their egg cases, as well as organic debris that drops behind appliances and furniture and feeds the pests. Chris Christiansen, owner of Urban Insect Solutions in Lexington, Kentucky, used a shop vacuum to clean out thousands of roaches in public housing units. He used the crevice attachment on the end of the hose to suck roaches out of cracks and the hose end alone to pull roaches out from under appliances, or from cupboards or upholstered furniture. Christiansen found that the dust that inevitably collected in the vacuum along with the insects apparently clogged the captured roaches' breathing apparatus and suffocated them. Thus, when full, the

A tiny parasitic miniwasp, *Comperia merceti,* is reared and released in research laboratories on the University of California at Berkeley campus to control brownbanded roaches. The tiny parasitoids lay their eggs in the roaches' egg cases. The parasitoid egg hatches into a hungry larva, which feeds on roach embryos. (Photo by Art Slater.)

vacuum bag could simply be removed and discarded. It would be prudent to enclose the vacuum bag in a sealed plastic bag prior to discarding it to prevent escapes by any roaches that did manage to survive the vacuuming process.

Treatment:
Direct Biological Controls

Cockroaches are fed upon by a host of natural enemies, including spiders, ants, rats, wasps, toads, beetles, bugs, mantids, dragonflies, geckos, scorpions, miniwasps and microbes. The real problem with our pest roaches is that they are exotic—they have invaded from elsewhere and have left their most serious natural enemies behind. As you will see repeatedly throughout this book, natural enemies that control insect populations are often the host-specific predators and parasitoids that evolved along with the pest in its natural area and depend solely or heavily upon it for their own survival. They exercise good control because there is no other way they can exist.

Occasionally, when a pest species invades a new area, the predators or parasitoids of closely related species

in the new area can feed on the invader. In fact, in some areas roach parasitoids are caught in traps along with the pest. Yet rarely do they exert the kind of control that the exotic roaches' true natural enemies would. If you have a roach problem, clearly the parasitoids that are present are not providing enough control.

Sometimes when a parasitoid is imported from the native area of an exotic pest, it actually does a better job of controlling the pest than it did in its homeland. This is because the parasitoid or predator is freed of its pests, the secondary carnivores, in the new area. The major pest roaches in the United States are believed to have come originally from East Africa. Thus, it seems like a good idea to collaborate with African entomologists in studying what lives on roaches there, with the idea of importing these natural enemies into the United States. In fact, quite a few people have been investigating the natural enemies of roaches, and a body of literature already exists on the subject. The parasitoids that attack the egg stage of the roach have received the most attention.

One such parasitoid has been used in a precedent-setting project to control the brownbanded cockroach in a large research building on the campus of the University of California at Berkeley. Because laboratory animals were being raised in this research facility, pesticides could not be used, and the roach population had become a big problem. Researchers in the Division of Biological Control imported the egg parasitoid *Comperia merceti* (see the photo at left) from Hawaii, where it was known to be effective against the brownbanded roach. The parasitoids are so tiny—less than half the size of the roach egg capsule—that even the periodic releases of 20,000 at a time went unnoticed by the people who worked there. The fact that the building contains animal-rearing labs where there is always food, water and animal fecal matter for roaches to feed on makes the high degree of control achieved in this project even more impressive.

Comperia merceti only attacks the brownbanded roach, but another parasitoid, *Tetrastichus hagenowi*, has been found to be effective against the American and three other roach species. Unfortunately, financial support for applied research on biological control of cockroaches is nonexistent at this time. If this is an area of research you would like to see supported, you might request that your representatives make this known to the congressional agriculture committees that control the Department of Agriculture research budget.

The use of natural enemies of roaches cannot by itself be expected to solve cockroach problems. Roach control must always involve habitat modification as described above, and, in most cases, the judicious use of least-toxic chemical controls.

Treatment: Direct Chemical Controls

Many conventional insecticides are ineffective against roaches. There are two main reasons for this. Sometimes the solvents used as carriers for the active ingredients in pesticides—and sometimes the poisons themselves—repel rather than kill roaches. When such materials are sprayed in a roach-infested room, the insects are repelled by the odors and escape into wall voids and other harborages for a day or longer. The second reason is that roaches have developed resistance to many insecticides (see pp. 95-96 for details on resistance). Thus, when the repellent odor from the spray has dissipated and the roaches return to the previously infested area, they are often unaffected as they walk over the residue of poison.

It is important, therefore, to resist the temptation to turn to an insecticide as an easy way to avoid necessary but more time-consuming habitat modifications. If you make the permanent changes in the environment first, you are more likely to get the results you want when you use

Where to Apply Boric Acid and Sorptive Dusts

German cockroaches live in cracks and crevices in warm, dark environments (A). Sorptive dusts can be applied in a thin layer under and behind stoves, refrigerators, washers, dryers and cabinets (B) with the pointed tip of the plastic squeeze bottle. Aerosol sprays with straw-type nozzles (C) make it easier to treat crevices where roaches hide.

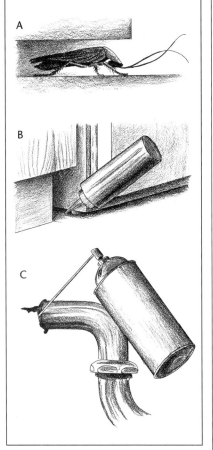

A

B

C

an insecticide. Safety to humans and effectiveness against roaches are the main factors you should consider when choosing an insecticide. (Before applying any insecticide, follow all the label directions and review the information on safety provided on pp. 97-103.)

When an insecticide is needed, there are three types of least-toxic materials available for roach control: insecticidal dusts, insecticidal baits and insect growth regulators. An important fact to bear in mind about these materials is that they take a week or longer to kill substantial numbers of roaches, and it can take a month or two to suppress very large populations to the point you cease seeing any roaches. However, once this point has been reached, and if you have taken parallel steps to reduce roach food and harborage, you can expect long-term relief from roach infestations.

1. Insecticidal Dusts. Boric acid, diatomaceous earth and silica aerogel are effective insecticides for use against roaches.

Boric Acid. Boric acid, which acts as a stomach poison, is one of very few materials that does not repel cockroaches, so they are not able to avoid it as they do other compounds. Moreover, roaches have not developed resistance to boric acid. It is also the safest roach control product to use around humans and pets. Boric-acid powder does not vaporize into the air as do conventional sprays. Thus you do not breathe it or its degradation products (although caution should be taken not to breathe in the dust when applying the material). Furthermore, if kept dry, it remains effective for the life of the building. Therefore we recommend boric acid as the major chemical control tool within an integrated program against roaches. The drawing at left shows where and how to apply it.

Despite its record of safety and effectiveness, however, boric acid is rarely used by pest control operators (PCOs) unless they are specifically requested to do so by the customer. There are two likely reasons for their reluctance to use boric acid. First, boric acid is generally applied as a dust, and most PCOs have little experience with dusts and dust-application equipment. They find dust applications messy and time-consuming compared to the more familiar liquid and aerosol formulations of conventional pesticides. Recent availabilty of more efficient dust-application equipment together with aerosol and paste formulations should help overcome this reluctance.

A second explanation has to do with boric acid's slower killing action. Since it takes five to ten days for roaches to feel the full effect of the poison, an occasional roach may be seen up to a week after the compound has been applied. Some PCOs insist that this is a major obstacle because their clients do not tolerate such sightings. Now that there are new baits and attractants available that give more immediate kill, these can be combined with boric-acid use to overcome this objection.

Because of its permanent effect we strongly recommend boric acid when an insecticide is needed. For detailed information on boric-acid products, see pp. 112-114; for sources of products and application equipment, look in the Resource Appendix under "Insect Management: Chemical Controls" on pp. 686-687.

Diatomaceous Earth and Silica Aerogel. These materials (discussed in detail on pp. 111-112) are nontoxic to humans and pets, and effective against roaches when used as dusts. Both diatomaceous earth and silica aerogel kill roaches by abrading their outer coverings, allowing metabolic sap to leak out, causing them to dehydrate and die.

A diatomaceous-earth product called Shellshock® contains ingredients that help it adhere to the insect's cuticle. As they lose body moisture, roaches become frantic in their search for water. This may make them more visible for a week or so after Shellshock® is applied, but within two or three weeks most of the roaches should be dead. Another product containing diatomaceous earth and pyrethrin called Diacide® has been blown into sewers and successfully controlled various roach species. Products such as Drione® and Re-

venge® that combine silica aerogel and pyrethrin in an aerosol formulation are also available and easy to apply in cracks and crevices. For sources, consult the Resource Appendix under "Insect Management: Chemical Controls" on pp. 686-687.

2. Insecticidal Baits. In general, baits help to reduce the amount of pesticides used against a pest because they rely on the pest to move to the poison and take it in, rather than spreading the poison around in the environment. Boric acid (discussed above), hydramethylnon and avermectin are available as baits.

Hydramethylnon. Hydramethylnon is the active ingredient in Combat® and Maxforce®. It is a slow-acting stomach poison that must be ingested to be effective. Roaches die within 48 to 96 hours after feeding on the bait. Hydramethylnon shows relatively low toxicity to mammals, and is packaged in small, square plastic discs or bait stations that reduce the risk of access by children or pets. The discs come with a double-sided tape so they can be glued to various surfaces out of view, which further reduces the likelihood that children will come into contact them. The tape also facilitates placement of the bait stations on the undersides of kitchen drawers, on walls and on other surfaces where roaches hide or travel. Like traps, the bait stations are most effective when placed on the edges or corners of rooms where roaches travel. If possible, place them between roach harborage and the sink or other sources of food or water.

If there are lots of roaches in your dwelling (e.g., you see about 20 in the kitchen), set out 10 or more bait stations. Two to three discs per 100 sq. ft. of horizontal surface area is recommended. When roach numbers are high, the bait will be used up fairly quickly—within a few weeks. The bait may last for several months if roach numbers are low to moderate. Be sure to check the plastic discs four to six weeks after installing them. If you see roaches inside, the bait may

have been used up and roaches are using the discs as harborage. If so, discard the discs and set out fresh bait stations. Combat® bait stations are sold in most hardware stores; Maxforce® discs are sold only to commercial pest control companies.

Avermectin. Avermectin (Avert®), an extract from the naturally occurring soil microorganism *Streptomyces avermitilis,* is another effective, fast-acting bait. This new product is registered by the EPA, but not yet in all states. It has relatively low toxicity to mammals, but at this time can be applied only by a commercial pest control operator. Avermectin works both as a lethal internal toxicant and as a contact insecticide when roaches groom themselves and ingest the bait. It takes a week or longer to kill 70% to 90% of the roaches, and it may take 12 weeks to produce 100% kill. Its high degree of effectiveness, coupled with the small amount required when applied as a bait in cracks and crevices, makes avermectin a valuable tool. For a source of Avert®, see the Resource Appendix under "Insect Management: Chemical Controls" on pp. 686-687.

3. Insect Growth Regulators (IGRs). Another recent development in cockroach control is the EPA registration of the IGRs fenoxycarb (Torus®) and hydroprene (Gencor®). IGRs are synthetic versions of the juvenile hormones insects produce to regulate development from their immature to adult stages. Because humans and other mammals don't produce these hormones, IGRs appear unlikely to pose human hazards.

Although they do appear to be safe for use around humans, IGRs have a major limitation: They do not kill insects directly. Their most important effect is to cause immature roaches to become sterile adults and eventually die without reproducing. But those roaches that are already adults before they come in contact with an IGR will keep on reproducing. Furthermore, many of the worst cockroach infestations occur in set-

Summary: Least-Toxic Cockroach Control

• Use traps to determine the locations of heaviest infestations and evaluate the effectiveness of treatments.

• Reduce the roach carrying capacity of the environment by placing food and organic wastes in sealed containers, fixing water leaks, etc.

• Reduce roach harborage through the use of caulk and paint. Give priority to cracks and crevices where you have found the highest roach densities.

• Screen vents and windows through which roaches travel.

• Use boric acid, diatomaceous earth or silica aerogel as a dust in areas where habitat modification is not feasible.

• Use boric acid tablets, paste or water washes where dusts are not appropriate.

• If necessary, use hydramethylnon or avermectin baits for quicker kill of roaches.

• Apply an insect growth regulator such as fenoxycarb or hydroprene as an adjunct to boric-acid and trapping programs.

• Teach the program to others who share the problem.

tings where migration from one infested area to another takes place. Thus, new adults can continue to move into areas where IGRs have been applied and will not be affected. As a result, use of IGRs makes sense only if they are combined with other tactics of roach exclusion, reduction of access to water, food and harborage, and boric-acid application.

IGRs are best applied after heavy infestations have been reduced to low levels and every effort has been made to eliminate harborage or opportunities for roaches to migrate in from other areas. When used this way, the small number of immature roaches that survived suppression efforts (perhaps because they were still inside egg capsules when the cleanup took place) will encounter the IGR and fail to mature and reproduce. Adults that survived the cleanup may produce young before dying, but their young will be sterilized by the IGR. Theoretically, the IGR will eventually eliminate the remnant cockroach population.

Assuming you have followed the other steps of the roach control program outlined in this chapter, you may want to spray an IGR where it is not possible or desirable to apply boric acid, such as on vertical surfaces where roaches are known to travel. Because of apparent low toxicity to humans and other mammals, an IGR might also be used on the wood surfaces of cabinets where dishes or food are stored, but it should not be used on dishes and surfaces where food will be placed. It can also be sprayed under shelf liners and on the undersides of horizontal shelves. It must be reapplied every three months to ensure effectiveness.

To monitor the effectiveness of IGR use, place small cardboard monitoring traps in areas where roaches are known to travel. When immature roaches that have been exposed to an IGR mature, they are darker in color and somewhat distorted in appearance (they have twisted wings) compared to normal adults. When darker, odd-looking roaches begin to appear

in the traps, you know that the roaches have absorbed the IGR and that the reproduction rate is being lowered. If you have carried out other parts of the roach program faithfully, the IGR will soon begin to demonstrate its impact.

Many products containing IGRs are packaged as foggers. We urge you to avoid foggers, because they waste a great deal of material and unnecessarily expose occupants of the house to the compound. Instead, look for a liquid aerosol formulation of the compound. For sources of IGRs, consult the Resource Appendix under "Insect Management: Chemical Controls" on pp. 686-687.

ANTS
(Order Hymenoptera, families Dolichoderinae and Myrmicinae)

Ants become pestiferous when they invade the home searching for food or when they hollow out decayed areas in buildings, a common behavior of carpenter ants. Occasionally, stinging ants—fire ants, for example—invade the first floor of houses built on cement slabs through cracks in the cement. Fortunately, stinging ants do not enter houses often and are most commonly a problem when they come into contact with people outside the house. Other ant species become problems outdoors when they protect aphids, scales and other insects that damage plants from attack by their natural enemies.

Regardless of the direct or indirect damage various ant species inflict, it is important to realize that the same species that are pests can also be beneficial. Like spiders in the house, they are likely to kill and eat any insect they find, including flea and fly larvae, bedbugs and other insects. Even such pestiferous species as the Argentine ant *(Iridomyrmex humilis)*, a notorious house invader in the western and southern states, kill numerous other pest insects such as subterranean termites in and around the house. Argentine ants also aerate the soil outdoors and recycle dead animal and vegetable material. From that point of view, ants provide an ecological cleansing and fertilization service of considerable importance. The fact that home-invading ants are generally a mixed blessing means that the approach to their management should aim to keep them out of the house without eliminating them from all other environments in which they are found.

It is difficult to arrive at generalizations about ants because there are so many different species. Some are strictly parasitic on other ants, others are herbivores, many are predators on other insects and still others can be considered omnivores since they eat plant material (e.g., pollen, nectar) as well as the dead or living flesh of vertebrates or invertebrates.

Numerically, ants are the most abundant social insects. There are an estimated 1,000,000,000,000,000, or 1 quadrillion, of them on earth at any time. This is estimated to be roughly 0.1% of the total number of insects. But because of their virtually ubiquitous presence, ants are probably the dominant form of life on earth in terms of the number of food chains with which they interact. There are probably 12,000 to 14,000 species of ants on the planet, but at present only 7,600 species in 250 genera have been described; 455 of these species are found in North America. Table 14.4 on pp. 230-233 describes and depicts the identifiable characteristics and distribution patterns of the major house-invading ant species.

Biology

All ants are social insects and live in colonies. Usually there are three distinct castes: workers, queens and males. Some species also have a soldier caste. Castes are colony groupings that usually look different from each other, perform different functions within the colony and are recruited at birth or later during their

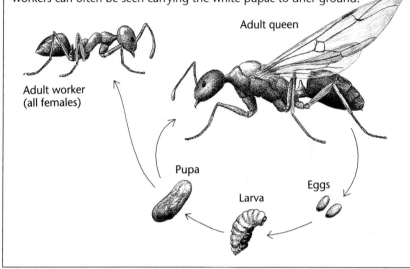

The Life Cycle of the Argentine Ant
Argentine ant colonies have many queens, each of which lays hundreds of eggs. About 30 days later, the eggs hatch into larvae that are cared for by the all-female workers. In 11 to 61 days, the larvae pass into a pupal stage before becoming adults 12 to 25 days later. If ant nests are flooded, lines of workers can often be seen carrying the white pupae to drier ground.

Adult queen

Adult worker (all females)

Pupa

Larva

Eggs

development. In some species, the worker caste is polymorphic, usually taking two forms: large-bodied and small-bodied. But in other species, only one form is found. The workers ordinarily enlarge and repair the nest, forage for food, care for the young and the queen and defend the colony. In some species, workers can also lay eggs that develop into males or females.

Some species have only one queen per colony, whereas others have multiple queens. In some species, colony reproduction occurs with a nuptial flight; in others, queens do not fly but walk off with some workers to start a new colony, a process known as budding.

The larvae, which hatch from microscopic eggs, are blind, legless, segmented and shaped like crooknecked squash (see the drawing of the Argentine ant above). The larvae are carried about by nurse-workers, who feed them with regurgitated liquid, partially masticated flesh or, in the case of fungus-eating ants,

parts of fungi. The pupal stage varies in length from species to species and according to conditions in the colony and the broader environment. For example, Argentine ant pupation may range from about a week and a half to several weeks or more. When flooded from their nests, adults transport the pupae to drier ground. Argentine ant pupae are white and conspicuous, and are easy to mistake for eggs. The primitive ants have pupae that are enclosed in parchment-like cocoons, whereas the higher ants have naked pupae.

The more primitive subfamilies Ponerinae and Dorylinae are largely carnivorous and live on insects and other invertebrates. Many dorylinids prey on other ants. They include the army or driver ants, which are particularly vicious and kill a wide range of ant species. The genus *Neivamyrmex* represents this subfamily in the southern parts of the United States, but these ants present no pest problem. The higher ants in the subfamilies Myrmicinae, Doli-

Table 14.4
Common House-Invading Ant Species

	Species	Color	Size/Body	Habits
	Argentine ant (subfamily Dolichoderinae: *Iridomyrmex humilis*)	light to dark brown	1/10 in. (2.5 mm)	walks in lines; multiple queens; reproduction by budding; lives under boards, stones and concrete; seldom bites, does not sting; prefers sweets
	big-headed ant (subfamily Myrmicinae: *Pheidole bicarinata*)	yellowish or light to dark brown	1/16 in. to 1/8 in. (1.5 mm to 3 mm); large head	nests in rotting wood and under objects; indoor foods are meat, grease and bread; outdoor foods are insects, seeds and honeydew
	carpenter ant (subfamily Formicinae: *Camponotus* spp.)	black, reddish brown or yellowish, depending on the species	5/16 in. to 3/4 in. (8 mm to 19 mm); large compared to other ants	nests in decaying wood, including lumber in buildings, but does not eat wood; primary foods are honeydew derived from other insects, as well as fruit juice, meat, grease, fat and dead insects
	harvester ant (subfamily Myrmicinae: *Pogonomyrmex* spp.)	red to dark brown	1/5 in. to 1/4 in. (5 mm to 6 mm)	never invades homes, but nests in lawns, paths, around door steps, etc.; primarily an agricultural pest; removes vegetation from around nest; fierce stinger
	imported fire ant (subfamily Myrmicinae: *Solenopsis geminata*)	yellowish-reddish to blackish (highly variable)	1/10 in. to 1/4 in. (2.5 mm to 6 mm); sharply incurved mandibles	highly predacious, especially on fly larvae; painful sting; large mounds
	little black ant (subfamily Myrmicinae: (*Monomorium minimum*)	jet black	very small, 1/32 in. to 1/16 in. (0.8 mm to 1.5 mm)	nest openings marked by craters of fine soil; occasional house invader
	odorous house ant (subfamily Dolichoderinae: *Tapinoma sessile*)	dark reddish brown to black	1/10 in. (2.5 mm); soft-bodied	similar to Argentine ant; does not sting; frequent house invader; nests outdoors or in foundations; rotten coconut odor when crushed

Distribution

Washington, Oregon, California, Maryland west to Illinois, Texas, Arizona, Mexico, South America (native), Europe, South Africa, Australia, Hawaii

New York to New England, south to Florida and Arizona; native to U.S.

most areas of United States, particularly the Pacific Northwest and other areas with high humidity

arid southwestern U.S., Mexico

South Carolina and Florida to Texas, south to Costa Rica, Brazil and Peru

throughout U.S.; genus originated in southern Asia

throughout U.S. (native), particularly West; driven out by Argentine ant

(continued on page 232)

choderinae and Formicinae are mostly herbivores, yet many eat animal tissue as well.

Damage

Although most ant house invaders do not sting, the species that do sting severely can cause distress and medical problems. The harvester ants *(Pogonomyrmex)* and fire ants *(Solenopsis)* inflict severe stings, but the former do not enter homes and the latter do so only rarely. Other species bite and inject a secretion into the wound. However, even among the biting ants, those that invade the house are not likely to be aggressive, and you are not likely to get bitten unless you accidentally crush one against your bare skin. Even this requires that you crush it slowly enough to get bitten before it dies.

There have been very few verified cases in the United States of large numbers of ants seriously harming humans. Where this did occur, victims were generally babies or other people too weak to defend themselves. The vision of humans being attacked and overwhelmed by ants is largely the stuff of science-fiction movies rather than of real life. Unfortunately, such images make a lasting impression and engender unwarranted hysteria in people who are uneducated about the natural world.

Certain species, such as the pharaoh, thief and Argentine ants, are particularly prone to getting into food. The most vulnerable foods are those standing in open containers, such as scraps of meat sitting in a pet dish. Food packaging thrown into the wastebasket without rinsing is also a strong attractant.

Ants that find their way into sugar, butter or other foods can often be sifted or washed out. They are unlikely to have caused deterioration of the food, and there is little evidence that they carry pathogens of humans. However, as you cannot be sure where these ants visited last, you might feel justifiably cautious about letting them crawl over your food. A

good rule to follow—if you can afford to—is to assume that any food ants have swarmed over has also been exposed to ant fecal matter and/or organisms that cause spoilage, and should therefore be thrown away.

Although human pathogens have been collected from pharaoh ants found in hospitals, in most home invasions the problem is largely aesthetic. People do not like to see ants crawling on the floor and other surfaces, and they especially do not like to see ants crawling on their own skin. Even where home owners are not particularly alarmed at seeing ants in the house, they may feel embarrassed, fearing that the ants reflect negatively on their housekeeping skills. We solve this problem in our own home by reminding ourselves that a few ants around the house are helpful in cleaning up any flea larvae or other insect pests that might have been missed by the vacuum. But we get away with a lot, since our visitors already know we like bugs!

Ants help illustrate how the IPM concept of injury or tolerance level can be very useful. We recommend that you begin with the assumption that ants in the house (with the exception of carpenter ants) provide benefits as well as annoyances. Because many species have been shown to prey on the young of far more pestiferous species, one can assume that a wide variety of other house pests, such as young silverfish or clothes moths, are also being preyed upon by the ants. In addition, ants also clean up small stray particles of organic debris from cracks and crevices—organic material that constitutes food for more pestiferous insects. In other words, you should not panic when you see a few ants.

Even species that regularly nest in houses are unlikely to become pests in large numbers if our recommendations for habitat modification and physical controls are followed conscientiously—particularly the suggestion that all stored foods attractive to these pests be kept in tightly sealed

Table 14.4 (continued from page 231)

	Species	Color	Size/Body	Habits
	pavement ant (subfamily Myrmicinae: *Tetramorium caespitum*)	light to dark brown or blackish; parallel lines on head and thorax	1/10 in. (2.5 mm)	common in lawns, under stones and along the edge of pavement in sandy or rocky places, and in woodwork and masonry; practically omnivorous
	pharaoh ant (subfamily Myrmicinae: *Monomorium pharaonis*)	yellowish to red	1/16 in. (1.5 mm)	nests in any secluded spot; frequent house invader
	red imported fire ant (subfamily Myrmicinae: *Solenopsis invicta*)	reddish	up to 1/4 in. (6 mm)	nests in mounds 1 ft. to 2 ft. (0.3 m to 0.6 m) in diameter and 1½ ft. (0.45 m) high; painful sting
	southern fire ant (subfamily Myrmicinae: *Solenopsis xyloni*)	brownish red, brown to black abdomen and head	1/16 in. to 1/4 in. (1.5 mm to 6 mm)	can nest in house structure (fireplaces, foundations, rotted wood); nests consist of loose soil with craters 2 ft. square; painful sting
	Texas leaf-cutting or fungus growing ant (subfamily Myrmicinae: *Atta texana*)	light to dark brown	1/16 in.to 1/2 in. (1.5 mm to 13 mm)	deep nests 10 ft. to 20 ft. (3 m to 6 m) below ground with 6-ft. square growing chambers; large excavations; occasionally invades homes for cereal products
	thief ant (subfamily Myrmicinae: *Solenopsis molesta*)	yellowish	very small, 1/32 in. to 1/16 in. (0.8 mm to 1.5 mm)	rarely stings; lives in or on other ants as predator of brood; omnivorous, prefers grease or high-protein foods over sweets; frequent house invader, may nest indoors in cracks and cupboards
	velvety tree ant, (subfamily Dolichoderinae: *Liometopum* spp.)	glistening velvety-black abdomen, red thorax and brownish black head	1/10 in. to 1/5 in. (2.5 mm to 5 mm)	predacious and honeydew feeder; lives under bark or in tree cavities (in oaks and poplars along stream banks); has rank odor when crushed; highly pugnacious; bites and injects poison into wound

Distribution

U.S., sporadic in Midwest; originated in Europe or Asia

throughout U.S. and Old World tropics; originated in tropics or in Egypt

southern North Carolina through Texas

Gulf Coast, and from Carolinas to California

northern Texas and Louisiana, other southern states

throughout U.S.

California east to Colorado and south to Mexico

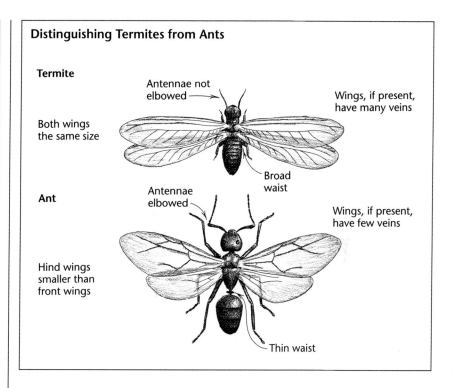

Distinguishing Termites from Ants

Termite

Antennae not elbowed

Both wings the same size

Wings, if present, have many veins

Broad waist

Ant

Antennae elbowed

Hind wings smaller than front wings

Wings, if present, have few veins

Thin waist

containers. Just as with cockroaches and other pests of the kitchen and pantry, if access to food and organic wastes is severely limited, the size of the pest population will also be limited. And, if you can tolerate a few ants here and there, you will simplify your task considerably.

But what should you do if you see hordes of ants swarming over the dirty dishes or taking up residence in the soil of a favorite potted house plant? In such emergencies, you can either opt for a quick fix (see the sidebar on p. 234) or follow the treatment strategies discussed below that offer more permanent solutions.

Detection and Monitoring

Ants are often confused with termites, and vice versa. The first step in management, therefore, is to determine which is present. First, examine the waist and antennae—you don't need a magnifying glass, and the insect need not be perfectly still. Then compare what you see to the drawings above. Ants have narrow waists and "elbowed" or bent antennae. Termites have thick waists and straight antennae. Note that the presence or absence of wings won't help you distinguish termites from ants. Both have winged forms when colony reproduction occurs. After mating, the males die, and the females or queens lose their wings.

If you determine that your invader is a termite, turn to Chapter 23. If it is an ant, your next task is to determine whether it could be damaging your house. This means distinguishing between carpenter ants (*Camponotus* spp.) and other common house-invading ants. We tell you how to do this in the sidebar on p. 235. Because carpenter ants can harm the house structure, their presence should be taken very seriously. Carpenter ant management is discussed in Chapter 24, along with the management of other pests of the house structure.

If you have determined that the ants are not carpenter ants, you can try to figure out exactly which species you do have, or you can sim-

A Quick Fix for an Ant Emergency

If a trail of ants is marching along your kitchen counter or swarming out the spout of your bathtub, here are few quick steps you can take to get the situation under control until you can implement the more permanent long-term solutions described in the text.

1. Observe the ants and try to determine what they are after (usually left-over food) and where they are entering the room (usually a crack in the wall). Mark the entry point.

2. If the ants are in one or more lines leading to food, don't remove the food until after Step 4. Ants are easier to kill if you keep them in line. (They are in lines because they are following a chemical trail excreted by the original scout.)

3. Fill a basin with soapy water, dip in a sponge and wipe up the ants (A in the drawing at right). Keep rinsing the sponge in the soapy water and wiping the surface until you have killed most of the ants. Alternatively, you can squirt a teaspoon or so of liquid soap or detergent into a plastic quart-size spray bottle, fill it the rest of the way with water, spray the trail and wipe up the dead ants with a sponge.

4. If the ants continue to appear, squirt a small amount of a pyrethrum/silica gel into the hole or crack from which the ants are emerging (B in the drawing).

5. Once you have killed most or all of the ants, block their point of entry by making a temporary

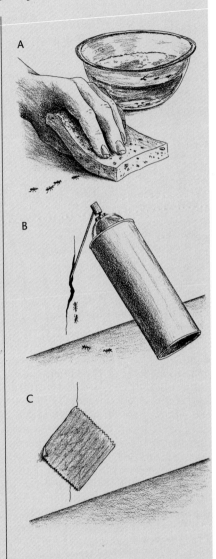

closure with a smear of petroleum jelly or duct tape. Later, you can buy a tube of silicone caulk and permanently close cracks and other openings in the wall along moldings and baseboards, and around pipes and ducts (C in the drawing).

ply observe the ants closely enough to understand their habits without worrying about their scientific name. In either case, try to answer the following questions:
• What are they feeding on?
• How are they getting into the house?
• Are they nesting in the house or coming in directly from outdoors?
• Are they biting or stinging ants?
Having a specific name for the ant will be appreciated only if initial attempts to manage it based on observations of behavior are unsuccessful. In that case, you will need more extensive information on your particular pest for clues to appropriate management strategies. Several readable and informative basic texts that can provide this information are listed under "References and Readings" on pp. 252-253.

Treatment:
Indirect Strategies

The recommendations presented in this section are based largely on our many years of practical experience in attempting to suppress the Argentine ant *(Iridomyrmex humilis)*. With a few modifications, these are virtually the same recommendations we suggest for managing cockroach problems in the kitchen. Experience has shown us that these very practical tactics work against crawling kitchen pests in old wooden Victorian structures (such as the one housing the BIRC offices and labs in Berkeley, California), in large apartment complexes in Washington, D.C., and in old brick homes in midwestern towns, such as Flint, Michigan.

We have also learned that reducing ants to an acceptable level is like doing dishes: even when the task is completed satisfactorily, it is only a temporary achievement. Another batch will come along by and by, and the effort must be renewed. Fortunately, each permanent change you make—caulking a crack, obtaining another good storage jar or educating your fellow housemates about proper kitchen and waste-management procedures—makes subsequent management efforts less strenuous.

Like all pests, ants need food, water and shelter to survive; by denying them access to any or all of these, you can reduce or eliminate them. The following methods are based on this principle. If your house is regularly invaded by hordes of ants, or even if the few ants that are around annoy you intensely, you should follow these recommendations religiously. If ants are rarely a nuisance, you will probably want to wait until you have a more noticeable problem before taking the steps suggested.

Remember that any measures you take to eliminate ants from the house simultaneously reduce the possibility of problems with cockroaches, flour beetles, moths and other common kitchen pests. Reducing these insects, in turn, reduces the number of spiders, centipedes and other predators that depend on household insects for food. Knowing this should encourage you to make the considerable initial investment of energy required for ant management.

1. Proper Storage of Food. Ants, like a number of other stored-food pests, can travel up the threads of a screw-top jar, and, if there is no rubber gasket or liner, the ants will enter the jar freely. Small ants sometimes enter refrigerators even when the seal appears intact, but refrigerator storage is usually safe. Of course, the freezer is completely safe, thanks to its extremely low temperatures. Two types of containers have proven completely successful in excluding ants: glass jars with rubber seals or inner rubber or plastic gaskets attached to the lid (see the drawing at right), and plastic containers with tight-fitting, snap-on lids. Given the wide range of long-lasting, tightly closing plastic containers on the market, you should be able to find one to fit every need. When you return from shopping, inspect all packages carefully to make sure you aren't importing storage pests, then transfer ant-attractive foods to appropriate sealed contain-

ers. Use the same kinds of containers to store non-refrigerated leftovers.

2. Waste Management. Ants are major decomposers of organic matter and will seek out food wastes on counters, in garbage pails and elsewhere. Here are some tips for discouraging ants from finding these food sources.
• Clean all kitchen surfaces and sweep or vacuum the floor thoroughly and frequently to get all scraps. If you are like us, you will find it hard to keep the kitchen floor clean enough to avoid ants, because the cats carry food away from their feeding dishes and leave tiny bits around for ants to feast on. The most convenient solution, if you don't want ants constantly combing the floor, is a quick daily vacuuming with an easy-to-empty machine such as a Dustbuster II™.
• Rinse glass, metal, plastic and paper food containers thoroughly before tossing them in waste receptacles. Take an appropriately shaped brush and wash off every edible particle.
• Clean wrappings of meat, fast foods, and delicatessen items by plunging them into the dishpan and cleaning them as if they were laundry before throwing them into the recy-

Pest-Proof Jars for Bulk Grain Storage
The most pest-proof containers for the storage of sugar, flour, rice and grains are glass jars with rubber seals and lids that are held closed under pressure with metal clamps. Such lids make a far better pest barrier than screw-top lids, which contain grooves insects can travel along. Foodstuffs can also be stored in plastic containers with tight-fitting snap-on lids.

cling or waste receptacle. Remember, if there is nothing left to eat on or in these items, you don't have to worry about ants in the wastebasket. The most difficult part of this step is getting other members of the household and house guests to accept the idea of washing garbage. Signs, demonstration lectures, admonitions, rewards and other strategies may help in winning their cooperation. It's either that...or ants.

• Separate organic wastes from all other materials. These include the parings and pieces left over from food preparation, plate and pot scrapings, sink-strainer accumulations and crumbs. This will be at least as difficult as the previous step, but once you are in the habit, you'll start feeling disgusted when you see organic wastes thrown together with other materials in a basket in your own or another household.

• Place all organic wastes in a separate container for composting or other disposal (as shown in the drawing on p. 222). We recommend using gallon-size plastic storage containers with snap-on lids. You will need at least two so one can be aired out while the other is in use. We have many storage containers, since we dig our organic wastes into our food garden as fertilizer. We let waste accumulate until it is worth transferring to the garden, then place it in a fresh hole more than a foot deep, cover it with earth and firmly tamp the soil to prevent rats or raccoons from getting at it.

If you must put organic waste in an outdoor garbage container for municipal collection or in an apartment-house incinerator, we suggest lining the plastic containers with plastic bags and folding the edges of the bags over the rim of the container before the top is snapped down. When the bag is full, tie it securely and dispose of it. Rinse out the plastic can and let it air out while you use your alternate can for the next batch. For parties or special situations where much food waste is generated, use a larger five-gallon can. Note: Much has been written about composting, but rarely by people who pay attention to the associated pest problems likely to arise. If you are storing organic waste to make batches of hot aerobic compost, it is important that you do it right so you don't create a fly, roach or rodent problem (see the sidebar on p. 644). For detailed instructions on the "hot" composting process, see *The Integral Urban House Book* (Olkowski et al., 1979).

3. Permanent Sticky Barriers. Ants will not cross barriers made from sticky materials. Commercially available sticky barriers include Stickem®, Tanglefoot® and Sticky Stuff®. If these materials are applied to a groove around the turned legs of freestanding tables, for example, ants are denied access to plants or other items above the barrier. We use this method in our own laboratory to prevent ants from reaching and killing the beneficial insects we raise. Directions for making an ant stand for large indoor or patio plants or beehives are provided on pp. 356-357.

4. Caulking Cracks. Find out where the ants are entering the house, then use a good-grade silicone caulk to block their passage. Silicone seal is less likely than other materials to crack, shrink or pull away from structural surfaces when the house shifts. Although it is more expensive than other caulks, it is well worth the additional expense. Silicone seal is also available as a paint-on sealer, for large-scale applications.

Many species of ants are seasonal invaders, coming in for warmth or a dry nesting place when the cold or rainy season starts. Sometimes the precise places to caulk cannot be found until the invading ants show the way. Where ants are already nesting in cracks, in wall voids or behind cupboards, the closing of cracks should be combined with use of a sorptive dust, boric-acid dusts or a desiccant such as silica aerogel or diatomaceous earth (see "Direct Chemical Controls" on pp. 237-240).

Treatment:
Direct Physical Controls

The following are the direct physical controls that we have found useful in managing ant populations.

1. Mopping up Ants. Killing individual worker ants will have little effect on the size of an ant population, because new ants are added to the colony so quickly. Nevertheless, after you have caulked entryways and nesting areas, if ants survive in large numbers you can mop them up with a soapy sponge; you can also use a mop or a wet vacuum.

2. Detergent Barriers. In the kitchen, you can make "moats" of detergent that are very effective in excluding ants from edible materials that cannot be placed in tightly closed containers. Water alone is insufficient, since most ants can float across using the water's surface tension. But if you mix in a little detergent, it breaks the surface tension of the water and the ants will sink.

In our own household, we place the sink-side container of organic wastes inside a shallow Pyrex™ pie pan filled with detergent and water; for the dish of cats' food, we use a concave saucer. We only go to this trouble, however, when threatened by a new ant invasion. The moats solve the problem very nicely as long we don't inadvertently lean something against the food containers, providing the ants with a bridge over the moat.

3. Flooding. Flooding can be used to drive ants out of flower pots and to force ants to move their nests away from an area. When ants built a nest in a large philodendron in our second-floor bathroom, we brought in a bucket of compost and set it down next to the infested pot. We placed the flower pot in a deep, wide pan and bridged the gap between the rim of the flower pot and the bucket of compost with a stick. Then we began watering the philodendron.

Repeated floodings of the potted plant forced the ants to pick up their pupae and make for the rim. A certain number climbed up the stem into the plant itself, but most traveled over the bridge to the compost. Those that climbed into the plant were allowed to descend while we ceased watering for an hour or so. Then we started the flooding again, forcing most of the remaining ants over the bridge. In the course of an afternoon, we got most of the ants out of the pot and into the compost. Then we moved the bucket of compost outside. A bucket of loose, dry soil undoubtedly would have worked as well as the compost.

Repeated flooding has been used successfully to force ants, including fire ants, to move their outdoor nests. A number of ants nest outdoors close to the house and then wander inside—the pavement ant is a good example. Therefore, it is sometimes desirable to move their nests farther away from the structure. Plain cold water from the garden hose works fine; if your object is to kill some of the ants, hot water or water mixed with detergent or other chemicals (see below) can be used. Flood the area where you observe the ants every few days until you no longer see ant activity.

4. Exposure to Heat and Cold. Ants, like all other life forms, have minimum and maximum temperatures beyond which they cannot survive. Research into the use of temperature for controlling pests of structures, including ants, has recently yielded a practical technology and associated equipment for delivering heat or cold where it is needed. It should be noted that this strategy is applicable to any ant that nests within the walls of a structure; however, the method does not work for most pest ants, because they nest outside, coming indoors only temporarily to exploit food and/or water sources.

Walter Ebeling, professor emeritus at the University of California at Los Angeles and author of *Urban Entomology*, has been at the forefront of this research. Initially, a method using liquid nitrogen to freeze insects in the walls, carpets and furnishings was shown to be practical. However, as it is easier to raise the temperature of a structure enough to kill all insects within, the most recent research has focused on bringing portable heating technology to the marketable stage. The use of heat is particularly effective for controlling species such as carpenter ants that nest within the walls of a structure.

Treatment:
Direct Biological Controls

Ants are attacked by a number of natural enemies, but only one, the pyemotes mite, is currently marketed for this purpose (see the Resource Appendix under "Insect Management: Biological Controls" on pp. 683-686). Pyemotes mites have been used successfully to control fire-ant nests outdoors and could be used to control carpenter-ant nests in trees. Because they also become temporary pests of humans (as their common name, itch mite, implies) and are very small and difficult to see, their use demands special skills. In our opinion, these mites are not suitable for general use in structures or near people.

Treatment:
Direct Chemical Controls

Creating a chemical barrier around the house foundation to keep it ant-free is a traditional strategy used by pest control professionals. However, you should bear in mind that certain species of house-invading ants are important enemies of termites. If there are no ants patrolling the perimeter of your house, you have lost an important living deterrent to the establishment of new termite nests. If you need a barrier against ants, first try one of the nontoxic alternatives discussed above that prevent ant access to living spaces.

Where caulk and sticky barriers are not enough, you may want to augment their use with a poison. In this section, we recommend a number of least-toxic chemical control strategies. Before using any insecticide, however, review the information on protective clothing and equipment on pp. 97-103.

1. Dusts. Sorptive dusts such as diatomaceous earth and silica aerogel have a drying effect on insects. They are particularly effective when blown into cracks and wall voids before the voids are sealed. Boric-acid dust, which poisons the ants when they clean themselves, can be used in the same way.

If kept dry, these materials should retain their killing power in the wall for years. If all cracks are well sealed, the dusts should not affect human residents. However, because no dusts should be inhaled, not even relatively "nontoxic" ones, you should either hire a professional to blow them into place or obtain your own professional safety equipment, including a dust mask and goggles for protection for your lungs and eyes.

2. Silica Aerogel/Pyrethrum Combination. Used alone, dusts are certain to kill ants and last a long time. But they can be slow-acting. To provide a quick knockdown of ants, silica aerogel is often combined with pyrethrum.

It is important to purchase this mixture in a container with an applicator that allows you to place the dust within the crack or hole without blowing it into the room air. Two aerosol formulations that come with excellent applicators are Revenge® and Pursue®. Drione®, a non-aerosol formulation, comes in a plastic container with a pointed applicator tip resembling a plastic ketchup dispenser (see the Resource Appendix under "Insect Management: Chemical Controls" on pp. 686-687). Although colorless when first applied, these materials dry to thin films of white silica-aerogel dust. This visible film, as well as the well-devised applicators, helps you place the material accurately within cracks and crevices rather than on exposed surfaces.

Because of its very low hazard to mammals, ease of application and quick effectiveness, the silica aerogel/pyrethrum combination is a very sat-

Moving an Ant Nest away from the House

Most of the following information was suggested to us by Dr. John French of the Commonwealth Scientific and Industrial Research Organization in Australia. It was originally recommended for use against the Argentine ant, but is likely to work against a number of other species as well. Repeated treatments will kill many ants, but it is unlikely that the nest will be completely destroyed. However, you will probably succeed in getting the ants to move their nest some distance from the spot under attack.

1. Follow ant trails to locate the nest entrance; there may be several for one colony. Small mounds of dirt may help locate the entrance(s), but these are not always present.

2. Drench the nest area thoroughly. As a first choice, we recommend a mixture using insecticidal soap. Follow the directions on the label for dilution rates. More than one drenching may be necessary to force the nest to move.

3. If you have given the soap a reasonable try and it is not adequate, try pyrethrum insecticides or one of their derivatives as the next-best choice. Although some of the laboratory-synthesized derivatives are quite toxic, natural pyrethrum or pyrethrins are relatively less toxic.

EcoSafe Laboratories, one of the suppliers of powdered pyrethrum flower heads, recommends soaking 1½ oz. of pyrethrum powder and 1 teaspoon of coconut oil soap in 1 gallon of water overnight for use as a drench. Always wear rubber gloves and use a respirator when handling pesticides of any kind, even comparatively nontoxic ones like pyrethrum. Launder contaminated clothing thoroughly and separately from the family wash.

4. Bait the trail and nest areas with the homemade bait described in the sidebar below.

How To Make a Boric-Acid Ant Bait

Commercially formulated boric-acid baits such as Drax®, which is made of mint jelly and boric acid, have recently become available for use against the pavement ant, thief ant, pharaoh ant and little black ant. They are sold under various labels, and all essentially consist of boric acid plus a sugary attractant. So far, we have had very mixed results using these formulations in field trials with Argentine ants, the principal pest ant in California and other western states. Apparently the ants are not sufficiently attracted to the jelly, although the commercial baits may be very effective against the ant species listed on their labels. We still prefer to make our own bait.

1. Mix 3 cups of water with 1 cup of sugar and 4 teaspoons of boric acid or borax. For the boric-acid component you can use one of the commercially available mixes already prepared for cockroach control. If sugary solutions don't attract your ants, try high-protein foods such as canned cat food.

(Note: The trick is to use enough boric acid to eliminate the ant colony but not so much that the first ants to try the mixture are killed before they pass it on to other members of the colony. If many ants die in or around the bait station, the bait is too strong; if they keep coming in undiminished numbers for more than a week, it is too weak.)

2. Pour 1 cup of bait into each of three to six small screw-top jars.

3. Loosely pack cotton wool to half the depth of the container, then saturate it with the bait solution.

4. Screw the lids on tightly, sealing them with adhesive tape.

5. Pierce the center of the lid with two or three small holes.

Caution: Label the containers with a skull and crossbones. Baited solution should be kept away from youngsters and pets.

isfactory instant remedy to an ant invasion. But it is far from being a cure-all. Most house-invading ants soon find a new route to the food or water they are seeking. Only if you make food sources inaccessible and place permanent barriers such as caulk and silica gel throughout wall voids will you get long-lasting relief.

The same type of product can be used outdoors to discourage ants from climbing certain plants. In recent studies at the BIRC's field station in northern California, we used a silica aerogel/pyrethrum spray in the experimental control of the native fire ant. The fire ant girdles eggplants and peppers and severely injures pole beans. The handy applicator makes it easy to put a protective barrier around the plant stems and on critical intersections of the bean trellis.

We have not yet determined how long such a barrier lasts in our dry Med terranean climate with an underground watering system. Undoubtedly, it will not be as long-lasting as a well-protected sticky barrier would be, but in some cases sticky barriers are not feasible. Our limited experience to date suggests that where summer rains or sprinkling irrigation does not wash the silica aerogel/pyrethrum off, it may last as long as the plant needs to be protected.

3. Insecticidal Soap. A drench of insecticidal soap or a household soap/pyrethrum mixture will kill some ants directly and cause the remainder to move their nests. The drench is most effective for moving outdoor ant nests away from the house. As explained in the sidebar at top on the facing page, a complete program for nest-moving involves the use of a soap/pyrethrum mix to flood the nests, combined with a boric-acid or borax-containing bait.

4. Boric-Acid Baits. Baits by nature have advantages over sprays or other broadcast application methods. Less poison is used overall, and the little that is used is applied directly to the target insect rather than to the environment. Essentially, we count on the pest species to find the toxicant and apply the poison to itself.

Ant baits work on the principle of trophallaxis (the exchange of food). A low dose of a poison in a favored food is provided to some scouts or workers. They not only eat the bait themselves, but bring it back to share with other members of the colony. If it does not kill too quickly, this shared feeding behavior ensures that all members of the colony, especially the developing brood, eventually obtain a lethal dose.

The queens may survive for a short time after all the workers have been killed, as they are larger and require a larger dose of poison. However, surviving queens are very vulnerable since they usually require workers to forage for them and nurse their young. Workers in the pupal stage during the baiting period are also likely to survive, since they have not eaten any bait. Depending upon the size of this group and the term of survival of the queen, the colony may be able to replenish itself over time.

Species whose workers are capable of laying eggs that develop into other workers and reproductives will be very difficult to eliminate entirely. They can rebuild a colony without the queen if some of them are in the pupal stage during the baiting period. Thus, you can see why it is possible to reduce the size of a colony with bait, but it is not always possible to eliminate the pestiferous ants completely. Periodic retreatment will probably be necessary.

One BIRC member reported to us that she used a homemade boric-acid bait to combat Argentine ants in her office: "Although the least-toxic ant bait [described in the sidebar at bottom on the facing page] seemed to work at first…they disappeared for about 2½ days, and then they came back. I keep putting out freshly soaked cotton balls saturated with the bait, and it does seem to keep them in check. I have ants in the office every day at the same location, but as long as the bait is there, they don't go any farther than the bait, and so far we do not have large numbers of ants." The letter reflects our own experience, although we found that after a week or two the ants going to a particular bait bottle disappeared.

The Argentine ant has extensive intercommunicating colonies, and is therefore impossible to wipe out entirely. On the other hand, it might be possible to wipe out an entire colony of another species that has more isolated nests.

5. Arsenic Baits. If boric-acid baits are too slow to work or do not work at all against the particular ant species you are battling, you may be tempted to fall back on arsenic baits (arsenic trioxide). Arsenic was used extensively as a pesticide at one time, but most arsenic compounds have been withdrawn from the American market because of the potential health hazards now understood to exist. Where arsenic baits are still available, they should be used only as a last resort.

6. Insect Growth Regulators (IGRs). IGR products have recently become available for control of two specific pest ants. They contain a synthetic analog of an insect juvenile hormone that inhibits the maturation of ants by interfering with the molting process. Pharorid® is available for pharaoh ants, long considered extremely difficult to control. The treatment program recommended by Zoecon, developers of the IGR, combines the use of this product and boric-acid baits. Logic® is available for the management of fire ants. For sources, see the Resource Appendix under "Insect Management: Chemical Controls" on pp. 686-687.

When workers feed the bait to developing young, it halts normal development, thus killing the next generation. The action is slow, taking 12 to 16 weeks to reduce a colony; however, there is no persistent residue in the environment and the material is relatively safe for the operator and other vertebrates, since vertebrates do not molt. Most important, the IGRs work very well against the ants. For a more thorough discussion of IGRs used to control pharaoh ants, see the article by Helga Olkowski listed under "References and Readings" on pp. 252-253.

Summary: Least-Toxic Ant Control

• Try to tolerate some ants—ants are beneficial as well as pestiferous.

• Use soapy water sprays or a soapy sponge to kill invading ants until you can undertake more permanent solutions.

• Store food and organic wastes in tight containers.

• Use barriers made from sticky materials or water and detergent moats.

• Caulk cracks where ants may nest or enter the house.

• Use sorptive dusts in cracks, wall voids and similarly inaccessible places before caulking.

• Flood with water to move ants from flowerpots and to move outdoor nests away from the house.

• Select the least-toxic poisons, such as insecticidal soap, boric acid and pyrethrum, for baits and sprays before turning to more toxic compounds.

PESTS OF STORED FOOD: BEETLES AND MOTH LARVAE
(Orders Coleoptera and Lepidoptera, families Anobiidae and Cucujidae)

Many of the pests discussed elsewhere in this book (including cloth and paper pests, cockroaches, mice, rats and houseflies) can become pests of stored foods. But clearly the most important visible pests of stored foods in homes, stores, bakeries, warehouses and flour mills are beetle and moth larvae. These are the pests we will focus on in this section.

People are generally unaware of the fact that most food products are perpetually contaminated by insects to some degree. There are overlapping food chains or communities that feed on and inhabit whole grains, broken grains, legumes, meats, cheeses, dried fruits, nuts, sugar, candies, spices, tobacco, vegetables, drugs and other products. At the very least, it is known that 102 species of beetles, 77 species of moths, 46 species of mites, three species of "wasps" (Hymenoptera), two species of ants, two species of silverfish, one species of psocids and one species of fly live in stored-food products. There are also nine natural enemy species —parasitoids and predators of the pests listed—associated with grains and bulbs in storage. No exhaustive investigation of this community has been conducted, so the number of pest species may be even greater.

According to Walter Ebeling, the majority of stored-product pests appear to have evolved from one or more of the following sources: seed-infesting species, scavengers that feed upon dead vegetable or animal material, scavengers or semi-predators that live under bark, and scavengers or predators that inhabit nests of bees, wasps or other similar Hymenoptera, or inhabit vertebrate (bird, rodent, bat) nests.

An ecological view suggests that the conditions under which grain is stored are critical in determining which pest species are present and how severe the infestation is. We see a succession of different organisms, beginning with the fungi and bacteria that grow on whole, cracked or milled grains. Next come the mites that feed on the fungi, followed by beetles and moths. In reality, the microbes, mites and insects may be imported on the backs of rodents that attack the same stored products. Or, if the insects get there first, their residues may create conditions favorable for molds and mites. Regardless of which pests arrive first, however, the most significant pests of stored grains and flours might well be the microbes that make conditions more favorable for later invaders. They are discussed in greater detail below. This well-studied stored-grain ecosystem can serve as an illustrative model for pest development in other stored-food systems as well.

The United States Food and Drug Administration is responsible for monitoring the contaminants—including the pests just mentioned—in foods distributed through the retail trade. Inspectors subject random samples to microanalysis. Identification of contaminants is frequently made from fragments of various insect, fungal and rodent parts. The number of these fragments determines whether a product batch is fed to livestock or destroyed rather than sold. (It is worth noting that the FDA also tests for biocide residues in foods, since most foods are treated with some sort of biocide—such as an insecticide, fungicide or fumigant —after harvest. Periodically, arguments arise about the amount of a particular biocide that can be tolerated in food. Most of this occurs without public scrutiny unless a particular pest or pesticide issue is being covered by the news media concurrently due to some catastrophic event.)

In 1988, Arrowhead Mills, a major grain processor in Herford, Texas, decided to try controlling stored-grain pests with beneficial insects rather than pesticides. Arrowhead contracted with Biofac, Inc., an insectary that rears natural enemies of insect pests, to release tiny parasitoids and predators into their grain bins to control insect pests. The beneficials were extremely effective, but when FDA inspectors learned of their use, they condemned the grain shipment, arguing that it had been "contaminated" with insects, even though the amount of insect parts found was well within the official tolerance limits.

Following the appearance of Biofac's Buddy Maedgen on CBS TV's "60 Minutes," the FDA in June, 1990, finally proposed that an "exemption from the requirements of a tolerance for parasitic and predacious insects" used to control stored-grain pests be established by the EPA. In the meantime, pesticides continue to be the predominant method used to protect stored-food products.

Biology

The life cycles of two common stored-product pests, the lesser grain borer, *Rhyzopertha dominica* (Coleoptera: Bostrichidae), and the angoumois grain moth, *Sitotroga cerealella* (Lepidoptera: Gelechiidae), are shown in the drawings at right Most pests of stored foods are imported into the house with foodstuffs that are already infested. Because the pests may be present only in the egg stage, they may not be noticeable. If the materials they infest are not transferred to tightly sealed containers, once the pests hatch, feed, pupate and become adults they can infest other foods and non-food materials. If the foods are properly stored, however, the infestation will be confined to the container. Then, when the infestation is discovered, the insects in that container can be killed by freezing or heating, as described below.

The pests discussed in this section can infest a wide range of foods, including flour, whole grains, crackers, peas, beans, nuts, dried fruit and spices. Many pests can bore through commercial wrappers or containers,

The Life Cycle of the Lesser Grain Borer

The adult female (A) lays 300 to 500 eggs in loose grain. The eggs hatch in a few days, and the whitish larvae (B) bore into kernels of wheat to feed, then enter the pupal stage (C). The period from egg to adult lasts about 30 days. (Actual size of adult: ⅛ in./3 mm)

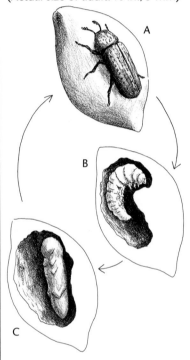

leaving holes through which other pests can enter. Some stored-food pests, the Mediterranean flour moth for example, will, unless sealed inside a container, leave the food when it is time to pupate. They spin their cocoons in crevices in cupboards or in corners, such as where the wall meets the ceiling. Once pests are at large in the room, some individuals may live out their life cycle on spilled foods and loosely bagged materials, becoming regular inhabitants of pantry and cupboard areas.

Adult female stored-food pests can lay more than a hundred eggs (and often more than several hundred), so

The Life Cycle of the Angoumois Grain Moth

The female moth lays an average of 40 eggs on kernels of wheat (A). The larva that hatches from the egg gnaws into the kernel (B), then feeds and grows, enlarging the cavity. The full grown larva (C) is almost as large as the kernel. It then enters the pupal stage (D) and emerges as an adult (E). The period from egg to adult is completed in five to eight weeks. (Actual size of adult: ½ in./13 mm)

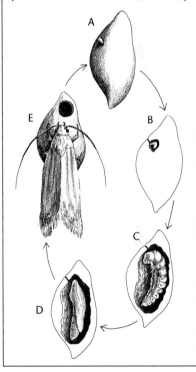

one female can infest a great deal of food. Depending on the species and the temperature, many generations usually occur during a single year. Some species feed in the adult stage, others do not. Because of the diversity of life cycles and behaviors among these pests, it is difficult to generalize about their habits. From the housekeeper's point of view, however, it is not always necessary to generalize, as management is pretty much the same for all pests of stored food.

Mycotoxins in Foods[a]

Mycotoxins are toxic substances produced by fungi. Although many mycotoxins have been known for hundreds of years, the discovery in the 1960s of the role of the fungus *Aspergillus flavus* in producing the highly hepatocarcinogenic (liver-attacking) toxin called aflatoxin B1 has accelerated research on the problem. Judging by the reactions of test animals, the aflatoxins, particularly aflatoxin B1, are among the most toxic substances known. Concentrations of aflatoxin B1 as low as 50 parts per billion in the diet have produced liver damage in laboratory animals.

Additional *Aspergillus* species have since joined the list of fungi that produce this toxin, and other genera of fungi also produce dangerous toxins. Foods consumed in the United States in which some aflatoxin contamination of marketplace samples has been found include peanuts, Brazil nuts, pistachio nuts, almonds, walnuts, pecans, filberts, cottonseed, copra, corn, grain sorghum, rice and figs. Outside the United States, aflatoxin-contaminated foodstuffs apparently are more common, and there is good evidence associating contaminated foods with primary liver cancer in humans.

Storage conditions in the home influence the development of fungi on foods. In general, warm temperatures and high humidity favor fungi and other food-spoiling microbes. If a stored food is suspected of being contaminated with food-spoilage organisms, do not taste it. Discard it immediately without contaminating other implements. Even extremely low doses of such contaminated food can be dangerous. The only exceptions are the molds (fungi) that grow on cheese. These may be cut off the cheese, and the unaffected part of the cheese may then be eaten.

In their studies, Benjamin Wilson and A. Wallace Hayes found that many microbial toxins are heat-stable. Therefore, you should never attempt to reclaim infested foods by cooking or otherwise heating, although it may be advisable to heat them before discarding them to kill insects that might otherwise infest other materials in the house.

Bulk purchases of nuts and grains can be stored for months in dry ice (solidified carbon dioxide, or CO_2—this procedure is described in the sidebar on p. 250). CO_2 vapors protect against the development of aflatoxin-producing fungi. All mycotoxin-producing fungi need oxygen, which the CO_2 displaces.

[a] From Wilson and Hayes, 1973.

However, if you decide to use the pheromone traps described below, you will need to know exactly which species are present. Tables 14.5 (pp. 244-247) and 14.6 (pp. 248-249), which list the most common beetles and moths infesting stored-food products, will help you distinguish among species. The information in these two tables was abstracted primarily from Arnold Mallis's *Handbook of Pest Control,* which we recommend you consult for greater detail.

Damage

Stored-product pests spoil the aesthetic appeal of infested foods and may impair their flavor. These pests and the foods they infested were, of course, eaten in large numbers by people in the United States before refrigeration and storage were developed to modern-day standards. Unfortunately, they still are eaten in many parts of the world where hunger is commonplace and storage methods remain primitive.

We strongly advise you not to eat food that has been contaminated by stored-product pests. Insects and other pests can introduce microbes into the food, and there may be an association between pest insects and the development of mycotoxins. These poisons, discussed in the sidebar at left, are particularly dangerous, because they are not destroyed by cooking. Ways to discard infested food are discussed on p. 251.

There are also a number of minor pests of stored-food products. Although they may be a major problem where they occur—in stores, warehouses, cheese factories and other commercial establishments—they are rarely encountered in home settings. Therefore, we will not discuss them at length here. Among these minor pests are mites, which may be present in various types of stored food and on furniture built out of or stuffed with grasses and other fibers. These mites cause a temporary itchy rash, which is discussed in the sidebar on the facing page.

Detection and Monitoring

Often an infestation of stored-food pests is detected by opening up a package and discovering the pests or signs of their damage inside. If the package has just been brought into the house, we suggest you keep the store receipt, place the package in a plastic bag and place it in the freezer until you have time to return it. If you have frozen the package for a few days, you have killed the pests, and there is no chance of causing further contamination by carrying it around. By returning it, you may be performing a valuable service for the store manager, since an entire batch may be contaminated and the supplier can be alerted.

If the infestation is found in a stored product that has been in the house for some time, the problem becomes more complicated. You have no way of knowing whether the pests were inside the package when it arrived or whether it became infested subsequently. The simplest course of action is to dispose of the infested product (see p. 251) and clean the area thoroughly with soap and water and/or water-vacuum the areas where the food was stored.

If the infestation is extensive or you have reason to believe the pests are in the house outside the packages, you will want to know whether the cleaning you have carried out has been effective. If you are protecting all susceptible materials in tightly sealed storage containers, it will probably not matter as much if there are still a few pests around. But many people find it difficult to follow this policy, either because the amounts of food to be stored are too extensive —large bags of pet food, for example —or because they cannot get other household members to cooperate.

Recently, a number of pheromone traps (see the drawing on p. 144) have become available that enable you to determine whether some of the pests we have described here, as well as a few less common ones, are present in your home even after you

have cleaned up the infested areas you know about.

Santa Cruz Horticultural Supply sells inexpensive traps that attract moths that infest stored grains (see the Resource Appendix under "Insect Management: Physical Controls" on pp. 682-683). These moths include the Indianmeal moth, Mediterranean flour moth, raisin moth, almond moth and tobacco moth. The moth traps can be suspended from the ceiling or placed on a shelf. A box trap for grain beetles can be placed on shelves or floors. The lure is effective for four to six months. You can use one or two traps for monitoring, or you can hang more out as control tools. Ask the supplier for advice about the number of traps to use and proper placement. Santa Cruz Horticultural Supply also sells a good booklet on ways to use pheromone traps and other nontoxic controls in health-food stores and other commercial establishments (see Stewart, 1986).

Tables 14.5 (pp. 244-247) and 14.6 (pp. 248-249) should help you sort out the common beetle and moth

---

Dermatitis Caused by Stored-Product Mites[a]

A number of mite species that develop in stored products can cause dermatitis in humans. *Glycyphagus domesticus*, the grocer's itch mite (also called the house or furniture mite) is a small white mite that can cause itching. However, it does not establish itself on humans; it leaves the skin after feeding. This worldwide species develops in flour, wheat, hay, linseed, tobacco, sugar and cheese. It has been found in cupboards, beehives, birds' nests and barns, among other places. Occasionally it is found in large numbers on rush furniture and upholstered chairs stuffed with Algerian fiber.

The straw itch mite *(Pyemotes tritici)* is a small, almost invisible mite that is a parasite of a variety of insects, particularly those that infest straw, hay, grasses, grains, beans and peas. A prickly sensation may be felt at the time of the bite, but no other immediate reaction is usually experienced. A delayed reaction up to 28 hours later produces a dermatitis on clothed portions of the body. The attacks produce wheals (welts) with inflammation that varies with the individual. Up to a thousand wheals have been observed 12 to 16 hours after exposure. In severe cases, headache, loss of appetite, nausea, vomiting, mild diarrhea and joint pain may occur.

Interestingly, this same mite, *P. tritici,* has been shown to be an effective biological control against a variety of stored-food pests. We do not recommend releases of this species in the home, however; it is better distributed in grain-storage bins in mills. A related species, *P. ventricosus,* is known to attack the furniture beetle, but causes little or no irritation to humans. A third species, *P. boylei,* parasitizes crop and stored-product pests as well as termites. It is known to have caused dermatitis in humans after fumigation of a storage area killed the original pest, forcing the mite to seek alternate hosts.

[a] From Harwood and James, 1979, and Ebeling, 1975.

Table 14.5

Common Beetle Pests of Stored Food and Other Products[a, b]

	Species	Color	Size/Features
	cigarette beetle (Anobiidae: *Lasioderma serricorne*)	light brown	small (⅛ in./3 mm long), oval; head and prothorax (the segment of the thorax nearest the head) bent downward, giving humped appearance[c]
	drugstore beetle (Anobiidae: *Stegobium paniceum*)	uniformly reddish to reddish brown	small (1⁄10 in. to 3⁄20 in./2.5 mm to 4 mm long); fine hairs in longitudinal rows on wing covers
	sawtoothed grain beetle (Cucujidae: *Oryzaephilus surinamensis*)	brown	small (⅛ in./3 mm long), slender, flattened with six sawlike teeth on each side of thorax
	confused flour beetle (Tenebrionidae: *Tribolium confusum*)	reddish brown	small (3⁄20 in./4 mm long); antennae gradually enlarged toward tips with four segments; sides of thorax straight; used as experimental lab animal
	red flour beetle (Tenebrionidae: *T. castaneum*)	reddish brown	similar to *T. confusum*; abruptly club-like antennae with three-segmented club; sides of thorax curved
	yellow mealworm (Tebrionidae: *Tenebrio molitor*)	shiny dark brown to black	adults medium large (½ in./13 mm long); larvae with hard, shiny cuticle; used for fish bait and as a lab animal

[a] Listed in approximate order of importance.

[b] Abstracted primarily from Mallis, 1982.

[c] This characteristic is shared by other anobiids and the bostrichids (see Chapter 25) as well as by the ptinids.

Foods	Biology	Monitoring and Treatment
paprika and dog food commonly infested, but many other products attacked, including other spices and dried foods, seeds, cigarettes, yeast, drugs, pyrethrum insecticides, dried insects, leather, cloth and books	adults strong flyers, active in subdued light above 65°F (18°C); life cycle about 70 to 90 days; adults live 34 weeks; in warm areas there may be five or six overlapping generations per year	all stages killed by freezing; store in freezer at 25°F (−4°C) for one week.
many household foods, spices, wool, hair, leather, horn, museum specimens and drugs; can perforate books and wood, tin and aluminum	life cycle takes seven months; may produce four overlapping generations per year in warm localities	all stages killed when exposed to temperatures of 140°F to 176°F (60°C to 80°C) for several hours; kill by burning or heating in oven
cereals, bread, macaroni, dried fruits and meats, nuts, sugar; nearly omnivorous; readily penetrates many packaged foods	not observed to fly; life cycle may last from 27 to 52 days, with six or seven generations per year; dry conditions are unfavorable; the optimum relative humidity for development is 70% or higher; female may lay 250 eggs	pheromone trap available for monitoring; all stages killed at 0°F to 5°F (−18°C to −15°C) for one day, or at 125°F (52°C) for one hour; kill by putting in freezer or heating in oven
flours, crackers, cereals and similar foods (but not undamaged grains), also peas, beans, shelled nuts, dried fruits, milk chocolate, spices, drugs, museum specimens	females may lay 300 to 400 eggs; life cycle can be completed in seven weeks or may require seven months or longer, depending on temperature	pheromone trap available for monitoring; all stages killed by freezing; store in freezer at 0°F (−18°C) for four days
same as *T. confusum*, above	similar to *T. confusum*; more a pest of warm climates	pheromone trap available for monitoring; all stages killed by freezing; store in freezer at 0°F (−18°C) for four days
grains, straw, cereals	usually one generation per year, although some individuals may require two; average of 276 eggs per female; eggs sometimes eaten in breakfast cereals and larvae passed in human feces	all stages killed by freezing; store in freezer at 0°F (−18°C) for four days or dust with 2% (by weight of grain) calcium carbonate

(continued on page 246)

Table 14.5 (continued from page 245)

	Species	Color	Size/Features
	cadelle (Trogositidae: *Tenebroides mauritanicus*)	shiny black	elongate, oblong, flattened adult; large (³⁄₁₀ in./7.5 mm long)
	granary weevil (Curculioniae: *Sitophilus granarius*)	polished chestnut brown or blackish	⅛ in. to ⅙ in. (3 mm to 4 mm) long; size of adult beetle may vary greatly according to size of kernel of grain in which it matured
	spider beetles (Ptinidae: many species)	variable; reddish brown, brown and black, with various markings	small (¹⁄₁₆ in. to ³⁄₁₆ in./1.5 mm to 4.5 mm long), oval or cylindrical; long legs, constricted prothorax; head not visible from above; long filiform antennae; resemble small spiders

pests of stored food products. Adult beetles are relatively easy to distinguish from adult moths. The moths have wings with scales, whereas the beetles have hard, shell-like wing covers over a membranous pair of wings. To the uninitiated, adult spider beetles resemble ticks; they often infest neglected sacks of dry pet food or old pelleted rabbit food stored indoors or outdoors. Adult weevils can be distinguished from other beetles by their long snout.

The larval forms of these pests are more difficult to differentiate. Larval moths usually have more than three pairs of legs, whereas beetle larvae have only three pairs. The additional larval legs on the lepidopterans, called prolegs, are attached to the abdomen. They look like miniature elephant legs and have small hooks on their bottoms called crotchets, which can be seen with a hand lens. They aid the lepidopterans in movement. These crotchets, as well as the hair patterns on the body, can be used to distinguish among larval species.

It may be worthwhile to learn to recognize adult Mediterranean flour moths and the angoumois grain moth so you can distinguish them from clothes moths. Notice their size, wing shape, color, markings and, particularly, their way of flying. Clothes moths have a fluttery flying pattern; they land and walk considerably between their short flights. They prefer clothes storage areas and places with low light intensity. Dermestid beetles can be pests of stored foods as well as of fabrics. Discovery of adult beetles in places other than the kitchen most likely indicates a fabric rather than a food problem. (Management of carpet beetles and clothes moths is discussed in Chapter 13.)

Treatment: Indirect Strategies

Indirect strategies for controlling pests of stored food focus on inspection and proper storage. These and other strategies are discussed below.

Foods	Biology	Monitoring and Treatment
flour, maize, oats, breakfast cereals of all kinds, shelled and unshelled nuts, spices, dried fruits; gnaws through packages and even through wood, making large holes through which other pests can enter	long-lived—females live up to a year; females lay 10 to 60 eggs in a batch but can lay over 1,000 in a lifetime; will migrate from food source to pupate in unusual places in the house; usually about two generations per year	larvae and adults resistant to low temperatures—can survive 15°F (–9°C) for several weeks; all stages killed by a week's storage at 0°F (–18°C) in freezer
whole grains	female deposits single egg in kernel of grain; can lay up to 254 eggs; life cycle from 30 to 146 days; adults can live from seven to eight months; believed to have no poisonous qualities	all stages controlled in 10 days in grain with a 2% (by weight of grain) dust of calcium carbonate; all stages killed by heating to 120°F (49°C) for one hour; kill by heating in oven or dusting with calcium carbonate
dung, wood, wool, hair, feathers, seeds, grain and grain products, flour, animal remains, pet and animal foods, dried fruit, spices, museum specimens	eggs are laid in the larval food; larvae develop at different rates in different species; larvae leave the larval medium and pupate; wingless adults mate and spread by crawling; cosmopolitan, can tolerate cold climates	can be killed by placing infested food on tray in 150°F (66°C) oven for one hour, stirring materials occasionally, or store in freezer for one week at 0°F (–18°C)—these beetles are very cold-resistant

1. **Inspection and Proper Storage.** Prevention is the simplest and best way to deal with stored-product pests. Since most problems begin when the insects are transported into the house with the product, it is wise to inspect all food packages before purchase. Wrappers should be checked for damage that might permit the entry of small insects. Bulk grains, fruits and similar foodstuffs should be examined carefully while being loaded into bags for weighing; inspect the contents again immediately upon bringing the package into the house.

Uncontaminated food should be stored in the freezer or in sealed glass jars or other tightly sealed containers made of a material tough enough to prevent beetles from boring through them. Glass jars that pressure-seal with rubber gaskets are ideal. Most of the pests described here can crawl down the threads of ordinary screw-top jars and enter the food unless prevented by a barrier at the top. To store large amounts of food, obtain 5-gallon buckets of the type bakeries use. These buckets usually have tight-fitting plastic or metal lids that are pushed on; insects cannot penetrate them. When storing grain in bulk (e.g., in 50-lb. amounts), divide it into 5-lb. or 10-lb. containers so that only smaller amounts will be lost if some of the grain becomes infested.

2. **Dehumidification.** When storing large amounts of grain, keep the area cool and dry to discourage pests. A dehumidifier may be useful. Most stored-product pests will not infest foodstuffs when the humidity is below 6%; an exception is the Mediterranean flour moth, which can live in a grain environment with a humidity of 1% or less. However, all these pests multiply faster at higher humidity, and low moisture is very important in reducing contamination by fungi as well as by insects. Therefore it is worthwhile to do all you can to dry grains, nuts and legumes before storage, even if the ideal level of dryness cannot be achieved.

Table 14.6
Common Moth Pests of Stored Food and Other Products[a]

	Species	Color	Size/Features
	angoumois grain moth (Gelechiidae: *Sitotroga cerealella*)[b]	buff to greyish or yellowish brown	adults small (wingspan ½ in./ 13 mm); hindwings narrow to a point apically; heavily margined with long hairs; size varies depending on volume of larval food
	Mediterranean flour moth (Pyralidae: *Anagasta [=Ephestia] kuehniella*)[b]	pale grey forewings transversely marked with two zigzag black lines; hindwings dirty white	wingspan ⅘ in. (20 mm); at rest, forebody distinctly raised
	Indianmeal moth (Pyralidae: *Plodia interpunctella*)[b]	pale grey wings; outer forewing reddish brown with coppery luster; often mistaken for clothes moths; larvae take color of food, with brown head	wingspan ⅝ in. (16 mm)
	tobacco moth (Pyralidae: *Ephestia elutella*)[c]	forewings brownish grey crossed with two oblique light-colored bands; hindwings uniformly grey	wingspan ⅗ in. (15 mm)
	almond moth (Pyralidae: *E. cautella*)[c]	similar to Mediterranean flour moth; forewings mottled grey on most individuals, but some with fawn-colored scales	wingspan ¾ in. (19 mm)
	raisin moth (Pyralidae: *Cadra figulilella*)[c]	forewings greyish, hindwings satiny white; larvae with four rows of purple spots along back	wingspan ⅖ in. (10 mm)

[a] Abstracted primarily from Mallis, 1982.
[b] Most common and destructive species.
[c] Somewhat less common in the home.

Foods	Biology	Monitoring and Treatment
attacks grain in the field and whole grains in storage	female can lay from 40 to 300 eggs; in warm climates life cycle may be completed in five to seven weeks, in colder climates it may take six months	all states killed by freezing; store in freezer at 0°F (−18°C) for four days; grain can be protected by dusting with diatomaceous earth
flour, cereals, bran, biscuits, dog food, nuts, seeds, beans, chocolate, dried fruit	female can lay 116 to 678 eggs; young larvae constantly spin silken tubes in which they remain while feeding, so infested materials and packages are eventually filled with webs as well as with frass (waste) from the larvae	pheromone trap available for monitoring; all stages killed by freezing; store in freezer at 0°F (−18°C) for four days
very general feeders on dried fruit, seeds, crackers, nuts, powdered milk, spices, candies, bird seed, dried pet food	female can lay up to 400 eggs; larvae feed in silk case and crawl out to pupate; braconid parasitoid (*Bracon hebetor*) often seen in infestations; life cycle varies from 27 to 305 days depending on type of food and temperature; very common in houses	pheromone trap available for monitoring; all stages killed by freezing; store in freezer at 0°F (−18°C) for four days
larvae feed on cereals, chocolate, cocoa beans, coffee, cotton seed, dried fruit, flour, nuts, seeds, spices	larvae leave their food sources to pupate in sheltered spots; create webs in food; may be two to three generations per year	pheromone trap available for monitoring; all stages killed by freezing; store in freezer at 0°F (−18°C) for four days
raisins and other dried fruit, nuts, seeds	female lays an average of 114 eggs; an average of 82 days required to go from egg to adult; moths fly with rapid wing vibration and dart about quickly	pheromone trap available for monitoring; all stages killed by freezing; store in freezer at 0°F (−18°C) for four days
most common pest of dried fruit; infests during drying in orchard or vineyard on injured grapes in storage less than one year; can also feed on grain, rice, corn, oatmeal	females can lay up to 350 eggs; moths overwinter as grown larvae outdoors in topsoil or under bark in mild winter climates	pheromone trap available for monitoring; all stages killed by freezing; store in freezer at 0°F (−18°C) for four days

Preserving Foods With Dry Ice[a]

Dry ice, or carbon dioxide (CO_2), is an extremely safe material for preserving small amounts of grain, flour, nuts, seeds, lentils, soybeans, dried fruit and related products. It is heavier than air, and when placed in a jar full of grain fills all the air spaces in the jar, forcing out the oxygen. Since the pests cannot live without oxygen, dry ice is a very effective control. It can be obtained from ice suppliers, which are listed in most Yellow Pages.

A word of caution: Although carbon dioxide gas is not toxic, do not handle dry ice with your bare hands—it is extremely cold and freezes skin very quickly. Wear gloves, then follow these steps:

1. Put a single layer of nuts and grains in the bottom of a mason-type jar.

2. Chip or saw the dry ice into 1-in. cubes. A 5-lb. dry-ice slab 10 in. by 10 in. by 1 in. makes 100 pieces.

3. Add one cube to a quart jar, and proportionately more or less to larger or smaller jars. Do not allow the ice to touch the sides of the jar, as the cold may break the glass. For much larger quantities of grain, use 14 oz. of dry ice for every 100 lb. of grain.

4. Fill the jar with the rest of the food product and shake gently to settle the contents.

5. Screw down the lid just until it begins to tighten, then turn it back a bit until it is slightly loose. The slightly loosened lid allows excess carbon dioxide to escape.

6. Allow the jars to sit undisturbed for a day or two until all the dry ice has disappeared. Then tighten down the lids and store the jars in a cool place.

[a] From Davis et al., 1974.

Drying Grain at Home

Dropping grain through a stream of air from an electric fan or heater helps dry it and cleans it of debris. This is an electrified version of the ancient process known as winnowing.

To dry grain, drop it slowly through the air stream of a fan, as shown in the drawing at left, or past an electric heater with a strong fan. Let it collect in a clean, high-sided container to reduce bouncing-out of the grain. The blowing has the added advantage of removing broken kernels, chaff and fungal spores. Sieving or hand-picking extracts the remaining contaminants. Do not wash grains until just before use. To make sure you have reduced the level of moisture sufficiently, use the test procedure described in the sidebar on the facing page.

3. **Diatomaceous Earth.** Another method for protecting grains from insect infestation is to add diatomaceous earth, a sorptive dust, directly to the storage container. The powder kills insects by physically disrupting their skins and causing them to dehydrate. (See pp. 111-112 for a detailed discussion.) It should be rinsed off the grains prior to cooking. Be sure to get the grade of diatomaceous earth used for treating grains and not

How To Determine the Moisture Content of Grains at Home[a]

Stored grains should be as dry as possible to discourage beetle and moth infestation. To test the moisture content of purchased grains, take the following steps:

1. Place exactly 20 oz. of grain taken from the middle of the bag or bin in a large baking dish so the grain will not exceed 1 in. in depth.

2. Heat the grain in an oven at 180°F (82°C) for two hours, stirring occasionally.

3. Weigh the grain again when cool. A 1-oz. loss in weight indicates roughly 5% moisture, a 2-oz. loss indicates 10% moisture, a 3-oz. loss 15%, and so on.

[a] From McAllister and Roberts, 1980.

the type used in swimming-pool filters. The latter is not edible, because it has been heated to 2000°F (1093°C) and has crystallized like glass.

4. Treatment with Desiccants. Calcium carbonate has a drying effect on insects and has been shown to be effective in preventing infestations of the granary weevil and the yellow mealworm. It does not need to be rinsed out before cooking. Silica aerogel is another desiccant that protects against a broad range of insects. Eating small amounts of it is not harmful. Note, however, that even grains stored with desiccants or sorptive dusts should be inspected occasionally for signs of infestation.

5. Sanitation. Because many pests of stored products can live and reproduce in spilled foods, spills should be cleaned up promptly. Crumbs lodged in cracks are feeding and breeding sites for insects. Use caulk to seal cracks and crevices where crumbs accumulate. Avoid cutting boards or bread drawers that are built into cupboards, since they have spaces through which crumbs may fall into areas that are difficult to clean. Cupboards and shelves should fit flush with walls or be movable so that cleaning behind them is easy. Select styles of toasters and other crumb-producing appliances that open easily for cleaning.

6. Caulking. The same modification of the environment suggested for cockroach management works in preventing stored-food pests from establishing themselves. Holes, cracks and crevices in the kitchen and pantry should be caulked or repaired.

7. Storage in Dry Ice. Grains and nuts can be stored in a dry-ice (CO_2) atmosphere to protect them from stored-food pests. Storage in CO_2 also protects grains and nuts from fungi that produce aflatoxins. The procedure for CO_2 storage is described in the sidebar on the facing page.

8. Disposal of Infested Stored Products. All infested products should be burned, heated or frozen to destroy any organisms that may infest other products. To use heat, spread the grain or other material to be sterilized on a tray. Heat it in the oven for 20 minutes at 150°F (66°C), or for two to three hours at 120°F to 130°F (49°C to 54°C). This procedure also dries grains prior to storage. Freezing grains for four to seven days at 0°F (−18°C) also kills most common stored-product pests.

Treatment: Direct Biological Controls

There are three natural enemies of stored-product pests available for control. The use of the first two may be cost-effective only for relatively large amounts of stored grains.

1. *Bacillus thuringiensis* (BT). BT is a naturally occurring bacterium that kills the larval stage of moths; it is

Summary: Least-Toxic Beetle and Moth Larvae Control

• Inspect foodstuffs for possible infestation at the time of purchase and/or when they are first brought into your home.

• Store susceptible foodstuffs in as dry a place or container as possible, for example, in pressure-sealed jars with rubber gaskets, in CO_2 from dry ice, in sorptive dust or in the freezer.

• Either freeze or heat infested food to kill live pests.

• Discard infested food after freezing.

• Clean up food spills promptly.

• Design or redesign kitchen and pantry areas to make it easy to clean up spilled foods.

• Use pheromone traps to detect pests that remain in the house after cleaning.

• Caulk or repair cracks and crevices that may harbor food pests.

• If a pesticide is needed, use silica aerogel, diatomaceous earth or pyrethrin.

nontoxic to humans (see pp. 132-136 for details). It is available in most retail plant nurseries under the trade names Dipel®, Thuricide® and Caterpillar Attack®, or in a formulation designed for stored-food pests called Topside Dipel® (for sources, see the Resource Appendix under "Insect Management: Biological Controls" on pp. 683-686). BT can be applied to stored grains for protection against the larval form of the Indianmeal moth and the almond moth (and probably the larvae of other moths as well). These insects seldom feed below a surface layer more than 4 in. (10 cm) thick in grain bins, so BT can be applied to the surface.

2. Parasitoids. The parasitoid *Bracon hebetor* has been used successfully against the almond moth in relatively small storage bins in a commercial mill. The insectary-reared *Trichogramma evanescens*, a parasitoid of caterpillars, has proven effective in controlling a number of moth pests of stored products in a variety of large and small grain-storage sites. These parasitoids kill the egg stage of the moth. This approach could be very helpful for controlling long-standing infestations in the home (or grocery store) that have proved resistant to the normal physical and sanitary methods already described. For sources of these parasitoids, see the Resource Appendix under "Insect Management: Biological Controls" on pp. 683-686.

Treatment:
Direct Chemical Controls

The use of poisons should not be necessary in the management of stored-food pests in the home. However, if the measures described above have not solved the problem, remove the contents from cupboards and drawers and apply an insecticidal dust such as silica aerogel or diatomaceous earth to cracks where pests congregate (see Chapter 7 for details on these materials).

Cover the bottom of drawers and shelves with shelf paper to keep the chemical dust off dishes and utensils. Where this does not provide adequate control, spray empty cupboards with pyrethrin. When the insecticide has dried, cover surfaces with shelf paper and replace food, dishes and utensils. Do not apply insecticides to food, food packages, dishes, utensils or any surface with which food comes in contact.

REFERENCES AND READINGS

Davis, C.S., A.S. Deal, V.E. Burton and J.E. Swift. 1974. *Common pantry pests and their control.* Berkeley: University of California Cooperative Extension (Publication No. AXT107). 6 pp.

An excellent summary of the subject with an emphasis on least-toxic control. This was the source of information on the dry-ice treatment for stored-grain pests.

Ebeling, W. 1975. *Urban entomology.* Berkeley, California: University of California Press. 695 pp.

Excellent drawings and photographs, extensive references and a readable text distinguish this book on all the household pests. The section on ants emphasizes ants found in California, but many of these species also occur widely in the United States and elsewhere. The chapter on pests of stored-food products was an important source of much of the information in this chapter. It is a good source for information about species not covered in this book.

Gorham, J.R., ed. 1977. *Training manual for analytical entomology in the food industry.* Washington, D.C.: Food and Drug Administration (FDA Technical Bulletin No. 2). 174 pp. (Available from: The Association of Official Analytical Chemists, Box 540, Benjamin Franklin Station, Washington, DC 20044.)

This bulletin contains procedures for detecting, inspecting and analyzing insect and rodent fragments and other materials, as well as a series of short articles that public-health technicians should be acquainted with.

Harwood, R.F., and M.T. James. 1979. *Entomology in human and animal health, seventh edition.* New York: Macmillan. 548 pp.

Information on the health effects of the itch mite on humans was taken from this source.

Mallis, A. 1982. *Handbook of pest control.* Cleveland: Franzak and Foster. 1,101 pp.

This is the sixth edition of the standard reference work on household pests used by the professional pest control industry. The chapter on ants was drawn on heavily for much of the information on ants in this chapter, particularly the descriptive table. The book also includes a long chapter with good drawings and color photographs of the stored-product pests. It was a major source of the information in tables 14.5 and 14.6.

McAllister, D.R., and R.S. Roberts. 1980. *Home storage of wheat and grain products.* Logan: Utah State University Extension Service. 9 pp. (Available from the university's extension service in Logan, UT 84322.)

A short but very useful pamphlet with practical methods for storage of wheat and grain products. This was the source of the information on cleaning, bulk storage and moisture control.

Moore, W.S., and T.A. Granovsky. 1983. Laboratory comparisons of sticky traps to detect and control five species of cockroaches (Orthoptera: *Blattidae* and *Blattellidae). Journal of Economic Entomology* 76(4):845-849.

This is the technical paper from which we obtained information on the effectiveness of various traps in catching different roach species.

Munro, J.W. 1966. *Pests of stored products.* London: Hutchinson. 234 pp.

This text discusses stored-product insects and mites, and contains chapters on inspection, prevention and physical, chemical and legislative control measures. It primarily covers pests found in the United Kingdom, but it is also useful in the United States and elsewhere, as many stored-product pests are cosmopolitan.

Olkowski, H. 1986. How to control pharoah ants. *The IPM Practitioner,* 8(5):9-12.

A description of a complete IPM program for pharoah ants.

Olkowski, W. 1989. New developments in non-toxic pest control for stored products. *The IPM Practitioner* 11(2):1-9.

This article documents the FDA action in condemning grain treated with biological control agents and reviews the latest developments in nontoxic controls.

Olkowski, W., H. Olkowski and S. Daar. 1983. *The German cockroach.* Berkeley, California: Bio-Integral Research Center (Technical Bulletin No. 4). 22 pp. (Available from: BIRC, Box 7414, Berkeley, CA 94707.)

A paper written for pest control professionals from which the cockroach section of this book was abstracted. It contains full references for the information discussed here.

Olkowski, W., H. Olkowski and T. Javits. 1979. *The integral urban house book.* San Francisco, Sierra Club Books. 494 pp.

Includes a description of methods for "hot" aerobic composting systems for recycling organic garbage.

Owens, J.M., and G.W. Bennett. 1983. Comparative study of German cockroach (Dictyoptera: *Blattellidae)* population sampling techniques. *Environmental Entomology* 12:1040-1046.

This technical paper presents information comparing the effectiveness of different traps in sampling populations of roaches.

Rodriguez, J.G., ed. 1979. *Recent advances in acarology,* Vol. 1. New York: Academic Press. 631 pp.

The short review article by R.N. Sinha entitled "Role of Acarina in the Stored Grain Ecosystem" (pp. 263-272) indicates the types and effects of granivorous, herbivorous, fungivorous, scavenger, saprophytic, parasitic and predacious mites found in stored-grain systems. It suggests that over 50 species are granivores.

Shejbal, J. 1980. *Controlled atmosphere storage of grains.* New York: Elsevier Scientific Publishing Co. 608 pp.

An innovative book that reports on alternatives to chemical grain fumigation. It describes the use of CO_2, nitrogen and other nontoxic gases, as well as modification of temperature and humidity to discourage pests.

Sinha, R.N., and W.E. Muir. 1973. *Grain storage: part of a system.* Westport, Conn.: Avi Publishing. 481 pp.

An excellent introduction to grain storage, including economics, storage techniques, policy and pests. A chapter by H.A.H. Wallace on the fungi and other organisms associated with stored grain provides a worldwide view of the microbial species that inhabit grains.

Slater, A., M. Hurlbert and R. Lewis. 1980. Biological control of brown-banded cockroaches. *California Agriculture* 34(8/9):16-18.

This short paper describes a project that used biological controls alone to manage the brownbanded roach problem in the University of California animal-rearing laboratories.

Stewart, T. 1986. *Control of the Indianmeal moth and other pantry pest insects in natural food stores.* Self-published. 30 pp. (Available from: Santa Cruz Horticultural Supply, P.O. Box, 1534, Morro Bay, CA 93442.)

This excellent booklet describes an IPM approach to managing common insect pests found in natural food, pet and feed stores. It describes all the available pheromone traps and gives storage tips to prevent infestation. It is well referenced and illustrated.

Swan, L.A., and C.S. Papp. 1972. *Common insects of North America.* New York: Harper and Row. 750 pp.

This reference book contains excellent line drawings and a large selection of ant species, with good field descriptions for quick identification.

Wilson, B.J., and A.W. Hayes. 1973. Microbial toxins. In *Toxicants occurring naturally in foods,* 2nd ed. Washington, D.C.: National Academy of Sciences. 624 pp.

This chapter on microbial toxins advises against reclaiming infested foods because of the strong probability of microbiological contamination of the food if insects or other organisms have defecated in the food.

Wilson, E.O. 1971. *The insect societies.* Cambridge, Mass.: Belknap Press of Harvard University Press. 548 pp.

A classic text that provides basic information on ant ecology and ant taxonomy.

CHAPTER 15

Fleas, Ticks, Heartworms and Mites

INTRODUCTION

When you decide to become responsible for a pet, you also decide, knowingly or not, to adopt its plant, animal and microbe companions. It is no more possible or desirable to attempt to sterilize your pet's body and environment than it is to do this to your own. Most of the organisms that come with the pet are quite benign and go unnoticed by humans. However, at least one of these organisms, the cat flea, causes almost as much misery to humans as such other major pests as cockroaches and termites. This chapter covers fleas, ticks (including the two types commonly found on dogs), the dog heartworm and ear mites of cats and dogs. These are pests people usually manage at home, sometimes with unnecessarily toxic materials.

FLEAS
(Order Siphonaptera)

They say a reasonable amount o'fleas is good for a dog—keeps him from broodin' over bein' a dog, mebbe.

Edward Noyes Westcott

All of the 2,000 known species of fleas worldwide are in the order Siphonaptera. The species most commonly a problem in the home is the cat flea *(Ctenocephalides felis)*, but other species can be troublesome. Table 15.1 at right lists common fleas and their known hosts.

The cat flea (see the drawing at right) occurs on both cats and dogs and bites humans as well. The dog flea *(C. canis)* and the human flea *(Pulex irritans)* are less commonly encountered. Cat fleas are also known to feed on rats, chickens, opossums, raccoons and other species.

The cat flea can carry or transmit various organisms, such as the bacterium *Yersinia pestis,* the causal agent of bubonic plague. It is also suspected of vectoring murine typhus, which is caused by *Rickettsia typhi (=R. mooseri).* The cat flea often causes se-

Table 15.1
Common Flea Species and their Known Hosts

Common Name	Scientific Name	Known Hosts
cat flea	*Ctenocephalides felis*	cat, dog[a]
chicken flea	*Ceratophyllus gallinae*	fowl, bird nests
dog flea	*Ctenocephalides canis*	dog, cat[a]
human flea	*Pulex irritans*	man, pig[a]
mouse flea	*Ctenopysllus segnis*	house mouse, rat
northern rat flea	*Nosopsyllus fasciatus*	Norway rats, roof rats
oriental rat flea	*Xenopyslla cheopis*	rat, mouse[a]
rabbit flea	*Cediopsylla simplex*	rabbits
sand flea	*Tunga penetrans*	humans outside U.S.
sticktight flea	*Echidnophaga gallinacea*	poultry, cat, dog[a]

[a] These fleas have also been detected on other hosts.

rious allergies (discussed further on p. 257) in infested animals and humans. This flea can also host the double-pored dog tapeworm *(Dipylidium caninum),* which can live in dogs, cats or humans. If you have pets, you should read the sidebar on p. 256 on these tapeworms.

Biology

All fleas are associated with warm-blooded hosts and pass through four developmental stages: egg, larva, pupa and adult. Optimal conditions for egg hatching and flea development are 65°F to 80°F (18°C to 27°C) with a relative humidity of 70% or more. Dryness is fatal to larvae because they cannot close their spiracles (breathing holes) to retain moisture. Thus, hot, dry summers reduce flea populations and rainy summers produce larger populations. Temperatures over 95°F (35°C) are also unfavorable.

Under optimal conditions, a female can lay about 25 eggs a day, 3 to 18 at a time after each blood meal for at least three weeks. Peak production occurs at six to seven days. She can produce over 800 eggs during her lifetime. Eggs are laid either on the pet or off the pet where it sleeps. Eggs laid on the host fall off and accumu-

The Life Cycle of the Cat Flea
The adult cat flea lays several hundred eggs that incubate off the host and hatch within 12 days into legless larvae. The larvae feed on organic debris for 8 to 24 days and become pupae. The pupae emerge into adults in five to seven days. When conditions are unfavorable for emergence, larvae can live for 200 days and pupae for up to a year. (Actual size: ⅟₁₆ in./1.5 mm)

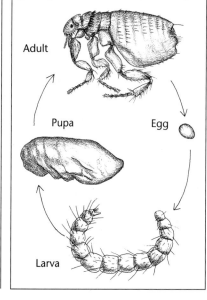

Adult

Pupa

Egg

Larva

Dog Tapeworms[a]

Pet owners should be aware that fleas can transmit the dog tapeworm *(Dipylidium caninum)*, an intestinal parasite. It is not cause for major concern, however, since a cat, dog or person must *eat* an infested flea to become infested. Even if this should happen, infestation by one worm discourages the attachment of others. Additionally, the nutritional requirements of the tapeworm are minimal, so an infested animal, if otherwise healthy, is in no immediate danger. A large number of flea larvae that ingest tapeworms die from the infestation before becoming adults.[b]

The signs of tapeworm infestation are easy for the pet owner to see. The broken-off segments of the worm that pass through the anus of the animal look like wriggly white squares. Later, these dry and resemble grains of brown rice. They can be found in places the pet sleeps, along with the salt-and-pepper-looking flea eggs and feces. Examination of a stool specimen by a veterinarian confirms the diagnosis, and the tapeworm can be killed with medication.

[a] From Marshall, 1967.

[b] The idea that the tapeworm acts as a biological control against the flea has not yet been adequately evaluated.

late in bedding, floor cracks, rugs, furniture, dust and damp soil.

Eggs hatch in 2 to 12 days. The hairy, worm-like, white larvae, which are $\frac{1}{16}$ in. to $\frac{1}{5}$ in. (1.5 mm to 5 mm) long, have a distinct brown head. The larvae go through three stages in 8 to 24 days; in unfavorable conditions, they may develop more slowly, taking up to 200 days. The larvae live wherever the eggs have fallen; they do not live on the pet nor do they bite pets or humans. Their food is the dried blood copiously defecated by the adults, who feed on the host. The "salt and pepper" found where the pet has been sleeping is a mixture of flea eggs (white) and dried blood (black). The larvae then spin a cocoon and transform themselves into pupae, which often become camouflaged among the debris.

Under favorable conditions, the pupal stage lasts one to two weeks, but in adverse conditions it may last nearly a year. Adverse conditions may occur in the absence of a host. Emergence takes place in response to host warmth and vibrations, as well as to carbon dioxide emitted from the host during respiration. Massive flea populations can result from the simultaneous emergence of accumulated generations of unhatched flea pupae triggered by the presence of a host. If you have ever moved into a residence that has been vacant for some time but was previously occupied by dog or cat owners, or if you have returned to your own residence after a vacation with Fido, you know what such an accumulated, hungry, newly emerged adult flea population can be like.

Once emerged, the male and female fleas immediately seek a blood meal. These adults are quite small and black in color, but after feeding, they expand and appear lighter brown. Adults can live one to two months without a meal and can survive seven or eight months with one. Adult fleas jump onto hosts, usually from the floor or furniture. Once on the host, they can hitchhike considerable distances.

Wide variations in development time account for the sudden appearance of large numbers of adult fleas in "flea season," late summer and fall. The population has been building up all year long in the form of eggs, larvae and pupae, but rapid development into biting adults is not completed until the temperature and humidity rise to requisite levels.

Because cat fleas prefer cat and dog hosts, humans are not likely to be attacked unless the flea population is high, the host pet is absent for a brief period or the pet is no longer in residence.

Damage

Fleas are serious pests for the reasons already mentioned. In addition, some fleas can carry disease-causing pathogens, such as the bacterium that causes bubonic plague. Since bubonic plague is endemic among certain small wild rodents in some parts of the United States, there is always the danger that fleas and the bacteria they carry will be passed from host to host, and that the disease ultimately will be transmitted to humans through contact with domestic animals. One case of bubonic plague reported not too long ago was suspected of having been transmitted by fleas from a cat to the veterinarian who was treating it. The cat was believed to have picked up plague-infested fleas from wild rodents driven out of their habitat by wildfires.

Other cases of plague in humans have been traced to contact with fleas from ground squirrels as a result of camping near infested squirrel nests. A serious plague outbreak among squirrels in Lassen State Park, California, was responsible for the temporary closure of the park a few years ago.

Occasionally, flea bites on humans are frequent and extensive even where there have never been pets in the home. Such infestations can usually be traced to wild animals living under the house, in the attic or in the eaves. The only way to solve this problem is to have the fleas identified by a professional so you know which animals are hosts to that species and then to locate and remove them.

Despite compelling public-health reasons for being concerned about various flea species, it is the cat flea that generates the most pesticide use in the vicinity of humans. The most common reason for the concern is an allergic response either by a pet or a human. Fleas secrete saliva during feeding to prevent clotting and aid in the uptake of ingested blood. There is great variability in reactions to this flea saliva among humans and pets. Four different classes of skin reactions to flea bites have been recognized: immediate (in minutes), delayed (hours to days), immediate as well as delayed and no reaction. Any allergy is an overreaction by the immune system, in this case to substances in flea saliva. A person who is allergic to flea bites may develop a variety of skin lesions. Itching and other symptoms may last weeks or longer. You can see why there might be disagreement among members of a household as to the severity of a flea infestation. Some members will never notice any bites and may be convinced that they are not being bitten, which may or may not be true. At the same time, others may be suffering greatly.

An allergic animal will lose hair, frequently around the base of the tail, and may repeatedly bite and scratch the area, sometimes until it becomes raw. Thus, even though humans are not bothered at all, the family pet may be in distress.

Two basic factors account for the variations in response to flea bites. One is the differential attractiveness of the hosts. This is probably due to skin secretions and emanations, particularly carbon dioxide. The other is physiological differences in immune systems, complicated by differences in exposure patterns to flea saliva. Thus, some people really are more attractive to fleas than others, and are bitten frequently. Others are allergic to the flea saliva and experience distress even though they are not getting bitten any more often than anyone else.

Desensitization through prolonged exposure to small doses of the irritant is a common medical means of reducing the reaction of sensitive individuals to many allergenic substances. Flea saliva allergen is available for hypersensitive humans and pets. With humans, more immediate relief can be obtained by using an ice cube, menthol, camphor or calamine lotion on the bite.

Some of the trigger mechanisms for immune system hypersensitivity in pets are known. One mechanism that cannot be avoided is aging. But others, such as emotional stress or inadequate protein, may be alleviated. Keep cats on a full-protein diet and make sure dogs have adequate protein. Give pets extra attention during stress-inducing times such as moving, introduction of a new pet or the birth of a human baby.

Detection and Monitoring

Monitoring can be as simple as noting when fleas attempt to bite humans or watching how much your pets scratch themselves. A more rigorous monitoring program attempts to correlate the number of bites of humans with an annoyance level. We described this kind of monitoring program in Chapter 3.

The key component of a good monitoring program is the use of a specially manufactured flea comb as frequently as necessary to determine whether the flea population is going up or down. It is important to score and record each day's "catch," so you do not have to depend on memory. (For a description of the combing technique, see pp. 258-259.)

Flea sock traps can also be used to sample flea populations. These are knee-high white flannel booties or leggings that fit over a person's shoes and lower pant legs. The adult fleas get entangled in the nap of the flannel, at least temporarily, and can be counted and usually caught. Such socks can also provide protection from bites if an allergic person must enter a severely flea-infested area for a short period.

Treatment:
Indirect Strategies

If you are experiencing a "flea emergency" as you read this, use the tactics described in the sidebar on p. 258 to reduce the problem to a tolerable level. Then follow the largely nontoxic methods described in this section to prevent flea populations from building up again.

Because reinfestation from other animals or outdoors is likely, it is usually impossible to have a flea-free pet for long. However, with sound management, flea populations can be held to tolerable levels (most pets can tolerate a moderate number of fleas without undue annoyance). In addition to direct reduction of all stages of fleas, flea-management programs should include efforts to decrease host attractiveness and reduce food and habitats available for larval flea development. A complete program for cat fleas includes monitoring, environmental modification, preventive maintenance and direct intervention.

1. Restricting Pet Access. Do not allow pets to enter areas where the resulting flea population will be particularly annoying to humans or where cleaning to remove fleas is difficult. For example, you can use screen fencing to keep pets from scrambling under porches. Exclude them from basements or workshops that are filled with objects that are difficult to vacuum. Don't let pets into bedrooms or regular work areas of those in your household who are disturbed by flea bites. Design your pet's designated or favorite sleeping areas so bedding materials can be moved and washed easily.

How To Handle a Flea Emergency

If a high flea population is driving you and your pets crazy, use the following tactics to get the emergency under control in the least-toxic manner. You should see a significant reduction in flea numbers within a day or two.

1. Fleas reside in carpeting, so remove all carpets and wash them or have them cleaned. If you have wall-to-wall carpeting, call in a steam-cleaning company. Give the technicians a container of insect repellent to apply to their pant legs and footwear, and remember to use some yourself for a measure of relief while combatting the fleas.

The steam will kill most of the adult and pre-adult fleas in the carpeting, although some eggs will survive and hatch afterwards. An alternative is to hire a pest control company to apply an infrared heat treatment to your carpets.

2. Whether or not you steam-clean or heat-treat, vacuum carpets and upholstered furniture every day for a week or more. The vacuum picks up all stages of the flea, but is best at capturing adults and eggs. Also vacuum floors, particularly along the edges, in corners and under furniture where dust gathers. Be sure to vacuum less-traveled areas of the carpet—behind doors, for example—because that is where fleas tend to deposit their eggs. Either discard the disposable vacuum bag or wrap it in plastic and store it in the freezer between vacuumings to kill captured fleas (even though most would be killed by the dusty conditions within the bag anyway).

3. Spray carpets and floors with the insect growth regulator methoprene.

4. Once you have followed the first three steps, the flea population is usually low enough to give you the breathing room you need to undertake the longer-term controls described in the text. If the problem is still not under control, apply diatomaceous earth or a borate product to the carpet or spot-treat with insecticidal soap or an insecticide containing limonene/linalool.

If after these efforts you are still getting bitten by fleas, treat those areas where you notice the fleas with a stronger insecticide, that is, one containing pyrethrin or a synthetic pyrethroid.

5. Shampoo your dog with insecticidal soap or a limonene/linalool product and then use a flea comb to remove surviving fleas. Also use a flea comb on cats, but be cautious about treating them with insecticides. Let pets roam the house, since they will attract fleas hiding in carpets and elsewhere, and comb them for a few minutes each day to remove fleas they have picked up.

If you have a dog or cat, flea infestations are most likely to occur during the warm, moist months of the year. Assume long before you notice the problem that the flea population is building up where your pet normally rests. Remember that the young flea larvae are not found on the animal; they are on the floor, rugs and cushions. No doubt this is why cats and dogs periodically change their favorite resting spot. By restricting your pet to a regular sleeping space, you can concentrate the flea population and focus cleaning efforts in fewer areas.

2. **Using Washable Pet Bedding.** In pet sleeping areas, use pet bedding or a cloth that can be gathered up easily and laundered every few weeks — weekly in peak flea season. Be sure to pick up the bedding by the four corners to avoid scattering flea eggs and larvae, then carry it to the soapy water that will be used to wash it. Washing in hot water with soap or detergent destroys all stages of the fleas.

Treatment:
Direct Physical Controls

Combing and bathing your pet, vacuuming, and exposing fleas to extremes of temperature are effective controls of flea populations. These and other physical treatment strategies are discussed below.

1. **Combing.** A flea comb (see the photo on the facing page) is a very effective tool in the suppression of adult fleas (for sources, see the Resource Appendix under "Insect Management: Physical Controls" on pp. 682-683). It removes the fleas themselves as well as the flea feces and dried blood, or specks, that provide food for larval populations. If you have both a cat and a dog, it's usually sufficient to comb just the cat to suppress the overall flea population, including that on the dog. If you do comb a dog with a thick coat, brush it well first to curry out the snarls and arrange the hair so that it is easy to pass the flea comb through.

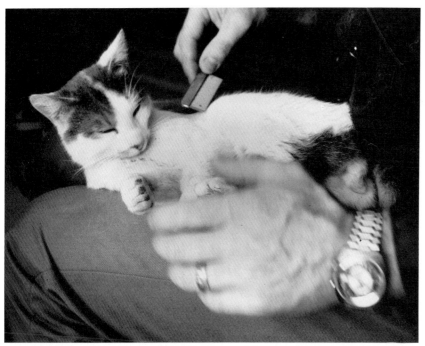

A fine-toothed metal flea comb is an excellent tool for removing fleas from cats, dogs and other furry pets. The comb is pulled in the direction of the fur, and fleas caught in the tines are flicked into soapy water, where they drown. (Photo by Helga Olkowski.)

The metal combs designed for catching fleas have their tines set to allow passage of hair but not fleas. If pressed for time, you can focus combing on those parts of the pet where the most fleas congregate, usually the neck or tail area. Observation often tells you which areas are the most infested.

Combing works best when the pet is resting and relaxed. Initially, it is probably best that two people carry out the process, one to hold, stroke and distract the pet, the other to begin combing. With time, the animal will likely grow to enjoy the combing and hold still for it, making it possible for just one person to perform the task. If you start when the animal is young, it will soon become accustomed to the process. Reluctant animals can be rewarded to encourage a tolerance for combing.

Inspect the comb at the end of each pass through the hair. Pull captured fleas from the comb and flick them into a container of soapy water. The fleas quickly sink to the bottom and drown. It's a good idea to keep a small cloth nearby to wipe your fingers on so the animal's coat does not get soapy.

The number of fleas captured at each combing is one indicator of the effectiveness of the other techniques being used to reduce flea numbers. If you correlate the flea catch with other indicators of flea presence—the number of fleas visible on the pet, rugs or furnishings, the degree of pet scratching, the number of flea bites on humans, and so on—you can decide what your personal tolerance level is at the moment. In this case, the tolerance level is the maximum number of fleas caught by combing that still allows an acceptable level of comfort for humans and pets. If the catch goes above this level, you know it is time to increase the frequency and intensity of management practices or institute other techniques.

In a system used in the Olkowski household, a flea comb, a sturdy old ceramic marmalade jar filled with detergent and water almost to the brim and a little booklet for keeping tally are kept close to the table where the cats like to stretch out in the sun. Once they are warm and sleepy, we run the comb over each cat about ten times and see how many fleas we have caught. It takes only a few minutes, and by the time the cats are fully awake, the combing session is usually over for the day.

2. Bathing. Giving your pet an occasional bath in soap and water can be useful in suppressing a flea population, particularly on dogs, which are generally more amenable to bathing than cats. Bathing works by drowning fleas; it is not necessary to use a soap impregnated with an insecticide, although more fleas will be killed if an insecticide is used. The least-toxic insecticidal material available is Safer's Flea Shampoo™, a soap made from fatty acids derived from vegetable oil. Shampoos containing pyrethrins are somewhat more toxic but produce a higher level of direct flea kill (see pp. 262-263 for more details, and consult the Resource Appendix under "Insect Management: Chemical Controls" on pp. 686-687 for sources of these products).

3. Vacuuming. Vacuum carpeting, upholstered furniture and floors with a machine with strong suction and a removable, easily closed disposable bag. Use vacuum attachments to clean cracks and crevices, or, better still, seal these openings permanently. After vacuuming, close the bag quickly and take it directly to the garbage, burn it or place it inside a sealed plastic bag. You can freeze the plastic bag for a few days or place it in the sun to kill the fleas with heat. Alternatively, you can use a water vacuum, as described on p. 163 for control of house dust mites; the same techniques apply.

Follow this procedure on a regular basis throughout the year to keep developing flea populations low. If populations are increasing noticeably, vacuum more frequently, as often as every day. Vacuuming is very effective at picking up adult and egg-stage fleas. In fact, adult fleas can be stimulated into emerging from the pupal stage by vibrations caused by such things as vacuum cleaners. Thus, they are caught by the vacuum before they bite pets or people.

Unfortunately, vacuuming is less effective at capturing flea larvae in carpeting. Research at Virginia Polytechnic Institute indicates that flea larvae concentrate in carpets where pets usually rest or travel. As the pets move about, they shed the dried feces and blood that adult fleas produce while feeding on the pet. The larvae depend on this food for survival. Although vacuuming helps remove this food source, the larvae respond to vacuuming by coiling around the base of a carpet fiber and hanging on. This behavior begins almost immediately after the larvae sense the disturbance. Thus, while up to 59% of flea eggs have been documented as being removed by vacuuming, only about 20% of flea larvae are removed. Consequently, when infestations are severe, you should supplement vacuuming with steam-cleaning or shampooing.

4. Steam-Cleaning. The services of a steam-cleaning firm may be warranted when flea populations are high. The process kills adult and larval fleas and probably some eggs as well. However, the warmth and humidity produced by the steam also triggers hatching of remaining flea eggs a day or two after the cleaning has occurred. So don't be surprised if some fleas reappear. Nonetheless, if the other steps recommended in this section are followed—regular vacuuming and flea-combing the pet—the few fleas that hatch out after steam-cleaning should represent the flea population's last gasp.

5. Heating and Freezing. In the late 1980s, scientists Walter Ebeling and Charles Forbes developed techniques that kill fleas by raising or lowering the temperature in a room to the point that insects die. The heat treatment involves a common heating unit that is modified to include special blowers and flexible ducts. This unit raises the temperature within a structure enough to kill fleas and other insects, such as termites, cockroaches and ants, without damaging either the structure or its contents. Tests indicate that cat flea larvae die after exposure to a temperature of 103°F (39°C) for one hour.

These heating units and a training program in their use are being marketed to pest control companies by Isothermics, Inc., in Anaheim, California. Since this system is designed primarily as an alternative to chemical fumigation for wood-damaging pests, the cost of using it against fleas may be warranted only by a severe flea infestation in a building where occupants cannot tolerate exposure to any pesticides.

Another tool based on the heat principle—and one that is more cost-effective—is the Sanix system, which resembles a vacuum cleaner. It releases heat generated by infrared rays that kills fleas and mites in carpeting. It is available only to pest control professionals. For sources of heating units, see the Resource Appendix under "Insect Management: Physical Controls" on pp. 682-683.

At the other end of the temperature scale, Ebeling and Forbes found that liquid nitrogen can be used to lower the temperature at floor level for a short time until fleas die. An interesting side benefit is that the extreme cold crystallizes dirt and stains on carpets and upholstery so they can be vacuumed up. At the time of writing, however, the liquid-nitrogen method for flea control is not commercially available.

6. Ultrasonic Collars and Machines. In the past few years a number of ultrasonic flea collars and area-wide machines have been marketed for flea control. To date, however, there is no scientific evidence that any of these products are effective. In a recent study (listed under "References and Readings" on pp. 283-285), veterinarian Michael Dryden and colleagues reported, "98.6% and 97.4% of fleas were still on the cats after treatment and control periods, respectively. The ultrasonic flea collars were ineffective in reducing flea numbers on these cats."

7. Drying or Flooding Infested Areas Outdoors. Outdoors, organic matter can temporarily harbor fleas while they are off the host. Either drying out or heavily watering these areas kills the eggs and larvae. These areas may also be treated with insecticidal soap or pyrethrins (see pp. 262-263).

Treatment:
Direct Chemical Controls
Insecticides for flea control are available as liquid solutions, aerosols, foggers and powders. Dry formulations are safer to use on pets than are liquid solutions because they contain no solvent to carry the toxicant into the skin. However, powders may be breathed by pets and are distributed wherever the pets travel. Liquid sprays are frequently used on pet bedding and in other areas where fleas breed, although dry powders such as diatomaceous earth are also used in carpeting and similar flea-breeding sites. For sources of all materials mentioned in this section, see the Resource Appendix under "Insect Management: Chemical Controls" on pp. 686-687.

1. Repellents. A repellent can be useful in some situations. The standard mosquito repellent DEET (diethyltoluamide) used in Cutter's® Insect Repellent, Off® and similar products is widely available in pharmacies and sporting goods stores. It is applied to clothing (avoid direct skin contact) and provides protection from fleas for several days. It is an effective interim measure when you are waiting for an insect growth regulator (described below) to take effect.

A number of pet sprays now contain DEET as well as an insecticide. Veterinarians caution those using such products to follow label directions carefully, because overuse can harm pets. In one study cited by research veterinarian David Dorman, a product containing 9% DEET and 0.09% fenvalerate, a synthetic pyrethroid insecticide, was implicated in 476 complaints about dog and cat sickness reported to the Illinois Animal Poison Information Center during 1987. By comparison, only 22 calls were received for all other DEET-containing insecticides.

A number of other repellent materials, such as pennyroyal, eucalyptus, rosemary and citronella, have traditionally been used in flea collars or in pet bedding. However, their strong odors can be irritating to pets. Although there are few, if any, scientific studies on the efficacy of these materials on fleas, recent interest in the pesticidal effect of natural plant oils is providing some clues. One study found that the volatile oil ecalyptol (1,8-cineole), which is found in eucalyptus and other plants in the Asteraceae, Magnoliaceae and Rutaceae families, has a strong repellent effect on mosquitoes, cockroaches and Colorado potato beetles. Although this material has not been tested against fleas specifically, its reputation for flea repellency may be warranted.

Cedar chips also have a reputation as a flea-repellent bedding material. One difficulty with such bedding is that it loses its distinctive odor as it ages and may soon become a convenient home for flea larvae, which cannot be vacuumed up or washed out effectively from the wood chips. It is better to use bedding materials that can be washed.

2. Vitamin B₁. Vitamin B_1 (thiamine hydrochloride), taken orally in the form of brewer's yeast, has also been used as a flea repellent. Entomologist F. Pearlman reports the results of a study in which 24 of 33 patients who took 50 mg of vitamin B_1 three times daily counted fewer flea bites while on the treatment.

You can also give vitamin B_1 to your pets. However, you might want to follow the advice of Judy Kahle (see the chapter references), who cautions pet owners to give yeast (a source of vitamin B_1) in small doses or with dry pet food, since it can cause undigested food to swell, leading to gas and cramps. She suggests that a better source of vitamin B_1 is B-complex vitamins, and recommends a dose of ¼ to ½ a 10-mg B-complex vitamin pill twice daily. She suggests that the vitamin be used only when the flea population is high and the animal is showing an allergic reaction to the fleas.

3. Limonene/Linalool. D-limonene and linalool are citrus-peel extracts that have been used for years as food additives and are considered quite safe for use on mammals. Products that contain d-limonene kill larval and adult fleas, while those containing both ingredients kill all flea stages. They are available as EPA-registered insecticides from pet stores under various trade names. Flea Stop® Pet Spray contains both active ingredients, and Flea Stop® Shampoo contains d-limonene alone. There are also some non-EPA-registered pet shampoos and coat conditioners that contain crude citrus extracts. At least one of these was implicated in the death of a cat dipped in it, presumably because a lack of refinement of the extract resulted in excessive exposure to the active ingredients.

EPA-registered citrus products can be used directly on pets, but veterinarians caution that some cats may be sensitive if the material is applied at excessive concentrations. For example, cats sprayed with a refined active ingredient extract at 5 to 10 times the recommended dose exhibited hypersalivation, tremors and other discomfort, although they recovered within six hours. These materials can also be applied against fleas in bedding, but should not be used to spray entire rooms. Nor are they registered for use outdoors.

4. Sorptive Dusts. The most common sorptive dusts, silica aerogel and diatomaceous earth, are chemically inert materials that kill insects by dehydrating them. Silica aerogels are made by reacting sodium silicate and sulfuric acid to form fluffy aerogels. These aerogels can absorb three times their weight in oil, including the oils covering the outer cuticle of insects. Diatomaceous earth is composed of finely ground fossil materials that kill insects by abrading their outer coverings, causing them to dehydrate and die. Although these materials are not poisonous to mammals, the fine dust can travel freely through the air and irritate the lungs (diatomaceous earth less so than silica aerogel). It is wise to wear a dust mask when applying these dusts, and to avoid getting them in the animal's face.

University of California researcher I.B. Tarshis reported great success using silica aerogel (Dri-Die®67) to control fleas on cats and several breeds of dogs. He used a small bulb duster or his hands to apply 1 oz. (28 g) of dust on cats and small dogs and 2 oz. (57 g) on larger dogs. According to Tarshis, "The dust should be applied on the ears, around the neck, over the back, around the anus, over and under the tail, over the genitals, on the abdomen and over the legs, with particular attention to the placement of the dust between the toes of the animals."

One dusting is sufficient to treat cats and short-haired dogs. Long-haired dogs may require two treatments. The dust is more effective if the dog is bathed and combed first. Severely matted hair should be clipped before the dust is applied. Tarshis found that shortly after the dust was worked into the animal's coat, large numbers of dust-covered fleas begin moving out from beneath the fur. Their movements were erratic, and within minutes they started falling off the treated animal, dying within an hour.

Tarshis recommends leashing the pet for several hours to allow time for all fleas to come in contact with the dust before the dust is partially removed through the normal activities of the animal. The dust should remain on the pet for as long as possible—at least a week—before regular bathing and other wetting of the animal resumes.

After treating the pet, apply silica aerogel or diatomaceous earth to areas where the pet sleeps or roams. Thoroughly powder all sides of the pet's bedding, including boxes or baskets where the pet sleeps. If the pet roams inside the house or is kept in a doghouse or kennel, first vacuum, then apply dust to cracks in walls, floorboards and other locations where fleas may lodge once off the animal. In the home this includes carpeting, upholstered furniture, bed frames and mattresses. Outdoors, dust can be applied to lawns, paths used by pets and to the runways of kennels. An average-size home and yard can usually be treated with 8 oz. to 12 oz. (227 g to 340 g) of dust.

Silica aerogel and diatomaceous earth are also available in combination with pyrethrin (discussed below) for faster killing of fleas. Drione®, Revenge® and Roach Attack® combine silica aerogel with pyrethrin and come in aerosol cans. Diacide® contains diatomaceous earth plus pyrethrin, and is packaged as a dust.

5. Insect Growth Regulators. Insect growth regulators (IGRs) are not poisons in the traditional sense of the word. They kill insects by inhibiting some crucial aspect of their physiological development, such as molting. Because these physiological processes are foreign to humans and other mammals, IGRs are generally regarded as extremely safe for pest-management purposes.

The IGRs methoprene (FleaTrol®, Precor®) and fenoxycarb (Torus®) are applied in liquid solution or as an aerosol to areas of potential flea development (such as carpets and pet bedding). They arrest the growth of the flea at or before the pupal stage, preventing development of adult fleas for months after a single application. However, IGRs do not kill fleas that reach the adult stage before the material is applied. Liquid spray solutions last longer, 210 days versus 75 for the aerosol fogger.

If adult fleas have already become bothersome by the time an IGR is used, you should immediately begin a twice-daily routine of combing your pet. You may want to combine this procedure with occasional use of an insecticidal spray in carpeting to kill existing adult fleas (see below).

Unfortunately, there is a temptation to use IGRs in the manner of traditional pesticides, which is to overuse them. Some insects have already developed resistance to IGRs. If home users and professionals can be convinced to apply these new products in moderation, and only as part of a complete integrated pest-management program, their useful life will be extended considerably.

IGRs such as FleaTrol® and Torus® are available without added ingredients, but the current trend is to market an IGR in the same container with a conventional insecticide aimed at adult fleas. This use is likely to speed up the development of resistance.

6. Insecticidal Soap. The insecticidal properties of the naturally occurring fatty acids used to make soaps have been refined in a number of products that are useful in the battle against fleas. These soaps are virtually nontoxic to mammals, and they biodegrade rapidly after application. Safer® Insecticidal Flea Soap can be used to bathe flea-infested animals and to wash bedding. Another product, Safer® Entire Flea and Tick Spray, composed of insecticidal soap plus 0.01% pyrethrins, can be used to spray pets, rugs, pet bedding, floors and other areas where the pet may have shed flea eggs or where young fleas may be living as they mature into adults.

Outdoors, fleas may live in the pet's favorite sleeping areas during warm weather. These areas can also be treated with an insecticidal soap to reduce adult populations. Although the soap is not hazardous to humans or mammals, it can kill a wide variety of arthropods, many of which are beneficial. Therefore, insecticidal soap should be used outdoors as a spot treatment only, and only during periods of truly high flea infestations.

To find out where the adult fleas are, you can wear a special pair of white flannel socks (see p. 257) or regular knee-high white sport socks while walking about the lawn or other areas you suspect contain fleas. If adult fleas are present, they will hop onto the socks and become visible against the white background. You should spray only those areas where you have determined that fleas are numerous.

7. Pyrethrum. The safest effective insecticide powder for use on animals is the botanical pyrethrum, a product made from the crushed flowers of the pyrethrum chrysanthemum (*Chrysanthemum cinerariaefolium* and related species). However, you must take care when using any powder to avoid getting the insecticide into the pet's eyes, nostrils or mouth. When powdering cats, remember that they will take some of the materials applied to their fur into their digestive system when they lick themselves in grooming, so powder only if necessary, and take care not to overapply the material. Put pets outside after powdering them, or better yet, powder them outside. Always wear a dust mask and goggles during application. See the remarks under pyrethrins, below, for further cautions.

8. Pyrethrins. These are the active insecticidal components in pyrethrum that are extracted and used in insecticide products. They are available from pet stores under many brand names, and are among the most effective and least-toxic products available for flea control. There are, however, some caveats concerning the use of pyrethrins.

First, most pyrethrin products contain the synergist piperonyl butoxide, which has been found problematical in some studies of chronic human exposure. We are aware of one pyrethrin product, Safer® Entire Flea and Tick Spray, that does not contain the synergist, and there may be others. Check the label. Second, pyrethrins may be safer to use on dogs than on cats. In a recent study published by Kenya's pyrethrum producers organization, it was reported that cats treated with liquid solutions containing more than 0.04% pyrethrins showed severe reactions, including convulsions and vomiting. If you use pyrethrins, look carefully at the label and make sure the product contains no more than 0.04% active pyrethrin; if the level is higher than that, you can dilute it to that level.

9. **Synthetic Pyrethroids.** These are synthetic versions of the pyrethrins described above, but with enhanced toxicity. Compared to conventional organophosphate and carbamate insecticides for fleas, the pyrethroids have the advantage of more rapid breakdown, reducing their impact on the larger environment.

Consider using a pyrethroid if the flea problem in your household is serious and chronic but nobody can or wants to take responsibility for managing it with the methods described above. First, call in a professional house-cleaner or rug-shampooer. While the house is receiving a thorough cleaning and all the rugs are being steamed or shampooed, have the pets bathed or combed at a pet clinic. Immediately upon the pet's return to the clean house, use an IGR to prevent further flea emergence. If even that doesn't work and you decide you must call a pest control operator, specify the use of a pyrethrin or synthetic pyrethroid.

10. **Flea Collars.** The most common flea-control method currently in use is the flea collar, a plastic strip impregnated with an organophosphate or methylcarbamate poison. Collars work by emitting pesticide vapors constantly over one to three months. The vapors kill fleas by contact and/or fumigation. They are also breathed into the lungs by pets and nearby humans.

The active ingredients in the collars are cholinesterase inhibitors,

Summary: Least-Toxic Flea Control

• Establish a single pet sleeping area that can be cleaned easily and regularly.

• Restrict pets' access to bedrooms, attics, basements or wherever the flea population may be particularly annoying or where cleaning is difficult.

• Vacuum areas frequented by your pet on a regular weekly basis during the year, more frequently in late summer and fall when flea populations increase. Dispose of collected material by burning, composting or sealing in a plastic bag and placing it in the freezer for a few days or in a sunny location to "cook."

• Regularly remove and wash all bedding and rugs that the pet comes into contact with.

• Flea-comb your pet regularly.

• Monitor the flea population by keeping records.

• Bathe the pet if the flea population starts to build up.

• If the above procedures are insufficient, use an insect growth regulator in a liquid spray formulation to prevent adult flea emergence.

• Spot-treat pet resting areas outdoors with insecticidal soap.

• If a flea collar is considered necessary, place it on your pet as briefly as possible. When it is off the pet, keep it in a tightly closed container in a cool location.

• If other poisons are used, follow the instructions carefully and protect yourself while applying them. If you must use poisons at all, use them for the shortest time possible and only during the most troublesome periods.

• Consider using professional services for extremely large flea populations when the above procedures do not solve the problem. But try a professional steam-cleaning and rug-shampooing service first, or ask a pest control operator to apply a heat treatment before resorting to a pesticide.

which interfere with normal nerve transmission. Because the collars emit poison whether fleas are present or not, it is our opinion that they create unnecessary environmental contamination. In addition, some flea collars are known to cause severe irritation to the neck regions of pets exposed, particularly cats. Dichlorvos-impregnated collars can also produce hypersensitive reactions such as dermatitis in some humans.

Flea-collar dermatitis has been recognized on small pets by H. Muller, who suggests a treatment regime for animals damaged by the collar and

recommends that pets not be exposed to other insecticides, such as those in hanging pest strips or worm medicines, while the collar is being worn. On larger dogs, the collars frequently are ineffective, probably because the poisonous vapor cannot reach as far as the tail end.

If, despite these drawbacks, it seems necessary to use a flea collar, follow the procedures in the sidebar on p. 264. Wear gloves when putting the collar on the animal and examine the pet's skin underneath the collar frequently, particularly when it is worn for the first time.

Flea Collars

We believe flea collars create unnecessary environmental contamination, since they emit poison whether or not fleas are present. Nonetheless, if you feel you must use these collars, you should follow these procedures:

• On dogs, fasten the collar loosely to allow as much space as possible between the skin and the collar.

• On cats, fit the collar snugly to avoid possible strangulation when the cat is climbing. Allow enough slack to permit three fingers to be inserted between the cat's neck and the collar.

• When you feel the collar must be used, put it on the animal for six days or less. Then remove it, place it in a jar with a tight-fitting lid and store in a cool place. Do not allow the collar to get wet, as this may weaken the insecticide. This on/off method applies insecticide only when needed, either when the flea population is high or just before it reaches numbers that are felt to cause a problem. This approach also extends the effective life of the collar, since a resistant population of fleas will not develop so quickly, and it reduces the potential hazard, because less toxicant is inhaled by pets and people.

TICKS: OVERVIEW
(Class Arachnida)

Many people know that Rocky Mountain spotted fever is transmitted by ticks, and, recently, tick-transmitted Lyme disease or Lyme arthritis has been very much in the news. But few people are aware of the important role that ticks have played in the history of medicine.

Ticks were the first animal discovered to be vectors, which are carriers of a pathogen that causes disease in another animal. The disease was Texas cattle fever, caused by the protozoan *Babesia bigemina,* which is transmitted by the cattle tick *Boophilus annulatus.* Soon after the relationship between tick, mammal and pathogen was discovered in 1893, the disease was eradicated from the United States.

Following that discovery, it was learned that ticks are also vectors of other disease-causing pathogens, some of which are listed in Table 15.2 on the facing page. Eventually, the major scourges of humankind, such as malaria, bubonic plague and oth-

ers, were found to be transmitted by insect or arachnid vectors. More than 65 pathogens are now known to be transmitted by ticks, making them collectively one of the most important groups from the perspective of human and domestic-animal health.

In addition to transmitting pathogens, some ticks can cause a type of paralysis in humans and other animals that results from compounds the tick injects into the host as part of its saliva when it feeds.

It is the blood-sucking behavior of ticks that helps account for their seriousness as disease vectors. Because ticks are relatively slow feeders, they can imbibe more pathogenic organisms from an infested host (such as ground squirrels and other mammals that serve as reservoirs for the disease organism) than can rapid feeders. Because they use different hosts for separate blood meals, ticks can spread disease organisms from one individual to another.

Despite their role as disease vectors, there is no need to panic at the sight of a tick. Although many species

are capable of carrying pathogens, not all individual ticks are infected. Also, the average healthy person would have to be bitten several times by infected ticks, and the ticks would have to feed for several hours before infection would be passed to humans or pets.

Ticks attach firmly to a host and may go unnoticed for long periods of time, which makes them difficult to control. They have few natural enemies, are relatively long-lived and have high reproductive rates. Some ticks, such as the deer tick and western black-legged tick that carry the Lyme arthritis disease pathogen, are so small they are very hard to detect before they fill with blood.

Ticks are not insects; they belong to the class Arachnida, which also includes mites, spiders and scorpions. Ticks differ from insects in that they have one body region whereas insects have three: head, thorax and abdomen. Ticks have eight legs and no antennae; insects have six legs and one pair of antennae.

Ticks are divided into two groups: hard ticks in the family Ixodidae, and soft ticks in the family Argasidae. Hard ticks have a shield on their backs and are tapered at the head end; they are the ticks readily recognized by most people. Soft ticks lack the shield-like plate on their upper surface, have a blunt head end and look like animated pieces of bark or debris. Both groups can swell to considerable size after a blood meal.

Tick/Host Relationships

Tick species differ from each other in longevity, reproductive powers, preferred habitats, ability to transmit various pathogens, choice of hosts and responses to environmental conditions. There are four general tick-host categories: one-host, two-host, three-host and many-host ticks. These designations refer to the number of times a tick feeds during its lifetime—a one-host tick feeds once, a two-host tick twice, and so on. Because the categories can be misunder-

Table 15.2
Human Diseases Transmitted by Ticks in the United States[a]

Disease	Causal Agent
Colorado tick fever	virus
human babesiosis	*Babesia* spp. (protozoan)
Lyme arthritis	*Borrelia burgdorferi* (bacterium)
Powassan encephalitis	virus
Q fever	*Coxiella burneti* (rickettsia)
relapsing fevers	*Borrelia* spp.
Rocky Mountain spotted fever	*Rickettsia rickettsii* (rickettsia)
tick paralysis	salivary neurotoxin
tularemia	*Pasteurella tularensis* (bacterium)

[a] From Centers for Disease Control, 1979.

Differences between the Adult Female Brown Dog Tick and the American Dog Tick
The brown dog tick (⅛ in./3 mm) is about half the size of the American dog tick (¼ in./6 mm) before feeding. The brown dog tick is a uniform red-brown with no white mottling; the American dog tick is dark brown with a shield that is mottled with white.

American dog tick

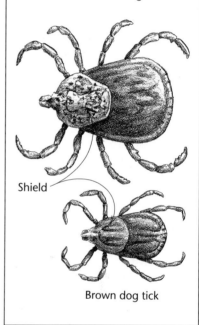

Shield

Brown dog tick

stood to mean how many different species of animals a tick feeds on, the terms are somewhat confusing. A one-host tick may be able to take its single blood meal from one of many species of animals and birds.

From a management standpoint, the number of different species a particular tick can feed on may be more important than the number of times it feeds during its lifetime. If a particular tick species can obtain suitable nourishment from many different species, it is less likely that the tick population in an area can be reduced by removing hosts. This is the reason Lyme disease cannot be tackled by focusing on the deer host alone—ticks that transmit Lyme disease can feed on many different species of animals in the same area. Conversely, the success in eradicating the cattle tick in Texas was due largely to the fact that this tick feeds primarily on cattle, so only the movements of cattle had to be manipulated to solve the problem.

How Humans Encounter Ticks
It is becoming clear that humans encounter and are bitten by certain disease-carrying ticks far more fre-quently than was previously thought. With the human population growing and its enthusiasm for outdoor recreation in wild and semiwild areas increasing, it is inevitable that human/tick encounters will increase.

The most common human encounter with ticks is through pets. Dogs and cats that run freely in wild or semiwild vegetation frequently bring ticks into the home or surrounding vegetation. Pet owners may become quite accustomed to seeing or searching for ticks, especially after a dog has had a run in the country or a cat has disappeared from home for a period of time. Ticks often attach themselves to the pet in areas around the head or neck or on the feet between the toes, where they cannot be disturbed so easily by the scratching or biting pet.

The second most common avenue of human encounter is through recreational activities such as picnicking, hiking and camping. Where residential areas are interwoven with wild or semiwild country, ticks may also be encountered in the garden. In areas such as Westchester County in New York State, where deer are very common, ticks can even be found on well-manicured lawns.

The sidebar on p. 266 provides a quick key to recognizing common ticks that transmit disease.

Two tick species common on dogs are discussed in this chapter: the brown dog tick and the American dog tick. Both are hard ticks. Although other ticks are known to feed on dogs, these are the two you are most likely to encounter on your pets. The drawing above shows you how to tell them apart. The easiest way to distinguish the two is by the color of the shield on the tick's back. If it has conspicuous white lines or mottled markings, you have an American dog tick; if it is reddish-

How to Recognize Common Ticks That Transmit Disease

American dog tick
(Dermacentor variabilis)

This is the species most likely to be found both on humans and dogs in the eastern United States, but it also inhabits pockets of the Midwest and West. It is a fairly large tick, about ¼ in. (6 mm) long before feeding, and its egg-shaped body is dark brown with a mottled white shield on the back. It transmits Rocky Mountain spotted fever.

Brown dog tick
(Rhipicephalus sanguineus)

This species, found in most areas of the United States, rarely attacks humans, but it can cause various diseases in dogs. Its reddish-brown, somewhat elongated, teardrop-shaped body is about ⅛ in. (3 mm) long (unfed) with an unornamented shield on the back.

Northern deer tick
(Ixodes dammini)

This tick, found primarily in the northern United States but also in the Midwest, is the primary vector of Lyme disease in these areas. It is very small, with nymphs about the size of a printed period and adults (unfed) about ⅛ in. (3 mm) long.

Lone star tick
(Amblyomma americanum)

This species inhabits all of the southern United States, and its range extends into the North. Its name comes from the white spot that is clearly visible on its dark shield. It is fairly large (about ⅓ in./8.5 mm long) and can transmit Rocky Mountain spotted fever and tularemia.

Rocky Mountain wood tick, Rocky Mountain spotted fever tick (Dermacentor andersoni)

This tick, common throughout western North America, is similar in size and appearance to the American dog tick but is slightly paler in color, with ornate markings on the back and shield. The adult bites humans and can transmit Rocky Mountain spotted fever and other diseases.

Western black-legged tick
(Ixodes pacificus)

This tick is the primary vector of Lyme disease in the western United States. It is teardrop shaped, and the adult (unfed) female is reddish-brown with black legs and about ⅒ in. (2.5 mm) long. The male is smaller and brownish black.

dog ticks, the brown dog tick is the species that becomes a problem indoors, because it favors a drier and warmer environment than the American dog tick.

Biology

The adult female brown dog tick is a uniform red-brown in color and is approximately ⅛ in. (3 mm) long prior to feeding. She is fertilized on the host by the male. After feeding and engorging, she falls from the dog and searches for a place to lay her eggs. Engorged females are sometimes seen crawling on walls or around baseboards and cracks in the house looking for a place to deposit eggs. The female lays her small brown eggs in a sheltered spot in one mass over a 7 to 17-day period. Because this tick likes warm, dry areas, it may climb to porch ceilings or roofs in kennels. These places are often relatively unfinished, offering many cracks and crevices in which the tick can hide.

The reproductive rate of ticks is prodigious. Females lay 1,000 to 5,000 eggs, depending upon temperature and food availability. The greatest number of eggs are laid between 78°F and 82°F (25°C and 28°C). After laying the eggs, the female does not survive long, usually only one or two days. The eggs hatch in 19 to 60 days and the young larval ticks, which are six-legged, climb walls and attach to a passing dog. If no dog or other host is available, the ticks can survive up to eight months without a blood meal.

Ticks at this stage feed on dogs for three to six days, fall off, molt to the nymph or eight-legged stage, then feed and molt again before becoming adults. After each blood meal while the tick is preparing to molt, it climbs up to a sheltered hiding place. After three or four additional days and another blood meal, mating occurs and egg laying begins. The full life cycle (shown in the drawing on the facing page) takes two to four months. Adults can live up to 18 months without feeding.

brown without markings, you are looking at a brown dog tick.

Since the brown dog tick is found primarily indoors and the American dog tick primarily outdoors, monitoring and management methods for these two differ considerably. For this reason, we discuss the brown dog tick separately from the outdoor American dog tick and the Lyme-disease-carrying ticks.

THE BROWN DOG TICK
(Order Acarina, family Ixodidae)

The brown dog tick (Rhipicephalus sanguineus) is one of the most widely distributed tick species on earth, particularly in temperate regions. It feeds primarily on dogs but may also feed on other animals, such as rats and mice. It feeds on humans only infrequently. Of the two most common

The Life Cycle of the Brown Dog Tick

Adult female brown dog ticks mate on the dog, then fall off and lay 1,000 to 5,000 eggs in cracks and crevices. Eggs hatch in 19 to 60 days. Larval ticks attach themselves to a host, feed for three to six days, fall off, and molt into the nymph stage, which lasts about a month. Adults can live over 500 days without a meal. (Actual size of adult: ⅛ in./3 mm)

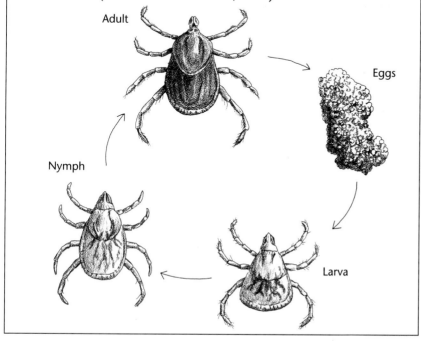

Adult

Eggs

Nymph

Larva

Damage

The brown dog tick causes irritation, anemia and paralysis in dogs. It can transmit the causal organisms of canine piroplasmosis (a lethal blood disease) and malignant jaundice in dogs, and is a vector of Rocky Mountain spotted fever in humans in parts of Mexico.

Detection and Monitoring

Adult brown dog ticks are most commonly found in the ears and between the toes of the dog. Larvae and nymphs are most often found in the long hair at the back of the neck. In southern states, the tick is found in outdoor kennels, animal hospitals, sheds, outbuildings and yards, as well as in various indoor places. In cooler northern states, it is rarely found outdoors and is common inside homes where there are pet dogs.

This tick has a strong tendency to climb upwards, so searches and treatments for the pest should be conducted around window moldings and trim and around picture moldings. Also look in cracks and crevices in areas where the dog sleeps or rests. These might include various indoor areas, as well as on the porch, near sheds and near wooden fences.

The brown dog tick has also been found on lawns in Florida. This is an indication of the tick's preference for the hot, dry conditions that a mowed lawn provides. The American dog tick, by contrast, prefers tall grasses.

You may find attached or unattached ticks on the dog when combing for fleas (see pp. 258-259 for details on combing). This is another benefit of making regular grooming, first with a brush, then with a flea comb, part of your dog's twice-week-ly schedule year-round. Be very careful not to break off attached ticks with the comb. This leaves their mouthparts embedded, which, in turn, can lead to infection. If monitoring has not been regular and you find ticks during combing or while petting the dog, expect to find ticks in areas of the house the dog frequents. Inspect the animal's ears and toes, especially after it has returned from being boarded in a kennel or visiting where other dogs reside.

Treatment: Indirect Strategies

Indirect strategies for controlling brown dog ticks focus on modifying the dog's habitat. Dogs pick up brown dog ticks from harborages such as cracks in baseboards rather than from other dogs. Thus, cracks and crevices, miscellaneous loose boards and other debris that can harbor resting and egg-laying ticks should be eliminated in dog runs and sleeping areas. Indoors, the same habitat modifications you carry out to reduce cockroach, carpet beetle and mouse infestations should be applied to the areas where the dog normally sleeps and rests. You should:

- Prepare the area by vacuuming (see p. 268), and by blowing sorptive dusts into wall voids (see pp. 277-279).
- Use steel wool to fill large cracks, then repair them with wood, plaster or other permanent materials.
- Seal small cracks, including those around repaired areas and between wall and baseboard, with a good-quality silicone caulk and one or more coats of paint.

You might also consider constructing a tick- and flea-free doghouse. By confining the dog to this sleeping area, you reduce the areas that can become infested. The doghouse should be tightly constructed. In one study, doghouses made of steel drums set on their side and raised slightly above the ground on sturdy legs provided good protection for the dog with the fewest possible crevices for ticks and fleas. The drum could be insulated for cold climates. If an inside liner is provided for the dog to lie on and to increase the warmth of the interior, it should be removable so it can be washed frequently.

Treatment: Direct Physical Controls

Two physical control strategies unique to the brown dog tick, which is found primarily indoors, are vacuuming and the use of carbon dioxide traps indoors.

1. Vacuuming. Vacuum the walls and surfaces around the dog's sleeping quarters regularly. Use a crevice tool to apply a strong suction to cracks where ticks may be hiding. It is important to avoid reinfesting the house with ticks that may have been sucked into the vacuum but crawl out while the vacuum is being stored. The contents of the vacuum should be destroyed by burning, heating in a plastic bag in the sun or freezing. The contents of a water vacuum can be flushed down the toilet.

2. Carbon Dioxide Trapping of Ticks Indoors. A strategy that merits testing is the use of carbon dioxide (dry ice) traps against brown dog ticks. Such traps have been used against many other tick species outdoors with great success. The ticks are attracted to carbon dioxide (this is how they find their host animals) and get trapped by a sticky band around the trap. Those that do not actually get caught in the trap can be vacuumed up from the periphery where they congregate. To our knowledge, no one has studied the use of these traps indoors, but they may have a place in a program to eliminate brown dog ticks from a room in which they are known to be hiding. Details on constructing and using a carbon dioxide trap are provided in the sidebar on p. 278.

When experimenting with a carbon dioxide trap indoors, we suggest you follow the following procedure.
• Plan to exclude people and pets from the room being treated for the entire day.
• Screen all windows in the room.

• Place the carbon dioxide trap in the middle of the room and partially open the windows (but not the screens).
• Close all passageways from the treated room to the rest of the house and place a throw rug or other cloth barrier snugly across any cracks at the base of doors.
• After 24 hours, open the door to start airing out the room.
• Slip the bucket that contained the dry ice (frozen carbon dioxide) into a plastic bag. If there is any dry ice left, you can save it in the freezer.
• Remove the tape containing trapped ticks. Place the ticks in soapy water or rubbing alcohol. Flush away the liquid with the ticks.
• Make sure the room is well aired before it is reused by humans and pets.

The biology of the brown dog tick suggests that this procedure might have to be repeated a number of times at two- to three-day intervals.

3. Additional Strategies. Some of the methods used to manage outdoor ticks are also useful against brown dog ticks when they are found adjacent to buildings. See the treatment recommendations for managing outdoor ticks on pp. 274-277. For a discussion of how to remove ticks attached to an animal or person, see the sidebar on p. 277.

The direct chemical controls for suppressing brown dog ticks are the same as those for outdoor ticks; see the discussion on pp. 277-279.

THE AMERICAN DOG TICK (Order Acarina, family Ixodidae)

The American dog tick (*Dermacentor variabilis*) is common on dogs, but also feeds on horses and cattle. In the eastern United States, it is the species most likely to be found on humans. Unlike the brown dog tick, it does not become established in the house, although it may be found there occasionally if it happens to drop off the pet. The American dog tick is an efficient vector of Rocky Mountain spotted fever, which is most prevalent in the eastern United States, even though its common name suggests otherwise. The American dog tick is most common east of the Rocky Mountains. It was accidentally intro-

---

Summary: Least-Toxic Brown Dog Tick Control

• Inspect the dog regularly, particularly the ears and between toes. Perform special inspections when the dog returns from woods and other areas where ticks might be encountered.

• Comb to remove ticks elsewhere on the dog's body, but be careful not to break off the mouthparts of any attached ticks.

• Remove embedded ticks by gently pulling with tweezers. Do not twist the tick, and avoid using your bare fingers.

• Clean wounds made by ticks with soap and water, then apply an antiseptic to prevent infection.

• Use a tick drag (see pp. 273-274) to help detect and collect local infestations.

• Confine the dog to specific sleeping areas to reduce the area likely to be infested.

• Reduce hiding places, primarily cracks and crevices, where ticks may hide between blood meals.

• Vacuum and use sorptive dust in cracks.

• Where above methods are insufficient to control infestations, apply insecticidal soap, d-limonene/linalool or pyrethrin in areas where ticks may be hiding.

Tick Paralysis[a]

Causal Agent

In the United States and Canada, tick paralysis is caused mainly by three species of ticks. The American dog tick *(Dermacentor andersoni)* is the primary culprit in the midwestern part of the continent, particularly in Canada. Two closely related species, *D. variabilis* in the eastern part of the United States and *D. occidentalis* in California, also inflict paralysis when they attach to their host for a blood meal. The salivary secretions they inject to aid in the process of sucking in the blood are believed to cause a neuromuscular block, resulting in paralysis of the whole body. This can lead to death.

Distribution and Prevalence

Tick paralysis occurs worldwide; it is more common among humans and livestock in Canada than in the United States. In British Columbia, April is the peak month in the southern part of the province, May and June are the peak months in the north. In the United States, human cases have been reported in northern Montana, Idaho and Washington, the mountains of Colorado and Wyoming and in northeastern Oregon. On the East Coast, paralysis has been reported in seaboard portions of Virginia, North Carolina, South Carolina and Georgia; a few cases have been reported in western Kentucky and Tennessee.

Symptoms

Children are the most likely victims. Patients typically start to show symptoms four to six days after visiting a tick-infested area. The first symptom is fever and difficulty walking, which progresses during the day to complete loss of coordination and numbness of extremities. Within 24 hours the patient becomes completely paralyzed; difficulties in speech follow, and finally respiratory paralysis and death may occur.

There are several records of ticks being found on the bodies of dead victims in funeral parlors; these findings allowed diagnosis of the cause of death. The lack of familiarity of medical personnel with this disease and the covert nature of the problem may preclude proper diagnosis and treatment. Misdiagnoses have included poliomyelitis and heart attacks. In pets, the syndrome also occurs more widely than is appreciated.

Where tick paralysis is suspected, you should search the body completely for hidden ticks. Thorough combing of the scalp with a fine-toothed comb may help detect and remove a tick hidden in the hair. Medical help should be obtained in all suspected cases, especially if difficulty with breathing or paralysis is evident.

Treatment

Once the tick is removed, paralysis disappears and most patients recover.

[a] From Gregson, 1973.

duced into the northwestern part of the country, where local populations established themselves along river valleys in Washington, Idaho and Oregon. It is now also found along the Pacific Coast.

Biology

The American dog tick is considered a two-host tick. The adult tick is most common on dogs, but adults and immature ticks are also found on raccoons, opossums, skunks and grey squirrels. Adult female ticks are ¼ in. (6 mm) long (½ in/13 mm long when engorged) and are dark brown with a mottled white shield on their backs. The life cycle is similar to that of the brown dog tick (see pp. 266-267).

All stages can live for long periods without blood meals, and unengorged adults have been shown to go for more than 500 days without feeding when they cannot find a suitable host. In Virginia, there are two peaks in the tick population each year: the spring peak is due to survivors from the previous season, and the late summer peak is the result of eggs laid in spring and summer. Nymphs usually engorge on field mice in the genera *Microtus* and *Peromyscus,* and the ticks are found in fields and meadows where these rodents live.

Damage

The American dog tick is a common cause of tick paralysis in humans, dogs and wildlife species, as discussed in the sidebar above. Besides vectoring Rocky Mountain spotted fever (described in the sidebar on p. 270), this species is also a vector of tularemia, a bacterial disease of rodents, particularly rabbits, that can be fatal in humans.

(Note: Monitoring and treatment for the American dog tick and the ticks that follow are discussed together on pp. 272-279.)

Rocky Mountain Spotted Fever[a]

Common Names
Tick-borne typhus, Mexican spotted fever, Tobia fever, Sao Paulo fever.

Causal Agent
Rocky Mountain spotted fever is caused by the microorganism *Rickettsia rickettsii*.

Vectors and Reservoirs
Ticks, especially in the genus *Dermacentor (D. andersoni, D. variabilis)*, carry the pathogen. Female ticks pass the pathogen to their young through the eggs. Thereafter, the pathogen is carried within the tick's body. Overwintering ticks carry the pathogen in an inactive state; it reactivates a few hours to a day or more after feeding. If ticks are removed within a few hours after attachment, the likelihood of pathogen transmission is greatly reduced. Other animal reservoirs of the pathogen include eastern chipmunks, grey squirrels, meadow voles, opossums, raccoons, skunks, white-footed mice, woodchucks and woodland jumping mice. A tick vector is needed to carry the pathogen from these reservoirs to humans.

Distribution and Prevalence
Rocky Mountain spotted fever occurs from Canada to South America, but is most common in the eastern United States (not in the Rocky Mountains, as the name implies). At present it is not prevalent, but it is increasing. In 1976 over 900 cases were reported in the United States.

Route of Infection
Any stage of the tick can transmit the pathogen. Tick tissues carrying the rickettsia are highly infectious when they come into contact with abraded skin. This is why we advise you not to crush ticks with your bare fingers.

Symptoms
The first symptoms are frontal and occipital headaches, intense lumbar itching and general malaise. Between the second and fifth day a characteristic rash appears on the wrists, ankles and, less commonly, on the back; it later spreads to the entire body. The body temperature may rise to 104°F (40°C) or higher in more pathogenic forms. In fatal cases, death occurs 9 to 15 days after the first symptoms appear. Formerly, mortality was high, but now it is infrequent.

Treatment
Broad-spectrum antibiotics. Commercial vaccines are available.

[a] From Harwood and James, 1979.

THE NORTHERN DEER TICK
(Order Acarina, family Ixodidae)

The northern deer tick *(Ixodes dammini)* is found primarily in the northeastern United States, although it is also seen in areas of the Midwest where deer herds are abundant. This tick is the primary vector of Lyme disease (discussed on p. 272) in the northeastern and midwestern United States. Although found on 12 mammalian and 18 bird species, the deer tick derives its common name from its close association with the white-tailed deer *(Odocoileus virginianus)*. Some researchers hypothesize that this tick was once widely distributed across the entire northeastern quadrant of the United States, but when deer herds were decimated by overhunting and deforestation, the tick died out except in isolated pockets where deer herds remained.

It is ironic that the resurgence of deer populations in recent years resulting from successful programs by wildlife agencies has brought with it a public health emergency. But as National Park Service naturalist James Northrup points out, "While there is strong evidence that the abundance of *I. dammini* is limited largely by the abundance of deer, ecologists warn against the apparent quick fix of reducing or eliminating deer herds. By eliminating the preferred host, ticks may seek out another mammalian host, increasing the incidence of Lyme disease even further." Nevertheless deer exclusion is one tactic that may be justified as part of an IPM program to reduce ticks in places where Lyme disease is prevalent and human/tick contacts are very likely.

Biology
Deer ticks are extremely small. Immature ticks are no larger than a period on this page and unengorged adults are about ⅛ in. (3 mm) long. They live about two years, during which they feed three times (see the drawing at left on the facing page). Adult ticks mate in the fall on the host animal, usually a white-tailed deer. The adult male dies and the female drops from the host, lays approximately 2,500 eggs in the soil in the spring, and dies about three weeks later. Larvae emerge in about a month, and sometime in the late summer or early fall attach themselves to a host, usually a white-footed mouse, and take a blood meal for two days.

After feeding, the larvae drop off the host, often in a mouse burrow, molt, and enter the nymph stage the following spring. Nymphs feed once for three or four days in early summer. The white-footed mouse, which is the main reservoir of the Lyme disease spirochete, is again the preferred

The Life Cycle of the Northern Deer Tick

After feeding once—deer are the preferred host—the adult female deposits about 2,500 eggs in the soil in spring, then dies about three weeks later. The eggs hatch into larvae after one month. The larvae feed once in summer, preferring mice as their hosts. In spring of the next year they become nymphs, which also feed on mice once before becoming adults in the fall. The entire life cycle takes about two years. (Actual size of adult: ⅛ in./3 mm)

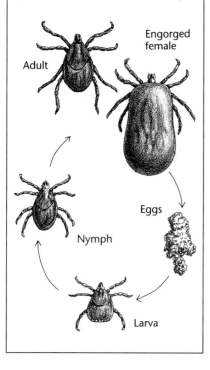

Adult

Engorged female

Nymph

Eggs

Larva

host, and many tick nymphs spend most of their time in mouse burrows. Nymphs molt into the adult form in the fall. Adults feed once in fall or winter, preferably on white-tailed deer hosts. Adults die after mating and egg deposition.

Damage
The deer tick is the most important vector of Lyme disease in the northeastern and midwestern United States. Lyme disease, which causes serious rheumatoid arthritis-like symptoms and many other medical problems in humans, livestock, pets and other mammals, is discussed in the sidebar on p. 272. Ticks in the nymph stage are most likely to transmit the disease. Their seasonal peak feeding extends from May until mid-July.

The deer tick is also the agent of a malaria-like disease called babesiosis, caused by the protozoan *Babesia microti*. In general, this is a mild disease and victims usually recover without treatment. But the elderly and persons whose spleens have been damaged by alcohol-related cirrhosis are at risk and can die if infected.

(Note: Monitoring and treatment for the northern deer tick are discussed on pp. 272-279.)

THE WESTERN BLACK-LEGGED TICK
(Order Acarina, family Ixodidae)

The western black-legged tick *(Ixodes pacificus)* is found in California, Idaho, Nevada, Oregon, Washington, Utah and the province of British Columbia. It prefers humid coastal areas but is also seen on the western slope of the Sierra Nevada. Although all stages of the black-legged tick can be found in urban and rural areas year-round, in California adult ticks are most active between November and May, whereas larvae and nymphs are most commonly found from March through June.

Immature stages (larvae and nymphs) of this three-host tick feed on small rodents, rabbits, lizards, birds and occasionally on large mammals. Adult ticks mount grasses and brushy vegetation to await a passing host. They feed on over 80 species of vertebrates, particularly large mammals, including deer, dogs and humans. All stages feed by embedding their mouthparts in the skin of the host and taking a blood meal.

The western black-legged tick is the major vector of Lyme disease in

The Life Cycle of the Western Black-Legged Tick

The adult female attaches herself to a host, such as a dog or deer, between November and May. She feeds and mates on the host, then drops off, lays several thousand eggs and dies. The larvae find another host—usually a small rodent or lizard—then drop off and molt into nymphs. Similarly, the nymphs find a host, drop off and molt into adults. Larvae and nymphs are most commonly found from March to June. (Actual size of adult: ⅒ in./2.5 mm)

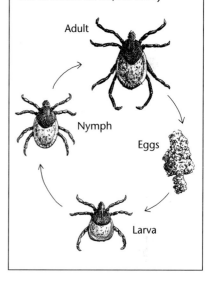

Adult

Nymph

Eggs

Larva

California, Oregon and British Columbia, although only 1% to 4% of the species appears to be infected, compared to a 30% to 80% infection rate among deer ticks found east of the Rockies.

Biology
The adult female tick is red-brown with black legs and is about ⅛ in. (3 mm) long, swelling to two to three times that size when engorged with blood. The adult male is smaller and entirely brownish black. Both sexes are teardrop shaped. Mating occurs on a host animal. Females then drop off the host, lay several thousand eggs and die (see the drawing above).

Lyme Disease

Common Name
Lyme disease takes its common name from the town of Old Lyme, Connecticut, where it was first reported in the United States in 1975.

Causal Agent
The disease is caused by the spirochete *Borrelia burgdorferi,* a corkscrew-shaped bacterium.

Vectors and Reservoirs
The bacteria may be carried by a number of different ticks, but the most important vectors to humans appear to be the northern deer tick *(Ixodes dammini)* and the western black-legged tick *(I. pacificus)*. These ticks are so small they often go undetected on humans and domestic animals. When left to feed at will, the tick is more likely to infect its host with the disease. *I. scapularis* in the South and Southwest, the lone star tick *(Amblyomma americanum)* in the Southwest and Southeast and the Pacific Coast tick *(Dermacentor occidentalis)* have also been shown to carry the bacterium, but it is not yet known how frequently these and other species of ticks are responsible for spreading the disease.

Distribution and Prevalence
Lyme disease has existed in Europe for the past 100 years, and has begun to spread through China and the Soviet Union. In the United States infected individuals have been reported in 43 states, including most of the Northeast and Midwest, as well as Georgia, Florida and Kentucky in the South, and California and Oregon in the Northwest. Cases have also been reported in British Columbia. Migrating birds appear to play a major role in transporting the tick to new areas. Over 14,000 cases have been reported nationally since 1980, most in the Northeast and Midwest. Because of the difficulty in diagnosing this disease, these figures are probably gross underestimates of actual disease incidence.

Route of Infection
An individual is infected through a bite from a spirochete-bearing tick, usually in the nymph stage. The infection rate in ticks varies from 30% to 80%.

Symptoms
The first sign may be a raised red rash called erythema migrans (see the photo on the facing page) that appears three to ten days after an infected tick bites. The rash, which expands outward around a clear central area, often (but not always) resembles a bull's-eye. The rash is red on light skin and appears as a bruise on dark skin. Rashes may occur at the bite site or at other locations on the body. Unfortunately, almost 25% of victims never develop a rash, which slows diagnosis of the disease. Therefore, if you know you have been bitten by one of the ticks that can transmit the disease, you may want to get a blood test to determine whether the bacterium is present.

The larvae feed on a host, then drop off to molt into the nymph stage. Nymphs again feed on a host, then drop off and molt into the adult form.

Damage
Bites from this species may produce painful sores that are slow to heal. Occasionally their bites are followed by sensory disturbances near the affected area. The black-legged tick is the primary vector of Lyme disease in the Western states (see the sidebar above) and has been implicated in the transmission of tick paralysis in dogs and of a rickettsia of the spotted fever group in other animals.

Detection and Monitoring
To detect western black-legged ticks, northern deer ticks and American dog ticks, it is important to monitor people, pets and the environment. You should inspect your own body and those of your companions, young and old, each night you have been in an area in which ticks are likely to be. It is unusual to pick up ticks in late autumn and early winter, even in tick-infested country. But, starting in December in areas with mild winters (such as the Pacific, Gulf and Florida coasts) and from early spring to early fall in most of the rest of the United States, you should make a body check at night if you or your pets spend time outdoors in tick-infested areas.

It's unlikely that you'll experience any sensation while a tick is biting you, so you need to check all the parts of your body that you can see and have someone else check the parts hidden from your view. Then you can return the favor. If there is no one who can help you, use a mirror to check yourself thoroughly. Pay special attention to the groin, back, armpits and head. Refer to the sidebar on p. 277 for instructions on removing attached ticks.

Monitor your pets by combing them with a flea comb regularly at the end of the day. Check closely be-

Flu-like symptoms (fever, headache, stiff neck), fatigue and joint pain may accompany the rash. These symptoms may disappear within a few weeks with or without treatment. Then, weeks to months following the infection, other, more serious symptoms may develop, including facial palsy, severe headaches and arthritis-like pain in the knees and other joints. The disease can mimic multiple sclerosis, brain tumors, strokes and mental disorders. Any of the symptoms may come and go, and diagnosis and treatment become more difficult with each recurrence.

Treatment

In the early stages, antibiotics such as tetracycline, amoxicillin or penicillin can arrest the disease. If neurological or arthritic disorders develop, ceftriaxone or penicillin is administered intravenously. A vaccine is under study at the University of Massachusetts and is currently being tested on dogs. A human vaccine is still some years away.

Prompt diagnosis and administration of antibiotics in the early phase of the disease are critical if later, more serious symptoms are to be avoided. Infected humans and animals produce antibodies to the disease, but blood tests are not yet reliable enough for accurate diagnosis, and physicians may choose to begin antibiotic therapy even before test results are available.

Note, however, that the administration of antibiotics before blood tests are conducted can mask the presence of the disease, leading to a falsely negative test result. Therefore, we recommend that the patient always be tested first, even though the tests are not completely reliable. If the test results are negative and the patient shows no rash, some doctors might elect to wait for clearer symptoms before treating so massively with antibiotics. This also allows for a second test that has not been disqualified by antibiotics.

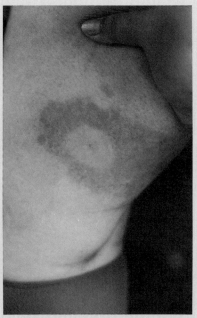

The first symptom of Lyme disease is often a raised red rash typified by a red outer ring with a clear center much like a bull's-eye. (Photo by Ross Ritter.)

hind the ears, around the neck and between the toes. A masking-tape roller (with the sticky side of the tape up) can be effective in picking up unattached ticks from cats. Your pets often give you an early warning that tick season has arrived, or that you have entered an area where ticks are abundant. In other words, your pets can serve as monitoring tools for you.

American dog ticks and the Lyme disease-vectoring black-legged and deer ticks are usually picked up when dogs or people roam into woods, brushy areas or meadows with abundant seed-producing vegetation that feeds mice and other rodents that are common tick hosts. Adult ticks are commonly found in the spring in their waiting positions on grass and low brush. Their third pair of legs is used to cling to the grass while the other legs are waved about, ready to grasp any host that comes by. Young ticks do not assume a waiting position, but actively seek out hosts, often by residing on the undersides of leaves or in leaf litter on the ground, where they attach themselves to passing mice and other small mammals. Ticks are attracted by the scent of animals, and thus are most numerous along roads, paths and trails. Blood-engorged ticks drop from animals, further increasing the concentration of ticks along these passageways.

Two tools can be used to monitor an area for the number, species and location of ticks: a tick "drag" or "flag," and a trap that attracts the ticks with carbon dioxide. The drag/flag is simple enough to construct (see the sidebar on p. 274), carry and use to take along on a picnic or camping trip to help you select relatively tick-free sites. A trap is more complex to make (see the sidebar on p. 278), but can be used to monitor an area throughout a season.

A word of caution: By concentrating the ticks on a drag, the person doing the collecting increases his or her risk of being bitten. This is of particular concern where Lyme disease is

Constructing and Using a Tick Flag or Drag

A tick flag or drag can be used to monitor and/or control ticks in an outdoor area. The difference between the two has to do with their size and construction.

A Tick Flag

To make a small, simple tick flag useful for dragging over medium-height brushy vegetation, staple or thumb-tack a 1 sq. yd. (0.84 sq. m) piece of white flannel cloth to a stick that is approximately 4½ ft. (1.37 m) long, creating a small flag. In Lyme disease areas, this tool may be preferable to the larger drag described below, because, in use, the flag precedes the person, so ticks encounter the flag first.

A Tick Drag

To make a larger drag appropriate for grassy areas or low brush, follow these steps:

1. On a 4-ft. by 6-ft. (1.2 m by 1.8 m) piece of white flannel cloth, attach one strip of a mated pair of Velcro™ strips along the edge of one of the narrow ends. Attach its mate 6 in. (15 cm) below the first. Sew lead fishing or curtain weights to the opposite end of the cloth to improve the performance of the drag. Make two or three of these sheets if you

are planning to use the drags as a tick control rather than simply for monitoring.

2. Drill a hole in each end of a 5-ft. (1.5 m) length of 1-in. (2.5 cm) diameter rigid plastic water pipe and insert a 6-ft. (1.8 m) length of clothes line through each hole. Knot each end of the rope behind the hole to form a rope handle.

3. Wrap the end of the flannel drag with the Velcro™ strips around the pipe and secure it by pressing the strips together.

4. Sweep the cloth portion of the drag over shrubs, grasses or ground suspected of harboring ticks, particularly along paths or trails where dogs or other animals regularly travel, or where your dog rests. The movement of the cloth simulates a passing host, and the ticks cling to it.

5. Check the drag, particularly the side facing the ground, for captured ticks, which show up well against the white cloth. You can pick the ticks off the cloth with tweezers and drop them into a jar containing soapy water or rubbing alcohol. Or you can detach the flannel cloth and soak it in soapy water to kill the ticks.

present. Anyone using a drag should follow the precautions about proper clothing described below and should apply insect repellent and/or a permethrin-based insecticide such as Permanone® to clothing and footwear from the thighs down.

If you find that outdoor dog ticks are numerous, you should check your dog several times a day. Combing will make the searching process more effective than a simple search through

the fur with your fingers. Also check yourself all over, using a mirror to view the rear of your legs and your back after walking in tick country.

Treatment:
Indirect Strategies

Indirect management strategies for outdoor ticks include avoidance of tick-infested areas, wearing protective clothing and clearing vegetation along paths and roadsides.

1. Avoiding Tick-Infested Areas. Disease-transmitting ticks prefer certain kinds of vegetation, depending on the species and stage of tick, and are more prevalent in some seasons than in others, depending on species and region. We discussed these characteristics in the biology sections on the various ticks. Consider them in regard to the places you live, work and engage in outdoor recreation, and make sure that maintenance supervisors, summer-camp directors and others are also knowledgeable about ticks. In public parks this information is increasingly presented as part of visitor orientation. Elsewhere you should enquire about ticks at state and local public health departments. These agencies generally keep track of where and when the tick "hot spots" occur.

When in tick-abundant areas during tick-active seasons:
• Stay clear of narrow animal trails where you cannot avoid brushing against vegetation.
• If you must move through vegetation, check your clothing immediately afterward for crawling ticks.
• Avoid brush or trash piles that are likely to harbor rodents.
• Use a tick flag or drag to clear areas in which you will be temporarily working or playing (see the sidebar at left). Research suggests that a properly used drag can temporarily reduce tick numbers by 70%.
• Don't sit or lie on the ground unless a tick drag or flag has shown that the area is clear.

2. Protective Clothing. You should wear light-colored shoes, socks, long pants and a long-sleeved shirt in tick-infested areas so ticks stand out readily. Since ticks climb upward, tucking your pant legs into your socks (as shown in the drawing at left on the facing page) will cause them to move on the outside of your garments where you can see them and pick them off.

3. Repellents on Clothing. If ticks are abundant, or you are operating tick drags or traps, you should treat

Protecting Yourself against Ticks

Tucking your pant legs into your socks makes a continuous "seal" that prevents ticks from reaching your skin. Wearing very light-colored socks and pants enables you to spot and remove ticks as they crawl up the outside of your clothing.

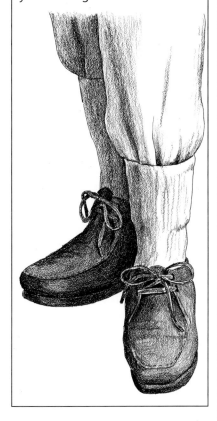

How Ticks Find a Host

Many ticks climb to the tops of grass and low brush to await a passing host; mowing vegetation prevents them from doing so.

your clothing (not your body) with a repellent or insecticide. A number of repellents are available for treating clothing, including DEET, indalone, dimethyl carbate, dimethyl phthalate, benzyl benzoate and M-1960. These are sold in pharmacies and sporting-goods stores under various trade names as sprays and liquid solutions. Treat clothing from the ground to the hips. Soaking clothing in a solution of repellent until it thoroughly impregnates the fabric and then air drying garments before wear-

ing can extend the effectiveness of the repellent for several weeks and through several washings.

The only material shown to be 100% repellent to ticks that carry Lyme disease pathogens and other disease organisms is permethrin (Permanone®), a synthetic pyrethroid insecticide that immobilizes or kills ticks shortly after they touch clothing sprayed with it. In a study conducted by University of California tick specialist Robert Lane, Permanone®, which contains 0.5% permethrin as its active ingredient, was sprayed for 14 seconds onto the front and back of white overalls between the waist and cuffs. Once the spray dried, researchers put on the treated overalls and walked in areas infested with the western black-legged tick (a Lyme disease carrier). All adult and pre-adult ticks that crawled onto the clothing fell off within seconds to minutes after contact with the insecticide, and most died. Other studies with permethrin have shown similar repellency and toxicity to the American dog tick, lone star tick, northern deer tick and Pacific Coast tick. In comparison, DEET, the active ingredient in most

insect repellents, provided only 85% to 94% protection against ticks.

Syrupy oil from the plant *Commiphora erythraea*, a close relative of *C. abyssinica* (the source of the biblical myrrh delivered to the wise men), has been shown to repel American dog, lone star and deer ticks. In laboratory studies, fewer than 1% of lone star larvae and adult ticks, and fewer than 16% of the dog and deer adult ticks crawled into a section of cloth soaked in a dilute hexane solution of this oil extract. By comparison, 73% to 83% of the ticks crawled the same distance on another piece of cloth treated with hexane alone. We hope that a commercial tick repellent based on this oil will become available in the near future.

4. Cutting Brush and Weeds along Roads and in Fields. Ticks tend to congregate on medium-height vegetation along paths and roadsides to gain access to hosts (see the drawing above). If these areas are kept mowed below ankle height, ticks do not have an adequate vantage point for attachment, and there will be fewer opportunities for them to latch onto passing humans, dogs, deer and other mammalian hosts. Mowing also reduces the vegetative cover needed by the wild rodents upon which young ticks feed. A mowed strip 4 ft. to 6 ft. (1.2 m to 1.8 m) wide along the sides of pathways is recommended.

Reducing the brushy habitat that provides cover for small mammals such as raccoons, skunks, foxes and opossums may help reduce ticks when mowing along paths and roads proves insufficient. Skunks and raccoons living under structures and in abandoned outbuildings can be sources of ticks that are picked up by mice and later by dogs from the mice. In such cases, forcing wildlife to den further away from the house or dog run helps reduce ticks.

Ticks require fairly humid conditions. Thus, if you live in a wooded area, prune trees to encourage sunlight to penetrate to the ground. This helps reduce the available moisture in the leaf litter. Keep grasses in woodlots mowed.

5. Removal of Mouse Nesting Sites. Because wild mice are the main reservoirs of Lyme disease and play a major role in the transmission of other tick-borne diseases, it is important to reduce mouse nesting habitats in areas where humans or dogs reside. Stack firewood and lumber away from the house. Remove piles of stones and other debris that harbor mice. Keep grasses mowed. Rake up leaves and let them decompose in a "hot" compost.

6. Locating Bird Feeders away from the House. You should avoid hanging bird feeders near to the house as many bird species carry ticks. In addition, the seeds birds drop from bird feeders can attract the mice that carry ticks.

Treatment:
Direct Physical Controls
Physical controls recommended for managing ticks include removal of ticks, tick dragging and use of carbon dioxide traps.

1. Removal of Ticks. Ticks roam around the bodies of humans and pets for a time before attaching themselves. On humans, free-roaming ticks can be brushed off the skin, although capturing them with a pair of tweezers and killing them in a bowl of soapy water or flushing them down the toilet is preferable. Showering after an outing in a tick-infested area is another good way to rid the body of unattached ticks.

A fine-toothed flea comb can be used to help capture unattached ticks on pets. Adult and nymphal ticks are caught in the teeth of the comb and can be flicked into a bowl of soapy water. A masking-tape lint roller, available at hardware stores, can be rolled over the body and head of cats and small dogs to capture unattached ticks. Medical researchers in New York found this method to be particularly effective at picking up tick nymphs, the stage most likely to carry Lyme disease, from cats.

The sidebar on the facing page suggests a procedure for removing ticks once they have attached themselves to an animal or person.

2. Tick Dragging. The tick drag or flag described in the sidebar on p. 274 can also help reduce tick populations. Dragging of severely infested areas can be done daily until numbers are reduced or no ticks at all are collected. To keep tick numbers low in an area, the dragging must be repeated roughly every two weeks throughout the spring and summer, since there will be overlapping generations of ticks throughout this period (i.e., sequential hatches of eggs and the emergence of larval and nymphal stages). Refer to the relevant sections above to determine when ticks are most active.

Where Lyme disease is present, persons using this method should take great care to protect themselves with proper clothing and insect repellent, because the person doing the dragging is under increased risk of tick bites.

3. Carbon Dioxide Traps. Ticks are attracted to hosts when they detect carbon dioxide emanating from them. This fact has been exploited in the design of the carbon dioxide (dry ice) tick trap described in the sidebar on p. 278, which has been used effectively to sample an area of 225 sq. ft. (21 sq. m) Its effectiveness depends on temperature and other variables.

Many tick nymphs will collect within a 4-ft. (1.2 m) radius of a CO_2 trap. If you wear knee-high rubber boots, these ticks will crawl up on them. The smooth rubber provides an ideal surface from which to vacuum the ticks with a portable insect vacuum cleaner (for sources, see the Resource Appendix under "Insect Management: Physical Controls" on pp. 682-683. You can find more information on how to design and use a portable vacuum cleaner in the books cited in the "References and Readings" on pp. 283-285.)

Where the tick problem is serious, CO_2 traps, combined with vacuuming of tick nymphs from boots, may be useful in reducing the tick population around a suburban home or woodlot. The traps can draw ticks from as far as 60 ft. (18 m) away. However, because young ticks will hatch as the season progresses and others will enter the area on wild animals, keeping the population to a tolerable level requires that a series of traps be set out periodically, starting when ticks are first noticed in the spring. You will need to work out an appropriate grid for placement of the traps based on the configuration of your property, bearing in mind that one trap will collect ticks for about a 225-sq. ft. (21 sq. m) area.

We do not know of anyone who has used traps and vacuuming from boots for tick management around a home; thus, we cannot give you more precise advice. However, in tests using the CO_2 technique, researchers collected an average of 5,000 lone star tick (*Amblyomma americanum*) nymphs per researcher per hour. This is a considerable number, and it suggests that such traps may be useful in small areas to reduce tick populations locally. You

How To Remove a Tick

Ticks must be removed in a manner that does not allow the head and mouthparts to break off and remain in the skin.[a] You can brush off an unattached tick with your bare hands, but you should not use bare fingers to remove an attached tick since this exposes you to possible disease. The following steps are recommended by medical authorities.

• Protect your hands with a tissue or gloves.

• With blunt, curved tweezers, grasp the tick as close to the head as possible and exert gentle, steady pressure until the tick withdraws and can be destroyed. Do not twist the tick. Tick mouthparts have harpoon-like barbs; they do not screw into the skin. Avoid crushing the tick during its extraction. The tick's body fluids, which potentially include Lyme spirochetes or other disease organisms, can enter your body through punctured skin or mucous membranes.

• If you want to save the tick for identification, drop it into a small vial of rubbing alcohol; otherwise you can drown it in soapy water or crush it with the tweezers (but not with your bare hand).

• Clean the site of the tick bite with an antiseptic. If the head of the tick is left embedded in the skin, try to remove the remaining parts with tweezers. Removal helps prevent an infection in the wound. If you cannot remove the mouthparts, apply an antiseptic and monitor the site regularly for complications. Seek medical help if the site darkens, becomes inflamed, fills with pus or develops a rash.

Unattached ticks such as this American dog tick can be grasped on any part of the body and removed. Ticks attached to the skin should be grasped close to the head and pulled gently but with increasing pressure until they withdraw. (Photo courtesy USDA/ARS.)

[a] A handy pocket-sized "tick solution kit" containing tweezers, magnifier and specimen storage bag is available from REI (listed in the Resource Appendix under "Suppliers" on pp. 690-696).

must do a little experimentation of your own to learn if and how this idea can work for you. Although carbon dioxide traps and dragging can remove large numbers of ticks, these procedures may not be adequate for outdoor tick control in many areas.

Treatment: Direct Biological Controls

A minute wasp, *Hunterellus hookeri,* that parasitizes deer and dog ticks was imported from Europe in the 1920s and released on Naushon Island off the coast of Massachusetts. Harvard School of Public Health researchers recently found that half the ticks sampled were infected with the wasp but were free of disease-causing microbes, suggesting that when the wasp is present, the disease-causing microbes are absent. Entomologists at the University of Massachusetts are exploring the possibility of mass-rearing this beneficial wasp and releasing it where Lyme disease is endemic.

A certain tolerance for the presence of fire ants also may help reduce tick numbers, because these ants prey on ticks. Researchers in some areas have reported that ticks disappeared after fire ants moved in.

Treatment: Direct Chemical Controls

If non-chemical methods have failed to control the tick problem, you may need to resort to chemical tools to reduce the degree of infestation. The

How To Make a Carbon Dioxide Tick Trap

1. Find a covered ice bucket or other styrofoam container measuring 6 in. x 6 in. x 12 in. (15 cm x 15 cm x 30 cm).

2. Cut four ¾-in. (19 mm) holes in the sides near the bottom. This will allow the dry ice described in the next step to vaporize outward and attract ticks.

3. Drop 2 lb. (454 g) dry ice (CO_2) into the bucket. It will last about three hours, depending on the temperature. The majority of ticks in a 75 sq. ft. (7 sq. m) area around the trap will be captured within the three hours.

4. Place the dry ice-filled container over a 1 sq. yd. (0.84 sq. m) piece of flannel or a piece of plywood with a masking tape

barrier. The tape can be stapled to the board sticky-side-up, or you can fold it in half to make it adhere to the plywood. (A very thin layer of Stickem™, Tanglefoot™ or Tack Trap™ might also work, although we have never tried them. These substances would be easier to work with if they were placed on paper and the paper stapled to the board, as with the tape.)

5. If you use flannel, inspect both sides of it for ticks one to three hours after the trapping begins. If you use plywood and masking tape, remove the tape to which ticks have adhered and replace it as often as necessary during the three-hour trapping period.

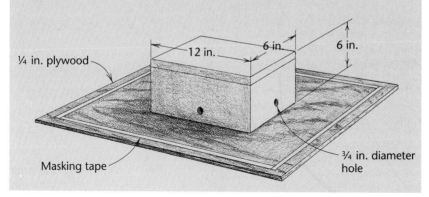

¼ in. plywood

12 in. 6 in. 6 in.

Masking tape

¾ in. diameter hole

insecticides discussed in this section are among the least toxic registered for ticks. You may need to treat a house or dog kennel infested with ticks, or the dog itself. However, it is rarely effective to spray entire yards. If you feel the need to treat vegetation, confine the spray to paths and places where dogs run and rest, because this is where the ticks congregate. Use a tick drag to identify other areas in the yard where ticks might be located and spray only those areas. Animals that attract ticks tend to follow well-defined paths or routes, and

ticks seldom wander far from an area where their host animals roam.

Before you apply any insecticide, read the label and refer to pp. 97-103 for details on protecting yourself and the environment.

1. Sorptive Dusts. Sorptive dusts such as silica aerogel and diatomaceous earth have a drying and abrasive effect on insects. They can be blown gently into cracks and crevices where ticks hide before the cracks are caulked shut permanently, or they can be applied where caulking is not possible. Silica aerogel plus pyrethrin

(Drione®) can be used in cracks as well as on the dog. Techniques for applying the dusts or a pyrethrum powder to pets are specified in the discussion of flea management on pp. 260-263.

2. Insecticidal Soap and Limonene/ Linalool. These products kill ticks yet are safe to use around humans and animals. See pp. 114-116 and 123-124 for details.

3. Insect Growth Regulators (IGRs). The IGRs methoprene (FleaTrol®, Precor®) and fenoxycarb (Torus®) inhibit the maturation of ticks and can be applied in dog kennels and bedding (see p. 262 for application details). Precocene, a new and very effective IGR for ticks, is currently undergoing commercial development.

4. Pyrethrum and Pyrethrin. These materials kill ticks but biodegrade within hours or days. Micro-encapsulated forms of pyrethrin such as Sectrol™ prolong the active life for a week or more. See the discussion of these materials on pp. 121-122 and 262-263.

5. Synthetic Pyrethroid. The most effective material for use against ticks in Lyme disease areas is permethrin, or Damminix®. This product packages permethrin-soaked cotton in small cardboard tubes that are placed in tall grass, wood or rock piles, dense shrubbery and other areas where the mice that host ticks are likely to nest. The mice, which only range about 10 yd. (9 m) from their nests, collect the cotton, take it back to their burrows and lie in it. The permethrin kills the ticks but it does not appear to harm the mice.

Placing these tubes on a 5-ft. or 10-ft. (15 m or 30 m) grid throughout your yard provides the best protection (up to 97% kill of ticks has been reported), but you can also derive some effect by placing the tubes along pathways and around the perimeter of the lawn. Complete instructions come with the product. For a source, see the Resource Appendix under "Insect Management: Chemical Controls" on pp. 686-687.

The greatest benefits of this technique are obtained the second and following years of the program, because the biggest impact the first year is reducing the number of adult ticks available to lay eggs for the next spring. Since the ticks feed on other species as well as on mice, this technique is limited in the extent to which it can reduce tick populations by itself.

In other studies, 6-in. (15 cm) lengths of 2-in. (5 cm) diameter PVC pipe were baited with peanut butter to attract rodent hosts of the American dog tick, an important vector of Rocky Mountain spotted fever. Three strips of felt weatherstripping were placed inside the tubes, and the felt was thoroughly soaked with pesticide dissolved in vegetable oil. The researchers used carbaryl, but a permethrin-based material such as Permanone® could be used instead. Rodents coming for the bait thoroughly coated themselves with the pesticide, which substantially reduced the target tick population in the study areas. Fifty treatment stations in a 2,448 sq. yd. (2,047 sq. m) area used only 0.5 grams of pesticide, posing little hazard to the environment.

6. Tick Collars. Flea and tick collars may be useful in reducing the degree of tick infestation, but they should be used intermittently to make them last longer and reduce canine and human exposure to their toxic substances, such as carbaryl (Sevin®). These collars should not be expected to work against ticks or fleas on large dogs, because the areas of the body farthest from the collar may not receive enough toxicant to deter the insects. For further directions and cautions on the use of these collars, see pp. 263-264.

7. Systemic Insecticides. Ectoral® tablets with the active ingredient ronnel are fed to animals, thus moving the insecticide throughout the animal's body. This can produce serious side effects and represents a risk to the animal. Taking the drastic step of feeding a systemic pesticide to a dog

Summary: Least-Toxic Tick Control

• Inspect your dog and other free-roaming pets regularly for ticks. Search particularly around the ears and toes, especially after pets have visited areas where ticks are common.

• Remove embedded ticks with tweezers by pulling gently without twisting. Avoid touching ticks with your fingers; instead, use a leaf, paper tissue or gloves.

• Comb to remove ticks elsewhere on the pet's body, but be careful not to break off the mouthparts of embedded ticks.

• Clean wounds made by ticks with soap and water, then apply an antiseptic.

• Indoors, designate specific sleeping areas for dogs to reduce the size of the dog-tick infestation.

• Vacuum and use sorptive dusts in cracks, then caulk cracks shut.

• Outdoors, use repellent, wear light-colored clothing and tuck your pants into your socks when walking in tick-infested areas. Thoroughly inspect your own body and your children's after an outing where ticks are common.

• Use a tick drag or carbon dioxide trap to locate ticks in an area and reduce their numbers.

• Remove woodpiles and other mouse habitats, and keep bird feeders away from the house. Mow vegetation below ankle height to reduce tick harborage.

• Where the above methods are insufficient, apply limonene/linalool or insecticidal soap indoors, or insecticidal soap, pyrethrin or permethrin (Damminix®) outdoors in specific areas where ticks may be hiding.

can be justified only by the failure to control the infestation through other means. These tablets must be prescribed by a veterinarian.

THE DOG HEARTWORM
(Order Spirurida, family Filariidae)

The dog heartworm (*Dirofilaria immitis*) is a filarial worm, or nematode, that infects dogs and to a lesser extent domestic and wild cats. It has also been found in the timber wolf, red fox, grey fox, coyote, bear, beaver, sea lion, harbor seal, muskrat, otter, nutria (well-known in the southern states, where it is a major pest) and humans. Humans are a "dead-end," or accidental, host for the worm, since the worm cannot complete its life cycle in humans; it is not clear exactly

what role the other wild animals play as reservoirs for dog infections.

Severe infections in dogs can kill the animal. Unfortunately, the drug program used to kill the worms can also kill the dog. This occurs through an immune reaction to the dead worms, not by a reaction to the drug per se. Death is caused by blockage of the pulmonary artery with emboli (masses of debris) resulting from the action of the drug on the worms. Thus, heartworms are a difficult problem to manage. A new drug, avermectin, promises to change this picture, although it may not be appropriate for use on all dog breeds.

The infection is spread by mosquitoes. The mosquito species most likely to be a vector (carrier) of the parasite varies regionally—some 60 species are believed to carry the nematode. This accounts for part of the difficulty in controlling the spread of the worm, because many of these mosquitoes are themselves difficult to manage.

Dog heartworm is found worldwide. In the United States, it is very prevalent in dogs on the eastern and southern seaboards and within the Mississippi Valley. However, it appears to be extending its range to the Midwest, and now is often found in California.

Biology

The small worms found circulating in the peripheral blood near the skin surface of infected dogs are called microfilariae. These are produced by adult female worms that live in the right side of the dog's heart and the pulmonary vessels associated with it. Microfilariae are taken in by mosquitoes during a blood meal. After 10 to 11 days in the mosquito, an infective-stage nematode develops. It is then injected into a dog with the mosquito's next blood meal. Mosquitoes require a blood meal for every batch of eggs the females lay.

Within the dog's body, the nematode passes through a period of development and growth in the subsurface and deeper tissues. After 70 to 90 days, the young adult worms migrate to the heart for an additional period of about three months. After mating, small microfilariae are produced, then circulate in the bloodstream. The life cycle (see the drawing at right) has started over again when the mosquito picks up these microfilariae in a blood meal.

Damage

Adult worms lodge in the dog's heart and pulmonary vessels and block blood flow. Their dead bodies can lodge in capillaries and arterioles. The first sign of infection is usually either a chronic cough that is aggravated by exercise when there is no evidence of upper respiratory infection, unusual tiring after exercise, or both. As the disease advances, chronic coughing

The Life Cycle of the Dog Heartworm

Infected heartworm larvae pass through the mouthparts of mosquitoes as they suck a dog's blood. The larvae burrow into the dog's skin and develop in tissue for 70 to 90 days, penetrating blood vessels and moving to the dog's heart. In five months they become adult worms in the heart and blood vessels. Females give birth to mobile embryos called microfilariae. Mosquitoes that bite the dog ingest these microfilariae, which then develop inside the mosquito and become infective larvae in 10 to 11 days. The cycle repeats when these mosquitoes bite another dog.

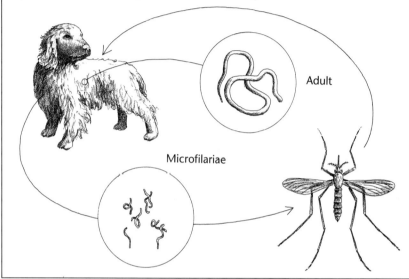

and shortness of breath even without exercise may become evident. Eventually collapse and even death of the dog may occur after heavy exertion. Sometimes these symptoms appear suddenly; death may occur 24 to 72 hours after the first signs of an infection. This sudden death syndrome, due to kidney and liver failure, usually occurs in young dogs.

Infections occur in humans only rarely, and involve an immature worm or worms lodged in the lung, where they are unlikely to cause noticeable symptoms. The coin-shaped lesion, or cyst, made by the worm is most likely to be detected accidentally when a person is receiving a chest X-ray for another purpose. There is the possibility that the cyst will be mistaken for a cancerous tumor, and this could lead to unnecessary surgery with all the trauma and expense that it entails. Occasionally, the human

response to an infestation by these worms may be more serious, such as a persistent cough or chest pain.

Detection and Monitoring

Based on the history of symptoms exhibited by the dog, one can make a presumptive diagnosis of heartworm. However, this should be confirmed through the detection of microfilariae in a blood sample under the microscope, which usually can be done by a veterinarian. Note that another filarial species, *Dipetalonema reconditum,* which is benign, is also common in dogs. Mixed infections are sometimes found, so it is important that the species be separated by their microscopic characters.

Ask your veterinarian if dog heartworm is common in your area. If it is, biannual or annual blood tests should become a routine part of the care of your pet. Successful treatment depends on catching the infection in its early stages before symptoms like coughing or fatigue show up.

Treatment:
Indirect Strategies

Indirect treatment strategies for the dog heartworm include:

1. **Screening.** Screening kennel areas or keeping dogs indoors during mosquito seasons can reduce the number of mosquito bites received by the dog.

2. **Use of Repellents.** Mosquitoes have a difficult time biting through fur and are most likely to attack the dog on the lower abdomen or wherever the skin is accessible. These are the areas that should be treated with repellents.

3. **Mosquito Management.** Management programs for mosquitoes in your area should, of course, be part of the suppression of any mosquito-borne disease. For more information on mosquito control, see the discussion on pp. 669-675.

Treatment:
Direct Chemical Controls

At present, chemical prophylactic treatment is the only certain way to prevent the heartworm problem. The major approach to curing an infection is also through the use of drugs. These drugs are aimed at killing the adult worms in the heart or the vessels leading to it. The chemical cure is much more problematic than chemical prevention, so emphasis should be placed primarily on prophylaxis.

There are three antibiotic treatments for managing the nematode. The first involves the preventive use of an antihelminthic in the food, the second uses a filaricide to remove the circulating microfilariae from the bloodstream and the third uses the filaricide to remove adult worms from the heart and pulmonary vessels.

The latter two antibiotics must be prescribed by a veterinarian. Of the two, the more hazardous is the one aimed at adult nematodes in the heart and pulmonary vessels. The

worms can be killed without direct toxic effects to the dog from the drug, but the release of their body contents and other tissue debris may cause the death of the dog from immunologic shock. During treatment to remove these worms, the dog should be under the daily surveillance of a veterinarian, which may require that the animal be confined for three to four weeks. An arsenical, thiacetarsamide, is used for the removal of adult worms.

If a dog is found to have microfilariae circulating in its bloodstream, the recommended procedure is to eliminate the adult worms producing the microfilariae as indicated above, then remove the microfilariae with dithiazanine or fenthion medications.

The preventive drug, which is used as a food additive, should not be used if microfilariae are circulating, because toxic shock can result when the microfilariae die. Only after the dog has been cleared of microfilariae should it be placed on the preventive program described below.

1. **Diethylcarbamazine (DEC).** The material used for preventive chemotherapy is diethylcarbamazine (DEC). In detailed studies with deliberately infected dogs, complete protection was obtained with 5 mg/lb./day for 30 days after infection. At half that dose, DEC was not effective if given for only 30 days, but was effective if given for 60 days. The half-dose — 2.5 mg/lb./day — also was protective if given every other day for 60 days. Although the lower dose is effective, the rationale for telling dog owners to use the higher dose is that they may forget to provide the medication.

Daily feedings should start one month before the mosquito season and continue for two to three months after the season ends. For example, if your mosquito season starts in June and continues until September, treatments should begin in May and continue until November. (Note that in tropical areas the mosquito season may last all year.) It is better to attempt to prevent the infection with

Summary: Least-Toxic Dog Heartworm Control

- Suspect heartworm if your dog develops a chronic cough without evidence of respiratory infection, or if there is sudden exhaustion after exercise.

- In areas where heartworm is common, annual or biannual blood tests are advisable for dogs that spend time where there are many mosquitoes.

- Have a veterinarian examine the dog and perform a blood examination for heartworms.

- If the examination is positive, have the veterinarian treat the dog with prescribed drugs.

- After successful therapy, begin the use of a chemotherapeutic drug in the dog's daily food for one month prior to and two to three months after the mosquito season.

- In areas where heartworm is prevalent, puppies should be started on preventive treatment as young as recommended by your veterinarian.

- During mosquito season, use very low doses of a preventive nematocide in your dog's food.

relatively low doses of a low-toxicity material than to risk having to kill adult worms later when the animal is under greater stress.

2. **Avermectin.** A new drug with the active ingredient avermectin is now available from veterinarians. Avermectin is a derivative of the actinomycete *Streptomyces avermitilis,* and an oral dose, administered just once a month, prevents development of microfilarial populations. The dose is based on the weight of the dog.

Initial studies of the mode of action of avermectin indicate a wide margin of safety to mammals. Although many dog breeds appear to tolerate avermectin without harm, collies have been known to die from the treatment, according to Charles Berger, a Berkeley, California veterinarian. The reason for this breed's susceptibility to avermectin has not been established. Clearly, testing on a wide range of breeds is necessary before the safety of this experimental material can be determined.

EAR MITES
(Order Acarina, family Psoroptidae)

The ear mite (*Otodectes cynotis*) is a blood-sucking mite that infests the ears of cats, dogs, ferrets and foxes. The condition of being infested with ear mites is called otocariasis or parasitic otitis. Recent information indicates that about 100 million U.S. households have cats. About half these cats are infested with ear mites at one time or another during their lives. That is a lot of mites!

Biology

Although ear mites infest both cats and dogs, they are more common in cats. Vigorous ear-scratching and head-shaking distributes the mites and a crumbly black wax outside the ear. The wax is a mixture of normal secretions produced in the inner ear and fluids resulting from mite bites. The mites can infest both ears and sometimes extend as far as the external areas of nostrils. Occasionally, secondary infestations may occur on the feet and the tip of the tail.

Mites are believed to be able to live away from the host for two or three months. This estimate is based on the observation that a mite-free cat introduced into a previously infested environment will become infested in about that time.

Damage

Mites feed by piercing the skin and sucking lymph. This may cause irritation, inflammation, exudation and crust formation. Heavy infestations may also produce fever and depression in the pet. Excessive scratching and rubbing may lead to a hematoma, or blood clot, and severe infestations can cause damage to the middle ear. Animals with this problem often hold their head to one side and turn in circles.

In a 1981 paper in *Annals of Allergy*, Larkin and Gaillard suggest that ear mites may be a contributing factor in producing allergies in humans similar to and possibly more important than those produced by the house dust mite (see pp. 160-162). Their argument is strengthened by laboratory evidence indicating that seven human patients tested in a skin-prick test for house dust mites and the ear mite (*O. cynotis*) showed similar reactions. Since about 15% of the American population is allergic to dust mites, and ear mites are so common and produce cross reactions in house-dust-allergic persons, Larkin and Gaillard feel more attention should be paid to ear mites and other mites of dogs, birds and horses.

Detection and Monitoring

If you notice a grey or black deposit in your pet's ear and the pet constantly shakes its head, you should suspect ear mites. The mites themselves can be detected by examining the ear exudate with a hand lens or under a low-power regular or dissecting microscope. Veterinarians using an otoscope (a lighted magnifier for examining ears) will see small white or flesh-colored mites moving on the dark exudate.

Because the least-toxic method of managing these mites hinges on not allowing the mites to build up a large population, regular inspection of the pet's ears is a good idea. You should comb your pet for fleas on a regular basis; this is also a good time to check the ears for mites. If you take your pet to the veterinarian for other purposes, have the vet examine the pet's ears for mites at the same time.

Treatment: Direct Chemical Controls

Mineral oil kills ear mites by smothering them. It also softens and removes accumulated ear wax and other debris. An eyedropper can be used to apply the oil. Follow with a gentle massage of the ear, placing your fingers on the furry side of the ear. Let the animal shake out the oil. This procedure is best done outside or after newspaper has been spread over the floor to catch the drops of oil. Small-animal specialists advise us that no other medication is superior to mineral oil for this purpose.

If, after following the above process, considerable debris remains visible within the ear, use cotton swabs to remove it. Do not clean deeper than you can see, because you may damage the animal's ear. If the animal will not hold still, a second person can hold and calm it while the first person cleans. If mineral-oil treatments do not seem to clear up the problem even after repeated attempts, take your pet to a veterinarian for an examination.

Summary: Least-Toxic Ear Mite Control

• Apply mineral oil to the animal's ear with an eyedropper.

• Massage the ear gently with your fingers on the fur side of the ear.

• Let the animal shake the mineral oil out of its ear to clear the debris.

• If necessary, use cotton swabs to remove the remaining softened wax deposits.

• If several treatments fail to clear up the symptoms, take your pet to a veterinarian.

REFERENCES AND READINGS

Cat Fleas

Bennett, G.W., and R.D. Lund. 1977. Evaluation of encapsulated pyrethrins (Sectrol™) for German cockroaches and cat flea control. *Pest Control* 45(9):48-50.

This research paper provides the results of the authors' tests with Sectrol™.

Dorman, D.C. 1990. Diethyltoluamide (DEET) insect repellent toxicosis. *Veterinary Clinics of North America: Small Animal Practice* 20(2):387-391.

This study discusses insecticides that also contain this repellent, indicating that most appear safe; however, one that combines the synthetic pyrethroid fenvalerate with DEET was implicated in complaints from over 400 pet owners.

Dryden, M.W., G R. Long and M.G. Sayed. 1989. Effects of ultrasonic flea collars on *Ctenocephalides felis* on cats. *J. Am. Vet. Med. Assoc.* 195(12): 1717-1718.

These veterinarians tested two brands of ultrasonic flea collars on cats and found that the collars failed either to repel fleas or to inhibit reproduction. Other studies of additional brands of ultrasonic collars have reached the same conclusions.

Hooser, S.B. 1984. Citrus insecticide hazardous to cats. *J. Am. Vet. Assoc.* 184:236.

This study points out that refined extracts of d-limonene and linalool used as pet sprays appear safe on cats as long as they are not applied in excessive concentrations. Crude extracts, often found in non-EPA-registered shampoos and coat conditioners, have been known to cause sickness in cats, and the death of at least one cat was attributed to one such product.

Kahle, J. 1980. Fleas and how to control them. *NCAP News* Winter/ Spring:46-51.

This article discusses the use of yeast and B vitamins to repel fleas.

Marshall, A.G. 1967. The cat flea, *Ctenocephalides felis* (Bouche, 1935) as an intermediate host for cestodes. *Parasitology* 57:419-430.

This is the source of the information in the sidebar on p. 256.

Muller, H. 1970. Flea collar dermatitis in animals. *J. Amer. Vet. Med. Assoc.* 157:161-626.

This article reviews and documents the occurrence of flea-collar dermatitis in response to dichlorvos-impregnated polyvinyl chloride pet collars.

Pearlman, F. 1962. Treatment for severe reactions to bites and stings of arthropods. *Med. Times* 90(8):813-820.

This paper provides results of an experiment in which humans were given 50-mg doses of thiamine hydrochloride three times a day to increase their resistance to flea bites.

Tarshis, I.B. 1959. Use of sorptive dusts on fleas. *California Agriculture* 13(3):13-14.

An article documenting the effectiveness of sorptive dusts applied to dogs and cats.

Ticks

Adams, S. 1988. Oil from myrrh's cousin repels ticks. *Agricultural Research* 36(8):4-5.

Presents results of studies showing that myrrh oil is a tick repellent.

Anderson, J.F. 1989. Preventing Lyme disease. *Rheumatic Disease Clinics of North America* 15(4):757-766.

This review updates knowledge about Lyme disease and its prevention.

Anderson, J.F., and L.A. Magnarelli. 1984. Avian and mammalian hosts for spirochete-infected ticks and insects in a Lyme disease focus in Connecticut. *Yale Journal of Biology and Medicine* 57:627-641.

This is a source for tick-host information.

Centers for Disease Control. 1979. *Ticks of public health importance and their control.* U.S. Department of Health, Education, and Welfare (Publication CDC788141). 15 pp. (Available from: Centers for Disease Control/Tropical Diseases, Atlanta, GA 30333. Attn: Publications.)

This excellent publication provides an introduction to ticks of public-health significance, with an emphasis on their effects on humans.

Collins, D.L., and R.V. Nardy. 1951. *The development and application of spray procedures for controlling the tick Dermacentor variabilis Say.* Albany: University of the State of New York (Circular No. 26). 37 pp.

An early paper discussing the use of DDT. This was the source for the information in this chapter on spot treatment.

Drummond, R.O., J.E. George and S.E. Kunz. 1988. *Control of arthropod pests of livestock: a review of technology.* Boca Raton, Fla.: CRC Press. 245 pp.

Surveys the history and current practices in all major livestock pest groups, with chapters on the most important pests.

Fish, D., and R.C. Dowler. 1989. Host associations of ticks (Acari: Ixodidae) parasitizing medium-sized mammals in a Lyme disease endemic area of southern New York. *Journal of Medical Entomology* 26(3):200-209.

This paper provides information on tick hosts in the northeastern United States.

Furman, D.P., and E.C. Looms. 1984. The ticks of California (Acari: Ixodidae). *Bulletin of the California Insect Survey* 25:63-64.

A basic source for tick biology.

Gregson, J.D. 1973. *Tick paralysis, an appraisal of natural and experiment data.* Ottawa: Canada Department of Agriculture (Monograph 9). 109 pp.

A detailed summary of observations and research on a rare but dangerous problem.

Hair, J.A., A.L. Hoch, R.W. Barker and P. J. Semtner. 1972. A method of collecting nymphal and adult lone star ticks, *Amblyomma americanum* (L.)(Acarina: Ixodidae), from woodlots. *Journal of Medical Entomology* 9(2):153-155.

The vacuum-collecting procedure mentioned in the text is described in this article.

Harwood, R. F., and M. T. James. 1979. *Entomology in human and animal health,* 7th ed. New York: Macmillan. 548 pp.

This publication contains an excellent chapter on ticks, including veterinary information.

Lane, R. S. 1989. Treatment of clothing with a permethrin spray for personal protection against the western black-legged tick, *Ixodes pacificus* (Acari: Ixodidae). *Experimental and Applied Acarology* 6:343-352.

This was the source of the recommendations on protective clothing in the text.

Leahy, M. G., and K. S. Booth. 1980. Precocene induction of tick sterility and ecdysis failure. *Journal of Medical Entomology* 17(1):18-21.

A research report on the effects of the insect growth regulator precocene.

Loomis, E.C., and D.P. Furman. 1970. *Common ticks affecting dogs.* Berkeley: University of California Extension Service ("One-sheet Answers"). 2 pp.

The recommendations for the use of Drione® and Ectoral® came from this source.

Magnarelli, L.A., L.F. Anderson, R.N. Philip and W. Brugdorfer. 1982. Antibodies to spotted fever group rickettsiae in dogs and prevalence of infected ticks in southern Connecticut. *American Journal of Veterinary Research* 43(4):656-659.

This study reports that 11% of 1,576 blood samples from dogs contained antibodies for different *Rickettsia* spp. The authors suggest that dogs may serve as indicators of rickettsial activity.

Magnarelli, L.A., J.F. Anderson, R.N. Philip, W. Brugdorfer and W. A. Chappell. 1983. Rickettsiae-infected ticks (Acari: Ixodidae) and seropositive mammals at a focus for Rocky Mountain spotted fever in Connecticut, USA. *Journal of Medical Entomology* 20(2):151-156.

Dermacentor variabilis was found to be most prevalent on white-footed mice and raccoons. Of ticks taken from hosts, 14% were infected with rickettsia-like organisms, and 4.6% of the specimens were confirmed to have spotted fever group antibodies. Other animals that tested positive for the antibodies were eastern chipmunks, grey squirrels, meadow voles, Virginia opossums, a short-tailed shrew, striped skunks, woodchucks and woodland jumping mice.

Northrup, J.G. 1987. Biology and public policy of Lyme disease at Fire Island. *Park Science* 7(2):10-11.

This article was the source of the quotation on p. 270 about the northern deer tick/deer relationship.

Olkowski, W., H. Olkowski and S. Daar. 1990. Managing ticks, the least-toxic way. *Common Sense Pest Control Quarterly* 6(2):4-25.

This article reviews the biology and control of major pestiferous ticks of North America, with an emphasis on practical techniques useful for the general public and professional pest managers. It is fully referenced.

Sardey, M.R., and S.R. Rao. 1971. Observations on the life-history and bionomics of *Rhipicephalus sanguineus* (Latreille, 1806) under different temperatures and humidities. *Indian Journal of Animal Science* 41(6):500-503.

A major source of information on the biology of the brown dog tick.

Smith, R.L. 1982. *Venomous animals of Arizona.* Tuscon: Cooperative Extension Service, College of Agriculture, University of Arizona (Bulletin No. 8245). 134 pp. (Available from: University of Arizona, Tuscon, AZ 85721.)

Provides a good short summary on detection and treatment of the brown dog tick.

Steere, A.C., R.L. Grodzicki, A.N. Kornblatt, et al. 1983. The spirochetal etiology of Lyme disease. *The New England Journal of Medicine* 308(13):733-740.

This is the first report indicating that a spirochete causes Lyme disease.

Sweatman, G.K. 1967. Physical and biological factors affecting the longevity and oviposition of engorged *Rhipicephalus sanguineus* female ticks. *Journal of Parasitology* 53(2):432-445.

A report on laboratory research conducted in Beirut, Lebanon, on the longevity of brown dog ticks in various temperature and humidity conditions. Maximum egg production was 5,414 per female.

Wickelgren, I. 1989. At the drop of a tick. *Science News* 135(12):184-187.

A succinct review of the first case of Lyme disease in the United States and investigations into its origins.

Wilson, J.G., D.R. Kinzer, J.R. Sauer and J.A. Hair. 1972. Chemo-attraction in the lone star tick (Acarina: Ixodidae), Vol I. Response of different developmental stages of the tick to carbon dioxide administered via traps. *Journal of Medical Entomology* 9(3):245-252.

A description of the carbon dioxide trap and its use.

Zimmer, G.M. 1974. *Pest facts No. 20: dog ticks.* Providence: University of Rhode Island. 2 pp.

Contains information about tick repellents.

Dog Heartworms

Beaver, P.C., R.C. Jung and E.W. Cupp. 1984. *Clinical parasitology,* 9th ed. Philadelphia: Lea and Febiger. 825 pp.

A good summary of the biology of the heartworm within the dog, mosquito, other hosts and humans. Closely related filarial species are also covered.

Harwood, R. F., and M. T. James. 1979. *Entomology in human and animal health,* 7th ed. New York: Macmillan. 548 pp.

This text has a short section on the heartworm and should be consulted for biological information about the worm and its vectors.

Pacheco, G. 1973. Synopsis of Dr. Seiji Kume's reports at the first international symposium on canine heartworm disease. In *Canine heartworm disease, the current knowledge,* R.E. Bradley and G. Pacheco, eds., pp. 137-144. Gainsville: University of Florida. 148 pp.

This report summarizes various chemotherapeutic approaches to the management of canine heartworm.

Siegmund, O.H., and C.M. Fraser, eds. 1973. *The Merck veterinary manual: a handbook of diagnosis and therapy for the veterinarian,* 4th ed. Rahway, N. J.: Merck and Co. 1,600 pp.

This authoritative reference work discusses the heartworm and its diagnosis and makes recommendations for treatment.

Ear Mites

Baker, E.W., T.M. Evans, D.J. Gould, W.B. Hull and H.L. Keegan. 1956. *A manual of parasitic mites of medical or economic importance.* New York: National Pest Control Association. 170 pp.

A useful manual for the identification and treatment of pest mites.

Harwood, R.F., and M.T. James. 1979. *Entomology in human and animal health,* 7th ed. New York: Macmillan. 548 pp.

This text has a short paragraph on ear mites and should be consulted for biological information about related mites. Treatment information is mentioned only briefly.

Larkin, A.D., and G.E. Gaillard. 1981. Mites in cat ears: a source of cross-antigenicity with house dust mites, preliminary report. *Annals of Allergy* 46:301-303.

The authors indicate that there is cross-reactivity between house dust mite and ear mite allergens. They suggest that house dust samples in other countries may be different from American samples because in the United States the cat is largely an indoor animal, whereas elsewhere it exists predominantly outdoors.

Siegmund, O.H., and C.M. Fraser, eds. 1973. *The Merck veterinary manual: a handbook of diagnosis and therapy for the veterinarian,* 4th ed. Rahway, N. J.: Merck and Co. 1,600 pp.

This authoritative reference work discusses the ear mite and makes recommendations for treatment, including various medications. It should be consulted if the animal's ears become inflamed or if hematoma develops.

Weiss, J. 1980. *The people's emergency guide.* New York: Dell. 288 pp.

This general reference work has good suggestions on ear cleaning and treatment for ear mites.

CHAPTER 16
Mice, Spiders and Bats

INTRODUCTION

In addition to the fabric, food and pet pests we have already described, there are other large and small animals that commonly share human dwellings and cause moderate to severe problems. Wild animal fleas, ticks, bedbugs and conenose bugs are transitory migrants into the house, but the wildlife we discuss in this chapter—the house mouse, spiders and bats—are more frequent and more permanent house companions.

Some of these animals lodge temporarily under the house and become annoying primarily because their own pests may leave them to bite humans. There are accounts of people being plagued by flea infestations they could not suppress or trace to any past or present pet occupancy. Eventually, through the identification of the flea species and a site inspection, it became apparent that the fleas were coming from a wild animal resident in, under or on the house, or in the attic and eave spaces. To solve a flea problem such as this, the suspected host must be trapped and/or excluded. We have heard similar reports of ticks and bedbugs that have left their wild rodent or bird hosts to feed on humans in the house. And in Chapter 12, we discussed the conenose bug, which may move impartially between wild rodents beneath or adjacent to buildings and the humans within.

Of the three most important urban rodents, the largest, the most ubiquitous and the most dangerous is the Norway rat *(Rattus norvegicus),* also called the brown, wharf or sewer rat. Although often found in the house, the Norway rat is rarely controlled completely by focusing treatment on one house alone. It is almost always a neighborhood-wide problem, and must be tackled from that perspective. Therefore, we discuss it in Chapter 33, where we cover community-wide pest problems.

THE HOUSE MOUSE
(Order Rodentia, family Muridae)

If a man can...make a better mousetrap...the world will make a beaten path to his door.
Ralph Waldo Emerson

Of all the mouse species that invade human structures, only the house mouse *(Mus musculus)* usually becomes a long-term inhabitant unless controlled. However, in some areas, other species often abandon their outdoor habitats and invade the house in fall, so it is important to determine which species you are dealing with. Table 16.1 on p. 288 helps you separate the true house mouse from related species; the house mouse is shown in the drawing below.

Management strategies for wild mice and the house mouse are slightly different. If the mouse you see in the house is merely a temporary invader, the major focus should be on trapping, exclusion and management of outdoor food and water sources close to the house. These include wood and debris piles, compost

---

The House Mouse
The house mouse is light brown to grey and reaches 3½ in. (9 cm) in length, with a tail as long as the body. Its large ears and pointed nose help distinguish it from a young rat, which has small ears and a blunt nose.

---

heaps and sacks of seeds or pet food in sheds or outbuildings. By contrast, management of the house mouse, which can live happily indoors without ever returning to the wild, must focus on food sources within the house as well as on trapping.

It is tempting to think of the house mouse as a small version of the rat. They are so closely related that a hybrid has been produced by artificially inseminating a white mouse with the sperm of a white rat. Thus, there is some debate as to whether both should be placed in the same genus rather than being separated into *Mus* and *Rattus,* as has been done traditionally. Some scientists speculate that mice developed from rats under conditions where it was less important to be large and ferocious than to be able to get into a smaller hole. Table 33.1 on p. 626 will help you distinguish a mouse from a small rat.

Mice are more acceptable to humans than rats, possibly because of what we call the "Disney influence." But Mickey Mouse doesn't transmit pathogens and physically damage your house and its furnishings. House mice do.

According to Walter Ebeling, writing in *Urban Entomology,*

The house mouse is indigenous to the arid grasslands of Southwest Asia, where prehistoric man first harvested the early forms of wheat and barley. Long droughts are characteristic of that region. Small rodents of the area had to adapt themselves to survival for long periods without drinking water, just as in the cases of those in the southwestern United States, such as the kangaroo rat *(Dipodomys).* Thus, mice are admirably suited to be ubiquitous commensals [associates] of man, capable of being transported for long periods in closed containers, such as boxes, trunks or barrels. The man-made environments they now occupy are often low in humidity and contain only dry food, much as in their original environments.

Table 16.1
Distinguishing the House Mouse from Related Species

House Mouse	Related Species
feet and head proportional to body; semi-naked tail as long as body and head combined	young roof or sewer rat, *Rattus* spp.: head and feet large for body
lacks distinct bicolored tail; upper body brown or grey, feet and venter same color as back	deer mouse or whitefooted mouse, *Peromyscus* spp.: bicolored tail, white venter (underside)
body more slender and smaller than vole, long tail, large ears and eyes in proportion to head	meadow mouse or vole, *Microtus* spp.: body plump, short hairy tail, small eyes and ears in proportion to head
flat, notched (not grooved) upper incisors	harvest mouse, *Reithrodontomys*: grooved upper incisors

The house mouse is found throughout the world from the tropics to the Arctic regions. At least two subspecies of mice were brought to this continent with the early European explorers and settlers. One subspecies came to the Southwest, California and Latin America on Spanish and Portuguese ships; the other arrived on the north Atlantic Coast and in southern Canada on English, French and Dutch ships. These subspecies have interbred extensively, and today there are believed to be more than 300 separate varieties of house mice in the United States.

The literature concerning the biology and physiology of *M. musculus* is immense, since the mouse is the most widely used laboratory animal. However, as most of the literature addresses only those strains derived from laboratory cultures, there is very little information on reducing mouse populations in the house or elsewhere.

Biology

The reproductive rate of house mice is formidable. Mice become sexually mature when two to three months old. The females are polyestrous, meaning they have menstrual periods every four days. Mating takes place over the entire estrus period and at other times as well. A postpartum estrus with delayed impregnation while the female is nursing her young can also occur. With an average litter size of 6.7 and a gestation period of 20 days plus an eight-day period during suckling when estrus does not occur, one pair of mice can theoretically produce 87 young per year. Table 16.2 on the facing page summarizes the reproductive biology of the house mouse.

Some laboratory-reared females have produced as many as 100 young per year. In urban mouse populations, the average proportion of females found pregnant during the year was 22%. A female stops producing young after about 15 months, but she may live much longer. Males can live up to three years.

Given such a high potential reproductive rate, one can see that in most indoor populations, environmental factors are limiting the actual population. These factors include availability of food and shelter, as well as competition from other species. Because rats prey on mice and compete for the same food and shelter, removing the rats often makes mouse populations more visible. This is important, because the prior presence of rats in a structure may foretell a later mouse infestation.

Water is seldom if ever limiting, since this species can fill its water needs from the food it eats—even from dry cereals. As for shelter, in northern climates the house mouse can establish itself outdoors during favorable seasons, returning to buildings when conditions become severe. In addition, the house mouse has a protective mechanism that responds to environmental stress—excessive heat, for example—by inducing a torpor or dormancy that conserves its physiological reserves.

Damage

Mice damage food, clothing, documents and other human artifacts and structures through gnawing, urination and defecation. The damage to food stores from mice waste is probably ten times the damage attributed to direct feeding. Many fires of "unknown cause" undoubtedly occur when mice or rats chew through electrical wires. Although the complete role and extent of mice involvement in human diseases is not yet known, Table 16.3 on the facing page points out some of the connections that have come to light.

The fact that many pathogens of humans have been isolated from house mice does not confirm that they are transmitting these diseases to people. For example, although bubonic plague is a notorious killer of humans, it is not known to what degree the house mouse is involved in its transmission. However, there is no doubt that there is transmission of a virus in the arenavirus group called LCM virus, because it causes lymphocytic choriomeningitis. It is one of the very dangerous pathogens isolated from house mice. This virus is also one of the causal agents of acute aseptic meningitis, which has been known to cause human death, although cases are usually mild.

The routes of transmission of LCM virus are probably dust contaminated with mouse urine, contaminated food and drink and direct contact. Surveys of mouse populations indicate that up to 69% are infected with LCM and are probably long-term carriers. Up to 9.1% of humans tested have been found to carry antibodies to the virus, indicating previous exposure. Outbreaks of this disease in humans in the United States and West Germany probably originated in laboratory animals, especially the Syrian hamster. However, the house mouse continues to be the major known reservoir.

LCM virus alone justifies mouse control from a public health standpoint. But the association of mice with many other human pathogens suggests that a potential hazard exists wherever mice come into contact with people, their pets or other laboratory animals. Unlike rats, house mice are often pests to rich and poor alike; they should be considered at least as serious a problem as rats, because they probably cause more economic damage and present a greater nuisance. In our opinion, one mouse in the house is one too many.

Detection and Monitoring

The sight of a mouse running across an open space is often the first sign of an infestation; droppings, nest material or gnawing damage are other common indicators. In kitchens, pantries or wherever food (including pet food) or grains are stored, you should anticipate a mouse invasion. Preventive inspections and the setting of traps help curtail the mouse population before it becomes serious.

Sometimes the first sign of an increasing mouse population in the neighborhood is sightings of mice in areas adjacent to houses. You may see mice dashing between shelters, or you may notice that cats and other enemies are catching them in greater numbers. You may also find mice in water-filled pails. Since mice move indoors with the onset of cold weath-

er, you can anticipate an invasion at certain times, especially where they have invaded successfully before.

Because they secrete themselves in wall voids and other protected areas, indoor mouse populations are difficult to assess. This probably accounts for the paucity of useful documented studies of mouse numbers in buildings. The easiest, most accurate way to estimate the population is by snap-trapping. The snap trap is also an efficient first step in managing small infestations of one or two mice. In such cases, by the time you know how many mice you have, the infestation is over—at least temporarily.

Treatment: Indirect Strategies

Preventive maintenance that limits mouse habitat and access to food is the best approach to control. If exclusion strategies are not undertaken

Table 16.2
The Biology of the House Mouse

Sexual cycle	polyestrous, every 4 days all year
Litter size	average of 6.7 (based on field studies)
Litters per year	up to 10, depending on food available
Age at weaning	21 days
Gestation period	20 days
Age at mating	6 to 10 weeks
Lifespan	1 to 2 years average; maximum 6 years

Table 16.3
Mouse Involvement in Diseases of Humans[a]

Disease	Causal Agent	Transmission
bubonic plague	Yersinia pestis	infested fleas, e.g. Xenopsylla cheopis
salmonellosis	Salmonella spp.	contaminated food
lymphocytic choriomeningitis	LCM virus	contaminated food, dust on fecal particles
rickettsial pox	Rickettsia akari	house mouse mite, Liponyssoides sanguineus
leptospirosis, or infectious jaundice	Leptospira icterohaemorrhagiae	contaminated food, water, etc.
ratbite fever	Spirillum minus	bite
tapeworms	Hymenolepis nana, H. diminuta	droppings, contaminated food
favus, ringworm	Trichophyton schoenleini	direct contact, mites
dermatitis	house mouse mite, Liponyssoides sanguineus	bite

[a] In approximate descending order of seriousness.

Filling Mouse Access Holes

Seal gaps or holes where pipes, wires or similar objects enter buildings with materials resistant to rodent gnawing. You can use steel wool or wire mesh (A) as a temporary seal in holes. For a more permanent seal, fasten a sheet-metal plate over wood surfaces (B), or cement or mortar over masonry (C).

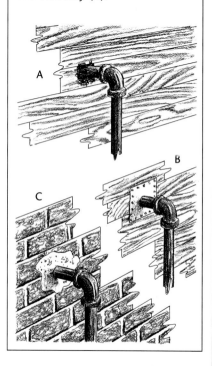

Mouse Traps

The traditional snap trap (A) is effective and inexpensive but can be messy. The metal lever trap (B) is easier to use, because there is no need to touch the trapped mouse, and it is equally effective, though more expensive. Place traps near mouse nests. Five to 10 traps per hole is best, spaced 2 ft. to 3 ft. (0.6 m to 0.9 m) apart at right angles to the wall (C).

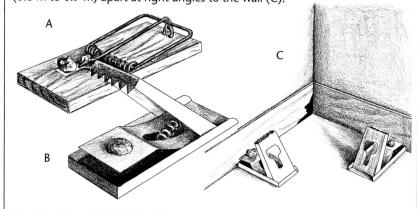

reduce mouse access. If you have already protected your edibles and organic wastes against cockroaches, you have adequate barriers for mice. Even if roaches are not a problem for you, you should read the suggestions for habitat modification for roaches on pp. 222-223. Protect food and garbage as suggested there until you have had a chance to eliminate indoor mice by trapping, repairing broken screens and filling cracks and crevices around doors and anywhere else mice have been entering.

3. Barriers. Vertical barriers of galvanized sheet metal 18 in. to 24 in. (46 cm to 61 cm) high placed around grain stores excluded mice during the great Australian mouse plagues in the early part of this century. If you have a problem with mice around rabbit hutches, dog enclosures or similar outdoor structures, you should consider a similar modification.

Treatment:
Direct Physical Controls

Of the procedures available for suppression, trapping is preferred. Traps provide physical evidence of capture, whereas poisoning shows no such evidence; moreover, poisons may result in flies and unpleasant odors from hidden decaying mouse carcasses.

1. Snap Traps. The simple, widely available "breakback" or snap traps are effective, particularly if they have expanded triggers so they snap when a mouse runs over them even when it does not reach for food. (Homemade expanded triggers are discussed on p. 636.)

Traps should be handled infrequently and with gloved hands, since mice can detect human smells on the traps. Coating traps with bacon grease helps mask human odors. The best snap traps are metal with a closing mechanism similar to that of a clothespin (see B in the drawing above); for sources, see the Resource Appendix under "Vertebrate Management: Physical Controls" on p. 688. Metal traps last well, particularly if lubricated and protected from rusting. The clothespin-type traps can be set rapidly and easily, compared to wire-spring-type traps, which require more time and skill to set. This is an important consideration, because trapping mice requires the setting of numerous traps. The traps work best indoors when set at right angles to the wall where mice travel. The bait and

along with direct action, the habitat is left open to new invaders, and sooner or later you will have another mouse in the house.

1. Filling Access Holes. Due to the small size of mice, mouse-proofing a house is rather like weatherproofing it. A fully grown mouse can squeeze through openings the size of a dime. Consequently, even small holes must be searched out and stuffed with steel wool, covered with sheet metal and/or filled with caulk, plaster or similar materials (see the drawing above).

2. Mouse-Proof Storage. Storage of foods, particularly grains, in tight-fitting metal or glass containers helps trigger end of the trap should be facing the wall.

Snap traps work best when baited. The bait should be sticky to ensure that the mouse will disturb the trigger mechanism even if it touches the bait only lightly. Commonly used baits include peanut butter mixed with rolled oats, raisins, gum drops and other mixtures. Alternatively, you can attach a small piece of cotton to the trigger instead of edible bait. The mice pull the cotton for use as nesting material, and the cotton does not spoil as food baits do.

In a Philippine study that evaluated snap-trap bait materials, baked breads had the highest trap catch rates for rats and mice. Trap-shyness was minimized by alternating different breads. The traps caught significantly greater numbers of females than males, and more adults than young. However, over an intensive six-month trapping period, the trapping efficiency decreased, probably due to the survival of trap-shy mice.

The food preferences of outdoor-living house mice are whole canary seed, pinhead oatmeal and wheat. This suggests, among other things, that the spill from bird feeders could be a significant source of food for mice.

Because mice are suspicious of new objects, place traps out baited but unset for a few days to get mice used to them. Once you see they are taking the bait, you know the traps are in the right place. Replace the bait and set the trap.

Most trapping efforts that don't work fail because too few traps are used. Indoors you should place at least one trap every 2 ft. to 3 ft. (0.6 m to 0.9 m) along a wall, since mice have relatively small home ranges. Five to ten traps per hole or more may be needed. Extensive trapping efforts carried out by the British Bureau of Animal Population during World War II indicate that keeping high densities of traps in place for two to three days is the most efficient approach. However, small mice are seldom killed by these traps because they escape the killing wire spring and survive to re-establish the infestation. We suggest setting a large number of traps for a few days, removing them, then resetting them two weeks later. This captures any young (and now larger) mice that were missed during the first trapping.

If you are trying to catch field mice, a slightly different technique should be used. Fresh scats (mouse fecal droppings) will indicate currently used runways. The traps should be placed on recognizable runways in grass or under bushes and hedgerows. "Breakback" or snap traps should be placed at right angles to the runway rather than in line with it. This places the bait and trigger where mice are most likely to encounter them.

Metal traps used outdoors will last longer if coated with wax. They also require oil to keep the moving parts in working condition. Petroleum oils are likely to be repellent; it is better to wipe the trap with bacon rinds to prevent rusting and make the trap more attractive to mice. Traps soiled with blood should not be cleaned since they are more effective than a clean, unused trap.

2. Glue Traps. Glue boards or sticky box traps can also be used to catch mice. However, many people find sticky traps inhumane because they do not kill the mice immediately and may trap nontarget species. Furthermore, if forgotten, the traps produce odors after the death of a rodent. No data comparing the efficacy of glue boards with snap traps is available. However, it is commonly known that glue traps catch large adults as well as smaller mice that may be missed by snap traps. Rats are more difficult to capture with glue boards because they sometimes pull themselves from the glue. Such traps are easy to put in place, but, like snap traps, they require follow-up in order to prevent unsightly and odoriferous decomposition of trapped animals.

If glue boards are baited, the bait —peanut butter, jam, nutmeats, cake crumbs, sweets—should be placed in the center of the board. Enclosed glue boards guard against moisture and dust, but may not be as effective, because mice are cautious about entering an unfamiliar enclosed space. Keep glue boards in place for at least five days to allow mice to become accustomed to the new object in their environment. If no mice are trapped after a week, move the trap.

Sweeping traps with their catches into a plastic bag is an easy way to pick them up. Place the bag in the garbage. If you find a live mouse in the glue, you can submerge it in soapy water until it is dead. Traps and carcasses can be buried or wrapped in a bag and disposed of. Pets should be confined during periods of mouse-trapping or excluded by temporary fences or other barriers.

3. Repellent Sound Devices. Ultrasonic devices that claim to disrupt the sound communication between rodents have captured the imagination of consumers. However, there is no research that demonstrates their effectiveness, except perhaps in very confined quarters when careful attention is paid to their placement.

It can be assumed that any positive effects are likely to be short-lived for two reasons. First, mice and rats are extremely adaptable, so it is hard to imagine that they would not soon learn to ignore vibrations that did not directly harm them. Moreover, it seems that the device would have to emit sound at irregular intervals to prevent the habituation that occurs with continuous sound. But even if they operated this way, it is likely that the mice would eventually grow accustomed to this, too. Second, if the habitat is not modified at the same time the device is used, it seems likely that the repelled rodents would soon be replaced by new ones, since the entry points and food supplies would still exist as they did before.

Recently, the Federal Trade Commission has taken a stand against misleading advertising used by the makers of some of these ultrasonic devices. The FTC has stated that the devices are ineffective in controlling rodents and insects, that they do not prevent pests from entering an area and that the sound does not cover the area advertised.

Although no technique should be overlooked in pest control, one should not expect panaceas, either. The appeal of repellent sound devices is their apparent simplicity. You plug in the machine and the rodents go away. As with other simple solutions to complex problems, you should retain a sense of skepticism if you experiment with them. We suggest that if you have mouse problems, do what it takes to keep the mice from entering your premises in the first place. Any that have already entered should be removed with traps one by one until there are no more in the house to cause damage.

Treatment:
Direct Biological Controls

Many people feel immune to mouse invasions because they have a cat. In our experience, cats can be very useful in picking off an individual mouse after a period of patient stalking, but it is entirely possible to have two alert cats and still have an occasional mouse visitor. Often, the mouse may be in the house for several days to a week before it is finally caught, and that is plenty of time for it to spread pathogens over clean dishes, contaminate food and/or destroy furnishings.

Female cats tend to be more predacious than males. Few cats are "good mousers" unless trained as young kittens to recognize mice as prey. This is not an inherent skill. Mother cats may bring in live mice they have injured for their kittens to play with, or for their own amusement. Sometimes these are species of outdoor mice that normally would not have come inside. Eventually the cats kill these, but in the meantime human occupants are exposed to the mouse fleas and other pathogens.

We suspect that the cat's most important role is in preventing, detect-

ing and removing new colonizers rather then in suppressing an established and regularly occurring mouse population. And even though we are cat lovers with cats of our own, we must admit there are two sides to the question of the value of cats in mouse control. Cats bring the cat flea, a major pest of humans, dogs and cats, plus a lot of hair and dander to feed dust mites and cause allergic reactions in sensitive people. Furthermore, in the garden, cats scratch up the newly planted beds so that seedlings must be protected by chicken wire or other constructions. They also catch birds and kill snakes— themselves mouse predators—and other wildlife. In short, there must be many people for whom exclusion and trapping of mice are preferable to acquiring a cat.

Outdoors, there are many natural enemies of mice. In urban settings, some of these can be encouraged deliberately by leaving certain areas wild within parks. Native hawks, owls, snakes, mites, ticks, fleas, flies, nematodes, bacteria and viruses all help keep mouse populations in check.

In the Soviet Union specific strains of Typhimurium-like salmonellas (bacteria) have been used to control outbreaks of small field rodents. Much remains to be explored about the use of microbes to control mice and rats; unfortunately, there are as yet no practical microbial controls available to the home owner.

Treatment:
Direct Chemical Controls

If there are just a few mice in the house, they should be handled with traps, not poison. A poisoned rodent is too likely to run off and die in some hidden or inaccessible place, eventually causing odor and fly problems. Chemical controls should be considered only after trapping or physical changes have proven ineffective.

1. **Rodenticides.** Two chemical approaches are available: baits and tracking powders. Tracking powders are too hazardous for use by the

home owner and should be left to professional pest control companies. Table 16.4 on the facing page lists some common rodenticides. We have included information that is generally not available on the product label.

Some poison-containing baits used for rat control (except red squill and norbormide) can also be used against mice. However, because mice nibble rather than eat large quantities at a time, a higher concentration of the poison is needed. This requires proportionately more care by the pest control operator to prevent human, pet and wildlife exposure, particularly with single-dose materials like zinc phosphide, strychnine, arsenic trioxide, fluoroacetamide (commonly called "1081") and sodium fluoroacetate (commonly referred to as "1080"). These are all restricted materials that require permits, and can be applied only by professionals.

Anticoagulants. Because they are less hazardous to humans and wildlife, the multiple-dose anticoagulant poisons are preferable. With these, the rodent takes many smaller doses over several days. The anticoagulant prevents blood clotting, and the stricken rodent bleeds to death internally. The chief symptom of this poison is extreme dehydration. An attractant or bait, usually a food item, is the key to the formulation, because it masks the poison. The preparation of an impregnated bait requires an acceptable solvent. Glycerin, corn oil, peanut oil and mineral oils have been found to be more palatable than olive, linseed or cod liver oil.

The multiple-dose anticoagulants, warfarin, diphacinone, fumarin and others, are relatively safe for the operator and other humans. Directions for use of these materials are widely available. However, widespread resistance to warfarin in household mice has developed in the United States and Canada. In some areas, resistance is seen in over 75% of the housemouse population.

Warfarin-resistant mice also show resistance to chlorophacinone and a

Table 16.4
Some Common Rodenticides[a, b]

Rodenticide	Characteristics
Multiple-Dose Anticoagulants	
brodifacoum (Talon®, Havoc®)	may kill with a single dose; unknown risk of poisoning nontarget species[c]
broma-diolone (Maki®, Contrac®)	may kill with a single dose; unknown risk of poisoning nontarget species[c]
chlorophacinone (Rozol®)	widely used by pest control companies; low toxicity to humans and other mammals; risk of poisoning to nontarget mouse predators[c]
diphacinone (Ramik®, Contrax-D®)	widely used by pest control companies; low toxicity to humans and other mammals; risk of poisoning to nontarget mouse predators[c]
coumafuryl (Fumarin®, Fumasol®)	relatively new material; a few resistant rodent populations reported
warfarin (d-Con®, others)	most widely available rodenticide; widespread resistance reported, thus it may be ineffective in many areas; comparatively nontoxic to humans
warfarin + sulfaquinoxaline (Prolin®)	warfarin plus antibacterial agent to kill intestinal bacteria that produce vitamin K_1; it has been difficult to prove superior effectiveness
Single-Dose Non-Anticoagulants	
zinc phosphide	very widely used material; has garlic-like odor; available as a dark grey powder, insoluble in water; slightly hazardous to nontarget species
strychnine	extremely hazardous to nontarget organisms; **do not use this material**
cholecalciferol (Quintox®, Rampage®)	mobilizes calcium from bone matrix to plasma; death is from hypercalcemia three to four days after eating a fatal dose
Fumigants	
carbon dioxide	useful in small, enclosed spaces; the safest of all rodenticides; kills by excluding oxygen

[a] From Timm, 1983.

[b] More toxic materials can be used by licensed pest control operators only.

[c] Nontarget species refers to any animal that may pick up a dying rodent or eat the bait directly. Examples are cats, owls and hawks. Because rodenticides kill slowly, the rodent may wander from its burrow in a weakened state and be particularly easy prey for predatory animals.

tolerance for the newer anticoagulants brodifacoum and broma-diolone. The rapid development of cross-resistance to these newer materials is significant, because it may have the unfortunate effect of encouraging the pest control profession to shift to more toxic materials.

You should suspect resistance to baits if bait blocks (poisoned paraffin blocks), bait packages or loose bait is regularly eaten without a corresponding reduction in mouse sightings, holes or other signs of mice. The best evaluation of resistance in a local mouse population is performed in a laboratory by trained professionals, but serious cutbacks in federal funding have meant that this kind of work is no longer available in most parts of the country.

The use of traps, alone or in conjunction with baits, increased emphasis on preventive habitat maintenance, and habitat alterations will help extend the useful life of existing baits. Efforts to make existing baits or baiting procedures more effective also may reduce the speed with which resistance develops.

2. Bait Boxes. These plastic or metal boxes with the bait placed inside (see the drawing on p. 294) have certain advantages over other delivery systems. The bait is protected from the elements, humans and pets are protected from inadvertent exposure and the amount taken by the mice can be monitored more carefully than when bait is broadcast. Bait boxes can also increase the amount of food taken by the mouse. For sources of bait boxes, see the Resource Appendix under "Vertebrate Management: Physical Controls" on p. 688.

There is always a temptation to increase the amount or concentration of poison in the bait. That way a mouse can take a smaller piece of bait and still receive a lethal dose. Moreover, a higher dose kills mice that are beginning to show a tolerance for bait with lower levels of poison (and thus ensures that they don't reproduce and contribute to a new mouse

A Tamper-Proof Bait Station

If you use poison, it should be placed in a tamper-proof bait station. These plastic containers hold the bait and lock with a metal screw. A small hole allows mice to enter, but denies access to children, pets and wildlife.

Summary: Least-Toxic House Mouse Control

• Mouseproof your house as you would weatherproof it by repairing all small holes through which mice might enter.

• Store grain and other foodstuffs in tight-fitting glass or metal containers.

• Trap mice that have already entered the house.

• Use a large number of traps, one every 2 to 3 linear feet (0.6 m to 0.9 m) of wall.

• Set the traps at right angles to the wall with the bait pan and trigger facing the wall.

• Handle traps with gloves to avoid contaminating them with human smells.

• Bait traps with a mixture of peanut butter and oats, or use cotton, which provides nesting material. If one of these substances doesn't work, try another.

population with an enhanced poison tolerance). But you should also be aware of the serious potential disadvantage. There may be a few mice that tolerate even the higher level of poison. If these survive, you have actually helped create or speed up the development of a highly poison-resistant mouse, and your infestation is suddenly much harder to get rid of than it was at the outset. This is why rodenticides should be used with great restraint by the home owner and the pest control professional.

SPIDERS: OVERVIEW

Few other "creepy crawlies" engender as much hysteria as spiders. We are very sympathetic to those people who recoil in fear, usually involuntarily, from any spider they see, since one of us (William Olkowski) had to overcome a serious phobia regarding these animals. Such phobias can be conquered. It takes determination, a willingness to learn about the feared animal and a readiness to force yourself to observe the animal ever more closely in controlled situations designed to be nonthreatening. (Of course it helps to realize that generally spiders are very nearsighted. Most can't see more than a few inches. If they are running toward you, they probably don't know it!)

As with the hysterical reactions to many of the organisms discussed in this book, a fear of spiders encountered in the United States is largely unwarranted. This is not only because spiders are beneficial to the larger interests of humans, and not just because they are so important in catching pest insects, but also because they rarely cause direct injury to us. Even the most dangerous spiders in the United States are not aggressive; they can be provoked to bite only under certain circumstances. Sadly, most spiders that are seen and killed by people pose no danger at all.

Willis J. Gertsch, curator of the Department of Insects and Spiders at the American Museum of Natural

History in New York for more than 35 years, has written a wonderful book called *American Spiders*. In it, he discusses at length the ways in which spiders are maligned and the true facts concerning the threat they pose.

People imagine that they have been bitten by spiders when the actual culprits are fleas or bedbugs or biting flies. The responsibility for mysterious skin eruptions acquired during the night is often laid to a spider seen scurrying over the rug at the bedside, or serenely spinning its web in a corner of a room. It is not uncommon to attribute many types of dermatitis to spider bites. All mistakenly. What are the facts?

Spiders are shy animals that run away from pursuers whenever they can. Almost without exception, they will walk over the skin of man and make no effort to bite, regarding his body merely as a substrate....By far the majority of spiders are relatively helpless creatures....Indeed, many of them must be forced by extreme means to bite when their venom is required for experiment.

In Chapter 5 we discussed some of the beneficial aspects of spiders as biological control agents. Beneficial or not, many people are upset by the presence of spiders in the house, or even the sight of their webs. Webs in the house have been associated with slovenly housekeeping, the mistaken assumption being that in a well-cared-for home, all insects and spiders should be killed.

We take a different view. Usually webs become visible only when they are old, no longer used and gathering dust. Furthermore, the only potentially dangerous web-building spiders occasionally found in the house—the black widow and the brown recluse or violin spider—are found in dark, hidden corners, usually near the floor, and not in light airy spaces along the ceiling or around windows where spider webs call attention to themselves and embarrass the housekeeper. Therefore, we suggest that you clean away webs you see in the open, but leave the web-building spider herself intact. There are exceptions, however, and we note them under the various spider genera discussed below.

Another general strategy for the management of spiders in the house is reducing their food supply. Because they feed on insects, study the situation to see if you can determine where the insects are coming from. Are too many flies getting into the house? If so, install or repair window screens and doors.

But what if you don't want spiders in the house, beneficial or not? You can of course kill spiders by stepping on them or vacuuming them up. However, if you are not the bloodthirsty type, there are alternatives. If you are tracking a very fast-moving hunting spider and cannot catch up with it, use a broom to herd it in the direction of an open doorway. If the spider is not moving too swiftly, use the following procedure.

First, invert a large-mouthed jar —a mayonnaise jar, for example— over the spider. Slowly slide a piece of stiff paper or thin cardboard large enough to cover the mouth of the jar under the jar while keeping the jar pressed against the surface on which the spider is standing (as shown in the drawing at right). A 3x5 index card works well. Work slowly so the spider is not harmed. The spider will end up standing on the paper, or will move to the side wall of the jar. Keeping the card over the mouth of the jar, turn the jar over and tap the paper so the spider falls into the jar. The spider cannot climb the sides of a clean jar. Holding the paper over the top as a cap, carry the jar outside and release the spider there, or shake it out the window. (Note: If you have a fear of spiders, you can practice this procedure on other less frightening species before taking on spiders.)

Although most bites for which people blame spiders are really in-

Capturing and Moving a Spider
To capture a spider, invert a glass or jar over it, slip an index card underneath, carry the spider outside and release it.

flicted by other organisms, some spiders do bite humans if provoked, and the bites can have painful consequences. In this section we deal briefly with three types of spiders whose bites cause the most concern in the minds of the public: tarantulas, black widows and brown recluse or violin spiders.

Reactions to arthropod bites are often due not to the poisonous quality of the animal's venom, but to foreign proteins in the animal's saliva. The reaction varies from person to person. One individual may have a serious response, whereas another experiences no painful reaction at all. For more information on these "autopharmacological responses," see the sidebar on p. 300. The problem of biting and stinging insects outdoors is discussed in Part 9 of this book.

If you are bitten by a spider, capture it if you can. That way, should your reaction become serious enough to warrant medical attention, you can bring the specimen to your doctor. Proper treatment may depend on identifying the species that gave the bite. Even the squashed remains of the spider can be useful for identification purposes.

TARANTULAS
(Class Arachnida, family Theraphosidae)

Tarantulas are the largest spiders in the United States, and are fascinating creatures that are often kept as pets. They are not very common, except in certain parts of the Southwest. If you live or travel in any part of the Southwest, from Texas through California, or north through Oklahoma, Colorado, Utah and Nevada, you should read *Venomous Animals of Arizona,* written by Robert L. Smith and illustrated by Joel Floyd. Smith describes the ecology and management of tarantulas and other spiders in greater and more interesting detail than we have space for here.

Biology

Tarantulas that live in the United States can grow to a size of 5 in. (13 cm), including the legs. They are relatively long-lived (20 years or more) and don't reach maturity until they are 10 years old. Many males do not live much longer than that, partly because they are vulnerable to natural hazards, including humans, as they search for female mates, and partly because the female may kill

The Tarantula

Tarantulas are light to dark brown, and their abdomens and legs are covered with hair. Despite their large size—with a typical body length of 2½ in. (6.5 cm)—they are basically harmless.

them once mating is over! Presumably this act of killing and eating one's mate, not uncommon among spiders, helps provide nourishment for the production of eggs by the inseminated female.

Young tarantulas either burrow in the ground or find a suitable hole to occupy in a protected location. They line their tunnels with silk, and camouflage the opening with plant debris or soil that sticks to the web. Once they have found a good nest, they do not stray far for the many years it takes them to mature. Emerging at night, they hunt within a few yards of the nest. In winter, they are inactive and plug the opening to their hole more securely.

The male wanders in search of the female upon maturity. Smith reports that in Arizona this takes place from June to October, the time when tarantulas are seen on roads and paths and when they may enter houses and cause concern. After mating, the female creates a nest of silk and remains with the eggs for the six to seven weeks it takes them to hatch. After hatching, the young spiders remain with their mother for a short time, then move off to settle in burrows of their own nearby.

The mortality rate of young tarantulas is tremendous. As Smith points out, on average, only two spiders of the 150 per egg sac live long enough to reproduce themselves. Birds, lizards, snakes, frogs, toads, skunks, coatimundis and javelinas are among the natural predators cited by Smith. The spiders are also parasitized by flies and wasps. The best known of the latter are the "tarantula hawks," large black wasps with orange wings that paralyze the spider, drag it to their own burrow, lay an egg upon it and leave the drugged spider as food for the hatching wasp larvae.

Smith refers to these magnificent spiders as "gentle giants." However, if severely provoked they have several ways of responding. The first is to rear up on their hind legs and look fierce. If that doesn't work, they may attempt to bite. They also have specialized urticating hairs on their abdomen that are tipped with venom. The spider can brush these loose with its hind legs.

Damage

Apparently, there are no recorded deaths or serious reactions to bites of the tarantulas in Arizona, where they are common. In *Urban Entomology*, Walter Ebeling describes a researcher who was bitten twice, and said that the bites felt like pinpricks, with mild pain lasting only 15 to 30 minutes. However, tarantulas do have strong jaws and powerful fangs, and we do not advise our readers to investigate the statements about the mildness of the bites. Smith suggests that if bitten, you should encourage the bite to bleed, wash it well with soap and warm water, then apply an antiseptic. If severe pain results, you should consult a doctor.

The urticating hairs, which may cause intense itching or sores on the skin, can be removed with cellophane or masking tape. If the hairs accidentally get into your eyes or lungs, they can cause more severe symptoms that require the immediate attention of a doctor. Apparently

the spider must feel very provoked to cause these hairs to be shed, since many people have had tarantulas walk on them without this happening.

Treatment: Indirect Strategies

Learning more about any animal is often the key to overcoming a fear of it. Because tarantulas are so mild-mannered, they make interesting pets for the school or home.

Ebeling suggests using an aquarium as a cage. An otherwise useless, leaky aquarium will serve, since it doesn't have to be watertight. Place sand in the bottom, and in one corner partially bury a small flowerpot on its side as a hiding place. Make the sand flow into the pot as a floor. You can sink a jar lid to hold drinking water in another corner. Feed the tarantula live insects. Ebeling suggests crickets. Although insects can be caught especially for the purpose, you may want to purchase them from a pet store or supplier of fish bait or grow your own to ensure a steady supply. Various flour beetles are relatively easy to rear.

Ebeling points out that your spider can live many years if well cared for, but Smith advises against handling it. If you insist on doing so, Smith suggests that you always allow the spider to walk onto your hand by itself—do not try to pick it up by grabbing it from above as it may bite you.

Treatment: Direct Physical Controls

If one of these "would-be Casanovas," as Smith refers to the searching males, should come wandering into your house, we suggest that you follow his recommendation: Gently sweep the tarantula into a dustpan, drop it into a large grocery bag and release it outside. Smith concludes, "No control procedures are recommended for tarantulas and none should be taken."

BLACK WIDOWS
(Family Theridiidae:
Latrodectus spp.)

There are at least five differently marked species of the much-feared black widow in the United States. In *American Spiders,* Willis Gertsch generalizes about them as follows:

> Our black widows are shy, sedentary creatures, largely nocturnal in habit, which live retiring lives in the small world of their coarse web. The females rarely leave the snare voluntarily and are clumsy creatures when not in intimate touch with the lines. Much more venturesome are the males, which, only about a third as large as their mates, must search for them during the brief mating season. In this weaker sex the chelicerae [mouthparts] are very small, and the males are reputed never to bite. To the female credit must be given for all poisonous injury to animals and man.

Biology

All the adults of the three most common species of black widows in the United States, *Latrodectus variolus, L. mactans* and *L. hesperus,* are shiny black with a red design on the underside of the abdomen that usually resembles an hourglass (see the drawing above). There is a red form of this genus in the sandy scrub pine areas of central and southeastern Florida, and a tropical brown widow that also has established itself in southern Florida. The young spiders of the black widow are whitish when they leave the egg and darken gradually, passing through stages in which the black is mixed with white, yellow and red spots and bands.

The black widow spins a small web of coarse silk with a tunnel in the center. She spends the day in this web and retreats into the tunnel when disturbed. Generally these webs are spun close to the ground. The most notorious behavior of this spider is the consuming of the male by the female after mating. The result

is extra nutrients for the female when she lays her eggs. However, she does not always end the courtship as a widow, because the male occasionally leaves the web quickly enough to avoid being eaten.

The female then lays up to 150 eggs and places the spherical egg sacs within the web. The young spiders (spiderlings) hatch in about 30 days. They undergo one molt in the egg sac before using their saliva to melt an escape hole into the web. As with many spiders, the young engage in "ballooning" to find a place to settle down. This consists of climbing to the top of a plant or other projection and spinning out a strand of silk that is caught by the wind. They may be carried many miles. Upon landing, the spiderling looks for a suitable spot, then settles down. In the laboratory, the life cycle takes about four months, but it may be shorter outdoors when temperatures are above 70°F (21°C).

Damage

The black widow produces a powerful venom that is neurotoxic (it affects the nerves). According to Gertsch:

> The females are timid. They ordinarily make no effort to bite, even when subjected to all kinds of provocation. They are never aggressive and make no effort to attack, preferring instead to retreat or lie perfectly still. The danger lies in the fact that, because they live in abundance near man, they may be accidentally squeezed against his body in some way. They lie hidden in the folds of clothing, in shoes, or under objects in corners. When body contact is established under normal or exceptional circumstances, the black widow bites in self-defense.

Within half an hour sharp pain develops at the site of the bite. This pain is the prime symptom. Gradually, it may move to other parts of the body and the person may experience a wide variety of other symptoms as

The Black Widow
Adult female black widow spiders have shiny black bodies that are about 9/16 in. (14 mm) long. A distinctive red hourglass-shaped marking is located on the underside of the abdomen. These spiders are not aggressive and seldom bite; when they do, their bites are rarely fatal.

the poison affects the nerves. Alcohol should be strictly avoided by anyone bitten by this spider.

If you suspect you have been bitten by a black widow, call a doctor immediately. Those particularly at risk are the very young, the elderly and sick or hypertensive persons. An antivenin (Lyovac) is available, and pain medication will probably be needed. An intravenous injection of calcium gluconate can help the victim overcome symptoms of muscle spasticity and hypertension. Hospitalization is advised for high-risk persons sensitized by earlier bites or the bites of other arthropods; they should remain under observation for at least a day. Although the illness can be serious, death from black widow bites is very rare. Where the outcome is fatal, it is often the result of secondary complications, such as when pathogens like tetanus bacteria enter the wound.

In the 227 years between 1716 and 1943, approximately 1,300 bites by various black widow species were reported in the United States, nearly half of them in California. Virginia led the eastern states, followed by

Florida. A total of 55 deaths were recorded, according to Gertsch, about 4% of the total number of bites. He concludes: "This percentage of fatality is low, but would have been even lower had all the bite cases been available for the record. Many people who are bitten are not sufficiently affected to receive medical treatment; therefore, while fatal cases are usually reported, non-fatal ones do not often find their way into the record. It is also known that some deaths were the result of improper treatment." Gertsch plainly feels that the medical significance of the black widow spider has been overemphasized.

We should add that when outdoor privies were common, black widows often built their webs across the opening just under the toilet seat. Thus, the outhouse was a common place for black widow bites. With the advent of indoor plumbing, however, this hazard has largely disappeared.

Detection and Monitoring

Black widows like to make their homes in specific locations. If they are common in your area, a new spider is likely to move in not long after the previous occupant is removed from the same spot. Because black widows prefer to build nests within a few feet of the ground, they pose a risk to children who are mobile and curious yet unable to understand the risk of poking a finger into a web. In fact, this is probably the sole justification for concern about these spiders.

Monitor for black widows at night with a flashlight or head lamp, because this is when they move to the center of their webs; during the day they conceal themselves. The best places to check are: small crevices around the foundations of the house, garage, sheds and outbuildings; on the undersides of outdoor wooden furniture (for example, beneath the seats in the corners where the legs are braced); between stones and flower pots that are accessible to children; and around the edges of woodpiles or other materials stored outdoors.

Children who are old enough to differentiate between spiders and insects can be very helpful to you in spotting black widows, as their eyes are at about the right height to notice them.

Smith recommends checking every two weeks in summer and once a month in winter. This applies to Arizona and similar climates; of course, in areas where black widows are rarely seen or no toddlers are at risk, such frequent surveillance is not necessary. In addition to periodic monitoring, we advise the following precautions to keep from getting bitten: Look where you are placing your hands when doing outdoor work; wear gloves and a long-sleeved shirt when working around woodpiles and other items stored outdoors that are likely to harbor the spiders.

Treatment: Indirect Strategies

Teach young children and others what black widows look like and the kinds of locations they prefer. Urge them not to tease spiders in their webs by poking at them and not to put their hands in dark crevices in garages, storage buildings and the like without looking first to make sure they are not inhabited by black widows. Explain the dangers of the bite without exaggerating so the child does not develop an unnecessary fear of all spiders. Children should learn that "black spiders" they see walking around are not likely to be black widows, since the widows are not seen away from their webs. Again, in some urban areas in the Southwest, these spiders are extremely common, but most people in the rest of the country will probably never see one.

If you find places where black widows typically build their webs, see if you can modify the area by increasing light, caulking crevices or taking other steps to make it less attractive to the spider or the insects it traps.

Treatment: Direct Physical Controls

A black widow is easy to crush with a stick or similar tool. Simply press the spider against one of the surfaces to which it has attached its web. If the web is in a small crevice, it is a lot easier to kill the spider by crushing it than to try and get it out of the web without injuring it.

We do not think that killing these spiders is always the best way to deal with them. Black widows are very shy and will not bite unless provoked. Like other spiders around human structures, they are doing an important job of suppressing insect populations. Furthermore, killing one spider without changing the habitat merely leaves vacant a spot that another spider is likely to occupy. Therefore, if you find a black widow living where it is not likely to be touched by humans, we suggest leaving it alone.

BROWN RECLUSE OR VIOLIN SPIDERS (Family Loxoscelidae: *Loxosceles* spp.)

Occasional media articles have exaggerated the dangers of being bitten by members of the brown recluse spider family and have created a certain amount of hysteria. Nevertheless, the bite may be painful when it occurs, and it can cause a distinctive-looking sore that is slow to heal.

As the common name "recluse" suggests, these spiders are similar to black widows in their shyness, retreating when possible, and preferring dark, undisturbed places near or on the ground for their webs. Unlike the black widow, however, the *Loxosceles* spiders hunt some distance from their webs, and it is usually when they have taken temporary refuge in clothing or bedding that humans are bitten.

At least six species of *Loxosceles* spiders are found in the United States. Table 16.5 on the facing page provides information about their distribution and female adult size.

Table 16.5
Size and Distribution of Adult Female *Loxosceles* in the United States[a]

Species	Approximate Size of Adult Female Body[b]	Distribution in United States
Loxosceles arizonica	up to ⅜ in. (9.5 mm)	Arizona, New Mexico and Texas; south into Mexico and Baja California
L. devia	⁵⁄₁₆ in. (8 mm)	southern Texas; south into Mexico
L. laeta	up to ½ in. (13 mm)	southern California, occasionally reintroduced to East Coast from South America
L. reclusa	up to ½ in. (13 mm)	Ohio, Indiana, Illinois, Missouri, Kansas, Nebraska and south to Gulf of Mexico
L. rufescens	⁵⁄₁₆ in. (8 mm)	introduced from Europe; occurs in a number of places from New York to Illinois
L. unicolor	up to ⅜ in. (9.5 mm)	California, Arizona, New Mexico, Nevada, Utah and Texas; south into Mexico and Baja California

[a] From Ebeling, 1975.
[b] Not counting the length of the legs.

Biology

The spiders in this family are distinguished by legs that are long and thin, a body that is smaller in relation to the legs than a black widow's, a light tan to dark brown color and a very distinctive violin-shaped mark on the back (see the drawing at right). This violin design gives rise to the other common name for members of this genus, violin spiders. The base of the fiddle fills a portion of the cephalothorax (the head/thorax segment of the two-segmented body), with the neck of the instrument appearing to extend toward the spider's waist. The legs are longer than the body, giving the spider an approximate overall span two and a half times the size of the female's body alone. The males are always slightly smaller than the females.

Loxosceles spiders have six eyes (which are arranged in a semicircle), unlike most spiders, which usually have eight. The sticky web is without a definite pattern. The spider spins a thicker tube or mat in the center of the web as a retreat. *L. laeta,* the South American member of the

The Brown Recluse or Violin Spider
Adult brown recluse spiders are tan to brown with a distinctive violin-shaped darker marking on the top of the body near the head. They have a typical body length of ⅓ in. (8.5 mm). They can deliver a painful bite, but it is nowhere near as dangerous as some media articles have suggested.

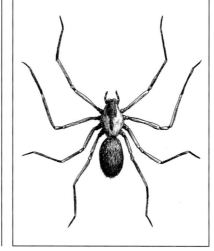

genus occasionally found in the United States, is known as "la araña de los rincones," the spider of the corners, because of this species' habit of spinning webs in corners. The webs are not used specifically for trapping prey, but rather as a protected place for the spider to hide.

Laboratory egg production in a female *L. reclusa* may range from as few as 31 to as many as 300. The spiders may take from eight months to two years to mature, and may live for another year after that. Observations of color changes in *L. unicolor* indicate that to some degree these colors hinge on the food last eaten. Fruit flies cause the spider's abdomen to turn orange-red, house flies turn it grey, grasshopper nymphs, light green and cockroaches, violet.

Damage

The bite of the brown recluse spider is rarely fatal. However, as Smith points out, neglected bites can cause a disfiguring scar or, in rare cases, renal failure. The principal problem is that bites sometimes cause ulcerous wounds called necrotic lesions in the

Is It Really a Spider Bite?

The following information is taken from a June, 1982, letter entitled "Facts and Fallacies on Araneism," written to the editor of the *American Arachnology Newsletter* by Findlay E. Russell, M.D., and Willis J. Gertsch, Ph.D.

"In our experience, chiefly at the Los Angeles County General Hospital, University of Southern California Medical Center, and more recently at the University of Arizona extending over a 30-year period we have found...solpugids [wind scorpions], ticks, assassin bugs, and even Jerusalem crickets, grasshoppers and other orthopterons...brought into the hospital as 'spiders,' along with a patient bearing a necrotic lesion....One must learn to entertain serious doubts about implicating a spider (particularly *Loxosceles* spp.).

"...Of approximately 600 suspected spider bites seen by us, 80% were found to be caused by arthropods other than spiders or by other disease states. Most often implicated were ticks, particularly *Ornithodoros coriaceaus* and the kissing [conenose] bug *Triatoma protracta*. Vesicating beetle and lepidopteran blisters, infected flea bites, imbedded tick mouthparts, mite, bedbug and fly bites (sometimes infected) and even hymenopterous stings...were seen in this series of cases. Since the patients came to the hospital as spider bite cases, 'probably brown recluse' and...the 'brown recluse' (*L. reclusa*) is not found within a thousand miles of the hospital, the diagnosis was held as suspect.

"It is known that other genera of spiders can produce lesions in man....In fact, we believe that almost 60 spider species in the United States have been implicated in medically significant bites on man....And, if the physician persists in relating every case of 'necrotic arachnadism' to *Loxosceles*, it may be another decade before the other culprit(s) can be positively identified....We hope that arachnologists will be the voice in the wilderness to the medical fraternity: BRING IN THE SPIDER.

"Another difficulty...is the significance of what the medical profession calls 'autopharmacological responses.'...Fundamentally, these reactions represent a response by the host (human or animal) to the presence of a foreign substance. The body reacts by releasing (or failing to release) certain normal cellular components contained within certain of the body's tissues. These components may have several physiologic functions under normal conditions. However, in response to the presence of a foreign material, usually a protein, the cells producing these substances respond abnormally and release larger than physiological amounts, which, in turn, produce a deleterious reaction in the host. This reaction may vary from mild anxiety and hives to shock and death.

"In some cases, a bee sting, rather than displaying mere swelling and redness, may break down at the site of the bite and display vesicle-pustule-ulcer-eschar [a dry scab], not unlike that seen following *Loxosceles* bites, or it may produce shock or death. We have also seen such lesions following tick, *Triatoma*, water bug (*Lethocerus* and relatives), deer fly bites and possibly flea bites. In every case so far examined, the patient was subsequently shown to be sensitive to the toxin of the particular arthropod. We have no idea how may cases of 'necrotic arachnidism' or 'loxoscelism' can be attributed to this phenomenon.

"...[A] number of medical diseases show lesions very similar to those of 'loxoscelism' and...are frequently diagnosed as 'brown recluse bites.'...[Examples are] erythema chronicum migrans, Stevens-Johnson Syndrome, Lyells' syndrome or toxic epidermal necrolysis, erythema nodosum, erythema multiforme, chronic herpes simplex, infected herpes simplex, arthritis dematitis, pupura fulminans, diabetic ulcer, bed sore, poison oak, poison ivy.

"A final important point, overlooked by the public (and some physicians), is the presence of an underlying, subclinical disease state, with cutaneous manifestations, which can be brought to a clinical state (and diagnosis) through what is known as a stress reaction....This phenomeon...may account for some of the bizarre reactions one sees following a spider or arthropod bite or sting."

kidney that may take a very long time to heal. Similar reactions may also result from the bites of some other spiders as well as other arthropods such as ticks and conenose bugs (see the discussion in the sidebar on the facing page, which should be of particular interest to physicians and other health professionals). Young children, the elderly and the infirm are most likely to be affected severely. Bites are usually the result of pressing the spider between the body and either clothing or sheets.

Detection and Monitoring

The brown recluse spider wanders at night searching for prey. It seeks dark areas for protection. A detailed study of *L. reclusa* by Hite and others at the University of Arkansas (see "References and Readings" on pp. 312-313) revealed that 92% of recluse spiders in the home were found in the following places: boxes 52%, papers 14%, bedrooms 10%, attics 7%, halls 5%, utility rooms 2% and kitchens 2%. The remaining areas in which 2% or fewer were found were, in descending order, living rooms, bathrooms, front porches, window wells, cellars and basements. Outdoors, 82% were found under rocks, 17% under inner tubes and less than 1% under houses or bark. Information on *L. laeta* indicates that it is usually found on floors and baseboards; only rarely is it seen on desks and tables, and it is never found on walls.

This information suggests that searches for this spider should concentrate close to the floor, particularly in boxes, around piles of paper and debris, in bedroom closets and under furniture. Outdoors, periodically check around debris and woodpiles, sheds and similar areas, particularly if small children play in those places (see the recommendations for the black widow spider).

Summary: Least-Toxic Spider Control

• When spider webs become noticeable on ceilings, walls and windows, clean away the web without harming the spider.

• To remove small and medium-sized spiders from the house, trap them in a jar and shake them free outside.

• To remove wandering male tarantulas, sweep them gently into a dustpan, then drop them into a large grocery bag and release them outside.

• Eliminate black widows and brown recluse or violin spiders by thorough, regular cleaning of floors, baseboards and accumulations of debris indoors, particularly in bedrooms, closets, storerooms and where children play. Black widows seek dark crevices for their webs. Violin spiders hide in shoes, clothing and bedding left on the floor during the day, as well in boxes and piles of paper left on or near the floor.

• Monitor for black widow spiders at night with a flashlight, both indoors and out, checking the small crevices and corners these spiders prefer around foundations, woodpiles, sheds and other outbuildings.

• Use a tool to squash black widows or violin spiders; you can also use a vacuum.

• If you think you have been bitten by a spider, catch and save the specimen, even if it is partially destroyed, for later identification in case your response to the bite requires medical care.

Treatment:
Direct Physical Controls

These are the direct physical strategies we recommend for controlling brown recluse spiders.

1. Removing Clothing from Floor Areas. Because most bites are received when putting on shoes or clothing that has lain on the floor, clothes stored near the floor should be moved elsewhere. Hanging shoes or placing them in sealed plastic bags reduces the likelihood of being bitten. Wearing leather gloves while searching through stored items can help prevent bites.

2. Freezing. Boxes of goods or papers suspected of harboring brown recluse spiders can be placed in a bin-type freezer for 48 hours to kill the spiders before they are unpacked.

3. Vacuuming. Keep the floor, baseboards and corners of the bedroom well-vacuumed. Boxes of paper and other items stored in closets or anywhere else that is dark and undisturbed should be handled carefully when first inspected. A small hand-held, battery-run vacuum may be the ideal tool for checking through stored items. If a spider is vacuumed up, slip the vacuum bag into a plastic bag, then place it in the freezer to kill the spider before emptying it.

4. Shaking out Clothing. Because most bites are received when the spider is squeezed between clothing and the body, it is a good idea to shake out thoroughly any clothing that has sat at ground level overnight. Blankets or other bedding that remain in contact with the floor and are undisturbed for long periods should also be checked for spiders and shaken clean.

BATS

Do cats eat bats?...Do bats eat cats?
Lewis Carroll

With no other species do myth and reality diverge so significantly. The film media are partly the cause of this problem, with their steady flow of horror movies associating bats with evil. The biological facts about bats differ greatly from these fancies, but unfortunately they are largely unknown. Healthy bats do not attack people, do not tangle in women's hair and do not transmit tuberculosis. Although bats can vector rabies, probably less than 1% of them become infected with the disease. Bats are extremely valuable as predators of insects and as pollinators of night-opening flowers.

Merlin Tuttle, in his excellent book *America's Neighborhood Bats: Understanding and Learning To Live with Them*, points out that all bats in the United States and Canada are insectivorous except for three species of nectar-feeders found along the Mexican border of Texas and Arizona. Tuttle writes:

Although 70 percent of bats eat insects, many tropical species feed exclusively on fruit or nectar. A few are carnivorous, hunting small vertebrates such as fish, frogs, mice, and birds. Despite their notoriety, vampire bats make up only a small portion (there are only three species) of all bats, and they live only in Latin America.

In many parts of the world the value of bats in insect control is recognized and they are conserved and protected. If people learned that bats were not dangerous, they might even begin to enjoy having them around their homes. Because loss of natural habitat may be driving bats into urban sites, protecting, restoring and building bat habitats should be part of area-wide wildlife planning. Since hawks, owls, eagles and wolves now receive a measure of public respect once again, perhaps there is hope for

The Little Brown Bat

Many bats are insect-eaters, and some can consume more than 500 mosquitoes in an hour. They catch their prey while flying, using their wings—which are really elongated fingers that serve as supports for their gliding membranes—to transfer captured prey to their mouths.

a more realistic and appreciative attitude towards bats, too.

However, like squirrels, birds, deer and many other species of wildlife living close to humans, bats can become annoying when they attempt to share our structures. Under certain conditions, they may require management. Although these situations require careful attention, they are by no means license to destroy bats wherever they are found. The soundest long-term solution to a bat problem in the house is "bat-proofing," described below.

Biology

Bats, the nocturnal equivalent of birds, are the only mammals capable of sustained flight. They are probably the most prevalent group of mammals in numbers of individuals (rodents have the greatest number of species). There are about 900 species in 18 families of bats, but only 400 species in three families are found north of Mexico. Most species are tropical. Table 16.6 on pp. 304-305 depicts and lists common bat species in the United States (for more extensive descriptions of these bats, see Tuttle's *America's Neighborhood Bats*).

Caves and trees are the natural roosting sites for most bats, but some have adapted to human-created habitats, such as mines and buildings. Solitary bats live alone in trees—never in caves—and may enter buildings, much like their relatives who live in colonies. George Scott, writing in *Pest Control* magazine, calls the emergence of bat swarms from caverns or large buildings "one of the most dramatic sights on earth." In the last century, James Larkin White investigated a "cloud of smoke" on the New Mexico desert and found instead the Carlsbad Caverns. The smoke turned out to be the mass flight of bats from the cave's entrance.

Bats mate in fall and winter, but females are capable of retaining sperm in the uterus until spring, when ovulation and fertilization occur. Births occur from April to July. Usually one young is produced, although some species are capable of producing two to four per litter. Within three weeks the young bats are flying. Weaning occurs in July and August, when colonies disperse. In preparation for winter, some species migrate and others hibernate. Most temperate species are nonmigratory, and hibernate in winter. Bats often live more than 10 years. Two little brown bats were captured some 30 years after first being banded.

Bats emit high-frequency sounds inaudible to humans that enable them to avoid obstacles and detect flying-insect food. They emit sounds that are audible to us when they are communicating with other bats. They catch prey while flying, using their "wings," which are really modified hand structures, not modified arms as many people assume, to transfer prey to their mouths. They must alight to eat larger insects. They forage over ponds and streams, along the forest edge, beside cliffs and ravines and among buildings. Sometimes they can be seen around outdoor lights, which attract insects. The pallid bat *(Antrozous pallidus)* feeds while on the ground. Tuttle's book has a dramatic color picture of one consuming a scorpion. Bats drink in flight by scooping up water with their lower jaws.

The widely distributed little brown bat *(Myotis lucifugus)* feeds on midges, mosquitoes, caddis flies, moths and beetles. A colony of 500 bats can easily capture half a million insects nightly. The Mexican free-tailed bat forms the largest colonies of any mammal. A colony of 20 million individuals consumes over 100,000 lb. (45,000 kg) of insects each night. Bats, in turn, are preyed on by hawks, kites, falcons, owls, cats and snakes. Humans kill untold millions of bats through habitat destruction, food reduction and direct poisoning; bats are also destroyed indirectly by agricultural pesticides.

Damage

As useful as bats are in catching mosquitoes, grasshoppers and other insect pests of humans and crops, they make poor housemates. Their presence, odors from fecal matter and urine, and ectoparasites are all of concern. Bat guano—their fecal matter, which is high in nitrogen—and urine attract roaches, mites and other species. Although insect parasites of bats such as ticks, mites, fleas and bat bugs rarely bite humans, they may become a pest problem for a brief period after a structure has been altered to exclude bats, because the pests wander away from the empty roost in search of a replacement host.

Fecal droppings and brown stains from urine, feces and glandular body secretions may stain the outside of buildings, particularly beneath eaves, entrance and exit holes, and elsewhere below roosts. In old buildings where an attic roost or a space between a wall and a chimney exists, excreta may seep through cracks and stain interior surfaces.

The main human disease threats from bats come from rabies and histoplasmosis. Rabies is a potentially fatal viral disease of man and other mammals transmitted between animals by bites or through contact with saliva or body tissue. Although this pathogen is usually associated with dogs and other carnivores, bats are known to become infected with and die from rabies. In 1986, bats accounted for 14.2% of all reported animal rabies in the United States, third behind skunks (42.9%) and raccoons (28.4%). Dogs accounted for only 1.7%.

Attacks by rabid bats are extremely rare; healthy bats do not attack people. Only 12 to 15 cases of rabies traceable to bats have been reported in the United States in more than 30 years, and only a single case was reported in Canada during the same period. The rabies problem is best managed by having pets and valuable domestic stock vaccinated against the disease. Cats and dogs stand the greatest chance of becoming infected by picking up a diseased bat. Most human run-ins with bats come from careless or accidental handling of sick, partially paralyzed, grounded individuals. (For this reason, any diseased bats floundering on the ground should not be handled. Instead, they should be shoveled into a container and transported to public health authorities.)

At one time, bats were thought to be frequent carriers and reservoirs of rabies, but laboratory studies do not support this. Transmission of rabies by airborne particles is known to have occurred only twice. Thousands of people explore bat caves each year without harm, so one can conclude that this route of transmission is not common. Still, if you do spend considerable time in caves, attics or other roost sites with large bat colonies, it might be a good idea to get immunized for rabies, since bats can carry the disease.

The sidebar on p. 306 is taken from a Centers for Disease Control report on rabies prevention. If you are interested in learning more about the subject, we refer you to the original document from which these paragraphs were abstracted.

Histoplasmosis is a systemic fungus disease of humans that may be contracted through the inhalation of dusty bat manure (guano) containing the causal organism *Histoplasma capsulatum*. But bats are far from being the only source of this pathogen. It is widespread in soils and bird droppings and is distributed by wind. Human infections are very common. As much as 80% of the population is infected in large portions of the Americas, Europe, Africa and the Far East. Almost 90% of the human cases in the United States occur in the Ohio and Mississippi River drainages and eastward into Virginia and Maryland. The pathogen is considered endemic in 31 states. Most infections are either asymptomatic or appear as benign respiratory illness.

Because histoplasmosis is extremely common, other mechanisms besides bat transmission must be operating. An inner-city source that probably accounts for far more cases is pigeon droppings. Still, if you are cleaning up bat manure or collecting it for garden fertilizer, it makes sense

Table 16.6
Bat Species Most Commonly Encountered in Houses[a]

	Species	Color/Features	Wingspan
	little brown bat (Myotis lucifugus)	rich brown, dense, fine, almost bronze fur; ears and membranes glossy dark brown	8.9 in. to 10.8 in. (226 mm to 274 mm)
	big brown bat, house bat, barn bat, dusky bat (Eptesicus fuscus)	light to dark brown, with most copper-colored; each hair bi-colored, with bottom almost black and upper half brown; face, ears and membranes dark brown, nearly black	13 in. to 14 in. (330 mm to 356 mm)
	Mexican free-tailed bat, free-tailed bat, guano bat (Tadarida brasiliensis)	dark brown, but fur may be bleached to grey or pale brown by ammonia fumes from guano (fecal) deposits	11.3 in. to 13 in. (287 mm to 330 mm)
	Yuma myotis (Myotis yumanensis)	light tan to dark brown; underparts white to buff-colored; membranes darker than body	about 8.7 in. (220 mm)
	pallid bat, desert pallid bat (Antrozous pallidus)	light yellow on top, hairs tipped with brown or grey; underparts pale creamy, almost white; membranes tan	13 in. to 14 in. (330 mm to 356 mm)
	red bat, leaf bat, northern bat, tree bat, New York bat (Lasiurus borealis)	bright rust-colored with short, rounded ears and long pointed wings, usually with a white shoulder spot; wing membrane thickly furred on entire upper surface; long tail membrane extends straight out in flight	11.4 in. to 13.1 in. (290 mm to 332 mm)
	hoary bat, frosted bat, great northern bat, twilight bat (Lasiurus cinereus)	dark and heavily furred, tips of many hairs white, giving frosted appearance; ears short and edged with black, usually white shoulder spot; membranes brownish and upper surface completely furred	15.2 in. to 16.4 in. (386 mm to 417 mm)

[a] From Tuttle, 1988.

Habits and Habitats	Distribution
most common of mouse-eared bats that inhabit buildings; breeding colonies of several hundred or more reside in attics, barns, etc.; in winter they hibernate in caves and mines, returning every year; colonies common near lakes and rivers; feed on mosquitoes and other insects	found in most of United States, Canada and sierran Mexico; absent in Texas, Oklahoma, Louisiana and Florida, portions of eastern New Mexico, eastern Colorado, western Missouri, central Kansas and the coastal lowlands of the Carolinas
flies at night to roost, favoring porches, brick houses, garages with open doors; eats many kinds of insects	widely distributed in Canada, the United States and Mexico
most colonial of all bats, inhabiting buildings on the West Coast and in the Southeast; primarily a cave bat in the Southwest; large colonies in caves may be a hazard to humans exploring because of the danger of airborne rabies; an important insect-eater	across the southern half of the United States from the Pacific to the Atlantic, and extending into Mexico
always found near open water; roosts in buildings, attics, porches, abandoned cabins, church belfries; feeds on many insects	southwestern United States
roosts in open shelters such as rafters in open garages; feeds on many pest insects	found primarily in the western United States, Canada and northern Mexico
only occasionally enters buildings (during migration); well-developed annual flyways; copulation begins in air and sometimes ends on ground; produces large litters of up to five young; rarely encountered unless sick, which explains relatively high incidence of rabies in those sampled; very important in control of crop pests	common throughout United States and Canada, extending into Mexico
one of the largest bats in North America; almost never enters homes; solitary, often in evergreen rather than in deciduous trees; feeds on many insects	common in United States, eastern Canada and northern Mexico, except in Rockies and Mexican sierra

Rabies and Rabies Immunization[a]

Rabies in humans has decreased from an average of 22 cases per year between 1946 to 1950 to only 15 cases a year since 1960. The number of cases of rabies in domestic animals has decreased similarly. In 1946, for example, there were more than 8,000 cases of rabies in dogs; in 1978 there were only 122. The likelihood of human exposure to rabies from domestic animals has decreased greatly, although bites by dogs and cats continue to be the principal reason for anti-rabies treatments.

Rabies in wildlife—especially skunks, foxes, raccoons and bats—has become increasingly prominent in recent years, accounting for more than 70% of all reported cases of animal rabies each year since 1968. Wild animals now constitute the most significant source of infection for humans and domestic animals in the United States. Rabies is present in animals throughout the United States, with only Hawaii and the District of Columbia reporting no cases between 1974 and 1979.

There are two types of rabies immunization products. The first consists of vaccines that induce an active immune response. Antibodies take seven to ten days to develop, but the immunity can persist for a year or more. The second, globulins, provide rapid immune protection that persists for a short period—they have a half life of about 21 days. Both products should be used concurrently for post-exposure prevention of rabies.

[a] From *Morbidity and Mortality Weekly Report*, June 13, 1980.

to avoid inhaling the dust by wearing a tight-fitting respirator capable of filtering particles as small as two microns in diameter (for sources, see the Resource Appendix under "Vertebrate Management: Chemical Controls" on pp. 688).

Detection and Monitoring

Bats are usually detected in structures by their droppings, urine or noise-making. A high-pitched squeaking or rustling and an acrid, musty odor indicates their presence.

So does their guano. Bats defecate from their permanent roosts and at temporary roosting sites (on porches, for example) where they rest between nighttime foraging periods. The droppings can be distinguished from those of mice because they can be crushed easily into fine, shiny fragments. These fragments are undigested insect parts. By contrast, mouse droppings are firm and do not disintegrate readily. Close inspection will reveal a variety of insect body parts in the feces. The pallid bat, for example, leaves remains of Jerusalem crickets. Dark or black droppings and a fresh appearance suggests an active or recently active colony. No white color appears in bat feces; if it is present, you have birds, not bats.

If you suspect you have bats in your house, the best way to find entry and exit holes is to conduct a "bat watch." This involves stationing one person on each side of the building a half hour before dark, when bats begin to leave their roosts, or just before dawn, when they return. Generally, they are somewhat easier to see at dawn than at dusk.

Bat watchers should have a clipboard with a sketched elevation (vertical drawing) of that particular side of the building. As bats exit or enter the building, the watcher should mark the locations of the holes on the diagram. A count of bats using each hole will help determine how many bats are roosting in the building and which holes are the major access points. Bats frequently enter a building at the ridge cap, so pay special attention to the roof. A watch of an hour or so should be sufficient to identify all the major holes.

You can use a flashlight to find the entries. But be sure to aim the light beam to one side of the suspected hole so only the edge of the light falls on the hole. Bats will enter and exit as long as the light is dim. Therefore it is also advisable to use a flashlight with a red filter. You can find sources for these in the Resource Appendix under "Vertebrate Management: Identification and Monitoring" on p. 688, or you can make one yourself by affixing several layers of dark red cellophane over the head of a flashlight with a rubber band. Once the entry/exit points have been located, you can focus your management efforts on those locations.

Treatment:
Indirect Strategies

Indirect strategies include constructing bat houses as alternative roosting sites to human dwellings and designing buildings that are bat-proof. In addition, individual, neighborhood and community education can play an important part in solving any bat-management problem.

1. Education. Largely because bats were closely associated with witchcraft in Europe, people retain superstitions and fears about them. Other cultures, however, hold different beliefs. In China, for example, bats are considered symbols of good luck, and many American Indian cultures consider them powerful deities.

One way to combat misinformation about bats is to encourage your

Artificial Bat Houses

A bat house that attracts and supports bats but discourages rodents and other animals from nesting must meet several criteria. Studies show they should be located within 1,000 ft. (305 m) of a river, lake or pond, and should be oriented toward the east or southeast so they warm up quickly in the morning. The best designs provide crevices of different widths to attract different species. Boards that have rough surfaces make the crevices easier for bats to cling to.

Because different species prefer different-sized crevices, temperatures and heights above the ground, a serious bat-management project involves the erection of several houses around a property at various heights between 6 ft. (1.8 m) and 40 ft. (12.2 m) high. They should be placed where they are sheltered from the wind and where the entrance is not obstructed by tree branches or other obstacles. The house should have an open bottom, since bats enter from below. An open bottom also discourages occupation by non-bat wildlife.

A number of small and large bat houses are described and pictured in Merlin Tuttle's *America's Neighborhood Bats*. Bat Conservation International, the nonprofit organization Tuttle founded to educate the public and carry out research on bats, sells different sized bat houses that are ready to mount (see the Resource Appendix under "Vertebrate Management" on p. 688). We purchased one of these handsome structures and have installed it at the Bio-Integral Resource Center's field station to attract bat residents that eat mosquitoes and other pestiferous insects. Tuttle says a year may elapse before bats occupy the bat house, so patience is important. Tuttle's book provides further details on bat houses, anecdotes on their successful use to reduce mosquitoes in parks and resorts and a summary of what has been learned by researchers.

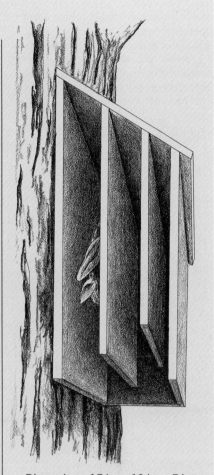

Dimensions: 17 in. x 10 in. x 7 in.

local library to carry books about them. You can also write letters to the editor of your local newspaper during outbreaks of public hysteria over bats; mention the literature in the library. If you want to know which books to recommend, consult the references at the end of this chapter.

Teach children that bats are beneficial predators of insects, and, like many wild animals, should not be handled. Children should be taught to be particularly cautious with wild animals that seem tame. An animal lying on the ground that allows humans to approach it may be ill, and should not be picked up. (This applies to squirrels and other small animals as well.)

The issue of bat conservation should be brought before public bodies, particularly parks and recreation agencies. Wherever possible, natural bat roosts should be conserved. Interpretive programs can encourage rational bat management. If bats are roosting on a structure where they are not wanted, the possibility of shifting them to an artificial roost should be considered. Humans and bats must learn to live together on this planet. We will have to change some of our attitudes and behavior to make this possible.

2. Bat Houses. Bats are important insect predators; therefore they should be encouraged to roost in structures other than those in which people are living and working. Trees and outbuildings, for example, can support bat populations without causing problems for nearby humans. You should consider erecting a bat house, such as the one shown above, as a means of encouraging bat colonies, especially if you are simultaneously excluding them from your own house.

3. Bat-Proof Initial Design. During the design and construction of buildings, all openings to the outside should be sealed. This is particularly important for spaces under the eaves, openings where electrical conduits and water pipes enter, spaces around windows and window trim, vent holes and where the chimney and house meet. Vents that must be left open for air circulation should be screened with a fine ½-in. by ½-in. (13 mm by 13 mm) or smaller mesh.

All new construction or remedial work should explicitly specify the various pest-proofing measures to be incorporated. An ounce of detail work specified in advance will eliminate the need for a pound of remedial work later. Nonetheless, do not expect contractors to follow these measures automatically. It is critical that you make on-site inspections to ensure that the work is being carried out properly.

Treatment:
Direct Physical Controls
Closing off points of entry to the building is the best way to solve bat problems. This strategy and other physical controls are discussed below.

1. Sealing Points of Entry. Some bats can pass through spaces as small as ¼ in. by 1½ in. (6 mm by 38 mm), but cannot pass through holes smaller than ⅜ in. (9.5 mm) in diameter. Although the job of finding and sealing entrance holes for bats can be tedious, it has the fringe benefit of tightening up the structure and reducing heat loss. Furthermore, the cost of energy-saving improvements is tax-deductible in some states.

Simple homemade air leak detection devices can be used to find holes in the outer skin of the house (see the drawing at right). A piece of thin-film plastic or bathroom tissue taped to a clothes hanger can serve as a flag whose movement indicates an air leak. On a windy day, move the detector around doors and window frames, attic storage areas and any other place you suspect is not airtight. The direction opposite the deflection of the flag or the movement of smoke indicates the source of the

Bat-Proofing a House[a]

The following areas are parts of the house exterior that should be caulked to prevent bat entry:

• between drip caps above windows and doors and the house siding

• between sills below windows and doors and the house siding

• at joints between window frames and house siding

• at building corners

• at the house sills where the frame meets the foundation

• around outside water faucets and other breaks in the exterior house surface

• where pipes and wires penetrate the ceiling and walls in unheated attics

• between porches and other additions and the main body of the house

• where chimneys and other masonry meet the side of the house

• at roof edges, ridge caps, soffits and fascia boards

• where storm windows meet window frames, except for drain holes at window sills, which must be kept free

• where walls meet the eaves at the gable ends of an attic

[a] From Greenhall, 1982.

leak. More formal tools, including air testers, smoke generators and smoke sticks, are available for the same purpose from energy conservation centers. As mentioned earlier, a "bat watch" can also pinpoint entry and exit holes.

Seal small openings with a high-quality caulk that resists weathering, responds to house movement without cracking and is long-lasting. You can usually judge its quality by the length of the manufacturer's guarantee. Buy caulk that matches the background color of the house or that can be painted.

Larger spaces can be filled with self-expanding urethane foams applied from pressurized aerosol containers. Polycell™ and Great Stuff™ are two brand names that are widely available. If you haven't worked with these products before, experiment first so you don't apply so much that the pressure blows out interior or ex-

A Simple Air Leak Detector
A sheet of tissue paper taped to a clothes hanger helps locate bat entrance holes by finding air leaks. Movement of the paper indicates a leak. It is best to perform this test on a windy day.

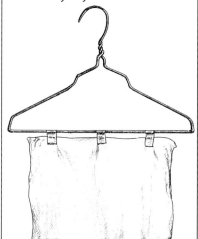

terior wall components. Lath, sheet metal, hardware cloth and window screening can also be used to seal holes. Bats do not gnaw their way through barriers, but they will push loose barriers out of the way. The sidebar on the facing page lists areas that commonly need sealing. Generally, it takes a few days to block all the minor holes. Monitor the structure until it is finally bat-proofed.

All bat-proofing should take place after young bats have been weaned and left the structure to avoid sealing them in and killing them inside. The best times to undertake the job are in spring before migratory bats return to the roost or in fall after all the young have been produced (but before the cold weather starts). If you need to perform exclusion work while bats are still in the structure, close the entry points only after the bats have left the roost for the night to forage. This can be difficult and even dangerous, since it often requires high ladder work after dark.

2. One-Way "Valves." To help solve the problem of sealing the last few holes when bats may still be inside the structure, one-way valve-like devices such as the EX100 Hanks Bat Excluder (see the Resource Appendix under "Vertebrate Management: Physical Controls" on p. 688) can be installed during daylight hours. The valves allow bats to exit but prevent re-entry. They are not as appropriate where there are large, diffuse or widely distributed entries.

3. Bird Netting. Stephen Frantz, vertebrate vector specialist at the New York State Department of Health, has developed a check-valve technique that uses polypropylene bird netting as a bat-proofing tool. The stiff, structural-grade netting with a diagonal hole opening of ⅝ in. (16 mm) is available in rolls 14 ft. (4.3 m) wide and up to 3,000 ft. (914 m) long. It is sold in hardware and garden stores; you can also find sources in the Resource Appendix under "Vertebrate Management: Physical Controls" on p. 688.

Removing Bats with Bird Netting

To exclude bats from a building, hang bird netting over entry points so that it extends at least 3 ft. (0.9 m) below and to each side of each entry. The bottom edge should hang loosely one to several inches away from the building. This enables emerging bats to crawl under and out, but returning bats can't find their way back in.

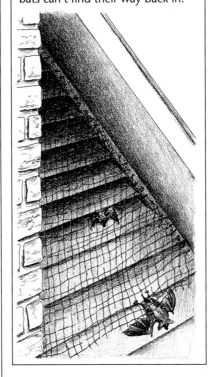

The netting is stapled or duct-taped to the structure above the exit hole. Its stiffness allows it to project clear of the hole without impeding the bats' exit. The side portions of the netting are also stapled to the structure, forming an open-bottomed box, sleeve or skirt (as shown in the drawing above). The width of the check valve depends largely on the number of holes to be covered; the length is approximately 3 ft. (0.3 m).

When bats leave the net-covered exit hole, they tumble down to the open bottom and fly off. Upon re-

---

turn, however, they are unable to find their way back through the net into the structure. After flying around the netting for a short period, they leave to find a new roosting site. After three to five days when no more bats are seen exiting the building, the netting can be removed and the holes permanently sealed. Again, always perform such work before the young have been born or after all the young can fly to avoid trapping bats inside.

4. Removing Stray Bats from the House. When a stray bat wanders into your house, before you take action it helps to understand its movements —and some of the popular misconceptions about bats. These are discussed in the sidebar on p. 311. The sidebar on p. 310 suggests two methods that should help you lead the bat back outside.

5. Traps. A wide variety of traps can be used to capture and remove resident bats from buildings before bat-proofing begins. Although all traps require assembly, many are quite simple. We recommend that you first construct artificial roosts to attract displaced or excluded bats after bat-proofing, then use traps. Various traps and their use are described further in the publication by A.M. Greenhall listed in the references.

6. Physical Repellents. Ultrasonic repelling devices are sold widely as solutions to many vertebrate pest problems. However, studies show them to be ineffective. In attic areas, floodlights that illuminate roosting sites may cause bats to leave. Drafts produced by powerful fans have also proven effective in repelling bats from established roosts.

Fiberglass insulation is one of the best materials for repelling bats, because it apparently irritates their skin. Blown-in insulation is also effective, but fiberglass batting is easier to use in areas such as between attic rafters.

7. Glue Boards. Rodent glue boards have been used effectively to capture and kill bats, but we do not recommend them, because they do nothing to adjust the habitat and

How to Remove a Stray Bat from Your House

Occasionally, a bat wanders into a room through an open window, door or damper-less fireplace. There is no cause for alarm. Migratory bats may temporarily enter buildings during their spring and fall migrations. Young bats can wander in from regular roosts in unused chimneys or elsewhere and make an appearance in rooms that are otherwise screened and closed. Bats may also come into rooms through cracks under doors and similar spaces. If a stray bat should enter a room in your house or apartment, follow this simple procedure:

I. Passive Method

1. Close the doors to other rooms, confining the bat to just one room.

2. Open all doors and windows to the outdoors. The bat will likely follow the smell of fresh air.

3. Reassure those in the room that there is no danger to them as long as they do not touch the bat.

4. Sit down, near the walls if possible, and wait for the bat to leave. Ask others in the room to remain still so the bat can leave without running into anyone.

5. If the bat is still in the house at nightfall even though you have opened all exterior doors and windows, keep the lights down low since they frighten and confuse the bat (but leave enough illumination so you can see whether the bat has left). If all else fails, the bat can be captured and actively removed from the room, as described below.

II. Active Method

1. If the passive method fails, net the bat or capture it in a small box or can (as shown at right). Place the container over the bat, then slide a stiff piece of cardboard under the bat, enclosing it in the container. However, take note: If the bat is on the ground and permits you to walk right up to it, it is probably sick, since healthy bats are not found in this position.

Don't use your hands to pick it up; use a shovel.

2. If you think that the bat is healthy, take it outside in the box and release it just as you would any other wildlife that wanders into the house by mistake. Wear thick leather gloves if the situation requires placing your hands near the bat. A frightened bat may panic and bite, even if it is not sick.

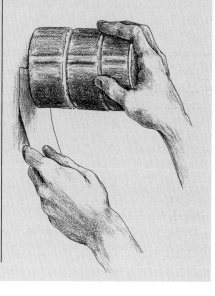

consequently do not provide permanent control. In our opinion, glue boards used against bats are inhumane, since the captured animals struggle until dead and the process of starvation may take several days. In addition, if these traps are used and forgotten or put in inaccessible places, odors and insect pests may arise from dead animals.

8. *Sticky Bird Repellents.* Sticky bird repellents (glue materials used in a manner that repels rather than traps) can play a role if used according to directions provided by vertebrate vector specialist Stephen Frantz. He recommends placing thin beads of sticky repellent in two bands an inch or so apart around or below a vertically oriented entrance hole so that bats are forced to land on the material when re-entering. Because there is only a small amount of the material, bats do not become stuck; instead they get "annoyed" by the stickiness and eventually leave the roost.

Treatment:
Direct Chemical Controls

Naphthalene, or moth flakes, is frequently recommended as a bat repellent for use in remote areas of the house. Because naphthalene fumes are quite toxic, use moth flakes only if other methods fail. Apply 5 lb. (2.25 kg) for every 2,000 cu. ft. (56.6 cu. m) of space to keep bats away, or 10 lb. (4.5 kg) to drive existing bats out. The fumes that arise from evaporation repel the bats. However, the naphthalene must be replaced every three to four weeks, so it is at best a temporary measure to force bats from a structure just prior to bat-proofing.

The convenience of naphthalene over the slower procedure recommended under habitat management should be weighed against the likelihood of vapors making their way into living quarters. And, because such a large amount must be used, the

The Logistics of Bat Flight

In his book *America's Neighborhood Bats*, Merlin Tuttle offers an explanation for why some people insist that bats have swooped down and attacked them indoors.

"In a lifetime of studying bats, I have caught and handled many thousands of individual bats, and never once have I been attacked by one—no matter how long I chased it! Although a bat flying around a room often appears to be attacking, anyone who simply stands still for a moment will quickly learn better.

"To understand the underlying reason for the bat's apparent swoops at your head, just put yourself in the same situation and imagine that you are the pilot of a small airplane. You cross the room, having to make a U-turn each time you come to a corner. When you make the turn you must virtually stop, causing a stall; and, as any pilot knows, you must quickly swoop downward to regain flight speed and control. The bottom of the swoop will occur near the middle of the room, where observers are most likely to be standing. This, of course, gives the false impression that the bat is attacking, and, given most people's preconceived ideas of bats as vicious, they run before discovering that the bat would have steered around them if they had just stood still."

Fleeing the house altogether, a common response, is not very satisfactory, as Tuttle points out. If you flee, you have no way of knowing whether the bat has found its way out of the house or wandered into another room. Some people who fear bats enough to flee have spent several apprehensive weeks wondering if the bats are still there. The best strategy is to open the windows, sit along a wall of the room, stay still and wait for the bat to leave.

Summary: Least-Toxic Bat Control

• Consider the role of bats in the biological control of mosquitoes, wasps, moths and other pestiferous insects when discussing management. The loss of bat predation on these and other pests should be weighed against killing bats or disturbing their roosts.

• Construct or remodel buildings to eliminate holes where bats can enter.

• Allow a migrating bat that enters a house temporarily to fly out by itself through open windows or doors.

• Seal out bats roosting in a structure at night after they leave to forage. Use bird netting check valves, which allow them to exit but not to re-enter.

• Bat-proof the house in spring before bats return to the nest, or in late fall, when the young and adult bats leave each night to hunt insects.

• Conserve bats to encourage insect control. Provide bat houses and help educate the public about the beneficial contributions bats make to community and agricultural pest management.

---

odor persists for a long time. Generally, the netting check valve discussed on p. 309 is more effective.

DDT and Rozolin are more hazardous chemicals that should not be used to kill bats. Such lethal materials are sometimes resorted to when "bat hysteria" is in the air. In such cases, an educational program is more cost-effective, less environmentally damaging and less of a health hazard. Toxicants applied to roosts in a home may create a hazard when the sprays, dusts or powders seep into living areas. Furthermore, using a pesticide may cause poisoned bats to scatter over a wide area before they die. This increases the potential for encounters with people and pets.

DDT, now banned in the United States, has been observed to kill bats for up to six years after a single application to an area. Some pest control professionals have attempted to use Rozolin in place of DDT. Rozolin is the trade name for an anticoagulant "tracking powder" used to kill mice and rats. Its active ingredient is diphacinone, a restricted material sold only to pest control professionals. Another rodenticidal material, chlorphacinone, is also used. The powder is applied to roosting areas, which means that bats either get it on their bodies and are killed by contact, or ingest the powder during grooming. These materials are hazardous to humans and are not regis-

tered by the EPA for bat control, although some states have authorized their experimental use.

If you want bats removed but don't want to deal with the problem yourself, we suggest that you employ pest control firms and construction personnel experienced in bat-proofing without the use of lethal controls.

REFERENCES AND READINGS

House Mice

Ebeling, W. 1975. *Urban entomology.* Los Angeles: University of California. 695 pp.

This classic text contains an excellent description of mouse biology and nontoxic control measures.

Frantz, S.C. 1980. *Integrated pest management: philosophy and basic guidelines.* Albany, N.Y.: National Association of Housing and Redevelopment Officials, September 3 and 4, 1980. 55 pp.

An excellent discussion of an IPM approach to rodent control emphasizing sanitation, pest-proofing structures and trapping.

Howard, W.E., and R.E. Marsh, 1974. Rat control manual. *Pest Control* 42(8):1-21 (also reprinted as University of California Division of Agricultural Sciences Leaflet 2896, 1976).

A pamphlet on the control of rats.

Marsh, R.E., and W.E. Howard. 1977. *The house mouse: its biology and control.* Berkeley: University of California Division of Agricultural Sciences (Leaflet 2945).

A pamphlet on the control of house mice.

Pratt, H.D., B.F. Bjornson and K.S. Littig. 1977. *Control of domestic rats and mice.* Washington, D.C.: United States Department of Health, Education and Welfare (Publication CDC77-8141). 47 pp. (This publication is no longer available from the U.S. Government. A photocopy is available from: BIRC, P.O. Box 7414, Berkeley, CA 94707.)

An excellent publication explaining how to operate a community-wide control program for suppression of rats and mice.

Pratt, H.D., and R.Z. Brown. 1976. *Biological factors in domestic rodent control.* Washington, D.C.: United States Department of Health, Education and Welfare (Publication CDC76-8144). 30 pp.

This short booklet describes the biological factors that support urban rodent populations and how control programs use this knowledge to reduce their numbers.

Timm, R. M. 1983. House mouse. In *Prevention and control of wildlife damage*, pp. B27-B44. Lincoln: University of Nebraska.

This was the source of the information on rodenticides in Table 16.4.

Spiders

Ebeling, W. 1975. *Urban entomology.*

This was the source of much of the biological description of spiders in this chapter.

Gertsch, W. J. 1979. *American spiders.* Princeton, N.J.: Van Nostrand Reinhold. 274 pp.

This book is a scholarly but never dull treatment of the spiders of North America, and includes a discussion of public-health aspects. Although the book is largely unillustrated, its two sections of brilliant color photographs are quite adequate for identifying the basic body types of different spiders.

Hite, J.M., W.J. Gladney, J.L. Lancaster and W.H. Whitcomb. 1966. *Biology of the brown recluse spider.* Fayetteville: Division of Agriculture, University of Arkansas (Bulletin 711). 26 pp.

A very useful survey of the sites where the brown recluse spider is found, and a good general study of its biology.

Smith, R.L. 1982. *Venomous animals of Arizona.* Tuscon: College of Agriculture, University of Arizona (Bulletin 8245). 134 pp.

This outstanding, well-illustrated and concise book is useful for travelers and visitors to the southwestern states and California. Alternative controls are suggested.

Bats

Barbour, R.W., and W.H. Davis. 1969. *Bats of America.* Lexington: University of Kentucky Press. 285 pp.

An authoritative text on the biology, ecology and management of bat species in North America.

Caire, W., and M.A. Ports. 1981. An adaptive method of predation by the great horned owl on Mexican free-tailed bats. *The Southwestern Naturalist* 26(1):70-71.

A short note on the behavior of the great horned owl in attacking a swarm of bats; it also lists other papers on predation on bats.

Centers for Disease Control. 1980. *Morbidity and Mortality Weekly Report* 29(23). United States Department of Health and Human Services.

This report contains data about rabies vaccinations and their effectiveness against the disease.

Clark, D.R. 1981. *Bats and environmental contaminants: a review.* Washington, D.C.: United States Department of the Interior Fish and Wildlife Service (Special Scientific Report, Wildlife No. 235). 27 pp.

A thorough review of the effects of pesticides on bats, including the direct effects of residential pesticide use and the side effects of agricultural pesticide use.

Constantine, D.G. 1979. Bat rabies and bat management. *Bulletin of the Society of Vector Ecology* 4:19.

A review of rabies in bats and methods of excluding and repelling bats. Fiberglass batting is mentioned as a repellent.

Corrigan, R.M., and G.W. Bennett. 1982. Bats, part II: exclusion provides permanent control. In *Pest Control* 50:43-46.

This article discusses exclusion as a strategy, including specific tactics and materials. It also discusses the advantages and drawbacks of repellents (naphthalene) and anticoagulants.

Frantz, S.C., and C.V. Trimarchi. 1983. Bats in human dwellings: Health concerns and management. In *Proceedings of the First Eastern Wildlife Damage Control Conference, September 27-30, 1983.* Ithaca, N.Y.: Cornell University.

A review article with numerous original observations and health-related data from New York State. This was the source for the bird netting check valve technique.

Greenhall, A.M. 1982. *House bat management.* Washington, D.C.: The United States Fish and Wildlife Service (Resource Publication 143). 33 pp.

This was the primary source for much of the information on bats. It includes good line drawings (from which excluders and traps can be constructed), keys and descriptions for identification, an excellent discussion of bat-proofing that mentions materials and sources, and a good list of references.

Greenhall, A.M. 1983. Bats. In *Prevention and control of wildlife damage,* R. M. Timm, ed., pp. D9-D22. Lincoln: University of Nebraska. (Available from: Wildlife Damage Handbook, 202 Natural Resources Hall, University of Nebraska, Lincoln, NE 68583-0819.)

This article is a shortened version of Greenhall's 1982 booklet, with some important additions, including sources for the EX100 Hanks Bat Excluder and some good black-and-white photographs. The book containing the article is the most comprehensive source currently available on managing wildlife pest problems. The groups covered include rodents, carnivores, other mammals (antelope, bats, deer), birds, reptiles, amphibians and others. Each entry covers a particular species in one or a few pages with good graphics; all entries are fully referenced. Three additional sections discuss 35 registered vertebrate pesticides, with sample labels. The book also covers exclusion devices, repellents, traps and other tools for bird and mammal control, as well as trapping techniques.

Kunz, T.H., ed. 1982. *Ecology of bats.* New York: Plenum Publications: 425 pp.

An authoritative account of the major topics in bat ecology: roosts and roosting behavior, reproduction, development, physiology, activity patterns, morphology, echo-location, foraging strategies of plant-visiting bats, coevolution of bats and plants and the ecology of bat ectoparasites.

Pratt, H. 1958. Ectoparasites of birds, bats and rodents and their control. *Pest Control* 26(10):55-56, 58, 60, 94, 96.

A discussion of bedbugs, mites and fleas that originate on bats, birds and rodent inhabitants of the home and that can attack or annoy humans.

Scott, H.G. 1961. Bats, public health importance, identification, and control. In *Pest Control* 29(8):23-26.

A short review article that lists the different diseases bats are associated with. It also contains a species list and a pictorial key to the 20 species found in the United States.

Tuttle, M.D. 1979. Twilight for the gray bat: haunted by human ignorance and superstition, an endangered species struggles to survive. *National Parks and Conservation Magazine* Oct. 1979:12-15.

This article includes a description of how vandals setting off fireworks in Alabama's Hambrick Cave probably helped destroy one of the largest colonies of the endangered gray bat, *Myotis grisescens.*

Tuttle, M.D. 1988. *America's neighborhood bats: understanding and learning to live in harmony with them.* Austin: University of Texas Press. 96 pp.

The best book on bat biology and management currently available. Tuttle is a worldwide authority on bats and heads the nonprofit Bat Conservation International in Houston.

Tuttle, M.D., and S.J. Kern. 1981. *Bats and public health.* Milwaukee: Milwaukee Public Museum Press. 11 pp.

An excellent short review of public-health concerns with bats that puts to rest the inordinate fear most people carry about them.

PART 6

Pests of Indoor Plants

CHAPTER 17
Detecting Symptoms of Indoor Plant Problems

OVERVIEW OF PART 6

For many of us, our degree of success with house plants contributes significantly to our sense of whether or not we have a "green thumb." The optimism we feel when buying or receiving a new container plant often gives way to dismay as its leaves yellow and drop or an insect infestation appears. The plant may be in as much shock as the owner. Most likely it has just been transported from the near-tropical commercial greenhouse environment in which it was nurtured to the very different world of the owner's living room or window sill.

The environment inside the house or home greenhouse not only represents a change from the conditions under which the plant had been growing, but it is also usually very different from the plant's native habitat, which is the natural environment in which the plant evolved. Even the commercial greenhouse, operating as it does under economic and production constraints, can usually only imperfectly mimic the species' original environment. Furthermore, horticultural varieties are often bred for color, size and perfume—characteristics other than those that help it tolerate adverse conditions. Pest-repellent traits such as hairy leaves are often sacrificed for more cosmetic qualities. Thus, indoor container-grown plants are often stressed in ways that make them especially vulnerable to pest problems.

Until the early 1980s, when we started to publish information based on our own experiences in controlling pests of plants indoors, there was no publication that attempted to describe precisely how an integrated pest management (IPM) program might work in such a setting. The standard work on control of greenhouse pests, *The Pests of Protected Cultivation* by Hussey, Read and Hesling (see "References and Readings" on p. 325), relies almost exclusively on toxic pesticides for control.

Even now, although a number of small booklets and two major books have appeared on the subject of biological control methods for plants indoors, none covers all the most common worldwide pests and ways you can manage them when they occur together. And, with only one exception *(What's Eating Your Houseplants?* by W. Jordan), this literature is all oriented toward the greenhouse manager, not the house-plant owner.

We mention this at the start of this part of the book so you will understand that there are few tested answers to many of the questions about how to interpret or apply results from work with large indoor plant collections to the relatively small collections of plants we grow in our homes and offices. However, by reading the background material we provide here, you should be able to tailor these procedures and concepts to fit your own setting, as we have for ours.

In our experience, successful management of plants indoors means re-creating as suitable an environment as possible and compensating where this cannot be done with various modifications of the environment. The key to creating a suitable environment is combining a basic understanding of the plant's biological requirements with a correct diagnosis of the symptoms of distress.

To help you do this, Chapter 17 describes the most common symptoms of environmental stress and attack by disease pathogens, mites and insects. Chapter 18 focuses on treatment strategies and tactics that maintain the overall health of plants indoors, since the care indoor plants receive is sometimes the deciding factor in how well they can withstand soil pathogens and infestations of insects and mites. Chapter 19 discusses various ways in which you can prepare yourself and your home, sun porch or greenhouse for an IPM program that de-emphasizes toxic chemical controls and replaces them with less toxic methods. Chapter 20 covers in detail each of the common insect and mite pests of plants grown indoors.

INTRODUCTION

When a house plant begins to look sickly, most people want to know why. The answer is often complex. The visible symptoms, even large numbers of insects, may be the result of more than one factor affecting the overall health of the plant. Unfortunately, by the time these symptoms are really obvious it is often too late to do anything to save the specimen. But you can learn from the experience and avoid a similar disaster the next time.

The most important thing that you can learn is to inspect every new plant that enters your household or greenhouse; the next most important thing is learning how to monitor your plants on a regular basis for symptoms of distress.

PLANT INSPECTION

You should inspect each new plant at the time of purchase; follow this with a more thorough inspection when you get home. Gifts from friends and relations should receive the same scrutiny as specimens you buy or grow yourself (although not in front of the donor if that might endanger your relationship).

Begin at the top of the plant and work slowly downward, checking the undersides of the leaves, crevices in the bark, leaf axils and other places favored by insects, mites and plant pathogens. Use a hand lens or other magnifier to examine more closely anything that appears suspicious. It is a good idea to wash off new plants with water. You can use a hose outdoors, set the plant in the shower or invert it at the sink and dunk it (see p. 344 for details on this procedure). Then set the new plants off by themselves for a few days, even if they pass the first inspection. Check them again before adding them to your established collection.

Many experts advise regular monthly or bimonthly rinsing of all house plants. This is a good idea not only because it keeps plants looking

Symptoms Caused by Horticultural or Environmental Conditions

To use this key and the keys on pp. 319-323, read through the symptoms until you find one that matches the plant problem you are observing. The information below each symptom tells more about the problem, then refers you to the section in this or the next three chapters that can help you solve it.

Symptoms: Lower leaves turn yellow and drop off one by one. Algae form on clay pots and soil surface.
Probable Cause: Too much water for the amount of drainage and light. Waterlogged soils low in oxygen, which plant roots need. (Plant pathogens that cause root rot multiply under these conditions.)
What to Do: Increase light by moving plant closer to window. Improve drainage by removing crockery or any other obstruction from hole in bottom of pot and by elevating pot above drainage saucer. Increase intervals between watering. Repot and prune back.
See: Habitat Modification: light (pp. 327-328), drainage (pp. 330-331). Horticultural Controls (pp. 332-341).

Symptoms: Many leaves fall off suddenly.
Probable Cause: Sudden temperature change.
What to Do: Protect plant from open windows. Move away from heating vents and air conditioners. Repot and prune back.
See: Habitat Modification: temperature (pp. 331-332).

Symptoms: Leaf tips turn brown and dry. White crust appears on soil surface and outside of clay pot.
Probable Cause: Too much fertilizer or chlorine salts building up in growing medium, the latter resulting from drainage water re-entering pot and evaporating from soil surface after watering.
What to Do: Water thoroughly to dissolve and flush away salts. Clean pot; repot in fresh soil medium. Elevate pot above drainage water. Fertilize less frequently with weaker concentration of nutrients. Let water stand overnight before watering to evaporate chlorine, or distill or boil water (but make sure you cool water before using).
See: Habitat Modification: drainage (pp. 330-331), salts (p. 331). Horticultural Controls: fertilizing (pp. 332-336).

Symptoms: New growth pale green, stems weak.
Probable Cause: Not enough light or too much nitrogen.
What to Do: Move plant closer to light. Decrease fertilization and select fertilizer with less nitrogen (N) in proportion to phosphorus (P) and potassium (K). Prune back weak growth.
See: Horticultural Controls: fertilizing (pp. 333-336).

Symptoms: Leaves look dry and papery, some edges curled under, some leaves yellow, some brown spots between leaf veins or along edges where tissue has died.
Probable Cause: Too much heat and/or not enough humidity. If symptoms are worse on side toward light, too much direct sun.
What to Do: Increase humidity by misting periodically and placing free water in pans between plants or under pots. Elevate pots on pebbles so roots don't drown. Group plants together. Move plants out of strong light or create some shade for them.
See: Habitat Modification: humidity (pp. 328-330).

Symptoms: Small water-soaked blisters develop randomly over leaf surface, most noticeable on older leaves. Blisters eventually become corky.
Probable Cause: Nonparasitic oedema.
What to Do: Move plant to more shaded location, since condition is probably reaction to overly intense sunlight.
See: Habitat Modification: light (pp. 327-328).

Symptoms: New leaves distorted, sometimes yellow. Older leaves may be yellow in spots, brown areas of dead tissue may appear at tips and along sides of leaves.
Probable Cause: Phytotoxic response (the reaction of a plant to something it finds poisonous) to soap, oils or other chemical controls used on plant.
What to Do: Rinse plant thoroughly with plain water. Reduce concentration of phytotoxic material in future applications and rinse off sooner after use. Apply chemical controls when temperatures are cool.
See: Direct Chemical Controls (pp. 343-344) and the appropriate pest insect or mite discussion in Chapter 20.

clean and shiny, but also because it helps rid their foliage of dust that clogs stomata (pores) on the leaves. These pores allow the plant to take in oxygen and give off carbon dioxide during respiration and carry out the opposite exchange when using sunlight to make sugar and build tissues during photosynthesis.

Regular bathing of plants also provides the perfect opportunity to monitor for overall health and check for any new insect or mite populations. If you catch these populations at the early stage, you can usually eliminate them by pruning out the affected part of the plant, modifying environmental factors or horticultural routines, or destroying the insects by squashing them or dabbing them with alcohol or soap and water. Also check for salt buildup on the pot or soil and see whether the plant shows good leaf color.

PLANT MONITORING: DIAGNOSTIC KEYS

To help you determine which of many possible factors may be causing the suspicious symptoms you observe during monitoring, we have devised three symptom keys. These keys treat: (a) problems caused by the way you care for the plant, including the environment in which you have placed it; (b) problems caused by observable insects and mites; and (c) problems caused by certain plant pathogens (which cause disease). We have made a somewhat artificial distinction between the first category and the other two, since plant care and the general environment are inevitably involved in the other two categories of problems. The keys are followed by a sidebar on pp. 323-324 on the biology and dissemination of plant pathogens.

To use the keys, read through the symptoms until you find one that matches the plant problem you are observing. The information below each symptom tells more about the problem, then refers you to the section in this or the next three chapters that can help you solve it.

Symptoms of Mite and Insect Presence[a]

Symptoms: Stippling on leaves in the form of tiny yellow or white spots (but no brown or black spots). Leaves turn pale green or yellowish. Webs appear in leaf axils, between leaves or in branch crotches. Hand lens reveals tiny moving dots.
Probable Cause: Spider mites.
What to Do: Isolate infested plant from other plants. Wash off thoroughly with soap and water or insecticidal soap. Purchase and release predatory mites periodically.
See: Mites (pp. 358-363).

Symptoms: Leaves silvery with brown flecks or stippling. Leaf surface looks as if top layer of cells has been scraped away. Hand lens reveals very small dark brown or cream-colored insects with straight bodies and no easily visible wings or legs.
Probable Cause: Thrips.
What to Do: Mist plants frequently. Moisture on greenhouse floor is helpful in controlling some species. In the greenhouse, use blue sticky traps to capture adults. Wash periodically with insecticidal soap or soap and horticultural oil in morning or evening when temperatures are cool (check product label for specifics). Purchase and release commercially available mite predators of thrips.
See: Thrips (pp. 363-367).

Symptoms: Small green, black, brown, yellow or pinkish insects with or without wings clearly visible on buds, undersides of leaves, at leaf base and along stem. Leaves glisten with sticky honey-like material, which may attract ants.
Probable Cause: Aphids.
What to Do: Wash plant with insecticidal soap or use growth regulator, if available. Exclude ants, or poison with baits. In well-screened greenhouses, introduce commercially available lady beetles, lacewings or aphid-eating gall midges (*Aphidoletes* spp.). Or establish colony of gall midges by collecting larvae from outdoors in summer. To improve egg-laying rate of predators, feed yeast and sugar-based bee food to lady beetles and lacewings on stands protected from ants. The artificial diet (Wheast™, Formula 57™) augments their diet of aphids.
See: Aphids (pp. 367-375).

[a] For a full discussion of each organism, see Chapter 20. Note that when the use of natural enemies is mentioned, the recommendation may require placing house plants in a gauze tent (see p. 343) or screening greehouses, sun porches, conservatories or other enclosed "plantscapes."

Symptoms: Brown, white or yellow oval bumps along stems, branches, leaf midribs or undersides. Leaves glisten with sticky honey-like material, which may attract ants.
Probable Cause: Scales.
What to Do: Gently rub off scales with finger or cotton swab. Use hand lens to determine when scale crawlers (young scales) are ready to migrate away from mother scales. Use insecticidal soap or summer-weight dormant oil spray when crawlers are out. Exclude ants or poison them with baits. Have the scale identified. For species in the black-scale group, release commercially available black-scale parasitoids.
See: Scales (pp. 375-378).

Symptoms: Cottony fuzz appears in leaf axils, along stems or in leaf midribs. Leaves glisten with sticky honey-like material, which may attract ants.
Probable Cause: Mealybugs.
What to Do: Use cotton swab or small brush with rubbing alcohol to kill small localized infestations. Prune off severely infested areas. Wash plant with insecticidal soap. Exclude ants or poison them with baits. Periodically purchase and release mealybug predators.
See: Mealybugs (pp. 379-384).

Symptoms: Small white-winged insects cluster on leaves and fly up when leaves shaken.
Probable Cause: Whiteflies.
What to Do: Wipe or vacuum off adults when temperature is low and flies are cold and relatively immobile. Wash plant with insecticidal soap or use growth regulator. In the greenhouse, put up yellow sticky traps to catch adults. Periodically release commercially available whitefly parasitoids.
See: Whiteflies (pp. 384-388).

Symptoms: Wriggly, irregular, pale lines or blotches on leaves.
Probable Cause: Leafminers.
What to Do: For small plantings, hand-pick to remove infested leaves. Catch adults with yellow sticky (whitefly) type traps or Pherocon® leafminer traps. Release commercially available parasitoids. For large plantings, spray neem oil, methoprene or horticultural oils to supplement trapping and parasitoid release in "hot spots" where infestations have survived parasitoids.
See: Leafminers (pp. 388-393).

Symptoms: Bulb plants, corm plants or other plants wilt suddenly, although soil is moist. Plant may be loose in pot because roots have been eaten off (afflicted cyclamen plants, for example, can be lifted clear of their pots by wilted foliage). White grubs may be seen in soil or among roots.
Probable Cause: Black vine weevils.
What to Do: Discard infested plant. Usually by the time the symptoms are noticed, plant is beyond saving. To prevent future infestations, screen and weatherstrip porches and greenhouses, place sticky barriers on greenhouse table legs and/or place pots above specially constructed ant stands. Where infestations are common, treat pots four times a year with insect-eating nematodes.
See: Black vine weevils (pp. 393-395).

Symptoms: Small, fragile, mosquito-like flies hover around plants when plants are disturbed or collect at windows. There may be some wilting of seedlings grown in soil with organic material added.
Probable Cause: Fungus gnats.
What to Do: Drench soil with *Bacillus thuringiensis israelensis* (BTI), methoprene or insect-eating nematodes. Use "trap crop" of sprouted wheat to attract gnats; dispose of it outside or by immersing in boiling water.
See: Fungus gnats (pp. 395-398).

Symptoms of Disease[a]

Symptoms: Spots with angular margins appear on leaf. Initially spots are water-soaked and yellowish, later turning dark brown with reddish-brown margins and diffuse chlorotic (pale yellow-green) halos. Small spots may merge and become large, angular blotches between veins. Affected leaves appear rotted and wilted. Stems not affected.
Probable Cause: Bacterial leaf spot *(Pseudomonas, Xanthomonas* spp.).[b]
What to Do: Prune off infected leaves and discard carefully so spores are not spread. Improve air circulation around plant to reduce humidity. Keep irrigation water off leaves, since pathogen needs wet foliage to infect plant. Water early in day so foliage dries before nightfall.
See: Sidebar (pp. 323-324): bacterial leaf spot. Habitat Modification: humidity (pp. 328-330). Horticultural Controls (pp. 332-341). Physical Controls: pruning and discarding infected plant debris (p. 342).

Symptoms: Leaves reduced in size and pale yellow in color; may have small, irregular, water-soaked areas. Spot enlarges rapidly, develops water-filled blisters, then leaf and petiole tissue may collapse into soft, slimy mass. Stems have lesions that are water-soaked, soft and greyish at first, becoming pale brown and sunken later. Clear line between infected and healthy tissues on stem.
Probable Cause: Bacterial leaf and stem rot *(Erwinia* spp.).
What to Do: If symptoms appear over large area of plant, it probably cannot be saved and should be discarded carefully so spores are not spread. If only a small part of plant appears infected, prune back infected stems to healthy tissue and dispose of infected parts so spores are not spread. Increase air circulation around plant. Water early in morning, keeping water off foliage. Keep plant on dry side. Keep insects off plant, since they spread the disease.
See: Sidebar (pp. 323-324): bacterial leaf and stem rot. Habitat Modification: humidity (pp. 328-330). Horticultural Controls: watering (pp. 337-341). Physical Controls: pruning and discarding infected plant debris (p. 342).

Symptoms: Brown, water-soaked spots on flowers or leaves. Spots may become covered with coating of woolly grey fungus spores, especially if humidity is high.
Probable Cause: Grey mold *(Botrytis* spp.).
What to Do: Prune off infected flowers or leaves and discard carefully so spores are not spread. Increase spacing between plants. Provide cross-ventilation or use fan to improve air circulation. Raise temperature above 70°F (21°C), reduce humidity below 80% to 85%. Use immersion watering method to avoid splashing water on leaves, since spores are spread by water. Make sure soil mix is well-drained.
See: Sidebar (pp. 323-324): grey mold. Horticultural Controls: soil mixes (p. 333), watering (pp. 337-341). Physical Controls: pruning and discarding infected plant debris (p. 342). Chemical Controls: fungicidal soap, sodium hypochlorite (bleach) solution (pp. 343-344).

Symptoms: Leaves develop small, yellowish round spots. Spots enlarge, develop prominent reddish-brown centers and yellow halos.
Probable Cause: Fungal leaf spot. Spots irregularly shaped with reddish centers and yellow halo: *Fusarium moniliforme.* Spots on young leaves with reddish-brown to yellow border and centers that become grey and papery, spots on older leaves with concentric ring patterns: *Cephalosporium* spp. Spots minute, slightly elevated on undersides of leaves: *Cercospora* spp. Spots irregularly shaped, tan or straw-colored, surrounded by water-soaked margins: *Phytophthora* spp.
What to Do: Prune off infected leaves and discard in a way that does not spread spores. Repot in pasteurized, well-drained soil mix. Avoid fertilizer with excessive nitrogen, because it stimulates disease spread. Irrigate so water does not splash onto leaves, spreading fungal spores. Improve air circulation. Syringe leaves with household bleach solution or fungicidal soap.
See: Sidebar (pp. 323-324): fungal leaf spot. Habitat Modification: humidity (pp. 328-330). Horticultural Controls (pp. 332-341). Physical Controls: pruning

[a] Descriptions of symptoms are adapted primarily from McCain, 1979.
[b] For information on the biology and dissemination of the plant pathogens mentioned here, refer to the sidebar on plant pathogens (pp. 323-324).

and discarding infected plant debris (p. 342). Chemical Controls: sodium hypochlorite (bleach) solution, fungicidal soap (pp. 343-344).

Symptoms: Plant wilts, stem tissue at soil line or just below looks water-soaked, then turns brown or black. Stem becomes completely girdled (the surface tissues are damaged or removed).
Probable Cause: Fungal stem rot. Brown threads visible on leaves or soil: *Rhizoctonia* spp. No hyphae (thread-like branching bodies of the mycelium of a fungus) visible: *Phythophthora* or other spp.
What to Do: If symptoms are visible on stem, plant probably cannot be saved. Discard in a manner that does not spread spores. If plant is not rotted around entire circumference, you might be able to save it by gently removing from pot and letting roots air-dry until root ball is barely moist. Prune off dead or discolored roots, repot in pasteurized, well-drained soil mix. Set plant in area with good air circulation. Water with household bleach solution. Adjust regular watering to keep root ball barely moist, not soggy.
See: Sidebar (pp. 323-324): fungal stem rot. Horticultural Controls: soil mixes (p. 333), fertilizing (pp. 333-336), watering (pp. 337-341). Physical Controls: pruning and discarding infected plant debris (p. 342). Chemical Controls: sodium hypochlorite (bleach) solution (pp. 343-344).

Symptoms: Leaves, stems and/or flowers have surface coating of grey-white powdery substance (mycelium) that can be rubbed off. Black specks may later develop in grey-white powder. Plant tissue under powdery coating may remain green, while the surrounding leaf tissue is yellow, creating green-island effect.
Probable Cause: Powdery mildew, many species.
What to Do: Prune off infected plant parts and discard carefully so spores do not spread. Improve air circulation—e.g., move plants farther apart or use fan—to reduce humidity at leaf surface, or syringe leaves with soapy water early in morning to drown mildew spores. Dust leaves with sulfur or spray with lime sulfur, an antitranspirant, a fungicidal soap or sodium hypochlorite (bleach) solution.

See: Sidebar (pp. 323-324): powdery mildew. Horticultural Controls (pp. 332-341). Physical Controls: pruning and discarding infected plant debris (p. 342). Chemical Controls: sulfur, antitranspirants, fungicidal soap, sodium hypochlorite (bleach) solution (pp. 343-344).

Symptoms: Plant wilts despite moist soil; leaves yellow and/or drop off, roots turn watery, then blacken and rot.
Probable Cause: Fungal root rot (*Pythium* spp.).
What to Do: Gently remove plant from pot and examine roots. If brownish or black, cut off damaged roots, leaving white-colored roots intact. Let remaining root ball air-dry overnight. Repot in pasteurized soil mix in sterilized porous container. Water once or twice with household bleach solution. Avoid extremes of wet or dry soil when watering.
See: Sidebar (pp. 323-324): fungal root rot. Horticultural Controls: soil mixes (p. 333), watering (pp. 337-341). Physical Controls: pruning and discarding infected plant debris (p. 342). Chemical Controls: sodium hypochlorite (bleach) solution (pp. 343-344).

Symptoms: Surface of leaves or flowers covered with black powdery material growing on sticky drops of honeydew (the secretion of aphids, mealybugs, etc., derived from plant sap).
Probable Cause: Sooty mold (*Capnodium* spp.).
What to Do: Wash leaves with soapy water to remove honeydew and mold. (Sooty mold does not feed on plants, only on mold; thus, it does not harm plants except indirectly by filtering sunlight from leaf surfaces and impeding photosynthesis.) Identify insect pest producing honeydew and reduce insect population. Ants that may be present (they collect honeydew produced by the pest insects) should be excluded, since they protect pest insects from natural enemies.
See: Sidebar (pp. 323-324): sooty mold. Appropriate pest insect in Chapter 20.

Symptoms: Plant wilts, stem water-soaked and discolored brownish-black at soil line, lower leaves rotted. Mass of white thread-like strands (mycelia) visible at or below soil line.
Probable Cause: Southern blight *(Sclerotium rolfsii)*.
What to Do: Discard plant in a manner that does not spread spores. Improve air circulation around remaining plants. Make sure soil mix is well drained. Consider reducing amount and frequency of watering to prevent re-occurrence of blight.
See: Sidebar (pp. 323-324): Southern blight. Horticultural Controls: soil mixes (p. 333),

fertilizing (pp. 333-336), watering (pp. 337-341). Physical Controls: pruning and discarding infected plant debris (p. 342).

Symptoms: Young leaves look distorted. Concentric yellowish rings, sometimes with dead tissue in center, appear on leaves.
Probable Cause: Ring spot virus.
What to Do: No treatment. Discard plant.
See: Physical Controls: discarding infected plant debris (p. 342).

Biology and Dissemination of Plant Pathogens[a]

Bacterial leaf spot
(Family Pseudomonodaceae:
Pseudomonas and *Xanthomonas* spp.):
Small, rod-shaped organisms with polar flagella (whip-like appendages) that are mobile in water. Live in soil or water as saprophytes (decomposers), becoming parasitic when they enter plant tissue. Land on wet leaves, multiply in film or drops of water and penetrate leaf through stomata and wounds. A circular, yellowish-green halo surrounds each lesion. Affected tissues in center of each lesion collapse and die. Overwinter in soil, on plant debris and on seeds.

Bacterial leaf and stem rot
(Family Enterobacteriaceae: *Erwinia* spp.):
Small, mobile rod-shaped organisms with multiple flagella. Usually enter plants through wounds made by insects. Multiply and spread intercellularly, excreting enzymes that break down cellular tissue resulting in rot; characteristic "rotten" smell is associated with this disease. Overwinter in soil in pupae of insects or in plant parts, and can be spread by infected insects or tools.

Grey mold
(Family Moniliaceae:
Botrytis cinerea and other *Botrytis* spp.):
Egg-like, one-celled spores forming grape-like clusters on branched conidiophores (hyphae, or filaments, that bear asexual spores). Spores require cool

temperatures (45°F to 61°F/7°C to 16°C) and high humidity (93% RH and above) to germinate. The fungus overwinters on plants or in soil as hemispherical black sclerotia (hardened masses of hyphae). Spores develop from sclerotia when conditions are optimal, and are moved by wind or splashing water onto blossoms or young leaves, where they germinate and enter plant.

Fungal leaf spot
(Family Tuberculariaceae: *Fusarium moniliforme):*
Brightly colored spores and mycelium (the body of a fungus, made of a mass of hyphae). Branched conidiophores form slimy masses. Spores germinate when temperatures are warm, humidity is high and free water is present on leaf. Spores are moved by splashing water.

Fungal leaf spot
(Family Moniliaceae: *Cephalosporium* spp.):
Single-celled, transparent spores collected in a slime drop. Mealybugs may carry the fungus from plant to plant; fungus enters plant through wounds caused by the insect.

Fungal leaf spot
(Family Dematiaceae:
about 2,000 described *Cercospora* **species):**
Transparent to pale green or brown spores that appear attached together as a chain. Spread by

[a] Adapted in large part from Agrios, 1968, and Horst, 1979.

water, wind, tools and insects. Migrating spores land on undersides of leaves, germinate and grow into the leaf through the stomata. Two to eight weeks later, new spores develop on undersides of diseased leaves and the cycle repeats. Infections are most severe under conditions of high temperature (77°F/25°C and above) and humidity that keep stomata open. Growth is encouraged when cool nights alternate with warm days.

Fungal leaf spot, fungal root rot
(Family Pythiaceae: *Phytophthora* spp.):
Slender, branched sporangia (fungal organs that produce asexual spores) emerge from stomata on lower side of leaf. More sporangia are then formed, some of which infect leaf when germ tube (the early growth of a mycelium) is inserted through leaf cuticle or stoma. Some of these sporangia become zoospores (spores with flagella capable of moving in water) that swim about as they are splashed by water onto other leaves, finally settling on a leaf and infecting it by inserting the germ tube. Requires warm temperatures (60°F to 70°F/16°C to 21°C) and high humidity (90% RH) to germinate. Overwinters on infected plants or in the soil, especially in southeastern states. Note: Irrigation water drawn from a pond may be contaminated with this organism.

Fungal stem rot, fungal root rot
(*Rhizoctonia solani*), fungal stem rot
(Class Peronosporales: *Phytophthora* spp.):
Young mycelium colorless, with branches constricted at points of origin from main axis. Older mycelium colored reddish-brown and highly visible as mass of spiderweb-like strands. Sclerotia made up of short, irregular barrel-shaped cells. Requires high temperatures and humidity and free water to germinate. No spores are produced.

Powdery mildew
(Order Erysiphales: *Erysiphe* spp.):
Spores colorless, borne in chains on upright conidiophores, which have a characteristic white powdery effect. Mycelium appears as thick white felt made of criss-cross tangle of hyphae. Spores do not require free water to germinate. Some species require high humidity, usually provided at the leaf surface when cold nights become warm days or when plants are grown in crowded, low or shady locations without sufficient air circulation. When a mildew spore lands

on leaf and inserts its germ tube, it produces a tangle of threads on the surface. Then special sucking organs penetrate the leaf surface in search of food. Conidiophores growing at right angles from the mycelium produce one-celled spores in rows or chains. These spores are dislodged from the top of the chain and are disseminated by wind. Overwinter on living or dead plants, including bark and buds; drown in the presence of free water on leaf surfaces.

Fungal root rot, damping off
(Family Pythiaceae: *Pythium* spp.):
Smooth-walled sporangia are borne terminally, or along the mycelium. Spores occur naturally in soils as saprophytes, overwintering as mobile spores. High soil moisture stimulates germination. The optimum temperature for germination and multiplication varies depending on host-plant characteristics; in general, low temperatures (48°F/9°C and below) favor spread of fungus in warm-temperature crops, and high temperatures (65°F to 70°F/18°C to 21°C) favor its spread on cool-season crops. Rapidly growing seedlings with thin cell walls are particularly susceptible to penetration. Spores transmitted by splashing water, tools, infested soil, etc.; growth enhanced by both excessive and insufficient nitrogen.

Sooty mold
(Family Capnodiaceae: *Capnodium* spp.):
Dark-black mycelium. A saprophyte that feeds on insect excretions (honeydew) and does not infect the plant directly; damage to plant occurs when mold covers sufficient leaf area to inhibit photosynthesis.

Southern blight, crown rot
(Agnonomycetes: *Sclerotium rolfsii*):
Sclerotia very small, round, tan, about the size, shape and color of mustard seed. White mats of mycelium form at base of stem, spreading upward in somewhat fan-shaped fashion, sometimes out over the ground in wet weather. Sclerotia formed in mats are first white, later reddish tan or light brown. They may form white crust over the soil for several inches around a stem, or may be sparse and scattered. In white stage, droplets of liquid form on sclerotia; the oxalic acid in this liquid is assumed to kill plant cells in advance of the fungus hyphae; thus, the pathogen never has to penetrate living tissue, which explains why so many different kinds of plants succumb so readily.

REFERENCES AND READINGS

Agrios, G.N. 1988. *Plant pathology,* 3rd ed. New York: Academic Press. 803 pp.

This is the standard text in the field, and includes lucid descriptions of the ways in which pathogens enter plant tissue, the means by which some plant species are able to resist the attack of pathogens and other information useful in managing plant diseases.

Gill, R.J. 1982. *Five photo recognition keys to the families and common species of whiteflies, mealybugs and soft and armored scale insects of California.* Sacramento: Department of Food and Agriculture. 10 pp. (Available from: R. J. Gill, 1220 N Street, Sacramento, CA 95814.)

Five fold-out charts with color photographs and a key that is very easy to use help you identify the species of these pests you are likely to encounter in greenhouses or on house plants anywhere in the country, with the exception of a few exotics in southern Florida. This is a wonderful introduction that helps beginners recognize these insects.

Horst, R.K., ed. 1979. *Westcott's plant disease handbook.* New York: Van Nostrand Reinhold. 803 pp.

This handbook (as well as Gill's photo recognition keys mentioned above) was consulted in the preparation of the sidebar on plant pathogens on pp. 323-324. The book is very good for diagnosing a plant disease but is poor in suggesting alternatives to toxic materials.

Hussey, N.W., W.H. Read and J.J. Hesling. 1969. *The pests of protected cultivation.* New York: American Elsevier Publishing. 404 pp.

For many years this has been the standard overview of pest problems of plants in indoor environments. The biological information and photographs are quite inclusive and very useful. The control information is oriented strictly toward conventional pesticides used between 1955 and 1970, many of which are still in common use in commercial greenhouses.

Jordan, W. 1977. *What's eating your houseplants?* Emmaus, Pa.: Rodale Press. 229 pp.

This book, originally published as *Windowsill Ecology,* provides a comprehensive discussion of biological control of indoor plant pests in a straightforward and entertaining style. Excellent photos and line drawings illustrate the insects, equipment and methods described. The book is an invaluable tool for people who are serious about nontoxic pest management of indoor plants. Unfortunately, as of this writing, it is out of print. Look for it in your library.

Kono, T., and C.S. Papp. 1977. *Handbook of agricultural pests: aphids, thrips, mites, snails, and slugs.* Sacramento: California Department of Food and Agriculture (Available from: Laboratory Services-Entomology, 1220 N Street, Sacramento, CA 98514). 205 pp.

This handbook, primarily for specialists, is very helpful in identifying common thrips, spider mites and aphids encountered on indoor plants. It also makes suggestions on how to prepare specimens for identification.

McCain, A.H. 1979. Disease of foliage plants. *California Plant Pathology,* No. 45. Berkeley: University of California Cooperative Extension. 13 pp.

A useful pamphlet for recognizing symptoms of plant diseases.

Smith, M.D. 1982. *The Ortho problem solver.* San Francisco: Ortho Information Services. 1,022 pp.

The section on house plants has outstanding photographs that help you identify pest problems, and the appendix contains a good list of house plants that are sensitive to salts. Not surprisingly, the management recommendations serve primarily to promote the use of Ortho products, but a great deal of useful horticultural information is also provided in a concise format.

CHAPTER 18
General Management Strategies for House Plant Problems

INTRODUCTION

A house plant living in splendid isolation in its own flowerpot experiences an environment that is extremely simple compared to its natural habitat. Consider the reduced range of climate and the smaller number of plant, insect and microbial competitors in the container's soil. This lack of ecosystem diversity indoors may actually aggravate pest and disease problems, since the natural enemies of plant pathogens, insects and mites are usually not present. For this reason, effective pest and disease management inside a house may be more difficult to achieve than in the greenhouse or garden.

If a house plant is suffering from insect or mite infestations, the fastest way you can introduce naturally occurring biological controls is by moving it outdoors. If the plant is small enough and you have a protected outdoor environment where it can spend a few weeks or even months, you are fortunate. The spot should be semishaded, warm, sheltered from winds and, if possible, surrounded by other plants.

The conservatory of the Victorian era represented an attempt to restore some of this environmental diversity indoors. The modern greenhouse, whether attached to living quarters or located in the garden, also offers an opportunity to diversify the environment and simulate the natural habitat of the plants. Tropical and semitropical species can flourish almost as well in greenhouses as in their native homes when given adequate humidity, planted in deep containers or in the ground itself and given the appropriate level of shade or light.

Low levels of plant-feeding insects and mites are more easily tolerated in large plant collections in conservatories and home greenhouses than they are on individual plants on home windowsills or in greenhouses that raise potted plants for sale. In large collections the pests are less visible among abundant foliage; they are also present at more stages of their life cycle because of the variety of plants available at various points in their annual cycles. These plant-feeding insects and mites can support a correspondingly complex population of the predators and parasitoids that feed upon them. The result is less toxic, more consistent suppression of the pest population than can be achieved with pesticides alone. Botanic garden display greenhouses, such as the San Francisco Conservatory of Flowers in Golden Gate Park, that have stable, long-lived plantings among which more ephemeral seasonal displays are rotated can arrive at a remarkably diverse and stable system indoors if managed properly.

Because it is often inconvenient to move every house plant outdoors for the warm parts of the year, management strategies must address the plant's indoor environment. The limiting factors for plants indoors are usually light, drainage, humidity and temperature, in that order (see the discussion of limiting factors on p. 49). But the amount of habitat modification that can be carried out has limits, too. Since different species and varieties within species show variation in their adaptability to less-than-perfect conditions, it is wise to give some thought to house plant selection initially.

Since light and temperature are the most energy-consuming and costly of the limiting factors to modify, you should select plants that are by nature suited to the light and temperature levels of the areas in which you plan to grow them. Tables 18.1 and 18.2 on pgs. 328 and 329 list common house plants that can endure the low light conditions in most homes. To learn the requirements of plants you already have, consult a good house plant encyclopedia such as the *Book of House Plants* by Joan Lee Faust, *Foliage House Plants* and *Flowering House Plants* by James Crockett and the editors of Time-Life Books, or *Rodale's Encyclopedia of Indoor Gardening* by A.M. Halpin.

HABITAT MODIFICATION

Only certain varieties of plants grow successfully under the reduced light conditions of the average room interior or windowsill. Those marketed commercially for such settings are often plants that developed originally on the forest floor or in the shade of other plants. Cacti and certain succulents that need fairly strong light appreciate low humidity. The venus flytrap and other bog plants suitable for terrariums and semiaquatic greenhouse settings can endure waterlogged soils. But these are exceptions. In general, the native shaded forest floor environments of the typical house plant are high in humidity, have excellent drainage, are low in soluble salts (such as those found in commercial fertilizers and chlorine-treated tap water) and like an even temperature. These are the conditions you must attempt to reproduce if you want to relieve some of the stress experienced by the average container-bound house plant. Let us look at how you might meet these typical requirements, starting with the management of light levels.

Light

In *Foliage House Plants*, James Crockett describes the difference between natural light outside and light likely to be encountered inside the home:

> Outdoors, the summer sun at midday may produce as much as 10,000 or 12,000 foot-candles of light....Inside a house, however, plants in a sunny window may receive only 4,000 or 5,000 foot-candles, and a few feet from the window the level may drop to 200 footcandles or less. Still farther away the average light may range between 10 and 100 footcandles (a book can be read comfortably in illumination of 50 footcandles or less).

Skylights raise the light level in a room significantly, and a greenhouse with glass or translucent plastic paneling for walls and ceiling can come

Table 18.1
Common House Plants that Tolerate
Very Low Light Levels (50 to 150 footcandles)[a, b]

Scientific Name	Common Name
Aglaonema commutatum var. elegans	silver Chinese evergreen
Aspidistra elatior	cast iron plant
Chamaedorea elegans	neanthe bella palm; parlor palm
Cordyline terminalis var. Baby Ti	baby-doll dracaena
C. terminalis var. Ti	Hawaiian good-luck plant
Crassula argentea	jade plant
Dracaena deremensis var. Janet Craig	Janet Craig dracaena
D. deremensis cv. Warneckii[c]	Warneckii dracaena
D. fragrans cv. Massangeana	corn plant
D. surculosa	gold-dust dracaena
Epipremnum aureum (*Scindapsus aureus*)	devil's ivy; golden pothos
Fatsia juponica	Japanese aralia
Hedera helix	English ivy
Maranta leuconeura var. kerchoviana	green prayer plant
M. leuconeura var. massangeana	red prayer plant
Monstera deliciosa	split-leaf philodendron
Nepthytis afzelii (*Syngonium podophyllum*)	nepthytis
Philodendron miduhoi	silver-sheen philodendron
P. scandens subsp. oxycardium	cordatum philodendron
P. scandens subsp. scandens forma	velvet-leaf philodendron
Spathiphyllum cv. Clevelandii	white anthurium, peace lily
S. wallisii	peace lily
S. cv. Mauna Loa	white flag

[a] Compiled from Gaines, 1977, and Pierce, 1977.

[b] One footcandle is equal to the amount of light cast by a candle on a surface 1 ft. (30 cm) away.

[c] cv = cultivated variety

very close to duplicating outdoor light conditions. Crockett describes how to use the exposure meter of a camera to gauge the light level in footcandles; he also provides several useful charts for calculating the light levels produced by fluorescent lamps and incandescent (regular nonfluorescent) bulbs at different distances from the bulbs. Artificial lighting may be justified under certain conditions, such as when you are starting seedlings indoors during a dark, rainy spring, or when you want to force plants to bloom at specified times by extending the period of light in imitation of the longer days of late spring and early summer.

However, neither incandescent nor fluorescent light begins to approximate the full light spectrum of the sun. To some extent, the two complement each other and are usually used together (at one watt of incandescent light for every two of fluorescent). You can use full-spectrum light fixtures where their extra cost and energy consumption are justified, but even these really do not duplicate the natural light conditions of the outdoor garden.

Thus, all other aspects of indoor plant environments must be adjusted to the decreased light conditions. Particularly during the darker months, other factors that favor rapid plant growth—temperature, soil moisture and plant nutrients, especially nitrogen—should be modified. In general, when light intensity is very low, plants should be grown very slowly and kept close to the resting state. Therefore it should be cool—68°F to 70°F (20°C to 21°C)—and the soil should be slightly drier than during the active growing season. Regular fertilization should be omitted during darker seasons.

Buying plants already acclimatized to low light conditions can minimize or prevent shock, including dropping of leaves and other visual symptoms experienced by plants that are moved from the greenhouse into darker residential environments (see the discussion of horticultural controls on pp. 332-341).

Humidity
Inside the greenhouse, especially where automatic mist systems are used, excessive humidity can be a problem because it can cause fungus diseases to multiply. With the extra moisture, small flies, fungus gnats, fungus-eating mites, snails, slugs and millipedes may all begin to increase noticeably. In the house, however, quite the opposite is true. Generally the home environment is very dry, ranging between 10% and 30% hu-

midity. There are exceptions to this low indoor humidity, such as when it is raining or it is very humid outdoors and the house is unheated.

Presumably, until the invention of central forced-air heating, humans experienced indoor humidity that was more similar to the natural humidity outdoors. Thus, it was fairly damp indoors during rainy or cold periods. Moist conditions indoors encourage many common pests of people, clothes and pets. House dust mites, fleas, silverfish, other insects and molds all thrive where humidity is high.

If you have been reading the chapters of this book consecutively, you will know that we have been urging you to reduce indoor humidity to reduce indoor pest problems. One potential problem, however, is that humans are among the living organisms that suffer in extremely dry environments. The low humidity caused by many home heating systems in winter is thought to influence susceptibility to colds in humans. The mucus membranes of the nasal passages may dry and become irritated by the air, making them more vulnerable to virus invasions. And low humidity indoors can produce annoying discharges of static electricity when one walks across a rug and then touches metal—a doorknob, for example.

The dry conditions that cause difficulty for humans may put even more stress on house plants. With the exception of cacti and other true desert-dwellers, most common house plants prefer humidity between 70% and 90%. How can you create a more humid environment for plants indoors? Usually, increased watering is not the answer (see the discussion of drainage on pp. 330-331). An equally important question is how to create a more humid environment for plants without simultaneously increasing humidity in areas where indoor pests —such as immature flea larvae and silverfish—thrive. The answer is spot treatment. You must create a suitable environment for the plants where

Table 18.2
Common House Plants that Tolerate Low to Medium Light Levels (150 to 500 footcandles)[a, b]

Scientific Name	Common Name
Araucaria heterophylla	Norfolk Island pine
Brassaia actinophylla	schefflera, umbrella tree
Caladium bicolor	fancy-leafed caladium
Chamaedorea erumpens	bamboo palm
C. seifrizii	reed palm
Chlorophytum comosum	green spider plant
C. comosum cv. Vittatum	variegated spider plant
Chrysalidocarpus lutescens	areca palm
Cissus antarctica	kangaroo vine
Cissus cv. Ellen Danica	oak-leaf ivy
C. rhombifolia	grape ivy
Coffea arabica	Arabian coffee plant
Cycas circinalis	queen sago palm
C. revoluta	king sago palm
Cyperus alternifolius	umbrella plant
Cyrtomium falcatum Rochfordianum	holly fern
Davallia trichomanoides	rabbit's-foot fern
Dieffenbachia amoena	giant dumb cane
Dracaena amoena var. Tropic Snow	tropic snow cane
D. angustifolia var. honoriae	honoriae dracaena or pleomele
D. marginata	Madagascar dragon tree
D. reflexa	dracaena pleomele
Ficus benjamina	weeping fig
F. elastica cv. Decora	broad-leaved Indian rubber plant
F. lyrata	fiddle-leaf fig
F. retusa	Indian laurel
Howea forsterana	kentia palm
Nephrolepis exaltata cv. Bostoniensis	Boston fern
N. exaltata cv. Fluffy Ruffles	fluffy-ruffle fern
Pandanus utilis	common screw pine
Philodendron selloum	tree-like philodendron
P. x Red Emerald	red emerald philodendron
Plectranthus australis	Swedish ivy
Podocarpus gracilior	fern pine
Polyscias balfouriana	Balfour aralia
P. filicifolia	fern-leaf aralia
P. fruticosa	Ming aralia
Rumohra adiantiformis	leatherleaf fern
Sansevieria trifasciata	snake plant
Soleirolia soleirolii/Helxine soleirolii	baby's tears
Tolmiea menziesii	piggyback plant
Tradescantia albiflora	wandering Jew

[a] Compiled from Gaines, 1977, and Pierce, 1977.
[b] One footcandle is equal to the amount of light cast by a candle on a surface 1ft. (30 cm) away.

they are located without raising the overall humidity of the house. Several techniques are helpful in increasing humidity around plants:

• Cluster potted plants. Since each plant releases water vapor from its leaves, a group of plants multiplies the amount of air moisture in the immediate environment; the combined foliage helps contain that moisture.

• Set pans or bowls of water among the potted plants, on radiators or in front of heating vents. The purpose is to have free water evaporate into the air as the temperature rises each day without having the water pass through the medium in which the plants are set. Note: Placing the pots in saucers of water is not advisable, because it encourages root rot and the accumulation of chlorine and other salts from the water and fertilizer. However, as long as the pot containing the plant is elevated above the water on gravel or other supports so that the water in the pans cannot enter the soil, the pans of water can be located beneath the plants (see the drawing at right).

• Mist the plants once or twice a week. Water drops on the leaves not only increase the humidity, they also help reduce populations of spider mites and thrips, which prefer drier conditions. During very dry periods, an automatic cold-mist unit, such as the one sold for sickroom use, may be focused on a group of plants that are particularly susceptible to dryness.

Whereas low humidity can be troublesome in winter, high humidity can be a problem in summer in certain regions of the United States. Plants may contract leaf, stem or root diseases unless the humidity around the plants is lowered. Most fungal and bacterial disease organisms need free water to germinate and infect the host plant. This free water is usually present on the surfaces of leaves or stems or in soggy soil where the soil oxygen has been displaced by surplus water molecules. However, the rapid movement of air across the leaves causes them to dry off and encour-

ages evaporation of surplus water in the root zone. Thus, the most effective way to lower humidity is to increase the flow of air around and through the plant foliage. This can be done by widening the distance between adjacent plants so air can pass between them, by setting plants where they can get cross-ventilation from at least two windows or by using a small electric fan to speed air passage through the plants.

Drainage

With very few exceptions (for example, bog plants), a key requirement of container plants is good drainage. Drainage should not be confused with soil moisture. Plants differ greatly in their need for soil moisture, some preferring a constantly moist growing medium, some moderate in their water requirements and others needing a dry period between each watering. You can learn more about the best watering regime for your plants by consulting an encyclopedia of house plant care, such as those mentioned on p. 327.

Drainage refers to how quickly the water can move through the soil. This depends on several factors: the porosity of the soil medium (how many spaces there are between soil grains and how large the spaces are), whether the hole at the bottom of the pot allows the water to leave the pot freely and how high the pot is above the saucer provided to collect the leachate (the water that seeps out). If adequate drainage is not provided, sooner or later the plant will die from root disease or salt buildup. There are several steps you can take to ensure adequate drainage.

• Use well-draining potting soil (see p. 333 under "Soil Mixes").

• Press the potting soil firmly against the open hole at the bottom of the pot. Do not use broken crockery, gravel or any other coarse material in the bottom of the pot. Contrary to advice frequently given, this impedes rather than enhances drainage, since all the larger spaces between the

Elevating Indoor Plants on Pebble-Filled Trays
To prevent plant disease caused by excessive moisture, elevate your plants on pebble-filled trays. Water the plant from the top down to leach out salts, and remove surplus standing water from the saucer with a baster.

pieces fill with water before the pot begins to drain. This leads to standing water in the pot and provides the ideal environment for pathogens that cause root rot. Waterlogged soils also directly inhibit the free exchange of gases from the roots, which must breathe, giving out carbon dioxide as a by-product of their cell metabolism and taking in oxygen to fuel the same process. A plant may actually smother to death if there is inadequate oxygen in the soil.

• Elevate the pot above the container that is to receive drained water so none of it can re-enter the pot and evaporate from the soil surface (see the drawing above). Some ornamen-

tal pots have legs especially designed to elevate them. Gravel or marbles placed under the pot achieve the same effect if they raise the pot above the level of the standing water.
• Use an unglazed pot whenever possible. Plastic pots may seem appealing because they are lighter, are less likely to break and reduce the need for watering since, unlike clay pots, they are nonporous. Some people also find them more attractive than clay pots. But there is one serious drawback. The incidence of plant root disease in container plants in plastic pots is higher than in clay pots. If you are offended by the look of an unglazed clay pot, place it inside a larger decorative outer pot of any type, but make sure there is enough room for water to drain out between the two. Unglazed clay allows water to evaporate from the soil on all sides. The water is replaced by air, and in well-aerated soil the plant has the upper hand against the many pathogens in the soil that cause root rot.

Salts
Most common house plant species cannot tolerate soils high in soluble salts. Sodium salts are occasionally a problem where water-softening devices are used. Some water softeners substitute sodium for the calcium and magnesium salts that make water hard. Fortunately, many devices then pass the treated water through a de-ionizer, which removes the salt and leaves water that is excellent for plants. If the sodium is not removed, however, the water is not safe for house plants, and outdoor unsoftened tap water, rainwater or bottled water (including distilled water) should be collected for this purpose.

In areas where the water is heavily chlorinated, chlorine salts build up quickly and are seen as white crystals on the sides of clay pots. When the pot sits in a saucer that collects the drainage water and the water is allowed to re-enter the pot and evaporate from the soil surface, the crystals can be seen there as well (see the

Salt Buildup
Excessive fertilization and failure to leach plants with water periodically results in a buildup of salts that damage plants. When the drainage water backs up in the saucer, it prevents salts from leaching out.

Browning of leaf tips

White crust on soil surface and on sides of porous clay pot

Drained water backing up into root zone

drawing above). Even before the crystals appear, however, plants particularly sensitive to this condition—certain ferns, for example—may show a browning or drying of the leaf tips.

If salt crystals form on the soil and/or the plant shows tip burning:
• Remove the plant and clean out the salty pot before reusing it by soaking it in a bucket of clean water and scrubbing with a brush.
• Repot the plant in fresh soil.
• Elevate the container with the plant above the saucer containing drainage water so that water leaching from the pot cannot re-enter the soil. Use small stones to elevate the container.
• When watering, allow a small amount of water to flow through the pot into the saucer below at each watering. The rule of thumb is that one-third of the water should pass through. The saucer should be large enough to accommodate this unless you water your plants by taking them to the sink or bathtub.

• Check the directions on your fertilizer container to make sure you are not overfertilizing the plant. Also see "Watering" on pp. 337-341.

Temperature
The comfort zone for humans ranges between 60°F and 75°F (16°C and 24°C); with few exceptions, common house plants do best between 70°F and 90°F (21°C and 32°C). From this information, you can see that it may easily get too cold in the house or too warm in the greenhouse for many plants. Sudden cold, such as cold air drafts or very cold water, is probably more of a problem than a steady temperature, even if it is a little warm or cold. Symptoms of chilling include sudden loss of most of the leaves, or spotting of the leaves where droplets of cold water hit them.

Extremes of temperature in the greenhouse will be even greater than those in the house. If the greenhouse is attached, warm air from the heated house may circulate through it in the winter, helping to moderate temperatures for the plants. Freestanding greenhouses present a bigger challenge. They lack the wall and ceiling insulation of houses and are therefore subject to much wider temperature swings in response to changes in the outdoor temperature. As a result, conventionally constructed glasshouses are notorious for the energy they consume for heating and cooling while trying to maintain an even temperature. Fortunately, there are now numerous greenhouse designs that use large masses of rock or water that absorb, store and then release heat—often cost-free solar heat—to help even out temperature extremes without the substantial expense of supplying artificial heat. This subject is covered in our book, *The Integral Urban House,* along with tips on growing food in attached and freestanding greenhouses that consume little nonrenewable energy.

If plants become overheated, they may wilt; their leaves can dry and curl along the edges, and lower leaves may turn yellow with brown spots and drop (see the symptom key on p. 318). Scorched patches may appear on the leaves if the sun is too bright. In summer, it may be desirable to whitewash clear greenhouse window panes to reduce the amount of sun entering. Air vents (which should be screened to retain beneficial insects released inside the greenhouse) that open and close automatically in response to temperature changes also can help. Fans will probably be required, too, unless the greenhouse has been especially designed to lose excess heat passively.

To avoid chilling or overheating in the house or greenhouse:
• Place plants in rooms where the temperature comes closest to their requirements.
• Use barriers to protect plants from chilling drafts, particularly if you move them outside in warm weather.
• Water temperature-sensitive plants, such as African violets, with water

that feels mildly warm to the fingers.
• Moderate the heat in the greenhouse in summer by opening vents, running fans and whitewashing. In winter, you can store heat in water drums or ponds, or you can artificially heat the greenhouse.

HORTICULTURAL CONTROLS
The major purpose of horticultural controls is to minimize or reduce stress placed on indoor plants caused by improper practice of plant culture, because plants under horticultural stress are more susceptible to pests. In this section we describe cultural practices that maximize plant health and thus serve as preventive pest management strategies.

Plant Selection
Many pest problems of indoor plants occur because the wrong plant is in the wrong place and receives the wrong amount of care. To minimize these problems, the plant species should be suited to the room in which they are placed, to the level of horticultural skill of the owner and to the amount of time the owner has to care for them.

Some plant species are tolerant of a wide range of environments and levels of care. These include philodendrons, sansevierias, crassulas, scheffleras, aglaonemas, dracaenas, cissus and some of the ficus. Others, such as fittonias, aphelandras, dizygothecas, columneas and peperomias, are less tolerant of poor lighting, over- or under-watering and other common environmental and cultural limitations.

It is important to resist the impulse to buy an indoor plant until you are relatively certain the environment in your home is suited to the plant and you have enough knowledge and time to give to it. If these are limited, stick to species that require minimal care. Seek advice from a good nursery or indoor-plant store, or consult a book on house plants to find out which are suitable.

Another thing to consider is whether the plant has been acclimated to the low light levels in most homes. In the commercial nursery, plants are usually grown in bright light and fertilized heavily to induce rapid growth. Once they reach marketable size, they are delivered to the retail outlet and sold to the consumer. Often the interval between the time the plant leaves these conditions and the time it arrives at your door is quite short. The radical change in environment usually puts it in shock, and symptoms such as leaf- and flower-drop and fading of leaf color appear.

Knowing this, more conscientious wholesale growers allow a transition period during which their plants are held for a few weeks or even longer in heavily shaded lathhouses and are given lower levels of fertilizer to prepare them for the environmental conditions common in residences and commercial buildings. However, this acclimatization is almost always restricted to large specimen plants whose selling price is high enough to justify the extra time taken. If you are considering the purchase of a large, expensive specimen plant, ask if it was acclimated to lower light levels before being delivered to the retail nursery or plant store. If it was not, or if the retailer doesn't know, look elsewhere for your plants. With an inexpensive plant you will have to take a chance, giving it the closest approximation of its ideal environmental conditions, as suggested by a good house-plant book, once you get it home.

Our final advice on plant selection may seem obvious, but it is often overlooked by house-plant owners struggling to get their plants to grow: Give away or dispose of plants that are not thriving under your care. Plants that grow poorly usually are not adapted to your indoor environment or your level of care, and they are prime candidates for pest problems. Give them to someone who has more expertise or a better-suited environment. Do not replace plants that have not done well in your home with the same species. It is tempting to keep trying to get a certain plant you really like to grow. However, if that African violet or Swedish ivy just isn't happy despite your loving attention, chances are the species will never grow well in the conditions of your home. Find another species that grows better.

Soil Mixes

The plant you bring home from the nursery is probably growing in a "soil-less" mix, usually a combination of pulverized peat and fine sand, that may be hard as rock by the time it arrives at your door. Commercial growers favor these mixes because they are partially sterile and theoretically harbor fewer soil pathogens than more expensive mixes containing loamy soil. The fact that the components in these mixes do not hold nutrients for long and become compacted within a few months is not a problem in the commercial nursery, where soil is simply used as a medium for supporting the plant in the container, not as a reservoir for nutrients and water. In the nursery, nutrients are supplied daily or weekly in the irrigation water. The fact that they quickly leach out of the containers is offset by the high frequency with which they are supplied. By the time soil in the containers shows signs of compaction from the constant impact of irrigation water, most house plants are on their way to retail outlets.

And by the time the typical house plant arrives in your home, the "soil" may have become a fairly hostile habitat for the roots. Compacted soil restricts the ability of oxygen and other gases to move in and out of the root zone and inhibits the ability of roots to absorb the water and nutrients needed to sustain growth. Add to this the other stresses the plant has undergone since leaving the original greenhouse—radical lowering of light, different temperature and hu-midity levels—and you have a situation ripe for pest problems.

Given the limitations of commercial soil mixes, it is often a good idea to repot plants in a better soil mix soon after acquiring them. Choose a potting mix that contains a high percentage of coarse organic matter, because it holds nutrients until plant roots need them. The mix should also contain coarse sand (its large particle size ensures good drainage and air movement). To improve drainage even more, include perlite (a silica derivative) or vermiculite (expanded mica).

The addition of a moderate amount of pasteurized (not sterilized) loamy soil is often recommended in garden literature. This is because most garden soils contain a broad spectrum of major and minor nutrients, as discussed under "Fertilizing" below, some of which may not be present in the organic portion of the mix. The loam does not decompose as the organic matter does, and thus may serve as a longer-term nutrient reservoir. If garden loam is pasteurized properly (which you can do yourself—see the sidebar at right), it will be free of soil pathogens. The addition of the loam to the soil mix contributes an array of beneficial microorganisms that help move nutrients into plant roots and deter pathogens trying to establish themselves in the soil.

In his succinct but comprehensive book, *Greenhouse Grow How*, John Pierce describes in detail various standard soil mix recipes that are tailored for specific types of plants. If you don't have his book, you can make our tried-and-true mix described in the sidebar on p. 334. We've found that it works for most house plants.

Fertilizing

People tend to fall into one of two groups when it comes to fertilizing house plants: those who do nothing at all and those who fertilize with a vengeance. People in the latter category often use too much of the wrong product. We must stress that

---

How To Pasteurize Soil in Your Oven[a]

A. Temperatures Required

140°F (60°C)—Kills worms, slugs, centipedes, many pathogenic fungi and bacteria.

160°F (71°C)—Kills all plant disease-causing bacteria, most plant viruses and soil insects.

180°F (82°C)—Kills most organisms, including weed seeds.

B. Soil Treatment in Conventional Convection (Non-Microwave) Ovens

(Note: Soil cannot be pasteurized reliably in a microwave oven because ungerminated fungal spores are not affected by the microwaves.)

1. Place soil in a pan 3 in. to 4 in. deep and add enough water to moisten it thoroughly.

2. Cover the pan with aluminum foil or put it in into a roasting bag pierced in two places and tied at the end.

3. Insert a meat thermometer through the foil or bag into the soil. It should not touch the pan bottom.

4. Set oven on low or at 200°F (93°C). Begin timing when the thermometer temperature reaches 150°F (66°C).

5. Keep the temperature between 150°F and 180°F (66°C and 82°C) for 30 minutes. If the temperature exceeds 180°F, turn the oven off; higher temperatures kill beneficial organisms.

6. Remove the soil from the oven and allow it to cool.

[a] Adapted from Halpin, 1980, and Pierce, 1977.

"Never-Fail Potting Mix"

A. Mix:[a]

1 part garden compost or shredded fir bark

1 part pasteurized loamy garden soil

1 part sharp builder's sand

1 part perlite

B. Add the following amounts of fertilizer to each cubic yard of potting mix:[b]

2 lb. hoof and horn meal or blood meal with 13% N (nitrogen)

2 lb. superphosphate with 18% P (phosphorus)

1 lb. potassium sulfate with 48% K (potassium)

1 lb. calcium carbonate (dolomite lime)

[a] If your local garden supply store, hardware store or nursery doesn't stock these items, you can obtain them from one of the catalog mail-order sources listed in the Resource Appendix under "Suppliers" on p. 690.

[b] Recommended by the John Innes Horticultural Institute of Great Britain.

A Diet for Plants...And How To Remember It

Plants acquire energy for growth in two ways. First, they manufacture sugars and starches in their leaves through the process of photosynthesis, and second, they take up inorganic gaseous and mineral nutrients through their roots. Students of plant nutrition use the following mnemonic to remember the long list of essential plant nutrients:

See Hopkin's Cafe, mighty good club, Cousin Moman.

Or, written out in the letters that stand for the chemical elements:

C, H, O, P, K, N, S Ca, Fe, Mg, Cl, B, Cu, Zn, Mo, Mn.

If you can remember that, you can begin decoding. The letters stand for the chemical symbols:

C = carbon, H = hydrogen, O = oxygen, P = phosphorus,

K = potassium, N = nitrogen, S = sulfur, Ca = calcium, Fe = iron, Mg = magnesium, Cl = chlorine, B = boron, Cu = copper, Zn = zinc, Mo = molybdenum, Mn = manganese.

The nutrients are listed in order of importance. Carbon, hydrogen, oxygen, phosphorus, potassium, nitrogen, sulfur and calcium are called major nutrients, because plants use them in relatively large amounts; the others are minor nutrients, or trace elements, since they are essential to plants, but only in small amounts. Bear in mind that every few years scientists discover that other naturally occurring elements play key roles in plant nutrition, so we can assume that in time, other nutrients will be added to this list.

the goal in raising plants indoors is to have them stay healthy while growing them *slowly*. The lush, quick growth that is desirable in the vegetable patch is not the objective here. Quick growth increases the amount of care required in pruning, repotting and watering plants and makes them more susceptible to many problems.

Improper fertilization also causes nutrient deficiency or toxicity symptoms that are often mistaken for pest problems. Therefore, some understanding of plant nutrition is useful in preventing or treating pest and other plant problems. The sidebar above lists the nutrients required by plants.

The major plant nutrients that are most often deficient in existing soil or are removed through subsequent plant growth are nitrogen (N), phosphorus (P) and potassium (K). These are the nutrients featured on the labels of fertilizer products, appearing in an N-P-K number formula, such as 5-10-5 or 12-6-6. The numbers indicate the percentage of each of these ingredients in the overall mix. If there are four numbers, the fourth is the sulfur content. For example, 10-10-10-10 = % N-P-K-S.

As Pierce explains it, "If you purchase 1 pound (16 oz.) of a 20-20-20 formula you have 20 percent, or 3.2 ounces, each of N, P and K for a total of 9.6 ounces (60%) of actual fertiliz-er. The other 6.4 ounces (40%) in the package is filler, often composed of organic material, chelating compounds (agents that make metal ions more available to plants), or other material to assist the nutritional process." Some fertilizer formulations contain minor, or trace, elements in addition to major nutrients. These, too, are listed on the package. It is also possible to buy minor elements singly or in mixes to add to a fertilizer.

In natural settings, plants can take nitrogen, oxygen and carbon from the air. Carbon is absorbed as carbon dioxide through openings in plant leaves. Nitrogen taken from air in the soil is transformed by soil microorganisms into organic ammonium and nitrate compounds. Also, organic nitrogen compounds from dead plants, animals, microbes and manures in the soil are broken down

How Nutrients Cycle

In the natural environment essential plant nutrients available as gases in the air or within organic matter require the action of microorganisms to convert them to soluble forms that can be absorbed by plant roots. The cycling of nitrogen by microorganisms is illustrated here. Physical and chemical action within the soil releases nutrients from mineral layers for uptake by plants. The addition of manufactured fertilizers also contributes to plant nutrient sources.

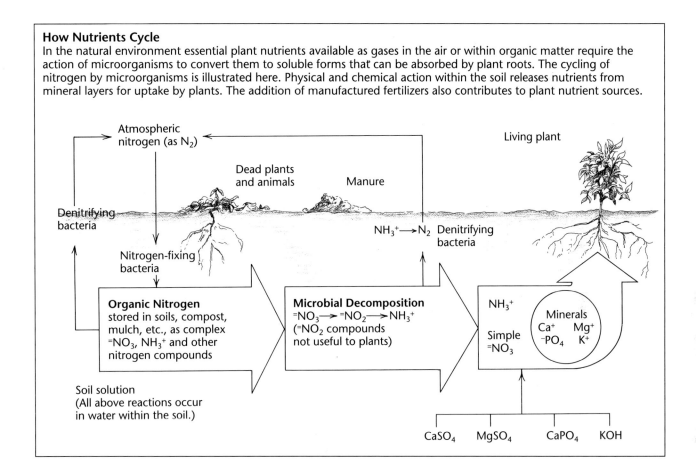

Atmospheric nitrogen (as N_2)

Living plant

Dead plants and animals

Manure

Denitrifying bacteria

$NH_3^+ \longrightarrow N_2$ Denitrifying bacteria

Nitrogen-fixing bacteria

Organic Nitrogen
stored in soils, compost, mulch, etc., as complex $=NO_3$, NH_3^+ and other nitrogen compounds

Microbial Decomposition
$=NO_3 \longrightarrow =NO_2 \longrightarrow NH_3^+$
($=NO_2$ compounds not useful to plants)

NH_3^+

Simple $=NO_3$

Minerals
Ca^+ Mg^+
$^-PO_4$ K^+

Soil solution
(All above reactions occur in water within the soil.)

$CaSO_4$ $MgSO_4$ $CaPO_4$ KOH

by other soil microorganisms and converted to nitrates, which are absorbed by roots. The other major nutrients, including calcium and sulfur, as well as the trace elements available from minerals in the soil are dissolved in the soil water solution and are absorbed by roots. Oxygen dissolved in the soil solution is also absorbed by roots.

Plants grow best when their roots can absorb small concentrations of nutrients at frequent intervals. Clay minerals have bonds that hold nutrients and restrict their movement in water, reducing their tendency to leach out of the root zone. A complex relationship exists between the soil medium and the soil microorganisms that act upon organic matter to transform nutrients into forms available to plants (see the drawing above). This

relationship ensures that a slow, constant stream of nutrients makes its way into plant systems rather than into the groundwater.

The nitrogen sources—the hoof and horn meal or blood meal in the "Never-Fail Potting Mix" described in the sidebar on the facing page, for example—are formulations that will not release their nutrients to plants without the intervention of the microorganisms in the compost/fir bark and garden loam components of the mixes. Thus, the mixes mimic natural systems by releasing nutrients in a slow but steady stream, enabling plant roots to absorb just the amount of fertilizer they need at any one time.

This fertilizing concept differs greatly from that followed in commercial nurseries, where highly soluble, quick-acting liquid fertilizers are

provided at low but frequent doses in order to force plants into rapid growth. These synthetic chemical fertilizers—ammonium nitrate, for example—are formulated in highly soluble forms that do not rely on microorganisms to make them available to plants. With these products, timing and dosage must be precise and consistent. They can injure plants if the dosage is too high, and they provide insufficient nutrients when the amount is too low.

A "feast or famine" fertilizer regime, such as results from the use of these highly soluble products, stresses plants, making them susceptible to various pests. For example, surplus soluble nitrogen can enhance aphid populations. The plant concentrates the nitrogen at its growing tips, where it is used to build cellular tissue. Aphids are attracted to this lush, succulent tip growth where they can acquire nitrogen (in the form of amino acids) for their own growth.

According to plant pathologist George Agrios, author of the superb text *Plant Pathology*,

Abundance of certain nutrients, e.g., nitrogen, may result in the production of young, succulent growth and may prolong the vegetative period and delay maturity of the plant, making it more susceptible to pathogens that prefer to attack such tissues and for longer periods. Conversely, lack of nitrogen would make plants weaker, slower-growing, and faster-aging and would make them susceptible to pathogens that are best able to attack weak, slow-growing plants.

The best way to avoid stress and pest problems associated with fertilizing practices is to stick to slow-release forms of plant nutrients, preferably those derived from inorganic rock minerals, such as rock phosphate, granite dust and dolomitic limestone, and those derived from plant or animal by-products, such as decomposed plant material, fish bodies and animal bones.

The designation "organic" appeals to the public, which assumes that organic means natural and good. This use of the term "organic" drives fertilizer chemists crazy. The definition of organic in chemistry is anything that contains a carbon atom, including synthetic chemical fertilizers. Concern over proper terminology aside, the so-called organic fertilizers offer two major advantages over quick-acting synthetic chemical fertilizers: They release their nutrients slowly, preventing burning of the roots, and they contain a good balance of major and minor nutrients, presumably including some whose identity and role are not yet understood by scientists. Most synthetic fertilizers do not contain the full range of known essential nutrients, even when the label describes them as "balanced" fertilizers.

Three types of fertilizers that we recommend are discussed below.

1. Fish Emulsion or Seaweed. These are good liquid fertilizers that supply nutrients in slowly soluble forms. Fish emulsion is made from ground-up whole fish, such as herring, in an emulsion that contains major nutrients as well as the necessary minor, or trace, elements. Emulsified seaweed is processed in a similar way.

The label often recommends mixing one tablespoon of these fertilizers per gallon of water once every month for most plants in 6-in. or 8-in. pots. By dividing the recommended dose into smaller portions distributed over the course of a month—for example, ¼ tablespoon per gallon in each of four weekly waterings—the fertilizer will be available to the plant roots through the entire month. There is a slight fishy odor when the fish emulsion is first mixed with water, but diluting the dose as recommended above makes the odor dissipate in a few minutes.

2. Compost Tea. Compost tea is another good slow-release liquid fertilizer. Mix one part finished compost (compost that has cooled down and in which the original components are no longer recognizable—it should be dark brown and crumbly) with four parts water in a covered bucket. Let the mixture stand outdoors for two weeks while nutrients from the compost leach into the water. When the liquid is a medium-brown color, it is ready for use on your house plants. It should be applied at every fourth watering in place of water. If it is very dark brown or black, dilute it with more water first. Strain the "tea" into bottles and store in a cool place until needed. Because the gases may expand in the bottles, cap them with aluminum foil or cotton rather than with tight-fitting lids.

3. Encapsulated Synthetic Fertilizers. In recent years, soluble synthetic fertilizer formulations have been given polymer resin coatings. These are semipermeable membranes that release nutrients slowly into the soil. In

composition and function they resemble the timed-release cold capsules that relieve flu symptoms. According to Pierce, these coatings "...meter out the nitrogen, phosphate and potassium in relation to temperature. The release rate increases in warm soils, decreases in good soils, and stops completely in cold soils. The type and thickness of the coating can be varied to create tailor-made formulas and products for a wide range of growing requirements." These products are available as Osmocote®, Precise®, Ortho® and Rainbird® timed-release fertilizers.

The proper amount and frequency of fertilizer application varies from season to season. During warm periods with long days, plants grow rapidly and have a high demand for nutrients. During cooler, darker seasons, growth is at a very low ebb. At such times, little or no fertilizer should be applied since plants will not absorb it; moreover, the roots can be damaged by unused fertilizer if it is highly soluble.

Correcting Nutrient Problems

Most plants will show visible signs of over- or under-fertilizing. Because these symptoms are often confused with pest problems, we have included the key in the sidebar on p. 339, which helps you identify nutrient deficiency symptoms. Table 18.4 on pp. 340-341 advises you how to correct these deficiencies. Toxicity problems can be solved either by leaching the soil in the pot with sufficient water to wash out the surplus fertilizer or by repotting the plant in fresh soil.

pH

The degree to which potting soil is acid or alkaline is a factor in determining whether a plant will grow vigorously or be subjected to stresses leading to pest problems. The relative acidity or alkalinity of soils is determined by the percent hydrogen (pH) in the soil solution.

A logarithmic (pH) scale is used to measure the range of acid or alkaline conditions of the soil (see Table 18.3 at right). A pH of 7 is neutral, pH 1 to 6 is acid and pH 8 to 14 is alkaline. Most house plants grow best in slightly acidic soils with a pH between 5.5 and 7.5. If the pH of the soil is not within this range, certain nutrients may remain bound up in the soil and unavailable to the plants. The lack of these nutrients stresses plants, stunts growth and produces visible symptoms such as chlorosis (yellowing of the tissues), malformed leaves and/or other signs that may be mistaken for pest problems.

Areas with heavy rainfall tend to develop acidic soils, those with little rain are often alkaline. Thus, in the tropical forests where most house plants originate, soils tend to be acidic. The explanation for this is somewhat technical.

A water molecule (H_2O) is composed of two atoms of hydrogen and one of oxygen. When water enters the soil solution, this molecule often splits into two parts: a hydrogen ion, which is small and contains a positive electrical charge (H^+), and a hydroxyl ion (OH^-), which contains a negative electrical charge. The free, small hydrogen ion is able to slip in close to the surface of clay or organic soil particles and knock off other minerals, or bases, such as calcium and magnesium, that are attached to the particles. Thus, in high-rainfall areas, soils may slowly become acidic as other minerals are replaced by hydrogen ions from the rainwater. The rainwater combines with carbon dioxide to form carbonic acid (H_2CO_3), a weak acid that also contributes to acid conditions by adding hydrogen ions and leaching out calcium and related positive elements. Where little water is available to wash them away, calcium, magnesium and sodium ions that create alkaline soils may be present in high numbers.

The sidebar on p. 338 describes two methods for testing the pH of your soil.

The pH level can be raised (made more alkaline) by adding various

Table 18.3
pH Values of Hydrogen and Hydroxyl

	pH	Hydrogen Ion Concentration (moles/liter)[a]	Hydroxyl Ion Concentration (moles/liter)[a]	Acidity of Common Solutions
Acid	0	10^0	10^{-14}	
	1	10^{-1}[b]	10^{-13}	
	2	10^{-2}	10^{-12}	
	3	10^{-3}	10^{-11}	lemon juice
	4	10^{-4}	10^{-10}	beer
	5 Normal	10^{-5}	10^{-9}	boric acid
	6 Soil	10^{-6}	10^{-8}	milk
Neutral	7 or	10^{-7}	10^{-7}	pure water
	8 Plant	10^{-8}	10^{-6}	seawater
	9 Range	10^{-9}	10^{-5}	soap solution
	10	10^{-10}	10^{-4}	milk of magnesia
Alkaline	11	10^{-11}	10^{-3}	trisodium phosphate
	12	10^{-12}	10^{-2}	lye
	13	10^{-13}	10^{-1}	
	14	10^{-14}	10^0	

[a] One mole of any substance is a quantity of grams equal in number to its molecular weight, and is equivalent to 6×10^{23} molecules of that substance.

[b] 10^{-1} is a notation for $1/10^1$ or $1/10$; $10^{-7} = 1/10^7$ or $1/10,000,000$ or 0.0000001.

forms of calcium carbonate. One form is dolomitic lime, which contains both calcium and magnesium and counters the acidic properties of ammonium sulfate fertilizer. To lower the pH, add fertilizers containing sulfur—garden sulfur or iron sulfate, for example—to the irrigation water. Refer to the package labels for guidance as to the amount to apply to correct the pH in your specific situation.

Watering

Overwatering is probably the major cause of disease and death of indoor plants. Waterlogged soils exclude oxygen from the root zone, and the lack of oxygen impedes plant respiration, causes formation of carbon monoxide (no less toxic to plant roots than to humans) and creates a habitat ideal for disease-causing microorganisms. Thus, the watchwords in watering are "when in doubt, don't water." Symptoms of overwatering are:
• Leaves that turn yellow or light green.
• Leaves that have brown edges, tips or spots.
• Small roots at the edge or bottom of the pot that are dark brown or black, and a lack of white roots. (Note: If the first two symptoms are present,

Testing the pH

There are two simple methods for testing the pH of your potting soil. The less expensive is to purchase pH test paper (A in the drawing at right), available from pharmacies. It comes in a two-tape roll in a cellophane-tape-type dispenser. One tape covers pH 0 to 9.0, the other, pH 9.0 to 13.0.

To conduct the test, mix one part potting soil to two parts water in a small glass container. Stir thoroughly and let the solution settle for a few minutes. Dip one piece of tape from each roll into the solution an inch or less for 30 seconds, then withdraw the tape and match the resulting color with the colors on the dispenser to get

the pH reading. Handle the tape with tweezers rather than your fingers so your skin oil does not influence the reading.

A more expensive but faster and more convenient tool for determining pH is the pH meter (B in the drawing at right), which eliminates the need for making a solution of water and soil. It consists of a probe that is inserted directly into the soil and a gauge mounted on top of the probe that registers a pH reading. These meters are available from nurseries and mail-order sources.

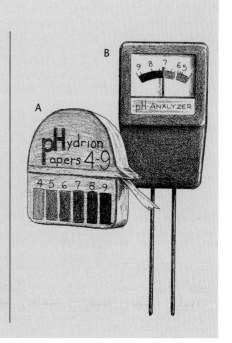

A Victim of the Watering Can
This plant shows the typical symptoms of overwatering. More house plants die from this easy-to-correct problem than from any other. A moisture meter can help you prevent overwatering if you have trouble judging soil moisture without it.

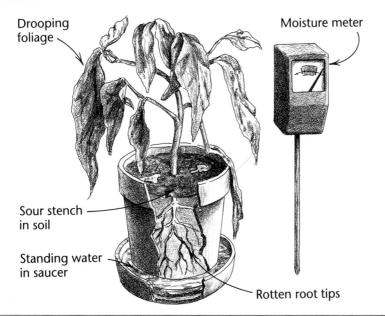

Drooping foliage

Moisture meter

Sour stench in soil

Standing water in saucer

Rotten root tips

but roots look white and healthy, check for other causes.)

Symptoms of underwatering are:
• Young foliage that is limp and has a greyish tinge.
• Soil from the pot that is powder-dry and dusty when rubbed between the fingers.
• Dry roots at the edges and bottom of the pot.

To determine how much water you should give and how often to water, you need to consider a number of variables, including plant species and size, type of soil mix, type of container, the environment in the room and the season. This number of variables makes it impossible to give pat "recipes" for correct watering. However, some general guidelines do apply.

Stick your finger into the top inch of potting soil. If it feels dry and no damp soil particles are visible on your finger when you withdraw it, then it is probably time to water. If you are still unsure, invert the plant and gently tap the root ball out of the pot to see if it looks dry. Never water just because the soil surface looks dry — water evaporates rapidly from the surface, but there may still be plenty of water left underneath.

An alternate method is to use a moisture meter to determine watering needs. These meters, which are similar in form to the pH meters, operate by passing a weak electric current through the soil water. The meter measures the salt content of the water and makes a correlation between the salt content and moisture. Its gauge then indicates whether or not water is needed. Although these meters are useful, they are subject to error and should be used in conjunction with the visual and physical inspections just described.

It is important to pour on enough water to wet the root ball thoroughly; the surplus should be allowed to drain away. If the root ball is not thoroughly wetted, particularly in "soil-less" mixes, the mix will begin to shrink away from the edges of the container. This eventually allows water to move to and along the sides of the pot and pass through the drainage holes without ever wetting the interior of the root ball. If this has already happened with your plants, follow the immersion method described below. If the soil is high in peat moss, it may be difficult to rewet it adequately once it has dried out, and repotting may be in order.

If your plant containers are sitting in saucers, it is important to check them 15 or 20 minutes after you water to see whether surplus water has drained out of the pots into the saucers. If so, empty the saucers, since most house plants will develop root diseases if allowed to sit in water. Pebbles can be used in saucers to avoid this problem (see p. 330).

It is a good idea to augment tap-watering with monthly immersion watering. This system works best with plants in unglazed clay containers, and is the only method that ensures complete wetting of the soil mass. Dip the potted plants in a larg-

How To Recognize Nutrient Deficiency Symptoms in Higher Plants[a]

I. Symptoms appear first or most severely on youngest leaves.

A. Interveinal chlorosis (paling or yellowing) on young leaves.

1. Black spots adjacent to veins at base of leaflets; smallest veins remain green (the mosaic pattern of chlorosis); grey specks on grasses: manganese deficiency.

2. Black spots absent; small veins do not remain green: iron deficiency.

3. New leaves very small: zinc deficiency.

B. Interveinal chlorosis absent; young leaves remain rolled and appear needle-like in grasses; failure of growing points.

1. Necrotic (dead) spots sharply delimited and sunken: copper deficiency.

2. Tissues brittle, especially stems; saw-toothed edges on leaves of grasses: boron deficiency.

II. Symptoms appear uniformly throughout plant or most severely on oldest leaves.

A. Chlorosis generally present, but not confined to the tissue between the leaves.

1. Veins of lower leaf surface purple; petioles (leaf stems) tend to be more vertical: sulfur deficiency.

2. First symptom is yellowing of oldest leaves, spreading to entire plant; growing point may remain green in less severe cases; oldest leaves drop off: nitrogen deficiency.

B. Interveinal chlorosis, appearing first on oldest leaves.

1. Chlorotic areas bright yellow or orange, turning brown and becoming necrotic; oldest leaves affected most: magnesium deficiency.

2. Chlorotic areas pale yellow, affecting whole plant; leaf edges curl upward: molybdenum deficiency.

C. Chlorosis absent.

1. Scorching and sunken brown spots appearing at edge of oldest leaves; veins remain green (some chlorosis may appear): potassium deficiency.

2. Purpling in the veins and between the veins of lower leaf surfaces, also sometimes on stems and lower stalks of plant: phosphorus deficiency.

3. Bronze-colored necrosis of leaves; plants prone to wilt: chlorine deficiency.

[a] Originally developed with assistance from Dr. James Vlamis, Department of Soils and Plant Nutrition, University of California, Berkeley, and modified from the version printed in Olkowski, Olkowski and Javits, 1979.

Table 18.4
How to Correct Plant Nutrient Deficiencies[a]

A. Nutrients Required in Large Amounts

	Role in plant growth	Materials for correcting deficiencies
Nitrogen N	Leaf and stem production; builds proteins. Food for microorganisms; green in color. Too much causes tip burn on leaves, weak growth, susceptibility to insect and disease attack, lack of flowers; too little stunts growth, causes yellowing.	fish emulsion (1 tbs./gal. water); blood meal (¼ tsp./6-in. pot); timed-release fertilizer (see label)
Phosphorus P	Flower, fruit and seed production: root and stem development, resistance to cold and disease. Too much causes weak, floppy appearance; too little causes stunted, short internodes, purple foliage, poor flowering and seed sterility.	bone meal (1 tsp./6-in. pot); granite dust; timed-release fertilizer (see label)
Potassium K	Formation of carbohydrates, proteins, cell membranes, root and stem development, flower production, resistance to cold and disease. Most plants require large amounts of this nutrient. Too little stunts roots, weakens stems, shrivels fruit, deforms and burns leaves.	wood ashes (1 tsp./6-in. pot); muriate of potash (1 tsp./gal. water); seaweed fertilizer (see label)
Calcium Ca	Cell wall formation, cell division and elongation. Enzyme catalyst; neutralizes certain organic acids; too little causes yellowing, weak growing tips and stems, short, dark roots.	gypsum (1 tsp./6-in. pot)
Magnesium Mg	Chlorophyll production, protein formation, utilization of N, P and S. Too little causes lower leaves to yellow between veins and gradually die.	Epsom salts (magnesium sulfate) 2 tsp./gal. water
Sulfur S	Protein synthesis, water uptake from soil, fruit and seed maturation, speeds up decomposition. Too little causes lower leaves to yellow, and leads to smaller-diameter, hard, brittle stems and roots.	gypsum (1 tsp./6-in. pot); timed-release fertilizer (see label)

[a] Adapted from Pierce, 1977.

er container of water, such as a sink, bathtub or large bucket, until the water comes at least half way up the outside of the pot. Don't let the water flow over the rim of the pot or you may drown the roots. Roots that are completely immersed for long periods can be damaged. Let plants sit in the water until the top of the soil is moist, then remove them from the water bath and allow them to drain thoroughly before replacing them in their usual locations.

The immersion method is also recommended for plants highly susceptible to the leaf diseases. Many leaf diseases can be prevented by keeping water off foliage, particularly with hairy-leafed plants such as African violets, gloxinias, etc. If you can't avoid wetting the leaves when watering, water in the morning so the leaves are thoroughly dry before the temperature drops at night.

A word about water quality: Most urban water contains chemicals, pri-marily chlorine, and in some areas, fluoride. The amount of chlorine in city water is probably not enough to harm most plants, but as a precaution you can fill your watering pail and let it sit overnight. By morning most of the chlorine will have decomposed to chloride ions that bind harmlessly with the organic matter in the potting soil when water is poured into the flower pot. Moreover, the water will have reached room temperature, which is better for plant

Table 18.4 (continued)

B. Nutrients Required in Small Amounts

	Role in plant growth	Materials for correcting deficiencies
Boron B	Cell division, nitrogen and carbohydrate metabolism, flowering, fruiting. Too much quickly kills growing tips, roots and makes fruit corky, flowers do not form.	complete chelated trace elements (see label); boric acid (H_3BO_3), 17% B (6 fine crystals/gal. water)
Iron Fe	Chlorophyll and carbohydrate production, respiration of sugars to provide growth energy. Too little causes leaves to yellow between veins starting on young leaves, stunts growth.	complete chelated trace elements (see label); sequestrene 330, 10% Fe (.004 oz./gal. water)
Zinc Zn	Chlorophyll formation, respiration, nitrogen metabolism. Too little causes small terminal leaves, poor bud formation and dead areas in leaves.	complete chelated trace elements (see label); zinc sulfate, 20% to 30% Zn (.001 oz./gal. water)
Manganese Mn	Catalyst in growth process, formation of oxygen in photosynthesis. Too little causes tissue between veins to turn white, dead spots on leaves, dwarfing of plant.	complete chelated trace elements (see label); manganese sulfate, 25% Mn (.001 oz./gal. water)
Molybdenum Mo	Nitrogen metabolism and fixation. Too little drops ascorbic acid levels in plant, leading to stunting and yellowing of leaves.	complete chelated trace elements (see label); sodium molybdate, 22% Mo (.0001 oz./gal. water)
Copper Cu	Component of enzymes, involved in respiration and utilization of iron; regulates soil nitrogen. Too little causes new growth tips to die.	complete chelated trace elements (see label)
Chlorine Cl	Exact function not known.	pinch of table salt in 1 gal. water

roots than cold water directly from the tap.

Fluorides can cause tip burn as well as chlorosis (paling or yellowing of leaves) on plants in the genera *Cordyline*, *Dracaena*, *Maranta* and *Yucca*. If you see symptoms of burn on the margins of the leaves of these species and your water is fluoridated, try distilled water or place a rain barrel in your garden and use this water for your plants. De-mineralized water can leach important elements out of the soil over a long period, but they are easily replaced through mulches and light fertilization. If you must use tap water, increase the pH of the soil mix to deactivate the fluoride ions. (See the discussion of pH on p. 337 for a description of how to do this; you will have to experiment with the dosage of the amendment, since no precise figures are given in the literature).

Water softening devices replace calcium with sodium salts. Over time, these sodium salts can harm plants. If possible, tap into your water line before it reaches the water softener and use the "hard" water for your plants. Although the hard water will not injure plants directly, the excess calcium (lime) in the water will eventually raise the pH of the soil. To offset this, water the plants once a month with a solution of 1 tbs. (15 ml) of vinegar to 1 gal. (3.8 l) of water.

DIRECT PHYSICAL CONTROLS

The management strategies discussed so far have emphasized preventive care. Once your plants have symptoms of disease or insect and mite presence, your primary focus must change from maintaining plant health to assessing the degree of damage and the possibilities for control.

Regular monitoring of plants allows you to catch most problems before they become severe. For example, if you spot the symptoms of root disease early, there is usually time to modify the habitat or horticultural practices so that you keep the problem to a tolerable level. Sometimes diseased upper portions of plants can be pruned off and discarded. If the disease has advanced throughout the plant, however, the best procedure is to dispose of the entire plant in a manner that does not spread pathogenic spores to other plants.

With insect and mite problems you usually have a wider range of management options than are available for diseases. Management tactics generally fall into one of three categories: physical, biological and chemical controls. We look at physical controls first.

1. Hand Pruning. Leaves or larger portions of the plant that show disease symptoms should be pruned off and discarded by placing them in a closed paper bag and burning them, by composting them in a hot compost or by burying them in garden soil. If you do not have access to a garden, place the pieces in a sealed plastic bag and put them in the garbage. Always try to avoid scattering spores of the plant pathogens.

All tools used for pruning diseased materials should be sterilized. You can do this by letting them soak for 10 to 15 minutes in a 5% solution of bleach and water (approximately ½ tbs./7.5 ml of bleach to 1 pt./0.47 l of water), or you can boil them for 15 minutes in plain water.

2. Squashing, Vacuuming, Traps. A variety of physical controls can be used on pests of plants indoors. For example, squashing or picking off pests by hand is a direct approach that works well for small infestations of aphids and scales. Whitefly adults can be caught on yellow sticky traps, and resting adults can be vacuumed up during the cool hours of the day. Barriers can be used against slugs and snails, ants and the black vine weevil. Control procedures are discussed in much greater detail under the individual discussions of these pests in Chapter 20.

Insects captured live can be killed by putting them in a container inside the freezer overnight, or they can be dropped in a bucket of soapy water. However, where biological controls are being used, it is worth learning to recognize parasitized pests and the insects that are preying on them so that the latter can be saved when infested materials are thrown out.

In some cases, such as with the use of the beneficial aphid-eating gall midge (*Aphidoletes aphidimyza*) or insect-attacking nematodes, it is the soil you want to save. The aphid-eating gall midge pupates in the soil, and thus the entire pot should be set aside in a place where the newly emerged adult can re-enter the plant collection to find new aphids. The soil containing beneficial nematodes can also be reused. These biological controls are discussed further on pp. 140-142.

DIRECT BIOLOGICAL CONTROLS

In home, public and commercial greenhouses it is possible to manage almost all insect and mite pests using biological controls in conjunction with the physical tactics just discussed. Chemical controls can complement this approach as an occasional backup, particularly the use of relatively benign chemical materials, such as soaps and oils, which we discuss next. We can say confidently that this integrated approach works, since we have first-hand experience with successful programs. But we should add here that one key to success is the careful preparation of yourself and your greenhouse, which is the subject of the next chapter.

There is growing interest in the use of biological controls on a smaller scale, such as in sun porches. There is a good reason for this. Because many sun porches have been modified to store solar heat and then circulate it through the living space, any toxic materials used to control plant pests on the porch also circulate through the house. This danger can be avoided by using biological controls.

The application of biological controls to house plants within the actual living space is more problematic for several reasons. First, fear of insects and mites is so strong that most people must overcome this psychological barrier before they deliberately release beneficial insects within the house. Second, although certain predators such as mites are effective on isolated plant specimens and do not fly to light, many adult beneficial insects leave the plants and congregate around windows. Third, it is difficult to obtain beneficial insects, mites and other predatory and parasitic organisms in such small numbers, because the commercial insectaries and distributors that handle them are oriented toward customers who purchase at least garden-sized quantities.

Nevertheless, if you are interested in trying biological controls on individual house plants, by all means experiment. If you are releasing crawling predators such as the lacewing larvae that control aphids and young scales or the predatory mites that control pest mites or thrips, the beneficials can simply be shaken onto or placed upon the infested plant as they come from the package by using a small paint brush. The more plants you have, the closer the affected plants are placed together, and the larger the individual plants, the better the chance you will provide enough prey, hiding places and humidity to maintain the predators.

Insect-attacking nematodes are applied to the soil. They can be applied on a pot-by-pot basis and are suitable for use inside homes. Even the aphid-eating gall midge can be released indoors. Although the adults can fly, they avoid light and stay close to the undersides of the plant leaves. Most likely they will pass unnoticed by the human occupants of the house.

However, if you are planning to release flying insects such as lady beetles in the house, you should tent individual plants to contain them; otherwise they will wind up dead on your windowsills and beneath lamps, because they are attracted to light. The sidebar at right tells you how to make a plant tent.

DIRECT CHEMICAL CONTROLS

A horticultural oil can be used against scales; sulfur works for mites and powdery mildew; pyrethroid compounds are effective against aphids, mites, thrips, mealy bugs and scales in the crawler stage; and mild cases of powdery mildew and pythium root rot can be treated with bleach solutions. Table 18.5 at right summarizes which materials are effective against which pests. Chapter 7 discusses the use of soaps, oils, sulfur, bleach and the botanical pyrethrum. Chapter 8 discusses insect growth regulators and microbials. For details on how to integrate these materials into a program against a specific indoor plant pest, see Chapter 20.

House plants are often more tender and succulent than plants grown outdoors because of the lower light conditions and/or overfertilization. Depending on the species, they may be more susceptible to damage from chemical controls, even controls that are not harmful to humans and other mammals. Do not apply any chemical, especially oils or mixtures with oils, when the temperature is high and/or plants are sitting in bright sunlight, as the pesticides may damage leaves. Early morning, when tem-

How To Make A Plant Tent

To make a plant tent, fashion a rectangular bag out of cheesecloth or mosquito netting by doubling the cloth over and sewing the edges together, leaving the bottom open. Drive bamboo stakes into the soil in the pot to hold the tent away from the plant's leaves, then slip the tent over the plant until the open end of the bag surrounds the pot.

After introducing the beneficial insects, tie the open neck of the cloth bag securely around the pot to prevent the insects from escaping. William Jordan, an entomologist and highly skilled science writer, has written a delightful book (*What's Eating Your Houseplants?*, originally published as *Windowsill Ecology*) that discusses his experimentation with this technique in detail.

If making your own tents seems too time-consuming, you can buy ready-made mesh tents with zippers from the W.C. Batiste Company (see the drawing below). They and other entomological equipment companies, such as BioQuip and Pest Management Supply, can also make cages to your specifications. For their addresses, see the Resource Appendix under "Suppliers" on pp. 690-696.

Table 18.5
Chemical Controls for Common House Plant Pests

House Plant Pests	Chemical Control Tools
aphids	soap wash, oil, pyrethroid
leafminers	growth regulator
mealybugs	soap wash, oil, pyrethroid
mites	soap wash, oil, pyrethroid, sulfur
powdery mildew	soap wash, sulfur (lime sulfur also effective)
pythium root rot	bleach
scales	soap wash (on crawler stage), oil, pyrethroid
thrips	soap wash, oil, pyrethroid
whitefies	soap wash, oil, pyrethroid

peratures are coolest and plants are dry, is the best time to use chemicals.

1. Insecticidal Soaps. Plain water baths alone may hold back small mite and thrip infestations, but the addition of insecticidal soap is far more effective. It has been known for a long time that soap can be used to clean house plants without harming most of them. A newly synthesized soap material has been registered as a pesticide effective against a wide range of insects and some plant diseases. These soap-based products are described in greater detail on pp. 114-116. When and how to use them on indoor plants is discussed in a sidebar (p. 350) in the next chapter. They are also mentioned where appropriate in the discussions of various pests in Chapter 20. Sources of insecticidal soaps are listed in the Resource Appendix under "Insect Management: Chemical Controls" on pp. 686-687.

To make an insecticidal-soap bath for dunking small plants, fill a bucket with water just barely warm to your hands. Wrap a cloth around the plant stem so that it also covers the soil surface. Placing one hand on each side of the stem (palm toward the soil), spread your fingers to keep the soil in the pot while your thumbs steady the outside of the pot (see the drawing below). Vigorously slosh the plant through the soapy water until the leaves and stems are clean. Then empty the bucket, refill it with fresh water and soap and repeat the entire procedure.

After 15 minutes, rinse the plant thoroughly, again with tepid water. You can do this in a shower. Then inspect the plant to see how effective the washing has been in knocking off pests directly as well as in killing them chemically. The insecticidal soap kills insects upon contact. Detergents and soaps formulated for laundry, dishwashing or other cleaning purposes can be tried, but they may be more variable in their impact.

Pest infestations that cannot be rubbed off plants that are too big to move can be daubed with a flexible cotton swab or small brush dipped in soap and water or alcohol. If a sheet or cloth or a plastic painter's tarp is used to protect adjacent rugs and furniture, soap spray and rinsing water can be spot-applied with a hand-operated spray gun such as might be used for misting the plant. With extremely large plants that are too difficult to treat in this manner, the repeated release of natural enemies may actually be easier than treating with chemical controls (see Chapter 19 for a discussion of the appropriate biological controls for your pest problem).

2. Sulfur/Soap Mixtures, Bleach, Pyrethrum. Powdery mildew can be reduced by applying the sulfur/soap mixture in Safer's™ fungicide/miticide. A solution of sodium hypochlorite (bleach) and water can be used on mild cases of pythium root rot and other damping off diseases. Make a 1% solution by mixing 1 tbs. (15 ml) of bleach to 1 gal. (3.8 l) of water. Drench the soil.

If you plan to use a botanical pesticide such as pyrethrum or anything more toxic, move plants outdoors for treatment. Use cotton coveralls, neoprene rubber gloves and a cartridge-type respirator designed to absorb chemical odors with activated charcoal (see pp. 97-103 and the Resource Appendix under "Insect Management: Chemical Controls" on pp. 686-687). Spray when winds are calm to prevent drift of the chemicals. Clean equipment and clothing after each use, and be sure to wash garments separately from the the family wash. Swab the gloves and respirator with detergent and paper towels or disposable cotton rags. Place the swabs in a plastic bag, seal it tightly and put it in the garbage. Store safety equipment and clothing individually in plastic bags.

Rinsing Plants in Insecticidal Soap

Rinsing plants in soapy water is a good way of preventing the buildup of pests on plants and of getting rid of existing pests. Place a hand over the base of the plant so it can't unseat itself from the pot and move it back and forth in the water until the pests have been dislodged.

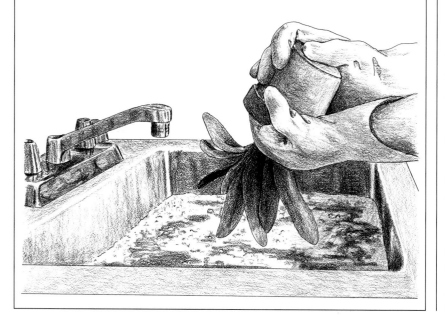

Summary: Least-Toxic House Plant Management Strategies

- Select plant species that are appropriate to the light levels and temperatures in your home.
- Inspect and quarantine all new plants.
- Provide adequate humidity, drainage, air circulation and protection from drafts and overheating.
- Push a finger into the soil to test the moisture level.
- Water sensitive species with dechlorinated, defluoridated, room-temperature water. Avoid artificially softened water that contains sodium.

- If water does not move easily through the soil, repot plants in a pasteurized, well-drained soil mix.
- Monitor plants for general health and pest presence during your monthly or bimonthly cleaning of the foliage.
- Prune off and discard foliage or roots that have been discolored by disease.
- Remove small insect infestations by hand-picking, squashing, rubbing, spot-application of alcohol or soap and water or pruning out affected areas.
- Treat moderate infestations with soap sprays, rinsing the plant well afterward.

- For large plant collections or where physical controls or washing with soap and water are inadequate, consult the detailed discussions under the specific pests in Chapter 20.
- If insect infestations cannot be controlled by physical controls, biological controls or relatively nontoxic soaps, oils, sulfurs or IGRs and the plant must be kept at all costs, move it outdoors and use a botanical insecticide. Make sure you protect yourself from drift and inhalation of the pesticide by using a respirator and by changing your clothing immediately after application.

REFERENCES AND READINGS

Conover, C.A. and R.T. Poole. 1982. Acclimatizing tropical foliage plants for sale and shipping. *Foliage Digest* V(2):7-9.

This article contains many good suggestions for acclimatizing foliage plants.

Crockett, J.U. 1971. *Flowering house plants.* New York: Time-Life Books. 160 pp.

A visually beautiful book with many good ideas.

Crockett, J.U. 1972. *Foliage house plants.* New York: Time-Life Books. 160 pp.

Includes a good discussion of proper environmental conditions for foliage plants indoors.

Faust, J.L. 1973. *Book of house plants.* New York: New York Times Books. 274 pp.

A well-illustrated book with many good suggestions for plant care.

Gaines, R.L. 1977. *Interior plantscaping: building design for interior foliage plants.* New York: Architectural Record Books. 182 pp.

This book includes professional tips on selecting the right plant for the right spot inside the building. The discussion of light requirements of plants is particularly thorough.

Halpin, A.M., ed. 1980. *Rodale's encyclopedia of indoor gardening.* Emmaus, Pa.: Rodale Press. 902 pp.

A beautifully illustrated book that explores the use of indoor space to extend the growing season and the range of home gardening activities.

Jordan, W. 1977. *What's eating your houseplants?* Emmaus, Pa.: Rodale Press. 229 pp.

This book, originally published as *Windowsill Ecology,* provides a comprehensive discussion of the biological control of indoor plant pests in a straightforward yet entertaining style. Excellent photos and line drawings illustrate insects, equipment and methods described in the text. Unfortunately, the book is out of print —look for it in your library.

Olkowski, H., W. Olkowski and T. Javits. 1979. *The integral urban house.* San Francisco: Sierra Club Books. 493 pp.

This book discusses building and using a solar greenhouse.

Pierce, J.H. 1977. *Greenhouse grow how.* Seattle: Plants Alive Books. 241 pp.

An excellent reference book on greenhouse management.

CHAPTER 19
Preparing for Least-Toxic Pest Control

INTRODUCTION

Least-toxic management methods for the most common pests of plants indoors are well developed; the strategies we recommend here come from published descriptions of the integrated management of greenhouse pests and from our personal experience with the design and implementation of such programs. The pest management techniques applicable to house plants, particularly the use of biological controls, were worked out in large-scale indoor plant collections first. Only later did we and others tackle the question of how to scale down the technology for use on small plant collections in homes, offices and other indoor locations.

Some pests may be easier to control in large plant collections than in smaller ones. For example, in biologically controlling pest mites in a small plant collection, predatory mites may eliminate the pests on a single house plant but then starve to death for lack of additional prey before the eggs of the pest mites have a chance to hatch. When the eggs do hatch, the pest population returns unchallenged by the predator. For this reason, small plant collections may require more frequent releases of predatory mites than do larger ones.

Our initial opportunity to explore this aspect of pest management came in 1982 when we were asked to design and help implement an IPM program for the extensive collection of orchids and other plants at the San Francisco Conservatory of Flowers in Golden Gate Park. The program was very effective in controlling pests, primarily through biological controls and insecticidal soap. An article, "IPM for a Conservatory and Greenhouses," describing our overall approach, the pests encountered and the IPM strategies we recommended appeared in *The IPM Practitioner* 5(8): 4-6, 9 (Olkowski, W., S. Daar and H. Olkowski, 1983).

Since the Conservatory of Flowers program, we have advised the maintenance staffs of interior landscapes of numerous office buildings, hotels, research greenhouses and commercial greenhouses.

Where our recommended methods have achieved the goal of substantial or complete reduction of toxic pesticide use, the success must be credited to those in charge (in the case of the Conservatory of Flowers, this was former director Tom Bass) and to the motivation, innovation and perseverance of the staff in removing toxic materials from the workplace and patiently fine-tuning new methods of pest management. It is relatively easy to describe a less toxic control program, but implementation is a complex task that usually takes several years to accomplish. The motivation to make the necessary effort often comes from the realization that pesticides applied in enclosed spaces present higher exposure risks to humans and pets than when they are applied outdoors.

Not only does least-toxic management of plant pests indoors require more than one strategy, many of the problems have to be tackled together because the management of one influences the handling of the others. For example, in some areas of the country, the successful use of biological controls to manage scales, aphids, whiteflies and mealybugs can be achieved only if ants are excluded. Ants protect these pests from their natural enemies and harvest the honeydew excreted by them. Moreover, certain ant species regularly invade houses and other structures. They may take up residence in flowerpots, where they can become directly destructive when their nests cause deterioration of the growth medium supporting the potted plant.

Often when conventional pesticides are used to control pests of plants indoors, people are conscious only of the major pests they are treating. However, after they stop regular preventive use of the pesticides, other pest problems may emerge. Then the true complexity of the task is revealed.

SETTING REALISTIC OBJECTIVES

As we emphasized earlier, the elimination of every last pest is not the objective of an IPM approach, because beneficial insects must have at least a few pests around as food. When all pests are eliminated, the beneficial insects die, too. A more realistic objective is to keep pest populations below the injury level, or the level where they cause unacceptable aesthetic or economic damage to plants. Such suppression keeps the offending population small enough that it is rarely seen.

The injury level for any pest is not an absolute number. Different plant species and varieties can tolerate different numbers of the same pest before they show symptoms. The genetic makeup and current health of an individual plant also influence the numbers of a particular pest it can tolerate, and plant owners or managers differ in their tolerance of insects and signs of their presence. Only you can determine when injury levels are being approached and what treatment is needed to halt the damage. A regular monitoring program is the key to deciding whether treatments are needed, which ones to use and how to apply them.

Inspection and Monitoring

Inspection means looking thoroughly; monitoring is inspection on a regular basis, such as once every week or two. A monitoring frequency of twice a month is probably the minimum necessary for keeping pest populations below problem levels in large plant collections. Monitoring has three main objectives:
• noting whether the population of any specific pest species is approaching the point where action is required,
• observing where in the building and on which plants pest problems are most serious, and
• checking to see whether natural enemies of the pest are present and whether other treatment actions have been effective.

Making and Using A Monitoring Map

1. Draw a map of your plant collection (similar to the one at right) and make several copies.

2. Clip or staple these sheets together to form a booklet, and keep it on a clipboard with a pencil attached.

3. Each time you make your observations, use a fresh map sheet and note the date.

4. When you observe large numbers of pests or predators on a plant, note the species name and the approximate number on the map at the problem plant's location.

5. If plants of the same species are numerous or are shifted around frequently, paint an identifying number on each pot. Record the pot number at the appropriate location on your map.

6. Use the same map sheet to record other important information, such as temperature extremes and treatment actions taken. Make note of the release of beneficial insects or mites, the addition of new plants in the greenhouse and other significant events. These records enable you to spot the times in the season when pest populations begin to rise; they also help you evaluate the effectiveness of your management effort over the long term.

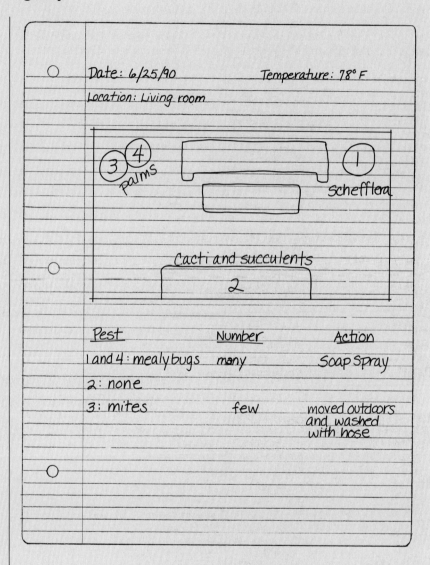

Proper monitoring means that you must recognize the pests and their natural enemies. You can teach yourself to do this by studying the illustrations of pests in books and pamphlets recommended in the reading lists and by closely examining individual predators and parasites purchased from an insectary. Inevitably, a few individuals sent by the insectary die during shipment—save them for comparison with insects and mites you find on your plants. You can also take specimens from your plants to your local cooperative extension office for help in identification.

Because many common insects are small, particularly in the early stages, and because mites are even smaller, it is often necessary to use a magnifying device to view them properly. A small but very useful 10- or 15-power hand lens can be obtained from museum gift shops, book and school supply stores serving college communities and other stores that provide books and equipment for naturalists (see the Resource Appendix under "Insect Management: Identification and Monitoring" on pp. 681-682).

How can you tell whether there are enough beneficials on your plants to control the pest? There is no single answer for all situations, since each pest, beneficial organism, plant variety and/or set of environmental conditions can be different. In some cases the producer of the beneficial organisms can guide you, particularly if you are growing a type of plant for which there is a fairly well-understood biological control program. The producer may say, for example, that on greenhouse tomatoes there should be so many predators per so many plants or pests. Nonetheless, the most valuable information is usually developed by you in your own plant collection through monitoring and recording what you see.

Good record-keeping is the key to fine-tuning a general IPM program to your specific conditions. If your monitoring shows a slight rise in the pest population, you can order beneficial insects and mites in time to prevent severe plant damage. If you keep records on temperature, humidity, pest abundance, releases of beneficials and the use of least-toxic pesticides, you will build an invaluable guide to keeping pest problems below the injury level as seasons and plant collections change. A fast, comparatively easy method of record-keeping is to write your observations on a sketched floor plan of the plant collection, as described in the sidebar on the facing page.

MAKING THE TRANSITION TO LEAST-TOXIC METHODS

Making the transition from conventional pesticides to least-toxic controls requires that you avoid introducing new pests to your collections and ward off potentially damaging infestations through careful monitoring before they become established. Learn what is the best time to release beneficials, and determine what temperature and humidity are best for the maintenance of the beneficials.

If you are currently using conventional toxic pesticides to control insect and mite pests on plants indoors, we do not recommend that you suddenly stop all treatments and order biological controls. You must detoxify your plants and their surroundings before you start releasing parasitoids and predators, and generally it takes about a month for residual pesticides to lose their toxic effect. During this time, you can make periodic applications of insecticidal soap or horticultural oils (for sources, see the Resource Appendix under "Insect Management: Chemical Controls" on pp. 686-687) to keep pest populations down, as described in the sidebar on p. 350.

STRATEGIES FOR PREVENTING PEST PROBLEMS

The best and safest way to handle pest problems is to prevent them from occurring in the first place. Establishing a plant quarantine area and erecting barriers to pests are two practical preventive steps that can be taken in homes and greenhouses.

Quarantining

Set up a quarantine area for new or infested plants that is separate from the main greenhouse or your house plant collection. We cannot overemphasize the importance of doing this. The quarantine applies to plants new to the collection or those that are badly infested with pests but are worth saving. No plant from any source should be allowed into the permanent collection without a period of isolation and inspection in the quarantine area. Considering the problems caused by certain almost invisible but very damaging pests, such as broad mites (*Polyphagotarsonemus latus* and related species), or certain diseases transmitted by aphids or other piercing and sucking insects, no effort is too great to keep these pests from infesting the collection in the first place.

With new or severely infested plants that have received treatment, allow an observation period of a week or more. Using a hand lens, examine the plant for any suspicious lumps, marks or other indications of pest presence. Inspect the root ball by lifting the plant from its pot and gently probing the root area. While holding the root ball, look for pests inside the pot itself. Depending on what is found during this inspection, a number of actions, including repotting, physical removal of the pests by pruning off infested sections and/or treatments with insecticidal soap, may be needed before the plant can be placed in the larger collection.

It is best to locate the quarantine area well away from the main collection, because certain pests such as mites travel on air drafts. Use a back

Using Soaps and Horticultural Oils on Plants Indoors

The use of soap for controlling insects and mites has an extensive history. Ivory® soap has long been a favorite of organic gardeners, and Acco® Highway Spray has been used by city and state agencies to control a variety of pests of trees and shrubs outdoors. However, the products specifically devised for controlling insects on plants are the insecticidal soaps marketed by Safer, Inc., and by Ringer Co. (see pp. 114-116 for details). Because these soaps have been formulated specifically for pest control rather than for laundry purposes, you can expect them to be reliable at the doses recommended by the manufacturer on the label.

The new, highly refined horticultural oil sprays discussed on pp. 116-119 are highly effective against many indoor plant pests and can be sprayed safely on many plant species. These new oils differ from the older "dormant" oils that would burn plant foliage.

Soaps and oils are regarded as nontoxic to humans and pets. However, some plants are sensitive to them. Each plant species or variety may react differently. A few may show a brown burn or distortion of the leaves in reaction to soap washes or oil sprays; in others where the leaves are unaffected, the buds may show a burn. Therefore, you should follow the procedure outlined below before using a soap or oil.

• Read the product label to see if any cautions apply to the plant species you are planning to treat.

• Test a small portion of each plant for sensitivity to the soap or oil the first time you treat that variety. Record your findings.

• Treat when the temperature is cool and preferably out of direct sunlight. This may limit treatments of sensitive plants to the early morning (which is best, since excess moisture from soaping and rinsing will have a chance to dry during the day) or early evening.

• On plants that are sensitive, wash off the soap spray shortly after application (you do not have to rinse off oil sprays, however). You should do this within 5 to 30 minutes, depending on the degree of sensitivity. The soap kills the pest after only a short period of contact, but it can persist and damage the plant. Fortunately both Safer's and Ringer's insecticidal soap products are tolerated by a wide range of plants without damage.

• Spot-treat with soaps or oils, but do not use them routinely in all areas. As with any other pesticide, the more you use soaps and oils, the sooner there will develop a population of pests that is no longer killed by the material. Use soap or oil sprays only when and where needed, particularly in a plant collection in which you are trying to establish biological controls. Although certain beneficials such as adult lady beetles are highly tolerant of the soap or oil, others, including many parasitoids, are damaged or killed by them.

porch or outbuilding, if light and temperature conditions can be modified to allow plant survival. A less desirable alternative is to use sheets of plastic to screen off a space in a corner of the house or greenhouse.

Ideally, you should never walk from the quarantine area to the main collection, since pest mites and insects can hitch a ride on your arms or clothing. Keep a smock in the quarantine area to cover your regular work clothing when you enter. Before you leave, remove the smock, wash your hands and brush off your pant legs and shoes with a whisk broom. Other techniques that have been used by researchers to prevent the spread of pests from area to area include putting plastic bags over footwear while in the quarantine area and walking through a shallow pan of soapy water upon leaving the infested area.

Barriers

Whereas some pests are imported into the house, greenhouse or other indoor areas on newly acquired plants, many gain entry through broken or poorly fitting window screens, vents, cracks in siding and floors or other openings. If these points of entry can be sealed, many pests will be prevented from entering.

Yoder Brothers Nurseries, one of the largest wholesale greenhouses in the United States, excludes certain pests by screening greenhouse openings and by using a system of double doorways separated by a type of airlock common on houses in cold climates (see the drawing on the facing page). In addition, the interior doorway is hung with thin vertical strips of lightweight plastic that brush the clothing of workers passing through, knocking off any hitchhiking pests. A small fan, mounted near the door, creates a current of air that blows insects back outside. These simple modifications can be made to a home greenhouse, an indoor atrium or other indoor structures where plants are cultivated and displayed.

Excluding Pests from Greenhouses

In the greenhouses at Yoder Brothers, a large wholesale nursery, strips of plastic hung from doorways brush hitchhiking pests from workers' clothing, while a current of air from fans facing doors further repels the pests. Tight-mesh screens are placed over vents. Similar modifications can be made to home greenhouses.

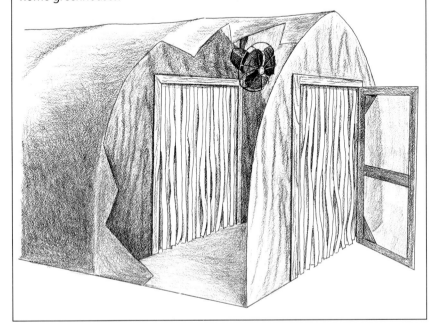

Careful screening more than pays for itself in the number of pests kept out as well as in savings on purchases of beneficial insects when biological controls are begun. Besides, your house should be completely screened anyway to keep out fabric pests and pests of stored food.

Screen all greenhouse vents with a mesh fine enough to exclude gnats. A white polypropylene screen with a mesh of 22 by 24 squares per inch works well (for sources, see the Resource Appendix under "Insect Management: Physical Controls" on pp. 682-683). Using the screen may require some modification to the structure or readjustment of the ventilation system, since it reduces air circulation somewhat. In some cases, additional vents will be needed to offset the reduced air flow.

Slugs, snails, ants and black vine weevils enter the greenhouse through cracks, by crawling under doors and/or by walking up the sides of the greenhouse and crawling in through unscreened vents. If you are troubled by these pests, caulk cracks and fit doors snugly against their frames and thresholds. Use weatherstripping where appropriate. For more specific information on barriers to these pests, see the discussion of the relevant pest in Chapter 20.

BIOLOGICAL CONTROLS

The key to a least-toxic program for controlling insect and mite pests of large plant collections indoors is the regular release of beneficial organisms. This hinges on creating an environment that encourages their permanent residence. As discussed in Chapter 4, biological control involves the use of predators, parasitoids (which are parasite-like in that they kill their host rather than just live on or in it) or pathogens (microbes that cause disease in the pest). As a group, these organisms are often referred to as natural enemies of the pest.

Beneficials available commercially in the United States are discussed throughout this book under the pests they control; they are also discussed at length in Chapter 5. But many more are known. A number of these are now available in other countries, although not yet in the United States, and even more have been raised for research purposes. So we can look forward to a wider range of species, improved strains, greater commercial availability and, perhaps, lower prices.

As you plan to use biological controls, there are some basic points you should keep in mind. Most people are more familiar with the use of nonliving pest control materials, such as pesticides. Biological control requires that you pay close attention to the special needs of each organism used against pests. Here are some hints that will help you obtain good results when releasing biological controls.

• Monitor the pest situation before and after releases, making estimates of the number of pests.

• Release sufficient numbers of controlling organisms. We recommend talking with the insectary (insect-rearing facility) to obtain advice on how many to release. If they do not sell directly to the public, they may recommend that you speak to a distributor of the organisms in your area.

• Release beneficials on a regular basis. Keep up the monitoring to see whether they are still around in sufficient numbers, and try to anticipate pest buildup so that you can order in time. Alternatively, you can make arrangements ahead of time for delivery at set intervals recommended by the producers.

You will know that the pests are building up when you see their numbers increase and/or the damage begins to annoy you, meaning the pest population is approaching the injury level. But there is no simple recipe that tells you when you have released enough predators. Although distributors may have some suggestions, in the last analysis you will have to experiment yourself. We tend to err on the side of too many predators by making releases on a regular (e.g., weekly) basis because we are often in the position of having to prove to an unconvinced client that alternatives work. Even where the number of releases of specific beneficials has become a standard recommendation for certain crops under certain commercial conditions, there may still be very little guidance for the keeper of a small collection of plants in the house or home greenhouse because these environments vary so much from case to case.

• Confine beneficials to the problem area by screening windows, vents and doors, or by tenting house plants (see p. 343 for a discussion of tenting).

• Prevent ants from interfering with the activities of predators and parasitoids by building barriers and by using baits.

• Reduce high pest infestations by pruning or by spraying plants with insecticidal soap or horticultural oil before the initial releases of beneficial organisms.

• Don't use residual pesticides for a month before releasing beneficial organisms (the exceptions are insecticidal soap and horticultural oil, which can be used up to two days before releasing beneficials).

Ordering Beneficial Organisms

There are over two dozen insectaries in the United States and Canada. Distributors are more numerous, and include many mail-order businesses. U.S. distributors can order from Canadian insectaries, and vice versa. Some beneficials are now ordered from Europe, and there are companies in the United States that hope to import beneficials from China, where species not yet reared in North America or Europe are available.

The availability of beneficial organisms is changing very rapidly, with new species being raised and new strains of others that have long been in commercial use now available. You can get the best information about the current state of the technology by contacting the producers directly. They can tell you how many beneficial organisms to release for the numbers of plants you have, the amount of greenhouse space or the severity of the infestation. For a list of producers, see the Resource Appendix under "Insect Management: Biological Controls" on pp. 683-686.

If you have only a small greenhouse or house plant collection, you will probably need to order from a distributor. Insectaries generally require very large orders before they sell to the consumer, but they can refer you to distributors in your area, or you can buy through most major garden supply catalogs. Beneficials generally cost less per unit when ordered in large numbers. Therefore you may want to get together with others in garden clubs or neighborhood groups to place a larger order. When you contact the insectary or distributor, ask:

• what is the smallest order they ship,

• how many organisms must be ordered to get a price break,

• what developmental stage of the insect is shipped,

• by what means they ship,

• how long shipping takes, and whether they guarantee delivery within a certain number of days,

• how to store beneficials that are not used immediately (usually the answer is refrigeration), and how long they can be expected to stay viable under those conditions.

There are often other questions you should ask the seller about specific beneficials; we mention some of these in the individual discussions of pests in the next chapter.

The Cost of Beneficial Organisms

When comparing the cost of beneficial organisms with conventional pesticides, you must consider several things. When you rely on conventional pesticides, sooner or later the pest population becomes resistant and you must use more or different pesticides to suppress it. This process gets progressively more hazardous, more bothersome and usually more expensive. In the large plant collections in conservatories, malls and other indoor locations, there are always some natural enemies of the pests that eventually make their way indoors to help control the pests; this sometimes happens in houses, too. Conventional broad-spectrum pesticides, which kill many different species, also kill these stray beneficials, making pest control even harder and more expensive. In the long run, even when the potential human health hazards and costs from pesticide exposure are not considered (and they should be), exclusive reliance on conventional pesticides is often expensive and troublesome.

The initial cost of predators and parasitoids is almost always higher than buying a can of insecticide. But the long-term maintenance of plant collections under biological controls becomes very economical. As a better balance of beneficials is achieved within the plant collection, there is a less violent fluctuation of pest numbers. Eventually, only periodic small releases of the predators and parasitoids are required. In large collections, where undisturbed areas are available, some beneficials may actually establish themselves indoors and propagate without much additional help from humans.

For example, at the Conservatory of Flowers in San Francisco's Golden Gate Park, whiteflies ceased to be a problem after only two seasons of releases of the parasitoid *Encarsia formosa*. The parasitoid became established and kept whitefly numbers low without further releases, and the total IPM program at the conservatory was 75% cheaper to operate than the chemical pest control program in use formerly.

As you keep your biological control program going over many years, there will be times when you are faced with pest "hot spots," local areas in the greenhouse, sometimes confined to one or two plants, where pest numbers climb beyond the ability of the predators or parasitoids to suppress them. Usually there is an environmental explanation for this; determining what the explanation is will help you avoid the same problem in the future.

Once the hot spot is there, our advice is either to spot-treat it with soap or simply prune out and dispose of the infested material. Note: Don't dump insect-infested material into a waste receptacle in the greenhouse or near the door; drop it in a bucket of insecticidal soap first so the pests have little opportunity to fly, crawl or hitchhike their way back into the greenhouse.

Summary: Preparing Yourself and Your Indoor Plant Environments for a Least-Toxic Pest Control Program

• Set up a monitoring and record-keeping program to help determine the level of pests that causes intolerable damage (known as the injury level), when and where treatment is needed and the effectiveness of biological controls after releases.

• Use screening to keep pests out and beneficial insects in. Build barriers to crawling pests.

• If residual pesticides have been used routinely in the past, substitute soap sprays or horticultural oil for several weeks to detoxify the plants and the environment.

• Establish a quarantine area for new or severely infested plants.

• Release beneficial insects on a regular basis and in sufficient quantities.

• Spot-treat infested plants with soap or oil sprays or prune out "hot spots" to prevent insect pest populations from becoming numerous in any one area or as a backup while you wait for beneficials to arrive.

CHAPTER 20
Controlling Pests of Indoor Plants

INTRODUCTION

When you stop using conventional pesticides in the house, greenhouse or other indoor space, you will probably find that a host of new pest problems emerge. This is because broad-spectrum conventional pesticides kill many beneficial organisms as well as the pests for which they are intended. It is wise to anticipate some of these new problems and prepare yourself accordingly.

In this chapter, we discuss ants, slugs, snails, mites, thrips, aphids, scales, mealybugs, whiteflies, leafminers, black vine weevils and fungus gnats. We begin with ants because they often exacerbate other pest problems by moving pests to new plants and protecting pest species from their natural enemies. Thus, controlling ants can be critical to a successful pest control program.

Not every indoor plant setting will be plagued with all the pests listed here. The presence or absence of the last three pests depends largely on which plants you grow (leafminers), your geographic location (black vine weevils) or what kind of growing medium you use (fungus gnats). But there is a very good chance that most of the other pests listed will show up sooner or later wherever you are located and no matter what plants you have.

If you already know which pest is causing your plant problem, you may elect to turn to the particular section describing that pest and ignore the rest of the chapter. You should bear in mind, however, that a totally nontoxic indoor plant environment involving large collections usually can be achieved only through the careful integration of control methods for all potential pests. If you focus on just one pest, there is a good chance you may later have a problem with another, and controlling it may require the emergency use of pesticides. This, in turn, could disrupt the program against the first pest by killing its natural enemies; it will also contaminate the environment for future releases

of beneficials. With this in mind, we recommend that you at least scan the sections describing control of the other major pests.

ANTS
(Order Hymenoptera, family Formicidae)

The general biology of ants, as well as the damage they cause and various means of detecting them, are discussed in greater detail under pantry pests in Chapter 14.

Ant control indoors, around house plants and in greenhouses is essential if you want to control aphids, scales, mealybugs and whiteflies. These insects all produce honeydew, a sugary exudate prized as food by various ant species. Ants kill or repel the beneficial insects used to control these pests.

Treatment: Direct Physical Controls

If your plants are in containers, the most effective means of denying ants access is to use barriers. Constructing ant barriers requires an initial expenditure of time and money, but the effort is repaid quickly, since the same devices can be used to exclude other crawling pests such as slugs, snails and black vine weevils. The sidebar on pp. 356-357 describes how to make barriers for freestanding and attached greenhouse benches.

Inspect all plants and containers for ants, slugs, snails and other pests before placing them above the barriers. Gently lift out the root ball and examine it and the pot for pests, particularly around the drainage hole. Do not place pots containing pests on the stand.

If ants are nesting in some of the containers, put the pot outside and flood it repeatedly with water to force the ants to relocate. Sometimes this process can be accelerated by setting a pail of dry soil or compost next to the infested pot and using a piece of wood to create a bridge between the flowerpot and the pail. During the flooding, the ants will use the bridge

to move their pupae (the young within cocoons) to the drier habitat. Once no more ants appear in the flooded pot, the pail can be moved outside. This process takes patience because the flooding must be repeated until all the ants have left; its benefit is that it is effective and totally nontoxic.

Treatment: Direct Chemical Controls

Another way to flood ants from infested containers is to use an insecticidal soap drench. Soap drenches do not generally hurt plant roots, but you should check the label to make sure the soap is compatible with the plant species you are treating.

If you lack the time or patience to flood ants from the infested containers, you can use poison baits to kill many species. For many decades arsenic trioxide mixed with a sweet attractant as a bait was used against the Argentine ant and other species. But the toxin is easily absorbed through human skin; those interested in a less-toxic material may want to experiment with boric-acid baits (see pp. 238-239) or hydramethylnon (Combat®).

SLUGS AND SNAILS
(Order Stylommatophora, families Limacidae and Helicidae)

The biology and monitoring of slugs and snails are discussed in detail in Chapter 31.

Slugs and, to a lesser extent, snails can both become problems on plants indoors. They may be present on the plant when it is purchased, they may enter a pot when it is set outside temporarily or they may gain access to the plant collection through a crack in the building, most commonly at ground level, where dampness persists after rains or irrigation.

Damage and Detection

The slimy and/or shiny trails snails and slugs leave behind are the first clue to their presence. Potted plants

Making Barriers for Greenhouse Benches

I. Barriers for Freestanding Benches or Tables

1. Push the legs of the bench or table through the center of downward-facing aluminum pie pans as shown in drawing A below. It helps to cut a starter hole or snip out a portion of the pan slightly smaller than the diameter of the leg (as shown in drawing B below). If the bench is too large or heavy to lift, cut the pans and reform them around the bench legs.

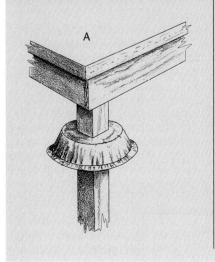

2. Pleat, fold or bend the pie pans so they form neat, downward-facing cups, tightly encircling the legs. They shouldn't protrude so far into the aisle that they become a nuisance.

3. Coat the undersides of the pie pans with one of the commercially available sticky materials used by entomologists as barriers to crawling insects. These are listed in the Resource Appendix under "Insect Management: Physical Controls" on pp. 682-683.

4. Check the pie pans once a month to make sure the coating is still sticky. Pests that attempt to crawl up the legs of the benches

either become stuck on or are repelled by these barriers. If the sticky coating is amply protected from dust and debris by the sides of the pan, it should last several years before a new layer is needed.

II. Barriers for Benches or Shelves that are Attached to Walls

Where the surfaces supporting the plants are not freestanding, you must build separate ant stands that sit on these surfaces and support the plants.

1. Cut exterior-grade plywood pieces to fit the area that is to support the plant (drawing C). The plywood should be at least ½ in. (1.3 cm) thick; ¾-in. (1.9 cm) plywood serves better where you are building a stand for a long greenhouse bench or the pots are heavy. The plywood stands should not be so wide that they touch the walls or any other structure that ants can climb up.

---

added to your collection should always be checked for slime tracks or the slugs themselves, which often gather around the hole at the bottom of the pot. When repotting, check the root ball for signs of slugs. Some slugs feed only on roots and can be devastating to bulb plants. Others browse on foliage, the young rasping away at surface tissues while the older ones eat irregularly shaped holes in the plant.

Treatment:
Direct Physical Controls

Slugs and snails generally avoid crossing copper barriers, because the metal is poisonous to them. When ant barriers are installed, it may be worth running copper strips around the legs of freestanding benches or ant stands to exclude slugs and snails as well. The strips should be at least 2½ in. (6.5 cm) wide. A copper strip called Snail-Barr® can be used to exclude snails from citrus trees and garden beds; it would also work well on table legs. For a source, see the Resource Appendix under "Insect Management: Physical Controls" on pp. 682-683.

In an article that appeared in *The IPM Practitioner*, Michael Roling, professor of agriculture at Southwest Missouri State University, describes the successful exclusion of a very common *Limax* species of slug in a commercial greenhouse. Copper barriers were placed around the wood blocks supporting benches where slug damage had been observed. Then beer was used as a bait in Garden Sentry® traps (see the Resource Appendix under "Insect Management: Physical Controls" on pp. 682-683) placed under the benches. The greater number of slugs found in some traps suggested possible points of entry. On the north side of the greenhouse, aluminum flashing was installed on the outside of the wooden baseboard to seal points where the traps indicated slugs were entering.

In applying the flashing, a trench was dug to the original depth of the curtain wall. A 7-in. (18 cm) wide band of aluminum flashing was inserted into the trench, aligned evenly

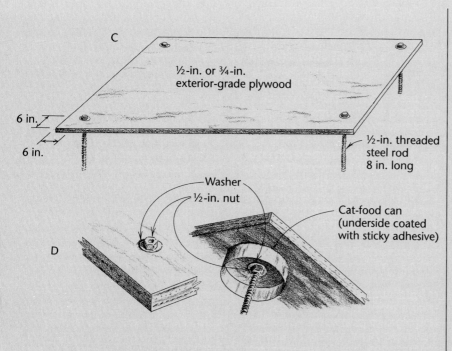

C

½-in. or ¾-in. exterior-grade plywood

6 in.

6 in.

½-in. threaded steel rod 8 in. long

Washer

½-in. nut

D

Cat-food can (underside coated with sticky adhesive)

3. Make the legs for the stands by drilling a ⁹⁄₁₆-in. (1.4 cm) hole through the plywood 6 in. (15 cm) from the edges in each corner. Place a ½-in. (1.3 cm) threaded steel rod through each hole and bolt the rods in place with washers and nuts above the plywood.

4. Thread the steel rod legs through upside-down tuna-fish or cat-food cans so that the cans encircle the rods tightly. The cans should open downward and be flush against the underside of the stand. Thread another washer and nut onto the leg on the underside of the stand to hold the can against the plywood (drawing D).

5. Coat the inside of the cans with Tanglefoot™, Stickem™ or other sticky adhesive.

Note: Small, decorative ant stands can be built to display one or two pots at a time on a patio or other area by using redwood instead of plywood.

Leave a gap of 1 in. (2.5 cm) between the ant stand and the wall to prevent ants from crossing. Although we have not found drainage to be a problem on these stands, you can drill holes in the plywood to allow water to drain through in greenhouse settings.

2. Protect all the wood surfaces from moisture by applying exterior paint before the wood gets wet.

with the bottom edge of the curtain wall, and stapled along the entire length of the north curtain wall. Once the flashing was attached, the trench was filled with soil to the original level. Then the copper barrier was stapled in place approximately 2 in. to 3 in. (5 cm to 7.6 cm) above the soil level to block the entry points that existed at the junction of the curtain wall and the plastic covering of the greenhouse. Greenhouse workers were advised that plants on the barrier-protected benches must not touch the plastic wall, because this would allow slugs to climb directly from the wall onto the foliage.

Professor Roling writes: "Once these minor problems were ironed out, the project was concluded on a very satisfactory note. The greenhouse operator was very pleased with the results: no complaints from customers, no slug damage, no regular application of chemicals, and no additional toxic substances in the greenhouse environment."

The copper-barrier installation method described here was created to repair an existing structure, but a similar method can be used in other structures. The drawing on p. 358 provides details on a barrier design for a standard greenhouse concrete-block footing.

According to the *Rodale Encyclopedia of Indoor Gardening*, slugs can be baited with raw potato. If you build the copper barrier described here, you might place some slices of raw potato above the barrier to attract and capture any mollusks that were hiding in the plant foliage before the barrier was installed. We suggest leaving the potato out overnight, then checking in the early morning. Any slugs or snails drawn to the bait can be picked up by hand or with tweezers and put outside or dropped into soapy water. Beer also attracts snails and slugs, as do the decomposing bodies of other slugs and snails. For more details on physical controls, see the discussion of slugs and snails in Chapter 31 on pests of food and ornamental gardens.

A Copper Slug and Snail Barrier for Greenhouses

Copper sheeting can be affixed to the baseboard atop a greenhouse footing to serve as a barrier to slugs and snails.

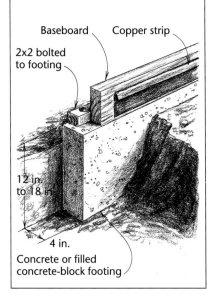

Baseboard

Copper strip

2x2 bolted to footing

12 in. to 18 in.

4 in.

Concrete or filled concrete-block footing

Treatment: Direct Chemical Controls

If chemical controls are considered necessary, a salt-impregnated vinyl barrier called Slug and Snail De-Fence™ is available that can be stapled around table legs or along the edges of plant stands. According to the product literature, slugs and snails sense the salt and are repelled by it; if they try to cross the barrier, the salt dehydrates them and they die. Although we have not tested this material, we can see how it might be useful where the salt is unlikely to wash into the soil in which plants are growing.

If telltale mucus trails above plant barriers suggest that not all slugs and snails were discovered before the pots were set on stands, commercially available baits can be placed on the stands briefly to kill the remaining individuals. To use these baits, cut the end off a soup can, place the bait inside and lay the can on its side on the surface of the bench to protect the bait from moisture. Alternatively, you can use a plastic trap to hold the bait. Dead slugs and snails remain in the can or trap and can be disposed of easily.

MITES
(Order Acari, families Tetranychidae, Tenuipalpidae, Tarsonemidae and others)

Until recently, mite infestations of indoor plants were extremely difficult to manage. This problem was due primarily to the excessive use of pesticides, which kill not just the pest mites but also their natural enemies. The pesticides also encouraged the development of strains of mites that were resistant to the chemicals. Fortunately, predatory mites that kill common pest mites of plants indoors are now available. Their use can be coupled with insecticidal soap to cool down occasional mite hot spots. The success of this two-part approach has made mites among the easiest of pests to control without the use of materials toxic to humans or other nontarget animals.

Biology

For many gardeners, the primary connotation of mites is "pest." This is unfortunate, because many mite species are directly beneficial to humans and human pursuits. Those that live in the soil help decompose organic matter, returning it to its constituent elements in forms essential to plant growth.

The spider mites, so-called because of the webs they build, are among the most common mite pests of plants. Outdoors in late fall and winter, the reduced hours of light, lower temperatures and shortage of suitable food plants cause the two-spotted mite (the most common spider mite pest of indoor plants) to go into a resting phase called diapause, which might be compared to hibernation in mammals. The mites seek out cracks and crevices in the soil, under bark and on structures. But not all spider mites diapause in this fashion. In the artificial environment of a warm, lighted greenhouse or residence, some mites may be active periodically throughout the winter.

Even though some relatives of the two-spotted mite balloon through the air like spiders spinning a web, the two-spotted mite itself is most likely to drop off one plant and crawl over the ground surface to the next. Two-spotted mite development is suppressed by high humidity. Predatory mites, on the other hand, are more tolerant of humid conditions. In the greenhouse, two-spotted mite populations can be diminished or prevented by periodically hosing down plants, especially the undersides of the leaves, with plain water, as described under "Physical Controls" on p. 360; a good rinsing under the shower provides the same benefits to potted house plants.

Damage

You can detect the presence of mites indirectly by their damage. This shows first as needle-like puncture marks where mites have sucked the sap from plant parts. Initially the tops of damaged leaves are stippled with tiny silvery or yellowish dots; later the punctures become brown and sunken. Broad mites cause a distortion of the new growth of leaves and buds. Because these mites are so small, early detection is relatively difficult, and a large infestation may develop before symptoms appear. Once a plant with distorted new growth is detected, it is prudent to isolate it in the hope that the infestation can be confined to that plant. The infested plant should be treated and kept isolated until additional new growth appears normal, indicating that treatment has brought the infestation under control.

Most indoor plants can tolerate a low level of pest mites without sustaining noticeable damage, particularly during winter, when low light

Mites in the Quarantine Area

Infestations of mites and other plant pests usually begin with a few pests settling on one or two plants. The pests can arrive on recently purchased plants, wind currents or clothing. To keep these initial pest infestations from spreading throughout the collection, establish a quarantine area where newly purchased plants can be held for inspection and where infested plants can be isolated for treatment. For details on how to set up and manage this quarantine area, refer to p. 349.

Because mites can travel on air currents, the quarantine area should be physically separated from the main plant collection. Obviously a separate room is best; however, within the greenhouse, plastic sheets suspended from the ceiling also create effective isolation areas. You can discourage mites from traveling from plant to plant within the isolation area by applying sulfur dust to the plant benches. Spider mites can cling to your arms and clothing, so avoid going directly from the quarantine area to the main collection. Try to schedule your work in the quarantine area as the last task of the day.

Keep each new plant in quarantine for at least one week, and use a 10x hand lens to examine its foliage. Inspect several times during this period, since mite eggs hatch over several days. If spider mites or their silken webs are observed on the new plants, release predatory mites if pest mite numbers are relatively low, or spray with insecticidal soap if many pests are observed. Discard severely infested plants that do not respond to treatment.

If a specimen is too valuable to discard but is too severely infested to clear of mites with insecticidal soap, you may decide to spray a conventional miticide (a pesticide specifically designed to kill mites). If so, do it outdoors and protect yourself with a respirator and other gear designed for use when applying toxic materials. Be sure to read all label directions. After treatment, hold the plant in the quarantine area for a month to see whether the miticide has worked. The holdover also ensures that the pesticide has dissipated enough to avoid harming any beneficial mites you have already released in the main plant collection.

---

and cool temperatures restrict mite maturation and reproduction. If you see one or two mites on four or five leaves during winter, it may not be necessary to rush in with treatment since environmental conditions alone will keep the population low. Move the infested plant to an isolated area to prevent the mites from spreading and monitor it weekly.

Bear in mind that a number of fungus-eating mite species you may find on stems and foliage do not damage the plants. So don't panic just because you see mites—you are looking specifically for mites associated with damage. But also remember that when temperature and humidity levels are optimal, pest mite populations can increase to damaging levels very rapidly. Thus, if you spot a few spider mites on a plant during spring or summer, it is wise to begin treatment right away. If you act while the pest mite population is relatively low, you have a broader range of nontoxic options open for control.

Monitoring and Detection

Regular monitoring enables you to detect mite problems before they become serious. We recommend that you inspect your plant collection weekly or biweekly during the growing season and monthly during the winter. Check new plants carefully before you add them to the collection, preferably in the type of quarantine area described in the sidebar above. If you do find mite hot spots, you still have time to order and release beneficial predatory mites (see "Biological Controls" on pp. 360-362) before the problem becomes more serious. Monitoring also enables you to decide whether or not these beneficial mites are keeping pest mites at tolerable levels. If not, you know it's time to use insecticidal soap or horticultural oil.

Checking for mites involves regular examination of the foliage. You must learn to recognize mites, the damage they cause and/or their webbing (shown in the drawing on p. 360). A 10x hand lens is invaluable for this, since mites are very small. Those referred to as spider mites, the type most commonly found on indoor plants, are about the size of a period on this page. They may be yellowish, greenish, pink or shades of red, depending on the species. Their eggs may be round and translucent, pale white or ivory in color (these are the true spider mites in the family Tetranychidae); or they may be oval and bright orange-red (these are the "false" spider mites in the family Tenuipalpidae). Pest mites grouped under the general names broad or cyclamen mites (Tarsonemidae) are

Spider Mite Webbing

Spider mites produce large amounts of webbing. The presence of webbing helps distinguish spider mites from predatory mites, which do not produce webs.

one-fourth the size of spider mites and almost impossible to see even with a hand lens. They are primarily a problem on cyclamens, gerberas, begonias and African violets.

Inspect the undersides of leaves, particularly along the main ribs. Check the middle-aged leaves first, since mite infestations seem to begin on such leaves. If the infestation becomes severe on these leaves, the mites move to new growth. Also check where the bases of the leaves join the stems and where branches attach to the main trunk of the plant.

True spider mites may form large colonies on a single plant. You will see mites of many sizes, which means many ages, running over their webs; over time, they will expand the web. Webs of the true spider mite can be seen by allowing sunlight to fall at an angle across a leaf when it is turned over. You can also try shining a flashlight beam across the leaf's midrib, or misting it with water so the light catches droplets clinging to the web. Note, however, that web-making is not characteristic of all mites, and mite-inflicted damage may be the only clue that other pest mites are present on your plants.

Treatment: Direct Physical Controls

One effective nontoxic means of preventing mite problems or reducing the severity of an existing mite population is manipulating the environment of the house or greenhouse to make it unsuitable for mites. To understand how to do this, you must have a basic notion of the environmental conditions that mites thrive in. A review of the "Biology" section on p. 358 will provide some clues.

In general, mites prefer high temperatures and low humidity. Thus, make sure there is adequate moisture in the air around your plants and protect them from heat. (Desert plants are the exception. Cacti can live at high temperatures in a dry atmosphere without any danger of mite infestations.)

In the house, misting plant foliage periodically increases local moisture, and clustering plants together prevents the water vapor from evaporating too quickly. But don't overwater the soil in the container. Set pots above, not in, larger containers of water. Alternatively, you can place pots containing plants into larger pots and pack moist sphagnum or peat moss between the two pots. The objective is to keep the soil containing the roots well-drained while humidifying the air surrounding the foliage. For more on this subject, review the discussion of habitat modification on pp. 328-331. A thorough hosing with a strong jet of water knocks off mites and destroys their webs. Increased humidity may also trigger a disease of the mite.

Protect house plants from hot late-afternoon sun with blinds or curtains, and place them away from the direct blast of heating vents in winter. In greenhouses or on sun porches you can reduce the brightest light with shade cloth or whitewash, both of which are available from garden suppliers, or with window blinds. Be sure to provide adequate ventilation to avoid overheating.

Predatory Mites

A predatory mite (A) is shown here attacking a pest two-spotted mite (B). Predatory mites arrive from the insectary in small vials and can be tapped out onto the leaves of mite-infested plants (C).

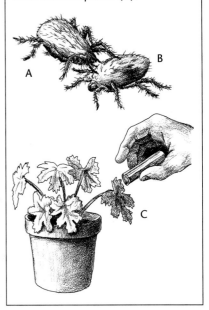

Treatment: Direct Biological Controls

In the long term, the simplest means of preventing a buildup of pest mites or of "knocking down" an incipient outbreak is to release beneficial predatory mites that eat pest mites.

Predatory mites are suitable for release on mite-infested plants in the house and greenhouse. They are very tiny, often smaller than the mites they prey upon (see the drawing above); once you release them on the plant, they are essentially invisible. They cannot bite people and they do not leave the plants and become a nuisance in the house or greenhouse. When they have killed off the pest mites, they may survive for some time by feeding on pollen and nectar from plants, but they will not injure the plants. If pest mites remain unavailable, the predatory mites eventually starve to death.

A number of predatory mite species can be purchased from commercial sources (see the Resource Appendix under "Insect Management: Biological Controls" on pp. 683-686); those most commonly available are listed in the sidebar at right. Predators vary in the prey they favor, the temperatures and humidity at which they function best and the height in the plant at which they feed on prey. For example, the predatory mite *Metaseiulus occidentalis* may not be as voracious as other mites in its consumption of pest mites, but it can go longer without food. This better enables it to survive the period when pest mites have all been eaten and the predators must wait for more eggs of the pest to hatch.

Given the variations among predator mites, we recommend buying a mix of the first three predators listed in the sidebar. Some producers ship this mix as a matter of course. A fourth spider-mite predator, *Phytoseiulus longipes,* which tolerates high temperatures, has recently become available. We have no personal experience with its use, but we suggest you ask that it be added to the mix as extra insurance.

Most of the predators listed are regularly available, particularly if purchased in large quantities. However, new producers of beneficial organisms enter the trade each year and long-established insectaries continually expand their offerings. Many other species are raised for research and could constitute valuable additions to the currently marketed selection. Lack of demand is the main reason they are not available.

There is every reason to believe that as more people learn about the ability of these organisms to control pest mites and certain pest insects, an expanded assortment will be marketed. You can help make this happen by purchasing the species that are currently available and requesting of suppliers that species not currently produced in large numbers be raised for the marketplace and publicized.

Predatory Mites Available for the Control of Pest Mites in Greenhouses[a]

For spider mites:
Phytoseiulus persimilis. A major predator of the two-spotted spider mite. Most efficient in mild humidity and temperatures up to 80°F (27°C).

Amblyseius californicus. Most often used in greenhouses on interior plants and outside ornamentals. Efficient at temperatures up to 85°F (29°C).

Metaseiulus (Typhlodromus) occidentalis: Used against the two-spotted mite, Pacific mite and tomato russet mite. Tolerates temperatures of 90°F (32°C) and above.

Phytoseiulus longipes: A recent import from Africa. Preliminary applications show it remains an effective spider-mite predator after *P. persimilis* succumbs to high temperatures. Tolerant of low humidity and temperatures up to 90°F (32°C).

For broad mites:
Amblyseius limonicus. This predator, which is occasionally available from Biotactics, was periodically released by the authors in a large conservatory to control broad mites on gerberas grown on greenhouse benches, in hanging baskets of columnias, in a permanent ground cover of ruella and on large scheffleras. One or two releases of the predator seemed to provide lasting control of the broad mite, except on gerberas. For the gerberas, frequent supplemental soap sprays were needed. The effectiveness of the predators may have been lessened by the high temperatures and low humidity in that particular greenhouse. Also, the mobility of the predators may have been hampered by the wide spacing of the plants on benches. The predators were very effective in the more humid, partially shaded and somewhat cooler areas where the other infested plants were located.

Euseius stipulatus, E. hibisci, Typhlodromus rickeri, T. porresi, T. annectens: These predators were tested in the laboratory against the broad mite and they show promise. None is yet produced commercially, but producers may be willing to rear them if asked.

[a] The comments in these listings are abstracted from materials produced by Biotactics, a major producer of predatory mites. For a complete list of producers see the Resource Appendix under "Insect Management: Biological Controls" on pp. 683-686; for updates on any mite predators that may have become available since this book was published, contact BIRC, P.O. Box 7414, Berkeley, CA 94707.

If you use predatory mites, here are some basic guidelines that you should follow:
• Phone or write the closest producer to ask which predatory mites are best for the control of the particular pest mites infesting your plants. A mix is often recommended.

• Ask how many mites you should order. This is usually based on the number of plants or the square footage of greenhouse. Typical recommendations are 20 predators per sq. yd. of bench space, two predators per damaged leaf or two predators per plant if the plants are small.

• Avoid using conventional pesticides during the month prior to releases. It takes a minimum of 30 days for residues of many of these materials to leave the plant and its environment. If residues are present when beneficial mites are released, the mites will probably be killed. Observe newly released predatory mites for signs of poisoning if pesticides have been used previously.

• Adjust the temperature to favor the predatory mites.

• Begin introducing beneficial mites at the first sign of pest mite damage. If pest mite infestations are already severe by the time the predatory mites arrive in the mail, spray the plants with insecticidal soap or horticultural oil 48 hours before releasing the predators.

• Keep the predators cool, but not refrigerated, after they arrive—on the north side of the building or in the basement, for example—and release them the next morning.

• Distribute predators on the middle or upper leaves throughout the plant collection. Visibly infested plants should receive more predators than those that show no damage, but try to ensure that most plants receive at least one or two predators. The easiest way to distribute the predators is to shake a little of the sawdust-like carrier out of the vial or cup containing the mites onto the plants. The mites will crawl off the sawdust and move rapidly over the leaves in search of prey.

• Set a few predators aside for later examination with a hand lens. This helps you learn to recognize them. Examination is easier if you kill the predators first by chilling them overnight in a freezer.

• Introduce the next batch of predators two weeks later, then release them at regular monthly intervals during the warm season. The later batches should be concentrated where monitoring indicates pest mite numbers are rising.

• Monitor every week once pest mites are coming under control and no new areas are being infested. In cool weather when the pest mites may hibernate, a warm spell may temporarily bring them out again. Check for outbreaks near doors, windows, support posts and other structural features that have cracks and crevices where they may hibernate.

Treatment:
Direct Chemical Controls

Direct chemical controls for mites on plants indoors include the use of insecticidal soap, horticultural oil and sulfur.

1. **Insecticidal Soap.** We recommend insecticidal soap for reducing severe infestations and for management of susceptible plants while you wait for shipments of predators to arrive. If specialized broad mite predators are not available, you may be able to control an infestation by applying insecticidal soap at four- or five-day intervals. We suggested using soap with hot water at these intervals to control broad mites on a large number of gerberas grown for display in the San Francisco Conservatory of Flowers, and very satisfactory control was achieved. Of course, it is preferable to get the right species of predator even if the supply is intermittent, and save the soap sprays for hot spots.

2. **Horticultural Oil.** There are reliable reports that a 2% solution of horticultural oil in water is highly effective in suppressing spider mite populations. Tests on over 50 species of mite-infested plants have been successful. Phytotoxicity is not a problem on most plants, even at daily temperatures above 95°F (35°C) and relative humidities below 90%.

Such oil treatments lack the residual activity of traditional insecticides but provide comparable short-term mortality. Considering their low mammalian toxicity, horticultural oils should become widely used alternatives, particularly during the transition to complete biological control. For further information on horticultural oils, see pp. 116-119 and the article by Grossman, listed under "References and Readings" on pp. 398.

3. **Sulfur.** Sulfur is toxic to mites but not very toxic to humans unless taken internally or inhaled. However, because it leaves a visible residue on foliage, few people like to use sulfur on infested ornamental plants; some people object to the smell. You should avoid using horticultural oils for a month after applications of sulfur since sulfur residues can cause the oil sprays to trigger phytotoxic reactions in plants.

Summary: Least-Toxic Pest Mite Control

• Isolate newly or severely mite-infested plants for treatment and observation.

• Adjust the indoor temperature and humidity to slow pest mite development and favor predatory mites.

• Release sufficient numbers of predatory mites often enough to obtain adequate control.

• Monitor with a hand lens at least once a week to determine the success of beneficial mite treatments and to catch increases in the pest mite population before they become serious.

• Use insecticidal soap or horticultural oil to spot-treat pest mite hot spots, to reduce high pest infestations prior to beneficial mite releases and to remove pest mites from new additions to your plant collection.

• Place sulfur on benches where there are broad mite infestations to reduce mite travel between plants.

Despite these shortcomings, we recommend the use of sulfur in the quarantine area, particularly if you are using this area to isolate plants infested with broad mites. These very tiny mites that distort new growth on plants move rapidly along shelves or greenhouse benches to reach new plants. A sulfur dusting of the surface on which the container plants sit kills the migrating mites. If you are applying sulfur as a dust, be sure to wear a respirator.

THRIPS
(Order Thysanoptera, many families)

Thrips are so insignificant to the naked eye that they are unfamiliar to the average person. They take the form of barely visible, slightly animated straight lines clustered along veins on the undersides of leaves. Usually their fecal spots and the damage they cause by scraping the surface of the leaf are more visible than the thrips themselves.

Some thrips are predators, feeding on other species of thrips or on mites, whereas others feed on plants. In this section, we will focus on plant-eating thrips that can reach damaging numbers on ornamental and vegetable plants grown indoors.

Biology

Thrips are tiny insects, ⅕ in. (5 mm) long or less. They occupy their own taxonomic order, Thysanoptera (for more about insect orders, see Chapter 1). Thysanoptera is divided into two suborders with distinctly different visual characteristics (unfortunately, visible only under a microscope) and an important behavioral difference.

Members of the suborder Terebrantia, which includes many common indoor pest thrips such as the greenhouse thrips and the onion thrips, make a slit in the surface of a plant's epidermis and insert their eggs into the plant tissue. Members of the suborder Tubulifera—which includes the black hunter *(Hap-lothrips mali)*, an important and common predator of mites, small aphids and other thrips—lay their eggs on plant surfaces, in cracks and in other protected areas.

The process of metamorphosis in thrips falls midway between the kind of change that takes place in grasshoppers, in which the young look very similar to the adults but are

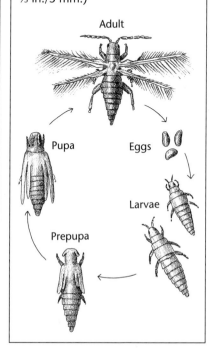

The Life Cycle of Thrips
Adult female thrips insert several hundred eggs into the tissues of flowers, leaves or stems. The eggs hatch within days in warm weather, or weeks to months in colder weather. They become wingless larvae (nymphs), which feed on plant sap. After two or more nymphal stages, many thrips drop to the soil, where they pass the prepupal and pupal stages. Emerging adults fly to the plant and repeat the cycle.
Development from egg to adult takes about two weeks in warm weather and a month in cooler weather. (Actual length of adult: ⅕ in./5 mm.)

Adult

Pupa

Eggs

Larvae

Prepupa

smaller, and the full metamorphosis of caterpillars, which change their appearance completely during the pupal, or cocoon, stage and emerge as butterflies or moths. The life stages of thrips include the egg, two larval stages, a prepupal stage, the pupa and the adult, as shown in the drawing below. Adults have two pairs of fringed wings, which normally are held back over and parallel to the body.

Only the two larval stages and the adults are active feeders; thrips rest during the prepupal and pupal stages. Because many pest thrips descend to the ground to spend this resting period, these species can be controlled if they are prevented from finding suitable pupation sites or if they are attacked in the soil during pupation by nematodes or pathogens. The latter are encouraged by the presence of moisture (these tactics are discussed further below).

In many species males are rare; in some species they seem to be absent altogether. Thrips apparently can rely almost entirely on parthenogenetic reproduction, in which the females produce young without mating. The process, which is also common in aphids, permits a very rapid population buildup since no time is lost finding a mate.

Damage

Thrips are rarely serious pests where conventional pesticides are used. They can become troublesome on indoor plants when efforts are made to reduce pesticide use and rely on biological controls. The difficulty occurs in part because thrips are often found in the same places as aphids and whiteflies. The common insecticides used to control these pests also kill thrips. Thus, thrips may go unnoticed indoors because insecticides keep their numbers so low.

When pesticides are replaced by biological controls specific to whiteflies and aphids, thrips often rise to damaging numbers, and it becomes tempting to use an insecticide to control them. However, unless this is done with great care, there is a danger of killing the predators and parasitoids that have been introduced against the other pests. Thus, if you are planning to develop a complete program of nontoxic biological pest control for your plant collection, choose a method of thrips control at the same time that you plan for control of the more obvious aphids and whiteflies.

Thrips feed by scraping the surface of plant tissue and sucking up juices that leak out. Heavily infested leaves appear brownish or silver and dried rather than wilted. The growing points of the plant may become distorted. Certain species, such as the greenhouse thrips *(Heliothrips haemorrhoidalis)*, leave copious amounts of their soot-like fecal matter on the leaves (see the photo at right). These black spots may be more noticeable than the insects themselves.

These leaves, which are silver in color, show the soot-like flecks of fecal matter characteristic of a heavy infestation of the greenhouse thrips *(Heliothrips haemorrhoidalis)*. (Photo by Max Badgley.)

Monitoring and Detection
A blue sticky trap that attracts thrips is now available for use in greenhouses. The design of the trap is based on research by AgCanada entomologists David Gillespie and Bob Vernon. Starting with yellow sticky traps such as those used to catch whiteflies, they tested a range of colors and found that a light shade of blue was most attractive to thrips. Depending on the manufacturer, these traps are coated with sticky adhesive on one or both sides.

The traps are available as lengths of thin blue sticky ribbon used to monitor large greenhouse crops and as cards that can be attached to stakes and placed in individual plant pots or hung above groups of plants, as shown in the drawing at right. Gillespie recommends that when using the ribbon traps in greenhouses, they be hung vertically so that the top of the trap is 2 ft. (61 cm) above plants, with the bottom of the plastic strip an inch or two above the plant canopy. This recommendation is based on the fact that most adult thrips fly within a 2-ft. zone above the plants.

The natural enemies of the thrips, discussed on pp. 365-367, should be released as soon as the first adults are spotted on a trap. When you see adult thrips stuck to the trap, you can get the species identified and search your collection for infested plants.

Treatment: Direct Physical Controls
Numerous studies on managing thrips on agricultural crops outdoors have demonstrated that dry plants are most likely to suffer thrips attack, although it is not clear why this is so. Thus, where thrips are a problem indoors, adequate water use may be the first and most important control strategy. Other strategies include maintaining diverse vegetation in areas prone to thrips and using mulches to control thrips.

1. Moisture. Thrips were rarely a problem in old-style greenhouses, where plants were watered with ordinary garden hoses and were grown above slowly decomposing beds of manure, which contributed heat and moisture to the growing medium.

Monitoring Thrips with Sticky Traps
Blue sticky cards, either hung above the plants or placed on stakes in the plant pots, are used to detect thrips and help reduce their numbers. The traps should be positioned within a 2-ft. (61 cm) zone above the plants.

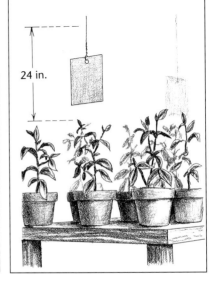

24 in.

The walkways were usually sodden, and the moisture content of the air and soil was very high. The high moisture helped kill thrips by spreading fungi to which they are very susceptible and by drowning the thrips when they attempted to pupate near the soil surface.

In addition to ensuring that plants receive adequate soil moisture for desired growth, two other tactics that can be used to reduce thrips damage are regularly misting plants with water or delivering all irrigation from overhead, and periodically flooding earthen greenhouse floors to drown pupating thrips.

2. Maintaining Vegetation. Because a number of pestiferous thrips species are common on weeds outdoors, one might think that weed control around lathhouses or unscreened greenhouses would reduce infestations on indoor plants. In fact, it has been documented that destroying weeds, particularly when the remaining desired plants are susceptible to thrips, can have the opposite effect since it causes the thrips to migrate onto cultivated plants. Because plant-eating thrips have many natural enemies in undisturbed areas, probably the best strategy for controlling them is to maintain diverse vegetation around such outdoor lath structures and greenhouses rather than undertaking zealous weed control in the immediate environs.

3. Mulches. Mulches have been used to control thrips on a small scale on high-cash crops outdoors. They might be tried in indoor settings. In his discussion of agricultural thrips control, researcher T. Lewis observes that aluminum foil mulches closely surrounding the stems of plants are suspected of disorienting thrips by creating a "bright, highly reflective vegetation or surface beneath them instead of the usual duller, less reflective vegetation or earth." Additionally, aluminum foil mulches may prevent those species of thrips that pupate in the soil from finding suitable pupation sites.

Other mulches may also decrease infestations of thrips by interfering with pupation. In greenhouse settings, plastic sheets, roofing paper, newspapers or kraft (brown) paper can be unrolled over the soil beneath the benches. These mulches have the added benefit of preventing weed growth. The coverings must be lifted periodically and shaken free of soil and other debris that accumulates on them. Alternatively, new coverings can be laid on top of the old ones to provide a fresh, soil-free surface.

Some important pest thrips of plants indoors do not return to the soil to pupate, however, and in such cases biological control may represent the best tactic.

Treatment:
Direct Biological Controls

Several natural enemies of thrips are available commercially, but they are not yet commonly used in greenhouse control programs because their potential is not well-known and their precise method of application has not been spelled out. However, since experimenting with biological controls of this type presents no hazards to the user or to the environment, it is exactly the type of new technology that the small grower or amateur gardener can explore independently. From our reading of what little scientific literature there is, we conclude that biological control will be the best method of indoor thrips control in the future; in many cases, it is the best method now.

The most promising organisms are thrips-eating mites, lacewings and nematodes. Because few studies have been made on the use of these predators and parasitoids, you must do your own experimenting to find out how many and how often to release, and which environmental conditions promote their effectiveness. It may be worth consulting suppliers, since they are often the first to hear of successful applications of their products. You will probably find that some suppliers are more interested in acquir-

ing and providing this kind of information to the small-scale user than others. For sources of the natural enemies described in this section, see the Resource Appendix under "Insect Management: Biological Controls" on pp. 683-686.

1. Predatory Mites. Two predatory mites, *Neoseiulus (=Amblyseius) mackenziei* and *Amblyseius cucumeris,* appear to have substantial potential for thrips control. They can be mass-produced easily, which is critical in making any biological control organism available, and they can coexist with other predators released in the same settings to control other pests, although the predators will prey on each other to a limited extent. When they temporarily run out of thrips to eat, these same predatory mites can survive on spider mites, which are serious pests of indoor plants. Like the mite predators of spider mites, they are suitable for release on plants in the home or office.

In *Biological Pest Control, The Glasshouse Experience,* N. W. Hussey describes the successful control of thrips on greenhouse cucumbers over 8 to 10 weeks after an initial release of only 28 predator mites on 2 out of 17 plants. Note how long it took for the control to become evident. Be patient! Adult thrips are long-lived. The mites apparently prey primarily upon the egg and larval stages. Therefore you are likely to see adult thrips on the leaves long after the overall pest population has been substantially reduced. Yet the new foliage should show progressively less damage. You should begin to notice control two to three months after the first predator release. If you make periodic releases after that, particularly in the driest, hottest times of the year, you should keep the thrips population in check.

These predatory mites are known to prey on a number of common pest mites, but the data are incomplete as to how many different species they can control. Therefore, if control is not achieved within the time suggested here and you are certain that the mites were alive when you released them and that you released enough according to the producer's advice, you can assume that the predatory mite is ineffective against your species of thrips.

2. Lacewings. Lacewing larvae are among the most voracious predators of thrips. Some of the many thrips species they prey on are particularly difficult to control because they pupate in the foliage and do not descend to the ground where they would be vulnerable to a variety of other control tactics. One such example is the greenhouse thrips *(Heliothrips haemorrhoidalis),* which is preyed upon by the green lacewing, the lacewing predator most commonly available commercially.

Lacewings are general predators. If you release them for control of other pests such as aphids on the same plants, they will undoubtedly help reduce thrips populations, too. However thrips are not their preferred food, so if you are relying on them for thrips control, you must pay special attention to where and how frequently you release them.

Lacewings are most commonly sold in the egg stage to make shipping easier, but we have had little success in releasing lacewings at this stage, and recommend instead that they be purchased as larvae. Ask that they be sent in the packages they are raised in, in which each larva has its own six-sided compartment. This is necessary because lacewing larvae attack their own kind as readily as they prey on pests. You may have to negotiate with the supplier, because not all suppliers are willing to make the extra effort. The special packaging is also more expensive, but, in our estimation, worth it. One company that uses these hex cell units is Rincon-Vitova Insectary (see the Resource Appendix under "Insect Management: Biological Controls" on pp. 683-686).

You can transfer the lacewing larvae to each plant with a fine-pointed paint brush. Use water to wet the brush (avoid using saliva, which can be toxic to the insects). Alternatively, you can hold the individual hex cell over the plant and tap it with a pencil so the larva drops to the foliage. In controlling aphids on cyclamens and similar small, individually potted ornamental plants, we have found that one larva per plant is enough; we also recommend starting with that ratio for thrips control if the pest population is small.

You can release lacewing eggs or larvae on plants in your home or office without tenting the plants. But you must be willing to vacuum them up or capture them in a jar and release them outside when they finally mature and become flying adults that are attracted to light. For a description of this procedure, see pp. 371-372; for details on tenting lacewings, see the sidebar on p. 343. Commercially available lacewing species are discussed further under aphid control on pp. 370-372.

3. Nematodes. Because most thrips pupate in the soil, they are potentially susceptible to control through the release of insect-eating nematodes. An important exception is the greenhouse thrips *(Heliothrips haemorrhoidalis).*

Field experiments conducted at Hydro-Gardens, a large commercial nursery in Colorado Springs, Colorado, indicate that it is possible to control some thrips species indoors using commercially reared nematodes. In the experiment, six million nematodes were added to the fertilizer water of a quarter-acre greenhouse in which European cucumbers were being grown. Each cucumber flower contained about four to six thrips of all ages (there are about 8 to 10 flowers per plant). The watering was repeated three times during July. Within a month there was a major reduction in thrips, and after two months they had virtually disappeared. In a separate greenhouse on the same site, conventional insecticides were used. They failed to control the thrips, and the entire cucumber crop was lost.

Mike Morton, who conducted the experiment, told us that it was his impression that the nematodes killed the immature thrips and pupating larvae while they were in the plant-growing medium. He described that medium as rock wool, which is similar to fiberglass insulation but without additives. Although adult thrips were present on the foliage and continued to lay eggs there for many weeks, eventually the population was dramatically reduced because the young did not survive the nematode attack in the pupation stage.

Hydro-Gardens distributes these nematodes throughout the United States under the name Guardian™. For other sources of insect-eating nematodes, see the Resource Appendix under "Insect Management: Biological Controls" on pp. 683-686.

This experiment gives no indication of how useful nematodes would be if applied in a foliage spray, and we have found no information on field tests using them this way in greenhouses. Nematodes are very susceptible to drying out, which would seem a major obstacle to aerial applications. High humidity would probably aid in short-term nematode survival, and some immediate pest reduction might presumably be achieved by applying nematodes in a water spray to the undersides of the leaves where the thrips congregate. Considerable research is now underway to find an application medium that would prevent the nematodes from drying out. If it is successful, foliage applications may become a useful tool for controlling thrips that do not descend to the ground to pupate.

4. Damsel Bugs and Pirate Bugs. Other organisms commonly found in gardens in the United States during the warm season can also be captured and brought indoors to aid in thrips control in small greenhouses and sun porches. These include predatory bugs (Hemiptera) in the family Nabidae (the damsel bugs) and in the family Anthocoridae (the flower or minute pirate bugs). They are good

Pirate and Damsel Bugs

The minute pirate bug, *Orius tristicolor* (A), and the western damsel bug, *Nabis alternatus* (B), can be collected outdoors and moved into the greenhouse, where they prey on thrips. (Actual sizes: pirate bug, 1/12 in./2 mm; damsel bug, 5/16 in./8 mm)

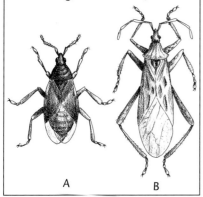

A   B

general insect- and mite-eating beneficials to have in indoor plant settings, as they also feed on a wide variety of pests besides thrips. Examples of species that have been observed to prey on common indoor thrips are the minute pirate bug *(Orius tristicolor)* and the western damsel bug *(Nabis alternatus),* shown in the drawing above.

These bugs are large enough to be easily visible to the gardener and slow-moving enough to catch outdoors. But don't count on being able to tap or shake them loose from the substrate on which you find them —they have a remarkable ability to cling to whatever they're on. Try inverting a wide-mouthed glass jar over a bug as it walks over the leaves, and quickly bring the jar lid up underneath it. Use the pressure of the lid on the jar rim to tear off the small amount of foliage on which the bug sits, trapping it inside the jar. Or you can clip off the part of the leaf with the bug and let it drop into a wide-mouthed container. Cap the jar. Indoors, shake the bugs out onto the foliage of your plants.

Treatment: Direct Chemical Controls

Thrips, like whiteflies, are very likely to become resistant to insecticides that are used regularly. For this reason, alternatives to chemical controls should be used whenever possible.

Insecticidal soap or horticultural oils can be used to provide temporary relief from thrips while you are waiting for predators to arrive. They can be used to reduce the pest population somewhat before release of biological controls, a strategy we recommend if the pest population is high, or for spot treatments if hot spots develop within the greenhouse from temporarily uneven distribution of predators.

APHIDS
(Order Homoptera, superfamily Aphidoidea)

With ants excluded and biological control of mites and thrips planned or underway, you are ready to tackle the common homopteran pests of plants indoors: aphids, scales, mealybugs and whiteflies. The winged forms of these four groups and the newly emerged young all look similar, and it is easy to see why taxonomists group them together. But in the stages that are likely to catch the eye of the gardener or greenhouse manager, only certain scales and mealybugs are obviously similar. This is largely because some species of both groups are able to produce copious amounts of wax, often extruded from the body in highly ornamental filaments.

Like all the other homopterans discussed in this chapter, aphids are small, no more than about 1/8 in. (3 mm) long. And, like the other homopterans, they are soft-bodied, sap-sucking insects that produce honeydew, a sugary protein mixture fed upon by many organisms, including ants and many natural enemies of aphids. Because ants often kill or disturb these natural enemies, ant control is an integral part of managing aphids and other pests that produce honeydew.

Honeydew may be the first sign you notice when homopterans are present. If you see a sticky shine or dark dust of spores on the upper surfaces of the lower leaves of your plants, you can guess that you have aphids or one of the other honeydew-producing insects on the undersides of the leaves above. Honeydew is thought to be the "manna from heaven" of the Bible. It is still collected and sold as sugar candy in bazaars of the Middle East. If you lick some fresh deposits off leaves, you will find the taste reminiscent of maple sugar. This is not surprising since both are essentially concentrated plant sap. Unfortunately, honeydew is frequently host to a black sooty mold that feeds on it, making the leaf appear dirty and unattractive. Avoid tasting mold-blackened honeydew in case you are hypersensitive to molds.

Biology

Aphids are frequently called plant lice because of their superficial resemblance to human lice. However, these two insects are not closely related and differ in many important ways. Most of the more than 4,000 aphid species in the world feed only on a few closely related plant species. The rose aphid, for example, attacks only plants in the rose family; it does not attack oleanders or birch trees. Only 10% of aphid species attack many species of plants.

With so many different aphids, many feeding on only certain types of plants or in certain environments, it is very difficult to make generalizations about them. Some do no more than take a little sap from the plant and are hardly ever noticed. Others have saliva that is toxic to certain plants or spread viruses and mycoplasmas into the host, causing disease. Such aphids can be serious problems even when they occur in small numbers. Table 20.1 on p. 368 lists the distinguishing characteristics and favorite host plants of some species frequently found indoors.

Table 20.1
Some Important Indoor Aphid Pests

Common Name	Scientific Name	Likely Host Plants
fern aphid	*Idiopterus nephrolepidis*	ferns, pteris
glasshouse potato aphid	*A. solani*	caladium, calceolaria, dahlia, cineraria, many other species
green peach aphid	*Myzus persicae*	cacti, cineraria, orchids, roses, mums, carnations, many other species
melon or cotton aphid	*Aphis gossypii*	schefflera, Dioscorea, many other species
mottled arum aphid	*Aulacorthum circumflexum*	caladium, cyclamen, arums, amaryllis, azalea, begonia, schizanthus, tulip, many other species
potato aphid	*Macrosiphum euphorbiae*	Roseaceae, many other species
rose aphid	*Macrosiphum rosae*	Roseaceae and plants in Dipsaceae, Umbelliferae and Valerianaceac

The Life Cycle of Aphids

A stem mother (A) hatches from the overwintering egg and gives rise to 60 to 100 females, which produce other females (B) 6 to 10 days after birth without mating. Males (C) arise in the fall and mate with egg-laying females (D), which produce the overwintering eggs (E). Aphids can overwinter as eggs for months, but once they hatch they complete their life cycle within 30 days.

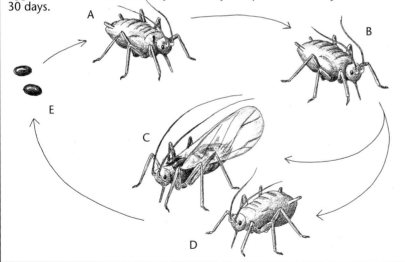

Aphids develop gradually through stages that resemble the adult in appearance (see the drawing above). They live throughout the winter as shiny black eggs in the crevices of bud scales and bark and in other protected locations on the plant; the eggs are visible with a 15x or 20x hand lens. A female called the "stem mother" hatches in the spring from an overwintering egg. She does not lay eggs, but instead gives birth to live young, which are all females. Unfertilized females produce other females for most of the season, a process called parthenogenetic reproduction. But in the fall, due primarily to changing light conditions, the females produce winged males and females, which mate. The fertilized females lay overwintering eggs.

All sorts of variations on this basic cycle are possible. The egg is the form in which aphids withstand inclement weather in temperate and northern climates. Indoors, with more even temperatures and artificial light extending the season, there is no need for an overwintering egg. Thus, in aphid species found on plants indoors or in tropical areas outdoors, males, which are necessary only to fertilize the egg, may never be produced at all or are rare and difficult to find.

Some aphid adults are winged while others are not, depending on the species and the environment (see the drawing on the facing page). The same species that does not produce winged adults when conditions are very favorable will begin to produce winged forms when the situation for survival is less promising. Conditions that are colder, hotter, drier or wetter than preferred by a species, or crowding and changes in the physiology of the plant, particularly in the amount

Physical Features of Aphids

Adult aphids can be winged or wingless, and can produce living young at various times of the year without mating. The paired tubular structures on the abdomen are called cornicles, which produce an alarm substance when the aphids are disturbed by predators. The size and shape of the cornicles help distinguish aphid species. (Actual size of adult: ⅛ in./3 mm)

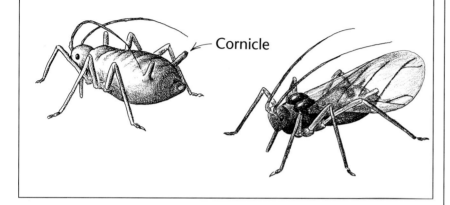

Cornicle

---

of nitrogen, may all trigger the birth of winged individuals capable of flying off to more comfortable locations. Aphids are weak flyers, however, and they are really blown away by the wind. One might think of them as aerial plankton.

The ability of females to give live birth to other females without being fertilized is the reason so many aphids can appear so quickly on a leaf or stem where there were few before. There is no time wasted finding and courting a mate! If you slide a female aphid into some lightly salted water and examine it under a low-power microscope, you can usually see the living babies within the abdomen, their red eyes shining through the skin.

The green peach aphid (*Myzus persicae*) is a worldwide pest of many agricultural crops. It is probably the aphid most frequently encountered indoors, and it is the most difficult to control of all the indoor plant pests. The same species can have pale green, yellow or pink forms, even on the same branch. Live young and both winged and nonwinged adults are produced all year long. A single female gives birth to 60 to 100 nymphs (young) during its 20- to 30-day lifetime. The young can begin reproducing 6 to 10 days after birth. The lack of a need to mate and the potential for extremely high reproductive rates help make this species so difficult to control.

You can distinguish green peach aphids from other species indoors by the dark irregular blotch on their backs and the black head and thorax of the otherwise green winged adults.

Damage, Detection and Monitoring

Like other aphids, the green peach aphid causes damage by sucking plant sap. This may result in wilting, deformed and stunted growth, chlorosis (yellowing), loss of leaves and/or accumulations of honeydew. The honeydew often supports a black sooty mold that darkens leaves and makes them look dirty but does not cause other noticeable damage.

Fortunately, if you monitor your indoor plants regularly you can spot these aphids before they cause much damage. Winged aphid adults enter the house through unscreened windows and lay eggs on indoor plants that suit them. Because aphid eggs and young are so tiny, they can easily be imported into the house or greenhouse accidentally with new additions to your plant collection. Examine every leaf on each new plant. If you find aphids, treat them with several washes and soil drenches of insecticidal soap. Keep the plant under observation until you are sure you have eliminated the infestation. Even if no insects are found, isolate the plant for several weeks in a separate room or greenhouse before adding it to the collection. See p. 349 for a detailed description of establishing a quarantine area.

Treatment: Direct Physical Controls

Direct physical controls for aphids include screening, pruning and washing and the use of barriers.

1. Screening. Some indoor aphid species are also common outdoors, so you should make sure that windows in the house or vents in the greenhouse are adequately screened. Screens are also useful for containing the beneficial insects you release to control the aphids.

2. Pruning, Washing. Heavily infested leaves or plant sections can be pruned or pinched off. During warm weather, some plants can be moved outdoors and hosed off with a stream of water. Although both approaches result in only a temporary reduction of the aphid population, they may be useful just prior to the release of biological controls (smaller initial pest populations make it easier for the beneficial insects to catch up with the pests).

3. Barriers. Ant exclusion is critical to the successful use of biological controls against aphids indoors. The isolation of plants above ant barriers is described on pp. 355-357.

Treatment: Direct Horticultural Controls

Like many other pests of plants indoors, aphids are very sensitive to nitrogen levels in plants. Sometimes a pest outbreak can be triggered by the use of a potent quick-release fertilizer on plants where no aphids were previously noted.

Encouraging the fast growth of plants indoors, especially through the use of high-nitrogen fertilizers, is undesirable for several reasons. The growth achieved is likely to be weak and susceptible to plant disease, partly because of the higher temperature and lower light indoors compared with more natural settings. Furthermore, rapidly growing plants outgrow their containers and require frequent transplanting and adjustment of the indoor landscape.

Your objective should be to grow plants as slowly as possible while keeping them healthy. Our recommendations for fertilizing plants indoors with regard to aphid control are the same as they are for reducing problems with scale pests: Switch to a slow-release fertilizer with a moderate proportion of nitrogen, such as fish emulsion or liquid seaweed. If label directions recommend one feeding per month, it might be preferable to apply one-quarter of the recommended dose once a week. For a more detailed discussion of fertilizing, see pp. 333-336.

Treatment:
Direct Biological Controls

Three aphid predators available commercially are the green lacewing (Chrysoperla carnea), the convergent lady beetle (Hippodamia convergens) and the aphid-eating gall midge (Aphidoletes aphidimyza). These predators can help substantially in controlling aphids on plants indoors.

Before discussing each of these aphid predators, we list some of the basic rules and procedures (adapted here for aphid control) that you should follow when releasing most beneficial insects:
• Reduce pest numbers before your initial introduction of the beneficial insects by pruning, applying soap or oil sprays or using a selective insecticide, such as pyrethrum or pyrethrins, with a short residual life.

• In greenhouses, or in any large plant collection, begin monitoring weekly before releases are made. Get a rough count of the size of the pest population. Note how many insects are on how many leaves in what part of the greenhouse and/or how many leaves are infested out of a sample of 5 or 10 leaves within a group of plants. Write down your observations as described in the sidebar on p. 348 so you can determine the success of releases. Written records also help you identify hot spots that may require further attention.
• Release large numbers of beneficials initially. Subsequent releases can be smaller.
• Continue monitoring weekly or even more often to see whether the pest population is being suppressed and whether the beneficials are present. Use predator/prey ratios to correlate the number of predators with damage and aphid visibility.
• Plan to make periodic releases during the year. The frequency of releases should be based on what you learn from monitoring. One release per year is rarely sufficient; on the other hand, one release per month may be unnecessarily frequent.
• Exclude or kill ants with barriers, baits, soap or pyrethrin drenches.
• In greenhouses or conservatories, feed aphid predators the artificial diet described in the sidebar on p. 372 when aphid numbers are low to maintain them year-round. The sidebar on p. 373 describes construction of a feeding station for the predators.
• If you have been using insecticide or fungicide sprays regularly and now want to switch to biological controls, use soap or oil sprays to reduce the pest population while you are waiting for the poison residues to degrade.
• If the reason you are switching from pesticides is that the aphids have become resistant to the sprays, proceed under the assumption that the sprays were successfully suppressing spider mites. Thus, if you don't also release spider mite predators when you switch to biological con-

trols, you may have a mite outbreak on your hands. Also be prepared to release natural enemies of other pests such as thrips that may have been kept under control by the pesticides.
• Keep records. A sample record sheet is shown on the facing page. By analyzing what happens over a full year you can develop a cost-effective biological pest-suppression program.

1. Green Lacewings. The green lacewing (Chrysoperla carnea), now mass-produced and released for control of aphids on many greenhouse and agricultural crops, has become an important commercial product in recent years. For details on the biology of this beneficial insect, see pp. 66-68.

Lacewings are commonly released in the egg stage. Commercial insectaries produce and distribute lacewing eggs that have been de-stalked (detached from the silken stalks on which they are laid by the female). The eggs are counted by volume. Food (in the form of moth eggs) is included in the package in case the lacewings hatch in the mail. You can also special-order lacewings as already-hatched larvae. This is more expensive since the insectary must keep a special batch of eggs for you, feed the young larvae and pack them in hex cell packages. These cardboard sheets are divided into individual compartments that isolate the larvae and keep them from consuming each other en route.

In our own work we have found that the greater cost of larvae versus eggs is more than repaid by their enhanced effectiveness at suppressing aphids, even in a medium-sized commercial greenhouse. Because you may not always be able to purchase lacewings in their larval stage, we describe the use of both stages here.

The eggs usually arrive mixed with rice hulls. Pour the mix back and forth three or four times between two containers until the eggs are evenly mixed with the hulls. Roll a clean sheet of 8½ x 11 paper to form a cone with a small hole at one end and pour the egg mixture into the cone, as shown in the drawing below.

To estimate the distribution density for the eggs, divide the number of eggs by the number of sites. For example, with 1,000 eggs and 100 sites, 10 eggs should be distributed at each site, meaning each pot, plant or area of ground in an indoor "plantscape." Then, using the cone-shaped applicator, gently tap out about 10 eggs per plant or site at a place where the young can hatch, such as at the base of a plant or in a crotch between branches. Avoid surfaces that will be watered in the next two or three days, since the eggs may be washed away. Note: If you cannot distribute the eggs right away, they can be kept safely for several days at room temperature (but not in the refrigerator or freezer).

Lacewing larvae are very tiny when they first emerge from the egg. Generally, they can tackle only young, tiny aphids. Use a hand lens to find the small aphids when you distribute the eggs.

If you are using lacewing larvae that have just hatched rather than the eggs, refer to the discussion of lacewings in the section on thrips (p. 366). To apply the larvae, peel back the paper covering on the hex cells in which they arrive bit by bit, tapping out the larvae with a pencil while holding the cell unit upside-down over the plant. The larvae can be moved around with a small pointed paint brush or pencil tip; wetting the brush may help (but avoid the temptation to use saliva, as it is toxic to some insects).

With small potted plants such as cyclamens, one larva per plant should be sufficient. The larger the plant and the more heavily infested it is, the more larvae you should release. This will take some experimenting. If more than one larva is released on each plant, spread the larvae as far apart as possible so they have a chance to clean up the aphids before they discover and attack each other.

Sample Record Sheet for Releases of Beneficials

Date	Plant	Pest	# of Pests	Beneficial	# released	Notes
1/16	coleus (12 plants)	aphids	20+ on 15 leaves	lacewing eggs	200	sprayed with soap then released eggs
1/23	"	"	same	—	—	damage tolerable
1/29	"	"	only 1 or 2 on 15 leaves	—	—	no new damage

Distributing Lacewing Eggs

After pouring the eggs and rice hulls from the delivery container into a paper cone, gently tap the cone to distribute the eggs over the infested plant.

Artificial Diets for Lacewings and Lady Beetles

Artificial diets simulate the sugar/protein secretions of honeydew produced by aphids and scales, the prey of many lacewings and lady beetles. These food mixtures can be sprayed onto plants or wooden posts, and have been used to retain, arrest, attract and feed lacewings, especially *Chrysoperla carnea*. When the desired species of lacewing already occurs in the area, the artificial food is used to prevent it from leaving. The simulated honeydew can arrest lacewings on their way through an area or attract them into an area they might not otherwise visit. Some diets do all three, or can be composed to attract and nourish specific species.

The ability to increase the numbers of predators artificially by spraying food substances was first observed when sucrose or molasses solutions were applied to plant crops. Subsequent work with Wheast™ (the yeast *Kluyveromyces fragilis* plus a milk whey substrate produced as a by-product of the cheese-making industry) and sugar mixtures were shown to augment necessary protein supplies and increase lacewing egg production in field tests. Other substances such as acid hydrolysates of casein and rehydrated beef blood can have the same effect.

Wheast™ and other similar mixtures, such as Formula 57™, that are composed of dried yeast, whey products (casein protein), sugar and water (with no more than 10% salts) are sold in bulk by a number of companies primarily for use by beekeepers as a winter supplement in the hives (see the Resource Appendix under "Insect Management: Biological Controls" on pp. 683-686). If you buy the mixture in bulk, you must add sugar and water. The ratio of Wheast™ or Formula 57™, sugar and water is 1:1:10.

A number of commercial insectaries that sell lacewing eggs also sell smaller amounts of Formula 57™ that is already mixed with sugar. The mixture can be applied to wood with paintbrushes or sprayed on plants or wood with standard hand-held garden spray equipment (see the sidebar on the facing page).

Normally, *C. carnea* carries over enough food from the larval stage to produce about 30 eggs. However, when fed artificial honeydew, lacewings are able to produce up to about 1,000 eggs, or about 30 eggs per day. Field applications of simulated honeydew have been shown to attract adult green lacewings, the lady beetle species *Coccinella tranversoguttata* and *Scymnus post-pinctus*, the predatory bug *Georcoris pallens* and the pest plant-feeding bug *Lygus hesperus* (which is also predacious on the eggs and larvae of other insects).

Species such as the convergent lady beetle, although attracted to the artificial honeydew, will not lay eggs unless some prey are present. By contrast, *C. carnea* is one of about 15 species of lacewings known to lay eggs with the artificial diet alone.

The use of lacewings in conjunction with artificial diets has been shown to provide pest control comparable to that of insecticides in preliminary field tests on cotton and alfalfa crops; however, no studies have been done on a smaller scale or on different pests and plants. We mention this work because the technique shows promise and may encourage other efforts to refine the approach. Studies are needed to improve the diet, determine the best application strategy and gauge the effect on pest ant species. For more information on artificial diets, consult "References and Readings" on pp. 398-401.

Lacewings will fly toward light when they are adults. If you are releasing eggs or larvae onto large potted plants inside the house, viable adults on the windowsills (you can vacuum them up) are a sign that it is time to release more eggs or larvae on the plants.

2. Convergent Lady Beetles. The convergent lady beetle *(Hippodamia convergens)* is the best-known commercially available lady beetle. For details on its biology, see pp. 62-65. We have released adult lady beetles in the active feeding stage in greenhouses and were impressed with the large num-ber of aphids they ate. However, the beetles have characteristic searching patterns that result in their leaving large numbers of aphids untouched among the vegetation. These patterns vary with the type of plant, the size and arrangement of its leaves, its height and other factors. Furthermore, as soon as the size of the remaining aphid population drops below a certain level, the adults fly off through unscreened windows and other openings to look for new food sources. If prevented from leaving, they tend to collect around windows and die. Thus, our recommendation is that in large plant collections, you combine the use of lady beetles with other natural aphid enemies.

If you have just a few house plants with aphids, try capturing lady beetle larvae in the garden for use indoors. These young cannot fly. Use a glass jar and a small, moist paint brush to transfer the lady beetle larvae. You can use adults if you enclose the plant in a tent of cheesecloth or netting to prevent them from flying away (see the sidebar on p. 343). Adults can be collected by tapping the leaf they are on over an open jar.

Like lacewings, lady beetles can be encouraged to reproduce more abundantly and remain in the greenhouse longer if their insect diet is supplemented with sugar/protein food sources. The same tips discussed on p. 370 under lacewings apply to lady beetles.

3. Aphid-Eating Gall Midges. Although flies are considered a nuisance or worse, there are a number of fly families that contain species directly beneficial to humans. The aphid-eating gall midge *Aphidoletes aphidimyza* is one example.

The adult midges are small, fragile flies with very long legs. They look more like very small mosquitoes or fungus gnats than houseflies. One advantage these insects have over lacewings and lady beetles in aphid control is that the adults are not attracted to light. Thus, they will not congregate and die on window sills, nor will you see them during the day. They tend to collect under the leaves in any dark area, usually holding on with only one of their long thin legs. The more moisture in the air, the better they like it.

These valuable predators can be found outdoors during late spring

Constructing Feeding Stands for Lacewings and Lady Beetles

A feeding stand can be as simple as a flat board attached at a right angle to a stake (as shown in the drawing at right). Anchor the stake into a 5-gal. can of earth or directly into the ground. Construct an ant barrier around the stake using a downward-facing aluminum pie pan (see the sidebar on pp. 356-357 for directions). Place a sticky adhesive on the undersides of the pan, where it will impede ants traveling up the stake and be protected from dust and leaves. The inverted pan also prevents the sticky adhesive from getting on people working around the feeding station. For sources of sticky adhesives, see the Resource Appendix under "Insect Management: Physical Controls" on pp. 682-683.

The artificial diet can be painted on the upper surface of the flat board by brush, or it can be sprayed on with hand-held garden spraying equipment. The feeding station above the sticky barrier must be kept isolated from surrounding vegetation, walls or

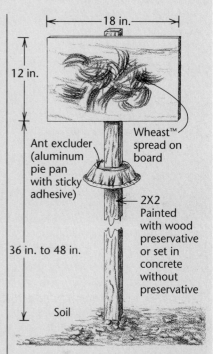

18 in.

12 in.

Ant excluder (aluminum pie pan with sticky adhesive)

Wheast™ spread on board

36 in. to 48 in.

2X2 Painted with wood preservative or set in concrete without preservative

Soil

any structure that might allow the ants to gain access to the food. Since the beneficial insects can fly in the adult stage—the only stage in which they need the protein mix to lay eggs—they can get the food by flying to the feeding stand.

and summer wherever aphid colonies are abundant. You can collect them in the larval stage and bring them indoors. If enough are introduced, they do an excellent job of suppressing aphids so that neither predator nor aphid is noticed.

Where we live, we can nearly always find gall midges in midsummer on weeds of the Compositae family, which have dandelion-like flowers. These are abundant in abandoned areas and vacant lots. Fortunately, the gall midges eat many aphid

species (see the photo on the next page), not just those that feed on Compositae plants. Our own colony of gall midges was initially collected from an aphid-infested loquat tree in Berkeley, California; we have also collected them by the hundreds as they attacked aphids on a common weed, *Sonchus oleraceus,* sometimes called annual sowthistle.

The eggs and young larvae are very difficult to see without a microscope, despite the fact that the larvae are a bright orange-yellow. The fol-

This worm-like larva of the aphid-eating gall midge has injected a toxin into an aphid to paralyze it and is sucking out its body fluids, distorting the aphid's body. (Photo by Helga Olkowski.)

lowing collection method, described by Gilkeson and Klein in *A Guide to the Biological Control of Aphids,* has worked very well for us.

Place the leaves and stems of plants heavily infested with aphids into large, clear plastic bags. Inflate the bags like balloons and tie their necks with a rubber band or wire, capturing as much air as possible. Set the bags in a shady place for a day or two, then examine them under good light. If there were any gall midges in the aphid colonies, they will be seen as tiny, orange, worm-shaped fly larvae clinging to the inside walls of the bag. As you turn the bag over, they tend to lift off the leaves and stick to the plastic. Often you find them trapped in the moisture drops that form as the plants wilt inside the bag.

Using a very fine paintbrush moistened with water, pick up the gall midge larvae and transfer them to your plants where you have aphid problems. The larvae take about five days to mature at 65°F to 75°F (18°C to 24°C). Each larva molts four times and kills many dozens of aphids. If aphids are abundant, the larvae will kill more than they eat. In con-

trast to the younger larvae, the mature larvae are quite visible to the naked eye on the leaf once you learn what to look for.

You can tell when the full-size larvae are ready to pupate by their restlessness. If you touch them with a brush they hunch up in an upside-down "U" and spring off the leaf into the air, often landing many inches from where they started. Eventually they burrow about ½ in. (1.3 cm) under the soil and make a fragile cocoon, in which they pupate.

In usual warm-season temperatures the pupae remain in the soil for two to three weeks, then emerge as winged insects ready to start another generation. They mate the night they emerge. By the second night they have begun laying orange eggs wherever they find aphids, sometimes gluing them to the top of the living aphids, but usually laying them on nearby leaves and stems. In three or four days the eggs hatch and the larvae begin to feed. Since egg production has been found to be somewhat responsive to the number of aphids present, we sometimes spray a weak solution of honey and water on the

leaves. This seems to fool the adult predators into thinking there are lots of honeydew-producing aphids and encourages them to lay many eggs.

The gall midge has a diapause, or resting period, triggered by the shortening days of autumn. Gall midges that begin their diapause under these conditions do not emerge from the soil until late spring or early summer. To benefit from these predators during the short days when temperatures are lower and when aphids are likely to be very active, you must either place artificial lights above the plants to postpone diapause or purchase the predators from a supplier who is raising them under long-light conditions and has larvae available in winter and early spring.

Recent research suggests that if a 100-watt bulb is used for illumination, more than half the larvae within a radius of 60 ft. (18 m) of the bulb can be prevented from going into diapause. The light should be used when there are fewer than nine hours of light per day and the temperature drops below 70°F (21°C) during the day and below 59°F (15°C) at night. Using a light bulb to prevent diapause in the predator on extremely light-sensitive crops such as poinsettia may be undesirable, however, since excessive light delays production of the colorful red bracts.

The alternative is to purchase gall midges periodically. There are a number of commercial suppliers in the United States, Canada and Europe (listed in the Resource Appendix under "Insect Management: Biological Controls" on pp. 683-686), but the demand is not great enough to bring down the high cost. If the cost of regular gall-midge releases is beyond your means, you can combine their use in the late spring and summer (when the larvae can be captured outside and there is likely to be a second rise in aphid populations indoors) with releases of commercially purchased lacewings in the winter and early spring when aphids first become active. The larvae of the aphid-eating gall midge can be released on plants in a home or office. Those that manage to make it to adulthood are unlikely to cause a problem, because they eat only aphids, stay close to the undersides of the plants and are unlikely to be noticed.

Treatment:
Direct Chemical Controls

Spot treatment is the important concept underlying the integration of chemical controls with biological and other nontoxic controls in greenhouse or house-plant pest management. You should confine the use of any pesticide, no matter how benign, to just those plants where the problem is reaching intolerable levels. Always use pesticides that are as nontoxic to mammals as possible.

1. **Insecticidal Soap.** The least-toxic chemical control available for aphids is Safer™ Insecticidal Soap. It is nontoxic to the user and leaves no poisonous residue. Unfortunately, these same good qualities limit its usefulness. It kills aphids on contact but does not have a lasting preventive effect. It is ideal for use while you switch from conventional pesticides to biological controls and for spot treatment where the aphid population has risen temporarily.

2. **Horticultural Oil.** Horticultural oil in a 2% solution in water is an effective least-toxic treatment for aphids. For more information, see p. 362 and Grossman (1990), listed under "References and Readings" on p. 398.

3. **Neem Oil.** If spot treatment with insecticidal soap is not sufficient to control an aphid infestation and you feel you must use a pesticide, we recommend the use of neem oil (see pp. 122-123).

4. **Pyrethrum or Pyrethrin-Based Pesticides.** This naturally occurring botanical and its laboratory-synthesized analogs (see pp. 121-122) are more toxic to humans than is insecticidal soap but are more benign than other commercial products available for use against aphids. The difficulty with using pyrethrum products is that they

must be applied with a spray, because they are contact insecticides. Spraying requires careful use of an appropriate protective mask and clothing (as described on pp. 97-103). Furthermore, it is very difficult to confine any spray to a small area. Because pyrethrum-type pesticides kill many species of insects, it is difficult to use the spray without seriously disturbing other biological controls operating in the enclosed space.

SCALES
(Order Homoptera, superfamily Coccoidea)

Scales are sucking insects closely related to aphids, mealybugs and whiteflies. The mouthparts of all these insects are fused into a slender tube, or stylet, that is used to pierce the plant surface. After hatching, the young scales wander over the plant searching for a spot in which to settle and begin producing their distinctive shell coverings. As adults, they are sedentary; only a few species have the ability to move once mature.

Biology

The scales that attack indoor plants fall into two common families: the armored scales (Diaspididae) and the soft scales (Coccoidae). It is useful to be able to distinguish these families if you plan to use biological controls. Telling the difference is not difficult with a magnifying glass or hand lens and penknife; it also helps to refer to

---

Summary: Least-Toxic Aphid Control

• Use screens and other physical techniques to prevent pest entry and keep beneficial insects in.

• Establish a quarantine area for newly or severely infested plants.

• If ants are present, build sticky barriers between the plants and the pests. If necessary, kill any ants that remain above the barriers with poison baits.

• If residual pesticides have been used routinely in the past, substitute soap sprays for several weeks to allow the plants and the environment to detoxify.

• Use slow-release fertilizers with moderate proportions of nitrogen.

• Pinch or prune off heavily infested leaves or other plant parts. Hose off plants that can be moved outdoors with a strong stream of water.

• Prior to releasing beneficials, reduce very large aphid populations by spot-treating with insecticidal soap sprays.

• Release a mix of beneficial predators regularly and provide supplemental feedings of artificial sugar/protein diets to increase the egg-laying of lacewings and lady beetles.

• If you release aphid-eating gall midges, increase artificial lighting when light levels and temperatures drop below critical levels in the fall or winter.

• Spray honey and water on leaves to increase egg-laying of gall midges.

• Monitor regularly to keep track of any growth in pest populations and evaluate the effectiveness of beneficials.

• If you must use pesticides, spot-treat with insecticidal soap or horticultural oil.

one of the excellent color-illustrated keys listed in the "Readings and References" on pp. 398-401.

Armored scales are small (about ⅛ in./3 mm long) and do not produce the copious amount of protein/ sugar exudate (honeydew) that is common to soft scales and their homopteran relatives, the aphids. But perhaps the most important identifying characteristic of armored scales is their habit of remaining attached to the host plant when their shells are lifted up and away with a sharp knife (see the drawing at right).

Armored scales are known to carry viruses that cause plant disease even when the scales are present in low numbers. Examples of armored scales commonly found on plants indoors include the oleander scale (*Aspidiotus nerii),* the cymbidium scale (*Lepidosaphes machili)* and the latania scale (*Hemiberlesia lataniae).* The boisduval scale (*Diaspis boisduvalii)* is particularly common on orchids and palms.

Although one might logically suppose otherwise, the shells of the soft scales are every bit as hard or even harder than those of the armored scales; at maturity, their shells are generally larger and darker as well. The most common soft scales on indoor plants have semicircular profiles in the adult stage. Soft scales secrete honeydew, some more than others, and thus are very attractive to ant species that collect the honeydew to feed their young.

One of the most important characteristics of soft scales, and one that you can use to distinguish them from armored scales, is that the shell does not lift off the body of the insect. When you slip a knife under an armored scale and flip it over, you will see the body of the scale inside the shell like a turtle, its legs and antennae waving about and clearly visible through a hand lens. If the scale is dead, its remains lift away cleanly with the shell, they are not left on the plant.

Common examples of soft scales that attack many plants indoors are

The Armored Scale
The female armored scale and her eggs are protected by an outer shell-like covering. When the eggs hatch, the larvae migrate out from this covering, attach themselves to the plant and feed, gradually developing their own armor.
(Actual size of scale: ⅛ in./3 mm)

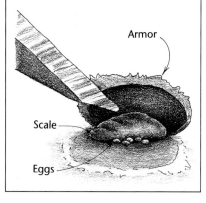

the hemispherical scale (*Saissetia coffeae),* the black scale (*Saissetia oleae)* and the brown soft scale (*Coccus hesperidum).* These three scales are light grey-brown and flatter in profile when young than when mature. Each matures into a shiny hemisphere; the shell of the brown soft scale is lighter in color and somewhat less humped in profile than the others. The young of all three species have marks in the form of the letter "H" on their backs, the crossbar running along the ridge of the shell. These markings are visible in adults of the brown soft scale only; the other two scales mature to a dark brown, which obscures the markings.

Scales are most vulnerable to low-toxicity chemical controls such as insecticidal soap and horticultural oil at the crawler (young scale) stage. Thus, one objective of monitoring is to check plants for crawlers. You will need a hand lens, since the young scales are small and flat, like minute animated pancakes.

Damage, Detection and Monitoring
A few scales on a plant will not cause problems, although some people regard their presence as unsightly. A plant badly infested with scales may turn yellow, however, and branches ringed with scales may die. Because adult scales are highly visible and the honeydew produced in large quantities by some species is highly noticeable, it is unlikely that one would let a plant reach a severely infested state without attempting to do something about it.

If you are in doubt as to whether what you see on the plant is a scale or merely a botanical feature, look at it through a hand lens while scraping it gently. If it is part of the plant, you will see green tissue beneath; if it is a scale, you can disturb its cover. The shine of honeydew on the leaves beneath the spot is a telltale clue. If ants are attending the spots, you can be certain you have sucking insects.

To tell whether scale numbers are rising or falling, count the number of adults on a given length of branch or crotch, or on a given number of leaves. Use the tip of a penknife to flip off the scale's cover to see if there is a live insect underneath. (Scales may die, but their covers remain attached to the plant for a time, leading one to think there are more scales than ever.) If the scale population is actively growing, you will first detect a mass of eggs surrounding the mother's body underneath the shell. A week or so later you will see the eggs hatch and become active under their covers. At this point you should check their development every day. When the young fan out over the plant, they are most vulnerable to sprays of insecticidal soap, horticultural oil or pyrethrum. Record your observations as described on p. 348.

Treatment: Direct Physical Controls
Scales can be rubbed off of plants by hand, using garden gloves, a toothbrush or a dry or alcohol-dipped cot-

ton swab. Once the mature scales are rubbed off, their mouthparts are broken and they will not survive to reinfest the plant.

When there are only a few scales on a few plants, rubbing off the adults may be enough to keep the scale population in check. Removing the shells also reduces the chance that you will mistakenly interpret the population as rising when it is stable or shrinking (often you are counting shells of species whose shells remain on plants long after the scale is dead).

Unfortunately, in the early stages of infestation the immature scales are so small that they are hard to see without magnification. Thus physical removal may not be feasible until the scales have partially matured.

Treatment:
Direct Horticultural Controls

Efforts to save plants that are already infested should include pruning out leaves or stem sections that have been attacked severely. Be sure to flip over the shells of soft scales with a penknife and examine them with a hand lens for signs of the live, plump bodies of the female scale.

Scales can also be controlled by moderating the amount of nitrogen in plant fertilizer. Like their close relatives the aphids, mealybugs and whiteflies, scales increase their population as the nitrogen level in plants increases. Therefore, the aim of a fertilization program for plants susceptible to any of these pests should be to provide just enough nitrogen to keep the plants healthy.

Sometimes switching to a slow-release fertilizer with a moderate proportion of nitrogen—fish emulsion, for example—can make a big difference in the number and frequency of occurrence of these pests. If the directions on the fertilizer label recommend one feeding per month, it might be better to apply a quarter of the recommended monthly dose each week. That way, instead of receiving a fairly concentrated dose of nitrogen,

An *Aphytis* parasitoid is shown laying her egg in the body of a scale. The parasitoid's larva hatches within the scale's body and feeds on scale tissue, killing the host. (Photo by Max Badgley.)

the plants take in smaller amounts over a longer period (see pp. 333-336 for more tips on fertilizing).

Treatment:
Direct Biological Controls

Beneficial parasitoids and predators that control many scales in greenhouses are available from commercial sources. The key to success in using these scale controls is to:

• Release sufficient numbers.

• Release on a regular basis.

• Keep the flying stage of the beneficial organisms on plants by tenting or by screening vents and doors in the greenhouse.

• Prevent the Argentine ant or other ant species that feed on honeydew produced by scales from interfering with the activities of the beneficials.

• Provide an auxiliary protein food such as Wheast™ to maintain predatory lacewings and lady beetles when other food sources are low. These sugary foods should be placed on stands protected by ant barriers. See the sidebar on p. 373 for instructions on how to build a feeding stand.

• Provide free water in the form of droplets on plant foliage if parasitoids are released.

• Keep the temperature between 70°F and 85°F (21°C and 29°C) and maintain moderate to high humidity. This simulates the semitropical native climates of indoor plants and the insects associated with them.

1. Parasitoids. Adult scale parasitoids feed directly on scales and lay their eggs inside the bodies of living scales (see the photo above). The eggs hatch and the larvae of the parasitoid eat the body of the scale from the inside. When a larval parasitoid matures into an adult, it cuts a small hole in the shell of the scale and emerges. It then flies off to mate and seeks new scales to parasitize. (For more on parasitoids, see pp. 33-34.)

It is difficult to tell when a parasitoid is inside a scale without dissecting the scale. However, it is easy to spot the pin-sized exit holes that indicate a parasitoid has emerged. The dead scale shell will remain on the plant for a long time unless brushed away. Thus, you must periodically examine the scales for these holes. Initially you will need a hand lens, but once you become familiar with the appearance of the holes you should be able to detect them without the aid of magnification.

It takes two to three weeks for parasitoids to develop from eggs into adults at room temperature, so the earliest you can expect to see exit holes is two weeks after you have released them. When your monitoring shows that the proportion of shells with exit holes has diminished relative to the number of intact shells, it is time to order more parasitoids.

Scale parasitoids are generally released at the rate of 10 per sq. yd. of greenhouse floor space, or 5 to 10 per infested plant (see p. 343 for advice on tenting house plants for the release of parasitoids). However, it is probably a good idea to purchase greater numbers of parasitoids when releasing for the first time. When plants are heavily infested, make several releases two to three weeks apart. The scale problem should be under good biological control within, at most, two or three months after beginning the releases. Thereafter, one or two releases per year should suffice. Integration of insecticidal soap or horticultural oil with biological controls will hasten control.

Before ordering parasitoids it is important to know which scale families are attacking your plants. If armored scales are the problem, order *Aphytis melinus,* a tiny yellow miniwasp that lays her eggs on the soft body under the outer waxy shell of young scales. If soft scales are present, order the tiny black and yellow miniwasp, *Metaphycus helvolus.* In many cases, scales from both families are found, so a mix of parasitoids should be released. Sources of scale parasitoids are listed in the Resource Appendix under "Insect Management: Biological Controls" on pp. 683-686.

2. Mealybug Destroyers. There are two commercially available predators that feed on scales when their preferred hosts are not abundant. The first is *Cryptolaemus montrouzieri,* a species of lady beetle more commonly known as the mealybug destroyer (see the photos on the facing page). This orange and black beetle is used to control mealybug pests on a wide variety of plants. But it also preys on scales, particularly the boisduval scale, a common pest of orchids, palms, cacti and bromeliads indoors. The waxy cover of the male boisduval scale is similar to the waxy covering on the egg masses and backs of many mealybugs, which may account for this scale's attractiveness to the beetle. The larvae suck out the body contents of young scales, and the adult beetles force the shell off the scales and devour the body.

Although the mealybug destroyer can be useful in keeping boisduval scale numbers low, it cannot by itself provide complete control because it cannot pursue scales that establish themselves under the sheaths of leaves, under light bud scales and in other scale hiding places. For these scales, an additional predator, the green lacewing, is required.

3. Green Lacewings. In its adult form, the green lacewing (*Chrysoperla carnea*) is a delicate-looking, winged insect that feeds only on nectar and pollen (see the photos on p. 67). In its larval form, the lacewing resembles a rapidly moving little alligator and has a large appetite for many common pests, including aphids, mealybugs, mites and scales. Lacewing larvae eat young and mature scales alike, puncturing their shells to gain access to their bodies. Very young lacewing larvae are small and thin enough to pursue scales under the sheaths of orchids and other plants and fit into other tight spaces where very small young scales may settle. Lacewings are discussed in greater detail on pp. 370-372; sources are listed in the Resource Appendix under "Insect Management: Biological Controls" on pp. 683-686.

Treatment:
Direct Chemical Controls

Effective as beneficials are at keeping scale numbers down over the long term, it has been our experience that if scale populations are already high and rapidly reproducing when beneficials are released, the parasitoids and predators may not be able to work quickly enough to prevent plant damage. There is a lag of days or weeks before the released beneficials have eaten enough of the pests to reduce their numbers significantly.

Thus, when monitoring shows more than 10 scale crawlers on leaves or stems of a plant, spot treatment with insecticidal soap or horticultural oil a day or two before beneficials are released is wise. (Spot treatment refers to applications of pesticides to only those plants where pests are present. This technique contrasts with the use of sprays, which are broadcast throughout the greenhouse. By confining the pesticide to local infestations, human exposure to the material is kept to a minimum and better pest control is usually achieved.)

By reducing a portion of the pest population with a soap or oil spray before releasing biological controls, the beneficials are given an edge over the scales. It is safe to apply insecticidal soap or oil a day before releasing beneficials because, unlike other pesticides, they leave no toxic residue. Once a heavy scale infestation has been reduced to a low level by the combined use of insecticidal soap or oil and beneficial insects, periodic releases—meaning once or twice a year—of the beneficials alone should be sufficient to keep scale populations below the injury level.

A second reason for using insecticidal soap or oil is to wash off the honeydew that scales and related pests secrete onto the plants. When soft scale populations are high, there is usually a large amount of this sticky exudate covering the leaves and stems. Beneficials searching for prey get stuck in the honeydew and spend a lot of time cleaning themselves off, which reduces their effectiveness at finding and destroying scales.

Insecticidal soaps are discussed in detail on pp. 114-116. For more information on horticultural oils, see pp. 116-119, p. 362 and Grossman (1990) listed under "References and Readings" on p. 398.

MEALYBUGS
(Order Homoptera, family Pseudococcidae)

Mealybugs are a common problem on plants indoors. They can usually be recognized by the copious cottony wax they produce. A plant infested with the common citrus mealybug *(Planococcus citri)* may appear to have small puffs of cotton in the joints where the stems branch, on the undersides of leaves or in other protected areas or crevices. The presence of this wax and the fact that mealybugs hide in hard-to-reach places makes it difficult to kill them with conventional insecticides. Moreover, mealybugs rapidly develop populations that are insecticide-resistant.

Biology

Mealybugs are soft-bodied sucking insects in the large insect order Homoptera, which also includes aphids, scales and whiteflies. There are many species of mealybugs—at least 193 species are known to exist in California alone—and they are very common on a wide variety of plants in almost every environment above and below ground. Some species are specialists, found exclusively on one genus of plants, whereas others are generalists with a wide range.

Mealybugs are extremely sensitive to temperature and humidity since they have no hard outer covering to prevent moisture loss. As a result, a seasonal succession of species may occur, with certain species becoming more prominent than others as the weather changes.

Although mealybugs are widely distributed, their preference for tiny, snug spaces makes them hard to find at a glance. Fortunately, species commonly found on indoor plants are easier to spot. They produce an abundance of wax and are more likely than other species to be found feeding on leaves, usually the undersides. Mealybugs commonly found indoors include the citrus mealybug *(Planococcus citri)*, the long-tailed mealybug *(Pseudococcus longispinus)* and the ob-

Both adult (top) and larval (bottom) mealybug destroyers *(Cryptolaemus montrouzieri)* feed on all stages of mealybugs. Notice that white cottony mealybug destroyer larvae superficially resemble the mealybugs themselves. (Top photo by Jack Kelly Clark; bottom photo by Max Badgley.)

scure mealybug *(Pseudococcus obscurus).* Their pancake-shaped bodies are pinkish lavender, which shows faintly through the white wax. The wax appears powdery and covers hairs around the edge of the body, giving the body a fringe of wax streamers. The wax around eggs is cottony in appearance.

An important predator of the mealybug, called "crypts" or the mealybug destroyer *(Cryptolaemus montrouzieri),* is shown in the top photo. It also produces white cottony wax on its body in the wingless larval stage (bottom photo). This camouflages the young predator, which is easily mistaken for its prey. Initially, you will need a 10x magnifying glass or hand lens to see the difference between the two. With practice however, you should be able to distinguish crypt larvae from mealybug larvae with the naked eye.

Like the scales, aphids and white-flies to which they are closely related, mealybugs also excrete honeydew. The ants that are attracted to the honeydew protect the mealybugs from their natural enemies. Many unusual ant-mealybug relationships have been described in the scientific literature. For example, some ants move mealybugs around and create underground refuges for them.

The number of eggs each female can produce varies by species, but 1,000 have been recorded for one species that holds the eggs within the body before they hatch. Less than half that number is probably more usual for mealybug species common on indoor plants. The number of generations per year also varies greatly among species. Some outdoor types at high elevations have a single generation each year, but the common citrus mealybug has been shown to have at least eight cycles per year under warm, moist conditions. The life cycle of the citrus mealybug is shown in the drawing at right.

Female mealybugs go through four stages, or instars, after hatching from the egg; this means that they molt, or spit their skin, three times. To the eye, each stage looks similar to the one before. This is referred to as incomplete metamorphosis. This contrasts with the crypt predator, which looks similar to the mealybug when it is young, but passes through a pupal or cocoon-like stage and emerges completely metamorphosed into a small red and orange lady beetle. Table 20.2 on the facing page provides data on the developmental times for various stages in the life cycle of the mealybug destroyer. In contrast to the females, the winged male mealybugs are rarely seen by the uninitiated since they are very small and live only a few days.

To learn more about mealybug biology, we recommend Howard L. McKenzie's *Mealybugs of California*. Despite the book's title, all mealybug species common on indoor plants worldwide are included.

The Life Cycle of the Citrus Mealybug

The adult female mealybug deposits over 500 eggs within the cottony mass that covers most of her body. The eggs hatch in a week or more, giving rise to nymphs, which migrate over the plant until they find a suitable spot to feed on the plant's sap. Within four weeks, those nymphs that will become males form a mass of cottony filaments, within which they transform themselves within two weeks into winged adults. Female nymphs reach adulthood in four weeks. (Actual size of adult: 1/16 in. to 1/8 in./1.5 mm to 3 mm)

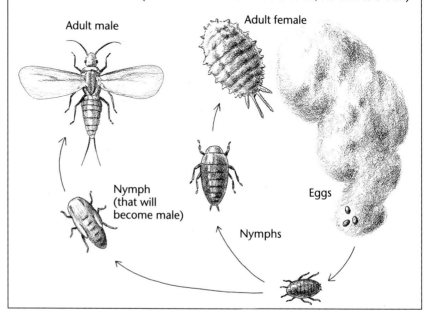

Adult male

Adult female

Nymph (that will become male)

Eggs

Nymphs

Damage

A large mealybug population can cause many species of common indoor plants to shed their leaves, become stunted or even die. Mealybugs can walk fairly quickly from plant to plant, and they multiply rapidly in the absence of natural enemies. Though many natural enemies of mealybugs exist outdoors, they rarely find their way inside.

For the above reasons, you should act immediately when the telltale signs of mealybug infestation are seen on indoor plants. In large plant collections, eradication of all mealybugs is usually neither possible nor advisable; instead, you should reduce them to the point where serious damage does not occur.

Treatment: Indirect Physical Controls

A few mealybugs on a plant can be killed directly by rubbing them off with your fingers or a cotton swab. This strategy is not adequate, however, when mealybugs are present in large numbers. In such cases, physical controls are more effective when used indirectly to prevent ants from tending and protecting mealybugs. Ants seeking the honeydew produced by the mealybugs can increase the numbers of these pests by killing or disrupting the natural enemies you release. The ants must be controlled before adequate control of mealybugs can be achieved.

The best way to control ants is to place potted plants above ant-proof barriers. For details on constructing barriers for the house, porch or greenhouse, see pp. 355-357.

Table 20.2
Developmental Stages of the Mealybug Destroyer[a]

Stage	Developmental Period[b]	
	70°F (21°C)	**81°F (27°C)**
egg	8 to 9 days	5 to 6 days
larvae	17 to 24 days	12 to 17 days
pupae	14 to 20 days	8 to 10 days
egg to egg	53 days	33 days

[a] Compiled from Steiner and Elliott, 1983.

[b] Minimum temperature for development is 48°F (9°C); optimum development occurs at 72°F to 77°F (22°C to 25°C).

Treatment:
Direct Horticultural Controls

Fortunately, there are a number of simple ways to make sure that mealybugs do not become a serious problem on your house or greenhouse plants. The first and most important is preventive: Inspect all new plant arrivals to the collection and quarantine any that appear to be already infested, as described on p. 349. Severely infested plants should be disposed of. Treated plants should be allowed into the general collection only after a quarantine of several weeks has indicated that mealybugs are no longer present.

Mealybug populations thrive on plants with high nitrogen levels or overly succulent growth. Overwatering, overfertilizing and/or too much humidity and warmth relative to the available light may encourage succulence in some species. This, in turn, can lead to severe mealybug damage. If plants are not excessively succulent they may be able to tolerate large numbers of mealybugs without showing significant damage.

When conditions are unfavorable for mealybugs during cold or dry periods, or when nitrogen levels are just high enough for the plant to grow slowly but not succulently, the mealybugs may slow their reproduction and retreat to the roots or crown of the plant (the parts of the plant about 2 in./5 cm above and below the soil level). When conditions favor mealybugs again, their population expands and they become more visible on the upper portions of the plant.

Thus, if you alternate your horticultural activities between benign neglect and periods of oversolicitous attention, you may find that mealybugs appear and disappear from the leaves and stems of certain plants, as if they were coming in from somewhere else. In fact, they are probably moving in and out of more noticeable areas on the plant or in the soil.

Infestations of cacti and certain other succulents are the exception to this pattern. Mealybugs may be more noticeable on these plants when the plants are drought-stressed. When the soil and roots are dry, the main water source is the stem. At such times, mealybugs that are usually hidden below the soil move up to feed on the main body of the plant and suddenly become visible.

Two conclusions can be drawn from these observations. First, a mealybug population can sometimes be kept at low levels by certain horticultural practices. Under the right conditions, species of potted plants such as cacti and some other succulents can tolerate small mealybug populations for years without noticeable damage. Second, you should aim for a fertilizing and watering regime that is just adequate to keep each plant species growing slowly, since excesses encourage the succulence that attracts mealybugs.

Treatment:
Direct Biological Controls

Biological controls currently available for mealybug control include mealybug destroyers, green lacewings and the parasitoid *Leptomastix dactylopii*.

1. Mealybug Destroyers. The mealybug destroyer *(Cryptolaemus montrouzieri)* is a small black and orange lady beetle commonly known as "crypts." The beetle feeds on certain stages and species of scales and on the young of some aphids, but its fame as a biological control agent rests upon its ability to keep mealybugs under control in settings as diverse as citrus orchards and greenhouses.

The female lays her eggs near groups of prey. The eggs hatch in eight to nine days when the temperature is around 70°F (21°C). The distinctive coloring of the adult beetles makes them easy to recognize, but the larval stages can be confused with pests such as mealybugs because of their similar white waxy coating. It is important to become familiar with the appearance of the larval beetles so you don't confuse them with pests.

When adult beetles are released indoors, they tend to fly toward light. Therefore, you should screen windows or vents to keep the beetles inside. Where individual plants will receive releases of crypts, enclose them in separate tents or cages to prevent the lady beetles from escaping.

When releasing crypts or any other predators or parasitoids, inspect plants regularly. We recommend weekly checks. Physically remove any hot spots not caught in time by the natural enemies by pruning or spot-treating with insecticidal soap or horticultural oil (see "Chemical Controls" on pp. 383-384).

Accurate monitoring may be difficult, because young larvae of the lady beetle look similar to the mealybugs they are preying on and very much like the mealybug egg masses that they destroy with gusto. Furthermore, the destroyed egg masses remain white, cottony and visible on the leaves until watering or physical cleaning of the leaves with a soft cloth wipes them off. So don't make the mistake of thinking you still have a large infestation when in fact there are no viable eggs left. The clue that the egg masses have been destroyed is that the wax filaments are spread out or strewn about, no longer forming a compact, undisturbed mound.

If on initial inspection you find that there is a very large mealybug population, use soap or oil sprays to knock it down before you begin releasing crypts. It is unreasonable to expect initial releases to suppress a runaway pest population.

Finally, it is desirable to keep the greenhouse temperature as close as possible to that favored by the crypts. M. Steiner and D. Elliott in *Biological Pest Management for Interior Plantscapes* provide guidance on the temperatures best suited for crypts as well as suggestions on how and how many to release. We can add a few comments of our own, based on our experience designing IPM programs for the San Francisco Conservatory of Flowers and the Marin County Civic Center Building.

• Adjust the temperature to 72°F to 77°F (22°C to 25°C) to favor crypts.

• If overhead skylights provide intense glare, which attracts crypts, use shade cloth (available at hardware stores and nurseries).

• Order five or more crypts for each infested plant or for every square yard. When ordering, bear in mind that you can release too few crypts but never too many (though some larvae may cannibalize others). Thus, release a large number initially; once good control is achieved, you can make smaller releases.

• Distribute live adults at the various infested sites, preferably in the early morning or late evening so they settle down more readily on the plants. Spread them among the plants by gently shaking a few at a time from the plastic mailing carton. Alternatively, you can lay pieces of a food-and-water-impregnated paper towel to which the crypts are clinging on the leaves of infested plants. Given the opportunity, the crypts will move onto a paper towel from the mailing container. Do this inside a larger cage or container. The crypts will then disperse throughout the plant collection in search of mealybugs.

• Avoid wearing white clothing while distributing the beetles — they are attracted to light colors and will move to your clothing instead of the plants.

• Monitor the plants at least once a week by checking new growth on all susceptible specimens.

• If you keep a shipment of crypts for several days before releasing them (they are mailed with enough food and water to sustain them for several days), store them in a cool place but not in the refrigerator. Adult beetles become inactive below 48°F (9°C) and die from the cold in the refrigerator.

• Repeat releases as often as necessary. In small home greenhouses or enclosed porches, one or two releases a year may be adequate. In the Conservatory of Flowers, which contains approximately 30,000 sq. ft. of greenhouse, some 2,000 crypts are released once a month for eight to nine months of the year.

2. Green Lacewings. The green lacewing (*Chrysoperla carnea*) is another commercially available insect that eats mealybugs. It can also be very important in the biological control of aphids and scales indoors, and captures and sucks dry almost any other insect or mite it encounters, including caterpillars larger than itself, crypts and other lacewings. Because of their voraciousness, lacewings are difficult to integrate into biological control programs where the plant collection is small and other beneficial insects are being released. Thus, we recommend that lacewings be reserved for settings where aphids are the primary problem. For details on this predator, see pp. 370-372.

3. *Leptomastix dactylopii*. The citrus mealybug is probably the most common mealybug on indoor plants. Where this species is the primary pest, the tiny parasitoid *Leptomastix dactylopii* (see the photo on the facing page) can be a valuable addition to the control program. The miniwasp is about the size of the head of a pin and has a deep yellow color. It attacks both the adult and the larger immature stages, or instars, of the citrus mealybug. Females lay eggs within the body of the pest; after hatching, the wasp larvae kill the mealybugs by eating their insides.

Once the wasp has consumed the edible portions of the mealybug, it forms a small cocoon, called a mummy, from the wax-covered remains. A colony of mealybugs that has died in this fashion looks like a bunch of tiny, cotton-covered grapes attached to the plant. Within the mummy the wasp changes from a worm-like larva into the adult form. When ready to emerge, the tiny wasp cuts a neat hole into the mummy and climbs out to look for a mate. Once fertilized, the female searches out more mealybugs in which to lay her eggs.

According to Steiner and Elliott, "*Leptomastix* prefers a sunny, warm, and humid environment; however, it has been used successfully in low-humidity situations. Development time is 28 days at 75°F [24°C] and 18 days at 81°F [27°C]. Females lay an average of 80 eggs."

The size of releases and the ideal conditions for release are the same as for crypts. Remember, however, that crypts are effective against many species of mealybugs, whereas *Leptomastix* is a specific parasitoid of the common citrus mealybug. At present, this beneficial is only intermittently available on a commercial basis in North America and Europe (for sources, see the Resource Appendix under "Insect Management: Biological Controls" on pp. 683-686) and is used mainly in citrus orchards.

A tiny miniwasp, *Leptomastix dactylopii,* uses her antennae to locate a larval mealybug, into which she will insert her egg. The hatching larva will eat the mealybug from inside, killing it. Shortly thereafter, the larva will complete its life cycle and emerge from the dead mealybug as an adult miniwasp. (Photo by Max Badgley.)

Treatment:
Direct Chemical Controls

Rubbing alcohol, insecticidal soap and horticultural oil are effective chemical controls of mealybugs.

1. **Rubbing Alcohol.** If only one or two plants are lightly infested, a cotton swab dipped in ordinary rubbing alcohol can be used to kill the visible mealybugs. Alcohol dissolves the wax around the insect and its egg masses and kills them. If this method is used, be sure to check carefully every few days for several weeks for young mealybugs that were too small to see initially but have now matured. Spot treatment with alcohol can sometimes be combined with pruning of infested areas. If the collection is large, the infestation is more serious or the mealybugs are entrenched in the crown or root areas of the plant, then spot treatments with alcohol will not be adequate.

2. **Insecticidal Soap.** There are four important uses for insecticidal soap in mealybug control: treating infested, newly acquired plants during quarantine before adding them to your main collection; reducing high mealybug populations before introducing predators and parasites; treating hot spots where pests have not responded to the predators; and controlling root mealybug infestations in susceptible plants, such as African violets.

Insecticidal soaps are generally regarded as nontoxic to humans and pets, but some plants are particularly sensitive to them. Each species and variety may react differently, a few showing a brown burn, or distortion (check the label on soap products to find out which plants are affected). Sources of insecticidal soap are listed in the Resource Appendix under "Insect Management: Chemical Controls" on pp. 683-686.

Mealybugs that feed on plants below the soil line are a special problem because mealybug predators and parasites cannot pursue them there. We asked Michael Atkins of Safer, Inc., to recommend a method for managing this particular problem. According to Atkins, Safer™ Insecticidal Soap will control mealybug infestations in the roots of African violets. Mix the soap

Summary: Least-Toxic Mealybug Control

• Use screens and other barriers to prevent pest entry and retain beneficial insects. Individual plants in the house may be tented to contain beneficials temporarily during treatment.

• Establish a quarantine area for newly or severely infested plants.

• Regularly monitor the mealybug population to evaluate the effectiveness of beneficials. Keep records of what you find.

• If residual pesticides have been used routinely in the past, substitute insecticidal soap or oil sprays for several weeks to suppress the mealybugs while the toxic residues dissipate.

• Where plants are few and the mealybug infestation is light, prune out the infestation or dab the visible insects with alcohol.

• Where plant collections are large, release the mealybug destroyer, *Cryptolaemus montrouzieri,* as often as necessary. Where the citrus mealybug is the primary problem, augment these releases with the parasitoid *Leptomastix dactylopii.*

• Control ants in settings where beneficials are being released.

• Spot-treat infested plants with soap or oil sprays to keep pests from becoming too numerous or as a backup when the arrival of beneficials is delayed.

as a drench in the proportions recommended on the label and pour it slowly through the plant and soil. Let the plant sit in a soap-filled saucer until the soil is thoroughly wet. Bacteria in the soil are able to break down the soap fairly rapidly, so it is safe and desirable to repeat this treatment in seven days. If you try this method, check the root ball a week later for the third time. If you see mealybugs, drench the plant again.

According to Atkins, the only side effect from repeated drenchings is a gradual increase in the alkalinity of the potting soil. To restore the proper soil acidity after several soap treatments, he recommends watering with a solution of ordinary black tea.

3. Horticultural Oil. Spray treatments with a 2% solution of horticultural oil in water can provide effective least-toxic control of mealybugs. For further information on horticultural oils, see pp. 116-119 and p. 362.

WHITEFLIES
(Order Homoptera, family Aleyrodidae)

Whiteflies are not true flies in the sense of the housefly (*Musca domestica*), but are closely related to scales, mealybugs and aphids. Although whitefly adults may not resemble these close relatives, the newly born or just-hatched stage, called the first instar, looks a lot like those of closely related insects.

Whiteflies share a number of characteristics with other organisms in the order Homoptera. They are sucking insects that secrete a white wax at certain stages of their life cycle. They also produce honeydew, a sugar/protein exudate made from the sap of the plants on which they feed. As with scales, to which they are most closely related, the mobile young nymphs soon settle down to several stages of immobility. Unlike true scales, however, the whitefly adult emerges from its pupal stage as a flying insect, the form with which most people are familiar.

Biology

The most widely distributed whitefly found on indoor plants is the greenhouse whitefly *(Trialeurodes vaporariorum)*, whose life cycle is shown in the drawing below. It is particularly pestiferous on begonias, coleus, fuchsias, pelargoniums, primulas, poinsettias, salvia, verbena and greenhouse cucumbers and tomatoes. The greenhouse whitefly is a subtropical species; in areas with mild winters it is found on outdoor plants as well. The species is largely parthenogenetic, meaning that the birth of young may occur without mating. Interestingly, some unfertilized females lay eggs that produce only males and fertilized females produce only females.

The Life Cycle of the Greenhouse Whitefly
Adult female whiteflies deposit 200 to 400 eggs in circular clusters on the undersides of leaves. The eggs hatch in 5 to 10 days into larvae (nymphs), which go through several stages over the course of three to four weeks until they pupate. Within a week, adults emerge and repeat the cycle.
(Actual size of adult: ¹⁄₁₆ in./1.5 mm)

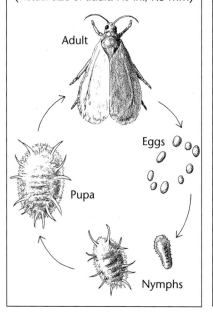

Adult

Eggs

Pupa

Nymphs

The adult female whitefly lays 200 to 400 eggs on the underside of a leaf. She pivots her abdomen so that the eggs cluster together in a circle. The egg itself is cigar-shaped, greenish white at first and then translucent grey once hatched. It sits upright on a small stalk.

Although the newly hatched whiteflies resemble small mealybugs, scales or aphids, once they move a short distance from the egg they change their appearance entirely. After three or four days during their first molt, they lose their legs, and for the next three stages remain attached tightly to the leaf like a scale. These stages are actually called scales, even though they are not true scales. The scale form produces white wax filaments that surround its periphery with decorative rays.

At room temperature, it takes a newly laid egg about 25 days to grow into an adult. At 81°F (27°C) the full cycle is completed in 18 days, but high temperatures reduce the number of young laid by the female. The optimal range for population increase is 64°F to 75°F (18°C to 24°C).

Damage

Some plants tolerate large numbers of whiteflies and show very little damage. In such cases, people may be more upset by seeing the adult insect fly up from the plant than they are by the effect on the plant itself. Human tolerance varies greatly. On other plants where whitefly populations are very high and/or the plant is very susceptible, these insects can cause wilting, chlorosis (yellowing), loss of leaves or stunting. In addition, the honeydew that whiteflies produce may grow a black fungus called sooty mold; the mold does not damage the leaf, but it may make the plant look dirty.

Detection and Monitoring

Whitefly adults are very easy to see, whether flying or resting on plant leaves (see the photo on the facing page). They are most likely to be

Encarsia formosa Preying on a Whitefly

Encarsia formosa is very effective at keeping whitefly numbers low. First a female finds a larva and drums on it with her antennae (A) to ensure it is at the right stage (the third or fourth instar) for egg-laying. Then she deposits her eggs inside the larva (B). The eggs hatch into a worm form, which eats the larva from the inside. Encarsia can also kill whitefly larvae by direct feeding through the ovipositor wound (C).

A

B

C

When monitoring for whiteflies, it is important to check the undersides of leaves, where whiteflies develop. The adult whiteflies shown here are surrounded by spherical, scale-like larva and empty pupal cases whose skins were split open as adults emerged. (Photo courtesy USDA/ARS.)

found near the tops of the plants or on stem ends, since they are attracted to the lighter yellow-green of this foliage. Adult males are slightly smaller than the females. The eggs, laid in a circle usually on the leaf undersides, can also be seen with the naked eye.

The pre-adult or larval and pupal stages are found on the undersides of the lower leaves. If only a few adults are present, they may not be a problem, since most plants can tolerate low numbers of whiteflies. But if the undersides of the lower leaves are covered with immature whiteflies, adults seen on top of the plant will soon be joined by hundreds more.

Whitefly scales are normally hard to see since they are almost translucent and blend with the color of the leaf to which they have attached. However, after they have been parasitized by Encarsia formosa, one of their natural enemies (see the drawing at left), they turn black. This makes it easy to recognize and monitor the presence of this beneficial parasitoid, which is discussed further under "Biological Controls" on pp. 386-388. If the whitefly scale is not parasitized, it forms a pupa after four molts, remaining in the same place.

Finally, the winged adult emerges from a T-shaped slit it cuts in the outer skin and flies toward the light yellow-green of the youngest foliage.

To find larval and pupal stages that have not been parasitized, you must look on the undersides of the older, lowest leaves. A hand lens will help; the lens also helps you distinguish between molted empty skins and live insects.

Treatment: Direct Physical Controls

Vacuuming and trapping are effective physical controls of whiteflies.

1. Vacuuming. In the early morning when whiteflies are cold and slow-moving, the adults can be sucked up with a small, hand-held, battery-operated vacuum, such as a Dustbuster Plus™. Vacuuming is a particularly valuable strategy when you discover the adults before they have done a great deal of egg-laying.

Making Your Own Whitefly Traps [a, b]

In small plant collections where releases of the beneficial parasitoid *Encarsia formosa* to control whiteflies are not feasible, the use of traps may be an effective control.

Traps can be made by cutting ¼-in. plywood, Masonite or cardboard into rectangular pieces (approximately 1 ft. by 2 ft.) and painting them on both sides with Rustoleum Yellow No. 659. Wait for the paint to dry and then coat both sides with a sticky adhesive over the yellow paint. This particular shade of yellow has been shown in laboratory tests to be a superior whitefly attractant. Drill holes through the plywood for wire hangers, and hang the boards or cards as close as possible to the plants with adult whiteflies.

The type of adhesive you use is very important. Stickem Special™, Tack Trap™ or Tanglefoot™ are all effective.

These products, while excellent adhesives, are difficult to handle because of their stickiness. Allow extra room for plants near traps with these adhesives. Special solvents are needed to clean off the whiteflies, fungus gnats and other flying insects caught on the traps. The solvents also remove the sticky substances, so the adhesive must be replaced before the traps are reused.

An adhesive that is easier to remove from the traps is made from two parts petroleum jelly (such as Vaseline®) or mineral oil and one part household detergent or insecticidal soap. Apply a thin coat of the mixture to the boards so that it will not run when temperatures are high. Although this mixture has been used successfully by Applied Bionomics, a commercial insectary in British Columbia, Canada, it has not been tested under a wide variety of conditions.

[a] The effectiveness of yellow sticky traps on whiteflies was first reported by Webb and Smith, 1980.

[b] The petroleum jelly-mineral oil idea comes from Steiner and Elliott, 1983.

same tests suggest that the traps begin to catch beneficials as the pest population drops. Therefore, use traps when whiteflies first start to appear, but remove them when the population seems to be decreasing. You can judge this by how many adults are present and how many new larvae show up on older leaves.

Commercially available traps should be quite adequate for greenhouse use, but for home use you may want to make your own sticky traps, as described in the sidebar at left, because they can be tailored to the location where they will be placed. Moreover, you can make them with surfaces that are somewhat larger than those available commercially.

Treatment: Direct Biological Controls

The use of biological controls against whiteflies is most likely to be practical in plant collections where screening of vents and windows keeps the beneficial insects indoors and where the temperature, humidity and, in winter, light can be adjusted to favor the pest's natural controls over the pest itself. This generally means warmer and more humid conditions than most people would care to have in a home or office. Enclosed sun porches, greenhouses and conservatories are more suitable settings for the release of biological controls.

1. *Encarsia formosa.* The parasitoid *Encarsia formosa*, which lives only on the greenhouse whitefly, is a tiny golden-yellow miniwasp that has been used effectively for over 50 years in whitefly control. It is called a parasitoid because, unlike true parasites, it kills its host.

Although smaller than the head of a pin, *Encarsia* is a true hymenopteran, related to the larger wasps with which most of us are more familiar. It is in the superfamily Chalcidoidea, which provides its other common name, the golden chalcid. The species is native to North America and is available from commercial suppliers in the United States and

It is also helpful when combined with other approaches, such as trapping and/or the release of the beneficial parasitoid *Encarsia formosa*. If much egg-laying has already taken place, vacuuming alone usually does not stem pest population growth.

After vacuuming up the adults, enclose the section of the machine containing the bag in plastic and put it into a freezer for 24 hours to kill the insects before shaking it out. (Caution: If you put the entire vacuum in the freezer you may have a problem with moisture condensation

on the motor when you bring it out into the warm air again.)

2. Trapping. Whiteflies are attracted to a specific shade of yellow, so they can be trapped on boards painted that color and coated with a nontoxic sticky material. Such traps are sold commercially and come with simple directions (see the Resource Appendix under "Insect Management: Physical Controls" on pp. 682-683).

There is some evidence that traps catch more whiteflies than natural whitefly enemies as long as the pest population is high; however, the

The Life Cycles of the Greenhouse Whitefly and its Parasitoid

Encarsia formosa inserts its egg into a whitefly larva (nymph) that has reached its third or fourth developmental stage, or instar. The egg hatches into a tiny worm that eats the whitefly larva from within, turning its body black. Within three to four weeks, the adult parasitoid emerges from the dead whitefly and repeats the cycle. Unparasitized whiteflies give rise to second-generation adults.

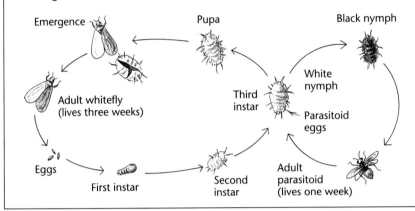

Emergence · Pupa · Black nymph · Adult whitefly (lives three weeks) · Third instar · White nymph · Parasitoid eggs · Eggs · First instar · Second instar · Adult parasitoid (lives one week)

Canada (see the Resource Appendix under "Insect Management: Biological Controls" on pp. 683-686).

The *Encarsia* female is only slightly larger than a spider mite. She has a dark head and thorax and a yellow abdomen. The female feeds on and kills the young whitefly instars, but she inserts her eggs into only the third and fourth instars of young whiteflies (see the drawing above). (Thus, to be precise, *Encarsia* is both a predator and a parasitoid.) Within two weeks the whitefly scale turns black. At 70°F (21°C), the adult parasitoid will take about 20 days to develop within the whitefly. At higher temperatures development is faster: It takes 10 days at 86°F (30°C).

The parasitoid wasp develops faster than its whitefly host, especially at higher temperatures; it also lays twice as many eggs in the same time. Although each female lays between 50 and 100 eggs, only one parasitoid develops in each young whitefly.

Here are some recommendations for using *Encarsia formosa*:

• Avoid using insecticides (except insecticidal soap or oil) for one month prior to releasing *Encarsia*.

• Reduce existing whitefly populations with insecticidal soap or oil before releasing beneficials. A good rule of thumb is that by the time the parasitoids are released, there should be an average of no more than one adult whitefly per leaf.

• Adjust the environmental conditions to favor *Encarsia* over the whiteflies. Optimum conditions include a temperature of 80°F (27°C), 70% relative humidity and a light intensity greater than 650 footcandles (7,000 lux). Below 390 footcandles (4,200 lux) the whitefly parasitoid suffers great mortality. (See the discussion of light intensity indoors on pp. 327-328.) Many winter settings require supplementary light to maintain optimum conditions.

• Order *Encarsia* after reducing a high whitefly population with insecticidal soap or oil, or when you see the first whiteflies appear in the greenhouse; do not wait for the situation to become serious.

• Release one to five *Encarsia* per plant, or one for every 10 sq. yd. (8.4 sq.m) of plant area. The first release should err on the side of too many rather than too few *Encarsia*. Later, as

you become more familiar with the predator-prey relationship, you can adjust the dosage downward.

• Carefully read the instructions that come with the package containing parasitized whiteflies. The black parasitized scales of the whiteflies will probably arrive attached to leaves, which in turn are glued to a paper or cardboard backing. These should be distributed around the plantings where whitefly control is desired.

• Introduce *Encarsia* at 10- to 14-day intervals, timed so that the parasitoid can attack the third and fourth whitefly instar stages. Usually, one series of releases in early spring is sufficient to protect plants through spring and summer. Where year-round plantings are maintained, releases can be repeated as needed.

• Spot-vacuum or spot-treat with insecticidal soap or oil those locations where whiteflies build up despite releases of *Encarsia;* do not treat the rest of the greenhouse. Spot treatment should be done carefully and sparingly since it may damage adult parasitoids or deny the parasitoids food by killing too many whiteflies.

• Watch for blackened whitefly scales two to three weeks after you release the *Encarsia*. Good control should be achieved in two to three months. If after less than one month fewer than 20% of the developing whitefly scales are parasitized (blackened), make additional releases.

• If plants that already have the parasitized whitefly scales must be removed from the greenhouse, strip off those leaves containing black pupae and scatter them around. This will allow the *Encarsia* to emerge. Distributing leaves containing parasitized larvae is one way of introducing the parasitoid into other greenhouses that have whitefly problems.

2. Mycotal®. In the past, the fungus *Verticillium lecanii* was commercially available in the United States under the name Mycotal®. Mycotal® (which is still used in Europe) is a naturally occurring pathogen of whiteflies. Although the parasitoid *Encar-*

sia is somewhat susceptible to the same fungus, it is much less susceptible than the whitefly. *Encarsia* and the fungus have been used in combination on European greenhouse tomatoes and gerberas. With interest in microbial insecticides such as Mycotal® now on the rise, this microbial may return to the U.S. market. For more information about Mycotal®, see pp. 137-138 and Hussey and Scopes (1986), listed in "References and Readings" on pp. 398-401.

Treatment:
Direct Chemical Controls
Least-toxic chemical controls for whiteflies include insecticidal soap, kinoprene and horticultural oil.

1. Insecticidal Soap. Insecticidal soap is effective against whiteflies, but it also kills the parasitoids. For this reason, we recommend that you reserve insecticidal soap for spot treatments of flare-ups on specific plants or to reduce high pest populations before parasitoids are released. For more details on insecticidal soap, see pp. 114-116; for sources, see the Resource Appendix under "Insect

Summary: Least-Toxic Whitefly Control

• Check the undersides of the lower leaves of the plant for immature stages of whitefly.

• Spot-treat with insecticidal soap, oil and/or kinoprene where populations are becoming intolerable.

• Vacuum up adults when low temperatures make them slow-moving.

• Release adequate numbers of the parasitoid *Encarsia formosa* in screened greenhouses where favorable temperature and light conditions can be maintained.

Management: Chemical Controls" on pp. 686-687.

2. Kinoprene. The insect growth regulator kinoprene (Enstar®) is available for whitefly control. It is comparatively nontoxic to humans and is highly selective, affecting only whiteflies and aphids.

We had very good results with this product while establishing biological controls in the San Francisco Conservatory of Flowers. For more details on IGRs, see pp. 145-148.

3. Horticultural Oil. Horticultural oil as a 2% solution in water is reported to be an effective treatment for whiteflies. For further information, see pp. 116-119 and p. 362.

LEAFMINERS
(Order Diptera, family Agromyzidae)
Leafminers are insects that tunnel between the upper and lower surfaces of leaves, each species making its own characteristic pattern. Although very high populations of some leafminers can seriously restrict plant growth, it is the highly visible tunnels, or mines, in leaves that make most people want to control these insects. A certain amount of tunneling can be tolerated in home plantings, but in commercial settings tunneling severely affects the market value of the plants, so the problem cannot be ignored.

A number of conventional insecticides are registered for use against leafminers, but they have become largely ineffective. Overuse has resulted in wide-scale development of leafminer populations that can detoxify the synthetic chemical insecticides. This resistance problem, together with concerns about the safety of conventional insecticides, has led to a search for less-toxic alternatives to control the pests.

Fortunately, a number of methods that are nontoxic to humans and other mammals are available. These include traps, biological controls and less-toxic insecticides.

Biology
Although the term "leafminer" can be applied to the immature stages of many insects in the orders Lepidoptera (moths and butterflies), Diptera (flies) and Hymenoptera (ants, bees and wasps), the occurrence of mines on the leaves of indoor plants is most often caused by dipteran flies in the family Agromyzidae and the genus *Liriomyza*.

There are over 300 described species of *Liriomyza;* 23 are economically significant. The most pestiferous species worldwide is the serpentine leafminer *(L. trifolii),* which attacks many plant species and is resistant to a large number of insecticides. It is the worst pest of greenhouse-grown chrysanthemums. Four other species in this genus cause minor to substantial damage on indoor and outdoor crops in North America. They are *L. huidobrensis, L. sativae, L. brassicae* and *L. trifoliearum.* In the past, there has been confusion about the identification of some species because they often mix together on the same host plant. To add to the confusion, there is also a caterpillar that mines the leaves of azaleas indoors.

Fortunately for the non-specialist, identification of the leafminer species is generally not necessary for control. The exception is when damage is widespread and severe and nontoxic controls are ineffective. In such cases, one may suspect an uncommon or exotic species, and good control may be achieved only by identifying the species, researching its biology, origins and parasitoids, and tailoring a control program with this information in mind.

In general, if you see leafminers for the first time on a plant that has not been treated with insecticides, you should suspect the serpentine leafminer, *L. trifolii.* The adult *L. trifolii* is quite attractive, with a yellow head, plum-red eyes, a greyish-black thorax and an abdomen with a noticeable yellow patch at the upper hind end of the mid-thoracic segment. The adults are small ($\frac{1}{12}$ in./

2 mm long), but they can be seen with the naked eye as they search for feeding and egg-laying sites on leaf surfaces during daylight hours.

The female *L. trifolii* feeds on leaf mesophyll cells (cells in the middle leaf layer) after cutting a hole in the leaf surface with her ovipositor. Males are unable to cut the leaf but can feed at holes cut by females. The female tastes the leaf to determine whether it is a suitable plant in which to lay eggs. Although females feed throughout the day, most feeding occurs about midday. Adults of both sexes also feed on nectar and honeydew.

The female fly inserts her eggs through ovipositor punctures just below the epidermis of the leaf. When first laid, the oval eggs are translucent and very small (about 0.01 in./0.2 mm long). Later they become cream-colored. They hatch in 2 to 5 days (see the drawing at right). The larvae, originally colorless, darken as they pass through their three stages. They feed on the palisade parenchyma tissue within the leaf below the upper surface, and complete their development in 4 to 7 days. The last stage leaves the interior of the leaf by cutting a hole in either the lower or upper surface, and drops to pupate in the soil or the darkest accessible area. The pupa is orange-yellow and turns brown as it ages. Pupation lasts 10 to 15 days.

The duration of the *L. trifolii* life cycle is highly variable. At warm temperatures the egg-to-adult cycle can be completed in less than 20 days. The males live only an average of two days, while females are reported to live up to seven days. The sex ratio is 1:1. Adults can fly up to 300 ft. (91 m) within a few hours of emergence.

Mating occurs during the day of emergence. A single mating is enough to ensure fertilization of all eggs. Unfertilized females are unable to oviposit. Females lay an average of 17 eggs per day, and a maximum of 250 eggs during their lifetimes. Several generations of leafminers may be produced each year.

The Life Cycle of the Leafminer

Leafminers such as *Liriomyza trifolii* lay up to 250 eggs just under the surface of the leaf epidermis. Hatching larvae tunnel through the mid-leaf tissue, feeding as they go and leaving characteristic wavy lines that are visible on the top of the leaf. When ready to pupate, the larvae leave the leaf and drop to the soil or other dark places, emerging in 10 to 15 days as adult flies. (Actual size of adult: ½ in./2 mm)

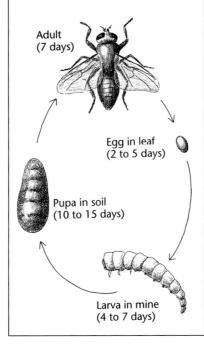

Adult
(7 days)

Egg in leaf
(2 to 5 days)

Pupa in soil
(10 to 15 days)

Larva in mine
(4 to 7 days)

Although *L. trifolii* is now found in many parts of the world, Florida is thought to have been its original home. From Florida, leafminers spread northward through the eastern United States as far as Ontario, Canada, and southward to the Bahamas, Venezuela and Guyana. They later spread to Colombia, California, Kenya, Britain, Germany, Denmark, the Netherlands, the Canary Islands and Malta. Although they can survive in areas with sub-zero temperatures, they thrive only in subtropical and tropical conditions.

Damage

As leafminers invaded each new area, the absence of natural enemies allowed their numbers to grow. Heavy use of insecticides was the common reaction to their presence, producing the resistance that is common today.

L. trifolii has been found on 120 plant species in 47 plant genera in 21 families, although it primarily attacks species in Compositae and Leguminosae. Among the economically important plants that it attacks are melons, cucumbers, squash, beans, peas, onions, peppers, tomatoes, eggplants, potatoes, celery, lettuce and carrots. Among the ornamental crops are asters, calendulas, chrysanthemums, cineraria, gerbera, baby's breath, snapdragons, gypsophila and marigolds. Thirty weed species have also been listed as host plants.

Crops can be severely stunted or killed by leafminer damage, especially in the seedling stage. Tunneling larvae that disfigure leaves are the primary source of injury, particularly of ornamental crops and food crops that emphasize the plant's leaves. Feeding and egg-puncture sites also add to leaf disfigurement.

Detection and Monitoring

Cost-effective management of leafminers requires that you establish a monitoring program to determine if and when treatment is needed. In small plant collections, removing any infested leaves as soon as you notice them may solve the problem.

Regular inspection enables you to detect leafminers at an early stage of infestation and determine whether their numbers are rising or falling. If the population is falling, it indicates that local natural enemies, including disease-causing pathogens, are active and further control may not be necessary. If parasitoids are released, you should monitor them to see whether they are establishing themselves.

In large plantings you can monitor leafminer adults, larvae or pupae. To monitor adults you can use the same yellow sticky traps that are widely used for monitoring and controlling whiteflies (see p. 386). The traps do not seem to attract the commercially available leafminer parasitoids, so trapping and biological control can occur simultaneously. Adult emergence from the soil can be monitored by inverted funnels capped with a vial, as shown in the drawing below. The vial is removed at regular intervals to count captured flies, and then replaced.

Larvae can be counted by selecting leaves and counting the number of mines. In greenhouses in Europe, 10 plants or more are selected in each house and are marked with colored tape for season-long inspection. On each plant, an upper, middle and lower leaf are also marked. Each week both the number of leaflets showing feeding marks and the number of mines per leaf are recorded. As the plants grow and lose lower leaves, a replacement upper leaf is marked. At that point, the previous upper and middle leaves become the middle and lower leaves, respectively. To tell whether larvae have been parasitized, individual infested leaves are placed in small cotton-stoppered vials or gelatin capsules and watched to see if parasitoids emerge.

Pupal numbers can be estimated by placing 9 in. x 11 in. x ⅝ in. (23 cm x 28 cm x 1.6 cm) Styrofoam trays on the ground under foliage to capture larvae as they fall to the soil to pupate. This technique is also used outdoors on tomato crops in Southern California.

Monitoring enables you to determine just what size pest population causes enough leaf damage to require treatment. This is known as the injury level. (For a full discussion of this concept, see pp. 40-41.) Bear in mind that successful biological control requires at least some tolerance of damage. Also remember that when using biological controls there is usually a lag between the time you make your decision to treat and when the treatment is carried out, since it generally takes a week or more for parasitoids to arrive by mail. Monitoring gives you an early warning so you have time to order beneficials.

Because every site and plant maintenance regime is different, separate injury and action levels must be established. The first growing season with nontoxic controls is usually something of an on-site experiment, so it comes as no surprise that many commercial growers are reluctant to switch. Initially, the attention and time required to fine-tune the nontoxic program are greater than with more toxic conventional insecticides; later the reverse is true.

You can use the experience of others as a starting point, then fine-tune releases and other controls to suit your particular conditions. For example, research has shown that on greenhouse tomatoes infested with the leafminer *L. bryoniae,* it wasn't until leaves adjacent to a truss of swelling fruit contained 15 mines per leaf that yields were reduced. Thus, a fair degree of leaf damage can be tolerated without significant crop loss. Unfortunately, commercial growers usually react prematurely to aesthetic damage caused by only three or four mines per leaf by spraying insecticides. A simple method for keeping records of your observations during monitoring is described in the sidebar on p. 348.

Treatment:
Direct Biological Controls

A range of environmentally sound management techniques is available, so you can select a mix that fits your situation. If only a few indoor plants are being attacked, simply pruning off infested leaves or moving plants outdoors to attract natural enemies from the surrounding environment may solve the problem. But with large indoor plant collections, a full range of methods should be considered.

1. Natural Enemies. Leafminers are eaten by such predators as ants, true bugs, flies, lacewings, birds and spiders. Adults are killed by various predatory flies in the families Empididae, Muscidae and Dolicopodidae. The insect-attacking parasitoid nematode *Steinernema (=Neoaplectana) carpocapsae* may be effective against soil-occurring stages.

Monitoring for Leafminers
Yellow sticky traps (A) capture adult leafminers flying to plants in a planter box or greenhouse bed. The emergence of adults from the pupal stage in the soil can be monitored with an inverted kitchen funnel capped with a plastic vial (B).

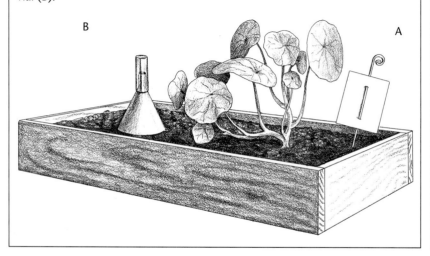

On a worldwide basis, 28 parasitoid species that attack *L. trifolii* have been identified. The most important are *Diglyphus isaea, D. begini* (see the photo at right), *D. intermedius, D. pulchripes, D. websteri, Dacnusa sibirica* and *Chrysocharis parksi*. The two parasitoids that are available commercially belong to two different superfamilies. One, *Diglyphus isaea,* is a chalcid. Chalcids frequently kill their hosts by opening a hole through which they feed upon tissues. Such feeding is essential for the adult females to obtain protein for egg development. In fact, they may kill many more leafminer larvae by host feeding than by parasitizing them.

Diglyphus isaea is abundant in Europe, North Africa and Japan, and is a natural enemy of 18 leafminer species in five genera. The female paralyzes the host with her ovipositor and usually lays one egg, although she occasionally lays two to five eggs near or on the host. The parasitized leafminer becomes brown and flaccid after a few days. Before pupation, the developing larva consolidates its pupal chamber with fecal pillars, presumably as a structural support for protection when the leaf dries out. At constant temperature of 68°F (20°C), *D. isaea* develops from egg to adult in about 17 days. In comparison, the host serpentine leafminer develops in about 20 to 30 days, depending on the plant upon which it is feeding.

The other commercially available parasitoid is *Dacnusa sibirica*, which attacks a wide variety of leafminer species besides *L. trifolii*. It is a braconid, meaning that is does not host feed. *Dacnusa sibirica* is widely distributed in Europe and Siberia, and has been introduced into North America. Females of this species oviposit into all larval instars, and the eggs develop inside the host while it is in the leaf. At room temperature, egg-to-adult development takes about 16 days. The adults live only six days, and females deposit 72 eggs.

As part of our work in preparing reports for *The IPM Practitioner*, we

Diglyphus begini miniwasp is shown drinking from a droplet of water on a leaf. The female *Diglyphus* inserts her sharp egg-laying appendage, or ovipositor, into a leafminer while it is in its tunnel and deposits an egg. The egg hatches into its worm stage and feeds within the leafminer's body. An adult female miniwasp can also feed directly on larval tissue through puncture wounds made with her ovipositor. (Photo courtesy Michael Parella.)

talked with R. C. Gerhart, whose firm is importing into the United States two leafminer parasitoids from Koppert B.V. in Holland. The firm is known throughout Europe for the high quality of its beneficial insects, mites and microbial pesticides, as well for as its impressive technical support.

A rule of thumb that evolved from the European work is that parasitoids should be introduced at the rate of one adult for every 10 new mines seen on the plant each week during the first six weeks of an infestation. This approach achieved 72% to 80% parasitism of second-generation leafminers. However, since 90% of the leafminers must be parasitized in the first generation to prevent large buildups later, larger numbers of parasitoids should be released initially.

Reports on the use of leafminer parasitoids on commercial crops in European greenhouses indicate that a single release of parasitoids is insufficient for control. Thus, where relatively large numbers of plants are involved, several releases are required during the growing season. The specific number and frequency of the re-

leases depend on a variety of factors, including number and species of plants, temperature and humidity, number of leafminers and time of year. You should discuss your particular situation with the supplier.

Ideally, repeated releases of the parasitoids will eventually lead to their permanent establishment in the greenhouse, atrium or plant-decorated shopping mall. Chances of this happening are enhanced if you tolerate a few leafminer-susceptible permanent plantings such as cineraria. These support a few leafminers on a permanent basis, which is desirable because the parasitoids also die out if all the leafminers are killed.

If biological controls are introduced, you must monitor to determine whether the desired level of parasitism is being achieved. This can be done by placing a certain number of infested leaves in individual vials and waiting to see how many parasitoids and how many leafminer flies emerge. Since the desired level of parasitism is 90%, careful and regular monitoring is needed.

Treatment:
Direct Physical Controls

Currently available beneficial insects alone are not likely to keep leafminer numbers low enough to suit competition-oriented amateur horticulturalists or growers of commercial crops. Integration of additional techniques and products compatible with biocontrols will probably be necessary. Physical controls include the use of screens, mulches and traps.

1. Screening. If regular releases of natural enemies are being made, it is best to screen all openings to the greenhouse to keep the beneficials inside and exclude their natural enemies, the hyperparasitoids.

2. Plastic Mulches. In experiments conducted by J. L. Keularts at Ohio State University, tomato plants were protected from leafminer damage by covering their soil with plastic mulches (available at local garden stores). The soil covering prevented leafminer larvae from reaching the soil to pupate. Larvae that dropped to the plastic were subsequently removed by ants.

3. Trapping. In some settings trapping alone may be effective, particularly if enough traps are used. For example, paper plates painted yellow and coated with a sticky adhesive kept leafminer populations below economic injury levels in greenhouse studies conducted by M. van de Veire at the University of Ghent in Belgium. Van de Veire found that the traps originally set out for whiteflies were also effective against leafminers. However, the plates were not attractive to the beneficial parasitoids *Diglyphus isaea* and *Dacnusa* spp., nor to the whitefly parasitoid *Encarsia formosa* because sufficient hosts were available to prevent the adult parasitoids from extensive searching and subsequent capture in the traps.

The number of sticky traps to use in a particular setting will have to be determined by on-site experimentation. If large numbers of parasitoids are caught on the traps, the quantity of traps should be reduced.

The larvae of leafminer flies can be captured without traps, since they drop to the soil when they are ready to pupate.

Treatment:
Direct Chemical Controls

Least-toxic chemical controls of leafminers include neem oil, methoprene (effective only on leafminer larvae) and horticultural oils.

1. Neem Oil. The commercialization of Margosan-O®, a neem oil product, is one of the most important developments in botanical insecticides. For details on this material, see pp. 122-123. Neem oil's principal active ingredient, azadirachtin, operates as a repellent to adult leafminers and as a systemic insect growth regulator (IGR) on larvae. (An IGR is a juvenile hormone that prevents insects from reaching maturity and reproducing.) The fact that these effects can occur simultaneously gives neem oil products an edge over other commercial IGRs such as methoprene (Minex®), which has no effect on adult leafminers.

Neem extracts have proven effective against the leafminers *L. trifolii* and *L. sativae* on chrysanthemums in both laboratory and field studies. They can be applied as foliage sprays or as soil drenches. Foliage sprays act as repellents against adult leafminers, and treated leaves show fewer feeding and egg-laying punctures than untreated leaves. When used as a drench, the insecticide is taken up by the roots and translocated (distributed) throughout the plant. Insects that subsequently eat plant tissues containing the extract are prevented from further development. The insecticide remains active within the plant tissue for three weeks. To get the greatest value from neem oil extracts, both foliar applications and soil drenches should be used.

2. Methoprene. Minex®, or methoprene, is an IGR manufactured by Sandoz Crop Protection. A methoprene soil drench applied 7 days after planting cuttings and repeated 30 days later is recommended for greenhouse-grown crops. The second drench protects new tissue as the plant grows, since the systemic action does not apply to new plant growth. Mature plants should be treated at 30-day intervals.

Since Minex® does not affect adult leafminers, the product literature recommends that it be used in conjunction with an insecticide that kills adults. It recommends that the level of treatment be based on the number of catches in a leafminer trap (a flat yellow card coated with a sticky ad-

Summary: Least-Toxic Leafminer Control

• Remove infested leaves in small plantings by hand.

• Use yellow sticky (whitefly) traps or Pherocon™ leafminer traps to catch adults.

• Consider combining periodic releases of commercially available parasitoids with trapping.

• Screen all greenhouse vents, windows and other openings to retain released organisms.

• Use IGR sprays of neem or methoprene or horticultural oils to supplement parasitoid releases and trapping.

• In large and/or commercial plantings, establish a monitoring program to determine when to take action and whether treatments are effective.

hesive—see the Resource Appendix under "Insect Management: Physical Controls" on pp. 682-683). When up to 20 adult flies are caught in each trap each week, applications of an adulticide and Minex® should begin, if they are not already underway. Adulticide spraying should continue until trap catches decrease to fewer than 20 flies per trap per week.

3. **Horticultural Oils.** Recent work with horticultural oils by USDA scientist Hiram Larew indicates that oils may work against leafminers. The oils are Sunspray 5E™, Sunspray 6E™, Ortho Volck Oil Spray and Natur'l Oil, which is derived from soybean oil. All were used in 2% concentrations in a spray applied to three-week-old "Iceberg" chrysanthemums placed for 24 hours in cages with 50 to 75 adult serpentine leafminers. All worked equally well in reducing both egg-laying leaf punctures and the number of eggs laid. Although the most effective methods of integrating such oils into IPM programs have yet to be determined, we are reporting this work to encourage others to begin experimenting with these and other oils. For more information on horticultural oils, see pp. 116-119; for sources, consult the Resource Appendix under "Insect Management: Chemical Controls" on pp. 686-687.

BLACK VINE WEEVILS
(Order Coleoptera, family Curculionidae)
The black vine weevil *(Otiorhynchus sulcatus)* is a pest of ornamentals throughout much of the United States. Outdoors it attacks the roots of rhododendrons, azaleas, yews, hemlocks, many berry species and other ornamental and wild plants. It is closely related to the strawberry root weevil *(O. ovatus)*, an agricultural pest. Indoors the black vine weevil infests begonias, ferns, carnations, orchids and other common container-grown plants, but it is particularly damaging to cyclamens and is often called the cyclamen grub.

As revealed by the discussion of its biology below, several characteristics of this beetle and its life cycle make it difficult to control with insecticides.

Biology
The black vine weevil is a large black insect that cannot fly. Most weevils tend to stay within 30 ft. (9 m) of where they hatch, though a few individuals in every batch may travel considerably farther. They avoid grassy areas, preferring cement walkways and other cleared spaces, and they frequently enter greenhouses by walking up the sides and coming through open vents near or on the roof, or simply by sneaking under a poorly fitted door. They can enter

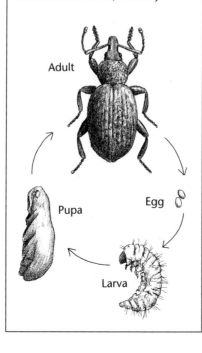

The Life Cycle of the Black Vine Weevil
Adult black vine weevils *(Otiorhynchus sulcatus)* lay up to 1,000 eggs over a four-month period. Eggs hatch in three weeks and grubs feed for two to three months before pupating. Adults emerge seven weeks later. (Actual size of adult: 7/10 in./18 mm)

Adult

Pupa

Egg

Larva

house plant pots when they are set outdoors temporarily.

Black vine weevils are active at night but hide in crevices in the soil by day. The adult weevils' habit of crawling down into the soil each day makes them particularly vulnerable to attack by beneficial nematodes. The nematodes can also attack the larval stage of the weevil. When fully grown, the larval weevil is a fat white grub that assumes a semicircular position when disturbed.

N. W. Hussey, W. H. Read and J. J. Hesling reported on the life cycle of the weevil in British greenhouses in the standard reference work on pests of plants indoors, *The Pests of Protected Cultivation:*

Reproduction is parthenogenetic, no males being known, and begins about 10 weeks after maturation from the pupa. Under glass, weevils mature in greater numbers in the late autumn. As individuals...[lay eggs] for at least 4 months, producing about 1,000 eggs at an average rate of 7 per day, eggs will generally be found in spring and early summer. They are deposited near plants in the surface soil. Eggs are spherical, white at first but becoming pale brown within a few days. They hatch in about 3 weeks to legless, yellowish-white grubs with markedly wrinkled bodies and brown heads (0.7 mm [3/100 in.] in diameter). They feed for about 80 days throughout the spring and early summer before pupating in earthen cells about 12 mm [½ in.] in diameter within an inch or so of the soil surface. Hence eggs laid in mid winter give rise to full-grown larvae which may cause extensive damage the following autumn. The adults emerge about 7 weeks later. Though there is only one generation per year there is much overlapping as outdoor populations lay eggs in early autumn, so that, at any time, all stages may be found.

The top photo shows wilting on a cyclamen caused by black vine weevil larvae, which feed on its roots (middle photo). To control the problem, a solution of insect-attacking nematodes is applied to the soil (bottom photo). The nematodes swim to the weevil larvae, enter their bodies and kill them. (Photos by Helga Olkowski.)

Damage

When black vine weevils attack a container-grown plant, the result is dramatic and usually fatal. The plant wilts despite the presence of moisture in the soil. This is caused by weevil grubs, which tunnel into the roots and may eventually destroy the entire root ball. If you place your hand on a wilted, infested cyclamen and lightly tug the plant, the entire plant—or what remains of it—will come out of the pot with ease. Usually it appears as if the tuber has been sheared off just below ground level. Close examination reveals the white grubs either snuggled into tunnels they have made in the tuber or lying curled up in the soil to which they have dropped during removal of the plant.

Treatment:
Direct Physical Controls

As non-flying insects, weevils travel from plant to plant by walking. It stands to reason, then, that physical barriers form the first line of defense. The adult weevil generally walks into greenhouses, sun porches and other structures through unscreened windows, doors and vents, or by crawling through cracks around doors that lack weatherstripping or sturdy thresholds. You can make the structures tight by using caulk, screens or whatever other means are appropriate. This has the added benefit of keeping out mice and other pests and retaining beneficial insects.

Another approach is to place all susceptible plants, particularly cyclamens, on stands that have sticky barriers around their legs. We offer complete instructions for making these stands in the sidebar on pp. 356-357. Plants should remain above such barriers at all times, even while being stored during dormancy. The only exception is when they are temporarily displayed within the home itself. Living areas of the home should be sufficiently bug-tight.

Treatment:
Direct Biological Controls

The most recent breakthrough in the control of black vine weevils is the use of certain nematode species that kill insects and some related arthropods by entering the victim's body. Two species are commercially available: *Steinernema (=Neoaplectana) carpocapsae* and *Heterorhabditis heliothidis*. Both have been proven effective at killing black vine weevils in greenhouse settings. *H. heliothidis* is more effective than *S. carpocapsae* at the same dose, presumably because it actively penetrates the insect cuticle. As it is more difficult to rear, however, it costs more for equal numbers.

H. heliothidis also has been shown to be more effective against the early stages of the weevil at greater soil depths. The depth of the container or bed in which the plants are growing should offer you some guidance as to whether the differences between the nematode species is something you need to consider.

There are two techniques for applying nematodes. They can be mixed with water and simply sprayed on the soil beneath the foliage (see the photos on the facing page). Alternatively, where only a few pots are involved, the nematodes can be mixed with soil and the mixture added to the pots. This second method was suggested to us by Dr. Albert Pye, of BioLogic Insectaries in Pennsylvania, who has had extensive experience in rearing and applying beneficial nematodes in the United States and in Sweden. The pots should be watered after applying the mix since the major limiting factor in the use of these beneficial nematodes is that they cannot survive in dry conditions for long.

Timing of applications is considerably less critical when using nematodes than when using conventional synthetic insecticides. Nematodes are effective only on certain growth stages of weevil grubs, even though adult beetles may be entering the greenhouse and laying eggs at almost any time during the growing season or during the year in areas with mild winters; thus more than one application of nematodes per year may be required. Nematodes can last three months in the soil, so quarterly applications should be adequate to handle even the most severe infestations.

FUNGUS GNATS
(Order Diptera, family Mycetophilidae and others)

If you raise plants indoors you are probably familiar with fungus gnats, even though you may not know what to call them. They are tiny, dark, slender, fragile-looking flies that flit through foliage or lie dead on window sills. Most are merely a nuisance, but a few species harm plants by feeding on the roots. Among the common plants attacked by the larval stage of the gnats are poinsettias, gerberas, daisies, gloxinias, most bulb crops, cyclamens, hybrid impatiens, salvia, geraniums and ornamental peppers. All bedding plants and vegetables grown in plugs are highly vulnerable, and tender tissue-culture plugs are particularly susceptible.

Biology

The term "fungus gnat" refers to a very large group of insects, most of which have not been studied extensively. Many questions regarding their taxonomy (physical characteristics) and biology remain unanswered. It appears that their primary food is the organic matter and fungi in the soil or planting medium, and it seems probable that all or most species that are true pests can feed on organic matter or on plant roots.

As used by a horticulturalist, "fungus gnat" could mean any species in the following families: Phoridae, Mycetophilidae, Sciaridae, Sphaeroceridae (small dung flies), Psychodidae (moth flies) and Cecidomyiidae (gall midges), as well as any species in related but more obscure families. They are all small flies, as the term gnat connotes; in fact, fungus gnats in the genus *Megaselia* (family Phoridae) are tiny enough to penetrate typical window screening. A more conservative use of the term "gnat" limits the organism to about 2,000 species of flies in the family Mycetophilidae (which, depending upon the researcher, sometimes also includes the Sciaridae). The adults of this family superficially look like mosquitoes, although upon closer inspection they are distinctly different. Mosquitoes, for example, have long piercing mouthparts, whereas gnats do not.

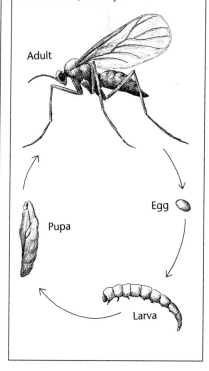

The Life Cycle of the Fungus Gnat
Adult fungus gnats live about one week and lay up to 200 eggs. Eggs hatch in about four days into larvae that damage plant roots during their two-week larval period in the soil. The pupal stage lasts three to four days before adults emerge. (Actual size of adult: 1/8 in./3 mm)

Adult

Egg

Pupa

Larva

Under natural conditions fungus gnat larvae inhabit wild fungi, leaf mold, manure piles and rotting wood, feeding on dead organic matter and fungi—hence their name. Adult gnats like moist areas. Although there are many highly specialized species within the broad assemblage of fungus gnats, they generally have similar habits. The information provided below is based on the biology of a specific pest species, the well-known North American greenhouse and mushroom pest *Lycoriella mali* (*L. solani* is its counterpart in Europe), which is a member of the family Sciaridae.

Lycoriella mali adults are all very small, sooty grey or nearly black, long-legged, slender flies about 1/10 in. to 1/8 in. (2.5 mm to 3 mm) long. They are not swift flyers. Adults live about one week, during which time they mate. The females are attracted by soils and soil mixes that have a high organic content; they lay their eggs on top of the soil near plant stems. Eggs hatch in about four days, and the larvae are clear with black heads. They feed on fungi and algae on pot surfaces and on or under benches. In containers, the larvae feed on root hairs and roots in the upper inch of soil. Later they burrow into stems and leaves, causing eventual destruction of the plant.

Damage

Where root-feeding by fungus gnat larvae is negligible, no ill effects are observed. But when it becomes more extensive, plants show signs of wilting (we could not find data on the number of pest larvae that cause noticeable injury). After the roots have been injured, root rots may attack the plant. In commercial greenhouses entire crops of poinsettias —300,000 to 600,000 pots—have been destroyed this way. Growers may not even associate the damage with gnats unless the larvae are noticed when the roots of the wilted plants are examined. Fortunately, when damage is severe, indicating that a large number of damaging species are present in the greenhouse, there are safe management methods that prevent recurrence.

Detection and Monitoring

Light/electrocution traps and sticky traps are the most efficient monitoring tools (for sources, see the Resource Appendix under "Insect Management: Physical Controls" on pp. 682-683). If you are growing only a small number of plants, these tools may be so effective at catching the flies that they also function as controls. The expense of light/electrocution traps is likely to limit their use in homes and small plantings. You may have to experiment, taking a unit on a trial basis to determine whether it is appropriate for the size of the plantings and the seriousness of the infestation. (Note that advertisements for these light/electrocution traps often suggest that they can rid your outdoor patio of pests at barbecues. We strongly advise against using light traps outdoors. They are relatively indiscriminate in the species they attract and kill, and you run the risk of causing more pest problems than you cure by eliminating the beneficial insects that control pests.)

An innovative, convenient sticky trap for monitoring mushroom fly populations was recently developed in Australia. No doubt it will eventually become available in the United States. It uses sheets of plastic cut from a roll and coated with a sticky adhesive as a collection surface. As each sheet fills it is discarded, and a new length of plastic is pulled out and treated with the adhesive. Aerosol cans with adhesive can be used to speed up the application process when many traps are being used. A word of caution, however: In the past the propellant used in these cans was methylene chloride, a carcinogen that should not be inhaled. This material is widely used as a paint remover and as a liquid fumigant against gophers. You should avoid aerosol cans with this propellant.

Since there are no published reports on the number of gnats that cause intolerable damage, you will have to establish your own correlation between the gnat population and damage. Start by checking traps biweekly, then modify the frequency of checking according to the temperature and light conditions. Longer, warmer days increase fly breeding; darker, cooler periods retard them. In greenhouses, fly production will also vary according to the crops grown. If catches are initially very high and then fall off dramatically, you can assume that the trap itself is acting as a control; it may be all you need.

If trap catches remain high, however, you must turn to one of the controls suggested below. Continue checking the traps to see whether the population is dropping. If not, you may need to try another treatment or even combine treatments. Remember that elimination of all gnats is not your goal, especially if you are releasing predators, since you want low numbers of the pests around to feed the beneficial organisms.

Treatment: Direct Biological Controls

Some fungus gnats have become resistant to conventional pesticides, which has encouraged testing of a number of less-toxic approaches. Because these approaches have only recently been developed, however, the literature on their use and effectiveness is not extensive. You will probably have to do some experimenting to match the methods to your specific problem.

1. *Bacillus thuringiensis. Bacillus thuringiensis israelensis,* or BTI, has been used very effectively to control fungus gnats in mushroom culture by treating the compost used to grow the mushrooms. Recent unpublished information indicates that there has been an important advance using BTI to control gnats in containers of ornamental plants as well.

BTI is a widely available biological control that is a highly effective and safe agent for suppressing the larvae of mosquitoes and blackflies (see pp. 135-136). Because BTI acts as a stomach poison, it must be applied so that the targeted stage of the pest consumes it. Bear in mind that adult fungus gnats do not eat, or, if they do, their consumption is negligible. Thus, for fungus gnat control, the bacterial spores must be placed in the potting soil where larvae feed. The easiest way to do this is to mix BTI with water and drench the soil. Directions for such applications are provided by the manufacturer.

At present we are aware of only one company that has studied the use of BTI for fungus gnat control: Abbott Laboratories. They report 100% success in controlling the gnats at several field sites. They market BTI in two formulations, Vectobac-AS® and Vectobac-12AS® (see the Resource Appendix under "Insect Management: Biological Controls" on pp. 683-686).

2. Methoprene. The insect growth regulator methoprene is labeled for fungus gnat control in mushroom culture under the trade name Apex 5E®. (For details on this and other IGRs consult pp. 145-148). It is available from Zoecon Corporation. As of this writing, horticultural and pest control professionals can purchase unmixed methoprene by itself from chemical suppliers; consumers can only purchase it mixed with a conventional insecticide.

IGRs work on young, growing insects; they have no effect on those that are already mature. Thus, some adults will survive after you use the IGR even though the pest population is ultimately doomed since no more young can survive. Because of the lag between the time you use methoprene and the time the adults are dead, it is usually sold in combination with a "knock-down" insecticide such as a synthetic pyrethroid. This satisfies the consumer's desire for immediate, visible results.

We suggest using methoprene alone and letting the adults die off naturally, or catching them in traps. In controlling gnats in mushroom culture, methoprene is added in liquid form to the compost or casing material; directions are on the product label. Since methoprene has proven effective for this purpose, it will undoubtedly be available for more general use in the near future. For sources of methoprene, see the Resource Appendix under "Insect Management: Chemical Controls" on pp. 686-687.

3. Nematodes. Commercially available neoaplectanid or steinernematid nematodes are reportedly effective against fungus gnats (for further information on insect-attacking nematodes, see pp. 140-142; for sources, see the Resource Appendix under "Insect Management: Biological Controls" on pp. 683-686). One important advantage of nematodes is that they can remain active in the soil mix for up to 90 days, a much longer period than BTI survives.

The staff of Hydro-Gardens in Boulder, Colorado, a supplier of products to the vegetable and greenhouse industries, has used these nematodes successfully against fungus gnats (which they also refer to as algae gnats). They report that applications of nematodes against the gnats also eliminated a thrips problem in one greenhouse, apparently because the species of thrips troubling them pupates in the soil.

Because we could not find published studies on the use of nematodes for gnat control, we spoke with Mike Morton of Hydro-Gardens to learn more about their experience. He recommends using nematodes every 30 to 60 days in drip irrigation and nutrient film (liquid growing medium) systems. The exact frequency depends on how dry the growing medium becomes, since nematodes must have adequate moisture. Thus, home owners who keep their house plants on the dry side may need to apply nematodes more frequently.

The nematodes are mixed with water and sprayed or poured on the soil. The recommended dose is 24 million nematodes per acre for large operations; in smaller operations, a rule of thumb is one million nematodes for about 200 sq. ft. (18.5 sq. m) House plant owners should use approximately 5,000 nematodes per pot. Because sunshine kills nematodes, it is important to avoid exposing nematode-containing water to sunlight or any other light source for any length of time. The nematodes can be kept in the refrigerator—but not below freezing—until used.

We offer one very important caveat regarding the use of nematodes in greenhouses that are managed entirely through biological controls. The aphid predator *Aphidoletes aphidimyza* pupates in the soil (meaning that it goes through a cocoon-like stage while the larvae change into the adult flies). So if you are depending on this predator for aphid control, nematodes should be avoided since they kill the aphid predator during that stage of its life cycle.

4. Predatory Mites. A short news item in *The Nursery Manager*, a trade magazine, alerted us to the possibility of using a predatory mite (*Hypoaspis* spp.) for the control of gnats on greenhouse plants. We discussed this recently with Dr. David Gillespie of Canada's Agassiz Research Station in British Columbia. He told us that the mite is really a species of *Geolaelaps* —you may see either name being used—and that it has been shown in controlled studies to be an excellent predator of fungus gnats.

The mite was first noticed at relatively high levels in British Columbia greenhouses that had switched to biological controls. In these greenhouses there were no fungus gnat problems, whereas in other greenhouses where conventional pesticides were used there were high gnat populations. The mite is now being reared and tested as a supplementary control in greenhouse environments. Applied Bionomics, an insectary in Sydney, British Columbia, plans to produce the mite for sale.

Treatment:
Direct Horticultural Controls

If you have a small house plant collection you may want to adapt the agricultural strategy of "trap-cropping." A plant known to be particularly attractive to the pest is either grown close to or planted earlier than the main crop or plant. When pests are drawn to the "trap crop," they are destroyed, often by spraying with a pesticide (outdoors), leaving the main crop or plant unsprayed.

A Cooperative Extension pamphlet written by A. L. Antonelli of Washington State University suggests that since fungus gnats are attracted to sprouted grain, a pot of sprouted wheat be used as a trap crop. Antonelli recommends setting the pot among the plants to be protected. Female gnats should be given a few days to lay their eggs on this moist material, then the pot can be submerged in boiling water to kill the eggs and larvae. Alternatively, its contents can be discarded outdoors. This procedure must be repeated every two weeks until the flies are no longer pestiferous.

Summary: Least-Toxic Fungus Gnat Control

• Monitor with yellow sticky traps or light/electrocution traps.

• Depending on your setting, apply an insect growth regulator such as methoprene, a biological insecticide such as BTI or natural enemies such as insect-attacking nematodes or predatory mites for control.

• Use wheat sprouts as a trap crop on small collections.

REFERENCES AND READINGS

General

Clausen, C.P., ed. 1978. *Introduced parasites and predators of arthropod pests and weeds: a world review.* Washington, D.C.: USDA (Agricultural Handbook 480). 545 pp. (Available from: Superintendent of Documents, U.S. Government Printing Office, Washington, DC 20402.)

This comprehensive document is an excellent starting point for those who need information on the biology of many pests and their natural enemies. Previous cases of successful biological control are described.

Grossman, J. 1990. Horticultural oils: New summer uses on ornamental plant pests. *The IPM Practitioner* 12(8):1-10.

This review summarizes new information showing that horticultural oils have a wide range of effectiveness. Pest populations in the following groups were suppressed: aphids, scales, mealybugs, whiteflies, spider mites, psyllids, caterpillars, rusts and mildews.

Heie, O.E. 1980. *The Aphidoidea (Hemiptera) of Fennoscandia and Denmark, Vol. I.* Klampenborg, Denmark: Scandinavian Science Press. 238 pp.

This book is recommended for serious students who want an introduction to the Aphidoidea.

Hussey, N.W., W.H. Read and J.J. Hesling. 1969. *The pests of protected cultivation.* New York: American Elsevier Publishing Co. 404 pp.

For many years this has been the standard overview of pest problems of plants in indoor environments. The biological information and photographs are quite inclusive and very useful. The control information is oriented strictly toward conventional pesticides used between 1955 and 1970, many of which are still in use in commercial greenhouses.

Hussey, N.W. and N. Scopes, eds. 1986. *Biological pest control, the glasshouse experience.* Ithaca, N.Y.: Cornell University Press. 240 pp.

Includes a description of successful biological pest control programs in European greenhouses.

Jordan, W. 1977. *What's eating your houseplants?* Emmaus, Pa.: Rodale Press. 227 pp.

A comprehensive discussion of biological control of indoor plant pests in a straightforward and entertaining style. Excellent photos and line drawings illustrate the insects, equipment and methods described. This book, unfortunately out of print, is an invaluable tool for people who are serious about nontoxic pest management of indoor plants.

Kono, T., and C. Papp. 1977. *Handbook of agricultural pests. Aphids, thrips, mites, snails, and slugs.* Sacramento: California Department of Food and Agriculture. 205 pp. (Available from: California Department of Food and Agriculture, Division of Plant Industry, 1220 N St., Sacramento, CA 95814.)

Although aimed primarily at California users, the keys in this book give useful general information on those pests listed in the title. A dissecting microscope is usually necessary to determine species, and microscope slide-mounting techniques are discussed.

Steiner, M.Y., and D.P. Elliott. 1983. *Biological pest management for interior plantscapes.* Vegreville, Canada: Alberta Environmental Centre (Publication AECV83E1). 30 pp. (Available from: Alberta Environmental Centre, Vegreville, Alberta, T0B 4L0, Canada.)

This excellent pamphlet describes the life cycles and provides other biological information about indoor plant pests and their natural enemies, including details on when and how to purchase and release natural enemies in indoor environments. Color photographs aid in recognizing pests, parasitoids and predators.

Streets, R.B., Sr. 1979. *The diagnosis of plant disease: a field and laboratory manual emphasizing the most practical methods for rapid identification.* Tuscon, Ariz.: University of Arizona Press. 150 pp.

A very useful introduction to the diagnosis of plant disease with good photographs and simple line drawings. The opening discussion is particularly appropriate for someone starting out as a consultant.

Ants

References and readings on the subject of ants are listed at the end of Chapter 14 on pp. 252-253.

Slugs and Snails

Grossman, J., and H. Olkowski. 1990. Stopping slugs and snails. *Common Sense Pest Control Quarterly* 6(1):7-18.

This comprehensive discussion of slug and snail management contains an extensive bibliography.

Roling, M. 1988. Non-toxic slug control in greenhouses: a case history. *The IPM Practitioner* 10(4):6-7.

This article describes the use of copper barriers against slugs in a southwestern Missouri bedding-plant greenhouse.

Mites

Helle, W., and M.W. Sabelis, eds. 1985. *Spider mites: their biology, natural enemies and control. Vol. A, The Tetranychidae. Vol. B, Natural enemies of the Tetranychidae.* Amsterdam: Elsevier. 400 pp.

A comprehensive review of the literature in the field.

Jepson, L.R., H.H. Keifer and E.W. Baker. 1975. *Mites injurious to economic plants.* Berkeley: University of California Press. 614 pp.

An excellent text covering the biology and ecology of pest mites, including those found on plants indoors. However, control is not the major focus, and, where control is covered, the emphasis is on conventional pesticides.

Thrips

Ananthakrishnan, T.N. 1984. *Biology of thrips.* Oak Park, Mich.: Indira Publishing House. 233 pp. (Available from: P.O. Box 37256, Oak Park, MI 48237-0256.)

An excellent introduction to thrips classification, biology, ecology, natural control agents and host-plant interactions.

Lewis, T. 1973. *Thrips: their biology, ecology and economic importance.* New York: Academic Press. 349 pp.

An important source that draws together the literature on thrips and provides an overview of the order. The primary focus of the control sections is on agricultural crop pests. The text cites studies showing the importance of adequate soil moisture and the use of aluminum foil to discourage thrips.

Aphids

Blackman, R. 1974. *Aphids.* London: Ginn and Co. 175 pp.

This book and that by Dixon, below, are suitable for readers with no previous training in entomology. Both books provide a very thorough treatment of the subject, although they are weak on the subject of biological control of aphids.

Blackman, R.L., and Eastop, V.F. 1984. *Aphids on the world's crops: an identification guide.* New York: Wiley & Sons. 466 pp.

An essential reference for anyone responsible for aphid control on a large scale. Includes an excellent illustrated field key for identifying common aphids on plants of commercial importance.

Dixon, A. G. 1973. *Biology of aphids.* London: Edward Arnold. 58 pp.

See Blackman, 1984.

Gilkeson, L., and M. Klein. 1981. *A guide to the biological control of aphids.* Newport, Vt.: The Memphremagog Group. 30 pp. (Available from The Memphremagog Group, Box 456, Newport, VT 05855.)

A good introductory pamphlet, containing information on finding and rearing the aphid-eating gall midge *(Aphidoletes aphidimyza)* in home greenhouses.

Heie, O.E. 1980.

See listing under "General."

Minks, A.K., and P. Harrewijn, eds. 1987-1989. *Aphids: their biology, natural enemies and control, vols. A, B and C.* New York: Elsevier Science Publishing. 450, 364 and 386 pp.

Essential references for anyone working with aphids. Volume A includes chapters on aphid classification and biology; Volume B covers techniques for working with aphids and discusses different natural enemy families and groups; Volume C considers damage caused by aphids as well as aphid control.

Olkowski, W. 1989. Biological control of aphids: What's really involved? *The IPM Practitioner* 11(4):1-9.

A summary of successful cases of natural enemy importation. The article also describes the process of importing natural enemies and covers current issues of concern to biological control workers. It includes recent work on the Russian wheat aphid and recommendations for improving the importation procedure.

Mealybugs

McKenzie, H.L. 1967. *Mealybugs of California.* Berkeley: University of California Press. 526 pp.

A scholarly text that discusses the economic importance, ecology, biology, taxonomy (including keys to North American genera), field collection techniques and slide preparation of these insects. California species are described in detail, including all those common on indoor plants. Many of these are also found in other states. In addition to the line drawings accompanying each species description there are wonderful color paintings of mealybugs in their native environments. Unfortunately, McKenzie does not tell much about the biological control of mealybugs.

Whiteflies

Costello, R.A., and D.P. Elliott. 1981. *Integrated control of mites and whiteflies in greenhouses.* British Columbia, Canada: Ministry of Agriculture and Food. 17 pp.

A simple, practical guide to using biological controls against the two most common pests of cucumbers and tomatoes in the greenhouse. Its excellent color photographs help you recognize the parasitized whiteflies and predatory mites.

Hussey, N.W., and N. Scopes, eds. 1986. *Biological pest control: the glasshouse experience.* Ithaca, N.Y.: Cornell University Press. 240 pp.

An excellent book on biological control of greenhouse pests in Western and Eastern Europe. Good short sections deal with whiteflies, the use of the parasitoid *Encarsia,* and the fungus *Verticillium lecanii.* European greenhouse biological control workers are leading the world in developing new commercial parasitoids and pathogens, and systems for using them. This book reviews the state of the art, citing many sources not easily available elsewhere.

Steiner, M.Y., and D.P. Elliott. 1983. *Biological pest management for interior plantscapes.* Vegreville: Alberta Environmental Centre. 30 pp. (Available from: Alberta Environmental Centre, Vegreville, Alberta, Canada T0B 4L0.)

A practical primer on the use of the most commonly available natural enemies of greenhouse pests, including whiteflies. Good photographs help you identify pest and beneficial insects and mites.

Webb, R.E., and F.F. Smith. 1980. Greenhouse whitefly control in an integrated regimen based on adult trapping and nymphal parasitism. *Bulletin SROP/WPRS* 3(3):235-246.

This was the first paper to show how yellow sticky traps could be used within an IPM program for whitefly control.

Woets, J., and J.C. van Lenteren. 1976. The parasite-host relationship between *Encarsia formosa* (Hymenoptera: Aphelinidae) and *Trialeurodes vaporariorum* (Homoptera: Aleyrodidae). Bulletin IOBC/WPRS working group on integrated control in glasshouses. *Antibes* 4: 151-164.

An early and excellent discussion of biological control of whiteflies.

Leafminers

Larew, H.G. et al. 1985. *Liriomyza trifolii* (Burgess) (Diptera: Agromyzidae) control on Chrysanthemum bay neem seed extract applied to soil. *Journal of Economic Entomology* 78: 80-84.

A report on the use of soil drenches with 0.5% crude neem extract, which produced insecticidal effects for three weeks in research and commercial greenhouses.

Larew, H.G. 1987. Repellency and toxicity of a horticultural oil against four greenhouse pests and oviposition by *Liriomyza trifolii. Journal of Economic Entomology* (submitted).

A description of the effectiveness of horticultural oils against this major whitefly pest.

Minkenberg, O.P.J.M, and J.C. van Lenteren. 1986. The leafminers *Liriomyza bryoniae* and *L. trifolii* (Diptera: Agromyzidae), their parasites and host plants: a review. *Agricultural University Wageningen Papers* 86:2. 50 pp.

This monograph was the principal source for much of the biological information about the serpentine leafminer and its parasitoids presented in this chapter.

Parella, M. P., and K. L. Robb. 1985. *Economically important members of the genus Liriomyza Mik: a selected bibliography.* Entomological Society of America (Miscellaneous Publication 59). 26 pp.

This bibliography contains 661 papers, a four-paragraph overview and a simple index listing the numbers of the papers in various categories, including biology, chemical control and systematics. The papers were compiled from computerized literature reviews back to 1969.

Wardlow, L.R. 1986. Leafminers and their parasites. In *Biological pest control: the glasshouse experience*, eds. N. W. Hussey and N. Scopes, pp. 62-65. Ithaca, N.Y.: Cornell University Press. 240 pp.

A short article about the use of leafminer parasitoids in European greenhouses.

Webb, R.E. et al. 1983. Evaluation of aqueous solution of neem seed extract against *Liriomyza sativae* and *L. trifolii* (Diptera: Agromyzidae). *Journal of Econ. Entomology* 76(2):357-362.

An early report on the use of water solutions of neem oil extracts applied to bush lima beans. The most effective treatment was a 0.1% to 0.05% solution applied to the leaves, which produced 91% to 100% mortality in larvae hatching from eggs.

Fungus Gnats

Cantwell, G.E., and W.W. Cantelo. 1984. Effectiveness of *Bacillus thuringiensis* var. *israelensis* in controlling a sciarid fly, *Lycoriella mali*, in mushroom compost. *Journal of Economic Entomology* 77:473-475.

The authors, who work at the USDA Vegetable Laboratory in Beltsville, Maryland, report that a 1:60 solution of BTI in water produced gnat mortality exceeding 99.5%.

Kielbasa, R., and R. Snetsinger. 1980. *Life history of a sciarid fly, Lycoriella mali, and its injury threshold on the commercial mushroom.* University Park: Pennsylvania State University (Bulletin 833). 14 pp.

A description of the life, culture and history of pest control practices of *Lycoriella mali*. Results from insecticide evaluation trials are also presented. The authors used a Pestolite Insect Killer trap for monitoring during their studies.

Larsson, S.F. 1986. A sticky trap for monitoring fly populations on mushroom farms. *J. Aust. Ent. Soc.* 25:87-88.

A description of an innovative trap for controlling fungus gnats.

Ogden, M.A. 1988. *Biological pesticides and plant growth regulators in greenhouses.* (An unpublished handout available from Abbott Laboratories, North Chicago, Ill. 60064.)

Dr. Ogden of Abbott Laboratories was kind enough to provide us with a brief summary of this unpublished material on work with BTI.

Richardson, P.N. 1983. A new approach to mushroom pest control. *Tenth International Congress of Plant Protection 1983*, 3:11-13.

Proceedings of a conference held at Brighton, England, November 20 to 25, 1983, on plant protection for human welfare. Tests conducted with the nematode *Howardula husseyi* reduced the lifespan of the fly *Megaselia halterata*. Trials with the nematodes *Steinernema (Neoaplectana) feltiae* and *Heterorhabditis heliothidis* against *Heteropeza pygmaea* and *Lycoriella auripila* showed that both nematode species killed both hosts, and that *H. heliothidis* was more effective than *S. feltiae*.

PART 7

Pests of the House Structure

CHAPTER 21
Identifying Structural Pests and Eliminating Moisture

OVERVIEW OF PART 7

Part 7 helps you identify and manage some of the pests that can damage the wooden components of your house. Chapter 21 gets you started by providing a key to the identification of the responsible organisms based on their appearance and/or the damage they cause. Because moisture is the single biggest invitation to virtually all major structural pests, this chapter also suggests where in the house you should monitor for moisture infiltration and how you can correct it.

Subsequent chapters provide more detailed discussions of structural pests. Chapter 22 examines the biology and control of wood-decay fungi. Chapter 23 looks at termites, the one pest about which we get more requests for advice than any other. Chapter 24 covers carpenter ants and carpenter bees, and Chapter 25 examines the wood-boring beetles.

INTRODUCTION

A house is our buffer against extremes of temperature, moisture and wind. It, rather than we, suffers directly from the effects of these elements. As the shell of the house ages, shingles fall off, cracks form and wood splits and shrinks. These events allow the elements access to the structural components of the house and eventually lead to microbial and insect attacks. The house structure is home for many organisms other than ourselves. Some of these organisms move in for a short time, others start a family and settle down. Those that find the structure to their taste eat as much as they can. Obviously these organisms, especially when combined with the effects of weathering, can create problems.

Ideally, the job of maintaining a house means detecting pest problems before they become severe and performing the necessary preventive maintenance. It also means deciding which organisms can be tolerated and which must go. This chapter will

Table 21.1
Major Groups of Organisms that Attack Wood

Common Name	Scientific Group	Examples
algae	Cyanophycota (blue-green)	*Gloeocapsa* spp.
bacteria	Bacteria	many species
moss	Cryptogamia	many species
lichens	Mycota (fungi)	many species
crustaceans	Crustacea	gribble
mollusks	Mollusca	teredo
fungi	Mycota (fungi)	white rot
insects	Insecta	
beetles	Coleoptera	powderpost beetles
termites	Isoptera	drywood termites
ants	Hymenoptera	carpenter ants
bees	Hymenoptera	carpenter bees

help you decide which pests are causing the problems and how to get rid of them.

In the United States most houses are constructed primarily of wood, even though they are often surfaced with other materials. Most of the pests that damage buildings attack wood. Table 21.1 above lists the major groups of wood-attacking organisms. The most serious are the fungi and insects, especially termites.

SOME PERTINENT FACTS ABOUT WOOD

To understand the true role of wood-destroying pests, you must keep in mind the large-scale planetary circulation of materials, called bio/geo/chemical cycling, that supports life on earth. The same organisms that are so eager to attack the wooden parts of your house and reduce it to dust are an integral part of the cycling of carbon, nitrogen, oxygen and other nutrients that make possible human existence—and, ultimately, the houses we build.

The cycling process begins with sunlight, air and chemical compounds in the soil that have eroded from rocks. Through photosynthesis, plants produce sugars from these soil chemicals in the presence of sunlight with the aid of chlorophyll in their leaves and carbon dioxide in the air. From these sugars, they produce cellulose, which forms the skeleton of plant tissue, including the walls of the plant cells.

Within these cells are the other chemicals of life drawn up by the plant from the soil. These chemicals are formed into and interact as complex plant-manufactured compounds, including sugars, proteins and fats. Eventually, the plant tissues die and are recycled by detritivores, such as insects and mites, as well as fungal and other microbial decomposers. These organisms physically and chemically convert the once-living tissues back to raw materials other plants can ingest and use to build their own tissues.

Trees are among the most important plants of the landscape, and locked up in their tissues are vast amounts of potential nutrients for other organisms. The wood in the tree provides the structure that enables the tree to outreach other plant types in the competition for sunlight; it also allows the transport and storage of nutrients. As the tree gets older, the tissues that previously conveyed sap turn over that task to younger tissue and form a core of heartwood with high mechanical strength (see the drawing at right). Because older trees contain more heartwood than younger trees, older trees provide stronger wood for building. Younger trees are composed primarily of sapwood formed by cambium cells just beneath the bark.

Some wood-decomposing organisms prefer sapwood to heartwood, whereas others prefer heartwood to sapwood; some organisms attack either. Knowing what kind of wood is under attack in a structure can help identify a pest. Naturally, correct identification of the pest is critical to effective management.

Wood-producing plants are divided into two groups: hardwoods and softwoods. Hardwoods belong to the dicotyledon group of flowering plants, so-called because they have two leaves that unfurl from the germinating seed. Examples are oak, teak and hickory. Softwoods are the naked-seed plants, or gymnosperms, almost all of which occur in the Coniferae. Most conifers bear cones and have needle-shaped leaves. Examples are pines and redwoods.

Cross Section of a Tree Trunk

The sapwood and phloem transport nutrients and water throughout a living tree. As trees grow, older sap-conducting tissue solidifies into heartwood with high mechanical strength, and is replaced by younger sapwood produced by cambium cells. Some wood-destroying organisms prefer sapwood, others attack heartwood.

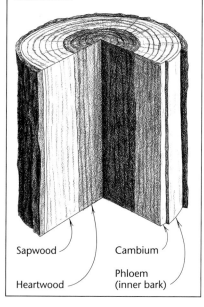

Sapwood   Cambium

Heartwood   Phloem (inner bark)

Softwoods are more commercially important than hardwoods for building purposes on a gross tonnage basis. This is because they grow faster, produce more lumber per unit of growing area and are easier to cut and work with. Today, softwoods usually form the major supports for wood-framed homes—the floor joists and wall studs, for example. Hardwoods are used for floors and other areas that undergo heavy wear or require greater strength. Plywood is usually made from softwood that is treated to resist decay. Pretreated, decay-resistant softwood lumber is also commercially available.

DIAGNOSTIC KEY TO WOOD-DESTROYING ORGANISMS

The sidebar on pp. 406-408 should help you identify the pest damaging the structure of your house based on the symptoms you see. Read through the "General Symptoms" until you find the one that best describes what you are observing, then select the most appropriate specific "Symptom" beneath it. A reference to the appropriate discussion of the pest causing the damage is provided at the end of each symptom.

Diagnostic Key to Wood-Destroying Organisms Based on Symptoms

GENERAL SYMPTOM:
Wood damaged and discolored with shrinkage and/or loss of structural strength.
Probable Cause: A fungus.
See: Fungi (pp. 420-423).

Symptom: Colored stains or dusty coating on underside of floor, on walls or on ceilings.
Probable Cause: Fungus.
What to Do: Determine the type of fungus and find and eliminate the moisture source.
See: Surface stainers (pp. 421-422).

Symptom: Blue stain visible in sapwood.
Probable Cause: Blue stain fungus.
What to Do: Nothing. The stain indicates the wood at one time contained more than 20% moisture, but there is no loss in strength. Check for possible water leaks.
See: Sap stainers (p. 422).

Symptom: Fan-shaped white fungal mat with large 1-in. (2.5 cm) wide dirty white, brown or black thread-like strands (mycelia).
Probable Cause: Poria fungus, or "dry rot."
What to Do: Eliminate the water source and replace wood in a large section around the damaged area.
See: Decay fungi (pp. 422-423).

GENERAL SYMPTOM:
Holes, tunnels, galleries or chambers on or beneath the surface of the wood.
Probable Cause: Insects.
See: Appropriate insect.

Symptom: Holes greater than ½ in. (1.3 cm) in diameter on the exterior of the structure or in the attic.
Probable Cause: Carpenter bees (see the drawing at right).
What To Do: There are several options, including home-owner toleration and wood treatments to prevent attack.
See: Carpenter bees (pp. 451-453).

Symptom: Holes less than ½ in. (1.3 cm) in diameter.
Probable Cause: Wood-boring beetles (see the drawing below: A shows damage caused by lyctid powderpost beetles;
B, old house borer damage;
C, bark beetle damage;
D, ambrosia beetle damage).
What to Do: Identify the most probable species and institute the appropriate management procedure.
See: Wood-boring beetles (pp. 457-464).

Brown Rot

Symptom: Soft decayed wood with white mycelia and checking (cracking) at right angles to the grain of the wood, particularly on floor or perimeter joists. Wood looks brown and crumbles to a powder when touched.
Probable Cause: Brown rot (see the drawing above).
What to Do: Remove the source of moisture and replace the wood.
See: Decay fungi (pp. 422-423).

Symptom: White mycelial mass covered with irregular specks or pocks.
Probable Cause: Fomes fungi.
What to Do: Nothing.
See: Decay fungi (pp. 422-423).

Carpenter Bee Damage

Symptom: Galleries or chambers in wood. The wood surface is easily penetrated with a screwdriver or ice pick.
Probable Cause: Termites (see the drawing below: E shows damage caused by subterranean termites; F, drywood termite damage).
What To Do: Deny termites access to structural wood and wood pieces in soil. Remove moisture sources. Kill or remove existing termites. Replace damaged wood.
See: Termites (pp. 433-443).

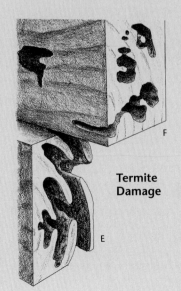

Termite Damage

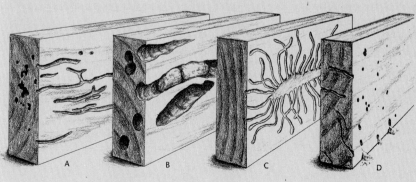

Wood-Boring Beetle Damage

GENERAL SYMPTOM:
Presence and/or signs of insects.
See: Appropriate insect.

Symptom: Surface tunnels running from soil to wood.
Probable Cause: Subterranean termites.
What To Do: Knock apart tunnels to see whether termites are still active by searching for workers traveling within them.
See: Termites, physical controls (pp. 438-439).

Symptom: Swarming winged termites at the base of a fence post, foundation or similar area.
Probable Cause: Subterranean termite nest.
What To Do: Destroy as many termites as possible with the least-toxic insecticide.
See: Termites, chemical controls (pp. 441-443).

Symptom: Swarming winged ants or foraging large black ants emerging from wall or floor area in search of sweets.
Probable Cause: Black carpenter ants.
What To Do: Locate the nest area and use bait to destroy the colony. Repair damaged structural elements and eliminate the source of moisture that invited the original infestation.
See: Carpenter ants (pp. 446-451).

Symptom: Very large, bumblebee-like organisms flying around the exterior of the house near eaves, some entering large holes. Damage mainly confined to the siding or outer boards.
Probable Cause: Carpenter bees.
What To Do: Coat the wood to discourage females from making new nests. Repair damaged wood.
See: Carpenter bees (pp. 451-453).

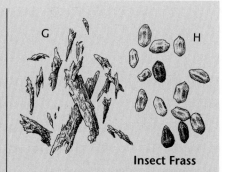

Insect Frass

Symptom: Sawdust or tiny wood scraps on floor.
Probable Cause: Carpenter ants (G in the drawing above: wood fibers mixed with fecal matter [frass] and fragments of ants or other insects) or drywood termites (H in the drawing: primarily fecal pellets).
What To Do: Follow the directions for the diagnosed insect.
See: Carpenter ants (pp. 446-451) or drywood termites (pp. 433-443).

MOISTURE CONTROL: THE KEY TO EFFECTIVE STRUCTURAL PEST MANAGEMENT

Moisture in or on wood is the single most important predisposing condition for wood damage and structural failure. Moisture attracts the major pests of structures, including fungi, subterranean termites, carpenter ants and certain wood-boring beetles. The only significant exception may be drywood termites, since it is believed they can attack completely dry wood. Therefore, the key to protecting wood structures is to use sound construction practices that minimize moisture buildup (see the top drawing on the facing page).

A simple "formula" describing the decay process in wooden structures might be written:

Wood + Moisture + Stress = Decay

The primary agents of wood decay are fungi, whose spores are present in the air and soil, and the major requirement for the development of decay fungi in wood is moisture. The decay process is illustrated in the bottom drawing on the facing page. Wood must contain at least 20% moisture before it will support the growth of fungi; dry wood does not rot. Lumber dried properly by air or kiln contains only 6% to 16% moisture. Thus, unless additional moisture is permitted to penetrate this lumber, decay does not occur.

In the early stages of decay, repairs that simply eliminate the source of moisture and allow the wood to dry out usually end the destruction without the need for application of toxic materials. (The U.S. Environmental Protection Agency's restriction of commonly used wood preservatives has increased interest in alternatives for stopping wood decay. Moisture detection and control, discussed below, are foremost among these, and in the next chapter we discuss some wood preservatives that do not contain the materials found hazardous by the EPA.)

Wood-decay fungi enter buildings three ways: in the air, through soil-wood contact and in previously infested lumber. In each case, the fungi must have temperature and moisture conditions sufficient for survival, and they must avoid or overcome molds and other organisms that prey on them or compete with them for food and habitat. Of these limiting factors, moisture is the most important. For example, even if lumber that is heavily infested with fungi is used in a

Sound Construction Practices that Minimize Moisture Buildup

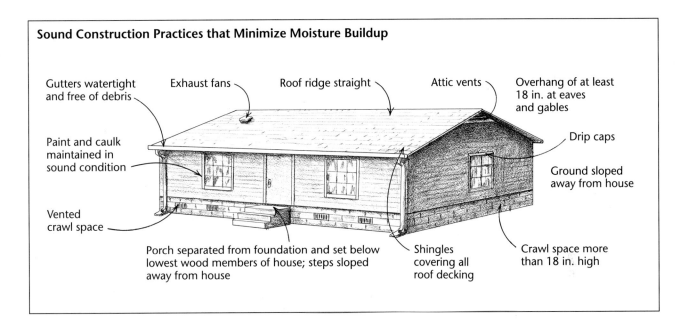

Gutters watertight and free of debris

Exhaust fans

Roof ridge straight

Attic vents

Overhang of at least 18 in. at eaves and gables

Paint and caulk maintained in sound condition

Drip caps

Ground sloped away from house

Vented crawl space

Porch separated from foundation and set below lowest wood members of house; steps sloped away from house

Shingles covering all roof decking

Crawl space more than 18 in. high

building, the fungi cannot survive and spread if the wood is allowed to dry out and is kept dry.

Wood swells and shrinks with changes in moisture content and the humidity of the surrounding air. Small changes in the dimensions of wood are unavoidable, but poor construction and inadequate maintenance can lead to excessive warping, checking and/or nail-pulling. These, in turn, provide avenues for the entry of rainwater and other moisture. Success in preventing decay depends on early detection of physical damage caused by the stresses that weaken wood or its paint, flashing, caulk or other protective materials.

Moisture can also penetrate the house structure where there are rain or plumbing leaks or when atmospheric water vapor condenses and is absorbed by the wood. Condensation occurs when warm, moist air is cooled sufficiently to become supersaturated. Excess vapor then condenses to liquid water, as when steam becomes droplets on a cool window pane. Condensation is a more frequent problem now that energy conservation measures have "tightened" many houses, blocking the escape of

Wood Decay by Fungi

When fungal spores carried by wind fall on moist wood, they germinate and produce thread-like strands that penetrate wood cells and feed on them. As large numbers of cells die, the wood becomes discolored and weakened. As decay becomes extensive, fungal fruiting bodies (mushrooms) appear on the outer surface and produce new spores.

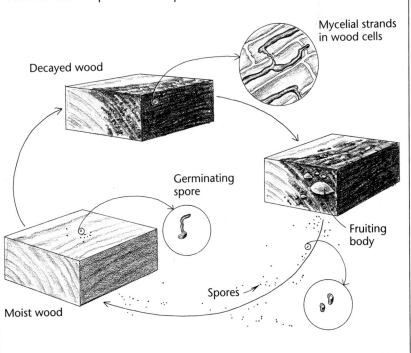

Mycelial strands in wood cells

Decayed wood

Germinating spore

Fruiting body

Spores

Moist wood

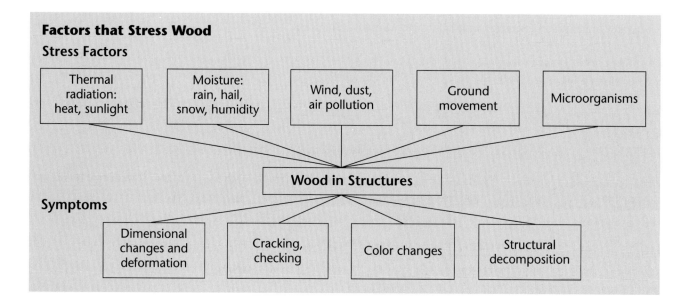

Factors that Stress Wood

Stress Factors

Thermal radiation: heat, sunlight | Moisture: rain, hail, snow, humidity | Wind, dust, air pollution | Ground movement | Microorganisms

Wood in Structures

Symptoms

Dimensional changes and deformation | Cracking, checking | Color changes | Structural decomposition

supersaturated air. Moisture can also enter from the soil through capillary action, a process known informally as "rising damp."

Detecting and Correcting Moisture Problems

The first step in managing wood decay is inspecting for conditions such as flaking paint, damaged siding, obstructed gutters, leaky plumbing or soil-wood contact that allow moisture to penetrate the wood. A sketch of the floor plan of the house that shows the location of problem areas and contains a record of repairs is often helpful during later inspections and for evaluating the long-term effectiveness of the repair work.

Ideally, inspections should be conducted twice annually, once at the end of summer to check for condensation from air conditioners, and again at the end of winter to look for condensation from heating and weather damage. If you check only once, do it well before the onset of the rainiest season so repairs will not be hampered by the weather.

The sidebar on pp. 411-416 is a guide to finding structural decay and the damage that can lead to decay. It tells you what to look for and what to

do about it. In undertaking the search, it helps to have a ladder, flashlight, ice pick (see p. 417) and moisture meter (see p. 417). Protective clothing, knee pads and a dust mask also make the job easier and safer. Detailed recommendations on correcting specific problems are provided in various chapters of this book. For additional how-to instructions, we recommend Verrall and Amburgey's illustrated booklet, *Prevention and Control of Decay in Homes* (listed under "References and Readings" on pp. 417-418). The Resource Appendix on pp. 681-696 directs you to suppliers of products called for in the checklist.

Recognizing Decay

While monitoring your building you may spot signs of fungus growth such as mushrooms or large mats of white thread-like material called mycelia (singular: mycelium). These growths indicate that the decay organisms have been active for at least a year and serious weakening of wood has probably occurred. However, this kind of decay in the early stage may not be as easy to spot. Be on the alert for discoloration of the wood. *Prevention and Control of Decay*

in Homes provides tips on discoloration and loss of strength that may help you catch decay before it advances to a serious stage.

On surfaced wood, the discoloration commonly shows as some shade of brown deeper than that of the sound wood. Some decays produce a lighter than normal shade of brown, and this change may progress to a point where the surface might be called white or bleached. If this bleaching is accompanied by fine black "zone lines," decay is virtually certain. Often, an abnormal variation in color creating a mottled appearance is more helpful in detecting early decay than actual hue or shade of discoloration.

Loss of wood toughness and hardness is another clue to the presence of decay organisms. Toughness is the strength property most severely reduced by early decay. The "pick test" (see the sidebar on p. 417) is a simple and widely used means of detecting diminished toughness. On surfaced lumber, the reduced toughness of wood with early decay is sometimes indicated by abnormally rough or fibrous surfaces. Similarly, the end grain of a board or timber may be rougher than usual after sawing.

Checklist for Detecting Structural Decay in Wood Buildings[a]

I. Roof, Overhangs, Gutters, Eaves, Trim, Attic

Roof surface

Check the roof for cracks, missing shingles and other openings where moisture can enter. Shingles should extend ¾ in. (1.9 cm) or more beyond the edges of the roof. They should form a continuous drip line at the eave and end rafters or at the rake boards that cover the end rafters.
• Remove leaves from the roof surface, and replace missing shingles. Install flashing or an aluminum drip edge under the first course of shingles to divert rainwater from the fascia board and wall of the house, as shown in the drawing below. (If the fascia board is slanted inward toward the house from top to bottom, the 1-in. x 1-in./2.5 cm x 2.5 cm wood strip can be eliminated).

Check for the formation of masses of ice on the roof near the gutters, which can lead to water infiltration and/or excessive condensation on interior attic walls.
• Insulate the attic beneath the ice dam and in the third of the roof nearest the gutter. Be careful not to block eave vents. Install flashing; it should curl over the forward edge of the fascia board for about 2 in. (5 cm) and then run about 6 in. (15 cm) beyond a vertical line drawn from the inside face of the wall studs (see the drawing below).

Overhangs

Make sure there is at least 18 in. (46 cm) of overhang to allow proper water runoff.
• Extend short overhangs.

Flashings

Make sure areas around vents, chimneys and dormers are flush and well sealed. Rusty or broken nails can cause problems in flashings. Aluminum or galvanized nails are required to prevent electrolysis, a chemical reaction between dissimilar metals that causes the nails to disintegrate.
• Seal these areas with marine-quality caulk or silicone latex (tar preparations are cheapest, but they crack after a few years in the sun). Replace iron nails with more resistant aluminum or galvanized nails or screws.

Gutters

Check for poorly sloped, clogged, rotted or leaking gutters that can lead to eave, overhang or siding leaks and rots.
• Remove leaves and twigs that absorb moisture and cause rot. In areas with low overall rainfall, flush gutters with a hose prior to the rainy season. Install downspout leaf strainers and gutter guards.

Damaged or discolored areas

Search for soft, tunneled, cracked, rotted or blistered exposed areas.

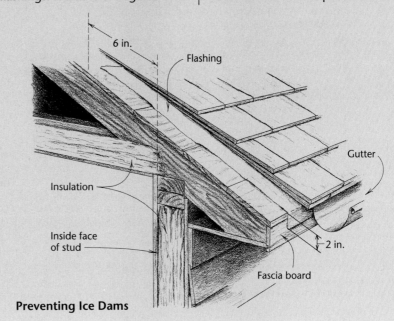

Roof deck
Underlayment
Aluminum drip edge
1-in. x 1-in. wood strip
Fascia board

Correct Roof Construction

6 in.
Flashing
Insulation
Inside face of stud
Gutter
2 in.
Fascia board

Preventing Ice Dams

Check where algae, moss, lichens or discoloration occur, since these areas indicate potential openings for fungi and/or insects.
• Locate the sources of moisture and make the necessary repairs. Use the pick test described in the sidebar on p. 417 to confirm suspected decay.

II. Outside Walls

Rusty nails
Check for rusty nails or nail-staining, which indicates moisture within the wall and/or the use of non-galvanized nails.
• Replace nails with aluminum or galvanized nails or screws.

Deteriorating paint
Loss of paint sheen or discoloration is probably due to poor initial surface preparation, or painting latex over an oil-based paint or vice versa. If you find bubbling or peeling paint, the paint was probably applied to a dew-drenched or otherwise moist surface.
• To correct either condition, prepare the surface by scraping and sanding. If the wood seems soft, weak or spongy, replace or scrape out the spongy parts and refill them with caulk (if holes are smaller than ½ in./1.3 cm in diameter).

House siding stained or buckled
Stained or buckled siding (with or without peeling paint) is a symptom of underlying moisture, rot or insects. Check for moisture caused by splashing rain or sprinklers.
• If possible, remove the source of the moisture and refinish or replace the damaged wood. In tropical, subtropical or heavy rainfall areas, such as Hawaii or the Gulf Coast, pressure-treated siding is usually recommended. You might also consider using a more durable material, such as aluminum siding.

Damaged wood junctions
Moisture and insect problems often occur where wood pieces join or abut, particularly when there is shrinkage, splintering or settling. Corners, edges of walls, roof-siding intersections and siding-chimney contacts are particularly vulnerable.
• Apply water repellent and caulk to these joints, and monitor them regularly for house movement.

Weathering of exposed lumber ends
See whether exposed ends have expanded, split or cracked, providing access for moisture and insects. Even previously treated wood is subject to attack if the openings are deep enough.
• Caulk cracks and monitor for further developments.

Loose stucco or cracks in stucco
Search for cracks, especially stress cracks around windows and doors.
• Caulk cracks. If they are large, you may have to replace the old stucco.

Moisture accumulation around the clothes dryer vent
Check for signs of moisture accumulation around the vent.
• Modify the vent to direct exhaust air away from the building.

Moisture associated with pipes and ducts
Check for moisture where the ducts pass through wood parts of building. Also check downspouts during heavy rains for leakage and proper drainage.
• Insulate ducts, install splash guards below downspouts, repair the spouts, direct water away from the house.

Moist window sills, windows or doors
Check for cracked sills and poorly fitting windows and doors. Badly fitting doors may indicate warping of the door or its casing from excessive moisture or uneven house settling. Moisture problems also commonly alter door jambs in garages.
• Caulk cracks and monitor for further developments. Warped door thresholds and jambs may need replacement, and casings may need repair if the cracks are too large to caulk effectively.

III. Foundation and Grade
(Note: If you are unfamiliar with building terminology, the top drawing on the facing page should help you understand the terms used in the next several sections.)

Soil surface
Make sure the soil surface slopes away from the house, especially at downspouts, so it carries water away from the foundation. Seepage under the foundation will cause it to crack and settle.
• Add fill to direct the water away from the house, making sure there is at least 8 in. (20 cm) between the top of the fill and the sill (see the bottom drawing on the facing page). If you do not have that much clearance, install foundation "gutters" (see p. 415).

Building Foundation Terminology

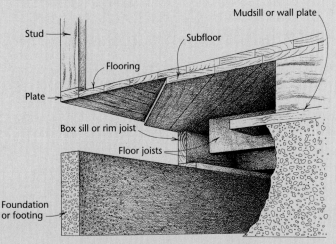

Stud
Mudsill or wall plate
Subfloor
Flooring
Plate
Box sill or rim joist
Floor joists
Foundation or footing

Directing Water away from the House

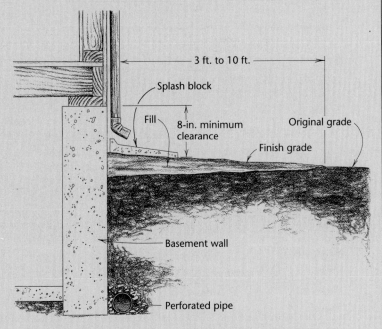

3 ft. to 10 ft.
Splash block
Fill
8-in. minimum clearance
Original grade
Finish grade
Basement wall
Perforated pipe

• Also install splash blocks and perforated pipe. Check their performance during rains or test the system with a hose. A sump pump can also be used to move water away from the foundation.

Wood-to-soil contacts

Check whether wood is in contact with the soil. It should be at least 8 in. (20 cm), and preferably more, above the soil surface.
• Remove wood that comes in contact with the soil and replace it with concrete.

Foundation cracks

Check for cracks that allow decay organisms access to wood. Cracking may also indicate uneven house settling. Monitor cracked walls for seepage during rains and look around cracks for discoloration.
• If the problem is serious, the foundation may need repair.

Brick veneer or stucco applied to the foundation

Check the bond between the veneer or stucco and the foundation wall. If it is failing, moisture and termites may have a hidden entrance to wooden portions of the house.
• Remove the loose covering and explore the extent of the decay.

IV. Crawl Space and Basement Vents

Make sure enclosed crawl spaces are vented to help moist air escape. Milder climates are especially vulnerable to dry-rot fungus. Inspect during late fall and winter, since during summer in humid climates the subfloor can be wet from condensation from interior air conditioning. There should be one vent for every 25 lin. ft. (7.6 m) of foundation. Make sure the vents are not obstructed by vegetation.
• Clean existing vents of dust, plants and debris. If more vents are needed, install 2 sq. ft. (0.2 sq. m.) of galvanized iron or copper mesh-screened venting for every 25 lin. ft. (7.6 m) of outside wall. Place vents within 5 ft. (1.5 m) of each house corner. The top edge of the concrete under all vents should be at least 6 in. (15 cm) above the finished grade to allow sufficient ventilation.

Corners of the building

Check for moisture accumulation and stains at junctions of wood surfaces in these areas.
• Install additional cellar or crawl space vents.

Enclosed areas

Check for proper ventilation under staircases, porches and other enclosed areas, since these are vulnerable to moisture buildup. Look for decayed, discolored or stained areas.
• Adjust or add venting.

Vapor barriers

Consult the map at right to see whether you live in an area of the United States where condensation is a potential problem. Check for condensation on the subfloor and/or sill, which may indicate the need for vapor barriers on the subfloor and on the soil surface in the crawl space. In some very moist areas, such barriers are required by code as a preventive measure; in others they are added to reduce the moisture that results from poor soil grading, unexpected seepage or high rainfall.
• Cover the crawl space soil surface with a 6-mil polyethylene vapor barrier. (See the drawing at right for installation details.) Make sure you use polyethylene, not roofing paper, which is subject to rotting. A slurry of concrete can be placed over the plastic to protect it from rodents. Where condensation continues, consider installing extra static vents or electric-powered vents whose fans and openings are operated automatically. You can also install a sump pump to remove any standing water.

The Condensation Zone in the United States

Winter condensation problems occur in the speckled zone, where the average January temperature is 35°F (2°C) or lower.

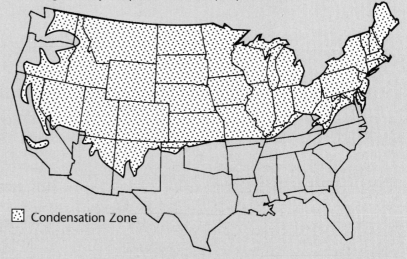

⬚ Condensation Zone

Installing a Crawl-Space Vapor Barrier

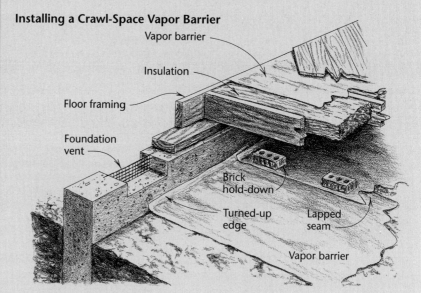

Vapor barrier
Insulation
Floor framing
Foundation vent
Brick hold-down
Turned-up edge
Lapped seam
Vapor barrier

Wood-to-stone or wood-to-concrete contacts

Check to see whether the wood is pressure-treated (it is usually colored green).
• Replace untreated wood with rot-resistant or pressure-treated wood. Be sure sealing material is used between the wood and stone or concrete, and place a metal washer between the post and the footing.

Leaky pipes or faucets

Even small leaks keep the wood or soil underneath continuously moist.
• Fix all leaks.

Problems Associated with Earth-Filled Porches

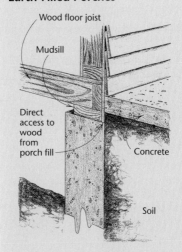

Wood floor joist

Mudsill

Direct access to wood from porch fill

Concrete

Soil

Foundation "Gutters"

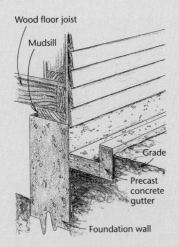

Wood floor joist

Mudsill

Grade

Precast concrete gutter

Foundation wall

Fixing a Decayed Post

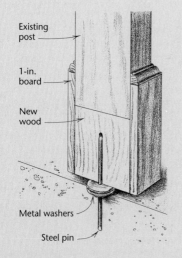

Existing post

1-in. board

New wood

Metal washers

Steel pin

Water- or space-heating units

Check to see whether the heating unit is insulated. If the soil near the flame is kept warm throughout the year due to lack of insulation, microbial and insect development will be accelerated.
• Insulate the heater, and cover the soil with concrete.

V. External Areas

Porches

Check to see whether the wooden steps touch the soil, and inspect for possible decay or termite access. The porch surface must slope away from the house to carry rain away quickly. Tongue-and-groove flooring is a water trap. If there is a space between the porch and the building, check for drainage problems.
• Caulk and repair cracks and early decay. Fill any spaces between tongue-and-groove floorboards with caulk or resurface and refinish with wood-sealing compounds and appropriate paint. You can also place another floor over the first.

Earth-filled porches

Check that the soil is at least 8 in. (20 cm) below the level of any wooden members. The drawing above left shows a typical problem spot.
• Remove the excess soil where possible, regrade to enhance drainage and redesign the porch to eliminate earth/wood contact.

Low foundation walls and footings

Check for wooden walls close to or touching the soil, since they provide access routes for subterranean termites and fungi.
• Repair these areas or install sub-grade concrete "gutters" where the house sills sit to close to ground level, as shown in the drawing above.

Planter boxes

Check to see whether the boxes are built against the house, since they allow direct access to unprotected veneer, siding or cracked stucco.

• Install a 2-in. to 3-in. (5 cm to 7.5 cm) thick protective concrete wall between the planter and the house.

Trellises and fences

Check to see whether the wooden portions of the trellis touch the soil and are connected to the house, since they provide a direct link to the house for wood rot and termites. Check fence stringers and posts for decay.
• Cut off the decay and install a concrete footing for trellises and fence posts. Replace decayed stringers and leave a small gap between the stringers to allow air circulation. Separate wood and concrete with metal washers, as shown in the drawing above.

Wooden forms around drains

Check to see whether wooden forms have been left in the holes of concrete slabs where bathtub drains, sink drains, etc., exit the building. They frequently provide a direct route for insects to inner walls. Areas around pipes rising

from slabs should be sealed with tar or other adhesive to prevent water and termite access.
• Caulk the holes, and monitor them for decay and wetness.

Gate posts, fence tie-ins, abutments, columns

Inspect areas of wood adjacent to the soil for weakness and rot.
• Cut the post tops at an angle to promote runoff and prevent water from penetrating the vulnerable end grain. The bottoms of posts in the soil should be cut and replaced with a concrete footing.

VI. Interior

Kitchen pipes

Look for condensation and leaks, especially where pipes enter walls.
• Repair leaks and insulate pipes where condensation is excessive.

Counter areas

Check around and below sink surfaces for moisture and decay.
• Caulk or otherwise protect wall surfaces from moisture. Subsurface areas damaged by water leaking from above may be tolerated if the surface leaks are repaired.

Exhaust vents

Check for moisture leaks from outside.
• Repair with caulk or water-resistant sealing material, or replace vent and the rotted wood areas around it. Use extra flashing to fill the gap.

Toilet

Check the integrity of the floor around the toilet base by thumping lightly with a hammer. Then check the wax seal for leakage at the floor/toilet pedestal intersection. Finally, check the cellar or crawl space beneath the toilet to see whether the leakage has caused damage.
• Replace the wax seal if necessary and repair the surrounding water damage.

Bathtub or tub/shower combination

Check the tub perimeter for a sound caulk seal. Look for splash-over on the bathroom floor from inadequate water barriers or user carelessness.
• Caulk cracks or gaps and install shower doors to prevent splash-over.

Shower

Fill the shower basin and check for leaks in the crawl space or the ceiling of the room below. If a leak occurs when the basin is full, it may be cracked. If a leak occurs when the shower is running, the leak could be in the drain pipe and/or delivery pipes. If it occurs when water from another container is poured down the drain, the drain itself may be leaking.
• Repair or replace the basin, pipes or drain as necessary. Sealing compounds may be useful when leaks are relatively recent and small, especially if termites have not been found. Regular monitoring is necessary if sealing materials are used.

Tile walls

Check for mildew stains. Make sure the grouting of tile walls has a silicone coating to prevent water penetration.
• Clean the walls regularly to remove mildew, and improve ventilation. Leave a heater on in the bathroom until the walls and ceiling have dried.

Ceilings

Check for blistered areas, since these can indicate moisture leaks in the area above or inadequate installation of a vapor barrier.
• Repair leaks and faulty vapor barriers.

Windows

Check for moisture accumulation on window frames, and water or water stains on walls.
• Wipe the window trim and glass dry, open the windows after the shower is used and install double- or triple-glazed windows. Use aluminum frames if the wooden frames are decaying.

Closets

Check for dampness.
• A light bulb left burning continuously in a damp closet will often generate enough heat to dry it out, but make sure you place the bulb far enough away from clothing to avoid any fire hazard. Containers of highly absorbent silica aerogel, activated alumina or calcium chloride also remove moisture from the air in enclosed spaces. These chemicals can be reused after drying in the oven. Small exhaust fans can also improve closet ventilation.

[a] The authors thank Mal Cafino, a specialist in construction repairs, for his expert assistance in developing this monitoring checklist.

Monitoring Tools

Signs of weakened wood can usually be spotted with the naked eye, but the presence of dampness inside interior walls, mudsills, joists or other hard-to-see areas is best measured with a tool of some kind. An ice pick can be used to probe structural wood that does not have a painted or finished surface. If the wood feels soft and has little resistance, it is probably decayed. When the wood looks dry and sound from the outside, but you feel the interior may be wet or decayed either because of a color change or because the wood is in an area you know has been moist, use the pick test described in the sidebar at right to test your suspicions.

A more elaborate and sometimes more revealing alternative to the pick test is a portable moisture meter. When the probes of the meter are placed on or into wood or a plaster wall, they detect moisture problems in areas hidden from the eye by measuring electrical conductivity. The drawback is that these meters cost from $75 to $140 (for sources, see the Resource Appendix under "Insect Management: Identification and Monitoring" on pp. 681-682).

The Pick Test

When monitoring your building, try using an ice pick or screwdriver to probe wood you feel might be decayed based on its color or other changes you detect. Insert the pick about ¼ in. (6 mm) into the wood and press sharply downward perpendicular to the grain. If the wood is sound, a long splinter will pull out of the wood along the grain (as shown at A in the drawing). If the wood is decayed, the splinter will be brittle and break into short pieces across the grain, especially at the point where the pick enters the wood and acts as a lever (B in the drawing). You can also detect decayed wood by its lack of resistance relative to sound wood.

Mudsills (wood installed on footings) can be pick-tested without producing excessive visual or structural damage, since they are not visible from outside

the crawl space. Sometimes wood treated with a preservative on the surface is decayed inside. The pick test can help reveal these hidden pockets of decay.

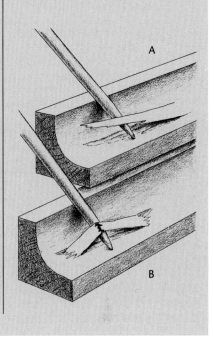

REFERENCES AND READINGS

Anderson, L.O. 1975. *Wood-frame house construction.* Washington, D.C.: USDA Forest Service (Agricultural Handbook No. 73). 223 pp. (Available from: Superintendent of Documents, U.S. Government Printing Office, Washington, D.C. 20402.)

A richly illustrated reference, essential for any person who works on or constructs wood-framed buildings.

Anderson, L.O., and G.E. Sherwood. 1974. *Condensation problems in your house: prevention and solution.* Washington, D.C.: USDA Forest Service (Agriculture Information Bulletin No. 373). 39 pp.

This booklet illustrates how to detect condensation-caused damage and describes how to install vapor barriers, vents and insulation.

Coggins, C.R. 1980. *Decay of timber in buildings: dry rot, wet rot and other fungi.* Stoneham, Mass.: Butterworths Publishing Co. 115 pp.

An authoritative source book on wood decay and its treatment, with excellent photographs that help in identification. It covers the structure of wood, the decay process, rot fungi and their incidence in Great Britain and the detection and treatment of fungal decay. One chapter is devoted to the wood-boring beetles and their associated fungi. Most of the information is also useful outside Britain.

Feist, W.C. 1984. *Protecting woodwork against decay without chemical preservatives.* Atlanta: Center for Architectural Conservation. 4 pp. (Available from: Preservation Tech Notes. P.O. Box 93402, Atlanta, GA 30377.)

A description of the U.S. Forest Products Laboratory's research on alternatives to wood preservatives.

Gorman, T.M., and N.C. Feist. 1989. *Chronicle of 65 years of wood finishing research at the Forest Products Laboratory.* Madison, Wis.: USDA Forest Products Laboratory (General Technical Report FPL-GTR-60). 81 pp. (Available from: FPL, 1 Gifford Pinchot Dr., Madison, WI 53705-2398.)

A summary of the Forest Products Laboratory's formation, history, research and accomplishments. Almost half the booklet is an annotated list of major reports produced by the laboratory since 1923.

Hickin, N.E. 1972. *The dry rot problem.* London: Hutchinson. 115 pp.

This short book depicts and documents the problem of fungal decay in English buildings. It reviews the nature of wood, the biology of fungi and how to identify wood-rotting fungi. It also discusses fungicides and corrective procedures, "rising damp" and its cure, wood preservatives and wood-boring beetles associated with fungal attack.

Johnson, S.M. 1965. *Deterioration, maintenance, and repair of structures.* New York: McGraw-Hill. 373 pp.

A well-illustrated book that covers deterioration of steel, concrete and wood. Methods for strengthening existing structures are included.

Levy, M.P. 1975. *A guide to the inspection of new houses and houses under construction for conditions which favor attack by wood-inhabiting fungi and insects.* Washington, D.C.: U.S. Department of Housing and Urban Development. 42 pp. (Available from: HUD User, P.O. Box 280, Germantown, MD 20767.)

Includes color photographs and line drawings indicating areas around a house where insects attack wood. This publication can be used by the home owner to establish a regular inspection procedure.

Mampe, C.D. 1974. *Wood decay in structures and its control.* Vienna, Va.: National Pest Control Association. 28 pp. (Available from: NPCA, 8150 Leesburg Pike, Vienna, VA 22180.)

Contains color plates and numerous line drawings of sample alterations to buildings illustrating how common problems can be repaired. The plates were reproduced from slides made by Dr. M.P. Levy of the School of Forest Resources of North Carolina State University at Raleigh; these slides are available on loan.

Moore, H.B. 1979. *Wood-inhabiting insects in houses: their identification, biology, prevention and control.* Washington, D.C.: USDA Forest Service. 133 pp.

This glossy paperback covers the different groups of wood-damaging insects and includes numerous line drawings of construction details and of insects and the damage they cause.

Oxley, T.A., and E.G. Gobert. 1981. *Dampness in buildings: diagnosis, treatment, instruments.* Boston: Butterworths Publishing Co. 123 pp.

This book on the causes of dampness in buildings includes directions for using moisture meters.

Smith, R.S. 1977. *Protection and preservation of wood against attack by fungi.* Vancouver, B.C.: Western Forest Products Laboratory (Information Report VPX170). 14 pp. (Available from: WFPL, V67 1X2, Vancouver, B.C., Canada.)

The information about wood decay in Canada is also useful in the United States.

United States Forest Products Laboratory. 1974. *Wood handbook: wood as an engineering material.* (USDA Agricultural Handbook 72, revised). 200 pp.

This book provides a wealth of information about construction lumber, including how to prevent decay.

Verrall, A.F., and T. Amburgey. 1975. *Prevention and control of decay in homes.* Washington, D.C.: USDA and the U.S. Department of Housing and Urban Development. 148 pp. (Available from: HUD User.)

This comprehensive volume, illustrated with black and white photographs, describes causes of damage to wood and remedies for moisture problems. It discusses inspection techniques, ways of preventing condensation and how to select and use wood preservatives. It is the best book for learning how to detect decay and potentially decayed areas.

Wilkinson, J.G. 1979. *Industrial timber preservation.* London: Associated Business Press. 532 pp.

A description of the timber preservation industry and its methods. There is a good introduction to the process of wood decay.

Wilson, F. 1984. *Building materials evaluation handbook.* New York: Van Nostrand Reinhold. 358 pp.

Covers all materials used in construction, with an emphasis on diagnosis and testing.

Young, E.D. 1976. *Training manual for the structural pesticide applicator.* Washington, D.C.: EPA Office of Pesticide Programs. 168 pp.

Includes good introductory information, drawings, keys and a detailed discussion of the use and abuse of pesticides. Note, however, that the laws and regulations in place when the book was published have since changed.

CHAPTER 22
Wood Decay and Preservative Treatments

INTRODUCTION

If you live in a region with high or moderate moisture conditions (as shown on the map below), you may spot signs of fungus attack while inspecting and monitoring your building for moisture. In this chapter we look closely at the fungi that cause decay in wood. We first discuss the biology and life cycle of fungi, then examine specific organisms that cause structural damage and the various options for controlling them. Foremost among the treatment options are the moisture-control measures surveyed in the previous chapter. Next in importance are chemical wood preservatives; we present some very important less-toxic alternatives to traditional chemical wood preservatives in this chapter. Finally, we discuss a few biological controls that are in the early stages of research and development.

THE BIOLOGY OF WOOD-DECAY FUNGI

Understanding a few basic facts about the biology and behavior of wood-dwelling fungi can provide important clues in the detection and/or prevention of wood decay.

Fungi probably evolved from the most primitive green plants, the algae. They reproduce from seed-like spores present in the air and soil (see the top drawing on the facing page). Stem-like structures called hyphae grow from the spore. They function as both the roots and branches of the fungal body. These "roots" (they are not true roots) penetrate directly into the wood substrate, while the "branches" appear as thread-like mats or fans called mycelia (singular: mycelium) on the surface of wood. These mats can become very large, and reproductive organs develop from them. Often these fruiting bodies, as they are called, take the form

of mushrooms and can be used to identify the specific fungus.

Optimum growth occurs at temperatures between 50°F and 95°F (10°C and 35°C) on a wood substrate containing at least 20% moisture. Since fungi do not contain chlorophyll and therefore cannot photosynthesize, they obtain food from the materials on which they grow. In the case of wood-attacking fungi, the hyphae penetrate into the wood to feed on cellulose, lignin or other wood constituents. It is this feeding that results in wood decay.

Three major groups of fungi attack wood: surface-staining fungi, sap-staining fungi and decay fungi. These fungi are commonly called molds, mildews, wood stains or wood rots. Other fungi, such as slime molds, also live on wood but do no structural damage. In moist climates, however, they serve as early indicators of decay-producing moisture. Details on the identification and treatment of the major destructive fungi and their early indicators are provided in the sidebar on pp. 406-408.

SLIME MOLDS
(Class Myxomycetes)

The first organisms to become visible in very moist areas of the structure may be the slime molds (see the bottom drawing on the facing page). Alexopoulos and Bold, in *Algae and Fungi* (listed under "References and Readings" on pp. 426-427), describe slime molds as follows:

> [They are] easily detected in the field and may be collected in one or the other of the two major phases of their life cycles: the plasmodium and the sporophores. The plasmodium, a free-living, multinucleate, naked creeping mass of protoplasm devoid of cell walls but enveloped by a slimy sheath...lives in moist dark areas [and] engulfs bacteria, various spores, and perhaps bits of decaying organic matter, feeding in an animal-like fashion. Eventually,

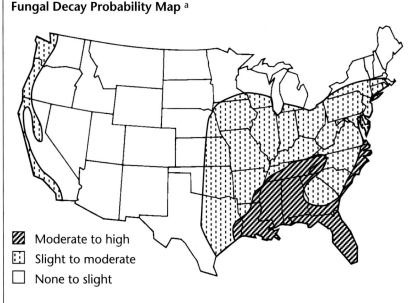

Fungal Decay Probability Map [a]

▨ Moderate to high

⬚ Slight to moderate

☐ None to slight

[a] Not shown on the map are Alaska, which falls in the none-to-slight category, and Hawaii, which has more decay on the "wet" side of the islands than on the dry side. Note also that decay severity in any category may vary, depending on local conditions.

the plasmodium emerges and in a matter of hours becomes converted into one large sporophore or dozens of small, intricately constructed fruiting bodies...12 mm [½ in.] tall....Spores are said to remain viable under unfavorable conditions for a very long time, as long as 60 or more years....In the presence of water the spores germinate.

Slime molds look like mushrooms in the sporophore stage, and are sometimes brightly colored. In the plasmodial stage they resemble egg whites.

Damage and Treatment

Slime molds do not damage wood directly; they feed upon other organisms, most likely bacterial species or other fungi that can start the decay process. They are more important as indicator organisms. Essentially, they are telling you that the area is damp and that wood-damaging organisms are already present or will follow if the moisture problem is not corrected.

Treatment should not be focused on the slime mold itself as much as on the source of the moisture that makes it possible for the mold to survive (see the sidebar on pp. 411-417). Once you find the moisture source, eliminate it so the area dries out and stays dry. With the moisture gone, the slime mold will die. Since the spores remain, it is very important that the change to drier conditions be permanent.

SURFACE-STAINERS: MILDEWS
(Class Ascomycetes)

If high levels of moisture are allowed to persist, slime molds are succeeded by stain-producing fungi. These fungi, often called mildews or molds, produce colorless hyphae that penetrate wood. Fruiting bodies, colored pink, yellow, orange, green, grey or powdery black, appear on the wood surface. Although they do not attack

How Fungi Attack Wood

A fungal fruiting body liberates asexual spores, which germinate when in contact with moist wood, producing hyphae that penetrate and feed on wood by producing enzymes that chemically destroy cell walls.

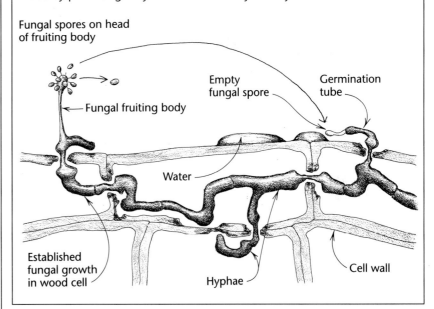

Fungal spores on head of fruiting body

Empty fungal spore

Germination tube

Fungal fruiting body

Water

Established fungal growth in wood cell

Hyphae

Cell wall

Slime Molds

This drawing shows the slime mold *Dictyostelium discoideum* in its amoeba-like and fungus-like stages. Slime molds begin life from spores, much as fungi do, but upon germination develop instead into amoebas that feed on bacteria. In the presence of sufficient moisture, heat and other variables, they aggregate, grow into a tube called a plasmodium and produce a fruiting body. Plasmodia and spore-producing sporophores are analogous to fungal fruiting bodies (mushrooms). The time it takes to pass from stage to stage depends upon environmental conditions.

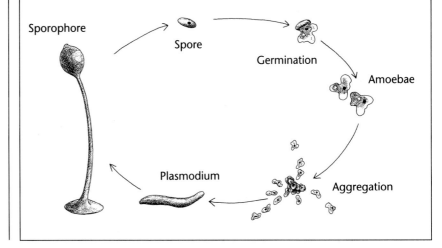

Sporophore

Spore

Germination

Amoebae

Plasmodium

Aggregation

dry wood, they indicate that the wood surface currently or in the very recent past contained at least 20% moisture, and thus may be susceptible to decay.

Mildews are common during wet periods, especially in warmer parts of the world. They develop best in temperatures around 60°F (16°C) and a relative humidity of at least 60%. They are often seen growing on the walls of showers or in other areas of the home where condensation regularly appears. But they also attack plaster, linoleum, linoleum and plastic tile, paper, plastic, asphalt and other materials.

Damage and Treatment

Mildews can increase wood's capacity to absorb moisture, setting the stage for further decay. Although they do not themselves reduce the strength of wood, mildews can stain it and can produce foul odors. They can also spread from infested wood to clothing, upholstery or other fabric and leather goods, on which they can cause severe damage, discoloring and weakening these softer materials.

Mildew growing on the surface of wood can be brushed off; then the wood can be sanded lightly to remove the discoloration. The mildew can also be scrubbed off with a solution of household bleach at roughly 1 part bleach to 16 parts water, or with a mild alkali such as washing soda or trisodium phosphate at 4 to 6 tablespoons per gallon of water (see the precise directions on the various containers).

If the mildew has grown underneath cracked paint or varnish, it may be necessary to scrub the surface with an abrasive cleaner. In *Wood Decay in Structures and its Control*, Douglas Mampe suggests removing mildews and molds by scrubbing them with a soft brush dipped in a solution of 3 oz. (85 g) trisodium phosphate, 1 oz. (28 g) household detergent, 1 qt. (0.95 l) household bleach and 3 qt. (2.84 l) warm water. We strongly recommend that you wear protective

goggles or glasses and good rubber gloves while handling this caustic solution, taking care not to splash it on your skin, clothing or non-mildewed surfaces. A gas mask with an activated charcoal filter is also necessary, since chlorine and ammonia gases are given off by this mixture.

The National Pest Control Association (NPCA) further recommends that after rinsing off mildew, the surface be covered with a zinc oxide paint or one containing a fungicide. We suggest that before you consider a fungicidal paint, however, you make every effort to discover the origin of the high moisture levels that encouraged fungal growth in the first place (see Chapter 21). Only if the moisture source cannot be eliminated and the fungal growth persists should you consider using a paint that contains a fungicide. Remember, however, that fungicides in paints will gradually volatilize out of the wood over time.

SAP STAINERS
(Class Ascomycetes)

Common sap-staining, or blue-stain, fungi in the genus *Ceratocystis* often attack trees before they are cut, dried and sold as timber. These fungi produce colored hyphae deep within the outer layers of wood. The stain may be visible on construction lumber, even though no moisture is currently present. However, blue stain can also develop on lumber subjected to prolonged soaking from chronic leaks or other water sources, and the surface of the wood may appear dry when the hidden interior is wet. Thus, if you spot blue-stain fungi on wood, only a moisture meter (see p. 417) can determine whether excessive moisture is present within.

Like the surface-stainers, these fungi cause no loss of structural strength; however, the discoloration they cause cannot be removed by brushing or sanding, as it can with the surface-stainers. Moreover, blue-staining fungi may cause structural

harm to chip board and similar materials. They also increase the capacity of wood to absorb moisture, setting the stage for future decay. If moisture is present, eliminate the moisture source, allowing the wood to dry out and stay dry.

DECAY FUNGI: THE ROTS
(Class Hymenomycetes or Aphyllophorales)

"Rot" or "dry rot" fungi consume the cellulose and lignin tissues of wood and cause structural weakness. Because they have colorless hyphae, the early stages of decay are not easily detected. However, advanced stages are quite evident from the gross changes in the wood's appearance.

Biology and Damage

Wood-rotting fungi can be grouped into five categories based on the type and appearance of the damage they produce in wood.

Brown rot fungi are the principal cause of building decay in the United States. Their mycelial mats are white; these fungi get their name from the brown color of the wood they have rotted. They cause wood to shrink and twist; the wood then cracks into small cubical pieces perpendicular to the wood grain. The wood rapidly loses its strength and eventually crumbles to a powder. Brown-rotted wood may already have weakened significantly before decay is visible; hence, a moisture meter is important for preventive detection.

Water-conducting rots, or "dry rots," are specialized brown rot fungi. They are most often found in new construction and can disperse rapidly throughout wood, destroying a large amount of it in one or two years. They are sometimes called dry rots because they can infest dry wood. Large tubes up to an inch in diameter (rhizomorphs) are formed; these can conduct water up to 25 ft. (7.6 m). The rhizomorphs allow the fungus to extend its growth into dry wood or wood containing less than 20% moisture. The fungus responsible for the most damage is *Poria incrassata*.

You should suspect the presence of water-conducting rots when you see large, papery, white-yellow mycelial fans with long tube-like rhizomorphs. These are dirty white to black and grow out and away from the moisture source. The decayed wood has much the same appearance as that affected by brown rot; the major difference is that the wood surface may appear wavy but sound when the interior is heavily decayed. The extent of damage caused by these fungi is often difficult to assess, because much of it may be occurring in dry wood some distance from the moisture source. Fortunately, these fungi are relatively rare, and it has been shown that once the moisture source is removed, they die after drying in air for 32 days.

White rots give wood a bleached appearance. The affected wood feels spongy when probed and is stringy when broken. The strength of the wood gradually diminishes, although there is no abnormal shrinkage.

Soft rot fungi attack wood surfaces and produce a gradual softening from the surface inward. They develop in marine habitats in wood that is too wet to be attacked by other decay fungi. They are seldom encountered in buildings, except where the wood is in contact with constantly wet soil.

A fifth class of wood-damaging fungi, pock rot *(Fomes pini)*, also known as pocket rot, white pocket or white speck, differs from the fungi just described in that it damages only living conifers, particularly Douglas-fir. Pock rot forms a white mycelial mat with characteristic small, ⅛ in. to ½ in. (3 mm to 13 mm) long, spindle-shaped white pockets that are filled with fungus and look like pock marks on the wood. Recently milled wood may still show evidence of this fungus. Because pock rot cannot survive in nonliving wood, no treatment is required.

Treatment

Elimination of the moisture source as described in Chapter 21 is the only long-term solution to problems caused by decay fungi. When the wood dries, the fungi die or become dormant. If the decay is minor, drying and exclusion of water may be all that is required. If it is extensive, the wood should be replaced.

Use lumber such as heart redwood or red cedar, if available, since these have high natural resistance to decay. However, recent studies indicate that second-growth redwood and cedar may not have the decay resistance of old-growth lumber. Unless treated with a preservative, they may not be adequate for moisture-prone areas such as mudsills. If the moisture source cannot be eliminated, replace decayed wood with concrete or other non-wood construction materials or with pressure-treated lumber.

WOOD PRESERVATIVES

Most woods exposed to moisture over long periods of time show decay within one to five years unless protected. Areas particularly prone to long-term moisture problems include mudsills or columns resting on concrete foundations that "wick" water up from damp soil; siding, window frames or decking exposed to the elements; posts or footings buried in the ground; and rafters where condensation forms.

Wood preservatives are usually recommended to protect such areas. Dipping wood for 5 to 15 minutes in a preservative provides better protection than a brush application. In fact, merely brushing wood preservative on lumber is rarely effective because it does not penetrate deep enough. Dipping the cut ends of lumber in a preservative is worthwhile for two reasons. First, the point where lumber is cut is usually where decay fungi initially attack. And second, the preservative can penetrate the ¼ in. to ½ in. (6 mm to 13 mm) into the wood necessary to provide a barrier toxic to fungi.

Until the mid-1980s, wood preservatives containing pentachlorophenol (often called "penta"), arsenates or creosote were widely recommended. However, in 1986 the EPA restricted the use of these materials in response to mounting evidence that all three can cause birth defects and other serious health problems. Wood that is pressure-treated with these materials at the mill is still sold in lumberyards, but consumers can no longer buy the preservatives over the counter.

If strong chemicals are used, precautions should be taken to minimize human contact with them. They should never be used in basements or other areas where vapors might circulate through heating vents or other openings, and they should never be applied to decks, floors or other surfaces with which people, particularly young children, come into regular contact.

Pressure-treatment forces the preservative to penetrate at least an inch into the wood, enhancing its protective action; thus, human exposure to it is reduced. However, when handling and particularly when cutting chemically treated wood, always wear gloves, goggles and effective respiratory protection—a dust mask at minimum—to keep sawdust out of your eyes and lungs. Remember, the freshly cut ends of pressure-treated lumber must be dipped or brushed with preservative before being nailed in place. Use stainless-steel or copper fasteners with pressure-treated wood to avoid the risk of galvanic corrosion of fasteners.

While the debate continues as to the precise health hazards posed by penta, arsenicals and creosote, common sense argues for using the less-toxic alternatives whenever possible. Table 22.1 on p. 424 lists some less-toxic preservatives, such as copper-8-quinolinolate, copper and zinc naphthenate, TBTO compounds and borate preservatives, that are avail-

Table 22.1
Some Least-Toxic Wood Preservatives

Type	Examples	Uses	Average Life
copper naphthenate	Cuprinol Green #10™	porch footings, fence posts, boats, decks	3.7 years for 1 coat 5.2 years for 1 dip
copper-8-quinolinolate	Woodguard™	siding, fences, shingles	8.0 years
polyphase (3-iodo-2-propynyl-butyl-carbamate)	Magicolor Natural Wood Preservative™	siding, fences, shingles, doors, windows	8.0 years
sodium octyborate (borates)	TIM-BOR®	wood above ground	20.0+ years
TBTO (bis-tributyl-tin oxide)	Sherwin-Williams Clear Wood Finish™	siding, fences, shingles, floors, furniture, decks	3.0 to 5.0 years
TBTO/polyphase	Minwax Clear Wood Preservative™	siding, fences, furniture, decks	3.0 to 5.0
zinc naphthenate	Cuprinol Clear #20™	siding, decks, furniture, shingles	2.9 years for brush 2.2 years for dip

An Alternative Wood Preservative

The USDA's Forest Products Laboratory (FPL) has developed an effective water repellent that contains no chemical preservatives. It can be applied to wood before it is painted. A comparable commercial product is Thompson's Water Seal™, available at most building supply and paint stores. If you want to mix your own water repellent, follow these directions:

I. FPL Water Repellent
Ingredients:
• 3 cups exterior varnish or 1½ cups boiled linseed oil
• 1 oz. (28 g) paraffin wax
• Enough solvent, either mineral spirits, paint thinner or turpentine at room temperature, to make 1 gal. (3.8 l)

Formulation: Melt the paraffin over water in a double boiler. Use an electric heat source such as a

hot plate. Do not heat the paraffin over a direct flame. Stir the solvent vigorously, and slowly pour in the melted paraffin. Add the varnish or linseed oil and stir thoroughly.

Application: The repellent can be applied before or after construction. Treatment is best done by dipping the wood for one to three minutes in the solution. If dipping is inconvenient, brush applications, with heavy treatment of all board ends and joints, can be substituted. The treated surface can be painted after two or three days of warm weather.

II. FPL Water Repellent plus Preservative
When wood is in contact with the soil, the addition of copper naphthenate or copper-8-quinolinolate to the water repellent gives added protection. "Copper-8," as it is often

abbreviated, is approved by the Food and Drug Administration for use on surfaces such as picnic tables where food is served and contact with human skin occurs.

Ingredients:
• 1½ cups boiled linseed oil
• 1 oz. (28 g) melted paraffin wax
• Enough solvent (paint thinner) to make 1 gal. (3.8 l)
• 9.6 oz. (272 g) copper-8-quinolinolate or naphthenate (if there will be wood/soil contact, use 19 oz./539 g copper material, either copper-8 or copper naphthenate; copper naphthenate, available as Cuprinol Green #10™, is another preservative that may be less toxic than pentachlorophenol, arsenates and creosote, the three materials restricted by the EPA).

Formulation and Application: As for #I, above.

able at most paint stores. Although they do not provide the length of protection afforded by the more toxic compounds when applied to wood that sits in the soil, they do provide significant protection to above-ground wood.

Nontoxic Water Repellents

The USDA's Forest Products Laboratory (FPL) has developed an effective alternative to most toxic wood preservatives. This simple water repellent is a mixture of varnish, paraffin wax and mineral spirits, as described in the sidebar on the facing page. The performance of this repellent versus a solution containing penta versus no preservative at all on painted windows and sashes was evaluated in a 20-year test in Madison, Wisconsin. One-third of the windows and sashes were treated with penta, one-third were treated with water repellent and one-third received no treatment. Then all windows and sashes were painted. The painted windows without preservative or repellent rotted within 6 years. At the end of 20 years, protection provided by the FPL's water repellent was equal to that provided by penta.

The FPL water repellent can be used to protect painted decks, siding, fences, furniture and other exterior wood surfaces. As long as the water repellent-treated wood is also painted, no chemical fungicide is necessary. Unpainted wood coated with water repellent alone may mildew, so it may be necessary to add copper-8-quinolinolate to the water repellent, especially in regions where warm temperatures and high humidity create optimal conditions for fungi. Application of a water repellent to the cut ends of lumber is particularly important because decay organisms initially become established in these locations.

Borax-Based Preservatives

Borax-based preservatives represent a bright spot in the search for safe and effective wood preservatives (for sources, see the Resource Appendix under "Insect Management: Chemical Controls" on pp. 686-687). Sodium borates are salts that are mined from deposits in various parts of the world, particularly in Death Valley, California. They have been used as wood preservatives for decades in Australia, New Zealand, Europe and, more recently, in Canada.

Borate is toxic to insects and fungi that damage wood (see Chapter 7 for more details on borax-based materials), but poses far fewer risks to humans than other preservatives. Borate preservatives also offer a number of other advantages:

• Borates are water-soluble. When wood is dipped in borate preservatives, the borate penetrates all the way to the heartwood without pressure treatment. And when the wood is cut, the cut portion is still protected by the borate. Other preservatives, such as penta, arsenates and creosote, do not penetrate wood this thoroughly even when applied under pressure; the cut ends must be re-coated with the preservative.

• When mixed with glycols, borates can be brushed onto dry lumber and penetrate well.

• Borates impart no color to the wood and leave it dimensionally stable, whereas other treatments leave a green or brown color.

• Borates act as fire retardants.

The major shortcoming of borate preservatives is their tendency to leach out of the wood when they come into contact with water. In one study in Mississippi, borax-treated posts in soil lasted only 6 years compared to 20 years for posts treated with penta. However, U.S. Borax and other companies are developing new borate formulations to overcome this problem, and products that protect fence posts and other in-ground wood can be expected in the future.

One borate wood preservative, TIM-BOR®, a product of the U.S. Borax Company, is registered by the EPA for use against wood decay and wood-boring beetles. In a series of tests in various parts of the United States, researchers found that by spraying TIM-BOR® on wooden posts, joists, rafters, subflooring and the soil surface in foundation areas of the house, the wood was successfully protected from attack by decay organisms and insects as long as the wood was not chronically wet. As we go to press, EPA registration of TIM-BOR® has been granted for all states except California, where registration is expected soon.

Summary: Treatment for Wood Decay

• Eliminate sources of moisture as described in Chapter 21.

• Replace wood where decay is extensive.

• Treat wood above the ground with a least-toxic wood preservative, such as copper-8-quinolinolate, copper or zinc naphthenate, a TBTO compound or a borax-based preservative.

• Apply a nontoxic water repellent to wood before painting.

• If conventional wood preservatives are used, take precautions to minimize human contact with them.

• When cutting or handling pressure-treated wood, always wear protective equipment.

BIOLOGICAL CONTROLS

Tests conducted in England and Scotland by the British Utility Board of two beneficial fungi antagonistic to the decay fungi that damage underground portions of utility poles are showing promise. Preliminary results from five years of testing the fungi *Trichoderma harzianum* and *Scytalidium* FY strain indicate they protect uncreosoted poles as well as extend the life of poles treated with creosote. *Trichoderma* fungi are already available from commercial sources in Europe as the product BINAB-B®, which was recently registered in the United States as well. The Eastman Kodak company has requested EPA registration for a *Trichoderma* formula called F-Stop™.

With the growing interest in and market for less-toxic preservatives, a greater variety of products should become available in the next few years. The alternative biological and chemical materials we have described here are but early portents of products to come. Through the Bio-Integral Resource Center (see p. 7), we promise to keep you informed about new preservatives as they are developed.

REFERENCES AND READINGS

Alexopoulos, C.J., and H.C. Bold. 1967. *Algae and fungi.* London: Macmillan. 133 pp.

Includes a good introductory discussion of slime molds.

Anderson, L.O., and G.E. Sherwood. 1974. *Condensation problems in your house: prevention and solution.* Washington, D.C.: USDA (Bulletin No. 373). 39 pp. (Available from: Superintendent of Documents, Washington, D.C. 20250, or as a photocopy from BIRC.)

The causes of condensation in houses and how to eliminate them are described. Includes excellent line drawings of proper vapor-barrier installation and many construction drawings of alterations that prevent condensation problems.

Baker, A.J. 1980. Corrosion of metal in wood products. In: *Durability of building materials and components: proceedings of the first international conference, Ottawa, Canada, 21-23 August, 1978,* eds. P.J Sereda and G.G. Litvan. Philadelphia: American Society for Testing and Materials. pp. 931-933.

This paper reports that damp wood causes metals such as nails, spikes, screws, bolts and plates used in construction to corrode because wood is slightly acidic. It works the other way, too: Corroding metals result in wood deterioration. The paper explains the chemistry involved in these corrosion processes and presents the results of three-year corrosion tests with 11 wood-fastening materials treated with copper-containing water-borne salt preservatives. It found that copper, silicon, bronze and stainless-steel (types 304 and 316) fasteners are suitable in moist ACA- (ammoniacal copper arsenate) and CCA- (copper, chrome and arsenate) treated wood where long service life is required. (ACA and CCA are the most commonly used wood preservatives in the United States.) Aluminum or zinc nails that are tin- and cadmium-coated are not suitable for use in moist ACA- and CCA-treated wood.

Barnes, H.M., D.D. Nicholas and R.W. Lander. 1984. Corrosion of metals in contact with wood treated with water-borne preservatives. *American Wood Preservers' Association, 80th Annual Meeting.* 80:110-125.

This work tested metal fasteners and found that carbon and galvanized steel showed the greatest amount of corrosion, whereas aluminum, copper and brass were relatively inert. Brass showed the least corrosion. Of the preservatives tested, ACA (ammoniacal copper arsenate) was the most corrosive and penta/P9 the least corrosive.

Bruce, A., and B. King. 1983. Biological control of wood decay by *Lentinus lepideus* produced by scytalidium and trichoderma residues. *Material und Organismen* 18(3):171-181.

A good summary of biological control experiments on pests that harm utility poles. The lessons learned are directly applicable to the home, and it is likely that this process will become available for protecting fence posts in the future.

Coggins, C.R. 1980. *Decay of timber in buildings: dry rot, wet rot and other fungi.* West Sussex, England: Rentokil Ltd. 115 pp.

This small hardcover book covers the structure of wood and how it decays. It introduces all the fungi, then discusses the major wood-rotting fungi in England, the wood-boring beetles associated with fungal decay and the detection and treatment of fungal decay. The information is also applicable outside Great Britain.

Feist, W.C., and E.A. Mraz. 1980. *Durability of exterior natural wood finishes in the Pacific Northwest* (Research Paper FPL 366). Madison, Wis.: Forest Products Research Laboratory. 8 pp.

The types of wood finishes and their durability are described in relation to the moist, cool conditions of the Pacific Northwest. The authors maintain that solvent-based penetrating finishes are aesthetically pleasing but do not offer the same degree of protection from surface checking as do film-forming impervious finishes such as paints. On the other hand, penetrating finishes do not blister or peel even in extremely moist areas, and can be refinished without scraping or other preparation.

Hickin, N.E. 1972. *The dry rot problem.* London: Hutchinson Benham Ltd. 115 pp.

This authoritative work covers the types of fungi that cause dry and wet rot and how to control them. One chapter addresses insects associated with fungal decay. Although focused primarily on the climate in Great Britain the book is also useful in other parts of the world.

National Center for Appropriate Technology (NCAT). 1983. *Moisture and home energy conservation: how to detect, solve, and avoid problems.* Butte, Mont.: NCAT. 36 pp.

This concise pamphlet contains illustrations, precise data and methods for altering moisture problems when "tightening up" a house to prevent energy loss. Appendices describe various tests used to evaluate moisture accumulation and list sources of information about materials and devices useful for moisture control in the home (including vapor retarders and breather materials, ventilators, drainage and waterproofing materials for foundations and wood finishes).

Oxley, T.A., and E.G. Gobert. 1983. *Dampness in buildings: diagnosis, treatment, instruments.* Boston: Butterworth's. 123 pp.

An excellent introduction to the evaluation and control of dampness in buildings. The approach is built around the three main sources of moisture-related problems: rain ingress, rising damp and condensation. A checklist for surveying the inside of a home for dampness is included.

Wheeler, Q., and M. Blackwell. 1984. *Fungus-insect relationships: perspectives in ecology and evolution.* New York: Columbia University Press. 514 pp.

Includes in-depth biological articles exploring both the fungi and fungal-associated insects.

Wilkinson, J.G. 1979. *Industrial timber preservation.* London: Associated Business Press. 532 pp.

"Industrial timber preservation" is the process of treating wood with preservatives on a large scale. This book covers the development of and recent advances in the process of injecting preservative solutions into wood. It discusses the boron-based wood preservatives that are presently being examined for use in the United States, as well as research into other types of preservatives.

Yousef, A., and J.F. Domson, eds. 1984. *Mold allergy.* Philadelphia: Lea and Febiger. 287 pp.

This book explains which fungi cause allergies and how to sample them, and provides biochemical details about hypersensitive responses. Clinical information is covered in three chapters, including incidence, characteristics, diagnostic procedures and a review of therapeutic procedures. Two additional chapters cover specific syndromes: aspergillosis and pneumonitis. The final chapter covers the climatic and microclimatic relationships to fungal growth indoors, including the role of man-made devices such as cold mist vaporizers, air-conditioners and evaporative coolers. Many black and white photographs, including scanning electron micrographs, illustrate the text.

CHAPTER 23
Termites

INTRODUCTION

Of the more than 50 million housing units in the United States, about 1% are treated annually for termites, and the cost of termite damage and treatment probably exceeds $1 billion per year. The cost of treating an individual structure ranges from hundreds to thousands of dollars. Many of the conventional treatments are extremely toxic to humans and other organisms and remain so for a very long time. Thus, it comes as no surprise that we receive more calls about less-toxic termite control than about any other single pest-related problem.

In this chapter we first look at the biology and interesting social behavior of termites, then discuss some of the specific tools and techniques that can help you find and monitor them. In case you don't want to do the inspection and monitoring yourself, we suggest what you should look for in a professional. Finally, we discuss the various strategies for managing the problem, some of them quite innovative and promising.

OVERVIEW OF THE PROBLEM

Termites are social insects in the order Isoptera—from the Greek "iso," meaning equal, and "ptera," meaning wing—so named for the equal length and similar texture of the wings of the reproductive termites. Termites are a favorite subject of biologists, who are fascinated by their social organization. E.O. Wilson's classic work, *The Insect Societies,* describes and compares ant, wasp, bee and termite social systems. Wilson emphasizes the evolutionary affinity of termites to cockroaches: "In an almost literal sense, termites can be called social cockroaches." Cockroaches are older, more primitive organisms from which termites evolved. We should be thankful the cockroaches did not adopt the termites' more advanced social organization!

Over 2,200 species of termites, most of them tropical, have been described by entomologists. Ecologically, termites are important recyclers of cellulosic materials, returning the carbonaceous and other compounds in trees to the soil for reuse. As soon as we humans began making things out of trees and other plants, termites became our competitors, since they damage our wooden structures and furniture, stored food and paper. In fact, much information about the early human history of South America and the rest of the tropics has been lost due to the wood- and paper-eating habit of termites.

The Toxicity of Conventional Termiticides

Approximately 30,000 professionals in 6,000 firms offer termite control services in the United States. Traditionally these services have emphasized or have been limited to applications of pesticides, particularly fumigants such as methyl bromide or termiticides such as liquid chlordane. There is growing concern about the health and environmental hazards associated with these and newer substances. Chlordane, for example, is now banned from use and has been withdrawn from the market. Accidents caused by poorly trained or irresponsible pest control operators, increased governmental restrictions and the availability of new techniques all suggest the need for a reappraisal of termite control procedures.

Professional Assistance for the Home Owner

Successful least-toxic termite management depends on a cooperative effort among residents and/or owners of structures and various professionals in the industry. A professional will probably be needed for the inspection because termite nests can be difficult to locate. Special carpentry skills are often needed to replace infested timbers with new wood. And if spot treatment with biological or chemical controls is necessary, special equipment and experience are required. Thus, in contrast to the management of many of the pests we discuss in this book, successful termite management usually requires at least some professional help. The most permanent, most effective and safest treatment of the problem at the most reasonable cost may require a careful integration of activities carried out by the home owner and a number of experienced professionals from more than one company.

Perhaps the most important guidance we can give you if you find termites in your house is not to panic. Although there may be severe consequences when a termite infestation is neglected for a year or more, this does not mean you have to act the minute you discover termites. Some termite control companies feel it is in their interest to scare you into making a hasty and often costly decision. In fact, termite species in temperate zones damage wood fairly slowly. You have ample time to learn about your options, then shop around for a company or companies that will deliver the best mix of least-toxic termite control and house repair. Moreover, you may find ways of cutting costs by doing some of the work yourself.

Buying a Termite-Infested House

To acquire a good house at a fair price you sometimes need to close on it quickly. The closing requires a clearance by a termite inspector, who won't sign off on the building unless it has been treated with a pesticide, but you don't want the house to be treated with toxic materials. If you want time to explore alternatives but don't want to lose the deal, what can you do?

Regulations covering structural pest control differ from one lending institution to another and from state to state. However, we can generalize from our experience. Your objective should be to arrive at an agreement where you, the buyer, assume responsibility for termite control. Do this by writing an "as is" condition into the contract with regard to the termite problem. This implies that you are buying the house in whatever state the termite inspector found it. In addition, add a clause to the purchase contract that explicitly transfers the responsibility for follow-up termite inspections to the buyer. The price of the house should reflect the savings the seller realizes by not having to undertake the repairs; better still, the money allocated for termite repairs by the seller can be released directly to the buyer for termite control.

Alternatively, if the conditions under which the the house can be sold and bought are such that the seller is required to add the cost of termite repairs to the selling price to ensure that the termite work is completed satisfactorily, this money can be put into escrow with the provision that the buyer has control over how the money is spent to achieve that end. Then you, as buyer, can select the mix of professional services and your own handiwork that will achieve the level of termite control specified in the report prepared by the inspector.

BIOLOGY

There are five major groups of termite pests in the United States: subterranean, drywood, dampwood, powderpost and Formosan. Table 23.1 below lists basic characteristics that will enable you to tell them apart. The map on the facing page shows the areas of the country that are most prone to termite infestations. Subterranean termites are found in every state and in Canada and are responsible for 95% of termite-related damage. Drywood termites have a more localized distribution, but are currently the most costly to treat.

Like their archenemies the ants, termites are social insects. Their colonies are organized similarly to those of colonial ants and bees. But termites have some special social qualities. For example, the king termite stays with the queen and fertilizes her periodically, whereas with ants and bees the queen is only fertilized once on the nuptial flight or during swarming.

Table 23.1
Distinguishing Major Termite Groups

	Distribution	Habitat	Behavior	Appearance
subterranean termite (*Reticulitermes* spp.)	throughout United States	ground-dwelling in moist sites	builds earthen tubes; does not form fecal pellets	workers and soldiers ¼ in. (6 mm) long; winged forms ½ in. (13 mm) long
drywood termite (*Incisitermes* spp.)	southern and coastal areas	dry sites	forms oval, six-sided fecal pellets; expels fecal pellets in sawdust-like piles from "kickhole" exits in galleries	larger than subterraneans but smaller than dampwoods; winged forms and soldiers up to ½ in. (13 mm) long
dampwood termite (*Zootermopsis* spp.)	western United States and from British Columbia to lower California	damp, decaying wood	produces large, oval fecal pellets; forms only reproductives and soldiers; no workers	largest termite in United States; winged forms 1 in. (25 mm) long, with wings twice the length of the body
powderpost termite (*Cryptotermes* spp.)	southern and subtropical areas; occasional invader elsewhere	dry wood, furniture, woodwork, floors	forms small fecal pellets	small; soldiers have strongly concave brown or black heads; winged forms ⁷⁄₁₆ in. (11 mm) long
Formosan termite (*Coptotermes formosanus* spp.)	along Gulf and southern Atlantic coasts, Florida, Hawaii	structural lumber, living plants; can penetrate noncellulosic materials such as soft metals and cracked concrete	builds earthen tubes; swarms on warm evenings after rain	soldiers have oval head with prominent horn-like gland; winged forms pale yellow brown, similar to drywood termites, with wings about ½ in. (13 mm) long

Termite colonies contain several castes, each with specific functions. A typical colony consists of one or more pairs of darkly pigmented, ant-like winged reproductives, and two nonreproductive castes known as workers and soldiers. New colonies are formed when reproductives ("kings and queens") swarm or fly away from overcrowded colonies, usually in the spring for subterranean termites and in summer or fall for drywood termites. After swarming, males and females pair off, seek nesting sites, discard their wings and mate (see the drawing on p. 432).

A pile of tiny wings discarded on the ground beneath doors or windows is a sign that a new colony has been established nearby. In general, the colonies grow very slowly and many die out in their early stages.

During the first six months, only 6 to 20 eggs are deposited by the queen. Drywood and dampwood queens lay only a few hundred eggs during their lifetimes, whereas subterranean queens can lay tens of thousands. Young nymphs hatch out in 6 to 12 weeks and are tended by the reproductives. As the nymphs increase in size and number, castes are formed. The workers maintain and feed the colony, damaging wood while tunneling for food. All termites depend on protozoa (one-celled organisms) in their intestines to digest the wood cellulose for them. Therefore, it is really termites and protozoa that attack wood. It is also possible that other microscopic organisms are involved.

The workers provide food for the young and other castes through regurgitation and excretion. Soldiers, with their large head capsules and strong mandibles, protect the colony but do not feed on wood; they are fed by the workers. When a queen ages or dies, a supplementary reproductive takes her place. In general it takes four to five years before the colony is large enough to promote swarming.

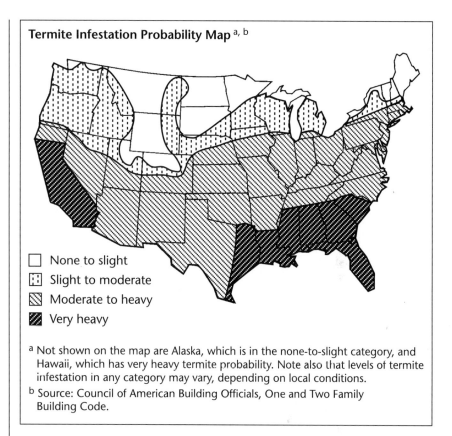

Termite Infestation Probability Map [a, b]

☐ None to slight

⊡ Slight to moderate

▨ Moderate to heavy

▧ Very heavy

[a] Not shown on the map are Alaska, which is in the none-to-slight category, and Hawaii, which has very heavy termite probability. Note also that levels of termite infestation in any category may vary, depending on local conditions.

[b] Source: Council of American Building Officials, One and Two Family Building Code.

The Ecological Differences Between Subterranean and Drywood Termites

Subterranean termites require very different ecological conditions than does the drywood group. Knowing these differences is critical to the successful detection and management of either group.

Subterranean termites (*Reticulitermes* spp.) must be in regular contact with moisture, which in most cases means they must stay in contact with the soil. (In rare cases, they live in the wood above the soil, getting their moisture from a leaky air-conditioner or some other constant moisture source.) In almost all situations, their need for moisture limits their attacks to wood that is within reach of the soil. They construct distinctive earthen tubes to bridge the distance between soil and susceptible wood. The passageways protect them from predators and desiccation (drying out) as they travel between the soil and the wood, and are important visible clues to subterranean-termite presence. The distance between soil and wood has been recorded at up to 3 ft. (0.9 m).

Drywood termites (*Incisitermes* spp.), by contrast, do not need much moisture. They can attack a structure at points far removed from the soil. In their natural forest habitat they are found in dead cottonwood, ash, walnut and cypress trees. In man-altered environments they also infest utility poles, piled lumber (including the sapwood of redwood) and posts.

After entering wood through a crack, drywood termites excavate a small gallery and plug the entrance with partially chewed wood and a cement-like secretion. They then drill small, round "kickholes" from the galleries to the outside for expulsion

The Life Cycle of Termites

Termite colonies are initiated when swarms of winged male and female reproductives leave a mature nest, usually in summer in warm temperate areas and during the rainy season in tropical and warm desert areas. Termites pair off, shed their wings and excavate a nest in or near a source of wood. After constructing a chamber, the pair mates and the female begins laying eggs, producing from a few hundred to tens of thousands (depending on the species) over her many-year lifetime. The eggs hatch within a few weeks or months (depending on the species), and the emerging larvae, or nymphs, mature over a period of two to six months. Most become workers or soldiers. When the nest reaches its maximum population, some of the nymphs mature into winged reproductives, and the cycle is repeated.

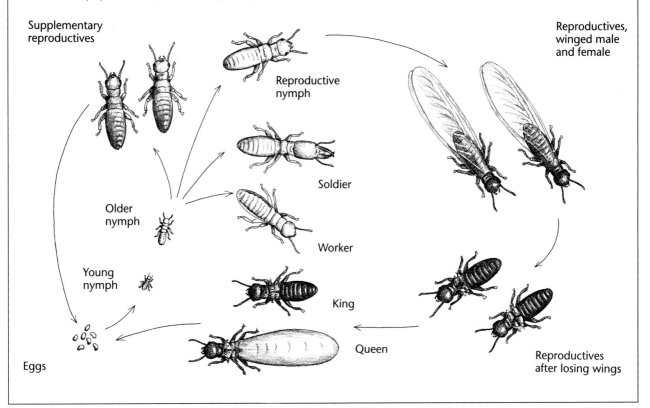

Supplementary reproductives

Reproductive nymph

Reproductives, winged male and female

Soldier

Older nymph

Worker

Young nymph

King

Eggs

Queen

Reproductives after losing wings

of fecal pellets. Piles of the sawdust-like pellets are distinctive signs of drywood termites. In spite of this wood-boring action, damage causing structural weakness is less common than with subterranean termites.

In some areas of the United States, termites from three other groups produce the most structural damage. The powderpost termites (*Cryptotermes* spp.) are tropical pests that can live in subtropical climates such as those found in Florida, Louisiana, southern California and Hawaii. They may occur elsewhere when brought in accidentally with infested goods im-

ported from the subtropics, but such cases are not common. When discovered, powderpost termites usually become the focus of government-sponsored eradication projects. State departments concerned with agricultural or environmental affairs in conjunction with federal authorities are usually responsible for such projects.

The dampwood termites (*Zootermopsis* spp.) are found primarily in wet, decaying wood (caused by a water leak), although they can extend their feeding activities into sound, dry wood. Once the leak is fixed, the rotted wood replaced and the ter-

mites destroyed, the problem is usually solved.

The Formosan subterranean termite (*Coptotermes formosanus*), long a serious pest in China (where it originated) and Japan, has recently invaded the United States. It is considered a serious threat at least in tropical and subtropical areas of the United States because it is so voracious, attacks a greater variety of materials, builds more extensive tubes and galleries than other subterranean termite species and is difficult to control with conventional methods.

INSPECTION: DOING IT YOURSELF

There are two parts to the identification process: discovering the damage and determining the organism(s) responsible. The best way to find and assess damage is through a regular inspection and monitoring program, which you can accomplish in three ways: you can do it yourself, you can hire a professional or you can do both. We begin with do-it-yourself inspection.

Detection and Identification

When inspecting for termites yourself, the first step is to look for signs of damage to the wooden parts of the structure. Damaged wood is often found where moisture collects. Since damp wood attracts many fungal species as well as a variety of wood-boring insects, it is important to determine exactly which organisms are present before deciding on treatment strategies. The diagnostic key in Chapter 21 (see pp. 406-408) should help you use these signs of damage or sightings of insects to determine which pest is causing the problem.

Once you determine that the primary damage-causing organism is an insect, you must decide which insect it is. Termites are often confused with ants, particularly in their winged stage. The drawing at right illustrates some of the major differences between ants and termites. It is extremely important that you learn to distinguish between the two. A termite infestation is usually a more serious problem than an invasion of a local ant species, such as the kind that sends a column or two into the kitchen for some sweets. Moreover, many ant species prey on termites, and, in general, anything that preys on termites should be viewed as a friend of the home owner. An exception is the carpenter ant, which although seldom as destructive as termites, is usually more difficult to locate and control (see pp. 446-451).

Once you have determined that termites are present, use Table 23.1

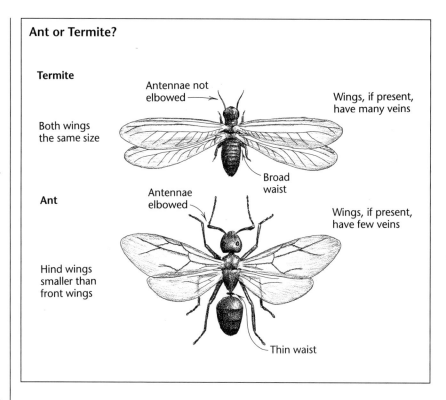

Ant or Termite?

Termite

Antennae not elbowed

Both wings the same size

Wings, if present, have many veins

Broad waist

Ant

Antennae elbowed

Hind wings smaller than front wings

Wings, if present, have few veins

Thin waist

on p. 430 to tell which of the five major types you have, since management differs substantially for each. If you are still uncertain, review the procedure for collecting specimens for identification in Chapter 1 (pp. 12-13). A professional from your local cooperative extension office, college entomology department or natural history museum, or from a pest control company, can then confirm your identification.

Monitoring

Anyone responsible for maintaining a wood structure should understand the basics of monitoring for wood-damaging organisms, because the conditions that invite their presence can often be discovered and corrected before the pests have made themselves at home. You should come to regard monitoring your house for structural pests in the same way you look at such tasks as brushing your teeth, doing the dishes and tuning up the car. They are never really done; to the contrary, they must be repeated at regular intervals.

Many people first become aware of the presence of termites by sighting swarmers, the fully winged kings and queens that aggregate around a small emergence hole in a wood or soil nest before taking flight. However, we strongly recommend that you do not wait until you see flying termites to discover their presence in your home.

The first step in monitoring is to walk around the exterior of your building and record its dimensions, including those of porches, garage and other outbuildings, on a piece of graph paper. You can make the map a plan (the view from above), an elevation (a side view) or any other perspective that clarifies the situation. The map helps you spot areas that might be overlooked when making the inspection of the interior. Make a number of copies so you can use a fresh map each time you check the structure.

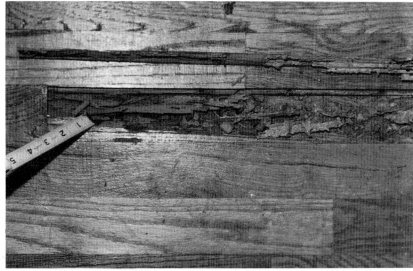

Subterranean termites can be detected by the telltale earthen tubes they construct to move from the soil to the wood. In the photo at left, exterior stucco has been stripped away to reveal the tubes; in many cases, the tubes are visible on the exterior surface of a wall. In the photo at right, the hardwood flooring looked sound but when probed with an ice pick, broke into small pieces due to extensive termite tunneling below the surface. (Photos courtesy NPCA.)

Termites around the Foundation

Subterranean termites are attracted by buried wood, including decaying tree roots and construction debris. They build earthen tubes through cracks or up the side of concrete foundations to reach moist wood above ground.

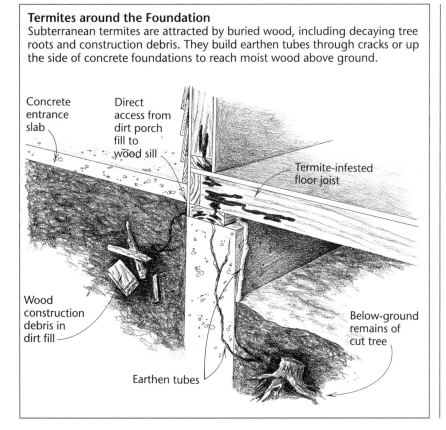

Concrete entrance slab

Direct access from dirt porch fill to wood sill

Termite-infested floor joist

Wood construction debris in dirt fill

Below-ground remains of cut tree

Earthen tubes

Look generally for:
• Conditions such as chronically damp wood or soil suited to subterranean termites (see the drawing at left) or dry, cracked wood, which provides openings for drywood termites.
• Signs of damaged wood, such as holes or tunnels, or wood that does not sound or feel solid when poked with a sharp instrument or hit with a hammer (see the photo above right).
• Signs of insects, including fecal pellets, piles of discarded wings and earthen tubes built by subterranean termites (see the photo above left).

The inspection checklist in the sidebar on the facing page itemizes specific major interior and exterior locations in and around wooden structures that should receive close attention. You can use it to guide your own monitoring or to check the thoroughness of an inspection performed by a professional. A compromise between doing your own work and using a professional might involve your checking the relatively accessible areas once or twice a year, and hiring a professional to check the harder-to-see places less frequently.

Termite Inspection Checklist[a]

Check the following locations for termites visually and by probing with a pointed tool, such as an ice pick. Look for signs of moisture, damaged wood and termite earthen tunnels and/or fecal pellets. Then refer to the sidebar on pp. 411-417 for details on identifying and correcting the conditions that may be encouraging the termite problem.

• **Cracks in the concrete foundation.** These give termites hidden access to house timbers.

• **Support posts set in concrete.** If these go all the way through the concrete to the soil, they invite termite attack.

• **Earth-filled porches.** The earth fill should be at least 8 in. (20 cm) below the level of any wooden members.

[a] From Beal et al., 1983.

• **Leaking pipes or faucets.** These can keep the soil underneath continually moist.

• **Wooden form boards.** These are sometimes left in place after the concrete foundation is poured. They are tasty termite food.

• **Shrubbery near air vents.** Anything that blocks air flow causes the air underneath the house to remain warm and moist, an ideal climate for termites.

• **Debris under and around the house.** Pieces of wood can support a termite colony and permit it to grow to the point where the house itself is attacked.

• **Low foundation walls or footings.** These often permit wooden structural members to come in contact with the soil.

• **Brick veneer over the foundation.** If the bond between the brick surfacing and the foundation fails, termites have hidden entrances.

• **Flower planters.** If built against the house, these allow direct access to unprotected veneer, siding and cracked stucco.

• **Wooden forms around drains.** As with wooden form boards, smaller forms left in holes in and around drains provide termites direct access to the wood within the walls above.

• **Porch steps that rest on the ground.** These literally offer termites a stairway into the house.

• **The area around the furnace.** The soil around and under the furnace unit is often kept moist year-round, accelerating termite development.

• **Paper collars around pipes.** Since paper is made from wood, it is very attractive to termites.

Pay particular attention to locations likely to harbor the type of termites most common in your area (see Table 23.1 on p. 430). Each time you discover something suspicious or obviously wrong during your inspection, mark it on the house map. When your inspection is complete you will have an overview of the extent of the actual or possible damage. Then you can use your notes and the map to plan how you and/or the person you hire will tackle the necessary repairs.

In an excellent booklet entitled *A Guide to the Inspection of Existing Homes for Wood-Inhabiting Fungi and Insects,* author Michael Levy lists tools and safety equipment for carrying out a professional-quality home termite inspection. His list, with some of our own comments, is presented in the sidebar at right.

Tools and Safety Equipment for Monitoring Termites

• **Coveralls.** You don't want to worry about your clothes while you crawl.

• **Safety helmet** or wool hat and gloves for crawl space and attic inspections.

• **Flashlight** with spare batteries and bulbs.

• **Screwdriver** or ice pick for probing wood suspected of being infested.

• **Hammer** or similar instrument for hitting wood and listening for any indication of hollowness.

• **Ladder** for inspecting roof trim and other off-ground areas.

• **Moisture meter** with a range of at least 15% to 24%. For details on moisture meters, see p. 417.

• **Pencil, clipboard, graph paper and measuring tape.** With these you can mark precisely on the floor plan or elevation of the house where moisture is evident or wood is damaged.

• **Good-quality caulk,** such as silicone seal, and a caulking gun to plug any suspicious exterior cracks and crevices. Silicone seal is also available in a thinner consistency that can be applied with a brush.

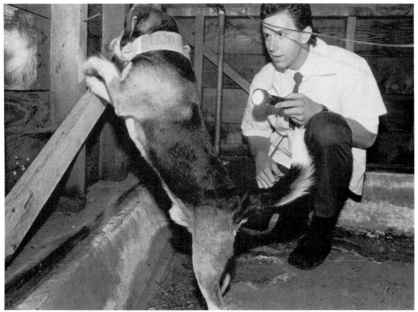

Specially trained beagles use their superior hearing and sense of smell to detect the presence of termites, wood-boring beetles and carpenter ants within walls and other inaccessible places where the pests might otherwise go unnoticed. (Photo courtesy TADD Services.)

INSPECTION: HIRING A PROFESSIONAL

Many people find they have neither the time nor the skill to do their own monitoring and prefer to hire a pest control company. Having your house inspected regularly by a professional skilled in detecting the sometimes subtle signs of termite presence is a good investment.

We strongly recommend that you shop around to find a pest control company willing to provide annual termite monitoring services for a fee separate and distinct from any treatments. In some parts of the country it is still common for pest control professionals to offer free termite inspections with the expectation that the inspection cost will be covered by the fees for treatments that follow. Unfortunately, there are unscrupulous companies that make false claims about the presence of termites or other wood-destroying organisms. Thus, there is a potential conflict of interest in having the inspection and treatments performed by the same company. By paying for inspection services separately, you are more likely to get an unbiased inspection.

It is also important to remember that most termite infestations are very slow to damage wood, so you should not let a company scare you into a hasty decision—you may sign up for treatments you will later regret. Use the inspection checklist on p. 435 to evaluate the thoroughness of the inspection report. Ask to see samples of damaged wood, and make sure infestations are current by asking to be shown live insects or fresh frass (fecal material).

Termite-Detecting Dogs and Other Innovative Techniques

Hiring a company that uses termite-detecting dogs will likely produce superior results. Like their bomb- and narcotics-detecting counterparts, these dogs, usually beagles, are specially trained to smell wood-damaging insects, particularly termites (see the photo at left). They can squeeze into places humans cannot reach. Where buildings have been inspected by both dogs and humans, the dogs have found every infestation noted by human inspectors and, in many cases, have detected infestations the inspectors missed.

The dogs are insured for errors, and the results of a dog-assisted inspection are admissible in court when claims are made against guarantees issued by pest control companies. Termite inspections with dogs cost more than inspections by humans alone (in our area the difference is about $100), but this cost usually is more than justified by the increase in thoroughness of the inspection and the added precision in pinpointing sites of infestation. The added precision can lead to enormous savings since you can focus treatment on the site of infestation rather than on the entire house.

Although clearly a superior detection system, such dogs are not yet widely available, primarily because consumers and many pest control companies are not aware they exist. For sources of inspection dogs, consult the Resource Appendix under "Insect Management: Identification and Monitoring" on pp. 681-682. The sources listed can tell you which pest control companies use the dogs.

Another inspection tool now coming into use by professionals is a fiber-optic scope that allows viewing of areas behind drywall and paneling. A small hole is drilled through the skin of the wall, and the long flexible neck of the scope is inserted. Light conducted through the filament provides illumination, enabling the inspector, who looks through the other end of the scope, to search for signs of termites. This tool may soon prove very important in reducing pesticide use in the termite control industry. Currently, laws in many states require that entire houses be fumigated or sprayed if termites are suspected. To the degree that inspectors can

Foundation Designs that Deter Subterranean Termites

A reinforced concrete cap on masonry walls or piers (shown at right) prevents hidden attack by termites. The minimum clearance of 18 in. (46 cm) under the floor joists allows inspection for termite tubes or possible cracking of the cap. The sand barrier provides extra protection. The monolithic slab-on-ground construction (shown at left) used in conjunction with a sand barrier also provides termite protection.

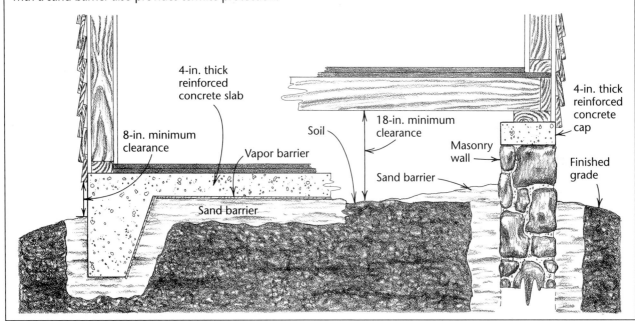

gain visual access to inaccessible areas and pinpoint infestations, the rationale for such laws will no longer exist, and spot treatment will become the main approach.

TREATMENT: INDIRECT STRATEGIES

No termite control program is complete unless the conditions that favor termite survival are modified. To the extent that the termite problem is associated with moisture or wood in contact with soil, these conditions must be corrected. The drawing above shows examples of foundation designs that discourage termite attack.

Indirect treatment strategies recommended for control of subterranean termites include:

1. Reducing the Moisture Level of the Wood. Any exterior feature that leaks moisture should be repaired. The investment in installing, fixing, or relocating gutters, siding, roofing, vents, drains, downspouts and vapor barriers will pay for itself in long-term protection against organisms that attack wood.

2. Eliminating Direct Contact between Wood and Soil. Ideally, wood should be at least 8 in. (20 cm) above the soil. Wood in contact with the soil must be replaced with concrete.

3. Installing Termite Shields. Metal termite shields composed of sheet-metal strips bent into an L shape along one edge (as shown in the drawing at left on p. 438) prevent hidden termite entry through masonry walls. If properly constructed and maintained, the shields force termites to build their tubes over the shield in the open where the tubes can be spotted and destroyed.

4. Removal of Tree Stumps and Wood Debris. Decaying stumps, construction debris and wood scraps near the house can be a source of ter-

mite infestation. The closer to the house they are, the greater the hazard. Wood stumps or debris within 10 ft. (3 m) of foundations and/or portions of a house with a history of termites should be removed. Do not bury wood pieces; they can become termite nesting areas.

5. Proper Storage of Wood Piles. Firewood or lumber piles should be constructed so that no wood rests directly on the ground. Use cinder blocks or other concrete as a base on which to pile lumber or firewood. Large piles should be as far from the house as is practical (this also protects against fire and wood-boring beetles); smaller amounts of wood can be moved closer to the house as they are needed.

6. Planting Trees away from the House. Because ornamental trees and shrubs are often planted when young, a common mistake is to site them too close to a wood structure to

Termite Shields

The crack in the masonry foundation shown here would normally allow termites hidden access to the wooden structural components of the house. Installation of a termite shield made from heavy-gauge galvanized sheet metal forces the termites to build their tubes out in the open where you can see and destroy them during your regular termite inspections before the termites damage the house.

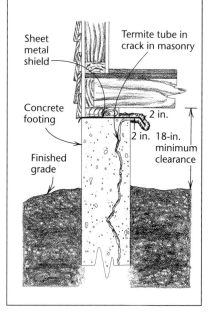

Sand Barriers

Sand barriers can be installed under concrete slabs (left), or inside or outside foundation walls (right). Sand barriers constructed outside walls should be covered with a concrete cap to minimize disturbance of the sand. Barriers on the inside can be placed on the soil surface next to foundation walls.

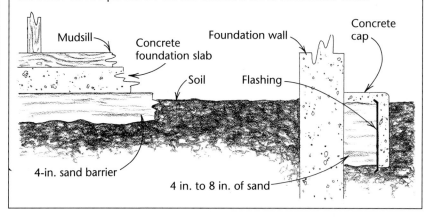

accommodate their size at maturity. Roots, branches and eventually decaying stumps all provide avenues for termite, carpenter ant and wood-boring beetle infestations. Trees and large shrubs may also provide roof rats, squirrels and other animals nesting places and access to the upper portions of your house.

7. Installing Sand Barriers. Research conducted by UCLA entomologist Walter Ebeling showed that termites cannot tunnel through a layer of dry or moist sand consisting of particles ranging in size from 10 to 16 mesh (the larger the number, the smaller the size). This finding led him to test barriers composed of the type of sand used in the sand-blasting industry, most of which falls within this size range. Ebeling found that barriers placed around the inside, outside or on both sides of existing foundations protected buildings from termite attack (see the drawing above). A 4-in. (10 cm) layer of sand or volcanic gravel in the critical size range placed on the soil prior to the laying of concrete slabs also protected against termites. After tests conducted by University of Hawaii researchers confirmed Ebeling's findings, this technique was written into the building code in Honolulu. For details on how to install the barriers, see the article by Ebeling and Forbes listed under "References and Readings" on p. 444.

The most effective indirect treatment strategy for controlling dry-wood termites is to keep the exterior of the house well-painted, sealing all cracks and keeping the outer skin in good repair to prevent termite entry.

TREATMENT: DIRECT STRATEGIES

In recent years a number of new developments have been made in the field of termite control. In this section we look at some of these innovative strategies, and also discuss conventional control practices.

Physical Controls

As with indirect treatment strategies, physical controls for termites differ depending on the species. However, regardless of the type of termite present, you should remove heavily damaged wood and replace it with sound wood. Small pieces of wood debris containing live termites can be soaked in soapy water to kill the insects; larger pieces should be taken to a landfill or other area where the natural decomposing abilities of termites are useful.

Direct physical controls recommended for the control of subterranean termites include digging out colonies and destroying the tubes.

1. Digging out Colonies. Very small colonies, such as those adjacent to buried wood scraps in crawl spaces, can often be dug out. Even if all the termites are not removed, the digging creates openings in the nest that allow natural enemies such as ants to enter and kill the rest of the colony (see "Biological Controls" on pp. 440-441). When digging, remove any pieces of wood or remains of termite tubes you encounter. Digging should be followed by regular monitoring to make sure the colony has been destroyed. This procedure may have to be repeated until the termites exhaust their food supply.

2. Breaking Open Termite Tubes. The highly visible earthen tubes of subterranean termites (see the photo at left on p. 434) can be broken open easily or removed with a trowel or other instrument. Since this type of termite requires daily contact with the soil, destruction of their protective tubes effectively cuts off the connection between the colony and the house. Furthermore, once the tubes are opened, ant enemies can enter the colony and kill the termites.

Physical controls for managing drywood-termite infestations include killing the termites with electricity or heat and applying desiccating dusts.

1. Electricity. The use of a tool called an Electrogun™, invented by Dr. L.G. Lawrence, to kill drywood termites is a recent development. The gun shoots pulses of electricity into the wood at low energy (90 watts), high voltage (90,000 volts) and high frequency (100 kHz), killing the insects in their galleries. This tool is safe for the operator and emits no microwaves, X-rays, ultraviolet rays or other potentially harmful radiation.

Existing drywood termite kickholes or holes drilled into galleries by the operator can be used as entry points for the electricity. In one study, current from the Electrogun™ was shown to penetrate into galleries located ½ in. (1.3 cm) below the surface, killing the termites within. Where the galleries are deeper, a nail can be used to conduct the current to the gallery.

The Extermax System, as the process is called, was tested in the laboratory by Walter Ebeling. He found that whereas some termites die immediately, others take weeks to die, but that they all die eventually. Why this happens and the precise way in which the gun causes termite death remain unclear.

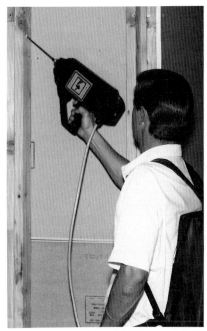

Drywood termites can be killed with a "gun" that shoots an electric current along termite galleries. Because it is used to spot-treat termite-infested wood, the gun serves as an alternative to fumigation of the entire structure with toxic chemicals. (Photo courtesy Etex, Ltd.)

Ebeling describes his findings in a paper available from Etex, the company currently developing and distributing the equipment. After observing technicians using the Electrogun™ in a number of buildings, Dr. Ebeling summarized the technique as follows:

The technical operator moves his probe over most surfaces rapidly...but when he finds a gallery close to the surface, based on the electric current's sound and appearance, he spends considerable time on that spot, recognizing that he has found one of the gateways to the gallery system. From that point the current can flow through the galleries at least as far as 18 inches [46 cm]....It is important not to push the probe so far into a [termite] kickhole that it

reaches the far side of the gallery, because in that case the current will carbonize a pathway directly to the effective electrode [the soil, a pipe, etc., diverting the current away from the termite gallery].

Of 35 Electrogun™-treated drywood termite infestations investigated by Dr. Ebeling, only three required follow-up treatment. A questionnaire sent to 13 pest control operators using the gun elicited nine responses, and all but one operator said they were getting fewer callbacks than with conventional pesticide drill-and-treat methods. One operator, who also does fumigation work, indicated that as his workers gained more experience with the gun, they reduced call-backs "to a very small percentage." One call-back was traced to aluminum-backed insulation in the wall that interfered with the electrical current. Another operator wrote, "We have completed over $400,000 of business using the gun... We issue full, two-year unconditional guarantees on the work. We are extremely satisfied with the gun [and] feel the potential is limited only by the expertise of the operator."

The Electrogun™ is distributed by a number of firms nationwide. Training is provided by the distributors. Contact Etex, Ltd. for further details (see the Resource Appendix under "Suppliers"on pp. 690-696).

2. Heat Treatment. Another new technology uses heat to kill drywood and powderpost termites as well as other pests such as cockroaches, ants, fleas and wood-boring beetles. Heat technology shows the greatest promise of any current alternative tool for displacing chemical fumigation for drywood termites.

The heat-treatment method was developed by scientists Charles Forbes and Walter Ebeling, who demonstrated that insects can be killed by raising the temperature to 120°F (49°C) or more. Special equipment composed of a heating unit, blowers and ducts (see the photos

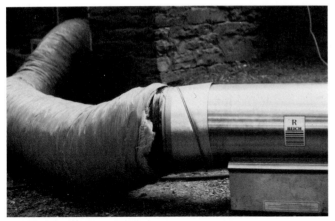

Heat can be used to control drywood termites, wood-boring beetles and other insects that infest buildings. Here, heated air is blown through flexible ducts into a crawl space to treat infested flooring. Insects die when the temperature in the wood is raised above 120°F (49°C) for a specified period of time. A tarp can be used to retain the heat in walls. (Photos by Pamela Griffen.)

Ants that Prey on Termites

Many ants are predators of termites. When ants gain access to termite nests, they are capable of destroying the entire colony. Here, an Argentine ant *(Iridomyrmex humilis)* is shown with subterranean termite eggs, a worker and a large-headed soldier, all of which are potential food for the ant if the soldier termite can be overcome.

above) carries the heat to the locations in the structure where the pests are causing damage. In several years of field tests in various parts of the United States, heat treatments have killed insects inside wood without damaging the building or furnishings, although certain sensitive appliances were removed as a precaution. For more details on heat treatment, see the article by Forbes and Ebeling listed under "References and Readings" on p. 444).

The technique called Thermal Pest Eradication™, marketed by Isothermics, Inc., is available nationwide.

3. Desiccating Dusts. These materials kill insects by drying them out, which technically makes them physical controls. The desiccant silica aerogel is registered for the control of drywood termites. It is usually combined with a pyrethrum insecticide, as in Drione®, for example. Therefore, we discuss all the dusts under "Chemical Controls" on pp. 441-443.

Biological Controls

Biological controls recommended for termite control include conservation of termite-eating ants living around the building's foundations and treatment with beneficial nematodes.

1. Termite-Eating Ants. Ants are among the most important enemies

of termites. We have seen the Argentine ant, common to California and many areas in the southern United States, kill a large number of exposed termites overnight (see the drawing at left). The scientific literature also contains reports of ants as natural enemies of termites.

We (the Olkowskis) conducted an informal experiment in our own home in the early 1970s. During routine monitoring of our unfinished basement crawl space, we discovered the tubes of subterranean termites crossing the foundations of the house from the soil to the wood supports. We remembered that we had found a large group of Argentine ants nesting in a old compost pile near the house —one that had ceased heating up— so we moved a bucket of this ant-infested compost into the basement. Next we broke open the termite tubes, since, in the case of subterranean termites, the tubes usually protect the termites from ant attack. Then we dumped the compost over the entire area where the tubes originated and where we assumed the termite nest was located. We poured a cup of honey and water on the ground near the broken tubes to attract the ants in the area. Since then, yearly inspections have revealed no new earthen tubes or other signs of termite activity. Eventually the ants disappeared from the area, too.

Although we know of no scientific studies of the use of ants to clean out termite nests this way, the experience has led us to believe that it should be investigated. Since many people have a phobia about ants, their use in deliberate biological control of termites would presumably be best in garages and outbuildings where their presence is less likely to be regarded as a nuisance. Argentine ants only rarely bite, but they regularly invade living spaces and become nuisances (see Chapter 14). Theoretically, the ant colony could be killed with poison baits after the ants have finished off the termites. (Note, however, that where pesticides are routinely applied to the soil at the perimeter of foundations to prevent ant and/or termite invasion, the beneficial effects of ant predation against termites are lost.)

Under normal circumstances, ants can be expected to have the greatest impact on a termite infestation when swarmers emerge from the soil or wood prior to flight, or after the swarmers have landed at a new site and are in the early stages of forming another colony. At such times the ants can attack the swarmers en masse and kill large numbers.

2. Nematodes. Scientists are currently investigating termite-eating nematodes as a biological control for subterranean termites. Although many people think of these microscopic worms primarily as plant-infesting pests, there are groups of nematodes that feed only on insects and do not attack plants, animals or microbes.

Termite-eating nematodes are currently marketed under various trade names (see the Resource Appendix under "Insect Management: Biological Controls" on pp. 683-686). The commercial products are composed of strains of a predatory nematode that are applied to infested wood or soil in a water solution much like a conventional termiticide. The nema-

todes seek out termites over short distances—a few inches at most—enter their bodies, and kill them. Because individual termites eat dead and dying termites and share food and feces, the nematodes are spread rapidly throughout a termite colony and destroy part or all of it.

Although laboratory studies have shown these nematodes to be effective at killing subterranean termites, there is a lack of extensive testing under real-life conditions in typical houses. However, a number of termite control companies on the East and West coasts and in the South that have been experimenting with nematodes for several years report good results.

One pest control operator reports that he regularly injects nematodes to treat termites under concrete slab foundations and finds them 95% to 100% effective. Another operator says the nematodes are about 50% effective with the first treatment. Still another, who is also a distributor of the nematodes, claims he finds the nematodes 80% effective the first time, compared to 92% effectiveness with chlordane, a long-lasting, highly toxic pesticide that has since been banned. These figures were based on annual inspections and the number of return visits, or call-backs, in that operator's own company, as well as reports from other pest control operators who purchase the nematodes from the company.

At present, follow-up repeat treatments with nematodes may be necessary, as is often the case when pesticides and other control techniques are used, particularly in the absence of habitat modifications. Since the nematodes pose no hazard to humans, pets or other organisms in the environment, re-treatment is considerably less of a problem than when toxic materials are used. Monitoring is also safer, because the soil beneath the structure is not contaminated.

Unlike the long-lived chemical pesticides used to control termites, nematodes live only a maximum of

two years under the best of conditions (depending on moisture). They cannot survive desiccation (drying out) and are more effective when applied to moist clay soils that hold water than to well-drained sandy soils. The fact that they dry out so quickly also means the nematodes die relatively soon after they have killed the termites. This underscores the need for regular monitoring so that re-treatment can occur as soon as any new infestations are detected.

Many pest control companies are not yet aware of the potential of this biological control agent. If the termite company you use is skeptical and wants more information, suggest that they contact the nematode distributors or write to us at BIRC (see p. 7) for more information.

Chemical Controls
There may be situations where the use of insecticides to control termites is warranted. In such cases, there are two ways to reduce potential health hazards associated with their use: select the least-toxic pesticide(s) that will work, and spot-treat, confining use of pesticides to only those areas where pests have been detected.

1. Conventional Pesticides. When you seek advice from pest control professionals about control of subterranean termites, you will likely find that the standard recommendation is to make routine applications of toxic, long-lasting pesticides in the soil and in the foundations around the entire perimeter of the affected buildings. This recommendation is made in the belief that the creation of an enduring chemical barrier in the soil prevents termite damage for a long time (for the counter-argument, see the discussion under "Spot Treatment" on p. 443). Chlordane was used for this purpose for decades but was banned due to the health hazards associated with it.

Chlorpyrifos (Dursban®), a member of the organophosphate chemical group, is now the most popular substitute for chlordane. It is used to protect wood from both drywood and subterranean termites and has been reported to last up to 11 years in the soil. Chlorpyrifos acts as a cholinesterase inhibitor (nerve toxin), killing insects by disrupting their nervous systems. Although its oral LD_{50} of 1,630 to 2,140 mg/kg in rats suggests moderately acute toxicity, there are reports in the toxicology literature about adverse human health effects, particularly when the substance is inhaled. If chlorpyrifos is being used to treat your home, be certain it is not applied in basements or other areas where fumes can rise through the heating or cooling system and move throughout the house.

The standard pesticides recommended for the treatment of drywood termites include highly toxic fumigants such as methyl bromide and ViKane® (sulfuryl fluoride), applied throughout the building. Residents are required to vacate the premises for two days to give the poison vapors time to dissipate. The use of these toxic materials gives the illusion of long-term security from termites without the need for regular monitoring or habitat modification. However, termites can and do appear or reappear in structures that have been treated with these materials, although at a much lower rate than in buildings that are neither treated nor monitored.

2. Least-Toxic Pesticides. Least-toxic materials for controlling termites include borax, desiccating dusts, synthetic pyrethroids and methoprene.

Borax. Borax-based products, such as TIM-BOR® or Bora-Care™ (disodium octoborate), can be used to protect building foundations from attack by many termite species. The borate acts as a protective barrier against termites that attempt to feed on treated wood. Currently available only to pest control professionals, it is sprayed on wood surfaces in the crawl spaces under structures.

When subterranean termites are present, pest control technicians first destroy all earthen tubes, then apply the borate spray, taking care to saturate the area where the tubes were found. Wooden joists, posts and subflooring are coated twice within a six-hour period. Subterranean termites are unable to rebuild their tubes on treated areas. Termites left in the wood after the tubes are destroyed die within a few weeks because they cannot return to the soil for moisture and other needs. For more information on borates, see the discussion on pp. 112-114; for sources, see the Resource Appendix under "Insect Management: Chemical Controls" on pp. 686-687.

Desiccating Dusts. Desiccating dusts are very safe and effective materials for use against drywood termites. As mentioned earlier, they act primarily as physical, not chemical, agents, but they are discussed here since they are commonly combined with pyrethrum, a relatively less-hazardous insecticide due to its short residual life (24 to 48 hours). The dusts can be applied either during new construction or after fumigation in older buildings to prevent infestation.

Desiccating dusts fall into two general categories, abrasive and sorptive, both of which are described at some length in Chapter 7. One dust, silica aerogel, is useful in confined areas such as attics, particularly when combined with pyrethrins as in the product Drione®.

Walter Ebeling, in his classic text *Urban Entomology,* writes:

If silica aerogel is dusted onto wooden blocks, even in such small quantities that termites placed on them can survive for 2 weeks, the insects do not feed on the wood, although non-treated wood is vigorously attacked. Silica aerogel is generally used at 1 lb. per 1,000 sq ft. (0.45 kg per 93 sq m) in dusting attics for prevention of [winged drywood termites], who generally gain access to a house via the attic and crawl about extensively before attempting to bore into the wood. In crawling about, they soon pick up a lethal dose of desiccating dust and may die in as brief a period as 2 hours....The particular advantage of the silica aerogel is that it is inorganic and not subject to decomposition, and should protect the dusted wood against termite attack for the life of the building.

If dusts are applied on a large scale, it is best to use special (but readily available) pressurized application equipment, which Ebeling describes in his book. If you use dusts of any kind in pest management programs, avoid breathing the material and getting it in your eyes by protecting yourself with goggles and a dust mask. Treated areas should be posted with durable signs that enable future inspectors, repair persons and owners to identify and avoid the materials.

Synthetic Pyrethroids. These compounds are analogs of the natural insecticide pyrethrum, a member of the chrysanthemum family, that have been made more toxic in the laboratory (see the discussion of pyrethrum products on pp. 121-122).

Synthetic pyrethroids are coming into wider use as termiticides. One pyrethroid registered for use against termites is fenvalerate (Pydrin®), with an acute oral LD_{50} in rats of 300 to 600 mg/kg. This suggests a fairly high acute toxicity. Another registered pyrethroid is permethrin (Torpedo®), which has an acute oral toxicity in rats of 430 to 4,000 mg/kg, depending on the formulation (presumably the formulation designed for use in soil is at the higher toxicity level). The advantage these materials have over chlorpyrifos from a health point of view is that they degrade rapidly in the presence of sunlight. Thus, if there is an improper application or accidental spill and some of the material becomes volatilized in the air, it dissipates within hours or a day; chlorpyrifos, by contrast, can remain active for months or years.

Methoprene. One new and truly less-toxic material on the horizon for termite control is an insect growth regulator called methoprene (discussed further on pp. 145-148). Methoprene is an insect juvenile hormone that prevents termite nymphs from maturing into reproductive adults. Since humans and other mammals do not metamorphose as do insects, it is unlikely that this hormone will have detrimental affects on mammals. Scientists have applied methoprene to termite bait blocks, which are decayed pieces of wood used to lure termites into range of the methoprene. One researcher told us that the methoprene remained effective against termites for five to six years in these tests. However, field tests must show equally good results before this technique becomes commercially available.

3. **Spot Treatment.** No matter what termiticide is used, spot treatment is an effective way to reduce human exposure. Spot treatment in this case refers to the application of the insecticide to only those areas where termites have been detected or are not accessible for monitoring.

Spot treatment is a controversial concept in termite control. The standard recommendation is that you apply long-lasting pesticides in any and all areas where termites might conceivably become established. We believe that thorough annual monitoring is a very effective way to spot and

Summary: Least-Toxic Termite Control

• Monitor your building once a year; keep records and compare observations from year to year.

• Be certain you have termites, not ants, and identify the species of termite present.

• Correct the structural conditions that are inviting termite attack.

• Try to find pest control companies that use new, less-toxic methods for termite control.

• Apply physical controls appropriate for the species of termite present (e.g., digging out subterranean termite tubes, using heat treatment to kill drywood termites).

• Conserve termite-eating ants.

• Spot-treat with chemical controls, if necessary.

• Check the effectiveness of any treatment and re-treat if necessary.

treat incipient termite problems before they become serious. The use of inspection dogs and fiber-optic scopes makes this approach more feasible since they enable inspectors to detect termites even in inaccessible areas. With a good monitoring program in place, it should not be necessary to use broad-scale applications of insecticides. Remember, however, that insecticides used for spot treatments are most effective when combined with habitat modification, wood replacement, heat treatments, electrical treatments and/or biological controls.

A second way in which chemical controls can be confined to actual or potential termite infestations is through the use of wood chemically pretreated with borates or other preservatives. Such wood may be used during initial construction or to replace damaged wood in sites where untreated wood might encourage re-infestation. Examples of such sites are areas where condensation or poor drainage cannot be corrected, where wood cannot be moved far enough above the soil level or where physical access for monitoring is limited. This subject is discussed further on p. 425.

REFERENCES AND READINGS

Beal, R.H., J.K. Maudlin and S.C. Jones. 1983. *Subterranean termites: their prevention and control in buildings.* Washington, D.C.: U.S. Forest Service (Home and Garden Bulletin 64). 36 pp.

An excellent, beautifully illustrated booklet on detecting termite damage. Prevention in the form of correct building design and maintenance is stressed, but the discussion of corrective treatments is limited to chemical controls.

Brown, R.W. 1979. *Residential foundations: design, behavior and repair.* New York: Van Nostrand Reinhold. 99 pp.

An excellent book with many line drawings that describes procedures for repairing foundations from the author's own experience. It contains information about repair procedures that is difficult to find elsewhere.

Ebeling, W. *The Extermax system for control of the western drywood termite, Incisitermes minor.* Las Vegas, Nev.: Etex Ltd. 11 pp.

This privately printed paper provides details on some of the first studies of the effectiveness of using electricity as applied with the Electro-gun™ for the control of drywood termites and other insects.

Ebeling, W. 1968. *Termites: identification, biology, and control of termites attacking buildings.* Berkeley: California Agricultural Experiment Station Extension Service (Manual 38). 74 pp.

This inexpensive booklet focuses primarily on subterreanean termites and their control through structural alteration and chemical treatment. It contains additional information not covered by the author's later classic text, listed next.

Ebeling, W. 1975. *Urban entomology.* Los Angeles: University of California Publications. 695 pp.

Discusses the biology, detection and treatment of subterranean and drywood termites, with detailed descriptions of silica aerogel treatments and drill-and-treat procedures.

Ebeling, W., and C.F. Forbes. 1988. Sand barriers for subterranean termite control. *The IPM Practitioner* 10(5):1-6. (Copies available from BIRC.)

A report on experiments using sand as a barrier to subterranean termite invasions.

Forbes, C.F., and W. Ebeling. 1987. Use of heat for elimination of structural pests. *The IPM Practitioner* 9(8): 1-5. (Copies available from BIRC.)

This article describes the methods used to test the effectiveness of heat against a wide range of pest insects, including drywood termites, carpenter ants, cockroaches and fleas. It includes data on the specific temperatures that kill various insect species.

Hickin, N.E. 1971. *Termites, a world problem.* London: Hutchinson and Co. 232 pp.

Provides a general introduction to social insects, then goes on to discuss the economic significance of termites, termite classification, anatomy, biology and collection methods, principles of termite control, soil treatment methods, control techniques for drywood termites, wood preservation, testing procedures and safety in wood preservation.

Hickin, N.E. 1972. *The woodworm problem.* 2nd ed. London: Hutchinson and Co. 123 pp.

An authoritative source, primarily on the wood-attacking beetles, that also includes short sections on other pests of wood, control recommendations and procedures (which need to be updated). The book is written for the United Kingdom, but most of its information is also applicable to the United States.

Levy, M.P. 1975. *A guide to the inspection of new houses and houses under construction for conditions which favor attack by wood-inhabiting fungi and insects.* Washington, D.C.: U.S. Department of Housing and Urban Development. 42 pp. (Available from: HUD User, Document 1083, P.O. Box 280, Germantown, MD 20767.)

Contains color photographs and line drawings indicating areas around a house where construction defects are likely to occur and recommends various types of pressure-treated wood for different areas of the country based on decay hazards in those areas. Most of the pamphlet comprises a long checklist. Wood damaged by fungi and various insects are indicated with color photos.

Levy, M.P. 1975. *A guide to the inspection of existing homes for wood-inhabiting fungi and insects.* Washington, D.C.: U.S. Department of Housing and Urban Development. 104 pp.

A longer version of the previous listing covering more pest problems.

Scheffer, T.C., and A.F. Verrall. 1973. *Principles for protecting wood buildings from decay.* Washington, D.C.: U.S. Department of Agriculture (Forest Service Research Paper FPL 190). 56 pp.

A pamphlet covering the biological and environmental causes of decay and ways to alter designs to prevent decay problems.

Young, E.D. 1976. *Training manual for the structural pesticide applicator.* Washington, D.C.: Environmental Protection Agency, Office of Pesticide Programs. 168 pp. (Available from: EPA, Office of Pesticide Programs, Washington, D.C. 20460).

This manual contains good introductory drawings, insect keys and much information about the use and abuse of pesticides, including the laws and regulations in effect at the time of publication. The latter are still useful to read.

Weesner, F.M. 1965. *The termites of the United States, a handbook.* Vienna, Va.: The National Pest Control Association. Volume 1, 28 pp., Volume 2, 71 pp. (Available from: NPCA, 8150 Leesburg Pike, Vienna, VA 22180.)

An authoritative source on the biology, classification and distribution of termites found in the United States.

CHAPTER 24
Carpenter Ants and Carpenter Bees

INTRODUCTION

In this chapter we discuss two quite different but closely related insects in the order Hymenoptera. The fact that their common names both begin with the word "carpenter" reflects their home-building activities. Unfortunately, when your home becomes host to theirs, they can cause unacceptable damage. The carpenter ant, the more troublesome of the two, can chew away within the structure for a long time before being noticed and can do significant harm. In defense of the relatively unaggressive carpenter bee, however, we should say that its highly visible behavior and nest entrances often elicit a reaction out of proportion to the overall damage it causes. Moreover, the carpenter bee is quite valuable as a pollinator. We discuss carpenter ants, the more common of the two pests, first.

CARPENTER ANTS
(Order Hymenoptera, family Formicidae)

Carpenter ants (*Camponotus* spp.) are among the most efficient wood-destroying insects in the United States. When confined to their natural habitats in forests, they act as important decomposers of decaying trees. But in our homes they become annoying and damaging pests.

Carpenter ants can nest in the structure of a house and invade interior rooms in their search for food. Unlike termites, they do not burrow into the wood to feed upon it, but to construct their nests within it. They usually prefer decaying wood that is easy to excavate or already hollow areas within walls, ceilings or other parts of a structure. Less often, they tunnel into sound wood. They are slow to cause harm, but seldom-used recreational structures and weathered, neglected portions of the house can be seriously damaged by the long-term activity of large colonies.

In forested urban areas the main nest may be located outdoors, often in nearby shade trees. From this nest the carpenter ants first send out scouts and worker groups to establish smaller satellite colonies in firewood, lumber or wood debris stacked against or inside the house. Once inside, they become nuisances by scavenging for sweets, much like other house-invading ants. They can bite, but it is their large size—up to ½ in. (13 mm)—that often causes greater annoyance than the wood destruction for which they are responsible.

Of the more than 500 species of carpenter ants in the world, only nine are common in various regions of the United States. Because these ants were originally forest inhabitants that nested in damp, decaying wood, it is not surprising that they are a structural pest equal in significance to termites in the moist, forested areas of the Pacific Northwest. The distribution of black carpenter ants in the United States is shown in the map below.

Fortunately, there are a number of controls for carpenter ants that pose little hazard to humans and other mammals. Before implementing these, however, it is important to make sure you have identified the pest correctly and have a basic understanding of its biology.

Biology

Of the nine species of native carpenter ants commonly found in the United States, the black carpenter art (*Camponotus pennsylvanicus*) is the most thoroughly studied. The other species have similar habits, so useful generalizations can be made.

Most adult carpenter ants are black, but some may be reddish brown to yellowish. The young are small, legless, white, grub-like and helpless; they must be fed and completely cared for by other colony members. The tan "ant eggs" are really cream-colored silken cocoons from which the adults emerge.

Usually there is one functioning wingless queen per colony. She can be up to 9/16 in. (14 mm) long. The swarmer females are winged and can attain a length of ¾ in. (19 mm), including wings. Winged males are up to 7/16 in. (11 mm) long. The wingless workers vary from 5/16 in. to 7/16 in. (8 mm to 11 mm).

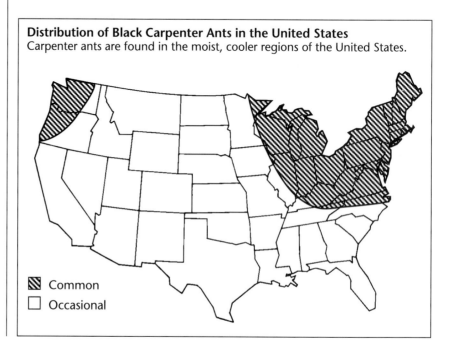

Distribution of Black Carpenter Ants in the United States
Carpenter ants are found in the moist, cooler regions of the United States.

▨ Common
☐ Occasional

Normally, carpenter ants nest in dead portions of standing trees, stumps or logs, or burrow under fallen logs or stones. A survey of 306 shade trees in urban areas in New Jersey indicated that 75% were infested with carpenter ant nests. Only white pine was free of these colonies. Each colony occupied several trees, with one tree containing the brood. The branches of a single colony were linked by tunnels under the soil surface. As many as eight trees were found to be linked this way, and the ants were active within them 24 hours a day.

Destruction of such ant-infested trees or the clearing of building sites with infestations is one reason colonies move into nearby structures. Carpenter ants attack both softwoods and hardwoods in human-made structures, often selecting soft, damp, partially decayed timbers for nest sites. Laboratory studies indicate that the black carpenter ant cannot establish a colony in wood containing less than 15% moisture.

Colonies also commonly nest in houses without attacking structural timbers. They use existing voids in walls, doors or other cavities in the structure, or they nest behind seldom-used shelves, inside stored furniture, in accumulations of debris, in fiberglass or foamed-plastic insulation or even in the open.

A carpenter ant queen lays about 15 to 20 eggs after finding, excavating and sealing herself into a small cavity. She feeds the developing young with fluids derived from stored fat and her own wing muscles, which she no longer needs. When the young are old enough to care for the next brood, the queen resumes her function as sole egg-producer for the colony.

The eggs develop into three adult castes: winged males, winged females and workers (see the photo above). Winged females, or queens, develop from fertilized eggs laid by mated queens; males develop from unfertilized eggs. There are two basic sizes of

The large queen at the center of the photo is flanked by the smaller winged king and wingless workers of various sizes. (Photo by Stennett Heaton, courtesy Van Waters and Rogers.)

workers, majors and minors, but overlapping intermediates also occur. The largest workers, all sexually undeveloped females, forage for food. They transfer the food to the smaller workers, who expand the nest and care for the young. The large workers guard the nest. These ants cannot sting, but they do inflict a painful bite if provoked.

The carpenter ant's primary food is believed to be honeydew derived from insects such as aphids, leafhoppers, mealybugs, scales and whiteflies. They also feed on dead insects, plant and fruit juices, sweets, most kinds of meats, grease and fat. The workers eat the food, carry it back to the nest and feed other colony members through regurgitation. Workers can live up to six months without food. If a colony is stressed by lack of food and water, the queen and a few workers can survive for long periods by resorting to cannibalism.

Colonies can contain up to 3,000 workers, with a peak population reached in three to six years. At this point, winged reproductive females are produced and establish new colonies. A colony can start with a single fertilized queen that flies into an area, or when part of a colony walks into a structure, a process called budding. Myrmecologists (ant specialists) consider budding the main mechanism for house invasions by carpenter ants.

Identification

A question we are often asked is: "How can I tell if the insects I see are ants or termites?" What they have in common is that both are comparatively large insects and are particularly likely to be noticed when swarming in the winged stage. But there are important differences in their appearance. Termites have broad, thick waists, whereas ants have narrow, thin ones; termites have slightly concave antennae, ants' antennae are bent at right angles and are referred to as elbowed. These differences are pictured in the drawing on p. 433 in Chapter 23.

Carpenter ants in the nonwinged stage are often found foraging for sweets or protein in the house. They are frequently first encountered when a light is switched on at night, particularly between 11 p.m. and 2 a.m. in the kitchen, pantry or other area likely to provide them with human or pet food and drinking water. In contrast, termites remain in their tunnels (except when swarming), since the wood itself supplies the nutrients they need.

Damage, Detection and Monitoring

To tell the difference between damage inflicted by carpenter ants and damage inflicted by other organisms, refer to the sidebar on pp. 406-408. The drawing below shows the areas of buildings where carpenter ants commonly cause problems.

The primary problem in the management of carpenter ants is finding the nest. The presence of large workers inside the house is the most obvious sign that the ants may be nesting indoors or, if the primary nest is not in the house, that a secondary colony has been established there. Tracing the ants back to their nest can be very difficult.

The time of year when the ants are found may give a clue to nest location. If the ants are active all year, the nest probably is located in the heated or warmest parts of the house. Winged ants migrating from nests to the indoors can be found congregating around the insides of windows in spring. If nonwinged ants first become noticeable when the weather warms up in the spring, then the nest is probably located in an area that experiences outdoor temperatures. This may mean that the main nest is in an unheated or generally cold part of the house such as under stairs or a porch roof, or near a cellar doorway. But it might also mean that the nest is located in nearby small buildings, fences or trees.

If ants are migrating into the house from outdoors, their trails may be visible in the grass or debris on the ground surface. If this is so, you can trace these trails to the nest. Dead ants caught in spider webs may also give clues to nest location, or, equally important, they may indicate access points to the house from a primary colony outdoors. Bear in mind that utility wires, phone wires and vegetation that touches the house often provide bridges for ants from the outdoors to the house structure.

Look for nest sites in areas most likely to have a regularly high moisture content. Check shade trees within 300 ft. (90 m) of the house for signs of ants, such as sawdust piles, hollowed or rotted areas or wind-blown branches. Inspect outside and inside attics, crawl spaces and basements. Carefully examine window and door trim, wall voids above windows and doors, the edges of floors and ceilings and the insides of hollow doors.

In a survey of pest control operators, it was found that the areas of a house most frequented by carpenter ants, in order of decreasing frequency, are: inside walls, in ceilings, under outdoor siding, in wood-soil contacts near foundations, along downspouts near the roof line, around roof gutter braces, under roofing panels, in hollow doors, in floors, in window sills, under bathroom floors and in padded ceiling insulation.

During very hot weather, the daytime activity of ants is reduced, so foraging workers are best detected late at night. When you find ants scavenging indoors, watch them long enough to tell where they are coming from. Baits such as jellies, jams or honey may be needed to bring enough workers out of a wall so you can follow them back to discover their entrance(s). An examination of the areas where they have left the wall to wander within the room may lead to nest sites.

Sometimes you can detect carpenter ants by the rustling they make within walls, which can be heard faintly by ear and becomes more obvious through a stethoscope (a good

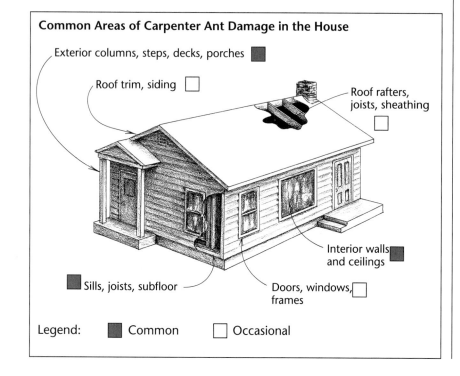

Common Areas of Carpenter Ant Damage in the House

Exterior columns, steps, decks, porches

Roof trim, siding

Roof rafters, joists, sheathing

Sills, joists, subfloor

Doors, windows, frames

Interior walls and ceilings

Legend: ■ Common ☐ Occasional

monitoring tool). The rustling increases if you pound the area, since ants are sensitive to vibration and respond with greater activity. Other indicators of a possible nest site are slit-like entrances to galleries and piles of loose, fibrous sawdust-like wood shavings and frass (insect feces) beneath the opening. The slit, called a window, is sometimes sealed over with a clear substance when it is no longer used to expel sawdust. Occasionally, rather than create a slit, carpenter ants use an existing crack in the woodwork.

You may also find frass in basements, in dark closets, in attics, under porches and in other areas subject to moist conditions. If the frass is produced by ants living within decayed wood, it will tend to be dark and square-ended. The shavings look like tiny wood chips that have been gouged out and cast away. Partial ant bodies are sometimes mixed with this debris.

Dogs trained to detect termite nests (see p. 436) can also help locate carpenter ant nests that might otherwise go undetected. As with termites, the use of dogs reduces the need to fumigate the entire house, since pinpointing the locations of all nests allows spot treatments at only those points. If the pest control companies in your community want to know more about the use and availability of trained dogs, and no local sources are known, refer them to the dog-training companies listed in the Resource Appendix under "Insect Management: Identification and Monitoring" on pp. 681-682.

Treatment:
Indirect Strategies
Few pest problems cause more panic and premature decisions among home owners than those involving wood-destroying insects such as carpenter ants or termites. Sometimes this sense of urgency is deliberately provoked by the pest control company undertaking the inspection of the premises, sometimes it is the result of

a prospective home owner's eagerness to close on a good house deal.

Whatever the reason, you should not feel pressured. None of these pests causes new damage at the rate you are probably imagining. You have plenty of time to find the least-toxic treatment and decide whether you want to do some of the work yourself and contract out the rest to a professional or turn over the entire job to a professional. If you decide to hire a pest control company, it is important that you find one that is familiar with the techniques you want used and willing to implement them in close consultation with you. We have found consistently that an educated consumer is a critical component in the successful application of least-toxic pest control technology.

Another word of advice: You should not get so carried away by the promise of a new less-toxic technological fix that you neglect the basic changes to the house that are almost always essential to long-term pest control. Moreover, a successful integrated pest management program does not rely on a single strategy. It is essential to combine strategies in an overall program that includes necessary structural modifications and post-treatment monitoring so you can determine whether treatments are effective or need adjustment.

1. Eliminating Moisture Sources. Carpenter ants are usually associated with moisture and wood rots unless they are just temporary invaders whose main nests are outside. Thus, the problem cannot be solved permanently until conditions allowing the wood to become damp and remain so are corrected. Structural defects and weather-damaged areas must be repaired and damp areas should be properly ventilated.

Inspect and clean gutters before the rainy season. Clogged gutters can force rainwater under the gutter and across the siding surface, where it may enter the outer envelope of the house and cause wood rot. These damaged areas may then attract car-

penter ants. For additional suggestions on moisture detection and management, see pp. 410-417.

2. Proper Storage of Firewood. Firewood piles should be elevated above the ground and as far from the house as is practical. Before bringing firewood indoors, knock it firmly to shake off any clinging insects and check that the logs do not contain small nests of wood-boring pests. Check again after the wood has been in the house long enough to warm up and activate any ants.

3. Pruning and Maintaining Trees. Tree branches should be pruned so they do not touch structures, because they can provide bridges to the structure for ants. Repair nearby damaged trees and remove tree stumps.

Treatment:
Direct Physical Controls
Direct physical controls for carpenter ants include removal of nests, use of sponge traps, treatment with electricity and exposure to heat.

1. Nest Removal. The most direct physical control involves determining where the carpenter ants are nesting and removing the wood, nest and stray ants (they can be vacuumed up) before repairs are made. The skills of a good carpenter should be sought.

As mentioned earlier, carpenter ants sometimes set up temporary nests, or "bivouacs," in voids rather than in the wood itself. If the bivouacs are eliminated and access points caulked, the problem may be solved at that site.

2. Sponge Traps. One researcher discovered that small groups of carpenter ants can be captured with a large-pored sponge soaked in a thick sugar solution. The ants collected in the sponge trap are then killed by dropping the sponge in a solution of detergent and water. Note, however, that although this procedure may help kill small colonies, it cannot be relied on to eradicate larger ones.

3. Electricity. Where the infestation is small or the colony has not caused much damage to the structure, the nest can be eliminated with electricity. The Electrogun™, discussed under termite control on p. 439, is a valuable, safe new tool for the physical control of many wood-boring insects, including carpenter ants. A pest control operator must be trained to use it effectively. So far only a few companies in each area of the country are offering the service; however, because of its wide applicability in the control of drywood termites, carpenter ants and, in some situations, wood-boring beetles, we expect Electrogun™ use to grow rapidly.

4. Exposure to Heat. A technique developed by researchers Charles Forbes and Walter Ebeling and marketed as Thermal Pest Eradication™ by Isothermics, Inc., uses elevated air temperatures to control carpenter ants and other structural pests. The heat-treatment technique is discussed in detail under physical controls for termites on pp. 439-440.

Treatment: Direct Biological Controls

The possibility of using insect-attacking nematodes in a bait is currently under study. This technique appeared to eliminate a carpenter ant nest in a pilot field test we conducted in a house in the Washington, D.C., area, but further work is needed to verify and refine this technique. If you would like to experiment, the following guidelines are recommended.

The nematodes should be mixed with a protein substance such as tuna or pet food and placed where foraging ants will find it. Pre-baiting, (setting out the food without the nematodes) tests whether the ants will eat the bait before any of the purchased nematodes are wasted (they keep for months in the refrigerator). A few teaspoons of the bait in a small can is enough. Although sugary foods are certain to attract the ants, a protein bait ensures that workers take the nematode-infested food back to the developing larvae and reproductives in the nest. For sources of insect-attacking nema-

todes, see the Resource Appendix under "Insect Management: Biological Controls" on pp. 683-686.

Direct Chemical Controls

Conventional organophosphate pesticides such as chlorpyrifos (Dursban®) and diazinon, are frequently used as stopgap substitutes for necessary structural changes and habitat modification. Economic reasons are generally the rationale for the failure to make building repairs. These chemicals alone will not solve your problem in the long run. However, several low-toxicity chemical substances can be used effectively as adjuncts to an overall program for carpenter ant control. If applied properly, they pose little hazard to the occupants of the house because of their low mammalian toxicity and, in the case of desiccating dusts and boric acid, their low volatility (volatility refers to the tendency to pass into the vapor phase).

For a more complete description of the least-toxic chemicals mentioned in this section, see Chapter 7. Sources for these products are listed

in the Resource Appendix under "Insect Management: Chemical Controls" on pp. 686-687.

1. Desiccating Dusts. Desiccating dusts can be blown into voids through small holes drilled in the wall. They fall into two general categories: abrasive and sorptive, referring to their ability to abrade or absorb the waxy layer on the outer coat of insect bodies, causing the insects to dehydrate and die from moisture loss.

If you use dusts of any kind in your pest management program, avoid breathing them or getting them in your eyes. Protect yourself with goggles and a dust mask, as described on pp. 97-103.

Diatomaceous Earth. Diatomaceous earth is a combined abrasive/sorptive dust made from naturally occurring deposits of fossilized diatoms. It is safe enough to be categorized among the "inert" ingredients in many products, yet has considerable killing power against a wide range of pests. It is allowed as an additive to grain in storage for control of insects, and it is also used as a feed additive

---

Summary: Least-Toxic Carpenter Ant Control[a]

• Prevent excessive moisture accumulation in wood through good maintenance of the house structure and surroundings. Repair existing damage, then cut off ant access routes.

• Eliminate potential ant-nesting areas by repairing damaged trees and removing decaying stumps and wood debris. Prune branches that touch the house and eliminate wood/earth contact of structural members.

• Locate nests by trailing workers, searching for frass piles or listening for the sound of ants moving in the walls. The aid of a stethoscope or specially trained dog is very helpful.

• Check firewood carefully for insects before bringing it indoors and monitor for insect activity after the wood warms up.

• Destroy nests through physical controls, desiccating dusts, boric acid and/or nematode or hydramethylnon baits.

[a] Adapted from Mallis, 1982.

for the control of intestinal parasitic worms in cows, horses and dogs. Note that the product we are describing here should not be confused with the glassified diatomaceous earth used in swimming pool filters.

Silica aerogel. Silica aerogel (Dri-Die®), a sorptive dust that kills insects by dehydrating them, can be blown as a dust into voids where ants nest. It is also sold as a spray in combination with pyrethrin, a botanical insecticide generally regarded as having low mammalian toxicity. We have had great success with this spray in controlling other ant species in wall voids and suspect it also works well against carpenter ants.

2. Boric Acid. After desiccating dusts, boric acid is the pesticide with the next-lowest toxicity to mammals; it, too, can be blown or sprayed into wall voids to kill ants.

3. Hydramethylnon Baits. If you decide to treat carpenter ants with conventional carbamate and organophosphate insecticides, use bait formulations rather than spray treatments, since baits reduce human and pet exposure to these toxic materials.

CARPENTER BEES
(Order Hymenoptera, family Anthophoridae)

In most situations, carpenter bees (*Xylocopa* spp.) are more of an annoyance than a threat to the integrity of a building. However, they can become a significant problem in some weathered or unpainted woods when female carpenter bees build or enlarge their nests. This damage can be exacerbated by woodpeckers, which sometimes attack the nests. Fortunately, the bees are most likely to be nesting in exposed trim or other easily replaceable, non-weight-bearing portions of a structure. Only if extensive tunneling occurs in the supporting beams or other critical members of a building should direct measures be used against these beneficial insects. In most situations, only an appreciation of their activities and an

effort to prevent further colonization of the site are warranted.

The fierce appearance and loud sounds made by carpenter bees often trigger unnecessary fears. The bees are large, iridescent and hairy, except on the upper abdomen, where they lack hair. The males are fast flyers and make a loud buzz. From a human viewpoint, this noise is all bluff, since male carpenter bees cannot sting. The females can, but they don't, although they have been known to bite if handled roughly.

The fact that these bees are able to penetrate wood can also be a source of fear for home owners, particularly since most people are unaware of how slowly they tunnel and how simple it is to curb their damage. On the whole, it seems that ignorance about carpenter bees has turned a desirable wildlife species into an object of fear.

Biology

Carpenter bees overwinter in wood as young adults. Those that survive the winter mate from April to June, then begin preparations for the next generation. The female may clean out a previously excavated gallery and use it without additional boring. Alternatively, she may lengthen an existing gallery, bore a new tunnel or chew a new gallery from an entrance shared with or started by other bees.

The female provisions her nest with "bee bread," a mixture of pollen and regurgitated nectar that serves as food when the eggs hatch. She then closes each cell with chewed wood pulp. There may be as many as six sealed cells in a row in one 4-in. to 6-in. (10 cm to 15 cm) gallery. The time required to complete development from egg to adult varies between one and three months. Newly formed adult bees usually emerge in late August but do not mate until the following spring. The males vigorously defend their territory in the vicinity of the nest. Their threat display consists of close hovering, aggressive buzzing and rapid flying.

Identification

You should suspect carpenter bees if you see large bees about 1 in. (25 mm) long flying vigorously around the exterior of the house or near plants. Other signs of carpenter bees are ½-in. (13 mm) round holes in wood siding, outdoor trim or other wood areas; sawdust-like debris below areas being tunneled; and woodpecker-damaged wood on the house.

If you see large bees, the next question is whether they are carpenter bees or bumblebees, with which they are often confused. The sidebar on the next page will help you tell the two apart.

Damage

In natural settings in North America, these large, harmless bees nest in dead but sound parts of living trees. They do not attack wood that is soft due to decay, and will not tunnel into wood with bark still on it. They have distinct preferences for certain species of softwoods, including southern yellow pine, white pine, California redwood, cedar, Douglas-fir and cypress.

Carpenter bees drill, or more precisely, chew, with their mouthparts into structures such as fences, telephone poles, bridges, wooden water tanks, stored lumber and various parts of buildings. The areas of a structure most commonly attacked are, in order of frequency, roof trim and siding, exterior columns, steps, decks and porch beams and railings.

The bees' entrance is usually against the grain, except where it starts on the end of a board. About 1 in. (2.5 cm) into the wood, the tunnel turns abruptly at a right angle, and in newly excavated areas travels with the grain from 4 in. to 6 in. (10 cm to 15 cm). However, a system of galleries developed by several bees working in the same area over a period of time can extend as much as 6 ft. to 9 ft. (2 m to 3 m), within a piece of timber. The drawing on the next page shows some common configurations of carpenter bee galleries.

Distinguishing Carpenter Bees from Bumblebees

Carpenter bees (*Xylocopa* spp.) are likely to be confused with bumblebees *(Bombus* spp.), because both are large and hairy and are often seen on flowers. However, you can tell them apart by studying their behavior and appearance.

Behavior

Carpenter bees fly and hover almost without regard to human activity. The males are noticeable as they zoom swiftly between buildings, sometimes rising to 60 ft. (18 m) or more in the air. The aggressive interactions between the males are obvious as the bees defend and challenge each other over their territories. Their flights are noisy and their wings hum in a way that conveys threat; some may even seem to be threatening humans. Female carpenter bees concentrate on provisioning their nests and are seen most readily as they enter and emerge from large entrance holes in wood, or while on flowers searching for pollen.

By contrast, most bumblebee behavior around humans appears sedate or cautious. Bumblebees do not hover for long periods or defend territories around a structure; most stay busy foraging for pollen and nectar, and are seen most often on flowers.

Appearance

The top of the carpenter bee's hairless abdomen is metallic and iridescent; it may reflect blue, blue-black, purple, green, bronze or buff colors, depending on the species. Males and females of the same species may be slightly different in coloration. The thorax and legs are noticeably hairy.

Bumblebees, in contrast, are not shiny. They are furry-looking with hair all over. Their hind legs may support loads of yellow pollen on special structures that carpenter bees lack.

(Note: Carpenter bees are not likely to be confused with honeybees, which are often seen on the same flowers visited by both carpenter bees and bumblebees. Honeybees are much smaller, have hair all over and are duller and lighter in color.)

Carpenter Bee

No hair
on abdomen

Bumblebee

Hairy
abdomen

Carpenter Bee Holes, Tunnels and Nests

(A) shows a typical carpenter bee entrance hole and tunnel; the hole appears very round and regular on the outside of the wood. (B) shows a complete nest in cross section.

Treatment: Indirect Strategies

Carpenter bees prefer unpainted or nonvarnished softwoods, which are easy to penetrate. Where carpenter bees are known to be active around a building, consider constructing trim or exposed rafters, roof and porch beams, window sills and other vulnerable elements from woods not favored by the bee (see the list under "Damage" on p. 451) and/or keep such elements heavily coated with paint or varnish. This means repainting as frequently as necessary to keep up with weathering. Pay particular attention to maintaining the paint on the undersides of siding or trim that is accessible to bees but not easily visible to humans. Because female carpenter bees are attracted to depressions in the wood, fill them in before painting.

Previously damaged or especially vulnerable areas can be covered or replaced with aluminum, asphalt or fiberglass materials. Holes in wood created during previous tunneling by bees can be filled with steel wool and then covered with metal window screening. (Note: Many wood fillers and caulks are too soft to prevent re-entry by bees.)

Treatment:
Direct Chemical Controls

Chemicals that have been used to control carpenter bees include kerosene, almond oil and pyrethrum-based insecticides.

1. Kerosene. The older literature mentions the use of kerosene applied to bee holes as a way to repel or kill developing bees and the females who bring food into the galleries. Although the idea of a chemical that repels but does not harm the bees is attractive, the subject has not been studied in any depth.

2. Almond Oil. M.J. Orlove (listed under "References and Readings" on p. 455) found that benzaldehyde, the almond oil or almond essence used in cooking, has bee-repellent qualities. But, he cautions, "concentrated benzaldehyde from the chemists may contain certain other poisonous chemicals and is itself quite toxic to humans if swallowed or if the fumes are inhaled repeatedly." Almond oil or almond essence is worth trying as a repellent during the active season until physical changes can be implemented.

3. Pyrethrum-Based Insecticides. A pyrethrum-based insecticide can be used to kill the bees directly. Pyrethrum products do not pose significant hazards to mammals due to their very short residual life of 24 to 48 hours. Revenge®, a pyrethrin plus silica aerogel mixture in an aerosol can, is effective at killing bees directly and leaves a long-term silica aerogel residue whose desiccant action on bees makes treated areas less attractive to these insects. See pp. 121-122 for details on pyrethrum products.

Many commonly available "bug bombs" contain synthetic pyrethroids as active ingredients. Some of these products are sold for wasp control and are designed for long-distance (10-ft. to 12-ft./3 m to 3.7 m) applications. They should be applied to carpenter bee galleries after the females have been observed leaving the nest. This approach kills developing bees but spares the females. Night applications may also be effective, particularly if temperatures are low and bee activity has ceased.

Summary: Least-Toxic Carpenter Bee Control

• Protect carpenter bees wherever possible, since they do not constitute a hazard to humans through stinging and are very valuable pollinators. If you must remove them, alter their habitat after they have emerged in the spring.

• Where carpenter bees are known to be a problem, keep exposed wood heavily coated with paint or varnish, or cover it with materials such as metal or fiberglass, into which the bees cannot tunnel.

• Where damage is already underway, replace damaged wood with painted wood or other materials that are not attractive to the bees. Or fill the holes with steel wool and staple on metal screening after the bees have emerged.

• If a pesticide is considered necessary, use one that is pyrethrum-based. Plug holes after treatment, or replace damaged wood with undamaged, chemically protected materials.

REFERENCES AND READINGS

Carpenter Ants

Downes, W. 1939. Derris for ants and wasps. *Journal of Economic Entomology* 32(6):883-884.

This short paper records the successful use of derris powder (4% rotenone) for extermination of hidden colonies of *Camponotus* spp. at Shawnigan Lake north of Victoria, B.C., Canada.

Ebeling, W. 1975. *Urban Entomolgy.* Los Angeles: University of California Publications. 695 pp.

Ebeling's classic text includes a discussion and good drawings of carpenter ant biology in general, with further details on species.

Fowler, H.G., and M.D. Parrish. 1982. Urban shade trees and carpenter ants. *Journal of Arboriculture* 8(11): 281-284.

This study showed that 75% of 306 shade trees examined in central New Jersey were infested with carpenter ants. Silver maple was the most commonly infested, white pine the least. Carpenter ants protected honeydew-producing insects.

Fowler, H.G., and R.B. Roberts. 1980. Foraging behavior of the carpenter ant, *Camponotus pennsylvanicus* (Hymenoptera: Formicidae), in New Jersey. *Journal of the Kansas Entomological Society* 53(2):295-304.

An ecological study indicating that smaller workers guarded aphid colonies while larger workers foraged on the ground and in trees. Some workers served as honeydew transporters, carrying it to the nest.

Fowler, H.G., and R.B. Roberts. 1982. Insect growth regulators in baits: Acceptability to carpenter ants, *Camponotus pennsylvanicus* (Deg.) (Hymenoptera, Formicidae). *Zeitschrift für Angewandte Entomologie* 94:149-152.

This article emphasizes the need for acceptability in a bait and suggests that some IGRs may have potential as baits.

Fowler, H.G., and R.B. Roberts. 1983. Behavioral and developmental effects of some insect growth regulators on carpenter ants, *Camponotus pennsylvanicus* (Deg.) (Hym.: Formicidae). *Zeitschrift für Angewandte Entomologie* 95:507-512.

An initial study showing some of the successful morphological effects of feeding the insect growth regulator RO 13-5223 (Maag Agrochemicals) to the black carpenter ant.

Hansen, L.D. 1984. A PCO's guide to carpenter ant control. *Pest Control Technology,* April:56-58.

A short article with a good table of common U.S. species.

Levy, M.P. 1975. *A guide to the inspection of new houses and houses under construction for conditions which favor attack by wood-inhabiting fungi and insects.* Washington, D.C.: U.S. Department of Housing and Urban Development. 42 pp. (Available from: HUD User, P.O. Box 280, Germantown, MD 20767.)

A short, illustrated pamphlet indicating areas around a house where carpenter ants make their nests and what the damage looks like.

Levy, M.P. 1975. *A guide to the inspection of existing homes for wood-inhabiting fungi and insects.* Washington, D.C.: U.S. Department of Housing and Urban Development. 104 pp.

A longer version of the previous listing, covering more pest problems.

Mallis, A. 1982. *Handbook of Pest Control,* 6th ed. Cleveland: Franzak and Foster. 1,101 pp.

A classic work on household pests. The sidebar on p. 450 is based on a list in this book.

Moore, H.B. 1979. *Wood-inhabiting insects in houses: their identification, biology, prevention and control.* Washington, D.C.: USDA Forest Service and the Department of Housing and Urban Development. 133 pp.

A glossy paperback covering the different groups of wood-damaging insects that contains numerous line drawings of construction details, insects and their damage.

Rudinsky, J.A., ed. 1979. *Forest insect survey and control,* 4th ed. Corvallis, Oreg.: Oregon State University Bookstores. 472 pp.

A good, referenced introduction to carpenter ant biology and control.

Sanders, C.J. 1964. The biology of carpenter ants in New Brunswick. *Canadian Entomologist* 96:894-909.

Relates observations of 35 colonies of three *Camponotus* species in about 150 trees, in a study that found that entrances were underground and tunnels connected a series of trees. Woodpeckers attacked one-third of the brood (nest) trees.

Sanders, C.J. 1972. Seasonal and daily activity patterns of carpenter ants (*Camponotus* spp.) in northwestern Ontario (Hymenoptera: Formicidae). *Canadian Entomologist* 104:1681-1687.

This study found that carpenter ant activity peaked in June and early July. Peak daily activity in June occurred in mid-afternoon in underground trails tunnels. As the season progressed, *C. pennsylvanicus* become virtually nocturnal. Nest temperatures were raised as much as 61°F (16°C) above normal by the ants' metabolic body heat.

Townsend, L.H. 1945. *Literature of the black carpenter ant, Camponotus herculeanus pennsylvanicus (Degeer.): a bibliography with abstracts.* Lexington: University of Kentucky Agricultural Experiment Station (Circular 59). 27 pp.

An excellent guide to the early literature on carpenter ants.

Young, E.D. 1976. *Training manual for the structural pesticide applicator.* Washington, D.C.: EPA Office of Pesticide Programs. 168 pp. (Available from: EPA Office of Pesticide Programs, Washington, D.C. 20460.)

This manual includes good introductory information, drawings of nest structure and recommendations for detection and control. It stresses the need to paint or varnish wood surfaces for prevention.

Carpenter Bees

Baker, N.W. 1972. Carpenter bees. *Pacific Discovery* 25(2):26-27.

This short article mentions California species and contains excellent black-and-white pictures of Brazilian and Malaysian species.

Barrows, E.M. 1980. Results of a survey of damage caused by the carpenter bee *Xylocopa virginica* (Hymenoptera: Anthophoridae). *Proceedings of the Entomological Society of Washington* 82(1):44-47.

This survey conducted in the Washington, D.C., area indicated that the bees nested in porches, houses, garages, sheds, fences, benches, trellises, and lamp posts, particularly in pine and redwood and on the south sides of buildings. Other characteristics of nest sites are also discussed. The survey found that the average cost of controlling infestations was $84.

Clausen, C.P. 1978. *Introduced parasites and predators of arthropod pests and weeds: A world review.* Washington, D.C.: USDA (Agricultural Handbook No. 480). 545 pp.

Describes an unsuccessful attempt during 1933-35 in Hawaii to establish biological control of carpenter bees with the parasitic meloid beetle *Cissites auriculata* from Guatemala. The information is useful to others interested in this approach.

Ebeling, W. 1975. *Urban Entomology.* Los Angeles: University of California Publications. 695 pp.

A good referenced introduction to bee biology, with emphasis on California species. The control recommendations need to be updated.

Hurd, P.D. Jr. 1978. *An annotated catalog of the carpenter bees (genus Xylocopa katreille) of the western hemisphere (Hymenoptera: Anthophoridae).* Washington, D.C.: Smithsonian Institution Press. 106 pp.

A good introduction to the biology of the bees in the genus *Xylocopa*. It is the authoritative source for taxonomic, biological and ecological information, but offers very little on management, apart from this observation: "In general, the continued nesting of carpenter bees usually causes little more than a great deal of noise and minimal damage."

Levy, M.P. 1975. *A guide to the inspection of new houses and houses under construction for conditions which favor attack by wood-inhabiting fungi and insects.* Washington, D.C.: U.S. Department of Housing and Urban Development. 42 pp. (Available from: HUD User, P.O. Box 280, Germantown, MD 20767.)

Contains color photographs and line drawings that indicate areas around a house where carpenter bees make their nests and cause damage.

Orlove, M.J. Undated. *A contribution to the biology of the great carpenter bee, Xylocopa virginica (L.)(Anthophoridae: Apoidea: Hymenoptera): geographic variation in courtship; mimicry; and rearing methods.* Ithaca, N.Y.: Cornell University College of Agriculture, Division of Neurobiology and Behavior. (Unpublished manuscript; copies available from BIRC.)

A detailed explanation of successful colonization in artificial nests, with mating and nesting observations and discussions about mimicry and speciation.

Rudinsky, J.A., ed. 1979. *Forest insect survey and control,* 4th ed. Corvallis, Oreg.: Oregon State University Bookstores. 472 pp.

A good, referenced introduction to carpenter bee biology and control that emphasizes the need to paint and repaint exposed wood and the advantage of using pressure-treated wood. It also points out that these bees do not disperse widely and probably originate from nearby trees.

CHAPTER 25
Wood-Boring Beetles

INTRODUCTION

After wood-rotting fungi, termites and carpenter ants, the wood-boring beetles are next in the amount of damage they cause to structures in the United States. Fortunately, as with the other pests of structures, the damage usually occurs slowly over a period of years, so there is no need for panic if the beetles are detected. In fact, by the time you spot beetle holes in the wood, the beetles may be long dead. Even if they are still alive, it is quite possible they are of the type that cannot reinfest wood after they have completed their development, and thus they pose no further threat. In this chapter we are concerned primarily with those beetles that can reinfest wood.

WOOD-BORING BEETLES
(Order Coleoptera)

Although some wood-boring beetles can cause serious damage and should be controlled, there is always time to identify the type of beetle present before taking any action. Proper identification tells you immediately whether you have the type that can infest your structure over and over again, causing extensive damage, or the type whose damage is limited to one generation. You also have time to determine whether the larvae are still active in the wood and to assess the extent of the infestation. This information is key to solving the problem with relative permanence through the least-toxic means available.

Biology

Two major groups of beetles reinfest wood once inside a structure: the true powderpost beetles in the family Lyctidae; and the deathwatch and furniture beetles in the family Anobiidae. A third group, the false powderpost beetles in the family Bostrichidae, can reinfest but rarely do. None of the beetles in the family Cerambycidae reinfest wood, with one notable exception—the old house borer. These and other wood-boring beetle families are described in Table 25.1 on pp. 458-459, and can be distinguished by the type of frass (waste) and the holes they produce.

When reading the table, bear in mind that the term "powderpost beetles" is commonly used loosely to refer to all members of the reinfester group of beetles. The term should really be restricted to one particular family, the Lyctids, because they are the only group to produce a true powder.

Lyctid Powderpost Beetles. Lyctids are the most common and widespread of the wood-boring beetles that reinfest wood in houses in the United States and Canada. They also attack furniture. (However, since most furniture is now stored in heated spaces whose temperature is unfavorable to the beetles, this damage is becoming less of a problem.)

Outdoors, lyctid beetle adults overwinter in the larval stage. With the coming of spring, they bore closer to the surface of the wood to pupate. About two to three days after emerging as adults and mating, the females start depositing eggs in the surface pores of wood, particularly the sapwood (the outer wood) of hardwoods, since it has larger pores than the heartwood (the inner wood).

The most susceptible woods are the ring-porous hardwoods, such as oak, hickory and ash. Diffuse-porous hardwoods that are often attacked include walnut, pecan, poplar, sweetgum and wild cherry. (Ring-porous and diffuse-porous refer to the distribution of pores within the growth rings of the particular wood.) The moisture content of the wood needed for egg laying ranges between 8% and 32%, but the greatest activity occurs between 10% and 20%. The moisture content of wood in most residences falls within this range.

Females lay an average of 20 to 50 eggs in exposed areas of the tree or in milled lumber. The hatched larvae bore down the vessels of the wood, making straight tunnels. Later, the tunnels become irregular, intersecting other tunnels. The larvae remain in the wood until the following spring. Most species complete their life cycle in 9 to 12 months but they can develop more quickly if the temperature and starch content of the wood are favorable. The larvae cannot digest cellulose, but they do metabolize the starch within the wood cells. Females taste the wood and do not lay eggs where the starch content is below 3%. They also prefer recently dried wood.

Because kiln-drying at the lumberyard retains more starch than air-drying, air-dried wood is less prone to beetle attack and therefore preferable for building. However, because it takes more time in storage, it also costs more. Older wood also has a lower starch content.

Anobiid Deathwatch and Furniture Beetles. The anobiid species common in the United States include the deathwatch and furniture beetles. The furniture beetles don't attack furniture nearly as often as their name implies. The deathwatch beetles get their name from the ominous ticking sounds they make late at night, which are probably the mating calls of the adults. In general, these beetles require a higher wood moisture content than the lyctids, and thus are more frequent pests in coastal areas, unheated dwellings or wherever the humidity is high. Furniture, generally kept in less-humid living spaces, is usually too dry for them to infest.

Some anobiids, for example those in the genus *Xyletinus*, attack both hardwoods and softwoods, and new as well as slightly older wood. They feed mainly on the sapwood, digesting the cellulose with the aid of yeast cells in their digestive system. Outdoors in trees they live in dead limbs or in bark-free scars on the trunks; in houses they may be common in humid crawl spaces.

The females lay their eggs on the surface of the wood in small cracks or crevices. When the larvae hatch, they bore a short distance into the wood, then turn at a right angle and tunnel

Table 25.1
Distinguishing among Major Groups of Wood-Boring Beetles

	Family	Features	Exit Holes
	Lyctidae (true powderpost beetles)	⅛ in. to 5/16 in. (3 mm to 8 mm) long; body somewhat flattened; light brown to black; prominent head, not covered by pronotum[a], 11-segmented antennae with apical 2-segmented club	circular, 1/32 in. to 1/16 in. (0.8 mm to 1.5 mm) in diameter
	Anobiidae (deathwatch beetles, furniture beetles)	1/16 in. to ⅜ in. (1.5 mm to 9.5 mm) long; body cylindrical; head hidden beneath hood-like thorax, 11-segmented antennae attached near eyes, last three segments somewhat enlarged, forming club	circular, 1/16 in. to ⅛ in. (1.5 mm to 3 mm) in diameter
	Bostrichidae (false powderpost beetles, branch and twig borers)	¼ in. (6 mm) long; body stubby; head not visible from above	circular, 3/32 in. to 9/32 in. (2.5 mm to 7 mm) in diameter
	Buprestidae (flatheaded wood borers, metallic wood borers)	¼ in. to 1¼ in. (6 mm to 32 mm) long; boat-shaped body, slightly flattened; many metallically colored	elongated and oval, like old house borer's; distorted in sawn wood
	Cerambycidae (roundheaded wood borers, longhorned beetles)	⅓ in. to 2 in. (8.5 mm to 50 mm) long or longer; cylindrical body; long antennae, sometimes longer than body	slightly oval to nearly round, size depending on species
	Scolytidae (bark beetles, engraver beetles)	⅛ in. (3 mm) long; small cylindrical body; brown, reddish brown, or black; head partially concealed from above	1/16 in. (1.5 mm) in diameter; adults tunnel out through bark
	Curculionidae (wood-boring weevils, snout beetles)	⅛ in. to 3/16 in. (3 mm to 5 mm) long; cylindrical body, wing covers heavily pitted; head prolonged into snout; black or reddish brown	raggedly round, 1/16 in. (1.5 mm) in diameter, or irregularly shaped to 1/12 in. (2 mm)
	Platypodidae and some Scolytidae (ambrosia beetles)	1/50 in. to ⅛ in. (0.5 mm to 3 mm) long	circular, 1/50 in. to ⅛ in. (0.5 mm to 3 mm) in diameter

[a] The pronotum is the dorsal aspect (the top) of the first part of the thorax. In other beetle groups, some of which are also called powderpost beetles, this segment covers the head.

[b] In hardwoods, pellets may be absent and frass packed tight.

Tunnels	Frass	Habits
circular, 1/16 in. (1.5 mm) in diameter	fine, flour-like, loose in tunnels	attacks only sapwood of ring-porous and diffuse-porous hardwoods with high starch content; reinfests milled lumber
circular, up to 1/8 in. (3 mm) in diameter, numerous and random	fine powder with elongate pellets conspicuous, loosely packed in isolated clumps of different sizes; tends to stick together[b]	some attack both softwoods and hardwoods, others attack only one or the other; reinfest milled lumber
circular, 1/16 in. to 3/8 in. (1.5 mm to 9.5 mm) in diameter	fine to coarse powder, tightly packed, tends to stick together	attacks sapwood primarily in hardwoods and less in softwoods; little danger of reinfestation after first generation
very flat and winding, three to four times as wide as high, tightly packed with sawdust-like borings and pellets, walls scarred with fine, transverse lines	tightly packed in tunnels	rarely emerges in buildings; damage potential low; not a reinfester
can tunnel through plasterboard, hardboard, hardwood flooring, insulation, roofing felt, shingles, plywood; tunnel size varies by species	tightly packed, coarse frass may be present, or may have fallen in from gallery wall	most are not reinfesters; the exception is the old house borer (Hylotrupes bajulus), which attacks softwoods, especially conifers such as pine and fir
larvae make characteristic fan-shaped engraving in cambial layer beneath bark; only the surface is etched; size of engravings varies	tightly packed	pest of minor significance in seasoned wood but very damaging in forest; damage is commonly found in houses built with infested wood; not a reinfester
honeycombed when population is large; common to find adults feeding in the wood	consists of very fine powder and tiny pellets packed in galleries; similar to anobiids', but smaller	attacks sap and heartwood of hardwoods, softwoods and plywood; damage potential related to amount of dampness and decay; can reinfest
holes bored straight for several inches across grain; inside the wood, sapwood tunnel may branch and follow annual tree ring; the fungus stains gallery walls black, blue or brown	galleries free of frass	inoculates wood with fungus, which it feeds upon; often seen in hardwood, but abandons wood below 30% moisture; dry wood safe to use

in the direction of the grain. They make larger and larger tunnels as they grow and pack them with their fecal pellets. Eventually the tunnels become so numerous that they intersect, and the wood becomes a mass of fragments. It may take two to three years for the larva to complete its development, but during that period a combination of heat and drying out of the wood may slow its maturation or even kill it.

When ready to pupate, usually in the spring, the larva cleans out a portion of the tunnel and enlarges it slightly. The adults bore holes straight out of the wood and seek mates, starting the cycle again. A large proportion of the females lay eggs in the same wood from which they emerged.

Cerambycid Old House Borers. Unlike other cerambycids, the old house borer *(Hylotrupes bajulus)* does not need a bark covering on the wood it attacks. It has been shown to attack lumber in new houses more than in older homes, and prefers pine, spruce, hemlock and fir; it cannot develop in lumber from deciduous trees. The old house borer occurs along the East Coast and the Gulf of Mexico to Texas.

The female lays her eggs in cracks and crevices on the surface of wood, and the hatched larvae sometimes crawl around before finding a place through which they can bore into the wood. They remain near the surface, feeding on the sapwood and only gradually penetrating deeper as they grow. Larvae do not attack the heartwood.

The larval period may be completed in two to three years, but it can take as long as 12 or 15 years in very dry wood, such as that found in attics. Old house borer tunnels have a very distinctive appearance, with ring-like striations on their walls that form a rippled pattern, like sand over which water has washed. Unless the moisture content is high, the tunneling proceeds very slowly. Unlike the anobiids, old house borers do not

need yeasts in their gut to help them digest the cellulose in the wood.

The adults may remain within the tunnels for some time before emerging to mate, usually in the mid or late summer. Because they may emerge one at a time over a period of years, they may cause more alarm than is justified by the amount of damage they do or the speed at which they do it. They also are very sensitive to temperature changes, a fact which appears to be limiting their spread in the United States to those areas without great temperature fluctuations.

Non-Reinfesters. It is worth learning something about the beetles that cannot reinfest wood after they emerge, because their presence is often mistakenly used as the justification for whole-house fumigation. These are the beetles that attack forest trees, usually weakened specimens, before they are harvested. The larvae, or "grubs," inside these trees remain inside the wood during milling and emerge later as adults. Some of these beetles lay eggs within bark crevices on freshly cut trees. If the wood is uncured or improperly cured at the lumberyard, the larvae of these beetles are then built into homes. Later they emerge as adults from ceiling beams and subflooring, sometimes boring their way through polished hardwood floors, other floor coverings, wall plaster and even ceramic bathroom tiles.

Beetles of this type are the flat-headed borers in the family Buprestidae, round-headed borers in the family Cerambycidae (the old house borer described above is an exception) and bark and timber beetles in the family Scolytidae (which are also called ambrosia beetles). These beetles are unable to reinfest because they must have either bark, the cambium layer or living xylem for the placement of eggs. This type of wood is not found within structures because the outer sapwood is trimmed off at the lumber mill. Once these beetles emerge, they perish without

laying the eggs that would start a new generation.

Some non-reinfesters may emerge over a period of weeks or months, leading to the erroneous conclusion that new infestations have occurred. But treatment for these beetles, other than repair or replacement of the damaged wood, is usually an unnecessary expense.

Detection and Monitoring

To identify the type of beetle, note:
• the size and shape of its exit hole,
• whether it has infested a hardwood or a softwood,
• whether the infested wood is new or old (all the beetles under discussion attack new wood, but only three of the reinfesting types attack old wood), and
• what its frass looks like in the tunnels or in piles nearby.

By comparing the damage characteristics and the age and type of wood in which the beetle was found to the information in Table 25.1 on pp. 458-459, you should be able to make an adequate identification of beetle type. To confirm your identification, take a specimen and/or a sample of the damaged wood with frass to your local cooperative extension office or to the entomology department at the nearest state college.

If wood-boring beetles are a problem in your area, inspect your house yearly; if you have an annual termite inspection, the beetle inspection should be part of it. Look for entry and exit holes made by the beetles, signs of sawdust, minute wood fragments and/or wood that does not appear to be solid (see the drawing on the facing page). You can detect weakened wood by knocking on its surface and listening for a hollow sound or by probing the surface with a sharp instrument such as an ice pick.

Again, we must emphasize that discovering beetle damage is not necessarily evidence of an active infestation. Exit holes or frass indicate only that beetles were there at one time. The adults that made the exit holes may have been the last beetles that will ever emerge. The condition of the wood and other environmental factors may not support another generation of beetles.

Signs that the infestation is still active include fresh frass the color of new-sawn wood and live larvae or adults in the wood. Where you suspect an infestation of beetles such as old house borers that do not emerge for several years, you can confirm their presence by listening, preferably with the help of a doctor's stethoscope, for the chewing sounds they make inside the wood. An alternative is to place a cloth or paper beneath suspicious areas for a day or two. A live infestation will produce fresh debris and feces.

With beetle species that reinfest, determining the extent of the infestation may be difficult. Some beetles have a long development time and may be within lumber or furniture when it is installed, making assessment of their presence and the extent of their damage more difficult. The true extent of the damage may not be revealed until some of the wood is removed and examined. Take this into account when you negotiate a contract for repairs. It may not be possible to assess the full size of the job until the work is underway; financial agreements should take that into account.

Determining the full extent of an infestation is the kind of job that is tackled best by the sensitive nose of a beagle or other dog trained to sniff out structural pests. The use of such dogs is described in detail under termites on p. 436.

Treatment:
Indirect Strategies

As with any pest problem, prevention is the best control. The preventive tactics discussed here have been adapted from an excellent booklet, *Wood-Inhabiting Insects in Houses,* by Harry B. Moore (listed under References and Readings on pp. 464-465).

1. Inspecting Lumber and Other Wood Items. Inspect each piece of lumber for small holes and sawdust or tiny wood fragments before using it. Antiques and imported wooden crafts should also be examined. The authors recently glanced into a gift shop window and saw sawdust and exit holes around an imported wooden bowl. This damage had gone unnoticed by the salespeople. Potential purchasers would very likely also have failed to detect it. If you purchase an object like this, it is important to determine whether the beetles are of the type that are likely to infest the house or shop, or whether the problem has ended with their emergence. Exposing the item to heat treatment (described under "Physical Controls" on p. 463) might solve the problem either way.

2. Using Seasoned Lumber. Although close visual inspection of

---

Wood-Boring Beetle Damage

Wood infested by lyctid powderpost beetles (A) is typified by long, cylindrical galleries about 1⁄16 in. (1.5 mm) in diameter and loosely packed with fine frass. Old house borer galleries (B) are about 1⁄3 in. (8.5 mm) wide and have a surface with a rippled pattern, much like sand washed by waves. They are filled loosely with frass. C shows a typical gallery of a bark beetle, which damages wood just under the bark before it is milled, but does not reinfest dried wood. Ambrosia beetle damage (D) is characterized by circular holes and tunnels between 1⁄50 in. and 1⁄8 in. (0.5 mm and 3 mm) in diameter. The darkly stained tunnels are free of frass and run mainly across the grain. These beetles do not reinfest dried wood.

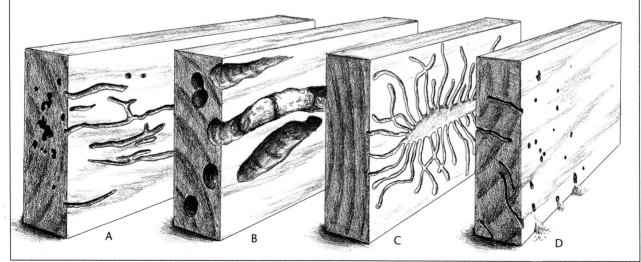

wood is essential, it is not a guarantee against beetle infestation. Some infestations can go undiscovered for years before damage is seen. You can guard against this by using kiln-dried or air-dried lumber in all construction projects. The drying process kills many types of beetles, including all stages of the lyctid or true powderpost beetle, considered to be among the most serious of the reinfesting beetles in the United States.

3. Sealing Exposed Surfaces. Another good preventive tactic, particularly against infestation by lyctid beetles, is sanding and coating susceptible woods with varnish, shellac or paint. These coatings fill the pores in the wood, eliminating the habitat necessary for egg laying.

By sealing surfaces in and outside the house with such materials, you make it difficult for powderpost beetles to find entry points. There is no need to coat storage containers or other wooden items around the house that are made from pine or other softwoods, because these are unattractive to powderpost beetles (they confine their attacks to bamboo and large-pored hardwoods such as oak, ash, hickory and mahogany). The furniture beetle, an anobiid, is also unlikely to lay eggs in painted or varnished woods.

4. Controlling Moisture. Reducing moisture levels within the house is also effective in preventing beetle infestations. Moore writes:

Good ventilation and drainage and proper clearance between wood and soil will tend to reduce the equilibrium moisture content of wood in the structure and thus render conditions less favorable for beetle development. The need for good clearance and ventilation is more important in the Gulf Coast areas, where high humidity and mild winter climates may allow wood framing in walls and attics, as well as crawl spaces, to retain relatively high moisture levels and support greater beetle activity.

5. Storing Firewood away from the House. Firewood infested with powderpost beetles when it is brought into the house can give rise to an infestation. It should be stored outdoors until just before use. If possible, make two outdoor piles, the main one at the greatest practical distance from the house and a much smaller, temporary one nearer by. The smaller pile can be eliminated during those seasons when no firewood is burned. Scrap pieces of wood should be burned and not allowed to accumulate around the house perimeter.

6. De-barking Logs. De-barking stored logs provides additional protection against wood-boring beetles that need bark to initiate their tunnels and egg laying. People who have elm trees are familiar with the need for storing elm wood in a de-barked state, since the beetles that spread Dutch elm disease cannot survive after the bark has been removed.

Treatment:
Direct Physical Controls

Direct physical controls for wood-boring beetles include replacing damaged wood, habitat modification and treatment with an electrical current or heat.

1. Replacing Damaged Wood. Replacing or repairing beetle-damaged wood is frequently the only step necessary after a beetle infestation is discovered, since many beetle species do not reinfest the wood after they have emerged. If the beetle species that caused the damage is identified as a reinfester, repaired wood should be coated with paint or shellac to prevent reinfestation.

2. Altering Moisture Levels and Other Environmental Conditions. Deathwatch beetles and old house borers are extremely susceptible to heat, fluctuating temperatures and, most of all, lack of moisture. The furniture beetle *(Anobium punctatum)* is one of the deathwatch beetles that causes serious damage in Europe and is also found in the United States. It infests only wood that has already been par-

tially predigested by fungi—a sure sign that there is a moisture problem where the beetle was found.

Deathwatch beetles are mainly a problem in unheated buildings in moist regions such as the Northwest. The same need for moisture is true of the old house borer. Laboratory studies indicate that the old house borer does not flourish where temperature and humidity fluctuate significantly. Wood blocks with larvae placed in attic, basement and laboratory areas in Virginia showed that average ambient conditions typical of attics (75°F/24°C, and a relative humidity of 66% to 86%) were not favorable to larval growth (although the fact that a Virginia attic experiences huge temperature extremes is probably a significant factor). In the laboratory, the conditions most favorable to larvae were 86°F (30°C) and a relative humidity of 72% to 92%.

In summary, Moore writes:

Alteration of environmental conditions in the house might one day be the only procedure necessary to eliminate some infestations of wood-boring beetles.... It is a well-established fact that no wood-boring beetles found in houses develop rapidly in wood that is very dry. There are indications that the most common anobiid beetles cannot establish an infestation in wood below about 15 percent moisture content. For the old house borer, the moisture requirement for establishment is probably more than 10 percent. If the use of vapor barriers, ventilation and central heat can dry wood out and keep it dry enough, the use of other control measures may not be necessary.

This method would not be a rapid means of control, and probably would not completely replace others. At the present time, it can only be recommended that every effort be made to reduce the moisture content of the wood to be protected. When the building is centrally heated, the drying process after construction is speeded up and the house becomes less susceptible to beetle attack more quickly, and it usually remains so as long as the house is regularly occupied and remains heated for extended periods.

Vacation or recreation structures tend to be more prone to extensive beetle attack because they often are not centrally heated or are heated only intermittently for relatively short periods. Leaving structures closed and unheated for long periods allows the moisture content of the wood to rise to higher levels than would otherwise be the case. Proper attention to good attic ventilation is even more important in the prevention of beetles than in the prevention of termites. If attics are well ventilated, in most regions they tend to dry out below the level of moisture needed for vigorous beetle attack. This is particularly true of the roof framing and sheathing.

3. Electrical Current. An important new tool for the control of wood-infesting insects is the Electrogun™, described in detail on p. 439 under the discussion of termites. In the hands of a trained operator, this instrument, which sends an electrical current with extremely high voltage at low wattage into the wood, kills insects within the wood without leaving toxic residues or harming the operator or the house.

Although initially resisted by some segments of the pest control industry who feared its use would take business away from companies long accustomed to providing more traditional fumigation services, the Electrogun™ is slowly gaining in popularity. Where it is necessary to kill a beetle infestation within paneling or other wood that cannot be removed and replaced, we suggest you investigate the use of this tool. If you find that local pest control companies are unfamiliar with it, refer them to Etex, Ltd., the manufacturer of the gun (listed in the Resource Appendix under "Suppliers" on pp. 690-696).

4. Heat Treatment. The use of heat to control infestations of wood-boring beetles has been proven effective in experiments by scientists Walter Ebeling and Charles Forbes. This technique is marketed as the Thermal Pest Eradication™ system by Isothermics, Inc. It is available through local pest control companies in many communities.

In field studies on historic buildings maintained by the National Park Service at Buffalo National River, Arkansas, the temperature in flooring infested with powderpost beetles was raised to 120°F (49°C) with a 90-lb. portable heater containing a fan and a propane-fueled heating unit. Hot air was blown into crawl spaces to heat severely infested floors from below, and reinforced aluminized heat-reflecting fabric tarps were placed over the floors to help retain the heat. It took three to six hours to bring the temperature in the wood up to the required 120°F, where it was held for 30 minutes. The treatment killed virtually all beetles in the heavily infested buildings.

Treatment: Direct Chemical Controls

Conventional chemical controls used against wood-boring beetles include fumigation with methyl bromide or sulfuryl fluoride and spraying with chlorpyrifos (Dursban®). Less-toxic alternatives include application of borates, pyrethrin/silica aerogel and synthetic pyrethroids. We discuss these less-toxic materials first.

1. Borates. Borax-based products such as TIM-BOR® or Bora-Care™ can be painted or sprayed on wood as a barrier to beetles. These materials have low toxicity to mammals but are lethal to beetles. For more details on borates, see pp. 112-114.

2. Pyrethrin/Silica Aerogel. An insecticidal dust that combines pyrethrin and silica aerogel is marketed as Revenge® (see the Resource Appendix under "Insect Management: Chemi-

cal Controls" on pp. 686-687). It comes in an aerosol can fitted with a tiny applicator tube, and can be applied in and around the exit holes of reinfesting beetles. This material can also be blown into wall voids, attics and crawl spaces where human access is limited.

Beetles that come into contact with the material soon after it is applied will be killed. After the pyrethrin has dissipated, the silica aerogel acts as a residual insecticide, killing later-emerging beetles by abrading their exoskeletons and causing dehydration.

3. Synthetic Pyrethroids. Synthetic pyrethroids are analogs of the natural insecticide pyrethrum, a member of the chrysanthemum family, that have been made more toxic in the laboratory (see the discussion of pyrethrum products on pp. 121-122). A synthetic pyrethroid registered for use against wood-boring beetles is cypermethrin (Demon® T.C.).

The advantage synthetic pyrethroids have over chlorpyrifos from a health point of view is that they degrade rapidly in the presence of sunlight. Thus, if there is an improper application or accidental spill and some of the material becomes volatilized in the air, it dissipates within hours or a day; chlorpyrifos, by contrast, can remain active for months or years.

4. Methyl Bromide. The fumigant methyl bromide is one of the most common chemical control agents for wood-boring beetles. In a typical application, the entire house is covered with a large plastic tent, and this highly toxic gas is released throughout the structure. Residents must vacate the premise for two to three days to allow the gas to dissipate. Confining fumigation to only those areas where beetle damage is evident has been tried, but with little success.

Among the shortcomings of this procedure are its high cost—in the thousands of dollars for a home—and the fact that although the treatment may reduce or eliminate an existing infestation, it does not provide protection from new invasions of beetles. Moreover, as Moore indicates, there is an unexplained 10% failure rate when using methyl bromide to control lyctid beetles.

5. **Sulfuryl Fluoride.** Even though this highly toxic chemical fumigant, also known as Vikane®, does not kill beetle eggs effectively, it is used widely at high dosages (to compensate for its limited ability to kill eggs). The high dosage necessarily increases the cost.

6. **Chlorpyrifos.** Spot-treating the surface of wood damaged by reinfesting beetles with the organophosphate insecticide chlorpyrifos (Dursban®) might reduce reinfestation by killing adults as they chew their way out of the wood and larvae as they emerge from eggs laid on the surface of the wood. This approach takes into account the fact that many woodborers tend to lay their eggs in the same wood from which they have emerged. For details on this material, see the discussion of chemical controls for termites on pp. 441-442.

7. **Pressure-Injection of Chemicals.** Some pest control companies have

---

Summary: Least-Toxic Wood-Boring Beetle Control

• Take steps to prevent beetle damage, including making annual inspections for beetles, building with kiln-dried or air-dried wood, sealing wood surfaces, reducing indoor moisture levels and de-barking and storing firewood away from the house.

• Identify the beetle species causing the damage. If it is a non-reinfester, there is no need to do anything; if it is a reinfester, follow the procedures below.

• Replace or seal damaged wood.

• Use electricity to kill beetles on a spot-treatment basis.

• Use heat treatments to kill beetles on a wide scale.

• If you must spot-treat with chemical controls, use borax-based products, a pyrethrin/silica aerogel mix, synthetic pyrethroids or chlorpyrifos.

---

tried pressure-injecting insecticides into damaged wood within the house structure. This procedure is not recommended, however, because wood absorbs the chemicals very erratically, the effectiveness is not predictable and the cost of the treatment is very high. But you might consider using pressure-treated construction lumber if you are replacing damaged wood in areas where chronic moisture problems cannot be corrected. This should be a last resort, however, since the less you use pressure-treated wood, the better. For more information on using pressure-treated wood, see p. 423.

REFERENCES AND READINGS

Cannon, K.F., and W.H. Robinson. 1981. Old house borer larvae: factors affecting wood consumption and growth. *Pest Control* 49(2):25-28.

This study suggests that in areas where the daily temperature and humidity fluctuate widely (ranges are specified), the growth of old house borer larvae and their wood consumption is reduced.

Ebeling, W. 1975. *Urban Entomolgy.* Berkeley: University of California Publications. 695 pp.

Includes a good general discussion of powderpost beetle biology.

Ito, T., and C. Hirose. 1980. Effects of certain insecticides on *Lyctus brunneus* Stephens (Coleoptera: Lyctidae). *Applied Entomology and Zoology.* 15(3): 293-298.

This study found that the synthetic pyrethroid permethrin was as effective at controlling beetles as were chlordane and other insecticides commonly used against these insects.

Levy, M.P. 1975. *A guide to the inspection of new houses and houses under construction for conditions which favor attack by wood-inhabiting fungi and insects.* Washington, D.C.: U.S. Department of Housing and Urban Development. 42 pp. (Available from: HUD User, P.O. Box 280, Germantown, MD 20767.)

A pamphlet with color photographs and line drawings showing those areas around a house where beetles often attack wood. Color photos also help identify the damage.

Levy, M.P. 1975. *A guide to the inspection of exising homes for wood-inhabiting fungi and insects.* Washington, D.C.: U.S. Department of Housing and Urban Development. 104 pp.

A longer version of the previous listing covering more pest problems.

Mallis, A. 1982. *Handbook of pest control.* New York: MacNair-Dorland. 1,101 pp.

This classic on household pests is still the best overall source for information on most structural pests, although it emphasizes the traditional use of pesticides.

Moore, H.B. 1979. *Wood-inhabiting insects in houses: their identification, biology, prevention and control.* Washington, D.C.: USDA Forest Service and the Department of Housing and Urban Development. 133 pp.

This paperback covers groups of wood-damaging insects, with numerous line drawings of construction details and insects and their damage.

Moore, H.B. 1978. The old house borer: An update. *Pest Control* 46 (3,4,5).

A three-part series describing the biology of the old house borer, as well as inspection, detection and treatment methods.

Moore, W.S., and C.S. Koehler. 1980. *Powderpost beetles and their control.* Berkeley: University of California (Cooperative Extension Leaflet 21017). 8 pp.

A short booklet on the detection and treatment of powderpost beetles. It discusses painting wood as an effective control.

Orsler, R.J., and M.W.S. Stone. 1972. Remedial spray treatments used against insect attack. Part I: permanence and distribution. *Material und Organismen* 17(3):161-180.

This study found that insecticides sprayed on wood damaged by beetle larvae were largely ineffective due to uneven and superficial penetration of the wood grain.

Rudinsky, J.A., ed. 1979. *Forest insect survey and control.* 4th ed. Corvallis, Oreg.: Oregon State University Bookstores. 472 pp.

A good referenced introduction to beetle biology and control.

U.S. Forest Products Laboratory. 1974. *Wood handbook: wood as an engineering material.* Washington, D.C.: USDA (Agr. Handbook 72, revised). 30 pp.

Includes a key that uses damage characteristics to identify certain beetle species.

Young, E.D. 1976. *Training manual for the structural pesticide applicator.* Washington, D.C.: U.S. Environmental Protection Agency. 168 pp. (Available from: EPA Office of Pesticide Programs, Washington, D.C. 20460.)

Good introductory information, drawings and recommendations for detection and control; the manual stresses the value of painting wood surfaces for prevention.

PART 8

Pests in the Garden

CHAPTER 26
Garden Design and Maintenance

INTRODUCTION

It seems to be human nature to respond to emergencies rather than to plan ahead and avoid them. Once a pest problem becomes intolerable, most people will seek and follow advice on pest control. But they are far less motivated to do so when there is no problem in sight. This is unfortunate because most pest problems in food-producing and ornamental home gardens can be prevented or greatly reduced during the initial design or regular maintenance of the garden.

When we speak of garden design, we mean the selection of the components of the system. These include the individual plants, their placement in relation to each other and the microclimate and soils of the site. There are two elementary rules of good garden design:

1. Select plants that are generally suited to the climate and soils of your area, require no more maintenance time and skill than you can give them and are most resistant to the common diseases or other pests of your area.

2. Place plants in relation to each other and the site in a way that provides necessary growing space, light, drainage and wind protection.

If you look at human-designed landscapes, you will discover that these two rules are often broken. Amateur and professional landscapers tend to focus on aesthetics to the exclusion of the practical problems of maintenance. In so doing, they build in pest problems from the start. If you want to manage your garden with a minimum of hazardous pesticides, you cannot afford to overlook these basic rules.

There are other considerations, too. Nearly everyone would agree that ideal garden design should preserve the balance of nature—the harmonious coexistence of plants, birds, insects and other organisms. Most of us also want as much beauty or food as possible from our gardens with as little effort as possible. Designing a garden system that largely maintains its own balance of pests and controls is the only way to achieve this goal.

THE DIFFERENCE BETWEEN HUMAN-DESIGNED AND NATURAL SYSTEMS

Without arguing whether a balance of nature still exists in natural areas undisturbed by human activities, you will doubtless agree that some very striking and relevant characteristics distinguish those environments from the ones we humans create. The most noticeable difference is that human-designed systems are greatly simplified in the number and arrangement of species they support compared to the complexity of undisturbed natural environments.

Ecologists may debate the extent to which species diversity contributes to ecosystem stability in specific settings. Nonetheless, it is very clear that the young, simplified systems typical of the common garden lack some of the protective mechanisms of more complex natural systems. Simplified systems are more subject to the wide fluctuations in pest and pathogen numbers we have come to expect in the cultivated plot. These fluctuations manifest themselves as pest emergencies that send us scrambling to the closest neighbor or plant nursery for advice on what to use to kill the offending organism.

This is the result of the simplified way in which we plan and care for our gardens. We assume that a healthy garden consists of a specific number of specimens of identifiable, desirable species of plants and animals. This notion, which focuses on individual organisms we recognize as desirable—for example, a rose bush, a cabbage plant, a honeybee or a lady beetle—inevitably leads to the assumption that all other organisms are undesirable and should be excluded. In our minds, these other organisms are now pests. As a consequence, we make a continuous effort to eliminate them, in most cases before careful observation and analysis suggest that they really deserve this fate.

Organisms live in communities. The complex interactions within these communities are the most reliable mechanisms for achieving and maintaining stability in an ecosystem. It is not just the presence or absence of a particular pest insect, plant pathogen or weed seed that determines the health of the garden. It is the composition and interaction of all these communities of organisms that ultimately determine the absence or presence of pest problems.

These communities are in the air surrounding the plants, on all the surfaces of the plants, above and below the ground, on the ground surface and between soil particles. Often they form extremely intimate internal associations with the plants, such as the relationship between plants and the mycorrhizal fungi or nitrogen-producing bacteria that assist plants in acquiring nutrients. A myriad of life forms, most too small to notice with the naked eye, most without common names and many difficult to identify, make up the true plant and garden environment. Any garden model that does not recognize the desirability of this natural complexity dooms the gardener to an endless battle against one plague after another.

DEVELOPING AN ECOSYSTEM PERSPECTIVE

A more complex, more realistic ecosystem perspective suggests a different approach to garden design and maintenance. It tends to evoke curiosity about and respect for the life forms encountered in the garden, and it fosters an innocent-unless-proven-guilty attitude toward new organisms. Ultimately, it leads to fewer pest emergencies and less frantic pest control.

This belief in the benefits of diversity is by no means a new discovery by modern ecologists. It was the intuitive agricultural practice of numerous "primitive" cultures, and today it is a basic tenet of the organic or biological agricultural movement. Unfortunately, recognition of this basic idea in no way lessens the disdain with which the latter movement has been regarded until recently by scientific horticulturalists and agronomists in the scientific community.

A 1960 USDA home and garden pamphlet pictures rows of vegetables spaced neatly apart in bare earth containing relatively little organic matter. A thin veneer of regularly applied preventive pesticide sprays ensures plastic-perfect foliage and the virtual absence of creepy-crawlies and nasty weeds. Now, by contrast, envision the heavily mulched, low-maintenance plots depicted in American organic garden literature or the densely planted beds of the much-publicized European and Asian intensive agricultural systems.

Consider also the native Latin American "dump heap" gardens so eloquently described by Edgar Anderson in *Plants, Man and Life*. In such native gardens, vegetables and flowers are mixed together and cover almost every available surface. After examining one Guatemalan plot in detail, Anderson concluded:

> In terms of our American and European equivalents the garden was a vegetable garden, an orchard, a medicinal garden, a dump heap, a compost heap, and a bee yard. There was no problem of erosion, though it was at the top of a steep slope; the soil surface was practically all covered and apparently would be during most of the year. Humidity would be kept up during the dry season and plants of the same sort were so isolated from one another by intervening vegetation that pests and diseases could not readily spread from plant to plant. The fertility was being conserved; in addition to the waste from the house, mature plants were being buried between the rows when their usefulness was over.

Even without the benefit of scientific research, these gardeners intuitively understood the importance of several basic assumptions that flow from an ecosystem perspective. We summarize them here and offer practical advice on how to achieve them.

1. Diversity in the garden should be encouraged (see the drawing on the facing page).
• Introduce a wide variety of flowering or fruiting plants.
• Select species so that something is in bloom at all times, even in the food garden.
• Protect and encourage a variety of recognizable predatory garden wildlife, such as toads, frogs, spiders, lizards, snakes and ground beetles.
• Avoid the area-wide use of any pesticide, no matter how selective or nontoxic it is to humans.

2. Bare soils are undesirable because they invite weeds, are subject to compaction by rain and foot traffic, and tend to lose organic matter through wind and exposure to sunlight.
• Mulch the soil surface.
• Shade the soil through correct plant spacing, cover-cropping, interplanting and multiple cropping strategies.

3. A variety of desirable macro- and microorganisms live in the soil.
• Incorporate organic matter — the microbes' food source — into the soil.
• Provide a residue of organic matter at the soil surface.

4. Plants influence one another in the garden.
• Plant one type of plant next to another to maximize pest control and other benefits derived from the association. Unfortunately, most information available on such "companion planting" is folklore that has never been proven or disproven scientifically (see p. 474). You will need to keep abreast of the horticultural literature to learn the results of new research.

5. Some damage from pests is natural and desirable.
• Take pest control action only if the amount of damage is or will become intolerable.
• Deliberately allow the presence of some pest insects so their natural enemies will also be present.

We look at these five basic ideas in greater detail below.

Encouraging Diversity in the Garden

It is desirable to grow a variety of flowering plants, even mixed among or bordering the vegetable patch, because of the many benefits a diversified garden community provides. Try to have one plant or another flowering throughout the growing season.

Many of the predatory and parasitic insects that feed on garden pests need nectar and pollen from flowers for nourishment in order to lay eggs. The California Department of Transportation capitalized on this fact in controlling a caterpillar pest on median strip plantings on roadways. The objective was to increase the number of parasitic miniwasp attacks on pest caterpillars. The parasitoids were already present in these plantings and did a good job of controlling the caterpillar through early June of each year, but after that the rate of parasitism fell dramatically.

In work carried out by Dudley Pinnock and James Milstead at the University of California in the early 1970s, several plants were examined for attractiveness to the beneficial parasitic miniwasp and for a tendency to flower from June through the summer months. Ultimately one plant was selected and tested in field trials. The increase in parasitism was dramatic and effective and the plants were added to the highway landscape at regular intervals where the pest problem occurred. This successful use of a flowering plant to enhance biological control of a pest insect was part of a larger biological control project that has saved the transportation

Healthy Gardens Have Great Diversity

Gardens with a high degree of ecological diversity are healthier and more productive than those with a limited number of plant and animal species. In this garden, a variety of flowering plants provides nectar to a wide range of beneficial insects. Birds help control pest insects, and mulch inhibits weeds and provides a rich organic medium for the growth of beneficial microbes that aid in nutrient uptake by plant roots and compete against pathogens.

department a considerable amount of money over the years.

Unfortunately, there has been too little research into which plants can be added to which settings to aid the home gardener in biological control of garden pests. But it is known that it is wise to include a number of shallow-throated flowering species in the garden, since many of the hymenopteran parasitoids of aphids, scales, mealybugs, caterpillars and other organisms are very tiny and compete poorly with honeybees and other larger hymenopteran insects for nectar from deep-throated flowers.

In his well-researched book, *Designing and Maintaining Your Edible Landscape Naturally,* Robert Kourik notes that plants in the parsley family (Apiaceae, formerly Umbelliferae) and in the sunflower family (Aster-aceae, formerly Compositae) are especially accessible to beneficial insects. Plants in the parsley family include carrots, celeriac, Florence fennel, dill, cumin, anise, coriander and caraway. Sunflower family plants include artichoke, lettuce, endive, daisy, dandelion, edible chrysanthemum, sunflower, yarrow, artemisia, marigold, zinnia, aster and gazania.

Table 26.1 on pp. 472-473 summarizes Kourik's suggestions for potential insectary plants (plants that feed beneficial insects). However, Kourik adds a caution: "While we may be able to somewhat shape the insect ecology of our yards by the types of flowering plants we grow, keep in mind that there is very little research on the subject, and I run the risk of starting new myths by mentioning specific plants and specific insects."

Kourik recommends that you observe flowers planted in your area to see which attract such easily recognized predators as syrphid or hover flies, which are important aphid controls, or the larger wasps that prey on caterpillars. A book like *Rodale's Color Handbook of Garden Insects* by Anne Carr that pictures each insect clearly and summarizes its habits and prey can be a great help. Leaf through the sections of the book devoted to those insect groups containing the largest number of important natural enemies of common insect pests. Gradually you can become quite knowledgeable about the various types of insects likely to be predators of pests, even if you never learn their scientific names or identify their species. You should also consult Chapter 5 of this book for further help in recognizing the beneficials in your garden.

If you live in an urban or suburban setting, you should be aware that protecting and maintaining a variety of wildlife in the garden is not always easy. Domestic cats that roam from yard to yard are likely to prey on lizards, snakes and toads, and they also hunt down larger insects, such as black ground beetles, that are very important predators of pests.

Table 26.1
Plants that Attract Beneficial Insects[a]

Common Name	Scientific Name	Beneficial Insects Attracted
alfalfa	*Medicago sativa*	minute pirate bugs, big-eyed bugs, damsel bugs, assassin bugs, lady beetles, parasitic wasps
angelica	*Angelica* spp.	lady beetles; lacewings; sand wasps
baby-blue-eyes	*Nemophila menziesii*	syrphid flies
buckwheat	*Fagopyrum esculentum*	syrphid flies
California buckwheat	*Eriogonum* spp.	sand wasps; tachinid, chloropid and syrphid flies; minute pirate bugs
California coffeeberry	*Rhamnus californica*	tachinid and syrphid flies; lady beetles; sand, ichneumonid and braconid wasps; lacewings
camphorweed	*Heterotheca subaxillaris*	tachinid and syrphid flies, lady beetles, ichneumonid and braconid wasps, lacewings
candytuft	*Iberis umbellata*	syrphid flies
carrot	*Daucus carota*	minute pirate bugs; big-eyed bugs; assassin bugs; lacewings; parasitic and predacious wasps
coriander	*Coriandrum sativum*	tachinid flies
coyote brush	*Baccharis pilularis*	syrphid, chloropid and tachinid flies; braconid, ichneumonid, sand, and chalcid wasps
evening primrose	*Oenothera laciniata* and *Oenothera biennis*	ground beetles
evergreen euonymus	*Euonymus japonica*	lacewings; chloropid, tachinid, and syrphid flies; chalcid, braconid, sand and ichneumonid wasps; lady beetles
fennel	*Foeniculum vulgare*	braconid and sand wasps; syrphid and tachinid flies

[a] From Kourik, 1986.

These larger predators also need protection from the sun and from their own natural enemies. Unfortunately, the gardener's desire to have the garden neat and clean-looking, like a room in the house, may lead to the elimination of miscellaneous organic debris that serves as hiding places for larger insects and other predators. In order to provide wildlife with a variety of habitats, garden borders can be designed with rocks, thick organic mulches or overturned flowerpots (particularly if their rims are uneven or they are placed on lumpy, uneven ground).

Avoid the area-wide use of any pesticide, no matter how selective or nontoxic it is to humans. Any material, even a fairly innocuous one such as soap or garlic spray, has the potential to kill organisms other than the target species. The sensible rule is to spot treat. In other words, confine your pest management action to only those areas and times where the pest population is rising to an intolerable level (see p. 44 for a discussion of this concept). As a rule, you should avoid preventive spray treatments.

Keeping the Soil Surface Covered

Mulching is one way to add diversity to the garden while protecting the soil surface. The advantages are many. Bare soils are subject to erosion from wind and water, extreme temperature fluctuations, rapid reduction in organic matter due to exposure to the sun and compaction from rainfall. As mentioned above, bare earth provides little or no habitat for a variety of permanently or periodically ground-dwelling natural enemies of plant pests. And it invites colonization by less-desired plants commonly called "weeds."

Mulches can be as simple as weeds pulled from the beds and left to die where they fall, or as elegant as purchased materials such as cocoa bean hulls. Either way, they serve to protect the soil surface from sun, rain

Table 26.1 (continued)

Common Name	Scientific Name	Beneficial Insects Attracted
goldenrod	*Solidago altissima*	predacious beetles, big-eyed bugs, lady beetles, spiders, parasitic wasps, long-legged flies, assassin bugs
ivy	*Hedera* spp.	flower and tachinid flies; braconid, sand, hornet and yellowjacket wasps
meadow foam	*Limnanthes douglasii*	syrphid flies
Mediterranean umble	*Bupleurum fruticosum*	tachinid flies; sand wasps
Mexican tea	*Chenopodium ambrosioides*	assassin bugs, big-eyed bugs, lady beetles
morningglory	*Convolvulus minor*	syrphid flies, lady beetles
oleander	*Nerium oleander*	minute pirate bugs, big-eyed bugs, assassin bugs, lady beetles, soft-winged flower beetles, lacewings, syrphid flies, parasitic wasps
pigweed	*Amaranthus* spp.	ground beetles
ragweed	*Ambrosia artemisiifolia*	lady beetles, assassin bugs, spiders
rue	*Ruta graveolens*	ichneumonid wasps
saltbush	*Atriplex* spp.	sand wasps
silver lace vine	*Polygonum aubertii*	tachinid and syrphid flies
snowberry	*Symphoricarpos* spp.	flower and tachinid flies
soapbark tree	*Quillaja saponaria*	syrphid and chloropid flies; lacewings; lady beetles; ichneumonid, chalcid and braconid wasps
tree-of-heaven	*Ailanthus altissima*	syrphid and chloropid flies; braconid and ichneumonid wasps; lacewings
white clover	*Trifolium repens*	parasitic wasps of aphids, scales and whiteflies
white sweet clover	*Melilotus alba*	tachinid flies; sand, hornet and yellowjacket wasps
wild lettuce	*Lactuca canadensis*	soldier beetles, lacewings, earwigs, syrphid flies
yarrow	*Achillea* spp.	lady beetles, parasitic wasps of aphids, scales and whiteflies

and wind, and discourage the germination of weed seeds, which generally need bright light and exposed soils. Consult Table 28.1 on p. 489 for a comprehensive list of mulch materials and methods.

There are many other ways to shade the soil surface. Examples are placing plants so they grow an arching mat of foliage either at ground level or above it, seeding in a fast-growing temporary cover plant where you plan to place another plant in the future or planting faster-growing annuals between slower-growing permanent plantings so they cover the soil until the other plants shade them out. A multitude of other planting strategies can be used to ensure that one annual plant follows another in succession so the soil remains covered continuously. These methods are discussed in greater detail on pp. 490-497.

The least desirable way of covering the soil surface involves the use of inorganic materials such as plastic sheets or synthetic fabrics. Although these materials do keep weeds down and unquestionably have a small role to play in the overall garden scheme, they introduce yet more nonrecyclable plastic into the environment and do not provide the benefit of the best mulches: contributing organic material to the soil.

Feeding the Soil Organisms

Fertile soil is teeming with simple life forms—yeasts, fungi, bacteria, actinomycetes, and others—which derive sustenance from the decomposition of organic matter. They in turn produce plant nutrients in the form of relatively stable compounds and are themselves the basis of many food chains within the soil. These organisms also compete with or actively destroy potentially destructive inhabitants of soil and root surfaces.

A complex soil community with many interlocking food webs provides the greatest resistance to invasion by exotic (non-native) organisms, including plant pathogens such as bacteria and fungi, root-feeding nematodes, soil-inhabiting insects and other plant-feeding arthropods. Exotics that are blown in by the wind or carried in by birds and other mammals or that travel in of their own will find a wealth of predators, parasitoids and competitors already established. These make it difficult for the strangers to survive and multiply. Thus, encouraging a diversity of soil life, even though most of it is hidden or too small to see, is an important part of creating diversity in the garden and protecting it from exotic invaders.

There is no better food for the communities of organisms that live on and in the soil than plant and animal waste. Manure, plate scrapings, vegetable peelings and plant prunings provide nutrients for plant growth and improve soil structure. These organic materials break down into humus, which has an electrical charge and can attract and release the basic mineral compounds in the soil needed for plant growth. For further discussion of these mechanisms, see pgs. 333-336 and 512-514.

To encourage this fertility, you can bury uncomposted organic kitchen wastes directly in the garden. But it is extremely important to bury waste quickly before it attracts flies, which lay eggs in it, and deeply enough so that it does not become a source of food for rats. Ideally, each day's waste should be taken to the garden and laid under 6 in to 12 in. (15 cm to 30 cm) of earth so it doesn't accumulate. However, if there are rat burrows in the neighborhood, it is better to save the waste and use it to make batches of hot compost in a bin.

Hot batch processing of organic wastes, in which the temperature rises to 160°F to 180°F (71°C to 81°C), is by far the best procedure for processing organic wastes that are high in nitrogen. If all parts of the batch are exposed to this temperature for a week or so, weed seeds, pathogens that cause plant disease and pesticide residues are broken down into useful compounds. Hot composting, however, takes some knowledge of the process and tight wooden, brick or cinder-block bins. For more on composting, see the sidebar on p. 644.

Companion Planting

Plants influence each other in the garden. They do this by producing substances that specifically inhibit or enhance the growth of other plants, by providing alternative food sources or habitats for beneficial insects and other organisms and by discouraging the buildup of undesired organisms. They may do the latter by reducing the attraction for certain pests or by repelling them.

In response to this realization, there has been a search for specific companion plants and an increase in tolerance among gardeners for some adjacent or interspersed weed or wild plants among the garden plants. Unfortunately, the search has not yet resulted in a list of species that produce reliable results outside the specific varieties of plants in the specific soils and climates and under the particular horticultural regimes used in the original studies.

Nonetheless, the organic literature abounds in recommendations, nearly all of them unsubstantiated. The most widely publicized of these schemes is derived from a misunderstanding. We often hear gardeners say, "I have planted marigolds, but they don't do any good." Will marigolds keep pest insects away? The idea that they do apparently arose from the fact that both small marigolds (*Tagetes patula*) and large marigolds (*T. erecta*) produce a root exudate or secretion that discourages certain plant-infesting nematodes, such as the meadow or root lesion nematode (*Pratylenchus penetrans*). But nematodes are not insects; they are long, thin worms. Moreover, the kinds that infest plants are microscopic and not that common. Usually they become a problem when highly susceptible plants such as strawberries are grown season after season in the same soil, so that the nematode population can build up.

A study by the Connecticut Agricultural Experiment Station showed that when soils are infested with nematodes, planting the field solidly with marigolds for an entire season, then plowing them under, provides good nematode control for two to three years, better than any other method used for this purpose. They also found that planting marigolds for shorter periods or merely interplanting them among the other crops does not have the same effect — it must be a solid planting, much as one would plant wheat. It should also be noted that while this technique has been proven effective against nematodes, there is no evidence that marigolds repel pest insects.

Because of growing interest in less-toxic controls, there have been various scientific studies of companion plantings. In *Designing and Maintaining Your Edible Landscape Naturally*, Robert Kourik has made an outstanding effort to render these scattered reports understandable and usable. Although he suggests what might be worth experimenting with in your own garden, he does not promise panaceas. All his recommendations are fully documented, so you can read the original study if you want to know more about the precise conditions under which the plant association was found to be effective.

Learning to Live with Some Visible Pest Damage

If you adopt the attitude that some visible effects of pest activity are tolerable, you can provide a garden environment that encourages the buildup of natural enemies of the pests, which in turn reduces pest populations and ensures that the damage remains within the tolerable range. This is one of the most important and basic considerations in pest control, since there can be no natural enemy populations without pests being present in some number (see the discussions of injury level on p. 40

and biological control on pp. 49-54 for a closer look at this concept).

The most critical time in the garden's life is when it is first established. Without the complexity of plants and animals that a mature garden provides, the newly planted area is likely to suffer severely from pest damage as the season progresses. However, stability can be established gradually by patiently introducing greater and greater diversity into the planting scheme, by encouraging insect and animal communities above and below the soil surface and by practicing a restrained form of spot treatment that uses hand removal and pruning as the primary tools for pest reduction.

It is particularly advantageous to leave the remains of heavily parasitized pests so that the beneficials can emerge to carry on their work. For example, a heavy infestation of aphids on Chinese cabbage is likely to be parasitized by beneficial mini-wasps and will probably attract large numbers of egg-laying syrphid flies. If these first plantings are left to crumble where they stand, they will become the nursery for natural enemies that will control aphids on cabbage family plants grown later in the season. The natural enemies will also eat other aphids that attack a wide variety of vegetables and ornamentals.

REFERENCES AND READINGS

Anderson, E. 1952. *Plants, man and life.* Berkeley: University of California Press. 251 pp.

This personal account of the author's travels, observations and philosophy made a deep impression on us when we were starting our professional careers. Every garden we have since designed for teaching, public demonstration or food production has been influenced by Anderson's accounts of the Central American gardens he visited.

Carr, A. 1979. *Rodale's color handbook of garden insects.* Emmaus, Pa.: Rodale Press. 241 pp.

Unfortunately, there is no single reference work that provides good color photos of the beneficial insects you should be looking for in the garden. But Carr's book includes many beneficials, and most of the photos are excellent. However, the book's emphasis is on pests; you will have to glance at every page and flag the beneficials for later reference, because they are not gathered in any one section.

Kourik, R. 1986. *Designing and maintaining your edible landscape naturally.* Santa Rosa, Calif.: Metamorphic Press. 370 pp.

This book, which we recommend highly, is an inspiring and reliable guide to practical methods of designing a healthy, beautiful garden that includes both ornamentals and vegetables. The book includes an excellent summary of the scientific literature on companion planting.

CHAPTER 27
Meet the Weeds

INTRODUCTION

Nature...knows no plants as weeds.
Liberty Hyde Bailey,
"Father" of modern horticulture

If we were asked to rank the garden pests we are most frequently asked about, weeds would be high on the list. No matter what the garden area —vegetable patch, lawn, path, fence line, drainage ditch or shrub bed —weeds usually manage to gain a foothold. If left unrestrained, some species seem to envelop a garden almost overnight, often out-competing cherished vegetables or flowers for the nutrients, water and sunlight necessary for vigorous growth.

The remarkable competitive edge that many weed species appear to have over edible and ornamental plants, coupled with their ability to intrude into even the most carefully placed brick pathways or other garden structures, mystifies and frustrates many gardeners and stimulates the "see 'em and spray 'em" attitude that is responsible for chronic overuse of herbicides.

A "weed" is commonly defined as a plant growing in a place where it is not wanted. Plants can be unwanted because they compete for resources with desired species, because they cause harm to people, pets or structures or simply because someone dislikes the way they look or smell. Thus, the designation "weed" can be quite subjective—the same species can be considered a weed in one setting and a wildflower or medicinal herb in another. When surveying the weed literature or discussing this topic with any group of gardeners, however, there appears to be some consensus on the weedy nature of certain plant species, such as thistles, docks, crabgrass, ragweed, poison oak, poison ivy and many others. These species tend to have common characteristics that enable them to "take over" certain garden habitats when conditions are right.

To the degree that gardeners gain a better understanding of conditions suited to weed growth and are able to design and maintain their gardens in ways that minimize such conditions, their battle with weeds will become briefer each year, and the need to resort to toxic weed control will be minimized or eliminated. To identify the conditions that promote weed growth, it helps to review some basic principles of weed biology and ecology. Because this information is usually omitted from conventional "recipes" for weed control, we cover it in detail here.

WEEDS: THE FIRST SOIL CONSERVATIONISTS

When a place where weeds grow is examined, a little detective work usually reveals that the soil has been subjected to a disturbance at some point. That disturbance may have taken the form of cultivation to prepare the ground for new plants, grading in connection with road maintenance, overgrazing of pasture, excessive trampling or close mowing of a lawn or repeated use of herbicides to clear vegetation.

The correlation between disturbed soil and the appearance of weeds is part of a natural process called vegetation succession, whereby the first plant species to colonize a patch of bare, open soil will be displaced over time by other plant species in response to changes in the soil microhabitat. Thus a meadow left undisturbed may eventually become a forest, as shown in the drawing below.

Plant ecologists explain the appearance of weeds this way. At the very beginning of the succession pro-

Vegetation Succession
This drawing shows a simplified sequence of vegetation succession. At A, bare, low-nutrient soil is colonized by broad-leafed plants such as thistles and some grasses. As the plants die and decompose, enriching the soil, grasses predominate (B). As the soil is further enriched, woody shrubs begin to appear (C), followed by trees (D). Eventually, the trees become the predominant vegetation type (E), shading out most competing vegetation.

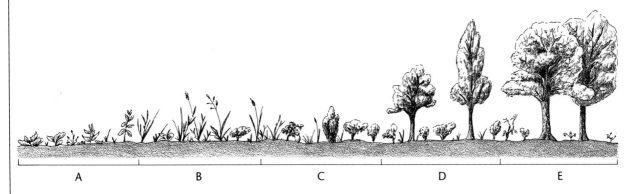

| A | B | C | D | E |

cess there is an earthquake, volcanic eruption, landslide, flood, fire or some other natural occurrence. Once the tremors stop or the floodwaters recede, an expanse of bare, exposed rock is left behind. After approximately 1,000 years of chemical and physical weathering, the rock is converted into an inch of topsoil. Left bare, these "young" soils are vulnerable to erosion by wind and water.

Certain plants have evolved to take advantage of these new or disturbed soils. As a consequence of their colonizing these areas, the soil is stabilized, erosion is reduced and the environment becomes more conducive to the growth of other plants with less-weedy characteristics. Since these disturbed soils tend to be hot, dry, unshaded habitats whose mineral nutrients are tied up in chemical forms largely unavailable to most vegetation, the plant species able to colonize such soils can do so only because they have developed special biological and behavioral mechanisms that enable them to migrate to new areas and survive in hostile locations. These plants are the very same garden nemeses that appear on every weed list: thistles, dandelions, docks, knotweeds, plantains, certain grasses and sedges, and many others.

WEED SURVIVAL STRATEGIES

One of the most important mechanisms many weeds utilize to compete against other plants is the production of large amounts of seed, which can give the weed a reproductive edge. A single curly dock plant *(Rumex crispus)* can generate up to 30,000 seeds in a single season! Table 27.1 above lists the seed production records of some familiar weeds. Moreover, weed seeds can remain dormant in the soil for many years, awaiting the right conditions for germination. In seed viability experiments conducted at the University of Michigan, curly dock seeds were found to be viable after 70 years of burial in sterile sub-

Table 27.1

Number of Seeds per Plant for Common Weeds[a]

Common Name	Scientific Name	Seeds per Plant[b]
barnyardgrass	*Echinochloa crus-galli*	7,160
black medic	*Medicago lupulina*	2,350
broadleaf plantain	*Plantago major*	36,150
Canada thistle	*Cirsium arvense*	680
common mullein	*Verbascum thapsus*	223,200
common ragweed	*Ambrosia artemisiifolia*	3,380
common sunflower	*Helianthus annuus*	7,200
crabgrass	*Digitaria sanguinalis*	8,246
curly dock	*Rumex crispus*	30,000
lambsquarters	*Chenopodium album*	72,450
mustard, black	*Brassica nigra*	13,400
mustard, white	*Brassica hirta*	2,700
Pennsylvania smartweed	*Polygonum pensylvanicum*	3,140
purslane	*Portulaca oleracea*	52,300
redroot pigweed	*Amaranthus retroflexus*	117,400
sandbur	*Cenchrus incertus*	1,110
shepherd's-purse	*Capsella bursa-pastoris*	38,500
spurge	*Euphorbia esula*	140
stinkgrass	*Eragrostis cilianensis*	82,100
wild buckwheat	*Polygonum convolvulus*	11,900
wild oats	*Avena fatua*	250
yellow foxtail	*Setaria glauca*	12,618
yellow nutsedge	*Cyperus esculentus*	2,240

[a] Data from Klingman et al., 1975; and King, 1966.
[b] Per year.

soil. But the viability record belongs to the seeds of the sacred lotus *(Nelumbo nucifera)*, found in the peat of a dried-up Manchurian lake and determined by residual carbon-14 dating to be over 1,000 years old!

Many weed species have developed special physical adaptations that allow them to use wind, water, wildlife, livestock, humans and even vehicles to travel to habitats suited to their growth and survival. The drawing at right on p. 479 illustrates some of these interesting adaptations. Perhaps the most important agents of dispersal are migratory birds, many of which fly thousands of miles in their seasonal travels. According to a report in Mea Allan's *Weeds—The Unbidden Guests in our Gardens* (listed under "References and Readings" on p. 484),

Alfred Newton, a professor of zoology at Cambridge University, sent Charles Darwin the leg of a partridge with a hard ball of earth weighing 6½ oz. [184 g] adhering to it. Darwin kept the earth for three years, but when he broke it up, watered it, and placed it under a bell glass, no fewer than 82 plants grew from it.

Annual vs. Perennial Weeds

Annual weeds reproduce only by seed and live just one season; perennial weeds reproduce both by seed and vegetatively and live two or more years.

Perennial

Annual

How Seeds Disperse

Physical adaptations enable seeds to disperse via wind and water, or by clinging to animals' coats, human clothing or other objects. The puncture vine punctures tires, shoes or feet, and becomes entangled in clothing, animal hair or fur. Cocklebur, sandbur and Spanish needle seeds cling to clothing and animal hair or wool. Dandelion seeds, with their parachutes, are carried by the wind. Curly dock seed pods are equipped with bladder-like floats.

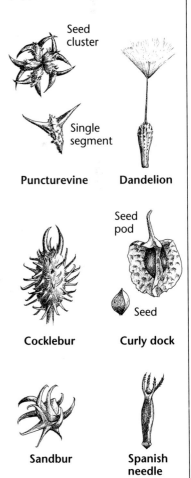

Seed cluster

Single segment

Puncturevine

Dandelion

Seed pod

Seed

Cocklebur

Curly dock

Sandbur

Spanish needle

(Adapted from Klingman, Ashton and Noordhoff, 1975.)

The most successful of the early colonizer weeds tend to be annual broad-leafed plants (shown at left in the drawing above), which have rapid life cycles that enable them to take advantage of brief periods of rainfall to germinate, shoot up, blossom, set seed and die, often within the space of a few weeks or months. Some desert species can accomplish this entire life cycle in a matter of days, often after lying dormant for years before adequate rainfall occurs. These rapid life cycles minimize the amount of nutrients and water needed for growth. The grey or grey-green foliage characteristic of many of these species reflects the heat of the sun from tender plant tissues. Such plants may also have other adaptations such as thick, waxy cuticles on leaf and stem surfaces that minimize water loss. Plants with these special characteristics include not only many of the common weeds listed in Table 27.1, but also many of the ephemeral wildflowers and herbs seen in abandoned fields and vacant lots.

Though perennial weeds (shown at right in the drawing above) also produce seeds, their main means of reproduction tends to be vegetative. They produce new top growth from buds located on the rootstalk. Using this method, a single perennial weed can cover large areas of soil in a short period. The vigorous underground rhizomes of Canada thistle (*Cirsium arvense*), for example, can spread laterally for a distance of 15 ft. (4.5 m) in a single season and produce dozens of new shoots.

Weeds and Vegetation Dynamics

When the early colonizing plants die, they are converted by soil microorganisms into organic matter. This material, called humus, improves the soil habitat by increasing overall water retention and helps make nutrients soluble and therefore available for uptake by plants. Organic matter also improves the physical structure of the soil, making it easier for plant roots to penetrate hard-packed ground in their search for minerals, water and anchorage. In sandy soil the organic matter acts like a glue, holding sand particles together and trapping water and nutrients that otherwise would be leached away.

Over time, the organic matter and shade provided by the early, primarily broad-leafed colonizer plants improves the soil microhabitat enough to allow slightly less hardy species such as annual grasses to move in. In the improved soil, grasses usually hold a competitive edge over broad-leafed plants and gradually displace them. As long as the soil remains undisturbed, the fertile organic matter produced by the constant recycling of dead plant roots and top growth continues to enrich the soil and increase water retention, creating a habitat capable of supporting longer-lived biennial and perennial grasses and broad-leafed species. Eventually shrubs and trees dominate.

This ecological process can be seen in contemporary gardens by comparing the abundance of weeds sprouting in freshly turned soil in the vegetable garden with the relative absence of weeds in perennial borders where a thick growth of shrubs, trees and groundcovers protects the soil from disturbance.

Sometimes this gradual process of succession gets stuck. For example, if the soil is frequently disturbed by flooding, cultivation or trampling, the habitat will continue to support only the hardiest of pioneering plant species. And if certain seeds, such as those of thistles, are uncovered and

exposed to sunlight or are the first to blow in and land on newly bared soil, they may become established for very long periods, refusing to yield to competing grasses or other plants despite improvement of the soil habitat. This is due to a variety of reasons, including the fact that certain plants, including many thistles, can release toxins into the soil that prevent seeds of other plants—and sometimes even their own offspring—from germinating and becoming established. This ability to inhibit the growth of potential competitors is called allelopathy, and is proving to be a promising new avenue in ecologically sound weed management. Allelopathy is discussed in detail in Chapter 28.

What does this discussion about vegetation dynamics have to do with the weeds in your garden? After all, you probably haven't had any landslides or major floods lately. However, your rototiller, lawn mower, herbicide sprayer, fenced-in dog and/or rambunctious children may be serving as surrogate acts of nature, trampling and compacting the soil, removing its vegetative cover, exposing it to the bright sun and drying it out. In other words, if weeds are a problem in your garden, it's probably because you or your family are creating the soil conditions that encourage weeds to grow. The mix of weeds that emerges is largely determined by the "seed bank" buried in your soil.

INTEGRATED WEED MANAGEMENT

Having learned about the connection between weeds and disturbed soils, you are probably wondering how you are supposed to maintain your lawn, ornamental beds, vegetable garden, orchard, pathways and fence lines without creating weed-favoring conditions. After all, isn't some tilling, mowing, hoeing or spraying required to plant and maintain such areas?

The answer is quite simple. If you want to minimize weeds in the first place or prevent their return once

you've pulled them out, dug them out or spot-treated them with herbicides, you must be certain that any tactic you use is combined with an action designed to modify the soil so it becomes unfavorable for future weed growth. It is this element of habitat modification that is missing from conventional weed control strategies (particularly those that rely exclusively on herbicides), dooming the gardener to an endless battle with weeds.

Habitat modification is a key element in an integrated approach to weed management that has three major components:
• Establishing realistic tolerance levels for weeds.
• Modifying the habitat to minimize conditions that produce more weeds than you are willing to tolerate (also called indirect suppression).
• Focusing direct suppression efforts on weed populations that threaten to exceed tolerance levels rather than on all weeds growing in the garden.

The first component of the integrated approach to weed management is discussed below; the other two components are described in detail in Chapter 28.

Establishing Tolerance Levels

Given the bad press that weeds have received over the years, many people find it difficult to develop realistic tolerance levels for weeds in their gardens. Although keeping weed populations to a minimum is definitely important to the growth and vigor of ornamental and edible garden plants as well as to overall garden appearance, complete eradication of all weeds from your garden now and forever is neither feasible nor desirable.

The oft-stated gardener's goal of a weed-free lawn, vegetable bed or flower border is fostered by a barrage of advertising with the objective of selling all kinds of hardware and chemical products that aid in the war on weeds. Take, for example, those photos of velvety-smooth "weed-free" lawns depicted in the herbicide ads. You can be 99.9% certain that if you examined random transects across those lawns, you would find that a number of weed species had set up housekeeping, staying low to the ground to avoid the mower and blending into the overall greensward captured by the camera lens. (A transect is a line drawn across an area. By identifying and recording the range of plant species along that line, you arrive at an estimate of the number of species present in a given area of soil. See p. 557 for details on the use of transects in lawn weed control.)

An annihilate-the-weeds ethic is also nurtured by much of the popular and scientific garden literature, which tends to apply to the residential garden the same economic and aesthetic standards established for agricultural crops and putting greens. Such rigid standards are not appropriate to the garden—nor, many would argue, are they realistic for agriculture or golf courses, given the large amounts of pesticides, fertilizers, water and other resources required to maintain such standards.

The bottom line is to recognize that the presence of some weeds is not only inevitable, but actually good for your garden. In *Weeds: Guardians of the Soil*, Joseph Cocannouer describes the way in which deep-rooted weeds such as thistles, pigweeds (*Amaranthus* spp.) and nightshades (*Solanum* spp.) penetrate the subsoil, increasing openings for water and root movement and absorbing minerals such as phosphorus and potassium stored in the lower soil horizons. These minerals are brought up to the topsoil, where they are made available to less aggressive plant species upon the death and decay of the weed that "mined" them.

In addition to improving soil fertility and water-holding capacity, certain weeds provide a habitat for beneficial insects and should therefore be tolerated to some degree. For example, in California the common blackberry provides nectar and shel-

ter for *Anagrus epos*, a tiny parasitoid of the grape leafhopper, which vectors a serious disease of wine and table grapes. It was discovered that by allowing hedgerows of blackberries to remain at the borders of vineyards, enough parasitoids develop to control the leafhopper. Moreover, at the East Malling Research Station in Kent, England, orchard specialists found that hedgerows of blackberries provide a habitat for a variety of beneficial organisms that control the two-spotted spider mite (*Tetranychus urticae*), a serious orchard pest.

Weeds in the sunflower (Asteraceae), parsley (Apiaceae) and mustard (Cruciferae) families are nectar sources for beneficial insects. These flowers have shallow throats whose pollen and nectar is easily available to beneficial wasp parasitoids that cannot compete with bees for these materials in deep-throated flower families such as the morningglories (Convolvulaceae).

Sometimes weeds help gardeners in unexpected ways. A good example is provided in Mea Allan's book:

F.C. King, for many years in charge of the famous garden at Levens Hall in England's Lake District, found that the best way to secure a good crop of sound onions was to allow weeds to develop in the onion bed after about the first week in July. The growing weeds, by denying the onions a supply of nitrogen, improved their keeping qualities, and by digging in the weeds in the autumn provided a supply of humus for the next crop.

Other weeds should be tolerated because they can assist the gardener by serving as "trap crops" for pest insects. By allowing these weeds to border your garden or grow in rows within the garden area, insects that otherwise would feed on your vegetables or ornamentals are attracted to the weeds instead.

For example, gardeners in South Dakota report that by encouraging

weedy grasses and broadleafs such as the annual kochia (*Kochia scoparia*) to grow as a barrier between the garden and adjacent open fields, grasshoppers that normally migrate from the dry pastures into irrigated gardens in the summer stop instead to feed on the weedy trap crop. The trap crop is irrigated occasionally to keep it lush, and is cut back lightly several times during the growing season to keep the weeds from going to seed. The grasshoppers often complete their life cycles and die off without ever leaving the trap crop. Some gardeners monitor their trap crops. When they detect large numbers of eggs or young pest insect larvae, they spray the trap plants to kill the pests. This approach allows the food crops to remain unsprayed but still protected.

These examples of the beneficial role some weeds play in gardens are offered not as rationalizations for tolerating all weed growth, but rather as counters to the barrage of media information that makes you feel that all sorts of horticultural havoc will result if weeds are tolerated at any level.

In setting weed tolerance levels you need to ask:
• Which weed species are growing in the garden?
• How aggressively are they growing and spreading?
• Where in the garden are they growing and how visible are they?
• How much damage are they likely to cause to other plants, structures or the overall aesthetics of the area?

For example, if the weed growing in your flower bed is the annual scarlet pimpernel (*Anagallis arvensis*), a relatively slow-growing, prostrate weed that competes poorly with established plants, there's no need to rush right out and remove it. You might even find its tiny scarlet flowers attractive and appreciate the fact that its spreading habit will protect the soil from desiccation (drying out) by the sun until your flower or vegetable seedlings are large enough to shade the soil (and shade out the scarlet pimpernel).

If, on the other hand, the weed is *Convolvulus arvensis,* commonly known as wild morningglory or field bindweed, quick action is required. This perennial plant can send out 30 sq. yd. (25 sq. m) of stolons (underground stems) in a single season. Each of the many buds on these stolons can produce new top growth with twining stems seemingly dedicated to the singular task of choking out your prize dahlias or zucchini.

Of course, if the bindweed happens to be growing not in your garden but in another of its habitats —say, on a south-facing hillside where the combination of harsh sunlight, steep slope, water runoff and little or no topsoil severely limits the growth of other plants—you should probably leave it alone and thank your stars that those bindweed roots are helping to hold the soil in place so your house does not go sliding downhill in heavy rains.

KNOWING YOUR WEEDS

The discussion of tolerance levels underscores the importance of identifying the weed species you are dealing with and knowing something about its biology. The more adept you become at recognizing garden weeds, particularly at the seedling stage, the better you can judge which weeds need immediate attention and which can be removed later or even allowed to stay.

For example, weeds that form deep, fleshy taproots such as dandelion *(Taraxacum officinale)* or sowthistle *(Sonchus arvensis)* should be removed in the seedling stage. If you wait until they mature, you will find the roots tenaciously anchored in the soil and the weed very difficult to pull out or kill. Moreover, if you fail to remove every piece of live root from the soil, new top growth is likely to emerge from dormant growth buds present on even small pieces of mature root tissue.

Quick action is not particularly necessary for weed species with shal-

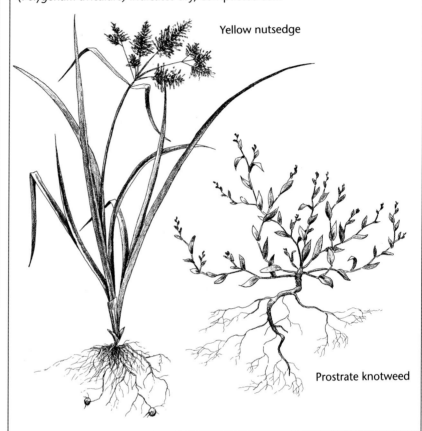

Indicator Weeds
Certain weed species are good indicators of soil conditions. Yellow nutsedge *(Cyperus esculentus)* indicates waterlogged soil, whereas prostrate knotweed *(Polygonum aviculare)* indicates dry, compacted soil.

Yellow nutsedge

Prostrate knotweed

low, fibrous root systems such as chickweed *(Stellaria* and *Cerastium* spp.) or lambsquarters *(Chenopodium album),* since these are easy to pull out of most garden soils even when approaching maturity. Still, it is very important that these weeds be harvested before they set seed.

Another good reason for learning to identify weeds is that some serve as excellent indicators of garden conditions, including soil pH (acidity), salinity and moisture (see the drawing above). For example, patches of nutsedge *(Cyperus* spp.) indicate the presence of excessive water perhaps due to a break in an irrigation pipe or the presence of an underground

spring. Conversely, prostrate knotweed *(Polygonum aviculare)* in your lawn indicates dry, compacted soil and suggests the need for improved aeration and irrigation.

Weed Names

A particular weed may have many common names, but it has only one scientific name, which consists of the genus and the species (see p. 11 for a review of scientific naming). The bad news is that even this scientific name can change, since botanists are forever moving plants from one genus or species to another as new information about them emerges. When looking up a particular weed, you may see it listed by different scientific names in different texts. For example, poison ivy is listed in some books as *Rhus radicans* or *Rhus toxicodendron* and in others as *Toxicodendron radicans*. If you want to know the scientific name currently in vogue, consult the most recent edition (1989, as of this writing) of the *Composite List of Weeds,* published by the Weed Science Society of America.

Helpful Literature about Weeds

Because there are thousands of species of plants that in one situation or another are considered weeds, describing all of them is far beyond the scope of this book. For aid in identifying your particular weeds and learning about their growth habits and other characteristics relevant to management, we offer the following suggestions.

The easiest way to identify weeds is to compare your live specimen with a good illustrated description of weeds common in your area. Such weed identification literature is often available from your local cooperative extension office.

Perhaps the best and most comprehensive photo-oriented identification tool is the *Grower's Weed Identification Handbook,* published by the University of California Cooperative Extension Service. This handbook is composed of individual weed identification sheets. The front of each sheet contains high-quality color photographs of the seed, seedling and mature stages of the weed, and the back provides information on the weed's biology and ecology. Over 240 weed species are described, and more are added periodically. The weed sheets come in a three-ring binder, which makes the book easy to use and supplement. It focuses on weeds in California, whose ecologically diverse ecosystems encompass weeds that grow as far away as Maine and Florida. No matter where you live, this superb identification tool is probably worth your investment.

Weed Keys

If you want to take the "Sherlock Holmes" approach to weed identification, you should acquire a key to the weeds or general flora of your region. First, however, we suggest you read Harrington and Durrell's gem of a book, *How to Identify Plants,* in which they write: "Keys provide a convenient shortcut method of determining plants by outlining and grouping related types. There is a particular 'knack' in using keys, gained partly by certain native ability in weighing evidence in order to arrive at a correct decision, but obtained mostly by constant practice and experience." The book provides the necessary background in botanical terminology and field collection for using plant keys. Without a reference such as this, working through keys can be extremely frustrating. The book also lists the major plant identification manuals available for each region of the United States, including Alaska, as well as for Canada. Two of the best keys for weed identification can be found in *Weed Identification and Control* by Duane Isely and in *Weeds* by W.C. Muenscher.

Bear in mind that if all efforts at identification fail, you can always prepare a sample of your weed and take or mail it to a weed identification expert (see pp. 11-12 for information on specimen preparation). Your local cooperative extension office or nearest state department of agriculture, university herbarium, community college botany department or natural history museum may offer such assistance.

Keeping Records

As long as you are taking time to identify the weeds in your garden and learn about their behavior and the beneficial and undesirable roles they play, it would be a shame not to record this information. Not only will it be useful in future seasons, but a written record means that the collected insights from your garden experience will not be lost due to the frailties of human memory. If you need a boost in getting your garden record-keeping underway, read *Vita Sackville-West's Garden Book.* Her sage advice is based on notes she kept on the evolution of her garden at Sissinghurst Castle in Kent, England.

One of the easiest and most practical methods we've seen for keeping a record of weeds and their management is to preserve samples on plastic-covered index cards in a ring binder. This simple method, described on p. 12, results in a portable, easy-to-use reference. Notes on the weed's identity, behavior and susceptibility to control efforts can be written on cards that are kept next to the specimen in the binder. By noting when weeds show up, how many appear and what effect they seem to have on the growth of garden ornamentals and food plants, you will, in a season or two, have a reliable means of determining which and how many weeds you can tolerate without harming the functional or aesthetic performance of the garden.

A written record also helps you keep track of whether you are winning or losing the battle with weeds over the long term. Unfortunately, most gardeners we've worked with have not been able to state with any certainty whether the weed populations that show up every season are increasing, falling or staying about the same. They are also unable to say whether the weeds are generally the same or are shifting to new species—a common result of weed control efforts. Without this information, it is impossible to determine the long-term effectiveness of your management methods.

Written records also minimize weed surprises. There's nothing more irritating than having weeds spring up and choke out the petunias, sugar peas or other plants you spent all weekend putting in the ground. By referring to your notes, you'll know which weeds to expect in various areas of your garden, and you will take preventive action accordingly.

REFERENCES AND READINGS

Allan, Mea. 1978. *Weeds—the unbidden guests in our gardens.* New York: Viking Press. 191 pp.

This work illustrates and describes over 200 common weeds of Britain and North America and includes discussions of how they migrate, why many immigrant plants are considered undesirable and why other weeds can be very useful.

Cocannouer, J.A. 1964. *Weeds: guardians of the soil.* New York: Devin-Adair. 179 pp.

Described by the publisher as "probably the first book ever written in praise of weeds," this folksy volume relates in anecdotal style observations of the positive roles weeds play in improving soils. The book, written by one of the first professors of conservation and botany at the University of Oklahoma, is based on several decades of study of weed behavior. While some observations about the benefits of weeds—for example, how certain weeds can make minerals available to shallow-rooted plants—have since been verified by contemporary researchers, Cocannouer presents little of his own data. Thus, the wisdom in this book too often must be taken as an article of faith rather than documented fact.

Fischer, B.B, A.H. Lange, J. McCaskill, B. Crampton and B. Tabraham. 1978. *Grower's weed identification handbook.* Oakland: University of California Cooperative Extension (Publication 4030). 250 pp. (Available from: ANR Publications, University of California, 6701 San Pablo Ave., Oakland, CA 94608-1239.)

The excellent color photographs of the seed, seedling and flowering stage of each of more than 240 weed species, together with pertinent biology and ecology, make this handbook the best weed identification tool currently available.

Harrington, H.D., and L.W. Durrell. 1957. *How to identify plants.* Chicago: Swallow Press. 203 pp.

This very well-written book takes the mystery out of botanical nomenclature. It includes a list of keys to plants in various regions of the United States.

Isely, D. 1960. *Weed identification and control.* Ames: Iowa State University Press. 400 pp.

An excellent key to the common weeds of the United States.

King, L.J. 1966. *Weeds of the world.* New York: Interscience Publishers. 526 pp.

One of the most thoroughly researched discussions ever written of the origin, botany, spread and control of agricultural weeds. Includes a good chapter on non-chemical methods for control of weeds (with an excellent bibliography).

Klingman, G.C., F.M. Ashton and L.J. Noordhoff. 1975. *Weed science: principles and practices.* New York: John Wiley and Sons. 431 pp.

A standard weed control text with descriptions of various chemical classes of herbicides.

Muenscher, W.C. 1980. *Weeds.* Ithaca, N.Y.: Cornell University Press. 586 pp.

An excellent reference tool for identifying weeds. It contains a key and descriptions for over 570 weeds found throughout the United States and Canada. Control information is limited to mechanical methods.

Nicolson, P., ed. 1983. *Vita Sackville-West's garden book.* New York: Atheneum. 250 pp.

This book is composed of garden columns written by Sackville-West in the *London Observer* from 1951 to 1958 chronicling her experience in her garden at Sissinghurst Castle, as well as her observations about other gardens and plants. She cautions against indiscriminate weed removal, since this eliminates survival of migrant seedlings such as the *Cotoneaster horizontalis* seedlings that improved the appearance of her garden in unexpected ways.

Stein, B. 1988. *My weeds: a gardener's botany.* New York: Harper and Row. 229 pp.

This delightful book, written by a botanist and gardener, spells out the history and ecological underpinnings of common weeds and describes how to design and manage gardens to minimize weed problems.

Subcommittee on Standardization of Common and Botanical Names of Weeds. 1989. *Composite list of weeds.* 112 pp. (Available from: The Weed Science Society of America, 309 W. Clark St., Champaign, IL 61820.

A very useful list of the most recent scientific names assigned to common weeds.

USDA Soil Conservation Service. 1981. *Cover crops in California orchards and vineyards.* 25 pp. (Available from: Publications, USDA Soil Conservation Service, 2828 Chiles Rd., Davis, CA 95616.)

Practical tips on how to select, plant and manage cover crops in orchards and vineyards.

CHAPTER 28
Safe and Sane
Weed Management

INTRODUCTION

Once you have acquired some biological background on the weeds that grow in your garden and have established realistic weed tolerance levels, you are ready to implement a variety of strategies that will rid your garden of weeds and prevent new ones from taking their place.

Preventive approaches, called indirect management strategies, focus on reducing or eliminating the habitat that supports weeds. A direct management strategy, by contrast, is one that attacks the weed itself and reduces or eliminates its population, but not the habitat that allowed it to grow in the first place. For the most permanent reduction of weeds (and weeding!) it is wise to use a combination of direct and indirect strategies, as summarized in the chart at right.

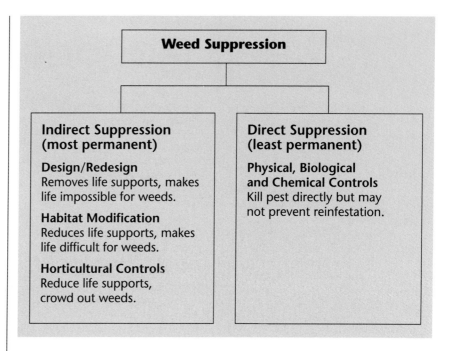

Weed Suppression

Indirect Suppression (most permanent)

Design/Redesign
Removes life supports, makes life impossible for weeds.

Habitat Modification
Reduces life supports, makes life difficult for weeds.

Horticultural Controls
Reduce life supports, crowd out weeds.

Direct Suppression (least permanent)

Physical, Biological and Chemical Controls
Kill pest directly but may not prevent reinfestation.

INDIRECT WEED SUPPRESSION

The three major indirect strategies are design/redesign, habitat modification and horticultural controls.

Design/Redesign

The design/redesign strategy focuses on prevention by removing weeds' life supports. It "designs" weeds permanently out of the system, first by identifying current or potential weed habitats, then by creating long-term weed barriers in those habitats.

Paths, Driveways and Patios. To reduce the likelihood of weeds growing through permeable pavings of gravel, brick or stone, place several layers of heavy building paper or roofing paper on the soil before installing the paving material (as shown at A in the drawing on the facing page). This type of paper is very durable and does not decompose rapidly, as does black plastic material. It will prevent weed growth for many years.

Algae on garden walkways or greenhouse floors can be minimized or prevented by using porous concrete rather than the typical impervious mixture. The porous mix uses no

sand, and therefore allows water to pass through by gravity. Because the pores are so large, this mixture also prevents water from moving upward through the concrete by capillary action. The formula for the mix (suggested by the staff of Cook College of Rutgers University) is given in the sidebar on the facing page.

Fences. The soil under and immediately adjacent to wooden fence posts and rails is usually colonized by weeds. Such areas are hard to reach with most weed control equipment, and herbicides can disfigure the finish on the fence and damage garden plants growing nearby. The best solution is to eliminate this weed habitat at the time the fence is constructed by creating a "mow strip."

To do this, lay an 8-in. (20 cm) wide strip of roofing paper in a line between the fence posts (you can also use brick pavers or pour a concrete strip). Cover the paper with decorative rock or bark mulch. Do this before nailing on the fence stringers and boards. The 8-in. width will cover the soil immediately under the fence and 3 in. (7.5 cm) either side of

it (shown at B in the drawing on the facing page). That way weeds cannot grow up the sides of the fence. If a flower border abuts your fence, the strip will provide an edge against which flowers or vegetables can grow. Stray weeds growing near this edge can be removed easily by pulling or other methods.

Similarly, if you are building a stone or masonry wall, simply add a 4-in. to 6-in. (10 cm to 15 cm) strip of concrete or brick at the soil surface adjacent to the sides of the wall to create a mow strip. The small concrete strip serves as a surface for one wheel of your lawn mower, as shown at C in the drawing on the facing page; it allows you to keep a neat, flush edge between the lawn and the wall.

Vegetable and Flower Beds. Instead of growing annual flowers and vegetables in a large patch that provides a habitat for weeds in the spaces not occupied by the plants, consider constructing raised beds with permanent paths between them. You can use wood, brick or stone to construct frames 8 in. to 10 in. (20 cm to 25 cm) high. Fill the beds with garden soil

Weed-Free Garden Design

Good garden design keeps weed habitats to a minimum. An underlayer of roofing paper (A) keeps weeds from coming up through gravel paths. Combining roofing paper and gravel (B) keep weeds from growing along fence lines, and a concrete mow strip (C) makes it easy to mow those plants that would otherwise spring up right alongside a wall.

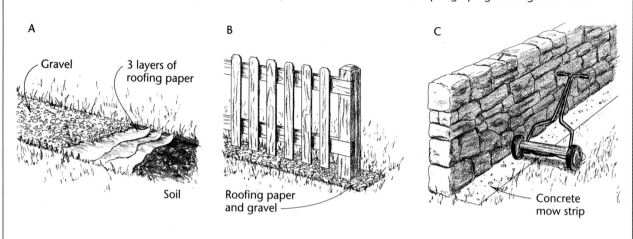

A — Gravel — 3 layers of roofing paper — Soil

B — Roofing paper and gravel

C — Concrete mow strip

---

with nutrient-rich compost or other soil additives so that flowers and vegetables grow rapidly, shading out weeds. The rich, friable (easy-to-crumble) soil can be covered with a mulch to discourage weeds further. Any weeds that do make an appearance are easy to pull out of this moist, organically rich soil.

When there are gaps in your garden activity (such as during winter or long vacations) the bare soil in these raised beds should be covered with plastic sheeting overlaid with mulch or fitted wooden covers. This helps keep wandering weed seeds from blowing into the soil. The paths between the raised beds can be "weed-proofed" by covering them with a deep layer of sawdust, wood chips or more permanent paving material (as described under "Paths" above). Our favorite mulch for paths is sawdust. Not only is it usually available free for the hauling, but microorganisms attempting to decompose the sawdust tie up soil nitrogen, rendering it unavailable for weed growth. In this sense, sawdust acts as an herbicide. Therefore, remember to use it only on paths, not on your planting beds.

(Note: For ways to design weeds out of lawns, see "Managing Weeds in Lawns," pp. 554-559.)

Habitat Modification

When permanent removal of the life-support systems for weeds proves impossible or prohibitively expensive, the next most permanent strategy, habitat modification, should be considered. Modifying the habitat changes the biophysical environment to reduce its carrying capacity for weeds. This is achieved primarily by limiting or manipulating the water, fertilizer and sunlight needed by weeds.

Limiting Water. Where feasible, use drip-irrigation systems that place water directly in the root zone of ornamental or edible plants. Drip systems apply water slowly enough for plants to absorb most of it soon after it reaches the roots, so little moisture is left over to support weeds. By contrast, overhead irrigation systems apply water indiscriminately over the soil surface, watering both garden plants and weeds.

A new subsurface irrigation system that relies on porous plastic hose has

Formula for Porous Concrete

To make 1 cu. yd. of mix, use:
- 2,700 lb. of ⅜-in. aggregate
- 5½ 94-lb. sacks of cement
- 22 to 23 gal. of water

The mix is stiff and sets up quickly, so it should be kept damp, particularly when temperatures are high. However, resist the temptation to add too much water. The material should be screeded (finished and leveled on its surface) with a 2x4 board; it should not be hand-troweled, since this works the cement to the surface and creates an impervious layer, just the opposite of what you want. When poured in a 3-in. slab, the working stress of this mix is 600 lb. per sq. in., more than enough to carry foot traffic and garden or other light vehicles.

recently become commercially available. This "ooze hose" is placed 6 in. (15 cm) below the soil in rows 12 in. to 18 in. (30 cm to 45 cm) apart. Garden transplants are set into the soil above the hoses. Because the moisture is released below grade, roots are encouraged to travel down to the water. The surface of the soil rarely becomes wet, and weed seeds in the top 2 in. (5 cm) of soil—the germination range—are unable to get the moisture required to germinate. Both drip and ooze irrigation supplies are carried in many garden supply stores.

The amount of water available to weeds can also be limited by planting vegetables on raised soil mounds and irrigating them via furrows dug beside the mounds. The furrows and the edges of the mounds where weeds get enough water to grow can be cultivated. Meanwhile, the tops of the mounds remain relatively dry, so few weeds germinate there. This technique may not be effective if the mounds are shallow—less than 4 in. (10 cm) high—or in clay soils where water may move upward by capillary action. When this happens, the tops of the mounds become wet after a furrow irrigation, a phenomenon known as "subbing."

Manipulating Soil Fertility. If you are trying to get a good stand of grass to grow to stop a slope from eroding or to improve the appearance of a weedy lawn, an application of high-nitrogen fertilizer—for example, 11 lb. (5 kg) of 16-20-0 mix per 1,000 sq. ft. (93 sq. m) of planting—is often just the thing to spur the grass into vigorous growth at the expense of broad-leaved weeds. If, on the other hand, you prefer to see a mix of wildflowers and clover, weedy grasses can be discouraged in favor of broad-leaved plants by increasing the amount of phosphorus in the soil—say, 11 lb. of single superphosphate 0-20-0 mix per 1,000 sq. ft.—but not adding any nitrogen. The subject of manipulating soil fertility is dealt with in an interesting bulletin by T.E. Adams and B. Kay, entitled "Seeding for Erosion Control" (listed under "References and Readings" on pp. 508-510).

Mulching to Limit Light. When weed seeds germinate, they have a finite amount of energy available to them to push up through the soil and reach sunlight. Sunlight is needed by most plants to manufacture, or photosynthesize, carbohydrates used to provide the energy for growth. If you can prevent the germinating seedling

from reaching sunlight, it will die without ever making an appearance above the soil. The most practical way to do this is to cover the soil with a mulch (as shown in the drawing below). Mulches can be composed of organic plant residues, gravel or manufactured plastic or metal products. Table 28.1 on the facing page lists the pros and cons of some common mulch materials.

To be effective in preventing or limiting weed growth, mulches must be applied immediately after soil cultivation or other soil disturbance—for example, after pulling weeds or readying the soil for planting. This timing is critical to prevent sunlight from reaching weed seeds brought to the surface when the soil was disturbed; it also prevents migrating seeds from settling in. Thus, it is best to have mulch on hand before you begin digging or weeding so you can periodically cover cleared sections before moving on.

Organic mulches must be applied deep enough to overcome the attempts of germinating seeds to get to sunlight. But too much organic mulch can smother the roots of desirable vegetation and impede water penetration and gaseous exchanges

---

Mulches

A variety of natural and synthetic materials can be placed on the soil surface as mulch to exclude light, inhibiting the growth of weeds. Organic compost (A) must be at least 4 in. (10 cm) deep. Sawdust (B) not only obscures light but also robs nitrogen from the surface of the soil, denying weeds critical nutrients. A synthetic weed mat (C) provides long-term protection from germinating weed seeds and is superior to black plastic in that it allows air and water to penetrate to the soil.

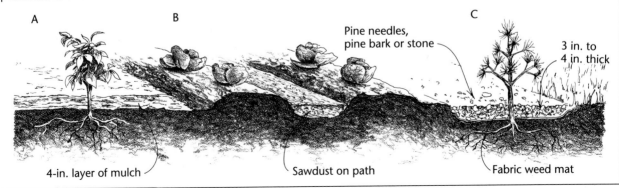

Table 28.1

A Comparison of Garden Mulch Materials Used for Weed Control

Material	Area	Advantages	Disadvantages
aluminum foil	beds	increases soil temperature, which may increase yields; may inhibit frost injury; repels some insects	expensive; may produce too much heat for ornamentals; must be weighted down or will blow away; tears easily
bark products	beds, paths	come in several sizes—medium and coarse grades best for weed control; can be slow to decompose; attractive	somewhat expensive; small sizes blow away in windy areas; can migrate onto pavement areas
black plastic	beds	easy to apply: lay on soil, cut slits, insert seeds or plants; use at least 6-mil grade for maximum longevity; irrigate soil before laying plastic	must be weighted down; weakened by ultraviolet sun rays, breaks down in one season; unattractive; somewhat expensive; roots of plants develop in thin layer beneath plastic, so they are poorly anchored and susceptible to drought; nonrecyclable
building/ roofing paper	paths	durable and long-lasting (use 80-lb. grade); tolerates some foot traffic; warms soil	expensive; somewhat unattractive (cover with bark or gravel to improve appearance); some types contain asphalt
cardboard/ newspaper	beds, paths	inexpensive, readily available; use 3 to 6 sheets thick	must be weighted down; unattractive; potential habitat for slugs; inks may contain PCBs toxic to plants
carpet pieces	paths	free or inexpensive; can be rolled up for tillage or planting; retain moisture; if laid with underside up, have brown, earthy appearance; decompose slowly	may become eventual disposal problem; can attract slugs and ants
compost	beds	improves soil as it decomposes; free if homemade; attractive	decomposes rapidly
gravel, crushed stone	paths	decorative; packs densely to exclude light; can be used to cover plastic or paper	expensive; can reflect excessive amounts of heat onto plants (use dark colors to reduce heat); semi-permanent, difficult to move
leafmold	beds	free, available, attractive	can be used only with plants suited to acid soils; decomposes rapidly
pine needles	beds, paths	free, attractive; good on paths since leaching stops most plant growth	on beds can only be used with plants suited to acid soils; can be fire hazard when dry
sawdust	beds, paths	free or inexpensive; excellent on paths since it depletes soil nitrogen, making weed growth difficult	must be stabilized with nitrogen when used on beds; decomposes fairly rapidly; blows away in windy areas unless kept wet; unstabilized sawdust should not be buried
straw/hay	beds, paths	inexpensive; enriches soil as it decomposes; lightweight, easy to apply; pleasant to walk on	can contain weed seeds; not easy to find in urban areas; unstable in wind; must be stabilized with nitrogen; fire hazard if dry
wood chips	beds, paths	slow to decompose; pack well to exclude light from soil; free from tree-care companies	can contain weed seeds; can be expensive to purchase; can be fire hazard; can migrate unless confined by retaining board
woven weed mats	beds, paths	allow water and air to penetrate soil but screen out light; available from nurseries	expensive if used on a large garden but worth the cost for long-term weed control

in the soil. Thus, on garden beds, you can apply lightweight mulches, such as straw, small-particle bark or compost, up to 6 in. (15 cm) deep. But heavier mulches such as wood chips, or mulches that pack densely such as sawdust or leafmold, should be limited to a maximum depth of 3 in. or 4 in. (7.5 cm or 10 cm). Be careful to keep the mulch several inches away from the stems of plants; when mulch is mounded against plant stems, moisture is retained and disease is promoted. You can apply mulch on paths to a depth of 8 in. (20 cm) or more. Organic mulches decompose over time, so they must be replenished periodically to maintain optimum depth.

Bear in mind that most organic mulches are high in cellulose and low in nitrogen. Soil microorganisms cannot get enough nitrogen from these materials to break them down to humus, so the microbes absorb additional nitrogen from the soil. This causes a reduction in nitrogen available to garden plants and stunts their growth. To avoid nitrogen deficiencies when using high-cellulose mulches such as raw sawdust on garden beds, add 1 lb. (0.45 kg) of available nitrogen per 1,000 sq. ft. (93 sq. m) of mulched area. This is the amount contained in 100 lb. (45 kg) of poultry manure or 200 lb. (90 kg) of cow, hog or steer manure, or in 10 lb. (4.5 kg) of commercial fertilizer such as a 10-10-10 or 12-12-12 mix. Spade the nitrogen source under with the mulch in the fall. On paths where no plant growth is desired, the addition of nitrogen is not recommended.

Horticultural Controls

Horticultural controls involve manipulating plant selection, planting techniques and cultural practices so that desired vegetation grows so densely and vigorously that weeds are crowded out.

Complementary Plantings. These are described by Oregon Extension Specialist Jim Green as plantings that are designed "to occupy an environment or space not occupied by crop plants which would otherwise be open for invasion...by weeds...and other uninvited 'guests.' As opposed to pathogenic or competitive organisms that would invade this environment, complementary plantings actively improve the environment of the neighboring crop plant."

Applications for this technique in typical gardens include:

1. Sod Aisles. One example of complementary plantings is the use of perennial grass, clover or other groundcover to provide a permanent cover on aisles between rows of trees, vegetable crops or flower beds. These plants are sown from seed in the aisles; they are then irrigated and fertilized to get them established quickly. Sod aisles should be mowed periodically to control their height and make it easy to walk or move garden equipment along them. Once established, the grass or other plant is an effective barrier to weeds that would otherwise colonize the cultivated soil separating rows of plants.

At one time, sod aisles were standard features in orchards, but the practice of using them was largely abandoned with the advent of herbicides. It is now gaining new popularity as the financial, horticultural and environmental limitations of herbicides become clearer. Larger agricultural systems, particularly the efficient polycultures still found in the Third World, have been the traditional settings for complementary plantings, but the use of this technique is also increasing in urban and suburban gardens in the United States and Europe. Many residential and community gardens in Europe have sod aisles as permanent paths between beds containing ornamental and vegetable plants. According to Dr. Green, these paths provide a verdant alternative to gravel, concrete or asphalt coverings, and they have additional benefits that include:

• minimizing freestanding water on the soil surface (the water can contribute to the spread of pathogens),

• facilitating biological control programs by providing host plants for predators and parasitoids and by serving as host sources for mycorrhizal inoculum (beneficial soil fungi that aid plant roots in absorbing mineral nutrients),

• contributing to the maintenance and renewal of soil organic matter and the soil structure, minimizing soil erosion,

• removing excess moisture from the root zone in the winter,

• conserving moisture in the summer through mulching action,

• providing, through the mulching effect, soil temperature modification, thereby protecting roots against freezing in winter and against high summer temperatures, and

• improving the load-bearing capacity of the soil, which facilitates year-round maintenance.

2. Overseeding. Another increasingly common application of the complementary planting technique involves heavily overseeding newly planted shrub beds or groundcover areas with fast-growing annual flowers. These include sweet alyssum (*Lobularia maritima*), farewell-to-spring (*Clarkia amoena*) and scarlet flax (*Linum grandiflorum* var. rubrum). Such plants are colorful temporary fillers that germinate quickly and occupy the soil spaces between the slower-growing shrubs or groundcovers. They later give way as the more vigorous landscape plants fill in. Consult your favorite seed catalog for fast-germinating annuals suited to your area.

3. Plant Succession. Perhaps the most imaginative use of the complementary planting concept in urban landscapes that we have observed is that developed by David Bigham, a landscape designer in Berkeley, California. Working almost exclusively with California native plants suited for use in ornamental plantings, Bigham has developed a unique planting procedure in which he installs an entire plant succession at once. For each area to be planted,

Bigham selects plant species that represent the major stages of a vegetative succession leading up to the final, or climax, planting designed for the site—usually a mixture of groundcovers, shrubs and trees. This approach takes into account what nature will do to a freshly cultivated planting bed—colonize it with weeds—and essentially outwits nature by including in the design aesthetically pleasing wildflowers or grasses to colonize the typical weed habitat.

For example, if the ultimate goal is a mature oak grove, Bigham plants the oaks and all phases of the understory at the same time. Such a planting might include a selection of ornamental grasses and wildflowers, semi-woody groundcovers, taller shrubs and the oak trees. The plants interact with each other much as they would if they were growing under natural conditions. Thus, in the first year or two, colorful grasses, wildflowers and groundcovers visually dominate. As the seasons pass and the shrubs and trees become well-established, they eventually overtop and shade out the lower-growing plants. Finally, the mature oaks largely shade out the understory trees.

Bigham's planting and maintenance techniques work for small- and large-scale landscapes. Since the planting design itself keeps the need for weed control to a minimum, his company is able to maintain plantings even on large private estates in a cost-effective manner, despite the fact that no herbicides are used. Although Bigham developed this method in California, the concept should work in any part of the country as long as the plant species used mimic the local vegetation succession patterns.

When designing complementary plantings, it is critical to select plant varieties that can out-compete weeds but will not unduly compete for the nutrients, light and water needed by the ornamental or food plants themselves. There isn't much documentation to guide the gardener through such selections, but a few useful resources do exist.

An exhaustive and delightfully written compendium of grasses and legumes (plants that cooperate with soil fungi to produce nitrogen) suited for use as complementary plantings in agricultural and ornamental systems can be found in *Feed the Soil* by Edwin McLeod. The description of each plant species includes a discussion of habit, uses, range, soil preferences and seeding rates. An excellent discussion of appropriate species and management programs for sod aisles in orchards appears in the pamphlet, "Cover Crops in California Orchards and Vineyards." Much of the information in this pamphlet appears to be appropriate to other areas of the United States as well.

Seed catalogs usually list appropriate times of the season to plant individual species, as well as the length of time it takes for seeds to germinate after planting. Using this information, you can select candidates for your complementary planting program.

Competitive Planting. Competitive planting entails growing a desired plant at a particular site (such as a garden) to reduce light, water, nutrients or space available to another plant, in this case weeds.

1. Shading out Weeds. Sometimes competitive planting is as simple as selecting a plant species that grows so large and rapidly that with just a little help in the beginning, it can shade out weeds. An example is corn and common summer annual weeds. If you destroy weed seedlings by running your hoe alongside young corn plants a couple of times in the first two or three weeks after they have germinated, the corn soon grows so rapidly that most remaining weed seeds can't get enough light to germinate, let alone grow. The same is true of ornamental plants such as the daisy-flowered marguerites (*Chrysanthemum frutescens*), euryops (*Euryops pectinatus*) and gamolepis (*Gamolepis chrysanthemoides*), which soon shade out competing weeds.

2. Using Smother Crops. One of the oldest competitive planting techniques uses smother crops to outcompete weeds. For example, large populations of perennial Canada thistle (*Cirsium arvense*) have been controlled by mowing or tilling and then planting the field in alfalfa or buckwheat. Alfalfa is a vigorous grower whose aggressiveness in exploiting the soil for moisture and nutrients provides severe competition even for the rugged thistles. The alfalfa's ability to colonize the soil environment is enhanced by periodic mowings. By cutting it several times a season, resurgence of thistle is prevented. Within as little as one season the thistle roots deplete their nutrient reserves and die. The alfalfa can be left in place or tilled under in late summer and allowed to decompose, enriching the soil with the nitrogen it produces. In the newly enriched soil other crops or ornamentals have a competitive advantage over many weeds.

If your garden is awash in perennial weeds, try mowing them down in early spring, irrigating and then using a seed drill (a tool that pokes seeds into shallow pockets in the soil) to plant a smother crop of alfalfa, buckwheat, clover or other legumes. Mow the smother crop twice during the summer to prevent it or any weeds that have managed to grow from producing seed. In the fall or spring, till the smother crop under and plant your garden.

3. Using Barrier Plants. One ingenious use of competitive plantings has been reported from the island of Mauritius, where bermudagrass (*Cynodon dactylon*) is kept out of sugarcane fields by planting a dense row of turf lilies (*Liriope* spp.) at the borders of the cane fields. The lily plant is apparently aggressive enough to keep encroaching bermudagrass out of the cane. This strategy might also be employed at the edges of lawns to keep grass from creeping into adjoining flower beds. A number of *Liriope* species are sold in nurseries throughout the United States, particularly in

the Southeast, where it is known as mondo grass.

4. Close Planting. If your garden soil is loose, well-drained and full of rich organic compost—which is easy to accomplish through the use of raised beds described earlier—you can plant your vegetables or flowering plants very close together without sacrificing yields. The close spacing will enable the transplants to occupy most of the soil habitat, inhibiting weed germination and shading out those weeds that do manage to lift their leaves above the soil line. This technique is clearly described in John Jeavon's interesting book, *How To Grow More Vegetables Than You Ever Thought Possible On Less Land Than You Can Imagine.*

5. Replacement Control. Replacement control involves manipulating the dynamics of natural vegetation to encourage desired species and discourage weeds. Plant ecologist Robert Piemeisel defines this method as that "which employs an indirect means of getting rid of pests through changes in vegetation." This concept has been employed on a large scale at a demonstration project conducted for several decades by the Connecticut College Arboretum in New London in an effort to reduce herbicide use in the management of vegetation growing under power lines and along other rights-of-way.

The focus of the project has been to remove selectively the tall-growing tree species such as oaks, poplars and maples found under power lines to encourage the development of dense, stable stands of low-growing native shrubs such as huckleberry (*Gaylussacia baccata*), low blueberry (*Vaccinium vacillans*) and greenbrier (*Smilax rotundifolia*), as well as herbaceous groundcovers such as little bluestem (*Andropogon scoparius*).

The project has been monitored for over three decades. Researchers have found that once existing trees are removed, there is little or no germination of new tree seedlings in areas where the shrub or grass cover

is dense. Where the density of the cover is moderate, only a few tree seedlings manage to germinate. The researchers hypothesize that competition for light, moisture and nutrients, as well as allelopathy (the ability of certain plants to produce toxic chemicals that prevent growth of other plants) probably account for the ability of well-established stands of shrubs and grasses to keep out trees. This pioneering concept was developed by researchers Frank Egler, William Niering, W.C. Bramble and W.R. Burns, and has been adopted by a number of northeast electric utility companies as a successful alternative to the blanket spraying of herbicides on rights-of-way.

If you live in the Northeast or other areas where tree seedlings seem to pop up overnight in your lawn or flower beds, replacement control might be a solution. Try covering these areas with a dense stand of attractive shrubs and/or groundcovers. Choose species that are adapted to the soils and climate and have a dense growth form. Many native shrubs that meet these criteria are very decorative and are readily available from commercial nurseries.

Plant the new shrubs 18 in. to 24 in. (45 cm to 60 cm) apart and apply 3 in. to 4 in. (7.5 cm to 10 cm) of mulch between them, keeping the mulch a few inches away from the stems to prevent moisture and disease problems. In the first season or two while the shrubs are filling in, pull out the seedlings that emerge in the spaces between the shrubs. The mulch will keep the soil moist and friable, making it relatively easy to remove the seedlings (and their roots) by hand. Once the shrubs have fully covered the planted area, tree seeds will find it very difficult, if not impossible, to germinate. You will have to sacrifice some lawn or flower beds to this strategy, but the tradeoff may be worth it if it means you don't have to battle tree seedlings every year.

If tree seedlings are a problem in a lawn area, instead of planting shrubs,

try planting an allelopathic grass species. These produce toxins that prevent or stunt the growth of certain tree species (see "Allelopathy" on pp. 493-495).

6. Competition on Ditchbanks and Swales. The collection and transportation of excess water is often achieved through the use of drainage ditches or swales. Water flow in the ditches is frequently seasonal, rendering the ditch a muddy eyesore part of the year and a weed patch the rest of the time. In sufficient numbers, weeds can reduce the carrying capacity of the swale as well as the speed with which water can move along it. Using herbicides in response adds toxicants to the water and creates environments for new weeds by only killing certain weed species.

A very innovative solution was designed by Mike and Judy Corbett and others at the Corbetts' award-winning solar subdivision, Village Homes, in Davis, California (see the photo on the facing page). Among the many energy-conserving features of this unique urban community is the use of swales and percolation ponds to conserve surface runoff and use it to recharge groundwater. This cuts down irrigation needs during the summer dry season, since many landscape plants can use groundwater for moisture.

There are many open swales and other catchment areas throughout the subdivision. Realizing these could become weedy eyesores, Corbett designed them to look like natural creeks and planted easy-to-manage ornamental vegetation that could out-compete weeds.

Varying grades of drain rock and sand were installed at the bottom of the swales to absorb and percolate runoff and recharge the groundwater. The rock layer is 12 in. to 18 in. (30 cm to 45 cm) thick, and serves as a barrier to weed growth. The ditch is intercepted at key points by intake pipes connected to the storm drain system, which acts as an emergency backup during peak water flows.

At Village Homes, an innovative solar subdivision in Davis, California, open swales that capture rainfall and irrigation runoff to recharge the groundwater have been designed to resemble natural creeks. The sides of the swales are gently graded to facilitate planting and mowing of grass, which out-competes the weeds that would otherwise spring up. (Photo by Sheila Daar.)

Allelopathy

Some plants exude toxic substances that inhibit the growth of competing vegetation, a phenomenon known as allelopathy. The source plant releases toxins that vaporize in the air, leach into the soil in rainwater or are exuded from roots or decomposing tissue. Nearby seeds or plants that are susceptible either fail to germinate or are stunted or killed after contact.

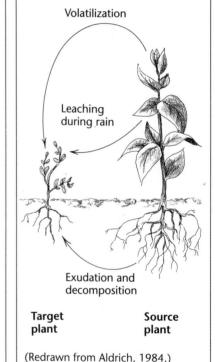

(Redrawn from Aldrich, 1984.)

The sides of the swales were graded at a gentle 4:1 slope to facilitate the planting and mowing of grass. The grass, which out-competes weeds that would otherwise colonize the ditch, is mowed to a height of 3 in. (7.5 cm) so it does not impede water flow and visually blends with the adjacent turf. Native riparian (stream-side) trees are planted in groves along the artificial creek to promote the effect of a natural stream and shade out undesirable plant species.

Allelopathy. The term "allelopathy" refers to the ability of certain plants to produce toxic substances in the soil that inhibit the growth of other plants. In other words, this is a kind of biochemical warfare. The drawing at right shows the movement of allelopathic substances from source plant to target plant.

Table 28.2 on pp. 494-495 lists some plants that are known to have allelopathic effects on weeds. For those who want to delve deeper into the subject, the sources of these findings are listed under "References and Readings" on pp. 508-510.

In her article, "Allelopathy: Chemical Conversation Between Plants," Linda Schenck describes allelopathy as "a process in which a plant adds a chemical compound to the environment that has a deleterious effect on others...." She goes on to say that the allelopathic chemicals include:

phenolic acids, flavenoids, coumarins, quinones and other aromatic compounds, terpenes, steroids, alkaloids, essential oils, and organic cyanides. They reach the soil by a variety of routes: release by rain wash and fog drip from leaf surfaces and glands, by volatilization from leaves, by excretion or exudation from roots, and by decay of above- and below-ground plant parts directly or through the agency of micro-organisms.

Early plants recognized as having allelopathic properties were walnut trees (*Juglans* spp.) and aromatic shrubs such as sage (*Salvia* spp.). As described by Schenck,

The principal allelopathic chemical of *Juglans* is juglone, found in a non-toxic form, hydroxyjuglone, in the leaves, fruits and other tissues. Washed by rain from living leaves and released with tannins from dead leaves and fruit, it is added to the soil in its oxidized form, juglone. It selectively inhibits many undergrowth species such as broomsedge, ericaceous shrubs and many broad-leaved herbs, while others, such as black raspberry and Kentucky bluegrass, are tolerant and may often be

Table 28.2
Plants Showing Allelopathic Effects on Weeds[a]

Allelopathic Plant		Weed Affected	
Common Name	Scientific Name	Common Name	Scientific Name
aster	*Aster pilosus*	common ragweed wild radish	*Ambrosia artemisiifolia* *Raphanus raphanistrum*
barley	*Hordeum vulgare*	common ragweed redroot pigweed purslane foxtail	*Ambrosia artemisiifolia* *Amaranthus retroflexus* *Portulaca oleracea* *Setaria viridis,* *S. lutescens*
besom heath	*Erica scoparia*	various grasses	
bracken fern	*Pteridium aquilinum*	barley	*Hordeum* spp.
broomsedge	*Andropogon virginicus*	pigweed Japanese bromegrass needlegrass bluestem	*Amaranthus palmeri* *Bromus japonicus* *Aristida oligantha* *Andropogon scoparius*
cereal ryegrass	*Secale cereale*	green foxtail redroot pigweed purslane common ragweed	*Setaria viridis* *Amaranthus retroflexus* *Portulaca oleracea* *Ambrosia artemisiifolia*
cucumber	*Cucumis sativus*	hog millet white mustard	*Panicum miliaceum* *Brassica hirta*
dropseed grass	*Sporobolus pyramidatus*	bermudagrass	*Cynodon dactylon*
eucalyptus	*Eucalyptus globulus,* *E. camaldulensis*	various forbs (broad-leaved plants) and grasses	
Italian ryegrass	*Lolium multiflorum*	various forbs and grasses	

[a] Data compiled from Anderson et al. (1978); Bokhari (1978); Fay and Duke (1977); Hoffman and Hazlett (1977); Larson and Schwartz (1980); Lockerman and Putnam (1979); Peters and Mohammed Zam (1980); Putnam and Duke (1974); Rice (1972); and Walters and Gilmore (1976).

found as ground cover under walnut trees.

The mechanism operating in the soft chaparral of low, aromatic shrubs is slightly different. In such an area, sage (*Salvia* spp.) and sagebrush (*Artemisia* spp.) often dominate, and some of the terpenes responsible for their fragrance (cineole and camphor) are allelopathic. They volatilize from the leaves into the atmosphere and from there into the soil, where they are adsorbed onto soil parti-

cles. Accumulated during the dry summer season, in the spring they show a strong inhibitory effect on the germination of grasses and herbs. By inhibiting respiration and the growth of seedlings that do germinate, terpenes increase the vulnerability of the seedlings to other environmental stresses.

The ability of some plants to inhibit others biochemically was reported as early as 1832 by Alphonse de Candolle, who observed that *Eu-*

phorbia was inhibitory to flax, thistles to oats and flax to wheat. That toxins accounted for this inhibition went counter to popular theories attributing plant competition solely to the cycling of soil nutrients. But scientific research that challenges conventional scientific or academic thought has often had a rough row to hoe.

L.J. King, in *Weeds of the World*, describes the battle over allelopathy:

The early work which touched off the controversy goes back to the early part of the twentieth century

Table 28.2 (continued)

| Allelopathic Plant | | Weed Affected | |
Common Name	Scientific Name	Common Name	Scientific Name
oats	*Avena sativa*	redroot pigweed wild mustard barnyardgrass	*Amaranthus retroflexus* *Brassica* spp. *Echinochloa crus-galli*
red fescue	*Festuca rubra*	various woody plants	
sage	*Salvia leucophylla*	wild oat	*Avena fatua*
sagebrush	*Artemisia tridentata*	wheatgrass spurge false pennyroyal pennycress yarrow bromegrass	*Agropyron smithii* *Euphorbia podperae* *Hedeoma hispida* *Thlaspi arvense* *Achillea millefolium* *Bromus inermis, B. rigidus*
sorghum	*Sorghum bicolor*	common ragweed redroot pigweed purslane foxtail	*Ambrosia artemisiifolia* *Amaranthus retroflexus* *Portulaca oleracea* *Setaria viridis, S. lutescens*
sudangrass	*Sorghum sudanense* 'Piper'	common ragweed redroot pigweed purslane foxtail	*Ambrosia artemisiifolia* *Amaranthus retroflexus* *Portulaca oleracea* *Setaria viridis, S. lutescens*
sunflower	*Helianthus mollis*	radishes, wheat	
sycamore	*Platanus* spp.	various forbs and grasses	
tall fescue	*Festuca arundinacea*	crabgrass various woody plants	*Digitaria sanguinalis*
wheat	*Triticum aestivum*	common ragweed redroot pigweed purslane foxtail	*Ambrosia artemisiifolia* *Amaranthus retroflexus* *Portulaca oleracea* *Setaria viridis, S. lutescens*

to the studies of Whitney of the United States Department of Agriculture. He believed that unproductiveness of cropped soils was due to the accumulation of toxic substances excreted by each crop plant, which proved injurious to that species of plant (truly an allelopathic action).

This was heresy to Cyril G. Hopkins, of the University of Illinois, who had reduced the soil fertility problem to a bank account system; and who held that nutri-ent depletion and reduction in crop yields would not occur if certain practices of rotating with leguminous crops, controlling the soil reaction with lime, and using fertilizers to replace the lost elements, were followed....The issue was so sharply defined that it led to a Congressional investigation of the teachings of Whitney and his associates.

Theories about the existence of allelopathy remained so controversial until just recently that research into ways to make use of this aspect of plant behavior for weed control has only begun to receive serious attention from researchers.

1. Ryegrass Mulch. One body of research that has reached the stage of practical use for gardeners is being conducted under the direction of Alan Putnam at the University of Michigan. First, a study was done to determine which species of cereal grains, such as rye, wheat and sorghum, would not harm vegetable

crops such as beans, peas, tomatoes, carrots and cabbage, but would exhibit toxic effects on weeds generally found with those crops.

Next, a plan for using annual cereal rye (Secale cereale) — the most successful of the experimental plants — as an allelopathic mulch for controlling weeds in vegetable crops was tested. Rye was planted as a fall cover crop, keeping the soil from blowing or washing away when the snow melted and emerging in the spring. When it was 12 in. to 16 in. (30 cm to 40 cm) tall, the ryegrass was mowed down or sprayed with a short-term herbicide; the residue was left on the soil as a mulch. After about a week, seeds of vegetables not affected by rye toxins were planted through the mulch with a seed drill.

Large-seeded crops such as beans and peas were found most compatible with the mulch. The vegetables germinate and grow up through the rye mulch. As the rye decomposes, toxins are released that inhibit the growth of such weeds as redroot pigweed (Amaranthus retroflexus), common ragweed (Ambrosia artemisiifolia), purslane (Portulaca oleracea) and green foxtail (Setaria viridis). Thus, the rye not only produces the usual benefits of mulch — increased soil moisture, greater microbial activity and buffered soil temperature — but also provides biochemical weed control.

Home gardeners with large seasonal vegetable gardens could plant rye cover crops following the procedure developed at the University of Michigan, or grow a crop of rye in the back area of the garden, mowing it monthly and spreading the clippings. Aisles between trees in home orchards might also be planted with rye and kept mowed.

The use of allelopathy for the control of weeds is at the cutting edge of environmentally sound pest management. In addition to looking at ways to use allelopathic plants as mulches, researchers are now trying to isolate the exact chemical toxin(s) responsible for the death of plants in the hope of developing plant-based organic herbicides.

2. Tree-Inhibiting Grasses. Other research projects have looked into the tendency of certain grasses to inhibit the growth of tree seedlings. Botanists Frank Egler, William Nierling and others in Connecticut and other parts of New England have observed the ability of little bluestem (Andropogron scoparius) to inhibit the germination of shrub and tree seedlings. This lovely perennial grass is native to the midwestern and northeastern United States, and is available from commercial suppliers of forage seed.

Recently, researchers at the University of Illinois have demonstrated that a common turfgrass, Kentucky 31 tall fescue (Festuca arundinacea), inhibits the germination of sweetgum (Liquidambar styraciflua) seedlings. In other studies conducted at the Ohio Agricultural Research and Development Center, tall fescue was found to inhibit the growth of black locust (Robinia pseudoacacia) and black alder (Alnus glutinosa) seedlings. Another turfgrass, Arizona fescue (Festuca 'Arizonii'), was shown by USDA Forest Service researchers to inhibit the germination of ponderosa pine (Pinus ponderosa).

Gardeners with unwanted tree seedlings sprouting in their lawns might experiment by seeding tall fescue in the problem areas. It is widely available from commercial nurseries. The research cited above was conducted with the wild species of tall fescue, which has a rather wide, coarse blade and is often considered a weed when found growing with finer-bladed turf grasses such as Kentucky bluegrass. Since the late 1970s, however, new tall fescue cultivars with narrow leaves have become widely available. Although these cultivars have not been studied for their allelopathic effects, given their parentage, chances are excellent that they carry the appropriate genes. Other advantages of these grasses are ability to survive drought, low soil fertility and heavy trampling.

Crop Rotation. The ancient agricultural technique of rotating crops probably developed because early farmers recognized that by growing the same crop in the same place season after season, soil nutrients were used up, crop yields decreased, populations of insects and soil pathogens built up and weeds became a problem. Weed species with life cycles most like that of the crop plant soon occupied any open soil niches. The same is true in small-scale plantings. Unless the crop plant or the management techniques are changed, weed populations become worse each year, seriously reducing crop yield.

As outlined in *Weed Control*, a report published by the National Academy of Sciences:

> Most habitat-management techniques [e.g., crop rotation] rely on sometimes subtle differences between weeds and crops. They usually require more sophisticated manipulations than the simple recognition of differences in appearance and the direct application of physical control methods. Important differences are the life cycles of weeds and crops, specific growth habits, variations in plant morphology and physiology, environmental influences that affect weeds differently than crops, and biotic factors.

Simply put, crop rotation involves following one crop with another that differs in its life cycle and associated cultural practices. This change in crop and culture reduces the habitat for weeds compatible with the previous crop. With the habitat reduced, those weeds are less successful competitors. Though rarely completely eliminated by rotations, their numbers drop to such low levels that they inflict no significant damage on the crop.

Classic crop rotation usually includes strongly competitive crops grown in each part of the rotation. For example, summer row crops such as corn are followed by winter or early spring grain crops, which are drilled

Summary of Horticultural Weed Controls

Complementary plantings:
• Using sod aisles.
• Overseeding annual flowers in spaces between immature groundcovers or shrubs.
• Installing an entire plant succession.

Competitive plantings:
• Shading out weeds.
• Using smother crops.
• Using barrier plants.
• Close planting.
• Replacement control.

• Maintaining grass swards in drainage ditches.

Allelopathy:
• Using toxin-producing plants to inhibit germination or growth of weeds.

Crop rotation:
• Rotating crops so that one crop is followed by a crop with a different life history and cultural requirements. Weeds suited to one crop will have difficulty growing with the following crop.

---

or broadcast. The grain crop and cultural practices associated with it suppress the summer annual weeds such as pigweed *(Amaranthus* spp.), lambsquarters *(Chenopodium album)* and common ragweed *(Ambrosia artemisiifolia),* which otherwise become pests in the corn. Likewise, the cultural practices used for the corn inhibit the growth of winter annuals such as wild mustard *(Brassica* spp.), wild oats *(Avena* spp.) and various thistle species that occur in the grain crops.

DIRECT WEED SUPPRESSION

Often you find yourself confronting a weed problem that is too far along to be managed by indirect suppression alone. When quick action is needed, the following direct weed suppression strategies are available: physical or mechanical controls, biological controls and chemical controls.

Before choosing a direct control strategy, determine whether you are dealing with young or mature weeds and whether they are annuals or perennials. All direct strategies are most effective on young seedlings generally no more than a few inches tall with only three to five leaves.

Seedling weeds, whether annuals or perennials, are easy to remove by hand and other non-chemical methods, roots and all.

If annual weeds have grown beyond the seedling stage, it is important to remove them before they produce seeds. At the stage where you can see unopened flower buds, you can often kill annual weeds simply by cutting off the top growth, by hand, with a "weed-eater" or with a lawn mower. This is because weeds at the bud stage have channeled most of their energy into the formation of flowers and seed embryos and have little or no carbohydrate left in their roots to use for regenerating new top growth.

If you wait until the flowers on annual weeds have opened before removing the weeds, there is a danger that the seeds will ripen on the plant even though it has been pulled out of the soil. Therefore, you should not allow mature flowering weeds to lie on the soil. Instead, throw them on a ground tarp or in a wheelbarrow. Put weed seeds in a compost only if you are operating a hot composting system (see p. 644), since cool, slowly decomposing compost piles will not

kill weed seeds. All areas of the compost pile must heat up to at least 160°F (71°C).

If perennial weeds have grown beyond the seedling stage, your efforts must focus primarily on the roots. This is because perennial roots—bulbs, tubers, rhizomes, stolons, crowns and taproots—produce new top growth if the existing leaves and stems are damaged or removed. Moreover, if the perennial roots are themselves broken apart by the gardener trying to dig them out, each piece may be able to generate an entirely new plant. This is the reason behind the admonition "get the roots" when pulling out perennial weeds.

The energy used to make new top growth comes from nutrients that are produced by the photosynthesizing leaves and sent down for storage in the roots at the end of the growing season. Every time the roots are called upon to initiate new top growth, this store is diminished. Thus, there is a limit to the number of times roots can initiate new foliage in a single season.

Once three or four new leaves have developed, they begin photosynthesizing and take over the job of supplying the energy needed for further growth. During the rapid growth phase of the new plant, the carbohydrates being manufactured by the top growth are used up in the production of leaves, stems, flowers, seeds and new root hairs. It is not until just after blossoming that surplus nutrients become available for storage in the roots. These nutrients are used to initiate new growth the next season.

This suggests that if your efforts to dig out or otherwise kill mature perennial weeds are insufficient, an alternative strategy is to exhaust nutrient reserves in the roots and prevent their resupply by repeatedly destroying new top growth as it emerges early in the growing season. This forces the roots to use up stored nutrients to develop new stems and leaves. Eventually the nutrient supply is exhausted completely and new top growth does not appear. Without leaves to photosynthesize and supply new food, the roots die.

To achieve the greatest effect, top growth should be removed before the weed begins to translocate (move) food reserves down to the root zone for storage for the following season. This translocation occurs just before or during the early stages of flowering. Removal of top growth at this point also takes advantage of the fact that root nutrient reserves are already low, and thus the plant is less able to generate new leaves and stems. Resupply of nutrients also can be reduced by limiting the access of plant leaves to sunlight, water or minerals.

Physical Controls

Physical or mechanical controls comprise such familiar methods as hand-pulling, cultivation with various tools, mowing and mulching, as well as some less familiar techniques such as flaming and soil solarization.

Hand Pulling. When removing weeds by hand, be certain to get a good grip so that when you pull you get the roots along with the tops. Grip the plant as close to the soil as possible, rock it back and forth a few times to loosen its roots, then pull steadily upward. Failure to pull up the roots usually means the weed will soon push out new top growth and your efforts will be wasted. It is also a good idea to water the soil the day before you intend to weed, because weed roots are very difficult to remove thoroughly when the soil is dry.

When hand-pulling weeds such as dandelions *(Taraxacum officinale)* that have long, fleshy taproots, a hand tool with a 12-in. (30 cm) long shaft and a V point (B and C in the drawing below) will help you get all the root. Remember that roots of perennial weeds usually have growth buds along their lengths, and even small pieces left in the soil can produce new plants.

Cultivation. The objective of cultivation is to cut or loosen the weed's roots and expose them to the drying action of the sun and air. If done properly, the roots desiccate (dry out) and die, providing a mulch for the soil. If rainfall or overhead irrigation is plentiful, however, you may be wise to rake up and remove the weeds so that their roots don't become re-established.

Cultivation is most effective on young weed seedlings. At that stage, weeds have not yet developed extensive roots or tops and are relatively easy to control. If you are preparing an area for planting, one effective cultivation technique is to dig out any existing weeds and then cultivate, level, rake and irrigate the soil where you intend to plant. Allow a new crop of weed seeds to germinate —this usually takes 7 to 10 days— then cultivate shallowly, about 1 in. (2.5 cm) down, and repeat the process, removing the weeds a second time.

A Weeder's Nontoxic Arsenal

A weed knife (A) is used for cutting and digging roots of perennial weeds, short- and long-handled dandelion knives (B, C) for removing taprooted weeds, a long-handled trimmer (D) for chopping annual and perennial weeds, hoes (E, F) for chopping and scraping out seedling weeds, a weed popper (G) for pulling roots of perennial weeds, a briar hook (H) for removing large weeds without bending, a gas or electric weed trimmer (I) for mowing weeds and a mattock (J) for digging out stubborn roots.

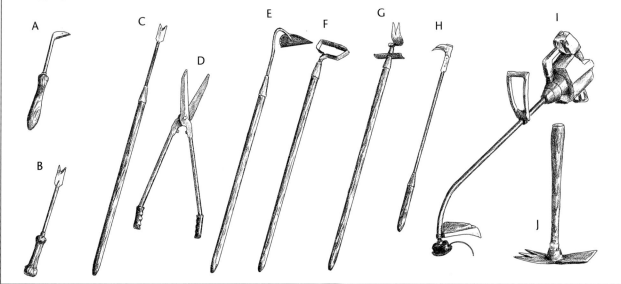

Plant your seeds or transplants after the second cultivation. This process decreases the supply of weed seeds in the top 2 in. (5 cm) of soil where weed seeds germinate, minimizing the need for subsequent weeding.

Another preventive cultivation method is described by Gene Logsdon, an organic farmer and regular contributor to *Organic Gardening* magazine, who recommends starting "preemergent rake cultivation" three to five days after planting seeds. According to Logsdon, you should:

...Watch the soil surface very closely after you have planted your seed. In about three days, you will notice (in most gardens) many tiny weeds beginning to sprout. A cursory cultivation with the steel rake will kill them....Just rake gently over the whole planted space, including the rows, to about an inch depth. You won't hurt your seeds if you don't rake as deeply as you planted. You can rake across corn rows even when the plants are coming up if you are gentle about it.

After the initial raking, rake again once a week for several weeks or until you no longer see the green "fuzz" of weeds. After that, your crop plants will be large enough to shade out any weeds that try to become established.

If the weeds in your garden have already passed the fuzz stage and are several inches tall, hoe them out or use one of the other weed cultivation tools illustrated in the drawing on the facing page (for sources, see the Resource Appendix under "Weed Management: Physical Controls" on p. 689). Be sure the tool is sharp. Power cultivating tools, such as The Green Machine™, designed for working among closely spaced plants are now available. The Green Machine™ has a ⅓-hp motor that runs on household current. It is a cross between a hoe and a rotary tiller and has two angled blades that move back and forth 1,555 times a minute in a "walking" motion. The blades

cut to a depth of 4 in. (10 cm), or deeper if you hold the tool in place.

In addition to physically removing weeds, cultivating tools can be used to throw several inches of soil into the row of growing vegetables or flowers that are 3 in. (7.5 cm) or more above the ground to bury small germinating weeds.

A stand of established weeds, either annuals with deep, fleshy taproots or perennials with extensive root systems, can be removed with a sharp, pointed shovel or a four-tined digging fork (available from garden centers). These tools help get all the root, reducing the likelihood of new top growth appearing from pieces left in the soil. If perennial weeds are covering a large area, you might be wise to mow off the tops and then rotary-till the area to bring up as many roots for drying as possible. The pieces of root left in the soil after tillage will soon sprout new tops. As soon as they do, till the area again. By repeating the tilling every time you see new flushes of top growth, you will eventually exhaust the food reserves in the roots and the roots will die.

Mowing. Mowing is effective for preventing seed production on medium- to tall-growing annual and perennial weeds. It can also be used to enhance the competitive edge of certain desired species over unwanted ones. A familiar example is using a mower to encourage tillering (the growth of numerous grass blades from a single bud) of lawn grasses, which enables them to out-compete broad-leaved weeds (see pp. 526-528 on lawn care for further discussion). In addition to suppressing weeds, mowing leaves a vegetative cover that reduces erosion and keeps the soil habitat closed to migrating weed species. The timing of mowing in the life cycle of the plant is roughly the same for annuals and perennials.

The objective of mowing annual weeds is to time the mowing to prevent seed production. This is achieved best by mowing just before

the weeds bloom to prevent seeds from forming. Just before blooming the weeds are well on their way to ending their life cycle and may not have enough energy left to produce a second flush of top growth. If you wait until after the blossoms have opened, you may be wasting your time, because many weed seeds are able to mature as long as pollination occurred prior to mowing.

Some weeds, such as yellow starthistle *(Centaurea solstitialis),* horseweed *(Erigeron canadensis)* or bitter sneezeweed *(Helenium tenuifolium),* are able to sprout new stems below the cut. With such species it is best to keep the blade high at the first mowing, then lower it enough at the second mowing to cut off the sprouted stems. By the second mowing the stem is often hard and woody and cannot put out new sprouts below the cut.

The prevention of seed production is one objective of mowing perennial weeds, but an even more important goal is forcing the roots to use up their nutrients, which leads to their death. This is done best by timing the first mowing to coincide with the bud stage of the weeds just before blossoms open. At this stage, nutrient reserves in the roots are lowest, making regeneration of new top growth more difficult. The second and, if necessary, subsequent mowings should occur after regrowth is halfway between your ankle and knee. The mower blade should be set low so that as much top growth as possible is removed.

The number of times you need to mow to kill the weed population depends on which species you are dealing with, how many weeds there are and how well established their root systems are. If you persist, even the toughest-to-control perennial weeds such as Canada thistle *(Cirsium arvense)* will succumb. Canadian botanist Dr. R.J. Moore, writing in the *Canadian Journal of Plant Science,* describes a study conducted on a large field in Kansas that was completely covered with this thistle. A series of systematic mowings with the blade as low as possible, one month apart and four times a season, exhausted root nutrients and resulted in the removal of practically all the thistle in two to three seasons.

Weeds can be mowed with rotary mowers (heavy-duty models are available), gas- or electric-powered "weed-eaters," which come with string or blade attachments, or small-scale riding tractors with mower attachments. For slicing weeds by hand, a well-made, inexpensive short-handled Japanese sickle called a "kama" is now available from mail-order suppliers in the United States.

If mowing is the only strategy used against weeds at a site, there is of course a good chance that weed species adapted to mowed areas will simply move into the area vacated by the weed species killed by the mowing. Examples are weeds with prostrate growth habits and a tolerance for bright sunlight, such as annual bluegrass *(Poa annua),* a lawn weed, or pigweed *(Amaranthus* spp.), a common garden weed. Thus, it is important that other tactics—smother-cropping and mulching, for example—be used in conjunction with mowing. See pp. 526-528 on lawns for suggestions on ways to integrate mowing with other tactics.

Flaming. This technique has been popular in residential gardens in Europe for over 50 years but has not yet received the attention it deserves in the United States. Before you conjure up an image of massive grass fires and "controlled burns," let us assure you we are not referring to these methods.

Flaming utilizes a gas- or oil-fired torch to sear the tops of young weeds, as shown in the photo above. The flame produces temperatures of 2,000°F (1,093°C), heating the sap in the cell walls of the plant tissue and causing the cells to expand and rupture. The weed wilts and dies. This technique is most effective on young annual and perennial weeds in the seedling (four- to five-leaf) stage, be-

Flamers can be used to control seedling-stage weeds. The heat from the flame causes weed cells to rupture. The weeds dehydrate and die within a few hours. (Photo courtesy Plow & Hearth.)

cause at that point the fragile root system is killed along with the top growth. Weeds growing in dry areas tend to respond more quickly to flaming than those growing in moist habitats, although the reason why is not known.

Mature perennial weeds such as johnsongrass *(Sorghum halepense),* Canada thistle *(Cirsium arvense)* and even wild morningglory *(Convolvulus arvensis)* also succumb to flaming, but only after a number of treatments spread over a season or two.

In the United States, flaming, or flame cultivation as it is called in agriculture, was used in cotton and corn fields in the 1930 before the advent of sophisticated herbicides. Its use petered out in the 1950s when the romance with herbicides was going strong. It experienced a revival in the mid-1960s when some of the shortcomings of chemicals, includ-

ing shifts of weed species, herbicide damage to crops and cost, made it attractive again. Today flaming is used to control weeds in row crops, orchards and along fence lines and waterways. A flamer has even been used to control stray weeds in the pavement in front of the Kennedy Center in Washington, D.C. In Europe, flamers are experiencing a renaissance, both on organic farms as well as in urban gardens and parks.

A number of hand-held and tractor-mounted flaming tools scaled to various garden sizes are available on the American market, but the best flamers are made in Switzerland and Holland. As we go to press, American distribution of these European flamers is being negotiated. Suppliers of American-made flamers are listed in the Resource Appendix under under "Weed Management: Physical Controls" on p. 689. In smaller gardens, weed infestations in confined areas such as pavement cracks can be killed with a flamer powered by a propane torch (of the type commonly used to remove paint).

There is an art and a science to flaming weeds. The mistake people often make is to assume that they must hold the flame on the weed until they see the plant burn up or at least look sizzled and scorched. Nothing could be farther from the truth. The whole point of flaming is to heat the cell sap, which is accomplished by slowly passing the flame over the plant. You may not see any evidence of wilting, let alone plant death, for several hours or even until the next day.

The process was stumbled upon by accident in the 1930s. As reported by Corkins and Elledge in the May, 1940, issue of *Reclamation Era,* it happened like this:

John Hendreschke, county pest inspector in the Eden Valley, Wyoming, was burning a patch of bindweed [morningglory] *(Convolvulus arvensis)* which had developed mature seed. The growth was heavy and thick and John was doing a good job of burning it up. In fact, he was doing such a good job that by the time it was half done, his burning fuel had been three-fourths used up. So it was a matter either of making a long trip after more fuel or taking a chance on getting the job done with a rapid, light burning. He chose the latter and proceeded to quickly sear the tops of the plants on the rest of the patch.

John got his surprise when he went back to treat this patch the next summer. The part which he had given a 'good job' of heavy burning seemed to have been stimulated by the treatment and the growth was heavier and ranker than before. The part that he had given the 'poor job' of light searing of the top foliage was thinned by at least half and the remaining plants were sickly and weak.

Leaves that have been heated sufficiently to burst cell walls will feel very soft to the touch and may turn a purplish color before wilting and dying. Thus, when you are first trying this technique, use this touch test on the weeds. With some experience you will learn how long to hold the flame to the plant. Remember that the hottest part of the flame is an invisible cone surrounding the visible portion—you should hold the flamer nozzle an inch or more above the weeds for optimum heating.

Broad-leaved weeds are far more susceptible to control by flaming than are grasses. The fact that grasses evolved in environments where fire was a natural component of the ecosystem may explain the relative heat resistance characteristic of many grasses. It is also important to note that flaming is most effective on seedling-stage weeds; older plants are more difficult to kill. A final point: annual weeds succumb to flaming more readily than perennials. One pass with a flamer may kill the tops of perennial weeds, but new growth will regenerate from the below-

Soil Solarization

Solarization uses trapped solar energy to raise the soil temperature high enough to kill germinating weed seeds. After cultivating the soil, removing the clods and irrigating, a plastic tarp is laid on as shown with its edges buried in the soil to seal in heat.

ground roots. Repeated flaming—several times in a season—eventually starves the roots and kills the weed.

Flaming is being used very successfully on organic farms in Europe as one element of an overall weed control program. European landscape gardeners also frequently use this technique.

Soil Solarization. Agricultural scientists in Israel have developed a practical way to use sunlight to generate soil temperatures hot enough to kill weeds. A clear plastic soil tarp is placed over weeds or cultivated soil containing weed seeds (see the drawing above). When daytime temperatures average 85°F (29°C) or more, the tarp traps solar energy, raising the soil temperature to 140°F (60°C) or higher, the thermal death point of the weeds. Black plastic is not used since it does not trap enough heat.

According to Hebrew University of Jerusalem plant pathologist J. Katan, possible mechanisms of weed control by solarization include "direct killing

of weed seeds by heat; indirect microbial killing of seeds weakened by sub-lethal heating; killing of seeds stimulated to germinate in the moistened mulched soil; and killing of germinating seeds whose dormancy is broken in the heated soil."

In the pamphlet "Vegetable Plantings Without Weeds," weed extension advisors Kathleen Hesketh and Clyde Elmore outline how this method can be used in cultivated beds in the home garden. First, they write:

Cultivate and rake the soil level, removing large clods. Irrigate the area 1 to 2 weeks before tarping to encourage weed seeds to sprout. An ideal irrigation method is to lay out a soaker hose because the plastic tarp can be placed directly over it as irrigation proceeds. Lightly work the soil to be sure it is level just before or while placing the tarp so that the soil is smooth enough that the tarp lies close to the soil surface. It is essential that the soil be relatively smooth: if there are furrows or large clods, poor control will result. A smooth, level surface maximizes the high soil temperatures necessary to render seeds unviable. Irrigate again to maximize soil moisture.

A clear plastic tarp should be [at least] 1 to 2 mils (.001 to .002 inch) thick and can be purchased at most hardware stores and many nurseries. Anchor the tarp by burying its edges in a small soil trench around the plot. If a soaker hose is not used under the tarp, or if the area was dry before the tarp was put down, place a hose under the tarp and thoroughly soak the soil with the water on at very low pressure. Because moisture loss by evaporation is minimal under plastic, one soaking is usually sufficient (unless the soil is very sandy). Wait 4 weeks while the sun heats the soil. If tears or rips occur in the plastic, repair them with tape for an air-tight cover.

Once the plastic is removed and the soil has dried somewhat, it is ready for planting. However, if the soil must be worked again before planting, be sure to work it shallowly to 1 inch [2.5 cm]. Weed seeds can be deep in the soil and if the soil is cultivated deeply—down to 4 inches [10 cm] where soil temperatures are not high enough to kill weed seeds—viable seeds may be brought to the surface.

Weeds usually controlled well by this method are annual grasses such as barnyardgrass (Echinochloa crus-galli) and wild barley (Hordeum leporinum) and some broad-leaved plants such as purslane (Portulaca oleracea), pigweed (Amaranthus spp.) and cheeseweed (Malva neglecta). Even bermudagrass has been controlled if the grass and soil are worked up (incorporated) and irrigated prior to placing the plastic.

Research has shown that soil solarization is effective during periods of high temperatures and high light intensity. This usually means keeping the treated area of your garden unplanted for four to six weeks during the prime growing season. However, this sacrifice may be more than offset by the high degree of weed control achieved and the bonus side effects: fewer disease problems and increased yields. It also is possible that solarization can be used in late fall to warm the soil sufficiently to germinate weed seeds. The tarps could then be removed and the weed seedlings left to freeze.

As well as controlling weeds, soil solarization also kills many disease-causing soil microorganisms and nematodes while leaving the beneficial soil fungi and bacteria unaffected. It also produces an increased growth response, a phenomenon noted at the turn of the century in soils disinfested of pathogens.

Katan found that solarization can result in plant growth up to 56% greater than in untreated controls. He writes:

A number of mechanisms, not related to pathogen control, have been suggested for explaining increased growth response in disinfested soils: increased micro and macro elements in the soil solution; elimination of minor pathogens or parasites; destruction of phytotoxic substances in the soil; release of growth regulator-like substances; and stimulation of mycorrhizae or other beneficial microorganisms.

Biological Controls

Biological control includes the use of herbivorous insects, pathogens, fish, geese and livestock to suppress weeds. These tactics have been used since the turn of the century, when the Argentine mothborer (Cactoblastis cactorum) was employed in Australia to control prickly pear cactus (Opuntia inermis and O. stricta), a pest introduced into that country by settlers from South America.

In the United States, beneficial insects have been used successfully to control a number of range and waterway pests, such as St. Johnswort (Hypericum perforatum) and waterhyacinth (Eichhornia crassipes). Recently a number of fungi that kill certain weed species have been produced commercially for use on range weeds. These pathogens are being called mycoherbicides, and within a few years they will probably be available for use in residential gardens. At present, however, practical use of the mycoherbicides as well as predatory insects and herbivorous fish is generally limited to large infestations of weeds in rangelands, pastures, open-space parks, rivers and lakes, rather than in residential gardens. In other words, these biological controls are good for use on a community-wide basis but are not yet cost-effective for individual gardeners.

We summarized current information about the most important mycoherbicides in Chapter 8; check there if you want to learn more about them. However, there are other biological control agents that are ready and waiting to help you weed the garden.

Goats. When we first mentioned goats as a possible alternative to herbicides for the control of brushy weeds such as poison oak, the suggestion was met with great skepticism. Weren't goats ornery critters that eat everything off the clothesline and then start in on the dahlias? Well, there may be goats like that, but not the ones we're talking about.

For years Spanish and Angora goats (Angoras are the small goats whose long shaggy hair is used by weavers) have been used to keep firebreaks cleared of brushy vegetation. These breeds prefer woody vegetation over grasses and forbs (broad-leaved plants), and, if managed properly, can convert areas covered with dense brush back to an earlier stage of vegetation, such as grassland. While goats do eat grasses and broad-leaved plants such as thistles, they look upon them as hors d'oeuvres, preferring for their main course the woodier species such as poison oak and ivy, bamboo, gorse, scotch broom, wild blackberry and coyote bush.

One pioneer in the use of goats for weed control in urban settings is Dick Otterstad, who formerly operated a goat-based brush-clearing service in the San Francisco Bay area. The primary weed control "tools" of Otterstad's company were small, 125-lb. to 175-lb. (57 kg to 79 kg) Angora and Spanish goats and lightweight, flexible fencing reinforced with electrified wire. (A brief flirtation with dairy goats in the brush-clearing operation was abandoned because Otterstad found them to be "goof-offs" when it came to eating and in need of more care than the other breeds.)

Otterstad discovered the effective role goats could play in urban weed management when searching for ways to respond to customer requests for cost-effective alternatives to herbicides. He was also concerned about reducing the hazards of mechanical and chemical brush clearing on steep slopes, where workers were more susceptible to injury from poison oak, falling brush, chemical spray drift, chain saws, gas-powered weed-eaters and other equipment. Since the majority of Otterstad's clients were residential property owners with large, steeply sloped, brush-covered lots who needed to comply with fire ordinances, the sure-footed goats were ideal.

Before moving the goats to the site, Otterstad's crew used chain saws, weed-eaters and brush hooks to clear a fence line and install lightweight, electrified plastic fencing called Flex-inet® (for sources, see the Resource Appendix under "Vertebrate Management: Physical Controls" on p. 688). The fence keeps the goats in and predators out. It is 30 in. (76 cm) high, augmented by 18 in. (45 cm) of plastic bird netting, all supported on nonconductive fiberglass fence posts. It is powered by a 12-volt car battery or a solar-fueled battery, and a two-person crew can install 150 ft. (46 m) of it in about half an hour. It proved so effective that only one goat was lost (to a dog) in the four years Otterstad worked with this method.

Once the fence was installed, the goats were moved to the site; up to 20 goats were carried in the back of a standard pickup truck. If wanted trees or shrubs were located inside the area to be cleared, they were surrounded with more electrified fencing to protect them from the goats. This was not always necessary, because goats that were not corralled in one place for too long often showed little interest in munching on established trees as long as there were still woody shrubs around.

The number of goats used to clear a site is determined by such factors as the size of the area, the species of vegetation, the age and density of weeds to be removed and the degree of brush destruction desired. By carefully manipulating the size of the herd and the length of time it is corralled at the site, the brush can be reduced in height and volume or can be completely killed so that the species composition is forced to revert to grasses and forbs—an ear-lier stage of plant succession. The odorless goat pellets increase avail-able nitrogen in the soil, which gives grasses a competitive edge over broad-leaved plants.

Otterstad usually put 10 goats to work at a typical residential site. He found this herd size to be sufficient to clear typical urban hillside lots and remain economically competitive with other brush-clearing methods. The herd and the state of the vegeta-tion were assessed every two to three days. Although goats get all the water they need from vegetation during the winter, supplemental water is neces-sary in summer and fall.

Experience has shown that al-though goats can eventually trample and consume even very dense, ma-ture woody vegetation in the initial clearing process, they are most cost-effective when clearing or suppress-ing one- to four-year-old regrowth of brush. When faced with mature brush, they defoliate twigs and strip off bark, but leave the plant's super-structure, which is too old and tough to tempt them. In such cases, the goats must be followed by human crews that cut the remaining plant parts with power saws. If, on the oth-er hand, you are removing a thick stand of young thistles or a patch of succulent poison oak or ivy, the goats will kill it quickly.

Once initial clearing has occurred, goats alone can be used periodically to keep the brush cover sparse, or to kill stump sprouts or young woody plants and encourage the growth of grasses and forbs. Some of Otterstad's clients wound up buying one or two goats as a more permanent means of keeping down the brush on their ur-ban and suburban lots.

A 300-goat herd operated by Ken McWilliams with the aid of Aus-tralian sheepdogs is currently em-ployed clearing firebreaks and trails for a number of large northern Cali-fornia regional parks and water dis-tricts that want to reduce their use of herbicides. For years, McWilliams' herd maintained the firebreaks in the Cleveland National Forest in South-ern California; local fire marshals are some of the strongest advocates of goats for brush control. Presumably, this is because much of the fire haz-ard in their communities comes from weedy vegetation on steep hillsides and other spots easily accessible only to goats.

Weeder Geese. Like many old tech-niques forgotten in the face of mod-ern technology, the use of weeder geese has made a comeback with farmers and gardeners looking for safe and effective ways to control weeds. Geese are grass-eaters, and when placed in a garden or orchard where the crop is a broad-leaved plant, they keep it clear of such aggressive species as johnsongrass (*Sorghum halepense*), bermudagrass (*Cynodon dactylon*), nutsedge (*Cyperus rotundus*), water-grass (*Echinochloa crus-galli*) and crab-grass (*Digitaria sanguinalis*). They have also been reported to eat puncture-vine (*Tribulus terrestris*), indicating that they're not total "grassetarians," and underscoring the fact that they must be managed properly so they don't damage the crop they're as-signed to weed.

Geese have been used extensively to weed cotton fields throughout the United States. Their use as weeders in vegetable and fruit crops and in tree nurseries is on the rise, particularly in organic farm and gardening systems. Any breed of goose can be used for weeding, but the preferred one is the white Chinese weeder goose, devel-oped 2,000 years ago in China pri-marily for weed control. These geese are lightweight, grow rapidly, are good egg-layers and appear to be more active than other breeds. More-over, their light color may make them more adaptable to hot weather.

Be forewarned, however, that all breeds of geese are noisy honkers, and some adults can be aggressive toward other animals, including humans. These qualities may make them good substitutes for watchdogs, but they also suggest that a degree of caution is advisable when handling them.

Young geese at least six weeks old and well feathered are considered the best weeders, because they eat their own weight or more in grass every day. Older geese require food only for body maintenance and therefore aren't as voracious. You don't need a lot of geese to get the job done. In very weedy fields, three to five geese per acre (0.4 hectare) are recommended; in areas with low to moderate infestations, one goose per acre may be all that's needed. Thus, in a residential garden, one or two geese ought to do the job. At the end of the season you can decide whether you want to keep the geese as permanent weeders and egg-layers, or eat them and buy new young ones next year.

One Missouri gardener keeps two adult Embden geese in a run adjacent to her 20-ft. by 60-ft. (6 m by 18 m) garden. The garden is divided by fencing into three areas connected by gates. In fall, the geese are turned onto the entire garden to eat the remains of the year's vegetables. What they don't eat, they crush, hastening the decomposition process. The geese remain in the dormant garden, keeping it weed-free until spring planting. They are excluded from one section of the garden while early crops are planted, then moved out of the second section into the run when the rest of the garden is ready for planting.

The geese spend the summer growing season in the run, with daily excursions on the grounds around the house. As soon as the seedlings are about 2 in. (5 cm) tall, mulch is applied between rows. When the crop is a foot tall, stray weeds are pulled and more mulch is applied. Any weeds that grow after that are left for the geese to deal with when they are turned into the garden in the fall. After several years of this routine, the soil in the garden is so friable that cultivation is rarely needed.

Geese are most effective if introduced into the area to be weeded just after weed seeds sprout and plants are still young and tender. They can be left in the field or garden until 75% to 90% of the weeds have been devoured, but should be removed at that point because there is the danger they will begin munching on the crop plant, seeking diversity in their diet. In fact, the provision of extra feed in the form of poultry or rabbit pellets or grain helps keep the geese healthy and growing. In an article entitled "Management of Weeder Geese in Commercial Fields," cooperative extension agent Clarence Johnson recommends that 1 lb. (0.45 kg) of feed supplement per 10 birds be provided daily. When geese are confined overnight, some feed should be provided before they go into the field, since they do not have a crop for storing food as do most other birds. If they are allowed to get very hungry, they may develop digestive troubles after gorging themselves on grass.

Geese also need clean, fresh drinking water and shade from the hot sun. By moving the location of the water and shade structure, geese can be encouraged to weed a given area more thoroughly. Although they don't absolutely need water to swim in, in hot climates they will probably develop leg or foot ailments if they don't have access to a pond or a ditch. In return, they help keep grasses from clogging the waters.

Geese need to be protected from predators such as dogs, which can "playfully" kill a whole flock overnight, and from wildlife such as raccoons, coyotes, weasels and foxes, which kill geese for food. The Flexinet® electric fence (described on p. 503) is an inexpensive means of protection, or you can construct a fence of chicken wire topped with barbed wire. A 2-ft. (0.6 m) high fence keeps the geese confined, but a 3-ft. or 4-ft. (0.9 m to 1.2 m) fence may be needed if dogs are a problem. The bottom 6 in. (15 cm) of the chicken wire should be bent into an L and buried at least 6 in. under the soil with the bottom of the L pointing outward. This helps prevent predators from digging under the fence.

White Chinese geese are available from hatcheries throughout the United States. An excellent source of weeder geese and information on their use for this purpose is the Permaculture Institute of North America (PINA), listed in the Resource Appendix under "Suppliers" on p. 695.

Chemical Controls

The use of herbicides in home gardens is usually unnecessary. As stated by cooperative extension weed scientists Hesketh and Elmore in their pamphlet "Vegetable Plantings Without Weeds":

> Chemical weed control is complicated. Most herbicides cannot be used to control all weeds safely in all crops....Residues of some herbicides may remain in the soil and affect the growth of a following crop....It takes much less time and effort in the small vegetable garden to hand-pull or hoe young weed seedlings than it does to read several chemical labels, decide on the proper chemical, check the sprayer, measure the needed amount of chemical, make the application and then wash the sprayer.

There are the added problems of washing the protective equipment and disposing of the extra herbicide.

It is a testament to the skill of the advertising industry that it has made herbicides seem so easy to use. However, anyone trying to understand the labels on herbicide containers or the recommendations given in weed control literature quickly runs into a bewildering array of herbicide terminology—contact, translocated, selective, non-selective, pre-emergent, post-emergent, soil-applied, foliage-applied, residual, pre-plant and so on. These and other terms (discussed in Chapter 6) refer, variously, to the ways in which the herbicide acts on the plant and to the point in the plant's life cycle at which the plant is susceptible to the herbicide. These concepts must be understood thoroughly in order to select the right chemical and apply it correctly.

But this is just the tip of the iceberg. An individual herbicide is usually effective only on a fairly limited range of weed species. Its ability to kill those species in a given location depends on a large number of variables, including soil type, climate, available moisture, equipment used and application technique.

Plant Resistance to Herbicides. If the same herbicide is used year after year on the same weed species, the weeds develop resistance just as insects develop resistance to insecticides. The resistance phenomenon in weeds has been documented primarily for species treated with the triazine class of preemergent herbicides, including simazine (Princep®), atrazine (AAtrex®) and prometon (Pramitol®), which are commonly used on flowerbeds, paths, baseball diamonds and roadsides. However, weed scientists are currently studying the resistance of certain weed species to other classes of herbicides. The failure of most people who use herbicides, including professionals, to understand the complexities of herbicide technology has no doubt contributed significantly to the chronic abuse of these chemicals that has exacerbated the resistance problem.

A brief but useful description of key herbicide terminology and explanations of the various classes of herbicides is provided in Chapter 6. The topic is explored in greater depth in Swan et al.'s *Weed Control on Rights-of-Way*. We recommend that you read and understand the information in this bulletin before you use any herbicides. We also recommend that you thoroughly protect yourself with gloves, goggles, a respirator and coveralls when applying these chemicals since they, like other pesticides, are poisons. See pp. 97-103 for a discussion of protective equipment.

Least-Toxic Pesticides. In those rare cases when herbicides are considered necessary, refer to pp. 114-119 for a discussion of soap-based herbicides such as Sharpshooter™ and weed oils, which we consider the least-toxic chemical materials available for managing weeds. Information on the many other registered herbicides is available from your local cooperative extension office. Unfortunately, most of these herbicides, in our opinion, have undesirable characteristics, and we try to avoid their use. Do not under any circumstances use herbicides containing arsenic compounds, 2,4-D or 2,4,5-T, because they have been found to pose serious hazards to humans and to the environment.

Integrating Chemical Controls. Once you have chosen the chemical, it is important that you apply it as selectively as possible; that is, do your best to restrict it to the target weeds and keep it off other vegetation and the soil. This is known as spot treatment, and it is most successful when integrated with other control strategies.

One of the most significant benefits of integrating chemical controls with other direct and indirect control strategies is that the amount of herbicide needed to control the weeds is reduced. Take, for example, the task of removing a large clump of wild berries, bamboo or other brush from your garden. Typically the gardener is advised to spray the entire clump of weeds thoroughly so the herbicide comes into contact with more surface area of each plant. But this approach makes it difficult to keep the herbicide from drifting onto nearby plants, including those located in neighboring gardens, or from coating the soil in which the weeds are growing.

An alternative method involves removing as much of the surface vegetation as possible by mechanical means and applying the herbicide to the remaining stems. This reduces the overall amount of herbicide needed to kill the weeds and enables you to use application techniques that confine the herbicide to the weeds. To do this, we recommend the use of a gas- or electric-powered "weed-eater" with a blade attachment to cut the brush as low to the ground as possible (see I in the drawing on p. 498). Rake away the severed plant parts to expose the stems left protruding from the ground. Use a hand ax to chop gashes in the stumps to expose more of the internal stem tissue that normally carries nutrients down to the plant roots.

Using an herbicide that translocates to the roots, apply the strongest solution permitted on the label to the cuts. For the most selective application, apply it with a paint brush or a wick applicator (for sources, see the Resource Appendix under "Weed Management: Chemical Controls" on p. 689) or with a standard one- or two-gallon herbicide sprayer available at nurseries or hardware stores.

For this technique to work, the herbicide must be applied within 30 minutes of cutting open the stumps, since you want the weed's internal plumbing system—the phloem cells—to absorb the herbicide and carry it to the roots. If you wait too long, the plant will place an invisible protective seal over cut surfaces. If you are treating a large area of brushy weeds, it might be difficult to chop down and rake all the foliage and get the herbicide on all surfaces within 30 minutes. Either work on small sections, completing all steps in one section before moving to the next, or simply hold off on chopping the stems with the ax until just before you are ready to apply the herbicide.

It will take several weeks for the underground parts of the plants to die. Some may send up new shoots, which will require spot treatment with the ax and/or herbicide. Resprouting can be prevented by covering the stumps with black plastic after applying the herbicide. However, it is not known to what degree, if any, sunlight is required by the plant to stimulate the phloem cells into translocating the herbicide to the roots. If you want to try this procedure, wait a few days after applying the herbicide before covering the treated area with plastic.

An Integrated Approach for Controlling Poison Oak and Poison Ivy

Dick Otterstad, owner of Otterstad's Brush Control Service in Albany, California (whose use of goats for clearing was discussed on pp. 502-503), has perfected a technique for cutting out poison oak *(Toxicodendron diversilobum)*, handling the debris and protecting the workers doing the job. The technique should also work for the control of poison ivy *(Toxicodendron radicans)*.

Overview of the method. After mechanically flailing (chopping) the plants during the dormant season, Otterstad follows in early spring with a spot treatment of the re-sprouts with small amounts of a translocating herbicide. In contrast to conventional poison oak control methods, which are applied in spring or summer when the plants are in full leaf, Otterstad's method is undertaken largely during the cool winter months when the plants have shed their leaves. Without leaves, there is less surface area from which workers might pick up the toxic oil. Also, the woody structure of the plants is quite visible at that time, enabling the crew to see what they are cutting.

Cutting. Poison oak is considered difficult to cut because of the springy nature of its many ½-in. (13 mm) diameter branches, which can whip up and fly against workers. Otterstad solves this problem by carefully removing such growth with power hedge shears. Next he cuts wood up to 2 in. (5 cm) in diameter with a heavy-duty Husqvarna® mechanical clearing saw (shown in the photo on the facing page) powered by a 65 cc, 2½-hp gasoline engine. Otterstad prefers this brand because it is well-balanced, maneuverable and rugged, and the variety of blades available increases the saw's versatility as a brush-clearing tool.

An experienced operator can clear a 5-ft. by 30-ft. (1.5 m by 9 m) stand in about 10 minutes. The flailed material falls to the ground in lengths varying from 1½ in. to 12 in. (4 cm to 30 cm), depending on the operator's technique and the needs of the client. The worker must be careful to cut plants as close to the ground as possible without damaging the sawblade.

Disposal of debris. Once the dormant plants are chopped, there are a number of options for handling the debris. Otterstad prefers to flail it into fairly small lengths, compact it firmly on the soil and leave it to decompose. In his experience, the woody stems do not sprout once they have been flailed, and the decomposing litter helps reduce erosion. It also saves clients hauling and dump fees, and eliminates the often fruitless search for a landfill that accepts poison oak.

To prevent pets or people from coming into contact with the still-toxic remains, Otterstad places logs on top of it or uses a 12-in. (30 cm) deep mulch of wood chips collected from tree-trimming. The litter can also be buried on the site. Debris that makes good contact with the soil will decompose completely in a season or two, depending on how finely it was chopped.

Subsequent treatment. In early spring, stumps left in the ground after winter flailing put out a flush of leaf growth. At this stage, the live clumps are easy to spot

The integrated methods described here work very well for the control of poison oak *(Toxicodendron [=Rhus] diversilobum)* and would probably also work on poison ivy *(Toxicodendron [=Rhus] radicans)*. The sidebar above describes how they can be used and what precautions must be taken. The sidebar on p. 508 tells you what to do if you are exposed to the sap of poison oak or poison ivy.

Methods for Applying Pesticides Selectively. There are a number of ways to apply herbicides to target weeds that minimize contact with nontarget organisms.

1. Wick Applicators. Wick applicators absorb the herbicide on a rope, sponge or carpet wick and permit the worker to wipe the herbicide directly onto the target weed. They can be designed or retrofitted with long handles, allowing the worker to stand some distance from the target weed. Hand-held or machine-mounted wick applicators can be purchased from commercial sources (see the Resource Appendix under "Weed Management: Chemical Controls" on p. 689).

2. Injection, Frill and Basal Application. When using herbicides to kill unwanted woody shrubs, trees or vines such as poison ivy, use injection, frill or basal spray techniques where possible. Frill application entails making shallow ax cuts around the circumference of the stem and applying herbicides in the cuts. Basal spraying involves coating the bark on

among the dead plant litter and are spot-treated once or twice with an herbicide. By limiting herbicide applications to spot treatments, workers' exposure to herbicides is minimized, and the danger to wanted vegetation from drift is virtually eliminated.

Once the poison oak is removed it is important to alter the habitat to discourage recolonization by poison oak seedlings, which can sprout from seed reserves in the soil. Deep wood chip mulches or vigorous alternative vegetation is recommended.

Protecting workers. Workers must be protected from the poison oak, as well as from accidents with power equipment and herbicides. To minimize contact with the poison oil in the sap, flailing is scheduled for cool, cloudy or foggy days when the air is less likely to contain the particulate matter to which droplets of the toxic plant resin can cling. Cool weather also makes workers more comfortable in the somewhat heavy protective clothing, and this in turn reduces exposure caused by wiping off perspiration with oil-contaminated sleeves or gloves. If the toxic oil

makes contact with the skin, it can be washed off with a special cleanser such as Tecnu®, available in hardware stores or pharmacies.

Following the maxim "keep covered but cool," crews wear only one layer of clothing. Shirts

and sleeves are fully buttoned, pant legs are tucked into boots and heavy cotton or leather gloves are worn at all times. A helmet with full-face visor protects against flying wood chips. Noise abaters on the helmet guard against hearing loss. Thigh and shin guards shield workers from poison oil and the occasional rocks and other debris thrown up as the saw moves through dense vegetation. The shin guards are the type made for baseball umpires, and contain a section that also protects the area between the ankle and the steel toe of the boot. The flexible covering over the kneecap is designed to move with the knee.

To protect the thighs, Otterstad and his crew developed a lightweight alternative to commercial equipment. Lengths of corrugated PVC drain pipe are cut with tin snips to fit the thighs of each crew member. Velcro™ is used to strap on the guards securely. These homemade devices are flexible and lightweight enough not to impede movement, yet strong enough to provide protection against sharp objects. They can be dropped in a bucket of soapy water to remove any poison oils that collect on them.

the lower 12 in. to 24 in. (30 cm to 60 cm) of trunk or stem with herbicide. Herbicide injection tools, which resemble either hatchets or hand guns and are attached by a tube to a pesticide container, are available from the forestry suppliers listed in the Resource Appendix under "Weed Management: Chemical Controls" and from other equipment sources.

3. *Large-Droplet Sprayers.* When foliage sprays are required, use spray nozzles that produce fairly large her-

bicide droplets to limit drift of the herbicide. It may be helpful to include an anti-drift product in the spray tank. Drift is also minimized by using moderate pressure, which produces relatively large spray droplets. High pressure produces smaller, lightweight droplets that can remain airborne for longer distances.

If herbicides drift onto wanted vegetation or sterilized soil you want to grow plants in, quick action is needed. Detoxifying methods differ,

depending on the type of herbicide used. Herbicides applied to plant leaves are less damaging to plants when they are on the soil than when they are on the leaves. Thus, rinse the plant thoroughly with plain water for 5 minutes to wash off the herbicide. To minimize damage, rinsing must occur within one to four hours of contamination. Lawns should be irrigated and then mowed as soon as possible after exposure. Remove contaminated clippings from the garden.

What To Do If You Are Exposed to Poison Oak or Poison Ivy Sap

Contaminated skin should be washed several times with water and a strong soap such as Fels Naphtha™, tincture of green soap, Dr. Brommer's Peppermint Soap™ or one of the new commercial poison oak and ivy preparations such as Tecnu®, available in hardware stores and pharmacies and from mail-order suppliers. Cold water is recommended for washing because heat tends to open the pores and allows the sap to enter the lower layers of skin. If soap is not available, you can use vinegar (2 tablespoons in 1 cup of water) or alcohol (½ cup of alcohol to ½ cup of water).

To avoid spreading the dissolved sap over wider areas of skin, dab the vinegar or alcohol onto the contaminated area with a piece of absorbent cotton. Promptly remove the dissolved oil with a dry piece of cotton, discarding each piece as used. Repeat this procedure a number of times. Calamine lotion or a paste of baking soda can be applied to the rash to relieve itching. (Note: Cortisone shots or creams may have dangerous side effects and should only be used with the advice and supervision of a physician.) Healing time varies from a few days to several weeks, and healed sites often remain hypersensitive to further contact with the sap for several months.

For soil-applied herbicides, if drift has just occurred, rinse off plants with water. If rain or irrigation has moved the herbicide into the soil, apply as much compost or other organic matter as you can. Organic matter attracts and binds up some herbicide residues, reducing their ability to damage plants. You can also cultivate into the soil powdered, steam-activated charcoal, which absorbs certain herbicides, particularly the triazines, such as simazine (Princep®).

Herbicide concentrations of 4 lb. (1.8 kg) of active ingredient or less per 100 sq. ft. (9 sq. m) can be counteracted with 1 lb. (0.45 kg) of activated charcoal over the same area. Thoroughly incorporate the charcoal to a depth of 6 in. (15 cm). This treatment should deactivate the herbicide, but it may take up to six months.

If these methods fail, it may be necessary to dig up and remove contaminated turf or soil. The contaminated soil should be composted in its own pile. Microbes will break down the toxicants to some degree, but there is no guarantee that the soil will again support plant growth. In any case, it should not be used to grow food plants.

REFERENCES AND READINGS

Adams, T.E., and B. Kay. 1982. *Seeding for erosion control in coastal and central California.* Davis: University of California Cooperative Extension (Leaflet 21304). 4 pp. (Available from: ANR Publications, 6701 San Pablo Ave., Oakland, CA 94608-1239).

This excellent booklet provides useful tips on ways to manipulate fertilization to encourage growth of wildflowers and/or clover versus grasses.

Aldrich, R.J. 1984. *Weed-crop ecology: principles in weed management.* Belmont, Calif.: Breton Publishers. 465 pp.

An excellent text on agricultural weed management from an ecological perspective.

Allan, Mea. 1978. *Weeds —the unbidden guests in our gardens.* New York: Viking Press. 191 pp.

A well-illustrated book of common weeds found in Britain and North America, including discussions of how the weeds migrate and why many immigrant plants are considered undesirable. The useful characteristics of many weeds are outlined, and over 200 weeds are illustrated and described.

Anderson, R.C., A.J. Katz and M.R. Anderson. 1978. Allelopathy as a factor in the success of *Helianthus mollis. Journal of Chemical Ecology* 4(1):9-16.

This is one of the sources of the information summarized in Table 28.2 on pp. 494-495; other sources are listed throughout this reference list.

Bokhari, U.G. 1978. Allelopathy among prairie grasses and its possible ecological significance. *American Botany* 42:127-136.

This is one of the sources of the information presented in Table 28.2.

Burger, A.A. 1925. Kill Canada thistles. *Wallace's Farmer* 50:822.

A delightful, first-person narrative of one of the earliest successful attempts at controlling Canada thistle using cultural methods.

Cocannouer, J.A. 1964. *Weeds: guardians of the soil.* New York: Devin-Adair. 179 pp.

This folksy volume presents in anecdotal style observations of the positive roles weeds play in improving soils. (For a lengthier description of this work, see p. 484.)

Corkins, C.L., and A.B. Ellegde. 1940. Continuous burning to eradicate noxious weeds. *The Reclamation Era* (May).

This is the source of the report on the accidental discovery of the flaming technique for weed control.

Daar, S. 1991. Vegetation management on rights-of-way: an ecological approach. *The IPM Practitioner* 8(2): 1-7.

This article describes techniques used by utility companies to establish low-growing, stable shrublands under power lines to replace problem trees. The techniques substantially reduced use of herbicides, and can be used along roads, park trails and other rights-of-way.

Egler, F.E. 1957. Science, industry, and the abuse of rights-of-way. *Science* 127:573-580.

A biting indictment of the headlong rush into the use of herbicides on roadsides and under power lines without consideration of the environmental consequences. It was written at the time synthetic herbicides were just beginning to be used widely and indiscriminately.

Fay, P.K., and W.B. Duke. 1977. An assessment of the allelopathic potential in *Avena* germ plasm. *Weed Science* 25(3): 224-228.

This is one of the sources of the information presented in Table 28.2.

Fischer, B.B, A.H. Lange, J. McCaskill, B. Crampton and B. Tabraham. 1978. *Grower's weed identification handbook.* Berkeley: University of California Cooperative Extension Service (Publication 4030). 250 pp. (Available from: ANR Publications, 6701 San Pablo Ave., Oakland, CA 94608-1239.)

Excellent color photographs of the seed, seedling and flowering stage of each of more than 170 weed species, together with summaries of pertinent biological and ecological information, make this the best weed identification tool currently available.

Green, J. 1982. Complementary field plantings: grass and nursery plants. *Ornamentals Northwest Newsletter* 6(3): 8-9. (Available free from: Horticulture Department, Oregon State University, Corvallis, OR 97331.)

Practical advise on the use of sod aisles and other complementary planting techniques.

Harrington, H.D., and L.W. Durrell. 1957. *How to identify plants.* Chicago: Swallow Press. 203 pp.

A well-written book that takes the mystery out of botanical nomenclature. It includes a list of keys to plants of the United States.

Hesketh, K.A., and C.L. Elmore. 1982. *Vegetable plantings without weeds.* Berkeley: University of California, Division of Agricultural Sciences (Leaflet 21153). 19 pp.

This concise booklet spells out procedures for reducing weeds through soil solarization. It also describes how cultivation and irrigation techniques can be used together to reduce weed growth.

Hoffman, G.R., and D.L. Hazlett. 1977. Effects of aqueous *Artemesia* extracts and volatile substances on germination of selected species. *Journal of Range Management* 30(2):134-137.

This is one of the sources of the information presented in Table 28.2.

Isely, D. 1960. *Weed identification and control.* Ames: Iowa State University Press. 400 pp.

An excellent key to common weeds of the United States.

Jeavons, J. 1974. *How to grow more vegetables than you ever thought possible on less land than you can imagine.* Palo Alto, Calif.: Ecology Action of the Mid-Peninsula. 82 pp.

This ground-breaking book introduced American gardeners to the French intensive method of gardening. It details strategies for maximizing yields on small garden plots using ecologically sound techniques.

Johnson, C. Undated. *Management of weeder geese in commercial crops.* Madera: University of California Cooperative Extension Service. 2 pp.

Includes a concise summary of the management of weeder geese together with a cost analysis.

Katan, J. 1981. Solar heating (solarization) of soil for control of soilborne pests. *Annual Review of Phytopathology* 19:211-236.

This paper describes the solarization technique for disease control. The same information can be extrapolated for use against weeds.

King, L.J. 1966. *Weeds of the world.* New York: Interscience. 526 pp.

One of the most thoroughly researched discussions of the origin, botany, spread and control of agricultural weeds ever written. Includes a good chapter on non-chemical methods for control of weeds (with an excellent bibliography).

Klingman, G.C., F.M. Ashton and L.J. Noordhoff. 1975. *Weed science: principles and practices.* New York: John Wiley and Sons. 431 pp.

A standard weed control text with explanations of various chemical classes of herbicides.

Larson, M.M., and E.L. Schwartz. 1980. Allelopathic inhibition of black locust, red clover, and black alder by six common herbaceous species. *Forest Science* 261(3):511-520.

This is one of the sources of the information presented in Table 28.8.

Lockerman, R.H., and A.R. Putnam. 1979. Evaluation of allelopathic cucumbers *(Cucumis sativus)* as an aid to weed control. *Weed Science* 27(1): 54-57.

This is one of the sources of the information presented in Table 28.2.

McLeod, Edwin. 1983. *Feed the soil.* Graton, Calif.: Organic Agricultural Research Institute. 209 pp. (Available from: AgAccess, P.O. Box 2008, Davis, CA 95617.)

This wonderful book tells you everything you need to know about dozens of nitrogen-fixing plants that improve the soil.

Moore, R.J. 1975. The biology of Canadian weeds: *Cirsium arvense.* *Canadian Journal of Plant Science* 55:1033-1048.

This is the source of the information on the mowing method used to virtually eliminate Canada thistle from a pasture within two to three seasons.

Muenscher, W.C. 1980. *Weeds.* Ithaca, N.Y.: Cornell University Press. 586 pp.

An excellent reference tool for identifying weeds. It contains a key to and descriptions of over 570 weeds found throughout the United States and Canada. Control information is limited to mechanical methods.

Nicolson, P., ed. 1983. *Vita Sackville-West's garden book.* New York: Atheneum. 250 pp.

This book is composed of garden columns written by Sackville-West in the *London Observer* from 1951 to 1958 chronicling her experience in her garden at Sissinghurst Castle. She cautions against the indiscriminate removal of weeds.

Niering, W.A. 1958. Principles of sound right-of-way vegetation management. *Economic Botany* 12:140-144.

Niering's was one of the early voices in opposition to strict reliance on herbicides for control of vegetation along power lines and roadsides.

Peters, E.J., and A.H.B. Mohammed Zam. 1981. Allelopathic effects of tall fescue genotypes. *Agronomy Journal* 73:56-58.

This is one of the sources of the information presented in Table 28.2.

Putnam, A.R., and W.B. Duke. 1974. Biological suppression of weeds: evidence for allelopathy on accessions of cucumber. *Science* 185: 370-372.

This is one of the sources of the information presented in Table 28.2.

Radosevich, S.R., and J.S. Holt. 1984. *Weed ecology.* New York: John Wiley and Sons. 265 pp.

An excellent introduction to weed management based on ecological principles.

Rice, E.L. 1972. Allelopathic effects of *Andropogon virginicus* and its persistence in old fields. *American Journal of Botany* 59(7):752-755.

This is one of the sources of the information presented in Table 28.2.

Schenck, Linda E. 1978. Allelopathy: chemical conversation between plants. *The Cornell Plantation* 34(2): 21-26.

A discussion of the mechanisms of allelopathy and how they are exhibited by various plant species.

Subcommittee on Standardizaton of Common and Botanical Names of Weeds. 1989. Composite list of weeds. (Available from: The Weed Science Society, 309 W. Clark St., Champaign, IL 61820.)

A very useful list of the most recent scientific names assigned to common weeds.

Subcommittee on Weeds. 1968. *Weed control.* Washington, D.C.: National Academy of Sciences (Publication 1597). 471 pp.

An excellent discussion of integrated approaches to weed control that focuses primarily on food crops.

Swan, D.G., L.E. Foote, T.M. Evans, R.L. Berger and W.E. Currie. 1980. *Weed control on rights-of-way.* Pullman: Washington State University Cooperative Extension Service (Bulletin 0669). 27 pp.

This well-illustrated booklet provides an overview of how herbicides affect plants, how to select them and how to time their use. If you plan to use herbicides occasionally, this is a good primer.

USDA Soil Conservation Service. 1981. *Cover crops in California orchards and vineyards.* 25 pp. (Available from: Publications, USDA Soil Conservation Service, 2828 Chiles Rd., Davis, CA 95616.)

A useful discussion of selecting, establishing and managing cover crops. The management techniques are applicable to orchards and vineyards throughout the United States. The particular plant species described are suited to California and similar Mediterranean climates.

Walters, D.T., and A.R. Gilmore. 1976. Allelopathic effects of fescue on the growth of sweetgum. *Journal of Chemical Ecology* 2(4):469-479.

This is one of the sources of the information presented in Table 28.2.

CHAPTER 29
Preventing Lawn Pests

INTRODUCTION

Most lawn pest problems can be solved safely by understanding which conditions favor the problem, then changing those conditions as much as possible. This approach—treating causes, not just symptoms—is not the traditional way of dealing with lawn pests. The technical literature or the expert being consulted more often focuses on the identity of the pest organism and on finding the "approved" pesticide for control. Thus, lawn pest control becomes a game of matching the pesticide to the pest organism. Unfortunately, this approach leads to the pesticide treadmill and associated problems outlined in the first chapter of this book and ignores the central question: Why is the pest problem occurring in the first place?

Unless this question is answered, any treatment, chemical or cultural, is likely to provide only short-term relief. If the conditions making the lawn hospitable to pests are not altered, the pests will return, requiring treatment again and again, season after season. The treadmill effect is worsened by the side effects on the lawn ecosystem of the pesticide regimens outlined in most lawn-care publications. Because the pesticide also damages soil organisms that benefit grass growth, grass vigor is reduced—and vigorous growth is the lawn's primary defense against pests, particularly weeds.

In order to explain what might be causing pest problems on your lawn and how you might alter the conditions conducive to pests, let's look at the evolution of a typical suburban lawn and see what lessons can be learned.

The Saga of the Suburban Lawn

Once upon a time there was a tomato field—or orchard or forest or pasture or hillside—that was converted into a residential or commercial development. First the topsoil was scraped off the land, sold and carted away. Then bulldozers and other heavy construction equipment ran across the bare subsoil, moving some of it and compacting all of it. The soil on the building pads (which include the area around the house that many people use for gardens) was compacted to a density of 90% or more to meet building codes.

Then construction began. Foundations were poured and innumerable supply trucks drove over the soil, compacting it even more. The soil became the local dump for debris generated during construction, including old crankcase oil from the bulldozers and pickups, leftover cement, paint, solvents, nails, mastic, drywall, "mud" (unused mortar and drywall compound) and a host of other exotic substances.

Upon completion of construction, the soil, including these various "amendments," was either left bare for the prospective home owner to tend, or a quick landscape "band-aid" was applied. Typically a few inches of imported loam are spread over the compacted subsoil, a layer of sod is rolled out, a few shrubs are planted and someone is paid to water these doomed plants daily in the hope that they will stay alive until the property is sold. The newly arrived residents are faced with the difficult task of trying to maintain a lawn essentially designed to die. Or, faced with bare soil, they often create their own version of a lawn band-aid in their eagerness to get something growing as soon as possible.

That lawns can, and often do, survive such careless installation results from their inherent ability as colonizing species to adapt to adverse conditions. However, lawns with such poor beginnings in life rarely thrive in the long run and require more maintenance than properly installed turf. Even with chemical help, the grass lacks vigor in soil abused by construction activities. It has few resources for warding off insect or disease attack or for competing with weeds. Next we look at why this is so.

HEALTHY SOIL: BUILDING BLOCK OF A HEALTHY LAWN

Grasses have descended from natural environments where they were constantly grazed. Thus, they can tolerate minor feeding by insects and fungi. If, despite this hardiness, your lawn lacks the color, density, vigor and pest resistance you hoped for, the soil is the first place to look for causes. Grasses, like other living organisms, need food, water and a hospitable habitat. Their habitat includes the soil in which roots can find the anchorage, air, water and minerals that support stem and leaf growth.

The most vigorous lawn growth occurs in friable (loose), loamy soils that are teeming with beneficial microorganisms, insects, worms and other invertebrates (see the drawing on the facing page). This active fauna is entertainingly described for the lay reader in Peter Farb's *Living Earth* and Friedrich Schaller's *Soil Animals* (listed under "References and Readings" on p. 528).

These organisms play critical roles in decomposing dead organic matter—such as blades of grass sheared off by a lawn mower—into an end product called humus. Humus increases soil aeration and water-holding and nutrient-exchange capacity, and it buffers the soil pH (its relative acidity or alkalinity). Soils rich in humus provide an environment with a wide margin for error in the growing of lawn grasses. The interaction of the soil flora and fauna with the decomposing organic matter creates a moist, nutrient-rich, buffered habitat where plant roots can survive short-term drought—such as when the family goes away for a summer weekend—or a lack of fertilizer.

Plant resiliency in organically rich soil is the result of abundant food, water and a protective habitat. All higher plants, be they lawn grasses or trees, acquire food in two ways. Organic foods are manufactured in the leaves through the process called photosynthesis, whereas minerals (there are at least 16 mineral nutrients required by plants) are obtained from the soil by the roots.

In order to "mine" these minerals from the soil, plant roots need help from other constituents of the soil ecosystem, primarily microbes. Most essential plant minerals are present in the soil in insoluble forms; plants cannot absorb them until microorganisms convert them into soluble states that can pass into the root hairs. Microbes produce many of the acid-forming compounds that break nutrient particles loose from bonds with other minerals, making them available for uptake by plant roots. Microbes are also necessary intermediaries in converting nitrogen from the gaseous state in which it is found in the atmosphere to water-soluble compounds that the plant roots can absorb.

Soil organisms growing in an organically rich soil substrate also play a key role in creating a favorable balance between soil air and soil water, both of which are essential to the growth of healthy plants. Grasses and other plants take water from the soil through their roots and rely on air spaces to support the exchange of oxygen and carbon dioxide that occurs in root respiration. Soils hold this water and air in openings between soil particles called pore spaces. These vary in size and capacity depending on the soil's texture and structure (see the drawing on p. 514).

Soil texture refers to the classification of the rock or mineral portion of a soil by particle size. The largest particles are sand; silt particles are next in size, and clay particles are the smallest. These particles impart physical properties to soils that affect water- and nutrient-holding abilities. Different soils have different proportions of sand, silt and clay, and thus vary in their moisture content and fertility. Knowing the basic texture of your soil (for example, "sandy," "silty loam" or "clayey") helps you determine fertilizing and irrigation needs. A simple procedure for determining

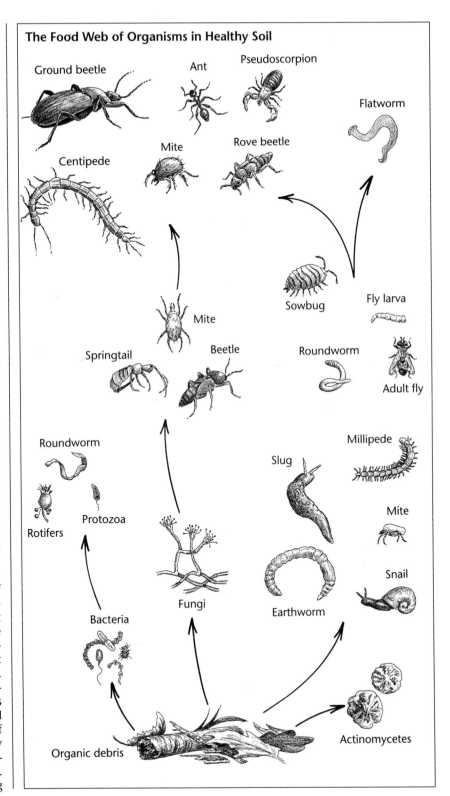

The Food Web of Organisms in Healthy Soil

Ground beetle

Ant

Pseudoscorpion

Flatworm

Centipede

Mite

Rove beetle

Sowbug

Fly larva

Mite

Springtail

Beetle

Roundworm

Adult fly

Millipede

Roundworm

Slug

Mite

Protozoa

Rotifers

Fungi

Earthworm

Snail

Bacteria

Organic debris

Actinomycetes

Pore Spaces in Soil

The openings between soil particles are called pore spaces, and serve as vital conduits for the passage of air and water. Clay soils have small pore spaces that contain little air but retain water, resulting in poor drainage. Sandy soils have big pore spaces that contain large amounts of air but allow water to drain away quickly. Loamy soils contain both large and small pore spaces, resulting in a better balance of soil air and water.

Clay

Sand

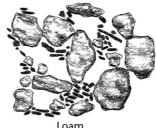

Loam

the texture of soil is described in the sidebar on the facing page.

Soil structure refers to the way in which the sand, silt and clay particles are clumped together in groups of grains, or aggregates. Soil microbes secrete complex sugars (organic gums and polysaccharides) that coat soil particles with a slime that helps cement the aggregates together. Unless the soil granules are stabilized by coatings of organic matter or by their own electrochemical properties, they gradually coalesce into larger and larger clods, creating lumpy, poorly drained soils that are inhospitable to plants. By adding compost to sandy soils, you can increase their ability to trap and hold water and nutrients. Conversely, compost can help break up clayey soils into larger aggregates that drain better.

Techniques for Soil Improvement

After the preceding discussion of soil composition, it should be clear why it is so difficult for lawn grasses to grow in the compacted, infertile, droughty soils found in typical subdivisions, condominium developments and other post-construction landscapes. Thus, one of the best investments you can make in your lawn is improving the soil. Below we discuss several ways of accomplishing this.

Planting Clover. If you've just moved into a newly constructed home and are faced with an expanse of bare, compacted soil, you should consider rototilling it, adding as much organic amendment as you can afford, and then sowing sweet clover (*Melilotus* spp.) over the entire area. The clover sends down deep roots, breaking up the compacted soil and raising mineral nutrients such as phosphorus to the upper soil levels, where they become available to later stands of lawn grasses.

The clover has a rich green appearance, produces surplus nitrogen and encourages the presence of beneficial soil microorganisms. After a season or two, it will improve the soil enough so that it can be rototilled under and replaced by lawn grasses. If you don't want to become a slave to the mower, you might even consider keeping the clover.

Top-Dressing. If you already have a lawn and don't want to dig it up in order to improve the soil, you should begin a program of top-dressing. This involves periodically spreading a thin layer—about ¼ in. (6 mm)—of composted organic matter mixed half-and-half with medium-grade sand over your lawn. The sand helps counteract soil compaction by increasing the number of pore spaces in the soil. The organic matter can con-

sist of composted manure, sewage sludge, sifted garden compost, pulverized fir bark or other material. Note, however, that if you use sewage sludge or manure, you should be certain they have been through the kind of "hot" compost system described in Chapter 34 that kills seeds. Otherwise, you may find small tomato plants and other "weeds" growing in your lawn!

The benefits of top-dressing are documented in a USDA study that found that a top dressing of composted sewage sludge applied to turf at a rate of 3,300 lb. to 6,600 lb. per 1,000 sq. ft. (180 to 360 metric tons per hectare) decreased the bulk density (compaction) of the soil, increased its water-holding capacity and air exchange and improved the rooting environment for grasses. Increases in pH, phosphorus and magnesium can also be expected with applications of sewage sludge. The sludge or other organic amendment is consumed by beneficial microorganisms, increasing their numbers and promoting all the benefits they provide, including suppression of weeds and diseases. Top-dressing is also the most effective method for reducing thatch (dead and dying roots and stems) in lawns. It should be applied at least twice a year—in spring and in early fall—particularly in combination with aeration (see pp. 521-522).

Pest-Suppressive Soils. By top-dressing your lawn with composted manure, sludge, garden debris or pulverized tree bark, you are quite likely inoculating it with insect and disease-fighting microbes. Plant pathologists are now paying more attention to the role beneficial microorganisms play in suppressing soil-borne plant disease. One aspect of this research involves the identification of "antagonists," usually beneficial fungi, that either out-compete disease organisms in the soil for food and habitat, keeping their numbers low, or attack and kill pests directly by producing antibiotics or other toxic substances. Soils containing high numbers of

The Touch Test for Soil Texture

With practice, you can tell soil texture (the proportions of sand, silt and clay) by touch. Try this touch comparison test with as many different soils as possible.

Preparation: Place about a tablespoonful of the soil in the palm of one hand. Then add a little water. (If water isn't handy, saliva works fine.) With the fingers of your other hand, work the water into the soil until the soil is thoroughly wet but still firm; don't use so much water that the mixture becomes runny. Now perform these two tests:

Test 1: Texture. Rub the mixture out thinly against your palm and note what you feel and see.
• Clay soil feels slippery and becomes shiny when you press down firmly to spread it out. It may also stick to your fingers.
• Sandy soil feels gritty; you may be able to feel individual sand grains. It does not shine. Make sure you take time to mix and knead the soil thoroughly so you won't be deceived into thinking you are feeling sand particles when you are really finding hard clay lumps.
• Silty soil has a greasy feel and slips easily through your fingers as you work it. But it lacks the plastic (moldable) quality of clay soil.

Test 2: Plasticity. The ability of moistened soil to maintain its shape is called plasticity. Roll the wet soil first into a ball and then into a snake as long and thin as possible. Let the last inch or so of snake overhang the edge of your palm. If the soil is very sandy, this portion of the snake will drop off due to its own weight. If this doesn't happen, try picking the snake up by the overhanging end. The greater the clay content of the soil, the thinner you can make the snake and still be able to pick it up this way. For example, when the clay content reaches about 35%, a snake ¼ in. (6 mm) in diameter can be picked up without breaking. Silty soil performs better in this test than sandy soil but not as well as clay soil.

To increase your understanding of how organic material influences soil performance, try mixing a small amount of sifted compost into the sample before you moisten it. The first thing you'll notice is how much more water it takes to moisten the more absorbent mixture thoroughly. If the soil is sandy, you'll see how the organic matter helps the soil maintain its shape; if it is high in clay, the organic matter will prevent it from becoming sticky and unworkable.

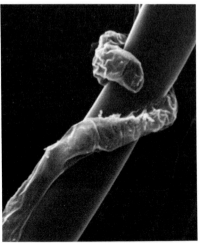

Beneficial fungi can keep the agents of plant disease at low levels. In this photograph, magnified about 1,000 times, the beneficial fungus *Gliocladium virens* coils around (and will eventually destroy) larger *Rhizoctonia solani,* a soil-borne pathogen that attacks more than 200 plant species. (Photo courtesy USDA Agricultural Research Service.)

Trichoderma controls a variety of soil-borne diseases, including *Rhizoctonia, Fusarium* and *Sclerotinia.* Many lawn diseases are represented by these genera. *Trichoderma* and other beneficial organisms have been isolated from aged compost (mostly from the centers of compost piles a year or more old) and from pulverized tree bark products (for example, Progrow®) sold in nurseries as soil amendments. A patented form of *Trichoderma* has received EPA registration and may be available soon as a natural fungicide.

A growing number of organic lawn fertilizers inoculated with disease-fighting beneficial microorganisms are becoming available in the United States (for sources, see the Resource Appendix under "Plant Disease Management: Biological Controls" on p. 687). For example, Lawn Restore™, produced by Ringer Corp., contains bone meal, feather meal, soybean meal and other protein sources plus actinomycetes and bacteria in the genus *Bacillus.* To increase the number of beneficial soil microbes, you

these antagonists are known as suppressive soils.

Current research is focusing on beneficial actinomycetes, fungi such as *Gliocladium* spp. (see the photo above) and *Trichoderma* spp., and bacteria such as *Bacillus subtilis* and *B.* *penetrans.* A commercial formulation of *Trichoderma* known as BINAB-B has been sold in Europe for a number of years and is used to treat a variety of plant diseases, including Dutch elm disease and utility-pole decay organism. Israeli studies have found that

Horticultural Characteristics of Common Cool Season Lawn Grasses[a]

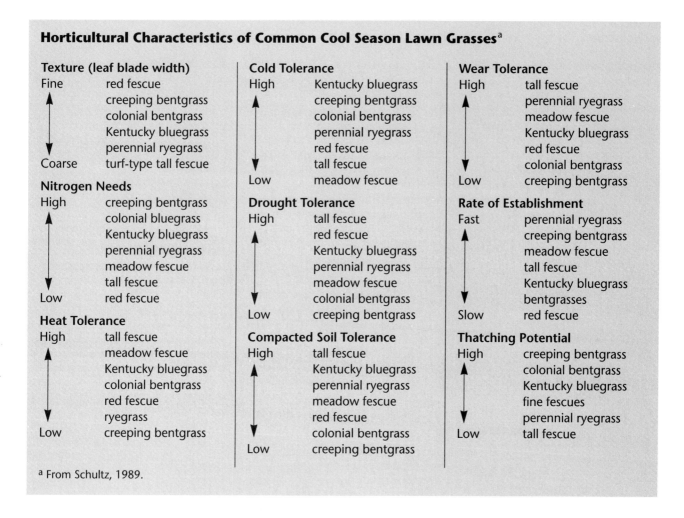

Texture (leaf blade width)
Fine — red fescue
↑ — creeping bentgrass
colonial bentgrass
Kentucky bluegrass
↓ — perennial ryegrass
Coarse — turf-type tall fescue

Nitrogen Needs
High — creeping bentgrass
↑ — colonial bluegrass
Kentucky bluegrass
perennial ryegrass
meadow fescue
↓ — tall fescue
Low — red fescue

Heat Tolerance
High — tall fescue
↑ — meadow fescue
Kentucky bluegrass
colonial bentgrass
red fescue
↓ — ryegrass
Low — creeping bentgrass

Cold Tolerance
High — Kentucky bluegrass
↑ — creeping bentgrass
colonial bentgrass
perennial ryegrass
red fescue
↓ — tall fescue
Low — meadow fescue

Drought Tolerance
High — tall fescue
↑ — red fescue
Kentucky bluegrass
perennial ryegrass
meadow fescue
↓ — colonial bentgrass
Low — creeping bentgrass

Compacted Soil Tolerance
High — tall fescue
↑ — Kentucky bluegrass
perennial ryegrass
meadow fescue
red fescue
↓ — colonial bentgrass
Low — creeping bentgrass

Wear Tolerance
High — tall fescue
↑ — perennial ryegrass
meadow fescue
Kentucky bluegrass
red fescue
↓ — colonial bentgrass
Low — creeping bentgrass

Rate of Establishment
Fast — perennial ryegrass
↑ — creeping bentgrass
meadow fescue
tall fescue
Kentucky bluegrass
↓ — bentgrasses
Slow — red fescue

Thatching Potential
High — creeping bentgrass
↑ — colonial bentgrass
Kentucky bluegrass
fine fescues
↓ — perennial ryegrass
Low — tall fescue

[a] From Schultz, 1989.

can also purchase a combination of products from Agro-Chem Corporation. These include Soil-Aid™, an enzymatic-type wetting agent that flushes out substances that inhibit high levels of microbial activity in thatch and soil. It is used in combination with either Green Magic™ or Strengthen & Renew™, both of which contain nutrients and extracts from plants and microbes.

Michigan State University researchers led by plant pathologist J.M. Vargas tested these products on Kentucky bluegrass lawns heavily infected with necrotic ring spot, which is caused by the fungus *Leptosphaeria korrae*. Plots treated with the microbe-boosted organic fertilizers three times

a year completely recovered from the disease, whereas plots receiving synthetic nitrogen fertilizer experienced a 300% increase in disease during the same period. For more details on this research, see pp. 550-551.

Dis-Patch™, a microbe-enriched product made by Ringer Corp., claims to help lawns recover from fusarium, dollar spot, brown patch and other fungal diseases. We hope that independent research will confirm the effectiveness of these and other products on common lawn diseases and that the number of such products will increase.

PEST-RESISTANT LAWN GRASSES

Once you have improved the soil, the next item on the pest-prevention agenda is the selection of grasses that grow vigorously in your climate and soils and therefore have the best chance of resisting pests.

Selecting the Right Species

The most commonly sold and advertised lawn grasses are varieties of Kentucky bluegrass *(Poa pratensis)*. These grow well in certain climates, but they are not suited to all situations, particularly where rainfall is low and summer temperatures are high, or where lawn maintenance is sporadic

Horticultural Characteristics of Common Warm Season Lawn Grasses[a]

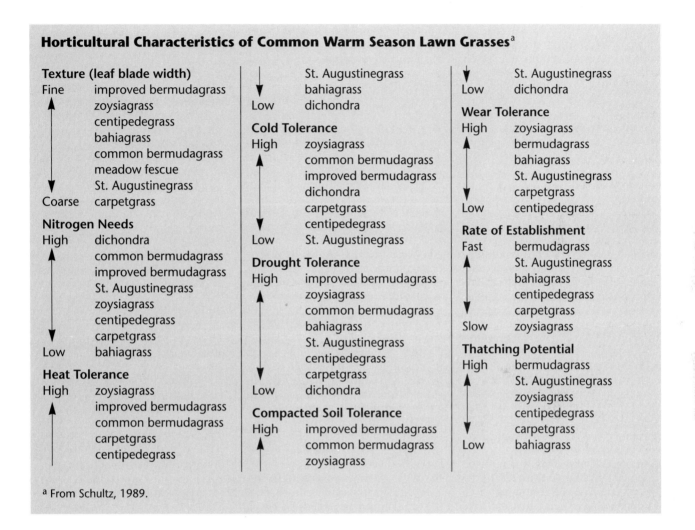

Texture (leaf blade width)
Fine	improved bermudagrass
↑	zoysiagrass
	centipedegrass
	bahiagrass
	common bermudagrass
	meadow fescue
↓	St. Augustinegrass
Coarse	carpetgrass

Nitrogen Needs
High	dichondra
↑	common bermudagrass
	improved bermudagrass
	St. Augustinegrass
	zoysiagrass
	centipedegrass
↓	carpetgrass
Low	bahiagrass

Heat Tolerance
High	zoysiagrass
↑	improved bermudagrass
	common bermudagrass
	carpetgrass
	centipedegrass

↓	St. Augustinegrass
	bahiagrass
Low	dichondra

Cold Tolerance
High	zoysiagrass
↑	common bermudagrass
	improved bermudagrass
	dichondra
	carpetgrass
↓	centipedegrass
Low	St. Augustinegrass

Drought Tolerance
High	improved bermudagrass
↑	zoysiagrass
	common bermudagrass
	bahiagrass
	St. Augustinegrass
	centipedegrass
↓	carpetgrass
Low	dichondra

Compacted Soil Tolerance
High	improved bermudagrass
↑	common bermudagrass
	zoysiagrass

↓	St. Augustinegrass
Low	dichondra

Wear Tolerance
High	zoysiagrass
↑	bermudagrass
	bahiagrass
	St. Augustinegrass
↓	carpetgrass
Low	centipedegrass

Rate of Establishment
Fast	bermudagrass
↑	St. Augustinegrass
	bahiagrass
	centipedegrass
↓	carpetgrass
Slow	zoysiagrass

Thatching Potential
High	bermudagrass
↑	St. Augustinegrass
	zoysiagrass
	centipedegrass
↓	carpetgrass
Low	bahiagrass

[a] From Schultz, 1989.

and the lawn is frequently walked or played on.

When a grass is ill-suited to the soil, climate, maintenance practices and other variables that affect lawn health, it does not thrive. Often, pesticides are applied with the mistaken notion that these chemical cure-alls will revive the grass. Also, even when grass varieties are bred for disease- or insect-resistance, these qualities may hold true only for certain climatic regions. Yet the grasses are often advertised as having these qualities no matter where they are planted. To make sure that the grass varieties you choose are pest-resistant in your area, contact your county cooperative ex-

tension office. The office is in touch with field stations throughout the United States that test the performance of lawn grasses.

Before selecting a species of grass, consider: which grasses are suited to the soils and climate in your area; how much maintenance effort you are willing to expend on the lawn; how much and what kind of use the lawn is going to get; what the common lawn pests in your area are; and how much time you are willing to spend on planting and maintenance.

The sidebars on this and the facing page rank lawn grasses on a relative scale according to various horticultural characteristics.

Plant Blends or Mixes of Species

To achieve a uniform lawn appearance, home owners often plant a single grass species. However, if that species happens to be susceptible to a particular disease or insect or cannot tolerate a sudden change in temperature or the availability of water or nutrients, the entire lawn can be lost. Furthermore, single-species lawns grow vigorously only under the seasonal conditions to which they are adapted. There are cool-season turfgrasses and warm-season grasses. If your grass likes the cool conditions of early spring and fall, it may not perform well in the heat of summer unless you maintain it within the narrow range of irrigation, fertilization and mowing regimens required to keep it growing when it would otherwise become partially or fully dormant.

If a uniform lawn appearance is extremely important to you and if you have the time and resources to maintain the lawn regularly, plant a blend of two or three varieties of the same species of grass. These blends are composed of varieties that have different levels of pest resistance, color, drought tolerance, and so forth. An interesting phenomenon concerning disease has been observed in such blends. When a disease-susceptible variety is planted with one or more varieties that are resistant to that particular disease, there is an overall reduction in disease that is greater than expected on the basis of the percentage of the varieties in the blend. Thus, if 'Merion' bluegrass, which is notoriously susceptible to stem rust, is planted 50/50 with a resistant bluegrass variety, rust infestations are very slight. Some researchers think the resistance is passed through the roots, but the phenomenon remains largely unexplained.

If you live in a climate with major seasonal temperature fluctuations, or if you don't have the time or resources for regular lawn maintenance, a mix of at least two different species of compatible lawn grasses may be a better choice. Combinations of bluegrass and perennial ryegrass, or tall fescue and perennial ryegrass are popular. With multiple grass species, a pest organism may attack one species but leave the other alone. The unaffected grasses will grow more vigorously, usually masking the damaged grass and providing the overall appearance of a healthy, green lawn.

The importance of planting multiple species where resources for lawn maintenance are low was demonstrated to us as we developed integrated pest management programs for the National Park Service and a number of municipal park systems throughout the United States. Park operators were often caught in the bind of ever-increasing use of lawn areas in the park while suffering budget cuts that reduced labor, equipment and supplies.

Most of the lawns we observed originally had been planted with Kentucky bluegrass. Although this species flourishes under optimum conditions, it is not very tolerant of neglect, particularly when subjected to heavy use. One of our first recommendations was to change the species of grass to types that could tolerate low maintenance, drought and heavy wear. One such mix is composed of a fine-bladed tall fescue (*Festuca arundinacea*) cultivar such as 'Rebel II,' 'Mustang' or 'Apache,' and a perennial ryegrass (*Lolium perenne*) cultivar such as 'Repell,' 'Derby' or 'Manhattan' in a ratio of 80% tall fescue to 20% ryegrass.

Since the parks' low budgets also reduced their use of fertilizer, we recommended adding white Dutch clover (*Trifolium repens*) or strawberry clover (*T. fragiferum*) to the grass mix. Clover, a plant that is maligned as a weed in most lawn-care publications, fixes nitrogen from the air and passes it to grasses via bacteria (*Rhizobium*) that live on its roots. Some turf researchers estimate that over 30% of the annual nitrogen needs of lawns can be provided by clover in the turf mix. Clover is far more drought-tolerant than most grasses and remains green under the droughty conditions that turn grasses brown.

There are, however, two potential drawbacks to clover. The first is that clover flowers attract bees to the lawn. However, regular mowing usually keeps flushes of bloom to a minimum. Turf specialist John Madison notes that strawberry clover has only a short season of bloom, and bees do not seem highly attracted to it. A second complaint is that clover usually grows in clumps, reducing the uniform look many people desire. Here, the use of strawberry clover may help. Madison found that when strawberry clover is grown with perennial ryegrass and/or tall fescue, it becomes loosely distributed throughout the lawn rather than growing in clumps. He attributes this to the fact that both perennial ryegrass and tall fescue are allelopathic; that is, they release toxins in the soil that weaken the clover enough to prevent it from forming clumps.

One of the most significant results of changing the park lawns from primarily Kentucky bluegrass to a tall fescue/perennial ryegrass/clover mix was significantly reduced weed problems. The drought tolerance, high resistance to wear and self-fertility of this mix enabled the grasses to grow vigorously. The tall fescue grew well in spring and summer. When it went into a resting stage in fall and winter, the perennial rye grew actively. Thus, there were few opportunities for weeds to invade the lawn despite low maintenance and high use.

Grasses That Repel Insects

In addition to out-competing weeds, certain tall fescue and perennial ryegrass varieties also resist insect attack. Called endophytic grasses, these varieties contain a symbiotic (beneficial to both organisms) endophytic fungus in their tissues that repels or kills common leaf- and stem-eating lawn insects such as sod webworms, armyworms, cutworms, billbug larvae, chinch bugs, certain aphids and Argentine stem weevil larvae. However, root-feeding lawn pests such as "white grubs," a blanket term that includes the larvae of the Japanese beetle and European chafer, do not appear to be repelled by endophytic grasses, probably because the endophytic fungi apparently do not live in the roots of grasses.

The endophyte phenomenon was first discovered by researchers in New Zealand, who found that certain forage grasses harbor fungi that maintain an intercellular relationship with the leaf tissue of the host grass. These endophytic fungi are felt to be the source of toxins that accumulate in infected grasses and cause physiolog-

Endophyte Levels in Perennial Ryegrasses[a]

Very High
Citation II
Repell

High
Commander
Pennant
Regal
Sunrise

Moderately High
Prelude
Cowboy
AllStar
Premier

Moderate
Dasher
Delray
Derby
Linn
Palmer

Pennfine
Vintage

Low
BT-1Gator
Citation
Diplomat
Elka
Manhattan
Omega
Ranger
Yorktown II

[a] Source: Dr. C.R. Funk, Department of Soils and Crops, Rutgers University, New Brunswick, N.J., and Turf Seed, Inc., Hubbard, Oreg.

ical disorders in grazing sheep and cattle. On the other hand, these same endophytic fungi do not harm the grass plant, and, in fact, contribute to the plant's resistance to attack by certain pests.

Scientists at Rutgers University, led by Dr. C.R. Funk, screened a number of commercially available perennial ryegrasses for levels of endophytes. Their findings are summarized in the sidebar above.

Product literature from the Lofts Seed Company, which markets the endophyte-bearing 'Repell' perennial ryegrass, contains the following comments on endophytes and the grasses they inhabit.

An endophyte is a fungus that lives within a plant but is not necessarily parasitic on another plant. The presence of an endophytic fungus produces no known adverse effects to the host plant, but provides many advantages which enhance turf grass performance. Upon seed germination the endophyte grows into the seedling and continues to live in the tissues of the mature grass plant....Resistance has been found with insects which typically feed on the lower stem and crown of plants, as these areas normally have the highest

concentration of endophytes. Plants containing endophytes may show improved disease resistance, drought tolerance, persistence and seedling vigor. Certified seed of 'Repell' perennial ryegrass is produced to insure that over 80% of seed will contain viable endophyte at the date of testing.

Other commercially available endophyte-bearing perennial ryegrasses (with the percentage of seed containing viable endophytes in parentheses) include 'Citation II' (94%), 'Commander' (86%), 'Sunrise' (85%) and 'Vintage 2Df' (65%). For sources, see the Resource Appendix under "Insect Management: Horticultural Controls" on p. 683.

Endophyte viability can be lost through normal seed storage within two years, so you should use only freshly harvested seed for insect-resistant turf. Seed of 'Repell' ryegrass is specially tagged to ensure the presence of the endophyte; to ensure the highest viable endophyte level, the seed should be used within nine months of the test date listed on the package. Cold storage at 40°F (4°C) prolongs endophyte viability.

Endophytes are often present in high numbers in the Kentucky-31 va-

riety of tall fescue *(Festuca arundinacea)*, and there is scientific documentation of this variety's resistance to sod webworms, armyworms and certain aphids. Unfortunately, the level of endophytes varies from one seed lot to the next, and the labels on the seed packages do not contain any information on endophyte content. Turf Seed, Inc., produces one commercial variety of tall fescue called 'Apache' that is known to contain approximately 25% endophytes (in other words, 25% of the seeds in the package are endophyte-bearing). Plant specialists at the company are currently breeding 'Apache' to increase the endophyte level to 100%, and they expect to market this improved strain within a few years.

Planting endophyte-bearing grass won't eliminate all insect pests from a lawn, but it will substantially reduce their numbers. As more endophytic grasses reach the market in the next few years, opportunities to reduce pesticide use on lawns will increase accordingly.

Disease-Resistant Grasses

Disease-resistant cultivars of most common lawn grasses, listed in the sidebar on p. 520, are available from seed suppliers and nurseries. However, resistance can diminish or be lost entirely in the presence of high numbers of disease spores and the temperatures and humidity levels that support them, particularly when these conditions are combined with poor horticultural practices.

Remember that lawn grass seed that shows disease resistance in one location may not retain it under the conditions in your area. To find out which diseases are prevalent locally and which grass cultivars appear to be resistant, consult your local cooperative extension office or a nursery. Their recommendations are based on real observations under local conditions. Note, too, that planting blends of one grass species or a mix of different species—discussed on p. 518— further enhances disease resistance.

Disease-Resistant Grass Varieties[a]

Brown Patch:
Perennial ryegrass: All Star, Barry, Citation, Delray, Manhattan II, Palmer, Pennant, Prelude, Premier, Yorktown II
Tall fescue: Brookston, Jaguar, Mustang, Olympic

Dollar Spot:
Fine fescue: Agram, Barfalla, Biljart, Checker, Encota, Famosa, Koket, Reliant, Scaldis, Shadow, Tournament
Kentucky bluegrass: Adelphi, America, Aquila, Arista, Bonnieblue, Bristol, Eclipse, Galaxy, Geary, Majestic, Midnight, Newport, Palouse, Parade, Park, Pennstar, Prato, Primo, Sodco, Windsor
Perennial ryegrass: Barry, Capper, Caravelle, Citation, Dasher, Ensporta, Exponent, Linn, Manhattan II, NK-100, NK-200, Regal, Rex, Sprinter, Venlona

Fusarium Blight Complex:[b, c]
Kentucky bluegrass: Columbia (adding 10% to 15% by weight of perennial ryegrass to Kentucky bluegrass seed mixes also results in resistant lawns)

Fusarium Patch:
Fine fescue: Barfalla, Biljart, Jade, Jamestown, Koket, Scaldis
Kentucky bluegrass: Adelphi, Admiral, Birka, Bonnieblue, Fylking, Glade, Lovegreen, Monopoly, Nassau, Shasta, Victa

Perennial ryegrass: Barenza, Diplomat, Eton, Game, Lamora, Manhattan, NK-200, Norlea, Omega, Pelo, Pennfine, Sprinter, Wendy

Leaf Rust:
Kentucky bluegrass: Aquila, Arista, Bonnieblue, Columbia, Delta, Enoble, Fylking, Geary, Georgetown, Glade, Kenblue, Majestic, Palouse, Parade, Park, Pennstar, Prato, Primo, Rugby, Sodco, South Dakota Common, Trenton, Windsor
Perennial ryegrass: Delray, Elka, Ensporta, Fiesta, Prelude, Wendy

Melting Out and Leaf Spot:
Fine Fescue: Reliant
Kentucky bluegrass: Bonnieblue, Challenger, Eclipse, Georgetown, Majestic, Midnight, Nassau
Perennial ryegrass: Belle, Blazer, Cowboy, Ranger
Tall fescue: Adventure, Brookston, Houndog, Jaguar, Mustang, Olympic

Powdery Mildew:
Fine fescue: Dawson, Fortress, Gracia, Reliant, Reptans, Ruby
Kentucky bluegrass: Aquila, Cello, Cougar, Kenblue, Mystic, Palouse, Primo, Ram I, Sodco, Welcome

Red Thread:
Fine fescue: Argenta, Atlanta, Barfalla, Biljart, Boreal, Cascade, Centurion, Engina, Ensylva,

Fortress, Gracia, Grello, Highlight, Jade, Pennlawn, Puma, Ranier, Ruby, Scaldis, Scarlet, Veni, Waldina, Waldorf, Wintergreen
Kentucky bluegrass: Adelphi, Admiral, Arista, Birka, Bonnieblue, Bristol, Campus, Cello, Challenger, Cougar, Delta, Dormie, Eclipse, Geary, Georgetown, Majestic, Monopoly, Nassau, Newport, Palouse, Primo, Sodco, Touchdown, Trenton
Perennial ryegrass: Acclaim, Barenza, Belle, Birdie, Blazer, Citation, Clipper, Dasher, Delray, Derby, Diplomat, Ensporta, Eton, Exponent, Fiesta, Goalie, Lamora, Linn, Loretta, NK-100, NK-200, Norlea, Perma, Player, Ranger, Regal, Score, Sprinter, Venlona, Wendy, Yorktown

Stripe Smut:
Kentucky bluegrass: Adelphi, Admiral, America, Apart, Aquila, Arista, Aspen, Banff, Barblue, Birka, Bonnieblue, Bristol, Brunswick, Campina, Campus, Challenger, Charlotte, Cheri, Columbia, Delft, Delta, Eclipse, Enmundi, Enoble, Escort, Geary, Georgetown, Geronimo, Glade, Holiday, Kenblue, Lovegreen, Majestic, Mona, Monopoly, Nassau, Nugget, Parade, Park, Pennstar, Plush, Ram I, Rugby, Shasta, Sodco, Sydsport, Touchdown, Trenton, Vantage, Welcome

Typhula Blight:
Perennial ryegrass: Regal

---

[a] Adapted from Schultz, 1989.
[b] Includes summer patch and necrotic ring spot.
[c] Most varieties of Kentucky bluegrass are highly susceptible to fusarium blight complex.

GRASS SUBSTITUTES

One important alternative to lawn maintenance is not having a conventional lawn at all. As mentioned earlier, if you want the look of a greensward without the maintenance of a typical lawn, you can achieve a lawn-like look with low-growing ground covers. Clovers, Irish or Scotch moss, creeping thyme *(Thymus serpyllum),* chamomile *(Anthemis nobilis),* Lippia *(Phyla nodiflora)* and creeping mint *(Mentha requienii)* are but a few of the many ground covers that can substitute for lawns.

Another possibility is to plant grasses that can remain unmowed and still look wonderful. One candidate is creeping red fescue *(Festuca rubra* 'Ruby'). Although its blades grow up to 14 in. (35 cm) long, they lie on their sides, creating glorious swirls and ripples when left uncut. Some people use a string trimmer to clip off the seed heads and cut the grass down to 4 in. to 6 in. (10 cm to 15 cm) every few years to reduce buildup of thatch; others just let the new blades of grass cover the thatch. The uncut tufts look particularly good on slopes, where they resemble tumbling ocean waves. Creeping red fescue can tolerate a moderate amount of traffic, and the tufts are wonderful to sunbathe on.

Before planting, you should cultivate the soil and irrigate it to germinate weed seeds. Hoe the weeds out and repeat the process to ensure minimum weed competition with the grass seedlings. Then sow 1 lb. to 2 lb. (0.45 kg to 0.90 kg) of fescue seed per 1,000 sq. ft. (93 sq. m). Once the fescue is well established, it can easily out-compete any weeds that attempt to germinate.

Another grass that can be left uncut is fountain grass *(Pennisetum setaceum,* often sold as *P. ruppelii).* It resembles a small-scale pampas grass, with 2-ft. (0.6 m) tall fountains of leaves and 3-ft. to 4-ft. (0.9 m to 1.2 m) pinkish flower plumes. Once established, it needs little or no summer water.

The most controversial alternative to the conventional suburban lawn is creating a "meadow" by letting an existing lawn go unmowed most of the year and incorporating wildflowers into the grass. You may have seen such meadows on highway median strips, where this technique has become popular of late. To achieve the meadow effect, cut the present grass as low as possible, or "scalp" it, in early fall or spring, rake up the clippings, scarify (scratch) the soil with a rake and sow wildflower seeds over the cut grass. The flowers will spring up in the spaces normally colonized by weeds.

You can either let the fall or spring rains germinate the flower seed or

Aerating the Lawn

Weeds and other pests thrive in lawns where there is excessive soil compaction and/or buildup of thatch. Foot- or gas-powered aerators (A) remove plugs of soil, improving aeration and drainage. Under these conditions, thatch (B) is decomposed more easily by soil arthropods and microbes.

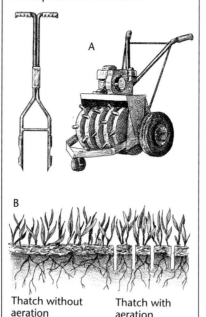

Thatch without aeration   Thatch with aeration

you can irrigate. In most areas the meadow will need only a few long, slow soakings during the summer. Mow the meadow down to a 6-in. (15 cm) height at the end of summer, or whenever the wildflowers lose their aesthetic appeal, and spread compost over the mown area in fall. Be warned, however, that some communities have ordinances that require that lawns be mowed and maintained in a conventional manner.

REDUCING STRESS ON LAWNS

If your lawn is attacked by insects, disease or weed pests, the first thing you should do is determine whether the lawn is under some kind of horticultural stress. A vigorous lawn can usually tolerate significant numbers of pest organisms without showing excessive damage. But if it is suffering from insufficient water or fertilizer, excessive compaction, improper mowing or other stresses, it generally lacks the resiliency to regenerate portions damaged by pests.

Most significant pest damage results from poor lawn maintenance. The following suggestions for general lawn care will help you keep pest problems to a minimum.

Aeration, Thatch Management and Interseeding

When lawns are used heavily or are simply mowed on a regular basis, the soil eventually becomes compacted, and the pore spaces that allow water and gases to pass through the soil become compressed. As a result, water is unable to penetrate easily to the root zone, and oxygen used by plants during respiration cannot escape from the soil. These adverse conditions in turn inhibit vigorous plant growth and create an environment that pest organisms exploit.

One way to counteract compaction is to punch holes in the soil once or twice a year using an aerator (see the drawing at left). Aerators remove soil cores ¼ in. to ½ in. (6 mm to 13 mm) in diameter approximately 3 in. (7.5 cm) deep at 4-in. (10 cm) intervals. These openings allow water and air to enter the soil. Such coring, or aeration, also cuts holes through thatch and helps relieve that problem as well.

Coring tools that are pressed into the soil by foot pressure are available from nurseries and hardware stores. They should have hollow tines that remove a core of soil, because spiking the soil with solid tines only worsens the situation by further compacting the soil. Power coring equipment can be rented or the work can be contracted for.

To avoid encouraging weed growth in the aerated lawn, aerate when the grasses in your lawn are growing most vigorously. Sow some grass seed over the lawn after coring, then drag the entire lawn surface with a metal door mat or piece of cyclone fence to break up the soil cores. This is also a good time to apply a top dressing of organic matter, as discussed on p. 514. The dressing helps fill the holes created by the coring and provides a good seed bed for the lawn grasses.

Thatch is an accumulation of dead but undecomposed roots and stems that collects in a layer at the soil surface. If the thatch becomes excessively deep—greater than ¾ in. (19 mm)—water and nutrients do not penetrate the soil adequately. When water puddles on thatch, it enhances the habitat for disease organisms. Regular aeration keeps thatch at an acceptable level, and the use of organic fertilizers such as composted sewage sludge promotes thatch decomposition. Synthetic chemical fertilizers, on the other hand, actually enhance thatch development. Excessive layers of thatch can also be removed with de-thatching rakes sold in garden centers, or with power de-thatchers available from the equipment rental firms found in most communities.

Wherever lawns are thinned by aeration, de-thatching procedures, insect or disease attack or environ-

Table 29.1
Water-Holding Capacity of Various Soil Types[a]

Soil Type	Water-Holding Capacity	
	In. per ft. of soil depth	Gal. per cu. ft. of soil
sand	0.8	0.5
loam	1.6	1.0
clay	2.4	1.5

[a] See the sidebar on p. 515 to determine what type of soil you have.

Table 29.2
Guide to Average Daily Water Use by Lawn Grasses in California

Irrigation Season[a]	Hot Interior Valleys	Coastal Valleys
summer	0.25 to 0.35 in.	0.15 to 0.20 in.
spring or fall	0.10 to 0.20 in.	0.10 to 0.15 in.

[a] Water use is slightly higher during dry, windy periods or when temperatures are abnormally high.

mental problems such as drought, it is wise to sow seed of desired turfgrasses. The seeds can be mixed into the top dressing of soil amendment or organic fertilizer that is customarily applied to thinned lawns. The grass seedlings usually out-compete weeds that attempt to occupy the openings.

Irrigation

Poor irrigation practices encourage a variety of pest problems. Too often, automatic sprinklers are timed to water lawns for brief periods on a daily basis. Although this may be a good idea during the first few weeks that a lawn is getting established, ongoing daily irrigation usually leads to problems. Light, frequent irrigations produce very shallow root systems that make grass completely dependent on artificial watering, and one or two missed irrigations can doom the lawn. In addition, daily irrigations may cause leaching of minerals, resulting in weakened grass plants with

a yellowish-green appearance that are more susceptible to invasions of weeds, insects and diseases.

It is best to irrigate only when the water supply in the soil has been depleted by the lawn sufficiently to require replacement. It is also a good idea to irrigate during the day in warm weather because nighttime irrigation encourages fungus diseases. Automatic systems can be set to start irrigating around dawn, when the disease hazard is less, the lawn is not in use, the water pressure is highest and most stable and there is usually less wind. The morning sun will dry the surface of the lawn before temperatures become high, reducing the likelihood of disease outbreak.

To determine when to irrigate and how much water to use, you must first understand a few basic facts about how soils hold and give up water. The following information is abstracted from an excellent pamphlet on this subject entitled "Soil and Water Management for Home Gardeners" by soil specialist B.A. Krantz.

The texture and structure of a soil determine the amount of available water the soil will hold at any one irrigation. Table 29.1 on the facing page gives the approximate water-holding capacities of various soil types.

The depth from which a plant normally extracts water depends on the rooting depth of the plant. Appropriately irrigated lawn grasses normally root in the top 6 in. to 12 in. (15 cm to 30 cm) of soil; lawns irrigated on a daily basis often root only in the top 1 in. (2.5 cm) of soil. The amount of water a plant uses in one day depends on the air temperature and the wind velocity. Table 29.2 on the facing page is a general guide to average daily water use in two typical climatic areas of California. Similar information for your area can be obtained from your county cooperative extension office or local weather bureau. Ask specifically for the evapotranspiration rate (the average amount of water that evaporates from the soil on a daily basis).

For example, during the summer, a lawn growing in loamy soil in an interior valley would use approximately 0.3 in. (8 mm) of water per day. Since the top 12 in. (30 cm) of a loam soil holds about 1.6 in. (4 cm) of water, the plants would deplete most of the available water from the main root zone in about five days (1.6 in. divided by 0.3 in.). Thus, irrigation would be required every four or five days.

If you have a sprinkler that applies about 0.5 in. (13 mm) of water per hour and no runoff occurs, a three-hour irrigation would be required to replenish the lost water. In spring and fall, the amount of water required per irrigation would be the same, but the number of days between irrigations would be almost twice as many in fall as in spring.

On vigorous, well-fertilized lawns, the first indication that you need to water is when the imprint of your foot remains visible in the grass for a

Calibrating Your Sprinklers

To determine evenness of water distribution from the sprinklers, place four or more straight-sided cans (all the same size) at regular intervals in a line running out from the sprinkler. Now run the sprinkler system for a period of time (a 1-hr. period simplifies your calculations). Ideally, when you shut the system off after that time, all the cans should contain the same amount of water, indicating that the water is being distributed evenly across the area served. If they don't, the problem could be any or all of three things: the sprinkler head(s) is spraying unevenly and needs cleaning; the spacing among sprinklers needs adjustment; or there is a drop in water pressure among the sprinklers in the system that must be corrected.

To determine how much water is reaching the lawn on average, add together the measurements you took for the depth of water in each can. Then divide by the number of cans to get the average depth of water per can. If you ran the sprinkler system for one hour and the total amount of water in all four cans was 1 in. (25 mm), the average depth of water in each can is ¼ in. (6 mm). Thus, if you wanted to apply ½ in. (13 mm) of water to the lawn, you would have to run your system for two hours. Generally the amount of water delivered by sprinklers ranges from ¹⁄₁₀ in. (2.5 mm) to 1 in. (25 mm) per hour.

few minutes or if the grass in areas that dry out fastest becomes dull and turns a bluish-green or yellow. You can also determine when to irrigate by poking a sharp metal rod such as a screwdriver into the soil. If it penetrates easily to a depth of 6 in. to 8 in. (15 cm to 20 cm), the soil is probably wet and irrigation is not needed. If you can't get the rod to sink more than an inch or so, the soil is probably dry. Tensiometers, available from garden suppliers, are more sophisticated tools that can be used to measure available water in the soil; some versions can be incorporated into an automated irrigation system. Hand-held models are available, but they are expensive and require some expertise to use.

To decide how long to leave your sprinklers on, you must know how much water they deliver over a given period. The sidebar above explains how to determine this.

You should irrigate a lawn slowly enough that the water soaks into the soil immediately without runoff. If runoff occurs, stop watering for an hour or two, then continue until enough water has been applied. Remember to irrigate thoroughly but as infrequently as possible. Frequent, shallow irrigation causes more water to be lost from the surface through evaporation than does infrequent, deep watering.

If your lawn is over- or under-watered it not only invites pest insects and diseases, it can also mask the symptoms of pests for a longer period than would otherwise be the case, preventing you from taking early remedial action. This is especially true of lawns that receive too little water.

In *Turfgrass Insects of the United States and Canada,* H. Tashiro writes:

Two groups of insects, the chinch bugs and sod webworms, do most of their damage during periods of high temperature and moisture stress, with the grass going into dormancy. The dormancy of the turfgrass makes it impossible or very difficult to detect early symptoms of damage. Only after heavy precipitation and greening of the healthy grass does the insect damage become apparent, often after irreversible damage has taken place....When the turf is growing steadily at adequate moisture levels, symptoms of early insect damage are much more readily detected in the form of yellow leaves and small patches of brown.

Fertilizing

The type and amount of fertilizer applied to a lawn plays a significant role in determining the presence or absence of pests. Because nutrition is such an important variable in lawn pest management, it is worth spending a little time learning about the below-ground food factory your grass relies on.

Calcium. Calcium is the key to balanced soil fertility. If you have read about basic lawn fertilization, your reaction is probably, "Hey, wait a minute! I thought nitrogen was the key to healthy lawns." It is true that modern lawn-care literature is dominated by an emphasis on nitrogen fertilization, but we do not agree with this approach.

Our emphasis on the key role of calcium is based upon the pioneering work of Dr. William A. Albrecht, microbiologist and soil scientist at the University of Missouri, who earned his Ph.D. in 1919 and whose career spanned more than 60 years. The fruits of his insights into soil fertility are collected in a volume entitled *The Albrecht Papers,* which we recommend for anyone who grows plants.

Albrecht studied the cation exchange capacity of soils. This is the process whereby plant nutrients containing positive electrical charges (cations) are held on particles of clay soil or organic matter that have a negative charge. Cations are loosened from their electrical bonds to the clay or organic matter particles only in the presence of hydrogen ions, which knock them off the soil colloid, enabling them to be absorbed by plant roots. For a more detailed discussion of plant fertilization and a diagram of the cation exchange process, see pp. 333-336.

Albrecht's study convinced him there was a critical proportion of calcium relative to other mineral nutrients. By artificially stripping all nutrient cations off a particle of clay soil in the laboratory and then slowly adding them back, he adjusted the proportion of the cations until he achieved optimum growth of laboratory plants. The proportion of cations that worked best was:

Calcium	60% to 75%
Magnesium	10% to 20%
Hydrogen	10%
Potassium	2% to 5%
Sodium	0.5% to 5%
Others	5%

To the degree that you can reproduce this balance of cations in the soil supporting your lawn, the healthier and more vigorously the lawn will grow. To determine the relative proportions of these cations in your soil, send a sample to a professional soil testing lab and request an analysis of the cation exchange capacity (CEC). Since most soil labs focus on the amounts of nitrogen, potassium and phosphorus (NPK) in the soil, be sure you make it clear you want to know the CEC in the detail described above.

Note that the proportion of calcium in Albrecht's guideline is as much as 10 times greater than the other nutrients. Many soils do not naturally contain that much calcium, particularly in areas of high rainfall or heavy irrigation. Under these conditions, calcium is leached out of the soil. When calcium is deficient, soils become acid, as represented by a pH level of less than 7 (for an explanation of pH, see pp. 336-337). When calcium is excessive, the soil is alkaline, with a pH above 7.

Lime. The common recommendation in conventional lawn-care literature that lime (calcium carbonate) should be added to soils on a regular basis is usually based on a desire to raise the pH of the soil. Albrecht maintains that this is far too simplistic a view of soil fertility. He suggests that it isn't the acidity of soils that should be of concern. Rather, we should recognize that acid soils are deficient in calcium, and the calcium balance should be restored as suggested in his formula. If this is done, he says, the soil pH will adjust itself to an appropriate level.

Viewed this way, the question of whether or not to add lime and which type to use becomes part of the overall question of soil fertility rather than merely a matter of tinkering with the pH. A soils laboratory report can tell you how much lime or other fertilizers to add to achieve the balance of cations recommended by Albrecht. Again, be sure to specify to the soil lab that you want this information, because it is not customarily spelled out.

Albrecht argues strongly in favor of using natural organic and inorganic forms of fertilizers when adding nutrients to the soil rather than the highly soluble synthetic forms that came into vogue in the 1930s and 1940s and still cause major environmental problems today. Limestone and gypsum (calcium and magnesium), rock phosphate (phosphorus) and bone meal (potassium) are mineral sources that have evolved with the microorganisms that break them down into forms that move first into the clay soil and organic matter soil particles and later into plants.

This highly efficient, symbiotic relationship is a system that conserves soil nutrients by keeping them bonded to soil particles (or in the bodies of microbes) until they are sought out and absorbed by plant roots. It minimizes leaching out of nutrients by rainfall or irrigation. By contrast, when synthetic chemical fertilizers are applied to the soil, they are in large part immediately available for uptake by plants. This can result in plant tissue being burned by toxic amounts of the nutrients, or in a rapid deficiency of nutrients after the soluble fertilizer is leached out of the soil.

Nitrogen. The greatest disservice you can do to your lawn is to load the soil with nitrogen, particularly the highly soluble forms such as nitrate or urea found in most commercial chemical fertilizer packages. Nitrate and urea forms leach easily from the soil. Studies at Alabama Polytechnic University showed that at least 50% of quickly soluble nitrogen applied to soil leaches out before it can be utilized by plants. The remainder, when taken up in large doses by plants, tends to encourage attack by insect pests such as aphids and various disease organisms that are attracted to the succulent growth resulting from excessive nitrogen.

Quickly soluble nitrogen also causes grass to grow more quickly, which means that you have to mow the grass more frequently. In addition, soluble nitrogen fertilizers are usually formulated with highly soluble forms of potassium and phosphorus salts. Many soils already have high natural levels of these nutrients, and when more are added, the natural nutrient levels are thrown out of balance. This imbalance can in turn reduce the availability of other nutrients to plants.

The best way to tell when to apply nitrogen to your lawn and how much to use is by watching it. When the lawn begins to look grey-green or yellowish, it is time to fertilize. Turf expert John Madison advises applying the least amount of nitrogen consistent with good results and use. He notes that one of the best ways to supply nitrogen and other nutrients is to allow grass clippings to remain on the turf after mowing. Microorganisms decompose the clippings, re-

turning the nutrients to the soil solution to be recycled by plant roots.

In experiments with grass clippings, Madison found that when starting new lawns on former agricultural soil in California, which presumably is severely nitrogen depleted, nitrogen fertilizer was needed the first year at a rate of 8 lb. to 10 lb. (3.6 kg to 4.5 kg) actual nitrogen per 1,000 sq. ft. (93 sq. m). ("Actual" nitrogen is the amount of nitrogen by weight in a fertilizer bag; for example, 10% N in a 25-lb. bag = 2½ lb. of actual N.) But the second year, with clippings left on the lawn, only 4 lb. to 5 lb. of actual nitrogen were needed, and the third year, 1 lb. to 3 lb. By the fourth year, the nitrates present in irrigation water alone were sufficient to augment the nitrogen available from the clippings. Madison also noted, however, that "sometime during the spring flush some rust will appear and a little nitrogen needs to be added to control rust. In October, another light application helps that spreading growth that enables the turf to compete with the germinating winter annual weeds."

If you plan to allow your clippings to remain on the lawn, be certain the mower you buy does not contain an automatic bagging device that forces you to collect clippings. In fact, consider buying a "mulching" mower such as the one manufactured by Toro, which automatically grinds clippings into fine pieces and spits them back out onto the lawn, where they quickly sift down into the turf and decompose.

When you must apply nitrogen, use an organic nitrogen source and split its application between fall and spring for best results. Irwin Brawley, groundskeeper at Davidson College in Davidson, North Carolina, uses only organic fertilizers to maintain the college's extensive lawns and athletic fields. He applies 7½ lb. (3.4 kg) of Zook and Ranck's Nitro-10™ (made from leather tankage, or dried animal residue), 2½ lb. (1.1 kg) of rock phosphate and 10¾ lb. (4.9 kg) of green-

sand (potassium) per 1,000 sq. ft. (93 sq. m) of lawn in the fall and spring. This is the organic equivalent of a 10-10-10 NPK fertilizer, and it provides approximately ¾ lb. (340 g) each of nitrogen, phosphorus and potash to the lawn. You can purchase organic fertilizer already blended at this ratio to avoid having to do the mixing yourself.

For warm-season grasses such as bermudagrass, centipedegrass and St. Augustinegrass, apply the 10-10-10 fertilizer when the grass begins active growth in May and again in late fall before it goes dormant. The fall application feeds the annual ryegrass that is usually overseeded to keep the lawn green in winter and also stimulates growth of the roots of the warm-season grasses long before new top growth is evident in late spring.

Other good organic fertilizers include stabilized, weed-free compost or stable manure, cottonseed meal, soybean meal, bloodmeal and castor bean pomace. Composted sewage sludge such as Milorganite, an activated sludge from the Milwaukee Metropolitan Sewerage District, has been increasingly used on turf. It has a 6-2-0 NPK ratio. Putting 1 lb. (0.45 kg) of nitrogen on the lawn means applying 12 lb. (5.4 kg) of Milorganite per 1,000 sq. ft. (93 sq. m). The one drawback of sewage sludge is that it may contain heavy metals, and therefore should not be used on or near food crops. Questions have recently been raised about a possible connection between Milorganite used on baseball fields and Hodgkin's disease contracted by several athletes. However, there is as yet no documentation of any connection.

If you use the proportions described above, watch your lawn for a few weeks after applying the organic fertilizers. If the lawn looks healthy and has a good green color, continue with the program. If it develops a yellowish look, it may need more nitrogen (see the key to nutrient deficiency on p. 339). Add more compost, or perhaps bloodmeal, which contains a higher percentage of nitrogen. Keep a record of your fertilizing program, and compare notes from year to year. After some experimentation you will find a nitrogen program that is right for your lawn.

In *Principles of Turfgrass Culture*, Madison cautions that a lawn's fertilizer needs change as the growing season changes and pest problems occur.

When seasonal stresses reduce growth, reduce [fertilizer] applications. When grass is thinned out, by insects for example, thin down the fertilizer applications until recovery is well along. Grass in shade can use a fraction of that in sun. Soil supplies much of the needed minerals. Your program only needs to supply the difference between what plants need and what the soil supplies. At times soil can supply minerals for heavy grass growth with no need for fertilizer.

Soil minerals are usually highest in spring, lowest in fall. When a steady fertilizer program has been followed for several years, soil reserves are often restored and needs decreased....If grass fails to respond to an application of nitrogen, don't add more nitrogen. First look for other problems.

If you do decide to use a synthetic nitrogen fertilizer, we suggest a slow-release form of urea or IBDU (isobutyldiene diurea) formulation used in combination with calcium. A recent study of synthetic lawn fertilizers conducted at Texas A&M University found that fertilization with four parts urea to one part calcium nitrate produced turf with better color, verdure (health) and root and rhizome production than did fertilization with various nitrogen sources that did not contain calcium. The researchers concluded that calcium enhanced the ability of grass roots to absorb nitrogen.

Clover can contribute as much as 30% of the yearly nitrogen needed by a lawn; by including clover in your lawn mix, you reduce the lawn's nitrogen requirement. Significant nitrogen amounts can also be obtained by allowing grass clippings to remain on the lawn after mowing (see the discussion of mowing below).

We should also mention that many professionals who manage golf courses and other high-maintenance turf keep the lawn looking good by simply fertilizing lightly and irrigating grass that shows signs of pest damage. We call this the "chicken soup" approach, because it is comparable to the attentive feeding of someone with an ailment. Since grasses are such resilient organisms, special but moderate feeding or watering when their roots or tops have suffered damage often gives them just the extra edge they need to recover. If you nurse the patient along with needed minerals, which, by the way, grass can absorb through its leaves when its roots are damaged, it will often put out a burst of new growth and repair the visual damage.

Mowing

One of the best ways to guarantee pest problems in a lawn is through improper mowing. Most lawns are mowed too short too often. As a result, the grass becomes weak and falls prey to invasion by weeds and infection by various pathogens. In fact, the USDA often lowers the cutting height of the mowers on its experimental lawn plots to incite lawn diseases for use in experiments!

In *Practical Turfgrass Management*, John Madison provides some explanations for our national penchant for closely mowed lawns:

Early mowing of ornamental turf was without doubt patterned after grazing and hay-making practices, cuts being made from three to four times a year to monthly during the growing season. Such a schedule is still followed in some European parks. In crowded U.S. suburbs, there is a kind of mind that finds even a little disorder disquieting. This, combined with an early 20th century passion for sanitary sterility, demands uniform lawns, free of weeds, evenly edged, and mowed as quickly as any new growth mars the uniformity of clipped ranks and rows.

Whenever a blade of grass is cut there are a number of predictable stress responses: root and rhizome growth temporarily stops, carbohydrate production and storage is reduced, there is water loss from the cut ends and water uptake decreases. As long as lawn grasses have enough nutrients, water and soil aeration, as well as moderate temperatures, most can tolerate the temporary stress caused by mowing and bounce back with new growth. The spurt of top growth occurs in two phases. The first ranges from three to four days and involves the elongation of existing cut leaves; the second includes the development of new leaves. In addition, under optimal horticultural conditions mowing also increases the number of individual grass plants in a lawn, making a tighter, more weed-resistant turf.

Unfortunately, few lawns are maintained under optimal conditions. If repeated close mowings occur in conjunction with one or more additional stresses such as drought, insufficient nutrients or a spell of unusually hot or cold weather, grass plants become smaller and fewer. This creates openings for weed invasion. Moreover, the cut ends provide ideal ports of entry for such disease organisms as leaf spot, rust and dollar spot.

Mowing Height. To minimize problems caused by mowing, cut the grass as high as is consistent with satisfactory growth and appearance and as infrequently as possible. (Note: To establish the height of the cut on a rotary mower, measure between the cutting edge of the blade and a smooth, level surface such as a pavement or patio. A small 2x4 wood block can be used to estimate height. For a reel-type mower, measure between the cutting edge of the stationary bed knife and the pavement.)

How high and how often you cut depends on the growth habit of the grass, the horticultural condition of the lawn, the climate and the purpose for which the lawn is used.

The key to judging appropriate mowing height is knowing something about the growth habit of the type(s) of grass in your lawn. Most lawns outside the southern United States are composed of a mixture of two or more grass species. Kentucky bluegrass (*Poa pratensis*) mixed with perennial ryegrass (*Lolium perenne*) or tall fescue (*Festuca arundinacea*) and perennial rye are popular in most parts of the Northeast, Midwest and West, where they are hardy. Bentgrasses (*Agrostis* spp.) are common in the Pacific Northwest. Bermudagrass (*Cynodon dactylon*), centipedegrass (*Eremochloa ophiuroides*), St. Augustinegrass (*Stenotaphrum secundatum*) and zoysiagrass (*Zoysia* spp.) are popular in the Southwest and southern states.

Prostrate, low-growing grasses such as bermudagrass and creeping bentgrass tolerate fairly low mowing heights—about ¾ in. to 1 in. (1.9 cm to 2.5 cm). Erect-growing grasses such as the fine-bladed, drought-resistant tall fescues or Italian ryegrasses respond better if cut higher, about 2 in. to 3 in. (5 cm to 7.5 cm).

Kentucky bluegrass lawns also fall within the latter mowing height range, depending on the cultivar. For example, 'Park,' 'Kenblue' and 'Baron' have a more erect growth habit and a higher growing point than the more prostrate 'Gnome,' 'Merit' and 'Rugby.' These prostrate cultivars can tolerate mowing as low as 1 in. to 1½ in. (2.5 cm to 3.8 cm), whereas the others should be mowed no shorter than 2 in. (5 cm).

Seasonal Adjustment of Mowing Height. The mowing height of cool-season grasses such as Kentucky bluegrass and the fescues, bentgrasses and ryes should be raised during periods of prolonged high temperature.

Table 29.3
Recommended Mowing Heights

Grass	Relative Height	Mowing Height (in Inches)	
		Spring/Fall	Summer
bentgrass	very short	0.75	1.0
bermudagrass		1.5	0.75-1.0
zoysiagrass		1.5	1.0
buffalograss	medium	2.0	2.5
red fescue		2.0	2.5
centipedegrass		2.0	1.5
carpetgrass		2.0	1.5
Kentucky bluegrass		2.0	2.5-3.0
perennial ryegrass		2.0	2.5-3.0
meadow fescue		2.0	2.5-3.0
bahiagrass	high	2.0	3.0
tall fescue		2.5	3.0
St. Augustinegrass		2.0	3.0 (West), 2.0 (South)
Canada bluegrass		3.0	4.0

Recent research at Mississippi State University with the increasingly popular tall fescue grasses found a noticeable advantage to raising the mowing height during midsummer, when tall fescue suffers most from heat and drought stress and is most susceptible to weed invasion and disease.

In the Mississippi study, the highest turf density and darkest color were obtained by using a split mowing schedule: a 2½-in. (6.5 cm) mowing height from September to May and a 5-in. (12.7 cm) mowing height from June through August. Raising the mowing height to 2½ in. to 3 in. (6.5 cm to 7.5 cm) during the summer is probably warranted on Kentucky bluegrass/perennial ryegrass mixes as well. However, grasses with very prostrate growth habits, such as the bentgrasses, probably should not be mowed higher than 1 in. (2.5 cm) to avoid drought stress, excessive accumulation of thatch and other problems.

Warm-season grasses such as bermudagrass or centipedegrass, which grow vigorously during periods of high temperature, can tolerate lower summer cutting heights. Bermudagrass should be cut as low as ¾ in. (1.9 cm) in summer when it is growing vigorously to prevent thatch buildup. During the cool season, when it is semi-dormant, the mowing height can be raised to 1½ in. (3.8 cm). Generally, when temperatures cool in fall, the mowing height of most grasses can be reduced. Seasonally adjusted optimum mowing heights are listed in Table 29.3 above.

Mowing Frequency. Most lawn-care books warn against long intervals between mowings because too much grass is cut off in a single cutting, leading to a severe setback in subsequent growth. Although there is some merit to this argument, studies by Madison and others indicate that as long as not more than 30% to 40% of the grass blades are removed at any one cutting, the setback is minimal. Thus, if the mowing height is set at 2 in. (5 cm), you can let the grass grow 3 in. (7.5 cm) tall before you need to mow it again.

In summary, lawn grasses can tolerate frequent mowing as long as the mowing height is not too low for the species of grass. Mowing must be more frequent when grasses are growing vigorously and less frequent when they are semi-dormant. An interval of 7 to 10 days between mowings may be appropriate for bluegrass or tall fescue/perennial rye mixes during their growing season; this extends to 14 to 21 days or longer when growth slows. The right interval between mowings allows grasses to recover from the previous cut and enter the second growth phase wherein new blades, called tillers, are produced from the growing points. "Tillering" keeps lawns growing in a tight, dense manner that discourages weeds.

REFERENCES AND READINGS

Albrecht, W.A. 1975. *The Albrecht papers.* Raytown, Mo.: Acres U.S.A. 515 pp. (Available from: AgAccess, P.O. Box 2008, Davis, CA 95617.)

This is probably the most important book on soil fertility currently available. If Albrecht's brilliant insights into the role calcium plays in soil and plant health and his cautions against wholesale adoption of synthetic chemical fertilizers had been heeded, American agriculture might not be facing some of its current problems with soil degradation and groundwater pollution.

Buckman, H.O., and N.C. Brady. 1969. *The nature and properties of soils.* Toronto: Macmillan. 653 pp.

This basic text provides a good overview of the components of soils and their interrelationships.

Dindal, Daniel L. 1978. Soil organisms and stabilizing wastes. *Compost Science* 9(4):8-11.

An interesting discussion of the role beneficial soil organisms play in processing organic matter.

Farb, Peter. 1959. *Living earth.* New York: Harper Colophon Books. 178 pp.

A wonderful book about life below ground, including an inside view of a termite colony, descriptions of predatory fungi attacking nematodes and a host of other entertaining insights into life in the soil.

Horts, G.L., L.B. Fenn and N.B. Dunning. 1985. Bermudagrass turf responses to nitrogen sources. *Journal of the American Society of Horticultural Science* 110(6):759-761.

A technical discussion of the impact of various forms of nitrogen on bermudagrass.

Madison, J.H. 1971. *Practical turfgrass management.* New York: Van Nostrand Reinhold. 466 pp.

This is still the best all-around text on proper lawn management.

Madison, J.H. 1971. *Principles of turfgrass culture.* New York: Van Nostrand Reinhold. 420 pp.

A scholarly text on the anatomy and physiology of turfgrasses and the principles of fertilization and irrigation.

Schaller, F. 1968. *Soil animals.* Ann Arbor: University of Michigan Press. 144 pp.

A highly entertaining discussion of the usually microscopic invertebrates that live in the soil, without which the planet would be covered with undecomposed garbage.

Schultz, W. 1989. *The chemical-free lawn.* Emmaus, Pa.: Rodale Press. 194 pp.

An excellent primer on lawn care without synthetic chemical products.

Tashiro, H. 1987. *Turfgrass insects of the United States and Canada.* Ithaca, N.Y.: Cornell University Press. 391 pp.

An excellent source for identifying common lawn insect pests and gaining background on their life cycles and behavior. Color photos show the pests and their damage.

Vargas, J.M., Jr., D. Roberts, T.K. Dannenberger, M. Otto and R. Detweiler. 1989. Biological management of turfgrass pests and the use of prediction models for more accurate pesticide applications. In *Integrated pest management for turfgrasses and ornamentals,* eds. A.R. Leslie and R.L. Metcalf, pp. 121-126. Washington, D.C.: U.S. EPA. (Available from: GSCAA, 1617 St. Andrews Ave., Lawrence, KS 66046.)

In addition to the paper by Vargas et al. documenting the effectiveness of the microbe-enriched organic fertilizers in fighting lawn diseases, this publication also includes research reports on other biological approaches to solving pest problems on lawns.

CHAPTER 30
Least-Toxic
Lawn Pest Management

INTRODUCTION

In this chapter we describe complete IPM programs for major insect, disease, weed and rodent pests of lawns. The solutions are based on the horticultural strategies for producing healthy lawns discussed in the previous chapter, so we encourage you to review that material before implementing the methods described here.

CATERPILLARS: THE SOD WEBWORM
(Order Lepidoptera, *Crambus* spp.)

The larval stages of butterflies and moths are called caterpillars or worms. Table 30.1 at right lists the major caterpillar species that are considered lawn pests. Although the list of potential caterpillar pests is long, only a few, including sod webworms, armyworms and cutworms, are serious pests of residential lawns. And of the 60 to 80 species of webworms in the United States, most are pests of grain crops and wild grasses, not of lawns. Since detection and management of all three are essentially the same, we confine our detailed discussion to sod webworms. If armyworms or cutworms are problems in your lawn, follow the recommendations here. For more detailed information on these and other insect lawn pests not covered in detail in this chapter, we recommend *Turfgrass Insects of the United States and Canada* by Haruo Tashiro (listed under "References and Readings on pp. 563-565).

Biology

A sod webworm (see the drawing at right) is the larval, or caterpillar, stage of a small whitish or dingy-brown moth. The caterpillar is ¾ in. to 1 in. (1.9 cm to 2.5 cm) long, and, depending on the species, greyish-brown to greenish to dirty white with four parallel rows of dark brown spots on the abdomen. The adult moths have a habit of folding their wings closely about their bodies when at rest, earning the group the

Table 30.1 **Caterpillars that Damage Lawns**[a]	
Common Name	**Scientific Name**
Lawn moths	
sod webworms	*Crambus* spp.
Skippers	
fiery skipper	*Hylephia phylaeus*
Essex skipper	*Thymelicus lineda*
Armyworms	
common armyworm	*Pseudaletia unipuncta*
fall armyworm	*Spodoptera frugiperda*
beet armyworm	*S. exigua*
Cutworms	
granulated cutworm	*Agrotis subterranea*
black cutworm	*A. ipsilon*
turnip moth	*A. segetum*
hart and dart	*A. exclamationis*
variegated cutworm	*Peridroma saucia*
yellow underwing	*Triphaena pronuba*

[a] From Madison, 1971.

name "close-winged moths." The two finger-like horns protruding from the head give them their other common name, "snout moths." If disturbed during the day, the moths fly erratically for a short distance before settling again on the lawn or adjacent shrubbery. The adult moths do not feed on grass.

Armyworms are larger than sod webworms in the moth and caterpillar stages. Mature armyworm caterpillars are 1½ in. to 2 in. (3.8 cm to 5 cm) long, and vary in color from grey to yellowish green. Light stripes run the length of their bodies. The fall armyworm usually found in the southern states has a characteristic white or yellow inverted "Y" on the front of its head capsule. Adult armyworm moths are three times larger than the sod webworm moth, with a 2-in. (5 cm) wingspan.

Cutworms are also larger than sod webworms, reaching 1½ in. to 2 in. (3.8 cm to 5 cm) in length, and vary-

The Sod Webworm

The larval stage (A) of the sod webworm feeds on blades of grass at night. When populations are high, larval feeding can cause browning and death of large areas of lawn. Adult moths (B) do not feed on lawns. (Wingspan: ¾ in./1.9 cm)

ing in color from pale grey to brownish black, often with a lighter-colored underside. Adult moths are brownish tan to greyish, with a wingspan of 1½ in. (3.8 cm). The front wings are darker than the hind pair and usually have various light and dark markings.

In late spring and early summer, female sod webworm moths fly over lawns at dusk, dipping down to drop as many as 200 eggs in the grass. The eggs resemble tiny cream-colored beads, and are preferentially dropped in humid areas of succulent grass. According to John Madison, writing in *Practical Turfgrass Management*,

The eggs need moisture to develop, and if the area dries, mortality will be high. The eggs hatch in about 4½ days at 75°F [24°C]. The small worm produced leads a precarious existence. With its small mouth it can only skeletonize the soft interveinal surface parts of a leaf. If the leaf is tough and hard it may starve to death at this stage. If a drop of rain or irrigation water hits the larva, it may wash off the leaf to the soil and be lost. The first and second instars [stages of caterpillar growth] are usually spent on a single grass leaf. By the third instar the worm is large enough to take bites from the edge of the leaf and leaves appear notched.

During the fourth, fifth and sixth instars, the worms construct little burrows or tunnels in the thatch layer of lawns. The burrows are covered with bits of dirt, lined with silk and reinforced with excrement and pieces of grass. Then the worms cut off the grass blades entirely and drag them into their burrows, where they feed in safety at leisure. When the larvae have completed their growth and are about ¾ in. (1.9 cm) long, they leave their burrows and construct cocoons of silk and bits of earth in the nearby soil. In 10 to 14 days the moth emerges from the pupa and forces its way from the cocoon into the open air. Within a few minutes the moth's wings have spread and dried and the moth is ready to mate and produce a new generation. Adult moths live only a few days. Since adults take no solid food, it is only in the larval stage that these insects are harmful.

Nearly mature caterpillars overwinter in the soil and resume feeding in late April to early May as soon as soil temperatures begin to rise. In northern and midwestern states, adults begin to emerge in early June and can be seen flying across lawns at dusk. Pupation occurs in late June to early July, and second-generation adults are observed shortly thereafter. New eggs are deposited and second-generation larvae reach peak activity in mid- to late August, which is when most damage is observed. As temperatures drop in fall, the larvae burrow deeper into the soil to overwinter. In warmer areas, webworms may produce up to three generations. In western and southern states, the generations may overlap, with all life stages occurring simultaneously.

Damage

All webworm feeding occurs at night. While the worms are small, the injury resulting from their feeding is likely to pass unnoticed. It appears first as small, irregular brown patches in the grass. As the worms grow older and begin eating entire leaves, often consuming twice their own weight nightly, large areas of grass can be severely damaged if the population is high. According to Madison:

A hundred larvae per square yard [or 11 per square foot] at this stage can thin turf out at a rate where it seems to disappear overnight. As green leaves are removed, the brown duff is exposed and the infested areas are straw-colored. The worms stay close to their burrows and so tend to thin the turf in a circular area the size of a quarter or half dollar. From above the turf, these feeding areas appear as pock marks in the lawn and can be readily recognized.

Detection and Monitoring

Because the brown patches caused by webworm damage can superficially resemble those caused by other pest insects or diseases, accurate diagnosis is important. Webworms live in the thatch layer of the lawn rather than in the soil, so you should check for them in the layer of dead grass just above the soil line. Webworms are present if: grass blades in the damaged area are actually missing and not just dead; there are green fecal pellets in the thatch; you find larvae in silk-lined tubes in the thatch (you can use a small hand trowel to loosen the thatch); or you find holes pecked by birds, which indicate the birds are searching for webworms.

Soap drenches, whose use as a monitoring tool is outlined in the sidebar on p. 532, can also help you detect thatch-dwelling insects such as webworms, cutworms and armyworms.

If your lawn is in good condition and growing vigorously, the presence of two or three webworm larvae per square foot is probably not cause for concern. If your lawn is under stress through compaction, infrequent irrigation or under-fertilization, the presence of as few as one larva per square foot usually indicates the need for treatment. Because factors such as grass vigor, temperature and moisture play major roles in the number of webworms a lawn can tolerate without significant damage, it may take a season or two for you to decide what the action level is.

Treatment:
Indirect Strategies

Indirect strategies for webworm control include planting resistant grass varieties, managing horticultural stresses on your lawn and conserving native biological controls.

1. Webworm-Resistant Grass Cultivars. The Kentucky bluegrass varieties 'Windsor' and 'Park' show some tolerance for webworms. If webworms are a chronic problem, however, you should consider replacing them with endophytic grasses (grasses that contain beneficial fungi within their tissues), discussed on pp. 518-519. Table 30.2 on p. 532 lists grass varieties with endophytic fungi that repel caterpillars, or "worms." Most lawn seed companies are introducing

Using a Soap Drench to Monitor for Webworms

Mark off two or three 2-ft. square (0.6 m by 0.6 m) sections of lawn in both damaged and undamaged areas. Mix 2 tablespoons of liquid soap or detergent in 1 gal. (3.8 l) of water in a sprinkling can, then pour the mix evenly over each area to be sampled. You can also make this kind of drench by mixing 1 tablespoon of 1% to 2% pyrethrin in 1 gal. of water.

The soap irritates the caterpillars, causing them to crawl to the surface. Keep a close watch on each test area for about 10 minutes, because brief movements alone may indicate webworms are present. Where the thatch is thick it may be necessary to pour several more gallons of soap solution on the test area to reach the webworms. If the thatch is saturated but no caterpillars appear, the damage is probably due to disease or another type of insect. If insects do surface, check to see that they are webworms.

Even if there is no damage, you can use the soap method to check your lawn periodically for developing insect problems. Since many such problems begin in the hot, dry edges of lawns, particularly near concrete driveways or sidewalks, it is a good idea to select several such areas and monitor them once a month during spring and summer with the soap drench.

Table 30.2

Endophytic Lawn Grasses that Repel Certain Insects[a]

Perennial Ryegrass[b]	Turf-Type Tall Fescue
Citation II	Apache (25% endophytes)
Commander	Kentucky 31 (variable levels)
Pennant	
Regal	
Repell	
Sunrise	

[a] These include sod webworms, armyworms, cutworms, billbug larvae, chinch bugs, certain aphids and Argentine stem weevil larvae.

[b] These varieties contain high levels of endophytes. Consult the sidebar on p. 519 for varieties with moderate to low levels.

endophytic fungi into a wide variety of their lawn grasses, so more varieties should be available by the time you read this. For commercial sources of these grasses see the Resource Appendix under "Insect Management: Horticultural Controls" on p. 683.

2. Habitat Management. Because webworms prefer to live in layers of deep thatch, you should reduce the thatch level if it is thicker than ½ in. to ¾ in. (1.3 cm to 1.9 cm). Refer to p. 522 for a discussion of dethatching procedures.

Webworms also like areas of the lawn that are hot and dry during the day. Damage may coincide with areas that are insufficiently watered or compacted (compaction interferes with the soil's ability to absorb water). Correction of these conditions enables the grass to resume vigorous growth and replace damaged blades (see Chapter 29 for a more detailed discussion of stress reduction methods). Once the grass is growing vigorously, a moderate amount of feeding by webworms will not be noticeable.

3. Conservation of Native Biological Controls. Good lawn management should encourage the presence of the natural enemies of webworms. Four species of ants, particularly *Pheidole tysoni,* and the mite *Macrocheles* feed on webworm eggs. The robber fly

(Erax aestuans) captures webworm moths. Spiders, vespid wasps, native earwigs, carabid beetles and rove beetles prey on various stages of the pest. Birds, including poultry, as well as a number of parasitoids and a pathogen eat the caterpillars.

For example, the parasitoid *Apanteles,* a small wasp-like insect in the family Braconidae, deposits its eggs inside webworms. The tiny parasitoid maggots emerging from these eggs feed on the internal tissues of their hosts, eventually causing death. Several parasitoids may develop in a single host larva. When full-grown, they emerge from the host and spin their small white ellipsoid cocoons in a mass on the ground. The adult parasitoids emerge from the cocoons to lay their eggs in other webworms. Two species of flies, *Phorocera claripennis* and *Zenillia caesar,* also parasitize webworms to some extent. These flies deposit their eggs on the skin of the webworm larvae. The maggots hatching from them burrow into the bodies of the host larvae and feed, eventually killing the worm.

Where moisture and temperature are high and infestations are heavy, the fungus *Beauveria bassiana* attacks webworms. The infected larvae turn dull pink and become flaccid. The fungus provides good control, but unfortunately only after the larvae have already caused significant damage to grass. The impact of the fungus is not really seen until the following year, when there are fewer overwintering webworms due to the kill of larvae the previous fall. Species of the protozoans *Nosema* and *Thelohania* also attack webworms.

Treatment: Direct Physical Controls

In areas where webworm presence has been confirmed, you can drench the soil under and adjacent to the damaged grass with the soap solution described in the sidebar on the facing page. As soon as the caterpillars wriggle to the surface, rake them into piles with a flexible lawn rake, scoop them up with a shovel and drop them into a bucket of soapy water.

Treatment: Direct Biological Controls

Poultry and the microbial insecticide *Bacillus thuringiensis* can be used to control webworm infestations.

1. Poultry. If you keep chickens, let them roam the lawn for a day or two. They can clean out a webworm infestation more quickly than any other method. After removing the poultry, irrigate the lawn thoroughly.

2. *Bacillus thuringiensis* (BT). For those of you who don't have chickens handy, *Bacillus thuringiensis* (BT) is the next best thing (see pp. 132-136 for a detailed discussion of this microbial product). Sold in nurseries and hardware stores under many brand names, this naturally occurring bacterium affects only caterpillars, acting as a stomach poison when ingested. It has no known damaging effects on other species.

Bear in mind, however, that BT also has no effect on the moth stage of sod webworms. Many people apply BT as soon as they observe large numbers of moths flying over the lawn. Moths do not feed on grass and therefore do not ingest the material. If you see moths and therefore anticipate a large infestation of caterpil-

lars, especially during abnormally hot, dry summer weather, wait approximately two weeks before applying BT to allow time for the eggs deposited by the moths to hatch.

It is the youngest caterpillars, the first and second instars, that are the most susceptible to BT. They ingest the BT spores when they eat grass sprayed with it. To maximize BT contact with the larvae, mow the lawn before you apply it; don't mow again until you absolutely must to delay removal of the sprayed leaves. It is recommended that you mix a good surfactant, sometimes called a "spreader-sticker," in the spray tank with the BT to ensure that the insecticide adheres to the blades of grass and/or penetrates the thatch.

3. Nematodes. Beneficial nematodes may also prove to be effective parasitoids of webworms. Research with commercially available *Heterorhabditis* and *Steinernema* nematodes indicates that they show promise for reducing webworm populations when watered into the thatch. For more information on these biological controls, see pp. 140-142 and the discussion of white grubs, below. Sources of nematodes are listed in the Resource Appendix under "Insect Management: Biological Controls" on pp. 683-686.

Treatment: Direct Chemical Controls

Natural pyrethrum and pyrethrin, as well as synthetic pyrethroids (see Chapter 7 for details) are effective against the sod webworm, although they also kill beneficial insects in treated portions of the lawn. Therefore, if you use pyrethrum products, confine them to those areas where you are certain webworms are present to minimize damage to the webworm's natural enemies.

Insecticidal soap shows promise for controlling webworms if the thatch layer is thoroughly saturated. Research to determine optimum dosage and frequency of application is now underway.

Summary: Least-Toxic Webworm Control

• Monitor for webworms by visually examining the thatch layer or by using a soap drench to flush them out.

• Plant webworm-resistant grass varieties.

• Reduce thatch and other horticultural stresses on lawns.

• Conserve native biological controls.

• Use soap drenches and raking to remove moderate populations.

• Apply the microbial insecticide *Bacillus thuringiensis* (BT) if high populations threaten the lawn. Beneficial nematodes may also control the infestation.

• If a chemical treatment is necessary, use a pyrethrum product or insecticidal soap.

BEETLES (WHITE GRUBS): THE JAPANESE BEETLE
(Order Coleoptera, family Scarabaeidae)

The larvae, or grubs, of a number of beetles can become serious lawn pests when present in high numbers. The most important of these are listed in Table 30.3 on p. 534.

Although the adults of various beetle species differ from one another in life cycle and appearance, the grubs of all species look very similar. Fully grown larvae are ½ in. to ¾ in. (1.3 cm to 1.9 cm) long, and white to greyish with brown heads and six legs. When you see the grubs in the soil, their bodies are usually curved in a characteristic C shape. The particular species can be identified on the basis of the pattern of hairs, or rasters, found on the underside of the

Table 30.3
Major Beetle Pests of Lawns

Common Name	Scientific Name	Native/ Exotic
black turfgrass ataenius	*Ataenius spretulus*	native
May or June beetles	*Phyllophaga* spp.	native
northern masked chafer	*Cyclocephala borealis*	native
southern masked chafer	*C. immaculata*	native
Asiatic garden beetle	*Maladera castanea*	exotic
European masked chafer	*Amphimallon majalis*	exotic
Japanese beetle	*Popillia japonica*	exotic
oriental beetle	*Anomala orientalis*	exotic

The Rasters of Some Common Grubs

A number of pest beetle larvae (grubs) attack lawn roots, and proper identification by species is necessary in order to choose the most effective management methods. Grubs are identified best with a hand lens by observing the raster on the end of the larval abdomen.

Grub

Bottom side of last segment bears the raster.

May beetle

Black turfgrass ataenius

Rasters

Japanese beetle

Masked chafer

European chafer

Aphodius spp.

(Redrawn from Niemczyk, 1981.)

United States, Japanese beetle grubs (one species of a number of lawn-dwelling beetle larvae known collectively as "white grubs") are considered the single most damaging insect pest on lawns.

As the name suggests, this beetle originated in Japan, where it is only a minor pest. It was first discovered in the United States at Riverton, New Jersey, in 1916. In the mid-Atlantic states, the beetles found a climate similar to that of their native Japan and large expanses of lawns and pastures in which to develop. But the natural enemies that kept the beetles below damaging levels in Japan were not present in New Jersey, and this allowed populations to build to extremely high levels. Their spread into neighboring states was rapid, despite concerted efforts to contain them. Today, the Japanese beetle is found in practically all states east of the Mississippi, and is a periodic invader in California and other states.

Biology

Adult Japanese beetles are approximately ¼ in. to ½ in. (6 mm to 13 mm) long. The head and prothorax are greenish bronze, and the wing covers are brownish bronze with green along the sides and center. Twelve white tufts of hair are present along the sides of the abdomen and at the tips of the wing covers. The adults' long legs have large claws. Adults live four to six weeks, and their maximum abundance occurs in early July in most infested areas. They are active during daylight, leaving their earthen cells to feed and mate in the morning and returning to the soil in late afternoon.

Mated females lay approximately 60 eggs during their lifetime, usually burrowing about 3 in. (7.6 cm) into the ground late in the afternoon to deposit the eggs. Favored egg-laying sites are grassy areas such as turf, pastures and meadows in close-cropped grass. Because the eggs must absorb water to support the embryo, moist soil is essential.

last abdominal segment, as shown in the drawing above. They are visible with a 10x hand lens.

Because prevention and treatment are quite similar for these various beetles, we will provide detailed instructions for the most widespread, the Japanese beetle *(Popillia japonica)*. If irregular patches of your lawn begin wilting and dying in late spring or summer, it might indicate the presence of the larvae, or grubs, of this beetle. Although the adult beetles are common, familiar feeders on leaves, flowers and fruits of ornamental and orchard plants, the grub stage prefers the roots of lawn and pasture grasses. In many parts of the

The white, elongate eggs hatch into grubs in about two weeks. The grubs feed approximately eight weeks until they are nearly full-grown. Most feeding damage on lawns is seen in September and October. Mature grubs are about 1 in. (2.5 cm) long, and have three pairs of legs. The thorax and most of the abdomen are white. The head is tan, with large, brown-black chewing mouthparts, or mandibles. The grubs hibernate over the winter, assuming a curled C position in earthen cells 4 in. to 8 in. (10 cm to 20 cm) below the ground.

The grubs feed in early spring, pupate in May or June and emerge as adults in summer (mid-May in North Carolina, mid-June in Maryland and Delaware, and by early July in New York, New Jersey, Connecticut, Pennsylvania, Ohio, Indiana and Michigan). The life cycle, which usually takes one year, is shown in the drawing at right. In high elevations and northern latitudes the cycle may take as long as two years.

Damage

The grubs inhabit the soil or subsurface layer of turf beneath the thatch (the accumulation of dead grass stems and roots at the soil line). They feed on the roots of a wide variety of grasses, cutting the roots and loosening the sod, which can then be rolled up like a carpet. Lawns attacked by grubs will show irregularly shaped patches of wilted, dead or dying grass in April and May and August to mid-October. The fall grub population is the most damaging because it feeds when all but warm-season grasses tend to be in a semi-dormant stage in the hot weather and moisture stress is common. Grass usually does not recover from severe grub injury, but it can regrow if the injury is moderate. An attack by even small numbers of grubs can cause yellowing and slowing of grass growth.

Once grubs complete their life cycle in the lawn, they emerge as adults in late spring and move to adjacent vegetation. They are known to feed

The Life Cycle of the Japanese Beetle
The Japanese beetle grub (A) overwinters in a cell 4 in. to 8 in. (10 cm to 20 cm) below the soil surface. The grub comes nearer the surface to feed in early spring (B), then pupates (C). An adult (D) emerges in summer, feeds on foliage and fruit (E), then lays eggs in the ground (F). The eggs hatch in about two weeks, and the young grubs (G) grow and feed rapidly. This is the stage at which they inflict the most damage on roots.

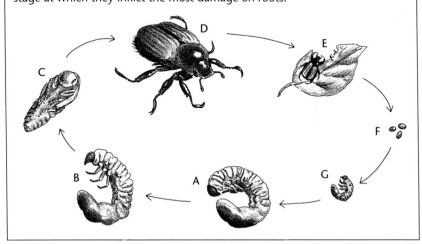

on close to 300 different species of plants. Generally, they consume leaf tissue between the veins, as well as portions of blossoms and fruits. Skeletonized leaves eventually wilt and fall from the plant. The beetles are most active and feed most extensively between 9 a.m. and 3 p.m. on warm, clear summer days, since they prefer areas exposed to direct sunlight; plants in densely wooded areas are rarely attacked.

Detection and Monitoring

The presence of large flocks of blackbirds, tunneling of moles or digging up of the lawn by skunks, raccoons and other mammals in search of grubs are signs that grub populations may be high. But the most accurate way to estimate grub populations is by examining several areas of soil underneath the grass. Since disease, adverse temperature and other factors greatly reduce the beetle population between the egg and adult stages, the most accurate surveys are made just prior to adult emergence in late May to mid-June (somewhat later farther north).

It is best to sample three or four locations on your lawn before you see any damage. This enables you to detect a developing problem and intervene. If you already see signs of damage, check those areas as well as undamaged grass nearby. Use a spade to cut three sides of a 1-ft. (30 cm) square of turf to a depth of 4 in. to 5 in. (10 cm to 12.7 cm). Carefully fold back the turf, using the uncut edge as a hinge. Pick the dirt from the roots and count the number of grubs exposed. Then fold the grass back into place, tamp it and water it with a small amount of fish emulsion or other fertilizer containing nitrogen and phosphorus.

Since there are several species of scarab grubs in turf that superficially resemble Japanese beetle grubs, it is imperative that sampled grubs be positively identified if species-specific controls are to be used successfully. Checking the rasters (see the drawing on the facing page) is one way of identifying the larvae; another is taking any large larvae found during sampling, placing them in a jar and waiting until the adults emerge. The jar can then be taken to a cooperative extension office for identification.

The number of beetle grubs your lawn can tolerate without showing significant damage is largely a matter of how well it is maintained and how vigorously it is growing. Well-maintained turf normally does not show signs of injury when spring grub populations are below 15 per square foot, whereas poorly maintained turf may show significant damage at that level. In late August or September, when grasses are semidormant and thus more susceptible to damage, as few as 6 to 10 grubs per square foot may call for some form of treatment. A couple of seasons of monitoring will enable you to gauge how many grubs per square foot your lawn can tolerate.

Remember that a low population of grubs may actually be advantageous, because the grubs ensure that a naturally occurring disease of Japanese and certain other pest beetles called *Bacillus popilliae* is maintained in the grass from year to year. The presence of this bacterium protects your lawn from extensive damage by infecting grubs, causing them to stop feeding and die without reproducing (for more information on these beneficial organisms, see "Biological Controls" on pp. 537-538). In addition, low populations of grubs help the lawn by decomposing the dead stems and roots of grass that accumulate at the soil line. When this layer of thatch is too thick, water cannot penetrate to the soil and lawns become drought-stressed.

Treatment: Indirect Strategies

Vigorously growing lawns can tolerate more grubs without showing damage. Thus, part of Japanese beetle control involves managing horticultural stresses on your lawn. Another indirect strategy is to conserve natural enemies of Japanese beetles.

1. Habitat Management. The first step in habitat management is to check for excessive thatch, compacted soil or other conditions that might impede proper flow of water and nutrients to the grass. These problems can often be corrected by aerating the soil. You can rent a power aerator that removes cores of soil from the lawn, or you can use a hand-operated aerator. You should then apply a top-dressing of 50% composted steer manure and 50% river sand, overseeding it with a mix of grasses suited to the microclimate of your yard (see Chapter 29 for details).

Appropriate irrigation can also help make lawns less hospitable to grubs and beetles. Japanese beetles prefer to lay eggs on soil that is constantly moist. When females are seeking a place to lay eggs—early July in most areas—deep, infrequent irrigation discourages them because the soil surface dries between waterings. Eggs that do get laid often desiccate (dry out) and fail to hatch. Deep, infrequent irrigation also encourages deep-rooted, drought-tolerant lawns and reduces lawn diseases fostered by heavy summer watering.

In the spring and fall (September), irrigation should be used to maintain sufficient soil moisture to keep the lawn from becoming drought-stressed. This watering regime encourages the spread of milky spore disease in grubs (see "Biological Controls" below) and encourages damaged grass to regrow. In many areas, spring and fall rains keep lawns sufficiently moist during these periods. In an unusually dry spring or fall, however, supplemental irrigation should be applied.

Beetles prefer to lay eggs in closely cropped lawns, so you should raise the summer mowing height to 2½ in. to 3 in. (6.4 cm to 7.6 cm).

2. Conservation of Natural Enemies. A number of native bird species, including grackles, starlings, cardinals, meadowlarks and catbirds, feed on adult beetles. Native insect predators include pentatomids such as *Podisus* spp. and wheel bugs *(Arilus cristatus)*. Between 1919 and 1936, soon after Japanese beetles were discovered in this country, a large-scale effort to import biological control agents was launched by the former U.S. Bureau of Entomology. Of the 26 species imported, five became established (see Table 30.4 at left). Two of these five, *Istochaeta aldrichi*, which parasitizes adults, and *Tiphia popilliavora*, which parasitizes larvae, show promise for providing good control in areas with

Table 30.4
Imported Natural Enemies of Japanese Beetles Established in the U.S.

Genus/ Species	Order/ Family	Association with Host	Adult Food Source
Istochaeta aldrichi (=*Hyperecteina alcrichi*)	Diptera/ Tachinidae	parasitizes adults	honeydew, nectar
Tiphia vernalis	Hymenoptera/ Tiphiidae	parasitizes larvae	honeydew
T. popilliavora	same	parasitizes larvae	wild carrot
Dexilla ventralis	same	parasitizes larvae	nectar
Prosena siberita	same	parasitizes larvae	nectar of umbelliferous plants

high beetle infestations. The best way to protect these natural enemies is by keeping the use of conventional garden pesticides to a minimum.

Treatment:
Direct Physical Controls

Direct physical controls for Japanese beetles include hand removal, vacuuming, trapping and spiking.

1. Hand Removal of Adult Beetles. Hand picking can be effective in reducing light infestations of adult beetles on shrubs bordering the lawn. Any method that reduces the number of adult females, particularly early in the season, will tend to reduce the grub population and therefore the adult population the following year.

One simple, effective method is to shake the beetles from plants before 7 a.m. on cool mornings when they are still sluggish. They will drop to the ground, feigning death. If a drop cloth is placed under the plants, large numbers can be collected quite easily. You can kill the beetles by immersing them in soapy water.

2. Vacuuming Adult Beetles. A small vacuum with a disposable bag can also be used to collect adult beetles. This method is commonly used by scientists to collect insects for research. See the Resource Appendix under "Insect Management: Physical Controls" on pp. 682-683 for sources of hand-held vacuums. Again, early morning is the best time for collection. You can place the paper vacuum bag in a plastic bag and leave it in the sun to kill the beetles or drop it in a bucket of soapy water.

3. Trapping Adult Beetles. Japanese beetle traps baited with food and/or sex pheromones have been on the market for many years. However, a recent study indicates that if only a few traps are used, they can actually attract more beetles than they catch. Researchers at the University of Kentucky tested the effectiveness of the traps in capturing adult beetles and reducing the number of grubs in the soil. They found that if only one or two traps are used in a garden, as

few as 54% of the beetles are captured and there is a net increase in beetles in the area around the traps. This is true despite the fact that a single trap often captures as many as 20,000 adult beetles in a single day. The experiment also revealed that the number of Japanese beetle grubs in the soil around the traps did not change, despite the large numbers of adult beetles found in the traps. The researchers concluded that the advice on the trap packages suggesting that only one or two traps are needed to protect an average-size yard is wrong.

Other studies have shown mass trapping to be effective at reducing adult beetle populations when large numbers of traps are used throughout an entire neighborhood. The traps should be placed every 200 ft. (60 m) around the perimeter of the area to be protected. In this way, the beetles are captured as they fly into the protected zone. Sources of these traps are listed in the Resource Appendix under "Insect Management: Physical Controls" on pp. 682-683.

4. Spiking Beetle Grubs. In studies at Colorado State University, a pair of Lawn Aerator Sandals, sold for use in lawn aeration by Mellinger Nursery (see the Resource Appendix under "Insect Management: Physical Controls" on pp. 682-683), was equal to or more effective than some insecticides at controlling Japanese beetle grubs. Called "Spikes O' Death" by entomologists Whitney Cranshaw and Rick Zimmerman, the sandals are fitted with 3 in. (7.6 cm) nails, and strap onto the wearer's shoes.

Wearing the sandals, the researchers walked over well-irrigated plots of lawn three to five times to achieve an average of two nail insertions per sq. in. (6.5 sq. cm). Two weeks later, flaps of turf in the plots were cut on three sides and pulled back so the grubs could be counted. Fifty-six percent of the grubs were killed by the spikes—a statistically significant level of control. The researchers concluded that this me-

chanical grub control technique, which can be used in late spring or late summer when grubs feed near the soil surface, shows promise. They plan to refine the method to increase penetration density, uniformity and the depth reached by the spikes. A mechanized aerator with spikes in place of plugs is another possible avenue of research.

Treatment:
Direct Biological Controls

By far the most important natural enemies of the Japanese beetle are the milky spore disease bacteria *Bacillus popilliae* and *Bacillus lentimorbus*. These bacteria, particularly *B. popilliae*, have been largely responsible for the widespread reduction in beetle populations over the last 40 years. These and other biological controls are discussed below.

1. Milky Spore Disease. *B. popilliae*, first isolated in 1933 from diseased grubs, was soon found to be virulent to Japanese beetle grubs and several other scarab grubs even though it is harmless to other organisms, including humans. Between 1939 and 1951, the USDA applied 178,000 lb. (80,740 kg) of spore dust containing 100 million spores/gram to 101,000 acres (40,875 hectares) in 14 states and the District of Columbia. To date, there is no evidence that beetle grubs have developed resistance to the disease.

Commercial formulations of milky spore disease such as Doom®, Japidemic™ and Grub Attack® are available for application to infested soil (for sources, see the Resource Appendix under "Insect Management: Biological Controls" on pp. 683-686). The commercial spore dust is made by inoculating beetle grubs with the disease and then extracting the spores, which resemble dust or powder when dry. Each commercial formulation contains 100 million viable spores of *Bacillus popilliae* (BP) per gram. The spores can be applied any time except when the ground is frozen or a strong wind is blowing. It makes sense to apply the dust as soon as you detect grubs in the spring or late summer.

One producer recommends using the material in early August when grubs are young, and sunlight, which can damage BP spores, is less intense. It is usually applied at a rate of 10 lb. per acre (11 kg per hectare) in spots 4 ft. (1.2 m) apart. Roughly speaking, this comes to about one level teaspoon per spot. At this rate, approximately 20 oz. (567 g) of the spore dust is enough to treat 5,000 sq. ft. (465 sq. m) of lawn.

If large areas are to be treated, a simple device can be constructed from a 1-lb. (454 g) coffee can and a broom handle. Using a 10-penny nail, punch 15 holes in an area about 1 in. square (2.5 cm by 2.5 cm) in the bottom of the can. Bolt the side of the can to the handle 4 in. (10 cm) from the bottom end of the handle. Fill the can three-quarters full with spore dust, then tap the lower end of the handle briskly against the ground at the spots to be treated. A pound (454 g) of spore dust treats about 225 spots. After application, light irrigation is recommended to wash the spores into the thatch and soil.

According to the Fairfax Biological Laboratory, which produces Doom® and Japidemic™, grubs become infected when they feed on the thatch or roots of grass where the spores have been applied. As the infected grubs move about in the soil, then die and disintegrate, they release one or two billion spores back into the soil. This spreads the disease to succeeding generations of grubs. Thus, tolerating a low population of grubs in your lawn helps keep the spores regenerating over the years, providing decades of protection.

How quickly milky spore disease alone brings a grub infestation under control depends on many factors, including the size of the beetle population, the amount of milky spore dust applied and the temperature of the soil. When grub populations are very high and feeding vigorously and the soil is at least 70°F (21°C) and very moist, the disease can spread through the grub population in a week or two. In general, however, the disease should not be thought of as a quick-knockdown insecticide. It may take a season or two before it has a substantial impact.

The high soil temperature required for rapid buildup of the spores makes the disease less effective north of New York City and through central Pennsylvania (latitude 40°N), where soil temperatures seldom reach 70°F (21°C) during the period when grubs are feeding. However, it should be noted that Fairfax Biological Laboratory collects its naturally infected milky grubs in the same area, so the disease works to some degree in this northern clime. If you live in this area, try quadrupling the dosage of spores to increase their effectiveness.

You can tell whether a grub has been infected with the disease by pulling off a leg and giving the grub a slight squeeze. If the blood has a milky color, the disease is present; if it is clear or slightly amber, the grub has not been infected.

Remember that adult Japanese beetles can migrate into your garden from as far away as ⅛ mile (0.2 km). They climb to the top of tall trees, then coast on wind currents until they find moist lawns on which to lay eggs. Thus, new generations of grubs can appear in your lawn in the fall even though the milky spore disease effectively suppressed grubs the previous spring. If the lawn is kept moist in the fall, the new grubs will probably become infected before they do much damage.

2. Parasitic Nematodes. The parasitic nematodes *Heterorhabditis heliothidis* and *Steinernema carpocapsae* are effective against grubs of the Japanese beetle as well as against the masked chafers (*Cyclocephala* and *Amphimallon* spp.). These beneficial nematodes attack only certain insects; they do not feed on plants or infest mammals. Recent field tests with *H. heliothidis* showed that over 70% of the spring grub population was killed by the nematodes. This is considered quite acceptable for control of low to moderate grub populations, meaning 10 to 15 grubs per sq. ft. (0.1 sq. m). It is not yet known whether the nematodes produce an acceptable level of control if grub populations reach high levels of more than 25 to 30 grubs per sq. ft.

The nematodes can be purchased from mail order suppliers, listed in the Resource Appendix under "Insect Management: Biological Controls" on pp. 683-686. They arrive in damp packing material. They should then be mixed with water and applied to the lawn with a sprinkling can or through an irrigation system. Adequate soil moisture is essential, because the nematodes need a film of water in which to migrate to and penetrate a grub. It is important to irrigate before and after applying nematodes. As much as ¼ in. to ½ in. (6 mm to 13 mm) of water may be needed to ensure that the nematodes are washed down through the grass to the soil, and that the soil is moist enough to provide a suitable habitat in the root zone.

Although nematodes can survive when grass is at the wilting point, they are far less mobile under these conditions. Proper irrigation is particularly critical when controlling grubs that appear in late summer and early fall when soil moisture deficits are common.

Treatment:
Direct Chemical Controls
The active ingredient azadirachtin, an extract of the neem tree (*Azadirachta indica*), has been shown in laboratory tests, to kill the grubs and some pupal stages of Japanese beetles, as indicated in Table 30.5 on the facing page. Pyrethrum-based products are also effective.

1. Neem. Neem has recently become available in the United States as the active ingredient in Margosan-O® (for sources, see the Resource Appendix under "Insect Management:

Table 30.5

Effects of Topical Applications of Azadirachtin on Immature Japanese Beetles[a, b]

Stages Treated	% Dead and Deformed
larvae (unfed from storage)	100
larvae (after feeding for 14 days)	100
larvae (feeding complete)	92
pre-pupae (immobile)	92
pupae (24 hours after molt)	79
pupae (72 hours after molt)	0
pupae (just prior to adult emergence)	0

[a] From Ladd et al., 1984.

[b] At 2 micrograms per insect.

Chemical Controls" on pp. 686-687). In a study by a major distributor of microbial and other pesticides with low toxicity to mammals, 99% of the adult Japanese beetles given leaves sprayed with neem oil refused to eat and starved to death. This suggests that neem acts as an antifeedant as well as an insecticide, so it could probably be used on foliage adjacent to lawns to discourage adult beetles from remaining in the area.

2. **Pyrethrum-Based Products.** Pyrethrins and synthetic pyrethroids can be used as soil drenches to kill grubs. See pp. 121-122 for details on these materials. A product containing insecticidal soap plus 0.01% pyrethrins extracted from the pyrethrum chrysanthemum flower is registered for use against adult beetles. Insecticidal soaps (see pp. 114-116) and pyrethrin extracts are among the safest insecticides for nontarget organisms currently available, and their combination in the new product promises to enhance their effectiveness against target pests.

The product, called Safer® Entire Yard and Garden Insect Killer, is available at garden centers. Safer's Michael Atkins says that this product will suppress adult Japanese beetles, preventing egg laying. This, in turn,

will reduce grubs in lawns the following year. But, Atkins cautions, the product is not very effective if applied to the soil to kill grubs. He points out that soil is a very biologically active medium, and when soap or pyrethrin is placed in such an environment, it is rapidly degraded by microorganisms.

CHINCH BUGS
(Order Hemiptera, family Lygaeidae)

Chinch bugs *(Blissus* spp.) are the most important of the "true bugs" (Order Hemiptera) that become pests on lawns. Many other insects in this family, especially the big-eyed bug *(Geocoris bullatis)*, are beneficial predators of pest insects such as the chinch bug.

Several species of chinch bug are serious pests of a variety of lawn grasses. The southern chinch bug *(B. insularis)*, prevalent in the warm climates of the Southeast, South and parts of the West, feeds primarily on St. Augustinegrass, but it also feeds on bermudagrass and zoysiagrass. The hairy chinch bug *(B. hirtus)*, a pest in the Northeast, particularly from New Jersey to Ohio, feeds on bentgrasses, bluegrass and red fescue.

Summary: Least-Toxic Beetle and Grub Control

• Ideally, begin monitoring your lawn before you see damage. Learn how many grubs your lawn can tolerate before treatment is necessary.

• Improve the soil to promote strong, healthy grass.

• Minimize irrigation to reduce the moist habitat preferred by the beetles during egg laying.

• Conserve the natural enemies of the beetle by minimizing use of conventional pesticides.

• Hand-pick, vacuum or trap adult beetles.

• Apply milky spore disease or beneficial nematodes to kill grubs.

• If chemical control is warranted, apply neem or an insecticidal soap/pyrethrin mix.

Biology

Adult chinch bugs overwinter in dry grass and other debris that offers them protection. In spring or early summer, depending on temperature and moisture, overwintering females lay from 200 to 300 eggs on leaves of grass, or push them into soft soil and other protected places. Young nymphs (the immature stages) emerging from the eggs are bright red with a distinct white band across the back. The red changes to orange, orange-brown and then to black as the nymph goes through five growth stages, or instars.

Nymphs range from about 1/20 in. (1.25 mm) long soon after hatching to nearly the size of the 1/4-in. (6 mm) long adult. The nymphs mature into adults, which are black with a white

The Chinch Bug

Chinch bugs are often found on drought-stressed lawns, where they suck juices from the leaves of grasses through needle-like beaks. Nymphs are easily recognized by their bright red color and white band across the back. Adults are black with shiny white wing covers. Big-eyed bugs feed on chinch bugs, which they superficially resemble. Their large eyes, wider bodies and rapid movements help distinguish them from the pests. (Actual length of adult bugs: ¼ in./6 mm)

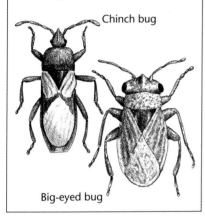

Chinch bug

Big-eyed bug

Counting Chinch Bugs

Flotation Method

If you see damage you suspect has been caused by chinch bugs but you cannot see the bugs themselves, try the flotation method. Cut the ends off a 2-lb. (0.9 kg) coffee can, then push one end of the can a few inches into the sod. If this is difficult, use a knife to cut the ground around the perimeter of the can. Fill the can with water; if it recedes, top it off.

If chinch bugs are present, they will float to the surface in 5 to 10 minutes. If you are monitoring before you see any sign of chinch bug damage, the flotation method should be used in four or five random locations around the lawn. If damage has already occurred and you are trying to diagnose the cause, place the can at the edge of the damaged area to detect nymphs that have moved to the perimeter of the damage to feed on fresh grass.

Soap-and-Flannel-Trap Method

Put 1 fluid oz. (30 ml) of dishwashing soap in a 2-gal. (7.5 l) sprinkling can and drench a 2-sq.-ft. (0.2 sq. m) area of lawn where you suspect there are chinch bugs. Watch the area for two or three minutes. Larger areas can be covered by putting the detergent in a hose attachment designed to hold pesticides for spraying the lawn. If chinch bugs are present, they will crawl to the surface of the grass.

Next, lay a piece of white cloth, such as an old bedsheet or a piece of nappy white flannel, over the area treated with the soapy water. Wait 15 to 20 minutes, then look under the cloth to see if chinch bugs have crawled onto it as they attempt to escape the soap. Their feet tend to get caught in the flannel's nap. Pick up the cloth and either vacuum it or rinse it off in a bucket of soapy water to remove the bugs. The vacuum bag should be disposed of so that the bugs will not return to the lawn.

This method can also be used to monitor for other insects such as lawn caterpillars, mole crickets and beneficial insects that feed above the soil, but it will not bring soil-inhabiting grubs or billbugs to the surface.

spot on the back between their wing pads. The adult stage of the southern chinch bug can live 70 days or more, whereas hairy chinch bug adults live only 8 to 10 days. Adult southern chinch bugs tend to move by walking, whereas hairy chinch bug adults fly. In spring the adults can be seen flying to new areas.

The development time of eggs, nymphs and adults is directly dependent upon temperature, and thus varies from one part of the country to another. Development of one generation, from egg to adult, can take six weeks at 83°F (28°C) and 17 weeks at 70°F (21°C). Chinch bugs produce up to seven generations per year in southern Florida, but only three to four generations in northern Florida, two generations in Ohio and one in New Jersey.

Damage

Chinch bugs suck the juices from grass leaves through their needle-like beaks. They also inject a toxic saliva into the plant that disrupts the plant's water-conducting system, causing it to wilt and die. Most damage is caused by nymphs that concentrate in limited areas together with the adults and feed on the same plants until all the available juice has been extracted from the grass. This

feeding pattern results in circular patches of damaged grass that turn yellow and then brown as they die. In the yellow stage, the grass superficially resembles grass that is drought-stressed. As it dies, the chinch bugs work outward from the center of the infestation, destroying a larger area as they advance.

Populations of chinch bugs are increased by hot, dry conditions. In wet, cool years, or when lawns are kept properly irrigated and not over-fertilized, the chinch bug populations decrease significantly.

Detection and Monitoring

You can best protect your lawn from damage by chinch bugs (or any other pest) through regular monitoring. The objective is to detect pests while their populations are still small and determine whether their natural controls —such as adverse weather, other insects and diseases—will keep the population low enough to prevent damage. Early detection allows you the option of using least-toxic controls.

Any lawn can tolerate a low population of chinch bugs and most other pests without sustaining significant damage. If the monitoring techniques described below indicate that there are fewer than 10 to 15 chinch bugs per square foot, generally no action is needed.

It is a good idea to begin monitoring as early as mid-April in south Florida, mid-May in Ohio and early June in New Jersey, before overwintering adults have laid their full complement of spring eggs. A quick check of the lawn once a month through September should be sufficient in most areas.

Chinch bugs produce an offensive odor that advertises their presence, especially when populations are high or when they are crushed by foot traffic. Since nymphs tend to congregate in groups, it is important to check several areas of the lawn. Infestations often begin on the edges of lawns, particularly in sunny, dry spots, so check these areas carefully. Spread the grass apart with your hands and search the soil surface for reddish nymphs or black adults. Chinch bugs may also be seen on the tips of grass blades, where they climb during the day. Be certain to distinguish between the pest chinch bugs and their predators, the big-eyed bugs, which they superficially resemble. The sidebar on the facing page describes two methods of counting chinch bugs.

Treatment:
Indirect Strategies

Indirect strategies for chinch bug control include planting resistant grass varieties, habitat management and conserving native biological controls.

1. Chinch-Bug-Resistant Grass Cultivars. If chinch bugs are a chronic problem, consider replacing your existing grass with a type that is resistant to chinch bugs. In southern states where St. Augustinegrass is the grass most often attacked by this pest, plant the variety 'Floratam' or switch to centipedegrass, which is not attacked. In other parts of the country, try planting an endophytic variety of tall fescue or perennial ryegrass (see the discussion of insect-resistant endophytic grasses on pp. 518-519).The 'Baron' and 'Newport' varieties of Kentucky bluegrass, and 'Score,' 'Pennfine' and 'Manhattan' perennial ryegrasses have shown the least damage from chinch bug feeding in a number of tests.

2. Habitat Management. Chinch bugs are attracted to lawns that have an excessive buildup of thatch, are insufficiently irrigated (often due to soil compaction) or have either too little nitrogen or too much in a highly soluble form that forces grass to grow too rapidly. Review the discussion of good lawn culture on pp. 521-528 for suggestions on overcoming these problems. Proper habitat management will go a long way toward controlling the bugs.

3. Conservation of Native Biological Controls. At least two beneficial organisms often move in to feed on chinch bugs. One is a predatory insect called the big-eyed bug (*Geocoris* spp.), which often appears where chinch bug populations are high, and feeds on them. Big-eyed bugs superficially resemble chinch bugs, so you must learn to distinguish between the "good guys" and the pests. According to Ohio State University turf specialist Harry Niemczyk, "the body of the chinch bug is narrow, the head small, pointed, triangular-shaped, with small eyes, while the body of

the big-eyed bug is wider, the head larger, blunt, with two large prominent eyes. Big-eyed bugs run quickly over the turf surface and are much more active insects than the slower-moving chinch bugs."

Recent research indicates that members of this genus can be reared easily and inexpensively, so commercial sources of these predators may surface in the near future.

In addition, a tiny wasp, *Eumicrosoma beneficum,* can parasitize up to 50% of the chinch bug eggs under favorable conditions. If the lawn is moist when the weather turns cool in fall, a beneficial fungus, *Beauveria* spp., often moves in and kills chinch bugs. Infected bugs become coated with a greyish cottony mass of fungal hyphae, which can be seen easily with the unaided eye. It should be noted that common insecticides such as chlorpyrifos (Dursban®) and herbicides such as simazine significantly reduce populations of these biological control organisms in lawns, thus triggering repeated pest outbreaks.

Treatment:
Direct Physical Controls

Small populations of chinch bugs can be removed from the lawn physically using the soap solution and white flannel cloth method described in the sidebar on the facing page. This is particularly appropriate when damage is just beginning to appear, since at this stage chinch bug nymphs are still congregated in specific locations and can be collected efficiently. Small vacuums may also be helpful.

Treatment:
Direct Chemical Controls

If pesticide use seems necessary to bring a serious chinch bug infestation under control, consider using insecticidal soap, or pyrethrin or synthetic pyrethroids. See pgs. 114-116 and 121-122 for information on these materials and the Resource Appendix under "Insect Management: Chemical Controls" on pp. 686-687 for sources.

Summary: Least-Toxic Chinch Bug Control

• Aerate your lawn in the spring and fertilize with a slow-release form of nitrogen. During hot summer months, irrigate as needed to maintain adequate soil moisture. Repeat the aeration and fertilization in fall.

• Monitor once a month beginning in May to detect developing chinch bug infestations. Check several areas of the lawn, particularly borders.

• Conserve native biological controls.

• Remove small infestations with soap-and-flannel traps.

• Treat large infestations with insecticidal soap or pyrethrum/pyrethroids.

• Begin a long-term program of replacing existing grass with varieties that show a high resistance to chinch bugs.

LAWN DISEASES: OVERVIEW

Lawn diseases are caused primarily by fungi that live in the soil or thatch layer. Over 400 species of fungi are known to live in the lawn habitat, but less than 25% are potentially harmful. Even the disease-causing fungi can live in association with grass plants without damaging them as long as environmental conditions and cultural practices do not create opportunities for attack.

The disease-causing fungi are often saprophytes, meaning they can feed on decaying organic matter. Thus, they act as decomposers of dead plant parts such as lawn clippings and thatch, helping recycle plant nutrients. Other fungi that cause disease can remain in the soil for a long time in the inactive spore stage; they attack only when the lawn ecosystem is thrown out of balance by various stresses, such as high temperature combined with excessive irrigation and fertilization.

This suggests why good cultural management, which involves proper irrigation, fertilization, aeration and mowing, and the avoidance of pesticides whenever possible, are the best defense against lawn disease. These preventive management practices are described at length in Chapter 29; if you want to avoid lawn diseases or solve an existing problem, read that chapter before proceeding.

Disease Identification

To manage a disease problem effectively in the least-toxic manner, it is essential that you identify the disease organism correctly. Often this can be done by learning to recognize the characteristic damage symptoms that pathogenic fungi cause on grasses. The sidebar on pp. 546-547 describes common lawn disease symptoms.

Photographic keys to common lawn diseases are often available from county cooperative extension offices. For example, the Nebraska Cooperative Extension Service publishes an inexpensive booklet called *Turfgrass Disease and Damage Prevention and Control: A Common-Sense Approach*. The O.M. Scott Company sells an excellent pocket-sized guide, *Scott's Guide to the Identification of Turfgrass Diseases and Insects*. The photos and descriptive information in these booklets are very useful for identifying common lawn diseases. A more scholarly disease atlas with excellent illustrations is the *Compendium of Turfgrass Diseases*. These and similar publications are listed under "References and Readings" on pp. 563-565.

One difficulty in disease identification is that attack by pathogens often occurs as a secondary affliction. That is, something else so weakens the grass that a pathogen is able to attack it. A classic example involves a leaf spot disease on Kentucky bluegrass caused by the fungus *Drechslera (=Helminthosporium) sorokinianum*. Normally this fungus is a very weak competitor with other microorganisms and is unable to get a foothold and attack plants. However, when the thatch layer of the lawn is allowed to dry out due to improper or nonexistent irrigation and is then re-moistened, the normal population of beneficial microorganisms drops, and the thatch leaks more sugars and amino acids than it normally would. *Drechslera* utilizes these nutrients in the absence of the competing microbes and rapidly becomes a problem. In this case, simply identifying the symptom — the disease-causing pathogen — would not give you enough information to solve the problem in the long term.

Another complication is that some disease symptoms resemble symptoms produced by insect damage. For example, damage by young sod webworms is often mistaken for a leaf spot disease. Alternatively, the disease symptoms can resemble cultural problems. The discoloration of large grass areas due to iron deficiency is sometimes mistaken for the disease caused by *Drechslera*. If you aren't certain how to identify the symptom you are observing, collect a sample of the damaged grass as described in the sidebar on the facing page and take or mail it to your local county cooperative extension office. Plant pathologists at the nearest land-grant university will culture the sample and determine whether a disease is present.

Keeping records is very important. In general, a lawn does not contract every disease it is susceptible to, nor is it attacked by a different disease every year. Usually, a single disease or a few diseases occur on a particular lawn from year to year. If your lawn has a disease now, chances are it has occurred before and that it coincides with certain weather patterns or lawn maintenance practices. Keep a record of when you water, mow and fertilize, and of weather just before and during disease outbreaks. It will help you identify the conditions triggering the disease so you can modify them to the degree possible.

Factors that Trigger Lawn Disease

Although disease spores may be present at any time in your lawn, an epidemic will not occur unless all of these factors are present:

• a host plant (i.e., the grass susceptible to attack by the specific fungus);

• a disease organism (i.e., the fungus that attaches itself to host plants and extracts nutrients from them);

• favorable environmental conditions (including the natural and man-made conditions and practices that encourage the development of disease, such as temperature, moisture, watering, fertilizing, mowing and soil compaction);

• a means of spore distribution (i.e., the means by which spores are transported from plant to plant, such as lawn mowers, foot traffic, wind, water and infected grass clippings).

Howard Ohr, plant pathologist with the University of California Cooperative Extension Service, lists the following factors as significant in whether or not diseases attack lawns:

1. **Water.** Most disease fungi need free water or very high relative humidity to germinate, grow and infect grasses. Water movement over the surface of the grass helps spread some pathogens. For example, the *Pythium* fungus thrives in warm, wet conditions, especially if the soil has been fertilized recently with nitrogen. It grows rapidly and releases its zoospores, which are capable of swimming in water to new plants. More important, the movement of water over the grass surface rapidly transports these spores over wide areas, where they infect more host plants.

The water or high relative humidity must be available over a long enough period to permit spores to germinate and infect grasses. This is

How To Collect and Prepare a Sample of Diseased Lawn for Identification

Take the sample from an area that is just beginning to show symptoms. Turf layers about 1 ft. (0.3 m) square and 2 in. (5 cm) deep are recommended. If the disease occurs in patches, half the turf in the sample should be from the diseased area, the other half from adjacent healthy turf. If large samples cannot be collected, cut several samples about 4 in. (10 cm) square and 4 in. deep. Do not soak the samples with water before or after collection or expose them to heat or sunlight.

If the sample is to be mailed, wrap it in several layers of paper or foil (not plastic, which retains too much moisture, causing the sample to rot). Pack samples tightly in boxes, and include a note providing as much of the following information as possible:

• species and cultivar(s) of grasses affected;

• age of the lawn;

• overall symptoms, answering these questions: Is the disease uniform throughout the area, or is it in low, wet areas only? Do symptoms occur in circular or irregular patches? How large are they? What color are they? Does the disease pattern suggest the involvement of your lawn mower or other equipment? Are there holes in the affected turf? Can the plants be pulled out easily, or are they firmly rooted?

• specific symptoms and signs on leaves of affected plants: spots,

yellowing, water-soaking, banding, shape and color of lesions, presence of fungal mycelia and/or fruiting bodies, color of fungal signs;

• general background information on the lawn environment: soil type; drainage; air movement (free or blocked by buildings?); the irrigation program for the past month; fertilization dates, types and amounts; the record of pesticide applications;

• weather conditions just before and at the time the disease symptoms appeared;

• dates symptoms were first observed and the date the sample was collected.

Take or mail the sample to the local cooperative extension office or state university plant pathology department. Remember that grass is a living system subject to decay as soon as it is removed from its "natural" environment. Accurate identification requires prompt examination so that secondary pathogens and other organisms present in the sample but not related to the problem will not overgrow the sample and make diagnosis impossible or inaccurate. Be sure to collect and mail samples early in the week so they will not sit in the post office over the weekend. Include your telephone number so the diagnostician can reach you.

usually 18 hours or more. Water applied in late evening or at night often remains on foliage for long periods, giving pathogens the maximum opportunity for infection, whereas water applied in the early morning usually dries rapidly, preventing pathogens from becoming established. Too much water on grass plants may also increase their succulence or stress them by preventing oxygen uptake by the roots, both of which result in increased susceptibility to disease. Too little water can trigger disease outbreaks as described above for *Drechslera* leaf spot.

2. Temperature. All grasses have a temperature range in which they grow most vigorously. Within this range they are most resistant to many pathogens; below or above it they become more susceptible.

The disease organism also has an optimum temperature range, but it may be able to grow sufficiently above or below this range to cause a serious problem. In addition, many lawn disease fungi are active at temperatures that may stress the grass. For example, several fungi known as snow molds are active under a blanket of snow. The fungus *Pythium* is capable of rapid growth and spread during 85°F to 95°F (29°C to 35°C) weather, when cool-season grasses such as Kentucky bluegrass and perennial ryegrass are under heat stress. The disease "spring dead spot" evidently occurs when bermudagrass is dormant. The most effective means of minimizing the effects of temperature on disease development is to choose grass species and varieties that are best adapted to your area.

3. Fertilizer. The effects of fertilizing on disease development vary with the disease. For example, when bentgrasses are grown with low but balanced levels of fertilizer, they are less susceptible to attack by *Pythium*. However, when calcium is deficient or out of balance in the soil relative to other nutrients, the plants are more susceptible to attack. Brown patch, caused by *Rhizoctonia solani*, is more severe if nitrogen levels are too high while phosphorus and potassium levels remain normal. If all three nutrients are lower than normal, disease severity increases. The effects of *Sclerotinia* dollar spot are more severe on nitrogen-deficient turf and may be reduced by increasing nitrogen fertilizer. This reduction is due to an increased growth response by the plants. (See the discussion of lawn fertilization in Chapter 29 for an overview of practices that ensure sufficient lawn fertility.)

4. Mowing. Mowing inflicts a large number of wounds on grass through which pathogens may enter. Brown patch is more severe on grasses that are cut short, possibly because the mowing wounds provide openings for pathogens. Mowing also appears to lower disease resistance by removing some photosynthesizing portions of the plant. The consequent reduced supply of sugars and starches results in a weakening of disease resistance. Kentucky bluegrass plants cut below 1½ in. (3.8 cm), for example, show a marked increase in incidence and severity of diseases caused by *Drechslera*.

5. Aeration. Coring the soil improves the ability of gases and water to move in and out of the soil. This reduces the anaerobic (oxygen-deprived) conditions in the soil that promote certain disease organisms. It also allows the grasses to grow more vigorously, enhancing their innate disease resistance.

6. Thatch Management. Thatch is the tightly intermingled layer of living and dead stems, leaves and roots of grass that develops between the green vegetation and soil surface. When the thatch is thick enough —greater than ¾ in. (1.9 cm)—grass roots develop in it rather than in the soil. Plants rooted in thatch are more subject to drought and inadequate nutrition, and thus become weakened. In addition, thatch is colonized by fungi that may, under suitable conditions, become pathogenic and attack growing plants, especially those in a weakened state. A reduction of thatch reduces the food base for disease organisms, thereby reducing the opportunity for pathogens to produce disease.

7. Pesticides. The application of common lawn pesticides can increase disease problems. For example, in a study at the University of Illinois it was found that frequent applications of two pre-emergent herbicides, calcium arsenate and bandane, increased the incidence of *Drechslera (=Helminthosporium)* disease on Kentucky bluegrass. The researchers concluded that the herbicides killed off earthworms. In the absence of these earthworm decomposers and the microorganisms that process thatch initially broken down by earthworms, the thatch layer grew, stressing the grass and making it more susceptible to disease. There are many other studies in the scientific literature describing how increased disease incidence is associated with the use of insecticides, herbicides and even fungicides.

General Biology of Lawn Disease Fungi

The fungi that cause most lawn diseases live in the soil and in the dead leaves, stems and decaying roots that form thatch. Fungi are low, thread-like forms of plant life that are incapable of manufacturing their own food. Instead, they live off living or dead plant or animal matter.

Most fungi produce spores (seedlike units) or other resistant forms (sclerotia or stromata), which can be spread by wind, water or mechanical means. Under ideal conditions, the spores germinate and produce branches (hyphae). These grow and multiply into masses of thread-like appendages called mycelia, which are sometimes visible with the naked eye. The hyphae penetrate the plant tissues through natural openings or wounds such as those caused by mowing. They grow, drawing their sustenance from the plant and breaking down its tissues until they destroy its normal functioning.

At maturity, the fungus gives off more spores (which are sometimes produced on mushrooms, the fruiting bodies of fungi). These spores start the life cycle over again. In a few cases, spores are not created, and perpetuation of the life of the fungus is carried on by parts of the mycelium scattered about the lawn or soil. The sidebar on pp. 546-547 describes the life cycles and damage symptoms of a number of the most common lawn disease organisms and indicates the seasons of the year each disease usually occurs. We have limited our discussion to lawn disease organisms that are common throughout most of North America for which there are effective management strategies that involve little or no use of conventional fungicides.

Given the major role temperature plays in the development of lawn diseases, specific turf diseases usually are associated with the cool, moderate or warm seasons of the year, depending on geographic location. Thus, we begin the following sections on treatment of lawn diseases with those associated with the warm season (generally June, July and August), and end with those that generally appear during the cool seasons (fall through early spring).

BROWN PATCH OR RHIZOCTONIA BLIGHT
(Rhizoctonia solani)

Humid weather with temperatures above 85°F (29°C) during the day and 60°F (16°C) at night, in combination with leaf surfaces that remain wet for six to eight hours, creates ideal conditions for the onset of brown patch. Unbalanced soil fertility and excessively low mowing heights exacerbate the disease. Susceptible grasses include bentgrasses, bermudagrass, bluegrasses, fescues, ryegrasses and zoysia. Damage symptoms are described in the sidebar on pp. 546-547 and are shown in the photo at right.

Treatment: Indirect Strategies

Indirect strategies for controlling brown patch focus on planting resistant grass cultivars or blends and on horticultural controls. See pp. 519-520 for details on resistant cultivars and pp. 521-528 for background information on the horticultural controls discussed in this section.

1. Water Management. Water only in the early morning to ensure that the grass dries before nightfall. During periods of drought or heat, give the lawn a long, slow irrigation to keep adequate water in the soil. Irrigate as infrequently as possible while temperatures are high and ripe for brown patch development. Improve the soil drainage by aerating and top-dressing (see pp. 521-522) so water does not puddle on the grass.

2. Fertility Management. High levels of nitrogen in combination with low levels of phosphorus, potassium or calcium exacerbate disease. Avoid heavy early spring and summer fertilization with highly soluble nitrate fertilizers. Apply only moderate levels of nitrogen, and make sure potassium and phosphorus levels are in balance with other nutrients, especially calcium. Use slow-release fertilizers and do not fertilize during hot periods.

3. Mowing and Thatch Management. Avoid frequent, low mowing of the grass. Raise the mowing height to 2.5 in. (6.5 cm) or higher and remove diseased grass clippings. A dull mower frays the edges of cut grass blades and serves as a point of entry for the fungus. Excessive layers of thatch favor the disease, so use the methods discussed on p. 522 to keep thatch in check.

4. "Poling" and Syringing. One study found that dew and other nutrient-bearing free water on grass leaves is a key factor in the development of brown patch. Dew or "guttation water" contains high amounts of nutritious sugars that wash out of grass leaves. This food source attracts fungi such as *Rhizoctonia*. Initial infection of the above-ground grass blades was observed to take place through a lower leaf that is in contact with the soil. The fungus then grew over and through this leaf to others, eventually reaching the uppermost clipped ends. During a brown patch attack, the fungus multiplied in the

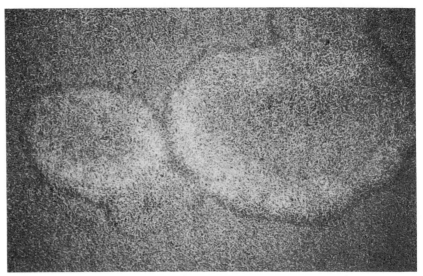

Brown patch symptoms include irregular brown areas ranging from a few inches to many feet across. The centers of the spots may recover, resulting in a darkened 'smoke ring' or 'halo' of diseased grass. (Photo courtesy Crop Science Society of America.)

Damage Symptoms and Life Cycles of Common Lawn Disease Organisms

Warm-Season Diseases (70°F to 100°F, 21°C to 38°C)[a]

Brown Patch *(Rhizoctonia solani)*

Brown patch generally appears as roughly circular brown patches from a few inches to several feet across. Infected leaves first appear dark and water soaked, then eventually dry, wither and turn brown. Brown-to-black fungal fruiting bodies may be found on stolons or under sheaths. The patch may be surrounded when humidity is high by a "smoke ring" of fungal mycelium. It disappears as the foliage dries. A musky odor may be perceptible 12 to 24 hours before the first appearance of the disease. In some cases, centers of damage may recover, resulting in a brown ring that surrounds healthy grass.

Brown patch can survive unfavorable periods as inert hyphal masses (fungal threads) or mycelia in infected plants and debris, or as growing saprophytic hyphae in soil. Under warm, humid conditions, hyphal masses germinate, and mycelia spread through leaf thatch or soil, infecting any roots or leaves contacted. Infected tissues collapse and shrivel rapidly when exposed to sun or wind. Hyphal masses (sclerotia) form on or in infected tissues, and are released into the soil as dead tissues decompose. The sclerotia are highly resistant to fungicides.

Fusarium Blight, Summer Patch *(Fusarium culmorum and F. tricinctum; Magnaporthe poae)*

The symptoms of these two diseases are so similar that we group them together. Infected turf has small, circular, 2-in. (5 cm) spots of dead and dying grass that often enlarge to 24 in. (60 cm) in diameter. Spots begin as dark blue to purple wilted turf and turn straw-colored to light tan when dead. The grass in the center of each spot may remain healthy and become surrounded by a band of dead turf—a symptom called "frog eye." Both leaf blades and the basal crown may be affected; summer patch tends to produce leaf die-back from the tip down, whereas fusarium blight tends to kill the basal crown. Pinkish fusarium mycelium can be seen on the surface of the crown when soil moisture is high.

These fungi overwinter as mycelia in infected plants and debris, and as thick-walled, microscopic chlamydospores in thatch or soil. When favorable conditions occur, mycelia grow rapidly and spores germinate. The fungi sporulate freely in moist thatch; spores are carried by wind and water to host plant leaves, roots or crowns, although main entry is via the roots. All parts of the plant can be infected. Sporulation may occur on infected plant leaves.

Pythium Blight *(Pythium spp.)*

Early symptoms are circular red-brown spots from 1 in. to 6 in. (2.5 cm to 15 cm) across. When dew-covered, infected leaves are water soaked, dark and may feel slimy. Leaves shrivel and turn red-brown as they dry. Dew-moistened spots may contain cottony purple-grey to white mycelium at the margins. Infected plants collapse quickly. In hot, moist weather, infected areas enlarge rapidly. The disease spreads along drainage patterns, thus it may appear in long streaks.

These fungi are soil saprophytes, and thus are common in soil, thatch and in the roots of mildly infected hosts. In the presence of high nitrogen, water and heat, motile zoospores or mycelia may penetrate host plants, producing new mycelia. The fungi spread from leaf to leaf by mycelial growth. Resting spores (oospores) are produced in or on dead tissues. All spore forms may be transmitted by water or in infected soil on shoes and equipment.

[a] Temperature ranges are approximate; some diseases may occur at higher or lower temperatures.

Moderate-Season Diseases (60°F to 80°F, 16°C to 27°C)[a]

Dollar Spot (Lanzia and Moellerodiscus spp., formerly Sclerotinia)

Dollar spot appears as round, bleached to straw-colored spots ranging from the size of a quarter to that of a silver dollar sunken in the turf. Individual spots may coalesce to destroy large areas of turf. Fresh spots may show fluffy grey-white mycelium in the early morning, while grass is wet. Leaf spots appear as bleached out or light tan lesions over the entire width of the blade, and have red-brown margins (in all hosts except annual bluegrass).

These fungi survive unfavorable periods as dormant hyphae in infected plants, and as mycelial masses (stromata) on the surfaces of leaves. When conditions become favorable, the hyphae begin growing out into humid air, infecting any moist leaf they contact (roots and rhizomes are not infected). No spores are formed by these fungi in nature, so that fungal distribution to new hosts is by movement of infected grass by people, animals, water, wind and equipment.

Necrotic Ring Spot (Leptosphaeria korrae)

Symptoms resemble those of fusarium blight and summer patch. However, necrotic ring spot occurs primarily in cool, wet weather, whereas the others are warm-season diseases. Dead patches of grass can reach 12 in. (30 cm) in diameter, with the characteristic "frog eye" frequently present.

Cool-Season Diseases (40°F to 75°F, 5°C to 18°C)[a]

Drechslera Melting Out, or Leaf Spot (Drechslera sativus, formerly Helminthosporium sativum)

Early symptoms are small dark purple or black leaf spots occurring primarily during cool weather in spring and fall. The centers of the spots may become light tan as the spots enlarge. The entire blade may become involved, appearing dry and straw-colored. Cool, drizzly weather promotes infection of roots and crowns, producing the "melting out" phase that can severely thin out turf. Similar symptoms can occur in summer when temperatures exceed 85°F (29°C), but this melting out is cause by another fungus, Bipolaris sorokinianum.

Fungi can survive unfavorable conditions as spores and dormant mycelium in infected plant tissue and debris. They are saprophytes, and will grow and sporulate when dry debris is moistened. During cool, wet weather, when moisture films can occur on leaf surfaces, spores produce germ tubes, which penetrate grass leaves. Lesions occur, and sporulation may occur on the larger lesions. Infection may continue until the cold weather returns.

Fusarium Patch, or Pink Snow Mold (Microdochium nivale, formerly Fusarium nivale)

In the absence of snow, fusarium patch occurs as reddish-brown, circular spots from 1 in. to 8 in. (2.5 cm to 20 cm) across in infected turf. Under snow cover the spots are tan to whitish-grey or red-brown and expand from 2 in. to 3 in. (5 cm to 7.5 cm) to 1 ft. to 2 ft. (0.3 m to 0.6 m) in diameter. Immediately after the snow has melted, pink mycelia may be visible at the margins of the spots.

Fungi survive unfavorable periods as mycelia in infected debris or as spores in the soil. Under cool, wet, overcast or shaded conditions, mycelium infects leaves, spreading rapidly in temperatures between 32°F and 61°F (0°C to 16°C). If overcast skies are broken by sufficient sun to keep up carbohydrate levels in grass, there is rarely a problem. Or, if the turf dries and warms up after a prolonged overcast period, the fungus becomes inactive.

Grey Snow Mold (Typhula spp.)

Infected turf develops circular, grey-straw to brown spots 3 in. (7.5 cm) to 2 ft. (0.6 m) across as the snow melts. Fuzzy, grey-white mycelia may be visible, especially at the margins of the spots immediately after the snow melts. The color of the mycelium gives the disease its name.

These fungi oversummer as dark-colored, small sclerotia on infected leaves. When temperatures reach 50°F to 64°F (10°C to 18°C), sclerotia may germinate if the humidity is high. Mycelium may be produced directly or may be preceded by sexual-spore production. Mycelia may infect grass plants under snow cover. When the snow melts, light causes the mycelia to go from the infective stage to production of sclerotia. New sclerotia are produced in infected leaves and crowns, and are released into the soil as dead plants decompose.

drops of dew and spread rapidly to adjacent plants by bridging the drops of water on grass blade tips in spider-web fashion.

Given the major role dew appears to play in the spread of this disease, it is wise to remove dew from the lawn in the morning, either by dragging a hose or a flexible bamboo pole across the lawn, a procedure called poling, or by squirting the dew off with water from a hose, which is called syringing. Studies at the University of Rhode Island indicate that spraying turf with a wetting agent such as soap or detergent helps prevent the accumulation of water drops on the grass blades for a number of days, thereby effectively controlling brown patch.

5. Hydrated Lime. On golf courses, hydrated lime is used to keep the surface of the leaves relatively dry, reducing *Rhizoctonia* damage. The procedure is described by Houston Couch, author of *Diseases of Turfgrasses*. According to Couch, at the first sign of the disease, you should broadcast the lime at the rate of 10 lb. (4.5 kg) per 1,000 sq. ft. (93 sq. m) of grass. To reduce the possibility of plant injury, apply the lime only when the grass is dry. Pole the limed grass immediately after application, and do not irrigate for 24 hours. Repeat the application at roughly three-week intervals as long as the disease is present.

Treatment:
Direct Physical Controls

The effectiveness of covering soil with thin sheets of clear plastic so sunlight heats it enough to kill disease organisms is well documented. This disease control practice, called solarization, is being adopted increasingly by farmers for the control of many agricultural disease organisms that also attack lawns. If a brown patch outbreak has killed extensive areas of your lawn, necessitating renovation of the lawn, we recommend solarizing the soil first. Details are provided on pp. 501-502.

Solarization, done in sunny, warm weather, heats the soil to tempera-

tures in the range of 113°F to 122°F (45°C to 50°C) at a depth of 4 in. (10 cm), and 100°F to 113°F (38°C to 45°C) at a depth of 8 in. (20 cm). Most lawn pathogens are present in the top 2 in. to 4 in. (5 cm to 10 cm) of soil, and are killed at these temperatures. Fortunately, many beneficial microorganisms such as *Trichoderma* (discussed below) can survive. Thus, solarization "pasteurizes" the soil, tipping the balance in favor of the beneficials. This contrasts with chemical fumigation, which sterilizes soils, killing virtually all microbes and creating a biotic vacuum that can be recolonized by pathogens just as readily as beneficials.

Israeli researchers have found that the beneficial *Trichoderma* is even more effective at suppressing *Rhizoctonia* and other pathogens if introduced into solarized soils. You can probably achieve the same effect by solarizing the diseased portion of your lawn, then incorporating large amounts of aged compost or pulverized tree bark into the soil before replanting the lawn.

Treatment:
Direct Biological Controls

Recognition of the important role played by beneficial microorganisms in suppressing disease organisms is growing (see the discussion of suppressive soils on pp. 514-516). The best-studied microbe antagonistic to species of *Rhizoctonia* is *Trichoderma*. This beneficial fungus is present in homemade compost and in the tree-bark-based soil amendments sold in nurseries.

Trichoderma is a very strong competitor in the soil habitat and has demonstrated its ability to outcompete a wide variety of disease organisms. In Europe it is being used to control problems ranging from Dutch Elm disease, caused by the fungus *Ceratocystis ulmi,* to decay organisms that attack utility poles. In Israel, scientists have demonstrated the ability of *Trichoderma harzianum* to control tomato fruit rot caused by

the same species of *Rhizoctonia* that attacks lawns.

In observing the behavior of *Trichoderma,* researchers found that when it moves into the vicinity of *Rhizoctonia,* it forms more branches (mycelia) and grows toward the disease organism. This directed growth is apparently the result of a chemical stimulus released by the *Rhizoctonia.* Once in contact with the *Rhizoctonia* fungus, *Trichoderma* coils around it. Scientists think that once *Trichoderma* is in the proximity of a host organism like *Rhizoctonia,* it produces antibiotics that damage or kill the other fungi.

This and other research linking *Trichoderma* to control of *Rhizoctonia* suggests that inoculation of a lawn with *Trichoderma* might slow or prevent development of brown patch. Although there are as yet no scientific studies of the effect of *Trichoderma* on lawns, we have some suggestions if you want to experiment on your own.

If a commercial source of pure *Trichoderma* is not yet available in the United States by the time you read this (marketing plans are underway as we go to press), your backyard compost pile or a bag of commercial pulverized tree bark will in all likelihood contain these beneficial organisms. Researchers at Ohio State University found that composted hardwood bark aged at least one year contains high numbers of *Trichoderma,* and that these beneficials suppress *Rhizoctonia* when compost constitutes 40% to 50% of the soil mix. *Trichoderma* have also been found to colonize compost piles.

Thus, if your lawn is showing damage from brown patch, you can try poking some holes in the damaged turf and adding a ¼-in. to ½-in. (6 mm to 13 mm) layer of composted tree bark (which is available from nurseries) or compost. Be sure that the bark you buy is well composted, since poorly aged bark does not work as effectively. If you are using your own compost, take it from the middle of an aged, stabilized pile. You can also try making a compost or bark "tea" by soaking a burlap bag full of the organic matter in a bucket of water for several days, then watering the damaged area with the solution. Laboratory studies have found that leachates of composted bark suppress disease, so we suggest trying the tea as a means of inoculating the lawn with *Trichoderma*.

If you try incorporating these compost materials or use the tea, leave at least one section of lawn untreated so you have a "control" to compare the treated area with. This will help you decide whether or not the method worked. Remember that lawn diseases are so temperature- and moisture-dependent that a sudden change in the weather can start or stop a disease outbreak. Keep records, and don't jump to any conclusions about the method until you have tried it a few times.

Inoculation of seeds with *Trichoderma* before planting has produced high levels of protection from the "damping off" forms of *Rhizoctonia* responsible for the death of many grasses at the seedling stage. Thus, you might also try coating grass seed with compost tea before sowing.

A number of organic fertilizer products enhanced with beneficial microorganisms (actinomycetes, fungi and bacteria) have been shown to prevent or halt some lawn diseases, including brown patch. These products are discussed on pp. 515-516. Dis-Patch™, specifically recommended for brown patch, is listed in the Resource Appendix under "Plant Disease Management: Biological Controls" on p. 687.

For additional information on microbial soil amendments, see the discussion of necrotic ring spot on pp. 550-551.

Treatment:
Direct Chemical Controls

Least-toxic chemical controls for brown patch include neem oil, garlic oil and fungicidal soap.

1. Neem Oil. Neem oil, a product extracted from India's neem tree *(Azadirachta indica)*, acts as a fungicide as well as an insecticide. Indian scientists testing the ability of neem oil to prevent or suppress diseases of gram, a type of bean, found that when soil is drenched with neem oil, *Rhizoctonia solani* as well as other pathogens do not form sclerotia and therefore do not reproduce.

In addition to other active ingredients, neem oil contains large amounts of sulfur compounds. Sulfur has been used as a fungicide for centuries, and it is thought that the sulfur compounds play a role in neem's toxic effects on certain fungi. Neem is available for use as an insecticide under the trade name Margosan-O® (see the Resource Appendix under "Insect Management: Chemical Controls" on pp. 686-687). It is hoped that additional EPA registration for its use as a fungicide is forthcoming. Household neem soap is sold in many import stores that carry products from India, and it might be worth experimenting with.

2. Garlic Oil. In laboratory studies in India, oil from the common garlic plant *(Allium sativum)* used as a soil drench at a concentration of 150 to 200 ppm (0.02 oz. to 0.03 oz. per gal.) completely inhibited sclerotium formation and mycelial growth in *Rhizoctonia solani*. In laboratory studies at the University of Hawaii, extracts from the roots of one-month-old garlic seedlings were ground up in water and diluted (1.5 grams wet weight of root per 1 milliliter of water). A solution of 30% garlic root extract applied to the soil (at 100 ml per 1,000 g of soil) held losses of papaya seedlings from damping off disease to only 3%, compared to 53% in the untreated soil.

To our knowledge, no field tests have been conducted with garlic, but these laboratory findings suggest that garlic oil is a promising subject for further research.

3. Fungicidal Soap. See the discussion under dollar spot below (p. 552).

FUSARIUM BLIGHT, SUMMER PATCH AND NECROTIC RING SPOT
(Fusarium culmorum and F. tricinctum; Magnaporthe poae; and Leptosphaeria korrae)

For many years a single disease called fusarium blight was thought to cause the symptoms shown in the photo on p. 550. Recently, however, it was discovered that fungi in three separate genera are involved, each of which has been given separate disease status as listed above.

Fusarium blight and summer patch are warm-weather diseases that can occur from late June through early September, depending on location. They usually appear after a week or two of dry weather following a heavy rain, and are associated with shallowly rooted grass, which is highly vulnerable to drought stress. Symptoms often appear first along sidewalks and in poorly drained areas, and primarily attack Kentucky bluegrass when it is kept in a lush, overfertilized state in summer. Necrotic ring spot is primarily a cool, wet-weather disease occurring in spring and fall, and attacks the roots of Kentucky bluegrass.

Damage symptoms for all three diseases are similar (see the sidebar on pp. 546-547). Kentucky bluegrass varieties 'Park,' 'Campus,' 'Fylking' and 'Nuggett' are particularly vulnerable. Annual bluegrass and fine-leaf fescues are also affected.

Treatment:
Indirect Strategies

Indirect strategies for controlling fusarium blight, summer patch and necrotic ring spot focus on planting resistant grasses and on various horticultural controls.

1. Planting Resistant Grasses. Consider modifying or replacing highly susceptible Kentucky bluegrass lawns with a mix of species such as the tall fescues, perennial ryegrasses or warm-season grasses (such as bermudagrass and St. Augustinegrass) that are less susceptible to the disease. 'Columbia'

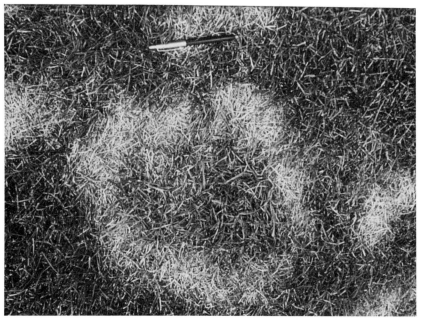

Fusarium blight and summer patch appear as small circular spots of dead grass that may enlarge to 2 ft. (0.6 m) in diameter. Grass in the center of each spot may remain healthy and become surrounded by a band of dead turf, a symptom referred to as 'frog eye.' (Photo courtesy Crop Science Society of America.)

is one bluegrass variety that is resistant to fusarium blight complex.

One study found that adding as little as 10% to 15% perennial 'Manhattan' or 'Pennfine' ryegrass to a 'Park' Kentucky bluegrass lawn eliminated summer patch. A seeding of 15% or more perennial ryegrass and 85% or less Kentucky bluegrass by weight resulted in approximately a 50/50 bluegrass/ryegrass plant count after three years. The increased drought- and heat-tolerance of perennial ryegrass, tall fescue and other varieties is one of the factors thought to explain the suppression of disease. Check with your local county cooperative extension service for cultivars that grow well in your area.

2. Fertility Management. If you have a Kentucky bluegrass lawn, remember that it naturally slows its growth during summer because it does not tolerate high temperatures well. So don't overfertilize; if you do, the lush, soft growth produced by the grass is more vulnerable to attack by these diseases. Maintain a moderate but balanced fertilizing program so the lawn can produce growth to cover damage. Slow-release fertilizers, especially composted garden material, sewage sludge or manure, should be used. Avoid the highly soluble fast-release nitrogen fertilizers. (Note: Important background information on lawn fertility is presented in the preceding chapter.)

3. Aeration. Fusarium blight, summer patch and necrotic ring spot are exacerbated by compacted soils, excessive thatch and soil layering, all of which inhibit the percolation (seeping) of water into the soil. Puddles of standing water create anaerobic conditions in the thatch that allow summer patch fungi to become active.

Diseased turf should be aerated with a coring tool (see the discussion of aeration on pp. 521-522) to reduce compaction and thatch and increase infiltration and soil air movement.

Coring also helps integrate the dissimilar soil layers that occur when imported topsoil or sod rather than seed is used to establish the lawn. When one soil type is laid on top of another, water tends to collect at the interface, moving laterally rather than vertically. Grass roots tend to stop growing when they reach this interface, and can be killed by the excessive water at that point. By coring into the layered soil and incorporating compost, both water and roots are encouraged to move more deeply into the soil, producing more vigorous grass growth.

4. Water Management. Supplemental irrigation will help drought-stressed grasses outgrow fusarium blight, summer patch and necrotic ring spot. You may need to water daily at the hottest times of the day until the grass resumes vigorous growth.

Thatch management and mowing are also effective controls; for information on these strategies see the discussion of melting out on p. 553.

For details on soil solarization, a recommended physical control for these three diseases, see p. 548.

Treatment: Direct Biological Controls

Because fusarium blight, summer patch and necrotic ring spot primarily attack roots, the more you can do to increase the number of beneficial soil fungi and bacteria antagonistic to the pathogens, the fewer problems you will have. In studies conducted by J.M. Vargas and colleagues at Michigan State University (listed under "References and Readings" on p. 565), several microbially enriched commercial soil amendments allowed existing necrotic ring spot patches to recover and prevented the development of new ones.

According to these researchers, when microbes are used for the biological management of soil-borne disease, two mechanisms are at work:

The first is competition for nutrients in the thatch and soil between the beneficial microorganisms and the pathogens. By utilizing available nutrients, they can deny the pathogens the nutrients needed to stimulate germination of resting structures (spores or sclerotia), and, after germination, they can deny them the nutrition needed to grow saprophytically to reach the root of the host plant for infection. The second feasible mechanism is the production by beneficial miroorganisms of substances that are antagonistic to the germination and growth of soil-borne pathogens.

Vargas et al. used two categories of commercial products to manage necrotic ring spot. The first improves the thatch and soil environment to encourage higher levels of beneficial microbial activity, whereas the second adds beneficial microbes to the thatch and soil. Products in the first category used in the study were Soil Aid™, an enzymatic wetting agent that flushes thatch and soil of substances toxic to beneficial microbes, and Green Magic™ or Strengthen & Renew™, which contain major and minor nutrients as well as extracts of plants and microorganisms. In the second category, the researchers used Lawn Restore™, an organic fertilizer consisting of bone meal, feather meal, soybean meal and other protein sources supplemented with actinomycete fungi and *Bacillus* spp. bacteria (see the Resource Appendix under "Plant Disease Management: Biological Controls" on p. 687 for sources of these products). These microbes have been shown in laboratory cultures to produce substances antagonistic to necrotic ring spot fungi.

In one series of plots on a condominium lawn in Novi, Michigan, Soil Aid™ plus either Green Magic™ or Strengthen & Renew™ was applied twice in summer and once in fall at a rate of 1 lb. per 100 sq. ft. (48 g per sq. m). In another series of plots, Lawn Restore™ was applied at the same frequency and dose. These treatments were repeated for three seasons. When the researchers compared the number of necrotic ring spots on the treated lawn at the end of the experiment in 1986 with the number of spots apparent in 1984 when the experiment began, they found 100% recovery of the lawn. In untreated areas of the lawn the number of ring spots had increased over 300% during the three-year period.

These researchers stress the importance of frequent treatment when using biological approaches to managing lawn diseases:

> These products are not like fungicides that can be applied one time, halting the spread of the fungus and allowing the grass to recover. In order to be effective, [such products] must be applied on a regular basis, either monthly or bi-monthly throughout the growing season to change the biological makeup of the thatch and soil environment.

For more on the use of beneficial microbes against lawn pathogens, see pp. 514-516 and the discussion of brown patch on pp. 548-549.

Direct chemical controls for fusarium blight, summer patch and necrotic ring spot include neem, garlic oil and fungicidal soap. For a discussion of the first two materials, see p. 549. The use of fungicidal soap is described under dollar spot on p. 552.

PYTHIUM BLIGHT (COTTONY BLIGHT, GREASE SPOT)
(*Pythium* spp.)

Pythium fungi survive in thatch and soil. They become active in warm, wet weather when daytime temperatures exceed 85°F (29°C), nighttime temperatures are above 68°F (20°C) and the relative humidity is close to 100%. The disease may occur to a limited extent under cooler conditions. Poorly drained, heavily used grasses are particularly vulnerable.

Disease symptoms are described in the sidebar on pp. 546-547 and shown in the photo below. All common turfgrasses are susceptible.

Pythium blight appears as roughly circular red-brown spots of dead grass from 1 in. to 6 in. (2.5 cm to 15 cm) across. Leaf blades tend to lie flat. They look greasy and stick together. (Photo courtesy Crop Science Society of America.)

Treatment:
Indirect Strategies

Indirect strategies for controlling pythium blight include:

1. Planting Resistant Grasses. For information on disease-resistant grasses, see pp. 519-520. Also, check with your local county cooperative extension office for recommendations on resistant grasses in your area.

2. Fertility Management. Grasses growing on soils with a calcium deficiency or excessive alkalinity are more susceptible to pythium blight. Make sure the soil nutrients are in balance, and avoid applications of highly soluble nitrogen fertilizers just prior to or during the onset of warm weather. (For an overall discussion of lawn fertility, see pp. 524-526.)

3. Water Management. Since pythium blight first appears where water forms puddles on the lawn, make sure all sprinkler heads are working properly. Fill in any low spots on the lawn where water collects. Irrigate the lawn infrequently and deeply during warm weather, and water early in the day so the grass dries before nightfall.

4. Aeration. Poor drainage exacerbates pythium blight, so aerate with a coring tool and top-dress with compost (see pp. 521-522).

5. Thatch Management. Reduce excessive thatch buildup. (See the discussion of thatch on p. 522.)

6. Mowing. Remove infected grass clippings to reduce sources of disease. Rinse the mower and the soles of your shoes with a bleach solution, as described below, before walking on undamaged parts of the lawn.

For information on direct physical controls, see the discussion of solarization on p. 548; for biological controls, see brown patch (pp. 548-549) and fusarium blight (pp. 550-551).

Treatment:
Direct Chemical Controls

In an experiment on a bowling green chronically infested with *Pythium* fungi, we found that drenching the affected areas with a solution of household bleach at 1 oz. bleach (5.25% available chlorine) per 4 gal. of water, or 100 ppm, reduced the incidence of the disease (but did not eliminate it). We got the idea when we learned that soils high in chloride ions suppress certain *Pythium* species. The bleach performed as well as did the fungicide chlorothalonil (Daconil®) in our experiments.

For information on the effectiveness of neem and garlic oil, see p. 549; for fungicidal soap, see dollar spot, below.

DOLLAR SPOT
(*Lanzia* and *Moellerodiscus* spp., formerly *Sclerotinia*)

Dollar spot overwinters in thatch. It is encouraged by nutritionally deficient grasses and by warm days and cool nights that produce dew. It is easily spread by infected grass clippings, foot traffic and mowers. Damage symptoms are described in the sidebar on pp. 546-547 and shown in the photo below.

Treatment

Indirect strategies for treating dollar spot are the same as those listed above for pythium blight. Similarly, direct physical controls (soil solarization) are identical to those given for brown patch (p. 548). For biological controls (microbial soil amendments), see brown patch (pp. 548-549) and necrotic ring spot (pp. 550-551).

Direct chemical controls for dollar spot include the use of bleach (see pythium blight, above), neem and garlic oil (see brown patch, p. 549) and fungicidal soap.

Field tests of a commercial fungicidal soap available from Safer, Inc. (see the Resource Appendix under "Plant Disease Management: Chemical Controls" on p. 687) against dollar spot and other lawn diseases look very promising. The soap kills the fungi; however, when used as a spray on lawns, the microbes break the soap down so quickly that there is little residual protection of the grass. Therefore, researchers are trying to develop a method for encapsulating the soap in a slow-release formulation that remains active on the lawn for some weeks. Using the soap as a drench spot treatment on discrete areas of damaged lawn, with repeat applications every four to five days, might work on home lawns, but there are no documented tests of such a procedure at present.

Dollar spot appears as a small, circular area of dead turf about 2 in. (5 cm) in diameter. Spots may merge to form large, irregular patches of dead grass. White cobwebby fungus threads may be visible in the early morning. (Photo courtesy Crop Science Society of America.)

DRECHSLERA MELTING OUT OR LEAF SPOT
(*Drechslera* spp., formerly *Helminthosporium* spp.)

A complex of leaf spot fungi survive in thatch and are most active during cool, moist weather. Symptoms of melting out are described in the sidebar on pp. 546-547. Overfertilized grass that produces lush, succulent growth is most likely to be attacked. Watering in the evening allows water to remain on grass blades for long periods, which provides disease spores with enough water for germination. Close mowing also stresses the grass and encourages the disease to move down to attack grass crowns and roots.

Treatment: Indirect Strategies

Indirect strategies for controlling melting out include:

1. **Planting Resistant Grasses.** Melting out primarily attacks Kentucky bluegrass. Check with your local county cooperative extension office for recommendations on resistant grass species that grow well in your area, or consult the sidebar on p. 520.

2. **Fertility Management.** Contrary to earlier recommendations against spring fertilizing, recent research at Michigan State University indicates that a good, balanced level of soil fertility in the spring helps protect grass during this potential infection period. For a more detailed discussion of this topic, see pp. 524-526.

3. **Mowing.** Grasses mowed at a height of 1½ in. (3.8 cm) or lower are more susceptible to melting out. If the disease is a problem in your lawn, raise the mowing height to 2½ in. to 3 in. (6.4 cm to 7.6 cm), keep the mower blades sharp and collect infected grass clippings. If only a small area is affected, drench the mower blades and wheels as well as the soles of your shoes with a 1% solution of bleach to disinfect them before mowing the rest of the lawn. Bleach reduces the spread of the disease.

4. **Thatch Management.** Since the fungus lives in thatch, management of this habitat is important in disease control. Turf scientists have discovered that by keeping thatch moist, large numbers of antagonistic microorganisms develop and hold *Drechslera* fungi at low levels.

It may seem strange to water the lawn during the season of spring or fall rains. But remember that we are not talking about irrigation, only a brief sprinkling to wet the thatch. If the thatch dries out, even for a few days, the beneficial organisms become inactive, the thatch begins leaking out highly nutritious sugars and starches from decomposing tissues, and the normally weak *Drechslera* fungi are able to grow in numbers great enough to damage the grass. A brief daily irrigation—just enough to keep the thatch layer moist but not enough to waterlog the soil—has been shown to reduce the incidence of the disease radically. If the thatch is excessively deep, aerate it in early spring or fall to reduce harborage for the disease.

Treatment: Direct Biological and Chemical Controls

Because this fungus is only a weak competitor in the presence of antagonistic fungi such as *Trichoderma*, careful lawn maintenance according to the directions in the preceding chapter, which are designed to enhance the habitat for beneficial organisms, should go far toward preventing or solving the problem of melting out. Regular application of organic matter (see the discussion under brown patch and necrotic ring spot, above), which enhances microbial diversity and activity, encourages the presence of antagonists of *Drechslera*.

Although there are no published studies of the use of neem, garlic oil or fungicidal soap against *Drechslera* species, they have proven effective against other lawn diseases that behave similarly. Thus, they are worth considering. Refer to the sections on brown patch and dollar spot for details on these chemical controls.

FUSARIUM PATCH (PINK SNOW MOLD) AND GREY SNOW MOLD
(*Microdochium nivale*, [formerly *Fusarium nivale*], and *Typhula* spp.)

Fusarium patch or pink snow mold (see the photo below) can develop whenever the temperature drops below 60°F (16°C), whether or not snow is present. The greatest activity occurs when snow falls on unfrozen ground. The disease is most serious in areas where air movement and soil drainage are poor, skies remain overcast for long periods and the grass stays wet for extended periods. Lush, tall growth in late fall and plant injury due to frost promote damage.

Grey snow mold occurs when the ground is unfrozen, soil moisture is plentiful and the temperature is between 32°F and 40°F (0°C and 4°C). Initial development takes place in the absence of light, which is usually brought about by snow cover.

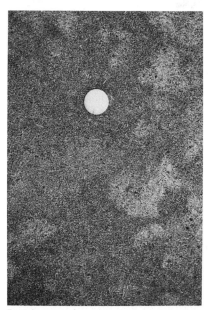

Fusarium patch occurs as reddish-brown circular spots 1 in. to 8 in. (2.5 cm to 20 cm) in diameter. White or pinkish fungal threads are sometimes visible in early morning or after snow has melted. (Photo by Arthur McCain.)

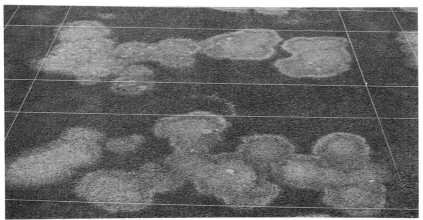

Grey snow mold appears as circular grey-to-brown spots 3 in. (7.5 cm) to 2 ft. (0.6 m) across. Fuzzy grey-white fungal threads may be visible after snow melts. (Photo courtesy O.M. Scott and Sons.)

Symptoms of grey snow mold are described in the sidebar on pp. 546-547 and shown in the photo above. Most turfgrasses that grow where temperatures are cool are susceptible. Such grasses include bluegrass, fescues and ryegrass.

Treatment:
Indirect Strategies

Indirect treatment strategies for fusarium patch and grey snow mold include:

1. Planting Resistant Grasses. For information on this strategy, see the discussion of disease-resistant grasses on pp. 519-520. Also, check with your local county cooperative extension office for recommendations on resistant grasses in your area.

2. Fertility Management. Lawns should not be allowed to enter cold weather in an actively growing condition. A light application of fertilizer in early fall encourages grass to grow and fill in bare spots, which is important for weed management. However, fertilization in late fall near the time of potential snowfall may encourage active growth too late in the season, leading to damage from cold or disease. (Note: Background information on cultural practices is provided in Chapter 29.)

3. Aeration. Since poor drainage exacerbates these two diseases, you should aerate in fall with a coring tool and top-dress with compost.

4. Thatch Management. Reduce excessive thatch buildup (see the discussion of aeration and thatch on pp. 521-522) and remove grass clippings at the last mowing of the season. These practices will reduce the nutrients from decaying organic matter available to the disease organism.

Treatment:
Direct Controls

Physical controls include soil solarization (see brown patch, p. 548) and the use of snow barriers. The latter entails the proper placement of barriers, snow fences or landscape plantings to reduce snow buildup on the lawn. Do not mulch the grass with straw, which is often done to try to prevent winter kill of the grass. The straw creates an ideal environment for the disease.

For information on biological controls for fusarium patch and grey snow mold, see the discussion of microbial soil amendments under brown patch and necrotic ring spot.

Chemical controls include the use of neem and garlic oil (see brown patch, p. 549), fungicidal soap (see dollar spot, p. 552) and iron sulfate. An iron sulfate solution made from ¼ oz. (7 g) of ferrous iron sulfate mixed in ½ gal. (1.9 l) of water (enough to cover 1 sq. yd./0.84 sq. m) is used by the Royal Horticultural Society in England to drench areas afflicted with snow mold. This mix must be used immediately, since it takes only 30 minutes for the ferrous form of the iron to change to the ineffective ferric form.

MANAGING WEEDS IN LAWNS

The good news about weed management is that if you follow the cultural recommendations for preventing lawn pest problems described in the previous chapter, you are not going to have significant weed growth in your lawn.

This statement is based on our many years' experience in lawn pest management. Every time we have been called in, we have been able to correlate the presence of weeds with stressful lawn maintenance practice —usually mowing too short and/or too frequently, fertilizing with excessive soluble nitrogen (or lack of any fertilization program) and irrigating too frequently. Soil compaction also contributes to weediness. Once cultural practices were improved, weed populations subsided, with many weed species disappearing altogether.

The direct relationship between optimum growing conditions for grasses and the relative absence of weeds results because vigorously growing grass can out-compete most broad-leaved weeds and many grass weeds. It is only when optimum conditions do not prevail that grass becomes stressed and thins out, enabling weeds to gain a foothold. More information on why this is so is provided on pp. 478-480.

When weeds invade lawns, they are responding to something that is out of balance in the lawn ecosystem. By identifying the weed, you can often tell what kind of stress is occurring. For example, prostrate knotweed (*Polygonum aviculare*) grows in compacted, droughty soils; yellow nutsedge *(Cyperus esculentus)* grows best in waterlogged soils. Table 30.6 on p. 556 lists soil or other stress conditions indicated by the presence of certain common lawn weeds. Use this information to help diagnose what is stressing the grass and enabling weeds to colonize your lawn.

Weed Tolerance Levels

Before proceeding any further, let's dispense with the notion of a "weed-free" lawn. This goal is rarely feasible or desirable. The lawn is a very dynamic ecosystem, and even under optimum grass-growing conditions, some weeds will become established. In many cases, weeds fill areas that simply cannot be made to suit vigorous lawn growth. Examples are a very shady spot next to a pine tree, whose leaf litter acidifies the soil, or an area with a very high water table.

As long as the weeds stay green, they blend in with the grass and help provide a uniform appearance. Some so-called lawn weeds, such as clover, move into compacted, insufficiently fertilized areas of lawn where the grass has thinned. The clover's deep roots break up the compacted soil and form associations with beneficial nitrogen-fixing soil bacteria *(Rhizobium)*. This enables the clover to provide surplus nitrogen to the soil, enhancing the growth of surrounding grass. After a time, the soil becomes so improved that the adjacent grass moves in and displaces the clover. The presence of some flowering weeds, such as dandelions or English daisies, also helps attract the beneficial insects that help control lawn and garden insect pests.

Thus, your goal in lawn weed management should not be to eliminate all weeds; rather, you should try to keep weed numbers low enough to prevent significant visual damage. Obviously this is a subjective aesthetic decision. Most people can and do tolerate 5% to 10% weed growth in their lawns without even knowing it. At those levels, weeds are hard to detect. Even when weeds are quite vis-

A length of rope or hose laid across the lawn can be used to mark a transect for estimating weed populations. By walking along the marker and recording the presence or absence of weeds, you can arrive at a 'ballpark' estimate of the percentage of weeds in the lawn. (Photo by Sheila Daar.)

ible, tolerance levels vary widely depending on the weed. For example, many people like the way English daisies *(Bellis perennis)* look and will tolerate high populations of this "weed." When confronted with plantain *(Plantago* spp.), however, these same people may show a very low tolerance because it has coarse leaves and lacks showy flowers.

How many and which type of weeds you are willing to tolerate in your lawn is up to you. If you have more weeds than you want, identify them. Two inexpensive, handy photographic reference tools are *Turfgrass Weed Identification and Control: A Common Sense Approach,* and *Turfgrass Pests,* which are listed in this chapter's "References and Readings" on p. 565. Other weed keys and photographic identification manuals are listed in the references for Chapter 27. You can also contact your local county cooperative extension office for publications and advice.

The next step is to estimate the percentage of lawn that is occupied by weeds. A good way to make this estimate and measure the rise and fall of weed populations from season to season is with a lawn transect (see the photo above). This is simply a line drawn through one or more representative areas of a lawn. By periodically recording the percentage of weeds vs. grass along the transect, the level of weed growth can be quantified.

The sidebar on p. 557 describes the use of the transect method to estimate weed populations on a home lawn. Once you know the percentage of weeds you are not willing to tolerate, you can begin management practices to enhance the competitiveness of grasses, thereby reducing weed growth to a level you can tolerate. For large lawn areas such as those in parks or athletic fields, several random transect lines should be used to ensure that the weed count is representative.

Table 30.6
Weed Indicators of Stress Conditions in Lawns

Common Name	Scientific Name	Stress Condition Indicated
annual bluegrass	*Poa annua*	low fertility, compaction, low mowing, high moisture
barnyardgrass	*Echinochloa crus-galli*	thinned, wet grass
black medic	*Medicago lupulina*	drought, low fertility
broomsedge	*Andropogon virginicus*	low fertility
buttercup	*Ranunculus* spp.	excessive moisture
carpetweed	*Mollugo verticillata*	drought, thin grass
chickweed	*Stellaria media*	thin grass, excessive moisture
clover	*Trifolium repens*	low nitrogen, drought, compaction
crabgrass	*Digitaria* spp.	compaction, low fertility, drought, thin grass, hot spots
cutleaf geranium	*Geranium dissectum*	droughty soils
dallisgrass	*Paspalum dilatatum*	low mowing, wet areas
dandelion	*Taraxacum officinale*	thin grass, low mowing, low fertility, drought
dock	*Rumex* spp.	excessive moisture
English daisy	*Bellis perennis*	low fertility, low pH, excessive moisture
goosegrass	*Eeusine indica*	compacted soils
ground ivy	*Glechoma hederacea*	excessive moisture and shade
hawkweed	*Hieracium* spp.	excessive moisture
kochia	*Kochia scoparia*	droughty soil
lambsquarters	*Chenopodium album*	disturbed soil, insufficient lawn seed
lippia	*Phyla nodiflora*	drought
mallow	*Malva* spp.	disturbed soil, thin grass
morningglory	*Convolvulus arvense*	disturbed, droughty soil, low mowing, low fertility
moss	various genera	low fertility, poor drainage, drought, low pH, compaction, heavy shade
mouse-eared chickweed	*Cerastium vulgatum*	low mowing
pennywort	*Hydrocotyle* spp.	excessive moisture, shade
pigweed	*Amaranthus* spp.	bare, droughty soil; low mowing, compaction
plantain	*Plantago* spp.	low fertility, low mowing
prostrate knotweed	*Polygonum aviculare*	compaction, drought, thin grass
puncturevine	*Tribulus terrestris*	dry, sandy soils
purslane	*Portulaca oleracea*	excessive fertilizer; thin grass
red sorrel	*Rumex acetosella*	low fertility, poor drainage, tolerates acidity
sandbur	*Cenchrus longispinus*	sandy soil, drought, low fertility
speedwell	*Veronica* spp.	low fertility, poor drainage, shade
spotted spurge	*Euphorbia maculata*	low mowing
thistles	*Cirsium* spp.	low fertility, drought, heavy clay compaction
wild garlic	*Allium vineale*	wet, heavy soil
woodsorrel	*Oxalis* spp.	drought
yarrow	*Achillea millefolium*	low fertility

Treatment: Indirect Strategies

The only way to achieve long-term weed control is to do everything you can to grow healthy, vigorous grass. If you succeed, the grass will perform its own weed control. The cultural methods for reducing stress on grasses outlined in the last chapter can produce an amazing turnaround in lawn weediness in a season or two.

It is dramatic what simply raising the mowing height can do to weeds. In a study at the University of Maryland on two-year-old lawn grass, crabgrass and broad-leaved weeds accounted for only 8% of the overall lawn cover in plots where the grass was mowed at a height of 2½ in. (6.4 cm), whereas weeds occupied 53% of the area in plots where grass was mowed at 1½ in. (3.8 cm). In this experiment, all other variables —such as watering and fertilizing— were the same.

Fertilization can also be used to reduce crabgrass incursions into lawns. A study by Ohio Extension Service researchers in the 1940s showed that an application of 20 lb. (9 kg) of composted poultry manure per 1,000 sq. ft. (93 sq. m) of lawn in late fall and early spring stimulated early spring growth of lawn grasses, enabling them to crowd out the crabgrass. In this study, crabgrass was reduced by up to 75% within one year. We have seen similarly dramatic reductions in weed growth in response to improved cultural practices in our work with parks departments throughout the United States and Canada. So before you consider other methods, revise your lawn maintenance practices to conform with the recommendations in the last chapter. That may be all that is required to solve your weed problem.

When designing a lawn area, install a mow strip—a line of bricks or a strip of concrete, for example—to separate the edge of the lawn from adjacent shrub beds or other planting areas. This prevents grass from growing into the planter bed and becom-

The Use of Transects To Monitor Weed Populations in Lawns

A transect is one line or a series of lines drawn across the surface of a lawn (or other surface). By walking along the line and recording the presence or absence of weeds, you can get a rough determination of the percentage of lawn taken up by weeds.

Step 1. Lay a length of rope or garden hose in a straight line across your lawn. Try to have the line cross all representative areas of your lawn (e.g., dry and wet spots, heavily used and lightly used areas, areas near concrete, shady areas). You may need to establish two or more transect lines if your lawn is large and conditions vary significantly. Place some sort of identifying markers such as small stakes or marks on a fence post at each end of the transect so you can repeat the process in the same location at the end of the season.

Step 2. Clamp a sheet of lined paper onto a clipboard and begin walking along the line. Each time you take a step, write a consecutive number on the paper to represent the step, then look down at the 3-in. by 3-in. (7.6 cm by 7.6 cm) area of lawn at the tip of your toe. Next to the number, write W if there is either a weed (even if it is mixed in with grass) or a bare spot (which is likely to become weedy even though there are no weeds yet). If you happen to know the name of the weed, write it down. Write G if all you see is grass. Continue taking this data until you reach the end of the transect. If you do more than one transect, use a separate column for each.

Step 3. Add up the total number of Ws in the column (or in each column, if there were several transects) and divide this number by the total number of steps you took on that transect. The resulting number represents the rough percentage of weeds in the lawn. Although this method would not satisfy a statistician, the data it yields is perfectly adequate for lawn care.

By collecting data from the transects at the beginning and end of each season, you can spot emerging problems. For example, if several steps in succession are marked W, a closer look at that area is warranted. Such a concentration of weed growth generally indicates compacted soil, heavy wear, too much or too little water (perhaps from a faulty sprinkler) or related conditions. If these conditions are spotted soon enough and corrected, the weeds will be displaced by grass.

ing a "weed." You can roll one wheel of the mower along the mow strip, cutting off the adjacent grass. Another benefit is the elimination of the need to edge the lawn.

If there are areas of your lawn that are chronically trampled and therefore prone to weeds (for example, where the dog customarily paces or where the neighbors cut across your lawn to get to the store), cover the area with turf blocks. These are concrete blocks with holes in them where grass can be planted. They are sold in most garden centers. The concrete reinforcement reduces the impact of the footwear while allowing the grass to grow.

In those instances where you feel you need to remove weeds more rapidly than can be achieved by improving cultural practices alone, consider the least-toxic options outlined below. If you are planting a new lawn, use the repeated cultivation technique described on pp. 498-499 to reduce weed seeds in the soil before you sow the grass seed.

Treatment:
Direct Physical Controls

Direct physical weed control focuses on cultivation, smothering, solarization, flaming and mowing.

1. Cultivation. Whenever people balk at cultivating out weeds we feel compelled to point out that even when an herbicide is used, it leaves a bare spot where the weeds die. This bare spot must be dug up and improved or another round of weeds will grow in the same place. So why not cultivate in the first place? You can dig out small groups of weeds with a trowel or sharp pointed tool — the Resource Appendix lists sources of good weeding tools under "Weed Management: Physical Controls" on p. 689). Large areas of weeds should be irrigated to loosen the soil first, then dug out with an appropriate tool. Incorporate compost and a slow-release phosphorus source such as bone meal to promote root growth in the bare soil. Level the area so it blends with the adjacent lawn, then sow lawn seed suited to your area.

If you are battling crabgrass (*Digitaria* spp.), consider planting a fine-bladed tall fescue or perennial rye cultivar. These grasses are reported to release toxins that repel crabgrass. Cover the seed with a very light dressing of compost and keep the area moist until the seeds germinate. This approach not only removes the weeds, it improves the soil, maximizing the chance of the new grass achieving vigorous growth.

2. Smothering. If you have large expanses of lawn weeds, irrigate and then cover the area with a layer of black plastic. Anchor the plastic with stones or bricks and leave it in place over the weeds for four to six weeks. This is usually sufficient to kill even the toughest perennials. You can cover the plastic with decorative bark mulch if you want to make the area look more aesthetically pleasing while the smothering is underway.

3. Solarization. If your lawn is so far gone that you need to renovate it completely, consider solarization. This technique not only kills the weeds, it kills the seeds buried in the top 4 in. to 6 in. (10 cm to 15 cm) of soil as well. Solarization takes about six weeks. It has the added benefit of killing many soil pathogens, while beneficial microbes are actually promoted through the process. Moreover, plants grown in solarized soil show better growth. Complete details on how to use this method are spelled out on pp. 501-502.

4. Flaming. This technique involves the use of a gas-powered torch to heat the cell sap of weeds enough to cause the plant cells to burst, killing the plant. Note that we are not talking about wildfires here! The flame is used only to heat — not burn — the weeds. Flamers are used widely in Europe for weed management in home and municipal gardens as well as on organic farms.

Flamers should also be considered for weed control on lawns. Grasses are far more heat-resistant than broad-leaved weeds, probably because grasses evolved on prairies, where fire is an integral part of the ecosystem. The growing points from which grass stems originate are contoured at the ground-hugging base of the plant, and are protected by leaf sheaths whose succulence helps protect the growing points from the heat of fire. Thus, even if the grass blades are damaged by the heat, the plant will bounce back.

Flamers work best on seedling-stage weeds, but can also be used to kill even deeply rooted perennials if several applications are made. They can also be used to spot-treat individual patches of weeds in a lawn, much as an herbicide is used. Both the herbicide and the flamer leave a dead patch of vegetation. The advantage of the flamer is that there is no toxic residue in the soil to pollute the groundwater and kill beneficial organisms. If the bare spot where the weed was killed is less than 12 in. (30 cm) in diameter, use a rake to scratch open the soil, then add some compost and irrigate. Adjacent grasses will soon grow in and cover the spot. If the spot is more than a foot in area, sow grass seed.

Information on buying and using flamers is provided on p. 500. For small jobs, you can use the type of small, hand-held propane torch sold in hardware stores for stripping paint.

5. Mowing. In addition to the suggestions made on pp. 526-528, you can use the mower to cut off flowers of lawn weeds before they set seed. That way you reduce the number of weed seeds in the soil.

Treatment:
Direct Chemical Controls

Safer Inc., producer of insecticidal and fungicidal soap, has recently introduced a nonselective herbicide based on the same soap technology. Called Sharpshooter™, the herbicide is made from fatty acids derived from plant oils and is nontoxic to people, pets and wildlife. When sprayed on plants, the cell membranes are disrupted, causing vegetation to shrivel and die. The fatty acids biodegrade, allowing replanting of grass 48 hours after application.

Sharpshooter™ can be spot-sprayed on seedling-stage weeds in lawns. Because it is a broad-spectrum herbicide, it damages or kills most vegetation it hits. To protect wanted grasses, you must apply it directly to weeds with a wick applicator (see p. 506). If you use the sprayer, cover the grass surrounding the weeds with cardboard or plastic. Once the weeds are dead, remove them and re-seed the bare spot with grass. Sharpshooter™

does not translocate to the roots, so it won't kill mature taprooted weeds such as dandelions, although it will burn their tops back. Repeated burning back of the tops ultimately starves the taproot and thus kills the plant. However, Safer is planning to introduce another soap-based herbicide that does translocate. It should be on the market by the time you read this.

Many annual weeds growing in lawns can be killed by spraying with a high dose of nitrate fertilizer (e.g., ammonium nitrate 20-0-0 NPK or ammonium thiosulfate 12-0-0-26 NPKS). The fertilizer acts as a contact herbicide, burning the tissue of the weed and killing it. This technique is most effective if used as a spot treatment on young weeds (the two- or three-leaved stage) in the heat of day when no moisture is on the leaves.

Weeds that can be controlled this way include mallow *(Malva* spp.), chickweed *(Stellaria media),* groundsel *(Senecio vulgaris),* London rocket *(Sisymbrium irio),* mustard *(Brassica* spp.), deadnettle *(Lamium* spp.), nightshade *(Solanum* spp.), purslane *(Portulaca oleracea)* and shepherd's-purse *(Capsella bursa-pastoris).* Many other weeds are no doubt also susceptible to this treatment.

MOLES
(Order Insectivora, family Talpidae)

Moles are much-maligned, delicate creatures that improve the soil, eat many pest insects and get blamed for damage they do not cause. At one time they were prized for their velvety fur, and a farmer angered by mole activity could sell the pelts for a good price. Although mole skin is no longer in vogue, killing moles is still popular. Yet it is best if moles can be tolerated, since in the long run their insectivorous diet is beneficial to the gardener. As discussed below, grass damaged by moles often recovers quickly, and moles rarely stay in lawns for long periods unless poor

cultural practices are encouraging high insect populations.

Moles are classified as insectivores, and the largest part of their diet is usually composed of insects. Of interest to gardeners is the fact that they eat many pestiferous beetle larvae such as the white grubs found in lawns. They may also eat earthworms, spiders and centipedes. Occasionally moles eat a small amount of vegetable matter, especially if it has been softened by water. Townsend's mole, found in the northwestern United States, eats more vegetation than do the other common mole species. Still, it has been shown that the mole will starve to death if offered only plant food.

People most often object to the sight of mole tunnels or molehills because they ruin their "perfect lawn." Certainly the tunnels make it more laborious to mow the grass. Mole runways may also be used by rodents, such as voles, white-footed mice and the common house mouse, that eat seeds, bulbs and roots, and do cause

> ### The Garden Mole
> Moles are insect eaters that 'swim' through the soil searching for prey. They are well adapted to life in narrow underground tunnels. Their large, outward-pointing claws and feet are designed for digging, and their dark brown fur can point forward or backward to facilitate movement. Their subterranean excursions often dislodge roots, damaging plants. (Average length, including tail: 7 in./17.8 cm)

direct damage to the garden. There may be the unfounded fear that mole tunneling will damage nearby trees or cause permanent damage to the turf. In fact, the only real damage caused by moles is indirect, as a result of their shallow tunnels lifting up the turf or garden soil and allowing the plant roots to dry out. The best immediate response while you are trying to decide whether mole control is warranted is to press back the soil with your foot and water the area thoroughly.

A great variety of folk remedies have been recommended. If they seem to work, it is largely by coincidence or because of indirect effects that could be achieved through other, less picturesque methods. For example, castor bean plants have been touted for mole control, the recommendation being that the plants be grown around the garden and the seeds, which are poisonous to people, be placed in the mole runways. But moles do not eat seeds. In an article that appeared in *Organic Gardening* magazine in July, 1949, Paul Scott suggested that if castor beans plants have any effect at all, it might be because they are fast-growing and quickly develop a large root system that requires large amounts of water. "This reduces the water content of the soil to such an extent," he writes, "that there are no pests, no earthworms, and, therefore, no moles."

Knowing something about the biology of moles and how to distinguish them from problem rodents such as gophers will help you in planning control strategies.

Biology

There are seven species of moles *(Scapanus* spp.) and shrew-moles *(Neurotrichus* spp.) in the United States, four on the West Coast and three on the East Coast. The lack of species in the Great Basin, Rocky Mountain and western Great Plains regions in part reflects the fact that these areas are largely too arid and rocky to provide good mole habitat. Moles require the

Mole Tunnels

Moles build two types of tunnels, or runways. Their permanent tunnels are often 1 ft. (0.3 m) underground and lead to nests that can be 2 ft. (0.6 m) deep. Connected to these permanent tunnels are runways that are closer to the soil surface, where moles can feed on root-dwelling insects. These runways may be used only once. Moles push excavated soil to the surface, creating their familiar molehills.

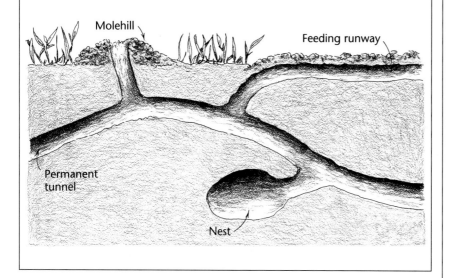

rich, moist, friable soil that also supports the insects and earthworms upon which they feed.

The mole's body shows many impressive adaptations to a life lived largely in narrow tunnels underground: a streamlined skeleton 5 in. to 7 in. (12.7 cm to 17.8 cm) long, fur that can point forward as easily as aft for ease of movement, a narrow snout, no external ears, eyes much reduced and covered with skin, and outwardly pointing claws and feet, with the front claws large and strong for digging.

These stout front claws are the mole's only means of digging through the soil. The mole uses them alternately to push the soil away from its face and along the sides of its body. A rodent's foot, by contrast, can be used to manipulate materials or dig like a dog. Since the rodent's feet can be placed flat against the ground when walking or running, the rodent is as agile above ground as

below. This is not so with the mole, which shows off its unique adaptations best when "swimming" through soft, moist earth.

If you compare the shape and arrangement of the mole's teeth with those of a gopher, a typical burrowing rodent, you will see that they also reflect important differences in digging style and abilities. The mole has pointy little incisors, or front teeth, that generally are too weak to dig through the soil or gnaw through vegetable matter, bulbs or roots. The gopher has sharp, strong incisors that continue to grow throughout its life. It uses these teeth to gnaw through tough materials. Behind these front teeth is a gap into which the rodent can suck its cheeks, preventing the entry of dirt into its mouth while it is gnawing and digging. A gopher uses its jaws to lift and remove rocks and pebbles from its path as it advances.

Whereas rodent skulls are comparatively tough, the mole's skull

is delicate. The mole cannot use its head in digging, which is why it prefers soft, uncompacted soil. In fact, the mole's head is so fragile and sensitive to vibrations that it can easily be stunned or killed by a sharp tap on the snout or by slapping the broad side of a shovel down on a tunnel where it is active.

Although the mole's eyes are virtually useless, probably only able to distinguish between light and dark, its hidden ears are remarkable in their acuity, making it possible for the mole to locate its prey through many inches of earth. Its sense of smell is also excellent. The mole with the most remarkable nose, the star-nosed mole *(Condylura cristata),* has a ring of 22 fleshy appendages at the tip of its snout, which it uses not for smelling but for feeling its environment. This mole, common on the East Coast in damp soils near swamps, streams and lake edges, wanders above ground more than many other species, and is also an excellent swimmer.

Moles build two types of tunnels (see the drawing at left). Their permanent tunnels may be quite deep and not detectable from the surface. Their nests, located in these permanent tunnels, may be 1 ft. to 2 ft. (0.3 m to 0.6 m) deep. Within these tunnels the moles are active year-round. It is their shallow feeding runways, sometimes used only once, that concern gardeners.

If you are faced with an elaborate series of tunnels in your lawn, it probably does not mean that you have more than one mole. Moles may tunnel extensively at any time of day or night just to obtain enough food to satisfy their enormous appetite. Most species are not gregarious; in fact, they are highly territorial and will fight to the death other moles attempting to enter their burrow system.

Moles also cause problems by throwing out excavated soil in large or small mounds or hills, depending on the species. These mounds can be distinguished from those of gophers by their shape and the texture of the soil used to build them. A Washington State University Cooperative Extension Service leaflet points out that a molehill is built like a volcano by the thrusting up of earth plugs through the center that then roll down all sides, whereas a gopher mound is built like a mine dump with loose dirt pushed out and away from the exit hole on one side. The characteristics that distinguish mole-hills from gopher mounds are shown in the drawing on p. 581.

Detection

If you are planning to use direct methods to kill the mole, you must determine which of the many run-ways are in use, since some of the shallow tunnels may be dug once for feeding and then abandoned. There is more than one method of doing this; which you use depends on the species you are dealing with.

East Coast moles do not leave tell-tale signs that betray the location of their deeper tunnels, so you must ex-amine the shallow surface ridges of soil they thrust up. Ignore ridges that twist and turn; instead, look for the straight runs, particularly those that seem to be connected to two or more other tunnels. Also look for ridges at the edge of the area along hedges or where the tunnels appear to enter the yard or garden from adjacent areas.

Moles repair their tunnels imme-diately if they are disturbed, so you can determine which tunnels are ac-tive by pressing down the earth with your foot and watching to see which ridges are rebuilt. Or you can poke a number of holes in the ridges you think may be active and check to see which are repaired. Repairs should be made within a few hours or at most within a day. Any tunnel that is not repaired is not active enough for use in direct mole control.

The larger mole species of coastal Washington, Oregon and California (*Scapanus* spp.) betray the presence of their deeper, permanent burrows by pushing up numerous molehills. You can locate the main runway leading away from these holes by probing the ground in a circle around them. Push a rod into the soil at 2-in. (5 cm) in-tervals 3 in. or 4 in. (7.6 cm or 10 cm) from the edge of the mound. When the rod is directly over a runway you will feel a sudden give as it breaks in-to the tunnel. These deeper tunnels are used year-round.

Treatment: Indirect Strategies

Because beetle larvae such as white grubs are a favorite food of moles, one strategy for reducing the attrac-tiveness of an area to the mole is re-ducing the number of these lawn pests. For ways to do this, consult the discussion of white grubs such as the Japanese beetle on pp. 533-539.

Another approach to managing mole pests focuses on the fact that they cannot dig through soil that is severely compacted, stony or heavy in clay. Consequently, building bor-ders of stone-filled, clay and/or com-pacted soil around the areas you want to protect discourages mole in-vasion. These barriers must extend at least 2 ft. (0.6 m) into the ground. In-troduced and compacted materials should be at least 6 in. (15 cm) wide, although 12 in. (30 cm) is even bet-ter. The barrier area can be paved over, creating a mow strip or a path around the lawn or garden.

Of course, there is always the chance that a mole will cross such a barrier above ground. A fence that is mainly buried but also reaches a short distance above ground helps prevent such crossings. If the barriers can be kept relatively dry all year they are even more effective. See the discussion of buried fences under "Physical Controls" below.

Treatment: Direct Physical Controls

Physical controls for moles include flushing with water, installing buried fencing and trapping.

1. Flushing with Water. Spring flooding, where it occurs in low-lying areas or along streams, is a natural control for moles. The adults may manage to climb out of their tunnels and wait for the water to subside on elevated ridges or drifting material, but the young are extremely vulner-able in their nests. Even a heavy rain can drown them.

Flooding can be used to a similar end by the gardener. It is probably most effective against West Coast moles that betray their deeper nests by pushing up large molehills. Flood-ing will likely have the greatest im-pact in the spring when the young are still in the nest. To drown them, open the molehill, poke a garden hose into the tunnel and turn on the water. Expect it to take about 10 or 15 minutes before there is enough water in the tunnels to flush out the adult mole. Watch for its emergence from one of the other exits; you can kill it with a small shovel. This method is likely to be effective only if the tunnel system is confined to a fairly small area.

2. Buried Fencing. Fencing a small area either with small-mesh, tightly woven hardware cloth or with low cement walls has been shown to pro-tect the area against the common eastern mole (it also protects against mice). The fence should begin slight-ly above the soil surface and extend into the soil at least 18 in. to 24 in. (45 cm to 60 cm). If it is bent out-ward underground in an L shape (as you would construct a similar barrier against rats—see p. 633) it is even more effective. The base of the L should point away from the area being protected. Joints or connec-tions in the fence should be over-lapped and tightly closed with staples or wire.

3. Live Trapping. You can capture moles live in a pit trap, then release them some distance away. First, dig through a mole tunnel that is likely to be in active use. Excavate deep enough so that the mouth of a large-mouthed jar or a 3-lb. (1.4 kg) coffee can will be flush with the floor of the mole tunnel when the container is

Mole Traps[a]

Trapping is the most successful and practical method of getting rid of moles. There are three excellent mole traps on the market. If properly handled, all give good results. All depend on the same type of mechanism for releasing the spring: the trap is triggered as the mole upheaves the depressed portion of the surface burrow over which the trap is set. Brand names of these traps are: Out O' Sight®, Victor® mole trap and Nash® (choker loop) mole trap [see the drawing at right]. The Out O' Sight® trap has scissor-like jaws which close firmly across the runway, one pair on either side of the trigger pan. The Victor® trap has sharp spikes which impale the mole when driven into the ground by the spring. The Nash® trap has a choker loop that tightens around the mole's body.

These traps are well-suited to moles because they capitalize on the mole's natural habits. They can be set without exciting the animal's suspicions by entering or introducing anything into its burrow, and they are sprung by the mole as it attempts to reopen obstructed passageways. Success or failure in the use of these devices depends largely on the operator's knowledge of the mole's habits and of the mechanism of the particular trap chosen.

Mole Traps

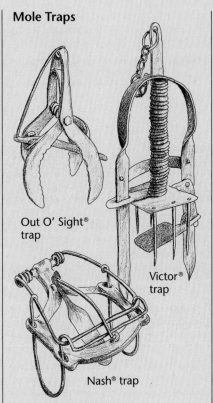

Out O' Sight® trap

Victor® trap

Nash® trap

Setting A Trap:

To set a trap properly, select a place in the surface runway where there is evidence of fresh work and where the burrow runs in a straight line. A satisfactory way to place the trap is to dig out a portion of the burrow, locate the tunnel [drawing A, above right], and replace the soil, packing it firmly beneath where the trigger pan of the trap will rest [drawing B, above right].

If the trap is the harpoon or impaling type, raise the spring, set the safety catch and push the

Setting a Scissor-Type Mole Trap

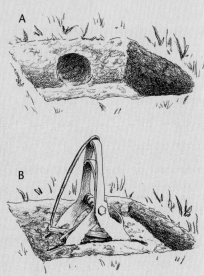

A

B

supporting spikes into the ground, one on either side of the runway. The trigger pan should just touch the earth where the soil is packed down. Now release the safety catch and allow the impaling spike to be forced down into the ground by the spring. This will facilitate their penetrating into the burrow when the trap is sprung. Set the trap and leave it. Do not tread on or otherwise disturb any other portion of the mole's runway.

[If a trap fails to catch the mole after two days, it can mean any of three things: the mole has changed its habits, the runway was disturbed too much during trap placement or the trap was improperly set and was detected by the mole. In any event you must move the trap to a new location.]

[a] Taken from the text by F. Robert Henderson, Extension State Leader, Wildlife Damage Control, Kansas State University, (*Prevention and Control of Wildlife Damage,* published by the University of Nebraska Cooperative Extension Service).

sunk into the hole you have just made. Then cover the top of the tunnel with a board so no light can enter. The mole will not be able to hoist itself out of the container.

Check the status of the trap daily by removing the cover board. Bear in mind that if you wait too long before checking, the mole may starve to death, defeating the purpose of the live trap. If several days pass with no sign of the mole, the runway has probably been abandoned and you should repeat the procedure in a different tunnel.

4. **Lethal Trapping.** The most effective method for removing moles from the garden is to use one of the commercially available mole traps. For a discussion of the three main types of traps, see the sidebar on the facing page.

Summary: Least-Toxic Mole Control

• Remember that moles are primarily beneficial—they eat pest insects and improve the soil through aeration. Do not kill them unless their damage is becoming intolerable. If the latter is true:

• Reduce the number of white grubs (beetle larvae) in the soil with the selective bacterial spray *Bacillus popilliae,* sold for Japanese beetle control.

• Where feasible, create dry, compacted and/or stony soil barriers.

• Use buried fencing or concrete barriers to protect small areas.

• Catch live moles in pit traps and release them away from garden areas.

• Flush moles out of their tunnels with water from a garden hose.

• Use strategically placed lethal traps.

REFERENCES AND READINGS

Lawn Insects

Bohart, R.M. 1940. Studies on the biology and control of sod webworms in California. *Journal of Economic Entomology* 33:886-890.

The classic study of webworms.

Gordon, F.C., and D.A. Potter. 1985. Efficiency of Japapese beetle (Coleoptera: Scarabaeidae) traps in reducing defoliation of plants in the urban landscape and their effect on larval density in turf. *Journal of Economic Entomology* 78:774-778.

This study indicates that if only a few traps are used, they may attract more adult beetles to the garden than are caught in the traps, actually increasing the problem.

Kennedy, K.M. 1981. *Sod webworm: biology and control.* East Lansing: Michigan State University Cooperative Extension Service (Extension Bulletin E-1480, File 27.36). 4 pp.

This pamphlet contains excellent color photos of the caterpillar and adult stages of sod webworm and the damage webworms cause.

Ladd, T.L., Jr., J.D. Warthen, Jr., and M.G. Klein. 1984. Japanese beetle (Coleoptera: Scarabaeidae): the effects of azadirachtin on the growth and development of immature forms. *Journal of Economic Entomology* 77: 903-905.

This study shows that leaves of plants sprayed with neem are protected from feeding by adult beetles.

Madison, J.H. 1971. *Practical turfgrass management.* Boston: PWS Publishers. 466 pp.

This is the best lawn management text yet written.

Niemczyk, H.D. 1981. *Destructive turf insects.* Wooster, Ohio: HDC Book Sales. 48 pp. (Available from: HDC, 2935 Smithville-Western Rd., Wooster, Ohio 44691.)

An invaluable tool for diagnosing pest problems on lawns. Includes a discussion of monitoring methods and excellent color photographs of turfgrass insect pests and typical damage symptoms.

Noble, W.B. 1932. *Sod webworms and their control in lawns and golf greens.* Washington, D.C.: USDA (Circular No. 248). 4 pp.

A wonderful pamphlet with lots of fascinating details on sod webworm behavior.

Tashiro, H. 1987. *Turfgrass insects of the United States and Canada.* Ithaca, N.Y.: Cornell University Press. 391 pp.

An invaluable guide to the biology and behavior of turfgrass insect pests. This excellent volume includes information on cultural and biological controls, monitoring data and other elements of an integrated pest management approach. Many color photos aid in identification.

Lawn Diseases

Bruneau, A.H., J.E. Watkins and R.C. Shearman. 1985. *Turfgrass disease and damage prevention and control: a common-sense approach.* Lincoln: University of Nebraska Cooperative Extension Service Publications (Publication EC81-1235). 28 pp.

Good color photos of lawn disease symptoms make this a handy tool for diagnosing lawn problems.

Chet, I., and Y. Henis. 1985. *Trichoderma* as a biocontrol agent against soil-borne root pathogens. In *Ecology and management of soil-borne pathogens,* Proceedings of Section 5 of the Fourth International Congress of Plant Pathology, American Phytopathological Society, St. Paul, Minnesota, eds. C.A. Parker et al. 358 pp.

This study describes the suppression of common soil pathogens by *Trichoderma* fungi.

Couch, H.B., 1973. *Diseases of turfgrass.* Huntington, N.Y.: Krieger Publications. 348 pp.

This is the most scholarly and comprehensive collection of information on turf diseases currently in print. There is a strong emphasis on understanding and changing horticultural management practices that stimulate turf diseases. Unfortunately, the book is somewhat dated and lacks the latest information on potential biological controls and newer, less-toxic fungicides.

Dernoeden. P.H. 1989. Symptomatology and management of common turfgrass diseases in transition zone and northern regions. In *Integrated pest management for turfgrass and ornamentals,* eds. A.R. Leslie and R.L. Metcalf, pp. 273-289. Washington, D.C.: U.S. EPA. (Available from: GSCAA, 1617 St. Andrews Ave., Lawrence, KS 66046.)

A useful review of cultural practices that prevent or cure common lawn diseases.

Gear, Alan, ed. 1986. *Trichoderma Newsletter.* (Available from: Henry Doubleday Research Association, Ryton-on-Dusmore, Coventry, CV8 3LG, England.)

This beautifully produced publication provides up-to-date information on the rapid developments in research on and use of *Trichoderma* as a biological control agent for many horticultural and agricultural disease organisms.

Gibeault, V.A., R. Autio, S. Spaulding and V.B. Younger. 1980. Mixing turfgrasses controls *Fusarium* blight. *California Agriculture* 34(10):11-12.

An excellent study demonstrating the effectiveness of planting a mix of grass varieties to increase disease protection.

Hoitink, H.A.J., and T.C. Fahey. 1986. Basis for the control of soil-borne plant pathogens with composts. *Annual Review of Phytopathology* 24:93-114.

This is a source of information on beneficial fungi in compost.

Katan, J. 1981. Solar heating (solarization) of soils for control of soil-borne pests. *Annual Review of Phytopathology* 19:211-236.

An important study documenting enhanced plant growth and suppression of disease in solarized soils.

Ohr, H.D. 1978. Management practices to minimize disease problems. *California Turfgrass Culture* 28(1):1-4.

A good review of cultural practices on lawns that help prevent disease.

Scott, O.M., and Sons. 1987. *Scott's guide to the identification of turfgrass diseases and insects.* Marysville, Ohio: O.M. Scott and Sons, Co. 105 pp.

Excellent color photos and line drawings make this pocket-sized paperback a handy identification tool.

Shurtleff, M.C. Jr., 1955. *Control of turf brown patch.* Providence: University of Rhode Island Agricultural Experiment Station (Bulletin 862). 25 pp.

A report on cultural practices that reduce brown patch.

Singh, H.B., and U.P. Singh. 1980. Inhibition of growth and sclerotium formation in *Rhizoctonia solani* by garlic oil. *Mycologia* 72:1022-1025.

One of the few scientific investigations of garlic oil as a fungicide.

Singh, U.P., H.B. Singh and R.B. Singh. 1980. The fungicidal effect of neem *(Azadirachta indica)* extracts on some soil-borne pathogens of gram *(Cicer arietinum). Mycologia* 72:1077-1093.

A discussion of the fungicidal properties of neem.

Smiley. R.W., ed. 1983. *Compendium of turfgrass diseases.* St. Paul, Minn.: American Phytopathological Society. 103 pp.

A scholarly overview of the biology and ecology of most common lawn diseases. The information helps you design cultural practices to prevent or stop the progress of lawn diseases.

Turgeon, A.J., R.P. Freeborg and W.N. Bruce. 1975. Thatch development and other effects of preemergence herbicides in Kentucky bluegrass turf. *Agronomy Journal* 67: 563-565.

This study documents ways in which repeated use of herbicides on lawns causes long-term turf damage.

Vargas, J.M., Jr., D. Roberts, T.K. Dannenberger, M. Otto and R. Detweiler. 1989. Biological management of turfgrass pests and the use of prediction models for more accurate pesticide applications. In *Integrated pest management for turfgrasses and ornamentals,* eds. A.R. Leslie and R.L. Metcalf, pp. 121-126. Washington, D.C.: U.S. EPA.

This paper documents the effectiveness of the microbe-enriched organic fertilizers in fighting necrotic ring spot on Kentucky bluegrass.

Lawn Weeds

Bowen, W.R. 1980. *Turfgrass pests.* Oakland: University of California Cooperative Extension Service (Publication 4053). 53 pp. (Available from: ANR Publications, 6701 San Pablo Ave., Oakland, CA 94608.)

A good source for identifying lawn insects, weeds and diseases; includes excellent color photographs.

Mansfield, R. 1977. *Weed control in North American ornamental and sports turf: an integrated approach.* Burnaby, B.C.: Simon Fraser University (Pest Management Paper No. 12). 98 pp. (Available from: SFU, Burnaby, B.C., Canada V5A 1S6).

This master's thesis contains a good discussion of primarily cultural approaches to weed management in turf. The bibliography is exhaustive for the period up to 1977.

Shearman, R.C., D.M. Bishop, A.H. Bruneau and J.D. Farrer. 1983. *Turfgrass weed identification and control: a common sense approach.* Lincoln: University of Nebraska Cooperative Extension Publications (Publication EC83-2241). 42 pp.

Color photographs and brief descriptions of symptoms make this a handy tool for identifying lawn insects, weeds and diseases.

Moles

Henderson, F.R. 1983. Moles. In *Prevention and control of wildlife damage,* ed. R. Trimm. Lincoln: University of Nebraska Cooperative Extension Service. 9 pp.

This publication contains the most comprehensive discussion of mole trapping techniques we have seen to date.

CHAPTER 31
Pests of Food and Ornamental Gardens

INTRODUCTION

The number of potential pest insects and other animals in gardens is so large that nothing less than an encyclopedia could begin to discuss them all. This contrasts with indoor environments, where only a limited number of serious pests are common in temperate climates.

Much of our garden wildlife falls into the pest category, but only because of limited human tolerance for minor plant damage and the visible presence of certain species. We prefer to think of these organisms as potential pests. Although some of them may be capable of eating garden plants, their presence does not necessarily mean they are causing damage worth worrying about. Other organisms may not be causing any damage at all; it's simply that the gardener finds them visually unappealing.

Even if we eliminate such cases from consideration, however, the list of pests that can become truly damaging remains enormous. The selection of books, pamphlets and magazine articles on garden pests is almost as large as the number of pests. Many take a partially or completely encyclopedic approach. Rodale's *Encyclopedia of Natural Insect and Disease Control,* edited by Roger B. Yepsen (listed under "References and Readings" on pp. 600-605), is among the best of these.

One difficulty with such an approach, however, is the simplification required to keep the book to a manageable size. This usually means reducing a problem's solution to a "recipe." It is a popular approach that most people welcome because it requires little thought. However, relying on recipes has two drawbacks in addition to the obvious one of limited information. One is that you may encounter new pests to which the instructions do not apply, since recipes tend to be very specific. The other is that if new developments in the control of a pest occur after the book has been produced, you have learned little that will help you judge

the merits of the new approach or its compatibility with the previously recommended procedure.

The solution to the first problem is to provide yourself with some basic information about the garden ecosystem and the role the specific pest plays within it. This is not so difficult, because information on the biology of these animals is usually available through a variety of educational materials. However, make sure you supplement your book research with first-hand observation, which we discuss below.

Solving the second problem takes the kind of time and resources most people do not have. The field of nontoxic pest control is changing so rapidly that you really need regular updates to keep abreast of the newest and best methods available. That is one of the main purposes of our periodical for the general public, *Common Sense Pest Control Quarterly.* Readers can look through its indexes to keep up with the latest developments in the management of whichever garden pests concern them.

Throughout this book we have tried to arouse your curiosity about the insects and other animals you find in your garden. We believe that learning about the species you are trying to control is the surest route to finding least-toxic ways of preventing the damage they cause. Another benefit of increased knowledge is decreased fear of pests.

Some of this kind of information can be found in books such as this one and the others we recommend in the chapter bibliographies. But often the most valuable insights are those you acquire through your own patient observation. You might even discover something about the pest or its natural controls that is not yet known to others.

This might strike you as fanciful, but it shouldn't. In our culture, professionals tend to guard their status by disdaining amateurs; as a result, many amateurs whose hobbies lead them to watch insects or other ani-

mals have a modest or self-deprecating attitude toward their own observations. In some countries, the observations of amateur naturalists, including entomologists, are highly valued. The world authority on fleas, Miriam Rothschild of England, and the former world authority on aphids, the late Hill Ris Lambers of the Netherlands, were self-taught "non-credentialed" individuals. A host of lesser-known amateur naturalists have also influenced and interacted with professionals in their countries.

So let us encourage you to spend some peaceful moments in your garden looking at the wildlife. You can learn to distinguish the plant-feeders from the carnivores, the potentially serious pests from those that are infrequent problems, and the beneficial organisms that are worth encouraging from those that are not.

In this chapter we have chosen to discuss a number of specific pests (organized alphabetically by group) of food and ornamental gardens for which our recommendations may be at variance with the abundant literature on the subject. For instance, we advise against importing lady beetles to control aphids, and suggest conserving rather than killing earwigs whenever possible. Sometimes we offer something in addition to the popular knowledge on the subject— we suggest, for example, that you use traps for catching cucumber beetles and a vacuum for collecting whitefly adults.

In each case, we hope you will keep in mind three things. First, basic information on the biology of the pest is crucial to successful control. Second, control efforts work best when confined to the precise time and place where the pest is a severe problem. And third, it is rare that you can do just one thing to solve a pest problem.

In our minds, there is a distinct difference between pests such as termites or mosquitoes that can have a serious economic or medical impact on the household, and those that are primarily an annoyance because, for example, they chew holes in cabbage or disfigure a few flowers. Our hope is that by refraining from pest control in the garden unless the situation is serious enough to warrant it, many more of the visitors to our gardens will be spared and allowed to establish a complex, stable environment.

Usually a mix of direct and indirect tactics is required to achieve the desired effect and derive a lasting benefit. You may want to review Chapter 4, which describes these general strategies for controlling pests and some criteria for selecting treatments. The discussion is particularly applicable to garden problems.

Assuming you have done your best to select and site the plants appropriately, we recommend that you apply physical controls first, particularly in emergencies. Squash the pest, pick it off the plant, prune it out, grub it out, trap it or create a barrier between the plant and the pest. Then examine the potential for modifying your horticultural practices such as fertilizing and watering. Next, decide whether releasing biological control organisms is appropriate. The Resource Appendix on pp. 683-686 provides a long list of commercially available beneficial insects and tells you which pests they attack. Finally, if none of the above is adequate by itself, follow the advice given in Chapter 6 on the use of chemical controls.

APHIDS
(Order Homoptera, superfamily Aphidoidea)

Aphids are a common garden problem, particularly at the beginning and end of each plant's growing season. Given that aphids have an abundance of natural enemies, you might wonder why this is so. Part of the answer is that the predators and parasites of aphids generally are not available to help control the pests until large numbers of their prey are already present. It makes good sense if you think about it. If the beneficial

insects arrived on the scene too early, they would starve to death before they had a chance to propagate themselves. The interval between the appearance of the aphids and that of their natural enemies may be as short as a day or two or as long as several weeks if the temperature is low. It is this predator-prey lag that you must bridge to control most aphids.

Since the potential for good biological control of aphids improves as the season progresses, the first rule of aphid management is to conserve the many natural enemies of aphids present in most gardens. You do this by confining any treatments against aphids to just those times and places where aphids are intolerable, and by using only methods that do not harm the beneficial predators and parasitoids when they do arrive in the aphid colonies.

Another reason aphids are so visible at certain times and not at others, and on certain parts of a plant but not elsewhere, is that they respond to nitrogen levels in the plant. When and where nitrogen levels are high, aphids can multiply very rapidly. Nitrogen levels are generally very high when a plant begins active growth. For most plants in temperate climates this is in the spring. Nitrogen is particularly high in the portions of the plant that grow the most rapidly, such as the buds and tips of the stems. The nitrogen level drops during the middle of the growth period, only to rise again to a smaller peak in the fall or when the leaves begin senescence (their decline) and prepare to drop off the plant.

Thus, the second rule of good aphid management is to follow horticultural practices that maintain nitrogen at a level just adequate for slow to moderate growth, just as we advised in Chapter 20 during the discussion of the control of aphid pests of plants indoors. Chapter 20 also contains a list of common indoor aphids and a short discussion of their life cycles as they relate to house plant and greenhouse management.

That information complements the information presented here, and you should read it to get the full picture.

Biology

At least 4,000 aphid species have been described, and probably many more remain to be discovered and named. Within each species there may be considerable variation in color, size, other aspects of appearance, response to environmental conditions and/or food preference. Thus, it is very difficult to generalize about aphids in a way that is useful for the particular species you find in your garden.

Most of the known aphid species are quite restricted in their host range; that is, they feed on one or a few closely related species of plants. On the other hand, approximately 10% of aphid species can and do feed on many different types of plants since they are blown from plant to plant by the winds, sometimes for hundreds of miles.

Some species alternate between two host plants each year, leaving their spring environments to fly to other species of plants during the summer, and returning to their initial hosts at the end of the growing season. For this reason it is not uncommon to find a heavy infestation on one type of plant and then, just when you think you must do something about it, the aphids disappear, as if by magic. They have gone off to their summer host. In many cases, the alternate hosts of common aphids have not yet been discovered. Other aphid species remain all season on the same species, although they may be lifted by the winds from one patch of it to another.

The superfamily of aphids is divided into two major groups. One of the differences between the groups is defined by the ability to bear live young. Although there are a number of root and conifer aphid pests that only lay eggs, the aphids seen most commonly in gardens are more unusual. Their remarkable life cycle helps explain how they can appear in

Aphids

Adult aphids can be winged or wingless, and can produce living young at various times of the year without mating. The paired tubular structures on the abdomen are called cornicles, which produce an alarm substance when the aphids are disturbed by predators. The size and shape of the cornicles help distinguish aphid species. (Actual size of adult: ⅛ in./3 mm)

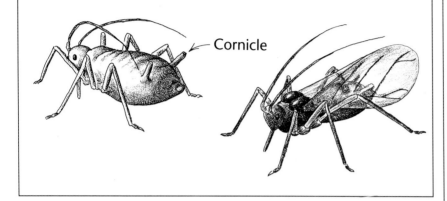

Cornicle

large numbers quickly when there were few before, and how variation within the species occurs.

In temperate climates, females lay their eggs toward the end of the growing season in protected places on their favorite plant species. Such places include cracks and crevices in the bark or bud scales. When spring arrives, a plump, distinctive-looking aphid emerges from these eggs. These are called "stem mothers," and they give live birth to daughters, and they to more daughters, all without mating. As each new female is born, she already has her partially formed daughters within her. This is called telescoping generations. Thus, each female can rapidly replicate any genetic peculiarities originally passed on by her. It is very interesting to take a 10x hand lens and watch the baby aphids being born alive. Meanwhile, the mother goes on calmly feeding on the host plant, her pointed, stylet-like mouthparts inserted into the leaf or stem from which she sucks nutritious sap.

At the end of the growing season, males are finally produced in the aphid colonies. Females born at the same time have eggs rather than live young inside them. Mating occurs, the eggs are fertilized, and the over-wintering eggs are again laid in protected areas on the plants. One exception occurs among those species that live in subtropical or tropical environments, including greenhouses. Such aphids may never produce either males or females that lay eggs. In fact, there are some species for which no males have ever been identified.

The sap that aphids imbibe from the plants is sweet, like maple syrup. They take more in than they can assimilate and excrete the excess, called honeydew. Honeydew is also produced by other common insects in the order Homoptera, including scales, whiteflies and mealybugs.

The honeydew, which is quite harmless in itself and is in fact tasty, soon grows a sooty mold, much like a black fungus growing in an old jelly jar. This may be considered undesirable because it makes the plant's leaves look sooty or dirty. Some tree-feeding aphids produce such copious amounts of honeydew that it falls off in great drops on cars parked beneath or on sidewalks, where it causes leaves and other debris to stick to the feet of pedestrians. In this way, honeydew can become a problem even when aphids are not doing any appreciable damage to a tree.

Other insects such as honeybees may feed on the honeydew. Certain ant species are so fond of this material that they jealously guard the aphid colonies producing it, killing such natural aphid enemies as the larvae of lady beetles, lacewings, syrphid flies and gall midges. This can lead to an aphid pest problem, and ant-exclusion measures become essential.

An aphid group often referred to as the woolly aphids produce filaments of fine wax around themselves, a trait shared with the closely related Homoptera. One common species, the woolly apple aphid *(Eriosoma lanigerum),* is found worldwide on some species of apple, pear, quince and closely related plants. The aphid is under such good control by its natural enemy, a chalcid wasp, that gardeners notice it only when large numbers of its parasitoid have been temporarily eliminated through pesticide use, ant interference or unfavorable environmental conditions.

Natural Enemies of Aphids

The natural enemies of aphids are so numerous and varied that it is as difficult to generalize about them as it is about the aphids themselves. The enemies fall into three major groups: pathogens, predators and parasitoids.

Certain aphids can transmit plant-infecting viruses from plant to plant, but the aphids themselves are not harmed by these. Fungi are the important pathogens causing disease in aphids, and close examination of any aphid colony often reveals the fruiting bodies of a fungus emerging from dead individuals.

Predators are the most familiar of the natural aphid enemies. They differ from parasitoids in that one predator consumes many prey, often of many different species. Examples are lady beetles, brown and green lacewings and various flies. The best-known of the flies are the syrphid flies and the aphid-eating gall midges. The latter are the gnat-like insects we discussed on pp. 373-375, where we recommended them for the control of aphids in greenhouses.

Numerous species exist in each of these families of predators, but, in the case of lady beetles, lacewings and gall midges, only one species is available commercially for aphid control, and thus is the only species familiar to most people. No species of syrphid or flower fly is commercially available. For more information about these beneficial insects see Chapter 5.

The difficulty in using aphid predators outdoors is that they tend to skim the top off whatever local aphid population is largest, then, because they can feed on so many different species of aphids, move on to find a more abundant colony elsewhere. Thus, rather than purchasing commercially available predators for outdoor use, we urge you to encourage native predators by growing a variety of plants so a variety of aphid species will also be present. That way the predators will stay nearby, feeding on each aphid population in turn according to which is most abundant. In addition, if you grow flowering plants you can attract those predator species such as syrphid flies in which the adult is dependent on pollen and nectar for egg laying.

The parasitoids of aphids generally are no larger than the head of a pin (about $1/10$ in./2.5 mm). They resemble parasites of mammals in that they reside either within the host or on its skin, living off just one host during their larval life. Unlike true parasites, however, parasitoids kill the host.

The most important aphid parasitoids—all members of the large order Hymenoptera to which the honeybees and paper wasps also belong—are highly species-specific. The significance of this fact is that they can keep the population of aphid hosts very low, because they live off no other species. The minute female parasitoid searches diligently for in-dividual aphids in which to lay her eggs. After the egg hatches inside the aphid, the larva of the miniwasp eats the aphid from the inside out, then pupates within or just below the dead body. Parasitized aphids are easy to detect, because their bodies become stiff, shiny and hard, with a color varying from black to tan, cream or brown.

If you discover such aphid "mummies" on your plants and would like to know what the responsible aphid parasitoid looks like, place the leaf with the mummy in a small pill jar stoppered tightly with cotton. Check it daily for the emergence of a small black, yellow or brown flying insect and the appearance of a small round hole in the aphid where it has emerged. Some parasitoids are very tiny and difficult to see without a hand lens, but larger ones are the size of a very small ant with wings. Since there are also parasitoids of the parasitoids (secondary parasitoids), you have no way of knowing whether the insect that emerges is a first- or second-level carnivore. One clue is that the common secondary parasitoids of aphids are very small, uniformly dark and fairly chunky looking. They also make ragged emergence holes, whereas primary parasitoids make smooth, round holes. Any small, light-colored or yellow miniwasps are probably primary parasites.

Once you have taught yourself what the parasitoids look like, you will begin to recognize them when you see them in the garden walking on leaves or flowers while hunting their prey. The ovipositor, or egg-laying apparatus, by which the female places her egg within the aphid can be seen clearly on the abdomen of the larger parasitoids.

In addition to laying larvae within the aphids, some of these miniwasps also feed upon the aphids directly, behaving like predators. Although it is difficult to quantify the effect of direct feeding by parasitoids on an aphid population, the combination of both methods of attack means that some of these beneficial insects can have a very significant impact upon the potential pest problem.

Detection and Monitoring

Since all plants can tolerate some number of aphids without sustaining significant damage, the trick is to determine what number that is. By carefully observing your roses or other plants in early spring, you can note when aphids first appear. Check the stem ends and buds weekly on those varieties that have proven most susceptible to aphids in the past. By watching the aphid colonies you locate, you should be able to spot the arrival of lady beetles, lacewing larvae and the tiny slug-like larvae of the syrphid flies. The aphid-eating gall midges, another species of small flies, are usually late to arrive in the colonies. They have a brilliant orange-yellow color, which may make them stand out from their surroundings in certain settings. Also watch for the mummies, described above, that signal the presence of parasitoids.

For each susceptible plant, you need to determine whether the amount of damage that occurs between the hatching of the aphids and the arrival of sufficient natural enemies—the lag time—is tolerable. For example, in a municipal rose garden in coastal northern California, our staff determined that most of the rose species could tolerate up to 10 aphids per bud before damage was significant. This tolerance was based on a number of factors, such as temperature, that affect how rapidly aphids multiply and how quickly beneficial insects appear. By making similar observations, you can determine your own aphid tolerance levels.

Treatment: Indirect Strategies

Indirect strategies for aphid control include nitrogen control, strategic pruning, allowing aging plants to decompose in place, the use of ant barriers and attracting predators and parasitoids with flowering plants.

1. Nitrogen Control. Since aphid reproduction is enhanced by high nitrogen levels in plants, you should avoid using heavy doses of highly soluble nitrogen fertilizer. Instead, use less soluble—for example, ammonium or urea-based—forms of nitrogen, and space the feedings over the growing season. Compost or decomposed manure is ideal for general garden use; fish emulsion or liquid seaweed can be used for individual ornamental plants. Timed-release urea-based formulations such as Ozmacote® can also be used for cole (cabbage family) crops, which require a substantial nitrogen input. If you are growing plants primarily for flowers or fruit, use fertilizers that are relatively high in phosphorus relative to nitrogen. For example, rock phosphate combined with composted manure provides adequate nourishment when supplied in a slow but constant stream over the growing season.

2. Pruning. Pruning can also play a role in encouraging aphids, because a flush of high-nitrogen new growth follows the old growth. If the plant is a variety that is susceptible to aphids in your area, encouraging an abundance of new growth early in the season before most of the aphids' natural enemies are present can cause a serious aphid problem. It may even lead to stunting or distortion of the new growth.

On such plants, prune more moderately in winter and early spring, saving more severe pruning for after the aphids arrive. Then plan your cuts strategically to remove heavily infested areas. Space out thinning and shaping over the remainder of the season, a very little at a time. End all pruning well before fall so you don't encourage a sudden flush of new growth and increased nitrogen when the plant should be starting its process of hardening off for the approaching cold season.

3. Letting Aging Plants Linger. When you observe an aging annual plant with aphid colonies that are heavily parasitized or are attracting many predators, save its foliage so natural enemies that are nonspecific in their aphid prey can move from it to younger foliage. When possible, as in the case of successive plantings of vegetables, simply let the aging plant linger until it falls over and decomposes in place. Where you find the appearance of the aging plant unattractive, you may be able to bend it down and out of sight behind other plants. Alternatively, you can cut off the aphid-infested material and use it as a mulch under other plants to build up the beneficial insect population in the garden.

4. Ant Barriers. As discussed earlier, in some areas of the country certain ant species protect aphids from their natural enemies to ensure that the aphids continue to excrete the honeydew the ants feed upon. If you see ants on aphid-infested plants, assume they are playing this protective role. The application of a band of sticky material (such as Stickem™ or Tanglefoot™, available at nurseries) to stalks of roses and other woody plants keeps the ants away. Be certain the foliage of the banded plant is not touching anything the ants can use as a bridge to the plant foliage.

Specimen plants particularly susceptible to aphids that are being protected by ants can be raised in large tubs or planters. Either the sides of the planter should have ant (and slug and snail) barriers built in, as recommended in Chapter 20 on the control of greenhouse pests, or the container should be placed on an ant stand that is similarly protected, as described in the sidebar on pp. 356-357. For more on ant control, see the discussion under "Chemical Controls" on pp. 572-573.

5. Encouraging a Continuum of Flowers. Try to ensure that there are some plants flowering in your garden all season long, because many predators and parasitoids of aphids are dependent on obtaining nectar and pollen for egg laying.

Treatment:
Direct Physical Controls

A time-honored physical means of controlling aphids is washing them off a plant with a strong stream of water. A certain number of aphids are destroyed by this process, and others are eaten by predators such as spiders once they are on the ground. The disadvantage is that water-washing must be repeated fairly often, sometimes every three or four days, until the natural enemies of the aphids make their appearance in the garden and take over. On the positive side, water poses no hazard to humans and leaves no toxic residue on the plants that might harm the beneficial organisms.

You can wipe small colonies of aphids from leaves and buds with your hands, which should be covered by a pair of cloth garden gloves. Severely infested sections can be pinched off or pruned out. If it is early in the season and no natural enemies of the aphids seem to have arrived yet, dispose of the prunings in a hot compost. They can also be dropped in a bucket of soapy water, then drained and left to decompose as mulch or in a slow compost pile. If the aphid colonies are already parasitized or are attracting lady beetles and other predators, cut the prunings to a small size and leave them in an inconspicuous place beneath a shrub to decompose.

Treatment:
Direct Biological Controls

Although lady beetles and praying mantids are listed in nursery and other mail-order catalogs for aphid control, in our opinion, they are not appropriate for outdoor control of garden aphids.

As far as we can tell, the "success" that people claim when using lady beetles and mantids for aphid control is really the result of their refraining from using conventional pesticides for fear of harming the beneficials. When you refrain from using conventional pesticides, particularly in the conventional manner—that is to say, spraying everything in sight—you allow the survival of a large number of native predators and parasitoids. These become active about the time the commercially available lady beetles and mantids arrive. The result is good biological control, but not particularly from the insects that were purchased and released.

Lady beetles sold commercially are collected in the areas where they hibernate in large numbers. In California, the popular convergent lady beetle *(Hippodamia convergens)* gathers yearly by the millions in the same sites along river valleys in the foothills of the Sierra Nevada. These are the beetles that are collected by the dealers. After collection, which is usually in winter, the beetles are placed in cold storage and sold in the spring. When you release them in your garden, they fly away, just as they would from their hibernation sites, especially when the temperature reaches 65° (18°C) or above.

Since releases of purchased beetles are usually made at the same time the native convergent lady beetles are flying in, and they all look the same, you have no way of knowing whether the beetles in the garden are the ones you released. This was demonstrated to us conclusively when we participated in a study in which the beetles purchased were marked with blue paint. A day after release, there were many beetles in the garden but very few with blue marks. If they had not been marked, we might have thought the release was a success.

While the beetles hibernate (more accurately "diapause," a state of arrested development often compared with the hibernation of mammals), they must burn up fat deposits in their bodies before they can feed again. Beetles collected after May from mountain aggregations may remain in the area where they are released, but their feeding activity is not normal, apparently because they are still subsisting on their stored fat.

Moreover, the process of collection and release results in the unavoidable death of large numbers of these beneficials through shipping and storage. For this reason, we discourage the practice of purchasing lady beetles for aphid control.

Praying mantids are a different story. They are fascinating insects and make good pets for children. You can keep one in a small terrarium and feed it flies and other insects appropriate to its size. Such close observance of a mantid may inspire a lifelong interest in insects. If you do this, one thing you will observe is that mantids are general feeders, totally indiscriminate in what they eat. They are as likely to feed on a beneficial insect as they are on a pest. In fact, if you release enough mantids they will eat each other.

Until recently we have generally discouraged people from releasing mantids in the garden for pest control. However, recent literature we have translated from the Chinese has broadened our sense of how these predators might find a role in a biological control program if the right procedure were followed. The mantids would have to be hatched in time to grow large enough to handle the pest in question. This might require purchasing them in advance and keeping them at a temperature that would enable you to predict their emergence. The Chinese are developing artificial diets to reduce cannibalism among newly emerged nymphs. If no artificial diet is available, then the cases containing the nymphs would have to be moved to plants with insects small enough for the young mantids to eat.

We will continue monitoring research on mantid use in China and elsewhere, hoping that our publication of these translations will encourage American research. In the meantime, we suggest purchasing mantids only if you have an interest in the insect itself and don't expect much pest control from random releases in your garden.

Treatment: Direct Chemical Controls

A variety of home brews for aphid control can be found in the organic gardening literature, but we do not recommend them. Now that reliable insecticidal soaps that are nontoxic to mammals are available commercially, we suggest you become familiar with their use. Other chemical controls focus on exclusion of the ant species that protect aphids.

1. **Insecticidal Soap.** When water alone is ineffective at reducing aphid numbers, either because the plant cannot sustain the force of a stream strong enough to wash them off or because the leaves are so sticky the aphids won't wash off, we suggest using insecticidal soap. First, however, make some careful observations. Treatments should be made only when and where aphid numbers are really intolerable and there is no sign that natural predators and parasitoids have arrived. If you feel you must apply insecticidal soap, read pp. 114-116 for details.

2. **Insecticidal Baits.** Where ants cannot be controlled with sticky barriers, you might want to try a boric-acid bait, available from hardware stores in plastic bait stations. You can also make your own boric-acid bait as described on p. 238. Ant species in the garden, and sometimes ant colonies within a species, may vary greatly as to what foods attract them, so the secret to baiting is discovering what attracts the colony you are trying to kill. Once you know what food they prefer over the other potential foods around them, mix this with the boric acid. The proportion of poison to food should be great enough to kill the colony, but the poison should not be so strong that the ant scouts die before they have an opportunity to carry the food back to their queen in the nest.

We suggest placing the bait inside a small, baby-food-type jar. Punch holes in the lid, then tighten it securely. The holes allow ants to enter and enable you to re-liquefy the bait with additional water as necessary, since the bait should be kept moist. Several containers will be needed to surround the plant or the entrance to the ant colony you are trying to kill.

If you mix the bait yourself, be sure to mark the containers "poison" with a skull and crossbones. Although boric acid is much less of a hazard than the commercial arsenic ant baits that have been popular for so long, it nevertheless can harm a child or pet that eats it. Warn your children of the danger; if they are simply too young to understand and have access to your garden, we suggest you tolerate the ants rather than take any risk.

Hydramethylnon (see p. 227) is also effective against ants. It is available as Combat® bait stations, which are sold in most hardware stores.

Insecticidal baits must be renewed periodically, since as fast as you kill one ant colony, another seems to replace it. Where the aphid-infested plant has one or only a few woody stems, we advise combining sticky barriers (see p. 571) with use of baits.

3. Silica Aerogel/Pyrethrin. If none of the techniques suggested above is adequate and the problem is serious, you can spot-treat with a silica aerogel/pyrethrin mix, as described on p. 111. This material is available in an aerosol can with an applicator tip (see the Resource Appendix under "Insect Management: Chemical Controls" on pp. 686-687) that allows you to confine the material to a small area such as a plant stem. The silica aerogel leaves a white residue so you can see exactly where it has been applied.

We have found this product to be extremely useful at the BIRC field station, where native fire ants *(Solenopsis xyloni)* are a problem. This ant kills eggplants and peppers by girdling their stems and branches. In as little as two days a mature plant can be injured beyond recovery. Usually the ants affect just one plant at a time or occasionally two adjacent plants.

When we discover an infestation early enough, we can usually destroy it by spraying the compound on about 6 in. (15 cm) of the stem beginning at the base, and in a circle about 12 in. (30 cm) in diameter around the plant. If lower branches touch the ground, we prune them off so the ants have no other access to the upper portions of the plant. Because the pesticide breaks down in a few days, it is often necessary to repeat the application several times at intervals of five to seven days before the attack subsides.

The fire ant is a problem only in extremely dry areas. Thus, an alternative to using this pesticide is watering plants by soaking the ground between rows as well as around the crops themselves. When we did this at the field station, fire ants were never a problem. But water is very scarce there, and we now use underground irrigation to minimize water consumption. In this case, we decided that water conservation was essential and elected to spot-treat periodically with the pesticide.

Remember, however, that ants are generally very beneficial, eating many pest insects and aerating the soil with their tunneling. So don't kill them wherever you find them in the garden, but confine ant control to those areas where they are a serious problem.

CUCUMBER BEETLES
(Order Coleoptera, family Chrysomelidae)

Cucumber beetles *(Diabrotica* spp.) are serious agricultural pests that also bother home gardeners, although not necessarily on the same crops. The adults feed mostly on pollens and floral parts, especially on corn but also on other garden vegetables, flowers, weeds and native plants. At certain times during the season they may be highly visible on members of the cucurbit family, as the name cucumber beetle implies. The adults of pestiferous species are a conspicuous yellow or green, some marked with black spots or stripes. They fly or drop from the plant quickly if the leaves are touched.

Farmers are primarily concerned with the damage these beetles inflict on corn. The adults lay their eggs in the ground and the larvae feed on the roots; thus, they are also called corn rootworms. They probably cause more agricultural loss than any other pest, and more insecticide is used against them than against any other pest. About $1 billion is lost each year to the beetle and its control in the United States alone. Recent research indicates that much of this insecticide use is probably ineffective, and new research is underway to develop other means of control. Some of the early results already have implications for the home gardener. We summarize them here.

Biology

Only seven of the 338 known beetle species in the genus *Diabrotica* occur in the United States; of these, six are serious pests (see Table 31.1 on p. 574). Overall, the most damaging species in the corn belt are the western corn rootworm and the northern corn rootworm.

Diabrotica are divided into two groups. Species in the *furcata* group overwinter as adults and have more than one generation per year (they are multivoltine) in the north temperate zone. Those in the *virgifera* group have only one generation per year (they are univoltine) and overwinter as resting or hibernating (diapausing) eggs. Thus, they would appear to be controllable through crop rotation. Recent research indicates, however, that at least one species, the northern corn rootworm, has eggs that can diapause in the soil for two years. This is discussed further below.

Adult cucumber beetles feed on more than 280 plants in at least 29 families. They have been reported as a pest of 61 different crops, but they primarily attack corn, cucurbits, sweet potatoes and legumes, including peanuts, common beans, cowpeas and broad beans.

Table 31.1
North American Temperate Zone Pestiferous Cucumber Beetle *(Diabrotica)* Species

	Common Name	Scientific Name	Distribution
	banded cucumber beetle[a]	*D. balteata*	South America, Central America
	western spotted cucumber beetle[a]	*D. undecimpunctata*	West Coast
	northern corn rootworm	*D. barberi*	Midwest to East, not South
	southern corn rootworm (spotted cucumber beetle)[a]	*D. undecimpunctata howardi*	Midwest to East, South and Southwest
	western corn rootworm	*D. virgifera virgifera*	Midwest and Southwest
	Mexican corn rootworm	*D. virgifera zeae*	Texas and Oklahoma, Mexico

[a] These beetles are in the *furcata* group, have more than one generation per year and overwinter as adults. The remaining species are in the *virgifera* group, have a single generation per year and overwinter as eggs.

Beetles developing on corn probably account for most of the *Diabrotica* in any particular area. The adults feed on corn tassels, leaves and silk, as well as on the pollen of corn, grain crops, legumes and weeds. The adults can keep the corn silks chewed back to the ear tip during the period of pollination, resulting in poor grain set; they can also feed directly on the terminal kernels of corn. The larvae can cause poor grain set through excessive root feeding, which reduces water intake and produces symptoms that mimic drought damage.

The yellow-orange rootworm eggs are deposited in the moist soil at the base of corn plants from about August to October. The larvae feed on the roots of grasses, legumes and six other plant families. They also transmit plant pathogens through their feeding. Larvae-infested plants grow slowly and can topple in wind or heavy rain. After leaving the roots, the larvae pupate in the soil.

Damage and Detection

A heavy rootworm infestation can completely destroy the roots of corn. The loss of primary and brace roots greatly weakens the support system of the plant and can reduce plant growth and production. Weakened or fallen plants should be pulled or dug out and inspected for larvae feeding on the roots. After feeding, the larvae can be found in small cells in the soil where they prepare themselves for pupation. Mature larvae are white, slender and about ½ in. (1.3 cm) long with brown heads. They can move at most 20 in. (50 cm) to another corn plant after hatching or during their larval lives.

Adults may tunnel into or completely destroy the corn tips, resulting in a browning and rotting of the injured areas. When present on the corn plant above ground, or on other vegetable plants, the adults are easy to spot because of their light color.

Treatment: Indirect Strategies

For many years it was believed that yearly crop rotations with legumes such as soybeans was completely effective in reducing the opportunities for these beetles to lay eggs and reproduce. It has now been found that annual crop rotations are not always helpful, apparently because at least one species, the northern corn rootworm, has eggs that can diapause in the soil for two years. Thus, a non-host crop would have to remain in place for two or more years if rotation were the only technique being used to manage the problem. This is not economically feasible for most large-scale growers, but it could certainly be used on a small scale.

Recent research has found that some corn cultivars show resistance to rootworm damage, but it may be some years before commercial seed is available for such varieties.

Treatment:
Direct Physical Controls

In years when adult beetle numbers are overwhelming, hand-picking may seem tiresome and ineffective. In most years, however, repeated hand-picking in small plots or vacuuming in larger plots can greatly reduce adult damage. Other physical controls include:

1. **Funnel-and-Bag System.** An effective way to collect relatively large numbers of adults is to adapt the funnel-and-bag system used by researchers. They use a bag measuring 16 in. by 24 in. (40 cm by 60 cm) that is sewn from plastic window screen (18 mesh) with a drawstring at the opening. A small #10 ½-in. rubber stopper is fitted to the base of the funnel. The bag is then tightened over the stopper with the drawstring. We have also used plastic bags and masking tape to hold the bag to the funnel. The small producer or gardener can set up a similar system with plastic bags and rubber bands.

The funnel is placed beneath leaves with beetles. With a slight jarring of the foliage, the beetles fall into the funnel and slide down into the bag. In corn fields, one person can collect 15,000 to 20,000 beetles in three or four hours. Daily collections when beetles are particularly numerous may help prevent excessive damage. Captured beetles can be kept in the freezer until they are dead or can be placed in the sun to "cook" in a tightly closed plastic bag.

2. **Sticky Traps.** Trapping may also be effective if enough of the proper type of traps are used. This is speculative, since no studies have been conducted yet, but the usefulness of traps as monitoring tools has been proven. Because trapping methods are currently being researched, it is possible that a cheap, convenient, mass-produced trap will soon appear on the market. Before that occurs, how-

ever, small-scale growers may want to experiment with their own models.

Researchers have used yellow sticky traps made from pieces of fiber board 6 in. (15 cm) wide and 8 in. (20 cm) high coated with an adhesive such as Tack Trap™, Stickem™ or Tanglefoot™. The traps can be attached to stakes at ground level or about 12 in. (30 cm) above. Researchers found that when these traps were baited with eugenol emanating from dental wicks (tube-shaped pieces of gauze) attached to the boards, the number of females captured was much greater than with unbaited boards. Eugenol, available in a pure form as a laboratory material, is also found in natural form in many plants. For example, allspice oil from *Pimenta dioica* is composed of 60% to 80% eugenol. Bay oil from the West Indian bay plant *(P. racemosa)* contains up to 56% eugenol. Similarly, clove bud oil from *Syzygium aromaticum* contains 60% to 90% eugenol.

These trap designs will undoubtedly go through many changes before a commercially available product is marketed. The small producer or home gardener may want to experiment to find designs that are easy to service and last many seasons. Plywood or Masonite pieces or plastic boards should be better than fiber board because they last longer, particularly after repeated exposure to sunlight, heat and the solvents used to remove the adhesive and trapped beetles. Alternatively, traps could be made from recycled cardboard painted yellow and covered with adhesive. When full of beetles, these traps could be discarded.

A trap with a detachable sticky yellow sheet may prove even more effective. Larger boards should capture more beetles overall than smaller ones. No studies currently indicate how large such traps should be, but there must be some point of diminishing return where further increases in trap size are not effective relative to the size of the plot being protected. Wind should also be considered

when sizing traps, since larger traps are more vulnerable to buffeting.

Although sticky traps generally are inexpensive and easy to construct, they are hard to manage unless designed so that the adhesive does not interfere with transport, servicing and storage. Anyone who has worked with these adhesives can attest to the nuisance factor. In addition, the trap described above is inherently limited in its effectiveness because eugenol primarily attracts the northern corn rootworm and not the western corn rootworm. Combinations of lures and traps may prove effective once sex pheromones that attract both major rootworm species have been isolated, identified and tested. For example, indole has now been identified as the active attractant in squash blossoms, which are highly attractive to rootworm adults.

3. **Attractant/Poison Traps.** Studies have shown that attractant/poison traps can be effective at catching beetles without broadcasting the poison into the environment. This type of trap uses the attractiveness of certain cucurbits with high levels of the bitter compound cucurbitacin. Cucurbitacin acts like an arrestant rather than a classical pheromone, causing beetles to stay where they are rather than pulling them in from a considerable distance, as classical sex pheromones do. The sidebar on p. 576 (aimed primarily at professionals) describes how these traps are made.

Treatment:
Direct Biological Controls

There are two promising new areas of biological beetle control, both involving nematodes. Recently, a mermithid nematode, *Hexamermis* spp., was discovered to be infesting and killing adults of *D. speciosa vigens* in Peru. Over a four-year period, parasitism rates varied, but included up to 90% of the adults in some samples. Laboratory testing indicates a relatively wide host range for this nematode, so it looks hopeful. After further evaluation, the beneficial nematode may be

A Less-Toxic Attractant/Poison Trap for Cucumber Beetles

The first step in making an attractant/poison trap is selecting the most bitter fruits of cucumber (e.g., 'Marketer') or bitter squash (e.g., 'Calabazilla' or 'Hubbard') that result from a cross of *Cucurbita andreana* and *C. maxima*. You can do this by touching small pieces of the fruits to your tongue. The most bitter fruits are then cut up into small pieces, air-dried and powdered in a food-processing mill.

The powder containing the active ingredient cucurbitacin is usually mixed with an insecticidal dust—only carbaryl seems to have been used to date. It is dusted onto sheets of 3M® infrared transparency film, which are cut into 21 strips per sheet. The arrestant/insecticide strips are then placed in small amber 16-dram vials 1 in. (2.5 cm) in diameter and 3 in. (7.6 cm) high. These vials have white locking caps that have had the solid bottom portions removed. The opening made in the cap is covered with 14 by 18 mesh wire screening to prevent water vapor from condensing inside the trap. Five ⅕-in. (5 mm) holes are then drilled at equal intervals around the vial.

The vials are hung over the corn ears with a piece of wire. The beetles enter the traps, and while attempting to feed on the cucurbitacin are killed by contact with the insecticide. These traps have been used successfully to trap both the northern and western corn rootworms. If a more benign poison than carbaryl can be used, this sort of trap could be very useful in the future for small producers and gardeners.

[a] From Krysan and Miller, 1986.

introduced into *Diabrotica* populations in North America.

With luck, this nematode will establish itself and become an important natural control of cucumber beetles. However, as with other classical biological control attempts, there is no guarantee that it will work.

The other nematode that shows promise is *Steinernema (=Neoaplectana) carpocapsae*. This species can be applied much like conventional pesticides. It is poured or sprayed in liquid solution onto the soil about the same time immature beetles are hatching. Although further research is needed to select the appropriate strains, dosages, application times and delivery systems, enough current information is available from commercial suppliers to enable home gardeners to use them.

Inoculation of the soil with 90,000 nematodes per linear foot at planting time has proven effective in controlling rootworm in small test plots. Since the susceptible rootworm stages are not present for up to three weeks after planting, even better results may be obtained if the nematodes are applied at that time. Current research indicates that the nematodes are lost from the root zone soil rapidly, so multiple applications may be necessary.

The comments in this section are based on our reading of preliminary results from small-scale field tests; we will monitor further research for additional developments.

Treatment: Direct Chemical Controls

Until recently, it was not possible to determine infestation rates for cucumber beetle eggs in fields accurately, because egg and larval numbers were difficult to obtain. Further developments now suggest that most previous insecticide use was probably ineffective. Although disturbing from the viewpoint of efficiency and environmental pollution, this news suggests that preventive drenches with insecticides aimed at the larvae in the soil probably represent a dead end, and that new approaches and techniques must be searched out, tested and applied.

CUTWORMS
(Order Lepidoptera, family Noctuidae)

Nearly all caterpillars encountered in the garden can be controlled either by simple hand-picking or with the use of a bacterial spray of *Bacillus thuringiensis* (BT), described at length in Chapter 8. The Resource Appendix contains a list of caterpillars susceptible to BT under "Biological Controls" on pp. 683-686.

One group of caterpillars, the cutworms (see the drawing on the facing page), warrant additional discussion, because you may not be able to use either hand-picking or BT against them. Cutworms are common in grassy areas and may become severe in a garden that has just been converted from lawn or wild grass. Certain species are particularly damaging to young seedlings, and these are among the hardest pests to control.

Cutworms are hard to control with hand-picking or BT because they are most likely to inflict their damage at night; they spend the day buried in the soil somewhere near the plants they have been eating. Often, gardeners plant their seedlings one day and return the next to find a row of little stems cut an inch or less above the ground. No doubt this is the source of the name "cutworm."

Cutworms

You should suspect cutworms (the larvae of moths) when seedlings have been snipped off near the ground (A). Search for them at night on the plants or during the day when they lie curled up nearby in the mulch (B). (Actual length: up to 1¼ in./32 mm)

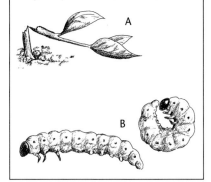

Table 31.2

Some Important Damaging Cutworm Species

Scientific Name	Common Name
Agrotis gladiaria	claybacked cutworm
A. ipsilon	black cutworm
A. malefida	pale-sided cutworm
A. orthogonia	pale western cutworm
A. venerabilis	dusky cutworm
Amathes c-nigrum	spotted cutworm
Chorizagrotis auxiliaris	army cutworm
Crymodes devastator	glassy cutworm
Euxoa auxillaris	army cutworm
E. detersa	sandhill cutworm
E. messoria	dark-sided cutworm
E. ochrogaster	red-backed cutworm
Feltia ducens	dingy cutworm
F. subterranea	granulate cutworm
Lacinipolia renigera	bristly cutworm
Loxagrotis albicosta	western bean cutworm
Peridroma saucia	variegated cutworm
Spodoptera eridania	southern armyworm
S. exigua	beet armyworm
S. frugiperda	fall armyworm
S. praefica	western yellow striped armyworm

Biology

The word "cutworm" is used loosely to designate about 200 species in the family Noctuidae, the largest family in the Lepidoptera. There are 2,925 species of this family in North America. Most of the cutworms occur in one of the 16 subfamilies, the Noctuinae. Table 31.2 at right lists some common species. The different groups of cutworms can be distinguished by their feeding habits.

Tunnel-making cutworms feed at or below the soil surface and eat only enough to topple the seedling. Examples are black, bronzed and clay cutworms. Climbing cutworms climb plants and eat buds, leaves and fruits. Examples are variegated and spotted cutworms. Army cutworms may move in large groups from field to field and can consume all parts of the plant. Examples are the several species of army cutworms. Subterranean cutworms remain in the soil and feed on underground stems and roots. Examples are the pale western and glassy cutworms.

There is an unfortunate overlap in the use of the common names cutworm and armyworm, and some-times "army cutworm." Some people call a particular species an armyworm, others may call it a cutworm. The term army cutworm refers to the characteristics of both groups: the cut-stem plant damage and the army-like larval foraging behavior. This can cause confusion unless the scientific name is used.

In general, cutworm larvae start feeding in early spring. They eat at night and spend the day under surface litter near plant stems or in burrows in the top few inches of soil. Pupation occurs in the soil. Eggs are laid mostly on broad-leaved weed stems and leaves. Some species overwinter as eggs, others as larvae or adults. There can be up to four generations per year.

Detection and Monitoring

If seedlings are cut off at ground level or slightly higher (as shown in the drawing at left), cutworms should be suspected. You can verify their presence by searching just below soil surface debris in concentric circles around several remaining stems. Frequently you will find the C-shaped cutworm. Searches should be made at night with a flashlight and pencil or small stick.

Farmers can use black light traps (as shown in the photo on p. 578) to capture adult moths to determine the peak periods of egg laying and subsequent emergence and growth. There are also numerous pheromone traps available for many adult stages of cutworm species that are used to determine peak activity periods. Light traps and pheromone traps should be evaluated as potential mass-trapping systems.

If these techniques are used by the small-scale gardener, however, there is a danger that the pheromones will attract more adults into the garden than would occur if no traps were set. This is more of a danger when too few traps are used. The position of the traps in relation to the potential food sources is also important. Traps should be as far away from the crop as possible to minimize the number of insects attracted into the core growing area. You will have to experiment. At this time we can give no clear guidelines for the small-scale producer and cannot yet recommend these traps for home gardens.

Treatment:
Indirect Strategies

One approach we have used successfully is starting seedlings inside on window sills, then transplanting them when they are large enough to withstand a little damage. On the West Coast where we garden, there are other pests that are particularly hard on seedlings, including birds, snails, slugs, mice and sowbugs. Putting in larger plants instead of seedlings reduces the time spent in the seedling stage and provides greater production per unit of area once transplantation shock has been overcome. Moreover, a new batch of seedlings can be started before the crop has been harvested. We realize, however, that this is not practical in many situations.

In large gardens you may reduce cutworm damage by minimizing the amount of weeds, particularly grass or grass-like weeds, where the seedlings will grow. The timing of spring cultivation is important. If you can eliminate all weed food for developing cutworm larvae for 10 days or longer (depending upon the cutworm species) before the emergence of crop seedlings, you will starve the newly hatched larvae. A weed-free period prior to planting also minimizes cutworm egg laying in the im-

Electric black light (ultraviolet) traps such as the BioQuip Universal model shown here attract a variety of night-flying insects such as moths and beetles. They are useful monitoring tools, and can be purchased from entomological suppliers or made from standard parts available at hardware stores. The trap consists of a fluorescent black light tube, a ballast and a cord from which is suspended a plastic bucket containing a funnel and a mesh collecting bag. (Photo courtesy BioQuip.)

mediate area. Small gardens may experience less benefit than larger ones from this tactic, since cutworms do migrate in the larval form, some species more than others. Cutworms can visit small gardens one evening, then retire to neighboring areas before morning.

Treatment:
Direct Physical Controls

The use of barriers to control cutworms may have potential for small-scale gardeners.

Although it is popularly recommended that you place tar paper squares flat on the ground around the plant, this control is only somewhat successful. This is probably so because modern "tar" or roofing paper is not actually impregnated with tar as it used to be, and the repellent

effect on caterpillars is considerably less than in the past.

Yet the general tactic of constructing barriers against these caterpillars makes sense due to the caterpillar's habit of biting off seedlings at ground level. In our experience, paper collars, such as the cardboard tube inside a roll of toilet paper, provide a bit more protection than tar paper squares. A foolproof method is to use seedling-sized or plant-bed-sized screened enclosures. These enclosures also protect against root maggots, the young of flies that burrow into the roots of cabbage family plants and onions (see the directions for constructing cone-shaped enclosures under "Root Maggots" on p. 584).

Although sticky barriers are of no help in protecting seedlings, on sturdier plants they prevent the larvae from moving up the stems to feed on buds, fruit and leaves. This is particularly true if the barrier is wide enough to prevent the passage of the worms en masse, if the particular species shows this behavior.

The possibility of success with sticky barriers in larger field applications has increased with the availability of two relatively new products. One incorporates Tanglefoot™ into an aerosol (for sources, see the Resource Appendix under "Insect Management: Physical Controls" on pp. 682-683), allowing the quick application of a sticky barrier to many stems in a short time. We have no experience with this aerosol on succulent plants, so we cannot recommend it without encouraging you to test it first on a few plants to make sure no phytotoxic reactions result. We should also caution that methylene chloride, the propellant in this product, poses a hazard to the user. If a substitute propellant can be found, this method of Tanglefoot™ application will find many uses.

Another sticky barrier product is Tack Trap™ (also listed in the Resource Appendix). It is relatively easy to work with and can be removed from tools, clothing and other surfaces with water. To use Tack Trap™, you heat the can until the adhesive is liquid, then apply it to surfaces with a paint brush. Again, we caution you to test it first on a few plants, since we do not know which, if any, plants may be damaged by this substance. We have used sticky barriers very successfully to deter crawling insects from moving onto shrubs, stems and tree trunks.

Treatment: Direct Biological Controls

Many organisms feed on cutworms, including microbes, birds, insect predators such as ground beetles, and hymenopteran parasitoids. Thus, any control aimed at cutworms must not pose a simultaneous threat to these species that prey on them. Fortunately, there are indications that baits containing BT as the active ingredient are effective specifically against caterpillars without harming these other organisms.

In the older entomological literature there are many references to bran baits for controlling cutworms. The arsenic compounds used in these baits are fortunately now obsolete and unavailable, but BT can be mixed 12% by weight with wheat bran and either grape or apple pomace, the residue left after juicing. The mixture should be placed on the soil surface or on boards or cardboard.

There is so little research on the use of baits for cutworm control that we cannot make more precise recommendations on bait placement and renewal. It is unclear from the present literature whether it is the bran or other ingredients that attract the cutworms, or whether these substances merely cause the cutworms to stop and feed. In any case, the bait should be broadcast around the entire plant to be protected, not just piled in one spot, to ensure that the cutworms encounter it before they reach the plant.

EARWIGS (Order Dermaptera, family Forficulidae)

Despite the fact that earwigs are now known to be largely beneficial, most of us are still trying to control them in our vegetable and flower gardens and occasionally in our homes. This is partly because of the damage they cause when they eat small holes in the leaf margins of seedlings of plants such as radishes. But the desire to kill earwigs is also due to the fact that people simply don't like the way they look, whether encountered in the garden or indoors.

The appearance of their posterior pincers seems frightening. These pincers, or forceps, are used by females to defend their families against predators. Earwig mothers are very protective of their eggs and young. If these are scattered, the mother collects them and stays to defend them with her pincers. Earwigs also use their pincers to fold away their wings after flight. Occasionally two adjacent females with young will use the pincers to fight over food. As threatening as they may look, however, the pincers are not a menace to people.

Perhaps the worst fear people have of earwigs, and the one that is least founded, is that they crawl into the ear and bore into the brain. The old Anglo Saxon word "earwicga" literally means "ear creature," and in nearly all European languages the name for earwig suggests a connection with the ear. Apparently, present-day Americans have inherited this ancient European fear. Perhaps when people slept on dirt floors, straw or hay, earwigs explored human ears as a place to hide. It is not inconceivable, though there are no records of this actually happening.

The European earwig *(Forficula auricularia),* which was accidentally introduced into North America in 1907, is native to Europe, western Asia and possibly North Africa. The species is omnivorous; it eats plants, other animals and decaying material. When it enters homes looking for a

nice dark place to hide, it becomes a household pest.

Recent research has demonstrated that earwig predation is significant in suppressing pests such as aphids in apple trees. It is our first-hand experience that, given a diverse soil surface of compost mulch on which to feed and hunt, earwigs can be present in the vegetable garden in enormous numbers and cause negligible damage to seedlings and larger plants. By contrast, when plants are set out in neat rows with bare soil between them and boards, pieces of broken sidewalk or other inedible debris that can serve as earwig hiding places nearby, the earwigs may feed on the seedlings because there isn't much else available.

When abundant, earwigs are often blamed for damage caused by snails, slugs, cutworms and other garden pests, since during the day when gardeners are active, the earwigs may choose damaged tomatoes or other fruits as handy, dark, moist hiding places. Nighttime checks with a flashlight reveal quite a different picture as the true culprits emerge to feed and the earwigs are busy foraging in the mulch.

We recommend that you keep in mind the beneficial predatory role earwigs can play in the garden, and make an effort to reduce their numbers only when nighttime checks definitely show them to be causing intolerable damage to your horticultural plants.

Biology

Earwigs are reddish-brown and approximately ¾ in. (19 mm) long (see the drawing on p. 580). The young are similar in appearance to the adults. The male's pincers are large and curved; the female's are smaller and nearly straight. As explained above, the pincers help females defend their eggs and clean their nests but pose no threat to humans. These insects have wings but rarely fly.

The female may lay up to 60 round white eggs in small nests in the upper

The European Earwig

Earwigs are small reddish-brown insects that feed both on plants and on insects such as aphids. The pincers on the rear of their bodies are used primarily to defend themselves against other insects. Earwigs do not attack humans. (Actual size: ¾ in./19 mm)

few inches of soil. Earwigs are often referred to as semi-social insects, since the female guards the eggs and tends the young during their first two weeks of life. The first batch of eggs hatches in the spring, and the insect takes about 70 days to mature. A second batch may be laid during the summer. Earwigs live about a year, and many die the winter following their birth. A few, mostly females, survive to the following spring to raise another generation.

Earwigs forage at night, eating the eggs, young and adults of small organisms such as insects, mites and nematodes, as well as algae, fungi and tender plant tips. During the day they hide in any tiny crevice they find near or on the ground, on plants, in piles of debris, in the cracks and crevices of the bark of trees, or in houses, sheds and other structures.

Damage, Detection and Monitoring

Earwig damage to plants can consist of small holes in the leaves or entire new growth on seedlings that is nibbled away. Because earwig damage is similar to that of other pests, night-time checks with a flashlight are the only sure way to determine whether

What To Do If Earwigs Are Getting into Your House

• Caulk cracks and crevices.

• Screen and weatherstrip windows and doors to eliminate access routes.

• Remove piles of debris or organic materials that lean against the house.

• Prune foliage that touches the walls of the house.

• Create a clean, dry border directly adjacent to the house foundation.

• Vacuum up stray earwigs found indoors, and plug entrance cracks.

If earwigs are clustering in damp basements and/or storage areas, follow the directions for moisture reduction provided on pp. 408-416.

earwigs are the cause. Check on a number of successive nights for actively feeding earwigs where you have noticed plant damage.

Rolled-up newspapers or other traps (see "Physical Controls," below) can catch large numbers of earwigs even when they are not causing a problem, so we do not consider trapping by itself a good monitoring strat-egy. However, where nighttime checks reveal that earwigs are causing damage, traps can indicate where they are most heavily concentrated.

Treatment: Indirect Strategies

The most frequent complaints we receive about earwigs come from gardeners planting a newly landscaped area and starting with relatively bare, unmulched soil. In such cases, we recommend putting down a mulch

of compost to provide a complex soil surface with many organisms on which the earwigs can feed.

Where earwigs are causing damage in an already mulched older garden, the best strategy is to raise seedlings indoors and transplant them to the outdoors when they are large enough to withstand some damage. You can also raise them outdoors on a protected surface such as a table with ant excluders around its legs (see p. 571). If you see earwigs eating flowers or damaging larger plants, trapping them to reduce their numbers may be the best approach (see below).

We also receive complaints about earwigs getting into the house. They do not cause any damage there, but people do not like to see them. For suggestions on what to do about earwigs in the house, refer to the sidebar at left.

Treatment: Direct Physical Controls

Earwigs are easy to trap. In the home garden, containers such as tuna-fish cans that hold ½ in. (13 mm) of vegetable oil or moistened bread crumbs can serve as traps without any poison. Because of the earwigs' predilection for crawling into small spaces, bamboo tubes or rolled-up newspapers are also good traps. The traps, baited or not, should be placed on the soil near plants just before dark and checked with a flashlight 12 hours later or in the morning. Shaking the trapped insects into a pail of soapy water drowns them.

Treatment: Direct Biological Controls

The European earwig, like may insect pests not native to the United States, left its natural enemies in its country of origin. Beginning in 1924, efforts were made to import a parasitic tachinid fly, *Bigonicheta spinipennis*, into the United States from Europe in the hope that it would control the earwig. Because the parasitoid depends upon the earwig alone for its sustenance, there was no danger it would attack other prey and become a nuisance itself.

This effort is considered to have been moderately successful in the northwestern United States and very successful in British Columbia. Today, one usually does not need to do anything to obtain the effects of this biological control except know that it exists. The predator has now spread widely, but there still may be places without it. In such cases, contact your local cooperative extension service or call us at the Bio-Integral Resource Center at (415) 524-2567 for assistance. Note also that specialists working on earwig control draw attention to the beneficial predatory habits of the earwig, and emphasize that control should be carried out only when earwig numbers increase beyond tolerable levels.

GOPHERS
(Order Rodentia, family Geomyidae)

Gophers feed on a wide variety of roots, bulbs, tubers, grasses and seeds, which makes these burrowing rodents a threat to cultivated gardens and lawns. The pocket gopher (*Thomomys* spp.) shown in the drawing above is the type most often found around the home. Gophers live alone in the extensive underground burrow system they create by tunneling through the soil and disposing of the excavated dirt above ground in fan-shaped mounds. The shape of these mounds can be used to distinguish gophers from moles, whose hills tend to be circular with a plug in the middle (see the drawing at right).

Biology

Pocket gophers are thick-bodied rodents that range from 6 in. to 12 in. (15 cm to 30 cm) long. In the western hemisphere there are some 33 species in five genera. The differences between them are discussed in an excellent article on gopher control by Ronald Case in *Prevention and Control of Wildlife Damage.*

The Pocket Gopher

Pocket gophers are burrowing rodents with fur-lined pouches inside the mouth that are used to carry foods such as roots, bulbs, grasses and seeds. (Actual length: 6 in. to 12 in./15 cm to 30 cm)

Gopher adaptations for life underground include powerful forelegs with long claws, small eyes and small ears set far back on the head. Their exposed chisel-like teeth are used for digging, and grow continuously 9 in. to 14 in. (23 cm to 36 cm) a year. Gophers keep dirt out of their mouths by closing their lips behind the exposed teeth. The name "pocket" refers to the external reversible fur-lined cheek pouches they use for carrying food and nest materials. Gopher fur is a mottled brown. This also distinguishes them from moles, which have very dark velvety fur, spade-like front paws and no visible ears. Gophers use their keen sense of smell to locate foods such as bulbs, tubers, roots, grasses, seeds and occasionally, tree bark.

Gophers do not hibernate, although they do spend most of their lives underground, coming to the surface only for brief periods to push soil out of their burrows, forage, disperse to new areas and seek mates. Except when mating or rearing a brood, gophers live alone in their burrows. They mate and produce young only in January to April, depending on the location. They generally have one litter per year, with an average of five offspring per litter. Their lifespan is up to 12 years.

Gopher Mounds and Molehills

A gopher mound is fan-shaped with an offset plug and an indentation in its circumference; a molehill is circular with the plug at its center.

Gopher mound

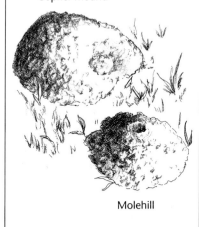

Molehill

Detection

Gopher control is not very successful when carried out at the mound, because the mound is located at the end of the lateral tunnel the gopher regularly plugs. Instead, you must locate the main burrow that runs perpendicular to the lateral tunnel below the ground at a depth of 4 in. to 18 in. (10 cm to 45 cm).

Probing for Gophers

A gopher's main burrow can be located by probing with a long screwdriver, wire or commercial probe, shown here. Look for a slight depression in the 'unfanned' side of the mound indicating the plug to the lateral tunnel, and begin probing 8 in. to 10 in. (20 cm to 25 cm) out from that point. The probe suddenly drops a few inches when it finds the burrow.

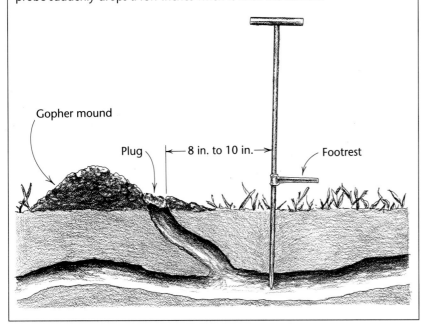

You can find the main burrow by probing the soil with a long, thin screwdriver, sharp stick or wire or with a probe sold commercially (see the drawing above). Locate a fresh mound and look for a small circle or slight depression on the "unfanned" side of the mound. This indicates the location of the plug in the lateral tunnel. Begin probing 8 in. to 10 in. (20 cm to 25 cm) from the plug side of the mound. Repeated probing may be required before you find the burrow. When the probe hits the burrow, it suddenly drops 2 in. to 3 in. (5 cm to 7.5 cm).

Treatment:
Direct Physical Controls

Direct physical controls for gophers include the construction of barriers, flooding and the use of traps.

1. Barriers. As with any pest problem, the safest and most effective management method is to "design the pest out" of the system. Sometimes gophers can be excluded from a garden by burying ½-in. (1.3 cm) mesh fencing 24 in. (60 cm) below ground and extending it the same distance above ground. This might be effective around raised vegetable beds or small flower gardens and lawns. Bulb beds or individual shrubs or small trees can be protected by ½-in. mesh wire if it is laid on the bottom and sides of the planting hole. Be sure to place the wire deep enough so it does not restrict root growth.

Barrier trenches that exclude gophers can be used to protect large lawns, gardens and orchards. They are steep, vertical-walled ditches 18 in. (45 cm) wide and 24 in. (60 cm) deep that contain open-topped 5-gal. cans spaced at 25-ft. (7.6 m) intervals and sunk so their tops are level with the ditch bottom. When gophers burrow or move on the surface, they fall into the trench and follow it until they tumble into the cans, from which they cannot escape. The trenches can be dug with a shovel or spade.

Because gophers occasionally feed on the bark of certain trees, particularly stone fruits such as almonds and cherries, it is wise to protect the trunks of these trees during planting with cylinders of ½-in. galvanized hardware cloth sunk 12 in. (30 cm) underground and rising 12 in. above the surface.

Encircling the garden with plants such as oleanders that are unpalatable to gophers is another exclusion tactic that might be tried. Foraging gophers that encounter oleander roots would presumably be deterred from tunneling into the garden. There is quite a body of anecdotal literature on the use of plant barriers against gophers, but there are no scientific studies confirming their effectiveness.

2. Flooding. Once you have located the main burrow, you can insert a garden hose into it. The water will flow in both directions in the burrow, and the gopher will try to escape from one of the mounds. When you spot it, you can kill it with a shovel. However, this requires fast action because gophers move quickly when above ground. A whole area such as a field can be flooded by raising dikes around it and filling it with water.

3. Trapping. You can trap gophers with a Macabee™ or other pincer trap, or a box trap such as the Gopher Getter™. You need two or more traps, and you must set them with care. Wear gloves to prevent human smells from contaminating the devices. You can also wash the traps in soapy water.

Open an active main burrow enough to allow insertion of two traps, one facing in each direction (as shown in the drawing on the facing page). This ensures that no matter which direction the gopher moves in, it will run over a trigger. Attach strong twine or rope to the trap and to a stake to prevent the rodent from pulling the trap deep into its burrow. Use a board, cardboard or other material to cover the traps, and be sure to sift dirt around the edges of this cover to exclude light. If the gophers see light, they will push soil toward it, tripping the trap without getting caught. If no gopher is caught within three days, pull out and reset the traps in a new location.

Treatment:
Direct Chemical Controls

Unfortunately, the most commonly available rodenticide for gopher control is strychnine-baited barley. In California, a licensed pest control operator or advisor must apply this if more than 1 lb. (0.45 kg) is used. Strychnine-baited grain for gopher control is placed underground, but it can cause secondary kill. This means that if another predatory animal such as a gopher snake, owl or hawk eats a gopher that has taken in strychnine-baited grain, then it too dies. Consequently, we do not recommend the routine use of strychnine-baited grains, especially around the home, since strychnine is so toxic.

One strategy we do recommend for gopher control is fumigation. Gopher burrows can be fumigated with the exhaust from a gas-powered riding mower, rototiller or other vehicle. This is done by slipping a 10-ft. (3 m) length of flexible metal exhaust pipe, available at automotive shops, over the rigid exhaust pipe on the mower. Be sure the diameter of the flexible pipe is such that it fits snugly over rigid pipe. Non-riding mowers may require addition of a metal elbow to the rigid exhaust pipe to facilitate attachment of the flexible pipe.

Before attaching the pipe, squirt a few drops of oil into the end to be fitted to the mower pipe. Place the free end of the pipe at the mouth of the excavated runway and pack soil around it to create a seal. To avoid the possibility of the heated pipe scorching the lawn or ground cover, prop it on a shovel. Let the mower engine idle for 5 to 10 minutes. The

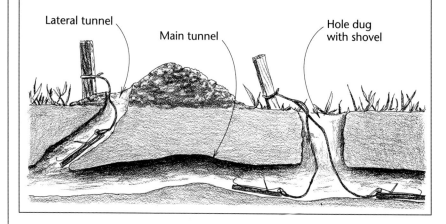

Trapping Gophers
Place two traps in opposite directions in the main gopher tunnel, and a single trap in the lateral tunnel. Stake traps so they can be retrieved easily and pack dirt loosely in the hole to exclude light. Check the traps daily.

Lateral tunnel — Main tunnel — Hole dug with shovel

carbon monoxide exhaust acts as a fumigant, killing the gopher quickly in the tunnel. Smoke created by the oil squirted into the mower end of the flexible hose will escape from any exit holes available to the gopher. If you spot escaping smoke, quickly seal the exit or kill the emerging gopher with a shovel.

ROOT MAGGOTS: THE CABBAGE ROOT MAGGOT
(Order Diptera, family Anthomyiidae)

Imagine that your seedlings of broccoli, turnips or other members of the cabbage family are growing nicely. Then suddenly one day, although no insects or other pests are visible, many of the young plants begin to wilt and die. When you pull them up you find small, fat, white, worm-like maggots tunneling into the roots. Or perhaps the roots are so damaged the plant appears not to have any at all. You have just had your first close encounter with the cabbage root maggot *(Delia brassicae)*, the larval stage of a small fly.

Closely related species attack carrots, onions and seed corn, which show similar damage. All the flies be-

long to the genus *Delia* (formerly *Hylemya)*, on which there is extensive literature. (We might also mention that another member of the genus, *Delia [=Hylemya] seneciella*, has been introduced into the Pacific Coast states from France to control the noxious weed tansy ragwort. This latest introduction is a supplement to the earlier establishment of another biological control against this same weed, the cinnabar moth *[Tyria jacobaeae]*. This is a classic case of human interests labeling one creature a pest and its close relative a beneficial.)

Biology

Cabbage root maggots are usually less than ⅓ in. (8.5 mm) long when fully grown. The head end is pointed and the rear is blunt with a dozen short, pointed, fleshy projections arranged in a circle around two brown, button-like spiracles, or breathing holes. The larvae are usually found eating feeder roots and boring into the taproot. As many as 100 larvae can be collected from a single root. The maggot attacks cabbages, brussels sprouts, cauliflower, radishes, rutabagas and turnips.

The adult is an ash-colored fly slightly smaller than a housefly. It has black stripes on the thorax and black bristles over its body. This is not the only species that may be found in the root zone of a cruciferous (cabbage family) plant—there are up to 30 others—but the cabbage root maggot *(Delia [=Hylemya] brassicae)* is the most common. Two other common and related species are *Delia (=Hylemya) crucifera* and *D. (=Hylemya) planipalpis.*

The females lay their small white eggs within 2 in. (5 cm) of the stem of a cabbage-like plant. They hatch in a few days and the larvae tunnel into the roots. They feed for three to five weeks, then pupate in the roots or surrounding soil. Later they emerge as adults and mate, and the females begin oviposition. There can be as many as three generations during a single season. Some pupae can diapause (hibernate) for more than one season.

The cabbage maggot is found throughout North America from Alaska to California and Manitoba to Newfoundland, and south to Illinois and North Carolina. It is also found in Europe. It was accidentally introduced into North America from Europe; fortunately, certain natural enemies were introduced at the same time. The discussion of control of these root maggots is applicable to any of the species that attack vegetable crops in the home garden.

Damage

Injury is seldom serious in the southern part of the cabbage maggot's range. Sometimes the maggots provide entry for decay organisms so that infested roots are rotten and riddled with burrows. Infested plants can appear yellowed, stunted and wilted, especially during the hottest part of the day. Young plants are the most susceptible; healthy, larger plants that are well established can tolerate moderate infestations and usually outgrow the damage.

Winter and spring crops suffer the most. The greatest damage is experienced during wet years, especially in cool, moist areas. Because cauliflower and brussels sprouts are less vigorous than the hybrid cultivars of broccoli that are now grown, they sustain more damage.

Detection and Monitoring

To sample for eggs, mark a circle 5 in. (12.7 cm) in diameter around the plant's stem. Dig out the soil within the circle to a depth of 1 in. (2.5 cm), then drop the soil in a container of water. After mixing and allowing the soil to settle, small white eggs will float to the surface if the maggots are present.

Although one source document indicates that adults are attracted to purple sticky traps, no further information about this monitoring technique is available.

Because injury levels are very site-specific, it is difficult to say what number of individuals at a particular stage of development will cause damage. However, *Integrated Pest Management for Cole Crops and Lettuce,* a manual published by the University of California, suggests that "when using the above-mentioned egg-sampling procedure, if [there are] more than 25 eggs per cauliflower plant or more than 50 eggs per cabbage plant, economic damage may occur."

Treatment: Indirect Strategies

One way to minimize losses of young seedlings is to start them on sunny window sills indoors or within tightly screened greenhouses or cold frames. It is essential that the seedlings be protected from ovipositing flies at all stages, particularly during the hardening-off period when they are between the house or greenhouse and the growing plot and are getting used to outdoor temperatures. When they are several inches tall, they can be transplanted into protective screened cones, as described below.

Treatment: Direct Physical Controls

The most effective reusable device for controlling root maggots in the home garden is a cone-shaped protective screen barrier that is placed over seedlings immediately upon transplanting. It is described in the sidebar on the facing page.

Tightly constructed cold frames or similar structures would also presumably be effective in preventing oviposition by root maggot flies, but we have no experience using them. A less permanent but simple barrier can be created by protecting plants with plastic row covers. However, where slugs are also a problem, unacceptable damage is likely to occur under the covers, making this approach impractical.

Although it seems reasonable to use traps to capture the flies before they have an opportunity to deposit their eggs near the plants, there are no studies documenting the efficacy of this approach. A few years ago some of our students tried unsuccessfully to attract adults into standard fly traps baited with various crucifers (cabbage family plants). We suspect that root maggot populations may have been too low at that time to provide enough adults to validate these initial tests, and we have not had the opportunity to pursue the matter further.

Treatment: Direct Biological Controls

One of the most important natural enemies of the cabbage root maggot and other related *Delia* species is the rove beetle *Aleochara bilineata* (family Staphylinidae). This small beetle is parasitic on the pupae of the cabbage maggot and predatory on its eggs. It was one of the species introduced into Canada probably at the time the cabbage maggot invaded; it now occurs widely throughout North America.

The staphylinid rove beetle attacks many *Delia* species, so it is important in helping to protect a number of

How To Construct a Cone Screen Barrier

Materials

To make a cone screen 18 in. (45 cm) tall and 12 in. (30 cm) in diameter, you need a pair of good household scissors or tin snips, a sturdy stapler, some aluminum screen (which is stronger than nylon and won't rust) and some short, thin wood strips, such as pieces of commercially available lath.

Procedure

Cut a length of screen into a rectangle approximately 18 in. (45 cm) by 24 in. (60 cm). Bend it into a cone shape, overlapping the edges, then close the two edges by stapling them together against the lath strip. Let the thin wood strip extend a few inches below the opening of the cone base so you can force it into the soil until the cone is flush with the ground, anchoring it firmly. The lower edges of the cone should be completely covered with mulch or soil. If you need multiple cone enclosures, make a paper model of the cone to facilitate duplication.

Once the seedlings are too big for the cones, their roots are tough enough to withstand any root maggot invasion. Remove the cones and place them over the second planting. At the end of the season, clean the cones and store them. They will serve you season after season and can reduce your root maggot losses to zero; the investment you make will repay you for many years.

---

crops. Recently there has been some work directed at developing a method of mass-rearing it. If there is enough consumer demand, perhaps one of the existing insectaries will take on the task. We would like to see this species become widely available by mail to the home gardener and the farmer.

At the time of writing, two species of beneficial parasitoid nematodes that can be used against the cabbage maggot are commercially available (for sources, see the Resource Appendix under "Insect Management: Biological Controls" on pp. 683-686). The nematodes are poured in solution around the base of the seedling stems so that they attack any maggots that hatch. The exact timing, dosage and frequency of application must, of course, be adapted to local conditions. Since there is no published literature to guide you at this time, we recommend that you con-tact the distributor or producer and ask how many nematodes to buy and how often to use them.

Treatment:
Direct Chemical Controls

There are many other natural enemies of the cabbage root maggot. Some of these are ground beetles (family Carabidae). Unfortunately, when most insecticides are applied to the soil in an attempt to control the cabbage maggot, they also kill these natural enemies. There are as yet no insecticides that kill only the cabbage maggot and leave these natural enemies. Consequently, we do not recommend the use of any insecticides for suppression of cabbage maggot populations.

ROSE DISEASES: BLACK SPOT, POWDERY MILDEW AND RUST
(Diplocarpon rosae; Spaerotheca pannosa; and Phragmidium spp.)

A few years ago, while strolling through our local municipal rose garden and enjoying the riot of colors and shapes of the hundreds of cultivars on display, we became aware of a strong, unpleasant odor that masked the roses' perfume. A chat with the rosarian revealed that the odor was the residue of 200 gallons of pesticides sprayed on the acre of rose shrubs each week from spring to fall. Since we knew that if we could smell the pesticide we were absorbing it into our lungs, we decided to leave.

As a result of this experience we pondered the unhappy fact that roses —one of the most aesthetically rewarding and popular flowering shrub groups in the world—are also among the most heavily sprayed. Is this heavy use of pesticides an unavoidable tradeoff for the enjoyment of roses, or are there less toxic ways to manage rose pests?

To answer this question, we reviewed the scientific literature on rose pests and talked with researchers, commercial rose growers, rosarians and rose gardeners in different regions of the United States. This investigation has produced a wealth of information on alternative methods for managing rose pests. Some methods have been used successfully for years, whereas others have proven effective in research programs but need further testing in the home garden. This book cannot be a manual for the cultivation of roses, but we hope that the information on aphids, snails and slugs in this chapter, plus the following summary of recent research on three rose diseases, will help reduce some of the pesticide load that both gardeners and gardens currently endure.

Three fungi top virtually any list of rose diseases: black spot, powdery mildew and rust. The sidebar on pp. 586-587 describes common

Identifying Rose Diseases[a]

Black Spot
(Diplocarpon rosae)
Optimum conditions for infection:[b] 64°F to 75°F (18°C to 24°C), 95% RH. Spores must be wet continuously for seven hours before infection can occur. Symptoms become visible 3 to 10 days after infection. New spores can be reproduced every three weeks.

Symptoms: Circular black spots 1/16 in. to 1/2 in. (1.5 mm to 13 mm) in size with fringed margins on canes and both leaf surfaces. Spots may coalesce to produce large, irregular lesions. Young leaves 6 to 14 days old are most susceptible. In mild infections, spots may remain as small black flecks, causing little damage. In severe cases, entire leaves may yellow and drop from plant, and plants may be defoliated by mid-summer.

Overwintering/dispersal: Spores overwinter on fallen leaves and in infected canes. Spores are dispersed in drops of splashing rain or irrigation water, by people during cultivation, by wind or by contact with sticky parts of insect bodies.

Distribution: Most common in Northeast, Southeast and some Midwestern states with warm, moist summer climates.

Monitoring: Begin in spring when temperatures approach the mid-60s and rainfall and humidity are high. Look for signs of dark-colored spots on the surfaces of leaves near the ground and on young leaves, stalks and flower buds at the top of the plant. If damage is seen, prune it off and/or begin treatments described in the text. Continue periodic monitoring during flushes of new growth.

Powdery Mildew
(Spaerotheca pannosa)
Optimum conditions for infection: Night—61°F (16°C) and 95% to 99% RH; day—81°F (27°C) and 40% to 70% RH. Drop-like humidity from fog or

[a] Compiled from Forsberg, 1975, and Horst, 1983.

[b] Some infection can occur at lower temperatures and humidity, but most occurs when conditions approach the figures cited here. Remember that if the leaf is in the sun, the temperature of the leaf surface will be higher than the ambient air temperature. If the leaf is shaded (e.g., when located in the interior of the bush), the temperature will be lower and the humidity may be higher than that indicated by garden wet and dry bulb maximum/minimum thermometers.

symptoms and provides other clues useful in identifying these diseases on your roses. All three diseases may occur in the same garden, but their severity usually depends on the prevailing climate. In general, black spot is most severe in the eastern United States, which has warm, wet summers. Powdery mildew grows best where summers are cool and dry, and is particularly prevalent in the coastal regions of the West. Rust is a major problem in areas such as the Pacific Northwest, where cool summers and high moisture levels prevail.

Biology
Studies of the life cycles of these three pathogens have shown that local temperature and humidity levels are limiting factors in disease development. Each disease begins as a microscopic spore that is transported by wind, water, animals or garden tools to a susceptible rose host. When enough heat, moisture and possibly light are available, the spores germinate, inserting a small germ tube into the plant tissue and absorbing nutrients from the plant. In the process, the plant tissue is damaged or killed.

Management of these diseases involves a mix of tactics designed to prevent spores from overwintering, prevent germination of those spores that survive the winter and kill germinated spores before they cause excessive plant damage.

Treatment:
Indirect Strategies
Indirect strategies for control of rose diseases include planting disease-resistant rose varieties, manipulation of moisture and nitrogen control.

1. Planting Disease-Resistant Roses. You should plant rose varieties with genetic features that make them resistant to or tolerant of (meaning they show only minor injury) the diseases prevalent in your area. For example, some species and cultivars have thick wax-like material in the outer layers of their leaves and stems. These coatings act as natural barriers against the penetration of plant tissue by pathogens. A high level of wax on leaves also repels water, limiting the germination of fungus spores with dew is more damaging, because germination and growth are inhibited by films of water on leaves. Powdery growth is visible two days after infection; thousands of new spores are produced every four days. Growth appears to be enhanced by low light levels that accompany cloudy or foggy periods.

Symptoms: Starts on young leaves as raised blister-like areas that cause leaves to curl, exposing lower surface. Infected leaves become covered with a greyish-white powdery fungus growth; unopened flower buds may be white with mildew and may never open. Disease prefers young, succulent growth; mature tissue is usually not affected.

Overwintering/dispersal: Spores overwinter inside leaf buds on canes and are dispersed by wind.

Distribution: Pacific Coast and other coastal areas with moderate temperatures, high cloud cover or fog and minimal rainfall in summer.

Monitoring: Begin in spring when temperatures are in the mid-60s without any rainfall. Check growing tips and young leaves for signs of powdery growth. Prune off infected parts. Begin water washes and other treatments and continue monitoring.

Rust
(Phragmidium spp.)
Optimum conditions for infection: Temperatures between 64°F and 70°F (18°C and 21°C) and continuous moisture for a period of two to four hours. Spores reproduce every 10 to 14 days in summer.

Symptoms: Small orange or yellow pustules appear on any green portions of the plant. First infections usually occur on the undersides of leaves and may be inconspicuous. Later, pustules develop on upper leaf surfaces and stems and are quite visible throughout the summer. Some cultivars drop infected leaves.

Overwintering/dispersal: Black overwintering spores are visible on leaves and canes in fall, and pass the winter inside the infected canes, which are distinguished by dark, corky blotches at points of infection. Spores are distributed by wind and water.

Distribution: Severe infestations are usually limited to the Pacific Coast; cold winters and very hot summers limit its development elsewhere.

Monitoring: Begin check for pustules on undersides of new foliage in early spring. Prune off damage. When temperatures optimal for rust coincide with heavy dew, rain, periods of cloud cover or periods of fog near the coast, preventive surfactant or other sprays may be needed.

high water requirements. It is also thought that some rose species produce toxins that repel or kill germinating spores.

Species known to have high levels of disease resistance include *Rosa majalis, R. multiflora, R. rugosa* and *R. wichuraiana*. These old variety roses can still be found in many public and private rose gardens, and are noted for their hardiness, profusion of blossoms once or twice a season, array of colors, petal arrangements and scents. A list of nurseries that sell old rose varieties by mail is provided in the Resource Appendix under "Plant Disease Management: Horticultural Controls" on p. 687. Many communities have old rose societies whose members open their gardens for public viewing. For help locating local societies, write the American Rose Society, PO Box 30,000, Shreveport, LA 71130.

The modern hybrid tea, floribunda and grandiflora roses have been bred to enhance the frequency and size of bloom, diversity of color, prominence of scent and other features rather than to increase pest tolerance. Fortunately, many modern hybrid roses have retained some of their ancestral resistance or tolerance of disease despite the indifference of breeders to these characteristics.

The degree of disease resistance of any cultivar can vary from site to site due to variations in environmental conditions or cultural practices. It can also vary over time, since disease pathogens sometimes develop new races able to overcome resistance factors. To identify roses with a long history of disease resistance in your area, talk to knowledgeable gardeners, members of rose societies or municipal rosarians. If you see a variety you like that seems to be disease free, ask if it has been sprayed. If it hasn't and it remains healthy throughout the summer, it's probably resistant to local pathogens. If roses in your garden have constant disease problems, consider replacing them with varieties you have observed to be resistant.

Bright spots for future rose research include the breeding programs underway at Canada's Ornamentals Research Service and the USDA's Science and Education Research Service.

The Canadians are crossing disease-resistant *R. rugosa* and *R. wichuraiana* stock with hybrid tea roses. USDA scientists have developed a black spot-resistant hybrid. These varieties should be on the market soon.

2. Manipulation of Moisture. Since black spot and rust spores must be immersed in a film of water for a number of hours before they germinate, disease prevention involves keeping susceptible foliage as dry as possible. This can be achieved in a number of ways: by planting roses in full sun and spacing them at least 3 ft. to 4 ft. (0.9 m to to 1.2 m) apart to encourage good air circulation; by pruning roses so that they have open centers, reducing the density of the interior foliage; by using bubbler heads or soaker hoses when irrigating to avoid wetting the foliage; or (if irrigating with sprinklers) by watering during periods of sunlight and ceasing irrigation in time for the foliage to dry before nightfall.

Powdery mildew, on the other hand, cannot survive if there is a film of water on leaves or stems. In one university study conducted in the 1930s, powdery mildew on the highly susceptible Dorothy Perkins rose was kept to very low levels simply by syringing the bushes with a heavy stream of water from a garden hose. The water was applied for a few minutes through an ordinary spray nozzle that raised the normal 40 psi household water pressure up to 70 psi. Care was taken to wash both the upper and lower surfaces of the leaves. The wash was timed for early afternoon, because that is when powdery mildew spores are most likely to be moving on air currents on their way to infecting new leaves.

This research demonstrated that if spores were wetted within six to eight hours after landing on a leaf, infection could be prevented or kept to a very low level. The washing was begun two weeks after spores were sprinkled on the leaves of test plants. The bushes were washed every three days for four weeks. At the end of the test period, 72% of the leaves on unwashed roses were infected with powdery mildew, compared to only 21% of the leaves on water-washed plants. When the mildewed leaves from washed and unwashed plants were compared, damage on washed leaves was much less severe than on unwashed leaves.

Water-washing appears to suppress mildew in several ways. First, the force of the water physically removes ungerminated spores resting on the leaf; it also removes spores that have already germinated and have inserted their tubes into the leaf tissue. Once the powdery growth is separated from the infective tube already stuck in the plant, the tube atrophies and causes no further damage. Spores that are not removed by the spray of water are prevented from germinating by the film of water left on the leaf. The bead of water may elevate the spore high enough to prevent the germ tube from reaching the leaf tissue for penetration.

For the home gardener, this research suggests that as soon as weather conditions are right for powdery mildew (see the sidebar on pp. 586-587), you should begin a program of hosing the foliage with a heavy stream of water for a few minutes once or twice a week, preferably in the early afternoon. Concentrate on tender new growth, since powdery mildew does not appear to attack mature foliage. Keep water-washing until the flush of new growth matures. Watch for the onset of new flushes of growth that coincide with optimal weather conditions for powdery mildew, and resume periodic water washes during the growth spurt. After a season or two of experimentation, you will be able to time your water-washing with increasing accuracy.

Since wetting the leaves can enhance black spot and rust in regions where these diseases occur along with powdery mildew, syringe the foliage in strong sunlight to speed drying. Fortunately, the temperature levels and other variables necessary for the development of black spot and, to some degree, rust often do not prevail in areas where powdery mildew is severe. The studies described above do not cite any secondary disease problems generated by water washes.

3. Fertilizing. Excessive application of highly soluble nitrate fertilizer should be avoided since it generates frequent flushes of lush, weak growth that is very susceptible to attack by powdery mildew and, to a lesser degree, black spot and rust. Moderate applications of compost, stabilized manure or slowly soluble ammonium-based fertilizers in late fall and early spring are recommended.

Treatment:
Direct Physical Controls

Pruning and mulching are effective physical controls for black spot, powdery mildew and rust.

1. Pruning. All three pathogens overwinter inside leaf buds formed on canes. In addition, spores of black spot and, to a moderate degree, rust also overwinter on or within the tissue of canes or fallen leaves. Thus, removal and destruction of infected leaves and canes is effective in limiting overwintering disease spores as well as in minimizing the spread of infection from spores active in spring and summer. Roses are fairly tolerant of heavy pruning and usually bounce back in the spring with strong new canes.

Researchers at England's Imperial College Field Station have found that powdery mildew spores tend to overwinter in leaf buds located just below infected flowers. They recommend that roses be lightly pruned in fall, with particular attention paid to the removal of infected flowers as well as stems and portions of canes directly below the damaged blooms. This removes newly forming buds that may already have become infected, preventing the carryover of inocula that might infect roses the next spring.

Overwintering black spot and rust spores are particularly common on fallen leaves; thus, proper disposal of all leaves and flower petals that have accumulated on the ground also helps prevent the spread of these diseases. The debris should be burned or composted. The spores will survive in compost piles unless they are hot-composted in systems such as the one described on p. 644.

Infected canes should be pruned off and removed from the garden as early in winter as the climate allows to ensure that infected buds are removed before an unexpected warm spell forces them open and activates the dormant spores. It is relatively easy to identify black spot infections by the dark blotches on the wood. Rust damage appears as dark, corky lesions on the canes, but powdery mildew is invisible inside protective leaf buds.

If your garden had high levels of disease the previous summer, it is probably wise to prune roses that showed severe damage to within 4 in. to 6 in. (10 cm to 15 cm) of the graft union. This increases the likelihood of destroying overwintering inocula. As with infected leaves, infected canes should not be composted unless you have a hot compost system.

Dr. Bob Raabe, plant pathologist at the University of California, Berkeley, notes that the level of rose disease in mild climates along the Pacific Coast is often increased by the fact that roses rarely go fully dormant. The pruning and garden cleanup that normally would reduce the carryover of disease spores from season to season does not occur. He recommends that in mild climates roses be "pruned into dormancy." Such pruning occurs in mid-January, and consists of removing all leaves and pruning off infected canes. This allows mild-climate gardeners to have the best of two worlds: a bloom for the winter holidays and reduced disease problems the following summer.

Some spores will evade removal despite all your efforts; others will blow in from adjacent gardens or may be imported on new rose bushes. Once the growing season has begun, watch for signs of infection when roses begin leafing out. Prune out damaged foliage, canes and flowers as they appear. Early removal of disease may reduce or prevent further outbreaks. Continue light pruning whenever you see signs of disease. As long as you do not remove enough foliage to hamper photosynthesis you can continue light, preventive pruning throughout the season.

One note of caution. If powdery mildew is the major disease in your garden, take care not to prune any single bush too heavily during the growing season, because the roses will respond with spurts of succulent growth that are particularly susceptible to mildew.

2. Mulching. Applying mulch under your rose bushes is another way to limit infection from disease spores that overwinter on fallen plant debris. After raking up the dead rose leaves in fall, apply a few inches of compost or other mulch material under the bushes. Apply another layer of mulch after mid-winter pruning. The mulch will form a barrier between the rose foliage and the black spot and rust spores overwintering on organic soil debris.

Treatment:
Direct Biological Controls

The potential for using natural enemies to control powdery mildew is under study in Israel and at the University of Oregon. These projects have been initiated in response to the growing resistance of pathogens to chemical controls as well as the tendency of fungicides to cause secondary outbreaks of pests such as mites. In Israel, the fungus species *Ampelomyces quisqualis* has been effective in destroying powdery mildew. In Oregon, eight species of fungi have shown considerable promise as biological disease control agents.

If a market among commercial rose growers can be developed for these organisms, home gardeners, too, may be able to purchase natural enemies for release on their roses.

Encourage your local land grant college to fund research on biological controls for rose pests and to assist commercial rose nurseries in using natural enemies in their pest management programs.

Treatment:
Direct Chemical Controls

The conscientious use of the non-chemical tactics described above will probably result in a significant reduction of disease in your roses. However, some cultivars may be so susceptible and some environments so optimal for disease development that these measures must be augmented by spot treatments with chemical controls. When such chemical controls seem necessary, it is wise to confine them to individual shrubs. Most roses can tolerate some level of disease without major damage. Experiment with spraying just those plants that you know from previous experience suffer intolerable damage.

Most of the available fungicides are more effective at preventing infections than at curing them. Thus, to protect roses and keep use of fungicides to a minimum, it is important to time treatments to coincide with periods of optimum temperature, humidity and rainfall, as well as with the growth stage of the rose. The sidebar on pp. 586-587 provides most of this information.

Remember that roses are most susceptible to infection when they are in a state of rapid growth. By becoming aware of the growth cycles of your plants—rapid growth in spring and early summer, moderate growth in mid-summer and a possible surge of growth in late summer—and by correlating these cycles with weather patterns that encourage disease development, you will learn how often it is necessary to apply fungicides.

1. Surfactants. Surface-active agents, or surfactants, are used daily in most homes in the form of dishwashing soaps and detergents. Gardeners know them as the wetting agents that are added to pesticide solutions to ensure even coverage of leaf surfaces and increase the ability of the pesticide to penetrate the waxy coatings on insect bodies. Chemically, surfactants are composed of fatty acid salts, and have been known to have insecticidal properties for 200 years. Studies in the United States, Canada and Great Britain indicate that surfactants show great promise as fungicides against powdery mildew and other plant diseases.

In the case of powdery mildew, researchers speculate that the surfactants work by disrupting the water balance inside ungerminated spores, by blocking certain fungal metabolic functions and by increasing the "wettability" of the leaf surface so that spores are either killed or fail to germinate due to the presence of too much water. The effects on other fungi are probably similar.

A commercial rose fungicide based on fatty acid technology has recently become available in the United States and Canada. In the United States the product is called Safer™ Fungicide and Miticide; in Canada it is known as Safer™ Natural Garden Fungicide.

According to Dr. George Puritch, Safer's chief research chemist, the fungicide prevents and eradicates powdery mildew or rust. For black spot control, however, it works only to prevent the onset of the disease. In areas where black spot is a problem, the soap must be applied to all new growth every 10 to 14 days to prevent infection. Once black spot symptoms have appeared, the fatty acid is unable to arrest its growth on the infected leaf. Dr. Puritch notes that the new product is not phytotoxic to roses, nor is it toxic to mammals. He said it also kills pest mites but does not harm beneficial mites.

If you want to experiment with household surfactants, we caution you to use a solution no stronger than 1%, or 2 tablespoons of surfactant per gallon of water, to minimize the chance of damaging the leaves. You can try liquid household soap or detergent or you can purchase a cation surfactant from a pesticide dealer. Apply the surfactant as soon as weather conditions for disease development are optimal or as soon as you spot the first symptoms.

If powdery mildew is the major problem, you should probably apply the surfactant every 7 to 14 days during cool, dry weather. Because powdery mildew tends to infest only immature plant tissue, you may need to spray only when roses are undergoing growth spurts. Black spot is generally most active in hot, rainy weather, and it is during these periods that you should make weekly or biweekly applications of surfactants. Rust appears to be most infective when temperatures are in the low 70s (about 20°C) and humidity is high. Treat the plants every 7 to 14 days when these conditions prevail.

2. Antitranspirants. These are waxes, silicones and other plastic polymers used on food crops and ornamental plants to decrease the loss of water (transpiration) through microscopic openings (stomata) in the leaves. They are also commonly used on agricultural products to delay desiccation (drying out) during storage or transportation.

In the early 1960s, Israeli agricultural scientists noted that sugar beets coated with antitranspirants remained largely free of powdery mildew. Recent tests by plant pathologists in Israel and Texas show that antitranspirants are effective at preventing infection of certain agricultural and ornamental plants by a number of mildew, rust, fusarium and other pathogens.

Antitranspirants work as disease-control agents by forming a barrier between the infective disease spore and the plant tissue that the spore must penetrate. When the stomata and other microscopic openings in leaf tissue are covered with air-permeable plastic or wax coatings, germ tubes from fungal spores seem to be discouraged from entering the leaf tissue. There is also evidence that the antitranspirants repel the film of water on the leaf surface needed by black spot, rust and other pathogens to germinate.

In one test, the antitranspirants Wilt Pruf® and Sta Fresh 460® were as effective as the fungicide benomyl (Benlate®) at controlling powdery mildew on wheat. In another test, control of powdery mildew on hydrangea and crape myrtle was as effective or better with the antitranspirants Vapor Gard® and Wilt Pruf® than with the systemic trizole fungicide Tilt®.

Although no experiments investigating the effectiveness of antitranspirants on roses have reached the scientific literature, experiments reported to us on greenhouse roses at Longwood Gardens in Delaware proved they were effective at preventing unacceptable levels of powdery mildew. Further experimentation is needed to determine when and how often the materials need to be applied. Dr. Bob Raabe notes that coatings applied to young foliage thin out or crack as the foliage expands, and lose their effectiveness as a barrier. Repeated applications may be required. Other researchers note that these materials may not be suited to humid climates with frequent cloud cover since photosynthesis may be unduly inhibited. Further research is also needed to determine the ultimate fate of the antitranspirants in the garden ecosystem. The fact that some are biodegradable is hopeful.

3. Baking Soda. The use of common baking soda, or bicarbonate of soda, to control powdery mildew is mentioned in old gardening books. Japanese researchers as well as members of the Henry Doubleday Research Association (HDRA) in Great Britain are pursuing this. We suggest you contact the latter directly to obtain the most recent information by writing, HDRA, Ryton-on-Dunsmore, Coventry, CV8 3LG, England.

4. Conventional Fungicides. In the 1950s, broad-spectrum rose fungicides were adopted with enthusiasm by rose growers. The fungicides seemed to protect roses from heavy damage most of the growing season and appeared less likely to burn plant leaves than some of the inorganic fungicides available, such as copper or sulfur. By the 1970s, however, it had become evident that fungi were developing a tolerance or resistance to many of these fungicides. It was also recognized that some fungicides were highly toxic to nontarget organisms, particularly predators of spider mites. As a result, mite outbreaks on roses were increasing following fungicide use. The lack of data on health effects of long-term exposure to fungicides also caused concern.

In an effort to overcome the negative effects on nontarget organisms, new selective fungicides have been developed. They are an improvement over the broad-spectrum materials, but the very mechanisms that make them selective also increase the likelihood of target diseases developing resistance. They will work for a while, but probably not for long.

Another development is the use of systemic fungicides to control rose disease. On many crops, systemics are applied to the soil. They are then absorbed by the roots and dispersed throughout the vascular system of the plant. Theoretically, this provides perfect coverage of the plant, avoiding the problem of rain or irrigation washing the chemical off and minimizing human exposure (although not that of beneficial microbes and insects), since the chemical is poured on the soil rather than sprayed in the air.

However, available systemics do not translocate readily in the woody tissues of roses. The major products used on roses are locally systemic on leaves, and are applied as sprays. Since roses put on rapid growth, the systemics become diluted by the expanding cell tissue and must be reapplied every 7 to 10 days to protect against disease. Information on the long-term health effects of these systemics on humans and beneficial organisms is difficult to obtain.

5. Sulfur-Based Fungicides. If you feel you must use a conventional fungicide, sulfur is probably safest to the applicator and beneficial organisms. When used in conjunction with the other tactics described in this section, sulfur should be quite effective in controlling the three rose pathogens. It has been used to suppress powdery mildew since at least 1820, and was probably used for hundreds of years before that. It also has a long history as a standard control for both black spot and rust. It comes in liquid or dust formulations and is easy to apply using conventional garden spray equipment. Both formulations are sold in garden stores, and directions for use, including the addition of surfactants, are on the label.

When applying the sulfur, be certain to cover the tops and undersides of leaves, paying special attention to the growing tips. It is best to begin applications early in the season, since sulfur is more effective at preventing disease than at curing it. Follow the directions on the label for dosage and timing. A word of caution: If the temperature exceeds 85°F (29°C), do not apply sulfur because it may burn the leaves. Fortunately, in areas where temperatures frequently reach that level, powdery mildew and rust are generally not significant problems as it is too hot for them. Although black spot can tolerate a fair amount of moist heat, disease growth is apt to come to a standstill when the temperature hits the high 80s (around 30°C). Thus, the temperature constraints on the use of sulfur may not unduly hinder disease control.

Some rose manuals recommend applying lime-sulfur sprays when roses are dormant. Presumably this kills overwintering spores lodged in unopened buds or on canes. Unfortunately, we could find no documentation of the efficacy of this treatment.

Summary: Least-Toxic Black Spot, Powdery Mildew and Rust Control on Roses

• Plant rose varieties that are tolerant of or resistant to the diseases prevalent in your area.

• Plant roses in full sun and space them a minimum of 3 ft. to 4 ft. (about 1 m) apart to encourage air circulation.

• In fall, rake up and discard all fallen leaves and other plant debris that may contain overwintering spores.

• In winter, prune off and discard all diseased canes and any remaining foliage.

• Before buds swell in spring, apply 2 in. to 3 in. (5 cm to 7.6 cm) of organic mulch under the bushes to cover any overwintering disease spores on the ground.

• When foliage emerges in the spring, monitor for signs of disease and prune off infected parts. Continue light pruning of infected parts throughout the growing season.

• If powdery mildew appears, apply weekly water washes during periods of active growth.

• If disease levels seem to be increasing despite your conscientious use of the tactics described above, spray with a surfactant, antitranspirant, baking soda or sulfur.

SNAILS AND SLUGS
(Order Stylommatophora, families Helicidae and Limacidae)

Snails and slugs are more closely related to shellfish, such as clams, than they are to insects. Where conditions are favorably moist, either or both animals may become serious garden and commercial crop pests. Some of the most troublesome mollusks (from "Mollusca," the phylum to which they belong) are those that have been introduced. One example is the brown garden snail *(Helix aspersa),* which was deliberately brought to California in the 1850s as a potential food source.

There are several hundred species of snails and at least 40 species of slugs in the United States. The native snails and slugs tend to be solitary in habit, whereas the introduced species are gregarious or colonial.

The use of poison baits is popular for controlling these pests, and it is possible to use baits in such a way that contamination of the environment is greatly reduced. However, the large number of snails and/or slugs in areas where they are a serious problem often leads to the use of large amounts of poison scattered widely and repeatedly. This may lead to the production of local populations of snails that ignore or are resistant to the baits, as well as the possibility of poisoning domestic pets and humans. Some predatory insects may also be damaged.

Whether or not you feel you must include poison baits in your campaigns against these pests, it is important to learn something about their biology. Then you can use a variety of tactics based on their behavior to reduce their numbers.

Biology

Both snails and slugs have shells. But the shells of slugs are much reduced and are hidden by the fleshy mantle on their backs. Snails and slugs rely on their large foot for locomotion and the secretion of a mucus, or

---

Snails and Slugs
Slugs and snails rely on a large, fleshy "foot" for locomotion and secrete a mucus or slime trail on which they glide. (Actual length: up to 2 in./5 cm)

Slug

Snail

---

slime, trail upon which they can glide. The snail's head has two pairs of retractable tentacles. The long pair has an eye on the end of each stalk, and the smaller pair is used to smell. The snail's mouth is below its tentacles and contains a horn-like rasping organ with which it scrapes away at food. The rest of the snail's body is curled up inside its shell. Variations in size, color and pattern are common within as well as among species.

One fascinating aspect of the biology of these animals is their hermaphroditism. Each animal has both male and female sex organs. Cross-fertilization is most common, though cases of self-fertilization have been reported. The brown garden snail may take from four months to two years to mature, depending on the abundance of moisture and food. Individual snails may lay up to 100 eggs, depending on the species, but usually the number is smaller. For example, the eggs of the brown garden snail, which are white and spherical,

are laid in masses 1 in. (2.5 cm) in diameter and contain an average of 86 eggs each. Slugs lay fewer eggs, which may remain unhatched for long periods under dry conditions. They hatch when they receive moisture.

Young snails remain in the nest for several days, then stay close to the area in which they hatched for a number of months. This is important in management, since a large number of young snails in one area is a clue to where the snails are laying eggs.

Both slugs and snails require a damp environment and fairly humid air to survive; they avoid the sun and come out primarily at night or on cloudy days. They are not pestiferous in dry climates. During the day, slugs pull themselves into the ground through crevices or available holes made by other animals such as earthworms, or they hide under boards and rocks or in other damp, shady places. The shady side of boards and rocks is favored by snails, too, along with damp leaves and other moist materials. They may return to the same place each night using the same route each time, unless their usual resting place dries out.

If the air or the substrate (the surface the snail is traveling on) becomes too dry, a snail can pull its entire body into its shell and seal the opening with a sheet of mucus, which then hardens, forming a secure closure. It can remain dormant in this condition for as long as four years (the brown garden snail normally is not active below 50°F/10°C).

Treatment: Indirect Strategies

Indirect strategies for slug and snail control focus on reduction of their favored habitat. Since both slugs and snails favor moist, shady areas for resting and laying eggs, a wise first step in their control is reducing such sites in the immediate neighborhood of the flower or vegetable garden. Remove boards, bricks and other piles of damp debris that are in contact with the ground. Either store them so that air can circulate around and under them, or place some moisture-reducing material under them (see the discussion of barriers under "Physical Controls" below).

Snails and slugs also favor certain vegetation, so check around your yard to find where the small young snails are. Ivy and succulents are among their favorites, particularly when grown as dense ground cover. Once you determine that certain planted areas are harboring snails or slugs, you have several options. One is to thin out the plants so sunshine can penetrate to ground level, wind can circulate and the bed has an opportunity to dry out.

However, thinning out may cause new problems in the form of weeds —probably the reason the ground cover was planted in the first place. In this case, mulches 6 in. (15 cm) thick or more can be used to replace plants removed from the beds. Some mulches do not seem particularly attractive to snails. For example, although brown garden snails are severe horticultural pests here in the Bay Area, rough-cut cedar chips are used in some of our city parks without much problem. We have also read anecdotal reports of crushed eggshells discouraging snails. You will have to observe conditions in your neighborhood to see which ground covers and which mulches are unattractive to these pests.

Where thinning is not appropriate, you can shift to a ground cover less favored by snails and slugs or surround the area with a barrier that discourages them from migrating into parts of the garden containing seedlings or other plants particularly attractive to them.

Treatment:
Direct Physical Controls

Direct physical controls for slugs and snails include hand-picking, trapping and the construction of barriers.

1. Hand-Picking. Hand-picking remains an important control that is usually combined with some other tactic. Despite the ability of slugs and snails to produce large numbers of young and migrate long distances in damp weather, conscientious hand-picking concentrated in the area to be protected and the immediate surrounding areas provides immediate relief. If hand-picking is combined with barriers, the relief is reasonably long-lasting.

Hand-picking is most productive at night, when these animals are active. The best time is two hours after sunset. Use a flashlight and carry a container for captured specimens. If you are squeamish about picking up slugs, use thin plastic gloves or tweezers with broad ends. If the captured mollusks are crawling out of the container before you have a chance to dispose of them, try adding a mixture of water and rubbing alcohol. A 3% to 5% concentration of alcohol anesthetizes them; you can throw them down the toilet once you get back to the house.

2. Trapping. If hand-picking at night is inconvenient, try trapping. Certain plants in the garden (for example, clumps of iris leaves) are excellent traps in themselves, because of their great attractiveness to snails. By observing which these are, you can focus your hand-picking effort on them in the daytime.

Overturned flower pots also make excellent traps for daytime collection. We use unglazed pots and are careful to place them on the shady sides of the plants. Snails will not retreat into pots that are heated and dried by the early sun; pots must make a cool, dark resting place. Make sure the ground beneath the pots is uneven so snails can crawl under the rim.

You can destroy the trapped snails by shaking them from the flower pot onto a board and stepping on them, you can scrape out the inside of the pot with a stick and dispose of the snails later or you can crush them against the sides of the pot with a stick and replace the pot without removing the bodies. Crushed snails and slugs make the pots particularly attractive to other snails and increase your catch.

Inverted grapefruit halves (after you have enjoyed the contents) can be used in a similar way. The animals like the citrus, moisture and shady refuge. Beer, as most people have heard, is an attractant for snails and slugs. Apparently the yeast is what the animals like, and many people have had success with a simple mixture of water and commercial yeast. The problem with these baits is that they must be monitored and renewed on a regular basis.

Garden writer Gene Logsdon describes an ingenious beer-baited pit trap made from a half-gallon-size coffee can. The entrance is a rectangular opening cut a third of the way up the side of the can. The can is sunk into the ground to the level of the opening, and the plastic cap, left on the can, cuts down on evaporation of beer and prevents larger animals from getting into the bait. (Those of us with beer-loving pets know this is not an unusual occurrence.)

Two other simple traps used by researchers, one for slugs and one for snails, can be adapted for home use. For monitoring slugs in grassy areas, use a white board or asphalt shingle covered on top with aluminum foil (as shown at A in the drawing on p. 594). The foil or white surface reflects light, which keeps the board cool. Moisture, which accumulates under the trap, attracts snails and slugs. The rough surface of the shingle is covered with the foil, and the foil edges are folded and glued to the smooth side. The shingles are then placed on the ground with the foil side up and a nail driven through the center into the ground to keep the shingle in position. Monitoring and collection must be done in the early morning because the high temperature and the evaporation of moisture force snails away later in the day.

Dr. Theodore Fisher of the University of California, Riverside, uses 12-in. (30 cm) square boards on 1-in. (2.5 cm) risers as monitoring traps in

Homemade Slug and Snail Traps

The simplest trap is a board or asphalt shingle (smooth side down) covered with aluminum foil and staked to the ground with a 3-in. (7.6 cm) galvanized nail in the center (A). Alternatively, a 12-in. square (30 cm by 30 cm) board can be elevated on 1-in. (2.5 cm) rails (B).

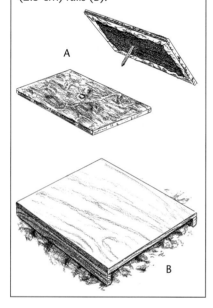

A

B

Strips of copper Snail-Barr® can be fastened around tree trunks and flower pots or stapled along the sides of planter beds as barriers. When slugs or snails make contact with the barrier, there is a toxic reaction—similar to an electric shock—and they are turned away. (Photo courtesy Custom Copper.)

his citrus orchard experiments (see B in the drawing above). He has found that when trap counts are above 300 snails per board, there is usually heavy damage to leaves and fruit; when there are fewer than 20, virtually no damage is evident. In a separate study of the effect of trap color in attracting snails, green was best, followed by red.

3. **Barriers.** A number of snail and slug barriers have been popular for some time. Testing by researchers at the University of California showed that hardwood and softwood ashes and diatomaceous earth were all effective if kept dry. This is a big "if," since snails and slug migrations are usually a problem when the ground is wet from rain, dew or irrigation. A commercial product, Snailproof®,

which consists of ground incense cedar by-products, did less well than other materials. However, this may be because in the tests the product was spread more thinly than it is by those who claim success. In these same tests, sand, which is sometimes suggested as a barrier, was found to be completely ineffective.

In our own vegetable gardens, we lay a 3-in. to 6-in. (7.6 cm to 15 cm) layer of fine sawdust on the paths surrounding each growing bed as a deterrent. Then, during our winter rainy season, we cover these paths with boards to walk on. This system has many advantages and we highly recommend it. The boards keep the sawdust dry and off your shoes; they also keep your feet dry when the ground is wet. The sawdust is an excellent herbicide. It shades the soil, and its slow decomposition takes nitrogen from the soil, depriving weed seedings of nutrients. The thick mulch prevents compaction of walkways, making reuse of those areas for planting easier once the sawdust has totally decomposed. Slugs and

snails do not like to cross the sawdust when it is dry, and they will not lay eggs beneath the boards. Best of all, we get the sawdust free from local cabinet shops and lumberyards. School woodworking shops are another good source.

The best barriers against these mollusks are strips of copper-backed paper stapled to boards around a bed, as shown in the photo above. This material is sold commercially for this purpose (see the Resource Appendix under "Insect Management: Physical Controls" on pp. 682-683) and is used extensively in California to ring citrus trees. You can make your own strips out of the thin sheets of pliable copper sheeting sold at hardware stores. Copper screening works well, too, but does not last as long. The eventual oxidizing of the copper, which turns green, does not affect its effectiveness as a barrier, however. The copper strips can be mounted on wooden frames or attached to existing benches with nails, glue or other materials. Make sure no foliage bridges the copper or the mollusks will cross over and colonize the protected area. This takes vigilance, since plants grow and lean more as the season progresses.

No barrier is effective against the snails and slugs already hiding in the area you want to protect. Snails are easier to clean out of an area than slugs, since slugs usually hide in soil crevices. Slugs can move down earthworm tunnels and openings left by root decay, and are sometimes found more than 1 ft. (30 cm) below the surface in soils high in clay. The only way to deal with this problem is to go out at night during the first weeks the barriers are in place and remove the slugs by hand.

Treatment:
Direct Biological Controls

Biological controls for slugs and snails include ducks and other animals, rove beetles, protozoans, snails themselves and humans.

1. Ducks and Other Animals. Many animals like to eat snails and slugs. A neighbor's dog crunches up the brown garden snail as if it were a chocolate-covered raisin; he likes to have them fed to him one by one. Many species of toads are very fond of slugs, as are other reptiles and amphibians. Ducks and chickens are often allowed to clear an area of snails. But chickens are so destructive to most plants that we do not recommend them for this purpose.

However, first-hand experience with ducks has convinced us that in certain settings they can contribute to easy, safe snail control. Because ducks eat seedlings, newly planted areas should be protected with chicken wire. Also, if they are kept too long in one spot the ducks mash down low vegetation. Rotation is the answer. The best system is to keep them in a pen except when being used for snail control. You can use low movable fences such as wooden picket fence sections for herding them around the property. They tend to stay near their water pans, so moving the pans encourages the ducks to

move, too. Because they eat tender weed seedlings, they can be used to weed among perennials while they are hunting for snails and slugs.

Some people object to the ducks' loud quacking, even though they are not quite as loud as geese. We happen to like the noises made by domestic animals such as ducks, chickens and geese and live in a city that is remarkably tolerant of most sorts of farm animals in its midst. After borrowing a neighbor's three ducks as often as she would part with them one summer, we decided that they make comical, charming pets as well as handy snail catchers. If you can provide the right circumstances, we recommend them. Be forewarned, however, that not all urban communities are as open-minded as ours.

2. Rove Beetles. Two natural enemies of these pests have been considered for rearing as biological control agents: a rove beetle predator and a ciliate protozoan. The rove beetle *Ocypus olens* was accidentally introduced into California from Europe and has been gradually increasing its range. It has been observed feeding on slugs in England. The beetle is large and dark-colored, with strong jaws that enable it to cut through a snail's shell. An empty shell with a telltale jagged hole in the side is evidence of beetle attack. Although the beetles are long-lived, they reproduce very slowly, which unfortunately makes commercial rearing less economically attractive. In addition, the rove beetle's large size (about 1 in./ 2.5 cm) may frighten people into killing the beetle.

3. Protozoans. The literature on the protozoan *Tetrahymena rostrata* indicates that it has potential as a biological control agent for certain species of slugs and snails due to its ability to persist in the environment and its virulency for the grey garden slug. However, this possibility has not yet been fully evaluated.

4. Snails as Snail Predators. An important snail predator is another snail: the decollate snail *(Rumina*

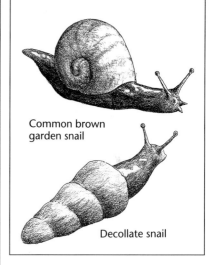

The Decollate Snail
The elongated decollate snail *(Ruminia decollata)* attacks the common brown garden snail *(Helix aspersa)*. It also attacks and kills other pest snails.

Common brown garden snail

Decollate snail

decollata) shown in the drawing above. It is currently being used for control of the brown garden snail in southern California citrus groves (for sources, see the Resource Appendix under "Insect Management: Biological Controls" on pp. 683-686). This predator evolved in North Africa and is found in countries around the Mediterranean. According to Ted Fisher, the University of California researcher who has studied this snail predator for many years, it was first reported in South Carolina in 1813, and has since been found in Alabama, Arizona, California, Florida, Georgia, Louisiana, Mississippi, New Mexico, North Carolina, Oklahoma, Texas and Virginia.

As efficient as this predator is in eliminating the brown garden snail, it is not entirely beneficial, because it feeds on seedlings and on a few succulent ground covers such as *Dichondra*, baby's tears and violets, as well as on flower petals. Once most plants are past the seedling stage, however, the snail shows no further interest. In some areas it may become a threat to native snails that are not pests and should be conserved. Therefore, it is difficult to recommend this snail for gardens outside the area in which it already occurs naturally.

5. **Humans.** For the brown garden snail, originally introduced here for food, and larger slugs such as the "banana" slug of the Northwest, humans are the ideal predator. Periodically the West Coast media blossoms with recipes for the preparation of these delicacies, and there are reports of cooking contests to judge the results. Rumor has it that many an escargot entree in high-priced San Francisco-area restaurants is actually composed of local snails stuffed into shells of the "the genuine article" imported from France.

At least one enterprising snail farmer sells his product in the United States and overseas in prepared form and ready to pop into the oven. Having tasted it, we can report that it is delicious; the snail meat itself is indistinguishable from the butter, garlic and other spices in the dish!

If you are planning to experiment with your own brown garden snails, be advised that culinary experts recommend that they be allowed to feed on clean lettuce for a few days before consumption to rid them of grit. This should be followed by washing in vinegar to remove the slime. Unfortunately, the amount of meat per snail or slug is not great in view of the effort expended, and one would have to be more inclined than are the authors to a diet heavy in melted butter to make snails and slugs a regular part of the fare.

Treatment:
Direct Chemical Controls

If you feel it necessary to use poison baits to control slugs and snails, we urge you to use baits rather than the broadcast treatments sometimes suggested by manufacturers. Even so, it is extremely likely that you will produce a local bait-resistant population. You are also faced with the problem of keeping the poison baits away from dogs and other pets. Place them in containers that allow access to slugs and snails only; position them in concealed locations where they cannot be picked up and played with by children.

SOWBUGS AND PILLBUGS
(Order Isopoda, families Porcellionidae and Armadillidiidae)

Sowbugs and pillbugs are the only crustaceans adapted to spending their entire lives out of water. In this way they are quite unlike their familiar relatives the crabs, shrimps and lobsters. On the other hand, they are

---

Sowbugs and Pillbugs

Sowbugs and pillbugs are small decomposers that closely resemble each other. However, sowbugs have two small tail-like appendages that pillbugs lack. The easiest way to tell them apart is by the fact that only pillbugs are able to roll up into a ball. (Actual size: ½ in. to ¾ in./13 mm to 19 mm)

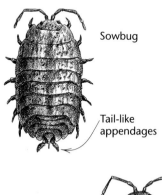

Sowbug

Tail-like appendages

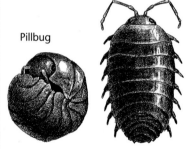

Pillbug

---

tied closely to damp environments and are not pestiferous where it is hot and dry.

In general, these animals are beneficial decomposers in the garden, breaking down complex plant material so its constituents are available to other plants as food. If you mulch your garden with organic matter, you are certain to see sowbugs in abundance because the decaying organic matter provides them with a source of food. Because they eat rotting material, these crustaceans can become a problem whenever garden vegetables remain damp and their outer cells begin decaying. This is particularly common where vegetables such as pumpkins and other winter squashes, or fruits such as strawberries rest on damp ground. These isopods may severely damage succulent bean and other seedlings that are slow to unfold and grow in cool, moist weather. Similarly, they quickly take advantage of damp seedlings that are kept covered with overturned flower pot too long after transplanting.

Biology

According to Dr. Arnold Mallis' *Handbook of Pest Control*, the common pillbug (*Armadillidium vulgare*) and the dooryard sowbug (*Porcellio laevis* and *P. scaber*) are worldwide in distribution. You can separate the pillbugs from the sowbugs by noting whether your specimen can curl into a ball that looks like a pill. The sowbug cannot manage this trick, but it does have two tail-like appendages the pillbug lacks.

The bodies of these crustaceans are oval when viewed from above. In cross section, they are convex above and flat or concave underneath. The head and thorax are small, but the abdomen is comparatively large and is composed of hard, overlapping plates. They have seven pairs of legs.

The female deposits her eggs in a membranous pouch called a marsupium or vivarium on the underside of her body. Here the embryos develop, the young emerging on their own about 44 days later for the pillbugs and in almost half that time for sowbugs. The females may have one or two generations per year, depending on the environmental conditions. Except in greenhouses, these crustaceans generally become inactive during the winter. Sowbugs may live as long as two years.

Treatment:
Indirect Strategies

Indirect strategies for control of sowbugs and pillbugs focus on modification of their favored habitat and horticultural controls.

1. Reduction of Favored Habitat. Try to create drier conditions where these animals cause problems. If sowbugs occasionally get into your house, this means there is damp, decaying vegetation adjacent to the building. Piles of wood, miscellaneous debris, decomposing leaves and clippings should be moved away from the structure. Prune vegetation back from the walls of the house so a space is created through which air can flow easily and dry out the area after a rain. Determine where the bugs are getting into the house and caulk or repair those cracks and crevices. Any space that gives sowbugs access to a house may also be a path for other undesired wildlife.

2. Watering. Water early in the day so plants have an opportunity to dry before evening. Select mulch materials that are coarse enough to let water pass through, particularly when you are mulching plants that are susceptible to damage from these animals. If you are using compost mulch, do not sift it; instead, use it in its coarsest state. Or use mulch composed of large bark pieces or other materials that do not pack down to create a constantly damp mat at the soil surface.

Seedlings such as beans that are particularly susceptible to sowbug and pillbug damage can be started indoors in peat pots or in open-bottomed cardboard containers. The seedlings can then be transplanted outdoors, container and all, which minimizes disturbance of sensitive roots. The level of the soil in the container should be slightly above the level of the garden soil after transplanting to ensure that the surface of the soil directly around the seedling does not collect moisture and promote disease. Pull mulch away from seedlings when you plant them, then return it after the plants have grown a few inches.

Many squashes can be grown on fences or trellises, where the drying effect of the wind is enough to reduce pest damage. Old leaves that are beginning to fade can be removed by hand to improve air circulation. Maturing squashes that are resting on the ground can be elevated slightly by placing a small piece of wood beneath them. If the skin on the squash or melon remains dry, it is unlikely to be attacked.

Strawberries grown over a mulch present a different kind of problem. In areas where dew is heavy or rains are frequent, the sowbugs have a tendency to move from the mulch to any ripe berries that lie directly on the ground. One solution for small gardens is to make several dozen supports for the stems with tie wire (sold in most hardware stores). These should be stuck into the ground directly below each fruit-bearing frond just before the berries turn ripe; it should hold them above the mulch through the picking phase. As you harvest the strawberries, you can move these supports to newly ripening stems nearby.

Another approach is to grow the strawberries in step-like tiers of narrow raised beds constructed of wood. This lifts the plants off the ground into breezier, drier air. If these beds are not much more than one plant wide, the ripening berries will hang over the edges and dry off after each shower or irrigation. This helps reduce slug and snail damage and makes the berries easier to pick.

Treatment:
Direct Chemical Controls

Sowbugs can be very damaging to bean and pea seedlings that are just emerging from the soil, particularly where heavy early morning condensation adds to the normal succulence of the seedlings. Thus a way must be found to protect them for the first day or two after they emerge.

A 2-in. (5 cm) wide strip of diatomaceous earth sprinkled directly over the row where the seeds have been placed will dry the area enough to discourage sowbugs if no rain or overhead irrigation wets the area in the meantime. One problem, however, is that too thin a layer of diatomaceous earth doesn't discourage the sowbugs, and a thick layer that becomes wet accidentally can harden to a plaster-like consistency that makes it very difficult for seedlings to poke through. Therefore, you must experiment with the thickness of the application, which will depend on the evenness of the soil surface and the likelihood it will get wet.

Where the mortality (death rate) of unprotected seedlings is high and diatomaceous earth is impractical because it cannot be kept dry, a 2-in. (5 cm) wide band of silica aerogel/pyrethrin spray (see p. 111 for more information, and the Resource Appendix under "Insect Management: Chemical Controls" on pp. 686-687 for sources) can be applied directly on the soil over the planted seeds. The white residue from the silica aerogel marks the treated area. Because this material breaks down rapidly, it must be renewed until the seedlings emerge. During the emergence and elongation period and until the true leaves have opened, you may need to spray the material at the base of the seedlings as well.

Usually two or three applications of the pesticide over 7 to 10 days confined to the narrow strip where the new bean or pea plants will emerge allows seedling survival even if sowbug populations are high in adjacent beds. Monitor for sowbugs in the daytime by disturbing the surrounding soil and mulch with your finger to see if they are curled up near the plant.

SYMPHYLANS
(Order Symphyla, family Scutigerellidae)

Symphylans are delicate small white creatures that resemble centipedes (see the drawing at right). But you should get to know the difference, because centipedes are beneficial predators that prey on many pest insects, whereas symphylans feed primarily on microbes and plant materials in the soil as well as the roots of horticultural plants. Symphylans can become a problem in moist soils that are high in organic material; thus, increasing soil fertility by adding large amounts of manure and/or compost may increase their presence and make a minor problem worse. An effective control program for these organisms still remains to be developed. Our efforts are summarized below.

Scutigerella immaculata, often called the garden centipede, is one of the better-known symphylan species and is a pest of many agricultural crops. However, just because you see symphylans in your garden soil, don't assume they are the cause of root damage unless there is clear evidence. The section on detection should help you make that determination. If the symphylans are not harming the plants you are trying to cultivate, leave them alone.

Biology

Symphylans are small, ⅓ in. (8.5 mm) long at most. You need a magnifying glass to distinguish them from the other soil-inhabiting animals with which they may be confused. These include springtails, young millipedes and centipedes. Symphylans are very active and very fragile.

The female symphylan lays about a dozen pearly white eggs in the soil and remains with them during the 10 to 23-day incubation period. The

---

The Symphylan
Symphylans are commonly called garden centipedes. This is a serious misnomer, because centipedes help keep pest insects under control, whereas symphylans are pests that eat plant roots. One way to tell them apart is by the number of legs they have: symphylans have 12 pairs, whereas centipedes have 15. (Actual length: ⅓ in./8.5 mm.)

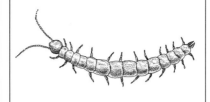

---

six-legged young mature after about three months into 14-segmented adults with 12 pairs of legs, long antennae and a pair of cerci (hair-like appendages) that arise from the last segment. They have a relatively long life, four years or more. Eggs and small larvae can be found in the soil year-round, but breeding is at its peak in the spring and early summer.

The vertical distribution of symphylans in the soil varies with the season. They are nearest the surface in bare soil in May and are deepest in July (in England, where most of the research has been done, although the findings apply to parts of America, as discussed below). Some individuals have been found as far as 5 ft. (1.5 m) below the surface. They do not tunnel; instead they follow earthworm tubes and natural soil crevices. In greenhouses, where they are commonly found near paths, walls, pipes and pillars, they can reproduce and cause damage all year. Their optimal temperature range is 59°F to 68°F (15°C to 20°C), and they prefer 100% relative humidity in the soil air.

The damage that symphylans inflict on roots and root hairs may initiate root rots caused by bacteria and fungi. Symphylans may also

---

eat yeasts, bacteria, fungi and dead soil animals. Among the crops they attack are tomato, lettuce, sugar beets, chrysanthemum, asparagus, beans, brassicas, celery, cucumber, parsley, peas, pepper, potato and strawberries. As mentioned earlier, they are primarily a problem where soils are moist, friable and high in organic materials.

Damage and Detection

Symphylan damage varies, but it is usually associated with the fact that symphylans, by eating the roots, have reduced a plant's ability to absorb water. The precise symptoms may be slightly different in different plant species.

Because the British climate and agricultural techniques yield growing conditions conducive to symphylan growth—plentiful rainfall and the use of animal manures and other organic materials for fertilizer— symphylans are a particular problem there, as they are in the American Northwest and in greenhouses worldwide. The damage is described in a bulletin of the British Ministry of Agriculture (listed under "References and Readings" on p. 605). Note that the bulletin uses "symphylid" when referring to symphylans:

Several crops are susceptible to symphylid attack; young plants can be killed but the survivors usually outgrow the damage. The main type of damage is the removal of root hairs from young growing roots, leading to the disappearance of many small roots and consequent stunting of the plants. In the glasshouse [greenhouse], severely damaged plants wilt readily. Damage is sometimes mistaken for that caused by other problems such as excess salts, water-logging or acidity.

On many crops damage shows as tiny black marks on the roots where a hemispherical piece of tissue has been scooped out. These small lesions may aid attack by fungi and other organisms, causing root rots. Where this occurs, the original cause is liable to be overlooked.

In addition to these general symptoms, there are some that are specific to the crop. The leaves of tomato take on a bluish tinge and the plants become very stunted. Lettuce plants do not develop a heart, and an injured plant often dies as a result of secondary root rots and botrytis. Chrysanthemum roots become thickened and gnarled, sometimes with a reddish tinge.

If garden plants appear to be suffering from root damage, there is only one way to determine whether symphylans are the source of the problem. The same British bulletin describes this technique:

The extent of symphylid attack can be determined by lifting poorly growing plants and quickly lowering them, together with the soil surrounding the roots, into a bucket of water. The soil should then be gently kneaded or stirred under the surface of the water, so that the symphylids come out of the soil and float up to the surface of the water where they can be counted.

Soil that is suspected of being infested before being sown or planted up can be examined by the same method. When there is no crop present the symphylids will be below the soil surface, so a few spadefuls of soil should be taken to a depth of about 18 in. (46 cm) and each dropped into a bucket of water. The numbers of symphylids coming to the water surface after the soil has been broken up will give a useful indication of the degree of infestation.

Be sure that you examine the floating animals carefully to distinguish symphylans from springtails and other organisms. Symphylans tend to have a spotty distribution in the soil. Some areas of the garden bed or field may have high populations, whereas others have few or none. Thus, you must sample soil in several areas to know where to direct control efforts and whether they are working. Several references suggest that 10 or more symphylans found among the roots of a single plant are enough to cause concern and may signal the need for control.

Treatment: Indirect Strategies

Although crop rotation is frequently suggested as an alternative to pesticides for controlling symphylans, the same literature is notably deficient in providing a list of specific rotations that have been shown to be successful. To the contrary, it was demonstrated that in some cases, a crop of tomatoes following a crop of lettuce actually made matters worse.

The University of California manual on IPM for commercial tomato production (listed under "References and Readings" on p. 605) suggests planting and then disking under a crop of sorghum prior to planting a tomato crop. Unfortunately, the manual does not provide references to the technical literature, and our effort to track down the source by telephoning the manual's editors were not successful.

Treatment: Direct Physical Controls

Because symphylans are so fragile, any technique that vigorously disturbs the soil is likely to kill them. Much of the literature on symphylan control contains the recommendation that you pulverize the planting area with a power disc when it is dry just prior to planting. A rototiller, used when the soil is not too soggy to be worked, might have the same effect. Populations are likely to build up again, but not in time to harm the crops before they are harvested and the soil is turned and mixed vigorously again.

In the USDA Cooperative Extension Office literature, artificial flooding is the most frequently mentioned non-pesticide control. The references they cite suggest flooding for three weeks in winter or in summer just before planting. One expert suggested that flooding even for as short a period as 24 hours is helpful. This is a difficult technique to carry out unless temporary dikes can be created around the infested area.

In one letter we received, an organic gardener pleaded for information on how to "fry the little critters." Doing so might not be so easy. Steam sterilization of the soil in the fall is reportedly ineffective, but spring treatment after crop removal does have some effect. Heating the soil by covering it with sheets of clear plastic, a technique called soil solarization that is discussed on pp. 501-502, has been used successfully against certain soil-borne pathogens, nematodes and weeds. Unfortunately, symphylans are more mobile than either weed seeds or microbes, and are likely to migrate away from areas made inhospitable to them.

Treatment: Direct Biological Controls

The most promising alternative control we have found is a reference to the fact that the nematode *Steinernema carpocapsae* may be effective against *Scutigerella immaculata*. This nematode is sold commercially and is listed in the Resource Appendix under "Insect Management: Biological Controls" on pp. 683-686. Initial field trials, however, were not successful.

(We would like to note that in researching the management of symphylans, we received helpful suggestions from R. Brendler and R. Van Steenwyk of the University of California Cooperative Extension Service, as well as from A. Michelbacher, Professor Emeritus at the University of California, Berkeley, and Dr. George Poinar at the same university.)

WHITEFLIES
(Order Homoptera, family Aleyrodidae)

Whiteflies are sucking insects that are more closely related to scales, aphids and mealybugs than to most other insects. They undergo a complete metamorphosis, meaning they make a complete transformation in appearance between their young and adult forms, passing through a pupal stage. You must use different strategies to control the different stages if you want to pursue least-toxic methods. These are discussed in detail in Chapter 20, since whiteflies are a more serious pest of plants indoors than in the garden, where they are more visible than damaging.

Control methods include the use of slow-release fertilizers to reduce nitrogen levels in the plant, hand-picking of older leaves to remove young whitefly stages and treating plants with insecticidal soap. The latter places particular emphasis on the undersides of the leaves. Adult whiteflies can be sucked off the tops of plants with a hand-held vacuum in the cool hours of the early morning. Or they can be trapped on yellow sticky boards that are hung or staked among the plants. Tapping the plants with a stick causes the whiteflies to fly up and into these boards. Construction of sticky traps is discussed in the section on whitefly control on p. 386.

Indoors, whiteflies can be controlled with commercially available beneficial insects. We do not recommend purchasing insects for the garden, however. If your garden is well diversified and you avoid frequent or widespread use of insecticides, there should be plenty of whitefly predators and parasitoids already present. Be patient, use soap or horticultural oil when you feel you must, and wait for the beneficial insects to catch up with the pests. An exception to this general advice concerns the recently introduced potato whitefly *(Bemisia tabaci)*. The reproductive rate of this species is so high that additional measures will be needed. This serious pest is the subject of intense research at this time. If the potato whitefly has entered your garden, contact us at the Bio-Integral Resource Center, P.O. Box 7414, Berkeley, CA 94707, for advice based on the latest research findings.

REFERENCES AND READINGS

General

Flint, M.L. 1990. *Pests of the garden and small farm: a grower's guide to using less pesticide.* Oakland, Calif.: ANR Publications, 6701 San Pablo Ave., Oakland, CA 94608-1239. 276 pp.

This beautifully illustrated publication summarizes IPM approaches to more than a hundred pest insects, weeds and plant diseases found in the United States and Canada.

Aphids

Blackman, R. 1974. *Aphids.* London: Ginn and Co. 175 pp.

A good introduction to aphid biology, ecology, behavior and methods of investigation, with illustrations (some in color) of common species and natural enemies.

Blackman, R.L., and V.F. Eastop. 1984. *Aphids on the world's crops: an identification guide.* New York: John Wiley. 466 pp.

This monumental work makes the identification of aphid pests of agriculture accessible to the pest manager for the first time. It contains illustrated keys to the more than 250 species of aphids that occur on commercially important crops, including some ornamentals. There are two alphabetized identification lists, the first by crop plant, the second by aphid species.

van den Bosch, R., P.S. Messinger and A.P. Gutierrez. 1982. *An introduction to biological control.* New York: Plenum. 247 pp.

This is the best introductory work on the subject. It covers the history, basic concepts and examples of pest control by natural enemies. The first-listed author of this book taught us and provided support for our work at a time when the university community was generally very hostile to our efforts. He was an expert in classical biological control; that is, the importation of natural enemies to control invaded aphids and other pests.

Cucumber Beetles

Branson, T.F., et al. 1983. Resistance to larvae of *Diabrotica virgifera virgifera* in three experimental maize hybrids. *Environmental Entomology* 12(5): 1509-1512.

Three experimental maize hybrids showed resistance to larvae of the western corn rootworm. This is the first report of resistance to larvae of corn rootworms.

Fielding, D.J., and W.G. Rusink. 1985. Varying amounts of bait influences numbers of western and northern corn rootworms (Coleoptera: Chrysomelidae) caught in cucurbitacin traps. *Journal of Economic Entomology* 78(5):1138-1144.

This study reveals that increasing levels of powdered squash bait caught higher numbers of western and northern corn rootworms in cucurbitacin traps. Details on trap use and construction are provided.

Fisher, J.R., et al. 1984. Use of common squash cultivars, *Cucurbita* spp., for mass collection of corn rootworm beetles, *Diabrotica* spp. (Coleoptera: Chrysomelidae). *Journal of the Kansas Entomological Society* 57(3):409-412.

Of nine cultivars of four *Cucurbita* species, the blossoms of the winter squash *(C. maxima* 'Blue Hubbard') attracted the most rootworm adults. More females then males were collected from all cultivars.

Jackson, J. 1986. Personal communication. Agricultural Research Service, North Central Region, Northern Grain Insects Research Laboratory, Brookings, South Dakota.

The information about the use of *Steinernema carpocapsae* was kindly provided by Dr. Jackson. However, the work is in the early stage and his results are preliminary.

Krysan, J.L., and T.F. Branson. 1983. Biology, ecology, and distribution of *Diabrotica*. In *Professional International Maize Virus Disease Colloquium and Workshop, Wooster, Ohio, August 26, 1982*, eds. D.T. Gordon, et al. pp. 144-150. (Available from: Ohio State University, Agricultural Research and Development Center, Wooster, OH 44691.)

A short review article summarizing the distribution, life cycles, host plant relationships and dispersal mechanisms of the diabroticites. Seven *Diabrotica* species in North America and 333 species worldwide are identified. The numbers and biology of the different groups are described.

Krysan, J.L., and T.A. Miller, eds. 1986. *Methods for the study of pest Diabrotica*. New York: Springer-Verlag. 260 pp.

This book is largely concerned with research methods. The preface by R.L. Metcalf provides economic estimates of the costs of beetle control and damage to corn, including the billion-dollar figure cited in this chapter. The introductory chapter reviews the biology, distribution, and identification of pest *Diabrotica*, and includes maps of the distribution of major pest species. The adult beetle collection technique described in this chapter (p. 575) came from Chapter 8, and the description of cucurbitacin baits (p. 576) came from Chapter 4.

Krysan, J.L., et al. 1982. Corn rootworm biology. In *Eighth Annual Illinois Crop Protection Workshop*, March 9-11, 1982, pp. 59-64. (Available from: Cooperative Extension Service, University of Illinois, Champaign/Urbana, IL 61820.)

This important review of the biology of the northern and western corn rootworm (then called *D. longicornis barberi*) also describes the early history of rootworm management. Early cultural practices were successful in controlling corn rootworms through crop rotation. The change in the status of the northern corn rootworm from non-pest to pest in the 1860s was associated with planting corn without rotation. Rotations at that time were long, with corn planted in only one of four years. More recent history is also reviewed.

Krysan, J.L., et al. 1984. Field termination of egg diapause in *Diabrotica* with new evidence of extended diapause in *D. barberi* (Coleoptera: Chrysomelidae). *Environmental Entomology* 13(5):1237-1240.

This article reports that a small percentage of northern corn rootworm eggs (less than 7%) hatched without exposure to field conditions in the laboratory. Some eggs, about 40%, showed an extended diapause that required two chill periods.

Ladd, T.L. 1984. Eugenol-related attractants for the northern corn rootworm (Coleoptera: Chrysomelidae). *Journal of Economic Entomology* 77(2): 339-341.

Two eugenol-related substances, 2-methoxy-4-propylphenol and isoeugenol, were comparable with eugenol in their ability to attract northern corn rootworm adults.

Ladd, T.L., et al. 1983. Eugenol, a new attractant for the northern corn rootworm (Coleoptera: Chrysomelidae). *Journal of Economic Entomology* 76(5):109-1051.

This was the first paper showing that eugenol was attractive to the northern corn rootworm and not the western corn rootworm.

Ladd, T.L., et al. 1984. Influence of color and height of eugenol-baited sticky traps on attractiveness to northern corn rootworm beetles (Coleoptera: Chrysomelidae). *Journal of Economic Entomology* 77(3):652-654.

Eugenol-baited sticky traps positioned outside cornfields were most attractive when painted yellow and placed 0 in. to 10 in. (25 cm) above the ground.

Ladd, T.L., et al. 1985. Corn rootworms (Coleoptera: Chrysomelidae): responses to eugenol and 8 R-methyl-2R-decyl propanoate. *Journal of Economic Entomology* 78(4):844-847.

Sticky traps baited with eugenol captured as many northern corn rootworm beetles as traps baited with eugenol and the sex pheromone 8 R-methyl-2R-decyl propanoate (MDP). Eugenol traps captured significantly more females than did traps baited only with the pheromone.

Leung, A.Y. 1980. *Encyclopedia of common natural ingredients used in food, drugs, and cosmetics*. New York: John Wiley. 409 pp.

This encyclopedia includes an extensive listing of plant sources for eugenol.

Lew, A.C., and G.R. Sutter. 1985. Toxicity of insecticides to northern corn rootworm (Coleoptera: Chrysomelidae) larvae. *Journal of the Kansas Entomological Society* 58(3):547-549.

This article reports that insecticidal resistance has been suspected by pest managers periodically over the last 10 years.

Olkowski, W. 1986. Integrated pest management for corn rootworms and cucumber beetles. *The IPM Practitioner* 8(11/12):1-8.

A short but in-depth review of the state of the art and research written for farmers and pest control advisors.

Cutworms

Bushing, M.K., and F.T. Turpin. 1976. Oviposition preferences of black cutworm moths among various crop plants, weeds, and plant debris. *Journal of Economic Entomology* 69(5): 587-590.

Of 14 crop and weed species and crop debris tested for oviposition preference, curly dock and yellow rocket mustard were found to be the most attractive; corn and soybeans were among the least attractive.

Bushing, M.K., and F.T. Turpin. 1977. Survival and development of black cutworm *(Agrotis ipsilon)* larvae on various species of crop plants and weeds. *Environmental Entomology* 6(1): 63-65.

Nineteen of 23 Indiana cornfields with cutworm damage showed moderate to heavy weed growth prior to planting. Of 16 possible food sources offered to larvae, survival was highest on bluegrass, curly dock and wheat, whereas no larvae survived on giant foxtail or debris.

Flint, M.L., et al. 1985. *Integrated pest management for cole crops and lettuce.* Berkeley: University of California Division of Agriculture and Natural Resources (Publication 3307). 112 pp.

This volume, like others in the series, contains summaries of work done by many investigators, as well as excellent color photographs by Jack Clark. It includes some useful information on cutworm biology and conditions in California cole and lettuce crops. Unfortunately, specific techniques and concepts are not traceable to source documents due to a lack of adequate citations.

Foster, M.A., and W.G. Ruesink. 1984. Influence of flowering weeds associated with reduced tillage in corn on a black cutworm (Lepidoptera: Noctuidae) parasitoid, *Meteorus rubens* (Nees von Esenbeck). *Environmental Entomology* 13:664-668.

Laboratory studies showed that when the major black cutworm parasitoid *Meteorus rubens* was provided with any of five flowering weed species it lived longer, attacked more hosts and produced more offspring than those not offered a food source.

Metcalf, C.L., and W.P. Flint. 1928. *Destructive and useful insects, their habits and control.* New York: McGraw-Hill. 918 pp.

This classic work contains much useful information about cutworms, including baiting techniques.

Redmond, J. 1982. Cutworm integrated pest management: an introduction. *IPM Practitioner* 4(7):5-8.

This short review article describes cutworm biology, monitoring systems, economic thresholds, weed management and biological control research up to 1982. We used it extensively in preparing the information on cutworms in this chapter.

Wilson, M.C., et al. 1980. *Practical insect pest management, Vol. 2, Insects of livestock and agronomic crops,* 2nd ed. Boulder, Colo.: Waveland Press. 198 pp.

This book contains a short section on the black cutworm *(Agrotis ipsilon)*.

Yepsen, R.B., Jr., ed. 1984. *Natural insect and disease control.* Emmaus, Pa.: Rodale. 490 pp.

Yepsen recommends using molasses in baits and as a sticky trap. He says that mixing equal parts of sawdust and wheat bran with enough molasses and water to make the mixture sticky will operate as a trap in which the cutworms will die after getting stuck.

Earwigs

Carroll, D.P., and S.C. Hoyt. 1984. Augmentation of European earwigs (Dermaptera: Forficulidae) for biological control of apple aphid (Homoptera: Aphididae) in an apple orchard. *Journal of Economic Entomology* 77:738-740.

This article describes methods for augmenting earwig numbers in order to increase predation on apple aphids.

Clausen, C.P., ed. 1978. *Introduced parasites and predators of arthropod pests and weeds: a world review.* Washington, D.C.: USDA (Handbook 480). 545 pp.

Includes information on parasitoid importations for control of earwigs.

Ebeling, W. 1975. *Urban entomology.* Berkeley: University of California Division of Agricultural Science. 695 pp.

Includes basic information on earwig biology and control.

Fulton, B.B. 1924. Some habits of earwigs. *Annals of the Entomological Society of America* 17:357-367.

A paper describing earwig behavior and other information at the time these insects were first found in North America.

Gophers

Golan, J. 1985. Personal communication.

Jack Golan of the Marin County Department of Parks and Recreation in San Rafael, California, provided information on the lawn mower carbon monoxide fumigation technique described on p. 583.

Logsdon, G. 1983. *Wildlife in your garden, or dealing with deer, rabbits, raccoons, moles, crows, sparrows, and other of nature's creatures.* Emmaus, Pa.: Rodale. 268 pp.

This book is for the suburban or rural home owner who wants to attract and understand wildlife around the house and yard. It also contains a discussion of tactics for excluding wildlife when it is pestiferous.

Olkowski, W., and H. Olkowski. 1980. *Managing the transition to an integrated pest management program on Department of Water Resources levees,* Final Report, July 1, 1979 to June 30, 1980. 289 pp. (Available from: BIRC, P.O. Box 7414, Berkeley, CA 94707.)

This report includes a 25-page review of the literature on gopher biology and management and a proposed IPM program for gopher management on levees maintained by the California State Department of Water Resources.

Salmon, T., and R. Lickliter. 1984. *Wildlife pest control around gardens and homes.* Berkeley: University of California Division of Agriculture and Natural Resources (Publication 21385). 90 pp. (Available from: ANR Publications, 6701 San Pablo Ave., Oakland, CA 94608-1239.)

Some of the methods described in this chapter were based on information from this excellent cooperative extension booklet.

Timm, R.M., ed. 1983. *Prevention and control of wildlife damage.* Lincoln: University of Nebraska. 250 pp.

This loose-leaf book is the most comprehensive source of information currently available on managing wildlife pest problems. The groups covered include rodents, carnivores, other mammals (such as bats, deer and antelope), birds, reptiles, amphibians and others. Three additional sections discuss 35 registered vertebrate pesticides, provide sample labels and list supplies and materials, including exclusion devices, repellent traps and other tools and materials for bird and mammal control. Each entry covers a particular species in one or a few pages with good graphics. Trapping techniques are covered in detail. All entries are fully referenced for further investigation.

Root Maggots

Brooks, A.R. 1951. Identification of the root maggots (Diptera: Anthomyiidae) attacking cruciferous garden crops in Canada, with notes on biology and control. *Canadian Entomology* 83(5):109-120.

Based on a field survey carried out in Canada during 1946 and 1947 and subsequent studies of collections, Brooks identified 30 species of Diptera associated with crucifer roots. A key to these species is provided.

Clausen, C.P., et al. 1977. *Introduced parasites and predators of arthropod pests and weeds: a world review.* Washington, D.C.: USDA (Handbook 480). 551 pp.

The review of root maggots indicates that *Aleochara bilineata* and the cynipid *Trybliographa (Cothonaspis) rapae* were already present in Canada when a relatively large importation program was conducted with the same parasitoids from Europe. Includes a short biological summary.

Colhoun, E.H. 1953. Notes on the stages and the biology of *Baryodma ontarionis* Casey (Coleoptera: Staphylinidae), a parasite of the cabbage maggot, *Hylemya brassicae* Bouche (Diptera: Anthomyiidae). *Can. Entomol.* 85(1):1-8.

B. ontarionis, now believed to be *Aleochara bilineata,* is pictured in the egg and adult stage. Rearing methods and biological details are described.

Finlayson, D.G., et al. 1980. Interactions of insecticides, a carabid predator, a staphylinid parasite, and cabbage maggots in cauliflower. *Environmental Entomology* 9(6):789-794.

Untreated cauliflower plants averaged 31%, 43% and 62% parasitism by *Aleochara bilineata* over the three-year period between 1976 and 1978. The article cites another paper where it was estimated that two carabid species destroyed more than 90% of the first-generation cabbage maggot eggs.

Flint, M.L., et al. 1985. *Integrated pest management for cole crops and lettuce.* Berkeley: University of California Division of Agriculture and Natural Resources (Publication 3307). 112 pp.

The sampling system and injury levels described in this chapter and the idea for using purple sticky traps came from this source.

Moore, I., and E.F. Legner. 1971. Host records of parasitic staphylinids of the genus *Aleochara* in America (Coleoptera: Staphylinidae). *Annals of the Entomological Society of America* 64:1184-1185.

Lists host records for eight of the 87 *Aleochara* species known to be from North America at that time. The *Hylemya* species listed as hosts of both *A. bilineata* and *A. bipustulata* are *brassicae, platura* and *floralis. H. planipalpus* is also listed as a host of *A. bilineata.*

Swan, L.A., and C.S. Papp. 1972. *The common insects of North America.* New York: Harper and Row. 750 pp.

An excellent general source book with short descriptions, line drawings, and brief notes about most agricultural pests and other common insect species.

Whistlecraft, J.W. 1985. Mass-rearing technique for *Aleochara bilineata* (Coleoptera: Staphylinidae). *Journal of Economic Entomology* 78(4):995-997.

Describes a mass-rearing system capable of producing 10,000 adults per week with five hours of labor. Further details on rearing *Delia* species are available in *The Handbook of Insect Rearing, Vol.II,* P. Singh and R.F. Moore, eds. New York: Elsevier. 1985. 514 pp.

Yepsen, R.B., Jr., ed. 1984. *The encyclopedia of natural insect and disease control.* Emmaus, Pa.: Rodale. 490 pp.

The use of diatomaceous earth or ashes around the base of plants is recommended here, but no information is provided on its efficacy.

Rose Diseases

Evans, E., J. Marshall, B.J. Couzens and R.L. Runham. 1970. The curative activity of non-ionic surface-active agents against some powdery mildew diseases. *Annals of Applied Biology* 65:473-480.

A research paper indicating the curative effect of soaps and detergents on powdery mildew.

Forsberg, J.L. 1975. *Diseases of ornamental plants.* Urbana-Champaign: University of Illinois College of Agriculture (Special Publication 3). 220 pp.

This publication includes concise descriptions of the biology of common disease pathogens such as rose powdery mildew.

Hartmann, H. 1984. Biological control of powdery mildew and grey mold on greenhouse cucumbers and tomatoes. *Ornamentals Northwest Newsletter* 8(3):12.

A one-page article with suggestions for the biological control of powdery mildew and botrytis mold.

Horst, R.K. 1983. *Compendium of rose diseases.* St. Paul, Minn.: American Phytopathological Society. 50 pp.

A scholarly text on the biology and ecology of rose diseases.

Kirby, A.H.M., and E.L. Frick. 1962. Greenhouse evaluation of chemicals for control of powdery mildews: Experiments with surface-active agents. *Annals of Applied Biology* 52:45-54.

This paper indicates that the interest in using soaps against mildews goes back many years.

Pears, P. 1985. Members' experiments for 1985. Experiment 1, 1985: bicarb. beats mildew. *Newsletter* 99:13. (Available from: Henry Doubleday Research Association, Ryton-on-Dunsmore, Coventry, CV8 3LG England.)

Anecdotal report of an experiment using baking soda to thwart mildew.

Perera, R.G., and B.E.J. Wheeler. 1975. Effect of water droplets on the development of *Sphaerotheca pannosa* on rose leaves. *Transcriptions of the British Mycological Society* 64(2): 313-319.

This paper discusses how water sprays can be used to drown spores of powdery mildew on rose plants.

Sztejnberg, A. 1979. Biological control of powdery mildews by *Ampelomyces quisqualis. Phytopathology* 69(9):10-47.

This study demonstrates the potential for using beneficial fungi to control powdery mildew.

Wheeler, B.E.J. 1973. Research on rose powdery mildew at Imperial College. *Journal of the Royal Horticultural Society* 98:225-230.

This paper contains excellent advice on cultural methods for preventing or controlling powdery mildew.

Yarwood, C.E. 1939. Control of powdery mildew with a water spray. *Phytopathology* 29:288-290.

This wonderful paper documents Yarwood's personal experience using water sprays to prevent powdery mildew outbreaks on roses.

Ziv, O., and H. Hagiladi. 1984. Control of powdery mildew on hydrangea and crape myrtle with antitranspirants. *HortScience* 19(5):708-709.

This paper documents the effectiveness of antitranspirants in preventing powdery mildew outbreaks. This technique has been used successfully on the lilacs at Longwood.

Snails and Slugs

Cole, H.N. 1984. Settling the score with snails *Helix aspersa, Rumina decollata. Organic Gardening* 31(3):86-90.

Includes suggestions for using barriers and other nontoxic control techniques.

Fisher, T.W., I. Moore, E.F. Legne and R.E. Orth. 1976. *Ocypus olens:* a predator of the brown garden snail *(Helix aspersa),* biological control. *California Agriculture* 30(3):20-21.

Describes the origin and effectiveness of this rove beetle against the garden snail.

Fisher, T.W., and R.E. Orth. 1975. Differential susceptibility of the brown garden snail, *Helix aspersa,* to metaldehyde. *California Agriculture* 29(6):7-8.

This paper reports that there are indications of snail resistance to metaldehyde.

Fisher, T.W., and S.C. Swanson. 1980. Snail *(Rumina decollata)* against snail *(Helix aspersa),* biological control. *California Agriculture* 34(11/12): 18-20.

Describes the effective control of the brown garden snail by the predatory snail.

Fisher, T.W., and S.C. Swanson. 1982. *Snail against snail: Rumina decollata against the vegetable garden pest Helix aspera, biological control in California.* Van Nuys, Calif.: Sunkist Growers. 2 pp.

Further evaluations of the use of the predatory snail in citrus groves in California.

Godan, D. 1983. *Pest slugs and snails.* New York: Springer-Verlag. 445 pp.

An authoritative volume on the biology and control of pest gastropods.

Orth, R.E., I. Moore and T.W. Fisher. 1975. A rove beetle, *Ocypus olens*, with potential for biological control of the brown garden snail, *Helix aspersa*, in California, including a key to the Nearctic species of *Ocypus*. *Canadian Entomology* 107(10): 1111-1116.

This publication contains information that is useful for identifying the different rove beetles.

Orth, R.E., I. Moore and T.W. Fisher. 1975. Biological notes on *Ocypus olens*, a predator of the brown garden snail *Helix aspersa*, with descriptions of the larva and pupa (Coleoptera: Staphylinidae) citrus pest. *Psyche* 82(3/4):292-298.

A discussion of the biology of *Ocypus olens*, an introduced predator.

Picart, F. 1978. *Escargots from your garden to your table: how to control, raise, and process common garden snails.* Santa Rosa, Calif.: F. Picart. (Available from: F. Picart, c/o Snails, 1550 Ridley Ave., Santa Rosa, CA 95401.)

This short book has numerous recipes and drawings as well as good information about snail management and rearing.

Symphylans

Edwards, C.A. 1958. Ecology of symphyla, Pt. I: populations. *Entomologia Experimental and Applied* 1:308-319.

This article suggests that symphylans are found in grasslands, forest litter, cultivated soils, and greenhouse soils. Up to 88 million per acre were found, with the greatest number seen in greenhouse soil.

Edwards, C.A. 1959. A revision of the British symphyla. *Proceedings of the Zoological Society of London,* 132: 403-439.

This taxonomic revision summarizes previous biological information on the order Symphyla and its two families. Keys and illustrations are included.

Edwards, C.A. 1959. Ecology of symphyla, Pt. II: seasonal soil migrations. *Entomologia Experimental and Applied* 2:257-267.

This article details results from greenhouse and field sites on vertical movement within the soil of two symphalans. One, *Scutigerella immaculata,* is an economic pest, the other, *S. vulgaris,* is believed to subsist on decaying matter and soil microorganisms. Even under adverse soil conditions, growing plants attracted *S. immaculata* to the surface.

Edwards, C.A. 1961. Ecology of symphyla, Pt. III: factors controlling soil distribution. *Entomologia Experimental and Applied* 4:239-256.

As well as summarizing previous work, this paper shows that symphylans migrate in response to soil moisture and cannot survive when the relative humidity is less than 100%. The most favorable conditions are soil temperatures in the range of 59°F to 70°F (15°C to 21°C) and a relative humidity in the soil of 100%, with growing plants at the soil surface.

Harpenden Laboratory. 1981. *Symphylids.* Northumberland, England: Ministry of Agriculture, MAFF Harpenden Laboratory Entomology Department (Leaflet 484). 6 pp.

This bulletin contains hard-to-find information on cultural management of symphylans.

Michelbacher, G.E. 1938. The biology of the garden centipede *Scutigerella immaculata* Newport. *Hilgardia.* 11:55-148.

An extensive work on the biology, ecology and control of *S. immaculata* under California conditions.

Rude, P.A. 1982. *Integrated pest management for tomatoes.* Berkeley: University of California Agricultural Sciences Publications (Publication 3274). 104 pp.

This booklet is the source of the recommendation to rotate symphylan-susceptible tomatoes with a crop of sorghum to reduce symphylan numbers.

Swenson, K.G. 1966. Infection of the garden symphylan, *Scutigerella immaculata,* with the DD-136 nematode. *Journal of Invertebrate Pathology* 8:133.

This study reports that *Steinernema feltia (=Neoaplectana) carpocapsae* DD-136) is capable of infesting the garden symphylan *(Scutigerella immaculata)* in the laboratory.

Whiteflies

Mound, L.A., and S.H. Halsey. 1978. *Whiteflies of the world: a systematic catalogue of the Aleyrodidae (Homoptera) with host plant and natural enemy data.* New York: John Wiley. 340pp.

This book lists the 1,156 Aleyrodid species in the world, and describes their taxonomy, geographical distribution, host plants and natural enemies. The introduction has a short overview of whitefly biology.

PART 9

Pests of the Community

CHAPTER 32
Pests of Shade Trees

OVERVIEW OF PART 9

Although certain pests may be fought valiantly by individual households, they are really community-wide problems that will be solved only when the community works together. The subject of community organization is too big to address here; instead, in Part 9 we discuss some of the more important community pests from the standpoint of what you can do around your own home. At the same time, we mention community-wide approaches appropriate for these problems, and we direct you to some excellent publications that can help you organize community-wide pest management efforts.

The pests discussed in Part 9 are shade-tree pests, rats, flies, yellowjackets and mosquitoes. All but the first of these pose serious public health problems for the communities in which they occur. Controlling rats, flies and yellowjackets involves the management of community and individual residential garbage; controlling mosquitoes requires management of water.

In many areas, the management of garbage and water are highly political issues. Garbage is a particularly serious problem in older cities where "sanitary" landfills are full or filling quickly. Water rights and management are powerful issues in the West and Southwest, where water is scarce. Water and garbage management programs often receive large amounts of public funding; where civic corruption exists, inevitably the quality of the management of the pests associated with these resources suffers.

Even at its best, traditional civic management of pest problems tends to be just that—traditional. Civil servants may be hard-working and conscientious, but they can rarely afford to be innovators. If you also consider the layers of state and federal programs aimed at controlling public health pests, you begin to understand why bureaucratic machinery is often cumbersome, insensitive to the needs of individual citizens and behind the

times in the technology it uses. The results are frequently confrontations, lawsuits and other disruptive community hassles in which both the citizen and good pest management often lose.

Shade-tree pests illustrate the range and kinds of problems that can arise in such situations. Insofar as these pests infest street trees as well as trees in individual back yards, they are community-wide. The problem is often the result of the sheer number of trees of the same species planted in a neighborhood, as well as the species of trees selected. This selection and mix is often dictated or recommended by municipal authorities. It becomes clear, then, that the severity of shade-tree problems in today's cities and suburbs is often a direct consequence of choices made in past decades. Present-day inhabitants have inherited pest problems associated with trees planted in an era when the price of labor for maintenance was cheaper, and when large quantities of highly toxic pesticides were used without reservation.

Community conflicts caused by the management of the pests described in this part of the book are often very similar, regardless of the particular community or pest species involved. The community-level solutions to these problems are also similar, although the specific tactics will naturally vary with the biological and ecological nature and requirements of the pest.

Essentially, the solutions involve a four-part process in which citizens:
• form ad-hoc groups to tackle what they see as the problem, such as fogging with insecticides for mosquitoes, foliar (leaf) spraying of shade trees and the use of herbicide on turf in public parks;
• educate themselves about less-toxic alternatives;
• identify the administrative units responsible for treatment action (for example, the public works department or the parks and recreation department), as well as points at which

political pressure can be exerted (such as the city council or the mayor's office); and
• devise a plan of action and obtain as much support from the general public as possible.

A number of good publications can assist you in this process. At the head of the list is a pamphlet published by Concern, Inc.: *Pesticides: A Community Action Guide* (see Bumstead et al., 1986, listed under "References and Readings" on pp. 622-624). It introduces the complex issues surrounding chemical pesticides and provides advice on how individuals and communities can take part in determining safe regulation of these materials. In addition to providing data on the problems associated with overuse of pesticides in agricultural, forest and urban areas, it offers detailed information on successful alternatives. This information is of particular value to citizens seeking to change pest management policy in their communities. The pamphlet also lists groups throughout the United States that work on pesticide and related environmental issues. The effectiveness of the organizing techniques spelled out in this pamphlet have become apparent to us as we help citizen groups and individuals provide scientifically based information on safe, cost-effective alternatives to conventional pesticides to local policymakers, agencies, farmers and pest control companies.

There are many examples of the increasing impact that citizens are having in reducing community pesticide use. The 4-J School District in Eugene, Oregon, has hired an integrated pest management coordinator to operate IPM programs for solving weed and other problems on school grounds with a minimum of reliance on herbicides. Citizens on Fisher's Island, New York, have succeeded in eliminating organophosphate insecticides from the community mosquito control program by substituting monitoring and spot treatments with a selective microbial insecticide (BTI) that is toxic only to mosquito larvae.

The State of Rhode Island has implemented legislation that funds IPM programs designed to reduce overall pesticide use, and the State of Massachusetts has hired a full-time biological control coordinator, who is accelerating adoption of biological controls. The city of Arcata, California, has implemented an IPM program for the turf in their city baseball park that has virtually eliminated herbicide use. IPM programs have been implemented at the Epcot Center at Florida's Disney World and at all the parks and facilities operated by the National Park Service.

All these programs reflect the increasing interest in finding less toxic methods for solving community-wide pest problems, and show that this goal is within the reach of local communities. For more information on communities that have developed forward-looking pest management ordinances governing pesticide use, you can write to: Concern, Inc., 1794 Columbia Rd., NW, Washington, DC 20009, or The National Coalition Against the Misuse of Pesticides (NCAMP), 701 E St., SE, Suite 200, Washington, DC 20003.

For a booklet that describes a model IPM policy for a city or school district and offers tips on how to get the policy and programs implemented, write to us at: The Bio-Integral Resource Center, P.O. Box 7414, Berkeley, CA 94707.

INTRODUCTION

Shade trees provide welcome protection from the sun and wind. They also humidify dry air, screen us from undesired sights and sounds and gracefully frame our homes and gardens. Shade trees are often the most significant landscape element in any neighborhood.

From a biological perspective, a shade tree is a world within a world. The birds, squirrels and tree frogs hosted by shade trees enhance the value of the trees to us. Along with these animals come a multitude of less appreciated forms of wildlife. But the microbes, fungi, other parasitic plants such as mistletoe, insects, mites and spiders, together with their more admired, better-recognized companions, the moths and butterflies, are integral and essential parts of the shade-tree community.

In a way, each shade tree mimics in miniature the larger ecosystem of the forest that was its evolutionary home. The vegetarians, or herbivores, include the birds and squirrels that eat berries and nuts, the mites and aphids that suck plant juices, the caterpillars, beetles and flies that eat leaves and the microbes and fungi that decompose the bark and wood itself. The carnivores, which include insect-eating birds, insects, spiders and mites, depend on the herbivores for their sustenance.

Unfortunately, several factors make it difficult for humans to take a calm, philosophical approach to the presence of all this shade-tree wildlife. One is the powerful image projected by the tree care and maintenance industries that a healthy, desirable tree is a sterile one with nary a bug or a blemish. Although a moment's reflection upon the natural forest scene tells us this is sheer nonsense, we may still fall for the misguided notion that complete elimination of these organisms is necessary, whatever the cost.

Then there is the fact that many people are afraid of insects or simply find them nasty—especially if they are overhead—whether they are causing problems or not. Or people fear that the life of the tree is threatened, or that the pests in the tree will spread to other plants in the garden. Finally, people who have lived through sieges of gypsy moths or Dutch elm disease understandably may have become gun-shy over new tree pest problems. Whatever the reason, the war against shade-tree wildlife has turned many a lovely, tree-shaded neighborhood into a battleground, with toxic materials being used as ammunition and, in some cases, citizens and their public officials in opposing camps.

To get a sound perspective of the problem of shade-tree pests, it helps to understand the role they play in the life cycle of the tree. It is also worth examining the natural rise and fall of pest populations and the special situation posed by exotic pest invaders. We examine each of these issues below.

THE RELATIONSHIP BETWEEN STRESS AND SHADE-TREE PESTS

Old trees in naturally wooded areas are decomposed and returned to the soil by certain insects, fungi, microbes and other organisms. In this way the minerals locked up in tree tissues are recycled for use by other plants, an essential natural process in the forest. But the spread of insects and diseases is a response to or symptom of stress or weakness in trees. In a way, this is analogous to our "catching" a cold. Under stress, the same cold-producing pathogens our bodies normally ward off may trigger a full-blown cold, paving the way for more serious secondary infections. Similarly, a tree may be showing signs of stress when it becomes pest infested. Stressed trees may not produce as many pest-repellent or pest-killing compounds in their leaves and other parts. Additionally, they may become more susceptible to wind injury, which can expose inner bark areas and invite pests. And when the pests attack, stressed trees may show a decreased ability to recover.

With this in mind, there are three questions to ask when faced with a serious shade-tree pest problem: Is the tree under stress? Can the stress be alleviated? How can the tree's vigor be restored?

Stress Reduction through Appropriate Species Selection

Stresses to shade trees can be grouped into two broad categories: those resulting from human activities and those caused by natural events. Of all the ways human activities adversely affect shade trees, none is more common or more tragic than the selection of the wrong species or the wrong variety of a particular species. Unfortunately, many landscape architects are more concerned with the appearance of a tree than with its ecological appropriateness to the site. They rarely take responsibility for maintaining the plants they design into a setting.

In addition, it is all too human to surround ourselves with vegetation that evokes childhood environments, status or romance. Thus, in the semi-arid, mild winter climate of many western states, people attempt to re-create the landscapes of well-watered English country estates or the cold-winter birch forests of the Great Lakes region. Conversely, residents of the East and Midwest often try to establish exotic plantings that are neither winter-hardy nor adapted to local soils.

The ideal approach to landscaping your home is to select tree species that are native to the area or to similar ecosystems elsewhere on the planet. Select species that are suited to your site's climate, soils, water-table level, winds and sun exposure. Avoid species that obviously do not do well in your neighborhood. This means looking around to see which trees are the oldest in your area; if you admire something planted locally, ask if it is comparatively maintenance-free. Seek advice from local arboricultural experts and horticultural manuals as to the tree varieties that are the most pest- and disease-resistant in your locale. Most county cooperative extension offices publish lists of trees suited to the area, and the "References and Readings" at the end of this chapter (pp. 622-624) provides

other useful references on appropriate tree selection.

When selecting a tree that is relatively pest-free in your area, consider not only the type of tree—*Acer,* or maple, for example—but also the species—*Acer saccharum,* or sugar maple—as well as the cultivar, which is the horticultural variety of that tree in the case of many commercially available plants. When purchasing trees from a plant nursery, you should ask for a cultivar that is best suited to the type of setting in which you intend to plant it.

Research has shown that the geographical origin of the tree seed affects pest management. Apparently through genetic selection, each species adapts to the climate and soils of its native area. These adaptations may not be visible, but they influence the tree's ability to withstand disease, insect pests, winter chill, summer scorch, different soil depths, varying soil moisture and other conditions. This native quality, or provenance, of the tree is not affected by the location of the nursery where the tree happened to be raised; it depends solely on seed origin.

If you live in a concrete-covered urban area, consider planting "pioneer" tree species. These are fast-growing trees with fairly short lifetimes. In nature, these are the first species to colonize arid, infertile environments, and they include the hawthorns *Crataegus crus-galli* and *C. phaenopyrum,* the tree-of-heaven (*Ailanthus altissima*), honey-locust (*Gleditsia*), cork tree (*Phellodendron*) and many others. Pioneer species can be quite attractive, and they tolerate the hostile planting sites of cities more readily than many popular shade trees grown in more horticulturally benign suburban settings.

There are fads in plants just as there are in fashion and popular music, so you may find it difficult to locate the trees most suited to your area if they are out of vogue. Even local nurseries frequently propagate unsuitable varieties if they are selling. A

classic example of this occurred in California, where the Modesto ash (*Fraxinus velutina* var. Modesto) was planted as a street tree in communities throughout the state long after it had been observed to be severely susceptible to the plant disease anthracnose and heavy infestations of the ash aphid (*Prociphilus fraxinifolii*). The result has been decades of heavy pesticide use in an attempt to control these two pests, which were "designed into" the neighborhoods when the tree species was selected. Ironically, an equally attractive species, the Shamel ash (*Fraxinus uhdei*), is quite resistant to both problems, but it was difficult or impossible to locate it in nurseries when the Modesto ash was first popular.

The lesson is that you must be persistent in your efforts to locate appropriate species. Do not overlook plant sales by local botanical gardens and arboretums, or catalogs from nurseries specializing in plants native to your area. The native plant societies found in many communities often provide lists of such nurseries.

We realize that many of you are looking for less-toxic ways of managing pests of trees already in your care. Nevertheless, if it takes pesticides to keep your current shade tree alive, you should consider whether replacing it with a tree more suited to the site might not be more satisfactory in the long run.

Stress Reduction through Proper Horticultural Care

Next in importance to appropriate species selection is proper care of the tree when it is young and as it grows. There are several horticultural factors you can monitor and control in this effort.

1. Drainage. Good drainage is essential. One common error is to sink a young tree in a hole to make irrigation easier. In fact, the top of the root ball should be elevated 1 in. to 2 in. (2.5 cm to 5 cm) above the soil grade when the tree is first planted to pre-

How Trees Respond to Wounds

Trees do not replace injured tissues as animals do. Instead, they compartmentalize or "wall off" injured tissue. After being wounded (see the drawing below), the tree reacts. Chemical barriers develop around the injured tissue, preventing many decay organisms from gaining a foothold in the damaged area. But some wood-inhabiting microorganisms surmount these barriers and begin to interact with the tree, moving from compartment to compartment. When the walls of the compartments begin to succumb to the invaders, the tops and bottoms of the compartment (Wall 1 in the drawing below) go first, followed by the inner wall (Wall 2) and then the side wall (Wall 3). But most of the time the barrier zone (Wall 4) holds up, confining the invaders to the wood present at the time of wounding. Eventually a ring of new, healthy wood surrounds the decayed area.

Recognition of this response mechanism was the outcome of a decade of research by Dr. Alex Shigo, a USDA forest pathologist. His insights into the response of trees to wounds has necessitated changes in the way trees are pruned and repaired (see text).

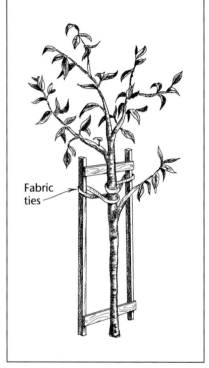

How to Stake a Tree
This method works well for staking young trees. Note that two stakes are used, spaced so they do not touch the trunk. The fabric ties are loose enough not to restrict growth and are arranged to allow the tree to bend in the wind.

Fabric ties

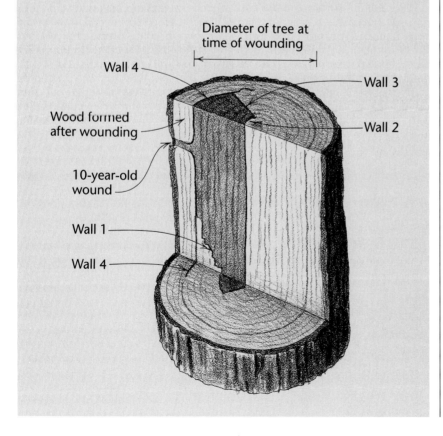

Diameter of tree at time of wounding

Wall 4

Wall 3

Wood formed after wounding

Wall 2

10-year-old wound

Wall 1

Wall 4

vent water from collecting around the base of the trunk as it settles. Otherwise, since there are no feeder roots close to the trunk to absorb the collecting water, the base of the trunk is kept moist and becomes susceptible to penetration by various disease-causing pathogens. Slope the soil away from the trunk in all directions, then place a trench for watering 12 in. (30 cm) or more out from the trunk.

2. Staking. Trees develop the strongest resistance to wood damage if the ties to stakes permit some movement of the young trunk when the wind blows. If the stake that comes with the tree is not replaced at planting time with a different staking system, the plant will tend to rub against the stake and sustain bark injuries. These injuries invite beetle damage or attack by microorganisms. The drawing above illustrates the proper staking of a tree.

3. Pruning. Improper pruning is also a major cause of tree decay and can trigger insect attack. The pioneering work of Dr. Alex Shigo, retired plant pathologist for the U.S. Forest Service, has demonstrated that trees have effective systems for defending themselves against disease organisms that enter the trunk through dead, dying or improperly pruned branches. His basic theory is presented in the sidebar on the facing page.

The front line of the tree's defense system is located in a swollen collar of wood located at the point where the branch grows out of its supporting limb or trunk (see the drawing at right). When a tree is wounded, tissues in this collar form the chemical barriers that wall off decay organisms. Not only does the collar tissue enable most trees to contain the decay organisms rapidly, it also appears to speed up the external closure of the wound by stimulating the cambium tissue into forming new bark and sapwood.

Thus, when tree branches are pruned off flush against the supporting trunk or limb, the branch collar is removed and the tree is less effective in implementing its defense system against the microorganisms that inevitably colonize the cut surface. Although compartmentalization does eventually occur in the absence of the collar, it is much slower and the extent of decay is greater. Delay in compartmentalization also occurs when a branch is not pruned close enough to the collar and a stub is left to die back.

Whenever sewer lines are dug, driveways renewed or house foundations built or repaired, the roots of nearby shade trees may be damaged severely. The tree needs its roots not only for anchorage but also to draw in the water it requires. This water is

---

The Shigo Pruning Technique
To minimize access of decay organisms to pruning wounds in trees, cut living and dying branches as close as possible to the branch collar, as indicated by line A-B. Do not leave stubs, and do not paint the cuts.

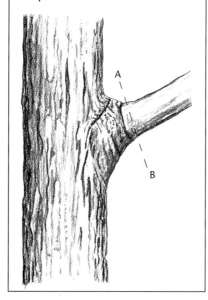

---

transpired largely through the leaves. If the roots are injured, the only way you can offset the fact that more water is being lost through the leaves than is being taken in through the roots is by promptly reducing the leaf area through pruning.

4. Soil Aeration. Tree roots need small empty spaces in the soil into which they can release carbon dioxide and from which they can obtain oxygen. Thus, a mulch of organic material should be placed over the soil to prevent compaction where human traffic passes beneath the drip line of the tree. Aeration in already compacted soils can sometimes be improved with a special probe powered by water pressure from a garden hose. Commercial tree care and landscape maintenance firms and suppliers have these tools; they are also available in some good hardware stores.

5. Weed Control. The application of herbicides to lawns and ground covers often harms nearby trees. Herbicides volatilize (vaporize) in warm temperatures and rise to damage the tree's leaves. Most herbicides are also water-soluble, and can move to lower levels of the soil where spreading tree roots, often located as far as 30 ft. (9 m) from the tree, absorb them.

New organic mulch "weed mats" can replace herbicides for weed control in ground covers under or around shade trees. Weeds can also be controlled through proper lawn care, including periodic soil aeration, proper mowing height and frequency, the use of grass species suited to the site, deep and infrequent irrigations and the use of slow-release fertilizers (see the discussion in Chapter 30 on lawn management).

6. Fertilizer. The overuse of nitrogen fertilizer can encourage the growth of aphid and scale populations. A slow-release fertilizer should be used, if one is needed at all. If you want to plant a ground cover beneath a tree, bear in mind that in natural areas a slowly decomposing mulch of leaves and other organic debris provides the fertilizer the tree needs. The requirements of any plants grown beneath the tree should not interfere with the needs of the tree itself.

7. Protection against Road Salt. Another serious stress results from the application of salt to icy roads in winter, which then burns nearby trees during spring thaws. The sidebar on p. 614 addresses this problem.

8. Protection against Natural Stresses. Stresses from natural causes also can reduce tree vigor. Most important among these are spells of unusual cold, periods of extreme dryness and heat, and successive years of attack by exotic (non-native) insects. Young trees can be wrapped to protect them against cold, and any tree benefits from periodic deep irrigation in unusually dry years. Whitewashing the bark of young trees helps prevent sunburn, which also invites insects and disease.

Protecting Your Plantings from Road Salt

In an excellent short article in the December, 1989, issue of *Horticulture,* Ellen M. Silva suggests these practical steps if you feel your trees and shrubs may be suffering from salt burn:

• Take a soil sample to your county extension service and request a soluble salt test. Silva notes that in sandy soil, salt levels greater than 1,000 parts per million indicate potential trouble. The clay, silt or humus portion of the soil has a higher water-holding capacity than the sand fraction. The presence of these non-sand components helps dilute high concentrations of salt. A pH of 7.5 or more may indicate a sodium overload.

• Find out whether local road maintenance crews can do anything to direct salty runoff away from your property.

• Leach the salt from the affected area in early spring. Apply 2 in. (5 cm) of water over a period of two to three hours. Wait three days, then repeat the procedure.

• Where salt spray from passing traffic is the problem, wash the affected leaves and branches with a large volume of water whenever the spray is heavy and again in early spring.

• When shoveling walks or driveways around your home, avoid piling up snow or ice that may contain salt where the melting water can run into the root zones of trees and shrubs. Leave this salt-containing material where the runoff can enter curbside ditches or rainwater catchments.

• Use sand or sawdust instead of salt to improve traction on your driveway and walks. Perhaps you can convince your local community to switch to one of these materials. Non-saline rock dust is popular in Europe for this purpose, but no similar product is as yet commonly available in the United States.

• Incorporate large quantities of organic material into salt-damaged soil to improve its texture and water-holding ability, counteracting the effects of the salt.

• Select salt-tolerant species for roadside plantings. Silva recommends honeylocust, juniper, Norway maple, roses, scotch pine and red or white oak; she suggests avoiding such salt-sensitive plants as black walnut, red or sugar maple and red or white pine.

• Build a low wall or grow a hedge of salt-tolerant evergreens along the road to deflect salt spray away from sensitive plantings.

UNDERSTANDING NATURAL CYCLES OF PEST ABUNDANCE

Even the most vigorous of shade trees experience fluctuating levels of insect pest abundance. These cycles occur during the season and from year to year. Each season there is a lag between the appearance and growth of the herbivorous (plant-feeding) pest population and the arrival and suppressive actions of these pests' natural enemies.

Even more dramatic, however, are the large yearly differences in the size of the pest population. Year-to-year changes in the weather and in the abundance of predators, parasitoids and pathogens that feed upon the pests play a significant role in these population changes. Periods of extreme winter cold or a very rainy or dry spring, for example, may cause high mortality among the overwintering forms of the pest. Or, even with small yearly differences in the weather pattern, the pest may increase in abundance for two or more years, then suffer a population crash, usually from an outbreak of a disease. After the crash, sparse pest populations for a year or two swiftly starve the natural enemies that rely on the pest for food. The lack of natural enemies enables the pest gradually to build up its population again, and the cycle repeats.

Such pendulum-like swings in the size of animal populations are common in the natural world. (We humans, with our world population doubling in ever-shorter intervals, are the only animal to have temporarily escaped this natural cycling.) These observations of natural cycles translate into several practical suggestions:
• Avoid preventive sprays, because it may be a year in which the pest population never becomes large enough to be a problem even if left untreated. Don't treat ahead of time because a certain problem occurred last year. In the case of gypsy moth infestations, treating high populations may actually prolong the outbreak (see the discussion on pp. 617-618).

• When the pest makes its appearance, don't panic. A small pest population does not constitute a crisis. If you cannot admire wildlife, at least tolerate a few insects—the birds will have something to feed their young, and the beneficial insects and spiders will have a chance to build up their numbers.

• Learn to recognize the natural enemies of pests, because you need to know when they are present and when their numbers are about to catch up with the pest population. Also, it is important not to mistake them for the pest organisms.

• When the pest population appears to be reaching levels you find intolerable, select methods of suppression that are the least harmful to the pest's natural enemies. Where possible, mimic nature, and use physical and biological controls first. Examples are pruning out the pest, crushing egg masses, using water washes and applying microbial insecticides. These and other techniques are discussed briefly below under the various categories of pests for which they are applicable. Use other insecticides as a last resort. By reducing the use of insecticides, you delay the development of insect populations that are resistant to them, and more natural enemies of the pest will survive to help suppress the pest population in future years. See the discussion of pest resistance on pp. 95-96.

• If toxic materials must be used, spot-treat; that is, confine treatment to just those areas where the pest problem is intolerable. For example, applying pesticide in a band around the trunk of an elm tree for the control of elm leaf beetle instead of spraying the foliage of the entire tree canopy is one way to confine pesticides to a specific location. Treating only those trees that are about to experience intolerable damage rather than spraying all the trees in an area is another example.

• Where you are dealing with a large number of trees of the same species, as on a city block or a large estate, initiate a monitoring system to keep track of the pest population over the season. It helps to design a monitoring sheet that contains such information as date, location of specimen, type of tree, number and type of pests per leaf and notes on treatments. Make photocopies of the blank form so you can use it repeatedly. You will probably find great differences between individual trees of the same species in natural resistance to pest attack. Only certain trees are likely to be so severely affected that treatment is warranted.

• Encourage city landscape planners to select a diversity of tree species for each neighborhood. This diversification reduces the likelihood of large numbers of trees simultaneously suffering high pest populations, and it reduces the amount of pesticide exposure in each neighborhood from street tree treatments.

ACCIDENTALLY INTRODUCED SHADE-TREE PESTS

The most notorious pests of shade trees in the United States are those that were introduced accidentally from other geographic areas, leaving their natural enemies behind. Freed from the restraints provided by complexes of predators, parasitoids and pathogens in their homelands and finding defenseless plant populations in the new environment, these exotic pests increased relatively unchecked.

The best-known examples of exotic shade-tree pests are the pathogens that cause Dutch elm disease and chestnut blight, as well as the gypsy moth, the elm leaf beetle and the Japanese beetle. There are many others, including the mimosa webworm, the smaller elm bark beetle (which carries the fungal pathogen that causes Dutch elm disease) and the European elm scale.

Although most people are aware of the large-scale disasters caused by these imported pests, it is still commonplace to find people attempting to circumvent the strict quarantine laws that regulate the movement of plant materials into the United States. A similar quarantine exists for the importation of plants into California, which is an "ecological island" separated by desert and mountains from neighboring states. The monthly reports from the agricultural inspection stations along California's borders with Oregon, Nevada and Arizona, provide insight into the unfortunate human affinity for smuggling, whether motivated by greed or by the excitement of taking a risk.

The breeding of genetically resistant plant materials has been the first line of defense against exotic plant diseases. But breeding is slow and uncertain, as those who have been following the progress of efforts to find resistant elms and chestnuts are well aware. More recently, direct assaults have been made against plant pathogens using other microbes that appear to be antagonists or competitors of the disease-causing organism. As the field of microbial controls develops, we can expect this technology to be applied to an increasing number of tree pathogens, including some of the exotic ones.

Biological Controls for Accidentally Introduced Insects

The most important, cost-effective and under-funded effort for suppressing exotic insects is the search for natural enemies of the pest in the area in which the pests originated. Projects in this kind of classical biological control of shade-tree pests are what gave us our first taste of pest management. In fact, all of our subsequent work in IPM began with the realization in the early 1970s that these imported biological controls of shade-tree pests could not succeed unless they were part of a larger, more systematic and environmentally sensitive approach to horticultural pest control. We describe one of these biological control projects briefly on p. 53.

Since the time when we were focusing exclusively on biological controls for urban shade-tree pests, there has been further work by others on finding natural enemies of the elm leaf beetle. An extensive effort to find natural controls for the gypsy moth *(Lymantria dispar)* has been ongoing since 1906; however, these efforts have not been spectacularly successful. For more information on the research of gypsy moth enemies, consult the "References and Readings" on pp. 622-624.

Pests of agricultural trees, including citrus, walnuts and olives, as well as pests of forest trees have commanded more biological control research dollars than urban shade trees (with some exceptions, since many forest trees are also common in cities). One notable example is the introduction of a parasitoid for the control of the winter moth *(Operophtera brumata)*, an accidentally introduced caterpillar pest of oaks, maples, fruit trees and other deciduous trees. It has been very successful on the east and west coasts of Canada.

Predators and parasitoids have a role to play in the biological control of certain native shade-tree pests, too. Recently the Canadians have been releasing a small wasp in the genus *Trichogramma* that parasitizes the eggs of the eastern spruce budworm *(Choristoneura fumiferana)*, which is a native caterpillar. Since the wasps do not overwinter in the Canadian release sites, they are reared in large numbers and put out each year as a biological insecticide. The Chinese also have many examples of rearing or collecting natural enemies such as parasitoids, spiders and nematodes and releasing them against tree pests (see the chapter references for more on this subject).

Perhaps future work on the biological control of shade-tree pests will follow along these lines. However, even as a private citizen you can protect the natural enemies of insect pests already on your trees, as well as additional pests that may be im-

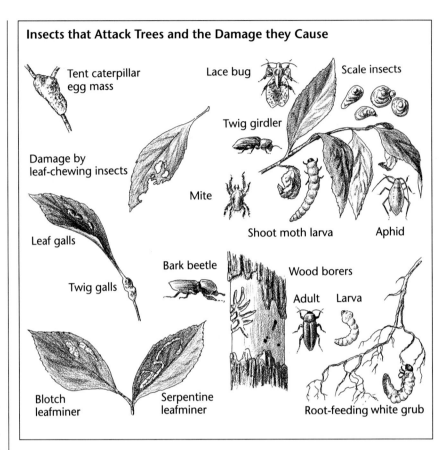

Insects that Attack Trees and the Damage they Cause

Tent caterpillar egg mass

Lace bug

Scale insects

Twig girdler

Damage by leaf-chewing insects

Mite

Shoot moth larva

Aphid

Leaf galls

Twig galls

Bark beetle

Wood borers

Adult Larva

Blotch leafminer

Serpentine leafminer

Root-feeding white grub

ported, by following conservation policies, and particularly by reducing or eliminating toxic and non-specific insecticides in your garden and neighborhood.

THE MOST SERIOUS SHADE-TREE PESTS

The following discussion of organisms that cause disease in trees focuses on arthropods rather than on pathogens. This is because the best management for tree pathogens is horticultural and involves proper species selection, watering practices and pruning techniques. By contrast, special techniques must be used in controlling arthropod pests. The exceptions are the non-native pathogens such as Dutch elm disease and chestnut blight. Finding a resistant variety of tree—one that has survived

the attack of the pathogen—and the selection and propagation of antagonist microorganisms both offer hope for restoring the American elm and the chestnut to urban landscapes. Anyone who is observant may come across resistant trees. In contrast, the selection and propagation of antagonist organisms is not a technique that is easily pursued by the average tree-lover, so we will not discuss it in this book.

An enormous number of species of plant-feeding insects and mites exist in shade trees (see the drawing above). Most are of no consequence in terms of their damage and visibility, and most of the rest cause only minor annoyance as a result of human fear or slight visible changes in tree foliage. Of those that have the potential to become pestiferous, most problems occur in response to improper species selection or tree management, environmental stress or human activities such as treatment of one pest with compounds that kill the natural enemies of another. These problems can be corrected thorough the horticultural and ecological practices suggested above.

However, there are a few pests that pose a serious danger to shade trees. These are often exotic insects or plant pathogens. Very little can be done to control them, even with the use of toxic materials. However, some are good candidates for classical biological control projects (as discussed on pp. 49-54).

Because shade-tree pest management is a field in which we have so many years of personal experience, we have accumulated a huge data base on the least-toxic management of specific shade-tree pests. It is now being computerized. If you have a deeper interest in this field, you can contact us at the Bio-Integral Resource Center.

Sapsuckers

The three categories of sapsucking arthropods are mites, aphids and scales. Management strategies for all three are discussed below.

Mites. In trees, mites are usually a secondary pest triggered by pesticide use against other pests or by dust from unpaved roads, which kills the mites' predators. They may also be a symptom of a lack of water due to inadequate rain, insufficient irrigation or plant pathogens that infect the tree's water-conducting tissues. In other words, a mite-infested tree can be presumed to be under some kind of stress if prior pesticide use is not involved.

For management of mites, switch to the selective microbial insecticides used in caterpillar control (see below). Increase irrigation, and try washing the tree periodically with water. It may gradually restore the balance between predatory and pest mites. Insecticidal soap may be helpful in emergencies. Use a hose-attached sprayer to get adequate water pressure for washing a medium-sized tree. A truly large specimen may require washing by professionals with special equipment. If washing with plain water or the insecticidal soap does not help, identify the mite or have it identified for you and ask the insectaries listed in the Resource Appendix under "Insect Management: Biological Controls" on pp. 683-686 about commercially available mite predators. Select tree species that are resistant to local soil-borne pathogens such as oak root fungus, armillaria and verticillium wilt.

Aphids. Aphids may be a symptom of excess nitrogen fertilizer, perhaps due to the use of lawn food. They can also be attracted to the succulent sucker growth that results from overly drastic pruning. The pesticides used against other pests can kill aphid predators and parasitoids, or there can be a temporary rise in aphid numbers in spring before the natural enemies catch up, a phenomenon called predator-prey lag. Sometimes the damage is primarily visual, such as black sooty mold growing on honeydew produced by the aphids or honeydew falling on parked cars and sidewalks. (Aphid infestation of indoor plants is discussed on pp. 367-375.)

To manage aphids, try to control the ants that protect aphids by ringing the tree trunk with a nontoxic sticky band (see the Resource Appendix under "Insect Management: Physical Controls" on pp. 682-683). Apply the band early in spring before the rise in ant activity. If ants are already in the canopy, use soap and water to wash as many ants as possible out of the tree before banding. Switch to slower-release fertilizers beneath the tree, and prune out the inner canopy if it is severely infested. Use water washes, horticultural oils or insecticidal soap to clean off aphids and honeydew.

Scales. Scales can be triggered by pesticides used against other pests (for example, fogging for mosquitoes), by excess nitrogen or by environmental stresses, such as too much or too little water.

Prune out severely infested limbs and switch to compounds that do not kill parasitoids. Since parasitoids are usually small wasps, select pesticides whose label shows no adverse effects on Hymenoptera such as honeybees. Control ants if they are protecting the scales (see aphids, above). Use dormant oils (see p. 117) during winter and/or insecticidal soap washes (see pgs. 114-116 and 378) when scale crawlers (the young stages) are moving over the bark. Horticultural oils (see pp. 116-119) are also effective against scales.

Leaf Chewers

Leafchewing insects include caterpillars and beetles.

Caterpillars. Most pestiferous larvae of moths and butterflies can be controlled with the selective microbial insecticide *Bacillus thuringiensis*, or BT (see pp. 132-136). Our recommendation for the control of the gypsy moth, however, is not to use any treatment at all. This approach maximizes the natural enemy population, which shortens the pest outbreak and lengthens the period between outbreaks. We recognize that this approach may cause changes in the composition of the forest, but in the long run it may be the most resource-conserving approach since repeated treatments will not be needed.

If you feel treatment is necessary on special trees or groups of trees surrounding homes or other areas, there are several things you can do. Where cocoons or egg masses are accessible on trunks or lower limbs, simply rub them off. Shake off larvae and sweep them up, then kill them by putting them in a sealed plastic bag in the sun. Use BT on the foliage during periods when larvae are feeding.

If you only need to protect a small number of trees from gypsy moth caterpillars, you may want to use special barriers that trap or exclude the pests from the foliage (see the draw-

Burlap Bands for Control of Gypsy Moth Larvae

Burlap bands wrapped around tree trunks trap gypsy moth larvae as they crawl down at night. The distinctive, hairy gypsy moth caterpillars collect under the bands and must be scraped off daily. They can then be stepped on or dropped into a pail of soapy water.

ing above). Using barriers is less expensive than having your trees sprayed with BT and other nontoxic materials recommended for large tree stands. However, maintaining barriers requires time and attention once they are in place.

An excellent pamphlet by K. Boyd (listed under "References and Readings" on pp. 622-624) describes exactly how to apply and maintain sticky barriers and burlap bands (both discussed below).

The sticky barriers deny access to the tree to the many caterpillars that drop out of the tree or crawl in from neighboring trees. Since sticky materials may injure the bark of some trees, it is prudent to use duct tape between the bark and the sticky band. Circle the trunk with the tape, then place the sticky material on the tape. Check periodically (every week or two) to make sure that squirrels

and other animals have not pulled the tape away from the bark or that dirt, other debris or silken strands deposited by the caterpillars have not adhered to the band so thickly that caterpillars are using them as a bridge across the barrier.

The burlap band provides an excellent trap for large caterpillars that crawl down from the tree to rest or pupate. Adult moths will also be attracted to the burlap as a protected place in which to lay eggs. Daily cleaning of this band is necessary if it is to remain effective.

The use of cloth bands to protect trees from caterpillar pests that seek such sheltered places to pupate or overwinter is a well-known strategy and was once widely used in this country. In a recent paper, Li Lianchang, a Chinese expert on pest control in fruit trees, commented that the Chinese have found the larvae that collect beneath such barriers to be heavily infested with a species of *Beauveria,* a fungal disease of insects. *Beauveria* is produced commercially in mainland China and is used to control a number of pests of agricultural, urban and forest trees. The Chinese are now studying ways to impregnate the bands with the fungus so that caterpillars pupating in the bands or laying eggs there become diseased and die.

If you decide that a pesticide must be used, we recommend neem or BT, the least-toxic products that are effective against caterpillars. An extract from the neem tree is marketed in the United States as Margosan-O® (see pp. 122-123) and is registered for the control of gypsy moths; it is listed in the Resource Appendix under "Insect Management: Chemical Controls" on pp. 686-687. Follow the directions on the label. Prune out tents of fall webworm or similar tent-making caterpillars when possible. Pyrethrin insecticides, although more costly than commonly used organophosphates and carbamates, are also safer for humans and degrade quickly (see pp. 121-122).

Elm Leaf Beetles

Elm leaf beetle larvae (A) scrape the tissue from the surface of leaves, whereas the adults (B) chew holes through the entire leaf. A 24-in. (60 cm) wide band of insecticide sprayed high up on the trunk kills migrating larvae, which must cross the band on their way down to the soil to pupate. (Actual size of adult: ¼ in./6 mm)

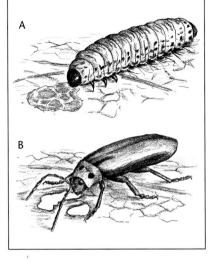

Beetles. The elm leaf beetle *(Pyrrhalta luteola)* travels down the trunk to pupate once during each generation. You can reduce pesticide use against this beetle by placing a 24-in. (60 cm) wide band of insecticide around a portion of the trunk high above the heads of passersby. This technique requires community-wide participation to be effective, and you can request that your local street tree department or professional arborists use it. Details on our experience in developing and evaluating this method are described in the *IPM Practitioner* (see Olkowski et al., 1986, listed under "References and Readings" on pp. 622-624).

Use traps and milky spore disease on turf areas to control the Japanese beetle (see pp. 537-538 for details). Neem (Margosan-O®) is also effective as a repellent against this beetle.

Table 32.1

Summary of the Shade-Tree System for the Urban Biological Control Project, University of California, Berkeley, at Completion of 1976 Season

City Name	Years in Program	City Population [a]	Tree Population	Trees Treated before IPM Initiated	1976 BT[b] Treatments	1976 Total Insecticide Treatment	% Reduction in Treatment Due to IPM Program[c]
Berkeley	6	107,500	35,000	11,500	32	35	99.7
San Jose	3	557,700	250,000	2,000	4,307	4,310	90.0
Palo Alto	2	54,900	80,000	1,600	369	375	77.0
Modesto	1	85,000	85,000	8,000	8	4,600[d]	91.0
Davis	1	32,800	12,000	10,000	0	817[e]	92.0
Totals		837,900	462,000	73,100	4,716	10,137[f]	89.3 (average)

[a] Census, January, 1976.

[b] *Bacillus thuringiensis.*

[c] Calculated by dividing total 1976 treatments by number of trees treated before the IPM program was initiated and subtracting from 100%.

[d] A total of 4,490 of these treatments occurred prior to the initiation of the IPM program. Only 350 trees were treated (twice) during the IPM program. These are estimates, since no records were kept prior to the IPM program.

[e] All these treatments, except 12, were carried out prior to the introduction of the IPM program.

[f] Only *Bacillus thuringiensis,* water-washing and pyrethrin treatments were used.

Bark Beetles and Trunk Borers

Bark beetles and trunk borers are the insects most closely associated with stressed trees. Extensive tunneling and/or holes can overwhelm a tree's defenses and kill it directly. Beetles and borers can also carry pathogens —Dutch elm disease, for example— that can kill trees.

Build tree vigor and reduce stress through the horticultural and ecological practices suggested earlier. Protect young bark from sunburn with whitewash. Prune and repair limb injuries by cutting back just to the outer edge of the shoulder ring of the limb (see p. 613). Provide deep irrigation during droughts. Arrange trees appropriately (for example, aspen, birch or eucalyptus should be grown in clusters and dogwoods should be grown as an understory to mimic their respective native forest conditions).

Sanitation is also very important in managing bark beetles and trunk

borers. If nearby trees are stressed and heavily infested, remove the infested limbs or dead or dying trees quickly. De-bark them (in case of bark beetles), and burn the debris. A solution of insect-eating nematodes can be injected into borer holes (for sources, see the Resource Appendix under "Insect Management: Biological Controls" on pp. 683-686). These nematodes are nontoxic to humans and do not feed on plants. Certain pine oil compounds have been found effective in repelling bark beetles and are being studied further for this use. Commercial products may show up in the marketplace soon.

IMPLEMENTING THE IPM CONCEPT FOR URBAN SHADE TREES

IPM is an ideal approach to tree pest management. You can apply it in your own back yard, professional arborists can use it in their work

and the city tree-maintenance department can make it standard operating procedure.

The great diversity of shade-tree species planted in most urban areas and the number of potential pest species in any one area precludes the quick development of integrated pest management programs for each species. What is needed is a template or model such as the flow diagram shown on pp. 620-621 for developing pest management programs for each problem. This device helps sort through pest problems very quickly. Over the years we have used it to develop many IPM programs for diverse and complex ecosystems across the United States. Table 32.1 above presents data on some of the shade tree systems for which we developed IPM programs, and shows how effective such programs can be.

The shapes in the flow diagram represent various processes. Diamonds pose questions, rectangles

An Ecosystem Management Model for Insects on Street Trees

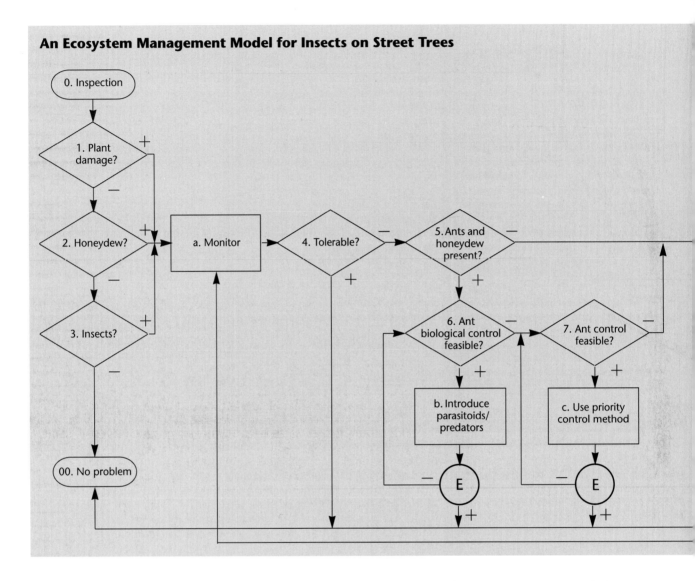

specify procedures, circles represent evaluation steps and arrows show the path of analysis. The path you take is determined by your answers to the questions. A plus sign means "yes," a minus sign, "no." To use the diagram, start at the top at "Inspection" and follow the arrows, answering the questions in the diamonds until you reach an appropriate solution.

To save space, we have used abbreviated notations on the diagram itself; once you become familiar with the process, these may be enough to guide you. Until then, refer to the more

complete descriptions given below; the numbers and letters correspond to those numbers on the diagram. (Note that the following is written for a professional pest manager who makes decisions after collecting information from a specific pest site.)

0. Inspection of the plant. This is the start of the analysis.
1. Is damage present? If so, go to "a" and begin monitoring; if not, go to 2.
2. Is honeydew being produced? If so, go to "a" and begin monitoring; if not, go to 3.

3. Are insects present? If so, go to "a" and begin monitoring; if not, go to 00.
a. Begin monitoring. Make observations, quantify them in some way, write them down and evaluate them. Then go to 4.
4. Is the plant damage, honeydew problem or insect presence tolerable? If so, no decision is required at this point. Make a note to check again in a week. If not, go to 5.
5. Are both ants and honeydew present? Since the Argentine ant

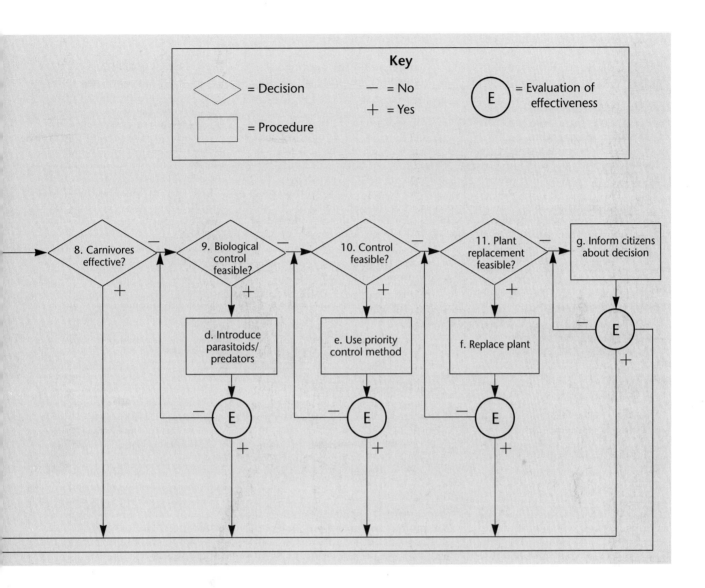

Key

◇ = Decision   — = No   Ⓔ = Evaluation of effectiveness

□ = Procedure   + = Yes

8. Carnivores effective?

9. Biological control feasible?

10. Control feasible?

11. Plant replacement feasible?

g. Inform citizens about decision

d. Introduce parasitoids/predators

e. Use priority control method

f. Replace plant

protects honeydew producers when both are present, go to 6.

6. Is importation of natural enemies of the Argentine ant feasible in your location? Some study of this complex question indicates that although importation of natural enemies is possible, it is probably not a good idea, since the Argentine ant kills the native fire ant, a more severe pest in many people's view. Also, the Argentine ant, although annoying and protective of aphids, scales and other honeydew producers, is also pre-

dacious and aerates the soil. Thus importation of natural enemies is not feasible and there is no need to go to procedure "b"; instead, go to 7.

7. Is ant control feasible? On most shade trees in the San Francisco Bay Area the Argentine ant forages in columns that can be excluded with Tanglefoot™ bands. Other methods of ant control are also possible. If ant control might be feasible, go to "c."

c. The principal control method is placement of a band of Tangle-

foot™ about 8 ft. (2.5 m) above the ground in a 4-in. to 6 in. (10 cm to 15 cm) wide band around the tree trunk.

8. Are carnivores effective? Because ants have been controlled and/or honeydew is present, it is reasonable to ask whether carnivores will now suppress the honeydew producer in a short time, meaning a few days or less, depending on how intolerable the situation is. If carnivores can be effective, go to 00 and wait for them to catch up; if not, go to 9.

9. Can importation of natural enemies be effective? If yes, go to "d"; if no, go to 10. Although the importation of a natural enemy is beyond the capabilities of a non-professional, the process can be initiated and supported by members of the public.

d. Begin the process of foreign exploration for natural enemies, development of rearing systems, etc., and import and establish natural enemies. Then evaluate the effectiveness of the importation. If it is successful, go to 00; if it is not, evaluate the feasibility of another importation (go back to 9).

10. Is control of the pest or honeydew feasible? For example, can high-pressure streams of water be effective in cleaning the leaves of honeydew while carnivores catch up to their prey? Can insecticidal soaps temporarily suppress the honeydew producers and/or the ants? If the answer to either question is yes, implement the control, then go to "E" to evaluate its effectiveness. If this or other controls is against city policy, or is possible but not acceptable to the home owner, or is undesirable for other reasons, then control is really not feasible. Go to 11.

11. Is plant replacement feasible? If this can be accomplished to everyone's satisfaction, the tree should be replaced. Go to "f."

f. Replace the plant and conduct an evaluation. Note that merely removing the plant without replacing it is not considered an option because such a tactic ignores the reason for originally planting and maintaining the tree. If replacement is not possible, go to "g."

g. This is the "do not treat" option. Since neither plant replacement nor other control tactics are feasible, you, the pest manager, must explain why the present problem must be tolerated. This explanation should be made in written form. Evaluating this "do nothing" option includes being sure that all previous steps have been carried out sincerely and vigorously; otherwise the whole process is threatened and the whole IPM may fail. The pest problem should be monitored on an ongoing basis.

00. No further analysis or action is necessary.

REFERENCES AND READINGS

Boyd, K. 1989. *Controlling gypsy moth caterpillars with barrier bands.* University of Maryland Cooperative Extension Service (Fact Sheet 476). 4 pp. (Available from: Room 1214, University of Maryland, College Park, MD 20742.)

An excellent illustrated guide.

Bumstead, C., A. Knaus and A. Jones, eds. 1986. *Pesticides: a community action guide.* Concern, Inc. 23 pp. (Available from: Concern, 1794 Columbia Rd., NW, Washington, D.C. 20009.)

An introduction to the complex issues surrounding chemical pesticides, with advice on the role individuals and communities can play in determining safe use and more effective regulation of these materials.

Davidson, J.A., S.A. Gill and W.T. Johnson. 1989. Foliar and growth effects of repetitive summer horticultural oil sprays on trees and shrubs under drought stress. *Journal of Arboriculture* 16(4):77-81.

This study reveals that the new, highly refined horticultural oils can be sprayed on many tree species while in full leaf and during high temperatures without causing significant damage. Former "dormant" oils were thought to be safe to use only when trees were dormant and without leaves.

Doane, C., and M. McManus, eds. 1981. *The gypsy moth: research toward integrated pest management.* Washington, D.C.: USDA, U.S. Forest Service (Bulletin 1584). 757 pp.

A detailed description of the first 90 years of American efforts to control this introduced pest.

Grossman, J. 1990. Horticultural oils: new summer uses on ornamental plant pests. *The IPM Practitioner* 12(8):1-10.

This article summarizes recent applied research using horticultural oils to kill common caterpillars and other pests on ornamental trees and shrubs. It discusses which oils to use and when to take precautions to prevent damage to the plants.

Harris, R.W. 1983. *Arboriculture: care of trees, shrubs, and vines in the landscape.* Englewood Cliffs, N.J.: Prentice-Hall. 688 pp.

An excellent, basic book on the proper management of trees.

Johnson, W.T., and H.H. Lyon. 1988. *Insects that feed on trees and shrubs, an illustrated practical guide,* 2nd ed. Ithaca, N.Y.: Cornell University Press. 464 pp.

A greatly expanded edition of a highly acclaimed work first published in 1976. Although there are no precise recommendations for management, this reference is a primary starting place place for identification, biological summaries and access to the literature, which is widely scattered and is seldom integrated. The IPM philosophy is advanced by the authors in the introductory section.

Miller, R.W. 1988. *Urban forestry: planning and managing urban greenspaces.* Englewood Cliffs, N.J.: Prentice-Hall. 404 pp.

This book does an excellent job of summarizing the value of trees in urban environments, and provides good models for intelligent tree management. The focus is on the "big picture," including discussions of tree ordinances, managing street tree planting programs, pruning schedules and caring for park and right-of-way vegetation. In our experience of developing IPM programs for municipal trees, the better organized the street tree department, the more likely the success of an IPM program.

(Note: All publications below by William Olkowski et al. are available from the author at BIRC, P.O. Box 7414, Berkeley, CA 94707.)

Olkowski, W. 1973. A model ecosystem management program. *Proceedings of the Tall Timbers Conference on Ecological Animal Control by Habitat Management* 5:103-117.

This paper presents a flow diagram of the components of an IPM program developed for the city of Berkeley, California. It also advances for the first time the concept of an aesthetic injury level.

Olkowski, W. 1989. Update: biological control of aphids: what's really involved. *The IPM Practitioner* 11(4):1-9.

This review article discusses important classic cases of parasitoid importation against aphids and the theory behind it. It summarizes efforts to import natural enemies.

Olkowski, W., and S. Daar. 1986. Biocontrol of winter moth on Vancouver Island. *The IPM Practitioner* 8(3):4-5.

A description of a successful Canadian program against this introduced tree pest.

Olkowski, W., and S. Daar. 1989. Chinese use insect-attacking nematodes against major pests. *The IPM Practitioner* 11(11/12):1-8.

A discussion of the innovative use of beneficial nematodes by the Chinese to control various pests, including an analog of the codling moth, an apple pest in the United States and carpenter worm borers of shade trees.

Olkowski, W., S. Daar, M. Green, D. Anderson and J. Hyde. 1986. Update: new IPM methods for elm leaf beetles. *The IPM Practitioner* 8(5):1-7.

This report summarizes work on the development of an IPM program featuring the use of insecticidal bands applied to tree trunks to reduce elm leaf beetle populations. The work was conducted over eight years in various cities in northern California. Previous work attempting to establish parasitoids against the elm leaf beetle is also summarized.

Olkowski, W., and H. Olkowski. 1975. Establishing an integrated pest control program for street trees. *Journal of Arboriculture* 1:167-172.

The practical aspects of establishing an IPM program with a street tree maintenance department are discussed. Examples are taken from working IPM programs in Berkeley and San Jose, California, which involved 300,000 street trees over 500 sq. mi. containing over half a million people. The discussion also covers the management of the program, including the operation of a foreign exploration component. It contains preliminary results from successful importation projects and comments on biological control.

Olkowski, W., and H. Olkowski. 1976. Entomophobia in the urban ecosystem, some observations and suggestions. *Bulletin of the Entomological Society of America* 22(3):313-317.

A summary from personal observations and published literature of the irrational fear of insects. The article discusses the need for education in IPM and how the educational program should be structured.

Olkowski, W., H. Olkowski and S. Daar. 1984. *Integrated pest management for tent caterpillars: a BIRC technical review.* Berkeley, California: Bio-Integral Resource Center. 20 pp.

This booklet uses an IPM framework to review the literature on tent caterpillars of the United States. It was originally prepared for the National Park Service.

Olkowski, W., H. Olkowski, T. Drylik, M. Minter, R. Zuparko, L. Laub, L. Orthel and N. Heidler. 1978. Pest control strategies: urban integrated pest management. In *Pest control strategies,* eds. E.H. Smith and D. Pimentel, pp. 215-234. New York: Academic Press. 334 pp.

This chapter reviews preliminary surveys on urban pests in California. It covers pesticide use, presents data on the aesthetic injury of street trees and summarizes pest problems faced by an urban biological control project managing street trees in five cities in the San Francisco Bay Area in 1976 and 1977. The need to include biological control importation in an IPM program is also discussed.

Olkowski, W., H. Olkowski, R. van den Bosch and R. Hom. 1976. Ecosystem management: a framework for urban pest control. *Bioscience* 26(6):384-389.

In addition to discussing how an IPM program fits into an ecosystem management framework, this paper summarizes pesticide use changes over a six-year period in Berkeley, California.

Olkowski, W., D. Pinnock, W. Toney, G. Mosher, W. Neasbitt, R van den Bosch and H. Olkowski. 1974. An integrated insect control program for street trees. *California Agriculture* 28(1):3-4.

This paper announced some of the results of a project then running for three years with the Berkeley Recreation and Parks Department that developed an IPM program for 30,000 street trees of 123 species. IPM had not previously been used in urban settings. The city saved about $22,500 a year by shifting from primarily foliar applications of insecticides to a system that stressed biological controls and required monitoring and the establishment of aesthetic injury levels before treatment was undertaken. This was the first IPM program for a city tree system in North America.

Olkowski, H., T. Stewart, W. Olkowski and S. Daar. 1982. Designing and implementing integrated pest management programs for cities. In *Urban and suburban trees: pest probelms, needs, prospects, and solutions,* eds. B.O. Parks, F.A. Fear, M.T. Lambur, and G.A. Simmons, pp. 149-155. Proceedings of a conference held at Michigan State University, Kellog Center for Continuing Education, East Lansing, Michigan, April 18-20, 1982. 253 pp.

A conceptual description of the IPM process, including a discussion of barriers to the adoption of IPM technology. Examples of psychological resistance are provided, with suggestions on how to plan for and overcome this resistance.

Shigo, A. 1986. *A new tree biology: facts, photos, and philosophies on trees and their problems and proper care.* Durham, N.H.: Shigo and Trees, Assoc. 595 pp.

This book is a collection of informative black and white photographs illustrating tree biology and practical management techniques. The corresponding text combines biological insights with inspirational vision. Shigo has devoted a lifetime to understanding how trees fight infections by organisms and damage from physical and human agents. The highly accessible, innovative format is composed of a picture followed by a paragraph or so of comment. This makes it easy to read and digest short sections at a sitting. There are no references or index, but the organization of the book is readily apparent and one can find subjects through the table of contents. This is an outstanding book on tree care.

Sinclair, W.A., H.H. Lyon and W.T. Johnson. 1987. *Diseases of trees and shrubs.* Ithaca, N.Y.: Comstock Publishing, Cornell University Press. 574 pp.

This basic resource on the identification and biology of diseases of shade trees and ornamental shrubs is already a classic in its field. The 247 color plates composed of 1,700 individual photographs are of great value in identification. The notes on the facing pages provide biological explanations of the pathogens or conditions pictured. Although precise directions for management are not provided, the biological information is critical for developing management programs. Everyone who works with trees and shrubs should use this book and its companion volume by Johnson and Lyon (see p. 623).

Tong, X.W. 1989. Enhancement of egg parasitization of pine caterpillars in China. *The IPM Practitioner* 11(2):12.

An English language abstract of important Chinese biological control work against this tree pest, reprinted from the *Chinese Journal of Biological Control.* The Chinese are far ahead of the Americans in using methods of biological control enhancement.

Xie, Q.K. 1989. Moving spiders to control pine sawfly in China. *The IPM Pratitioner* 11(3):14.

This paper was translated by BIRC's China Program staff. An English language abstract was published to encourage pest control researchers in the U.S. to place more emphasis on spiders in the control of pests and their potential use in biological control augmentation efforts.

Zhang, L.Q. 1989. Biological control of a wood borer in China. *The IPM Practitioner* 11(5):5-7.

Borers are extremely difficult to control, and the Chinese work rearing and releasing parasitoids is innovative and successful. This article reports on one example.

CHAPTER 33
Rats

INTRODUCTION

Rats are the object of widespread fear and revulsion, and they are considered pests for a variety of reasons. They damage structures, chew wiring and cause electrical fires, eat and urinate on human and animal food and serve as reservoirs or vectors (carriers) of human plague, infectious jaundice, salmonellosis, rat-bite fever, murine typhus, rickettsial pox and other pathogens. Thousands of rat bites are reported each year in the United States alone. In addition, there are accidental poisonings of humans and pets from poorly planned efforts to poison rats.

Rats are a community problem in that they are caused by community processes and must be managed through community-wide activities. Within urban areas, rats derive their life supports from waste-management systems and food-processing and storage areas. Waste management includes solid and liquid waste systems operated on a community-wide basis. Food-processing and storage areas are found in every living unit and also in public facilities such as restaurants, food stores, butcher shops, factories and canneries.

Although an individual rat and its associated family may first occupy a home by gnawing a hole in a door, wall or pipe, especially if it is broken, the original source of the rat is a population established somewhere else in the community. Consequently, control must focus on this reservoir rat population and the environment that supports it.

Of the three most important urban rodents—Norway rats, roof rats and house mice—the largest in the adult stage and the most ubiquitous and damaging is the Norway rat (Rattus norvegicus), also called the brown, wharf or sewer rat. Although it is often found in houses, it can rarely be completely controlled by focusing on one house alone. Serious Norway rat problems are doubtless also community-wide problems, and that is why we discuss them in this chapter. We also discuss the roof rat (Rattus rattus), sometimes called the black, ship or house rat, since it can also be a community-wide pest.

Contrary to popular belief, which associates rats exclusively with poverty and squalor, these rodents can be found virtually everywhere humans live. They are attracted to areas that provide a wealth of hiding places and easy access to food. This combination often occurs where garbage is poorly managed or where grains are stored improperly. These conditions are found frequently in low-income areas, but they also exist in prosperous residential and commercial developments. Rats have been found in penthouse suites atop skyscrapers, and we have seen them feeding and living in the lush ivy used to landscape expensive homes. One of the most serious infestations we ever encountered was in historic Lafayette Park, located across the street from the White House.

Table 33.1
Differences among Norway Rats, Roof Rats and Common House Mice

	Norway Rat	Roof Rat	House Mouse
Scientific name:	Rattus norvegicus	Rattus rattus	Mus musculus
Other common names:	brown, wharf or sewer rat	black, ship or house rat	
Adult size:	11 oz. (300 g)	7 oz. (200 g)	½ oz. (15 g)
Snout:	blunt	pointed	pointed
Ears:	small, short hairs	large, naked	large, some hair
Tail coloration:	dark above, pale underneath	all dark	all dark
Fur:	brown with black, shaggy	grey to black, smooth	light brown to grey
Droppings:	capsule-shaped	spindle-shaped	rod-shaped
Food requirement:	1 oz. (28 g)/day	1 oz. (28 g)/day	$\frac{1}{10}$ oz. (3 g)/day
Water source:	free water[a]	free water[a]	water from food
Climbing ability:	can climb	active climber	good climber
Nest locations:	mainly in burrows	walls, attics, trees	near/in stored material
Swimming ability:	excellent	can swim	can swim
Litter size:	8 to 12	6 to 8	6 to 7
Litters per year:	7	6	8 to 10

[a] Water present by itself and not simply a constituent of the food eaten by the rodent.

The same basic treatment methods work in high-income areas, low-income areas and nonresidential environments. Many of the safe, effective methods used to reduce rat problems in Lafayette Park are equally appropriate for homes, workplaces and community facilities everywhere. And no matter where the rats are found, an understanding of their needs and habits is valuable in designing an integrated management program for controlling them.

BIOLOGY

If you encounter a rat in your home or community, it is probably either the large Norway, or sewer, rat *(Rattus norvegicus)* or the smaller roof rat *(Rattus rattus)*. Wood rats *(Neotoma* spp.), like wild mice, can also invade homes, but generally do so when the weather gets colder and seldom if ever set up year-round habitations indoors. The first step in rat control is identifying the animal, and it is important to be able to distinguish Norway rats from roof rats (you should also be able to tell these from the common house mouse). Table 33.1 on the facing page and the drawing at right help you identify these rodents by summarizing their major physical characteristics and habits.

In general, Norway rats build their nests in burrows or at ground level, whereas roof rats make nests in trees, dense vegetation, walls or attics. In warm, subtropical climates, rats may breed all year; in cooler climates, they apparently have their peak breeding periods in spring and fall, with less breeding during the hottest periods of summer and nearly complete cessation in winter. The size and number of litters vary with habitat conditions, particularly food supply.

After mating, females gestate 21 to 23 days, producing litters of 6 to 12. Females may mate again a day or two after bearing the litter, and produce four to nine litters a year. However, not all embryos survive. Thus females may wean only 12 to 56

Norway Rats vs. Roof Rats
The differences between Norway and roof rats are subtle. The Norway rat *(Rattus norvegicus)* can grow to 16 in. (40 cm) long with a tail 7½ in. (19 cm) long, and weighs up to 12 oz. (340 g). The roof rat *(Rattus rattus)* can grow to 15 in. (38 cm) with a tail 8½ in. to 10 in. (22 cm to 25 cm) long, and it seldom weighs more than 8 oz. (227 g). The easiest way to tell them apart is to examine the tail. If it is shorter than the head plus the body and is dark on top and light on the bottom, it is a Norway, or sewer, rat. If the tail is longer than the head plus the body and dark on both sides, it is a roof rat. The lower drawing shows how to distinguish young rats from house mice.

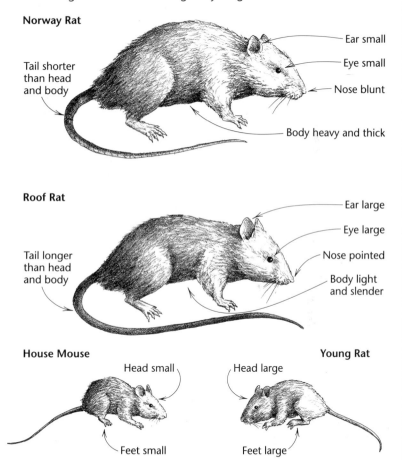

young per year. The young rats develop rapidly, eating solid food when they are three weeks old. Feeding preferences and aversions apparently are learned from the mother. At one month, the rats weigh about 1½ oz. (45 g), large enough to be snap-trapped. At three months they are sexually mature. Their normal life expectancy is one year.

Rat populations increase when there is ample food and shelter. Those that survive trapping or poisoning campaigns respond by increasing the size and frequency of litters. Apparently litter size and survival of young goes up when population size goes down. Thus, if food and shelter are not reduced, rat populations can rebound quickly from lethal control measures alone. However, although rat populations can grow to very high levels, there is an upper limit that they will not exceed even in the presence of ample food and shelter. The evolutionary process has produced mechanisms in rats that prevent environmental destruction as the result of overpopulation (for example, abortion of fetuses and eating of babies).

Rats rely predominantly on their senses of smell, taste, touch and hearing; apparently they have poor vision. They move around mainly in the dark, using their long, sensitive whiskers and the guard hairs on their body to guide them. They usually begin searching for food shortly after sunset, ranging up to 150 ft. (46 m) from their nest. When hungry or when living under crowded conditions, they may also be seen in daylight. Sometimes rats observed during the day are young or weak rats forced out of protected territory. Rats live in social hierarchies, and can become aggressive toward other rats when their territories are invaded.

To a large degree, rats are omnivorous, eating nearly any type of food, including dead and dying members of their own species. However, Norway rats are more likely to eat garbage than are roof rats, who seem to prefer fresh plant food, if available. Rats are cautious, and if their food is in an exposed area where it cannot be consumed quickly, they usually carry or drag it to a hiding place. Their excellent sense of taste enables them to detect certain compounds, including rat poisons, at extremely low concentrations very quickly. Therefore it is more important when trapping or poisoning to use a bait that is more attractive to rats than the other foods available. Experiment with foods with different odors, because rats rely on their sense of smell to locate food.

The physical abilities of rats are amazing. Understanding what they can and cannot do is extremely helpful when you are planning preven-

The Physical Capabilities of Rats[a]

When planning preventive measures, assume that rats can:

• Pass through any opening larger than ½ in. (1.3 cm) square.

• Walk along horizontal wires and climb vertical wires (roof rats).

• Climb the inside of vertical pipes 1½ in. to 4 in. (3.8 cm to 10 cm) in diameter.

• Climb the outside of vertical pipes up to 3 in. (7.6 cm) in diameter.

• Climb the outside of vertical pipes and conduits of any size if within 3 in. (7.6 cm) of a wall.

• Crawl horizontally on any type of pipe or conduit.

• Jump vertically at least 36 in. (0.9 m) above a flat surface.

• Reach about 13 in. (33 cm) above a flat surface.

• Dive and swim underwater for as long as 30 seconds.

• Swim up through the water seal, or trap, of toilets.

• Swim as far as ½ mi. (0.8 km) in open water.

• Gnaw and leave marks on almost anything, including wood, chip board, lead pipes, cinder blocks, asbestos, aluminum, sheet metal, glass and sun-dried adobe.

[a] Sources: Caslick and Decker, 1980, and Howard and Marsh, 1967.

tive measures and reducing existing populations. The sidebar at left summarizes these abilities.

DETECTION AND MONITORING

The first step in a good rat management program is regular monitoring of the locations rats are suspected of inhabiting. This includes determining where the rats are living and feeding, how many there are, how much and what kind of damage they are causing, which methods to use to suppress them and whether the methods you are presently using work.

Count rat holes and note their location on a hand-drawn map. Use an aerial view, approximating building sizes, showing garbage storage sites and clearly indicating rat holes. Make a thorough search of attics, basements, foundation perimeters and crawl spaces; also look behind and under stored materials. Once the holes are located and mapped, use soil, sawdust or crumpled paper to close them temporarily. Return 24 hours later to see whether they have been reopened or the paper has been chewed or moved. If so, you can assume the hole is in active use by one or more rats. Record this information on the map and use it when deciding where to focus management efforts.

Rats also leave characteristic signs, or signatures. The sidebar on p. 629 describes some of these. By considering the number of active holes along with the number of signs and visual sightings, you begin to get an idea of the number of rats to be managed and which areas deserve priority.

TREATMENT

Traditionally, poisons have been used for rat control. However, an overemphasis on the use of rat poisons usually leads to a poison-resistant rat population and neglect of other more permanent population suppression methods. In the long term, effective rat control can be achieved only

Signs of Rat Presence and What They Suggest about the Number of Rats[a]

Signs

• Droppings along runways, in feeding areas and near the rats' shelter. They may be as long as ¾ in. (1.9 cm) and up to ¼ in. (0.6 cm) in diameter. Fresh droppings are soft.

• Tracks, including footprints and tail marks, on dusty surfaces, in mud or in snow. You can make an artificial tracking patch with talcum powder. Sprinkle the powder wherever you suspect rats are gaining entrance but cannot be sure since other signs are indistinct. Examples include areas around doorways, broken windows and torn screens. Use as little powder as possible to minimize cleanup, and leave it in place overnight.

• Urine along traveled pathways or in feeding areas. Both wet and dry rat urine glows under ultraviolet light.

• Runs or burrows next to walls, along fences, next to buildings or under bushes and debris. Rats memorize these pathways and use the same routes habitually.

• Smudge marks, or rub marks, on beams, rafters, walls, pipes and other fixtures. These are the result of oil and dirt rubbing off the rats' fur along frequently traveled routes.

• Gnawing marks on doors or ledges, in corners, in wall material, on stored materials or on other surfaces. Fresh accumulations of wood shavings, insulation and other gnawed material indicate active infestations. Rats can also gnaw through rusty sheet metal. Rat gnawing can often be distinguished from mouse gnawing by the size of the associated entry holes, often 2 in. (5 cm) or more in diameter for rats, 1½ in. (3.8 cm) or less for mice. (Rats retain their paired incisor teeth, which grow continuously at the rate of about 5 in./12.7 cm per year and are worn down by gnawing on hard surfaces and by working them against each other. Consequently, rats have an ongoing need to reduce the length of their teeth through regular gnawing.)

• Noises in the walls caused by gnawing, climbing, clawing, squeaks and fighting, particularly at night when rats are most active. However, squirrels and other animals can make similar noises, so look for other signs.

The Number of Rats Suggested by these Signs

• **Few or no rats:** No signs detected, even though a rodent presumed to be a rat has been sighted in the area. There are probably fewer than five rats and they have invaded only recently.

• **A medium number of rats:** Old droppings and gnawing marks common; no rats observed in daytime, but one or more spotted at night. There are probably five or more rats in each area where one is spotted regularly at night.

• **Many rats:** Fresh droppings, tracks and gnawing marks, with three or more rats seen at night at any one time, or seen in daylight. There are probably more than 15 rats in the area.

Droppings

Norway rat

Blunt,
average length ¾ in.

Roof rat

Pointed,
average length ½ in.

House mouse

Pointed,
average length ¼ in.

Tracks

Mouse

Rat

Rub Marks

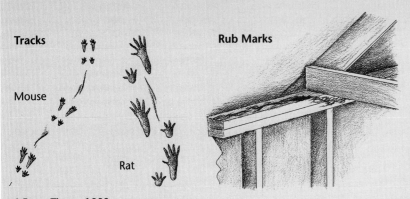

[a] From Timm, 1983.

through a combination of tactics, including removing food sources and debris, "rat-proofing" structures and treating locally with traps or rodenticides. Furthermore, if controls are to succeed over the long term, the entire community should be informed about the conditions that sustain and harbor rats. Education must be part of an integrated management program, and should involve neighbors, businesses and appropriate government agencies.

Indirect Strategies

If a public institution or local group is monitoring a neighborhood or community for rats, it is a good time for educating about rat management. Training programs for the general public and professional pest control personnel should focus on integrated pest management (IPM) concepts, including a survey of rat biology and behavior, as well as monitoring procedures, tolerance levels, sanitation,

habit modification and least-toxic control methods.

Rats can find stored foods in residences, restaurants, food-processing plants, warehouses, markets, grain mills and port facilities; thus, rat management programs must stress the removal of rat food and destruction of their harborage. Community members should understand that poisoning or trapping alone does not reduce rat populations over the long term because rats respond to population reduction by increasing the size and frequency of their litters. The young rats have greater appetites than the older ones, and thus are even more destructive. The community must also understand the critical importance of proper sanitation, which involves not only sound food storage practices, but also the hygienic removal and handling of refuse and sewage.

The key to successful long-term rat control, whether in a single building

or throughout a community, is reduction of the life supports that sustain rats. The importance of this, as opposed to simply poisoning some of the rats, is demonstrated in the graph below. Together, such supports are referred to as the carrying capacity of the area. For example, if you determine that one rat is living in your building, the structure must have a carrying capacity of at least one rat. If you kill the rat but do not change the environmental conditions that supported it, the carrying capacity does not change, and another rat will likely move in to take its place. However, by modifying your environment to reduce its carrying capacity, you solve both existing and potential future rat problems.

1. Food Storage. In homes or commercial establishments, foods, particularly grains and nutmeats, should be stored in rat-proof glass or metal containers. Fresh fruit and vegetables should be kept in refrigerators or in open-air coolers screened with ¼-in. (6 mm) wire mesh. Until rat problems are under control, you should consider temporarily storing any attractive food, even closed, packaged crackers or candy, in the refrigerator. Bags of grass seed, dry pet food and other materials sometimes stored in sheds and outbuildings should be checked regularly for signs of rodent entry. These may have to be moved indoors or put in metal or screened bins tough enough to foil rats and mice.

2. Management of Garden Waste. Fallen fruit, nuts and similar foods may be feeding rats in your neighborhood. Rake, sweep or scoop them up with a flat shovel as frequently as possible. Excess garden produce that will not be consumed or stored in a rodent-proof manner should be handled as described next.

3. Large-Scale Garbage Management. In most areas, improperly managed garbage is the main source of food for rats. How the organic component of the garbage is managed is critical to reducing rat problems, starting at the point where it

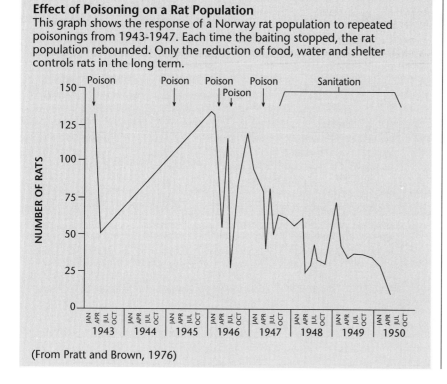

Effect of Poisoning on a Rat Population
This graph shows the response of a Norway rat population to repeated poisonings from 1943-1947. Each time the baiting stopped, the rat population rebounded. Only the reduction of food, water and shelter controls rats in the long term.

(From Pratt and Brown, 1976)

leaves the kitchen or other food-handling area. Electric sink disposal units may reduce cockroach and ant problems in the kitchen, but they can exacerbate rat problems by feeding rodents within the sewer system. Unfortunately, no matter how you get rid of this organic waste, there is the potential for increasing the rat population at every step along the way. This is true whether you incinerate, bury or place your garbage in a can for municipal pickup, and regardless of whether your community incinerates these wastes, buries them in a landfill, tows them out into the ocean for dumping or handles them in other ways.

In urban and suburban areas, free-roaming dogs or raccoons may overturn garbage cans, making the contents more accessible to rodents. If you bury your garbage but do not bury it deeply enough, rats can tunnel to it or dogs and raccoons can dig it up, exposing it for rodents. In addition, incompletely buried feces of dogs and cats, unfinished pet food and bird-feeder spill all provide sustenance for rats.

In commercial or other settings where garbage is stored in large metal dumpsters, lids should seal tightly when closed and be kept closed when the dumpster is not in use. Some dumpsters have drain holes to allow them to be hosed out periodically to remove organic material that sticks to the inside. These holes should be fitted with removable plugs or wire mesh screens; otherwise they turn the dumpster into a huge feeding station for rodents by providing easy access close to the ground.

It is important that no refuse falls next to the dumpster, particularly on school grounds and in other settings where people often throw waste in the general direction of the container. In such situations, the area around the dumpster should be monitored daily before dark. All misplaced material should be thrown in the dumpster and the lid closed for the night. Parents and other residents

near parks and schools should help ensure that the persons using and managing the waste receptacles are educated about the importance of doing this, and that these rat control responsibilities are written into custodial job descriptions.

Even after the garbage has left your neighborhood, the problem is not solved. When we examined the rat management system in the nation's capital in the early 1980s, we found the municipal incinerator to be a major reservoir for the rat population that regularly invaded the surrounding residential neighborhoods and parks. Elsewhere, we have visited landfills where rats feed on material underground that is sheltered within piles of partially buried concrete and other debris. On the periphery of the dump, these provide an ideal burrow environment. In cities, broken sewers and sewer gratings over rainwater catchments make available multiple dwelling places and highways for rats underground and give them access to almost any part of the community or any house or commercial building within it, since rats can come up through the water traps in toilets.

Ideally, organic garbage should be collected separately and recycled through municipal composting programs with very short storage periods. Unfortunately, at present the organic material is dispersed widely throughout the bulky municipal waste stream. People do not seem to enjoy thinking about garbage any more than they like to think about rats. Thus, it may take a major catastrophe, such as a recurrence of the "black death" (bubonic plague) or a similar rat-associated epidemic, to change priorities. In our opinion, adequate management of rats and garbage requires a willingness among citizens to fund the repair of sewer systems and large-scale recycling and composting systems in those areas where they are most needed.

4. Garbage Management around the Home. The list below outlines some of the steps you should take to reduce rat problems around your home.

• Separate organic garbage from metal, glass and plastic at the sink. Drain the organic material and wrap it in newspaper before placing it in the garbage can. If flies are also a problem in your neighborhood, follow the additional tips on preparing the organic waste for placement in the garbage can provided on pp. 642-644 in the chapter on fly management.

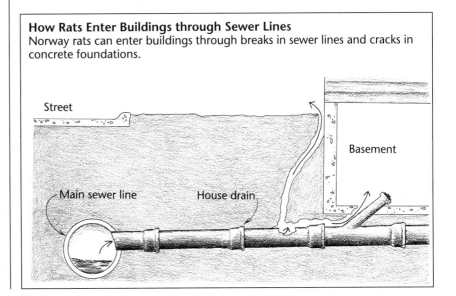

How Rats Enter Buildings through Sewer Lines
Norway rats can enter buildings through breaks in sewer lines and cracks in concrete foundations.

Street

Basement

Main sewer line   House drain

Rat-Proof Garbage Cans

You can protect your garbage cans against invasion by rats by setting them on a 12-in. (30 cm) high platform and equipping them with spring fasteners. The simplest way to make the fasteners is with elastic cords, available from hardware stores. Use two cords per can. For permanence you can bend the metal hook ends of the cords completely around the can and lid handles. This system has the extra advantage of keeping cans and lids together after the trash collector empties them.

How to handle organic garbage while it is being stored temporarily indoors is discussed on p. 222 on cockroach management. If you intend to process the material in an aerobic batch compost, store the wastes as described in the sidebar on p. 644.

• Replace or repair outdoor garbage cans that have holes or lids that do not fit tightly. Use spring fasteners that will keep the lid tightly closed when the can is pushed over (see the drawing above).

• Urge your city government or other public agencies to provide waste containers with self-closing lids in public areas.

• Place garbage cans in a rack that is elevated at least 12 in. (30 cm) above the ground (as shown in the drawing at left). Maintain a distance of at least 24 in. (60 cm) between the cans and structures from which rats might jump onto the cans.

• Use enough cans to hold all your garbage. Do not store surplus garbage in cardboard, plastic or paper bags that can be penetrated easily by rats.

• Wash out cans periodically so that no organic matter remains after the cans are emptied.

• Never leave garbage cans open during the night, and don't leave garbage outside in plastic bags.

• Pick up or bury fallen fruit and pet feces daily (see the discussion below on burying kitchen garbage and pet manure). Put away any food that pets do not eat between feedings.

• If you plan to bury organic kitchen garbage in the garden, store it in a closed container, such as a plastic carton with a snap-on top or a reclosable plastic bag. The object is to prevent flies from laying their eggs on the garbage before it is buried. Bury the garbage frequently, some each day if possible, and quickly. Once you open the bag or container, the smell attracts flies, so it is essential to cover the material before flies have a chance to lay eggs on it.

Bury garbage deep enough to prevent odors from escaping. Cover with at least 6 in. (15 cm) of earth and tamp it down firmly. Buried organic matter is subject to excavation by rats, raccoons and other urban wildlife, so monitor for signs of digging at the surface. If you see such signs, cover the surface with boards, wire screens or heavy objects for a month or so and do not continue to use this method of garbage disposal. For more information on composting organic kitchen wastes and pet manure, see pp. 642-645.

5. Habitat Modification. Studies conducted years ago showed that rodent control based primarily on sanitation and habitat modification through rat-proofing measures was successful. But these practices were largely abandoned when anticoagu-

lant rodenticides such as warfarin were developed. Now, as rats develop resistance to these anticoagulants, there is new impetus to promote habitat management. This means modifying the environment to reduce places for rats to roam and nest. Such places include deteriorated structures, outbuildings, cellars, attics, wall voids, false ceilings, street drains, unused sewer laterals (tunnels branching off from main lines), debris heaps, refuse dumps and wood piles.

Norway rats are good swimmers and often burrow along creek banks or into the rock embankments that line streams, irrigation canals and recreational lakes. These rats commonly use sewer and drain pipes and narrow passageways between buildings and fences. Roof rats find harborage and food in ornamental plants such as date palms and large-leaved ivy species. Important travel routes for the often arboreal roof rat include telephone, television and utility cables and poles, trees and service pipes on building exteriors and roofs.

The sidebar on pp. 633-635 describes some specific techniques that you can use to rat-proof your home and workplace.

To reduce rat harborage in landscaped areas, avoid large expanses of single-species ground cover that allow rats to run undetected for long distances. Break up dense plantings with exposed pathways, stretches of lawn or highly prostrate ground covers. These openings act as a deterrent because rats dislike moving across exposed areas. Avoid plants such as Algerian ivy (*Hedera canariensis*) and date palms that rats are known to live in or feed on.

You can make a rat-proof barrier to separate landscaping from the foundations of adjacent buildings by digging a small trench 8 in. to 12 in. (20 cm to 30 cm) wide, 8 in. deep and as long as the building, and filling it with pea gravel. Rats dislike burrowing in the loose gravel and will be discouraged from trying to penetrate the foundations.

Rat-Proofing Buildings

• Any hole a rat can fit its skull through, roughly ½ in. (1.3 cm) in diameter or larger, can provide entry. Plug such openings temporarily with tightly packed steel wool, then permanently seal them with 19-gauge or thicker galvanized metal sheeting, ¼ in. (0.6 cm) hardware cloth (strong wire mesh) or 22-gauge or thicker aluminum sheeting. Do not use plastic, wood or other chewable materials.

• Seal holes in foundations of buildings or entrances to rat burrows with a minimum of 2 in. (5 cm) of reinforced mortar mixed with iron filings (from machine shops) or broken glass pieces ⅛ in. to ½ in. (0.3 cm to 1.3 cm) long. (You can put some glass in a tough paper bag and smash it with a hammer. Shake out the broken glass pieces into the mortar as you are mixing it.) The glass or the filings deters rats from digging the filled holes out again before the mortar hardens. Use 3¾-in. (9.5 cm) thick mortar if you don't use the filings or glass. Specify portland cement when you purchase the mortar (from hardware stores, lumberyards or masonry supply companies). Another highly effective way to seal off such holes is to nail hardware cloth into the hole and then cover it with mortar.

• To prevent rat entry by burrowing, extend footings into the ground a minimum of 24 in. (60 cm) and make a concrete curtain wall with a horizontal extension that extends 12 in. (30 cm) outward (as shown in the

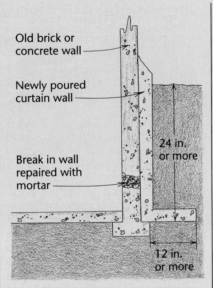

Old brick or concrete wall

Newly poured curtain wall

Break in wall repaired with mortar

24 in. or more

12 in. or more

drawing above). Ground floors should be 18 in. (45 cm) above the ground. Alternatively, they can be constructed of concrete, stone and mortar, or brick and mortar. Placing a termite shield between concrete and wood also helps prevent rodents from gaining access at these points.

• Ideally, you should construct floors of basements and outbuildings with reinforced concrete a minimum of 2 in. (5 cm) thick. If wood flooring is used, it should be lined underneath with ¼-in. by ¼-in. (0.6 cm by 0.6 cm), 19-gauge wire mesh or hardware cloth. If an existing structure has a wood floor either near or directly on the ground, bury an L-shaped length of hardware cloth 24 in. (60 cm) deep and bring it 24 in. up the outside wall and fasten it there (as shown at B in the drawing below). To prevent rat access to dog kennels, stables, storage sheds and other-dirt filled areas, lay metal hardware cloth on the ground and cover it with soil. The edges of the cloth should extend a minimum of 6 in. (15 cm) up from the soil and should be attached to the fencing (as shown at A below).

• On building exteriors, seal openings around pipes and wires that enter the structure through wood with metal collars (as shown

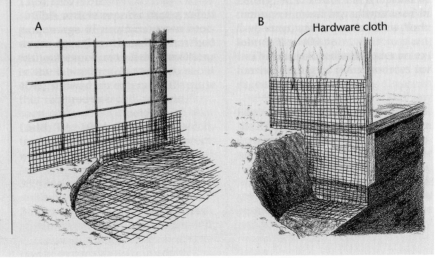

A

B   Hardware cloth

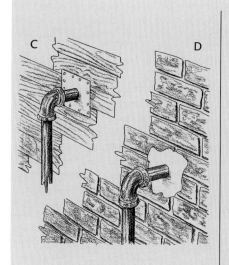

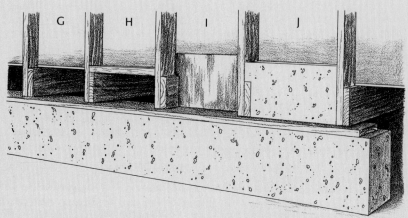

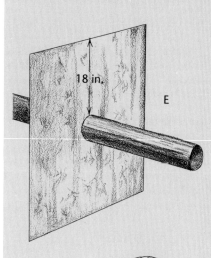

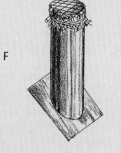

at C in the drawing at left). Use portland cement mortar where pipes pass through walls of brick or other masonry (as shown at D in the drawing at left).

• Install guards and barriers to prevent rats from climbing up or moving along pipes and wires. To prevent rats from entering a building at an open pipe, cut a piece of galvanized sheet metal 36 in. (90 cm) square with a pair of tin snips. In the center, cut a hole just large enough to fit the pipe snugly (as shown at E in the drawing at left); the 18 in. (45 cm) border is needed to prevent rats from jumping over the barrier. Vent pipes can be rat-proofed by bending a square of ¼-in.-mesh galvanized hardware cloth over the top and securing it with wire (as shown at F in the drawing at left).

• Cap drains in the floors of basements so rats cannot enter through them. Install a brass drain cover or a perforated metal cap held in place by a hinge so it can open for cleaning. Make sure the

unhinged type of cover is threaded so it screws in place; otherwise the rat can push it open. Place ¼-in. (0.6 cm) galvanized screen under existing drain covers to prevent rat entry if holes are larger than ½ in. (1.3 cm).

• Place barriers between and within walls to prevent rodent travel. An open space between floor joists (shown at G in the drawing above) gives rats free access to wall voids. Wooden 2x4 stops (shown at H) are sometimes used on upper floors, but a noncombustible material should be employed on lower floors. In old buildings, galvanized sheet metal (shown at I) can be cut to fit and nailed between studs, joists, floor and sill. In new construction, noncombustible stops of a good grade of cement are recommended (shown at J).

• Install flashing or metal channels on the lower edges of doors (see the drawing at top on the facing page) to prevent rat entry. The channels can be made by bending galvanized sheet metal in a

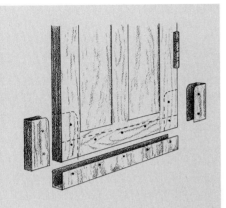

U-shape to fit the lower edges of the door. They are affixed with screws. The clearance between the door and its threshold should not exceed ¼ in. (0.6 cm). The door casing should also be protected with sheet metal to prevent rats from widening cracks by gnawing. Frequently used doors should be equipped with mechanical self-closing devices.

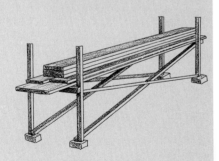

• Store lumber and equipment at least 18 in. (45 cm) above the ground on a rack (as shown in the drawing above). Set the length and width of the rack according to your storage needs, and prop the legs on concrete blocks to prevent decay from damp soil.

Direct Physical Controls

Traps or poison baits can be used to kill rats while sanitation and rat-proofing projects are underway. It may be wise to begin trapping or poisoning just before rat-proofing begins, because it reduces the likelihood that rats will become trapped inside rat-proofed buildings or move to neighboring areas.

Poison baits leave carcasses to rot in walls and other inaccessible areas, where they attract flies, carpet beetles and other pests. Trapping does not. Trapping is also more humane than poison baits because it kills rats faster. Therefore, it is the preferred method in homes, garages and other small structures, especially where there may be only a few rats. You and the other residents of your building can do the trapping yourselves or you can call a professional. Make sure you specify the techniques you want used.

Rat carcasses removed from traps can be disposed of by incinerating or by wrapping them in plastic and placing them in the garbage can. You can kill trapped rats that are still alive by drowning them in soapy water. Use a shovel to pick up the trap and rat to move them to the soapy water.

1. Spring-Operated Traps. Spring-operated traps can be purchased in supermarkets and hardware and farm supply stores. A square of cardboard fitted inside the wire deadfall as shown in the drawing below expands the trigger on the trap and increases its effectiveness. The trap should be baited with pieces of hot dog, bacon or liver tied securely to the trigger with string to ensure that the rat will spring the trap when feeding. Fruits, raisins, marshmallows or peanut butter mixed with rolled oats can also be used. If rats have been eating particular foods stored in cupboards, try these as bait.

Because rats are very wary of changes in their environment, leave the traps baited but unset for one to three days. This allows the rats to grow accustomed to the presence of the traps and allows you to see whether you have selected an attractive bait. Always use gloves when handling traps to protect yourself from pathogens and to prevent your skin oils from marking the trap. Rats may avoid traps with human smells on them.

Refer to your monitoring map to locate active rat holes, then set traps along walls or other runways leading to the holes. Other good locations are near droppings, gnawing marks or other signs of rat damage; under and behind objects likely to harbor rats; in dark corners; and along rafters or other protected areas where rats are likely to travel.

The drawing on p. 636 shows the best ways to position traps. The trig-

Making an Expanded Rat Trap Trigger

Rat traps with expanded triggers are available commercially, but you can also make your own. Cut a 1½ in. (3.8 cm) square piece of stiff cardboard or ⅛-in. (0.3 cm) thick wood and attach it to the existing trap trigger with wire or strong glue. Expanded triggers often catch rats without bait if the traps are placed well and are moved when necessary.

ger can be placed either next to or parallel to the wall, depending on the trapping method chosen. Traps can also be nailed to walls and rafters to keep them in position. Or, if they are being placed on the floor, they can be nailed to a larger supporting board if rats are knocking them over without getting caught.

To protect pets and young children, traps in living spaces should be covered. Lean a board against the wall where you have set the trap so that it shields the trap. Make sure the entrance and exit holes created by the leaning board are at least 2 in. (5 cm) wide so the rat can pass through and get to the trap. Use duct tape to fasten the upper edge of the board to the wall.

You can camouflage a trap by sinking it just below ground level on dirt floors or placing it in a shallow pie pan or other depression. Position the trap, then completely cover it with a thin coating of fine sand or sawdust. Leave the trap baited but unset. If rats take the bait from the camouflaged trap after a few days, rebait and set it. If there is no sign of rat activity, move the trap to a new location.

Traps should be checked daily and rebaited as needed. Move them after three or four days if there is no sign of activity. When most of the rats have been trapped, it may be difficult to catch the remaining few because of trap-shyness. Remove the traps for a week, then set them in new locations using the pre-baiting method described above. Use gloves or tongs to collect and remove rat carcasses for disposal. Before storing the traps, scrub them with a stiff brush soaked in detergent and water and coat their metal parts with a thin layer of oil to extend their useful life. Also see the discussion on trapping mice on pp. 290-291.

2. Glue Boards. Very young rats are small enough to avoid getting

Proper Trap Placement

Generally, traps should be placed with the baited trigger facing the wall. At A, two traps have been placed side-by-side to increase the chances of success. Alternatively, a double set of traps could be placed in line parallel to the wall with their triggers to the outside. A box placed a few inches from the wall creates a runway leading from the rat hole in the far wall to the traps. Where rats appear to be traveling along pipes, use copper U-shaped pipe clamps screwed into the bottom of the trap (B) on smaller-diameter pipes, and eye hooks and rubber bands as shown at C to secure traps to larger-diameter pipes. Where rats are moving along wooden studs and/or rafters, you can simply nail the trap into place (D).

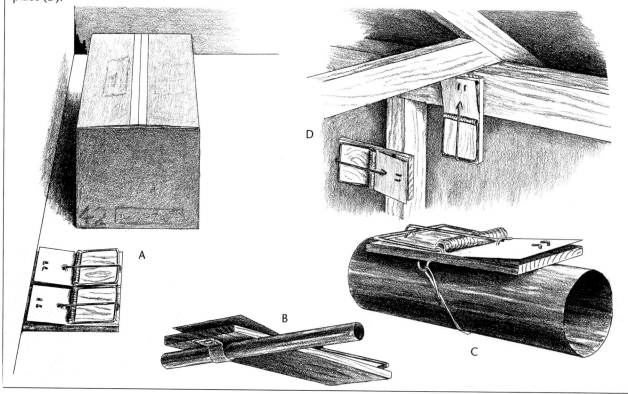

caught in spring-loaded traps. Glue boards, which are available in most hardware stores, are more effective for these younger rats. The boards should be set along runways as described above for snap traps. Although bait is not required, it can improve the chance of success. Rats that attempt to cross the boards are caught in the glue. The boards should be checked daily. Trapped rats can be disposed of by dropping the entire board with the rat in a bucket of soapy water. Move the board with a shovel. Glue boards lose their effectiveness in dusty areas unless covered, and temperature extremes may affect the tackiness of some glues. Do not use the boards where children, pets or wildlife may come into contact with them.

3. **Ultrasonic Devices.** It is unfortunate that ultrasonic devices are widely advertised, since there are no studies indicating they are effective at significantly reducing or eliminating rats or other rodents from an area. In 1984, the Federal Trade Commission ordered certain manufacturers of ultrasonic devices to stop making false claims about them and to provide substantiation for claims of effectiveness. Until such studies are available, we do not recommend the use of these products (see also the discussion on pp. 291-292). There are reports showing that certain ultrasonic devices are helpful when used in combination with other methods, but this still does not mean they alone will "eliminate" an infestation.

Direct Biological Controls

Owls can be important rat, mouse and gopher predators in urban areas, but they require protection and shelter in an area where no rat poison is being used. Such an approach could be a useful part of a preventive program. A number of snakes that are harmless to humans also have a suppressive effect on rats. However, it would take a considerable educational effort to teach enough of our population to tolerate them.

Domestic cats already serve an important function as urban rodent predators, especially for mice. Many cats also kill rats, particularly small ones. The presence of a cat can also act as a deterrent. Thus, cats should be considered along with other tactics as part of a rat control program. Stray cats have long been rampant in ghettos and other rundown areas and have always been considered a nuisance to be dealt with by animal control officers. The fact that they actually provide more of a service than a nuisance should be considered.

Direct Chemical Controls

If trapping is not effective, or if an emergency caused by a very high rat population occurs, poison baits can be useful. They may also be needed to prevent rats from migrating to neighboring areas while buildings are being rat-proofed or destroyed, or where rat fleas have been identified as transmitting bacteria that cause human plague. Although no large epidemic has occurred recently, plague bacilli live in wild rodents, and there is always the threat that the bacilli will pass to domestic rats and then to humans. If you decide that poisons are needed, we recommend that you hire a professional to apply them.

Many rats are resistant to warfarin (D-Con® and other products) and other familiar rat poisons, so we suggest use of the new anticoagulant rodenticide Quintox® (for sources, see the Resource Appendix under "Vertebrate Management: Chemical Controls" on p. 688). This product has not yet been used widely enough for rat populations to develop resistance. The active ingredient is vitamin D_3 (cholecalciferol). The poison should be placed in tamper-resistant bait stations (for sources, see the Resource Appendix under "Vertebrate Management: Physical Controls" on p. 688). The rats die two to four days after consuming a lethal dose.

Remember, however, that applications of poison baits must be accom-panied by habitat and sanitation modifications if a permanent reduction is to be achieved. If you call a professional to set out the poison but do not modify the habitat that is supporting the rats, don't blame the pest control company when the rat population increases again. Blame yourself for not making habitat changes along with the use of the poison.

Summary: Least-Toxic Rat Control

• Monitor to find out where the rats live, travel and feed. Record this information on a map or floor plan of your house or apartment.

• Improve sanitation and garbage management practices.

• Modify the habitat by rat-proofing buildings and altering landscaping.

• Use traps to reduce the existing rat population.

• If trapping is insufficient or if an emergency occurs, hire a professional to set out poison baits.

• Continue monitoring periodically to ensure that rats are not recolonizing.

REFERENCES AND READINGS

Caslick, J.W., and D.J. Decker. 1980. *Rat and mouse control.* Ithaca, N.Y.: Cornell Cooperative Extension Publication. Information Bulletin 163.

This was one of the sources for the the sidebar on the physical capabilities of rats (p. 628).

Davis, D. 1972. Rodent control strategy. In *Pest control: strategies for the future,* pp. 157-161. Washington, D.C.: National Academy of Science.

Davis reviews work on reducing the rat carrying capacity of residential areas in downtown Baltimore. The work showed that rodenticides alone are not enough to keep rat numbers low. He connects this field work with population regulation theory. Although the work is classic in terms of the practical demonstrations it includes, it is frequently absent from the literature on rat management.

Ebeling, W. 1975. *Urban entomology.* Berkeley: University of California Division of Agricultural Science. 695 pp.

This comprehensive work has an excellent section on rat biology and management.

Howard, W.E., and R.E. Marsh. 1976. *The rat: its biology and control.* Davis: University of California, Division of Biological Science, Cooperative Extension Service (Leaflet 2896). 22 pp.

A short booklet with excellent advice on habitat modification and the use of rodenticides.

Olkowski, W, and Daar, S. 1985. Update: plague on the rise. *The IPM Practitioner* 7(10):1-8.

A review of recent cases of human plague, including those transmitted from pet cats through what is believed to be respiratory transmission. The article includes background information on human plague and rodent plague and provides a decision-making procedure for organizing rat management programs.

Pratt, H.D., and R.Z. Brown. 1976. *Biological factors in domestic rodent control.* Department of H.E.W Publication CDC 76-8144. Washington, D.C.: Superintendent of Documents. 30 pp.

This was the source for the graph on reducing life supports for rat control (p. 630).

Redmond, J. 1984. IPM for rats: a case history. *IPM Practitioner* 6(3):2-3.

A summary of efforts to implement an IPM program for urban rats in Lafayette Park, across from the White House.

Scott, H.G., and M.R. Borom. 1976. *Rodent-borne disease control through rodent stoppage.* Atlanta: Centers for Disease Control. 33 pp. (Available from: BIRC, P.O. Box 7414, Berkeley, CA 94707.)

This is the best source of information on making the structural changes necessary to exclude rats from buildings.

Timm, R.M., ed. 1983. Norway rats. In *Prevention and control of wildlife damage,* pp. B-95 to B-120. Lincoln: University of Nebraska, Institute of Agriculture and Natural Resources. 250 pp.

Timm's chapter reviews literature about rat management and discusses and illustrates many rat management methods.

CHAPTER 34
Filth Flies

INTRODUCTION

Ogden Nash said that God made the fly and forgot to tell us why. In fact, the why of flies—the role they play in the overall scheme of things—turns out to be not so hard to understand and pretty fascinating, too. When you use the term "fly," you are talking about a big group of organisms. Individual species can be as different as the mosquito and the common housefly, or the cabbage maggot and the aphid-eating hover fly. This chapter addresses the so-called filth flies, which are associated primarily with human-generated garbage and domestic animal manure.

In the popular mind, "fly" nearly always conjures up the image of a pest. To some degree this is undeserved, because many species are predators, pathogens and parasitoids of pest insects or plant pollinators, and thus are directly beneficial to humans. In the larval stage they are often saprophytes, feeding on decaying vegetation or decomposing animal bodies and products, and recycling resources via decomposer food chains when they themselves are eaten.

Filth flies can be a menace to public health, although they pose less of a threat than blood-sucking flies such as mosquitoes (which can carry such serious pathogens as causal agents of malaria, yellow fever, dengue fever and encephalitis). Filth flies carry disease-causing organisms ranging from viruses and bacteria to helminths, or roundworms. There is unmistakable evidence for filth fly involvement in more than 60 human and animal diseases, including amebic dysentery, poliomyelitis, infectious hepatitis, trachoma, conjunctivitis, and salmonellosis. Fly management not only controls an annoyance; it is also an essential part of disease prevention among humans and domestic animals.

BIOLOGY

Of the more than 700,000 known species of insects, well over 85,000 are flies. This group of insects comprises the order Diptera, which itself contains 150 of the 1,000 or so families of the class Insecta. Diptera means two ("di") wings ("ptera"), and it is on the basis of this characteristic that all the species of flies are grouped together. At first glance, many wasps in the order Hymenoptera may be confused with flies. Wasps, however, have four wings arranged in two pairs, although the second pair is sometimes hidden by the first. Flies have small vibrating structures called halteres in place of the second pair of wings. The halteres aid in flying.

Flies pass through four distinct stages in their life cycle: egg, larva, pupa and adult (see the drawing below). The synanthropic (attracted to

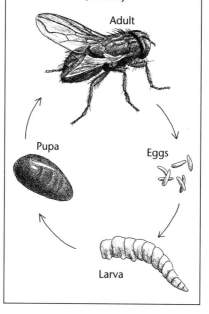

The Life Cycle of the Housefly
The housefly (Musca domestica) can go through complete metamorphosis, passing from egg to larva, pupa and adult, in as few as eight days. Other fly species have similar life cycles. (Actual size of adult: ¼ in./6 mm)

Adult

Pupa

Eggs

Larva

human habitats) filth flies look for a moist environment in which to lay their eggs, since their larvae feed and grow best under these conditions. An adult female housefly may lay up to 2,400 eggs in her lifetime, singly or in groups. The sarcophagids, or flesh flies, have a particularly interesting egg-laying pattern. Adult females lay eggs whose larvae are ready to hatch so soon after deposition that these species appear to lay larvae rather than eggs.

With all flies, it is the adult that determines the larval development site. Different stages of flies prefer different microenvironments in which to lay their eggs. Thus, proper identification of the adult is the key to finding the larval sources, and finding the larval sources is the key to fly management.

The primary food sources for synanthropic filth fly larvae as well as for common pest flies of homes, restaurants and urban areas are human food wastes, which we refer to here as garbage, and pet feces. This includes garbage in the can, garbage on its way to and at the dump and pet feces wherever they are found. Fly traps placed near garbage dumps, pet feces and garbage clearly demonstrate the attractiveness of these food sources to flies.

GREEN BOTTLE FLIES AND HOUSEFLIES
(Order Diptera, families Calliphoridae and Muscidae)

Green bottle flies, especially *Phaenicia sericata, P. cuprina* and the housefly *(Musca domestica),* are particularly prevalent in urban areas and are produced predominantly in household garbage. After the larvae have fed on the garbage or pet feces, they crawl out of the garbage can or away from the moist site in which they developed and look for a dry place in which to pupate. By setting a garbage can on a special trap, it is possible to determine how many flies are produced in the can by counting how many larvae leave to pupate. In a California study conducted from June 7 to October 20, 1958, a total of 378,889 larvae and 40,814 pupae were found in 697 specimen collections from 30 cans. This is equal to observing one can for 371 weeks with a production of 1,131 larvae and pupae per week. The greatest number of pupae found in one garbage can in one week was 19,614 (for a full report of this study, see Campbell and Black, 1960, listed under "References and Readings" on p. 649).

More than a thousand flies a week were produced by each garbage can —that's a lot of flies! This statistic is particularly interesting in light of the fact that the garbage cans studied were in a neighborhood of well-kept homes and tidy gardens. Presumably this was a neighborhood in which people took the trouble to wrap their garbage and place lids on cans that were in good shape (meaning they were not riddled with holes).

In rural areas, improperly managed feedlots, chicken or hog farms and general accumulations of agricultural waste are sources of food for larval flies. In suburban settings, horse stables and dog kennels may contribute to a community fly problem.

Like all insects, flies speed up their life processes in response to heat. The warmer the weather, the faster the garbage can produces its crop of flies. The study referred to above was done during warm—but not hot—weather. You can expect fly problems to worsen during or just after hot spells (although the cluster fly, discussed below, is an exception).

Although it is convenient to blame the presence of large numbers of filth flies around the home on other sources such as the city dump or suburban stables and kennels, the truth is that your garbage cans and those of your neighbors are the most likely sources of the problem. Thus, the key to solving fly problems is proper management of garbage and other organic wastes, particularly pet feces, that serve as breeding sites.

CLUSTER FLIES
(Order Diptera, family Calliphoridae)

We do not get many complaints about cluster flies (*Pollenia* spp.), but you should be aware of them since they may also become noticeable in the house during winter warm spells. These flies, which are neither garbage- nor manure-related, cluster characteristically in little groups around windows indoors, appearing suddenly when snow is still on the ground outdoors. They are slightly larger and darker than the housefly, and their thorax has a thick coating of short, golden, crinkled hairs among the larger bristles. They are sluggish fliers. During the warm season, the adults may be found on flowers.

In the larval stage, cluster flies are parasitoids of earthworms. Thus, soil containing many earthworms—for example, large lawn areas in nearby parks—are common sources of these flies. After feeding within the body of the worm for about 13 days, the flies tunnel out of the carcass and pupate in the earth. After emerging from the soil as adults, they seek mates and lay their fertilized eggs in the soil where earthworm hosts are likely to encounter them.

In the South, there may be four cluster fly broods in a single season. When autumn comes, the adults seek a protected place to spend the winter. They enter houses through open, unscreened doors and windows. They rest quietly, unnoticed in undisturbed areas indoors. When a warm spell suggests that spring has arrived, cluster flies look for a way to return to the outside to find more earthworms so they can lay eggs and produce another generation. Cluster flies are drawn to windows because of the light.

Cluster flies are not implicated in disease transmission, nor are they a community problem. In fact, they are really no more than a nuisance. Screens can prevent their entry to the house in late summer and fall. If they enter and cluster at windows period- ically, you can kill them with a fly swatter, vacuum them up or release them by opening the window.

MONITORING AND IDENTIFICATION

To find the source of flies and pinpoint their breeding site, you must capture a specimen. Once caught, if the fly is kept in good condition it can be identified by you (in the case of very common houseflies) or a specialist, who can usually be found at your local public health department. Table 34.1 on pp. 642-643 describes and illustrates some of the most common flies that pester people inside and around their homes.

Adult flies found near windows can be captured for identification by pressing an open jar against the window where the fly is resting, then sliding a piece of paper or thin cardboard over the end of the jar while holding it loosely against the window or sill. The fly can be left to die naturally, which it will do in a day or so, or it can be killed by placing the jar overnight in the freezer, which is faster and more humane. Releasing it outdoors is the most humane of all.

Outdoors, the best means of catching common pest house flies is a trap. Nuisance flies have a highly developed sense of smell, and most can be attracted to a trap containing bait with the right odor (discussed on pp. 646-647). Traps, whether homemade or purchased, can also be used to reduce overall adult fly numbers and to monitor the effectiveness of control efforts. If you follow the suggestions given below for traps, and the trap continues to catch as many flies as it did before you started your control measures, you may have fly species that do not fall within the common garbage/manure fly group and you should take a specimen to the local health department for identification. After the identification is made, the specialist should be able to tell you the type of breeding site you should be looking for.

Table 34.1
Filth-Fly Species and their Characteristics[a]

	Common Name	Scientific Name	Description[b]	Habits/Habitats
Endophilic Flies [c]				
	housefly	*Musca domestica*	medium-sized; grey; 4 stripes on thorax	enters houses
	vinegar fly	*Drosophila* spp.	small; yellow-brown	hovers over rotten fruit and vegetables
	drain fly	*Psychoda* spp.	small; gnat-like; wings held roof-like over body	larvae develop in sewage and kitchen drains
Exophilic Flies [d]				
	stable fly	*Stomoxys calcitrans*	medium; similar to housefly, long mouthparts	males and females suck blood
	green bottle fly	*Phaenicia* spp.	medium; green to bronze	seen on dog feces
	little housefly	*Fannia canicularis*	small; dull grey, yellow on upper abdomen	males circle in shady areas; larvae feed on garbage and pet feces

[a] Listed in order of importance and intimacy of human contact.
[b] Small = less than ¼ in. (6 mm) long; medium = approximately ¼ in. long; large = greater than ¼ in. long.
[c] Endophilic species readily enter homes and may develop within them.
[d] Exophilic species enter homes less readily.

TREATMENT

We do not recommend the use of pesticides for controlling flies in or around the house. Both aerosol applicators and constant-emission devices such as pesticide-impregnated hanging strips put poison into the air you breathe but do very little to control the fly problem. Instead, put your efforts into reducing fly production in the garbage can, installing and maintaining screens to keep flies out of the house, killing those flies that do get inside with a fly swatter and using fly traps outdoors where necessary.

Indirect Strategies

Indirect strategies for controlling filth flies focus on the proper disposal of garbage and pet feces.

1. **Disposing of Organic Kitchen Waste**. Organic garbage generated in the kitchen, whether destined for the garbage can or the compost heap, should be stored properly until it can be thrown out. This is critical in warm climates and warm weather. The object is to keep the stored material as dry as possible and to prevent odors from escaping and attracting egg-laying flies.

The California study cited on p. 641 found that well-wrapped garbage

	Common Name	Scientific Name	Description[b]	Habits/Habitats
	flesh fly	*Sarcophaga* spp.	large; grey checkered abdomen, 3 stripes on thorax	lay living young on dead animals
	black blowfly	*Phormia regina*	large; blue-black, hairy	seldom in homes
	black garbage fly	*Ophyra* spp.	small and slender; all black	predatory larvae
	drone fly	*Eristalis tenax*	large; bee-like; yellow markings	found in soupy fecal material and polluted water
	false stable fly	*Muscina stabulans*	medium; similar to housefly; red mark on back	found in decomposing organic matter
	cluster fly	*Pollenia rudis*	large; similar to housefly; hairy abdomen, yellow hair on sides	larvae parasitic on earthworms; adults enter houses

in suitable cans produced an average of about 92 larvae per can per week, compared to 877 larvae per can per week where the containers were unsatisfactory. This is a 90% reduction. Furthermore, whereas 46% of the unsatisfactory cans produced flies, only 26% of the satisfactory cans did.

Some basic guidelines for proper storage of organic wastes are given in the sidebar on p. 644.

2. Disposing of Non-Organic Garbage. The non-organic component of garbage—paper, metal and glass—should be recycled whenever possible to conserve landfill space and resources and to reduce the air pollution that occurs when these materials are incinerated. Rinse them free of any remaining food or liquid. Dirty beer bottles kept outdoors behind a restaurant, for example, can attract

flies because of the yeast remaining in the containers. The flies then enter the restaurant through unscreened back windows or service entrances that are left open. The same kind of problem can occur on a smaller scale around homes when unrinsed containers with organic residues are stored, even temporarily.

Obviously, elimination of the major sources of urban flies (see the

Proper Storage of Organic Wastes

• Separate organic wastes from paper, metal and glass; store the former for composting and recycle the latter.

• Let plate scrapings and other wet garbage drain so they are as dry as possible when stored.

If you are putting the organic waste in the garbage can:

• Wrap it in an absorbent material such as newspaper to dry it out after draining as thoroughly as possible.

• If the bulk of the organic kitchen garbage is too great for the option above, secure it in tightly wrapped plastic bags to prevent the entry of adult flies. We regard this as a second-best solution because it increases the amount of plastic sent to the dump or incinerator. As of this writing, no truly biodegradable plastic is available, despite manufacturers' claims to the contrary, and plastics give off undesirable fumes when burned.

• Place newspaper-wrapped organic waste in a paper bag, then fold the bag over securely or tape or tie it closed.

• Use a garbage can with a tight lid and a fastener that prevents its being opened by dogs or raccoons if it is pushed over. If your cans don't have this kind of fastener, the drawing on p. 632 shows how you can make one very easily.

If you are saving organic kitchen waste for a batch compost:

• Store it in sawdust to prevent odors from escaping and cover the material with at least 2 in. (5 cm) of sawdust.

• Make the compost in a bin with solid sides and a close-fitting lid. A closed bin keeps the heat in and the rain, flies and rats out.

• Turn the compost daily or every other day during the first week.

• Turn the compost so that the outsides of the pile are folded into the center, making sure all portions of the mix are subjected to the heat that develops in a properly constituted pile. (Note: We do not recommend placing organic kitchen garbage in a slow compost pile [one that is not turned regularly and does not heat up] or in compost bins without solid sides and a close-fitting lid. You will find that the popular literature on composting contains many designs for compost bins that permit passive air flow through the compost. If organic kitchen wastes are introduced into composts made in such bins, the process can produce large numbers of flies and become a neighborhood nuisance, although you may not be aware of it. If you want to compost your kitchen garbage or pet fecal material, use a hot, or aerobic, composting method. For detailed instructions on aerobic composting and plans for constructing fly-deterring compost bins, see Olkowski et al., 1979, listed under "References and Readings" on p. 649.)

If your apartment, home or workplace uses a dumpster:

• Follow the procedures recommended above for wrapping garbage for individual garbage cans.

• Communicate to the building's custodian the importance of keeping the dumpster closed between uses to reduce the odors that attract filth flies and prevent rat access (for more on the latter, see the discussion on p. 631).

• Ask that the custodian or caretaker hose out the dumpster thoroughly each time it is emptied by the refuse collector. Soap, a brush and a high-pressure stream of water should be used in hot weather. Using insecticidal soap helps kill any larvae hiding in waste residues left in the less accessible corners of the dumpster.

chart on p. 645) would require wide-scale employment of the same techniques described for the individual house or apartment dweller. Toward this end, public education about proper storage of garbage should be undertaken as part of municipal refuse management systems.

Unfortunately, municipal garbage collection is generally every seven days. Ideally, it should be more frequent. During hot months, garbage collection twice a week or every three days would significantly reduce fly production. One study showed that from June to October, only 11% of the fly larvae left the garbage cans during the first four days after refuse collection. Ultimately, an organic waste separation, storage and processing system must be developed to reclaim the minerals and calories present in organic waste. No such system is presently used by any city in the United States. Both earthworm and alcohol fermentation technology may ultimately become valuable components of such a system.

3. Disposing of Pet Feces. Dog feces that dry quickly may attract feeding adult flies, but it is unlikely that they will feed many larval flies. However, manure that remains damp due to humidity, rain or contact with other moist manure can become a larval development site. There are several disposal options open to pet owners or others who find animal feces on their property:

• Scoop up the manure with a utensil used for this purpose (available in pet stores), then flush it down the toilet. This approach has the advantage of avoiding the buildup of worm parasites in the soil that may infest your pet or be transferred from one dog to another.

• Store the manure in sawdust to dry it out before composting, then place it in a hot compost pile (see p. 474) that is turned regularly.

• Wrap the manure in newspaper to dry it out, place it in a well-closed paper bag, then deposit it in the garbage can.

• Place the manure in a plastic bag, close the bag tightly and put it in a garbage can. However, we object to the use of plastic bags because the plastic constitutes a serious environmental problem, so we don't recommend this method.

• Bury the feces immediately. Once larvae are within the manure, it must be buried at least 3 ft. (0.9 m) deep, and the earth above tamped down very firmly to prevent the flies from migrating to the surface. It is not likely that you will want to go through that kind of effort.

Direct Physical Controls

Direct physical controls for filth flies include the use of window screening, bead curtains, fly swatters, flypaper and traps.

1. Screens. Window screens are the best means of preventing the entry of flies into the home. To be effec-

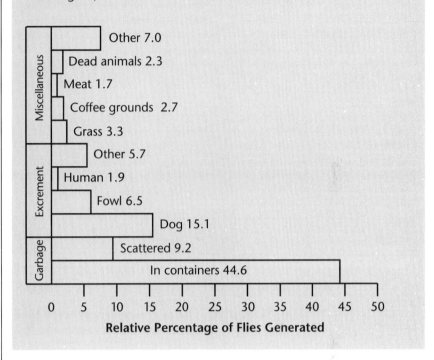

Major Sources of Urban Flies

This bar graph represents the relative percentages of flies generated by garbage and other media found in a study conducted in Charleston, West Virginia, in 1952.

Miscellaneous
- Other 7.0
- Dead animals 2.3
- Meat 1.7
- Coffee grounds 2.7
- Grass 3.3

Excrement
- Other 5.7
- Human 1.9
- Fowl 6.5
- Dog 15.1

Garbage
- Scattered 9.2
- In containers 44.6

Relative Percentage of Flies Generated

tive, screens must fit openings tightly, and any punctures or rips must be mended promptly. A clear caulk, such as silicone seal, does the job nicely, even for tears in the center of the screen. Screen doors should be fitted with springs that close them firmly after they are opened.

2. Bead Curtains. As an alternative to screens in areas of heavy traffic, bead curtains have proven moderately effective in deterring flies. The beads should be oval, with each string's beads offset from the next string so that the beads fit into each other's contours, eliminating gaps. The bead strings have the added advantage of brushing flies off people and pets so the flies don't piggyback a ride into the house. Bead curtains, which can be quite attractive, were often used in the past and are sometimes seen in old movies.

3. Fly Swatters. The old-fashioned fly swatter should not be overlooked as a way to dispense with flies in the house quickly and safely. The best types are flexible in the shaft and head. We have found that those with thin wire stems and natural fiber heads are superior to the more common plastic ones. The wire stems are less visible and seem to move more quickly through the air; the flexible, natural fiber heads provide the necessary coup de grace.

4. Flypaper. Rolls of sticky flypaper tape are available from most hardware stores. Although a length of paper peppered with dead flies is not the most attractive sight, flypaper has always been effective at catching flies and is suitable for use in areas such as back porches, garages and storage sheds where aesthetics are not of primary importance.

5. Traps. Traps can be used to reduce adult fly populations, capture specimens for identification and monitor the effectiveness of control programs. One very good fly trap comes with bait and a device that delivers water drop by drop from a bottle to keep the bait moist (shown in the drawing below). It is available from Beneficial BioSystems (see the Resource Appendix under "Insect Management: Physical Controls" on pp. 682-683).

The flies are attracted to the bait in the saucer or plate at the bottom of the trap. You can use any type of food or liquid that attracts flies—such as buttermilk, molasses and syrups, sweet-smelling fermenting foods and kitchen scraps. However, it is not a good idea to use meat or animal manure because they attract and produce blowflies, which usually are not pestiferous and don't need to be trapped; they also attract cats, raccoons and dogs, which can disturb the trap.

You may have to experiment to see which baits work best for your fly species, location and conditions. Typical houseflies are attracted to a wide variety of food wastes and animal manures. A mixture of cornmeal and molasses ferments and attracts houseflies, green bottle flies and others. The advantage of this mixture over others is that the flies cannot develop in it as they can in other baits. Yeast can be added to the mixture to speed up the fermenting process so you don't have to wait for the natural yeasts in the air to get the process going. When adding yeast, first dissolve it in water, as if you were making bread.

Keeping the bait moist is essential to successful baiting. You may have to moisten baits every day or so, or recharge the trap with fresh food, depending on the type of bait you use. The commercial traps listed in the Resource Appendix under "Insect Management: Physical Controls" on pp. 682-683 have water reservoirs that continuously moisten the bait; because keeping bait moist is such a problem, many people prefer these commercial traps. You can also purchase a liquid bait that uses yeast and ammonium carbonate as its main ingredients. This bait contains no protein, so the flies do not lay eggs in it.

When setting the trap, put the bait dish near the middle of the trap. If it is too close to the edge, the flies will find it easy to feed at the outer edges and escape the trap altogether. The object is to attract flies into the lower area of the trap, where the contrast between light and dark is greatest. You can also elevate the dish on bricks or boards to get the bait 2 in. or 3 in. (5 cm or 7.6 cm) up into the trapping area.

Since the cone of the trap is directly above the bait, flies land on the inside of the cone. Then, because the hole in the top of the cone is the brightest spot they see, they walk up to and through the hole after feeding. At that point they are trapped in the outer cylinder. They are not likely to go back down through the hole, since they are attracted to the light and will keep trying to fly up through the top of the trap until they die of exhaustion and starvation.

Gradually, dead flies will accumulate. When the upper portion of the trap becomes dark with fly bodies, the trap does not work as efficiently and should be emptied. You can kill live flies by covering the trap with a plastic bag and putting it in the sun. Dead flies can be composted, buried, flushed down the toilet or fed to chickens.

Once you understand the principle behind catching filth flies, you might want to design your own trap. After watching many of these novel homemade devices in action, we can say that they can work very well, no matter how bizarre the design. Keep in mind, however, that the most important factor in the design is to make the hole(s) through which the flies walk the brightest points they see after leaving the bait. If the design proves satisfactory, the usefulness of the trap depends upon how well you maintain the bait and where you place the trap.

A Cone-Type Fly Trap
Flies enter this simple Beneficial BioSystems trap through an opening in the top of the mesh cone, then cannot find their way back out again. The optional water bottle keeps the bait in the pan at the bottom of the trap moist for up to three weeks.

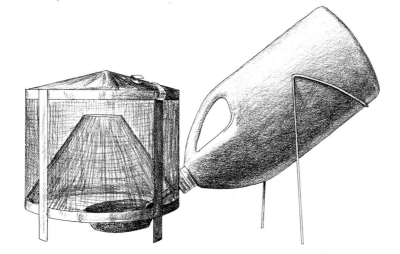

Trap location is important. The prevailing winds should blow from your trap toward the area where flies are most likely being generated. If you place the trap where the bait gets heavy competition from other food sources, you may not trap any flies at all. For example, if the garbage cans in the adjacent yard are poorly managed, and no amount of education, persuasion or rewards can get your neighbors to change their ways, you may want to place your trap on your side of the fence near the neighbor's garbage cans to prevent the flies from later coming to visit your patio barbecue. But the flies may find the garbage cans more attractive than your traps. The only solution in this case is to experiment with different baits until you find one so attractive it competes with the other source.

Ideal trap placement must be determined individually for each household, and will doubtless shift as the sun, prevailing winds and household activities change at different times of the year. Assuming that you are not producing flies on your own property because you are maintaining kitchen and animal wastes properly, the ideal place for your fly trap is near the property line, where flies first enter the area. Finding the best spot requires experimentation—you'll have to study the air currents and the direction from which most flies seem to arrive, based on the catches of the trap in different positions.

If possible, place the trap in a sunny area, because most flies are more active in sunlight. Traps should not be set near doorways and entrances to the house, and they should be located away from outdoor areas that people use for eating or recreation. In warm weather if flies are numerous, you can surround such areas with a ring of traps, drawing the flies away from the central area you wish to have comparatively fly-free.

6. Ultraviolet Light Traps. Contrary to the advice provided in the promotional literature for ultraviolet light or electrocuter traps, these traps should not be used outdoors. They are relatively nonselective in the insects they kill and can harm as many beneficial and other insects as pests. Indoors, electric light traps are useful in places where food is cooked and served, such as in restaurants, food stores and community facilities, but it should not be necessary to use them in ordinary homes since they can be protected adequately with window screens and screen doors.

The important thing to remember in selecting an electric light trap is that its size must correspond to the situation in which it is to be used. For more information on selecting traps, consult the article by D. Gilbert, listed under "References and Readings" on p. 649. Manufacturers of these traps are listed in the Resource Appendix under "Insect Management: Physical Controls" on pp. 682-683.

Direct Biological Controls

Where good garbage management exists, fly production will not be excessive, and the naturally occurring enemies of filth flies will do their best to hold down the number of flies to tolerable levels. Some of these natural enemies are listed in Table 34.2 below. Although many parasitoids of filth flies are available commercially, we do not recommend them for home yard use because the accumulation of manure is usually not very great. However, if you are raising chickens, horses or dogs, or are otherwise involved with the management of animal systems that produce a large quantity of manure, these commercially produced beneficial insects can be very helpful.

Both the design of the livestock housing and the management of the manure have been shown to have a critical impact upon the numbers of fly larvae produced and the effectiveness of natural enemies. The design of poultry housing is beyond the scope of this book; for a thorough introduction to this subject, however, see R.C. Axtell's article, listed under "References and Readings" on p. 649. The management of manure involves several variables: moisture, drying rate, depth, frequency of removal, removal technique and subsequent processing. Two of these are of particular importance. Moisture control involves good drainage and the fixing of any water leaks. It is also important that you leave behind at least 8 in. (20 cm) of manure when cleaning areas where manure has collected. This helps sustain a continuing population of natural enemies that will colonize newly deposited manure.

Predators and parasitoids are available for biological fly control and can be used in environments that have not been saturated with pesticides. The sidebar at left on p. 648 lists species of filth fly parasitoids now available from commercial insectaries in the United States and elsewhere (for sources, see the Re-

Table 34.2
Predators and Competitors of Filth Flies

Group[a]	Prey/Habits
beetles	histerid and staphylinids eat fly eggs and larvae
mites	macrochelid and uropidid mites eat eggs and larvae
soldier flies	can compete with houseflies for breeding media

[a] For species, see Axtell, 1981.

Commercially Available Filth Fly Pupal Parasitoids[a]

Spalangia endius:
The New Zealand strain
is currently in widest use.

Muscidifurax zoraptor:
Has replaced *M. raptor,* which was
used previously. The giant Denver
strain is now in common use.

Pachycrepoideus vindemiae
(shown in the photo at right[c]):
Has replaced *Sphegigaster* spp.
due to its greater effectiveness.

Tachinaephagus zealandicus:
Effective in cooler weather.
Attacks larvae but emerges
from pupae.

Nasonia vitripennis: [b]
A contaminant in insectary
cultures that is not effective in

poultry houses or feedlots. It
prefers to attack *Phaenicia* and
related species outdoors.

[a] All species listed are in the hymenopteran superfamily Chalcidoidea, family
Pteromalidae, except *T. zealandicus,* which is in the family Encyrtidae. All
species can also kill hosts by direct feeding.

[b] Some controversy exists concerning this species, but large-scale field studies
indicate it is ineffective in poultry houses and feedlots in hot dry areas.

[c] Photo by Max Badgley.

Summary: Least-Toxic Filth Fly Control

• Identify the adult flies to help determine where they are coming from.

• Dry and wrap organic garbage before placing it in the garbage can.

• Use tight-fitting lids held to garbage cans by spring fasteners to prevent dog, cat and raccoon access.

• Bury garbage deeply and swiftly if you decide to process it this way.

• Compost organic kitchen garbage using the hot aerobic method.

• Screen windows and doors to keep flies out.

• Use fly swatters or sticky tapes to catch flies indoors.

• Maintain baited fly traps outdoors to reduce the number of flies during warm weather.

• Dispose of pet feces in the toilet.

• Follow proper manure management practices and use commercially available natural enemies of filth flies to reduce fly production in animal facilities such as stables and kennels.

source Appendix under "Insect Management: Biological Controls" on pp. 683-686. By attacking the filth flies in their pupal stage, these parasitoids reduce adult fly populations without adding competitors to the existing naturally occurring enemy fauna. The latter are composed primarily of species that attack the earlier life stages of the fly.

When purchasing parasitoids from a producer or distributor, consider what mix of species (and strains within species) to buy, the dosage or number of parasitoids to be released and the frequency of releases. Fortunately, insectaries themselves can usually provide valuable advice about the parasitoids appropriate to your needs. Moreover, a substantial body of literature on this subject has developed, as reflected in the "References and Readings" on the facing page.

REFERENCES AND READINGS

Axtell, R.C. 1981. Use of predators and parasites in filth fly IPM programs in poultry housing. In Patterson et al., 1981 (see below), pp. 26-43.

This paper describes the impact of poultry housing design on pest management programs.

Campbell, E., and R.J. Black. 1960. The problem of migration of mature fly larvae from refuse containers and its implication on the frequency of refuse collection. *California Vector Views* 7:9-15.

Presents results of studies showing considerable fly production in urban garbage cans.

Drummond, R.O., J.E. George and S.E. Kunz. 1988. *Control of arthropod pests of livestock: a review of technology.* Boca Raton, Fla.: CRC Press. 245 pp.

This book thoroughly updates the history of and current work on the control of all pests of livestock, including filth flies.

Gilbert, D. 1984. Insect electrocutor light traps. In *Insect management for food storage and processing*, ed. F.J. Baur, pp. 87-108. St. Paul, Minn.: American Society of Cereal Chemists. 384 pp.

Gilbert's paper is the only known practical review of how to use light traps for capturing insects indoors. It includes some historical information and research work that has not been published elsewhere.

Greenberg, B. 1971. *Flies and disease, Volume I: ecology, classification, and biotic associations,* and *Volume II (1973): biology and disease transmission.* Princeton, N.J.: Princeton University Press. 856 and 447 pp., respectively.

These volumes are comprehensive sources of information on filth flies. They gather a vast amount of basic information on the dangers posed by these organisms and their ecology, but no control or management methods are discussed.

Kettle, D.S. 1984. *Medical and veterinary entomology.* New York: John Wiley and Sons. 658 pp.

This text has a relatively recent overview of the fly pests of medical and veterinary importance, including houseflies, stable flies and blowflies. Fly management is not discussed.

Oldroyd, H. 1964. *The natural history of flies.* New York: W.W. Norton. 324 pp.

Oldroyd manages to make what might normally be a dry technical work a highly readable yet authoritative exploration of fly biology and the relationships of flies to humans. He provides examples from all over the world. There are special chapters on compost and dung flies, the housefly and its relatives, and flies and man, including many informative black and white photographs and line drawings.

Olkowski, H., W. Olkowski and T. Javits. 1979. *The integral urban house.* San Francisco: Sierra Club Books. 494 pp. (Out of print, but available from BIRC, P.O. Box 7414, Berkeley, CA 94707.)

This book contains information about aesthetically acceptable storage of kitchen garbage, composting methods that minimize fly production and construction methods for a large filth fly trap.

Patterson, R.S., P.G. Koehler, P.B. Morgan and R.L. Harris, eds. 1981. *Status of biological control of filth flies,* Proceedings of a workshop, February 4 and 5, University of Florida, Gainesville. Gainesville, Fla.: Insects Affecting Man and Animals Research Laboratory. 212 pp. (Available from: Insects Affecting Man and Animals Research Lab., P.O. Box 14565, Gainesville, FL 32604.)

The 30 papers presented in this volume cover rearing methods for commercially available hosts and their parasitoids and those species in the research phase. They also discuss field evaluations of releases, the incorporation of mass-released parasitoids into IPM programs, foreign exploration for natural enemies, trapping and commercialization. Papers of particular importance include F. Legner's "Improving Commercial Biological Control of Filth Flies with Parasites" and "Commercial Production and Use of Predators and Parasites for Fly Control Programs," by Everitt J. Dietrick.

Patterson, R.S., and D.A. Rutz, eds. 1986. *Biological control of muscoid flies.* College Park, Md.: Entomological Society of America (Miscellaneous Publication 61). 174 pp.

Contains 19 papers discussing various aspects of the biological control of filth flies, particularly the housefly *(Musca domestica).* Topics include rearing of dung-burying beetles and microhymenopteran pupal parasitoids, as well as the use of mass-reared biological control agents in various parts of the world and in different types of animal facilities.

CHAPTER 35
Yellowjackets

INTRODUCTION

The threat of their sting makes yellowjackets unwelcome intruders wherever people are picnicking, hiking, camping, selling food, picking fruit, working at food-processing plants or depositing or collecting garbage. To people whose hypersensitivity to wasp stings is life-threatening, yellowjackets are among the most dangerous of common wildlife.

Although often lumped together with bees, yellowjackets (which are wasps) are a far more real and severe threat. They are more aggressive than bees; moreover, because they do not have barbs on their stingers, they can insert them repeatedly into a victim, whereas a single bee can sting only once, losing its barbed stinger and its own life at the same time.

Bees are widely known as extremely valuable pollinators, and we often make an effort not to harm them. Unfortunately, when people cannot tell them apart from their more aggressive and potentially harmful insect relatives, unnecessary destruction of critically necessary wildlife takes place. Furthermore, yellowjackets are also very valuable scavengers and predators of such insect pests as caterpillars. Thus, to avoid unnecessary ecological damage, it is important for people to learn how to protect themselves against yellowjackets and to decrease the likelihood of hazardous encounters with those insects while also preserving the insects themselves. Where you cannot protect yourself adequately against yellowjackets, they must be controlled. The latter part of the chapter is devoted to this topic.

BIOLOGY

It is important to be able to distinguish yellowjackets from other hornets and wasps, from bees and from their non-stinging mimics, the syrphid flies. Little confusion among these three groups is likely to arise at the picnic table, where the persistent intruder is most likely the yellowjack-

The Life Cycle of the Yellowjacket

Yellowjacket nests are begun by overwintering queens. In spring, the queen digs a cavity in the soil or enlarges an existing hole, constructs a nest from chewed cellulose fibers, and lays a dozen or so eggs. As new young are produced, the queen feeds them until they mature to workers and can forage for themselves. After this, she specializes in egg production while the workers feed her and care for the larvae and pupae. The colony reaches its peak in late summer. At this point, new males and queens mate, the males and workers die, and the fertilized queens seek a sheltered place to overwinter.

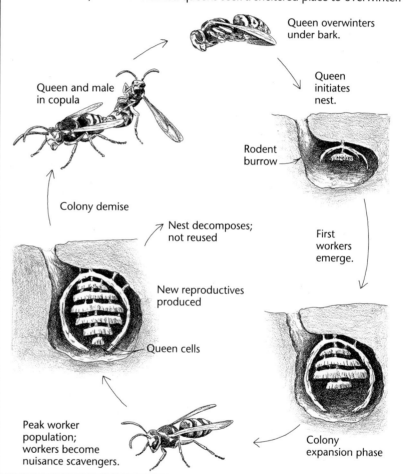

Queen overwinters under bark.

Queen and male in copula

Queen initiates nest.

Rodent burrow

Colony demise

Nest decomposes; not reused

First workers emerge.

New reproductives produced

Queen cells

Peak worker population; workers become nuisance scavengers.

Colony expansion phase

et searching out meats or other protein-rich or sugary foods and drink.

In other settings, such as the garden or wild areas, yellowjackets can be distinguished by one or more of three criteria: appearance, nest construction and behavior, as indicated in Table 35.1 on p. 652.

There are many types of large wasps, but only yellowjackets and pa-

per wasps (genus *Polistes)* are social, meaning that they are organized in colonies (see the drawing above). Within a colony, there are two castes: workers and reproductives. Reproductives include queens and kings. Two yellowjacket species, *Dolichovespula arctica* and *Vespula austriaca,* are parasitic and lack worker castes of their own; instead, they adopt the nests

Table 35.1
Distinguishing among the Stinging Bee-Like or Wasp-Like Hymenoptera

	Appearance	Habits	Nests	Feeding Behavior
Ants	thin waists; wingless except for reproductives structures; can bite or sting	workers search individually or in lines on soil surface, plants or structures; invade	ground nests under stones and sidewalks or in soil	scavengers; predators; herbivores
Bees	stout bodies with thick waists; hairy; workers and reproductives winged	noisy flight; sting mainly while defending nest; foraging workers seldom sting	in hives, trees or buildings	collect pollen and nectar; feed pollen to young and share food with other adults
Wasps	long bodies with thin waists; all winged	colorful, rapid fliers; solitary and social varieties	aerial or ground nests in ground or structures	scavengers and/or predators
Solitary wasps	thin- or thick-waisted	solitary; visit flowers and other vegetation; relatively docile	of mud, or in holes in ground	predators; provision nests with prey upon which young feed
Paper (umbrella) wasps	long bodies with thin waists	colonial; search vegetation for prey; visit flowers for nectar	single-comb nests attached to structures, fences, branches, burrows, boards; nests made from chewed vegetation (paper) in shape of upside-down umbrella	feed food to developing young in cells of combs
Hornets	large, wingspan up to 3 in. (7.6 cm)	not aggressive toward humans	multilayered aerial carton (cardboard-like) nest with brown envelope	predatory on cicadas, flies and bees
Yellowjackets	stout, colorful	rapid fliers, aggressive, with individuals capable of inflicting multiple stings; social in large colonies, which they defend vigorously	multilayered carton nests mostly in ground, although some aerial	mostly beneficial predators, but scavenger species become pestiferous

and workers of other yellowjackets after first killing the queen.

All colonies of yellowjackets are started in the spring by a single female, the queen, who has overwintered in a hibernating state in a protected location, such as under loose bark or in a decaying stump. When the weather warms, the queen begins feeding on flowers and other nectar sources, captures prey and searches for a nest site (common nest locations are described below). Her ovaries begin to enlarge. Once she has selected a nest site, the queen gathers fibers from weathered, decayed wood or living plants. She chews these into a pulp, from which she constructs a small nest.

The nest contains 20 to 45 cells covered by an envelope of the same paper-like material. The queen lays eggs in the cells and seeks food for the larvae. After 30 days the first five to seven workers emerge and assume construction, foraging and sanitation responsibilities. As the colony grows and the queen's duties are assumed by newly emerged workers, her function gradually shifts to just laying eggs. As the nest grows, a characteristic shape and structure with multiple comb layers develops.

Later in the season larger reproductive cells are formed, and new queens are reared from these. Still later the colony starts to decline, and workers pull larvae from their cells and discard them or feed them to other larvae. It is during this period—generally late summer to early fall—that workers are more likely to sting when away from the nest. The yellowjackets that remain in the nest shift their diet from an emphasis on protein to predominantly sweets. Before winter, the queens and males mate, the males die, the new queens and males leave the nest and the fertilized queens begin hibernation.

Yellowjacket species can be divided into two groups, the *Vespula rufa* group and the *Vespula vulgaris* group. Table 35.2 above lists the major pest yellowjacket species in both groups.

Table 35.2
Major Yellowjacket and Hornet Species in North America[a]

Species	Common Name	Distribution/Prey
Dolichovespula albida	none	boreal region (northern)
D. arctica	none	parasitic[b] on *D. arenaria;* transcontinental, boreal
D. arenaria	aerial yellowjacket	transcontinental, boreal
D. maculata	baldfaced hornet	transcontinental
D. norvegicoides	Norwegian yellowjacket	mostly Canadian
Vespa crabro germana	European hornet	eastern North America
Vespula acadica	forest yellowjacket	mostly Canada
V. atropilosa	prairie yellowjacket	western boreal
V. austriaca	cuckoo yellowjacket	parasitic[b] on *V. acadica;* transcontinental
V. consobrina	blackjacket	strict predator
V. flavopilosa[c]	hybrid yellowjacket	scavenger;eastern North America
V. germanica[c]	German yellowjacket	scavenger; eastern North America
V. intermedia	none	transcontinental; boreal
V. maculifrons[c]	eastern yellowjacket	scavenger
V. pensylvanica[c]	western yellowjacket	scavenger; western North America
V. squamosa[d]	southern yellowjacket	scavenger; parasitic[b] on *V. maculifrons*
V. sulphurea[d]	California yellowjacket	western North America
V. vidua	none	eastern North America
V. vulgaris[c]	common yellowjacket	scavenger; transcontinental

[a] From Akre et al., 1980, and Krombein et al., 1979.

[b] Parasitic without worker castes; they use the worker castes of other yellowjackets by destroying their queens.

[c] In the *vulgaris* group.

[d] Possibly in the *vulgaris* group.

Yellowjackets in the *rufa* group only forage for live prey, whereas those in the *vulgaris* group also scavenge around animal carcasses, picnic tables, garbage cans and other locations where their mere presence can make them bothersome and dangerous to hypersensitive individuals.

Although hikers and campers most frequently come into contact with the *rufa* group, most problems occur with members of the *vulgaris* group. The map on p. 654 shows the geographic distribution of the two most common species in the *vulgaris* group. This group has larger colonies

The Distribution of the Two Most Common Yellowjacket Species in the United States

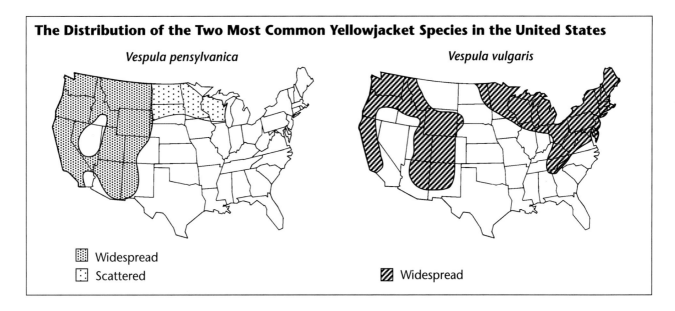

Vespula pensylvanica

Vespula vulgaris

▦ Widespread
⬚ Scattered

▨ Widespread

with larger nests and a longer colony duration, which makes their presence more common.

Both groups have members that can nest in or on human structures and can become very noticeable. Because all vespids defend their colonies, nest disturbance of either group can provoke a mass attack. This can occur when someone accidentally steps in an underground opening or hits an aerial nest. Swarm attacks from subterranean nests can also be triggered by ground vibrations that are detected by the wasps. Thus, mowing lawns, golf courses or athletic fields can be hazardous, and operators may need to wear protective clothing when mowing during the late summer season when colonies are large. Sometimes merely coming near a nest, especially if it has been disturbed previously, can provoke an attack by one or more yellowjackets.

MANAGING YELLOWJACKET PROBLEMS

There are two major objectives to yellowjacket management: protecting yourself from stings and reducing yellowjacket habitat in areas of human recreational activities. The latter objective (discussed under "Treatment" on pp. 656-660) has two elements: handling problems on your own property and managing community-wide problems or those at public facilities such as recreation centers and parks.

Avoiding and Treating Stings

Insect stings kill about 50 Americans each year and are the leading cause of fatalities from venomous animals; most of these bites are inflicted by yellowjackets. However, maintaining one's composure when confronted by a foraging yellowjacket can greatly reduce the likelihood of being stung. Slowly and carefully brushing off a yellowjacket that has landed on you, or waiting until it flies off is better than hitting or constraining it. We know from personal experience that it is possible to work near yellowjackets and not get stung by moving slowly and keeping calm when they land on your skin.

If you are hypersensitive to or especially fearful of these wasps, you should conduct a careful survey of lawns, gardens, eaves of buildings, chimneys and other areas for social wasp colonies before working in an outdoor area. The survey should be repeated once or twice during the warm season. The sidebar on the facing page provides some more specific advice on how to avoid yellowjackets in outdoor settings during warm weather, particularly in late summer. It also describes what you should do if you are stung.

Hypersensitive Reactions

A small percentage of the population—roughly two million Americans—are hypersensitive to wasp or bee stings. If you are wondering whether you or a family member is hypersensitive to such stings, we recommend that you go to an allergist for testing.

Hypersensitive reactions to yellowjacket stings include itching, flushing, hives and swelling distant from the sting site. Swelling of the tongue and closure of the small air passageways of the lungs can cause wheezing, choking and shortness of breath. Other reactions include hypotension (low blood pressure) with dizziness, unconsciousness, cyanosis (blueness), nausea, vomiting, chest pain, abdominal or pelvic cramps and headache. These symptoms can begin anywhere from a second after a sting to up to 30 minutes afterwards, and they can last for hours.

How to Avoid Stings, and What to Do if You Are Stung

Things to avoid include:

• Wearing perfumes and other scents, including scented hair spray, suntan lotion, cosmetics, deodorants and shaving lotions.

• Wearing brightly colored and patterned clothes.

• Going barefoot, especially in vegetation.

• Swatting at or squashing bees and yellowjackets. Squashing a yellowjacket releases a chemical alarm that signals other wasps and yellowjackets in the area to attack. Yellowjackets will not sting or bite (they can do that, too) a person at rest if they have not been disturbed by some agitation of their nest or threatened by swatting or other fast-moving movement of the arms or legs. They may land on your skin to inspect a smell or to get water if you are sweating heavily, but they will leave of their own accord if you stay calm and do not move quickly. If you lack the patience, you can brush them off gently with a piece of paper as long as you move slowly and deliberately.

• Drinking soft drinks from open containers. Use a lid with a straw.

• Carrying sugary or meat snacks in open containers.

• Sitting down on or handling wet towels, washcloths or clothes, without first checking to make sure no yellowjackets are drinking the moisture.

• Cooking and eating outdoors during yellowjacket season.

If a bee or wasp enters your moving car:

• Pull to the side of the road and stop, if possible.

• Open the car windows or doors and wait for the insect to leave by itself.

• If the yellowjacket is moving slowly and deliberately, guide it out of the vehicle with a piece of paper. Alternatively, you can invert a cup or jar over it, slip a piece of stiff paper under the open end of the container while it is still lightly pressed against the surface where the insect is trapped, carry the jar outside and point it away from your face and body as you slowly pull the paper away, freeing the insect. (This is the same method recommended for removing spiders from the house — see p. 295).

If you are *not* hypersensitive to bee or wasp venom and you are stung:

• Examine the site of the sting first to determine whether you have been stung by a yellowjacket or a bee. A yellowjacket does not have a barbed stinger that remains in the skin (see the drawing below),

Yellowjacket Stinger

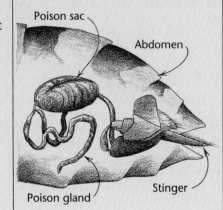

Poison sac

Abdomen

Poison gland

Stinger

whereas a bee leaves a stinger with a pulsating poison sac at the end of it in your skin. If you see such a stinger, do not grab or pinch it with your fingers, since it will only inject more venom. Unless your fingernail is very long, use some other tool, such as a knife, key or coin, that is thin and flat to scrape the stinger out with a side-to-side motion.

• Wash the wound and treat it. Non-hypersensitive individuals experience localized pain, itching, redness and swelling for a few minutes or hours after a bee or wasp sting. The most common treatments are ice, meat tenderizer, which contains enzymes that destroy the proteins in venoms (wet the powder and smear it on with your finger), and commercially available products like Sting Kill® that reduce the pain of the reaction. Aerosol or cream histamine preparations are also available. Some of these contain coolants, which can help reduce the spread of the venom in the tissues. Washing with soap and water also helps, because it removes some of the venom from the surface of the wound.

• Rest and don't drink alcohol.

• If the sting is to a limb and the limb swells, lower it below your body trunk.

• If the sting is to your throat or mouth, seek medical attention immediately, because swelling in these areas can cause suffocation.

• If the sting is followed by the severe symptoms described on p. 654 for hypersensitive persons, also seek immediate medical attention.

What to Do if You Are Hypersensitive to Stings

If you are hypersensitive to wasp or bee stings, or think you are becoming so, you should obtain a series of skin tests to diagnose the type of venom causing the reactions. Your physician should become familiar with the diagnostic and treatment systems offered by the Pharmacia Diagnostics Division of Pharmacia, Inc. (800 Centennial Ave., Piscataway, NJ 08854).

Treatment involves repeated injections of increasing doses of the appropriate venom extract. The whole-body extracts of wasps or bees that were used years ago are no longer believed to be effective; instead, desensitization with specific venoms of particular stinging groups of insects is the common practice.

If you are hypersensitive, we further recommend that you carry several pre-loaded epinephrine injectors as part of your first-aid kit. Have the kit with you when you go into areas where you are likely to encounter flowers, ripe fruit or garbage containers. The danger is greatest in August and September. The injectors are virtually painless to use and the needle is concealed, which helps when administering the venom extract to children. The injector is triggered when it is pressed against the thigh and delivers its dose into the muscle. The kits have a shelf life of about a year and come with instructions.

At least three versions of the injector are available; for sources, see the Resource Appendix under "Insect Management: Chemical Controls" on pp. 686-687. For further information on treatments for sting allergies, write to Pharmacia at the address given above, or to the North American Apiotherapy Society, 15621 Aitcheson Lane, Laurel, MD 20707. Ask for a copy of the article "Sting Allergy and Apiotherapy" by D.B.K. Golden, which appeared in Volume 2 of the *Proceedings of the North American Apiotherapy Society, 1979.*

If you notice that reactions to successive bee stings are becoming progressively more severe, this is a sign that hypersensitivity may be developing, and medical advice should be sought. However, the first allergic reaction is often preceded by many uneventful stings. It should also be stressed that the fact that you have other allergies does not predispose you to an insect sting allergy.

If tests indicate that you are hypersensitive, or if you suspect that you are becoming so because each sting causes a more severe reaction, we recommend that you carry an emergency kit containing pre-loaded syringes of epinephrine. These are available in an innovative system called the Epi-Pen® that can be self-administered as described in the sidebar above.

TREATMENT

Because of the beneficial role yellowjackets play in helping to suppress a wide variety of pest insects, the objective of a yellowjacket management program should be to reduce human encounters with pestiferous wasps, but not to eliminate the wasps from the entire area. The two most productive and least environmentally destructive ways to do this are modifying the habitat to reduce yellowjackets' access to food in the vicinity of human activities and using physical controls such as trapping and nest removal. Area-wide poison-baiting should be used only as a last resort when other methods have failed and stings are frequent.

Indirect Strategies

When a protein or sugar food source generated by humans is more or less constantly available, the yellowjacket queen may discover it early in the season and use the extra nutrients to increase the size of her colony beyond what she could sustain on naturally available foods such as insects. Subsequently, colony members may regularly scout the area for this handout. Although such food sources may seem insignificant to us, they are important. A good example is partially moist pet food regularly left outside between feedings. Pets should be fed indoors, on a screened porch or in other screened enclosures (this is also a good control against rats).

However, the most important human source of food for yellowjackets is garbage. This is true at home as well as in parks, other recreational facilities, shopping centers and schools. You should protect the home garbage can from the garbage-scattering of dogs and raccoons by using a spring-fitted lid as described on p. 632 on rat management (good garbage management is also essential for rat and fly control). Proper disposal of household organic wastes, either in a garbage can or by aerobic composting, is discussed on pp. 642-645. If you want to bury organic garbage in your back yard, follow the suggestions provided on p. 632.

Garbage cans in public areas should have removable domed tops with vertical spring-loaded swinging doors, and should be emptied frequently enough to prevent the contents from impeding the movement of the lid. The lid itself should be periodically cleaned of food wastes that adhere to it. Disposable liners can be used and replaced when soiled or damaged.

Where these practices are not followed, the public garbage can become a source of pestiferous wasps for the entire area. With a large number of wasps around the cans, people are afraid to place garbage all the way inside. Particularly with open-topped cans, this leads to standing at what seems to be a safe distance and attempting to pitch the garbage in. Inevitably, a certain amount of organic material never makes it into the can, which increases yellowjacket and rat access to the food.

In recreational areas, yellowjackets can become particularly pestiferous where concessions sell soft drinks in open-air settings. This is because most seemingly empty cups still contain enough sugary liquid to feed yellowjackets and give off an aroma that is particularly attractive to them. If you find yourself in a situation where there are many yellowjackets and soft drinks are being sold in uncovered cups, warn members of your party, especially children, to look into the cup before each sip, because there is a real danger that someone will accidentally drink in a wasp and get stung in the mouth or throat. But tell them not to panic if they find a wasp also taking a drink. They should wait patiently until the wasp leaves by itself, then place a napkin or similar barrier over the cup between sips. Alternatively, you can place the drink in a paper bag and poke a hole through it for the straw.

If such problems exist in your community parks and other recreational facilities, consider drawing the manager's attention to the importance of proper garbage can design and use—you'll be doing your entire neighborhood a favor.

One example of how effective habitat management can be is the case of Virginia's Great Falls National Park. We helped initiate an integrated pest management program in the park in response to the large number of yellowjacket stings experienced by visitors—as high as 1,000 per year before the program was started, according to park service estimates.

Lids and straws were added to soft-drink containers before they were served to customers. Wasp-tight garbage cans were substituted for open ones, and the frequency of garbage pickup was increased during the most severe period of infestation. Area-wide poison baiting was held in reserve largely because National Park Service policy excluded the use of insecticides against native animal or plant species, including the native yellowjacket *V. maculifrons*.

The IPM program achieved a 96% reduction in the number of yellowjacket stings; 48% of this reduction was achieved through more frequent garbage pickup and 48% through the use of lids on soft-drink containers and better garbage can tops. The most cost-effective tactics were the lids and wasp-tight can tops, since these were cheaper than increasing the frequency of garbage pickup.

It should also be mentioned that dumpsters behind restaurants and other food-handling establishments are another source of yellowjacket sustenance. These dumpsters should be cleaned regularly as described on p. 631 under rat management.

Direct Physical Controls

Direct physical controls for yellowjackets include trapping, nest removal and vacuuming.

1. Trapping. Picnickers who want to trap small numbers of yellowjackets during a meal can use small plastic traps that are sold commercially (as shown in the drawing at right). For sources, see the Resource Appendix under "Insect Management: Physical Controls" on pp. 682-683.

Alternatively, a variety of designs for homemade fly traps (see pp. 646-647) can be adapted to catch yellowjackets by using a bait that is more attractive to them than to bees or flies. Examples of such baits are dog food, ham, fish and other meat scraps, or, toward the end of the warm weather, sugar syrups, spoiled fruit and jelly. Detailed instructions for designing a large trap are provided in *The Integral Urban House* (listed under "References and Readings" on p. 661).

Mass trapping using an attractive bait and sturdy trap can significantly reduce the number of pestiferous yellowjackets if enough traps are available. One successful example of mass trapping took place in an Oregon peach orchard, where the pestiferous wasp was *V. pensylvanica*. This wasp is common throughout the western coastal, intermontane and southwest-

Yellowjacket Traps
The Seabright trap is inexpensive and very effective when used for wasp control for short periods; if used for more than a few hours, many yellowjackets escape. The IPC trap is constructed for use for short or long periods, and there are few escapes.

Seabright trap

IPC trap

ern states, and is a scattered nuisance in the north-central states as far east as Lake Michigan. Researcher H.G. Davis and coworkers used the synthetic lure heptyl butyrate in small carton traps placed around the periphery of a 21-acre (8.9 hectare) peach orchard. The trapping reduced yellowjacket populations to a level low enough to allow the resumption of harvesting.

V. pensylvanica seems to be fairly easy to trap. Using homemade fly traps baited with canned fruit preserves or cat food, we were able to reduce pest yellowjackets significantly in outdoor eating and food-preparation areas of a resort in the coastal mountains of central California. The trapping also proved educational, reducing the public's fear of being close to the wasps and increasing its tolerance of small numbers of them. We suspect that the knowledge that wasps can be controlled, approached and observed helped relieve some of the hysteria felt about them.

Another yellowjacket species, *V. germanica,* which invaded the East Coast of the United States and is spreading westward across the continent, is less easy to trap. The major problem is finding the right bait. The lure used in the Oregon orchard program is highly specific for *V. pensylvanica* but has not worked for other species. Ginger syrup bait is used in Europe to attract *V. germanica* and *V. vulgaris* but lasts only about two days; moreover, this syrup also attracts honey bees, so it cannot be used where commercial bees forage.

A horse-meat-based food has been found to be attractive to *V. germanica* and *V. maculifrons.* Further studies have indicated that boiled and ground ham is even more attractive. If it is kept sufficiently moist and is replaced regularly in a large number of traps for a number of weeks, mass trapping of the major eastern pestiferous yellowjackets may become a possibility; at present, however, trapping *V. germanica* works best for destroying a small number of scaveng-

A lightweight portable vacuum with a removable bag that can be closed tightly can be used to remove yellowjackets from their nests. It is best to have two people for this job. One vacuums while the other scoops out layers of the nest as the wasps are captured in the vacuum, and watches for escape holes near the nest. Protective bee veils and long-sleeved clothing must be worn. (Photo by Helga Olkowski.)

ing individuals during outdoor recreation events. Such trapping also serves as a monitoring tool for the evaluation of the other control techniques discussed here.

2. Nest Removal. You can destroy a nest by physically removing it or by using a toxicant. Either way, you must be extremely careful because any disturbance around a nest can trigger a mass attack. We recommend that you get professional help to remove yellowjacket nests. If you decide to do it yourself, you will need the special protective clothing described in the sidebar on p. 659.

3. Vacuuming. Vacuuming (see the photo above) can be particularly effective where nests occur in wall voids, in emergencies where nests have already been disturbed and in environmentally sensitive areas where nests should not be treated with insecticides.

A lightweight, powerful vacuum with a removable bag that can be stuffed closed with cotton or a rag while the machine is running is essential. We have successfully used a number of vacuums, but the Eureka

3-hp MightyMite™ proved particularly effective. It sells for approximately $140.

Before vacuuming underground nests, check for auxiliary nest openings in a 40-ft. to 50-ft. (12 m to 15 m) area around the main opening. Although these auxiliary holes are not very common, they do occur, and if not filled with soil before vacuuming begins, they provide outlets for angry wasps.

Vacuuming out an underground nest is a job for two people covered with protective clothing, as described in the sidebar on p. 659. While one person operates the vacuum, the other excavates the nest with a trowel. The vacuum operator doesn't actually insert the hose into the nest; instead, air is drawn in near (3 in. to 4 in./7.6 cm to 10 cm) the entrance so the vacuum sucks in yellowjackets as they fly out. In one study, two people experienced in handling bees but new to the vacuuming technique captured the adults from an underground yellowjacket nest and then dug up the nest in about an hour. Experience in handling bees is impor-

Protective Clothing for Nest Destruction

Whenever possible, nest destruction should be performed by someone experienced in handling bees and wasps. However, since we know that many inexperienced people are interested in eliminating yellowjacket nests without having to hire someone, we are including some details on methods here.

Protective clothing (as worn in the photo on p. 658) prevents unnecessary stings and provides greater freedom in manipulating the nest and wasps. Complete body coverage is extremely important, because these wasps can find even the smallest exposed area. The best protective clothing is the type made for beekeepers. This includes a bee veil or hood that fits over a lightweight pith helmet or hat, coveralls and long-sleeved gloves. At the very minimum, thick, loose-fitting clothing, gloves and a bee veil are necessities. The gloves should be extra long, with shirt sleeves secured inside them. This protects the wrists, which are bare if normal-length gloves are used. If these gloves are not available, you can substitute heavy leather gloves or double pairs of cloth gloves, since the hands are the part of the body most often attacked. Long-sleeved sweatshirts can help protect the wrists.

The strength of the fabric of bee suits makes it difficult for yellowjackets to penetrate, and zippers add protection by sealing pockets and other openings. If you cannot obtain a bee suit, you can use one-piece cloth coveralls sold widely for wear by mechanics, but you must first modify them by sewing closed all wasp access routes. You need a second layer of regular clothing beneath the bee suit or coverall because the suit can cling or stretch, allowing wasp stingers to penetrate to the skin. Be prepared to sweat heavily since this clothing does not allow ventilation; for this reason, we advise taking salt tablets in hot weather.

Stuffing pants legs into socks keeps wasps from walking up the leg inside the pants, but it also leaves your ankles exposed to stings. High-topped combat-style boots help solve this problem. Ankle-high leather work shoes are also used by some beekeepers, who secure the pant legs around the shoes at the ankle with Velcro™ fasteners or leg straps. Inserting a folded brown paper bag down each pant leg over the knee guards against stings when you squat or kneel. This or protective fabric can be held in place by the knee pads sold in garden and hardware stores.

Better-made bee veils either have a built-in hat or can be placed over hats. A metal-screen face plate that extends around the head for visibility is another desirable feature. Cloth screen, which is connected to the metal screen, comprises the remainder of the screening. Its long ties are passed under the armpits, around the back and across the chest for a snug fit. Make sure you inspect the veil carefully for tears before each use. Conduct nest removal jobs with two people and have each person inspect the other's clothing for openings before beginning the work. For suppliers of protective clothing, see the Resource Appendix under "Insect Management: Chemical Controls" on pp. 686-687.

tant because this operation requires that workers remain calm and move slowly even as buzzing, threatening insects land on their clothing and face nets. Wasps that escape initial vacuuming can be vacuumed off bee suits as they attempt to sting.

Once the nest is empty and no more wasps are seen entering or leaving, the underground nest structure is dug out to complete the destruction of the nest. Aerial nests and fragments of ground nests that still contain living larvae in the combs can be placed inside thick plastic bags and stored in an ice chest for transport to a freezer unit, where the cold will kill them. Bags full of angry adults should be removed from the vacuum and transported the same way. Yellowjackets frozen before they decompose can be sold to venom preparation companies (see the Resource Appendix under "Insect Management: Chemical Controls," pp. 686-687, for names of these companies).

Direct Biological Controls

Natural wildlife such as skunks, raccoons and badgers in parks, greenbelts and undeveloped areas help control yellowjackets by preying on their nests, primarily for the honey in the larval chambers. One naturalist with the East Bay Regional Park System in Oakland, California, put this predator-prey relationship to work. At closing time, he dripped honey over the entrance holes to the underground yellowjacket nests near picnic tables. When he returned the next morning, he found that all the nests had been dug out and destroyed. The somewhat indistinct footprints suggested that this was the work of either a skunk or a raccoon.

The same park system is also currently experimenting with the use of yellowjacket baits containing predatory nematodes. The bait is taken back to the nest. If the tests prove successful, the nematodes, which are already commercially available, may soon provide an effective alternative to poison baits.

Direct Chemical Controls

When an insecticide is considered necessary for the control of yellowjackets, the best approach is to confine it to the nest itself. Anyone applying insecticides should use special clothing that protects against the chemical as well as against wasps. This should include a respirator, goggles, coveralls and rubber gloves. For a more complete discussion of protective clothing, see pp. 97-103 and the sidebar on p. 659.

1. Pyrethrin/Rotenone Aerosol. One insecticide that is effective for spot applications and is not too toxic for use around the home is an aerosol product called Wasp-Stopper® (for sources, see the Resource Appendix under "Insect Management: Chemical Controls" on pp. 686-687). It contains the active ingredients pyrethrin and rotenone, as well as highly evaporative substances that "freeze" the wasps (they probably just stun them). The aerosol is designed to project its spray 6 ft. to 8 ft. (1.8 m to 2.4 m), and can be used safely around electrical equipment.

2. Pyrenone. Pyrenone contains pyrethrin alone, and is available as an aerosol for nest destruction. When purchased as a concentrate, it can be applied with a standard pressurized garden sprayer.

When nests occur in the walls of buildings, entrance holes should be plugged with steel wool after the insecticide has been applied to prevent

wasps from escaping before they die. In some instances, however, nests can be located as far as 90 ft. (27 m) from the openings. In such cases, John MacDonald, yellowjacket expert at Purdue University, advises that home owners hire a professional company with the proper equipment to blow an insecticidal dust into the entrance holes. Worker yellowjackets that fly into the treated opening will carry the dust to the queen and developing larvae in the nest.

3. Resmethrin. Where the nest is only a few feet from the entrance hole, an aerosol containing the repellent insecticide resmethrin can be used to force workers back into the nest. MacDonald recommends that steel wool treated with an insecticidal dust then be used as a plug for the entrance. The surviving workers inside and outside the nest chew on the steel wool and die from contact with the insecticide.

4. Carbaryl, Drione®. MacDonald has also tested the techniques described above using the insecticidal dust carbaryl (Sevin®), and it proved effective. A less-toxic product containing silica aerogel dust and pyrethrin, Drione®, should also work against yellowjackets, although we have not found any studies to confirm this. These two active ingredients are available in the aerosol Revenge®.

5. Diazinon Baits. Baiting utilizes the same attractants used in mass trapping but includes a nonrepellent toxicant. The most widely used bait/poison mixture contains encapsulated diazinon (0.5% by weight) mixed with tuna-flavored cat food. The encapsulation reduces the vaporization rate of the insecticide so it is not repellent to the wasps. It is marketed as Knoxout® and is available from pesticide distributors throughout the United States.

The insecticide/meat mixture is placed in a wire cage made from ½-in. (1.3 cm) hardware cloth and is suspended 6 ft. to 7 ft. (2 m to 2.5 m) above the ground from a tree branch. Foraging wasps carry the poisoned

meat back to their nests. When enough of the poison is eaten by their nestmates, including the queen and developing larvae, the colony dies.

6. Methoprene and Avermectin Baits. Research indicates that the less-toxic materials methoprene and avermectin B_1 are effective in baits. However, these studies were done only on the eastern yellowjacket (V. maculifrons); their effect on other species is unknown.

7. Gasoline. We know from conversations and from our reading that many people pour gasoline into underground nest holes. We do not recommend this practice. It is a fire hazard, can produce angry swarms of wasps and subsequent stings, contaminates the soil and prevents growth of vegetation for some time.

8. Area-Wide Poisoning. We strongly disapprove of area-wide poison-baiting. This opinion is shared by Roger Akre, a yellowjacket researcher at Washington State University who has considerable experience managing yellowjackets in the Northwest and whom we consulted while writing this chapter.

John MacDonald, who has studied various management techniques in and around West Lafayette, Indiana, where the German yellowjacket has invaded, told us that in his opinion mass poisoning is seldom if ever necessary. He says this technique is resorted to primarily by those unwilling to undertake more ecologically and economically acceptable methods such as proper garbage management. He indicates that area-wide poison-baiting programs are expensive due to the labor involved in the frequent mixing and replacement of bait. The effectiveness of bait mixtures is also questionable, since the baits face considerable competition from other food sources attractive to scavenging yellowjackets. Another reason to avoid area-wide baiting is the protection of beneficial foraging insect species that are attracted to the same bait and take it back to their nests.

REFERENCES AND READINGS

Akre, R.D., A. Greene, J.F. MacDonald, P.J. Landolt and H.G. Davis. 1980. *Yellowjackets of America north of Mexico.* Washington, D.C.: USDA (Agricultural Handbook 552). 102 pp.

This well-illustrated handbook contains a key to the North American yellowjackets, a review of the taxonomy of the yellowjacket family and related groups, descriptions of yellowjacket biology and discussions of the economic and medical importance and control of yellowjackets.

Davis, H.G. 1978. Yellowjacket wasps in urban environments. In *Perspectives in urban entomology,* eds. G.W. Frankie and C.S. Koehler, pp. 163-185. New York: Academic Press. 417 pp.

In this chapter, which covers the biology, taxonomy, importance and control of yellowjackets, the use of the lure heptyl butyrate is cited as being effective against *Vespula pensylvanica* populations when placed in small carton traps around the periphery of a peach orchard in Oregon.

Edwards, R. 1980. *Social wasps: their biology and control.* West Sussex, England: Rentokil Ltd. 398 pp.

This book covers the biology, behavior, population dynamics, classification and morphology of seven species of social wasps found in England in the genera *Vespula* and *Dolichovespula.* The effects of these wasps on human activities are documented, as are control methods. Experimental techniques are also covered.

Ennik, F. 1973. Abatement of yellowjackets using encapsulated formulations of diazinon and rabon. *Journal of Economic Entomology* 66(5):1097-1098.

This research paper shows that encapsulated formulations of diazinon mixed with food baits were effective in reducing *Vespula pensylvanica* populations.

Krombein, K.V, P.D. Hurd, Jr., D.R. Smith and B.D. Burks. 1979. *Catalog of hymenoptera in America north of Mexico,* Volumes I, II and III. Washington, D.C.: Smithsonian Institution Press. 1,198, 2,209 and 2,735 pp., respectively.

This compilation lists the hymenopteran species found in North America along with other important information about their biology, distribution and classification.

MacDonald, J.F. 1980. *Biology, recognition, medical importance and control of Indiana social wasps.* West Lafayette, Ind.: Purdue University Cooperative Extension Service (Publication E-91). 24 pp.

A pamphlet on the subject prepared for the general public.

MacDonald, J.F., and R.D. Akre. 1984. Range extension and emergence of subterranean nesting by the German yellowjacket, *Vespula germanica,* in North America (Hymenoptera: Vespidae). *Entomology News* 95(1):5-8.

This paper documents the spread of the newly introduced German yellowjacket *(Vespula germanica)* across North America.

MacDonald, J.F., R.D. Akre and R.W. Matthews. 1976. Evaluation of yellowjacket abatement in the United States. *Bulletin of the Entomological Society of America* 22(4):397-401.

A review of control methods in use up to 1976.

Olkowski, H., W. Olkowski and T. Javits. 1979. *The integral urban house.* San Francisco: Sierra Club Books. 494 pp.

This book contains a detailed description of a large A-frame trap useful for catching yellowjackets. It can be built with simple tools and materials.

Parrish, M.D., and R.B. Roberts. 1983. Toxicity of avermectin B_1 to larval yellowjackets, *Vespula maculifrons* (Hymenoptera: Vespidae). *Journal of Economic Entomology* 77(3): 769-772.

Avermectin, produced from a bacterial species, is shown to be an effective toxicant when mixed with meat baits.

Parrish, M.D., and R.B. Roberts. 1984. Insect growth regulators in baits: methoprene acceptability to foragers and effect on larval eastern yellowjackets (Hymenoptera: Vespidae). *Journal of Economic Entomology* 77(1):109-112.

This insect growth regulator was shown to be an effective toxicant when fed in meat baits to yellowjackets.

Ross, D.R., R.H. Shukle and J.F. MacDonald. 1984. Meat extracts attractive to scavenger *Vespula* in eastern North America (Hymenoptera: Vespidae). *Journal of Economic Entomology* 77(3):637-642.

Experiments indicated the effectiveness of various meat extracts as attractants.

Snelling, R.R. 1981. *Systematics of social hymenoptera.* In *Social insects, Volume II,* ed. H.R. Herman, pp. 370-454. New York: Academic Press. 491 pp.

This important paper clarifies the complexities of how the social hymenoptera, including the yellowjackets, are related to each other and other bees, ants and wasps.

CHAPTER 36
Mosquitoes

INTRODUCTION

Mosquitoes are among the most serious of insect pests that have a direct impact on humans. Judging by requests for help received by BIRC, the nonprofit institution with which we are associated, mosquitoes are also high on the list of pests that concern the general public. One major reason for this is that traditional chemical treatments for mosquitoes often unnecessarily expose large areas, including the people and wildlife that live there, to toxic materials.

Mosquitoes seriously affect the lives of vast numbers of people worldwide by transmitting microbial organisms that cause disease and death, especially in tropical areas. Mosquitoes continue to carry some of the most widespread and devastating human disease agents, including malaria, yellow fever, dengue and filariasis. Malaria is a constant threat even in the United States, where known vectors exist. Travelers returning from abroad can introduce the causal agents, which are protozoa in the genus *Plasmodium.*

In the United States, the primary reasons for controlling mosquitoes are to lessen the annoyance caused by their bites and to reduce the transmission of human and equine viral encephalitis and dog heartworm. The annoyance includes the itching, restlessness, loss of sleep and nervous irritation that people, pets and domestic animals suffer as a result of attacks. Sometimes this annoyance can be documented in terms of economic loss, such as decreased recreation income and lower milk and beef production due to blood loss and irritation. Mosquitoes are also reported to cause the death of domestic animals through blood loss and anaphylactic shock from reactions to mass injections of mosquito saliva, but these cases are rare.

Mosquito control agencies in the United States and Canada together spend in excess of $80 million annually to reduce the mosquito annoyance; the additional money spent by the public for aerosol insecticides, repellents, window screens and other controls easily exceeds this figure. Unfortunately, much of the money and effort is used ineffectively and serves only to put more toxic materials into the air people and pets breathe. Furthermore, these efforts often result in new pest problems, such as outbreaks of pests of shade and forest trees, when mosquito control activities kill the organisms that normally keep the pests under natural control.

The wasted money and time and the annoying or potentially dangerous side effects result because much of the control effort is directed against the adult mosquito instead of going to the source: the water where the larval stages of the mosquito are found. It is surprising to learn the extent to which routine aerial fogging with toxic chemical insecticides still occurs, even though source reduction techniques have been taught for decades. Although the spraying of insecticides that reduce adult mosquito populations can be an excellent emergency procedure where disease transmission problems exist, it is imperative that the spraying be followed with source reduction measures and the application of larvicides (insecticides that kill the larval stage of an organism).

As is common in many pest control situations, safe and effective management requires more attention, time and effort than the traditional spray-and-hope approach. Yet even good mosquito control programs can cause political problems. There may be acrimonious debate over mosquito control in parks and other less urbanized areas. Fishermen and naturalists understand that mosquitoes form an important part of the diet of fish and other wildlife. (Aquatic organisms that feed on mosquitoes are listed in the sidebar above). When you eliminate mosquitoes from a marsh or creek, you affect an important component of the aquatic food chain. And where you

Aquatic Organisms that Feed on Mosquitoes

amphipods
ants
backswimmers
bacteria
birds
crabs
dragonflies
fish
flatworms
frogs
fungi
giant water bugs
ground beetles
hydra
mites
parasitic nematodes
predacious mosquito larvae
predacious snails
rotifers
spiders
viruses
water scorpions
water striders

use persistent and/or accumulating poisons to kill mosquitoes, you can end up indirectly killing not only fish but birds as well, as happened with DDT long ago.

Politics: A Tricky Part of the Management Problem

Least-toxic mosquito management can become a political football, as the National Park Service has learned to its dismay on more than one occasion. What do you do when some residents want mosquito-free streamside golfing, while others depend for nutrition on the fish that feed on the mosquito larvae in the stream? How do you take a hands-off approach to the preservation of a natural marsh habitat when it is a breeding ground for mosquitoes that annoy people at nearby beaches and summer homes?

Some of these cases are reminiscent of the story about the king who was so enamored of the feel of leather under his bare feet that he ordered that the entire kingdom be covered in leather. Luckily, a wise person pointed out that the king could achieve the same effect by tying leather to his own feet. Surely screened windows and porches on summer homes and repellents on individual people in mosquito-prone areas are better than regularly wiping out entire wildlife food chains.

In wilderness areas where large mosquito populations occur, there is generally no justification for any treatment. Instead, many mosquito abatement districts that include wilderness areas would probably find it advantageous to establish a position for an ecologist, whose responsibilities would include citizen education about the role of mosquitoes in the natural world, least-toxic mosquito management and the need to tolerate some number of mosquitoes in order to preserve and enjoy the natural setting.

In many cases, the problem is not so clear-cut. Large numbers of pestiferous mosquitoes may be the result of disruptions to the natural environment that have killed off the mosquito's natural enemies. We were involved in one such situation in a town neighboring the C&O Canal outside Washington, D.C., in an area under the jurisdiction of the National Park Service. Local citizens put the blame on standing pools of water along the canal for their annual mosquito problems. The town government pressured the State of Maryland to undertake regular insecticide fogging along the canal, but this caused anger and apprehension among joggers, hikers and others who enjoyed the paths bordering the canal. They complained to the park service.

Subsequent investigations showed that the town was dumping sewage into one of the pools. This was polluting the water, encouraging mosquito development and reducing the number of natural mosquito predators. Even though the problem was now clear, the solution was not simple. Some pools needed draining. Other local bodies of water were mapped and monitored to make sure they weren't contributing to the problem, and various types of treatment were used. Politics and money were issues at every step. Our contribution in this case was to get the various factions talking to one another, teaching everyone involved about proper mosquito management and hoping that the local citizens' group would continue to follow the activities of all the bureaucracies concerned.

We want to emphasize that there are always solutions to these and similar community and individual mosquito problems. Sometimes they require a creative mix of approaches and considerable effort, but they are more effective in the long run than putting a lot of pesticide into the air.

Who Determines When Mosquitoes Become Intolerable?

How many mosquitoes are too many? Population growth has meant that many areas that were once pristine, healthy and wild have now been invaded by housing developments. These suburbs are inhabited by newcomers from cities where mosquito control is relatively easy; thus, they generally have a very low tolerance for mosquitoes. The desires of these new suburbanites may clash with those of long-time residents, who often have a higher mosquito tolerance level and a value system that places scenic and rustic beauty over the temporary or sporadic inconvenience of mosquitoes.

If a mosquito abatement district exists in the area, it can become a jousting arena. Good mosquito control may require greater expenditures, particularly during the transition from conventional methods to integrated pest management. Sometimes political expedience rules at the expense of ecologically sound management. Where citizens and mosquito abatement districts disagree about the proper course of action, it often helps to call in an expert who is well-versed in conflict resolution and ecologically responsible management strategies. But just as frequently, the single most important ingredient in the solution is an educated, persistent public.

In this chapter we examine what you as an individual can do to control mosquitoes around your home, and how you can judge the appropriateness of the treatment activities carried out by public agencies in your area. In both cases you must first learn about general mosquito biology and where to look for mosquito breeding grounds. Then you will have to make a judgment about injury level, that is, the point at which you find the mosquito population intolerable. And finally, you must chose safe control tactics. On the community level, this includes surveying for larval breeding areas and monitoring larval and adult mosquito populations. Professional managers must keep abreast of the latest news and innovations in the fast-developing field of least-toxic controls.

BIOLOGY

Mosquitoes belong to the family Culicidae in the order Diptera, the true flies. Worldwide, the mosquitoes, or culicids, are a medium-sized family, with over 3,000 species. The United States has about 160 species belonging to 13 genera, the most important of which are *Culex, Aedes, Culiseta, Psorophora* and *Anopheles*. All mosquitoes develop in water that is still or very slow-moving. However, each genus differs from the others primarily in the type of aquatic habitat (fresh-water or saltwater) in which it develops.

Adult mosquitoes are small (about ⅛ in./3 mm long), slender, long-legged insects with a single pair of membranous wings that are characteristic of all true flies. What distinguishes them from all other flies is the presence of a long piercing mouthpart called a proboscis and scales on the margins and veins of the wings. Morphologically, males differ from females in that they have feathery antennae, long feathery palps and smaller mouthparts, as well as other characters that are less visible to the naked eye.

Mosquitoes develop through four distinct stages: egg, larva or "wriggler," pupa or "tumbler" and adult (as shown in the drawing at right). Only adult females feed on human and/or animal blood; the protein helps bring their eggs to maturity. Not all female mosquito species feed on blood, however, and not all mosquito species feed on people. Some feed almost exclusively on birds, others on amphibians. Both males and females feed on plant nectar for energy.

Mosquito eggs can be classified into three groups (see the drawing at right): eggs laid singly on the water surface (Anopheles), with each egg having a series of "floats" along its perimeter; eggs laid in groups forming rafts that float on water surfaces (Culex and Culiseta); and eggs laid singly out of the water in the mud (Aedes and Psorophora).

The egg-laying, or ovipositing, adult females of the first two groups tend to seek out water sources that persist through the season. Females lay their eggs directly on the surface, sitting on the water and using its surface tension for support. Aedes and Psorophora females are most likely to lay their eggs in or on soil surfaces at the edges of more temporary water sites. When flooding occurs and the eggs are inundated, they hatch. The pasture mosquito (A. nigromaculis) in the West and the salt marsh mosquito (A. solicitans) on the East Coast use this egg-laying method.

The larvae of all mosquitoes are aquatic. They have adapted to a wide variety of habitats, including permanent ponds, marshes, woodland pools, tree holes and artificial containers. What these breeding sites have in

The Life Cycle and Key Characteristics of Common Mosquito Genera

The four stages of the life cycle of the mosquito are the egg, larva (wriggler), pupa (tumbler) and adult. One of the main differences among the three most common mosquito genera concerns egg-laying behavior and helps in identification. *Anopheles* mosquito eggs have fin-like structures that help eggs to float singly on the water surface. *Aedes* eggs are drilled individually into the mud; they hatch later when the mud is flooded. *Culex* eggs are laid in a mass that floats on the water surface and is subject to predation.

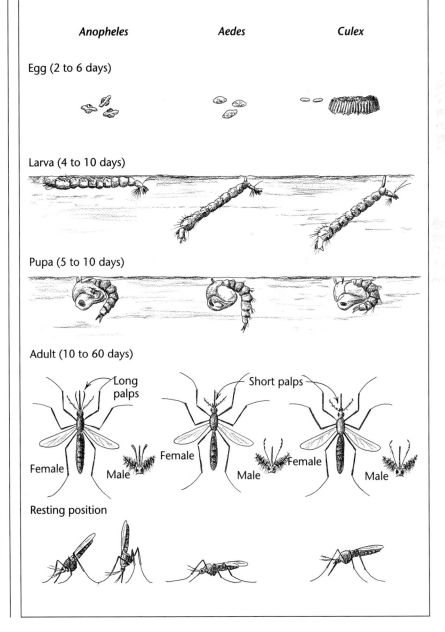

Mosquito larvae and pupae breathe by pushing tubes through the surface film of the water. Larvae and pupae move rapidly down into the water after being disturbed; the characteristic way in which they move gives them the names wrigglers and tumblers, respectively. (Photo courtesy USDA/ARS.)

common is that they are quiet pools of water that shelter the ovipositing female from wind and wave action. Thus, neither a flowing stream nor the open water of a river, lake or sea is suitable for mosquito breeding.

Mosquito larvae generally eat microorganisms and particles of organic matter by sweeping the food into their mouths with a pair of feeding brushes. They do not have gills for breathing; instead, most breathe directly from the surface of the water via a siphon tube located on the tip of the abdomen (see the photo above). There are a few exceptions to this, however. Some species in one genus obtain air through the underwater portions of plants.

Larvae take 4 to 10 days to complete their development, depending on the species, water temperature and other factors, passing through four separate developmental periods, or instars. Larvae move principally by jerking their bodies, hence the name wrigglers. After the fourth stage the pupa appears, and thereafter the adult emerges to mate, feed and lay eggs.

Although mosquitoes have a distinctive appearance, other flies are sometimes mistaken for them and are wrongly killed. When BIRC members call us frantically about "giant mosquitoes," usually they are worrying needlessly about the generally harmless and beautiful crane flies (see the drawing at right). Aphid-eating gall midges, which also resemble mosquitoes but are considerably smaller, are actually beneficial insects (see the discussion of gall midges on pp. 373-375).

Table 36.1 on the facing page lists some important ecological characteristics of mosquito species common in the United States.

DETECTION AND MONITORING

If mosquitoes are a problem around your home, scan the list of potential breeding sites in the sidebar on the facing page, then start a systematic survey of your premises for standing water in which the mosquitoes might be developing. Believe it or not,

Flies Often Mistaken for Mosquitoes

Flies that are often mistaken for mosquitoes include fungus gnats, dixa midges and crane flies. However, these flies do not bite and are harmless to humans. They generally develop in wet areas as part of the decomposer community. (Drawing not to scale.)

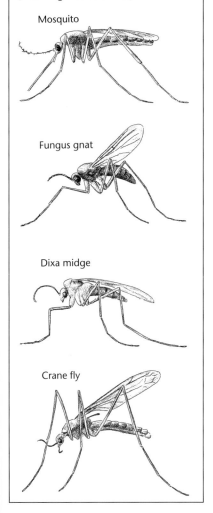

Mosquito

Fungus gnat

Dixa midge

Crane fly

chances are very good that the pests are being produced within a few yards of where you are being bitten.

Gradually working outward from the house, inspect the periphery of your own property. Then check nearby vacant lots and other neglected

Table 36.1
Ecological Characteristics of Some Common Mosquitoes of the United States

Species	Eggs	Larval Habitat	Flight Range (miles)
Aedes aegypti	laid singly; on container sides	containers	1 to 5+
A. albopictus [a]	singly	containers, tires	1 to 5+
A. taeniorhynchus	singly	salt-marsh soil	5 to 20+
A. triseriatus	singly	tree holes	½ to 1
A. nigromaculis	singly in ground	pastures	2 to 5
A. solicitans	singly in ground	brackish marshes	5 to 20+
A. vexans	singly in ground	temporary pools	5 to 20
Anopheles freeborni	laid singly on water	shaded water	1 to 2
A. quadrimaculatus	singly on water	shaded water	1 to 2
Culex pipiens	laid as rafts on water	polluted water	1+
C. salinarius	rafts on water	fresh and brackish water	1+
C. tarsalis	rafts on water	polluted water	2 to 10
Psorophora columbiae	singly	soil, rice fields, temporary pools	5+

[a] This mosquito, called the Asian tiger mosquito, has been found in the United States only recently. It is a vector of dengue fever.

Common Mosquito Breeding Sites around the Home

birdbaths
boats that have not been drained
cans, jars and other containers
catch basins at road corners
cisterns
clogged roof gutters
drain outlets from air conditioners
dripping outdoor faucets
leaf-filled drains
old tires
ornamental ponds
over-irrigated lawns and fields
poorly constructed cesspools
septic tanks
street gutters
leaky pipe joints
plastic wading pools
puddles from evaporative cooler drains
rain barrels
saucers under potted plants
standing water in tire ruts
stumps
tree holes
utility meters
watering cans, buckets
watering troughs
water-softening tanks
wells
wheelbarrows or tilt-up carts

areas. Old tires and similar water-holding objects behind garages and gas stations are frequent mosquito sources. Tires should be recycled or cut in half since it is very difficult to drain the water completely from an intact tire. (There is a real need for legislation requiring tire collection and recycling to help eliminate tires as breeding sources, particularly now that the Asian tiger mosquito, which carries dengue fever, is becoming more prevalent.) If the containers holding the water cannot be drained, filled in, removed or turned upside down so they no longer collect water, the problem will have to be addressed through one of the treatments discussed later in this chapter.

Field Surveys and Biting Counts

Field surveys are the foundation of any community-scale mosquito control program. They make it possible to determine which species are biting and, based on an identification of the species, where and when they are breeding. This information is necessary before control measures can be applied to only those sites where mosquitoes are present and causing a nuisance. The following discussion summarizes what kind of monitoring effort you should expect of your local mosquito management district or other local authorities who have responsibility for control of these pestiferous insects.

Community field surveys are of two types: preliminary surveys, which provide an overview of the situation and establish sampling locations; and ongoing surveys, made weekly or bi-weekly to monitor mosquito population growth and determine which species are present at different times of the season. Both types of survey generally include sampling for immature as well as adult mosquitoes; sampling for both stages must be carried out simultaneously during those parts of the year when mosquitoes are present.

Surveys that seek bodies of water containing immature mosquitoes should be carried out in concentric circles around inhabited areas, moving outward from the center as resources permit. Seasonal changes in the direction of prevailing winds must be factored into these plans, because such winds help carry mosquitoes away from their sources. A map record of mosquito sources should be kept since it may prove very informative in subsequent seasons.

If the larvae can be found before they emerge as biting adults, the problem can be solved before it becomes serious. The larvicides now available make it possible to treat mosquitoes with the least possible negative effect on humans, domestic animals and the larger environment.

Larval samples are most often taken from suspected aquatic development sites with a long-handled dipper (the drawing below shows this and other equipment used for mosquito monitoring). It takes some experience, however, since the larvae are sensitive to vibrations, shadows and ripples, and dive to escape the dipper. The number and instar (developmental stage) of larvae and the number of pupae should be recorded; the number and kinds of natural enemies of the larvae should also be noted. Pupae indicate that female adults are or will be biting soon.

Surveys of adult mosquitoes establish which species are biting, where in the community the bites are occurring and when during the day or night mosquitoes are the most troublesome. Because some species are specific to certain environments, these biting counts give you clues as to where you should look for the larvae, if that is not already known. After treatment actions have been executed, these surveys help determine whether they have been successful.

The term "biting count" is somewhat misleading because it suggests that the mosquitoes are allowed to bite humans; in fact, they are usually collected as they land to bite but before they actually pierce the skin. The advantage of this type of survey is that you can find out which of the various mosquito species in the area are doing the biting. You can then correlate this information with what has been learned about the species detected in the various bodies of water in and around your community. In some cases, this will show that certain bodies of water can be left untreated even though larvae are present, since these are not the mosquitoes causing the trouble. As stressed earlier, mosquitoes form a very significant component of wildlife food chains, and it is important to leave alone those that are not causing serious problems.

Biting counts must be taken after dark when female mosquitoes are flying and looking for blood meals (as mentioned earlier, only the females

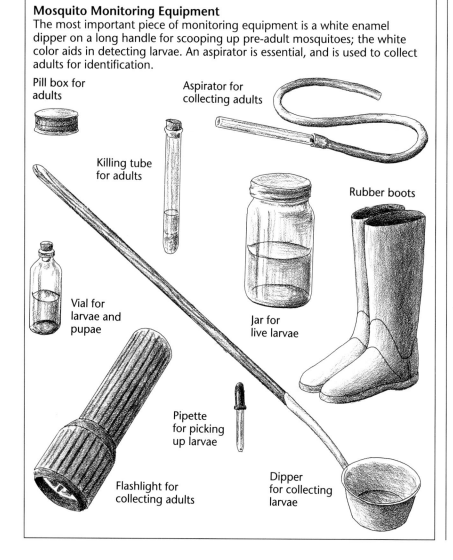

Mosquito Monitoring Equipment

The most important piece of monitoring equipment is a white enamel dipper on a long handle for scooping up pre-adult mosquitoes; the white color aids in detecting larvae. An aspirator is essential, and is used to collect adults for identification.

Pill box for adults

Aspirator for collecting adults

Killing tube for adults

Rubber boots

Vial for larvae and pupae

Jar for live larvae

Pipette for picking up larvae

Flashlight for collecting adults

Dipper for collecting larvae

bite). The count is made by exposing some portion of the body, usually a forearm or lower leg, for a specified time, usually 2 to 15 minutes, and capturing the insects as they land to feed. An aspirator (see the drawing on p. 668 and, for sources, the Resource Appendix under "Insect Management: Identification and Monitoring" on pp. 681-682) is used to suck up the mosquitoes. This clever device is comprised of a long flexible hose that you apply to your mouth and a stiff plastic or metal tube that is held close to the insect. Insects are sucked into the tube. A fine screen between the hose and the tube prevents the insect from being sucked into your mouth. Placing a finger over the end of the tube prevents captured insects from escaping. The aspirator can be manipulated with one hand by the same person who is exposing his or her skin during the biting count. When the tube is full, insects are blown into a small vial, which is capped with a wad of cotton wedged firmly in the opening, placed in the freezer to kill the insects and replaced with an empty bottle. Alternatively, the insects can be transferred to a container with rubbing alcohol or other lethal material.

Because the identification and counting of the mosquitoes must be performed by someone who knows how to use identification keys and has access to a dissecting microscope, most biting counts are made by mosquito control professionals. But, as you can see, almost anyone can learn to do the actual collecting; the insects can then be handed to a professional for identification.

Light traps (see the drawing at right), animal bait traps, resting stations and CO_2 traps are also commonly used for monitoring adults. Using these traps involves methods considerably more elaborate, inconvenient and expensive than biting counts. Traps are also less selective in the species they collect. Moreover, the direct measurements of biting frequency provided by biting counts

---

A Light Trap for Monitoring Adult Mosquitoes

The Centers for Disease Control has standardized the design of light traps used for mosquito monitoring. Such traps cannot be used for mosquito control, however, because their capacity is too limited. Mosquitoes are attracted to the light, enter the trap and are then blown downward by a small fan into a mesh bag, from which they cannot escape.

Plastic cylinder containing light, motor and fan blade

Plastic rain guard

Four size D batteries

Mesh bag

---

can be correlated with complaints from different areas called into mosquito control agencies much better than the less selective data collected from traps.

Although monitoring may be the most important component of a safe and successful mosquito control program, it can also be the most costly. However, one program we learned about used senior citizen volunteers for biting counts. Different people agreed to make counts at prescribed times during the night and then phone the results to a central office where the data was collected and analyzed. By using volunteers, the overall cost of the program was reduced and complete and effective mosquito control was the result.

Frequency and Timing

The frequency and timing of surveys or regular inspections is determined simply by when complaints arise. The number of complaints is a function of the mosquito species, the human population density and distribution, the tolerance level of the people affected and the type of management strategies and tactics practiced.

In the mid-Atlantic states, for example, monitoring should start in March for the salt-marsh mosquito (Aedes solicitans) and should continue at 10-day intervals until mid-May. This species is the major pestiferous mosquito on the East Coast where there are salt marshes (the major salt-marsh mosquito farther south is A. taeniorhynchus), which can travel 40 or more miles from its development site, depending on the wind.

TREATMENT

It is not realistic to assume that all mosquitoes can or should be eliminated from the area in which they are troublesome. The cost of environmental degradation in terms of wildlife loss would be too great, because mosquitoes are important prey in many bird, reptile, amphibian, fish and other food chains (see the sidebar on p. 663). The use of broad-spectrum insecticides reduces these and other populations by introducing toxicants that kill through direct and indirect action. Thus, before you embark on a mosquito control program, it is very important to consider how you can accomplish your goal in an environmentally safe, long-lasting manner.

Establishing Action Levels

The next step after establishing a monitoring program is determining how many mosquitoes are too many, and at what point treatment should be initiated. This is called the "action level," and it is often difficult for individuals and communities to agree on it. The action level is reached before the injury level, or the level at which pests become intolerable, because you must allow time to do something before pest numbers grow that large. This consideration is particularly important in least-toxic mosquito management, since it is the immature stage of the mosquito that must be treated. Once immature mosquitoes have developed into adults, it is often too late to use environmentally benign management methods.

Injury levels for a few nuisance and vector mosquito species are mentioned in the literature. A typical injury level for initiation of treatments might be 5 bites/15 minutes. But there is still a great need to establish injury and action levels for other species in various situations. The injury levels in areas far from population centers should be much higher —15 bites/15 minutes, for example— than those closer to such centers. Obviously, where there are few people for the mosquitoes to bother, larger numbers of these insects should be tolerated. This is true because all mosquito management programs have limited budgets and must use their funds to aid the most people. Also, in sparsely populated areas it is usually more important to protect the food chain than a few humans.

In order to establish an action level in an area where one has never been established before, you must start with some estimated or best-guess figure since you have to make a decision on whether and/or when to take action. You might decide, for example, that only if biting counts show one or more bites in 15 minutes, should treatment action be initiated. If possible this number should be based on the estimated or recorded number of complaints in previous similarly wet years. If good records of complaints, treatment actions, areas treated and results are kept for the current year, this initial "working" action level can be used as a base line and revised in subsequent years as more information is collected. There must be a working action level for the first year of the new program so that decisions can be made and results evaluated. This level will likely be adjusted as the program proceeds.

Organizing

The precise tactics to be used for mosquito treatment and prevention must be fitted to the source of the mosquitoes and must balance effectiveness, cost and environmental damage. Professional managers trained in mosquito identification, biology, ecology and management are usually required, due to the complexity of the biological and sociological situations involved. Throughout the United States, there are hundreds of local mosquito abatement districts (MADs) charged with mosquito control and financed by local taxes. They are primarily the legacy of programs that eliminated malaria as a transmissible disease in the United States in the 1950s. Although some MADs today are on the cutting edge of less-toxic mosquito management, not all are familiar with such technologies. Some areas lack mosquito control districts altogether.

If your city, county, other public agencies or private institutions are still dealing with mosquito problems individually, haphazardly and intermittently because no MAD exists, you should seriously consider trying to form one. This is particularly important where the mosquito problem traditionally has been handled by public agencies who lack mosquito control specialists and whose management consists primarily of fogging or aerial application of insecticides to suppress adult mosquitoes. In such situations the formation of a MAD helps prevent the problems from arising in the first place.

Forming a mosquito abatement district may involve getting interested friends and neighbors together with sympathetic local officials and attempting to educate the community as to the benefits of least-toxic control. A booklet entitled *Laws Relating to Local Agencies Engaged in Mosquito and Vector Control*, listed under "References and Readings" on p. 677, is based on excerpts from the California Health and Safety Code and the California Government Code. It provides sample language that can be adapted by other agencies elsewhere in establishing MADs.

Indirect Strategies

Elimination of all standing water is the key to preventing mosquitoes from breeding around the home. Even the smallest amount of water in a watering can or an old saucer used for pet feeding can be the source of a surprisingly large number of mosquitoes. Not even the tiniest amount of water should be allowed to collect.

1. **Promoting Good Drainage.** Keep roof drains and gutters clear of debris that can cause rain runoff to back up and collect, setting the stage for larval development. It is also very important that landscaped areas be graded so water does not stand on the surface in temporary pools between rains or irrigation. Drainage in large or small areas can be enhanced by gravity ditches, subsurface drainage tiles or sump pumps. You can also fill the low areas with imported soil. Unfortunately, storm sewer catch basins on the street cannot be drained easily, so they must be monitored and treated regularly.

2. **Managing Bodies of Water.** Woodland pools are shallow accumulations of water that last for weeks or longer after rains. They can produce enormous numbers of mosquitoes, sometimes near large population centers. Where spring and summer rains fill such woodland pools, inspection should be carried out in concentric circles of increasing diameter to the extent that resources permit. Only those pools found to contain live mosquito larvae should be drained or filled in. Keep in mind, however, that draining bodies of water can be highly disruptive to natural areas, food chains and ecosystems.

It takes good judgment to know when drainage is appropriate and when another less permanent procedure would be less environmentally damaging. With the development of selective and benign microbial products (discussed on p. 673), the choice has become easier because the microbes can be used for spot treatment with minimal damage to nontarget wildlife. Thus, where woodland pools are producing intolerable populations of biting mosquitoes, all such sources must be located, inspected at appropriate times, such as when rains or melting snow cause the pools to form each year, and treated in the least-toxic manner, for example with a BTI product. In some cases the same person can do the mapping, inspection and spot treatment on a single tour of the area.

Where there is sufficient motivation to treat in an environmentally sound manner, and where citizens are enlightened enough to support progressive mosquito control, there is little reason why coastal marshes cannot be managed in a manner that minimizes the use of toxic materials. Drainage ditches can be created so that high tides flush the marsh. The ditches link artificially created pools into which mosquito-eating native fish can retreat during periods of very low tide. When the water levels rise again, the fish fan out over the marsh, eating the mosquito larvae. There is a growing body of literature on techniques that have worked well in marshy areas on the East and West coasts (see, for example, the article by J. Redmond, listed under "References and Readings" on p. 679).

3. Managing Water-Collecting Tree Cavities. Certain mosquito species can breed in water-holding cavities in trees (see the drawing at left above). A common way of treating this problem is to drill a slanting drainage hole from the outside of the trunk up into the bottom of the cavity. Sometimes a metal pipe is inserted in this hole to ensure that drainage continues.

There are concerns about this technique, however. Although some very fine old specimen trees have survived this treatment—for example,

Tree Holes as Mosquito Breeding Areas

Trees with holes that catch rainwater can produce troublesome mosquito populations that are difficult to find and treat. *Aedes sierrensis* is a common tree-hole mosquito in the western United States; *A. triseriatus,* which is shown in the drawing, occurs in the eastern United States.

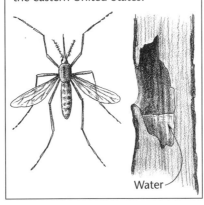

Water

on the historic Andrew Jackson Estate in Tennessee—recent research on how trees protect themselves from disease organisms indicates that in general this approach is not a good idea. Drilling can expose the tree to fungal and other invaders by breaking the seal the tree creates around such cavities. A better approach may be to insert an absorbent wicking material leading from the bottom of the hole over the lowest edge of the cavity and down the trunk to a level below the base of the cavity. The cavity is filled with a loose, porous material, such as sand or fiberglass insulation, that drains easily. Unfortunately, there is as yet no evaluative research on this technique.

Direct Physical Controls

The most important means of protecting yourself from mosquitoes in the house is also the most obvious: screens. You should screen windows, doors and porches where evening activities take place in hot weather. If an occasional mosquito bothers

A Simple Mosquito Net

Mosquito netting can be hung over a portable frame for protection when camping outdoors on a cot or in a sleeping bag. In this drawing, a T-shaped frame constructed from 2x2 (5 cm by 5 cm) wooden stakes is positioned at both ends of the cot. Three 12-gauge wires are fastened to the ends and middle of the "T." A rectangular mosquito bed net with a zippered closure at one end is suspended from the wires and tucked under the mattress or sleeping bag.

you at night, it probably slipped in through a doorway when someone entered the house. If this occurs regularly, however, you should suspect a hole in a screen or a crack around the edge of the door. Inspect screens each season and mend small holes or tears with dabs of clear silicone caulk. The screens should fit their openings tightly; any gaps around windows can be bridged with a soft, removable caulk such as rope caulk; door gaps can be filled with weatherstripping.

If you enjoy sleeping under the stars but are bothered by mosquitoes, placing nylon mosquito netting around your cot or sleeping bag is an excellent way to protect yourself. The nets can be purchased or made on a sewing machine. The netting is available in surplus stores, from some recreational equipment suppliers or repairers and by mail order.

To support a homemade net (see the drawing above), fashion a simple wood-and-wire frame that holds the net up over your head. Use Velcro™ tape to attach the net to the sleeping bag. If attaching the Velcro™ tape is too much trouble, buy the netting large enough so you can tuck its edges under sleeping pads. We have successfully adapted such a system from a commercially available model sold by an outdoor equipment store.

Head nets like those worn by bee-keepers can prevent mosquito bites around the neck and face in heavily infested areas. You should also wear a long-sleeved shirt and long pants fastened at the ankles with Velcro™ closures of the type bicyclists use. A sweatshirt is a good idea, even though it is uncomfortable in hot weather, because its thickness prevents bites. You can also buy net shirts, which you soak in repellent and wear over relatively light clothing or swimsuits. These allow the breeze to pass through. Net shirts also protect against many other biting flies. They are available in stores or by mail from suppliers of fishing and hunting gear.

Direct Biological Controls

Biological controls for mosquitoes include mosquito-eating fish, the bacterium BTI and nematodes.

1. Mosquito-Eating Fish. Small back yard ponds can be stocked with goldfish or the mosquito fish *(Gambusia affinis)* shown in the drawing below. Goldfish live longer, are generally hardier and are easier to find at pet stores. The fish must be protected from cats and raccoons by an overhang around the edge of the pool or an escape area where they cannot be caught. A 1-ft. (30 cm) section of 4-in. or 6-in. (10 cm or 15 cm) diameter clay drainage pipe, placed on the bottom of the pool, creates an excellent refuge from fish predators.

You should consider stocking any small, man-made body of water that has no natural drainage with some kind of mosquito-eating fish. Natural bodies of water, however, should not be stocked with exotic (non-native) species since they kill native fish either directly or indirectly by altering the habitat and competing for food. The exotics may also be killed by na-

tive fish. Fortunately, many native fish are good mosquito predators.

Unfortunately, the same man-made habitat alterations and pollution that make some bodies of water mosquito sources also reduce the ability of those areas to support native fish. For example, shallow streams and ponds often accumulate fertilizer. This encourages excessive aquatic plant growth, which competes with the fish for oxygen, reducing native fish numbers. As a result, mosquito populations rise. Proper management in this case means reducing the fertilizer input, then removing the excessive vegetation. If it is an artificial pond, it can usually be drained and cleaned.

The reduced oxygen content of some log ponds, sewage treatment ponds and dairy waste lagoons, for example, may limit survival of native fish species. These sites may be good candidates for the mosquito fish. Many mosquito control agencies already produce this species for use in such man-made habitats as back yard fish ponds, sewage treatment ponds and rice fields. You can call the nearest mosquito abatement agency to see whether these fish are available in your area.

There are other fish that may be useful in such troubled habitats. For example, some *Tilapia* species are used in sewage treatment ponds because they eat not only mosquitoes but some other pestiferous closely related species of flies as well. *Tilapia* are tropical species exotic to the United States that have been introduced here. But they die out where winter water temperatures drop below 45°F to 54°F (7°C to 12°C). Note that they are prohibited in certain areas, so fish and wildlife authorities must be consulted regarding any introductions.

Guppies *(Poecilia reticulata)* native to Central America have also been introduced into the United States and many other countries for mosquito control. They cannot survive below 52°F (11°C). Thus, the damage done to existing food webs can be mini-

The Mosquito Fish

Mosquito fish *(Gambusia affinis)* have been introduced worldwide for mosquito control. They are most appropriate in man-made bodies of water that do not connect with natural waters. The female is pictured here. When this or similar species are introduced into ponds or ornamental pools, they need protection from local predators. A piece of clay pipe at least 1 ft. (30 cm) long can provide such protection.

mized if this species is introduced where it will die out in winter.

2. BTI. The commercial development of *Bacillus thuringiensis israelensis,* or BTI, which is marketed as Teknar®, Bactimos® and Vectobac® (see the Resource Appendix under "Insect Management: Biological Controls" on pp. 683-686) offers the possibility of a least-toxic suppression agent that is also highly selective. BTI is one of several *Bacillus thuringiensis* strains now available for pest control. The species was first made commercially available as a potent and environmentally sound control for a large number of caterpillar species. For a more complete review, see the discussion on pp. 132-136.

BTI, like the other strains of BT, acts as a stomach poison, damaging cells of the mid-gut of mosquito larvae that have eaten the spores. The drawing at right illustrates how it works. Compared to other bacterial toxins and even many synthetic insecticides, BTI kills quickly. Studies show that a moderate to high concentration eliminates about half the test population of some *Culex* species in 15 minutes, and the rest after about an hour. Furthermore, a mere five-minute exposure causes eventual death. *Culiseta* and *Aedes* species require longer exposure times and higher doses than *Culex. Anopheles* appear to be the least susceptible of the mosquitoes tested.

In field studies, BTI has proven effective against several mosquito species in widely differing conditions, including irrigated pastures, storm drains, ponds, dairy lagoons and salt-marsh potholes. It has also been shown to kill many blackfly *(Simuliidae)* species, which are serious pests in some areas, while being nontoxic to most other aquatic species.

BTI can be applied with conventional spray equipment. Although it is more costly than more toxic, less selective products, the added cost should be weighed against the cost of the damage to nontarget wildlife caused by the other products. Since

How BTI Works to Control Mosquitoes

The bacterium *Bacillus thuringiensis israeliensis* infects and kills mosquito larvae. It is relatively safe and environmentally sound because it is highly selective, killing only mosquitoes and certain related water-inhabiting insects. The drawing shows the sequence of events that lead to the death of the larvae.

Larva

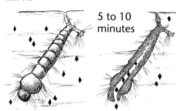

5 to 10 minutes

Larva feeds on BTI spores and crystals suspended in water.

Spores and crystals enter gut of larva; crystals dissolve.

Cross Section of Larval Mid-Gut

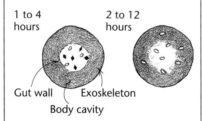

1 to 4 hours

2 to 12 hours

Gut wall   Exoskeleton
Body cavity

Gut wall breaks down from action of toxic crystals.

Crystals completely dissolve; spores escape into body cavity; larva dies.

BTI does not last beyond a few days in the environment after application, it must be released at more frequent intervals than conventional mosquito larvicides.

3. Nematodes. A commercially available mosquito-attacking nematode, *Romanomermis culcivorax,* was used in the United States for a number of years to control mosquitoes, but was then removed from the market due to poor sales. However, this nematode, which is discussed at length in the sidebar on p. 674, is a highly selective larvicide that lasts for a number of years because it reproduces on the mosquitoes and then dies out. We hope that it will be returned to the marketplace.

Direct Chemical Controls

A wide variety of chemical controls are available for the management of mosquitoes, including repellents, surface oils, insect growth regulators and superabsorbent polymers.

1. Repellents. Repellents provide excellent protection, even for people who are particularly sensitive to mosquito or other fly bites. Ideally such repellents should be displayed more prominently in recreation centers. If more people protected themselves on an individual basis, it would reduce the pressure on public service providers to spray insecticides over entire ecosystems.

DEET, or diethyltuolomide, is the most widely sold repellent, and is available in concentrations up to 75%. A word of caution: Apply repellents to your clothing rather than to your skin. Recent research suggests that repeated applications to the skin may be hazardous.

2. Suffocating Surface Films. One old but still effective method for killing mosquito larvae is to apply an oil to the surface of a body of standing water, where it forms a film. When the larvae try to break through the water surface to obtain oxygen from the air, the oil clogs their breathing tubes and smothers them. Enough oil should be applied so that the film covers the entire open surface. Although many oils, such as kerosene and number 2 fuel oil (used for home heating), have been used in the past, special mosquito control oils have recently come onto the market. These are more refined, cause less damage to nontarget wildlife and

Mosquito-Attacking Nematodes

The first nematode developed for commercial use in the United States was the mermithid *Romanomermis culcivorax* (shown in the drawing at right). It was used against pest mosquito species in the 1970s. Once mass-production of *R. culcivorax* within living hosts was achieved (in 1972), there was greater interest in the potential of mermithids as biocontrol agents. The mass-production techniques were improved so that infective pre-parasites were produced at a cost of $10 per million. Because the pre-parasites functioned like insect parasitoids, the Environmental Protection Agency determined that they were exempt from regulation.

Field trials using the nematodes against pest mosquito larvae were conducted in a number of locations, including ponds and grassy fields in Florida and Louisiana, rice fields and lakes in California and aquatic environments in Taiwan and Thailand. The results of these tests indicated that, under the right conditions—for example, a fairly warm temperature, the correct pH, low salinity and pollution, and the absence of nematode predators—*R. culcivorax* is a very effective biological control agent for mosquitoes.

This nematode species was produced and marketed by two commercial insectaries, Fairfax Biologicals in Clinton Corners, New York, which marketed the product under the name Skeeter Doom™, and by Nutralite in Lakeview, California. Unfortunately, this species is no longer available commercially. Apparently, the popularity of chemical controls for mosquitoes prevented the development of an adequate market for these products. However, current public

The Life Cycle of the Mermethid Nematode

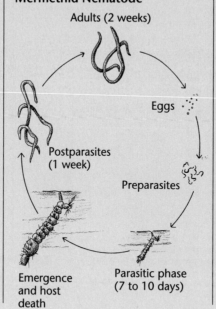

Adults (2 weeks)

Eggs

Postparasites (1 week)

Preparasites

Emergence and host death

Parasitic phase (7 to 10 days)

concerns about pesticide use, together with the growing interest in insect-attacking nematodes, may resurrect interest in mermithids.

Yet another stumbling block has been the lack of a technique for mass-rearing mermithid nematodes in an artificial medium, which is a less expensive technique than the use of live hosts. Although in vitro rearing could no doubt stimulate a mass market for mermithid nematodes, surely there is already a niche for smaller-scale production for specialty markets such as regional mosquito abatement districts and park systems with mosquito and black fly problems.

In the meantime, biological control workers are eagerly watching developments with the commercially available steinernematid and heterorhabditid nematodes, which reached the market in the 1980s. In vitro mass-rearing technology has significantly lowered their production costs so that treatments can compete economically with insecticide application. Commercial sources of these nematodes are listed in the Resource Appendix under "Insect Management: Biological Controls" on pp. 683-686.

plants and do not pollute water as the other oils do.

Another material aimed at killing larvae by disrupting breathing is a monomolecular surface film called Arosurf® (for a source, see the Resource Appendix under "Insect Management: Chemical Controls" on pp.

686-687). This product is safe to humans and wildlife, and it is effective at killing larvae, pupae, emerging adults, ovipositing females, resting males and egg rafts of some species.

The drawbacks of using this film are that its larvicidal action is not immediate and its effects are lessened if

the surface of the water is disturbed by wind or any other activity, although its ability to recover after disturbance is much greater than traditional oils. But a microbial product like BTI also has drawbacks. Although all three formulations of BTI mentioned earlier take rapid effect on larvae, they do not persist long enough to kill newly hatched larvae and they do not kill pupae. BTI is also ineffective against larvae that have ceased feeding prior to pupation. The good news is that field tests with Arosurf® and BTI in combination show 100% control of mixed larval and pupal populations of *Culex, Psorophora* and *Aedes* species in 24 to 48 hours.

3. Insect Growth Regulators (IGRs). Other new, less toxic chemicals are now being registered and are entering the marketplace. One example is the insect growth regulator methoprene (for a more complete review of IGRs, see pp. 145-148). This IGR, marketed as Altosid® by Zoecon (see the Resource Appendix under "Insect Management: Chemical Controls" on pp. 686-687), offers greater selectivity and less toxicity to nontarget wildlife than do conventional insecticides.

Altosid® induces damaging morphological changes in second, third and fourth instar mosquito larvae, resulting in the failure of adult mosquitoes to emerge from pupae. Packaged in slow-release briquettes, it is effective for 30 days in standing water. It can be coated onto sand particles for easier foliage penetration or applied as a spray solution from the air or ground.

Methoprene has an acute oral LD_{50} of greater than 34,000 mg/kg, indicating a high degree of safety to mammals (for more information on what the LD_{50} rating means, see pp. 89-92). This IGR is biodegradable and does not accumulate in food chains. It is far more selective in its action than the organophosphate or carbamate insecticides widely used as sprays for larval and adult mosquitoes.

4. Superabsorbent Polymers. A relatively new group of nontoxic synthetic materials called superabsorbent polymers have proven successful in field tests as larvicides and controlled-release substances. One of these polymers, Culigel™, has been patented by the Lee County Mosquito Control District in Fort Myers, Florida. Culigel™ introduced into a body of water

at 1 lb. to 5 lb. per surface acre (5.5 kg/hectare) absorbs water and swells to form a hydrogel or hydrogel complex from which microbial, insect growth regulator or other surface films can diffuse out.

Culigel™ in granular, pellet or briquette form could also be used in places such as tires, potholes, catch basins and pastures that are dry at the time of application but flood later, thereby activating the substance. When these areas dry out again, the hydrogel would persist until reactivated by the next flooding. It could be used with or without an additional larvicidal agent.

5. "New Jersey Larvicide." When the added cost of using more selective materials cannot be justified, or where there are minimal nontarget populations, an old traditional mixture called New Jersey larvicide, composed of diesel oil and pyrethrin, can be used. This combination degrades rapidly and is highly effective. However, it can kill a wide range of non-mosquito species, so its use should be carefully controlled.

6. Ground-Fogging and Aerial Applications. In general, we do not recommend that insecticidal chemicals be applied as ground fogs by air over populated areas. If broad-spectrum insectides must be used, it is less environmentally damaging to treat immature mosquitoes in their water sources than to pollute a much larger area by ground-fogging or aerial applications.

Ground-fogging is usually more selective than aerial application. And among aerial methods, helicopter applications are more selective than airplane applications, because helicopters can fly more slowly and closer to the ground, directing the material more accurately. Low-volume application methods are generally less damaging than high-volume applications. Among aerial application insecticides, some are more selective than others.

With so many environmentally sound tools to choose from, and the

extensive expertise already developed in least-toxic mosquito management, there is every reason to believe that citizen education, leading to citizen demand, will result in the reduction of the amount of toxic material applied to our communities and aquatic environments in the name of mosquito control.

To conclude this chapter, we present a case history showing how an IPM program for mosquitoes using some of the strategies and tactics described in this chapter was implemented in several cities in Arkansas.

CASE HISTORY: AN IPM PROGRAM FOR MOSQUITOES

For two successive years, University of Arkansas entomologist Max Meisch, and Allen Inman, director of the City of Stuttgart (Arkansas) Mosquito Abatement Program, compared the effectiveness of four different mosquito control regimes in five cities in the rice-growing region of Arkansas. Their data shows the superiority of an Integrated Pest Management (IPM) approach over the less sophisticated methods still used in many communities.

Good mosquito control in cities requires two steps that are difficult for city governments to take. The first is planning and financing control before a problem occurs. The second is orchestrating an IPM program that includes an area-wide survey of mosquito habitats, treatment of water sources that breed mosquitoes, and application of the most advanced control strategies. Usually, the best that city governments can do is provide an emergency response to citizen complaints. However, by the time citizens are bitten and call in complaints, it is too late to handle the problem through least-toxic methods.

A mosquito abatement agency is financed specifically to reduce populations of mosquitoes before they become pestiferous. It has access to the necessary equipment and expertise, and it can develop an IPM program for mosquitoes that includes monitoring before and after treatments. In the best programs, the entire area within and around a city is surveyed to determine when and where the pest species are hatching. With the sources pinpointed, a selective microbial insecticide can be used against larval mosquitoes before they fly and bite. This treatment is called "larviciding," and the best material for it is *Bacillus thuringiensis israelensis* (BTI). BTI kills the pest but is nontoxic to humans and other organisms in the environment.

In 1987, five cities in Arkansas' rice-growing area established the Grand Prairie Municipal Mosquito Abatement Program. Scientists in the Riceland Mosquito Management Program of the USDA cooperated with them to develop an IPM approach to mosquito problems in the abatement district. In Arkansas, rice fields produce large populations of mosquitoes. In 1987 and 1988, Meisch and Inman compared four different approaches to controlling the local pest mosquito species. The dark ricefield mosquito *(Psorophora columbiae)* develops in floodwaters. It usually becomes a problem in June and July; the common malaria mosquito *(Anopheles quadrimaculatus)* is a species that develops in permanent water. Its populations are usually largest in August.

The researchers monitored the size of the mosquito populations by using light traps, resting stations (at which counts of resting mosquitoes were made) and biting counts (which counted how many mosquitoes attempted to bite a human in a given period). Biting counts are the most direct measurements of pestiferousness. Because some species bite only at night, however, resting counts made during the day provide the best indication of their numbers.

In the city of Stuttgart, larval breeding areas received BTI applications, but no treatments were directed at adult mosquitoes. In Gillette, adult mosquitoes were treated and the surrounding rice fields were

Summary: Least-Toxic Mosquito Control

Home Mosquito Control:
• Repair window and door screens.

• Check carefully for standing water.

• Drain standing water. Where this cannot be done, add oil, BTI or mosquito-eating fish.

• Wear repellents and protective clothing outdoors during mosquito season.

Community Mosquito Control:
• Quantify mosquito activity by conducting biting counts.

• Identify the species.

• Establish tolerance or injury levels.

• Find the larval sources of the species identified in the biting counts, and map or record them for future reference.

• Educate members of the community about the role they can play in reducing larval sources.

• Eliminate larval sources by draining them, by stocking bodies of water with fish and through the use of other natural enemies as they become available commercially.

• Apply BTI or other least-toxic materials to larval mosquito sources.

• Return to breeding sites to evaluate all treatments.

• From the results of these evaluations, redesign treatments, if necessary, and develop plans for future management.

not. The other Arkansas cities received a mix of adulticiding and larviciding treatments over rice fields of varying sizes.

If adulticiding was necessary, resmethrin, a pyrethroid, was applied at carefully selected points around the perimeter of the city. Inman refers to this as barrier control, since it is designed to catch mosquitoes before they fly into the city. This contrasts sharply with community-wide fogging with organophosphate insecticides, an approach that is still used in many towns. Resmethrin is comparatively less disruptive of the environment. One reason is that it has a very short period of activity.

Because cattle are an important blood source for mosquitoes around these towns, the researchers also focused on them. At present, a method whereby cows rub up against bags containing a dust formulation of the synthetic pyrethroid insecticide permethrin is being used. The cows can administer this treatment themselves and the pesticide is confined to the target area (the cow's hide).

All the Arkansas cities experienced good mosquito control through this integrated mosquito management program, and Stuttgart achieved excellent control without using adulticides. Larviciding over 5,300 acres of rice located around that city was economically feasible because ultra-low-volume BTI sprays, applied by plane and truck, were used. The researchers were able to prove the effectiveness of the IPM concept under challenging circumstances.

REFERENCES AND READINGS

Busvine, J.R. 1980. *Insects and hygiene, the biology and control of insect pests of medical and domestic importance.* 3rd ed. New York: Chapman and Hall. 568 pp.

This volume includes a section on the biology and management of mosquitoes, with examples from Europe and some parts of the United States.

California Department of Health Services, Vector Biology and Control. 1985. *Laws relating to local agencies engaged in mosquito and vector control.* Sacramento: California Department of Health Services.

This booklet is based on excerpts from the California Health and Safety Code and the California Government Code. It contains language useful in establishing a legal entity that can raise funds through taxation for purposes of operating a mosquito control service.

Chapman, H.C. 1974. Biological control of mosquito larvae. *Annual Review of Entomology* 19:33-59.

An earlier review article emphasizing biological control, particularly microbial control, that is still worth reading today.

Chapman, H.C., ed. 1985. *Biological control of mosquitoes.* Fresno, Calif.: American Mosquito Control Association. 218 pp.

A comprehensive review of the current state of knowledge on biological control agents used against mosquitoes. The 23 papers in this book offer a rich set of possibilities for further commercial products. The microbial product *Bacillus thuringiensis israelensis* (BTI) has been used commercially for some years, but the current evaluation of another bacterium, *Bacillus sphaericus,* for its commercial potential is also described. Now that pesticide producers have learned to appreciate the market for the less-toxic and more selective microbial products, other groups of organisms may be developed. For example, among the fungi, *Lagenidium giganteum* is the next most obvious possibility for development.

In concluding the volume, Marshall Laird points out that for the immediate future, the best interests of biological control are served by devising practical integrated control methodologies in order to buy time for the development of additional least-toxic biological control products. He also notes that most of the current biological control research is conducted in an individual, uncoordinated manner in which workers too easily become sidetracked into fascinating paths that, although leading to advances in the academic sense, do little to provide practical new tools for mosquito management.

Christensen, J.B., and R.K. Washino. 1977. *Gambusia affinis and mosquito control: a review of the literature.* Unpublished manuscript. Department of Entomology, University of California.

An extensive review paper with bibliography on this important mosquito predator.

Darsie, R.F., Jr., and R.A. Ward. 1981. *Identification and geographical distribution of the mosquitoes of North America north of Mexico.* Fresno, Calif.: American Mosquito Control Association. 313 pp. (Available from: American Mosquito Control Association, 5545 E. Shields Ave., Fresno, CA 93727.)

An important source of information for anyone concerned with mosquito identification. It contains illustrated keys, distribution maps and an excellent introduction to mosquito morphology. The complementary volume for Canada is Wood et al., 1979 (see p. 679).

Furman, D.P., and E.P. Catts. 1982. *A manual of medical entomology.* 4th ed. New York: Cambridge University Press. 207 pp.

This manual includes a series of chapters with keys to the mosquitoes, as well as a wealth of information and keys on other animal species of medical importance. New chapters have been added in this latest edition. The chapter on mounting and dissection of mosquitoes is of particular interest.

Harwood, R.F., and M.T. James. 1979. *Entomology in human and animal health.* 7th ed. New York: Macmillan. 548 pp.

This is the standard graduate-level text for medical entomology in the United States. No recommendations for control are discussed. Although badly in need of updating, it is still an excellent source of information.

Kettle, D.S. 1984. *Medical and veterinary entomology.* New York: John Wiley and Sons. 658 pp.

A good introductory text emphasizing the Diptera (mosquitoes and higher flies) and Acari (mites and ticks). It updates (to about 1981) the major insect-vectored diseases such as arboviruses, typhus, malaria and onchocerciasis. Each of its 32 chapters is referenced. This text should be available in public health libraries and in the libraries of interested research professionals, since it adds a great deal to the available information by providing access to literature that is not readily accessible elsewhere and includes many management case histories.

Levy, R., M.A. Nichols, J.A. Hornby and T.W. Miller, Jr. 1989. Controlled release of mosquito larvicides and pupicides from a cross-linked polyacrylamide Culigel™ SP superabsorbent polymer matrix. In *Proceedings of the 16th international symposium on controlled release of bioactive materials, Chicago, August 6-9, 1989,* eds. R. Pearlman and J. Miller, pp. 437-438 (No. 222). Chicago: Controlled Release Society.

This was the source of the information on superabsorbent polymer matrices provided in this chapter.

Levy, R., C.N. Powell, B.C. Hertlein and T.W. Miller, Jr. 1984. Efficacy of Arosurf® and base formulations of *Bacillus thuringiensis* var. *israelensis* against mixed populations of mosquito larvae and pupae. *Mosquito News* 44(4):537-543.

This was the source of the information in this chapter about BTI and Arosurf®. For further information, contact Dr. Levy, c/o Lee County Mosquito Control District, P.O. Box 06005, Fort Myers, FL 33906.

Means, R.G. 1979. *Mosquitoes of New York, Part 1. The genus Aedes Meigen with identification keys to genera of Culicidae.* Albany: University of the State of New York (Bulletin 430a). (Available from: State Education Dept., State Science Service, N.Y. State Museum, Albany, NY 12234.)

A very important publication for New York and its surrounding states that is also useful elsewhere. It is practically oriented and includes pictures of collecting methods, habitats and mounting methods, as well as lists of New York State species and keys to the various genera and species.

Meek, C.L., and G.R. Hayes. 1978. *Commercial pesticide applicator mosquito control training manual.* New Orleans: Louisiana Mosquito Control Association. 152 pp.

Although this manual emphasizes mosquitoes important to Louisiana, it also incorporates information applicable to North America in general.

Meisch, M.V., and Inman, A. 1990. Surveillance results from mosquito abatement programs in the Grand Prairie. *Arkansas Farm Research* 3(2): 5-16.

This paper documents the effective use of IPM methods for mosquito management in five Arkansas cities, particularly the use of *Bacillus thuringiensis israelensis* instead of aerosol sprays against adult mosquitoes.

Merritt, R.W., and K.W. Cummins, eds. 1978. *An introduction to the aquatic insects of North America.* Dubuque, Iowa: Kendall/Hunt. (Available from: Kendall/Hunt, 2460 Kerper Blvd., Dubuque, IA 52001.)

There is no better manual for identifying the associates of mosquitoes, particularly the large number of predatory species that eat mosquitoes. It includes a chapter on mosquito biology and ecology.

Pennak, R.W. 1978. *Freshwater invertebrates of the United States.* 2nd ed. New York: John Wiley and Sons. 803 pp.

If you start looking at insects in fresh and brackish water, especially under a microscope, this book becomes essential. In addition to the insects, it also covers the protozoa, rotifers, the flatworms and other creatures.

Poinar, G.O., Jr. 1979. *Nematodes for biological control of insects.* Boca Raton, Fla.: CRC Press. 277 pp.

This is the source of the information on *Romanomermis culcivorax* in this chapter.

Redmond, J. 1984. Selective ditching for salt marsh mosquito control. *The IPM Practitioner* 6(7):4-5.

This short article discusses highly selective ditching practices for enhancing mosquito predation in salt marshes in the San Francisco Bay Area. Such recirculating ditches greatly aided mosquito control in a less damaging way than insecticide applications by enhancing predation and reducing water levels. However, this procedure decreases the diversity of aquatic invertebrates, so unnecessary ditching should be avoided.

Smith, K.G.V. 1973. *Insects and other arthropods of medical importance.* London: Trustees of the British Museum. 561 pp.

An introductory text with a world-wide perspective and excellent line drawings and keys.

U.S. Department of Health, Education and Welfare. 1979. *Mosquitoes of public health importance and their control.* Atlanta: Centers for Disease Control. 25 pp.

A pamphlet that contains good introductory information. it is no longer distributed by CDC, but we at BIRC (P.O. Box 7414, Berkeley, CA 94707) can make copies available.

Wood, D.M., P.T. Dang and R.A. Ellis. 1979. *The insects and arachnids of Canada. Part 6: the mosquitoes of Canada.* Hull, Quebec: Canadian Government Publishing Centre (Publication 1686). 390 pp. (Available from: Canadian Government Publishing Centre, Supply and Services Canada, Hull, Quebec, Canada K1A 0S9.)

This book has an excellent section on general mosquito biology, as well as high-quality line drawings. It contains detailed morphological, biological and ecological information pertinent to each genus, subgenus and species. With Darsie and Ward's 1981 book on hand, the reader can cover all of North America.

Resource Appendix

This Resource Appendix is divided into four management sections:

The products and services listed in each of these sections fall into one of five categories: Identification and Monitoring, Physical Controls, Horticultural Controls, Biological Controls and Least-Toxic Chemical Controls.

The products and the names of the companies that supply them are further grouped under appropriate subheadings. For example, Traps and Screens come under Physical Controls. To avoid cumbersome repetition, the addresses and phone numbers of manufacturers and suppliers of products and services are listed alphabetically under "SUPPLIERS" at the end of the Resource Appendix (pp. 690-697).

Two caveats apply to this information. First, to the best of our knowledge, the products and services listed here are effective and are produced by reputable companies. However, please be advised that you are using them at your own risk, and the authors and The Taunton Press make no guarantees or warranties regarding any product or service listed. We encourage you to write the authors at the Bio-Integral Resource Center (BIRC), P.O. Box 7414, Berkeley, CA 94707, with your comments on these or any other least-toxic pest management resources.

Second, this information was current at press time. But pest control is a rapidly changing field. Products come and go; companies change hands and locations relatively frequently. Therefore, if you fail to reach any of the companies listed here, contact BIRC at the address above. BIRC maintains a computerized data base of product information and can provide you with the latest sources of the materials you need.

INSECT MANAGEMENT

IDENTIFICATION AND MONITORING
Information and Identification
American Entomological Institute: pest identification service; ichneumonids only

CAB International Institute of Biological Control: information on biocontrol

Commonwealth International Institute of Entomology: pest identification service

Consulting Diagnostic Service: pest identification service

Note: The Cooperative Extension Service, located in every county in the United States, also provides pest identification services.

Collection and Identification
Arthropod Slidemounts: images for identifying arthropods

W.C. Batiste Co.: aspirators, beater trays, mesh cages

BioQuip Products: aspirators, hand lenses, beating cloths, sweep nets

Brody Enterprises: microscopes

Combined Scientific Supplies: insect collecting supplies

Dippers: mosquito larvae collectors

Great Lakes IPM: sweep nets

Oakfield Apparatus, Inc.: sweep nets

Pest Management Supply Co.: Macroscope™ portable microscopes

Wildlife Supply Co.: aquatic sampling equipment

Computers, Software, Instruments
Allen-Bradley Co.: Datamyte™ hand-held data collection computers

Automata, Inc.: Lynx Telemetry Systems (computerized monitoring and data collection equipment), traps and instruments for monitoring insects and soil moisture

Brody Enterprises, Inc.: moisture meters

Delmhorst Instrument Co.: moisture meters

Environdata: Environdata automatic weather station, Easidata microprocessor

NPIRS User Services: PEST-BANK™ software

Omnidata International, Inc.: Biophenometers, portable data recording equipment for monitoring temperature and climate

Insect Monitoring and Control

agAccess: pest management books

Brody Enterprises, Inc.: listening devices

Eriez Magnetics Pty. Ltd.: screens, vibratory feeders to separate insects from grain

Hogil Corp.: Innomed head-lice combs, Innoscan pediculosis detection kit

National Pediculosis Association: Pedicu-Sticks™ (head-lice, tick diagnostic tool)

REI: tick solution kit

Inspection Dogs For Termites

Beacon Dogs, Inc.

Industrial Discovery Systems

TADD Services, Inc.

Pheromones and Supplies

AgriSense: pheromone lures and traps for a wide variety of pests, Trappit™ (for crawling insects), Magnet™ (for flying insects), Decoy™ (mating disrupter for pink bollworm)

APMR: monitoring lures and traps for apple, blueberry and cherry fruit maggots, and European apple sawfly

Biocontrol Limited: Isomate-M™ for oriental fruit moth

Brody Enterprises: pheromone lures for cockroaches and other insects

Consep Membranes, Inc.: Biolure™ products, Checkmate-PBW™ for pink bollworm, Scentry, Inc. products, IPS Ltd. products

Frank Enterprises, Inc.: Grandlure™ for cotton boll weevil

Great Lakes IPM: full line of traps and lures for agricultural pests

Hercon Environmental: Hercon™ Luretape® lures

Insects Limited: full line of traps and lures for stored product pests

Monterey Chemical Co.: pheromone ropes

Pacific Biocontrol Corp.: Isomate-M™ for oriental fruit moth, GBM-Rope™ for grape berry moth, Isomate-C™ for codling moth

Pest Management Supply Co.: full line of lures and traps for garden and orchard pests

Phero Tech, Inc.: full line of lures and traps for orchard, vineyard, forest, field, greenhouse and some structural pests

Santa Cruz Horticultural Supply: stored product pest lures and traps, especially for Indianmeal moth

Scentry, Inc.: Scentry™ products for orchard, vineyard, forest, field and greenhouse pests

Summit Chemical Co.: Dispalure™ lure and trap for gypsy moth

Trécé, Inc.: Storgard™ and Pherocon™ monitoring systems for stored product insects

PHYSICAL CONTROLS
Barriers

L.L. Bean: cedar chests

C & L Labs.: fluon insect barrier

Coverplus: Ventflex™ furniture covers for dust mites

Custom Copper: Snail-Barr® copper snail barrier

Great Lakes IPM: gypsy moth barrier tape

ICI Americas: fluon insect barrier

Repel'm Distributors: gypsy moth caterpillar tape

Trump Masters, Inc.: Skips Stand copper snail barrier

Barriers (Sticky):

Animal Repellents, Inc.: Tack Trap™ sticky material

Great Lakes IPM: Tanglefoot™

Olson Products, Inc.: Sticky Stuff™

Seabright Enterprises: Stickem™

Tanglefoot Co.: Tanglefoot™

Electroguns:

ETEX Ltd.: for termites, wood-boring beetles

Flea and Lice Combs:

Breeders Equipment Co.: flea comb

Health Enterprises, Inc: MC-12 head-lice comb

Hogil Corp.: Innomed head-lice comb

JTLK, Inc.: Derbac head-lice comb

Petco Animal Supplies: flea comb

Heat Treatment:

Isothermics, Inc.: heat-based system for control of termites, wood-boring beetles, etc.

Town Enterprises (Sanix, Inc.): infrared heater for control of indoor fleas and mites

Plastic Bags for Cockroach Control:

Urban Insect Solutions

Screening:

BioQuip Products: for mosquitoes

Chicopea: for greenhouses

Hydro-Gardens: for greenhouses

REI: for mosquitoes

Tredegar Film Products: for greenhouses

Spikes:

Mellinger Nursery: spiked lawn aerator sandals for grub control

Traps
(see also Pheromones, above):

AgriSense: Trappit™ Roach Trap

Applied Bionomics: thrips trap

Baley's: pyramid fly trap

Bell Laboratories, Inc.: Trapper™ yellow sticky traps

Beneficial BioSystems: fly and yellowjacket traps

Brody Enterprises: cockroach and fly traps

Devpro Machine, Inc.: electric insect traps

Dewille Inc.: elm bark beetle, whitefly and gypsy moth traps; varroa mite detector

Gardener's Supply: Snailproof® slug and snail trap

Gilbert® Insect Light Traps: insect electrocuting light traps

Great Lakes IPM: complete line of insect traps

Growing Naturally: assorted insect traps

GTF Labs.: yellow sticky traps, cockroach traps, wasp and fly traps

Hansens Bio Systems: thrips and whitefly sticky traps

Insects Limited: stored product insect pheromone traps

Ladd Research Industries, Inc.: apple maggot trap

Monterey Chemical Co.: yellow sticky traps, cockroach traps, wasp and fly traps

Olson Products, Inc.: Sticky Stuff™ and Sticky Sleeve™ biting and filth fly trap, thrips trap

Phero Tech Inc.: forest insects, thrips, varroa mite, whitefly and yellowjacket traps

Safer, Inc.: complete line of insect traps

Scentry, Inc.: Scentry® pheromone lure traps

Seabright Enterprises: cockroach, yellowjacket and whitefly traps

Sound Merchandise: Garden Sentry™ snail trap

Sterling International: yellowjacket traps

Trécé Inc.: Pherocon™ leafminer traps

Vacuums:
BioQuip Products: hand-held insect vacuum

D-VAC Company: backpack and tractor-mounted insect vacuum

McCluney Manufacturing, Inc.: tractor-mounted insect vacuum

Rexair Inc.: Rainbow water vacuum

Ringer Corp.: Bug Sucker™ portable insect vacuum

HORTICULTURAL CONTROLS
Insect-Resistant Turfgrass:
Lesco, Inc.: 'Commander' perennial ryegrass

Lofts Seed Co.: 'Repell' perennial ryegrass

Turf Seed, Inc.: 'Apache' tall fescue; perennial ryegrass: 'Citation II,' 'Commander,' 'Sunrise' and 'Vintage 2'

BIOLOGICAL CONTROLS
Artificial and Natural Diets For Rearing Beneficial Insects:
Beneficial Insectary: *Sitotroga* larvae

Bio-Control Co.: Bio-Control Honeydew

CRS Company: Formula 57™ artificial diet for lacewings and lady beetles

Gardens Alive: Wheast™ for lacewings and lady beetles

Kunafin Trichogramma Insectaries: *Sitotroga* larvae

Merricks, Inc.: Ladybug Diet™

Rincon-Vitova Insectaries, Inc.: *Sitotroga* larvae

Beneficial Insects
Note: In this category, companies outside the United States and Canada are marked with an asterisk (*), and beneficial insects are grouped according to the pests they control.

Aphid Parasitoids:
Applied Bionomics: *Aphidius matricariae*

*English Woodlands Ltd.: *Aphidius matricariae*

*Hansens Bio Systems: *Aphidius matricariae*

*Koppert B. V.: *Aphidius matricariae*

*Polgar, L., Research Inst.: *Aphidius matricariae*

Aphid Predators:
Applied Bionomics: *Aphidoletes aphidimyza*

Arbico: *Aphidoletes aphidimyza*

Better Yield Insects: *Aphidoletes aphidimyza*

*English Woodlands Ltd.: *Aphidoletes aphidimyza*

Gerhart, Inc.: *Aphidoletes aphidimyza*

*Hansens Bio Systems: *Aphidoletes aphidimyza*

IPM Laboratories, Inc.: *Aphidoletes aphidimyza*

*Koppert B.V.: *Aphidoletes aphidimyza*

*Neudorff GmbH KG: *Aphidoletes aphidimyza*

*Polgar, L., Research Inst.: *Aphidoletes aphidimyza*

Beetle Parasitoids:
Arbico: *Podisus maculiventris* for mexican bean beetle

Biofac, Inc.: *Anisopteramalus calandrae*

Rocky Mountain Insectary: *Pediobius foveolatus* for Colorado potato beetle

Black Scale Parasitoids:
Foothill Agricultural Research, Inc.: *Metaphycus helvolus*

Caterpillar Egg Parasitoids:
Arbico: *Trichogramma minutum, T. platerni, T. pretiosum*

Beneficial Insectary: *Trichogramma minutum, T. pretiosum*

Beneficial Insects, Inc.: *Trichogramma pretiosum*

Biofac, Inc.: *Trichogramma* spp.

BoBiotrol: *Trichogramma* spp.

Foothill Agricultural Research, Inc.: *Trichogramma platerni, T. pretiosum*

Kunafin Trichogramma Insectaries: *Trichogramma* spp.

*Nordwestverband: *Trichogramma* spp.

Rincon-Vitova Insectaries, Inc.: *Trichogramma minutum, T. platerni, T. pretiosum*

Fly Parasitoids:
Arbico: *Muscidifurax zoraptor, Nasonia vitripennis, Spalangia endius*

Beneficial Insectary: *Muscidifurax raptorellus, M. zoraptor, Nasonia vitripennis, Spalangia cameroni, S. endius*

Beneficial Insects, Inc: *Muscidifurax zoraptor*

Biofac, Inc.: *Muscidifurax raptorellus, Spalangia endius* for stored grain beetles

BoBiotrol: *Goniozus legneri, Muscidifurax raptor, Spalangia endius*

IPM Laboratories, Inc.: *Muscidifurax raptor, Nasonia vitripennis*

Kunafin Trichogramma Insectaries: *Muscidifurax raptor, M. raptorellus, M. zoraptor, Pachycrepoideus vindemiae, Spalangia cameroni, S. endius, S. nigroaenea*

Rincon-Vitova Insectaries, Inc.:
*Muscidifurax raptor, M. raptorellus,
Spalangia endius*

Fungus Gnat Predators:
Applied Bionomics: *Hypoaspis* spp.
IPM Laboratories, Inc.: *Hypoaspis* spp.

Gypsy Moth Parasitoids:
National Gypsy Moth Management
Group Inc.: *Cotesia melanoscela*
(Korean strain), *Glyptapanteles
flavicoxis, Meteorus pulchricornis*

Lacewings:
Arbico: *Chrysoperla carnea*
Beneficial Insectary: *Chrysoperla
carnea, C. rufilabris*
Beneficial Insects, Inc.: *Chrysoperla
rufilabris*
Biofac, Inc.: *Chrysoperla carnea, C.
rufilabris*
*BIOLAB: *Chrysoperla carnea*
BoBiotrol: *Chrysoperla carnea*
IPM Laboratories, Inc.: *Chrysoperla
carnea, Chrysoperla rufilabris*
Kunafin Trichogramma Insectaries:
Chrysoperla spp.
M&R Durango, Inc.: *Chrysoperla
carnea, C. rufilabris*
Natural Pest Controls: *Chrysoperla
carnea*
Nature's Control: *Chrysoperla carnea*
*Neudorff GmbH KG: *Chrysoperla
carnea*
Rincon-Vitova Insectaries, Inc:
Chrysoperla carnea, C. rufilabris

Lady Beetles:
Arbico: *Hippodamia convergens*
Biofac, Inc.: *Hippodamia convergens*
Foothill Agricultural Research, Inc.:
Hippodamia convergens
Natural Pest Controls: *Hippodamia
convergens*

Leafminer Parasitoids:
Biofac, Inc.: *Dacnusa sibirica,
Diglyphus isaea*
*BIOLAB: *Diglyphus isaea*
*Biological Control Insectaries:
Dacnusa sibirica, Diglyphus isaea
*Brinkman B.V.: *Dacnusa sibirica*
*Bunting & Sons: *Dacnusa sibirica*
*Duclos S.A.: *Dacnusa sibirica*

Gerhart, Inc.: *Dacnusa sibirica,
Diglyphus isaea*
*Koppert B.V: *Dacnusa sibirica,
Diglyphus isaea*
*Natural Pest Control Watermead:
Dacnusa sibirica

Mealybug Parasitoids:
*Amos Rubin, Entomologist:
*Leptomastidea abnormis, L.
dactylopii, Pauridia peregrina*
*Biological Control Insectaries:
Leptomastix dactylopii
*Svenka Predator AB: *Leptomastix
dactylopii*

Mealybug Predators:
*Amos Rubin, Entomologist:
*Anagyrus pseudococci, Cryptolaemus
montrouzieri, Hyperaspis polita,
Nephus reunioni, Sympherobius
sanctus*
Applied Bionomics: *Cryptolaemus
montrouzieri*
Associates Insectary: *Cryptolaemus
montrouzieri*
Beneficial Insectary: *Cryptolaemus
montrouzieri*
Biofac, Inc.: *Cryptolaemus
montrouzieri*
*Biological Control Insectaries:
Cryptolaemus montrouzieri
*English Woodlands Ltd.:
Cryptolaemus montrouzieri
Foothill Agricultural Research, Inc.:
Cryptolaemus montrouzieri
Gerhart, Inc.: *Cryptolaemus
montrouzieri*
IPM Laboratories, Inc.: *Cryptolaemus
montrouzieri*
*Koppert B.V.: *Cryptolaemus
montrouzieri*

Mosquito Fish:
Natural Pest Controls: *Gambusa
affinis*

Navel Orangeworm Parasitoids:
BoBiotrol: *Pentalitomastix plethoricus*

Parasitic Mites:
Biofac, Inc.: *Pyemotes tritici*
Kunafin Trichogramma Insectaries:
Pyemotes tritici

Parasitic Nematodes:
Biofac, Inc.: *Steinernema carpocapsae*
BioLogic: *Steinernema carpocapsae*
*Biological Control Insectaries:
Heterorhabditis spp.
Biosys: *Steinernema* spp.
*De Groene Vlieg: *Heterorhabditis*
spp., *Steinernema bibionis,
S. carpocapsae*
*Hansens Bio Systems:
Heterorhabditis heliothidis
Hydro-Gardens, Inc.:
Heterorhabditis spp.
M&R Durango, Inc.: *Steinernema
carpocapsae*
Nematec: *Heterorhabditis* spp.
Phero Tech, Inc.:
Heterorhabditis spp.
Praxis: *Heterorhabditis* spp.
*Svenka Predator AB: *Steinernema
carpocapsae*

Praying Mantids:
Arbico: *Tenodera aridifoliasinensis*

Predatory Mites:
*Amos Rubin, Entomologist:
*Metaseiulus occidentalis,
Phytoseiulus persimilis,
Typhlodromus athiasae*
Applied Bionomics: *Phytoseiulus
persimilis*
Arbico: *Amblyseius californicus, A.
cucumeris, Metaseiulus occidentalis,
Phytoseiulus longipes, P. persimilis,
Pyemotes tritici*
Beneficial Insectary: *Amblyseius
californicus, Metaseiulus
occidentalis, Phytoseiulus longipes,
P. persimilis*
Better Yield Insects: *Phytoseiulus
persimilis*
Biofac, Inc.: *Amblyseius cucumeris,
Phytoseiulus persimilis*
*BIOLAB: *Phytoseiulus persimilis*
*Biological Control Insectaries:
*Metaseiulus occidentalis,
Phytoseiulus persimilis*
Biotactics, Inc: *Amblyseius
californicus, Metaseiulus
occidentalis, Phytoseiulus longipes,
P. persimilis*
*Brinkman B.V.: *Phytoseiulus
persimilis*

*Bunting & Sons, The Nurseries:
Phytoseiulus persimilis
*Duclos S.A.: *Phytoseiulus persimilis*
*English Woodlands Ltd.:
Phytoseiulus persimilis
Foothill Agricultural Research, Inc.:
Phytoseiulus persimilis
Gerhart, Inc: *Phytoseiulus persimilis*
*Hansens Bio Systems: *Phytoseiulus persimilis*
*Hawkaid Integrated Pest Management Service: *Phytoseiulus persimilis*
IPM Laboratories, Inc: *Metaseiulus occidentalis, Phytoseiulus longipes, P. persimilis*
*Koppert B.V.: *Phytoseiulus persimilis*
*L.O.G.: *Phytoseiulus persimilis*
*Natural Pest Control Watermead:
Phytoseiulus persimilis
Nature's Control: *Amblyseius californicus, Metaseiulus occidentalis, Phytoseiulus longipes, P. persimilis*
*Neudorff GmbH KG: *Phytoseiulus persimilis*
*Polgar, L., Research Inst.:
Phytoseiulus persimilis
Praxis: *Amblyseius fallacis*
Rincon-Vitova Insectaries, Inc.:
Phytoseiulus persimilis

Predatory Snails:
Associates Insectary: *Rumina decollata*
Foothill Agricultural Research, Inc.:
Rumina decollata
J. Harold Mitchell Co.: *Rumina decollata*
C.H. Musgrove: *Rumina decollata*

Scale Parasitoids:
*Amos Rubin, Entomologist:
Encyrtus infelix, Microterys flavus
Associates Insectary: *Aphytis melinus*
Foothill Agricultural Research, Inc.:
Aphytis melinus
Rincon-Vitova Insectaries, Inc.:
Aphytis melinus
*Svenka Predator AB: *Metapycus helvolous*

Sterilized Insects:
*De Groene Vlieg: *Delia antigua*

Stored Product Pest Parasitoids (see also Caterpillar Egg Parasitoids):
Biofac, Inc.: *Bracon hebetor*

Stored Product Pest Predators:
Biofac, Inc.: *Xylocoris flavipes*

Thrips Predators:
Applied Bionomics: *Amblyseius cucumeris, Orius tristicolor*
Better Yield Insects: *Amblyseius barkeri*
*Biological Control Insectaries:
Amblyseius cucumeris
*Brinkman B.V.: *Amblyseius barkeri, Amblyseius cucumeris*
*Bunting & Sons, The Nurseries:
Amblyseius barkeri, A. cucumeris
Foothill Agricultural Research, Inc.:
Thripobius semileuteus
Gerhart, Inc.: *Amblyseius barkeri, A. cucumeris*
*Hansens Bio Systems: *Amblyseius barkeri, A. cucumeris*
IPM Laboratories, Inc.: *Amblyseius barkeri, A. fallacis*
*Koppert B.V.: *Amblyseius barkeri, A. cucumeris*
Nature's Control: *Amblyseius barkeri, A. cucumeris*

Whitefly Parasitoids:
Applied Bionomics: *Encarsia formosa, Delphastus pusillus*
Beneficial Insectary: *Encarsia formosa*
Better Yield Insects: *Encarsia formosa*
Biofac, Inc.: *Encarsia formosa*
*BIOLAB: *Encarsia formosa*
*Biological Control Insectaries:
Encarsia formosa
*Brinkman B.V.: *Encarsia formosa*
*Bunting & Sons, The Nurseries:
Encarsia formosa
*Duclos S.A.: *Encarsia formosa*
*English Woodlands Ltd.: *Encarsia formosa*
Foothill Ag. Res., Inc.: *Encarsia formosa*
Gerhart, Inc.: *Encarsia formosa*
*Hansens Bio Systems: *Encarsia formosa*
IPM Laboratories Inc.: *Encarsia formosa*
*Koppert B.V.: *Encarsia formosa*

*Natural Pest Control Watermead:
Encarsia formosa
Nature's Control: *Encarsia formosa*
*Neudorff GmbH KG: *Encarsia formosa*
Rincon-Vitova Insectaries, Inc:
Encarsia formosa

Whitefly Predator:
*Amos Rubin, Entomologist:
Encarsia formosa for tobacco whitefly

Microbial Insecticides
BT (*Bacillus thuringiensis*) for Beetles:
Mycogen Corp.: M-One® for Colorado potato beetle and elm leaf beetle
Sandoz Crop Protection: Trident® for Colorado potato beetle and elm leaf beetle

BT (*Bacillus thuringiensis*) for Caterpillars:
Abbott Laboratories: Dipel®, Dipel® 4L
Biochem Products: Bug Time and Bactur®
Ecogen: BT products
Fairfax Biological Laboratory, Inc.: Larvo™
GTF Labs: Worm Ender®
Insects Limited: Topside Dipel®
PBI Gordon Corp.: Bactur®
Ringer Corp.: Caterpillar Attack®
Safer, Inc.: Caterpillar Killer®
Sandoz Crop Protection: Javelin®, Thuricide®

BTI (*Bacillus thuringiensis israelensis*) for Larvae of Mosquitoes and Blackflies:
Abbott Laboratories: Vectobac®
Biochem Products: Bactimos®, Bactimos briquets® and Bactospeine®
GTF Labs: Bactospeine®
Monterey Chemical Co.: Bactospeine®
PBI Gordon Corp.: Bactimos®, Bactimos briquets® and Bactospeine®
Ringer Corp.: Mosquito Attack®

Greenhouse Insects:
Koppert B.V.: Mycotal® for whiteflies and thrips; Vertalec® for aphids
Tate & Lyle: Mycotal® and Vertalec®

Insect Viruses:
Agricola "El Sol": VPN-80 and VPN-82
Association for Sensible Pest Control: codling moth granulosis virus
Forest Pest Management Institute: nucleopolyhedrosis virus for caterpillars
Sandoz Crop Protection: Elcar® (virus for *Heliothis* spp. caterpillars)
U.S. Forest Service: nucleopolyhedrosis virus for caterpillars

Milky Spore Disease:
All-Natural, Inc.: Milky Spore Disease™
Fairfax Biological Laboratory, Inc.: Doom® and Japidemic™ for Japanese beetle grubs
Ringer Corp.: Grub Attack®

***Nosema locustae* for Grasshoppers:**
Bozeman Bio-Tech: Semaspore™
M&R Durango Insectory: Nolo Bait®
Ringer Corp.: Grasshopper Attack®

Miscellaneous:
MSD AGVET, Merck & Co., Inc.: Ivomec (ivermectin for cattle grub control)
Sandoz Crop Protection: Gustol (a feeding stimulant)

LEAST-TOXIC CHEMICAL CONTROLS
Application Equipment and Protective Clothing:
B&G Equipment Co.: full line of pesticide application equipment and protective gear
BWS Distributors, Inc.: respirators
Dadant & Sons: beekeeping equipment and protective gear
Lab Safety Supply: full-hood respirator

Parker Pest Control, Inc.: P.E.S.T. Power Applicator for boric acid
Pristine Products: various powder/dust applicators
A.I. Root Co.: beekeeping equipment, protective clothing
Woodstream Corp.: Victor™ Pest Pistol powder/dust applicator

Aquatic Surface Coating:
Sherex Chemical Co., Inc.: Arosurf® mosquito larvicide

Boric-Acid Insecticides:
Copper Brite, Inc.: Roach Prufe®
It Works, Inc.: boric-acid cockroach bait
Organic Control, Inc.: Ant-T-Roach boric-acid cockroach bait
Perma Proof® Corp.: Permaproof® roach-proofing powder
R-Value: Drax™ ant bait; Roach Kill® cockroach bait
Seabright Enterprises: boric-acid cockroach bait stations
U.S. Borax: TIM-BOR® wood preservative

Botanical Insecticides:
W.R. Grace Co.: Margosan-O® neem oil extract
IFM: rotenone, ryania, sabadilla
Mulgum Hollow Farms: GreenBan™ botanical insecticides
Necessary Trading Co.: rotenone, ryania, sabadilla
Peaceful Valley Farm Supply: rotenone, ryania, sabadilla

Diatomaceous Earth:
Beneficial Biosystems
EcoSafe Products, Inc.
Dorsey, Inc.: Shellshock® for cockroaches
Insecto: for grain storage insects only
Nitron Industries
Pristine Products
Universal Diatoms Inc.

Horticultural Oils:
Mycogen Corp.: Sunspray™ (commercial quantities)
Safer, Inc.: Sunspray™ (retail sizes)
Valent USA: Volck Supreme Spray

Insect Growth Regulators:
Maag Agrochemicals Inc.: Torus® system for cockroaches
Paragon Inc.: Logic® for fire ants
PBI Gordon Corp.: Logic® for fire ants
Zoecon Corp.: methoprene products: Altosid® for mosquitoes, Apex® for fungus gnats, Dianex® for stored product pests, Gencor® hydroprene for cockroaches, Kabat® for pests of stored tobacco, Minex® for leafminers, Pharorid® for pharaoh ants, Precor® and FleaTrol® for cat fleas

Insect Repellents:
Mulgum Hollow Farms: GreenBan™ For People (an herbal mosquito repellent)
REI: Jungle Juice (DEET), Cutter's® (DEET)

Insecticidal Baits:
American Cyanamid Co.: hydramethylnon cockroach and ant bait (Combat®, Maxforce®)
Whitmire: avermectin cockroach bait (Avert®)

Insecticidal Soap:
*Koppert B.V.: Savona™ for garden insects
Ringer Corp.: Attack™ for garden insects
Safer, Inc.: Safer™ Insecticidal Soap for garden insects, Safer® Entire Flea & Tick Spray with pyrethrin, Flea Guard™, Flea Shampoo™

Limonene/Linalool (Citrus Oil Extracts):
Farnam Co.: Flea Stop® Pet Spray, Flea Stop® Pet Shampoo
Vet Express: d-limonene product distributor

Natural Nematicide:
IFM: Clandosan
Igene Biotechnology, Inc.: Clandosan
Safer Inc.: Clandosan

Pyrethrin:
Fairfield American Corp.: Pyrenone®
FMC, Inc.: Pyrenone®
GTF Laboratories: Pyrenone®
Monterey Chemical Co.: Pyrenone®
Safer, Inc.: pyrethrin products for
home and garden pests
Whitmire: PT 150®, PT 565®
(aerosols with piperonyl butoxide)

**Pyrethrin plus
Diatomaceous Earth:**
Pristine Products: Diacide®

Pyrethrin plus Insecticidal Soap:
Safer, Inc.: Safer® Entire Flea and
Tick Spray, Safer® Yard and
Garden Insect Killer (without
piperonyl butoxide)

Pyrethrin plus Rotenone:
IFM: Red Arrow™
Mine Safety Appliance Co.: Wasp-
Stopper aerosol

Pyrethrin plus Silica Aerogel:
Fairfield American Corp.: Drione®
Ringer Corp.: Roach Attack®
Roxide International: Revenge®

Pyrethroids:
E.I. duPont de Nemours & Co.:
Pydrin® for termites
Ecohealth, Inc.: Damminix®
permethrin for ticks
Fairfield American Corp.:
Permanone® Tick Repellent
Forestry Suppliers Inc.: Permanone®
Tick Repellent
ICI Americas: Demon® T.C. and
Torpedo® for termites and wood-
boring beetles
Sandoz Crop Protection: Mavrik®
3M Corp.: Sectrol™ for fleas

**Pyrethrum (Chrysanthemum
Seeds):**
J.L. Hudson, Seedsman
Johnny's Selected Seeds
Nichols Garden Nursery

Pyrethrum (Natural):
EcoSafe Laboratories: ZAP™
Pyrethrum Powder and POW™
Flea Powder
Pristine Products: Fossil Flowers™
natural powder

Silica Aerogel Products:
Fairfield American Corp.: Dri-Die®
silica gel; Drione® silica aerogel
plus pyrethrin
Roxide International: Revenge®
silica aerogel plus pyrethrin

**Wasp/Bee Sting Medication
(Anaphylaxis Kit):**
Center Laboratories,Inc.: self-
injected epinephrine
Hollister-Stier Labs., Inc.: self-
injected epinephrine
Pharmacia Diagnostics, Div. of
Pharmacia, Inc.: allergy
diagnostic and treatment systems
Spencer-Mead, Inc.: self-injected
epinephrine

PLANT DISEASE MANAGEMENT

IDENTIFICATION AND MONITORING
Agri-Diagnostics Associates: turf
disease detection kits
C.A.B. International Institute of
Biological Control: information
service
C.A.B. International Institute of
Parasitology: nematode
identification service
C.A.B. International Mycological
Institute: fungus identification
service

Note: The Cooperative Extension
Service, located in every county in
the United States, also provides pest
identification services.

BIOLOGICAL CONTROLS
Microbial Soil Amendments:
Agro-Chem Corp.: Soil Aid™, Green
Magic™, Strengthen & Renew™
New Era Farm Service: compost,
natural soil amendments

Ringer Corp.: Dis-Patch™, Lawn
Restore™ and other Restore™
products

Microbial Fungicides:
AgBioChem, Inc.: Galltrol-A® for
crown gall disease
IPM Laboratories, Inc.: NORBAC®
84-C for crown gall disease
New BioProducts, Inc.: NORBAC®
84-C for crown gall disease

HORTICULTURAL CONTROLS
Disease-Resistant Roses:
High Country Rosarium
Roses of Yesterday and Today

LEAST-TOXIC CHEMICAL CONTROLS
**Antitranspirants
(Barriers to Fungi):**
Aquatrols Corp. of America Inc.:
Folicote™ (paraffin wax emulsion)

Green Pro Services: Vita Coad™
(pine tar base)
Jonathan Green & Sons Inc.
Nature's Touch: Leaf Cote Clear™
PBI-Gordon Corp.: Transfirm™
(polyethylene/polyterpine base)
Precision Laboratories Inc.:
Preserve™
Safer, Inc.: Safer for Evergreen™
(polymer base)
Wilt-Pruf Products, Inc.: Wilt-Pruf™

Copper and Sulfur Fungicides:
GTF Laboratories: copper products
Monterey Chemical Co.: copper
and sulfur products

Fungicidal Soap:
Safer, Inc.: Safer™ Fungicide and
Miticide

Wood Preservatives:
U.S. Borax: TIM-BOR®

VERTEBRATE MANAGEMENT

IDENTIFICATION AND MONITORING

Brody Enterprises, Inc.: black light rodent detection device
Streamlight, Inc.: flashlights with special filters

Note: The Cooperative Extension Service, located in every county in the United States, also provides pest identification services.

PHYSICAL CONTROLS
Bait Stations:

Bell Laboratories, Inc.: Protecta®, RTV, Rodent Baiters
Brody Enterprises, Inc.
Woodstream Corp.

Bat Houses:

Bat Conservation International: booklet on how to build a bat house

Bird-Repelling Kites and Alarms:

Brody Enterprises, Inc.: alarms, hawk kites, alarm lighting
High As A Kite: kites
Pest Management Supply Co.: kites and balloons
Reed-Joseph International Co.: audio alarms

Bird-Repelling Strips:

Nixalite: stainless steel strips

Deer Reflectors:

Strieter Corp.: light reflectors to deter deer from crossing roads

Exclusion Devices:

Allen Special Products, Inc.: Stuff It™ copper mesh rodent hole filler
Bay Area Bat Protection: EX100 Hanks Bat Excluder
In-Tex Products, Inc.: Guard-All™ mesh metal rodent barrier

Fencing and Netting:

Advanced Farm Systems, Inc.: Techfence™ deer fence
Bluebird Enterprises: bird netting
InterNet, Inc.: bird/bat netting, rodent-proofing for trees
Net & Twine Co., Inc.: bird/bat netting
North Bradford Enterprises: Techfence®, electric deer fencing
Poultry Health Service: electric fencing
Waterford Corp.: Shock Tactics™ electric fence systems, Flexinet® fencing
Wildlife Control Technology: bird netting

Traps (Metal):

Brody Enterprises: rodent, bird and wildlife traps
Hadley Products: Trapper® clothespin mouse trap
Reed-Joseph International Co.: mammal and bird live trap
Seabright Enterprises: live traps for mice
Tomahawk Live Trap Co.: live traps
Woodstream Corp.: lethal and live traps for rodents and wildlife

Traps and Sticky Barriers:

Bell Laboratories, Inc.: Trapper® glue boards
Brody Enterprises: Roost No More™, 4 the Birds Gel™; live traps
Great Lakes IPM: Tanglefoot™ distributor
Olson Products, Inc.: Sticky Stuff™
Seabright Enterprises: Stickem™ whitefly traps and bird repellents
Streamlight, Inc.: Stickem™
Tanglefoot Co.: Tanglefoot™
Woodstream Corp.: Victor Holdfast glue boards

BIOLOGICAL CONTROLS
Guard Dogs (to Protect Sheep):

For assistance in obtaining a dog trained to protect sheep from predators, contact Jay Lorenz, Extension Wildlife Specialist, Dept. of Fisheries and Wildlife, Oregon State Univ., Corvallis, OR 97331; (503) 737-4531.

LEAST-TOXIC CHEMICAL CONTROLS
Applicators and Dispensers:

B&G Equipment Co.: dusters, sprayers and protective clothing
Diamond Shamrock Co.: cattle ear tags
Fermenta, Animal Health Dept.: cattle ear tags, oral fly larvicides
Norshore Distr. Co.: duster
Trebor Corp.: pressurized dust applicator

Fumigants:

U.S. Fish and Wildlife Service: CO_2 cartridges for gophers and other burrowing rodents available from county agricultural commissioners

Repellents:

Ani-Pel Silviculture Ltd.: deer and rabbit repellents
Bird-X, Inc.: bird repellent
Bonide Chemical Co.: deer and rabbit repellents
Hub States Corp.: Hubsco™ bird repellent
Intagra: Deer Away™ deer repellent
Necessary Trading Co.: blood meal for deer repellent
Reed-Joseph International Co.: deer repellent
Seabright Enterprises: Stickem™ bird repellent

Rodenticides:

Bell Laboratories, Inc.: Quintox® anticoagulant

WEED MANAGEMENT

IDENTIFICATION AND MONITORING

C.A.B. International Institute of Biological Control: information service

Valley Seed Service: weed seed identification kit

Note: The Cooperative Extension Service. located in every county in the United States, also provides pest identification services.

PHYSICAL CONTROLS
Crack Fillers:

Garon Products, Inc.: Crack-Fill™ asphalt crack filler

Flamers:

Ben Meadows Co.
Flame Engineering, Inc.
Forestry Suppliers, Inc.
Plow & Hearth

Girdlers:

Lee Valley Tools: Scorp
Vredenburg Industrial Packaging Products

Mulch:

Birkett Mills: MUL-TEX processed buckwheat hulls

Poison Oak and Ivy Cleanser:

Interpro, Inc.: Ivy Shield
Smith & Hawken: Tecnu®

Sun Barriers:

Aquashade, Inc.: algae control

Weed Mats:

Blunk's Wholesale Supply Inc.
E.I. duPont de Nemours & Co.
Geotex, Inc.: circular pads for use around trees, shrubs
Phillips Fibers Corp.

Weeding Tools, Flailers, Harvesters:

Aquamarine/Erectoweld
Beaird-Poulan/Weed Eater Div.
BeeTee Engine Sales: Husqvarna® mechanical clearing saw
Blackburn Manufacturing Co.: tree wrap (protects trunks from weed trimmer injury)
Bush Hog
Gardener's Supply: weed cultivators
HMC/The Green Machine™
Hockney Underwater Weed Cutters
Homelite Div./Textron, Inc.
Plow & Hearth: weed cultivators
Smith & Hawken

BIOLOGICAL CONTROLS
Beneficial Predatory Insects:

Bio Collect: field-collected insect and mite predators of thistles (bull, Canada, Italian, milk, musk, Russian, yellowstar), waterhyacinth, leafy spurge, St. Johnswort (Klamathweed), tansy ragwort, purslane, puncturevine, Mediterranean sage, rush skeletonweed, scotch broom, gorse and others
BioControl of Weeds: as above

Mycoherbicides:

Abbott Laboratories: Devine® for milkweed *(Morrenia odorata)*
Ecogen: Collego® for northern jointvetch *(Aeschynomene virgica)*
Mycogen Corp.: Casst® for sicklepod *(Cassia obtusifolia)* and coffee senna *(Cassia occidentalis)*

Weeder Geese:

Blohm Manufacturing: white Chinese geese
PINA: white Chinese geese

LEAST-TOXIC CHEMICAL CONTROLS
Application Equipment:

AG Spray Equip.
Bowman Manufacturing Co.
Chemihoe Inc.
Forestry Suppliers: Hypo-Hatchet Tree Injectors
Magnolia Spray Equipment Co.
Micron Corp.: Herbi micron sprayer
Performance Products, Inc.

Herbicides:

Safer, Inc.: Sharpshooter™ soap-based nonselective herbicide

SUPPLIERS

Many of the products listed in the Resource Appendix are available in local stores, but some must be ordered by mail. If you can't find a product locally, contact the manufacturer or distributor, listed alphabetically below.

They can either send the item by mail or direct you to the closest local distributor. You can also find many of the products in a number of farm and garden catalogs, available from the companies listed in the first three columns below.

CATALOG MAIL-ORDER SOURCES

Brody Enterprises, Inc.
9 Arlington Pl.
Fairlawn, NJ 07410
(800) 458-8727

Early's Farm and Garden Centre
Box 3024, Saskatoon
Saskatchewan S7K 3S9
Canada
(306) 931-1982

Gardener's Supply Co.
128 Intervale Rd.
Burlington, VT 05401
(802) 863-1700

Gardens Alive!
P.O. Box 149
Sunman, IN 47041
(812) 623-3800

Growing Naturally
149 Pine Lane
P.O. Box 54
Pineville, PA 18946
(215) 598-7025

Halifax Seed Co.
P.O. Box 8026
Station A, Halifax
Nova Scotia B3K 5L8
Canada
(902) 454-7456

Harmony Farm Supply
P.O. Box 460
Graton, CA 95444
(707) 823-9125

Hydro-Gardens
P.O. Box 9707
Colorado Springs
CO 80932
(800) 634-6362
(719) 495-2266

IFM
333 Ohme Gardens Rd.
Wenatchee, WA 98801
(800) 332-3179

Natural America
Box 7
Brentwood, NY 11717
(516) 435-2380

Natural Farm Products, Inc.
Rte. 2, Box 201-A
Spencer Rd. SE
Kalkaska, MI 49646
(616) 369-2465

Nature's Touch
11150 W. Addison St.
Franklin Park, IL 60131
(708) 455-8600

Necessary Trading Co.
8311 Salem Ave.
New Castle, VA 24127
(800) 447-5354

Peaceful Valley Farm Supply
P.O. Box 2209
Grass Valley, CA 95945
(916) 272-4769

Pest Management Supply Co.
P.O. Box 938
Amherst, MA 01004
(800) 272-7672

Plow & Hearth
301 Madison Rd.
Orange, VA 22960
(703) 672-1712

Le Reveil de la Nature
R.R. 1, St. Philbert, Beauce
Quebec G0M 1X0
Canada
(418) 228-0484

Ringer Corp.
9959 Valley View Rd.
Eden Prairie
MN 55344-3585
(800) 654-1047

T&T Seeds
Box 1710, Winnipeg
Manitoba R3C 3P6
Canada
(204) 943-8483

Weall and Cullen
400 Alden Rd.
Markham
Ontario L3R 4C1
Canada
(800) 387-9777

MANUFACTURERS AND DISTRIBUTORS:

Abbott Laboratories
1400 Sheridan Rd.
N. Chicago, IL 60064
(312) 937-5105

Advanced Farm Systems Inc.
Rte. 1, Box 364
Bradford, ME 04410

AG Spray Equipment
5121 Industrial Dr.
Hopkinsville, KY 42240
(502) 886-3182

agAccess
P.O. Box 2008
Davis, CA 95617-5009
(916) 756-7177

AgBioChem, Inc.
3 Fleetwood Ct.
Orinda CA 94563
(415) 254-0789

Agricola "El Sol"
30 Calle 11-42 Zona 12
Guatemala, CA
Tel. 760496

Agri-Diagnostics Associates
2611 Branch Pike
Cinnaminson, NJ 08077
(800) 322-KITS
(609) 829-6935

AgriSense
4230 W. Swift, Ste. 106
Fresno, CA 93710
(209) 276-7037

Agro-Chem Corp.
1150 Addison
Franklin Park, IL 60131
(708) 455-6900

Allen-Bradley Co.
14960 Industrial Rd.
Minnetonka, MN 55345
(612) 935-7704

Allen Special Products, Inc.
P.O. Box 605
Montgomeryville
PA 18936
(800) 848-6805
(215) 362-7515

All-Natural, Inc.
13600 Murphy Road
Stafford, TX 77477
(713) 499-8461

American Entomological Inst.
3005 SW 56th Ave.
Gainesville, FL 32608
(904) 377-6458

Amos Rubin
Entomologist
1 Keren Hayesod St.
Givat Shmuel
51905 Israel
(03) 357-469

Animal Repellents, Inc.
Griffin, GA 30223
(404) 227-8223

Ani-Pel Silviculture Ltd.
13550 106th Ave.
Surrey, British Columbia
V3T 2C5
Canada

APMR
P.O. Box 938
Amherst, MA 01004

Applied Bionomics
P.O. Box 2637
Sidney, British Columbia
V8L 1H1
Canada
(800) 663-2552
(604) 656-2123

Aquamarine/Erectoweld
1604 S. West Ave.
Waukesha, WI 53186-7434
(414) 547-0211

Aquashade, Inc.
P.O. Box 198
Eldred, NY 12732
(914) 557-8077

Aquatrols Corp. of
America, Inc.
1432 Union Ave.
Pennsauken, NJ 08110
(800) 257-7797
(609) 665-1130

Arbico Inc.
P.O. Box 4247 CRB
Tucson, AZ 85738
(800) 767-2847
(602) 825-9785

Arthropod Slidemounts
P.O. Box 185
Bluffton, IN 46714
(219) 824-4370

Associates Insectary
P.O. Box 969
Santa Paula, CA 93060
(805) 933-1301

Association for Sensible
Pest Control
P.O. Box 1154
Lafayette, CA 94549-1154
(415) 284-2775

Automata, Inc.
16216 Brooks
Grass Valley
CA 95745-8816
(916) 273-0380

B & G Equipment Co.
Applebutter Rd.
Plumsteadville, PA 18949
(215) 766-8811

Baley's
1206 N. 31st Ave.
Melrose Park, IL 60160
(312) 544-1850

Bat Conservation
International
P.O. Box 162603
Austin, TX 78716-2603
(512) 327-9721

W.C. Batiste, Co.
615 Peony Dr.
Grand Junction, CO 81503
(303) 245-4681

Bay Area Bat Protection
1312 Shiloah Rd.
Box 374, Sta. A
Sturgeon Bay, WI 54235
(414) 743-9049

Beacon Dogs, Inc.
1409 Bay Head Rd.
Annapolis, MD 21401
(301) 757-4999

Beaird-Poulan/
Weed Eater Div.
P.O. Box 9329
Shreveport, LA 71108
(318) 674-3596

L.L. Bean
Freeport, ME 04032
(800) 221-4221
(207) 865-4761

BeeTee Engine Sales
21075 Alexander Ct.
Unit H
Hayward, CA 94540
(415) 887-8301

Bell Laboratories, Inc.
3699 Kinsman Blvd.
Madison, WI 53704
(608) 241-0202

Beneficial BioSystems
P.O. Box 8461
Emeryville, CA 94662
(415) 655-3928

Beneficial Insectary
14751 Oak Run Rd.
Oak Run, CA 96069
(916) 472-3715

Beneficial Insects, Inc.
P.O. Box 40634
Memphis, TN 38174-0634
(901) 276-6879

Ben Meadows Co.
P.O. Box 80549
Atlanta, GA 30366
(800) 547-8813

Better Yield Insects
P.O. Box 3451
Tecumseh Station, Windsor
Ontario N8N 3C4
Canada
(519) 727-6108

Bio Collect
5841 Crittenden St.
Oakland, CA 94601
(415) 436-8052

Biochem Products
P.O. Box 264
Montchanin, DE 19710
(517) 694-2954

BioControl of Weeds
1140 Cherry Dr.
Bozeman, MT 59715
(406) 586-5111

Bio-Control Co.
Box 337
Berry Creek, CA 95916
(916) 589-5227

Biocontrol Ltd.
719 Second St., Ste. 12
Davis, CA 95616
(800) 999-8805
(916) 757-2307

Biofac, Inc.
P.O. Box 87
Mathis, TX 78368
(512) 547-3259

BIOLAB
Centrale Ortifrutticola
Alla Produzione
Via Dismano, 3845
I-47020 Pievestina di
Cesena (FO), Italy

BioLogic
P.O. Box 1777
Willow Hill
PA 17201
(717) 349-2789

Biological Control
Insectaries
Kibbutz Sde Eliyahu
D.N. Bet-Shean
10810 Israel
(06) 580-527 or
(06) 580-509

BioQuip Products
17803 South La Salle Ave.
Gardena, CA 90248
(213) 324-0620

Biosys
1057 East Meadow Circle
Palo Alto, CA 94303
(714) 783-2148 or
(714) 685-7681

Biotactics, Inc.
7765 Lakeside Dr.
Riverside, CA 92509
(714) 783-2148 or
(714) 685-7681

Bi-Pro Industries, Inc.
P.O. Box 998-845
El Segundo
CA 90245-3060
(213) 640-7648

Bird-X, Inc.
730 West Lake St.
Chicago, IL 60606
(312) 648-2191

Birkett Mills
P.O. Box 440
Penn Yan, NY 14527
(315) 536-3311

Blackburn
Manufacturing Co.
P.O. Box 86
Nelign, NE 68757
(800) 942-5826

Blohm Manufacturing
54 Blanca Way
Watsonville, CA 95076
(408) 724-6743

Bluebird Enterprises
6408 South Fig
Fresno, CA 93706
(209) 268-1200

**Blunk's Wholesale
Supply Co.**
8923 S. Octavia
Bridgeview, IL 60453
(312) 430-2025

BoBiotrol
54 South Bear Creek Dr.
Merced, CA 95340
(209) 722-4985

Bonide Products, Inc.
2 Wurz Ave.
Yorkville, NY 13495
(315) 736-8231

**Bowman
Manufacturing Co.**
Rte. 3, Box 705
Newport, AR 72112
(501) 523-2785

Bozeman Bio-Tech
1612 Gold Ave.
Box 3146
Bozeman, MT 59772
(406) 587-5891

Breeders Equipment Co.
Box 177
Flourtown, PA 19031
(215) 233-0799

Brinkman B.V.
Postbus 2,
2690 AA's-Gravenzande
The Netherlands
(01748) 11333

Brody Enterprises, Inc.
9 Arlington Pl.
Fairlawn, NJ 07410
(800) 458-8727
(201) 794-9618

Bunting & Sons
The Nurseries
Great Horkesley
Colchester, Essex CO6 4AJ
England, U.K.
(0206) 271300

Bush Hog
2501 Griffin Ave.
Selma, AL 36701
(205) 872-6261

BWS Distributors, Inc.
1849 Piner Rd.
Santa Rosa, CA 95401
(800) 862-4685

C&L Laboratories
7580 Chester Dr.
Salinas, CA 93907
(408) 663-5324

**C.A.B. International
Institute of Biological
Control**
Silkwood Park
Buckhurst Rd.
Ascot, Berks. SL5 7TA
England, U.K.
(0990) 872 999

**C.A.B. International
Institute of Parasitology**
395A Hatfield Rd.
St. Albans, Herts. AL4 0XU
England, U.K.
(0727) 33151

**C.A.B. International
Mycological Institute**
Ferry Lane
Kew, Surrey TW9 3AF
England, U.K.
(081) 940 4086

Center Laboratories, Inc.
35 Channel Dr.
Port Washington
NY 11050
(800) 223-6837

Chemihoe Inc.
P.O. Box 387
Plainview, TX 79073
(806) 293-3553

Chicopea
P.O. Box 2537
Gainesville, GA 30503
(404) 536-5972

**Combined Scientific
Supplies**
P.O. Box 1446
Fort Davis, TX 79734
(915) 426-3851

**Commonwealth
International Institute of
Entomology**
56 Queens Gate
London, SW7 5JR
England, U.K.

Consep Membranes, Inc.
P.O. Box 6059
Bend, OR 97708
(800) 367-8727
(503) 388-3688

**Consulting Diagnostic
Service**
992 Santa Barbara Rd.
Berkeley, CA 94707
(415) 524-9476

Copper Brite, Inc.
P.O. Box 50610
Santa Barbara
CA 93150-0610
(805) 565-1566

Coverplus
Hyde, Cheshire
England, U.K.

CRS Company
2909 NE Anthony Lane
St. Paul, MN 55119
(612) 781-3473

Custom Copper
P.O. Box 4939
Ventura, CA 93004
(805) 647-1652 (in CA)
(206) 676-5969 (in WA
and OR)

Dadant & Sons
51 S. 2nd St.
Hamilton, IL 64321
(217) 847-3324

De Groene Vlieg
Duivenwaardsedijk 1
3244 Lg Nieuwe Tonge
The Netherlands
(01875) 1862

Delmhorst Instrument Co.
51 Indian Lane E.
Towaco, NJ 07082
(201) 334-2557

Devpro Machine, Inc.
Insectocuter Div.
4595 Griswold
Middleport, NY 14105
(716) 735-7768

Dewille Inc.
61 S. Herbert Rd.
Riverside, IL 60546
(312) 442-6009

Dippers
P.O. Box 288
Roselle, IL 60172
(312) 894-2000

Dorsey, Inc.
136 Elm St.
South Williamsport
PA 17701
(717) 322-4885

Duclos S.A.
BP3, 13240
Septemes les Vallons
France
Tel. 91519056

**E.I. duPont
de Nemours & Co.**
Wilmington, DE 19898
(800) 441-7515

D-VAC Company
P.O. Box 2506
Ventura, CA 93002
(805) 643-2325 or
(805) 643-8541

**Early's Farm and Garden
Centre**
Box 3024, Saskatoon
Saskatchewan S7K 3S9
Canada
(306) 931-1982

Ecogen, Inc.
2005 Cabot Blvd.
N. Langhorne, PA 19047
(212) 757-1590

Ecohealth, Inc.
110 Broad St.
Boston, MA 02110
(617) 742-2400

EcoSafe Products, Inc.
P.O. Box 1177
St. Augustine, FL 32085
(800) 274-7387
(904) 824-5884

English Woodlands Ltd.
Hoyle Depot
Graffham Petworth
West Sussex, GU28 0LR
England, U.K.
(07986) 574

Environdata
719 Second St., Suite 12
Davis, CA 95616
(916) 757-2307

Eriez Magnetics Pty. Ltd.
P.O. Box 82
Terry Hills
New South Wales 2084
Australia
(02) 450-1988

ETEX, Ltd.
P.O. Box 80807
Las Vegas, NV 89180-0807
(800) 543-5651
(702) 382-3966

**Fairfax Biological
Laboratory, Inc.**
P.O. Box 300
Clinton Corners, NY 12514
(914) 266-3705

Fairfield American Corp.
201 Rte. 17 N.
Rutherford, NJ 07070
(800) 828-7941
(201) 507-4880

Farnam Co.
301 West Osborn Rd.
Phoenix, AZ 85013
(800) 343-9911

**Fermenta
Animal Health Dept.**
10150 N. Executive
Hills Blvd.
Kansas City, MO 64153
(816) 891-5500

Flame Engineering, Inc.
P.O. Box 577
LaCrosse, KS 67548
(800) 255-2469
(913) 222-2873

FMC, Inc.
100 Niagara St.
Middleport, NY 14105
(716) 735-3761

**Foothill Agricultural
Research, Inc.**
510½ West Chase Dr.
Corona, CA 91720
(714) 371-0120

**Forest Pest Management
Institute, Forestry Canada**
P.O. Box 490
Sault Ste. Marie
Ontario P6A 5M7
Canada
(705) 949-9461

Forestry Suppliers, Inc.
205 W. Rankin St.
P.O. Box 8397
Jackson, MS 39284-8397
(800) 647-5368
(601) 354-3565

Four Winds Farm Supply
Route 1, Box 206
River Falls, WI 54022
(715) 425-7037

Frank Enterprises, Inc.
1960 Birkdale Dr.
Columbus
OH 43232-3028
(614) 861-7010

Gardener's Supply Co.
128 Intervale Rd.
Burlington, VT 05401
(802) 863-1700

Gardens Alive!
P.O. Box 149
Sunman, IN 47041
(812) 623-3800

Garon Products, Inc.
1924 Hwy. 35, CN 20
Wall, NJ 07719
(800) 631-5380
(201) 449-1776

Geotex, Inc.
2783 Highway 54
Peachtree City, GA 30269

Gerhart, Inc.
6346 Avon Belden Rd.
N. Ridgeville, OH 44039
(216) 327-8056

**Gilbert® Insect
Light Traps**
5611 Krueger Dr.
Jonesboro, AR 72401
(800) 643-0400
(501) 932-6070

W.R. Grace Co.
7379 Rte. 32
Columbia, MO 21044
(800) 354-5414

Great Lakes IPM
10220 Church Rd., NE
Vestaburg, MI 48891
(517) 268-5693

Green Pro Services
380 S. Franklin St.
Hempstead, NY 11550
(516) 538-6444

Growing Naturally
149 Pine Lane
P.O. Box 54
Pineville, PA 18946
(215) 598-7025

GTF Laboratories
P.O. Box 2646
Fresno, CA 93745-2646
(209) 268-3417

Hadley Products
100 Products Lane
Marietta, OH 45750
(800) 848-9106

Hansens Bio Systems
Boge Alle 10-12
Horsholm, DK-2970
Denmark

Harmony Farm Supply
P.O. Box 460
Graton, CA 95444
(707) 823-9125

**Hawkaid Integrated Pest
Management Service**
P.O. Box 415
Richmond, New South
Wales, Australia

Health Enterprises, Inc.
15 Spruce St.
N. Attleboro, MA 02760
(800) 633-4243

Hercon Environmental
Aberdeen Rd.
Emigsville, PA 17318
(717) 764-1191

High As A Kite
691 Bridgeway Rd.
Sausalito, CA 94956
(415) 332-8944

High Country Rosarium
1717 Downing St.
Denver, CO 80218
(303) 832-4026

**HMC/The Green
Machine**
P.O. Box 4070
Medford, OR 97502
(503) 826-8900

**Hockney Underwater
Weed Cutter Co.**
913 Cogswell Dr.
Silver Lake, WI 53170
(414) 889-4581

Hogil Corp.
P.O. Box 1590
Port Chester, NY 10573
(914) 937-0551

Hollister-Stier Labs., Inc.
3525 Regal St.
P.O. Box 3145
Spokane, WA 99220
(509) 489-5656

**Homelite Div./
Textron, Inc.**
14401 Carowinds Blvd.
Charlotte, NC 28273
(704) 588-3200

Hub States Corp.
419 E. Washington St.
Indianapolis, IN 46204
(800) 428-4416

J.L. Hudson, Seedsman
P.O. Box 1058
Redwood City, CA 94064

Hydro-Gardens, Inc.
P.O. Box 9707
Colorado Springs
CO 80932
(800) 634-6362;
(719) 495-2266

ICI Americas
New Murphy Rd. and
Concord Pike
Wilmington, DE 19897
(800) 759-4500
(302) 886-3000

IFM
333 Ohme Gardens Rd.
Wenatchee, WA 98801
(800) 332-3179
(509) 662-3179

Igene Biotechnology Inc.
9110 Red Branch Rd.
Columbia, MD 21045
(800) 346-6421

Industrial Discovery Systems
P.O. Box 130
Kenner, LA 70063
(504) 466-9964

Insects Limited
10540 Jessup Blvd.
Indianapolis
IN 46280-1438
(800) 992-1991

Intagra
8500 Pillsbury Ave.
Minneapolis, MN 55420
(612) 881-6908

InterNet, Inc.
2730 Nevada Ave. N.
Minneapolis, MN 55427
(800) 328-8456

Interpro, Inc.
P.O. Box 1823
Haverhill, MA 01831
(800) 456-6489

In-Tex Products, Inc.
P.O. Box B
Cleveland, NY 13042
(315) 675-8471

IPM Laboratories, Inc.
Main St.
Locke, NY 13092-0099
(315) 497-3129

Isothermics, Inc.
P.O. Box 18703
Anaheim, CA 92817-8703
(714) 778-1396

It Works, Inc.
P.O. Box 972
Bridgeport, CT 06604
(203) 332-5856

Johnny's Selected Seeds
Foss Hill Rd.
Albion, ME 04910
(207) 437-9294 or
(207) 437-4301

Jonathan Green & Sons, Inc.
Squankum-Yellowbrook Rd.
P.O. Box 326
Farmingdale NJ 07727
(201) 938-7007

JTLK, Inc.
P.O. Box 427
Boonton, NJ 07005
(201) 334-2676

Koppert Biological Products (U.K.) Ltd.
P.O. Box 43
Tunbridge Wells
Kent TN2 5BX
England, U.K.

Koppert B.V.
Veilenweg 17
2651 BE Berkel en
Rodenrijs
The Netherlands
(01891) 4044

Kunafin Trichogramma Insectaries
Rte. 1, Box 39
Quemado, TX 78877
(800) 832-1113

Lab Safety Supply
3430 Palmer Dr.
P.O. Box 1368
Janesville, WI 53547-1368
(800) 356-0783

Ladd Research Industries, Inc.
P.O. Box 1005
Burlington, VT 05402
(802) 658-4961

Lawn & Garden Products, Inc.
P.O. Box 5317
Fresno, CA 93755
(209) 225-4770

Lee Valley Tools
1098 SW Marine Dr.
Vancouver
British Columbia V6P 5Z3
Canada
(604) 261-2262

Lesco, Inc.
P.O. Box 16915
Rocky River, OH 44117

Lethelin Products
15 MacQuesten Pkwy So.
Mt. Vernon, NY 10550
(914) 667-1820

Lofts Seed Co.
P.O. Box 146
Bound Brook, NJ 08805
(800) 526-3890

L.O.G.
Okern Torgvei 1
N-0580, Oslo 5, Norway

M&R Durango, Inc.
P.O. Box 886
Bayfield, CO 81122
(800) 526-4075
(303) 259-3521

Maag Agrochemicals Inc.
5690 N. Kings Highway
P.O. Box 6430
Vero Beach, FL 32961
(407) 778-4660

Magnolia Spray Equipment Co.
P.O. Box 6948
Jackson, MS 39212
(601) 372-6833

McCluney Manufacturing, Inc.
28 Morehouse Dr.
La Selva Beach, CA 95076

Mellinger Nursery
2310 W. South Range Rd.
N. Lima, OH 44452-9731
(216) 549-9861

Merricks, Inc.
Middleton, WI 53562
(800) 637-7425
(608) 831-3440

Micron Corp.
P.O. Box 19698
Houston, TX 77034
(713) 932-1405

Mine Safety Appliance Co.
P.O. Box 426
Pittsburgh, PA 15230
(412) 967-3000

J. Harold Mitchell Co.
305 Agostino Rd.
San Gabriel, CA 91776
(817) 287-1101

Monterey Chemical Co.
P.O. Box 5317
Fresno, CA 93755
(209) 225-4770

MSD AGVET
Merck & Co., Inc.
P.O. Box 2000
Rahway, NJ 07065
(201) 750-8231

Mulgum Hollow Farms
P.O. Box 745
Longview, WA 99164

C.H. Musgrove
2707 Monroe St.
Riverside, CA 92504
(714) 785-1680

Mycogen Corp.,
5451 Oberlin Dr.
San Diego, CA 92121
(619) 453-8030

National Gypsy Moth Management Group
RD 1, Box 715
Landisburg, PA 17040
(717) 789-3434

National Pediculosis Association
P.O. Box 149
Newton, MA 02161
(617) 449-6487

Natural Pest Control Watermead
Yapton Road, Barnham
Bognor Regis, Sussex
England, U.K.

Natural Pest Controls
8864 Little Creek Dr.
Orangevale, CA 95662
(916) 726-0855

Nature's Control
P.O. Box 35
Medford, OR 97501
(503) 899-8318

Nature's Touch
11150 W. Addison St.
Franklin Park, IL 60131
(708) 455-8600

Necessary Trading Co.
8311 Salem Ave.
New Castle, VA 24127
(800) 447-5354
(703) 864-5103

Nematec
P.O. Box 93
Lafayette, CA 94549
(415) 866-2800

Net & Twine Co., Inc.
RR 3, Bend Rd.
E. St. Louis, IL 62201
(618) 876-7700

Neudorff GmbH KG
Postfach 1209
3254 Emmerthal I
Germany
(05155) 63263

New BioProducts, Inc.
4737 NW Elmwood Dr.
Corvallis, OR 97330
(503) 752-2045

New Era Farm Service
23004 Rd. 140
Tulare, CA 93274
(209) 686-3833 or
(209) 686-5707

Nichols Garden Nursery
1190 N. Pacific Hwy.
Albany, OR 97372
(503) 928-9280

Nitron Industries
P.O. Box 1447
Fayetteville, AR 72702
(800) 835-0123
(501) 750-1777

Nixalite
P.O. Box 727
E. Moline, IL 61244
(309) 755-8771

Nordwestverband
Basel, Switzerland

Norshore Distr. Co.
P.O. Box 1122
Northbrook, IL 60065
(312) 272-7800

**North Bradford
Enterprises**
Box 364
Bradford, ME 04410
(207) 327-1237

NPIRS User Services
Manager, Purdue Univ.
Entomology Hall
W. Lafayette, IN 47907
(317) 494-6614

Oakfield Apparatus Inc.
P.O. Box 65
Oakfield, WI 53065
(414) 583-4114

Olson Products, Inc.
P.O. Box 1043
Medina, OH 44258
(216) 723-3210

**Omnidata
International, Inc.**
P.O. Box 3489
Logan, UT 84321
(801) 753-7760

Organic Control, Inc.
5132 Venice Blvd.
Los Angeles, CA 90019
(213) 937-7444

Pacific Biocontrol Corp.
719 Second St., Ste. 12
Davis, CA 95616
(916) 757-2307

Paragon, Inc.
P.O. Box 17167
Memphis, TN 38187
(800) 238-9254

Parker Pest Control, Inc.
1 Parker Pl.
Rte. 2, Box 37
Ponca City, OK 74601
(800) 654-4541

PBI Gordon Corp.
P.O. Box 4090
Kansas City, MO 64101
(800) 821-7925
(816) 421-4070

**Peaceful Valley Farm
Supply**
P.O. Box 2209
Grass Valley, CA 95945
(916) 272-4769

**Performance
Products, Inc.**
541 W. Coolidge
P.O. Box 417
Coolidge, AZ 85228
(602) 723-5294

Perma Proof® Corp.
1927 Howard St.
Chicago, IL 60626
(312) 764-5559

**Pest Management
Supply Co.**
P.O. Box 938
Amherst, MA 01004
(800) 272-7672
(413) 253-3747

Petco Animal Supplies
9151 Renco Rd.
San Diego, CA 92121
(619) 453-7845

**Pharmacia Diagnostics
Div. of Pharmacia, Inc.**
800 Centennial Ave.
Piscataway, NJ 08854
(201) 457-8162

Phero Tech Inc.
7572 Progress Way
RR 5, Delta
British Columbia V4G 1E9
Canada
(604) 940-9944

Phillips Fibers Corp.
P.O. Box 66,
Greenville, SC 29602
(803) 242-6600

PINA
4649 Sunnyside Ave. N.
Seattle, WA 98103
(206) 547-6838

Plow & Hearth
301 Madison Rd.
Orange, VA 22960
(703) 672-1712

Polgar, L., Research Inst.
Plant Protection Institute
Herman Otto ut 15
Budapest II, Hungary

Poultry Health Service
569 Stuart Lane
Jacksonville, FL 32205
(904) 786-5195

Praxis
P.O. Box 134
Allegen, MI 49010
(616) 673-2793

**Precision
Laboratories Inc.**
P.O. Box 127
Northbrook IL 60065
(312) 498-0800

Pristine Products
2311 E. Indian School Rd.
Phoenix, AZ 85016
(602) 955-7031

**Reed-Joseph
International Co.**
P.O. Box 894
Greenville, MS 38701
(601) 335-5822

REI
Box 88127
Seattle, WA 98188-0127
(206) 323-8333

Repel'm Distributors
303 Linwood Ave.
Fairfield, CT 06430
(203) 255-9042

Rexair Inc.
3221 West Big Beaver
Suite 2000
Troy, MI 48084
(313) 643-7222

**Rincon-Vitova
Insectaries, Inc.**
P.O. Box 95
Oakview, CA 93022
(805) 643-5407

Ringer Corp.
9959 Valley View Rd.
Eden Prairie
MN 55344-3585
(800) 654-1047
(612) 941-4180

**Rocky Mountain
Insectary**
P.O. Box 152
Palisade, CO 81526

A.I. Root, Co.
623 W. Liberty St.
Box 706
Medina, OH 44258
(216) 725-6677

**Roses of Yesterday and
Today**
802 Brown's Valley Rd.
Watsonville, CA 95076
(408) 724-3537

Roxide International, Inc.
P.O. Box 249
New Rochelle, NY 10802
(800) 431-5500
(914) 235-5300

R-Value/Redzone
P.O. Box 1812
Waterbury, CT 06722
(800) 845-3495

Safer, Inc.
(Consumer Products)
9959 Valley View Rd.
Eden Prairie
MN 55344-3585
(800) 654-1047
(612) 941-4180

Safer, Inc.
(Professional Products)
5451 Oberlin Dr.
San Diego, CA 92121
(619) 453-8030

Safer Ltd.
465 Milner Ave.
Scarborough
Ontario M1B 2K4
Canada
(800) 387-5306
(416) 291-8150

Sandoz Crop Protection
1300 East Touhy Ave.
Des Plaines, IL 60018
(800) 553-4833
(708) 699-1616

Santa Cruz Horticultural
Supply
P.O. Box 1534
Morro Bay, CA 93442
(805) 772-8262

Scentry, Inc.
P.O. Box 426
Buckeye, AZ 85326-0090
(800) 548-6531
(602) 233-1772 or
(602) 386-6737

Seabright Enterprises
4026 Harlan St.
Emeryville, CA 94608
(415) 655-3126

Sherex Chemical Co., Inc.
P.O. Box 646
Dublin, OH 43017
(800) 848-7452
(800) 848-5825

Smith & Hawken Tools
25 Corte Madera
Mill Valley, CA 94941
(415) 383-4050

Sound Merchandise
7903 E Fir St., P.O. Box 37
Manchester, WA 98353
(206) 565-2362

Spencer-Mead, Inc.
1730 Walton Rd., Ste. 307
Blueball, PA 19422
(800) 645-3696

Sterling International
15916 Sprauge Ave.
Veradale, WA 99037
(800) 666-6766
(509) 926-6766

Streamlight, Inc.
1030 W. Germantown Pike
Norristown, PA 19403
(215) 631-0600

Strieter Corp.
2100 18th Ave., Ste. 1
Rock Island, IL 61201
(309) 794-9800

Summit Chemical Co.
7657 Canton Center Dr.
Baltimore, MD 21218
(800) 227-8664
(301) 282-5200

Svenka Predator AB
Box 14017, S-250
14 Helsingborg, Sweden

TADD Services, Inc.
1617 Old Country Rd.
Ste. 4
Belmont, CA 94002
(800) 345-8233
(415) 595-5171

Tanglefoot Co.
314 Straight Ave. SW
Grand Rapids, MI 49504
(616) 459-4139

Tate & Lyle
P.O. Box 43
Tunbridge Wells
Kent TN2 5BX
England, U.K.

Thomson Publications
P.O. Box 9335
Fresno, CA 93991
(209) 435-2163

3M Corp
P.O. Box 3322
St Paul, MN 55133
(612) 733-1110

Tomahawk Live Traps
P.O. Box 323
Tomahawk, WI 54487
(715) 453-3550

Town Enterprises
(Sanix, Inc.)
11731 Sterling Ave., Ste. G
Riverside, CA 92503
(714) 689-2500

Trebor Corp.
4045-A Jonesboro Rd.
Forest Park, GA 30050
(404) 366-0957

Trécé, Inc.
1143 Madison Lane
Salinas, CA 93907-1817
(408) 758-0205

Tredegar Film Products
1100 Boulders Parkway
Richmond, VA 23225
(804) 330-1222

Trump Masters, Inc.
425 Merrimac, Suite D108
Costa Mesa, CA 92626
(714) 662-2431

Turf Seed, Co.
P.O. Box 250
Hubbard, OR 97032
(503) 981-9571

Universal Diatoms Inc.
410-12th St. NW
Albuquerque, NM 87102
(505) 247-3271

Urban Insect Solutions
1420 Jondymar Ct.
Lexington, KY 40517
(606) 273-6503

U.S. Borax
412 Crescent Way
Anaheim, CA 92801
(231) 251-5630

U.S. Forest Service, USDA
14th and
Independence Aves.
Washington, DC 27709

Valent USA
P.O. Box 4054
Richmond, CA 94804-0054
(415) 256-2724

Valley Seed Service
P.O. Box 9335
Fresno, CA 93791
(209) 435-2163

Vet Express, Inc.
P.O. Box 1168
Rhinelander, WI 54501
(800) 458-7656

Vredenburg Industrial
Packaging Products
P.O. Box 990
Eureka, MT 59917
(406) 889-3573

Waterbury Co.
P.O. Box 1812
Waterbury, CT 06722
(800) 845-3495
(203) 597-1812

Waterford Corp.
P.O. Box 1513
Fort Collins, CO 80522
(303) 482-0911

Whitmire
3568 Tree Court
Industrial Blvd.
St. Louis, MO 63122
(800) 325-3668
(314) 225-5371

Wildlife Control
Technology Inc.
2501 N. Sunnyside #103
Fresno, CA 93707
(800) 235-0262
(209) 294-0262

Wildlife Supply Co.
301 Cass St.
Saginaw, MI 48602
(517) 799-8102

Wilt-Pruf Products, Inc.
P.O. Box 4280
Greenwich
CT 06830-0280
(203) 531-4740

Woodstream Corp.
69 N. Locust St.
Lititz, PA 17543
(800) 233-0277
(717) 626-2125

Zoecon Corp.
12200 Denton Dr.
Dallas, TX 75234
(800) 527-0512

Index

Editor: Steve Marlens
Designer: Deborah Fillion
Layout artist: Jodie Delohery
Illustrator: Steve Buchanan
Copy/Production editors: Peter Chapman, Ruth Dobsevage
Art assistants: Mary Bresler, Iliana Koehler
Indexer: Harriet Hodges

Typeface: Stone Serif

Printer and binder: Arcata/Hawkins, New Canton, Tennessee